Winter '78

Carl B. Montano
6A Chittenden Hall
Michigan State University

TYPES OF ECONOMIC THEORY

VOLUME II

Also published in
REPRINTS OF ECONOMIC CLASSICS

BY

WESLEY C. MITCHELL

THE BACKWARD ART OF SPENDING MONEY AND OTHER ESSAYS [1937]

GOLD, PRICES AND WAGES UNDER THE GREENBACK STANDARD [1908]

THE MAKING AND USING OF INDEX NUMBERS [1915]

———————

WHAT VEBLEN TAUGHT. SELECTED WRITINGS OF THORSTEIN VEBLEN EDITED

WITH AN INTRODUCTION BY WESLEY C. MITCHELL [1936]

———————

BY

JOSEPH DORFMAN

THE ECONOMIC MIND IN AMERICAN CIVILIZATION
VOLUMES I AND II [1946], VOLUME III [1949],
VOLUMES IV AND V [1959]

THORSTEIN VEBLEN AND HIS AMERICA [1934]

TYPES

of

ECONOMIC THEORY

FROM MERCANTILISM TO INSTITUTIONALISM

By

WESLEY C. MITCHELL

EDITED BY

JOSEPH DORFMAN

VOLUME II

AUGUSTUS M. KELLEY PUBLISHERS
NEW YORK 1969

PRINTED IN THE UNITED STATES OF AMERICA

by SENTRY PRESS, NEW YORK, N. Y. 10019

CONTENTS

INTRODUCTION

Types of Economic Theory from Mercantilism to Institutionalism is the outgrowth of the demand for a printed version of the widely-used mimeographed notes of Professor Mitchell's lectures which bore the title, "Lecture Notes on Types of Economic Theory."[1] Since Professor Mitchell has so admirably set forth the scope, method and objectives in Chapter I, below, the editor feels that the most appropriate introduction would be one detailing the history and mechanics of the organization and composition of the treatise.

The original mimeographed version was prepared by a student, John Meyers, from stenographic notes in the academic year 1926-1927. New editions of the mimeographed lectures benefitted from his subsequent attendance of the course from time to time through the spring of 1935. Periodically when he had a substantial amount of new material he would run off the composite as a new edition. The result was that the last edition in 1935 was about thirty per cent larger than the original version. The demand for the notes not only at Columbia University but at other institutions both at home and abroad continued even after Professor Mitchell's death in 1948.

After Meyers gave up the venture, Augustus M. Kelley, the publisher, and a former student in the course, secured the consent of Mrs. Mitchell to resume mimeographing the lectures. Such was the stature of the material that this 1949 re-mimeographed manuscript was reviewed in such leading professional organs as *The Economic Journal* and was referred to in the professional literature as if it were a printed book. The continuing demand intensified the interest of

---

[1] Professor Mitchell gave the course at Columbia University from 1913 to 1937, except for the three years when he taught at the New School for Social Research (1919-1922) and the one year (1931-1932) when he served as Eastman Professor at Oxford.

The form of the course varied somewhat until 1922. In the first year it was a year course. In the next two years he gave it the second semester and a course on business cycles the first term. In 1916 it became once again a year course and it was mainly devoted to "current types," beginning with W. Stanley Jevons's *The Theory of Political Economy* (1871). Another change occurred when he taught the course at The New School beginning in 1919. He gave increasing attention to the classical school, so much so that the first part might have been called "The Ricardian Age." On his return to Columbia in 1922, he began to give the course in the form in which it appears in the mimeographed versions. The first term is exclusively devoted to the classical school and its forerunners and the second to the "moderns."

publishers in converting the mimeographed version into a more permanent form. Finally, in 1961, Mrs. Mitchell asked that I serve as the editor in the preparation of the lectures for publication.

To make the treatise as complete as possible, I used not only the 1949 mimeographed edition, but also the materials from previous editions of the mimeographed notes, from notes in my own possession, and from the vast collection of Mitchell Papers, including his diary, in the Columbia University Library. The last edition of the mimeographed version, which provides the framework and the basic segment, is given below in its entirety.

A substantial segment of the book is made up of extracts from a typescript of the lectures in the second half of the course in the 1918 spring term. This "1918 Typescript" is in some respects even richer than the mimeographed editions, especially in the reporting of class discussions. In the era of the mimeographed versions, the class required the largest hall used for the social sciences, and student participation was limited. Rarely were there more than two questions from the floor. The 1918 class, however, was very lively, for not only was it a small one of a dozen or so students—it was wartime—but it included two former students of Thorstein Veblen from the University of Missouri, a leading devotee of Karl Marx, and a student fresh from the halls of Alfred Marshall's Cambridge. It seems that every member participated in most if not all of the discussions. So animated were the sessions that at times the reporter was unable to identify a participant and was forced to record simply, "student."

Furthermore, unlike the mimeographed version, this transcript had the advantage of being arranged for, and at least in part supervised by Professor Mitchell. By 1917, he had definitely embarked on the preparation for publication of the lectures. To this end he had his secretary, Miss Ruth Bahret, attend the class beginning on October 1, 1917 and report the lectures in shorthand. The unpublished diary has from time to time such entries as "after lunch helped Miss Bahret to interpret her shorthand notes of yesterday's class discussion," or "helped Miss Bahret fill her lecture notes." Somehow members of the class obtained copies of the transcript of the second term. Fortunately these were passed on to members of succeeding classes and at least one batch of retyped copies was made from the original. As a consequence a few copies have survived, and the editor found himself in possession of two copies. So far no trace has been found of the transcript of the first term. The Mitchell Papers however con-

tain a few typed items, especially summaries of class discussions, that
may have been part of such a transcript.

Another large segment of *Types of Economic Theory* is composed
of extracts from a manuscript "The Classical Economics." This he
had planned as the first part of the treatise. He began writing it in
1916 and pursued this task vigorously over the next two years, and
then according to diary entries he made attempts at revision from
time to time down to 1923. He never completed the manuscript to
his own satisfaction, but he had hoped to do so in the days of his
retirement.[2] This manuscript covers a good part of what became the
first half of the course. It provides a fuller account of his views on a
number of episodes than does the mimeographed notes.

Still another large segment is drawn from the mass of relevant outlines and abstracts in the Mitchell Papers. These reach as far back
as the late 1890's when Professor Mitchell was a graduate student
at the University of Chicago and continue to his last days. They
cover not only the course in types of theory but also other courses,
conferences, addresses and his enormous reading. The outlines were
often so clear and full that relevant parts could be inserted in the
text in outline form. Some additional illuminating items have been
obtained from the notes of a student in the course in 1923-1924, and
from Professor Mitchell's correspondence. And of course, wherever
essential, his published works have been drawn upon and annotations have been provided by the editor. All these additions have so
expanded the coverage that *Types of Economic Theory* is approximately twice the volume of the last mimeographed edition.

The question may be raised why some theorists, notably Marx,
were not accorded the same comprehensive treatment that is given
other major figures. The answer lies partly in the fact that Professor
Mitchell wanted always to be most useful to the students, given the
total facilities available in the Columbia department of economics.
He had faced this problem first, it seems, when he was requested to
give a course in economic history in his last year at the University
of Chicago in 1902. He found that various areas in economic history
from 1750 on were covered adequately in other courses. He therefore
devoted his own lectures to the period from primitive times down to

---

[2] Two essays were published in revised form from the manuscript: "Bentham's
Felicific Calculus" (1918) and "Postulates and Preconceptions of Ricardian Economics" (1929). Both were republished in his *The Backward Art of Spending Money
and Other Essays,* ed. by Joseph Dorfman (New York: McGraw-Hill, 1937) pp.
177-224. All the essays in this volume are valuable as supplementary reading to
Types of Economic Theory.

1750. Now, at Columbia, in his day a one-year course on socialism was being given by Vladimir Simkhovitch. He felt, therefore, that he could leave the detailed, systematic treatment of Marx to his colleague. Yet while there is no single chapter on Marx in the treatise, the reader will discover considerable discussion of him in the book, especially in the chapters dealing with David Ricardo, Gustav von Schmoller and Thorstein Veblen.[3]

In some cases, changes in the course offerings of the department resulted in an enrichment of his course, an enrichment that found its way into the mimeographed editions. Thus, in 1922, when Professor Henry Seager dropped his course on readings in the economic classics, he suggested that Professor Mitchell provide an extended systematic discussion of Adam Smith. He accepted the advice and the result was the masterly analysis of the "father" of modern political economy with which he henceforth opened the course.

Sometimes students' suggestions accelerated the process of enrichment. This happened, for example, in the discussions on the mathematical type of theory. He had devoted considerable attention to Léon Walras's famous French treatise, *Élements d'économie politique pure,* as a representative of this type of economic theory. But since some students found themselves severely handicapped by its relatively highly mathematical form, Professor Mitchell turned, in 1914, for detailed exposition to Joseph A. Schumpeter's Walrasian *Das Wesen und der Hauptinhalt der theoretischen Nationalökonomie* (1908) which made limited use of mathematics. This book, like Walras's, still left the problem of the need for adequate knowledge of a foreign language. Professor Mitchell solved this when, at a student's suggestion, he included a discussion of Gustav Cassel's high level *Theoretische Sozialökonomie,* which had recently been translated into English as *The Theory of Social Economy* (1924).[4]

The documentation of *Types of Economic Theory from Mercantilism to Institutionalism* requires explanation. All material for which no source is supplied are from the mimeographed versions. Extracts from "1918 Typescript," from "The Classical Economics" Ms. and from "Student Notes 1923-1924" are referred to by titles. All the dated outlines of the course, "Types of Economic Theory," are referred to simply by date. For all other dated materials, titles and dates are

---

[3] Professor Mitchell lectured on Marx while teaching at the New School for Social Research, but the outline available is too schematic to add much.
[4] Professor Mitchell while preparing the revision of his *Business Cycles,* had already made notes in 1923 from the chapters on the subject in the original German edition.

supplied. Undated items, practically all of which were collected or prepared before 1919, are cited by title of folder, the number of the folder and the particular series in the Mitchell Papers in which it appears, such as "APP," "OPP," etc. Quotations from letters, the diary and from published works, and from unpublished manuscripts other than Professor Mitchell's have quotation marks. *All bracketed material, unless otherwise attributed, has been supplied by the editor.*

Because of the size of the present work, we thought that the convenience of the reader would best be served by issuing it in two volumes. The first is devoted to what Professor Mitchell called "the classical type of theory," the formation of the British classical political economy; and the second, to the "moderns", the heirs, both orthodox and heterodox that together comprise the leading dominant strains of theory today. The index appears in volume II.

In closing, I wish to thank Mr. Kelley who, besides executing the responsibilities of a publisher, applied his literary skill at all stages through which the mansucript passed.

JOSEPH DORFMAN

Columbia University
August 1966

INTRODUCTION

Addendum for Volume II

I should like to emphasize some statements which appear above. These volumes are more than a printed version of the entire mimeographed edition of Professor Mitchell's "Lectures." They include in addition a substantial amount of amplifying material drawn largely from the vast collection of his papers.

For volume II, I have also drawn from another set of student notes which differs somewhat from the "1918 typescript." While neither the name of the notetaker nor the date is indicated, an entry in Professor Mitchell's "Diary" suggests that the notetaker was William Howard Steiner who took the course in 1916-1917.

This volume reproduces one of the most distinctive, telling and exciting features of the course; namely, Professor Mitchell's practice, especially in the second term, of conducting the class by the question and answer method. He asked questions or called for questions, and the ensuing colloquy enabled him to present an intensive analysis of a writer's theory from different angles. For this exceptionally stimulating feature we are fortunate in having not only Meyers's mimeographed version of the lectures but also the "1918 Typescript" and a number of Professor Mitchell's summaries of interchanges at other times. He was very skillful in keeping the class room discussion moving in an orderly fashion from day to day. Thus his "Diary" records his procedure on three succeeding sessions in 1924 in dealing with Veblen's method: "April 22. Had class room discussion on applicability of Veblen's methods to problems of orthodox theory. April 24. Making notes on problem of economic method raised in discussion of Veblen's type of economic theory. April 29. Finished discussion of Veblen's method."

I have drawn, too, on many of Professor Mitchell's outlines because these are invaluable not only for purposes of clarification and summarization but also for relevant material which has not been recorded in the transcribed lectures. As every lecturer knows, limitations of time often impose such omissions. And of course it often happens that the transcriber may have inadvertently failed to catch all of the lecture and class room discussion.

Finally, I have drawn heavily on Mitchell's rich correspondence, especially with such leading thinkers as J. M. Clark, F. Y. Edgeworth, John A. Hobson, J. M. Keynes, Frank H. Knight, Joseph Schumpeter and Friedrich von Wieser.

We should like to thank Arnold Mitchell for making available to us the papers of his mother.

JOSEPH DORFMAN

Columbia University
July 1969

CHAPTER IX

The Rise of Utility Theory: W. Stanley Jevons; Carl Menger and Léon Walras

Economic theory is an intellectual product to be accounted for, something in which one's interest is not so much of a strictly scientific sort as of a philosophic order; that is, it is scarcely to be presumed that those seeking an understanding of economic activities would derive the best help from thinkers who lived a century or more ago. The scientifically valuable part of the work accomplished by Adam Smith, Malthus, Ricardo, and John Stuart Mill, for example, has been incorporated into the structure of economic science as it stands today, and can be found in actual use by later writers who have the advantage not only of the teachings of these theorists, but also of many others and of their own later reflection. Thus there was justification in looking back upon the great classics as representing the earlier stages of trying to understand rather than as yielding suggestions of great constructive value in contemporary life.

It would not be correct to assert that economics has made substantially no progress; the work of, say, a person who lived in the first third of the nineteenth century has been shown to be of great scientific value for people who are living in the twentieth century. We can, however, probably find someone in our own time who is of more value than the men who lived a hundred years ago. For as our discussion approaches the current era it is coming to people who represent more of the viewpoint of the present, whose ideas presumably are of greater scientific consequence. It is coming to the economists who have incorporated what was of lasting value in the work of the classical masters. In dealing with the later works we can advantageously try to use them in a somewhat different way from that in which we attempted to employ their predecessors' work.

Works of recent times are social products of the time quite as much as those of the earlier writers. For that matter the minds of economists today have been conditioned by the circumstances in which they have grown up, quite as truly as the minds of the theorists in

1

the past. If investigators had enough understanding of recent times they might treat the work of their contemporaries, in so far as they could free themselves from the inevitable personal equation, after the fashion in which I have endeavored to treat the works which are regarded as the cornerstones of modern economic theory. This would be an instructive thing to do, but with the sketch which already has been given of how economic theory is a social product, we had best

let matters stand as they are, merely reminding ourselves from time to time that we are children of our day and not the scientific intellects, free from preconceptions and prejudices and limiting special interests, which we are likely to think of ourselves as being.

In dealing with the classical type I had tried primarily to exhibit the development of economics as part of the social life of the times, to show the way in which economic problems arose, how these problems were formulated in scientific discussion, what conclusions the scientific writers reached, and how the ideas reacted upon the social process from which they arose. The centering the discussion on the theorists themselves more than on the circumstances which led to the formulation of their doctrines and the uses made of them in practical life does not mean that the development of economic theory is any less a social process nowadays than it was in the time of Adam Smith and Ricardo. On the contrary the work of Alfred Marshall or Thorstein Veblen or Frank A. Fetter, even the work which we ourselves may accomplish, is quite as much stimulated, characterized and limited by contemporary social life into which we are born and which we help develop, as in the case of earlier writers. That is an important point to realize—particularly with reference to ourselves.

But it is a point which is hard to make clear in detail. It is more difficult to get an objective view of the factors which are shaping our interests and limiting our insights than it is to get a similarly objective view of others. It is also harder to get such an objective view of our contemporaries than of our predecessors—partly because they are much like ourselves and partly because there is not available the lives and letters and histories which give insight into the mental development of men who lived a century ago. Our children and grandchildren will be able to formulate clearer ideas of Marshall, Veblen and Fetter and ourselves than we can. In the second place, one demonstration of the connection between the development of the social sciences and social life at large, as we have given in the case of the classical political economists, should suffice to make us realize that the vitality of our work is dependent upon keeping in close touch with practical problems and interests. A third reason for changing the method of approach is that we are more concerned with the results reached by our contemporaries than with those reached by Adam Smith or Ricardo or John Stuart Mill. To us the classical economists are not objects of scientific interest because of the light they shed on our practical and intellectual problems. Our problems are different in part and as far as the problems remain the same the later writers have made advances upon their predecessors. Thus, so far as we desire help in the effort at constructive work from writings of other men, it is rather to the later writers that we go.[1]

To repeat, it will be best therefore to take that basic conception of the forces which shape later economic theory as established, and try to become familiar somewhat more in detail with the views that are developed, thinking of them now as formulas which may in one way or another contribute to any theoretical work which we may accomplish. There is a certain value in learning how a man like Marshall or John Bates Clark or Herbert J. Davenport or Gustav von Schmoller attacks the problem of wages—this is much more important than what Adam Smith and Ricardo said on the subject.[1a] In other words, most of our time will be devoted to critical discussions which will aim: first, to develop exactly what the successive authorities have held; and, second, to discover what constructive value their ideas possess at the present time, and what are the limitations in their way of attacking the fundamental problems of economic theory. So the aim will be to become as familiar as we can with as many as possible of the recent writers of economic theory, seeing what they conceive to be the leading problems, how they attack them and what results they achieve.[2]

With that intent in mind, the method of conducting the discussion had also best be shifted. For I find it less successful to attempt to expound the views of any thinker to a class than to discuss those views with the class. An exposition which students listen to, even if it seems lucid at the time, is not likely to register in any prominent way in their minds; and anybody who is trying to explain a complicated set of intellectual propositions to a mixed group is certain to overlook many questions which will arise in the minds of the people who are endeavoring to understand. He may well make the error of expounding unduly on things which are obvious to the class, and, on the other hand, leave out matters which from their viewpoint require clarification. Class discussion is better because it shifts more or less the responsibility for what the students get from the course very largely from the instructor's shoulders to the shoulders on which it belongs. For the instructor puts himself by this scheme

---

[1] Outline, February 8, 1923.
[1a] Outline, February 8, 1923.
[2] Outline, February 8, 1923.

in the students' hands. He is putting on them the responsibility of being bold and free and coming out, however embarrassing it may be to him or them, to load him with any inquiries they may care to make.

The previous part ended with John Stuart Mill; this begins with W. Stanley Jevons (1835-1882) because he represents the most influential statement of marginal analysis.[3]

Between the time when John Stuart Mill published his *Principles of Political Economy* in 1848 and the time when Jevons published *The Theory of Political Economy* in 1871, the basic ideas of economics did not show any rapid development. During that period Mill remained the great English authority upon political economy in common estimation, just as between 1817 and 1848 Ricardo had been looked up to as the economist *par excellence*, and just as between 1776 and 1817 everybody had thought of Adam Smith as the supreme guide.

In some ways Mill's position was even greater than that which Adam Smith and Ricardo had enjoyed, for he was recognized not only as the foremost economist of the time but also as the leading English philosopher and as the most eminent writer on the theory of politics.[4] He was the first of the group of philosophical radicals to exercise considerable influence upon the universities, for at long last the great conservative strongholds of learning, especially Cambridge, found in this philosophical radical an authority whom they could admire. Indeed, Mill seems to have influenced the young intellectuals of the time in very large measure: men like Sir Leslie Stephen,

---

[3] Outline, February 8, 1923.

[4] [Mill also enjoyed a tremendous reputation in the United States, partly because of his strong espousal of the Union cause during the Civil War. Charles Sumner saluted him as "one of our best, truest & most disinterested friends in Europe, whose voice is that of history." (Sumner to Hugh McCulloch, September 28, 1865, McCulloch papers, Library of Congress.)

Sumner enclosed a clipping from a newspaper which summarized a letter from Mill to W. M. Dickson of Cincinnati, Ohio, which originally appeared in the Cincinnati *Commercial*. In the letter Mill emphasized that the ex-slaves must be allowed the franchise in the defeated southern states. He went on to say "I see no objection to requiring, as a condition of the suffrage, education up to the point of reading and writing; but on condition that this shall be required equally for the whites. The poor whites [of] the South are understood to need education quite as much as the negroes and are certainly quite as unfit for the exercise of the suffrage without it." (The original letter dated September 1, 1865, is now in the Yale University Libraries and is printed in J. E. Patterson, "A Letter of John Stuart Mill," *The Yale University Library Gazette*, April 1956, p. 165.)

Henry George summed up the general attitude in a letter to Mill: "You are regarded here as the supreme authority in the wide domain of political economy." (George to Mill, April 22, 1869, copy, George papers, New York Public Library.)]

Viscount Morley[5] and Henry Sidgwick looked up to him as their intellectual emancipator and guide. His standing with the public is clearly shown by such a simple objective test as the circulation attained by his books. In its expensive, elaborate form in two volumes, no less than seven editions of the *Principles of Political Economy* were published in his lifetime. At considerable financial cost to himself he made his publishers bring out a popular edition in one volume at a price which brought the book within reach of the working classes. Of that edition published in 1865 there were five reprints before Mill's death. The book was reprinted several times in the United States and made into an even more popular text book in 1884 as a one volume abridgement by J. Laurence Laughlin.[6] It was translated into all the leading languages of Europe.

The tremendous success of the book with the public on the one side and with men of striking intellectual taste on the other side is an exemplification of its outstanding qualities. As previously noted it was an admirable piece of exposition. Mill had the ability to set forth even the most difficult of his problems in a way in which it is comparatively easy to follow. Furthermore the treatise had a persuasive urbanity of tone, a sweet reasonableness,[7] and its popularity was doubtless increased by the temperate optimism with which Mill looked to the future, based upon his fundamental distinction between the laws of production as unchanging physical truths and the laws of distribution which are matters of human contrivance and might therefore be altered in such a fashion as to promote the happiness of the mass of the people. And by the spread of education, he held, people would become capable of exercising some measure of self-control in taking advantage of the widening democracy of the age to provide themselves a more representative type of government. The book is

---

[5] [John Morley (1838-1923) exercised considerable influence on the development of economics largely through his brilliant editorship from 1867 to 1883 of *The Fortnightly Review*, which was then the leading medium for economists. In 1883 he entered the House of Commons as a member of the Liberal party (the successor of the Whig party) and became an outstanding lieutenant of Gladstone.

Morley had been an unsuccessful candidate in 1872 for the chair of political economy at University College, London. (Morley to Frederic Harrison, May 1, 1872, in F. W. Hirst, *Early Life and Letters of John Morley,* 2 volumes (London: Macmillan, 1927) I, p. 214.)]

[6] [*Principles of Political Economy, Abridged, with Critical, Biographical and Explanatory Notes, and a Sketch of the History of Political Economy* (New York: Appleton, 1884).

Laughlin (1850-1933) prepared the abridgement while teaching at Harvard. In 1892 he became head professor of political economy at the newly opened University of Chicago. Among his first *protégés* there was Professor Mitchell.]

[7] The phrase is from Outline, January 10, 1933.

the culmination of classical political economy but it becomes in Mill very different from the political economy of Malthus and Ricardo.[8]

It is probable that the very authority which Mill enjoyed is particularly responsible for the fact that the science of economics made comparatively so little progress during this period. If a subject has been authoritatively expounded with a high degree of success, then the efforts to proceed further, to discover what is wrong with prevailing notions, to bring out the weaknesses of the accepted theories, to add to human knowledge, are likely to be less vigorous than when people are dissatisfied with prevailing statements.[9]

It is true that certain features of the economics expounded by Mill were attacked and Mill showed his customary candor in admitting the invalidity of at least one very important part of his body of doctrines; namely, the wages fund theory. The strange misconception that there exists a predetermined wages fund set by the amount of capital in existence and technological conditions was effectively challenged by F. D. Longe in 1866 and by Mill's friend William Thornton three years later. Upon reading Thornton's criticism in *On Labour*, Mill confessed in his review in *The Fortnightly Review* that he had shared in an idea that when it was critically considered appeared to have too little validity.[10] Yet, to repeat again, in the editions of his *Principles of Political Economy* which appeared in the short interval between his recantation of the wages fund fallacy and his death, Mill did not think it worth while to try to revise his theory in that respect.

One of his disciples, however, the able Irish economist, John Elliott Cairnes, whose chief book is *Some Leading Principles of Political Economy Newly Expounded* (1874), endeavored to show that Mill's recantation had been premature, that the wages fund theory may be restated in a somewhat different fashion than that adopted by the early classical masters, and in this elaborate form it still contained a very substantial element of truth.[11]

---

[8] Sentence from Outline, January 10, 1933.

[9] Mill's influence—pervasiveness of his authoritative restatement. As a leader of his group this widening influence was accompanied by a decline in efforts to further specific reforms. Contrast with Bentham and James Mill. Still the late years of John Stuart Mill's life saw the culmination of the Benthamite influence on British legislation. (Outline, January 10, 1933.)

[10] See Volume I. pp. 565-566.

[11] [Cairnes (1823-1875) was appointed in 1856 to a five year term in the Whately chair at Trinity College, Dublin. Three years later he became professor of jurisprudence and political economy at Queen's College, Galway. In 1866, he succeeded Waley as professor of political economy at University College, London, but ill health forced him to resign in 1872.]

Cairnes was Mill's leading disciple, reviser and a specialist on economic methodology. He was much concerned with emendation of details of doctrine and defense of the central positions of the classical school.[12] He was the supreme authority on method among the exponents of the classical school. His conception of the role of statistics was that of Mill. "According to the classical concept [as laid down by Cairnes], the business of the statistician is merely to verify conclusions established by deduction, and to discover disturbing causes that do not reveal themelves readily 'to a reasoner engaged in the development of the more capital economic doctrines.' "[13]

In any event, if the student had been talking with an Englishman acquainted with the subject in 1870 he would have said that the leading authorities of the day were disciples of Mill. Perhaps he would have set Cairnes above all but some might have looked to the less critical and constructive disciple, the blind Henry Fawcett of Cambridge University, who held the chief academic chair of political economy at the time, and who, in accordance with sound old utilitarian tradition, got into Parliament as a Liberal and served as postmaster general under Gladstone. He gave most of his attention to politics but he also wrote a very widely used text book, *Manual of Political Economy* (1863).[14]

Mill's disciples held practically all the important chairs, including the new ones. Thus when in 1871 the Merchant Company of Edinburgh set aside £10,000 for a professorship of commercial and political economy and mercantile law, the appointment went to W. B. Hodgson (1815-1880) [who spoke of "James Mill as the illustrious father of a still more illustrious son" and used John Stuart Mill's *Principles of Political Economy* as the textbook.][15] The course was intended for "the training of future merchants." The "patrons" included mercantile law in the chair with "the view of adding a practical side to the

---

[12] Sentence from Outline, January 10, 1933.

[13] Mitchell, "Quantitative Analysis in Economic Theory," 1925; reprinted in *The Backward Art of Spending Money and Other Essays,* edited by Joseph Dorfman (New York: McGraw-Hill, 1937) p. 33. The quotation is from Cairnes, *The Character and Logical Method of Political Economy* (London: Longmans *et al,* 1857; 2nd ed. 1875) p. 97.

[14] [Fawcett's wife, Dame Millicent Garrett Fawcett (1847-1929) was also a noted economist and her *Political Economy for Beginners* (1870) also enjoyed considerable Use in American colleges.]

[15] [Hodgson, *The True Scope of Economic Science* (London: Head, 1870) p. 14. The term of appointment was seven years but Hodgson was reappointed. His at the time was the highest paid chair in the United Kingdom, paying £450 a year.]

scientific and abstract theories of political economy."[16] [It was "believed by some of his friends that the chair would provide the effective forum for supplying the remedy for commercial panics," which "are at once so discreditable and so ruinous to the mercantile community."[17] He maintained in *The True Scope of Economic Science*, that "commercial crises" were due to men's neglect of "the exercise of intelligence, integrity, and forethought." One historian of the university wrote that "Hodgson did not strike out new paths, he was a sound and orthodox economist of the Bastiat and Stuart Mill school . . .; he was a representative of what may be called middle class ideas."[18] Hodgson's successor in 1880, Joseph Shield Nicholson (1850-1927) stated in the catalogue that "the Lectures will follow the order of arrangement of John Stuart Mill's *Principles of Political Economy*."][19]

Other types of thinking than that presented by the disciples of Mill had comparatively little hearing with the public. When the first vigorous innovator turned up in the person of W. Stanley Jevons, he promptly formed the opinion that progress in economics was held back by what he regarded as the "Mill despotism." Passages from different letters of his show how strongly he felt that the classical type

---

[16] [Sir Alexander Grant, *The Story of the University of Edinburgh During Its First Three Hundred Years,* 2 volumes (London: Longmans, Green, 1884) II, p. 149. Officially the divisions of the chair were: "1. Economics . . . 2. Commerce . . . 3. Mercantile Law . . ." *The Edinburgh University Calendar, 1879-1883,* (Edinburgh: Thin, 1879) p. 78. According to a student, two hours a week each were devoted to commercial history and political economy, and a fifth hour to a consideration of class essays; Hodgson had little enthusiasm for commercial history and would drop it after the Christmas holiday. J. M. D. Meiklejohn, *Life and Letters of William Ballantyne Hodgson* (Edinburgh: Douglas, 1883) p. 182.]

[17] [Meiklejohn, *Life and Letters of William Ballantyne Hodgson,* p. 168.]

[18] [Grant, *The History of the University of Edinburgh,* II, p. 468.

The French economist, Frédéric Bastiat (1801-1850) was described by Hodgson as "the most eloquent, noble and enthusiastic advocate of commercial freedom that has arisen since the time of Turgot." Hodgson, *Competition* (London: Head, 1870) p. 6. He first published this essay in the Manchester *Examiner and Times* in 1852 and then as a pamphlet which was frequently reprinted. It was a translation of the most famous of Bastiat's essays, *What is Seen and What is Not Seen; Our Political Economy in One Lesson.*]

On Hodgson, see "First Professorship in Scotland," APP 64-73, no. 66.

[19] [*The Edinburgh University Calendar, 1884-1885,* p. 63. "J. S. Nicholson. . . . Pupil of (Alfred) Marshall; Orthodox: Conservative" (William J. Ashley, to Edwin R. A. Seligman, September 15, 1889, in "The Seligman Correspondence." no. 4, edited by Joseph Dorfman; *Political Science Quarterly,* December 1941, p. 583.

After a separate lectureship in mercantile law was created, the title of the chair became "Political Economy." It was not until 1892 that "economic science" could be offered for the ordinary arts degree; and only in 1898 that it could be offered for "honors."]

of economics was being maintained by an interested party. In the first letter he says:

> I fear it is impossible to criticise Mr. Mill's writings without incurring the danger of rousing animosity, but I hope and believe you are right in saying that I have said nothing from petulance or passion.[20]

Again in a later letter to an admirer, Herbert Somerton Foxwell of Cambridge, he writes:

> There is much that is erroneous in his *Principles,* and he never had an idea what *capital* was, but the book is not the maze of self-contradictions which his *Logic* undoubtedly is.[21]

And then in still another letter to Foxwell:

> I am beginning to think very strongly that the true line of economic science descends from Smith through Malthus to Senior, while another branch through Ricardo to Mill has put as much error into the science as they have truth.[22]

Then too there is the celebrated passage in the Preface to the second edition (1879) of Jevons's *The Theory of Political Economy* in which he refers to Ricardo as "that able but wrong-headed man" who had "shunted the car of economic science onto a wrong line." Again, he says in another letter: ". . . the fact is my attack on Mill is as much a matter of the heart as the head . . ."[23] After perusing the writings which are devoted particularly to criticism of Mill, the reader can

---

[20] Jevons to W. Summers, December 16, 1874, *Letters & Journal of W. Stanley Jevons,* edited by Harriet A. Jevons (London: Macmillan, 1886) p. 329.

["Great as my respect for Mill's straightforward character is, I fear that his intellect if good originally was misused in youth." Jevons to Sir Anthony Musgrave, February 21, 1876, in Craufurd D. W. Goodwin, *Economic Enquiry in Australia* (Durham, N. C.: Duke University Press, 1965) p. 541.]

[21] Jevons to Foxwell, February 7, 1875, *Letters & Journal,* p. 331. [Foxwell (1849-1936) is best known as a famous collector of rare books on economics. He was appointed a lecturer of St. John's College in 1875; thirty years later he was also made Director of Economic Studies of the college. In 1876 he also began a lifelong connection with University College, London. That year during the illness of Jevons he gave the lectures on political economy and in 1881 he succeeded Jevons in the professorship. When the London School of Economics and Political Science was established in 1895 he also lectured there. In 1907 he and Edwin Cannan were made professors of political economy in the University of London. He contributed to the fields of money, socialism and economic history.

In 1886 Foxwell wrote "There is no doubt Mill is dead in this country. The mathematical for price theory, the historical for practical questions — this is what we are all coming to agree on." Foxwell to Léon Walras, November 26, 1886 in *Correspondence of Léon Walras and Related Papers,* ed. by William Jaffé, 3 volumes (Amsterdam: North Holland, 1965) II, p. 750.]

[22] Jevons to Foxwell, November 16, 1875, *Letters & Journal,* p. 344.

[23] Jevons to E. J. Broadfield, April 7, 1878, *Letters & Journal,* p. 385.

hardly avoid concluding that it is indeed true that Jevons's feelings were quite as much responsible for his attitude as his strictly intellectual convictions, and that doubtless his state of feeling was aroused by the fact that his own recognition had in considerable measure been delayed by virtue of the fact that the opinions which he formed were somewhat heterodox in color and so not readily acceptable. He says:

> The Mill faction never scrupled at putting their lecturers and examiners wherever they could, but I believe it only requires a little clear logic and a little time to overthrow them.[24]

Political economy at Jevons's time. High reputation among practical men— particularly statesmen (economists as statesmen—Cobden, Bright, J. S. Mill, Gladstone?). The triumph of free trade "proved" political economy. Reaction of the practical campaign for reform upon political economy as a science had been unfavorable. Theory had hardened into dogma. Spirit of inquiry, the skeptical frame of mind had yielded to desire to present a united front to the enemy. Exaltation of authority. Proper business of economists was not further investigation so much as inculcation and popularization of certain established "truths"—Malthusianism, *laissez-faire* in general and free trade and futility of trade unionism in particular. Mill's *Principles of Political Economy* the accepted authority: combination of pure theory learned from Adam Smith, Malthus, Ricardo, with slight modifications from Senior. Did not represent the best doctrine already expounded on all points; e.g., Mill's ideas about relation between supply and demand, and cost of production not as clear as Malthus's. Mill's social philosophy learned from Bentham with modifications from Comte. Distinguishing feature of *Principles* according to Mill is distinction between character of laws of production and laws of distribution. Important because it pointed to possibility and method of social reform. Allowed Mill to cherish hope of indefinite progress through education. Even sex instinct, which gave pessimistic note to Malthus and Ricardo, might be brought under control of reason. Popular success of the book: First edition (two volumes), 1848, seventh edition, 1870; popular edition in one volume, 1865, reprinted six times by November 1871. Brilliantly written. Mill taught as one having authority. Expounding a virtually completed system. Nothing in the theory of value remaining to be cleared up. Success reinforced by Mill's great reputation as a logician, ethicist and philosopher. He ruled the social sciences in the universities. Fawcett and Sidgwick at Cambridge were his pupils. Young liberals like John Morley and James Bryce looked to him for inspiration. "The Mill Despotism." It aroused Jevons's ire—in logic as well as in economics. Was beginning to yield a little. Mill gave up wages fund theory after attracks by Longe and Thornton. Cairnes had introduced non-competing groups in his *Leading Principles of Political Economy*. Jevons proposed far more fundamental changes.[24a]

This innovator in economic theory, W. Stanley Jevons, was a person with quite a different type of background and experience from any of

---

[24] Jevons to Foxwell, November 14, 1879, *Letters & Journal*, p. 409.
[24a] Outline, November 20, 1916.

the economists with whom we have dealt heretofore.[25] He came from a Welsh family. His father was an iron merchant, an ardent Unitarian, very much interested, it appears, in the affairs of his chapel. He was also a writer on legal and economic topics.[26] Stanley was the ninth of eleven children, only five of whom lived beyond babyhood. His mother died when he was ten years old. He was brought up by an older sister. When he was thirteen his father failed in business, largely as a result of the railway crisis of 1847, and the family circumstances suffered a serious change for the worse. The boy, when he was fifteen, was sent to London to prepare to attend University College, [where several of his cousins had also been pupils]. He came from a dissenting family—Unitarians—not the kind of people who usually sent their sons to Oxford or Cambridge. Moreover, the financial conditions resulting from his father's failure would presumably have made it difficult for him to attend one of the greater universities. He was a very studious young man. His family saw the importance of giving him the finest education within their power, and University College seemed to them to offer the best opportunities.

He spent a year in a preparatory school, University College School, and when he was sixteen entered University College where he stayed two and a half years.[27] Up to this time he had been interested in botany, but now he was attracted to chemistry. He did so well in the classes, especially in the laboratory work, that the professor of chemistry, Thomas Graham [who was also a consultant assayer and later master of the Royal Mint] recommended him as one of two assayers for the newly established branch of the mint at Sydney, Australia,

---

[25] The main source for biographical material is *Letters & Journal* (1886); consult also J. M. Keynes, "W. Stanley Jevons, 1853-1882; A Centenary Allocution on his Life and Work as an Economist and Statistician," *Journal of the Royal Statistical Society,* 1936; [reprinted in Keynes's *Essays in Biography,* new edition, edited by Geoffrey Keynes (New York: Horizon Press, 1951) pp. 255-309].

[26] His father wrote among other things a pamphlet *The Prosperity of the Landholders not Dependent on the Corn Laws* (1840). His grandfather on his mother's side was [William Roscoe of Liverpool, "the rediscoverer of the Italian Renaissance, a great collector and patron of the arts, a poet, and fervid social reformer, and a lawyer and banker by profession." (Mrs. Rosamond Könekamp, "William Stanley Jevons (1835-1883): Some Biographical Notes," *The Manchester School,* September 1962, p. 252) hereafter referred to as Könekamp, "William Stanley Jevons . . ."

Roscoe has an enduring claim as a historian for his *Life of Lorenzo de Medici* and *The Life and Pontificate of Leo X.* He made a large fortune which enabled him to retire early, but he was enticed back into business and lost his wealth in the crisis of 1816.]

[27] [He had previously gone for a time in 1846-1847 to the Mechanics Institute School in his native Liverpool where Hodgson was headmaster. Hodgson taught Jevons English and composition, and thought well of him; and Jevons would have liked to continue at the school.]

where gold had been discovered in 1850-1851.[28] Graham must have had a great deal of confidence in young Jevons, who was only eighteen years old at the time the recommendation was made. The job paid a handsome salary—from £600 to £700 per year. [This would be from £3000 to £3500 today (1962)].[29]

[It did mark some change in Jevons's plans. He had intended to leave University College at the end of the 1853 session and enter some business in Liverpool where he expected he could make a fortune rapidly and then retire to devote himself exclusively to his studies which in the interim he would continue at night.] The mint job had the disadvantage that Australia seemed so far away from civilization. But his father persuaded him to accept the post. It seemed to offer a much larger income than he could expect to make in any other occupation at the time, and a sum which was much needed inasmuch as there was a younger brother and sister to be helped with their education. He felt it his duty to the family to go. [He quickly finished his training as an assayer and by October Graham certified that Jevons was fully equipped to accept the responsibilities of the post. His departure, however, was delayed for a year, because the construction of the mint at Sydney was far from completed.] He used part of his time by taking a diploma in assaying at Paris. He came back to London, and sailed for Sydney just before his nineteenth birthday, June 29, 1854, and arrived at Sydney on October 16, 1854. He found his office very satisfactory, particularly, because after he had attained some technical skill in assaying he could do all the work that came to him in a comparatively short number of hours. He had no intention of staying permanently in the colony. He lived a secluded, studious life; avoided society systematically, worked hard, saved his money; and just as soon as his savings amounted to enough to give him some confidence in his ability to carry out the plan of life he had already set on, he planned to go back to London and start over again at the bottom of the ladder.

Meanwhile he developed a keen interest in meteorology. He was a

---

[28] [This was the first branch mint in Australia. It was closed in 1926. "Most of the initial appointments were of Royal Engineers and a few technicians from Town Hill; among them a youth, chosen for one of the two assayerships, threw in his hand after five years and returned to London and journalism, to win fame as the economist and statistician, Professor Stanley Jevons, F.R.S." Sir John Craig, *The Mint* (Cambridge: Cambridge University Press, 1953) p. 386.]

[29] [The position was not originally salaried. Each assayer would get a retainer of £100 a year and the rest was to be earned by piece-rate assaying, both for the mint and private persons. After Jevons reached Australia he agreed to work for the government exclusively at a fixed salary of £675. (Könekamp, "William Stanley Jevons . . .", pp. 256-257).]

boy of rather varied interests. When very young he had been much concerned with botany, and when he got to University College he was fascinated by chemistry. Then moving from England to Australia where the climate was different in character he became interested in another subject. In his characteristic fashion he began constructive work in the field that seemed to him very interesting. He got the necessary instruments and began to make careful day by day records of temperature and barometric pressure and precipitation. Presently he began publishing the results of his observations. His first considerable paper to be put into an Australian almanac just at the time of his leaving was called "Some Data Concerning the Climate of Australia and New Zealand," which appeared in Waugh's *Australian Almanac for the year 1859*.[30]

His other intellectual interests, however, were developing at the same time that he was working in the mint and making these observations on the weather. He came to the conclusion that he needed far more analytical training than he had so far had; and presently he began thinking about doing systematic work in political economy. We can date the time rather exactly from his letters. It was in 1857, when he was twenty-two years old. [He noted in his diary under the heading "work to be done during 1857," the following item: "Write work on Formal Economics." He had the previous year begun reading the leading works in classical economics, starting with Adam Smith's *The Wealth of Nations* and going on to Ricardo, John Stuart Mill, Harriet Martineau and others. In recording on February 13 the purchase of J. R. McCulloch's two volume *A Statistical Account of the British Empire*, he wrote that "in getting these as well as other expensive works, I wish to turn my attention to statistics."][31] As a result of this interest in economics he determined to shift his field from the natural to the moral sciences, as they were then called. In a characteristic letter in 1858 to his sister Henrietta, who had also begun studying economics, he writes:

> I am glad you find political economy tolerable. *The Wealth of Nations* is perhaps one of the driest on the subject. You will perceive that *economy*, scientifically speaking, is a very contracted science.

All this is very delightful to anyone who has just been reading Jevons's book, written some thirteen years later. In his early twenties he had

---

[30] [A sketch of Jevons's career in Sydney with a bibliography of his writings in Australia is in J. A. La Nauze, *Political Economy in Australia* (Melbourne: Melbourne University Press, 1949) pp. 26-44.]

[31] [Quoted in Könekamp, "William Stanley Jevons . . .," p. 258.]

the characteristic turn of mind which reveals itself sharply in his mature work. He continues:

> it is in fact a sort of vague mathematics which calculates the causes and effects of man's industry, and shows how it may best be applied. There are a multitude of allied branches of knowledge connected with man's condition; the relation of these to political economy is analogous to the connection of mechanics, astronomy, optics, sound, heat, and every other branch more or less of physical science, with pure mathematics. I have an idea, which I do not object to mention to you, that my insight into the foundations and nature of the knowledge of man is deeper than that of most men or writers. In fact, I think that it is my mission to apply myself to such subjects, and it is my intention to do so. You are desirous of engaging in the practically useful; you may feel assured that to extend and perfect the abstract or the detailed and practical knowledge of man and society is perhaps the most useful and necessary work in which any one can now engage. There are plenty of people engaged with physical science, and practical science and arts may be left to look after themselves, but thoroughly to understand the principles of society appears to me now the most cogent business.[32]

His lonely life led him to a good deal of introspection, and presently he made in a letter to both his sisters an analysis of his own aims and powers.

> I have but a poor memory, and consequently can retain only a small portion of learning at any one time, which great numbers of other persons possess. But I am not so much a storehouse of goods as I am a machine for making those goods. Give me a few facts or materials, and I can work them up into a smoothly-arranged and finished fabric of theory, or can turn them out in a shape which is something new. My mind is of the most regular structure, and I have such a strong disposition to classify things as is sometimes almost painful. I also think that if in anything I have a chance of acquiring the power, it is that I have some *originality*, and can strike out new things. This consists not so much in quickness of forming new thoughts or opinions, but in seizing upon one or two of them and developing them into something symmetrical. It is like a kaleidoscope; just put a bent pin in, or any little bit of rubbish, and a perfectly new and symmetrical pattern will be produced.[33]

That again seems to be a very just judgment upon himself.

At the end of approximately five years, as he had planned, Jevons resigned his position at the mint, rejected a promising business opening, and started home to resume his studies. On his way he visited the Australian gold fields, Peru, Panama, the West Indies and the United States. He came to the United States primarily to see his elder brother, Herbert, who had just taken up a claim of forty acres in Minnesota, and Stanley went out there for a brief visit. Finally

---

[32] Jevons to Henrietta, February 28, 1858, *Letters & Journal*, p. 101.

[33] Jevons to Lucy and Henrietta, November 17, 1857, *Letters & Journal*, pp. 96-97.

he reached Liverpool in September, 1859, when he was twenty-four years old. With his sisters he took economical lodgings and returned to his work at University College. He studied Greek, Latin, German, more particularly mathematics, and most of all moral philosophy and political economy—the latter mostly on his own.

The first definite idea of his theory of political economy occurred to him soon after his return to London while he was still a student. Fortunately we have definite knowledge of that, from a letter to his brother Herbert (June 1, 1860), who was still in the United States:

> During the last session I have worked a good deal at political economy; in the last few months I have fortunately struck out what I have no doubt is the *true Theory of Economy,* so thorough-going and consistent, that I cannot now read other books on the subject without indignation. While the theory is entirely mathematical in principle, I show, at the same time, how the data of calculation are so complicated as to be for the present hopeless. Nevertheless, I obtain from the mathematical principles all the chief laws at which political economists have previously arrived, only arranged in a series · of definitions, axioms, and theories almost as rigorous and connected as if they were so many geometrical problems. One of the most important axioms is, that as the quantity of any commodity, for instance, plain food, which a man has to consume, increases, so the utility or benefit derived from the last portion used decreases in degree.

There is already the fundamental tenor of his theory. This theory, he added, had "always been assumed by political economists under the more complex form and name of the Law of Supply and Demand." He went on: "I have no idea of letting these things lie by till somebody else had the advantage of them, and shall therefore try to publish them next spring."[34] That he did by sending a short paper "Notice of a General Mathematical Theory of Political Economy" to be read before Section F (Economic Science and Statistics) at the 1862 meeting of the British Association for the Advancement of

---

[34] Jevons to Herbert Jevons, June 1, 1860, *Letters & Journal,* pp. 151-152.

[J. A. La Nauze, through access to the diaries of Jevons, has been able to date the event a little more precisely. The first entry in February 1860 reads as follows: "3rd to 5th including Saturday and Sunday—was almost entirely engaged in commencing a work on Pol. Econ. to be established on a demonstrative basis, in the form of connected and distinct propositions. Value to be established on the basis of labour—and the problems of rent, wages, interest, etc., to be solved as mathematical functions. Am very sanguine of its success." On February 19, the entry reads: "At home all day, working chiefly at economy, arriving as I suppose at a true comprehension of *Value,* regarding which I have lately very much blundered." (Quotations are in La Nauze, "The Conception of Jevons's Utility Theory," *Economica,* November 1953, p. 356.)]

Science. He wrote in his journal that the paper was received "without a word of interest or belief."[35]

Meanwhile his university work had been prospering. He was awarded the B.A. and the Ricardo Scholarship in Political Economy, in 1860, and received a gold medal and the M.A. degree in 1863.[36] Before the completion of his formal studies, however, Jevons had already made another of his characteristic switches in occupation; he had become enamored of statistical researches. In October 1860, while working for his M.A., he began to make diagrams representing various economic statistics: the volume of trade, Bank of England returns, interest rates, etc. Presently he projected a statistical atlas,[37] but he could get no publisher. This led him to compromise by issuing at his own expense separate sheets, of which he managed to print two diagrams in 1862 and sell a few copies of each. He had hoped that this novel scheme of graphically representing fluctuations in reference to important economic processes of interest to the business community

[35] Entry, December 31, 1862, *Letters & Journal*, p. 175. The "Notice," an abstract of his paper was published the following year in the proceedings of the association ("Notices and Abstracts of Miscellaneous Communications to the Sections," *Report of the Thirty-Second Meeting of the British Association for the Advancement of Science*, 1862 (London: Murray, 1863) pp. 158-159.

The paper was printed in the June 1866 issue of the *Journal of the Statistical Society of London*, pp. 282-287, and is reprinted in *The Theory of Political Economy* (London: Macmillan, 1871; 4th ed., edited by H. Stanley Jevons, 1911) pp. 303-314, under the title, "Brief Account of a General Mathematical Theory of Political Economy." All references to *The Theory of Political Economy* are to the 4th ed.

[36] [Jevons received his M.A. in mental philosophy and mathematics. Mental philosophy, it appears, included logic and the other branches of philosophy and also political economy. At the time, the professor of political economy was Jacob Waley, who gave twenty lectures on the subject, on the basis of John Stuart Mill's *Principles of Political Economy*.]

[37] [Jevons to Herbert Jevons, April 7, 1861, *Letters & Journal*, p. 157. It was a common view in Jevons's day that "whether commercial revolutions be or be not as necessary and inevitable as are the flux and efflux of the tide, forms a curious and doubtful question. Certain it is that they make their appearance in the ordinary course of affairs, if not at periods exactly regular, at least in cycles of which it is not difficult to determine the average extent. Difficult though it be accurately to determine the principles which regulate them, they are usually found preceded by symptoms and followed by results bearing an analogy, if not a resemblance to each other. A close attention to them on the part of our business men would go far towards the dissemination of that sound information respecting the laws of trade, which would greatly mitigate the severity of commercial revulsions." (Quoted from the London *News* in Hodgson, *The True Scope of Economic Science*, p. 8.)

From the standpoint of statistical techniques, Jevons, in his use of diagrams, was reviving William Playfair's work in statistical graphics, or as Playfair called it, "lineal arithmetic." Jevons informed the London Statistical Society in 1879 that "Englishmen had lost sight of the fact that William Playfair who has never been heard of in this generation produced statistical atlases and statistical curves" that were worthy of serious critical attention. (Jevons's "Discussion on Dr. Guy's Paper," *Journal of the Statistical Society*, September 1879) p. 657; see also H. G. Funkhouser, "Graphical Representation of Statistical Data," *Osiris*, vol. 3 (1937) pp. 292-293.]

might find a ready market and yield him some income. But he was before the time of any keen general interest in such services.[38]

In September 1862, along with his mathematical theory, he sent to Section F of the British Association a second paper "On the Study of Periodic Commercial Fluctuations, with Five Diagrams," which the secretary wrote him was approved of.[39] That paper has considerable interest, because it is one of the earliest definite attempts to measure what now are called seasonal variations, one of the characteristic types of fluctuations of peculiar interest to all students of time series. This is perhaps an appropriate point to remark that Jevons never lost his keen interest in the technique of statistics, and that among the various services which he rendered to the development of economics perhaps his work in this field is as valuable as that which he accomplished in what we ordinarily think of and what he certainly thought of as the different field of economic theory proper. He made early studies not only of seasonal variations but also of secular trends, a subject which he dealt with very ably in *The Coal Question, An Inquiry Concerning the Progress of the Nation and the Probable Exhaustion of our Coal-Mines* (1865). His important work in developing the technique of making price index numbers (a rather technical matter) is widely known. He was one of the first economists to see that the general theory of probability which had been developed primarily by mathematicians and then applied to the study of such social phenomena as births and deaths and the reliability of witnesses by mathematicians, sociologists, and anthropologists might also be applied to the treatment of economic data.

Meanwhile in April 1863 Jevons published a pamphlet of less than 100 pages which attracted a great deal more attention than anything he had so far issued. This was the paper called *A Serious Fall in the Value of Gold Ascertained, and its Social Effects Set Forth, With Two Diagrams.* By 1863 the new supplies of gold from California and Australia had begun to produce a considerable change in the level of wholesale prices the world around, and several economists had been engaged in discussing this general subject, the influence of the new

---

[38] [The two were: *Diagram showing all the Weekly Accounts of the Bank of England, since the passing of the Bank Act of 1844, with the Amount of Bank of England, Private, and Joint Stock Bank Promissory Notes in Circulation during each week, and the Bank Minimum Rate of Discount;* and *Diagram showing the Price of the English Funds, the Price of Wheat, the Number of Bankruptcies, and the Rate of Discount, monthly, since 1731; so far as the same has been ascertained.*]

[39] A brief extract was published in the *Report of the Thirty-Second Meeting of the British Association for the Advancement of Science,* 1862, pp. 157-158; it is published in full in *Investigations in Currency and Finance,* edited by H. S. Foxwell (London: Macmillan, 1884) pp. 1-12.

gold upon price levels. He attacked the problem on the statistical side; it was for this purpose that he made his first index numbers. (He introduced the use of the geometrical mean.) He was able to demonstrate with a degree of certainty and precision which no one else working at the time had dreamed of attempting, not only that prices had risen in England since the late 40's and the early 50's, but he was also able to say approximately how great the rise had been—a notable contribution both to the monetary discussions of the time and to the technique of quantitative economics.[40] The monograph attracted considerable attention, because the subject interested so many people, and he was encouraged to believe that it might help him to obtain a hearing for his abstruse economic theory.

After receiving his M.A. in 1863, it became a question with him how he could make a living. He had been very careful of his money and still had some left, but he was unwilling to trench upon his savings further if he could help it, and the money he had saved in Australia would not enable him to devote himself to unremunerative scientific investigations. He tried writing for the popular magazines, but he was soon forced to recognize that neither his interests nor his literary style were adapted to such work. Then he tried setting up a literary agency. He offered to undertake researches in the British Museum on any subject for people who were unable or unwilling to do such work for themselves. But that scheme also brought him very slender returns and poor prospects for the future.

While he was in a very uncertain frame of mind, he received through a cousin an offer to go to twelve-year-old Owens College, Manchester (now Manchester University) in 1863 as a tutor.[41] The job was a humble one. [His specific duty was to "assist backward students, and to do this in any of the subjects taught by the six professors."[42] His income depended upon the number of students in his classes.]

Jevons disliked very much the idea of leaving the British Museum,

---

[40] [Jevons estimated that the value of gold had fallen at the least 9 per cent between 1845-1850 and 1860-1862. He thought that the gold standard should be left alone.

John Stuart Mill in testifying before the Select Committee on the Bank Acts of 1857 declared that it was a greatly "unsettled . . . point yet, to what extent general prices in this country have been raised by the gold discoveries." Mill's testimony reprinted under the title "The Bank Acts" in his *Essays on Economics and Society* ed. by J. M. Robson, with an introduction by Lord Robbins, 2 volumes (Toronto: University of Toronto Press, 1967) II, p. 516.]

[41] [The college, which was established in 1851, bore the name of its founder John Owens, a Manchester business man who acquired a substantial fortune, primarily as a merchant and cotton spinner. Like University College, London, it was non-sectarian.

The cousin was his fellow student at University College, Henry (later Sir Henry) Roscoe, professor of chemistry at Owens College.]

[42] [Könekamp, "William Stanley Jevons . . ." p. 264.]

where he would have been happy to spend all his days, but being unwilling to encroach further on his savings he accepted the offer with some reluctance. From 1863 to 1876, that is, for the thirteen most active years of his scientific life, he lived in Manchester as a teacher in a small college. [His income from classes for the first year was nearly £100, which with his private income of £70 gave a total of £170.] But his fortunes rapidly improved. [Jevons was soon teaching as a substitute or deputy for the professor of logic and the professor of political economy.[43] He supplemented his income by what he described as a "small professorship" of logic, mental and moral philosophy at Queen's College in Liverpool.] In 1866 he became professor of logic and of mental and moral philosophy and of political economy and Cobden lecturer at Manchester.[44] His total income from 1866 on from teaching was in the neighborhood of £300 a year and to this he could add £108 from investments, enough to enable him to marry, as he thought, and in 1867 when he was thirty-two he married Harriet Ann Taylor, the daughter of the founder and proprietor of the *Manchester Guardian,* the most famous of all English provincial newspapers.[45]

Jevons's duties as a teacher were very heavy; he overworked, in-

---

[43] [In 1854 the trustees created the chair of political economy and commercial science and to it appointed Richard Copely Christy, who a few months before had been given the chair of history and a few months later received also the chair of jurisprudence. He was primarily a lawyer, and not a specialist in political economy; he gave only a few lectures on the subject.

A benefactor of the college J. B. Smith stated that the failure to specify the teaching of political economy originally had been an oversight. He said: "There is one omission, if I know anything of the views of our late friend Owens, that he would have supplied; *viz.,* a course of Political Economy—a science of the highest importance to the welfare of every state, one with which the name of Manchester will be ever identified and one that is more than ever necessary to teach the rising generation as the best means of counteracting the dangerous spread of Socialist doctrine." (Cited from ms. in Manchester Central Library in Edward Fiddes, *Chapters in the History of Owens College and of Manchester University, 1851-1914* (Manchester: Manchester University Press, 1937) p. 149.]

[44] [In 1866 the Cobden Memorial Committee gave the college an endowment which eventually amounted to a chair in political economy on condition that the professor deliver each term a series of weekly evening lectures for teachers in the lower schools in order that they might afterwards "introduce the teaching of this important subject into elementary schools." Jevons, *Political Economy,* Macmillan's series of Science Primers (London: Macmillan, 1878) preface; Joseph Thompson, *The Owens College* (Manchester: Cornish, 1886) p. 288.

To the evening class, Jevons devoted one hour a week. The day class occupied two hours a week. In his last year at Owens 1875-1876, he was assisted by Elijah Helm. Originally Jevons used as a textbook McCulloch's edition of Adam Smith's *The Wealth of Nations.* Later he substituted John Stuart Mill's *Principles of Political Economy.*] On his use of orthodox textbooks see the amusing "Jevons and The Establishment" signed "Clovis" in *The American Scholar,* Winter, 1964-1965, pp. 109-111.

[45] ["His own capital was small, but his wife had some means of her own, and Jevons augmented their income by good investments of their savings." (J. M. Keynes, "W. Stanley Jevons . . ." *Essays in Biography,* p. 257.)]

jured his health permanently, and had to go at a slower pace for the future. He managed to accomplish a great deal both of teaching and writing, but at a heavy cost. His health was precarious for most of that time; and at frequent intervals he had to change the currents of his thoughts in order to provide mental rest. He was one of those men who are troubled by any interesting ideas which occur to them, and when these absorbing problems drove him nearly to desperation, the only way in which he could relax mentally was to go off on a trip somewhere, see new things, and force himself to think about matters of a less interesting kind. He was a person of intellectual passions.

In 1865 he published, as already noted, *The Coal Question*. It is to this day an extremely interesting and valuable treatise on a realistic problem of great social importance to England. The issue was how long the nation's coal deposits would last. English industry by that time had already taken on the features which have come to characterize it; it was centering upon coal and iron and their use. Coal supplies were remarkably ample for the extent of the country's territory, but people began to fear that the time must come sooner or later when the deposits which could be economically worked would be more or less depleted, and the question was how soon that would come and what effects would it have on England's economic problem. Jevons worked out the secular trends, the probable future trends of coal output in Great Britain, and discussed the whole problem in a thorough, scientific fashion. The treatise elicited the favorable notice of the great leader and financial expert of the Liberal party, William E. Gladstone,[46] and was favorably mentioned in Parliament by John Stuart Mill, and reinforced the position which Jevons had established by the publication of his earlier paper, *A Serious Fall in the Value of Gold Ascertained*.[47]

---

[46] [Gladstone served as chancellor of the exchequer as well as prime minister when the Liberal party held power.]

[47] [Jevons wrote in the preface of the second edition (1866) "The manner in which Mr. Mill mentioned this work in his remarkable speech on the National Debt (House of Commons, April 17th, 1866) was in the highest degree gratifying. I have found indeed, that most of what I said concerning the National Debt was unconsciously derived from Mr. Mill's own works. I have repeated it, unchanged in this edition, with the exception of adding references. The fact is that no writer can approach the subject of Political Economy without falling into the deepest obligations to Mr. Mill, and it is impossible as it is needless always to specify what we owe to a writer of such great eminence, and such widespread influence." (*The Coal Question* (London: Macmillan, 1865; 3rd edition 1906, edited by A. W. Flux.) p. xxxix.

Jevons proposed "to compensate posterity" for our present lavish use of cheap coal by reducing or paying off the national debt. "An annual appropriation towards the reduction of the debt would serve the three purposes of adding to the productive capital of the country, of slightly checking our present too rapid progress, and of lessening the future difficulties of the country." (*The Coal Question*, p. 448.)]

Meanwhile, the duty of teaching logic had turned Jevons's attention once more in a new direction, and for several years he gave most of his working time to elaborating a new logical system. He had been greatly impressed by George Boole's symbolic logic, *An Investigation of the Laws of Thought,* and he tried to work out Boole's ideas and elaborate them in a fuller form. In December 1863 he published *Pure Logic, or The Logic of Quality Apart from Quantity with Remarks on Boole's System and on the Relation of Logic and Mathematics.*

In 1865 he began working on "a reasoning machine, or logical abacus, adapted to show the working of Boole's Logic in a half mechanical manner."[48]

[As a leading disciple wrote, Jevons's system of logic is based upon the generally received axioms that "whatever is, is," that "a thing cannot both be and not be," and that "a thing must either be or not be." But to these he adds the principle of "the Substitution of Similars," that is to say, the axiom that whatever is true of A is true of everything that cannot be distinguished from A in the relation contemplated. Thus if B is identical with A then B may be substituted for A, in any assertion that has been shown to be true of A. The next and crucial step is to bring every proposition into the form of an assertion of an identity. . . . Having reduced deductive reasoning to a mechanical process, Jevons found no insuperable difficulty in constructing a syllogising machine; but he regarded this triumph as possessing little practical, though considerable theoretical significance.][49]

In 1866 he hit on "the great and universal principle of all reasoning," to quote from his own discussion; namely, "The Substitution of Similars," an idea that he developed at considerable length in a book of that title three years later.[50] All this work led up to his *Elementary Lessons in Logic* (1870) and to his far more important book, at least of his studies in logic, *The Principles of Science; a Treatise on Logic and Scientific Method* (1874).[51]

After he had satisfied himself about the fundamental importance of his great discovery that the substitution of similars is the fundamental principle in all reasoning, he turned back for a while to his economic

---

[48] Jevons to Herbert Jevons. May 25, 1865, *Letters & Journal,* p. 205.

[49] [Philip H. Wicksteed, "Jevons, William Stanley," *Palgrave's Dictionary of Political Economy,* 2nd ed. Edited by Henry Higgs, 3 volumes (London: Macmillan, 1925-1926) II, pp. 475-476.]

[50] Entry in Journal, December 4, 1866, *Letters & Journal,* p. 231. The full title is *The Substitution of Similars, or The True Principle of Reasoning, Derived From a Modification of Aristotle's Dictum* (1869).

[51] [It has been claimed that "because of his work and speculations in the field of mechanized reasoning, Jevons may be said to be one of the ancestors of modern computer theory." (W. Mays, "Jevons's Conception of Scientific Method," *The Manchester School.* September 1962, p. 223). Jevons's logical machine is in the History of Science Museum, Oxford.]

theory pure and simple. His wife says that the winter of 1870-1871 was devoted entirely to the writing of *The Theory of Political Economy*. The work was of such absorbing interest to him that he made rapid progress with it to the detriment of his health; it was published in 1871 when Jevons was thirty-six years of age. The reception of the treatise was once more grievously disappointing. Three years later on July 7, 1874, he wrote to the future Dutch economist, Johan Baron d'Aulnis de Bourouill, then a student in the faculty of law of the University of Leiden,

> It is quite true that what I have written on the subject has received little or no attention in England, and by those who have noticed it the theory has been generally rejected, or even ridiculed. ... While I am not aware that my views have been accepted by any well-known English economist, there are a certain number of younger mathematicians and economists who have entered into the subject, and treated it in a very different manner.[52]

George H. Darwin (later Sir George), the son of the great naturalist, was one of those who was interested in the book.[53]

But at the beginning the leading British economists were quite skeptical of its importance. Alfred Marshall whose first publication was an elaborate review of the book said "the main value of the book ... does not lie in its more prominent theories, but in its original treatment of a number of minor points."[54] Cairnes took a more critical attitude, [and John Stuart Mill informed his disciple:

> I have not seen Mr. Jevons' book, but as far as I can judge from such notices of it as have reached me, I do not expect that I shall think favourably of it. Jevons is a man of some ability, but he seems to me to have a mania for encumbering questions with useless complications and with a notation implying the existence of greater precision in the data than the questions admit of. His speculations on Logic ... are infested in an extraordinary degree with this vice. It is one pre-eminently at variance with the wants of the time,

---

[52] Jevons to d'Aulnis de Bourouill, July 7, 1874, *Letters & Journal*, pp. 309, 311. [Johan Baron d'Aulnis de Bourouill (1850-1930) received a doctorate from Leyden in 1874; he became, in 1878, professor of political history, statistics and economics at the University of Utrecht. In his doctoral dissertation, *Het inkomen der maatschappij* (1874), he embraced the doctrines of Jevons and his contemporary in the development of utility theory, Léon Walras (who is later discussed by Professor Mitchell). He had read Jevons's treatise at the suggestion of the leading Dutch economist of the day, N. G. Pierson (1839-1909) then a member of the board of directors of the Nederlandische Bank. (See R. D. Collison Black, "W. S. Jevons and the Economists of his Time," *The Manchester School*, September 1962, pp. 208-209.)]

[53] [Darwin became professor of astronomy at Cambridge University and served as president of both the Royal Astronomical Society and the British Association for the Advancement of Science.] He published an elaborate defense of Jevons's treatise ("The Theory of Exchange Value," *The Fortnightly Review*, February 1875, pp. 243-253).

[54] "Mr. Jevons' Theory of Political Economy," *The Academy*, April 1, 1872; reprinted in *Memorials of Alfred Marshall*, ed. A. C. Pigou (London: Macmillan, 1925) p. 95.

which demands that scientific deductions should be made as simply and as easily intelligible as they can be made without ceasing to be scientific.[55]

Jevons's old preparatory school teacher and then professor of political economy at Edinburgh, Hodgson, said of the book in a private letter that Jevons's view was sound but not new.

> It is the most usual tendency of ardent reformers in science— of men who think for themselves, and who, *in that sense,* are original —to fancy that they are more original, *in the other sense* of the word, than they really are. They magnify the differences, and underrate, perhaps ignore, the agreements. Jevons' doctrine of value is that of Whately, Bailey, Bastiat, M'Leod, and last, and least, your present correspondent. I frankly adopt Jevons' assertion: "I hold labour to be determined by the value of the produce, not the value of the producer, viz., that of the labourer."
> There is no real difficulty about the cost of production and its connection with value if only you begin at the right end of the question; the whole thing lies in a nutshell, as Whately has put it; he says, (I do not quote the exact words), "Men dive for pearls because they are valuable; pearls are not valuable because men dive for them." Once grasp that proposition, and the difficulties vanish. The cost of production is in the long run the limit of production, and for an obvious reason, that is to say, that if the cost of production rise above the value, or the value fall below the cost of production, production will be discouraged and suspended, or perhaps abolished. To make cost of production, on the other hand, the regulator of value, involves this absurdity, that, if you only increase the cost of production, the value will rise accordingly, which is no more true than that, if you lessen the cost, the value will necessarily (and in the absence of competition) fall. . . . Adam Smith, Ricardo, and De Quincey, and J. S. Mill have unravelled the whole question. There is much that is admirable in Jevons' book.[56]

---

[55] [Mill to Cairnes, December 5, 1871, in George O'Brien, "J. S. Mill and J. E. Cairnes," *Economica,* November, 1943, p. 274.] For Cairnes on Jevons see Cairnes, "New Theories in Political Economy," *The Fortnightly Review,* January 1872, pp. 71-75, and *Some Leading Principles of Political Economy.*

[56] [Hodgson to John Mills, November 30, 1871 in Isobel Mills. *From Tinder-Box to the "Larger" Light; Threads from the Life of John Mills, Banker* (Manchester: Sherratt and Hughes, 1899) pp. 325-326.

Whately said: "It is not that pearls fetch a high price *because* men have dived for them; but on the contrary men dive for them because they fetch a high price." Whately, *Introductory Lectures on Political Economy* (London: Parker, 1831; 4th ed. 1855) p. 167.

John Mills (1821-1896) was a friend and correspondent of Jevons as well as Hodgson. He helped stimulate Jevons's researches in business cycle theory through his famous paper of 1867, "On Credit Cycles and the Origin of Commercial Panics," (*Transactions of the Manchester Statistical Society,* 1867-1868, pp. 5-40.]

It elaborated on "the 'psychological' type of explanation . . . on this view, the fundamental cause of crises lies less in the character or abuse of economic institutions, than in the emotional aberrations to which business judgments are subject. Fair trade breeds optimism, optimism breeds recklessness, recklessness breeds disaster. In their turn, the disasters of a crisis breed pessimism and pessimism breeds stagnation. From depression business picks up only when men's spirits recover on finding that matters have gone less badly than they had feared." Mitchell, *Business Cycles, the Problem and Its Setting* (New York: National Bureau of Economic Research, 1927) p. 9.

The book, however, seems to have enjoyed considerable interest from the start in the United States. Henry Adams, then editor of the influential *The North American Review,* wrote to the famous astronomer and mathematical economist, Simon Newcomb in 1872 as follows: "Would you do for me a notice of Jevons's *Theory of Political Economy,* a book which requires some attention."[57] Newcomb wrote a very appreciative, perceptive review, which also called attention to the early but neglected study by the Frenchman A. A. Cournot *Recherches sur les principes mathématiques de la théorie des richesses* (1838). This review may have suggested Cournot's work to Jevons, who added it to the bibliography of the second edition of *The Theory of Political Economy* (1879); or Jevons may have run across the glowing review of Cournot's book in *The Canadian Journal of Industry, Science and Art,* May 1857, by J. B. Cherriman.]

Not only was comparatively little attention paid to the treatise at home, but also it turned out presently that others had presented the fundamental idea in an elaborate form, notably Hermann Heinrich Gossen (1810-1858) in 1854 in *Entwicklung der Gesetze des menschlichen Verkehrs, und der darausfliessenden Regeln für menschliches Handeln* ("Exposition of the Laws of Human Intercourse and of the Principles of Human Action Arising from Them").[58]

Jevons wrote to his brother Tom about this unpleasant find on August 21, 1878:

> . . . Within the last few days I have had rather a disagreeable incident in the discovery, of an unknown German book, by a man called Gossen, containing a theory of political economy apparently much like mine. There are, in fact, a whole series of books, hitherto quite unknown, even on the Continent, in which the principal ideas of my theory have been foreshadowed. I am therefore in the unfortunate position that the greater number of people think the theory nonsense, and do not understand it, and the rest discover that it is not new.[59]

When *The Theory of Political Economy* had appeared, Jevons turned back to his studies in logic and published in 1874, as noted previously, his chief work in the field, *The Principles of Science.* Meanwhile he had been recognized in a substantially gratifying way by several learned societies. He was made a fellow of the Royal Society

---

[57] [Adams to Newcomb, February 10, 1872, Newcomb Papers Library of Congress. C. S. Peirce, the eminent logician, as early as December 17, 1871, said in reference to his own mathematical formulations "this is all in Cournot." C. S. Eisele, "The Charles S. Peirce-Simon Newcomb Correspondence," *Proceedings of the American Philosophical Society,* October 1957, p. 414.]

[58] Gossen's book has become famous and was reprinted in Germany in 1889 and 1927. On Gossen see appendix three: [See also Emil Kauder, *A History of Marginal Utility Theory* (Princeton, N. J.: Princeton University Press, 1965) pp. 42-51.]

[59] *Letters & Journal,* pp. 387-388.

in 1872, an honorary member of the Political Economy Club of London in 1874 and (through the good offices of Herbert Spencer) he was elected to the Athenaeum Club—one of those special members chosen for distinguished accomplishments in letters and science. He received an LL.D. from Edinburgh in 1876. In that same year he returned to London as professor of political economy at his alma mater, University College, [as the successor of Leonard Courtney later Baron Courtney.[60] He informed the Owens College authorities that he had enjoyed his years at the college but he wished to leave because of a "desire to devote my time, under the most advantageous circumstances, to the literary and scientific work which presses upon me more and more urgently." He seemed to feel that his position in Manchester was "too isolated" and that he should move to London where contacts would be much easier to cultivate. Also his books were now providing a substantial income, especially *Elementary Lessons in Logic,* and he felt that he should write more such books.][61] Furthermore the London post enabled him to get back to the British Museum. Finally, the duties were light; he had to lecture but once a week.[62] Still he found this amount of teaching a strain and in 1881 he resigned his chair, resolving never to lecture again.

[60] [Courtney (1832-1910), lawyer and leader-writer for *The* [London] *Times,* held the post for three years and then resigned to begin a successful career in the House of Commons with the Liberal party.

He generally followed John Stuart Mill on policy matters as well as pure theory, emphasizing in particular that the problem of land policy falls within the proper sphere of government. On monetary policy, he expressed considerable sympathy with the view of the Democratic party candidate for the American presidency in 1896 for a restoration of the old bimetallic standard. So again he like Mill before him and Jevons after him was still "much involved in fears dating from Poor Law reform days. Courtney in 1885 made a long and deeply felt speech against the Medical Relief Bill, a measure to save the worker who sought parish medical relief from losing the franchise; he did so on the ground that such a concession would gravely weaken the character of those who received it." S. G. Checkland, *The Rise of Industrial Society in England: 1815-1885* (New York: St. Martin's Press, 1964) p. 377.]

[61] [Jevons to the Treasurer of Owens College, March 30, 1875 in Thompson, *The Owens College,* p. 569. Könekamp. "William Stanley Jevons . . .," p. 269.

His successor at Owens College was Robert Adamson (1852-1902), who had studied at Edinburgh and Heidelberg. It was Adamson who informed Jevons of Gossen's treatise in 1878. Adamson was much more interested in philosophy than in economics. In 1882 he was able to drop the subject with the appointment of J. E. Crawford Munroe as professor of law and political economy. Since Munroe was primarily interested in law, he gave up political economy in 1890. Political economy was put on a regular basis again in 1893 with the appointment as Cobden Lecturer of Alfred (later Sir Alfred) William Flux (1867-1942) who also taught geography. Five years later he became the first incumbent of the Stanley Jevons Professorship of Political Economy. He is best known for his statistical investigations while serving as Assistant Secretary of the Board of Trade in charge of statistics. Especially notable was his introduction of Jevons's geometrical average into the official index numbers of prices. See T. S. Ashton, *Economic and Social Investigations in Manchester, 1833-1933* (London: King, 1934) p. 98.]

[62] [The income, he estimated in 1880, was £70 a year, *Letters & Journal,* p. 420.]

Jevons's later years from 1875 to 1882 were devoted partly to elaborating his curious sun-spot theory of business cycles. He undertook to demonstrate on a statistical basis that there is a close correspondence between the periods of sun spots and the periods of severe commercial crises. His earlier meteorological studies in Australia may have led him to take up the idea that perhaps fluctuations in business, which he had been studying on a statistical basis, might be accounted for in changes of rainfall and other weather phenomena.[63]

The question as to the changes in the weather still had to be considered. In 1860 Sir William Herschel suggested that changes in sunspots may affect the weather, affecting crops and then prices. This idea, coupled with Samuel Heinrich Schwabe's discovery of 1843 (recognized by the Royal Astronomical Society in 1857) that sunspots are cyclical, "fascinated the speculative mind of . . . Jevons, and led him [beginning in 1875] to the hypothesis that business cycles are caused by solar cycles."[64] He hit upon the notion that weather changes were controlled by alterations in sun-spots. The average duration of the solar period at this time was taken as 10.45 years, and Jevons thought that he could prove statistically that the average period between crises in England for a period of nearly two centuries had been very nearly the same as the average period of the sun-spot cycle. Therefore, he connected the two phenomena in a characteristic and interesting speculation. The sun-spots controlled weather, and weather crops and the price and quantity of harvests are a factor of critical importance to business at large. [As he put this theory in his elementary treatise, *Political Economy:*

> Good vintage years on the continent of Europe and droughts in India, recur every ten or eleven years, and it seems probable that commercial crises are connected with a periodic variation of weather, affecting all parts of the earth, and probably arising from increased waves of heat received from the sun at average intervals of ten years and a fraction. A greater supply of heat increases the harvests, makes capital more abundant and trade more successful, and thus helps to create the hopefulness out of which a bubble arises. A falling off in the sun's heat makes bad harvests and deranges many enterprises in different parts of the world. This is likely to break the bubble and bring on a commercial collapse.][65]

It should be pointed out that,

> Unfortunately for this theory, since 1878 astronomers have revised their computations of the sun-spot cycle, (the average now

---

[63] [See Jevons, "Meteorological Report," *Empire,* March 17, 1858, and "Some Data Concerning the Climate of Australia and New Zealand," *Waugh's Australian Almanac for the Year 1859.* See quotations from these articles in La Nauze, *Political Economy in Australia,* pp. 42-44.]

[64] Mitchell, *Business Cycles, The Problem and its Setting,* p. 12.

[65] [*Political Economy* (London: Macmillan, 1878) p. 120. The treatise was published in Macmillan's series of Science Primers.]

commonly accepted is 11+ years), and commercial cycles have de-
pared still further from the decennial norm. . . .

[Jevons and other pioneering students of the business cycle]
quite naturally . . . overstressed its uniformity in . . . respect [to
duration.] . . .

Influenced by the dominant type of economic theory, these dis-
coverers thought of a "normal" cycle and so simplified their problem—a practice still common. . . . Even the early statistical workers
yielded to the lure of "normality." They were eager to establish the
"periodicity of crises," which was suggested by such crisis dates as
1815, 1825, 1836, 1847, 1857 and 1866. This desire warped their
selection and treatment of data. Jevons had an admirably candid
mind; yet in 1875, when the sun-spot cycle was supposed to last
11.1 years, he was able to get from [J. E.] Thorold Rogers's *History of Agriculture and Prices in England,* a period of 11 years in
price fluctuations, and when the sun-spot cycle was revised to
10.45 years he was able to make the average interval between
English crises 10.466 years.[66] To get this later result, Jevons pur-
posely left out from his list of crises, "a great commercial collapse
in 1810-11 (which will not fit into the decennial series"); he also
omitted the crisis of 1873 and inserted a crisis of 1878, which other
writers do not find.[67]

Another of his occupations in later years was preparing popular
books on logic and economics. On his textbooks in logic especially
Logic (in the Macmillan series of Science Primers, 1876) and *Elementary Lessons in Logic,* two generations of Englishmen and Americans were brought up, and his primer in economics, *Political Economy,*
was also widely used in introductory classes. He also devoted considerable time to new editions of his two most important treatises,
The Principles of Science and *The Theory of Political Economy.*[68]

[Up to 1936 British sales of his books on logic, published by Macmillan were as follows: *Elementary Lessons in Logic,* 130,000; *Logic,*

---

[66] [Jevons wrote to John Mills in 1880, "I now have complete confidence in the
cycle of 10.45 years, or thereabouts." (Jevons to Mills, January 7, 1880, in Isobel
Mills, *From Tinder-Box to the "Larger" Light,* p. 341.) Robert Adamson, Jevons's
successor at Owens College, wrote him in 1878 that "a very slight change in the period
would soon bring a discrepancy between the spots and crises." (Black, "W. S. Jevons
and the Economists of His Time," p. 219.)]

[67] Mitchell, *Business Cycles, The Problem and Its Setting,* pp. 13, 383-384. "Jevons's
leading papers on this topic, dating from 1875-1882 are reprinted in his *Investigations
in Currency and Finance,* . . . pp. 194-243."

Jevons's theory seems to have had much to do at least with the continued popularity of the notion of the ten-year business cycle. "The periodic recurrence of these
cycles of prosperity and depression has led certain economists to formulate a law
for their occurrence. That they are periodic the uninterrupted repetition every ten
years from 1815 down to the present time seems to indicate, although it is by no
means necessary to accept the fantastic conclusion drawn therefrom by Professor
Stanley Jevons of England, that they are dependent upon the decennial recurrence
of the spots upon the disc of the sun." (Frederic C. Howe, "Commercial Depressions
and Business Crises," *The American Journal of Politics,* November 1894, p. 457.]

[68] [The advanced *Substitution of Similars* was used as a textbook in logic at
Columbia College and by such teachers as the future president of Columbia, Nicholas
Murray Butler in the 1880's.]

148,000; *Pure Logic*, 1000; *Studies in Deductive Logic*, 6000; *The Principles of Science*, 9000.

In the field of economics, the *Political Economy*, which did not contain utility doctrine, had a sale of 98,000; *The Theory of Political Economy* sold only 7,000. *Money and the Mechanism of Exchange*, which first appeared in 1875, had a sale of 20,000, ("apart from a large sale in America where there was at one time a cheap pirated edition"; *The State in Relation to Labour*, 9,000; *The Coal Question*, 2,000; *Investigations in Currency and Finance* (posthumous collection of papers), 2,000; *Methods of Social Reform* (posthumous collection of essays), 2,000; *The Principles of Economics* (posthumous), 1000.]

Jevons was drowned accidentally while bathing in 1882, at the age of 46—a great loss, because he was in the full flood of his working power. He left several books partially written. One was a student's edition of *The Wealth of Nations* to which he planned to prefix an elaborate history of political economy. Another treatise, *The Principles of Economics*, was rather fragmentary, but in 1905 it was published with an introduction by Henry Higgs.[70] It adds comparatively little to knowledge. He also had in hand a book to be called "An Examination of John Stuart Mill's Philosophy." He had come to the conclusion by repeated reading that the chief characteristic of Mill as a philosopher was inconsistency; he could find inconsistencies on every page of every one of Mill's works. It would seem to a modern that he was building up a complex on the subject. Mill was the renowned political economist of the day, and with all his efforts to re-establish economic theory upon a new basis Jevons had succeeded in making scarcely any impression upon the followers of Mill. He thought that they descended to unworthy acts, to put people who accepted the orthodox doctrine into influential positions such as professorial chairs; and in general he was very much out of sympathy with the dominant trend in English political economy. This treatise, had he had time to elaborate it, would have been an exposure of the numerous errors which he found in Mill's philosophical and economic works.[71]

---

[69] [Keynes, "W. Stanley Jevons, . . ." pp. 299, 302. The primer, *Political Economy*, was hailed as providing teachers in Sunday Schools and the like with the best introductory work on the subject. (See H. S. Solly, "Political Economy of Questions of the Day," *The Theological Review*, December 1879, pp. 486-487.)]

[70] Higgs (1864-1940), a student of Jevons, is best known for *The Physiocrats* (1897). [The British sale of *The Principles* up to 1936 was 1,000.]

[71] Jevons's letters show that he was reacting vigorously against what he called the "Mill despotism," particularly in logic but also in political economy. (Outline, October 15, 1931.)

He also left unfinished a volume in the series called Bridgewater Treatises. Francis Henry Edgerton, the eighth Earl of Bridgewater, at his death in 1829 left a considerable sum of money [£8000] to be expended in publishing treatises to demonstrate the compatibility of the teachings of modern science with the teachings of religion; or, in the language of the half-title of the series, "On the Power, Wisdom and Goodness of God, as Manifested in the Creation." Nine volumes had been written by men such as William Whewell and Charles Babbage in the generation preceding Jevons. It was a subject which interested Jevons very much, and he was writing a tenth volume in the series.

All in all, Jevons's life and personality present a marked contrast with the economists with whom we have dealt so far. They were exceedingly interested in current affairs, wanted to make economics a great instrument for bettering the lot of mankind. They thought it should be a guide to public policy, and had definite schemes in mind for which each worked with full vigor. It was notably true in the case of Adam Smith that he wanted to change the general trend of economic policy in England. Ricardo was an even more militant reformer. At the height of his powers, he started excogitating a new economic system, entered Parliament and gave his greatest strength in his later years to his work there. Malthus was another reformer whose fundamental ideas about the best ways of checking a threatening increase to the population were embodied in the new poor law of 1834. The like was true of John Stuart Mill, although his most militant period was that of his younger years when he had still implicit faith in Benthamite philosophy. Later he saw the ineffectiveness of the philosophic radicals in Parliament and withdrew more and more from their active, practical, political work, but he was induced to accept election to Parliament and sat there as a member for a few years (1865-1868) in the latter part of his life. Still, no one can read his *Principles of Political Economy* without seeing how much of his heart was in the effort to develop those institutions for the improvement of which in the course of his book he offers numerous suggestions.

Opposed to these economists who wanted a system of economics which would show what ought to be done, who were themselves actively engaged in promoting certain specific reforms, stood Jevons. He felt temperamentally unfit for the work of practical reform and had little sympathy with, or interest in, the politics of his day. Indicative are two illustrative excerpts from his letters, one written in his youth in 1866 and the other written only four years before his death in 1878. In the first he says: "It is very difficult to know what view to take of the reform agitation." That was the time when John Bright was getting under way the tremendous campaign for the extension of the suffrage. The great Reform Bill of 1832, though it had made the suffrage in different constituencies uniform and had increased the number of voters, had still included a property qualification, which was sufficiently high to bar the bulk of the working classes from the exercise of the suffrage. Bright started an agitation to increase the number of male voters, an agitation, the aim of which was universal suffrage as it was then understood, nobody thinking that it could possibly include women.

This was the agitation on which Jevons says he found it very difficult to take any stand. He continued:

> I am not a democrat, as perhaps you know, and can't much care to adopt popular views to please the mob. However, I don't think any reform bill that is likely to pass will really upset our system here, while it may lead to many real improvements.[72]

In the second letter he says in reference to Benjamin Disraeli, the leader of the Conservative Party, who had recently (1876) accepted the title of the Earl of Beaconsfield:

> About politics, I confess myself in a fog. Sometimes I think Beaconsfield deserves hanging, and at other times I rather admire his cool and daring assertion of British power. But I prefer to leave *la haute politique* alone, as a subject which admits no scientific treatment. I have enough to think and write about which I can somewhat understand, without troubling myself about things which I cannot understand.[73]

[72] Jevons to Herbert Jevons, December 26, 1866, *Letters & Journal*, p. 232. [It was in keeping with these views that Jevons wrote Cairnes apropos the American Civil War and Cairnes's book, *The Slave Power* (1862), "I hardly go with you in your Northern sympathies, I am wholly neutral." (Jevons to Cairnes, April 23, 1864 in R. D. Collison Black, "Jevons and Cairnes," *Economica*, April 1960, p. 223.]
The Reform Bill finally passed in 1867 and gave the working classes the predominance which the middle classes had had since 1832. ("English Politics: 1820-1910," APP 84-91, no. 67.)
[73] Jevons to Tom Jevons, November 14, 1878, *Letters & Journal*, p. 393.
1874: General election—conservative victory—Disraeli wins with huge majority. In legislation attempted little.
1875: Suez Canal bought.
1876: Queen made Empress of India—Turkish question—reforms not carried out by Turkey. English supporting Turkey against Austria—Bulgarian atrocities [by Turkey]. Gladstone emerged from retirement to demand expulsion of Turkey [from Europe] 'bag and baggage." June: Servia and Montenegro [both now part of Jugoslavia] declared war on Turkey—Servia beaten.
1877: Russo-Turkish war—autumn—Plevna fell and Turkey collapsed. Disraeli sent fleet to Constantinople. War with Russia seemed likely. Bismarck obtained a conference from which Balkan treaty resulted. Disraeli claimed that he had gained "peace with honor." ("English Politics: 1820-1910," APP 84-91, no. 62.)
[With reference to above list, Professor Mitchell noted in his] diary September 9, 1919: "Began to compile a list of social movements [in England] year by year with a view to connecting it with development of economic theory."

Jevons was a professor (although one who hated lecturing), logician, man of scientific interest who got his views of how to improve political economy not from his dealings with the practical politics of the day but from his application in economics of ideas gained in other branches of learning.[74] In short, Jevons's valuable contributions to economics are those of a man who is basically interested in the subject as a science and not as a means of bettering economic organization. Doubtless he would have also contended that human advance in the field of social organization, as in all other areas, is most likely to be rapid and secure if it be guided by a thoroughgoing understanding of the fundamental laws involved; but he would have said that the principle of the division of labor should be applied in this field, as certainly for himself, at least, it was best to stick closely to the scientific task of trying to gain understanding and to leave to other people the task, for which he felt individually very little interest, of finding out how the scientific results could be best applied in practical fashion.[75]

What he did is also different from the work of Adam Smith, Malthus and John Stuart Mill, if not from the work of Ricardo, in the further respect that when he got a new idea he was immediately captivated by it, and proceeded to elaborate it only in a slight degree and then issue it to the world in suggestive but far from mature form. The contrast in this respect between Jevons and Alfred Marshall is even more striking than that between Jevons and his great predecessors. Marshall's temperamental feeling was in precisely the opposite direction. He was the kind of man who, when he had an idea, wanted to elaborate it fully, to reflect upon it at length, to let it lie by, come back to it, and not publish until he had fitted it completely into the framework of pre-existing knowledge. The result was that although he apparently came to hold much the same ideas regarding the analysis of utility which Jevons held, almost as early, he claims, as when Jevons published *The Theory of Political Economy*, he did not get round to publishing his *Principles of Economics* until 1890; and he was even more deliberate about his promised sequel volumes. His original plan had been to have a two volume treatise, but he never

---

[74] Sentence from Outline, February 23, 1916.

[75] Jevons was a mechanically minded logician and statistician not much interested in human beings (Outline, October 15, 1931). Primarily a logician who came to economics for a field in which to exercise his faculties. Practical results a matter of secondary interest. (Outline, November 20, 1916).

produced a real second volume though he did in the closing years of his life add two more books of economic theory.[76]

Jevons temperamentally was a person interested in suggestive ideas. We see that very distinctly in *The Theory of Political Economy;* we see it not less distinctly in the other very important side of his work, his statistical researches. As mentioned before, Jevons was one of the first investigators to attempt to study on a definite quantitative basis, fluctuations in price levels, variations in the seasonal amplitude of various economic processes, changes in secular trends of great industries, and business cycles. Perhaps the time is coming when people will regard the enormously suggestive work that he did in these several fields of statistical investigation as no less important in the development of economic theory at large than his rather fragmentary but nevertheless equally suggestive work in the field of what he considered to be theoretical political economy.[77]

[Jevons would doubtless have been pleased to hear that in 1883 provision was being made for lectures in statistics at University College.

> Economics met with some encouragement when in 1883, a fund raised in memory of William Newmarch was transferred to the college. The stipendiary was to deliver in each year at least six lectures on political economy as illustrated by statistics. Should the professor of Political Economy not himself deliver such a course in any year, there was for that year to be appointed a Newmarch Lecturer, and the endowment secured for the college the services of some notable economists.[78]

In a later period these included Edgeworth, A. L. Bowley, Udney Yule and J. M. Keynes.]

It is characteristic of the conception that men have entertained of economics as a whole that Jevons drew a line which economists are less inclined to draw nowadays between economic theory as such and the attempts to study on a quantitative basis certain economic processes.

---

[76] *Industry and Trade* (1919) and *Money, Credit, and Commerce* (1923). [Marshall wrote to Léon Walras in 1883 "following the lead of Cournot, I had anticipated all the central points of Jevons's book, and had in many respects gone beyond him. I was in no hurry to publish because I wished to work out my doctrines on their practical side. Latterly I have been hindered by illness. (Marshall to Walras November 1, 1883, in *Correspondence of Léon Walras and Related Papers,* I, p. 794)].

[77] His valuable contributions consist in brilliant suggestions rather than mature elaborated work.
Perhaps the stimulus he gave to quantitative work will some day rank higher than the stimulus he gave to what he thought of as economic theory. (Outline, November 20, 1916.)

[78] [H. Hale Bellott, *University College, London; 1826-1896* (London: University of London Press, 1929) p. 386.]

So much for Jevons as an individual and as an economist. The discussion of his *Theory of Political Economy* will be carried on at least as much by the class as by myself. Let me open the discussion by asking in what respect did the type of economic theory which Jevons developed differ from classical political economy? What are the outstanding differentiating characteristics of his kind of theory that contrasted with classical political economy?

S.[79] A different treatment of value.

M. Yes, that is the answer which most economists would be inclined to give at large; that is to say, they would put it this way: Jevons's important contribution was that he entered upon an analysis of demand as a factor in determining exchange values, whereas the classical writers had put their emphasis upon the analysis of cost. Is that all? Doesn't he go about this task of analyzing demand in a way which is different from that in which the classical economists had set about analyzing supply?

S. He introduced the psychological factor.

M. Yes. Do you find in any of Jevons's predecessors with whom you are acquainted a definite attempt, such as Jevons makes, to work economic theory upon the basis of psychology? Certainly none of them had made an attempt of that sort, though there were certain writers in the age of Ricardo, as we had previously noted, who had done the same thing. But they produced no influence at the time and were unknown to Jevons when he set about composing *The Theory of Political Economy.*

S. It seems that Jevons went back to Jeremy Bentham in a way.

M. Yes, the psychological foundation is supplied by Bentham. We may suppose—at least I am inclined to take that view—that the classical economists had been much influenced by the ideas of human nature similar to those of Jevons, but certainly among the classical economists it was not the practice explicitly to base economic theory on psychological doctrines. Is there any other difference? What about the method?

S. The scheme of his work is different. He does not deal with as complete a system as did John Stuart Mill. He is not interested in the same problems.

M. Yes, that is a difference of considerable interest for getting a clear view of Jevons's peculiarities. Adam Smith in *The Wealth of Nations* covered a wide range of subjects. Ricardo's range is contracted

---

[79] [In the discussion to follow the letter "M" will denote Professor Mitchell's remarks and the letter "S" those of the students.]

somewhat; he says that the most important problem in political economy concerns the shares in which the produce is distributed, but the discussion of distribution is prefaced by a thorough analysis of value and supplemented by chapters dealing elaborately with money and with taxation. John Stuart Mill has a more comprehensive scheme again. Presumably a classical economist would have said that Mill's treatment is a far more adequate representation of the field of economics than that about which Ricardo had written. In Mill there is the plan of successive books, he first deals with the production of wealth, a topic on which Smith had laid much stress but which Ricardo neglected. After the book on Distribution, comes one on Exchange, the subject in which both Smith and Ricardo were interested and with which they dealt fully, as under it comes the general theory of value. Then comes the book on the Influence of the Progress of Society on Production and Distribution which closes with the famous chapter on "The Probable Futurity of the Labouring Classes." The last book on the Influence of Government has a good deal not only on the functions of government but also on the revenue of the state. It covers a wide range of topics, all things considered.

Which of the subjects that Mill covered did Jevons take up? Does he discuss a theory of production? There is no real attempt to discuss production. Does he deal with distribution? Yes. Does he deal with exchange? Yes, that is the central feature of his treatise. Does he deal with public revenue and expenditures? No, except incidentally. What about the famous problem of population? Does that come into his discussion? No, he says explicitly that it has no place in his scheme. Why does he contract the field in this way? Is it because he thinks those other subjects are not parts of economic theory?

S. Jevons recognized the division of labor. He mentions about four divisions of economic problems.

M. Quite right. He confines himself to a narrow path not because he holds that to be the entire field of economic science. Quite the contrary, he takes a large, more catholic view of the field as a whole than most of his predecessors presumably would have done. [For example, he held that "Economic Statistics, comprehending the quantities of commodities produced, existing, exchanged, and consumed, constitute another most extensive body of science."][80]

In particular, instead of taking an extremely critical view of the work being done by the German historical school of economists, he

---

[80] [*Principles of Science; A Treatise on Logic and Scientific Method,* 2 volumes (New York: Macmillan, 1874) I, p. 386.]

regards that as a valuable contribution to the understanding of economic problems. He wrote that

> [The *historical method* must play a large part in economic science ... in such matters as land tenure, agriculture, and organization of industry, taxation, etc., theory must be applied with very large allowances for physical and historical circumstances. National character, ancient custom, political condition, and many other conditions, are economic factors of great importance.][81]

Contrast this with the prevalent attitude in the British Isles as illustrated by an admirer of Fawcett:

> He was an eminently practical man dealing with practical questions, and he sought in his economic studies for practical guidance. He found in Adam Smith a body of well-ascertained principles as to the course of trade and the laws of industry; which furnished him with an unerring clue through the sophistries of protectionism, and an unerring test by which to try every financial proposal and every industrial experiment. He found in Malthus the clear demonstration of a fundamental and unalterable law of human society which has baffled and must ever baffle every socialistic scheme for the improvement of the race, and which furnishes an unanswerable and the only unanswerable argument for the institution of private property. He found all these principles and many more equally significant and well established set out with admirable clearness and precision in the great work of Mill, brought into their mutual relations, and wrought into a harmonious system, applied to all the most pressing social problems of the time with a sobriety and calmness of judgment almost as conspicuous as the passionate vehemence of his sympathy for the suffering classes. And finding all this, can it be wondered that Fawcett should ask what the German [historical school] or any other school of economy had to teach him in place of this—or what results the new so-called historical method had to show that would bear comparison with these great triumphs of the much-decried method of analysis and deduction?[82]

As far as regards the great problem of the increase of population as compared with the increase of food supply, that is a matter of no concern to the theorist in Jevons's new economics. The area of production, public revenues and expenditures, consumption, were in his eyes not only legitimate but very important matters for the economist to work over; but he says that the development of the science as a whole would be more rapid if we practice the division of labor, and that his own particular contribution, the thing that he could do effectively, is to work out a very restricted but fundamental range of

---

[81] [Jevons, "Preface" to the English translation from the Italian of the second edition of Luigi Cossa, *Guide to the Study of Political Economy* (London: Macmillan, 1880) p. ix.]

[82] James Johnston Shaw, *Occasional Papers*, edited by Margaret G. Woods (Dublin: 1910) pp. 326-327. Quotation is in "Attitude of an English Economist toward German Historical School in 1886," APP 74-83, no. 61. [Shaw (1845-1910) was Whately Professor of Political Economy at Trinity College, Dublin, for the five-year term 1877-1882 and then devoted himself to the practice of law.]

problems. Those problems were concerned with what he called the "static state." That is, it was possible in his eyes to give a strictly scientific analysis of the fundamental problem of exchange value and also get additional light upon the problem of distribution if the theorist would work upon the assumption that the society to which his theory is applied was one in which no changes were taking place such as are brought about by an increase in population, accumulation of capital, changes in techniques of production, fundamental alterations in political institutions, or anything of the sort. That part of the field he thought could not be analyzed on a strictly scientific basis. Such an analysis would yield a set of economic theories the validity of which would not explain economic phenomena as we actually experience them, because the phenomena of practical experience are those encountered in a society which is changing in all sorts of ways.

To get the whole truth about economic phenomena, therefore, we should supplement these severe theoretical inquiries relating to the "static state" by all sorts of supplementary inquiries, including even those which the historical economists were carrying on, especially his Irish friend and contemporary, T. E. Cliffe Leslie (1826-1887). Leslie was a very able and extremely clever and attractive economist, who had a very critical attitude toward the Ricardian type of economic theory and who, in a series of delightful essays as admirably written as anything in economic literature, discussed a variety of topics which were treated in their theoretical aspects by the economist from what then seemed a novel historical viewpoint.[83]

General character of Leslie's *Essays in Political and Moral Philosophy,* as brief essays, brilliantly written, covering wide range of subjects from the ethical problem of the *summum bonum,* to the probability of future wars, armaments, international law, incidence of taxation, history of political economy, criticism of economic theory, distribution of the precious metals, and their effects on prices and wages, surveys of communities, and early history of institutions. The cement that binds all together is the his-

---

[83] *Essays in Political and Moral Philosophy,* 1879; 2nd edition, under the title *Essays in Political Economy,* 1888.

[Leslie was professor of jurisprudence and political economy at Queen's College, Belfast. He was also a member of the English bar and normally resided in London. John Stuart Mill wanted Leslie to succeed Cairnes at University College, London in 1872. (Mill to Cairnes, May 15, 1872, in George O'Brien "J. S. Mill and J. E. Cairnes," p. 274.) Leslie had served as Cairnes's deputy in the session of 1867-1868 (Bellott, *University College, 1826-1896,* p. 332.)

Mill in reviewing Leslie's famous *Land Systems and Industrial Economy of Ireland, England and Continental Countries* (1870) declared that Leslie was "one of the best living writers on applied political economy." ("Professor Leslie on the Land Question," 1870; reprinted under the title "Leslie on the Land Question," in Mill, *Essays on Economics and Society,* II, p. 535.)]

torical viewpoint. Learned historical method from Sir Henry Maine. He states in the preface that "Whatever differences exist between Mr. [John Stuart] Mill's treatment of some of these problems and his own—for example, in relation to the Utilitarian theory of morals, and the economic theories of profits and prices—are, he believes, in a great measure attributable to the fact, that whereas Mr. Mill in his youth attended the lectures of Mr. Austin, the author had the good fortune to attend those of Sir Henry Maine at the Middle Temple, and to learn first from them the historical method of investigation, followed with such brilliant success in *Ancient Law, Village Communities in the East and West,* and the *Lectures on the Early History of Institutions.* Holding a Professorship of both Jurisprudence and Political Economy, he was led to apply that method to the examination of economic questions, and to look at the present economic structure and state of society from Sir Henry Maine's point of view, as the result of a long evolution."

Leslie's leading ideas in systematic form. I. History of economic theory: derivation of the two opposing types of economic theory; Adam Smith—blending of the code of nature with natural theology; criticism of Ricardo.

II. Leslie's criticisms of *a priori* economic theory. 1. It starts from the individual; it should start from the community. 2. It neglects the family. 3. Motive which it recognizes—the desire for wealth—hides important problems from the economist. 4. Facts of human nature with which it starts are not ultimate facts but important problems. 5. Its practice of explaining discrepancies between theory and fact by "friction" is unscientific. 6. It misses the true problems of economics. 7. Its pretensions to apply to all times and to all countries are absurd. 8. Walter Bagehot's limitation of political economy to modern England cannot save it. 9. For its assumptions of a common rate of wages and a common rate of profits are invalid. 10. These erroneous assumptions might have been corrected by inductive verification, which the *a priori* economists preach but do not practice. 11. Their theories have wrought great harm. Adam Smith's assumption of identity between public and private interests led to neglect of study of consumption. Doctrine of a "natural" rate of wages led to passing of the corn laws. Doctrine of equality of profits has checked investition and facilitated maintenance of both exorbitant prices and low wages. Doctrine that wages vary inversely as profits has made enmity between capital and labor. *A priori* method has prevented men from attacking such problems as the differentiating characteristics of social groups. 12. Economic generalizations. Their seductiveness. Their dangers and their value. 13. Index numbers are not trustworthy.

III. Constructive suggestions. Leslie's basic conception of the problem of economics: The historical method: Can history be a science? Identity of the historical and inductive methods. Its bearing on the idea of what is good. Economics is properly a department of sociology. Multiplicity of motives facilitates prediction. Positive results reached by Leslie's studies: Incidence of taxation on the working classes. Effect of the new gold on prices in 16th century; in 19th century; causes of inequalities in agricultural wages. Cultural consequences of money making and towns. Causes of celibacy. Poor relief cheapens labor. Demand and supply regulate domestic as well as international values. Modern economic phenomena less easy to explain than mediaeval.

Note: General characteristics of Leslie's positive results. 1. On conventional topics, such as incidence of taxation, effect of gold on prices, etc., he generally concludes that it is impossible to state definitely what has happened; he finds inequalities instead of uniformities. 2. He introduces conclusions of an unconventional kind regarding the cultural consequences of institutions.[84]

Jevons, as said above, recognized in a systematic fashion, at least, that in order to get a comprehensive knowledge of economic behavior, it is necessary to discuss those aspects of the problems which interested Leslie. But he also added—and this is characteristic of the time— that to work out the theory of the subject, the inquirer must analyze a set of definite and restricted problems and handle them by themselves. Economists must proceed by a scheme of the division of labor. Let people interested and skilled in historical studies do as Leslie did; meanwhile, let the economic theorists go their own way. He seems to have deferred to an indefinite future the task of trying to bring the various sidelines shaped by historical, statistical, and theoretical investigations into a single focus.[84a]

There had been some references to a division of economics into static and dynamic problems before Jevons's time. You may recall that Mill had recognized this distinction, but undertook to treat them both, or at least to treat certain dynamic problems as well as certain static ones. Jevons as a theorist, however, confines himself to static problems. So far as the major lights in English political economy are concerned, he is perhaps the first who cultivated what is sometimes called pure economic theory. This is another characteristic of his investigations. How about the method by which he worked?

S. He employed a mathematical method.

M. Yes, Jevons undertook to carry on these severe fundamental theoretical inquiries by what he believed to be a mathematical method,

---

[84] "Leslie," APP 64-73, no. 47. Historical school: criticism of classical political economy. Cliffe Leslie's attack on assumptions of standard rate of wages and profits. J. K. Ingram's combination of historical viewpoint with Comtean sociology in his *History of Political Economy* (Outline, November 3, 1931).

[84a] [Jevons occasionally wandered off into ethnographic explanations of social phenomena. "The rates of mortality and the degrees of drunkenness of the northern towns were facts which could not be at present explained, and he believed the real explanation was to be found in the ethnographic character of the people. It would be found that the migration was going on to a greater extent than had been supposed. The Irish migrated into England, but it was doubtful whether they migrated out of it again. Now if the Irish should continue to migrate into England and the English migrated to Australia, and all parts of the world, the result would obviously be that our population would become Celticized." (Jevons, "Discussion of Mr. Ravenstein's Paper," *Journal of the Statistical Society of London,* September 1879, p. 640.)]

holding that economists have always dealt with quantities and that any science which deals with quantities is fundamentally mathematical in character, but that inasmuch as the economists had not recognized clearly that they were dealing with quantities they had been awkward in their method of procedure. We should be able to carry on these discussions far more effectively if, recognizing that we are dealing with quantities, we proceed to treat them by using that very powerful tool of mathematical symbolism, particularly differential calculus, not that mathematics would give different results, but experience in every scientific work has abundantly shown that the economist can think with less danger of falling into error if he uses mathematical symbols; and, by such use he also makes it possible to treat successfully a variety of problems which are too intricate to be handled by the methods of ordinary algebra.

S. Does Jevons confine himself to static problems?

M. Yes, to repeat, the leading characteristics of his type of theory as contrasted with classical political economy are the attempts to base economics explicitly upon a psychological foundation; the elaborate analysis of variations of utility—a matter that had been neglected by his classical predecessors; the use of mathematical symbolism as a tool of inquiry; and finally, the confining of the work to the bare theory of the static state.

None of these characteristics was original with him in the sense that it had no predecessors. That would not be true. But these notions were original with Jevons in the sense in which almost any scientific discovery is likely to be original with the man who makes it; simply that he was the first to make effective use of certain new ideas; that is, in a way that made them seem intellectually interesting and valuable to his successors.

S. What did Jevons conceive to be the relation between static and dynamic problems?

M. The static problems, to repeat, were economic problems which appear in a society that is not increasing in population or making appreciable additions to capital or effecting important changes in technique or altering its general political or economic institutions.

S. But if the institutions change, how do all his concepts hold true?

M. That is just it. Jevons does not hold that theories based upon the hypothesis of the static state are competent to explain phenomena that we experience. They do, however, give an important fundamental part of the whole truth. But to get the whole truth these basic static investigations must be supplemented with a series of dynamic studies to find out what modifications the results of the static inquiries must be subjected to, in view of the fact that say, population increases, capital is accumulated, methods of production are improved, some changes are made from time to time in the institutions of economic organization.

Hedonistic foundation: Jevons seeks to join economics to the wide field of speculation covered by the utilitarian school. In what respects does Jevons's treatise differ from Ricardo's? Psychological foundations laid expressly in Bentham's hedonistic functional psychology. Analysis of variations of utility—final degree of utility made foundation of the theory of exchange value. Mathematical formulation of the analysis and of results. Pure theory only. Includes consumption not population. Static not dynamic. Exclusion of problem of population. Are any of these features original with Jevons? His English predecessors had been utilitarians but their hedonism had been implicit rather than explicit. William Thompson, the Ricardian socialist, was explicit. Analysis of variations in utility was in W. F. Lloyd and Mountifort Longfield—1833-1834; marked in Richard Jennings, 1855, developed by the French civil engineer, Jules Dupuit, 1844.[85] Heinrich Gossen, 1854; Carl Menger, 1871; Léon Walras, 1873; John Bates Clark late in 1870s. Mathematical analysis developed to a high point by A. A. Cournot, 1838, for example. As for pure theory, Nassau Senior came close to giving in *An Outline of the Science of Political Economy* nothing but pure theory; Mill recognizes the distinction between "pure political economy" and its applications, but gives no book to it in his *Principles of Political Economy*. As for the distinction between statics and dynamics, the distinction goes back to August Comte; it was made use of by Mill, who endeavored to develop both branches. But if Jevons had forerunners in every one of these directions his work was still highly original, for he had hit upon some of the ideas afresh; he gives each of them a further development and he combines them most effectively for purposes of getting new results.

Relations between Jevons's and Ricardo's types of theory. Differences. 1. Jevons discusses psychological foundations of economics. His theory is more fundamental—if it is right at all, goes back of money and commodities to ultimate factors which both control behavior and constitute its success or failure. 2. Develops marginal analysis in all departments of economic theory whereas Ricardo developed it only with reference to cost of agricultural produce. 3. Narrow scope of economic theory. Pure theory only but brings in consumption; statics, not dynamics—excludes theory of population. Why? 4. Mathematical form of argument. 5. Professes to have a new theory of value. Similarities: Both start with a definite form of social organization, which they do not explain. Jevons clearly appreciated value of study of this organization, but thought that historical investigation should be a separate branch of economics. The remedy lies in subdivision. Both assume that economic behavior is directed by rational calculation. Jevons defines the calculation in terms of pleasure and pain;

---

[85] [Jules Dupuit (1804-1866), "On the Measurement of the Utility of Public Works," translation from the French by R. H. Barback in *International Economic Papers* no. 2 (London: Macmillan, 1952) pp. 83-110.]

Ricardo does not define it—to him it is economic interest. Hence both make economics a logic of self-interest—a statement not of how men behave, but of how it is to their interest to behave. Relation of theory to fact in both writers is vague; i.e., neither attempts a systematic verification or criticism of results. Method with both is reasoning on basis of premises, explicitly or implicitly assumed. Conclusion: The two types of theory are much more alike than Jevons thought. Made kin by sharing same fundamental conception of human behavior as calculating pursuit of self interest and same fundamental conception of economic method as reasoning about what men would do. The technical difference is that by extending the marginal concept from agriculture to other economic activities, Jevons found a way which Ricardo did not to apply Bentham's felicific calculus in economics. In terms of the levels analysis, Jevons works out most considerably the third level, the feeling level. His theory of exchange built frankly on a theory of pleasure and pain taken from Bentham, elaborated by discovery of significance of the margin, an idea familiar to classical economists in connection with land but not applied to sensations. Hedonistic foundation. Jevons seeks to join economics to the wide field of speculation covered by the utilitarian school.

How does Jevons's economic man differ from that of John Stuart Mill? Mill's economic man desired wealth as his leading motive, but this motive was opposed by (1) irksomeness of labor; (2) desire for present enjoyment; (3) desire of sexual gratification. Jevons's man simply desires pleasure and shuns pain, but the pleasures with which the economist deals are those obtained from commodities. The chief pains which the theorist considers are those of labor. Future pleasures and pains affect men less both because of uncertainty and of mere futurity; c.f., "a future feeling is always less influential than a present one." But on the other hand see statement "the enjoyment actually experienced at any moment . . . usually fails to answer to the anticipations which have been formed." Discounting for futurity and uncertainty is a more precise formulation of Mill's notion of the desire for present enjoyment. Desire of sexual gratification—doctrine of population [found in Mill] omitted by Jevons.[87]

Let us take up the discussion of the several characteristics of Jevons's theory one by one. We will begin with his attempt to base economic theory explicitly upon a hedonistic foundation. As was pointed out, the hedonistic foundation is borrowed directly from Bentham. But does Jevons use the felicific calculus in the form which Bentham had given it, or does he make modifications?

S. He is not concerned with the "greatest happiness."

M. The "greatest happiness" principle with Bentham is not so much part of his psychology as of his ethics. The important thing for Jevons was Bentham's explanation of men's behavior. Bentham's

---

[87] Outlines, November 20, 22, 1916; "Seminar in Economic Changes and Economic Theory," January 5, 1943. Quotations from Jevons's *The Theory of Political Economy,* pp. 34, 72.

notion as to the criterion for judging welfare, the "greatest happiness" principle, was an attempt to formulate a satisfactory basis for judging what is good. But the felicific calculus was an attempt to explain why men do certain things, according to the pleasure-pain scheme which we discussed in dealing with Bentham. To repeat the question, did Jevons use the felicific calculus in the form that Bentham had given it?

S. No, he omits several of Bentham's dimensions.

M. Yes. Let us go back to the first point. Bentham said that pleasure and pain had several dimensions which must be taken into account by people working in the social sciences; intensity, duration, propinquity, certainty, fecundity, purity and extent.[88] Which of these does Jevons leave out?

S. Fecundity, purity and extent.

M. In short, he deals only with the intensity of pleasures and pains, their duration, certainty and propinquity. Bentham himself did not make much of fecundity and purity. There is one very important difference; he does not propose to measure extent; that is, the number of people who enjoy a given pleasure or suffer from a given pain. How can an economist, who is concerned not with the individual as such but with social life, content himself with omitting any reference to extent, to the number of people who enjoy pleasures or suffer pains? Is not that a matter of fundamental consequence?

S. Not in motivating the individual to action.

M. Which implies that motivating the individual to action is the only problem that Jevons wants to throw light on by using the felicific calculus. That is true. Jevons is using the calculus in a spirit quite different from Bentham. To Bentham it was a scheme for showing both how people act and what the net results are. He was as a person interested in social affairs, more concerned with showing the effects or the detriments resulting from certain policies than he was in explaining why people act in a certain way. That goes with his lively interest in public welfare. Jevons, remember, had comparatively slight interest, as far as one can judge, in the general issues of welfare. He does refer to the matter once or twice incidentally in *The Theory of*

---

[88] Jevons quotes Bentham at length on pleasure-pain calculus. "To a person," he says, "considered *by himself* the value of a pleasure or a pain, considered *by itself*, will be greater or less according to the following circumstances: (1) *its intensity;* (2) *its duration;* (3) *its certainty* or *uncertainty;* (4) *its propinquity* or *remoteness.*" "Ultimate and complete result" also affected by (5) *fecundity*—chance a feeling has of being followed by feelings of the same kind ; (6) *purity*—chance of not being followed by feelings of opposite kind; (7) *extent*—number of persons affected. The last three, important in ethics but not in economics. ("Jevons" APP 64-73, no. 35.) Quotation from *The Theory of Political Economy,* pp. 28-29.

Political Economy, but does not think that it is a matter which is susceptible of strictly scientific treatment. He does try to explain certain types of economic activity, particularly why people exchange goods in certain ratios. To a person whose problem is limited primarily to this, in explaining why people do certain things, the question of the number of people who get commodities to consume, or the number who have to undergo the sacrifice of labor, can be set aside. The more limited range of the problem which Jevons has in view accounts for this important difference between his and Bentham's employment of the felicific calculus. As he puts it, the last three, fecundity, purity, extent, do "not enter into the more simple and restricted problem which we attempt to solve in Economics."[89]

M. I want to ask one or two more specific questions to bring out other differences. What units does Bentham employ for measuring the intensity of pleasures?

S. The least possible sensation that a man can have.

M. Yes, that is the unit, and pleasures and pains are to be counted in as many units as the intensity of the sensation contains multiples of this faintest pleasurable or painful sensation that can be distinguished. What units does Bentham employ for time, for duration of pleasures and pains? It is the moment of time itself. These are the more fundamental quantities.[90]

What units does Jevons employ for pleasures and pains, say for intensity and duration?

S. He says that it is impossible to measure the intensity of pleasure and pain in units.

M. He does not employ units, because he says the inquirer cannot measure these quantities. That leads to the next question. How can you use pleasure and pain to explain what people are going to do if

---

[89] Outline, November 22, 1916. Quotation from *The Theory of Political Economy,* p. 29. [Professor Mitchell's colleague, J. M. Clark explains Mitchell's view in the following extract from his notes. "Fecundity—deals with after effects, not immediate motivation; purity—qualitative—not measured by immediate action; extent, i.e., how many people as a normative standard, Jevons not interested. As explaining demand curves he should have been, one would think, but his analysis runs in different terms. Rejects 'cardinal' measure of utility and interpersonal comparisons. Does not need them for his explanation of behavior. Bentham's law-makers needed to measure utility to determine objectives and gauge sanctions. In free exchange area he could accept individual's choices; so did not need to 'measure' utility there. Jevons's theory is confined to that area. But Jevons's explanation seems to become mainly a tautology, without predictive value and what is left is: whatever happens is outgrowth of a more or less successful maximising of pleasure. (J. M. Clark, class notes, March 5, 1951.)]

[90] Certainty and propinquity are measured as fractions whose limit unity represents immediate actual enjoyment; for extent, the unit is the individual. (Outline, November 27, 1916.)

you cannot measure them? Presumably a man is going to follow the course which will give him the greatest pleasure, but if you cannot measure his pleasures how can you explain what he will do?

S. It is done indirectly, by its influence upon his actions.

M. That is, you do not measure the pleasure as a force which is going to push a person in a certain direction, but having observed that a person goes in a certain direction you infer the amount of pleasure he has gotten. Can you measure the amount of pleasure after you have seen what the man has done? What can you infer?

S. The differential between pleasures and pains.

M. That is, all that can be inferred, says Jevons, is that the man thinks that he will get greater pleasure by adopting this line of action than he could have obtained in going in any of the other ways that were possible to him. That is all the theorist can do. If the theorist cannot measure pleasure and pain units, how does the man himself measure the different pleasures which he may have the option of obtaining by different lines of action?

S. By results.

M. Yes, but the problem turns up as a problem of considering what lines of action a person had better choose, and he cannot tell what the results are until he has acted.

To repeat, Jevons's treatment of human nature differs from Bentham. Whereas Bentham found it necessary, for the kind of social science that he was trying to develop, to have a scheme for measuring pleasures and pains, Jevons thinks himself able to dispense with anything of that sort. In place of the elaborate and obviously artificial scheme called the felicific calculus, Jevons has a much more modest and persuasive way of showing how a man's conduct is influenced by pleasure and pain. He says that he, as a theorist, finds no occasion to determine in any units how great are the pleasures or the pains which influence the conduct of the people whose behavior he is trying to account for. Further, he says that he has no occasion to compare the amounts of pleasure or pain which a given stimulus will cause to different people. He even goes so far as to say that it is not necessary for his purpose to suppose that any given individual is capable of measuring the amount of pleasure which he can get from two alternative courses of action, or to measure the amounts of pain which two alternative acts of procedure or of abstinence will produce.

All that he supposes is necessary that an individual shall be able to do in order to afford a basis for a theory of value and of price is to tell which of the two pleasures is the greater; and further, when there is a balance between the two pleasures; similarly, to tell which of the two pains is the greater, or when two pains are equal to each other; or, finally, to tell whether a given pleasure is greater or less than the pain by which it may be purchased, and whether there is a balance of a certain promised pleasure and a certain pain in prospect.

In short, Jevons imputes to the human mind ability not to measure pleasures and pains but to discriminate among relations of equality or inequality among different pleasures, among different pains and among different pleasures as compared with different pains. The individual is supposed to be able to say whether the amount of satisfaction he will get from producing a bit more of a certain commodity will be equal to, in excess of, or less than the amount of pain which the act of production will cause. The individual is supposed to be able to tell whether an additional bit of a certain commodity which he may obtain in exchange will give him a pleasure equal to, in excess of, or less than the sacrifice which will be made by giving up something for what he gets. The modest ability to recognize relations of equality or inequality among pleasures and pains is sufficient. It is a use for economic purposes of a conception of human nature precisely the same as that which Bentham entertained, but it is a far more limited and modest use of the scheme. It is not an effort on the part of the theorist to do any calculating himself, but merely an assumption on the part of the theorist that the people whose behavior he is trying to explain are not able to measure but are able to tell whether pains and pleasures are equal to, or unequal to each other.

If Jevons simplified the application of the felicific calculus in this drastic fashion, it is equally true that he developed Bentham's scheme of analysis in one very important direction. Just what did he add to the idea of accounting for behavior in terms of pleasure and pain that Bentham developed?

S. The law of variation in utility.

M. Not that, because Bentham pointed out very clearly that if a man has increasing quantities of wealth, he will get diminishing satisfaction from each unit added to his supply. Perhaps you remember that Bentham in his discussion on the relation of the amount of pleasure the sovereign gets and the beggar gets, asks whether the sovereign's pleasure is fifty thousand times the beggar's, or a thousand times, or a hundred, ten, five times, or twice the beggar's. He distinctly developed and made use of the idea of diminishing utility.

S. Did he not use price as a measure?

M. The idea of using money measures of intensity of pleasure was in Bentham, but Jevons has no need to invoke it, because he is not trying to measure pleasures and pains.

S. Jevons added the idea of utility.

M. Yes: not total utility and final utility, but the *final degree of utility*. This is the important addition that Jevons makes to the analysis; that is, he recognized the significance of one particular point in the scale of declining utility. How he uses that concept we shall soon see. But before doing this, let me [restate the relation between Jevons's and Bentham's use of the felicific calculus.]

Bentham dreamed of using his calculus to measure total net utility or pleasure, for it was only by comparing happiness produced by various measures that he could determine on his principles what was the correct one. Jevons had a much more restricted aim. He did not try to measure total happiness or utility, but simply to show how men would behave with reference to the situations which he discusses. It is behavior which he explains, not the results of behavior which he measures. Further he holds that the behavior with which the economist is concerned turns not upon a comparison of total utility, but upon comparison of final degrees of utility. That is, the economist does not have to measure total utility in order to explain the behavior which is his business.

How this restricted use of the calculus simplifies the problem. Problem of units: Since Bentham was trying to measure pleasure he needed unit of intensity, duration, certainty, propinquity and extent. Jevons can get along without units. He does not measure—the minds of his subjects do that. Hence he needs no units. He need not even inquire whether the mind has such. What he does know is that the mind somehow makes comparisons and reaches decisions—that suffices for his purpose.

Problem of comparing the feelings of different men: Bentham admitted that "addibility of the happiness of different subjects . . . when considered rigorously" is "factitious"; but held nevertheless that it "is a postulation without the allowance of which all political reasoning is at a stand . . ." It was precisely this difficulty that prevented Ricardo from admitting utility as a factor controlling value. He said in *Principles of Political Economy* "Every man has some standard in his own mind by which he estimates the value of his enjoyments, but that standard is as various as the human character." "Value in use cannot be measured by any known standard; it is differently estimated by different persons." Perhaps would have admitted the comparability of utility to different men if without it all economic reasoning had been at a stand. But he thought he had an alternative: cost of production could be measured, and it could be treated as determinant of value. Hence, while he followed Bentham in politics and accepted his standard of welfare, he did not admit that utility cut a great figure in economics. Jevons avoids this difficulty altogether, by not measuring utility.

Problem of comparing pleasures of different kinds. Bentham, we know, made this problem more difficult by an elaborate analysis of pleasures into complex and simple, followed by discriminating fourteen different kinds of simple pleasures—pleasures of the senses, of wealth, of skill, of amity, etc.—

and twelve different kinds of simple pains. How then should he compare the different kinds? Sometimes he resorted to classification and thus avoided comparison. Sometimes used a money measure. Jevons on the other hand is more complex in general theory and more simple in economics. There is a "hierarchy of feelings." Higher ranks overbalance the lower ones. Bentham could not agree to this. "Pushpin is as good as poetry." What Jevons says is equivalent to Mill's admission of a qualitative difference between pleasures (see his *Utilitarianism*, which Jevons does not quote) and that is equivalent to surrender of the utilitarian standard in ethics. But economics [says Jevons] deals only with the coarsest rank and on that level he assumes that the mind compares different kinds of pleasure, of pain, and pleasure with pain—paying no attention to Bentham's list of simple pleasures and pains.

Problem of diminishing utility: Bentham grasped the fact of diminishing utility as clearly as Jevons. "The quantity of happiness produced by a particle of wealth (each particle being of the same magnitude) will be less and less at every particle; the second will produce less than the first, the third less than the second, and so on." Bentham, however, did not see clearly what to do with the observation. It was an obstacle to him—it meant that he could not assume that the same amount of wealth would mean the same amount of pleasure to different men. Instead the most plausible assumption was that a given amount of wealth would increase pleasure in a ratio equivalent to ratio by which wealth was increased. And he could not make effective use of these ratios. Jevons on the other hand, just because he was not trying to measure utility, found the fact of diminishing utility no obstacle. Rather it was a help. For it brought the most different kinds of wants down to a common threshold where they would be balanced against one another. Imperious needs like thirst became readily comparable with faint whims. Made orderly economic behavior possible and therefore made rational economic theory possible.

Conclusion: Credits man with power to compare pleasures and pains and to distinguish relations of greater, less, equality. Does not himself measure nor even suppose his subjects to measure in any more elaborate sense than this. Further most of these balancings are supposed to be not of total pleasures and pains but of marginal feelings.[91]

Before showing how he uses the concept of final degree of utility, let me point out broadly what the general scheme of Jevons's theory is. He says that the central problem of economics is the problem of exchange value. The theory of exchange value rests upon the theory of utility, which in turn rests upon the theory of pleasure and pain. Of this theory of pleasure and pain, his theory of labor is a special part. Let me call attention at this point to an awkward feature in Jevons's arrangement of chapters. He discusses the theory of exchange before he discusses the theory of labor which is logically a part of his theory

---

[91] Outline, November 27, 1916. For quotations from Bentham, see Volume I, pp. 207, 209.

of exchange.[92] He would have had a more orderly arrangement, if he had brought his theory of labor into his discussion of the theory of utility. In other words, he might have started more logically from a general sketch of pleasure and pain as the motive forces which control conduct, and then discussed the theory of utility as he does, then discussed disutility and pointed out that the disutilities that count most in economics are those connected with labor, and then said that we have here a theory, not of utility alone, but of utility and disutility. Then he could have proceeded to a discussion of the theory of exchange —and not, as he does in the book—the theory of pleasures and pains, then the theory of utility, then the theory of exchange value and finally labor.

Jevons's economics rests upon the theory of pleasures and pains as the controlling forces in conduct, upon an analysis of the utilities and disutilities which are important to an economist and which are his way of taking account of the pleasures and pains which different circumstances give us. Then, based on the theory of utility and disutility, comes his theory of exchange. His theory of pleasures and pains boils down to a few very simple propositions: pleasures and pains are quantities among which the mind of each individual is capable of recognizing relations of equality and inequality. Further, Jevons supposes that pleasures and pains vary continuously in intensity and duration, and they are susceptible of treatment in the ordinary mathematical symbolism employed in the differential calculus. Further, the pleasures and pains, he supposes, are discounted for futurity and uncertainty. Finally, he supposes that pain is the opposite of pleasure. Then he passes on to the theory of utility. Here his chief points are: utility is the pleasure which is derived from a commodity. The utility of which an economist takes account is the pleasure derived from the use of a commodity. This varies, declining with the amount of the commodity which a man has in his possession. It is, therefore, of the greatest importance to distinguish between total utility and final degree of utility. What is final degree of utility?

S 1. It is the pleasure derived from the last amount of the commodity in a person's possession.

M. The pleasure derived from the final increment of the commodity in your possession. Is there any member of the class who had gotten a different impression?

S 2. It is the measure of the pleasure a person would lose if deprived of a portion of his stock of a commodity.

---

[92] Sentence from Outline, December 6, 1916.

M. It is the amount of pleasure a person would lose if one unit of the commodity were taken away from him.

S 1. Is that not the same thing?

M. There is always a question about that, and since it is one which Jevons does not really discuss, I do not know precisely how he would answer. But are all agreed to accept the answer that final degree of utility is the amount of satisfaction which we derive from the consumption of the final increment of our supply of goods; or, to use an equivalent statement, the amount of utility that we would lose if deprived of one increment in our stock?

S. It is the ratio of that to the amount of the commodity involved.

M. Is there any difference between this statement of yours (S 1) that it is the amount of pleasure you get from the consumption of the commodity, and the other answer that the final degree of utility is a ratio?

S. Yes, because when we speak of ratios we are speaking in terms of exchange.

M. The ratio which is in mind is not an exchange ratio. When we are talking about the final degree of utility we must not undertake to explain it in terms of exchange. Exchange is largely, from his viewpoint, a matter which is built on the comparison of the final degrees of utility. If there is a ratio involved, it is not the ratio of exchange. Why is it a ratio?

S. It is the utility of the last increment divided by the quantity of the last increment.

M. du/dx—this is Jevons's symbol for it. Formally it is a ratio— one quantity divided by another; i.e., a ratio mathematically. Can a ratio be a quantity of feeling; can it be the amount of pleasure one gets from a commodity? Obviously not; that is, technically speaking, the final degree of utility is not the amount of feeling at all. It is a mathematical quantity; it is the ratio between increase in the amount of utility which a person derives from an addition to his stock of a commodity and the increase made to that stock when the addition is very small.

Now let me ask, what is meant by the marginal utility of any good? Is marginal utility a ratio or an amount of feeling?

S. The last added unit; the actual amount.

M. You must not speak of it as an amount of value, because that is a quantity we use in explaining value.

S. The pleasure then.

M. Pleasure of gratification or utility. The amount of utility which a person derives from the final unit of his supply. That is to say, the two conceptions of marginal utility and final degree of utility, while used for the same theoretical purpose are, from a strictly logical point of view, quite different things. One is an amount of feeling, and the other is a mathematical ratio.

This is a point at which I should anticipate some of the later discussion. The same year Jevons issued his treatise, Carl Menger in Austria, unknown to Jevons as Jevons was unknown to him, published *Grundsätze der Volkswirthschaftslehre* (*Principles of Economics*), in which he developed a similar analysis.[93] He pointed out that the amount of gratification which an individual derives from using successive increments in a supply of a commodity declines, and that there is in all his economic planning a critically important role played by one particular point in the series of declining utilities. To that point one of his disciples, Friedrich von Wieser, gave the name "Grenznutzen" (marginal utility).[94]

At the end of the 1880's there were a few Englishmen and Americans becoming acquainted with Menger's work, then almost twenty years old. Presently treatises of his two leading disciples who, along with Menger, are generally described as the founders of the Austrian School of marginal analysis, were translated into English; the two volumes of Eugen von Böhm-Bawerk's *Kapital und Kapitalzins* (1884-1889) were translated by William Smart as *Capital and Interest; A Critical History of Economical Theory* (1890) and *The Positive Theory of Capital* (1891); von Wieser's *Der natürliche Werth* (1889) was translated under the title *Natural Value* by a student of Smart,

---

[93] [The English translation in 1950 by James Dingwall and Bert F. Hoselitz was of the first edition. The second edition, which was published in 1923 two years after Menger's death, has not been translated. The translators of the first edition explained in the preface that they had "rejected the possibility of a variorum translation because it was the first edition only that influenced the development of economic doctrine, because of the posthumous character of the second edition and because the numerous differences between the two made a variorum translation impractical."]

[94] [Wieser, it has been argued, specifically introduced *"Grenznutzen"* as the German translation of Jevons's "terminal utility" or "final degree of utility" in his first book *Über den Ursprung und die Hauptgesetze des wirthschaftlichen Werthes* (Vienna: Holder, 1884) p. 128. In 1888 what amounted to a literal translation of the German expression into English "suddenly appeared" in Philip H. Wicksteed's *The Alphabet of Economic Science* (1888) as "marginal effectiveness." It has been well said that this change "from 'final' to 'marginal' became a permanent change in terminology after it caught on." R. S. Howey, *The Rise of the Marginal Utility School* (Lawrence, Kansas: The University of Kansas Press, 1961) p. 134.]

C. A. Malloch (1893).[95] Smart in 1891 wrote an intelligent, brief and skillful exposition of the whole Austrian theory of value in *Introduction to the Theory of Value.*[96]

After the translations appeared, the theory of marginal utility was adopted in varying degrees into the economic analysis which had been built up mainly on the classical model. At the present time, in the text-books in elementary courses, the idea of marginal utility is freely employed; and it is employed in contrast to the idea of marginal sacrifice or marginal disutility, as it is sometimes called. Most graduate students, therefore, are familiar with the marginal idea; it is part of the stock in trade of the text-book writers.

The notion of final degree of utility, however, despite the fact that it had the advantage of being in print first in England itself, the great source of orthodox economics, has not been taken over into current discussion. Presumably the reason is that the ideas of marginal utility and disutility have seemed clearer, more usable, more effective tools of thought to later writers than the concept of final degree of utility or the corresponding concept of final degree of disutility. There are certain marked advantages in the use of this mathematical way of defining the critically important idea which will be discussed later in more detail; that is, the use of the ratio has certain advantages over what seems to be the similar notion of a quantity of feeling. Do any of you see any advantage of talking about final degree of utility as the increase in the amount of satisfaction a person

---

[95] [In 1959, there appeared a new translation by G. D. Huncke and H. F. Sennholz of the German three-volume edition of 1921 of Böhm-Bawerk's work under the general title, *Capital and Interest*. Böhm-Bawerk's first book, in 1881. *Rechte und Verhältnisse vom Standpunkte der volkswirtschaftlichen Güterlehre* ("Legal Rights and Relations Viewed from the Standpoint of the Theory of Economic Goods") was, as he himself stated, a sort of introduction to the later volumes on capital and interest.]

[96] [Smart (1853-1913) received a B.A. degree in 1882, at the University of Glasgow, where he was deeply influenced by the famous Hegelian Edmund Caird, who taught economics as part of his professorship of moral philosophy, as in the days of Adam Smith. After giving university extension lectures in philosophy and political economy, Smart was appointed in 1886 lecturer in political economy at Queen Margaret College, which had been incorporated three years earlier as a woman's college. It was while teaching there that, at the suggestion of Caird, he produced or supervised the translation into English of the Austrians.

In 1896, he became the first occupant of the Adam Smith Professorship of Political Economy at Glasgow. "The chair was founded by the munificence of a great Glasgow iron master, Mr. Andrew Stewart. . . . As a young man when visiting Adam Smith's house in Kirkcaldy on one occasion, he had resolved to found a chair of political economy if ever the opportunity came. It came in 1896, and although some among the electors scented heresy in Smart's views on the gold standard, he was elected." Thomas Jones, "Biographical Sketch," in William Smart, *Second Thoughts of an Economist* (London: Macmillan, 1916; 2nd edition, 1924) p. xxx.

William Ashley played a large role in securing Smart's appointment to the University of Glasgow by getting for him testimonials from leading American economists.]

derives from a commodity divided by the increase in the addition made to his stock at the margin? Why should a person go through the division instead of merely talking about the amount of pleasure he gets from a stock of goods?

S. You must measure pleasure, according to Jevons.

M. Can you really measure that? To do so, you must have it in quantitative shape.

S. It seems to be implicitly stated, as the amount of pleasure derived from the utility of a commodity. You do not necessarily employ it.

M. It is employed. The amount of pleasure a person derives from a unit of a commodity of his stock being the given amount. That is, marginal utility varies with the amount of the supply. And this is an important feature of the notion. So the supply comes in there. On the same basis, supply comes into this quantity.

S. The comparison is easier.

M. What sort of comparison?

S. If you, the investigator can reduce pleasure to a ratio. You can always compare two ratios, but not two equal amounts or equal sizes of pleasures, without having them expressed in a ratio.

M. Yes. That is a point upon which later theorists have laid considerable stress. Put it this way: when the theorist thinks about the quantity of marginal utility, he sees that it has value; that is, mathematical value. What it really means is tied up with the size and nature of the unit, which he employs for a commodity. When he is thinking about the marginal utility of wheat, that is tied up with the final unit with which he measures wheat; namely, bushels, or sacks, or perhaps grains. And when he is thinking about the marginal utility of thread, it is tied up with the final, physical unit for measuring thread. He does not measure thread in bushels or grains, but presumably in diameters of the string itself and the length. If the inquirer talks about marginal utility and tries to get a series of quantities which are comparable he runs into various mathematical difficulties, arising from the fact that the physical units employed in dealing with amounts of different classes of commodities present the greatest variety, whereas if the individual goes through a simple operation of dividing the increase in the amount of satisfaction he gets from a given unit of a commodity, by the increase in the physical amount of that commodity that he has, and then throwing the concept into the form of a ratio, he will have a series of results which are mathematically strictly comparable with each other. One can compare any set of ratios in the world mathematically.

But that raises a question. What sense is there in dividing the increase in the amount of pleasure from consuming a certain commodity by physical commodities? How can you do it? Is not that nonsense? Doesn't it seem a little silly, perhaps, to divide the amount of satisfaction you get from eating bread by the increasing number of loaves? How do you perform an operation of that sort? This is an objection that arises in the minds of students. Is it an objection which is fatal to this whole procedure? Is it absurd to make a division of that sort?

S. As long as you measure pleasure at all, you might include that calculation. It is one simple fact. If anything is silly, the whole matter is and not that one fact. As long as you accept the whole matter, you might as well accept this fact too.

M. There is perhaps a simple way of reconciling your mind to this theory. You would say that it is logical to divide the number of people in the United States by the number of square miles in the country's area. Does that seem silly? It is just as silly as dividing the amount of pleasure by the physical units of the commodity. Yet that is exactly what is done when density per square mile is measured. We say there are so many people per square mile. We compare the density of population in the United States with the density in other countries. It is a legitimate procedure, to make a division of that sort and get a ratio for purposes of making comparisons.

S. That is not comparable.

M. Why not?

S. Units of quantity are definite—population is a definite quantity and area is a definite quantity; but utility is not measurable.

M. You are simply going back on one of the fundamental postulates in reference to our procedure which I mentioned in summarizing Jevons's theory of pleasure and pain; that is, he treats pleasures and pains as quantities which vary continuously. You may say that this is all nonsense. If you do, of course, you are quite right in drawing that conclusion. But granting Jevons's postulate that pleasures and pains are quantities that vary continuously, there is no reason why the investigator should not construct this ratio between the increase in the amount of pleasure and the amount of the commodity. Your criticism is against this whole type of work, and at a later stage of the discussion it must be faced. For the time being, we want to see what we can make out of this type of theory; and if this posture be granted there is nothing absurd in the procedure. The ratio between the increase in the amount of pleasure and the commodities can be handled in the same way as the ratio between the increase in the number of people in a certain territory and some artificial measure of extent.

Remember further that these ratios are regarded as significant by the theorist only for purposes of comparison, just like the figures of density per square mile. They are valuable primarily, because they help the investigator to compare conditions in different parts of the world; to say, for example, that the population situation is similar in perhaps Belgium and Holland and certain parts of England, and different in parts of Australia and Canada.

A member of the class objects to final degree of utility that it is illogical or rather nonsense to divide increase in utility by increase in commodity, as Jevons's symbols suggest. Analogy to clarify the concept afforded by increase of population. Suppose population of U.S. in 1910 was 100,000,000 and in 1920 will be 110,000,000. One cannot divide people by time but one can say that this increase takes place within a decade and amounts to 1,000,000 per year. That comparison of altogether dissimilar kinds is implied in such quantities as population per square mile, wealth per capita, wages per year, per week, per hour, etc. As for difference between final degree of utility and marginal utility, call increment in population marginal population. What is it? 10,000,000 or 1,000,000? What one should say is growth per some definite unit of time. So final degree of utility means increment added to utility per unit added to stock, say increase in population per decade, year, month or day. It does not measure value, it is not subjective value, but a proportion.[97]

---

[97] "Meaning of Final Degree of Utility and Marginal Utility," Outline, APP 44-53, no. 17.

[Professor Mitchell's friend, Allyn A. Young (1876-1929), gave a rather clear exposition of the point in his review of the fourth edition of *The Theory of Political Economy*: ". . . the concept of the 'final degree of utility' . . . is not precisely like the concept of 'marginal utility' with which it has usually been identified. For practical purposes both concepts come to about the same thing, and such difference as there is may be attributed to the fact that the concept of 'marginal utility' was not, in its origin, formulated mathematically.

The final degree of utility is, substantially, the quotient of marginal utility (conceived as the utility of the marginal increment) divided by the size of the marginal increment, where this increment is very small. More accurately, it is the *ratio* of the increase in total utility to the increase in the quantity of the commodity at the margin. 'Final degree of utility' is not only the more precise notion but it has the further advantage of being conceptually independent of the nature of the unit (pounds, bushels, yards, etc.) in which the commodity in question is usually measured. The latter quality made possible its convenient use in Jevons's 'equations of exchange.' But marginal utility is the less abstract concept and is undoubtedly better adapted to popular exposition . . .

The theorem that a person tends to adjust his expenditures so that the 'marginal utilities' of the various commodities consumed are equal, is, of course, true only when it is stipulated that the marginal increment is conceived as the amount of a commodity that can be bought with a dollar or other small unit of money. 'Marginal utility' is, for this reason, poorly adapted to the analysis of barter. 'Final degree of utility' is

To sum up this part of the discussion, the final degree of utility, as Jevons develops it, differs from the more familiar concept of marginal utility in that it is itself a ratio, whereas marginal utility is a quantity of feeling; that is, the final degree of utility is equal to the increase in the quantity of utility obtained by the addition of a final increment of a stock of a good divided by the increase in the physical quantity of the good. Marginal utility, on the other hand, is the utility derived from the use of the last added increment to the stock. This is a subtle but not unimportant difference. How does Jevons make use of this notion of final degree of utility? He supposes that all men utilize this conception in all their economic planning in their daily lives. He states that it can be employed to solve two problems: one is the problem of distributing a commodity among the different uses it may serve; the other is the problem of distributing over time a commodity which serves just one purpose. An example of the first problem, is distributing, say, wheat which can be put to several uses: as the basis for making ordinary white flour for bread or using it as a material for producing alcoholic liquor, or feeding it to poultry, and so on.

The easiest illustration for purposes of discussion is the distribution of a person's money income. For a person's objectives the chief advantage of money is that it can be converted into such a great variety of uses. How does he employ the notion of the final degree of utility in distributing the money at his disposal among the different uses to which it can be put? That is, he gets his newspapers, transportation, food, clothing, amusements and so on by spending money; and one of his chief economic problems is how he is going to use this common means, how much of it will he use in all these different avenues of expenditure. In solving that problem does he apply the idea of final degree of utility? What does Jevons say he does?

S. A person divides his money into these various classifications so that the final degree of utility of the money spent in each line is approximately equal according to his own judgment.

M. That is, a person divides the amount of money that he spends

the precise equivalent of Pareto's *ophélimité élémentaire* and of Walras's *rareté*." Young, "Jevons's *Theory of Political Economy*." 1912; reprinted in his *Economic Problems New and Old* (Boston: Houghton, Mifflin, 1927) pp. 222-223. For Vilfredo Pareto's term see his *Manuel d'economie politique* (1909); for Léon Walras's term see *Eléments d'economie politique pure,* 1874; definitive edition 1926; translation by William Jaffé under the title *Elements of Pure Economics* (1954).]

Total utility and degree of utility. Total utility represented by an area and degree of utility by a line. The final degree of utility equals degree of utility of last addition of a very small quantity to the existing stock. ("Jevons," APP 64-73, no. 35.)

upon satisfactions of different types in such a fashion that as nearly as possible the final degree of utility procured by the expenditure of one cent upon newspapers, subway trips, books, theatres, food and so on is equal. What is the reason for holding that? Why did Jevons take that for granted? Suppose a person says that he does not do that, how could you prove that he does?

S. I would go back to the assumption that individuals are trying to get the maximum utility from the expenditure of their money.

M. How does the adoption of the rule about equalizing the final degree of utility in all the different lines of expenditure maximize the utility a person can get from his income?

S. If a person spends money on one thing it is because he gets a higher final degree of utility from it than from some other thing. He expends his money for items that give him the highest final degree of utility.

M. Yes. There is a somewhat more effective way to explain this. The individual asks himself the question what would happen supposing he gets a higher final degree of utility from the money spent on newspapers than he got from the last cent he spent on food. Just as soon as he recognized that, he would increase his satisfaction by contracting his expenditure upon food and putting that same amount of money in newspapers. In other words, the proposition is readily proved by supposing its opposite, and recognizing that this presents a situation which no person, who endeavors to maximize the amount of utility he can get from spending money, would allow to continue, after he had recognized the situation. Clearly if he is getting more satisfaction from the money he is spending in one way, and that way is susceptible of ready increase, then he will cut down all expenditures that do not satisfy him in the same measure and increase expenditures in the other fashion.

In the case of the commodity wheat, first used as an example, Jevons supposes that a person will arrange the distribution of the quantities in each case in such a fashion that the final degree of utility derived from that article in each of its several uses will be as nearly as possible the same. If he secured a greater final degree of utility from the wheat which he fed to the fowls than from the wheat which he made into bread, it would be obvious that he had made a mistake in his distribution. He ought to have devoted more wheat to the feeding of his fowls, for by doing so he could have gained a larger degree of satisfaction out of the total stock.

The discussion will now pass to the second and the cognate problem: the use of the notion of final degree of utility in allocating the supply of a given commodity among the uses that it serves in time; that is, the distribution of the commodity in the same use over different periods of time. Take the case of Robinson Crusoe and his supply of wheat applied simply to making his own bread. Robinson Crusoe could get no increment added to his supply between harvests; therefore he faced the problem of so arranging the distribution of the wheat he made into bread so as to maximize his satisfaction. What role does the final degree of utility play in solving the problem? The question is in what way is Jevons's notion of the final degree of utility supposed to be invoked in order to guide the distribution of a commodity in the satisfaction of wants that recur through time?

Crusoe's wheat used for the making of bread was taken as a convenient stock example. After his harvest is over he has a certain supply and he must make it last for making bread. The question is how he will distribute, say, a stock of twenty bushels over the 180 days which elapse between harvests.

S. Jevons used the illustration of a boat at sea, and he said that they had a certain amount of food on board. If the boat reached the port within ten days they simply divided all the food by ten. If it was divided over a period of 30 days, it would be a hardship on everyone, for everyone would not get enough to eat. He gives the proportions as to how it should be divided.

M. And how should it be divided?

S. Jevons says that people value future wants less than present wants, and as the certainty of the event is less, so much less does one consider it.

M. Does he leave the matter there? Does it appear how these remarks bear on the use people make of final degree of utility?

S. We multiply the final degree of utility for each day's consumption by the probability, and the products for each day will be equal.

M. Does a similar remark apply to anything else about the future?

S. The remoteness.

M. That is, Jevons says that in practice, mankind discounts the gratification of the future in two ways; first, it discounts them just because they lie in the future and are not present; and second, it discounts them in accordance with their presumed degree of uncertainty. Granted that attitude, which is a familiar part of Bentham's felicific calculus—the discounting for futurity and uncertainty—what proposition remains that involves the final degree of utility? Can you equalize final degrees of utility? Does this mean that, if holding to the case of the bread on shipboard, we decided that we are providing sufficiently against the contingencies of a protracted voyage by laying in supplies for twenty days, we will take the stock we have now divided by twenty and assign the same amount for use in each of the twenty days? What does it mean?

S. It means, in a certain proportion; the first day's consumption will be the largest and provision for succeeding days will be less as they are more remote.

M. This is saying that the distribution would be made in such a fashion as to give rather larger consumption the first day than the second, a little more the second than the third, and so on throughout to the end. Do all the students agree?

S. Final degree of utility on each day is the same; but we consider futurity and uncertainty.

M. Yes. The future expected satisfactions are, he thinks, in practice discounted for their futurity and uncertainty; and then on the basis of the results left by the discounting, the person distributes the stock over the consumption of several days in such a fashion that the final degrees of utility will be equal. This means that the amount which he will consume in successive days is not equal but it starts at a maximum and then trails off slowly in the future. There is an equalization of final degrees of utility in solving this problem just as in solving the problem of the distribution of a good among several uses; but it is an equalizing of final degrees of utility as seen at the moment the distribution is carried out. As seen at that point the future satisfactions count as less important in a person's planning than immediate satisfactions. Therefore, they get assigned under a distribution of this sort smaller quantities of the commodity.

S. Is that because p and q are increasing fractions?

M. Yes. The discount for futurity and uncertainty becomes increasingly heavier as you get into the future. It is a theory which imputes to economic man a measure of what Irving Fisher of Yale has called "impatience."[98] It supposes, just as Bentham had, that because of lack of a sufficiently vivid imagination, men rate the satisfaction of present desires as more important than the satisfaction of future desires. And then it also supposes on top of that proposition, some irrational preferment given to immediate satisfaction over fu-

---

[98] See Fisher, *The Rate of Interest* (1907) and *The Theory of Interest* (1930). [Irving Fisher (1867-1947) was outstanding in mathematical economics and monetary theory.]

ture satisfaction. In addition, men are supposed to make as good a calculation as they can concerning uncertainties.

S. I should think that providing for the future would be more important.

M. There are circumstances. In later discussions it will be shown that, in general, solutions of this problem in the shape of supposing that all men discount the future or that nobody discounts for futurity are far from convincing. This general supposition has sometimes been replaced by an elaborate discussion to the effect that at certain times in his life the average man attaches more importance to providing for his future wants than for his present wants, and at other times in his life the opposite is the case. People in the stage of getting an education or professional training have a high discount on the future. Of most importance to them is what will happen to them in the next few years, and they will discount the years after they have secured their training very heavily. Men during their period of maximum earnings are supposed to discount the present in favor of the future; that is to say, the important thing for them is to make certain that they can remain tolerably comfortable during the years of declining earnings. And so it goes.

S. There is some mixup in Jevons's definition of intensity of feeling. He says that is the same thing as degree of utility—derived from an infinitesimal quantity of a commodity. Does he mean by that the units of intensity?

M. He professes to get on without units, and he supposes that a person in all his economic planning can go no further than to discriminate between quantities of feeling that are equal or unequal. He does suppose that every man can always tell which of two possible pleasures is the greater, and can also tell when he has achieved a balance of one pleasure over against another or of a pleasure against a pain; but Jevons has given up that artificial feature of Bentham's felicific calculus which called for setting up units in which a person could measure all the different aspects or phases of pleasure and pain; units of intensity, duration, fecundity, and so on.

S. From Jevons's discussion, just how much bread would be consumed the first day?

M. How much would the discount be? That is like asking just how many pounds of beef will a man give for a bushel of corn. The individual does not know. The theorist does not know. It depends on the *modus operandi* of the individual.

S. Does not Jevons deal with suppositions that are not true of any individual, but are true of the average individual?

M. He would say that the important thing for the purpose of the theorist is to deal not with the individual as such but with the characteristics which are common to large bodies of individuals. Jevons has not worked out that point completely, but he was a statistician and later in the discussion of the problem of the theory of exchange it will be seen that he has a device, although an awkward one, for meeting this condition.

Let us go on to what is from Jevons's point of view the central problem in the theory of political economy. This is the problem of exchange value. Jevons's solution of the problem of exchange is clearly stated in the following passage:

> The keystone of the whole Theory of Exchange and of the principal problems of Economics, lies in this proposition—*The ratio of exchange of any two commodities will be the reciprocal of the ratio of the final degrees of utility of the quantities of commodity available for consumption after the exchange is completed.* When the reader has reflected a little upon the meaning of this proposition, he will see, I think, that it is necessarily true, if the principles of human nature have been correctly represented in the previous pages.[99]

This means that Jevons here is proceeding to base his theory of exchange and the principal problems of economics on his preceding exposition of the principles of human nature. Later writers who have lost faith in hedonistic psychology believe this is one of his most serious, fundamental blunders. Many writers believe that his whole analysis is substantially valid, at least of great use, in accounting for the economic behavior of individuals, but that if it really did rest upon his preceding exposition of human nature, it would have to be discarded. They think the theorist can give it quite a different basis and still believe in its substantial solidity. But we will leave aside for the present, the question as to whether in fact the proposition is tied up with the correctness of the hedonistic psychology and try to get a clear view of what the proposition means and why anyone should believe it. Why does Jevons say that "the ratio of exchange of any two commodities will be the reciprocal of the ratio of the final degrees of utility"? Why the reciprocal? Why won't it be the ratio of the final degrees of utility?

S. The more of any commodity which is available for consumption at any one time, the smaller is the final degree of utility of any one unit of the commodity. Therefore if it is going to exchange with

---

[99] *The Theory of Political Economy,* p. 95.

something that has a higher degree of final utility, you will have an inverse relation there.

M. Cannot he put this simply and observe that the higher the importance the individual ascribes to a given commodity the less of that commodity will he give in exchange for anything else? That is obvious, is it not? Then let me ask another question. Jevons lays down this proposition with reference to the "final degrees of utility of the quantities of the commodity available for consumption after the exchange is completed." Why "after the exchange is completed"?

S. That is the point where it does not pay to exchange any more.

M. That is, we get the impression from the discussion as a whole that Jevons thinks perhaps (he is not clear on this) that trading might begin at some ratio other than that which is finally reached. The one proposition which the theorist can lay down concerns the ratio of exchange which will finally be arrived at, and that is the ratio with which dealing will come to an end. At that point, the two people who are exchanging commodities or two trading bodies have shifted the ownership of certain commodities, and then you can be sure on his analysis that the final degrees of utility are the reciprocals of the ratios at which the last trades have been effected.

Let us pass to a consideration of Jevons's way of demonstrating the grand conclusion. Who on his showing are the traders? Is he thinking about two large bodies of people who meet together? Do individuals compete for the goods exchanged? Who are the exchangers?

S. Individuals. We have their definite characteristics. He had in mind the idea of barter.

M. Yes, Jevons pictures the exchange which he is analyzing as carried on between two trading bodies; but the trading bodies, to all intents and purposes, act as two individuals. Consequently, what he gives here is an analysis of the case of barter between two aggregates of individuals acting as if they were single individuals. Observe in the first place, that this is a case of barter and not of buying and selling for money; and in the second place, that the trading bodies are pictured as individuals. Under these circumstances, can he conceive of this transaction as entered on under conditions of free competition?

S. There is no competition.

M. If two men are swapping a horse, is there any competition involved? (Just two men in one horse trade.) There is not, of course. Competition requires at least two men on one side of a possible bargain, so that there are two people who can compete against each other. If there are two men on one side and one on the other, this is a case of one-sided competition. If there be a large number of buyers and a large number of sellers, the buyers competing against each other, this is two-sided competition. Jevons's case of the two bodies acting as individuals eliminated competition. If there be no free competition can the theorist tell anything definite about the limits within which the price will fall?

S. The desire to part with commodities.

M. Take the case of two men trading a horse. Suppose this is a sale of a horse for money. Is there any basis for saying with any degree of certainty what price the two men will hit upon? Suppose one would be ready, if he had to, to give $100 for the horse, and the would-be seller would be willing to take $50. What will the price of the horse be?

S. Between $50 and $100.

M. But that is all the theorist can tell. If one of the traders happens to be a shrewd bargainer and can make successful guesses as to the limit to which the other man can be driven, he is likely to get the better of the bargain. If they are equally shrewd they will compromise somewhere within those limits. On the other hand, suppose there were a horse trade in which there were more individuals, an example which is common in modern text-books on economics. There are, say, ten men with horses for sale and ten who want to buy horses, and the horses are substantially alike. Suppose I set down the price that each one of the ten would-be buyers would be willing to give, those prices being different, and the prices the would-be sellers would be willing to accept, those prices also being different. Then the limits within which the prices for which the horses change hands would become much narrower than in the case of only the two men.

This illustrates the awkwardness of Jevons's treatment of this problem. The modern practice is to approach an exposition of the theory of price in the fashion that the illustration suggests; to begin with the case of buying and selling between two individuals and to suppose that the limiting prices are far apart; and then introducing more would-be buyers to show how that leads to a further narrowing of the price that can be realized in a market where all the people meet and compete against each other and every one of the buyers knows what everybody else is offering and every one of the sellers knows what each of the other sellers is willing to take. Under these circumstances the limits in which the price must fall become narrower. In making up an example the student should so arrange figures that the limits come precisely together and he will have a definite price. He can work out an example of that sort and he may find it instructive to get a contrast to Jevons's procedure.

Another remark is in order. The modern expositions almost always deal with buying and selling for money instead of dealing by barter. The problem of purchase and sale for money is technically a simpler problem than is presented by barter. Why?

S. The mere fact that the person who is trading the horse will be paid in a medium which he can use to purchase other commodities.

M. That is the point which theorists are likely to stress. They are dealing with stocks of commodities and want to give a picture which is realistic and convincing. They will have to introduce into their suppositions a rapid diminution in the final degree of utility of successive increments of the commodity. The horse trade is an exaggerated illustration of that. A farmer may want one or two horses, but after that the marginal utility of horses drops. On the other hand, for the reason just suggested by a member of the class, namely, that money is a means with which we can buy almost anything that we wish, it can be assumed without any radical departure from realism to have an almost or quite constant degree of utility for everyone in the market. That is to say, for two variables, there is substituted a problem that has but one; and that simplifies the problem.

Jevons, on the other hand, attacked the problem in a very hard form. He took in the first place, barter, and, in the second place, supposes dealings between two trading bodies, and that left him without the element of competition to help him in arriving at a decision. Yet he does seem to suppose that under these circumstances a definite ratio of exchange could be worked out, that without quite realizing what he was doing, he was thinking of these bodies not as individuals but as groups of people who would act more or less differently as individuals. It is hard to say; he does not make any remarks on the point. But later on, incidentally, in applying this theory of exchange to dealings in securities on the great stock exchanges, he does definitely take a situation in which there are many buyers and sellers, and in which one of the things which changes hands is money. If he had just taken that situation at the beginning instead of the one with the two trading bodies which he supposed was simpler, his exposition would have been more modern in tone, more convincing. If he limits himself to two trading bodies that act as individuals and are engaged in barter, then there is no telling at what specific prices exchanges will be made, unless the theorist has set up an exceptional supposition to the effect that one trading body will

give just one specific amount for the article held by the other and
vice versa, and supposes also that these bid and offer prices coincide.
It is only on that supposition, that the two trading bodies come to
market with their minds already made up to the same price, that
you can tell under Jevons's exposition—conditions taken literally and
strictly—what the ratio of exchange will be; or that you can lay down
his proposition to the effect that after trading is over, the final degrees
of utility of a commodity of the two parties separately will be the
reciprocals of the ratios on which the exchange was carried on.

Application of Jevons's law of ratio of exchange. Is it barter or purchase and
sale in money? Barter, but applies to money also in Jevons's eyes. Between
two trading bodies—which may be individuals or aggregates of individuals.
When taken as barter, Jevons uses not the concept of many dissimilar
individuals but a "fictitious man" who represents the average. Can there
be free competition between two individuals bartering with each other?
No. Can there be between two of Jevons's trading bodies literally interpreted? No. Jevons's conception of trading body keeps the cases in a
stage of barter between two individuals, where there are several or many
possible equilibrium prices.

How does Jevons's method of developing law of exchange value on basis of
marginal analysis differ from modern? The modern treatise begins with
case of two individuals bartering or buying and selling some commodity
for money; advantage of this supposition as opposed to barter. Simpler
because marginal utility of money is supposed to be constant. Shows that
there are *limits* within which ratios of exchange must fall. Then passes to
case of several buyers or several dealers or both, with different demand
and supply schedules and shows the limits within which ratios of exchange
are narrower. Jevons admits that the equations of exchange fail when
commodity is indivisible or even not infinitely indivisible. Hence, final
degree of utility merely sets limits for ratio of exchange. Within these
limits non-economic motives determine exact price. But he insists that
these cases harmonize with the perfect cases.[100]

S. Jevons says that stocks and prices of the two people are known
to all. What would be the consequence of that?

M. That is one of the things that suggests that he was thinking
more clearly than he wrote; that his trading bodies in his mind must
be conceived to be made up of different individuals. That is not the
way he writes it. It is a little curious that although his book went
through three editions in his lifetime, he left not a few ambiguities in it.

There is one other question for discussion by way of getting a clear
interpretation of the proposition as Jevons lays it down. He says,
to repeat, "the ratio of exchange of any two commodities will be the

---

[100] Outlines, December 4, 6, 1916. Refers to the discussion in *The Theory of Political
Economy,* pp. 122-126.

reciprocal of the ratio of the final degrees of utility of the quantities of commodity available for consumption after the exchange is completed." Suppose the commodities that he is talking about are corn and beef. We will call one trading body A and suppose that A had beef in the beginning and no corn; and the second trading body B, and suppose that it had corn and no beef. Does this mean that the final degree of utility of corn to A and beef to B will be in reciprocal relation to the final ratios of exchange? Jevons does not show whom he has in mind in his proposition about final degree of utility; yet final degrees of utility are feelings, and feelings have to be in someone's head. Does he mean that one trading body will value beef more than corn after the exchange is over in accordance with the reciprocals of the ratios of exchange?

S. He says merely that the final degree of utility is the reciprocal of the ratio of exchange after the transaction is over.

M. It should be recalled that Jevons said near the beginning that he was not going to institute any comparisons between the feelings of different individuals. Although he is not explicit at this point we must infer the result in the light of that earlier remark. He does not profess to know anything about how one trading body rates beef in comparison with the rating given to it by the other trading body, or how one trading body rates corn in comparison with the rating given by the second body. What he does hold is that to trading body A the final degree of utility of beef and corn is the reciprocal of the ratio of exchange after the transactions are over; and that the same is true with trading body B.

The suggestion has been made that Jevons's account gives an explanation as to why exchange does not occur rather than the ratio at which exchange takes place. Is that a comment which other members of the class accept? That is not what it purports to do. How do you justify the criticism?

S. Jevons speaks of what happens at the point of equilibrium. He explains conditions at which exchange would be incomplete.

M. In that sense you mean that he explains when exchange will stop. This is a just observation. That is not the sense in which I took your remark at the beginning. Jevons holds that exchange will cease when there is the inverse relationship established between the ratios in which the commodities are traded for each other and their final degrees of utility. Exchange goes on until an equilibrium is achieved and the interest of the theorist is in knowing how that equilibrium is attained and what bearing the attainment of the equilibrium has upon the ratios of exchange. Jevons himself might accept your comment in that form, without feeling that it was a stricture.

S. Does not Jevons's theory explain more adequately the exchange ratio for goods being purchased by consumers rather than goods being bought in the wholesale market for further sale to consumers?

M. To that all of us will agree. Jevons also might agree. He did not work out the problem, as the Austrians did presently, of how the exchange ratios of say, raw materials or producers' commodities can be explained on the basis of his analysis of utility. But the Austrians did complete the theory on that side. Their argument was that the utility of goods which are not in shape to satisfy human wants promptly is determined by the marginal utility of the finished products into which raw materials can be made or can be made by the use of things like machines.

These marginal utilities, on the Austrian type of analysis, are contributed ("imputed" is their technical term) by the commercial process, to the goods which are serviceable because indirectly they contribute to the satisfaction of people's wants; articles like hides, for instance, or, say, electrical energy which is used to drive machines, or machinery itself, or the equipment of a shop, a bank or mine. All these things can never directly gratify any human need; therefore they have no direct utility but have enormous indirect utility. The utility of such goods is derived from the marginal utility which they contribute indirectly to preparing goods which satisfy our wants.

S. What about the wholesale price of food products which are on the way to consumers in the hands of middlemen?

M. There the case, from the Austrian viewpoint, is comparatively simple. These goods are already in a shape to satisfy human wants. As such they have utility and marginal utility, but they are not capable of satisfying wants until they get distributed into the hands of the consumer. Further, you may regard them as goods of the second order; that is, they are closer to the satisfaction of wants than the raw materials out of which they are made, or machinery. But you impute the utilities which they are finally going to have in the present shape. Observe that they must go through another process, of being shipped to be distributed.

S. Jevons assumed that there is only one market. He does not consider, for instance, selling expenses, brokerage fees, commissions, etc.

M. Jevons says definitely in the beginning that his book is not an exhaustive treatise, but an effort to deal with the fundamental problems. He did not himself work out that question of what relation selling costs, etc., have to the price, the ratios of exchange of goods, any more than he worked out the problem of the way in which ratios of exchange are determined between raw materials or consumers commodities. But he would doubtless have said that anyone who would take up the problem could see that the fundamental fact in the whole situation must be the ratios between final degrees of utilities of the goods which satisfy desire; that just because goods satisfy desire, men are willing to take certain trouble, undergo the irksomeness of labor, in order to get hold of them. The painfulness of labor must be compensated for; it is part of the cost of production, and Jevons, as will soon be shown, has provided, even in his own logical discussion, a place for the influence of cost.

In his fundamental theorem of the inverse relationship which exists between ratios of exchange and final degrees of utility, nothing is said about cost of production. That meant formally, at least, a marked break from the traditional discussion of value. Ever since the days of Adam Smith, British theorists, in undertaking to explain at what ratios goods exchange for one another, had laid stress primarily upon cost of production. They had said that in the short run, exchange is determined by the supply of and the demand for the two commodities; but that in the long run (this is the best form which they had given to the theory) supply depends upon cost of production. Since the theorist is interested less in what happens in a given moment of time than over a considerable period, the economist, in analyzing the problem of value, finds that cost is the critically important factor in limiting supply. (See Appendix IV for elaboration.)

Jevons says nothing about this. On the first page of *The Theory of Political Economy* he states: "Repeated reflection and inquiry have led me to the somewhat novel opinion, that value depends entirely upon utility." Notice that he has put in the word *entirely*. Value depends *entirely* upon utility. Then when he lays down the proposition just discussed, which he asserts is the keystone of the whole "Theory of Exchange," again he makes no mention of cost of production; but a little later, when he is summing up the results of his discussion of exchange, he presents a different picture. This summary is introduced by the remark that *"Value depends solely on the final degree of utility."* But he goes on, *"How can we vary this degree of utility? By having more or less of the commodity to consume. And how shall we get more or less of it?—By spending more or less labour in obtaining a supply."* His own argument carries him back to the faith which the work of Ricardo and John Stuart Mill had rendered so familiar. He goes on to the particular point for discussion, which he represents in a *catena*.

>Cost of production determines supply.
>Supply determines final degree of utility.
>Final degree of utility determines value.[101]

[In a private letter to Cairnes, Jevons wrote: "In the chapter on Exchange, the dependence of value on supply and demand is treated wholly without regard to the mode of supply. It is when I pass in the next chapter, to the question of labour as yielding supply that values are found to be limited in the long run by the cost of production."][102]

Jevons's *catena* is a characteristically brief and brilliant summing up of his theory of exchange. Later economists have found various difficulties with the *catena*, the chain of reasoning. Are members of the class acquainted with any of the criticisms which have been made of the doctrine in this final formulation?

S. Alfred Marshall criticised that chain of reasoning.

M. Marshall has two criticisms. He says that the aim of science is to get back as far as possible to the factors which are ultimately responsible for the phenomena in which the theorist is interested. If this rule is followed and if Jevons is right in his *catena*, then the scientific thing is to do what Ricardo and John Stuart Mill had done; and say that cost of production determines value; that is, if cost of production determines supply, and supply the final degree of utility and final degree of utility determines value, then the conclusion must be drawn that in the last resort cost of production determines value. Thus Jevons's theory comes out at the same point at which Ricardo and John Stuart Mill had arrived. It is a more elaborate analysis of the process by which cost of production determines value—and that is all. There is no important change on Jevons's showing, according to Marshall.[103]

S. Would not Jevons's reasoning be that the final degree of utility determines cost of production?

---

[101] *The Theory of Political Economy*, p. 165.

[102] [Jevons to Cairnes, January 14. 1872 in R. D. Collison Black, "Jevons and Cairnes," *Economica*, April, 1960, p. 228. The *catena* reads in his primer of *Political Economy* as follows: "The labour which is required to get more of a commodity governs the supply of it: the supply determines whether people do or do not want some of it eagerly; and this eagerness of want or demand governs value." (*Political Economy*, p. 103.)]

[103] Marshall's criticism: why not leave out middle terms and say cost of production determines value? But note that Jevons says that value of products determine value of labor. (Outline, December 6, 1916.)

M. This leads to Marshall's second criticism. This is to the effect that the *catena* is a distortion of the facts. To understand the situation as a whole, the theorist must first recognize that all the factors determine one another; that is, cost of production and supply and final degree of utility and exchange ratios (value) are factors which do not stand in a single relation but in a relation of continual adjustment and readjustment. They all determine one another. The factors do not determine one another's variations but each helps in fixing the others.[104]

[Marshall says that Jevons's

> central doctrine . . . does not represent supply price, demand price and amount produced as mutually determining one another (subject to certain other conditions), but as determined one by another in a series. It is as though when three balls A, B, and C rest against one another in a bowl, instead of saying that the position of the three mutually determines one another under the action of gravity, he had said that A determines B, and B determines C. Someone else however with equal justice might say that C determines B and B determines A. And in reply to Jevons, a *catena* rather less untrue than his can be made by inverting his order and saying:—
> Utility determines the amount that has to be supplied,
> The amount that has to be supplied determines cost of production,
> Cost of production determines value,
> because it determines the supply price which is required to make the producers keep to their work.[105]

Later in the discussion of Marshall there will be a presentation of the analysis by which he tries to justify that view of the process as a whole, which is far more complex than the view that Jevons suggests. There is another criticism of the *catena* which has been made by Herbert Joseph Davenport.[106]

S. It is impossible to measure different kinds of labor or degrees of utility.

M. Of course, Jevons explicitly states not only that he does not attempt to measure utilities but that no one does. All that is necessary as the basis for his theory is that the people carrying on exchanges and producing can tell when one pleasure is greater than another or equal to another. What Davenport says is that it is by no means true that final degree of utility determines value directly. What is true if the theorist uses Jevons's theory is that every person who is engaged

---

[104] Sentence from Outline, December 6, 1916.
[105] [Marshall, *The Principles of Economics* (London: Macmillan, 1890; eighth edition, 1920) p. 818. All future references, unless otherwise specified, are to the eighth edition.]
[106] The specific criticisms are made in Davenport's *Value and Distribution: A Critical and Constructive Study* (Chicago: University of Chicago Press, 1908) pp. 336-337. On Davenport, see Chapter XIII.

in buying and selling makes a comparison between the final degrees of utility to him of both commodities which are subject of traffic. From this comparison of the changing final degrees of utility as stocks increase, every individual, Davenport explains elaborately in *The Economics of Enterprise* (1913), arrives at a set of demand prices—price offers—makes up his mind what it is worth his while to give for successive increments in the supply, and these scales of demand are what determine value. People do not connect final degree of utility directly with value, and the market does not do that. Values are determined directly by price offers and these price offers are determined by comparisons between final degrees of utility, and determined separately by every individual in the market.

S. Does that mean that the buyer has compared the final degrees of utility of several commodities offered for sale?

M. According to Davenport's analysis, a man would come into a market, say, for onions. He would be willing to pay a certain price for one, a lower price for a second, still lower for a third, and so on. That scale of demand prices—possibly a very high price for the first, maybe fifty cents, and perhaps when he gets down to the fortieth he would pay a cent or so for one—that scale of price offers he arrived at in his mind by comparing the marginal utility of successive onions added to his stock.

The last step in Jevons's *catena* is that final degree of utility determines value. Davenport's criticism is that we want to get final degrees of utility directly with value—value meaning rates of exchange in Jevons's treatise. What we can do is recognize that people compare final degrees of utility of the commodities being bought and sold and from this comparison they form their scale of prices for every successive unit of supply. And then when there is a market in which there are a considerable number of people who want to buy or sell and each one has his own scale of price offers, then there is the machinery for determining the rate of exchange, or price.

Davenport's criticism is that final degree of utility does not determine value, but for each man in the market separately comparison of the final degrees of utility of the two goods dealt in determines *his* marginal demand price. Market price falls within limits set by these marginal demand prices and corresponding marginal selling prices. Does Jevons confuse final degree of utility with marginal price offers? But there are also passages where there is a clear distinction.[107]

S. Cannot the same criticism be made of Davenport that Marshall makes of Jevons about the ultimate cost and intermediate steps?

---

[107] Outline, December 6, 1916.

M. This is not Davenport's full analysis but simply a point he makes in criticizing Jevons's theory of value.

S. I mean Marshall criticized Jevons for putting in intermediate steps. Davenport might be criticized for leaving out one.

M. Quite right. The first criticism of Marshall's is primarily a dialectical point. If there are intermediate steps between the influence which cost of production has upon value, then in the scientific analysis the inquirer wants to know what they are and if it is worth while to work out the process. Marshall's second criticism that the factors continually influence one another is scientifically much more important than the other. Now the *catena* means that Jevons does have occasion, though he started out by saying that the value depends entirely upon utility, to enter into a discussion of cost of production, which he proceeds to do immediately after the summary.

The next chapter in *The Theory of Political Economy* is on the theory of labor. In this he deals with labor as the most important factor in cost, in a manner analogous to that in which he dealt with utility. From his point of view, labor is most of the time irksome. He admits that when a man begins work, or at least after he has labored a bit and got into the swing of it, he may find the exertion actually pleasing for a time and derive some utility from it. But after he has continued toiling for a certain length of time he begins to find the work irksome and the pain imposed continues and grows greater as the working period is prolonged. So that the theorist can set up for labor a curve representing a gradually increasing pain cost just as he can set up for the consumption of commodities a curve representing the diminishing utility derived from consumption. Jevons says the increasing disutility of labor is what leads people to limit supply. The reason why people do not have more goods is that most of the goods they like to consume can be obtained only at the cost of labor; and the amount of the goods they can consume depends upon the time and energy they are ready to put into work. Since increasing labor time involves increasing pain, people continue to work up to that point at which the utility of the increment added to their supply of goods exceeds or just balances the increasing sacrifice involved in the work itself.

It would seem that Jevons here laid a basis for a highly systematic treatment of the whole theory of value. You might expect him, having arrived at this proposition, to go back to his *catena* and say that I have shown that the cost of production is a factor of precisely the same generic sort as utility, just as the reason why people value goods is a subjective one, in that the gratification they get from them was the limit upon their supply. Therefore, the ultimately important factor in determining value is a subjective matter: the sacrifices involved in producing goods. Thus Jevons writes:

> A free labourer endures the irksomeness of work because the pleasure he expects to receive, or the pain he expects to ward off, by means of the produce, exceeds the pain of exertion. When labour itself is a worse evil than that which it saves him from, there can be no motive for further exertion, and he ceases. Therefore he will cease to labour just at the point when the pain becomes equal to the corresponding pleasures gained . . .
>
> In this, as in the other questions of Economics, all depends upon the final increments, and we have expressed in the above formula *the final equivalence of labour and utility.*[108]

S. May we accept the theory that there is a certain constantly increasing pain cost? Does it follow that the second day's work is increasingly costly?

M. Jevons discusses this with reference to one day's work. The important factor, from his point of view, in determining how large the supply of goods will be is how many hours people are ready to work on the average, day by day.

S. Looking at it from another standpoint, not the cost to the individual but the judgment society has set on that expenditure of energy, the individual is not adjusting himself to his own individual valuation but to a valuation set in advance by many others, and he brings his own valuation into harmony with theirs.

M. I think you are implicitly criticizing Jevons's hedonistic view of people's whole procedure in working, a criticism you might extend to his theory of people's valuation of goods on the basis of their utilities. Any person acquainted in the least bit with modern psychological studies would agree with the criticism and say: no, it is a very artificial view of the situation to suppose that people are continually balancing the pains which labor involves against the utilities that they are going to get from the consumption of the goods they are producing. It was not long after Jevons wrote—a decade or so afterwards—when economists began to have serious doubts of exactly that sort, as to the validity of this whole theory of value. But that issue will be discussed at a later time. For the present we had better see how Jevons makes use of his artificial and indeed curious psychological notions for purposes of solving economic problems.

S. How does the theory apply when labor is not free?

M. Jevons says "A free labourer endures the irksomeness of work."

---

[108] *The Theory of Political Economy*, pp. 176-177.

Note that he is talking about a free labourer. A slave would not be in that position. Many of his later critics have said that this is false; that the modern business organization does not make it possible for the legally free laborer to stop when he wants to. He has to work until the whistle blows and it may be that the last hour of work to him will exceed in the sacrifice it entails the utility which he gets from his earnings in that last hour. If he wants the job at all he has to stay.

S. A man working for himself might be regarded as a free labourer.

M. Yes. A man working on his own behalf would be, from Jevons's point of view, a good case; say, a shoemaker working in his own little shop.

S. If Jevons's statement is taken as meaning that the man represents a social group in this theory of not working say an extra hour, then it probably has more value.

M. Yes. That is the answer to objections of this sort. Jevons in his discussion of labor, as in his discussion of the problems of exchange, talks about individuals or groups, and remarks every now and then that the one expression is for his purpose equivalent to the other. That remark is a little curious for if there is a group that is made up of different individuals, it could not be the same thing as one individual, unless the theorist had in mind a composite and he can do this only by summing up the feelings of different people. That is one of the minor slips of which Jevons's brilliant treatise is full.

S. What man gets as the result of his labor has little to do with the amount of labor he puts in. As things now stand, people can produce more than they do with not much more effort, but the prevailing system of exchange holds them back on that.

M. That is another legitimate line for criticizing not merely Jevons but everybody who has worked on the problem of value in this particular fashion. It is a type of theoretical approach which is exemplified in Thorstein Veblen, looking at the broader features of the prevailing economic organization and seeing how these institutions dominate men's behavior; how in large measure they act as they do not because of close individual calculation of what is to their advantage, but because people are in a great, big social system, which they have made for themselves and in the face of which each one is powerless and to which people have to adapt themselves.

In Jevons's treatise each individual is hunting for the greatest amount of pleasure at the expense of a minimum of pain; one is supposedly free to make his own choice. Of course, the theorist can reason on that assumption if he wants to. If he does, he ought to at

least carry the reasoning through and ask what relation it has to the
world in which people actually live. That is a consideration which
later theorists have put very vigorously. The answer they give to the
question is that this kind of analysis does not have a great deal to do
with the economic behavior of modern man. Jevons is a beautiful case
of a theorist suggesting a whole series of problems which some of the
later books on economic theory attempt to solve.

S. Jevons seems to say that a person considers the utility of a particular good to him. If we introduce money into that, as an inter-
mediary, are we to compare the pain of labor to money and then
from money go on to bread and so on?

M. From Jevons's point of view the individual compares the pain
which is involved in continuing to labor with the marginal utility
of whatever he would spend his additional earnings for. Maybe he
would buy periodicals with it and maybe someone else would buy
shoes or food. Whatever is of more importance to him that he does
not now have and he could buy with money, represents the addition he
compares with the sacrifice of continued work. This means that in
order to deal with any one problem of value, the theorist has to
consider the prices at which the individual can get other things; that
is, to solve the problem of exchange which the individual is ready
to make between work and money the theorist has to assume that a
whole set of other prices is already established. That means that to
solve one problem in value, the theorist supposes a great many other
problems in value have already been solved. If he pushes that kind
of analysis he comes to see that in a modern community every price
depends upon every other price; that the only satisfactory way in
which to handle the problem of price determination is to solve it in
a fashion that will allow the theorist to suppose that all prices determine one another at the same time. This is a line of analysis [general
equilibrium analysis] that certain theorists have taken up. This approach was followed three years after the publication of Jevons's
book, by his French contemporary Léon Walras (1834-1910) of the
University of Lausanne, and resulted in the brilliant development of
the mathematical theory of prices which Walras started in his
Éléments d'economie politique pure; ou theorie de la richesse social,
(1874-1877) [*Elements of Pure Economics, or the Theory of Social
Wealth,*] and which several economists are trying to complete.
Walras's theory of pricing presents most explicitly

> . . . the bewildering complexity of economic interrelations. . . . The
> classical economists felt justified in analyzing the factors that govern
> the price of one good in terms of a second, on the assumption that

other conditions remain the same. Léon Walras emphasized the unreality of this primitive procedure. Going to the opposite extreme, Walras insisted that the demand for every good in a market depends not only on its own price but also upon the prices at which all other goods in the market could be had, and that the supply of every good is similarly dependent not only on its own cost of production but also upon the cost of producing all other goods. On this showing, the proper way to study pricing is to consider the determination of the prices of n goods at the same time. Walras attacked this problem by using several sets of simultaneous equations of which the first will suffice for illustration [for the present]. Each of the n equations in this set represents the demand for one commodity as some function of its price and the price of every other commodity. Despite its formidable appearance, Walras demonstrated that the problem as he stated it is theoretically determinate, because the number of simultaneous equations that can be set up is equal to the number of unknowns.[109]

In one sense, Walras's approach is the line which Davenport has taken, although he has tried to present the problem without mathematical formulae, and it is largely because he did dispense with these symbols that the class should read his book representing that line of development, which will be discussed later.

Another attempt—and I suppose a theoretically more important attempt—to solve the problem of value analysis is represented by the Swedish economist Gustav Cassel in his *The Theory of Social Economy*.[110] [It is a simplified version of the Walrasian scheme, but represents such a development that the Walrasian model is now referred to as the "Walras-Cassel Model."] Cassel's treatise will also be discussed later in detail. (Chapter XVI).

Some theorists are trying to develop the whole scheme in a much more elaborate and satisfactory way than even Cassel has done. His book applies only to conditions that exist at a given moment. The theorist has to assume that no change takes place in the number of people, or the conditions under which the goods are produced, the desires that people have for different goods, the supply of labor of different kinds, and the quantity of capital available for investment;

[109] Mitchell, *The National Bureau Enters Its Twentieth Year* (New York: The National Bureau of Economic Research, 1939) p. 25.

[Mathematical economists while accepting Walras's scheme as substantially sound have found out that strictly speaking "Equality of the number of equations and the number of unknowns is neither necessary nor sufficient for the existence of a solution (let alone a unique solution) to a system of equations." Robert Dorfman, Paul Samuelson, and Robert Solow, *Linear Programming and Economic Analysis* (New York: McGraw-Hill, 1958) p. 350. The authors assert that "given reasonable assumptions, the existence of a competitive equilibrium can be proved and by methods which are essentially similar to the ones we have used, although necessarily more complicated." (p. 381).]

[110] Cassel's *Theoretische Sozialökonomie* (1918) was first translated into English in 1924; a later improved translation was made by S. L. Baron (1932).

all these things are taken as fixed and then the theorist can make a set of simultaneous equations equal to the unknowns in the problem, and he is justified in saying the problem can be solved. Some economists, for instance Henry L. Moore (1869-1958) of Columbia University in *Synthetic Economics* (1929), attempted to develop this line of treatment in such a fashion that they can apply it to dynamic problems. They do not have to suppose that the elements in the problem remain fixed; they can allow them all to vary as functions of time and still set up a series of equations which will be just equal to the number of unknowns in the problem. That is again simply an anticipation of another way of trying to solve one of the difficulties connected with the problem of the theory of value which John Stuart Mill, you may recall, says happily contains no elements which any "present or . . . future writer" will be required to clear up, and which, Jevons, in his turn, after he had wrought what he thought a fundamental change in methods of attack, presents as fundamentally simple to solve.

S. Is not Jevons's individualistic attack on the problem a development of the spirit of individualism at the time he was writing?

M. I suppose it is. Jevons comes finally to the statement that perfect freedom of exchange tends to maximize utility. He says that "in questions of this sort there is but one rule which can be safely laid down, namely that no one will buy a thing unless he expects advantage from the purchase." He might have added here that no one will work unless he expects advantage from his sacrifice. He continues with "and perfect freedom of exchange, therefore, tends to the maximising of utility."[111]

This is a very broad, sweeping statement of the fact that the people are going to get maximum satisfaction out of economic life if everyone is free. He can make his own decisions as to how much of a good he will give for another, as to just how long he will labor, because no one will give more of one commodity to secure a supply of a second unless the final degree of utility of the good he will get will be at least equal to the final degree of utility of the good he is parting with. No one produces anything unless he is sure the pleasures he gains by his consumption will fully compensate for the sacrifice involved in the toil.

The Jevonian scheme of analysis might be employed theoretically as a defense of that organization of society for which Adam Smith pleaded, for showing that *laissez-faire* is, from the point of view of economic welfare, the most advantageous method of organizing human

---

[111] *The Theory of Political Economy*, p. 145.

efforts. As a matter of fact, this type of analysis has been employed specifically toward that end. No one can read the Austrian writers, whose general scheme was similar to Jevons's, without feeling that they are interested in developing the concept of the maximizing of utility largely because they thought it answered Marx's socialistic critique of modern economic organization. It seemed at least at first blush, to show that, so long as interference with competition is repressed, theoretically the best possible organization of society results when everyone is left perfectly free to make his own decisions. On the other hand, there have been theorists who have utilized this type of analysis to a very different effect. One of the interesting and rather ironical developments of the generation after Jevons was that this line of economic theorizing which the Austrians used in answer to Marx was adopted by the Fabian socialists as their basic economic doctrine, and a new scheme of socialism, very different in character from Marx's, was erected on its foundation. But that is another matter for discussion.[112]

Jevons's most famous contribution to the development of economic theory was his discussion of value, but he also threw out, in characteristic fashion, a pregnant hint toward a theory of distribution. To appreciate this, it is necessary to recall a feature of the discussion of distribution in the treatises of Ricardo and John Stuart Mill. Ricardo was the first of the great economists who proceeded to make distribution the central problem of theory. It was in the preface to his *Principles of Political Economy* that the passage occurs in which he says that the chief problem of political economy concerns the proportion in which the wealth annually produced in a country is divided among the several classes concerned with production. But he opened the book by a long discussion on the theory of value. Judging by modern practice he would have been expected to treat the theory of distribution in terms of the concepts which he developed in his theory of value. But he does not do anything of the sort. He lays down a theory of value and then proceeds in successive chapters to develop the laws of wages, of profits, and of rent as though they have no formal organic connection with what he says about the principles of value.

In a genuine sense, John Stuart Mill followed Ricardo's example.

---

[112] Note Jevons's own discussion of *laissez-faire* in his *The State in Relation to Labour* (1882). Outline, December 6, 1916.

In so far as he deviated from Ricardo, he did so in a direction opposite from that of modern practice. His *Principles of Political Economy* begins with a discussion of the production of wealth. Then comes the distribution of wealth. Then he takes up the subject of exchange. This short section on exchange contains his exposition of the laws of value. This means that in his eyes, as in those of Ricardo, the principles of distribution are not derived from the theory of value.

Contrast that procedure with what is becoming standard practice in modern treatises. These begin, like Ricardo, with a discussion of value. Then they treat distribution; but all the problems in distribution are taken up as special problems to be treated in terms of the theory of value. The law of wages turns into a discussion of what determines the value of and the price paid for labor. The theory of rent turns into a discussion of what determines the value of and the price paid for the use of land. The theory of interest turns into a discussion of what determines the value of and the price paid for the use of loan capital; or, more at length, what it is that determines the value of the service rendered by capital in production. The theory of profits is similarly a discussion of what determines the value of and the price paid for the service of business management.

Jevons occupies a curious intermediate position between the attitude of his classical predecessors and that of his orthodox successors. He throws out in the preface of the second edition of 1879 this hint: "distribution is entirely subject to the principles of value," a remark which prepares a reader who has learned his economics from books written in comparatively recent years to expect that once his theory of value has been propounded, Jevons will go on and discuss in terms of final degree of utility, the value of the services rendered by labor, land, capital and management, and build up theories of wages, rents, interest and profits, corresponding in form to the celebrated proposition about the problem of exchange value. He, however, did not succeed in working out that hint. It was not less characteristic that he failed to follow up his curious bit of insight. Likewise the posthumous *The Principles of Economics* (1905) contains a better statement of the hint, but that is all. "The whole subject of the distribution of wealth is nothing but a result of the theory of value. Wages, profits, interest, rent, are but the prices at which the owners of diverse kinds of property are able to sell them."

When he goes on to discuss the theory of distribution he accepts explicitly the Ricardian law of rent, despite his rather vigorous anti-

Ricardian, anti-Mill complex, but Jevons translates it into his symbolic language and illustrates it by a diagram.[113]

When he discussed interest he gave a formula which his son, H. Stanley Jevons also an economist, interprets in the first appendix of the fourth edition to mean that he had at least a premonition or anticipation of the doctrine that the rate of interest is determined by the marginal productivity of capital. The passages on which that view might be based are:

(1) "consider that interest is determined by the increment of produce which it enables a labourer to obtain"; and (2) "the rate of interest depends on the advantage of the last increment of capital, and the advantages of previous increments may be greater in almost any ratio."[114]

It is easy to interpret these statements as a foreshadowing of the type of theory of interest which John Bates Clark of Columbia University (who will be discussed later, Chapter XI) elaborated in the 90's especially in *The Distribution of Wealth* (1899). Allyn A. Young pointed out that Jevons's ideas on interest were an adumbration of the theory which was shortly afterward developed by Böhm-Bawerk, and described by him as the theory of the technical superiority of present goods.[115] This theory, which connects the rate of interest not so much with the marginal productivity of capital as with the fact that by using capital men are enabled to adopt round-about methods of production. These methods are more efficient and produce a larger proportion to the total energy expended than the simple methods which alone can be carried on in a community where there is not a large stock of accumulated wealth which can be employed in producing additional wealth. In short, the most characteristic feature of Jevons's theory of interest is that we are left in doubt as to what he really did mean.

In dealing with wages he develops what perhaps may best be called the residual claimant theory. He says:

> The view which I accept concerning the rate of wages is not more difficult to comprehend than the current one. It is that the wages of a working man are ultimately coincident with what he produces, after the deduction of rent, taxes and the interest of capital.[116]

---

[113] Second clause in above sentence from Outline, December 6, 1916.

[Jevons also followed Ricardo on monetary and banking policy. He was a strong supporter of the Ricardian Peel's Bank Act of 1844.]

[114] *The Theory of Political Economy*, pp. 254, 256.

[115] Young pointed out that Jevons, along the line of Böhm-Bawerk's later theory, attributed diminishing productivity to the period of the investment rather than the capital invested. Outline, December 6, 1916. Young's statement is in his "Jevons's Theory of Political Economy," in *Economic Problems New and Old*, pp. 227-229.

[116] *The Theory of Political Economy*, p. 270.

This is not strictly a marginal productivity theory. He is saying that laborers get whatever is left after the shares of the landlord, the capitalist and the business manager have been paid. Labor is therefore the residual claimant; that is, it is the recipient of any surplus of production over and above the rewards which must be allocated to the three other factors.

Finally, on profits he has a simple doctrine: "We resolve profits into wages of superintendence, insurance against risk, and interest." The first part, wages of superintendence, is like wages; and so that element of profits is determined in accordance with the general law of wages as the residual share. The second part, insurance against risk "equalizes the result in different employments"; that is, it is simply a differential which is necessary to make sure that the results obtained in different employments of business management shall be in the long run substantially equal. The third part, "the interest is, I believe, determined as stated in the last chapter." As already noted it is difficult to make out how it is determined, but it is covered in a sense by that formula. The complete statement by Jevons is:

> If we resolve profit into wages of superintendence, insurance against risk, and interest, the first part is really wages itself; the second equalises the result in different employments, and the interest is, I believe, determined as stated in the last chapter.[117]

This constitutes the gist of Jevons's theory of distribution. He does not profess that the treatise gives a systematic view of economic theory as a whole. It does undertake the systematic statement of the theory of value, and then is supplemented by somewhat casual, random remarks about the shares in the produce which go to the various factors in production. The most valuable suggestion which Jevons makes about distribution is the hint which, as noted before, he inserted in the preface that "distribution . . . is entirely subject to the principles of value"; but he did not develop the hint.

Do the members of the class have any questions which they would like to discuss concerning any phase of Jevons's type of theory?

S. Is the residual claimant theory just the reverse of the discounted marginal [product] theory?

M. It is not the opposite. Perhaps it could be regarded as a twisted form of the marginal productivity theory. On the basis of the marginal productivity theory, as fully elaborated by John Bates Clark, all the factors of production have their shares in the net output determined by their several marginal contributions to the total. The product is

---

[117] *The Theory of Political Economy*, p. 270.

supposed to be divided up without residual among the several factors. The exponents of the residual claimant doctrine, of which the American General Francis A. Walker was a notable if not the most notable representative, took the ground that there was only one factor to which all the balance went.[118] Walker, like Jevons, put labor in that position. Walker, even more strongly and more effectively than Jevons, argued that the reason wages were on a higher level in the United States than in Europe, to give an example, was that in the United States the product of efforts spent in production was decidedly larger; and while the prices which had to be paid for the use of capital and managerial ability were higher than in Europe, they were not too much higher so that a considerably larger final share was not left to the workmen. Labor is the only claimant whose reward is not determined by some specific law. Others have set up residual claimant theories, only they represented other factors as the residual claimants. Particularly it is easy to represent profits as getting the residual share. That view is in a sense related to the marginal productivity notion, but not in any close and organic fashion.[119]

S. Is the work of John Bates Clark in the same class of theories as those of Jevons? Are there other theorists who come in that class?

M. I do not know whether Clark would feel quite satisfied with being put in the same class as Jevons. In several ways, he does not belong there. That suggests a question. What name can we give to the type of theory which Jevons developed? A name should be descriptive of it. We talk about classical political economy, meaning specifically the type of theory which is best represented in Ricardo and John Stuart Mill. Is there some other equally or even more descriptive phrase which could be applied to Jevons's type?

S.1. Hedonistic.

S.2. Psychological.

M. Psychological can certainly be spread over a great many other types of explanation. For that matter so can hedonistic. The classicists had a conception of behavior at least as hedonistic as Jevons. Furthermore, some of the later people worked on the basis of hedonistic assumptions.

---

[118] [General Francis Amasa Walker (1840-1897) while teaching at Yale published the most influential attack on the wages-fund doctrine. It began with newspaper articles in 1874 and culminated in *The Wages Question* (1876).

His residual claimant theory is best expressed in his *Political Economy* (New York: Holt, 1883; 3rd edition, 1888) pp. 248-251.]

[119] ". . . there is no evidence that he [W. Stanley Jevons] conceived of the idea of a general theory of distribution by marginal productivity." (H. Stanley Jevons, "Note by the Editor on the Author's Theory of Interest," in *The Theory of Political Economy*, p. 293). Quotation in Outline, December 6, 1916.

S. Mathematical.

M. Mathematical again is too wide. If that term is used at all, it belongs more properly to Walras who was stronger on the mathematical side than Jevons and whose type of theory was different. Jevons himself states the name for his theory.

S. Mechanics of utility.

M. Yes, he suggests that in his preface.

To go back to the question of whether Clark would feel altogether content to have his work described as the mechanics of utility, this is controversial. While some might feel that no injustice would be done to his accomplishments by applying that label to his works as well as to Jevons's, others would certainly take exception. Let us leave that difficult question alone for, at least, the present. Clark, so far as his fundamental notions concerning value are concerned, is more along Austrian than Jevonian ideas. He was one of the people who talked about marginal utility instead of final degree of utility; and his whole elaborate scheme of distribution on the basis of marginal productivity is technically much closer in line with the work of Menger, Wieser and Böhm-Bawerk than with Jevons.[120]

S. Please comment on the place of statistics in Jevons's theory. It seems that the use of statistics is more a supplement than a basis.

M. That is true. In a sense Jevons created difficulties for himself in using statistics; at least, in the fundamental groundwork of his theory. That is, if it is true, as he says, that the driving forces which the economist has to consider are pleasures and pains, that the theorist cannot measure these quantities and that people themselves do not measure them, but at most pay attention to the relations of equality and inequality, then it would appear that it is hopeless to get statistics concerning the fundamental forces. How can statistics be obtained unless there are units which can be counted? None the less, Jevons thought that by an adequate collection of statistical materials— which he thought might be available some day—it would be possible to subject the conclusions of economic theory to inductive verification. He did not go any length in that direction. Once again we have from him a pregnant hint of what might be possible, but it is something which might be possible in a vastly more effective fashion on the basis of a conception of human nature radically different from the one he employed. For the rest, Jevons's great service to the development of

---

[120] [Clark attributed the stimulus to the formulation of the marginal utility doctrine to suggestions of his teacher at Heidelberg, Knies. The doctrine of marginal productivity is generally considered to be a contribution of Clark. See Clark, *The Distribution of Wealth*, 1899 and Chapter XI below.]

quantitative methods in economics was more distinguished than that
of any other economist in the nineteenth century, with the possible
exception of Wilhelm Lexis and F. Y. Edgeworth.[121] Jevons's contributions to its development are contributions to the discussion of topics
which do not come into his scheme of fundamental economic theory.
They did not, to repeat, because he had the misfortune to build up
his plan of theory on the basis of the curious Benthamite viewpoint
that all that men do is controlled by the forces of pleasure and pain,
and this prevented him from making effective use of statistical procedure for the discussion of basic economic problems. Even today we
have not gone very far in using statistical devices in the discussions
of value and distribution.

S. Why are the classical economists called "classical"?

M. Probably because they were the representatives of that type
of economic theory which first got formulated in a fairly scientific
shape. Probably for the same reason that you can call, say, John
Milton's poems, classical; they are classical; they are representative
of their type. Needless to say, it is not because of any reference to
antiquity.

S. Is Adam Smith usually classed with or before them?

M. Usage differs. The application of the term "classical" is a little
loose. In Adam Smith economic theory was not very definitely formulated. *The Wealth of Nations* is a discussion, not of the problems
which have been put into the center of economics in the nineteenth
and twentieth centuries, but primarily of the old mercantilist problem
of how to increase the wealth of nations, yet in a spirit which had a
large share of modern admixture. The problems of the later day are
first definitely formulated in a systematic fashion by Ricardo.

I do not doubt my usage varies from time to time; I might include
Smith or exclude him. Stricter usage regards Smith as a forerunner
rather than as a representative of classical political economy in its
mature form; but it is always a little hard to know just how far one
will go in using a term like that, to include or exclude forerunners.
A bit of inconsistency of that sort is not very grievous.

S. Can you say that Smith is greater than the others?

M. Most people, if a vote were taken, would doubtless say that
Adam Smith is the greatest of economists.

S. Would Jevons regard the part of profits which goes to wages
of management as the residual share after all others?

---

[121] [Lexis (1837-1914) taught at a number of leading German universities. His
last post was the chair of economics at Göttingen where he began teaching in 1887.]

M. As a residual share in the sense that all wages are residual shares. That is all that he says about it, and I do not think on the basis of the text I can give any more detailed information than that. He leaves the specific question untouched.

S. The wages of management are always a proportion of profits?

M. Yes—it is certainly a casual and off-hand way of disposing of a difficult question. Jevons never thought out the question with any degree of thoroughness.

Summary of Jevons's theory. Restricted scope: Theory of value with some remarks on labor, rent, capital and population. Pure theory. Mathematical formulation. Developed utility analysis which had been neglected by classical political economy. That development followed Bentham. First and at least most elaborate attempt by one of the recognized economists to make use of Bentham's felicific calculus. Came at a time when hedonistic psychology was being superseded by changed conception of human nature. How Jevons's use of felicific calculus differed from Bentham's. What Jevons added is emphasis upon final degree of utility in determining economic behavior.

Jevons does not measure, nor even suppose his subjects to measure in any more elaborate sense than being able to tell whether pains and pleasures are equal to, or unequal to each other. Further, most of these balancings are supposed to be not of total pleasures but of marginal feelings, not of total utility but of final degree of utility.

Jevons holds to his ideal of pure theory rather strictly in *The Theory of Political Economy,* although he does occasionally offer advice (see for example pp. 87, 146). Aim, however, is distinctly to get clear insight into existing economic facts. How far does Jevons's type of theory carry back the explanation of value? Are there any facts assumed which themselves require explanation? Schedules of changing utility of commodities and of changing labor pains are taken ready made. And they determine final degrees of utility and ratios of exchange in a very simple fashion. It is only this last mechanical step in the process of determining value that Jevons's method attempts to account for. Even if he could get statistics to make empirically valid demand schedules for different commodities they would not explain how the ratios of exchange are fixed. Jevons's type of theory also takes for granted an elaborate set of institutions—private ownership, organized markets, habits of exchange and even, although Jevons is hardly aware of the fact, the use of money. Are we content to stop process of explanation at this point? Does economics hand over these problems to psychology and economic history? Do these sciences accept and solve these problems?[122]

The reception accorded *The Theory of Political Economy* was disappointing to the author. He made comparatively little impression

[122] Outline, December 6, 1916.

upon other students of economics, at the beginning presumably in good part at least because of the mathematical dress in which he clad his ideas. Anybody who reads the book nowadays, finds the mathematics simple enough, but it was an unfamiliar method of presentation in those days, though Jevons had had forerunners. Its fragmentary character in comparison with John Stuart Mill's *Principles of Political Economy* also limited its immediate influence.[123] This factor joined to the vigorous tone of criticism of Ricardo and the reigning classicists certainly restricted the influence which Jevons's ideas possessed.

Later, his influence was restricted also by competition, by the fact that similar ideas were worked out by the Austrian school led by Carl Menger (1840-1921). [Menger in 1867 got a Doctor of Jurisprudence degree from the University of Cracow. Then, after spending a few years as a journalist in Lemberg and Vienna, he entered the civil service, in the press department of the office of the Austrian prime minister. He began his teaching at the University of Vienna in 1872 as a *privatdozent*, that is, a lecturer who was paid by the fees of his auditors. In 1873, upon being made a *professor extraordinarius* (associate professor) he resigned his civil service post. Three years later he was appointed a tutor to the ill-fated Crown Prince Rudolph and accompanied him in his travels through most of Europe. Shortly after he returned to Vienna, Menger, in 1879, was given a full professorship at the university. "Menger took a lively interest in public issues and was highly influential in bringing about the Austrian currency reform in the 1890's which culminated in the adoption of the gold standard."][124]

Menger's *Grundsätze der Volkswirthschaftslehre* had for those who could read German two advantages over Jevons. One was that he employed the simpler conception of marginal utility and avoided mathematical forms of presentation, so that the ordinary reader who was not schooled in mathematics found it easier to grasp the nature and import of Menger's ideas than those of Jevons. The second advantage was more important. Jevons discusses in his illustrations only the valuation of consumers' commodities. He talks about the commodities which are subject to exchange as satisfying human wants. Men deal in the modern world largely in goods that are not yet ready to satisfy human wants directly and to a considerable extent in commodities

---

[123] Sentence from Outline, November 3, 1931.

[124] [Gottfried Haberler, "Joseph Alois Schumpeter, 1883-1950," 1950, reprinted in *Schumpeter: Social Scientist* (Cambridge, Mass.: Harvard University Press, 1951) p. 31.]

that never satisfy wants directly. More than that, a large part of men's transactions are carried on between people neither of whom is buying or selling in order to satisfy his own wants. When one merchant buys from another at wholesale he does not determine the value of the merchandise he buys by thinking about the way in which they satisfy his wants. Consequently the question remained open so far as Jevons's treatment was concerned as to what relevance a discussion which applied perhaps to the exchange of corn for beef had for the purchases of wheat by a grain miller, or what relevance it had for determining the values of goods that could be used for no other purpose than to make goods.

Menger attacked this problem and developed what came to be called a theory of imputation; that is a theory concerning the way in which men transfer their notions about the value of goods that will satisfy their wants, to the value of goods which are in the hands of merchants, bought by merchants for resale, then to the raw materials of which finished commodities for satisfying wants may be made, and finally to the means of production themselves—things like locomotives, factory machinery, buildings, and even to labor as an agent of production. The treatment of the problem of imputation was necessary to round out the theory which undertook to account for value in terms of utility.

On both counts, then, the work of Menger had marked advantages over that of Jevons. Menger was fortunate in having two extremely able disciples, Böhm-Bawerk and von Wieser who, as previously noted, developed his ideas further with much originality and vigor and had their works translated into English. As suggested before, Jevons also suffered from the competition offered by the great treatise of the patron saint of later mathematical economists, from Vilfredo Pareto to Gustav Cassel; namely, Léon Walras (1834-1910).

Walras was born in 1834 in Evreux in the province of Normandy, France. He came from a cultured middle class family. His father, Auguste Walras (1801-1866) was a teacher of literature and philosophy and a minor administrator in the secondary schools at various places in France, and achieved some reputation as an economist, especially for his *De la nature de la richesse et de l'origine de la valeur* (1831). His son, after twice failing the examinations for entrance to the École Polytechnique, finally was admitted [as a non-resident student] to the École des Mines, Paris, but he soon left the institution to try to win a place in literature. He worked as a journalist and tried his hand at novels but without much success. He informed his father in 1858 that he would devote himself to economics.

During the next twelve years, he made a precarious living in a variety of employments, including newspaper editor, railway clerk and bank manager. All the while he wrote and lectured on economics, especially in the area of the philosophy of social reform or what he called social economics. His lack of any formal preparation in economics did not help his chances for a position in the academic world in France. Fortunately he found an opportunity in Switzerland. In 1860, he had taken part in the international congress on taxation in Lausanne, [where he attracted the attention of a promising lawyer and politician, Louis Ruchonnet]. Ten years later, when in 1870 a chair of political economy was established in the Faculty of Law of the Academy (later the University) of Lausanne, Walras was appointed *professeur extraordinaire* (associate professor), and after a year's trial he was given a full professorship. After teaching for twenty-two years, he retired in 1892 because of ill health, and was succeeded by his *protégé*, Pareto.[125]

Léon Walras's *Éléments d'economie politique pure* was, to repeat, another exposition of the way in which one could treat the problem of value from the viewpoint of utility. He had an advantage over Jevons with a limited but highly influential class of people. Walras, like Jevons, used mathematical methods of inquiry, but he was a better mathematician, and mathematical economists of later days look back not to Jevons but to Walras. Walras, to repeat, also had the advantage of treating a problem which Jevons had not fully grasped and which no economist who does not proceed by mathematical methods can treat very effectively, the problem that is a genuine one to anybody who wants to understand price determination in the modern world. Jevons, like Ricardo and John Stuart Mill and their successors writing in English rather than in the language of mathematics, took up the problem of determination of the ratio of exchange between two commodities. His standard, it may be recalled, was corn and beef. Walras had the insight to see that in a modern community the prices of different commodities are all interdependent. It is strictly untrue that the ratio of exchange between corn and beef can be discussed without reference to the fact that there are a good many articles in the community, besides beef, which will satisfy men's appetites in much the same way. There is mutton, lamb, veal, pork,

---

[125] Outline November 3, 1931. Biographical paragraphs are a condensed version of the note in Outline, December 13, 1916. "Reading Walras, *Éléments,* and Cliffe Leslie, *Essays,* by turns." Mitchell, "Diary," November 19, 1916.

poultry, fish and all the other wide variety of beef substitutes; and it is untrue that the price of all kinds of meat is independent of other types of food.

It is also not true that the price of food is independent of the price of clothing. In the modern world where the purchaser is free to lay out his money in buying anything he wants, it is obvious that the demand prices which he will give for one thing are necessarily influenced by the prices at which he can get other things. Obviously the amount that one is ready to pay for a pound of beef is influenced by the prices at which he can get a vast variety of other commodities.

Enlarging upon this observation, Walras held that the problem which the economist ought to attack is that of the simultaneous determination of the prices of commodities in a market, quite literally the problem of the simultaneous determination of the prices of an indefinitely large number of commodities on the assumption that these prices all influenced one another. That seems at first blush an impossible undertaking, but Walras formulated a mathematical method of presenting that problem and of showing that the problem is theoretically solvable. When we come to discuss Cassel there will be an occasion to become acquainted with a somewhat simplified and considerably later version of this method of treating the generalized problem of prices. Meanwhile it should be observed simply that just as Menger and his disciples in Austria satisfied one set of people interested in economics better than Jevons by their presentation of the idea of marginal utility and the working out of their theory of imputation, so on the other hand Walras and his disciples satisfied more adequately than Jevons the intellectual needs of mathematical economists and of people who were ready to grasp the problem of prices in its generalized form on the assumption that all prices are interdependent.

In a certain sense Jevons fell between two stools and he had a further posthumous misfortune—not altogether posthumous, for the trouble was beginning in his lifetime. The Benthamite psychology on which he built his economics was being undermined in his own day and was progressively discredited by investigators who were trying to understand human behavior. Perhaps the most powerful single force undermining the hedonistic psychology was the publication of Darwin's *On the Origin of Species* (1859) with its theory of natural selection and emphasis on instincts. Not unnaturally it was a considerable time before economists began to realize that this biological treatise had any direct bearing upon their problems. That realization was prompted by Herbert Spencer who as the great philosophical exponent of the theory of evolution, as expressed through his multi-volume *Synthetic Philosophy,* came to write not only on biology but also upon metaphysics, psychology, ethics and sociology.

Spencer clarified the importance of the theory of natural selection to the social sciences. His effort, however, to unite hedonism with instinct of self-preservation an obvious begging of question. Spencer's *Principles of Sociology* contains nearest approach we have of a systematic treatise on the development of economic institutions, especially in the last two sections Professional Institutions and Industrial Institutions which deal with division of labor, exchange, regulation of labor, slavery, etc. Marred by Spencer's defective [hedonistic] psychology and in detail by careless use of comparative method.[126]

It came to be seen by those who were interested in problems of human behavior that the character of the species of animals whose behavior they were trying to account for was a fundamental one in their problem.

Jevons had recognized so much. But people who got to these problems of human behavior from Darwin's angle found that the great master gave a picture of behavior which made Bentham's psychology seem like a caricature. In *The Origin of Species,* Darwin was talking continually about the instincts as factors of dominant importance in controlling the behavior of animal species. In his later books notably the *Descent of Man* (1871) he implied that man has by no means escaped from the grip of these instincts that have developed in the course of evolution. The factors that govern men's behavior are not calculations of pleasures and pains; they are inherited drives that make men interested in certain goods, drives that lead them to certain activities the results of which men are scarcely conscious of when they engage in them, at least at the beginning.

The appearance of William James's *Principles of Psychology* (1890) reinforced the disintegration of hedonism, for he found that a factor of considerable importance in controlling human behavior had been overlooked, or at least had been inadequately recognized by the school of which Bentham was the great master; namely, the factor of habit. Habits were pictured by James as being in a certain sense the near brothers of instincts. They were the maturing of certain patterns of behavior, many of which had an instinctive basis. And

---

[126] Outline, November 3, 1937. Two outlines of "Introductory Lecture," for course "Economic Origins," OPP 1-6, nos. 70-71.

[Spencer began his great project, the multi-volume *Synthetic Philosophy,* with the publication of *First Principles* in 1862, and the other parts on biology, psychology, sociology and ethics, came out over the next thirty-five years.]

they had an enormous part to do with controlling the behavior of adults. The extent to which people's behavior is determined by anything that can properly be called calculation on James's showing is vastly less than would appear from the writings of Bentham, much less than one would judge from the exposition of Jevons.

Even the inheritors of the tradition of the philosophical radicals in England began to develop doubts about the adequacy of the picture which Bentham had given of the place that pleasure and pain played in controlling behavior. This was typified by Henry Sidgwick (1838-1900) and Alexander Bain. Sidgwick carried on the great utilitarian tradition in ethics, philosophy and economics; Bain carried the association psychology to its highest point.[127]

Sidgwick was an influential figure at Cambridge University and had a much greater intellectual keenness than Fawcett. He exercised a considerable influence on the development of Alfred Marshall and his generation of English economists. He was primarily a philosopher, interested in ethics, but wrote on political philosophy and on political economy. If any man was the lineal descendant of John Stuart Mill, it is Sidgwick who carried on the true old utilitarian position. He put his doubts of hedonism in a very simple form. He said that introspection convinced him that he ate dinner because he was hungery, not because he anticipated the pleasure that the food would give him. He had this inner desire or prompting to eat; that took him to the table, and pleasure came afterwards. His introspection found that it was not the association of pleasure with the idea of eating that sent him to dinner; he dined because he was hungry and the pleasure came with the eating.[128] From his point of view the scheme which Bentham had set forth in hard and fast terms, that people begin by getting an idea of pleasure which appeals to them, that they then proceed to calculate the amount of the pleasure, to compare it with the pains at which it can be attained, and thus arrive at a thought-out plan of action which was executed later, was a travesty of what goes on inside people's mind.

Henry Sidgwick—last of the great utilitarians—held that many of our acts are not directed by the search for pleasure. The question in his discussion concerns the relation of pleasure to desire. Is the desire aroused in all cases by pleasure? "Pleasure is a kind of feeling which stimulates the will to actions, tending to sustain or produce it,—to sustain it, if actually present and to produce it, if it be only represented in idea." (Does not this definition really imply the whole theory? No, pleasure it asserts is a kind of

[127] Sentence from Outline, November 3, 1931.
[128] Sentence from Outline, November 3, 1931.

feeling that moves to action.) Desire is "the felt volitional stimulus . . . when pleasure is not actually present, but only represented in idea." Sidgwick's answer, based on *introspection,* finds that "many pleasures,— especially those of sight, hearing and smell, together with many emotional pleasures,—occur to me without any perceptible relation to previous desires." (When they do occur they give rise to desire to attain them— implied?) But also finds "that throughout the whole scale of my impulses, sensual, emotional, and intellectual alike, I can distinguish desires of which the object is something other than my own pleasure. . . . The appetite of hunger, so far as I can observe, is a direct impulse to the eating of food. Such eating is no doubt commonly attended with an agreeable feeling of more or less intensity; but it cannot, I think, be strictly said that this agreeable feeling is the object of hunger, and that it is the representative of this pleasure which stimulates the will of the hungry man as such. . . . It is . . . obvious that hunger is something different from the desire of anticipated pleasure."[129]

Sidgwick's conclusion had a wide influence precisely because he continued to be regarded as belonging to the great utilitarian tradition, to be the prophet on whom John Stuart Mill's mantle had fallen.[130]

Sidgwick's *The Principles of Political Economy* (1883) was of a piece with his philosophy.[131] It was widely characterized as a commentary upon a treatise never written. It is full of discussions of points which one could regard as an effort to bring Mill up to date. The commentary is there although the text upon which the commentary is based is difficult to find unless the reader is skillful in reading between the lines. The book had considerable influence on some of the people interested in the development of economic theory.[132]

---

[129] Outline, "Final Lectures," April and May, 1914. Quotations from *The Methods of Ethics* (London: Macmillan, 1874; 7th ed., 1907) pp. 42, 43, 45.
As Professor Ernest Albee of Cornell University summarized Sidgwick on hunger, "It is a direct impulse to the eating of food. Of course, pleasure may be anticipated as a result of the satisfaction of this craving, and such is very often the case; but there could be no pleasure of satisfaction, and therefore no anticipation of such pleasure, were not the craving itself an original, objective tendency." Albee, *A History of English Utilitarianism* (London: Sonnenschein, 1902) p. 369. [Professor Mitchell recommended Albee's book along with those of Élie Halévy and Sir Leslie Stephen for an understanding of utilitarianism.] Later psychologists go further than Sidgwick and assert that pleasure is aroused by desire when thought of as fulfilled. (Outline, "Final Lectures," April and May, 1914.
[130] Sentence from "1918 Typescript."
[131] The third edition of 1901, a posthumous edition, was edited by John Neville Keynes, the Cambridge logician and economist, author of a standard work, *The Scope and Method of Political Economy* (1890) and father of J. M. Keynes.
[132] [The book was notable as the first attempt to incorporate in the classical tradition the work of leaders of the German Historical School. As Sidgwick stated in the "Preface," "Among the foreign writers I have derived most assistance from the works of Professors A. Held and A. Wagner especially from the latter's systematic treatise on the subject." Sidgwick also acknowledged receiving valuable suggestions from Francis A. Walker's *The Wages Question.* In recent years Sidgwick's treatise has been hailed as a landmark in the theory of policy.]

While Sidgwick was at Cambridge, Alexander Bain, the biographer of James Mill, the friend and somewhat younger contemporary as well as biographer of John Stuart Mill and the leading British psychologist of his day, was giving his exposition of the association psychology in those thick volumes on *The Senses and the Intellect* (1855) and *The Emotions and the Will* (1859) which are a mine of psychological information very much neglected at present.[133]

The important point about the work of Sidgwick and Bain for our purposes, which will be elaborated later, is that even in their reverent hands the conception of human nature which Bentham had expounded so vigorously and which Jevons had made the basis of political economy had begun to disintegrate.

People who had come to believe with Darwin in instincts, to recognize with James the enormous role that habit plays in driving behavior, to doubt with Sidgwick whether pleasures determine even such a simple action as sitting down to the table to dine, were inclined to question whether Jevons was a safe guide even in economics. If a person was to believe in the validity and usefulness of utility analysis as Jevons had developed it, one certainly must find some new psychological foundation to take the place of the discredited hedonism. The point is that James's psychology with its emphasis on habit was supplanting that of Bain with its emphasis on association.[134]

Economists as a rule have been no more learned in psychology than they are well trained in mathematics. When they were faced by the subtle questions concerning the way behavior is determined, and when on turning to books upon psychology for a clear statement of what controls human conduct, they found that different psychological writers held views that did not agree with one another any better than those the economists held on the theory of value at the time, and when economists had these bewildering experiences, they were inclined to agree that Jevons had made a blunder in seeking to base his economic analysis on psychological principles. They thought

---

[133] [Bain's biographies of the Mills are *James Mill* (1882) and *John Stuart Mill* (1882). He assisted John Stuart Mill in making substantial revisions of the third edition of *A System of Logic,* and in preparing a second edition of his father's *Analysis of the Phenomena of the Human Mind* (1867). Bain attenuated the older Benthamite utilitarianism along such lines as the following:

"In society, happiness is sought as the immediate end; there are other things that human beings engage in where happiness follows only as an indirect consequence in the pursuit of other ends. Such is the case in the all-important matter of occupation, profession, or the line of industry chosen as the means of subsistence, and the source of position in the general community." *The Moral Philosophy of Paley with additional dissertations and notes edited by Alexander Bain* (Edinburgh: W. and R. Chambers, 1887) pp. 60-61; see also p. 78.]

[134] Sentence from Outline, November 3, 1931.

that on the whole the precedent that had been set by theorists like Adam Smith, Malthus, Ricardo and John Stuart Mill in taking a rather offhand view of the principal drives in human nature was a better one to follow than that of a man who had made an ambitious attempt to show that the theory of value could be derived from solid psychological principles. So in this respect, also Jevons's influence was limited.

Jevons, however, had a notable successor for a time in this part of his endeavor. That was no less a person than F. Y. Edgeworth who has already been referred to especially in connection with Bentham.

Born in 1845 in Edgeworthstown, Ireland, where his family had lived since the reign of Queen Elizabeth. Nephew of Maria Edgeworth, famed novelist and friend of Ricardo. Education: home, Trinity College, Dublin, Magdalen Hall and Balliol College, Oxford. Called to the bar in 1877. In 1880 became lecturer in logic and in 1890 Tooke Professor of Economic Science and Statistics at King's College, London. In 1891 became Drummond Professor of Political Economy, Oxford, and first editor of *The Economic Journal*.[135]

In his younger days he had a view of the best way to work at the social sciences which was much of the same general character as Bentham's: the notion of developing a calculus in the moral branches like that which Newton had developed in physics. He set himself to see what he could do along those lines. For working purposes he adopted what he called the conception of man as a pleasure machine. Taking Bentham's fundamental notions of the forces that control conduct with as little questioning as Jevons had, he composed that remarkable volume, *Mathematical Psychics*. It is a charming performance. He worked out, as previously noted, a scheme showing that on the assumption that men are pleasure machines, each one tending to maximize his own satisfactions, it is theoretically possible to work up a maximization of satisfactions in society on the assumption that there is perfectly free competition. Economics "investigates the equilibrium of a system of hedonic forces each tending to maximum individual utility."[136] These forces will produce that maximum under conditions of perfect competition.

Having made the demonstration, he proceeded to observe that the trend of the times was in the direction of limiting free competition and thus making prices indeterminate. The great restrictive factors which he saw developing in English society were not those that an American economist would think of first. They did not consist in the

---

[135] Outlines, December 18, 1916, November 3, 1931.
[136] Outline, November 3, 1931. Quotation from *Mathematical Psychics* (London: C. Kegan Paul, 1881) p. 15.

group of great business enterprises (trusts) having a quasi-monopolistic position in the market. They consisted, on the contrary, in the development of trade unions limiting the freedom of competition among people offering their labor for sale; and second, in the rapid development of cooperatives—not the producers' cooperatives that John Stuart Mill had foreseen as rising rapidly to reform the organization of production, but the rapid development of consumers' cooperatives, represented particularly by the Rochdale Stores.[137] In a society where free competition was being increasingly interfered with by forces like trade unions and cooperative distributing agencies, Edgeworth argued that the maximization of utility in society as a whole cannot be achieved. By the limits which they place upon competition trade unions might increase the utility of their members at the expense of the utility of other people in the community; and, if certain groups of consumers bound themselves to manufacture and to produce for their own stores certain classes of commodities and gave their members particular advantages through the distribution of dividends on their purchases, then the organized groups might increase the utility to cooperators perhaps at the expense of the utility of members of the community at large outside their ranks. Consequently, Edgeworth argued there was need for some utilitarian calculus apart from the calculus which the economist would develop on the assumption of a theoretically perfect competition. This, as previously noted, he drew up on Benthamite lines, though on the assumption that all people are pleasure machines and some are better than others and that the maximizing of pleasure can be achieved only by feeding to the better pleasure machines a larger proportion of the raw materials of pleasure; that is, the income, the goods from which pleasures are derived. This was, in other words, a scheme which undertook to show that the members of the community who were by nature more capable of enjoying the good things of life ought to be on the principles of the utilitarian calculus in receipt of larger incomes than the others. On this ground Edgeworth justified not only the privileges of wealth and aristocracy but also those of the male as opposed to the female sex. For he held that men were better pleasure machines as a whole than women.

But Edgeworth, as he grew older, seems to have been increasingly sensitive to the doubts that the developments in biology, psychology and anthropology were casting upon the validity of the fundamental psychological notions which he had used. Consequently after pub-

---

[137] [This movement was started by a group of disciples of Robert Owen who in 1844 set up in Rochdale the Rochdale Pioneers' Cooperative Society.]

lishing this brilliant, exceedingly bold essay in his youth, he turned aside to other tasks. His later years were devoted to working out the beautiful series of papers on detailed topics in mathematical economics—that is, points in economic theory that could be treated mathematically—and to the long series of contributions to the theory of statistics for which he is famous. It was Edgeworth more than any other man who carried the theory of making index numbers far beyond the point at which Jevons had left it. Also on many other problems in the general theory of probability in particular he rendered notable technical service.[138] Though he may never have surrendered entirely the notions that he entertained in his youth concerning the factors which control conduct, he gave up the attempt to carry further his speculations upon mathematical psychics.

S. How does Edgeworth measure pleasure?

M. He thinks units can be used. It is in that respect particularly that he adheres to Bentham's viewpoint more than does Jevons. He also demonstrates that on a mathematical basis the theorist can arrive at certain broad conclusions like these without using measures but by using simply the conception of more or less.

S. The conception of final utility?

M. No. The view would be simply that before the pleasure which, say, an aristocrat can derive from the use of a given commodity is reduced to the level of the pleasure derived from the use of the same commodity by a farm laborer, the aristocrat would have to be given more of the commodity to consume because he is a more sensitive person, who can get more pleasure. The objective is to try to equalize the final degrees of utility on the part of all consumers but, if Edgeworth's hypothesis is correct, this is gotten by giving the more sensitive members of the community a larger amount of the commodities to be consumed.

Edgeworth in 1907 concluded that in place of the unit "the just perceivable increment" of pleasure which he presented in *Mathematical Psychics*—it might perhaps be "better to say with Professor A. Voigt,[139] that no such

---

[138] An annotated bibliography of his work in mathematical statistics is in A. L. Bowley, *F. Y. Edgeworth's Contributions to Mathematical Statistics* (1928).

"Both the economic and the more purely statistical part of the work [*Business Cycles*] are by me highly appreciated. You are no doubt right in seeking the cause of business cycles in a plurality of causes—avoiding the fallacy of simplicity." Edgeworth to Mitchell, July 27, 1914.

[139] "Zahl und Mass in der Oekonomie," *Zeitschrift für die Gesamte Staatswissenschaft*, 1893, no. 3; referred to in *The Economic Journal*, IV, [March, 1894] p. 202. [The reference is to an abstract of the article, doubtless by Edgeworth also, which reads, "Economics deals with quantities such as utility, which not being expressible in units, are measured only by *ordinal* numbers. As we may say of several sensations of heat that the second is more intense than the first, the third than the second, so the degree of advantage which a party to a contract would derive from various terms may be arranged in an order of magnitude."]

unit is required: quantities like utility are to be measured only by *ordinal* numbers. In confirmation of this conception, Professor Voigt refers to the view, now prevalent among mathematicians, . . . 'which sees in ordinal number rather than in cardinal the primary conception of number.' "[140]

[With this procedure is tied the use of indifference curves or maps of which Edgeworth appears to have been the first to make extensive use—in *Mathematical Psychics*—followed by Vilfredo Pareto, of whom more later.] According to Edgeworth,

> Professor Pareto . . . is in very good company when scrupling to designate utility as a function (say u) of quantities of commodities (say *x, y* . . .), he contemplates a family of successive *indifference-curves* (or generally surfaces in space of many dimensions) in the plane *x, y* (or corresponding hyper-surface); such that the advance from any one indifference-locus to the next in succession affords an *index*, rather than a measure, of the advance in satisfaction, or as Professor Pareto prefers to say, *ophelimity*. . . . The matter is well put by Mr. Johnson with reference to two commodities [*x* and *y*]: "There are no lines in the figure which measure the utility itself. The several utility-curves are arranged in a scale of increasing value as we pass to the right and above [in the plane of *x, y*]; and thus the 'distance' (measured arbitrarily) from one curve to another 'indicates' (without measuring) the increase in utility. But this impossibility of measurement does not affect any economic problem."[141]

How does Pareto's use of indifference curves differ from Edgeworth's? Simply in that Pareto takes them for data instead of for results.[142]

Recapitulation of Edgeworth's *Mathematical Psychics*. General character: Edgeworth as a disciple of Jevons in economics, of Bentham, John Stuart Mill and Sidgwick in ethics, and as a born mathematician, seeks to show that reasoning in the moral sciences is unsafe without the guidance of mathematics. Following discussion deals only with the points of chief interest for the purposes of students of types of economic theory.

1. Lack of numerical data not necessarily a bar to mathematical analysis for mathematical reasoning is possible, and may be indispensable where the data are quantitative though not numerical; i.e., "a quantity is *greater* or *less* than another, *increases* or *decreases*, is *positive* or *negative*, a *maximum* or *minimum*." Proved by examples from mathematical physics.

2. Mathematical psychics needs a unit as basis of calculation. Unit for economics confined to individual—like Jevons. Unit for ethics requires comparison of happiness of different people. The possibility of such comparisons. Argument is substantially that common sense admits compari-

---

[140] Edgeworth, "Appreciations of Mathematical Theories," *The Economic Journal*, June 1907, pp. 222-223.

[141] Edgeworth, "Recent Contributions to Mathematical Economics," *The Economic Journal*, March 1915, p. 58. Quotation is from W. E. Johnson, "The Pure Theory of Utility Curves," *The Economic Journal*, December 1913, p. 490. Brackets are those of Edgeworth. ["Mr. Johnson" was W. E. Johnson who taught not only logic but also advanced economic theory at Cambridge University. He was a mentor and friend of J. M. Keynes who said of the article that it "had carried the application of mathematical analysis to economic theory about as far as it was likely to be useful to carry it." Sir Roy Harrod, *The Life of John Maynard Keynes* (London: Macmillan, 1951) p. 8.]

[142] Outline, April 19, 1916 and "Edgeworth," APP 54-63, no. 71.

son of pleasures of individuals, and that estimate of other people's pleasures is not more difficult; [that is, that comparison of pleasures of different men is no more difficult than comparison of different pleasures of same man.]

3. Application of mathematics to psychics countenanced by an hypothesis which introduces close parallel with physics. Pleasure the concomitant of energy. Man conceived as a pleasure machine. On this hypothesis in the social sciences we may conceive and solve problems of maximizing pleasure on same lines on which problems of maximizing energy are conceived and solved in physics.

4. Resulting conception of calculus of pleasure has two branches—economics and utilitarian ethics. Difference is one of activating motive.

5. Economic calculus. The problem (all inclusive for economics?). Solution. Practical conclusion: Considerable degree of indeterminateness in economic contract is probable because of lack of perfect competition. Hence, as already noted, need a principle of arbitration [because of conflict of interests]. Need is present in social and political as well as economic contract. Where find this principle? One such principle is the contract dictated by utilitarian ethics and this principle has a special claim to acceptance. Transition from economic calculus to utilitarian calculus.

6. Utilitarian calculus. Problem: psychological assumptions: people differ in capacity for pleasure, for education and for work. Pleasure is measurable and pleasures of different people are commensurable. Rate of increase of pleasure decreases as its means increase. Rate of increase of fatigue increases as work done increases.

Solution: (1) Distribution of means. Those more capable of pleasure should have more means. (2) Distribution of labor. Those more capable of work should do more work. (3) The quality of the population required for greatest possible happines: those most capable of education (training in capacity for pleasure) should be best educated. Those most capable of pleasure should have more children. (4) The number of population requisite for greatest possible happiness. Since means increase at a decreasing rate, population should be limited.

Combining all four elements in the problem [we] reach following general solution. Corollaries: Equality is not the whole of distributive justice. Equal suffrage undesirable. Bentham's creed—greatest happiness of greatest number is inconsistent if not unnecessary. If pleasure is really the good then end is the greatest amount of pleasure irrespective of who gets it. (William Paley gives a better statement than Bentham in his *Principles of Moral and Political Philosophy* (1785): "The final view of all rational politics is to produce the greatest quantity of happiness in a given tract of country." Modern formulation of this economic ideal is maximum satisfaction.)

7. Practical character of the whole discussion. Stimulating effect: plenty of problems suggested by the book for further analysis. How far are differences in ability to produce pleasure and endure toil due to habit? If largely, do the conservative conclusions hold?

Conclusion: Technical discussion in part I of *Mathematical Psychics* has had considerable influence upon mathematical economics, especially suggestive of curves of indifference. Broader significance. It represents the indian summer of the great school of English utilitarians, which was vitally interested in happiness and cultivating social sciences as means towards this end. Shows most clearly how from this viewpoint economics merges into the largest conceptions of social science, but it also shows the uncertainty of conclusions drawn from the social sciences when cultivated from Benthamite point of view. With all its appearance of mathematical demonstration, the treatise's final conclusions rest on unproved assumptions about differences in human nature and how far those differences are inherited and therefore, presumably unchangeable, or acquired and therefore presumably capable of being affected by [habit]. As Edgeworth says, the notion of aristocracy vs. democracy "is still perhaps a subject more for prejudice than for judgment."[143]

Edgeworth increasingly considered himself a disciple of Marshall. Jevons was thus left with relatively few disciples. Among the people definitely enlisted under his banner, one may note particularly his most faithful disciple, Philip H. Wicksteed (1844-1927), a Unitarian clergyman, a brilliant lecturer and author of the admirable *The Common Sense of Political Economy* (1910). He explained there with great grace and charm and without the use of elaborate mathematics, a conception of the way in which values are determined, which follows Jevons's lines. [Wicksteed's earlier *Essay on the Coordination of the Laws of Distribution* (1894) was in a broad sense the application of Jevonian utility theory of value to distribution in the form of one of the earliest elegant mathematical demonstrations of the theory of marginal productivity. After criticisms by Edgeworth and Pareto, Wicksteed withdrew the demonstration as unsound. However, the *Essay* came to be considered a classic in the development of the marginal productivity theory.[144]

Wicksteed was originally attracted to the sustained study of economics by the American Henry George in *Progress and Poverty* (1879), a book which gave a tremendous stimulus to the revitalization of economic thinking throughout the western world that began in the last quarter of the nineteenth century. After giving an account of the way the material progress of the world is accompanied by increasing poverty, George proposed the taxing away of all rent as the instrument for obtaining substantial economic growth without the prevailing flagrant inequality of wealth and income, and recurring long,

---

[143] Outlines, "Final Lectures," April-May, 1914, December 18, 1916. Quotation from *Mathematical Psychics*, p. 76. [Bracketed word above is substituted for smudged word in original. Maffeo Pantaleoni also consciously based utility analysis on a hedonistic interpretation. See Appendix V.]

[144] [For Wicksteed's reasons for withdrawing his demonstration see Joseph Dorfman, "On Wicksteed's Recantation of the Marginal Productivity Theory," *Economica*, August 1964, pp. 294-295.]

severe depressions. In a letter to George in 1882, Wicksteed explained that he had been for years "an occasional student of Political Economy," but he had been unable to obtain either from his own reading or from "friends who were versed in the courses" any satisfactory explanation of the nature and cause of commercial depressions. But *Progress and Poverty* "has given me the light I vainly sought for myself" and "has made for me a new heaven and a new earth."]¹⁴⁵

Jevons also had considerable influence over the Fabian socialists. The Fabian Society was founded in 1884 and included among its founders and early members a notable group of young people: Sidney and Beatrice Webb, Graham Wallas, George Bernard Shaw, Sidney Olivier (later Baron Olivier), together with a small batch of highly intellectual and intelligent followers. H. G. Wells was also a member for a time. Shaw was then quite unknown to fame, a struggling and not very successful novelist, a journalist who was just beginning to attract attention. Graham Wallas withdrew but maintained friendly relations with the group. [Olivier, like Sidney Webb, was a civil servant in the colonial office, but unlike Webb, he remained in the government service. From 1899 to 1913 he served in Jamaica, becoming governor of the colony in 1907. He was Secretary of State for India in the first Labor government in 1924.]

These young people were highly critical of the economic organization in the England in which they grew up, and they were little disposed to accept the general economic theory of the classical economists which seemed to them to have altogether too apologetic a tone. There was much in John Stuart Mill which agreed with their sympathies, but they did not see how they could use his *Principles of Political Economy* very effectively for their purpose. In search for a basis on which to build their critical analysis of modern economic organization, they tried Marx but were repelled by the Hegelian metaphysics of *Capital*. As Graham Wallas put it,

> The chief significance of the society in the general development of social thought has been that it used the name and prestige of socialism for a movement which was free from and often opposed to Marx's analysis of history, industry, and human motive, and which therefore influenced non-socialist political opinion in Eng-

---

¹⁴⁵ [Wicksteed to George, October 26, 1882, quoted in Joseph Dorfman, *The Economic Mind in American Civilization*, 5 volumes (New York: Viking, 1946-1959) III, pp. 147-148

At a meeting of the Hampstead Liberal Club in 1884, "Henry R. Beeton, a member of the London Stock Exchange . . . spoke with emphatic approval of Henry George and his advocacy was immediately endorsed no less emphatically by Philip Wicksteed." After the meeting, the two men who had thus discovered each other "fell into each other's arms." C. H. Herford, *Philip Henry Wicksteed: His Life and Work* (London: Dent, 1931) p. 207.]

land, and helped to inspire the Revisionist movement in German social democracy.

Shaw joined the infant society in September 1884, Webb and Olivier in May, 1885, and I in April 1886. But from the beginning of 1885 we had all four belonged to a little reading circle in Hampstead for the study of *Das Kapital.* We expected to agree with Marx, but found ourselves from the beginning criticizing him. Webb and Olivier were civil servants who four or five years before had scored highly in political economy at the "Class One" examination owing to their ability to expound and apply the Ricardian law of rent. It was on this point that we first definitely disagreed with Marx. Instead of taking surplus value in the lump, we divided it into the three "rents," land, capital, and ability, and faced the fact that if he had worked with the worst land, tools, and brains, in "cultivation," the worst paid laborer might be producing no more wealth than he consumed. This led us to abandon "abstract labor" as the basis of value, and to adopt Jevons's conception of value as fixed by the point where "marginal effort" coincided with "marginal utility."[146]

While they were in this uncertain way, as Shaw has told in a charming essay, "On the History of Fabian Economics," he happened to get into a newspaper controversy with Wicksteed over a technical point in economic theory about which he says he knew very little. His lack of knowledge of the matter did not prevent him from writing frequently on the subject and even after he convinced himself that his knowledge was very slender, he asserts that he gave a good account of himself in the controversy.[147]

[While the debate was going on, Shaw appeared at a gathering of the Economic Circle, a group largely of university men led by Wicksteed, and meeting at the home of H. R. Beeton, a prominent stock broker, and like Wicksteed an ardent follower of Henry George. "The problem under discussion that evening was the element of

---

[146] Graham Wallas, "Socialism and the Fabian Society," *The New Republic,* June 24, 1916, p. 203. (Quotation is in "Marginal Theory as an Antidote to Marxist Socialism," APP 84-91, no. 24) [On margin of quotation Professor Mitchell wrote:] Wallas's statement that Marx had not divided up surplus is questionable. [Mitchell was referring to Marx's statement,] "Surplus value . . . splits up into various parts. Its fragments fall to various categories of persons, and take various forms, independent the one of the other, such as profit. interest, merchant's profit, rent, etc. It is only in Book III that we can take in hand these modified forms of surplus-value." *Capital: A Critique of Political Economy,* I, translated from the third German edition by Samuel Moore and Edward Aveling. and edited by Frederick Engels (1886); revised and amplified according to the 4th German edition by Ernest Untermann (Chicago: Kerr, 1907) pp. 118-119.

[147] Shaw "The History of Fabian Economics." in Edward R. Pease, *The History of the Fabian Society,* (1916; 2nd ed. New York: International, 1926), pp. 275-276. The newspaper articles are Wicksteed, "Das Kapital: A Criticism," 1884; Shaw, "The Jevonian Criticism of Marx," 1885; Wicksteed, "The Jevonian Criticism of Marx: A Rejoinder," 1885; [all reprinted in Wicksteed, *The Common Sense of Political Economy and Selected Papers and Reviews on Economic Theory,* edited by Lionel (now Lord) Robbins, 2 volumes (London: Routledge, 1933) II, pp. 705-733.]

choice in value, exchange, and purchase, and was carried on, as usual, with the help of the chalk and the blackboard." A member of the group recalled that Shaw "stood up with red hair and beard, in a grey suit (most of the company being in evening dress), and chaffed both Wicksteed and the rest of us with an audacious wit, sometimes too pointed to be entirely relished. 'You fellows,' he declared, 'have been talking a great deal about "choice." You would know better what choice is, if, like me, you had every night to "choose" between a bit of fire and a bit of supper before you went to bed. And as to curves the curves of supply and demand had much less to do with a man's control of the market, than the curves of his profile. He himself had earned only £100 in the previous twelve months, whereas, with our host's resolute curve of the chin, he would be making £10,000 a year.' And he proceeded to illustrate his point, amid the embarrassed laughter of the company, by drawing their own profiles in lively caricature on the blackboard."[148]

But Shaw also had the common sense to go to Wicksteed, according to his account, and put himself in Wicksteed's hands, and Wicksteed, he asserts, made a Jevonian of him.[149] Shaw in turn converted the Fabians to the Jevonian analysis of value; he got them away from the cost of production to an analysis of value in terms of utility. It seems that of these brilliant young people, the most promising were to get from Jevons a satisfactory basis for evaluating adequately the merits, and what was more for their purpose, the demerits of modern capitalistic economic organization.

Thus, Jevons found, curiously enough, his most active disciples in later years among a set of people whose attitude toward public life was more toward that of the philosophical radicals than his own. Jevons, remember, had comparatively little interest in practical affairs. He did not want to be bothered about politics. He was un-

---

[148] [Herford, *Philip Henry Wicksteed: His Life and Work*, pp. 208-209.]

[149] [Margaret Cole has argued that Shaw's essay, "The Economic Basis of Socialism" in the famous *Fabian Essays* (1889) took much from "Ricardo and Jevons, but also a good deal from Marx. *The Story of Fabian Socialism* (Stanford: Stanford University Press, 1961) pp. 27-28.]

Joseph Schumpeter points out that Marxians assert that marginal utility theory is nothing but a description of the enterprisers way of thinking ("Money in Economic Theory: Miscellaneous Notes" APP 84-91, no. 49. Statement from Schumpeter is from *Epochen der Dogmen- und Methodengeschichte* (1914). [In the English translation by R. Aris, *Economic Doctrine and Method: A Historical Sketch* (London: Allen and Unwin, 1954).] The full passage reads: "The assertion . . . is often made in Marxist quarters, that the theory of marginal utility is nothing but a description of the mentality of the employer and that by its individualist point of departure its representatives make it impossible for themselves to see the great objective conditions and results of the economic process" (pp. 190-191).

certain where his preference lay upon questions of the day. The Fabians, on the other hand, were a group who in intellectual capacity and in practical zeal can be compared, not to their disadvantage, with the great group of philosophical radicals who gathered around Jeremy Bentham. Just as the philosophical radicals were largely responsible for working out the logical case for that substantial series of reforms which took place in England from, say, the 1820's on to the 1880's, so the Fabians have been responsible for not a little of that further series of reforms moving in the direction that is loosely suggested by the term social legislation which has taken place in England since the 1890's.

But this is about all one can say concerning the obvious influence that Jevons exercised within a few years after his death upon the development of economic theory in England. So far as people were interested in the discussion of the elaborate analysis of demand and utility, they took up with the Austrian brand of the doctrine. James Bonar, who is best known as the author of *Malthus and His Work,* seems to have been one of the few English economists of the day who could read German readily enough to appreciate the significance of the books by Menger, Wieser and Böhm-Bawerk. He was the first to discover the Austrian writers and call the attention of English-speaking economists to them, in excellent articles in *The Quarterly Journal of Economics,* in October 1888 and April 1889.[150]

This Austrian theory did not frighten away readers by the use of mathematical symbols which played such an unduly large share in the mechanics of Jevons's exposition, and English economists seem to have grasped the importance of the idea much more readily in the Austrian form than in the one which was native to their country. This doubtless helped to deprive him of influence which he might have been expected to exercise. Furthermore, the Austrians had the advantage in their vigorous application of the idea in detail rather than with the grand flourish of Edgeworth.[151]

---

[150] [Largely because Bonar's articles appeared in an American journal, it was said that the British heard of the Austrians via the United States.

Alfred Marshall complained of the American acceptance of the Austrians, particularly of Böhm-Bawerk. "While he was still at school, I learned from the men whom he reviles everything which he has vaunted as a great discovery, and especially in America he has been taken at his own valuation by people who *have never studied the great men* on whose burial place he dances his war dance." Marshall to Knut Wicksell, December 19, 1904 in Torsten Gordlund, *The Life of Knut Wicksell* (Stockholm: Almqvist and Wiksell, 1958) p. 342.]

[151] Sentence from "Ostensible Dropping of Hedonism in Economic Theory After Edgeworth," APP 44-53, no. 5.

But this whole line of inquiry, the analysis of utility, the idea of using diminishing utility, etc., remained for a considerable time, esoteric doctrine. It made little impression on the intelligent public or even upon most English economists until the appearance in 1890 of Marshall's *Principles of Economics.*

In fact, from the point of view of technical economics, most important of all, Jevons's influence was limited by the success of Marshall in finding a way of uniting utility analysis on the one side with the cost of production analysis which Ricardo and his disciples had developed on the other side. To anticipate, from one point of view, Marshall's great achievement was that he found a way of integrating economic theory in such fashion that he could make effective use at the same time of the contributions which had come from his classical predecessors and also the contributions that had been made by the group of dissenters from the classical tradition represented by Jevons and the Austrians. His method of effecting the integration was simple. It was to observe that all problems of value can be treated in terms of supply and demand, when the case in hand was limited to a very brief time. The classical economists themselves had talked about problems of value in terms of supply and demand, but they had to say—at least Ricardo had—that when the theorist is discussing not the determination of values and prices in a market at a given moment but over considerable periods, he must resort to a different explanation; namely, that of cost of production (See Appendix 3). Jevons, however, had undertaken to show at least nominally that value depends solely upon utility. As our discussion of Jevons showed, despite this emphatic pronouncement, he recognized the influence of cost of production as limiting supply.

Amidst all the confusion and the lack of symmetry, Marshall said that the theorist should follow the scheme of demand and supply in all exchanges. He will recognize that the studies of cost of production explain the factors on which supply depends in the case of problems that cover a time long enough for new goods to be produced. And on the other side, he can use the utility analysis as an explanation of the factors on which demand depends. In this way, Marshall was able to find a place within one and the same body of theory for what Jevons had conceived to be, and what the Austrians continued in good part to believe, two more or less antagonistic elements: the element of cost analysis and the element of utility analysis. In short, Jevons's contribution was absorbed into a fuller analysis by Marshall.

Outcome: Economists became chary of hedonism and of psychology at large. Sought to show that validity of marginal analysis did not depend on Jevons's "principles of human nature"—but remained valid, when the latter discarded. Wicksteed, Jevons's most faithful follower, dropped hedonism. Jevons's economics was adopted by the Fabians, through Wicksteed and Shaw. Made basis for their assault on capitalism and privilege. Contrast to Edgeworth's aristocracy. Jevons's contribution absorbed into fuller analysis by Marshall.[152]

[Before going on to the next landmark in the development of economic thought, Alfred Marshall, it seems desirable to] compare and contrast the three great influential European strains in the formulation of utility theory—Jevons, Walras, Menger.

Similarity: Independently of each other, all three of these economists saw the necessity of analyzing demand as a factor in determining prices more fully than it had been analyzed by the classical type of economic theory. This analysis resolved itself into a study of variations in utility. The crucially important point in the variations of utility all three writers found to lie at the margin.

Differences in way of approaching the analysis of prices: Jevons began with theory of pleasure and pain. Derived theory of utility from theory of pleasure. Used final degree of utility—a ratio, not a quantity of feeling—as central concept in further analysis. Took exchange between two "trading bodies" conceived as individuals for this problem.

Explained exchange value as resultant of comparisons of final degrees of utility of different commodities in minds of each trader. Chief thesis: "The ratio of exchange of any two commodities will be the reciprocal of the ratio of the final degrees of utility of the quantities of commodity available for consumption after the exchange is completed."

Walras begins with an organized market where competition is perfectly free, where two commodities in definite quantities are brought for exchange, where there are numerous possessors of each commodity. He asks, what are the necessary and sufficient conditions that this market should be in equilibrium; that is to say, that there should be a distribution of the two commodities among the various exchangers such that no further exchanges should take place? Method of solving this problem: Defines his terms; price is the ratio of exchange per unit of the two commodities; effective supply and demand of one commodity are the quantities of that commodity actually given and received when an exchange is made. Certain conclusions are virtually implied by these definitions. 1. For every effective demand for one commodity there results an effective offer of the other commodity and a price. 2. Prices of the two commodities in terms of each other are reciprocals. 3. Quantities of the two commodities exchanged are inversely as their prices. 4. Effective demand for one commodity equals effective supply for the other times price of the latter in the former; and effective supply of one commodity equals effective demand for the other times its price in the latter. 5. Ratio of effective demand for one commodity to its effective supply equals ratio of effective supply of the other to its effective demand.

---

[152] Outline, November 3, 1931.

But these propositions hold true of every possible price at which an exchange is effected. Hence they do not show the equilibrium price. That market should be in equilibrium; i.e., that no further exchanges should occur, it is necessary that effective demand for each commodity should equal its effective supply. To know at which one of the numberless possible prices this condition will obtain, we must have another element; namely, demand curves. These curves are empirically determined [in principle]. Walras supposes each person in the market to make up his mind how much of the commodity he wants he will buy at each of the possible prices. He assumes that these quantities will vary with the price. He argues that in a market with many exchangers, the demand curves will be continuous. By definition, his curves of demand for each commodity are at the same time, curves of supply for the other commodity. Solution of the problem of equilibrium prices of two commodities: "Two commodities being given, in order that the market be in equilibrium with reference to them it is necessary and it is sufficient that the effective demand for each of the two shall be equal to the effective supply. When this equality does not exist, to arrive at equilibrium, it is necessary to raise the price of the commodity whose effective demand is greater than the effective supply, and to lower the price of the commodity whose effective supply is greater than its effective demand."[153]

[Let us repeat the discussion of the most difficult of writers up to this point, in a somewhat different form.] Walras begins with study of an organized market where competition is absolutely free, where two commodities are exchanged, where definite quantities of these commodities are present, where there are several buyers and several sellers of each commodity. He asks what are the necessary and sufficient conditions that this market should be in equilibrium; i.e., that there should be a distribution of the two commodities among the various exchangers such that no further exchanges should take place. Solution: Starts with an exchange made at some price. Points out that

1. This price equals the inverse ratio of the quantities exchanged. Prices are reciprocals; e.g., 60 bushels of oats exchange for 40 bushels of wheat; price of $1\frac{1}{2}$ bushels of oats equals one bushel of wheat; $\frac{2}{3}$ bushels of wheat equals one bushel of oats. 60 bushels : 40 bushels :: 3 : 2; or 40 bushels : 60 bushels :: 2 : 3.

2. Demand for one article in terms of the other equals supply of the other times its price in the first. Demand of wheat in terms of oats: 40 bushels of wheat equals 60 bushels of oats times $\frac{2}{3}$. Supply of one article offered for another equals demand for the other times its price in the first: 60 bushels of oats offered (for 40 bushels of wheat) equals 40 times $\frac{3}{2}$.

---

[153] [In the English translation (from the fifth edition of 1926) this passage reads: "Given two commodities, for the market to be in equilibrium with respect to these commodities, or for the price of either commodity to be stationary in terms of the other, it is necessary and sufficient that the effective demand be equal [to] the effective offer of each commodity. Where this equality does not obtain, in order to reach equilibrium price, the commodity having an effective demand greater than its effective offer must rise in price; and the commodity having an effective offer greater than its effective demand must fall in price." *Elements of Pure Economics or The Theory of Social Wealth* translated by William Jaffé (London: Allen and Unwin, 1954) p. 106. The italics of the original have been omitted.]

3. Ratio of effective demand for one article to its effective supply equals ratio
of effective supply of the other to its effective demand. Effective demand
for oats—60 bushels—divided by effective supply of oats—60 bushels—
equals effective supply of wheat—40 bushels—divided by effective demand
for wheat—40 bushels. But we do not know that this price with which
we start will be the equilibrium price; for there can be no equilibrium
unless at that price supply of each article equals demand for it in terms
of the other, and we do not know whether supply of wheat at price of ⅔
bushels for one bushel of barley equals 1 or greater or less than 1. To find
this out we need *curves of demand* for each article in terms of the other.
Suppose these curves are empirically determined; i.e., that each party
makes up his mind how much of the other commodity he will take at each
possible price. Walras tacitly supposes that quantity each exchanger will
give declines as price rises. He argues that in a market with large number
of exchanges, the demand curves will be continuous.

Remarks: Walras starts with fact of exchange of two commodities at a price.
Inquires what is price at which exchange will stop. Shows what data are
necessary to answer this question: quantities of the commodities on the
market; their curves of demand. Supposes not one pair but numerous pairs
of exchanges under conditions of free competition. Analysis of utility has
not been brought in so far. Argument has no psychological implications
beyond observation that demand varies with price. But now Walras asks:
How does an individual attain his curves of demand—still considering two
commodities? Method of answering: supposes that individual has a standard by which he can measure the intensity of his wants of the same and
of different kinds. Supposes further that intensities of want will decline
as stock acquired grows. On this basis he develops notion of final degree
of utility which he calls *rareté*. Walras shows then that: 1. Given a market
for two commodities at a given price, to maximise utility, each person will
trade until he has made his ratios of final degrees of utility equal the price.
2. Each person's schedule of demand prices for one commodity in terms
of the other can be determined directly from his curves of utility for the
two commodities. He concludes that: In a state of market equilibrium
prices of two commodities equal ratios of final degrees of utility; that is,
values in exchange are proportional to final degrees of utility.

Remarks: While Jevons begins with pleasure and works forward to arrive at
a price, Walras begins with price and works backward to find demand and
then analyzes relations between price and demand on the one hand and
utility on the other. Technically, his theory of prices depends directly on
demand schedules; he uses utility as a way of understanding demand
schedules and as an indication that the equilibrium price is also the equation of maximum satisfaction. Hence [his disciple and biographer, Etienne
Antonelli's] claim that Walras does not belong to the psychological school,
as do Jevons and the Austrians; that is, his theory of prices, of market
equilibrium, does not rest on his analysis of utility but upon empirically
determined curves of demand, which he afterwards explains, have the
form they would have if they were derived from curves of utility.

Treatment of problem of exchange of two commodities is clearer than that
of Jevons. But Walras's chief contribution was his treatment of problem

of equilibrium price in a market where *many commodities* are bought and sold. Of this later. What is needed for solution: 1. Demand and supply schedules for each individual for each commodity. 2. Quantities of commodities in every individual's hands at beginning. Conditions of equilibrium for each individual: (1) Realization of maximum satisfaction corresponding to equality between prices, final degrees of utility; (2) equivalence of purchases and sales or expenditures and receipts for each commodity balancing equivalence of supply and demand. Walras gives a general scheme for conceiving equilibrium in a large market where many buyers and sellers deal in many wares. Insists upon mutual interdetermination of all the factors. A criticism of use of category of cause and effect: ordinary logic is able to handle the problem only when conceived in that inadequate fashion. For treatment of the real problem mathematics is indispensable.

Before discussing Menger in particular, let us first attempt to formulate as succinctly as possible, the successive propositions of the essential points of the Austrian theory of subjective value. 1. Man has a vast number of desires of different kinds. These desires differ in degrees of intensity: (1) According to their kind; (e.g., desire for food is more intense than desire for amusement). (2) According to amount of satisfaction already bestowed upon them. The intensity of any desire diminishes with each successive draught of satisfaction. (This does not mean that an appetite for satisfaction of a given kind diminishes in intensity with indulgence, but that *at any given* time the appetite will slacken as number of draughts of satisfaction administered increases.)

2. Man always strives to satisfy his desires as completely as possible and in order of greatest intensity, so that desire last satisfied is always a desire of less intensity than any other desire previously satisfied. (It seems to be implicitly assumed that the reason why men try to satisfy wants is that an unsatisfied craving is a pain and satisfaction of any desire is a pleasure, and that the avoidance of the pain or attainment of the pleasure, or both, is the motive.)

3. (1) In order to satisfy most of his wants man must have at his disposal certain concrete things that exist in the objective world. (2) The term "good" ("commodity") is used to denote anything which has the capacity for satisfying any human want directly or indirectly.

4. (1) Man attaches importance to the possession of goods because they are indispensable conditions of the satisfaction of his desires. (2) When the satisfaction of no desire is dependent upon the possession of a concrete thing, no importance is attached to its possession. (3) The degree of importance attached to the possession of any good depends upon the degree of intensity of the desire whose satisfaction is conditioned by possession of the good concerned. The greater the intensity of the want, the more importance is attached to its satisfaction and the more importance consequently attached to the possession of the good which is needed to satisfy it.

5. (1) Value is the importance attached by men to goods arising from their recognized dependence upon possession of—disposal over goods for the satisfaction of their wants. (2) The value of any *single good* is determined by the intensity of the want whose satisfaction is dependent upon the

possession of it;—for men attach to the indispensable condition of a satisfaction an importance equal to that of the satisfaction itself. [c.f. 4(3).][154] (3) Value of any unit of a stock of precisely similar goods is determined by the intensity of the least pressing want which is satisfied by the use of a unit of the stock; for (a) the wants satisfied by the successive consumption of several similar goods differ in intensity, the last want satisfied being least intense [c.f. 1(2) and 2 *supra*];[155] (b) if one unit of the stock of goods is lost, making it necessary to forego the satisfaction of one want, it will be the least intense of the wants formerly met that will now remain unsatisfied; (c) therefore it is the least intense want whose satisfaction is dependent upon the possession of one unit of the stock.

In order to simplify the law, the term "marginal utility" is used to denote the degree of satisfaction derived from the consumption of that unit of a stock of goods which is employed to meet the least pressing want that is actually satisfied, by the possession of the given stock. The principle may then be stated as follows: the value of a commodity is determined by its marginal utility. According to the above, the process of subjective valuation seems to amount to this: an individual feels a definite desire of given intensity. He has knowledge of some thing which is capable of satisfying the desire. To that article he attaches an importance for his well-being corresponding to the intensity of the desire. This constitutes the "valuation" of the given article. In still briefer form the theory is: an article is valued for the sake of the definite state of feeling which it will produce in the given individual under the given circumstances. And the amount of value attached to it depends on the degree of satisfaction derived from the state of feeling, or the interest felt by the individual in experiencing this given state of feeling.

More specifically, Menger begins with a general theory of economic goods. Goods are classified into orders which are numbered in accordance with the immediacy of their relations to satisfaction of wants. Immediate [consumer] goods belong to the first order. Other goods to higher orders. Goods of higher orders depend for their quality of being goods upon: (1) possession of the complementary goods necessary to convert them into goods of the first order; (2) the quality of the goods of the first order into which they can be converted.

The economy. An economy is a system within which there is an orderly adjustment between wants and satisfactions—or an orderly application of resources to needs. Economic activity is directed mainly to satisfaction of wants. This requires (1) clear recognition of our needs—quantity of goods required; (2) knowledge of quantity of goods available for use. We economize only goods of which supply is less than need. Such goods alone are owned—property is a necessary result of the constitution of the world. Such goods alone are economic goods. The fundamental conception of economy is value. Theory of value—definition: "Value is the significance which concrete goods or quantities of goods attain for us because we recognize that the gratification of our wants depends upon disposal over

---

[154] [Brackets are Professor Mitchell's.]
[155] [Brackets are Professor Mitchell's.]

them."[156] Note: to Jevons value is a ratio of exchange: to Walras also value means exchange value—the property which certain goods have of being obtainable, not for nothing but only by exchange for other goods. To Menger value is a judgment; implies subjective matter; amount of value therefore dependent upon the intensity of the want, dependent upon having disposal over the good in question. Must therefore study wants. Wants have different orders. Some are more basic than others: must be satisfied before others receive attention. Diminish in intensity as stock available for satisfaction increases. Hence wants of first order may be no more intense under certain circumstances of supply than wants of tenth order. All this applies clearly to immediate goods. Goods of higher orders get their value at second hand from the contribution which they make in the end to gratification of wants by aiding in production of immediate goods.

Theory of exchange. Motive to exchange is to increase satisfaction of wants. Means is to give goods of less for goods of greater value. Limit of exchange. Gain usually greatest for exchange of first units of supplies on hand. Gain ceases and therefore exchange stops when A no longer has a unit of his commodity of less value to him than a unit of B's good for which it might be traded would have. Same conditions hold for B.

Theory of prices. (1) Isolated barter; limits within which price must fall are set by the respective valuations set by the two parties upon the two commodities. Demand schedules implied. Points within these limits at which price actually falls is determined by bargaining power. (2) Monopoly: demand schedules more definitely suggested. Monopolist can fix either supply to be sold or selling price. If he fixes supply, price will fall within limits set by the values set upon the monopoly good by the last included and the first excluded buyer. If he fixes price, it will be at point which he thinks to be the maximum revenue point. (3) Two-sided competition: general principle of price determination on basis of demand schedules which themselves run back to judgments of value still held. Competition affects prices only because it affects quantity of goods brought to market or schedules of supply prices.

Notes: Menger does not use term "marginal utility." That term introduced by Wieser. Lack of a definite name for this crucial element in Menger's analysis leaves it a little vague. His attention is devoted primarily to analysis of subjective value—men's judgments concerning the importance of goods to them—a subject little treated by Jevons or Walras.

Summary: Jevons built his theory explicitly upon hedonistic psychology. Neither Walras nor Menger put forward any explicit theory of why men are interested in goods. If their conceptions are hedonistic, they are tacitly so. Jevons and Menger put their analysis of utility forward first; then built upon it a theory of price; Walras developed theory of price from demand (and supply) schedules; then analyzes demand schedules and

---

[156] [In the English translation this passage reads: "Value is . . . the importance that individual goods or quantities of goods attain for us because we are conscious of being dependent on command of them for the satisfaction of our needs." *Principles of Economics,* translated and edited by James Dingwall and B. F. Hoselitz (Glencoe, Ill.: Free Press, 1950) p. 115.]

finds explanation in variation of utility. Jevons and Walras use idea of
final degree of utility—a ratio between amount of feeling and amount of
commodity; Menger uses idea of marginal utility although without giving
it a specific name. Jevons and Walras treat value as ratio in exchange;
Menger treats it as importance attributed to goods. Jevons and Walras
employ mathematical language largely to express their ideas—Walras more
effectively than Jevons; Menger goes no further in this direction than to
give simple, numerical examples. All three centered their interest in the
theory of prices; all three saw also that the theory of price might be made
a theory of distribution; none of them, however, worked out an elaborate
theory of distribution. Jevons's discussion of distribution is fragmentary
and not clear; Walras represents prices of productive services as simply
one of the problems solved in terms of supply and demand;[157] Menger
finds value of productive services by noting what is lost when one of the
factors drops out. Walras developed his analysis into a theory of general
equilibrium which went far beyond Jevons and Menger. Menger and
Walras develop a theory of money; Jevons does not [in his *The Theory
of Political Economy*].[158]

[The discussion will now turn to Marshall and his neo-classical type
of theory.]

---

[157] [Professor Mitchell it seems used the second edition of Walras's treatise, that
of 1889. In the third edition (1896), inspired in good part by Philip H. Wicksteed's
Essay on the Coordination of the Law of Distribution (1894), Walras presented a
formulation of what is now called the marginal productivity theory of distribution.]

[158] Outlines, December 11, 13, 1916, and "The Austrian Theory of Subjective
Value," APP 44-53, no. 9.

"Begin writing up lecture notes on relations between Jevons, Walras and Menger."
Mitchell, "Diary," December 10, 1916.

CHAPTER X

Alfred Marshall and Neo-Classical Economics

Before going on with Marshall it is desirable to discuss, even at the cost of some repetition, several developments in the social sciences that occurred between the publication of Jevons's treatise in 1871 and that of Marshall's *Principles of Economics* in 1890.

Though these movements did not occur in the field of economics proper, they did gradually come to exercise an influence over the minds of economists. Charles Darwin's *On the Origin of Species* appeared in John Stuart Mill's lifetime. He read the book and in his letters there is a brief note to a friend saying that it seemed to him that although Darwin had not proved his hypothesis, he had rendered it highly plausible, which was as much as anyone could hope to do in dealing with such a theme.[1] But neither Mill nor the other economists for a time seemed to grasp the notion that the new hypothesis formulated by a biologist had any special significance for students of the social sciences. It is true that presently Herbert Spencer, as part of his great *Synthetic Philosophy,* began to discuss the evolution of social institutions; particularly in his *Principles of Sociology.* But Spencer represented a curious transition period in the history of social thought. He was a follower in psychology of Bentham.

He tried to re-establish hedonism on an evolutionary basis—two forms of argument. 1. Natural selection would eliminate as unfit any stocks that did not take pleasure in beneficial forms of activity and feel pain in harmful ones— a fallacy. Takes hedonism for granted. 2. Natural selection eliminates stocks that are given to harmful behavior and preserves those given to wholesome behavior. But empirically the harmful is unpleasant and the wholesome is pleasurable. No proof of hedonism. From this the conclusion that follows is what men seek is generally pleasant and what they avoid is generally painful [and] *not* therefore man seeks pleasure and avoids pain. Spencer's effort to unite hedonism with instinct of self-preservation was thus obviously a begging of the question.

Evolutionary hedonism, in short, has not survived the struggle for existence among psychological theories. Spencer, furthermore, attempted to main-

---

[1] Mill to Alexander Bain, April 11, 1860, in *The Letters of John Stuart Mill,* edited by H. S. R. Elliot, 2 volumes (London: Longmans, Green, 1910) I, p. 236.

tain the hedonistic theory of human behavior and a highly individualistic attitude. Why Spencer failed to re-animate individualism: His antipathy to state action hard to reconcile with his view of society as an organism. Also he went to extremes, which alienated practical men.[2]

Consequently, the view of the evolution of institutions in his sociology seems, even after the lapse of only a generation or so, a curious one, containing elements which belong in the eighteenth rather than in the nineteenth century. Besides, he did not attempt to do much with economic institutions. His influence upon the development of sociology was prompt and great, but the economists seem not to have appreciated sufficiently the importance of his viewpoint to grasp the possibility of doing in their subject work of the sort that he was doing in sociology at large. Spencer was followed by a number of anthropologists who are now generally classed together as belonging to the historical or evolutionary school of that department of learning and as marking the great period of anthropological speculation.

Sir Henry Maine published *Ancient Law* in 1865.[3] He insisted that if the investigator wants to understand the differences among institutions, he must lay great stress upon habit. He especially stressed the influence of custom and evolution of custom.[4]

This did not mean that Maine was critical of the system of free contract. On the contrary, "the most formidable of the critics, from the historical side, of the individualist philosophy of the economists . . . in his work on *Ancient Law,* . . . seemed to put the principle of free contract on an even firmer basis than before by representing it as the inevitable outcome of an age-long historical evolution. *From Status to Contract* came in to supplement *Laissez-Faire.*" Does not this fact explain position of Thorold Rogers—an historical economist and a Manchester man in one?[5]

Walter Bagehot at the time was the editor of the influential London *Economist,* but he was writing on politics, sociology and anthropology about as freely as on economics. *Physics and Politics; or, Thoughts on the Application of the Principles of "Natural Selection" and "Inheritance" to Political Society* (1872), *The English Constitution, and*

---

[2] Outlines, January 9, 1918, November 3, 1931, "Ashley," APP 44-53, no. 99.

[3] [Maine whose influence on anthropology was immense has generally been considered a legal historian and political theorist.]

[4] "1918 Typescript." Outline, November 3, 1931.

[5] "Ashley," APP 44-53, no. 99. Quotation from Sir William Ashley, *The Economic Organization of England* (London: Longmans, Green, 1914) p. 167. [John Mills felt that Rogers would do the job of being the Bastiat of England if he "were not immersed in ultra-radical politics" in the sense of the philosophical radicals. (Mills to W. B. Hodgson, February 7, 1869 in Isobel Mills, *From Tinder-Box to the "Larger" Light: Threads from the Life of John Mills, Banker* (Manchester: Sherratt and Hughes, 1899) p. 322.]

Other Political Essays (1867) and *Lombard Street; A Description of the Money Market* (1873) are all classics. Bagehot's *Physics and Politics,* which like Spencer's work leaned heavily on Sir Henry Maine's *Ancient Law,* contributed especially to the disintegration of hedonism by its emphasis on custom. Bagehot tried to show that human behavior must be explained largely by imitation and by force of custom. Change is necessarily slow, he argued, because society is covered by a thick crust which is somewhat difficult to break, "a cake of custom."[6]

The greatest in the group of anthropologists, Edward B. Tylor, published *Researches into the Early History of Mankind* in 1865, and his most important treatise *Primitive Culture* in 1871, the same year in which Jevons's *Theory of Political Economy* appeared. An American member of the group, [the Rochester, New York, lawyer], Lewis H. Morgan published *Ancient Society* in 1877. All these works stressed the evolution of custom and its importance. The evolutionary school of anthropology gave clearer ideas about evolution of culture, of institutions. Modern social organization is seen not as a simple deliverance of common sense but as a complicated growth. What man is as an organism depends upon the culture into which he is born.[7]

These anthropologists, particularly Tylor and Morgan, had something to say about the early development of economic institutions, though that was not the central field of their interest; and they were throwing out suggestions which it seems now an economist might have seen had a definite bearing upon his conception of human nature.

Anthropology is under no professional obligation to explain why men do certain things but it does exhibit vividly the widely divergent behavior of men brought up in different cultures. Acquaintance with it is helpful to an economist not because it throws much direct light upon economic behavior in modern nations, but because it helps us to avoid the error that certain types of behavior common among ourselves are part of the established order of human nature.[8]

For the time being, however, the anthropologists were regarded as

---

[6] Paragraph from "1918 Typescript."

[7] Outline, November 3, 1931.
The period marked the rise of a more scientific anthropology and economic history (Outline, November 3, 1931).

[8] "The Problem of Human Nature in Economics," opening discussion with tutors in economics at Oxford, January 19, 1932.
Furthermore, "In these days when anthropology has superseded *histoire raisonné,* and we no longer imagine the institutions of our own time, with some small emendations, to be 'natural' and all others 'artificial', protests against the policy of leaving economic laws alone, are out of date, since that policy must be seen to be absolutely chimerical rather than simply erroneous. If any semi-somnolent individual still asks for *laissez-faire,* he can be sufficiently dealt with by an inquiry into what he supposes himself to mean by it." (Quoted from Edwin Cannan, review of Philip H. Wicksteed, *Common Sense of Political Economy,* in *The Economic Journal,* September 1910, p. 395; in "Wicksteed," APP 54-63, no. 23.)

cultivating a special field which had little to do with the problem of the economists. And that seems to have been the case despite the fact that there was also growing up within economics a group of people interested in discussing the historical aspects of economic problems, the historical school which later will be dealt with at length. The center of the historical school was in Germany; the great protagonist of it was Gustav von Schmoller of the University of Berlin.

The rise of the historical school, to repeat, led to a tremendous controversy which is generally known, even in Anglo-American universities by its German name, *Methodenstreit* (The Battle of Methods). The protagonists were Carl Menger on the one side and on the other Schmoller, who in his youthful days was a remarkably vigorous champion of the exclusive merits of the historical method of work, of the inductive method. As previously noted, Menger, who was a co-rediscoverer with Jevons and Walras of the marginal analysis, appeared as champion of the classical viewpoint, deductive economics, as far as method was concerned, [or, as his disciple Böhm-Bawerk called it, "the abstract-deductive method." Böhm-Bawerk also claimed for their school not only the name "Abstract-Deductive School" but also "Psychological School," a title which was later taken over by an American variant of the marginal analysis, led by Frank A. Fetter.][9]

Menger began the controversy in 1883 with *Untersuchungen über die Methode der Socialwissenschaften und der politischen Oekonomie insbesondere* ("An Inquiry into the Methods of the Social Sciences, Particularly of Economics").[10] Schmoller replied in the same year

----

[9] [According to Böhm-Bawerk, "if Schmoller rightly demands that political economy should provide itself with a sound psychological foundation, he will find his demand nowhere so nearly met as in the work of the so called abstract-deductive school, in the works of a Jevons or Sidgwick, a Menger or Wieser; indeed it would not surprise me if in the future this school should come to be called the 'psychological school of political economy'." ("The Historical vs. the Deductive Method in Political Economy," *The Annals of the American Academy of Political and Social Science,* October 1890, p. 206.) The article originally appeared in *Conrads Jahrbücher für Nationalökonomie und Statistik* (1890) and was translated by Henrietta Leonard.]

[10] [In 1963 there appeared an English translation by Frances J. Nock, under the title *Problems of Economics and Sociology.*

Menger's polemic was directed against Roscher, Knies and especially Albert Schäffle (1831-1903). It has been pointed out that Schäffle in his work, notably in *Die Quintessence des Sozialismus* (1874; translation under the title of *Quintessence of Socialism* 1892), "tentatively sketched out a scheme for a liberal-socialist economy with a centralized authority, plentifully supplied with statistical intelligence, and manipulating a system of taxes and subsidies, which would retain the freedom and stimuli of the competitive market. Schäffle's idea was essentially that later developed by Enrico Barone, Oskar Lange and others, but without the precise mathematical formulation and background of Walrasian and Paretian analysis." T. W. Hutchison, *A Review of Economic Doctrines: 1870-1929* (London: Oxford University Press, 1953) p. 294; see also p. 139 ft.]

with an equally intemperate review "Zur Methodologie der Staats-
und Socialwissenschaften" ("On the Method of the Political and
Social Sciences") in his influential journal.[11]

The tone of Schmoller's reply is not as angry as that of Menger's rejoinder,
Die Irrthümer des Historismus in der deutschen Nationalökonomie ("Errors of Historicism in German Economics") 1884. [Schmoller closed his
review with:] Menger admits that the theorist has to assume a specific
social environment as the basis for his exposition. Other environments are
to be treated as modifications necessitating some changes in statement of
the economic laws. Yes, but why not a theory of change as well as of static
west European society? Personally, Menger is a clever fellow, but lacks
a broad education—hence the one-sidedness of his economic views. He
fancies the one little room of theory with which he is acquainted is the
whole structure of Political Economy.[12]

In the heat of this controversy Menger took a position just about
as extreme as Schmoller. He declared vigorously that nothing can be
added to the knowledge of economics as a science by any other
method than that of deepening the process that Ricardo had developed, the same process that he and other theoretical-minded economists were trying to extend into new fields. Schmoller, on the other
hand, was inclined to deny practically *in toto* the usefulness of anything else than historical research and to say, moreover, that until
historical research had been practiced for a considerable time—he
even suggested several generations—we would not have a sufficient
body of data upon which to erect, by inductive methods, any science
of economics; that is to say, until this long historical lapse had resulted in piling up a great mass of detailed information regarding the
kind of economic life that people have lived in different stages of
development, in different parts of the world, until that time has
come, economists can have nothing like an economic theory. For
the time being they must merely accumulate economic data. They
waste their time if they try to theorize on the basis of such data as
are now possessed.

The controversy, to repeat, like many others, was carried on not
only in a bitter but in a very uncompromising and extreme spirit.
To read the most vigorous of Menger's pamphlets and articles, one
would have thought that there is no possibility of learning anything
about economics except by adopting the method of deduction from

---

[11] *Jahrbuch für Gesetzgebung, Verwaltung und Volkswirtschaft im deutschen Reich*
("Yearbook of Legislation, Administration and Economics"), generally referred to
as *Schmollers Jahrbuch*, n.s., vol. VII, pt. 3 (1883) pp. 975-994. [The same house,
Duncker and Hamblot, Leipzig, published Menger's attack and Schmoller's journal.]
[12] Abstract in "Scope and Method of Political Economy," APP 74-83, no. 54.
Abstract of Menger's rejoinder is in the same folder.

abstract premises; and, on the other hand, one might conclude from some of Schmoller's more extreme writings that nothing could be accomplished of value by that unreal method of procedure, and that the only possibility of arriving at valid decisions concerning economic behavior was to study history and statistical records.

The extremity of these positions was doubtless due in both cases in part to the mood of irritation into which the two writers fell. They called each other names which from the point of view of anybody but a continental controversialist seem rather rude, and this name-calling had the usual effect of making both the disputants distinctly intemperate in their frame of mind. The smoke of this controversy obscured the whole economic situation in Germany for a generation. As they lived with their problems the two parties began gradually to come a little bit closer together.[13]

Both extreme views are patently absurd and the controversy ran out, to the general satisfaction of the bystanders at least, to the conclusion that induction and deduction are both absolutely essential to successful work in economics and absolutely indispensable to solving the simplest problems of ordinary life. The majority of economists finally came round to a view which was not very different from that which prevailed among the English economists who had been interested in method, particularly people like that versatile genius Bagehot. As already noted, he had defended the methods which he attributed to Ricardo in a series of brilliant articles on "The Postulates of English Political Economy" in John Morley's *Fortnightly Review* in 1876, essays which are still read in courses on scope and method of economics.[14] The results of the controversy were summed up by John Neville Keynes (1852-1949), a logician at Cambridge, in an admirable and highly sensible book called *The Scope and Method of Political Economy* (1891). This Keynes has since become more famous by virtue of the fact that his son John Maynard Keynes [later Lord Keynes] attained such prominence.

It was also during these years that Marx entered the field with *Das Kapital*. One might have expected that alert-minded economists would have seen that in the first volume of the inquiry, the only one of the three volumes published during Marx's lifetime, there was a fresh approach to the study of some fundamental problems, perhaps a more brilliant example of how to combine analytical and historical

---

13 Last three paragraphs from "1918 Typescript."

14 [Alfred Marshall had these essays reprinted in a small volume under the title *The Postulates of English Political Economy* (1891) for which he supplied a preface.]

Bagehot defended the logic of political economy more in the spirit of Ricardo than John Stuart Mill (Outline, November 3, 1931).

research successfully in the treatment of theoretical problems than was afforded by any other writer. But Marx was not merely the author of a scientific treatise, he was also the great leader of the socialist movement, the most conspicuous figure in the First International. He was, therefore, a person whose conclusions were so unacceptable to economists that few of them had any will or patience to endeavor to profit by the aspects of his work which might have been serviceable to them.

So that, so far as theoretical political economy is concerned, the influence of Marx was, for a time at least, almost altogether indefinite. It was productive of further controversies, of many efforts simply to refute the socialistic conclusions at which Marx arrived, but of very few efforts to use that extraordinarily skilfull combination of study of recent records of the industrial development which England was going through with an analysis of economic processes similar in character and in intellectual temper to Ricardo's analysis. It seems to have been one of the cases where the feelings of a set of scholars regarding conclusions arrived at blinded them to the possible contribution of the underlying work. In England, Marx had no followers who made important scientific contributions to economics. His chief English disciple was the wealthy Henry Mayer Hyndman (1842-1921), a distinguished person on the socialist side, singularly gifted, persuasive as a public speaker. He wrote from time to time on economic topics but he was not scientifically-minded.

Another person who played a large role in the English socialist movement was William Morris (1834-1896). He was a good party man and spent a great deal of time and energy trying to recruit for the Socialist League [which he helped to organize in 1884]. It is a little hard to make out what his theoretical attitude on economic problems was, mainly for the reason that he was not interested in scientific questions; he was in all his dealings concerned with the world of the artist, the poet and the craftsman. It was primarily his hatred of the ugly side of English life, those effects upon character and surroundings which were concomitants of the industrialization of the country that made him so eager and so constant a supporter of socialism. When he attempted to make contributions of his own to the solution of social problems, these took the form primarily of beautiful allegories or fantasies—pictures of what might be accomplished, of how sweet and lovely life might be, if only men in their economic behavior could live under conditions similar to those which prevailed in the middle ages, which Morris idealized.

An earlier, influential exponent of Morris's aesthetic point of view was John Ruskin (1819-1900), whose condemnations of political economy were as stinging even as those of Carlyle. [John Mills, in congratulating his friend Hodgson on his educational work for sound economics, wrote:

> I am afresh from Ruskin's Lake papers, and have longed to pull him down from the fine-tinted cloud of sophisms on which he floats through the air with Jove-like mastery, glancing with supreme contempt on the poor economist below, whose feet cling to the *terra-firma* of fact and law. My fear is that, in proportion as the educational economists break down the barriers of indifference and ignorance, they will find themselves confronting a phalanx of imaginative men, whose pride of intellect rebels against any system ranging social facts under rigid laws. This is a case in which temperament has almost as much to do with conviction as logic has.][15]

Meanwhile there had been forming gradually that characteristically English group of socialists to whom reference has already been made, the Fabians. They were, to repeat, primarily reformers; they were not looking for a great social revolution of the Marxian kind, but they were working in an effective and intelligent fashion to bring about a series of cumulative changes in economic arrangements, which they expected would gradually, by an evolutionary process, substantially alter the organization and face of civilized life. Their theoretical doctrines, so far as economics is concerned, came to be that particular brand which ran in Jevons, the mechanics of utility. This they opposed not only to the orthodox Ricardo-John Stuart Mill doctrine, but also to the analysis of Marx. Thus there was a theoretical split within the forces which constituted the socialist movement as a whole in England. The Fabians regarded themselves as socialists and they were working for a reorganization of society, under which the state would assume a larger measure of responsibility than it had possessed in the past. But they were unwilling to accept, however, the Marxian doctrine of surplus value which was generally at that time put forth as the central feature of Marxian theory. Neither would they accept Marx's analysis of the process by which a transformation of society would be effected. Marx was counting on increasing misery of the laboring class, extension of the proletariat, increasing concentration of wealth and income in fewer hands, the growing frequency and intensity of commercial crises, to produce a situation from which there would be no escape except into the socialist state. The Fabians were, however, thinking that by working from the inside they could get

---

[15] [Mills to Hodgson, January 8, 1861, in Isobel Mills, *From Tinder-Box to the "Larger" Light*, p. 281.]

Parliament to adopt, one after another, carefully excogitated schemes which with their logical corollaries and concomitants would not suddenly but gradually raise the well-being of the country as a whole and effect sweeping changes in the end in economic organization. In temper and intellectual ability the Fabians make no unworthy comparison with the philosophical radicals of fifty or seventy-five years earlier.

During this time too the hedonistic view of human nature was gradually breaking down. The old tradition of utilitarianism was maintained at Cambridge, the great center of interest in social sciences, mainly by Sidgwick. He was, as noted, a good utilitarian and remained so to the end of his days, but as he thought about the problem of what makes men do things he came to be more and more skeptical concerning Bentham's simple assertion that pleasure and pain control all of men's actions. What made him doubtful was the discovery that he did not eat his dinner because he wanted pleasure, but because he felt hungry. This bit of introspection he went over and over again and in a period when introspection was relied upon as a satisfactory method of psychological inquiry; he attached considerable importance to the fact that he went to the table not because he was anticipating the pleasure to be derived from food but because he felt some kind of inner prompting of another sort which he called hunger. It followed that if people do not eat because they desire pleasure, it is doubtful whether people do other acts for that same reason. This introspective disintegration of the theory was supplemented gradually by a dawning appreciation of the role which instinct plays in determining behavior. Instinct had been one of the factors on which Darwin had laid much stress in his later books; and in those days instincts were listed and defined with a degree of confidence which people no longer feel. It was a comparatively simple thing to picture the lower animals as controlled in their behavior by methods of acting which they had inherited; that patterns of behavior were in them when they were born. When the psychologists accustomed themselves to thinking of men as a species of animals, they were inclined to see an important extension of the influence of instinct, which was supposed to control the behavior of the lower animals, into the behavior of man himself.

In this period also William James and other psychologists discovered the importance of habit, a factor in behavior which they readily allied with instinct, and which on the whole had been curiously neglected by Bentham and his school. One can tie the habit scheme into the Benthamite system of psychology by appealing to the association of ideas. But Bentham himself was inclined to argue that almost all actions are controlled by calculations and the easy explanation of the fact that many persons' actions are repeated frequently, from Bentham's viewpoint, was that the individual calculated that certain ways of doing things gave on the whole a maximum of pleasure and, having found by experience that the results answer calculations, he goes on acting in that way. But the people who were talking about habit did not consider it as based originally upon calculation of advantage so much as adding a sort of upper story of the instincts; as having a physiological basis in the human frame which had no simple counterpart in Bentham's scheme, though it might be traced in the more highly developed associationist psychology of Alexander Bain, a psychology which was being supplanted by that of James.[15a]

These doubts concerning the validity of the introspective argument for the hedonistic psychology, together with the other methods of explaining at least a large part of behavior which were suggested by appeal to instincts on one side and to habits on the other side, prepared investigators to take a new view of man's actions, to regard him less as a calculating animal and more as a creature who was ruled largely by characteristics which he inherited: by behavior and habit, imitation and other patterns in which the element of rationality was less conspicuous than in the Benthamite speculations.

The emphasis upon instinct meant that man's course of action is seldom thought out in advance, that by and large it is characteristic of all animal forms, including man, to do things first and reflect only when his action lands him in some kind of predicament out of which his instinctive methods of reaction cannot help him. Reflection came to be considered as a difficult, hesitating kind of mental exercise[16] in which man indulges very seldom, the greater part of his activity being controlled either by instincts or by habits which have been built up to such a point that thinking occupies comparatively little part in their immediate control. In short, the new conception particularly in its biological implications tends to discredit the older intellectualism and individualism of the Benthamite kind.

The Benthamite position, of course, had also been attacked in England, but on somewhat different grounds. It had been attacked by English philosophers who were themselves disciples of the important line of German philosophy (notably T. H. Green of Oxford and David

---

[15a]Clause from Outline, November 3, 1931.
[16] [This is the view developed by Mitchell's teacher in philosophy, John Dewey.]

Ritchie of Cambridge). This was a kind of neo-Hegelian philosophy—
I suppose its adherents would say it prevails today [1918] as the
dominant philosophy. This line of speculation, derived from German
philosophers, laid considerable stress upon the nature of society,
upon institutions, and much less upon the individual. These philosophers thinking largely upon ethical problems had begun contending,
before the first year of the twentieth century was out, that it is a
serious mistake to conceive of society as simply an aggregate of
independent individuals. This view leaves out of account the vital
feature of society; namely, the various factors which bind men together, which make each of us part of the others. The same view is
enforced by the study of biology, for any kind of animal species
lives as a group, and the behavior of individuals cannot be explained
unless the inquirer knows what the social habits of that particular
species are. Translate this to man, who is even more a socialized
being than the bee. Finally, as the German philosophers had been
saying, the inquirer is missing the great point of social organization
when he tries to account for it simply as so many separate individuals each more or less complete in himself. From the scientific
side the older view was undermined by biological study and still
more emphatically by ethnology.[17] This whole line of development
began to discredit in part at least the dependence upon introspection as substantially the sole method of prosecuting researches in
psychology. Introspection is a charmingly obliging instrument. The
user can ordinarily find in his mental processes just pretty much
what he expects to find in them; it is almost fair to say, pretty much
what he wants to find in them.

There was, again largely under German leadership, an important
supplement of the introspective method developed in experimental
psychology. Many of the experimental psychologists would readily
go to the length of saying that it was not a supplement but a substitute for introspection. Then recently [1918]—a further supplement has
been developed by the so-called behaviorists, the people who are
characterized not so much by the use of laboratory methods as they
are by the insistence on the need to study the actions of man from
the outside. The investigator must record the individual's muscular
behavior, and not depend upon guesses as to why an individual does
certain things, guesses which are necessarily colored by the views of
the investigator himself.[18]

---

[17] Sentence from Outline, March 11, 1918.
[18] Last three paragraphs from "1918 Typescript."

Also during the latter part of the nineteenth century the volume of statistical material available for exploitation by economists was accumulating in quantity and becoming very varied and more reliable. This meant that the economist found it easy to bring into his ken a far larger circle of observations for analysis than could Adam Smith, Malthus, Ricardo, John Stuart Mill or even W. Stanley Jevons. The earlier writers had had to depend for original materials largely upon their own observations of how men behave in economic conduct. The observations were eked out by current writings, but these studies were non-quantitative observations by their contemporaries. It is true that a certain amount of statistical material was in existence and had been for several centuries, but it covered no wide scope; and concerning much of it there were grave and legitimate doubts about its accuracy.

The increase in the volume of materials of the sort which economic theorists might use was another development which for the time being attracted comparatively little attention. Economists continued to rely upon old analytic methods in most of their work; but they found that to an increasing extent as they began the discussion of such practical questions as those touching the welfare of the wage-earning classes, the effect of alterations in the banking laws, of shifts in tariff duties, of depreciating and appreciating monetary units, figures were of the greatest use; and in dealing with these quasi-practical topics they accustomed themselves gradually to make an increasing use of and to place increasing reliance upon evidence of a quantitative order. The development of statistical methods (note Jevons's contributions) made possible a more positive and dynamic type of social science.[18a]

During the period too the whole perspective in which men saw population problems underwent a change. From the days when not only Malthus but almost all educated people, almost all economists, had thought of a rapid increase in population as the greatest danger to social welfare, a slow transition was being effected toward the time when President Theodore Roosevelt would regard race suicide as the greatest danger of the future. Ireland's population, which had been the stock example of the evils of an over-dense population, fell off by several millions—actually suffered an enormous decline, partly as a result of famine in 1845-1847, partly as a result of migration.[19] France,

---

[18a] Outline, November 3, 1931.

[19] [Between 1841 and 1851 the population of Ireland fell by 1,600,000 and since then the population has continued to decline. In 1881 the population of the twenty-six counties that now constitute Eire was 5,100,000; in 1946 it was 2,960,000. "... emigration is not the sole cause of the continuous and unique fall in the population of

which J. R. McCulloch saw bound to become the greatest pauper warren of Europe, suffered such a rapid decline in the birth-rate and so small a decline in the death-rate that the population became almost stationary; and in that country the pressing population question was not the danger of having to resort to more intense cultivation of the soil, but the danger to the nation's security arising from the fact that she would soon be far surpassed in numbers, and therefore in military effectiveness, by her rival across the Rhine. The change in the population question was one of the causes which definitely affected the minds of economists, and led them to take a different tone in discussions of what might happen in the future.

Brief mention must be made of a few alterations in social conditions. These stand in contrast with the changes in the realm of thought which were just discussed. To begin with, political economy had achieved, as noted before, its practical triumph with the abolition of the corn laws in 1846. There followed a period of very marked prosperity in England; the country enjoyed in the 1850's, 60's and early 70's a degree of material welfare which was almost unexampled, and redounded greatly to the benefit of political economy. The science as a whole profited by this fortunate turn of current affairs much as a political administration of the United States might, by the fact that times happen to be prosperous when its representatives are in office, and is just as logical.

In 1873, however, matters began to take a turn for the worse. The later 70's were a period of severe business depression; the 80's were somewhat better. But on the whole the rate of progress was believed by contemporaries to have been checked; agriculture in particular entered upon a long series of disappointing years, though not so much because the harvests were particularly poor—they alternated as usual—but it was because the development of the steamship in the Atlantic service and the expansion of the railroad on the North American continent were making it possible to sell in England wheat that was grown on new, rich, cheap American lands. So that the whole of English agriculture had to meet competition at prices which were by no means profitable. That reacted first on the fortunes of the farmers.

The system of land tenure had become one in which the bulk of good farms were rented to active cultivators, who supplied their own

Eire after 1841. The responsibility for that fall is shared by the spread of 'moral restraint,' by the steady rise in the proportion of men and women who did not marry." D. V. Glass, "Malthus and the Limitation of Population Growth" in *Introduction to Malthus,* edited by Glass (London: Watts, 1953) p. 32.]

capital and had leases for a considerable period of time. Men, who entered into long leases at high rents and found that they could not sell their produce profitably at the point where prices stood, were the first shock absorbers. But as the leases ran out or as the tenants were ruined and had to give them up the landlords who sought new people to take their places found it difficult to get as high rents as formerly.

Rents had been rising steadily and it had looked as if Ricardo's picture of the future when the landlords would reap double gains from an increase of the share of the produce which went to them as rent, plus an increase in the price paid for agricultural products in comparison with manufactured goods, was a picture that was valid in fact. But then the situation changed for the worse and the prospect was ever more gloomy; prices of English produce were going to be continually depressed by the further settlement of the western part of the United States, and it would be increasingly difficult for English agriculture to raise the great staples, in competition with men who had the benefit of land on which rents were almost nothing. In short the agricultural interests, first the farmers and then the landlords, had entered upon a period of great difficulty, which was particularly ascribed to the causes already suggested, but it was also connected in England as well as in the United States with the decline in the general price level.[20]

The general level of wholesale prices in both gold and silver standard countries had been rising from the end of the 1840's to 1873. At that time, for reasons which have been explained in a thousand different ways, among them being the perpetuation of the celebrated crime of 1873,[21] the trend of wholesale prices had taken a turn and began declining. The fall continued until the middle of the 90's. This brought to the forefront of practical discussion the monetary problem in a new form, the problem with which Ricardo's generation had been concerned, but primarily as the problem of the proper regulation of a bank note currency. It had been taken for granted in Ricardo's day that a metallic standard was desirable. The difficult technical problem was how to arrange the banking system so that the supply of bank notes would be properly adjusted to the needs of business and at the same time be continuously redeemable in gold—a problem that

---

[20] [In discussing the plight of the British farmer, Professor Mitchell referred to quasi-monopolistic industrial financial control, and gain of commercial and manufacturing influence at expense of landlord. Outline, November 3, 1931.]

[21] [This was the passage of the United States Coinage Act of 1873 which made no provision for the coinage of the old silver dollars and thus ended the bimetallic standard.]

it was believed had been satisfactorily solved by the reorganization of the Bank of England under Peel's Act of 1844, supplemented by the plan of permitting the Bank to issue emergency circulation in time of crisis.[22] But now it appeared that what had been believed to be a model monetary system was suffering grievously from a long period of decline in prices, and English economists took a prominent and effective part in the long drawn out bimetallic controversy which was at its height in the 80's and 90's and which lasted until the increasing output of gold largely from the South African [and later the Alaskan] mines gave a new direction to the secular trend of wholesale prices beginning in the latter half of the 90's.

Another feature of considerable importance was the rise of German and American competition which increased the severity with which the decline in prices affected the fortunes of English business men. There had been several generations in which England was almost the sole beneficiary of the great Industrial Revolution. In the 60's and 70's and 80's the new machine methods of production began to be developed on a great scale in Germany and perhaps to an equal extent in the United States. German competition was particularly difficult for the British to meet, but they also faced the prospect that the American market would be taken away from them by domestic manufactures aided by a high tariff wall and that the time might even come when American producers would be formidable rivals in neutral markets.

Finally, there should be mentioned that the trade union movement was gaining great strength and gradually acquiring government recognition—a matter of importance in its reactions upon political economy because the orthodox doctrine had been that a trade union can be of no real benefit to its members. Under the wages fund theory it appeared that the level of wages was fixed by dividing that part of the capital which was necessarily devoted to the paying of wages by the number of people who worked for wages, and if a trade union did succeed in getting a little more wages per head for its members it could do so only at the expense of the working class as a whole. Economists had thought that although the members of the working class were slow learners, they would gradually learn this fundamental truth and no longer submit to the useless expense of maintaining officers when they could in fact do no good for them. On the contrary

----

[22] [In times of a money panic, the government would authorize the suspension of the Bank Act of 1844 and allow the Bank of England to issue notes beyond the amount permitted under the Act, then secure an act of indemnity from Parliament absolving all parties of the suspension.]

the course of events proved that the trade union was an institution that came to have an increasingly strong hold upon the interests and maybe the affections of the British wage-earners. They proved to have a degree of rugged endurance which was altogether unexpected, and the time was close at hand when many economists would be forced to recognize that there was a new problem here presented for them. That time came the sooner because of the publication of Sidney and Beatrice Webb's pioneering *Industrial Democracy* (1897) in which they offered a new theoretical explanation of the trade union and its activities.[23] Other important social developments were increasing factory legislation, extension of the suffrage in 1867, rise of consumer cooperative stores on the Rochdale plan (not John Stuart Mill's producers' cooperatives).[24]

Summary: I am not trying to give an ordered account of relations between development of social science and development of social life within the period as I did of the generation that made classical political economy. I do not know enough to do that. But I am trying to suggest how complicated were the streams of thought and events that made up this modern world, how little events answered the simple projections of the economists.[24a]

Amidst the various changes in intellectual and practical affairs that were taking place in Marshall's youth, the subject of political economy lost much of the prestige and self-confidence which it had enjoyed in the period following Ricardo, and perhaps still more in the period following the publication of John Stuart Mill's *Principles of Political Economy,* when the triumph of the practical abolition of the corn laws was being achieved. The subject became more a specialty; something to be cultivated by people who devoted a great deal of time to it. It became a subject for specialists rather than for the man on the street; the man of affairs in business would have less to say. It became a mere academic discipline, technical, that is, refined in its details, and went through the subtle change which almost any department of learning goes through when it gets into the hands of specialists, and particularly of university professors.

---

[23] [For a critique of the Webbs' theory see Russell Bauder, "Three Interpretations of the American Trade Union Movement," *Social Forces,* December 1943, pp. 215-219. Webb at the time had "a sympathetic interest in Ricardo, Léon Walras and Jevons," especially in evidence in his astute "The Rate of Interest and the Laws of Distribution," *The Quarterly Journal of Economics,* January 1888, pp. 188-208. See footnote in Sidney Webb to Léon Walras, February 29, 1888 in *Correspondence of Léon Walras and Related Papers* ed. by William Jaffé, 3 volumes (Amsterdam: North Holland Publishing Co., 1965) II, p. 242.]

[24] Sentence from Outline, November 3, 1931.

[24a] Outline, November 3, 1931.

It became less confident in its claim to guide policy, less a weapon in the class struggle, although it was used by some in defence of the capitalist order against socialism, particularly by the Austrians. Vigorous development in Germany where it had a relation to public policy, not unlike the situation in the days of Sir Robert Peel. Vigorous development in the United States also, under combined German and English influence. Decidedly not so vigorous in France.[25]

All this is by way of background for the type of economic theory developed by Marshall.

[In short, on the continent (except for Germany) conditions were in a similar state of stagnation. Henri Pirenne, the Belgian economic historian of the University of Ghent, spoke of the domination of the "conception of political economy as a science regulated by immutable laws."[26] Likewise Henri Hauser of the University of Paris reported for France that the history of economic doctrine which provided the procedure or method of teaching economic theory had been treated "as if these doctrines had begotten one another after the fashion of the patriarchs of Scripture to end at last as 'sound doctrine,' that of Adam Smith, J.-B. Say and F. Bastiat; and in order to judge them more equitably, other doctrines were referred to this standard and considered either as anticipations or heresies. It was never considered that the mission of the historian is not to judge doctrines but to explain them. No one enquired whether these doctrines, although no doubt the product of human minds, were not largely the result of the economic situation at the moment of their appearance, whether the mercantilism of Burghley, the physiocratic theory of Quesnay, the economic theory of Gournay, Turgot, Smith, the nationalism of List, the materialism of Karl Marx, were not, like the neo-mercantilism of our own time, byproducts of contemporary economic evolution. Neither did it occur to anyone to consider whether these doctrines, once become popular, had not reacted on this evolution."[27]

The popular view in England, to repeat, expressed by *The Economist* in 1880 was: "The labour of the economic thinker is only suc-

---

[25] Outline, November 3, 1931.

[26] ["The Teaching of Economic History in Universities—Belgium," *The Economic History Review*, October 1931, p. 211.]

[27] ["The Teaching of Economic History in Universities—France," *The Economic History Review*, October 1931, pp. 203-204.

William Cecil, Baron Burghley (1520-1598) was Queen Elizabeth's chief adviser. Jacques C. M. V. de Gournay (1712-1759) the French economist best known for "his favorite maxim . . . *laissez faire, laissez passer* which may be freely translated as 'give free reign to production, give free reign to the circulation of goods produced'." G. Weulersse, "Gournay, Jacques Claude Marie Vincent de," *Encyclopedia of Social Sciences* ed. by E. R. A. Seligman and Alvin Johnson, 15 volumes (New York: Macmillan, 1930-1934) VII, p. 7.]

overlaid they may be by social habits, however unwilling social prejudice may be to admit that they are ultimately irresistible."][28]

Let us turn to Marshall. Marshall very distinctly marks the transformation into the stage of refined specialty. In a previous discussion
Jevons had been contrasted with the great figures among the philosophical radicals and even with John Stuart Mill, in that he had
much less touch with public affairs. Marshall lived, if anything, a
more academic life than Jevons did. Those students who are interested
are advised to read J. M. Keynes's charming memorial.[29]

It is an account of the extraordinary events of Marshall's life and
an analysis of his characteristics. He was born in 1842; his father was
one of the cashiers of the Bank of England, a strict evangelical who
trained his son in Hebrew and presumably planned that he should
enter the clergy. "In mingled affection and severity," says Keynes,
"his father recalls James Mill," who gave John Stuart Mill such a
thorough, even meticulous, education in his own study. But it happened that the boy's intellectual tastes, while very marked, were of
an altogether different character from those of his father. He had
little aptitude for theological studies but was from an early age fascinated by mathematics. One of the sources of satisfaction to him, he
said later, was that his father could not understand geometry. When
he got into that field he was free from paternal supervision.

Had he followed the line his father laid out for him, he would have
gone to Oxford and devoted himself primarily to the study of the
classics. But by great good fortune he managed, through a loan from
an uncle and a small scholarship, to get a chance to study at Cambridge, where the emphasis was upon mathematics in somewhat the
same fashion that the emphasis was upon the classics at Oxford.

At Cambridge his career was highly successful. He took his degree
as second wrangler—the rating in the honors course or tripos in mathematics—in the very year when the senior wrangler was Baron Ray-
leigh, the great mathematical physicist; Marshall then proposed to

---

[28] [Review of Alfred and Mary Marshall, *The Economics of Industry*, in *The
Economist*, February 28, 1880, p. 239.

The journal applauded the Marshalls for building upon John Stuart Mill "with a
skill and care which will render their volume of use to a class of readers who might
not be disposed to unravel the difficulties presented by the greater work of their
master." Marshall later disowned the book.]

[29] Keynes, "Alfred Marshall, 1842-1924," *The Economic Journal*, September 1924,
pp. 311-372. Reprinted in his *Essays in Biography* (1933; 2nd edition, New York:
Horizon Press, 1951) pp. 125-217.

For Marshall's bibliography, see *Memorials of Alfred Marshall* ed. by A. C. Pigou
(London: Macmillan, 1925) pp. 500-508; [and Royden Harrison, "Two Early Articles
by Alfred Marshall," *The Economic Journal*, September 1963, pp. 422-430].

devote himself to the study of molecular physics. He was distracted from this course by becoming interested in a theological controversy. John Stuart Mill had published his *Examination of Sir William Hamilton's Philosophy* in 1865, which included an attack on Hamilton's strongest disciple and a leading English theologian, H. L. Mansel.[30] Mansel replied and the controversy concerned Marshall greatly. After reading Mansel's defense of the theological position and realizing "how much there was to be defended" in the orthodox view, he decided that he must devote his attention to metaphysical problems if he wanted to understand the basis of knowledge. Metaphysics led him to ethics; and while thinking about ethics he became convinced that he would not be prepared to understand the important issues in behavior until he had studied political economy. So this mathematician, this would-be physicist, turned, fairly late in his career, to the reading of John Stuart Mill's *Principles of Political Economy*. He said "I . . . got much excited about it. I had doubts as to the propriety of inequalities of *opportunity,* rather than of material comfort."

What impressed him in Mill was the ethical bearing of the present form of economic organization. He was not interested in the technical questions; he was concerned with the way economic organization treated different classes; "then in my vacations I visited the poorest quarters of several cities and walked through one street after another, looking at the faces of the poorest people. Next, I resolved to make as thorough a study as I could of Political Economy." He turned to the cultivation of the new field. But when he once fairly got launched on the study of political economy, the mathematician in him reasserted himself and he began translating Ricardo into mathematical formulae, trying to see how he could put the propositions of economic theory into a stricter and more perfect form. In that connection he began to play with diagrams. He had already developed the use of diagrams as a method of representing the problems which economists up to that time had usually discussed without any such help, some time before Jevons's *The Theory of Political Economy* appeared in 1871. In fact, "the publication of this book," as Keynes says, "must have been an occasion of some disappointment and annoyance to Marshall," a disappointment which possibly accounts in some slight measure for the coolness and the severity with which he reviewed it in *The Academy* in 1872.

Meanwhile the question of how he should live had come to the fore. cessful when he explains the real working of natural forces, however

---

[30] [On this controversy see Joseph Dorfman, *Thorstein Veblen and His America* (New York: The Viking Press, 1934) pp. 19, 28.]

A friend in Cambridge got a special lectureship in moral science established for him. Moral science was in those days a very elastic term, and it enabled him to devote his courses primarily to economics.[30a] For nine years, from 1868 to 1877, he remained a fellow and lecturer of St. John's College, Cambridge, laying the basis of his system of economics but publishing no treatise.

Toward the end of that term, in 1876, he became engaged to be married. His fiancee was Mary Paley, a great-granddaughter of the famous Archdeacon William Paley. Miss Paley was a former pupil of his and was a lecturer in economics at Newnham College, the Cambridge woman's college.[30b] But in those days if he married a fellow had to give up his fellowship. Marshall left Cambridge and became the principal and professor of political economy of University College, Bristol, at a salary of £700 a year.

That college was a provincial school established by interested members of Oxford University in the hope that they might bring the advantage of modern learning home to the inhabitants of an industrial town. Marshall found his work as principal rather uncongenial, mainly because it involved him in the necessity of raising money. The funds for the school were not adequate, and the task of obtaining additional endowment was one for which he was not particularly fitted and which irked him grievously to perform. Moreover, his work there was very hard. His health suffered. Indeed, he became from this time a hypochondriac; his health all the time presumably seemed to him a good deal worse than it really was. Since he almost reached his eighty-second birthday, it is clear that his constitution had not been thoroughly undermined; but possibly his long tenure of life was due in part to the fact that he always took such excellent care of himself.

His relief from Bristol came when a vacancy was created at Oxford by the death of Arnold Toynbee (1852-1883), that admirable scholar whose posthumous *Lectures on the Industrial Revolution of the*

[30a] [He did for a time give a course on moral and political philosophy which was devoted chiefly to Bentham's and John Stuart Mill's utilitarianism. He contended that "not only is ethical well-being a portion of that well-being which any reasonable utilitarian system urges us to promote, but that it is much the more important element of that well-being." He also said that Bentham had more influence on economics than any other non-economist, his contribution being the stress laid on measurement. "When you have found a means of measurement you have a ground for controversy, and so it is a means of progress." Mary Paley Marshall, *What I Remember* with an introduction by G. M. Trevelyan (Cambridge: Cambridge University Press, 1947) p. 19.]

[30b] [While Eastman Professor at Oxford in 1931-1932, Professor Mitchell made the following entry in his diary: "Mrs. Holland [a student of Professor Mitchell at Columbia in 1917-1918 and then teaching at Cambridge] took me to tea with Mrs. Alfred Marshall at Balliolcroft. [The] Guillebauds there. Long talk. A charming woman." (Mitchell, "Diary," March 6, 1932).

Eighteenth Century in England (1884) was one of the first of the significant books on the Industrial Revolution in England.[31] That occurred in 1883, and Benjamin Jowett, the translator of Plato's *Dialogues,* who was then master of Balliol, got Marshall to go to Oxford. He succeeded to Toynbee's post as fellow of Balliol and lecturer on political economy to the selected candidates for the Indian Civil Service. He stayed there only a year, because in 1884 Henry Fawcett died and that opened the Cambridge professorship of economics. Marshall was appointed in January, 1885, and held the chair until he retired in 1908.[31a]

These are the leading events of his life. Of what an unexciting character they are! After he retired he tried to devote himself as exclusively as he could to the care of his health on the one side and the completion of his literary plans on the other side. In both aims he had a considerable measure of success. As said before he almost attained his eighty-second birthday, dying on the 13th of July, 1924.

Perhaps more important for the purpose of these lectures than the external details of his life are certain characteristics, upon which J. M. Keynes, as a man of rather similar gifts and a person who was closely associated with him as a pupil and whose father had been a colleague of Marshall for many years, is able to throw a good deal of light. In particular Keynes discusses in an interesting way the intellectual characteristics of Marshall. He began, says Keynes, "by founding modern diagrammatic methods"; but the more he thought on economics, the more skeptical he became about the value of the mathematical approach to the subject.

As Keynes put it:

> . . . Marshall, as one who had been second wrangler and had nourished ambitions to explore molecular physics, always felt a slight contempt from the intellectual or aesthetic point of view for the rather "potty" scraps of elementary algebra, geometry, and differential calculus which make up mathematical economics . . . Unlike physics, for example, such parts of the bare bones of economic theory as are expressible in mathematical form are extremely easy compared with the economic interpretation of the complex and incompletely known facts of experience, and lead one but a very little way towards establishing useful results.
>   Marshall felt all this with a vehemence which not all his pupils have shared. The preliminary mathematics was for him child's play.

---

[31] ["Arnold Toynbee—*very able,* more or less of a *socialist*" (Foxwell to Léon Walras, December 30, 1882, in *Correspondence of Léon Walras and Related Papers,* I, p. 738).]

[31a] ["Fawcett . . . is professor but most of the teaching is done by Mr. H. S. Foxwell." (Jevons to Walras, February 21, 1879, in *Correspondence of Léon Walras and Related Papers,* I, p. 599.)]

He wanted to enter the vast laboratory of the world, to hear its roar and distinguish the several notes, to speak with the tongues of businessmen, and yet to observe all with the eyes of a highly intelligent angel. So he set himself to get into closer contact with practical business and with the life of the working classes.

In Marshall's reaction against the mathematical methods which he had practiced with such great skill, Keynes thinks that he went too far. He believes that Marshall had no very remarkable gift for ascertaining and analyzing the facts of current business experience. That was the thing he wanted to do; he wanted to look at economic life more or less as Ricardo had, look at it through the eyes of a person who could appreciate the practical business problems—to give the kind of sober formulation, the sagacious judgments which could be pronounced by the great economic statesmen of the generation, Sir Robert Peel the younger and W. E. Gladstone, so far as Gladstone acted as chancellor of the exchequer. So, as Keynes puts it,

> Marshall, having begun by founding modern diagrammatic methods, ended by using much self-obliteration to keep them in their proper place. When the *Principles* appeared, the diagrams were imprisoned in footnotes, or, at their freest, could but exercise themselves as in a yard within the confines of a brief Appendix.[32]

Keynes also notes as characteristic of Marshall his unwillingness to publish any of his results until they had been twice or four times refined. Rather early in his life he had arrived at the main conclusions which were finally printed in the *Principles* that was published in 1890; but year after year he delayed bringing out his book, and after he had issued what he originally treated as the first volume he spent additional years in meticulous emendations of the facts in volume one, and it was not until many years after the *Principles of Economics* had appeared that he published his second book *Industry and Trade* (1919). Why was he so slow in publishing? Keynes thinks that in part he was deterred by the example of Jevons. As Keynes puts it,

> He depreciated Jevons' *Political Economy* . . . on the ground that it was no more than a brilliant brochure. Yet it was Jevons' willingness to spill his ideas, to flick them at the world, that won him his great personal position, and his unrivalled power of stimulating other minds. Every one of Jevons' contributions to Economics was in the nature of a pamphlet.

---

[32] [Marshall during his retirement became more sympathetic to the mathematical approach, more properly, the econometric approach. He had no sympathy for sociology and its practitioners. He complained that: "Sociology is a magnificent aspiration, but the greater part of sociologists seem to me to divide their time impartially between prehistoric institutions, without much knowledge of early history, and the latest new fashion in philanthropy, without a knowledge of economics." (Marshall to Lujo Brentano, August 18, 1903, in H. W. Macready, "Alfred Marshall and Tariff Reform, 1903; Some Unpublished Letters," *The Journal of Political Economy*, June 1955, p. 266.)]

But Marshall disliked the example. His plan was by keeping his wisdom at home to clothe it fully, making no mistakes, and then at last to give the world a completed product. He put his economics in the hands of his students, through his classes, long before he published them. But Keynes thinks that he probably kept the progress of economic theory from being as it might be by his forbearance concerning publication. Other reasons why he was so slow are suggested:

> First, Marshall was too much afraid of being wrong, too thin-skinned towards criticism; too easily upset by controversy even on matters of minor importance. An extreme sensitiveness deprived him of magnanimity towards the critic or the adversary. This fear of being open to correction by speaking too soon aggravated other tendencies.

Further, says Keynes:

> Marshall was too anxious to do good. He had an inclination to undervalue those intellectual parts of the subject which were not *directly* connected with human well-being or the condition of the working classes or the like, although *indirectly* they might be of the utmost importance, and to feel that when he was pursuing them he was not occupying himself with the Highest. It came out of the conflict, already remarked, between an intellect, which was hard, dry, critical, as unsentimental as you could find, with emotions and aspirations generally unspoken of quite a different type. When his intellect chased diagrams and Foreign Trade and Money, there was an evangelical moraliser of an imp somewhere inside him, that was so ill-advised as to disapprove.

For whatever reason, then, Marshall worked out his system and revised it several times, went over it with his pupils semester after semester, and not until 1890 did he publish his first volume. The book, when it came out, was exceedingly well received. Keynes thinks it was due particularly to the peculiar way in which it was written. He says:

> The way in which Marshall's *Principles of Economics* is written is more unusual than the casual reader will notice. It is elaborately unsensational and underemphatic. Its rhetoric is of the simplest, most unadorned order. It flows in a steady, lucid stream, with few passages which stop or perplex the intelligent reader, even though he know but little economics. Claims to novelty or to originality on the part of the author himself are altogether absent. Passages imputing error to others are rare; and it is explained that earlier writers of repute must be held to have *meant* what is right and reasonable, whatever they may have said. . . .
> By this stylistic achievement Marshall attained some of his objects. The book reached the general public. It increased the public esteem of Economics. The minimum of controversy was provoked. The average reviewer liked the author's attitude to his subject-matter, to his predecessors, and to his readers, and delighted Marshall by calling attention to the proper stress laid by him on the ethical element and to the much required humanising which the dismal science received at his hands; and, at the same time, could

remain happily insensible to the book's intellectual stature. As time
has gone on, moreover, the intellectual qualities of the book have
permeated English economic thought, without noise or disturbance,
in a degree which can be easily overlooked.

The method has, on the other hand, serious disadvantages. The
lack of emphasis and of strong light and shade, the sedulous rubbing
away of rough edges and salients and projections, until what is most
novel can appear as trite, allows the reader to pass . . . from this
douche of ideas with scarce a wetting. The difficulties are concealed:
the most ticklish problems are solved in footnotes; a pregnant and
original judgment is dressed up as a platitude. The author furnishes
his ideas with no labels of salesmanship and few hooks for them to
hang by in the wardrobe of the mind. A student can read the *Principles,* be fascinated by its pervading charm, think that he com-
prehends it, and, yet, a week later, know but little about it.

It is time to see whether that has been the students' experience. The
book begins by stating what economics is; and for once, the definition
that is given is important for an understanding of the author's attitude toward his subject. Here is a case in which the definition does
imply—of course, it does not fully express—the problem which the
writer sets himself to solve. The specific nature of the problem which
Marshall sets himself to solve leads the student on to see the pertinence of the stress which he lays upon a feature of economic life and
organization to which his predecessors had called very little attention.
Marshall's definition is: Political Economy or Economics is a study
of mankind in the ordinary business of life.[33]

Notice that Marshall does not want to have it an abstract subject.
Here comes out the driving inclination, on which Keynes comments,
to deal with things as they actually occur—not pure theory, but an
account of "mankind in the ordinary business of life." Marshall
continues:

> it examines that part of individual and social action which is most
> closely connected with the attainment and with the use of the mate-
> rial requisites of well being.

Marshall uses "well being" in the broad and casual sense of the
term. This is the first indication of that ethical interest which always
remained such a pronounced part of his concern for economics. The
beginning of his next sentence: "Thus it is on the one side a study of
wealth"—shows his reverence for his predecessors. They had usually
defined economics as a science of wealth. It never was merely that
with them, but Marshall adds:

> and on the other, and more important side, a part of the study of
> man. For man's character has been moulded by his everyday work,

---

[33] *Principles of Economics* (London: Macmillan, 1890; 8th edition, 1920) p. 1.
All references are to the 8th edition.

and the material resources which he thereby procures, more than by any other influence unless it be that of his religious ideals.[34]

Another definition much to the same effect is at the beginning of chapter II:

> Economics is a study of men as they live and move and think in the ordinary business of life. But it concerns itself chiefly with those motives which affect, most powerfully and most steadily, man's conduct in the business part of his life.[35]

He then proceeds at once to lay down a proposition that appears novel in the record of economic theory, something that deserves attention very strongly if the student wants to understand Marshall and to understand what is becoming to an increasing degree one of the most important theoretical issues. The proposition is that money is "the center around which economic science clusters."[36] That seems novel. This attitude is not found in Adam Smith, Ricardo, John Stuart Mill or Jevons. It seems a rather curious attitude for a man to take, who to the end of his days remained, at least in ethics, a good utilitarian, an avowed disciple of Bentham. His predecessors had seemed to feel largely a reaction against the emphasis put upon the importance of money by the mercantilists and by business men. They felt that talking about economics in terms of money was superficial; money does not count in a person's life except as a means to get something else. They believed that the theorist gets nearer to the heart of the laborer's position when he passes over money wages for real wages; that is, when he asks about the commodities that the individual is able to secure. He knows a great deal more about the wealth of a nation when he has figures which show fluctuations in the total amount of commodities that they can produce and consume year by year than he does when he has a row of figures that state that their income is so many million or billion pounds sterling.

The people who had been brought up on Bentham would say we must of necessity go further. The money level of analysis is more superficial than the commodity level, but commodities mean nothing in and of themselves. They are significant only in so far as they contribute to our pleasures or possibly pains. We are going to go to the matter which really concerns the economic man and the student of economic man when we get through to the psychic level. Real income does not consist of commodities but of pleasures. Then the moralists among the utilitarians—and here we found Marshall be-

---

[34] *Principles of Economics*, p. 1.
[35] *Principles of Economics*, p. 14.
[36] *Principles of Economics*, p. 22.

longing to that great tradition—would say it is not the pleasures of people as such with which we must be concerned but with their welfare.

From Bentham's point of view welfare consists in an amount of pleasure, but ever since the days of John Stuart Mill people had been inclined to criticize Bentham's dictum that one pleasure is as good as another. Marshall distinctly believed that there are qualitative differences in pleasures and that a man and the country is better off if the pleasures are of a noble sort. Marshall was drifting away from the fact that in a sense money is superficial, that commodities were more important than money, that the services the commodity renders are more important than the commodity itself. From his point of view the contribution which these commodities make to welfare is more important than the pleasure that they give. Yet he states that money is the "center around which economic science clusters." How can that be? What is the justification for taking that ground?

S. Everything starts with money.

M. That is not the reason Marshall gives. He has a reason that he thinks is more profound than that. This is in a passage which has been very little attended to by commentators, which exemplifies J. M. Keynes's remark that the easy flow of the style keeps it from making an impression on the reader. Have none of you observed Marshall's astonishing position and how he defends it?

S. He said that most of our economic ideals are pervaded by money.

M. No. He does not say that. Marshall thinks people's activities are motivated by the desire to get gratifications and avoid sacrifices.

S. Emphasis on consumption—measured by sacrifices.

M. Sacrifices and wants can be measured in terms of money. This is coming closer to the exact statement. Is there anything else that can be measured in money? Did you say satisfaction and wants?

S. Yes, sacrifices of consumption and wants.

2nd S. Economic motives.

M. Economic motives at large. Yes, suppose it is granted that money is the means by which Marshall starts out to measure not motives but the strength of motives. Suppose we say that the strength of motives can be measured by money. Why does that make money the center around which economic science clusters?

S. He provides a way of comparing a person's motives by the amount of money that measures them.

M. Yes. There is another implication that is contained in this definition of political economy.

S. I had an idea that money is the motive behind the economic activity.

M. Marshall would definitely say no. It is not the motive.

S. It is the motive of business.

M. Possibly in some cases it is; but Marshall would say that money is not the motive that concerns the economist at all; it is the center around which economic science clusters; it enables the economist to measure the strength of motives.

Consider what the implications of that statement are. Is the strength of motives the thing that a modern psychologist is talking about, when he is trying to explain why people act in certain ways? Not many of them take that ground nowadays. If you do not take that ground, however, that human behavior is controlled by motives, by considered motives, that what a person does depends upon the motive forces—motive is an excellent word to characterize it—that operate toward different lines of action, then the investigator is not going to be in a position to carry on a discussion of how people behave. He will be in no position to measure the propelling forces. To help clarify the matter, the definition with which the chapter starts will be again stated.

> Economics is a study of men as they live and move and think in the ordinary business of life. But it concerns itself chiefly with those motives which affect, most powerfully and most steadily, man's conduct in the business part of his life.

Note that Marshall does not say that economic behavior is controlled by motives. He does not say it, simply because it never occurs to him to question that this is the case. He takes it for granted: human behavior is controlled by motives—economics is concerned primarily with a certain set of "those motives which affect, most powerfully and most steadily, man's conduct in the business part of life." This conception of human nature is the one that was presented by Ricardo, John Stuart Mill and Jevons, that men are rational creatures; that what they do is determined by motives and motives are conscious affairs. To know what a man is going to do it is necessary to understand the motive that will bear upon it. Marshall would probably admit that what in his day people talked about as instincts are factors of consequence, but they do not seem such for him as an economist.

Man's behavior is then controlled by motives and the motives are from Marshall's point of view divided into two great categories. There are on the one side motives that impel men to exertion—the desire for satisfaction, gratification. On the other side, there are the great sets of motives that keep people from exerting themselves, more than a certain amount—the motives of avoiding the sacrifices involved in labor and the sacrifices involved in waiting. The equilibrium that Marshall studies throughout the greater part of the treatise is an equilibrium between the strength of motives which belong in the two opposing categories, desire for gratification—many different desires for gratification of many different sorts—on the one side; and disinclination to labor or to wait on the other side.

Since these are the forces that control men's actions, the economist who is going to make any progress in building up a theory about man's behavior in the ordinary business of life, must know some way of measuring the forces which control his materials. That measure is afforded by money. For Marshall goes on to argue that in the ordinary business of life nowadays, as a matter of practice, most of people's gratifications are obtained at a money price; and most of the sacrifices are undergone for a money reward. Life itself offers the individual these money measures. The theorist can study their records. They are significant because they show the strength of the inducement which must be offered to people to get them to work and to save, because they show the amount of sacrifice people must undergo in order to get the gratifications that they desire.

S. Granting that money is the measure of the motives, it does not follow that money is the center about which economics clusters but rather a measure of the center.

M. Yes, that might have been more accurate language. I was quoting Marshall. He makes that statement. What he meant is that this is the thing we have to be continually talking about. The theorist has to use the money measure continuously. Without making use of the money measure he could not get very far in dealing with the problem.

It is important to emphasize the observation that the money measure is Marshall's modern equivalent for Bentham's felicific calculus. Bentham's calculus was a scheme for measuring the strength of the motives that dominate man's behavior; he thought that there was literally a way of measuring the forces themselves. Marshall in effect says "I cannot measure the forces themselves, but money measures the strength of these forces. That is enough for my purpose." To repeat, Marshall is operating with substantially the same conception regarding the factors which control behavior, that were prevalent in the days of Adam Smith's contemporary, Bentham.

There are in Marshall, every now and then, insights into human behavior which presumably would not have occurred to Bentham, but fundamentally his notions are those of the philosophical radicals. Indeed, these psychological notions run much further back in time. The reader does not have any feeling of artificiality about Marshall's discussion, however, of the sort that he does about Bentham's or Jevons's discussion of behavior in terms of pleasures and pains, for Marshall uses modern terminology. The fact that he employs money measures, prices, wages and interest rates that are part of people's familiar experience today, makes it seem that he is actually talking about the human nature that people recognize in themselves and their fellows; and before the discussion of Marshall is completed we shall be in a position to answer the question whether he is or not, but more of that later.

Economics, Marshall thinks, deals on one side with the desires which are motives to activity and on the other side with the satisfactions which people derive from economic activities. The question is whether the amount of money which will induce people to take certain actions, say, to work at a certain task a certain length of time, should be regarded as a measure merely of the desires which prompt them to action or whether it can be used also for a second purpose, as a measure of the satisfactions which their actions procure for them. Marshall, taking the point up, says that the theorist assumes that the resulting satisfaction corresponds in general fairly well to that which was anticipated. Then he explains in a footnote that we do not measure even the desires directly.

> It cannot be too much insisted that to measure directly, or *per se*, either desires or the satisfaction which results from their fulfilment is impossible, if not inconceivable. If we could, we should have two accounts to make up, one of desires, and the other of realized satisfactions. And the two might differ considerably.

He goes on: we do not make direct measurement.

> . . . as neither of them is possible, we fall back on the measurement which economics supplies, of the motive or moving force to action: and we make it serve, with all its faults, *both* for the desires which prompt activities and for the satisfactions that result from them.[37]

So the money measures on his showing may be taken approximately. He is a little vague from time to time. In one passage he says "money measurements of the force of motives" and other times he says "approximate measures of the force of motives," and also a measure "for

---

[37] *Principles of Economics*, pp. 92-93.

the degree of satisfaction which is derived from the action taken
under the stress of the desires."

There is another aspect of Marshall's conception of human nature
that deserves mention, particularly because it is a point at which he
differs significantly from Bentham. This is the relative importance
which he, compared with Bentham, ascribes to the factor of habit.
One of the things that men had learned about themselves in the
hundred years between 1789 when Bentham published *An Introduction to the Principles of Morals and Legislation* and 1890 when
Marshall published the *Principles of Economics* was that in large
part men's actions are controlled not by calculation but by habit.
Bentham had taken the ground that actions are mainly of a calculating kind. To repeat a passage from Bentham

> When matters of such importance as pain and pleasure are at
> stake, and these in the highest degree (the only matters, in short,
> that can be of importance) who is there that does not calculate.
> Men calculate, some with less exactness, indeed, some with more:
> but all men calculate. I would not say that even a madman does not
> calculate. Passion calculates, more or less, in every man: in differ-
> ent men, according to the firmness or irritability of their minds:
> according to the nature of the motives by which they are acted
> upon. Happily, of all passions, that is the most given to calculation,
> from the excesses of which, by reason of its strength, constancy, and
> universality, society has most to apprehend: I mean that which
> corresponds to the motives of pecuniary interest.

That is, men are calculating animals; and in economic life this trait
is most pronounced. Marshall as the heir of a later period held that
action is largely ruled by habit, and especially as regards business
conduct. That might seem at first blush to mean that the measurement
of opposing motives, the calculating method of determining what individuals will do, is applicable only to a relatively small part of behavior.
But that is not the view that he takes.

> Now the side of life with which economics is specially concerned
> is that in which man's conduct is most deliberate, and in which he
> most often reckons up the advantages and disadvantages of any
> particular action before he enters on it. And further it is that side
> of his life in which, when he does follow habit and custom, and pro-
> ceeds for the moment without calculation, the habits and customs
> themselves are most nearly sure to have arisen from a close and
> careful watching the advantages and disadvantages of different
> courses of conduct.[38]

Thus, the most systematic parts of people's lives are those by which
they earn their living. It is also true that the habits and customs
themselves are nearly sure to have arisen from a close and careful
watching of the advantages and disadvantages of different courses

---

[38] *Principles of Economics,* pp. 20-21.

of conduct. So that habitual actions can be regarded as calculated actions at the second remove. By a sensible method of living, observing the results of different experimental lines of conduct, people find out that there are certain general rules of conduct they can follow in a good many cases with a given high degree of assurance that what has been proved in the past to be the wise choice will be the wise choice of action. When people merely do things from habit they are making use of what they had some time in the past thought out. Thus to all intents and purposes they are behaving as though they calculated.

Marshall sums up this general plan of procedure in the following passage:

> We cannot indeed measure motives of any kind, whether high or low, as they are in themselves: we can measure only their moving force. Money is never a perfect measure of that force; and it is not even a tolerably good measure unless careful account is taken of the general conditions under which it works, and especially of the riches or poverty of those whose action is under discussion. But with careful precautions money affords a fairly good measure of the moving force of a great part of the motives by which men's lives are fashioned.[39]

Consequently, a science which has real claims to credit can be built up. For, says Marshall, in putting forth the case for economics to be a science, economists

> deal with facts which can be observed, and quantities which can be measured and recorded; so that when differences of opinion arise with regard to them the differences can be brought to the test of public and well-established records; and thus science obtains a solid basis on which to work. In the second place, the problems, which are grouped as economic, because they relate specially to man's conduct under the influence of motives that are measurable by a money price, are found to make a fairly homogeneous group.[40]

Economics, as Marshall sees it, deals not with the behavior of some artificial creature but with the behavior of real men. It is concerned not with thinking out the possible consequences of a set of assumptions that may be contrary to fact. It is concerned instead with facts which can be observed and quantities which can be measured. It is subject to actual tests by comparisons between the results which it establishes and public records.

All this is reassuring to people who have often been troubled by a type of economics which professes to be abstract, to deal not with a real but an imaginary world, to be concerned with the conduct not of people such as we know and such as we are but with the conduct of a

---

[39]*Principles of Economics,* p. 39.
[40] *Principles of Economics,* p. 27.

non-existing tribe ruled only by a single motive, or possibly two
motives. From Marshall's point of view, economics gets its scientific
character not so much from the internal consistency of its propositions, not because it can claim some kinship with a subject like
Euclidian geometry; but from the fact that it is dealing with reality
and its propositions can be brought to the test of comparison with
factual records such as exist in public places and are known of all men.

This is advancing an ideal for economics different from that which
Ricardo set up. Remember how, in his discussion with Malthus,
Ricardo was led to say that questions of fact were not questions of
science. He says distinctly that the proper office of the economist is
to think out what will happen under certain assumed circumstances.
The question as to how closely the results correspond to the facts
of observation was one that was not of a scientific order. Ricardo was
extremely eager, as eager as any man, even as Marshall himself, to
have an economics that was serviceable for practical needs. But to
him the most serviceable type of science was built upon the foundation of definite assumptions and was concerned with finding out the
results which would follow in the world that the theorist imagined.
Even John Stuart Mill had said clearly that economics presupposes
an arbitrary definition of a man. Not so Marshall. To him it deals
with one side of the lives of real people. It is concerned to get measurements of the forces that actually control their conduct. Because it is a
mechanism for measuring these forces, it can achieve the stature of
a science. The validity of its conclusions can be brought to an objective test. It is an ideal different from that of his classical predecessors,
and needless to say, much more difficult of attainment.

It is on the basis of his ideas of human nature that the elaborate
structure of Marshall's theory rests. The motives which control economic behavior can be arranged in two great categories, two opposing
sets of forces; those which impel man to economic efforts and sacrifices
and those which hold him back, the desires which lead men to activities and the sacrifices which prevent men from carrying these activities beyond points which it is necessary for the theorist to investigate.
As he put it:

> While demand is based on the desire to obtain commodities,
> supply depends mainly on the overcoming of the unwillingness to
> undergo "discommodities." These fall generally under two heads:—
> labour, and the sacrifice involved in putting off consumption.[41]

In other words his conception of human nature called for a study
on the one hand of desires as the basis for demand; on the other

---

[41] *Principles of Economics*, p. 140.

hand for a study of sacrifices as limiting supply. Out of the comparatively simple opposition of desires and satisfactions, demand and
supply, he developed a theory of value with which in later parts of
the book he covers the peculiar problems presented by distribution.

Conception of human nature in Marshall. Differences [among people]: a continuous gradation—from actions of "city man" to those of ordinary people.
Theory of normal value applies to latter in same way, although not with
same precision of detail, as to bankers or merchants. Marked differences in
respect to saving. Racial differences in choice between leisure and productive work. Individual differences in reference to attitude toward taking
risks and aiming at large prizes. Preference for life in city at high wages
over life in country, and different ways of spending money. Differences in
marginal utility of money to poor and rich. Ways of escaping conflicts in
theory which those differences cause:
1. Using *groups* composed of large numbers of people.
2. Consideration of *normal* economic action.
3. Study of demand and supply *at the* margin. Use of cost of production
to a representative firm.
4. Ascription of differential advantages in consumption and production to
consumers' and producers' surpluses.
5. A statistical view of economic behavior implied. Certainty gives place to
probability.[42]

To repeat, Marshall's fundamental conception of human nature
determined the general framework of his theory, and in this sense is
fundamental to his whole exposition of economics. Human behavior
is guided by motives. These motives can be arranged in two opposing
sets: on the one side the desires to obtain satisfactions of many different sorts; on the other side the reluctance to undergo the sacrifices involved in labor, [etc.]. What a man does is determined by the outcome
of the two opposing sets of forces. Accordingly his system of economics
involves on the one hand, a study of demand; that is to say, of the
operations of the motives that make up desire, satisfaction. On the
other hand, it involves the study of supply; that is, the limitations
upon the abundance of commodities which are imposed by man's
reluctance to undergo labor for wages, [etc.]. From the study of the
demand for particular commodities and the limitations upon their supply, Marshall derived his theory of value, of price and of distribution.

He provides first in Book III a study of "wants and their satisfaction"; second, a study of "the agents of production: land, labor, capital, and organization," in Book IV which is concerned with supply. In
Book V which he points out is central to his whole body of theory,
he deals with the mutual interconnections among demand, supply

---

[42] Outline, January 17, 1917.

and value, value being the equated point between the demand for a good and the supply of it. It was called in the first edition The Theory of the Equilibrium of Demand and Supply With Some Considerations as to its Bearing on the Doctrine of Maximum Satisfaction. In the eighth, it becomes General Relations of Demand, Supply, and Value.

> What does Marshall discuss? "that part of individual and social action which is most closely connected with the attainment and with the use of the material requisites of well being."

> Division of discussion: Book III, Of Wants and Their Satisfaction. Wants grow out of action as well as action out of wants. Serves as theoretical basis for explanation of motives to action and also as theoretical basis for explanation of results of economic acts in satisfaction. Book IV, The Agents of Production—land, labor, capital and organization considered with reference to their bearing on physical volume of production—*efficiency*. Also with reference to the supply prices of each agent. Basis of theory of limitations of supply. Book V, General Relations of Demand, Supply [and Value]. Used demand prices from Book III and supply prices from Book IV and from these data constructs values. Stresses distinction between temporary and normal equilibrium between supply and demand. The backbone of economic theory. Distribution of the National Income, Book VI. Application of theory of Book V to special consideration of prices of labor, uses of land, loans and business ability.[43]

Several times attention has been called to the fact that the early types of economic theory are very imperfectly integrated; that is, the different parts do not have a close organic relation to one another that is demonstrated by the writer. Ricardo has at least three different laws of value: a law of supply and demand which is supposed to apply to the determination of the price of a commodity in a market at a given moment when there is not sufficient time allowed for increasing supply by bringing in new goods; second, a law of cost production, which is supposed to regulate the supply of readily reproduceable commodities in periods of time long enough to allow for further production; and third, a law of production costs [comparative cost] which applies to the exchange of commodities among different nations. One may even say that there is a fourth theory imperfectly worked out by Ricardo, scarcely more than suggested; the theory of monopoly price which takes the simple form that a monopolist charges the highest

---

[43] Outline, November 1, 1927. Quotation is from *Principles of Economics*, p. 1.

[Book, V, of all editions after the first includes also what was originally Book VI, The Cost of Production Further Considered. For explanation of the change see C. W. Guillebaud, "The Variorum Edition of Alfred Marshall's *Principles of Economics*," *The Economic Journal*, December 1961, pp. 679-680.]

possible price that he can get without any careful consideration of the limit to the prices that he may extort. The relations among the several laws of value are not clearly shown. And furthermore he even makes the slip in one of his letters of saying that the law of supply and demand has nothing to do with the law of cost production, that if the cost of production of a commodity were greatly reduced its price would fall promptly even though there had been no change in the supply of and the demand for it. The several laws of price or value in Ricardo have no close organic connection with his theories of distribution.

Marshall, however, succeeded in pulling the different parts of the Ricardian theory together by showing that all the problems which Ricardo treated can be discussed in terms of supply and demand. His framework can be utilized in discussing any problem of exchange whether the commodities being exchanged are goods for consumption, or whether they are human services or the services of capital or the services of land. The framework can be followed out, because it is possible to investigate in every case the conditions on which the demand and supply depend. There follows a series of closely related problems in prices including the prices of the various factors of production which can be differentiated from one another on logical lines. Thus the law of supply and demand, which Ricardo represented as applying only to the particular case of market supply and demand without the possibility of increasing production, is extended by Marshall over the whole field.

To say that the price of anything depends upon demand and supply, however, is no more than the barest of beginnings of an investigation if one has to study what are the factors that control at a given time the demand and the supply. If the theorist considers the problem to which Ricardo applied his law of supply and demand, he arrives at Ricardo's result: that in cases when it is not possible to add to the supply on the market, cost of production does not come into the picture. But when the theorist extends the period under consideration, then cost of production comes into the picture not as a new element, not as something strange and different from demand and supply, but as the chief factor determining the supply itself, limiting the amount that will be forthcoming for sale. When still longer periods of time are taken into account, not merely the cost of producing additional units of the goods the price of which the theorist is trying to make out must be considered, but also the cost of producing the factors of production which are used in making the goods.

Marshall also says it is feasible to treat the problem of wages in terms of the price that is commanded by labor. This price can be discussed in terms of supply and demand just as effectively as the price paid for some inorganic commodity. The problem of interest also comes into the picture on the same basis. For now the theorist is merely investigating the factors which give rise to the demand for the use of capital and the factors that limit the available supply of capital in periods of varying length; and this investigation of the supply and demand for capital constitutes the theory of interest, the price paid for this particular good. The problem of rent can also be treated in terms of the study of the peculiar conditions that determine the demand for the use of land and the peculiar conditions that limit the available supply of land of various sorts.

In short, Marshall organized economic theory in a much more effective fashion than his predecessors, in a fashion that is logically much simpler. It is one of the great strides forward which he took; and it is what usually comes to mind immediately, when his services to economic theory are considered. He also integrated the general body of economic theory more closely than his predecessors, by showing how the elaborate analysis of cost of production which had been built up by Adam Smith, Ricardo, John Stuart Mill and their co-workers, as the classical theory of cost of production, can be treated by the type of analysis of which Jevons was the first great British exponent, the utility analysis. Integration is effected by using the utility analysis to give an account of demand, and the cost of production analysis to give an account of supply.

The feat of utilizing in a single homogeneous body of doctrine the supposedly opposing value theories of the classical economists and of Jevons and the Austrian school attracted a great deal of comment among economists, when the *Principles of Economics* appeared. It was one of the points at which Marshall was attacked by critics. They said that he after all is an eclectic; he simply takes elements that he has derived from the Ricardians and from Jevons and the Austrians, and puts them together in a system which has the disadvantage of using two sets of forces. The Jevons-Austrian analysis, on the other hand, is represented by critics as being a monistic exposition of value; it invokes only one set of forces, those of supply. For in the later forms of the utility analysis developed by Böhm-Bawerk in particular an attempt is made to show that cost of production in any other sense than the sacrifice of utility is not a factor in limiting supply. Mankind had developed a system of production to such an extent that the real cost nowadays in producing goods is not a certain amount of pain or in Marshall's terminology, of sacrifices, in the sense of undergoing something disagreeable. It is only that if production is carried beyond a certain point then certain alternative pleasures or satisfactions must be surrendered. If a person stops work at the end of eight hours, what leads him to stop is not the fact that a ninth hour of labor would be disagreeable beyond the amount of satisfaction from the goods produced in the hour. It is the fact that if he worked nine hours per day, the time he can spend in enjoying the many things which the efficiency of modern production puts at his disposal is limited. The sacrifice is an alternative pleasure. The ultimate elements even in cost, therefore, are elements of utility, not of sacrifices.

The charge that he was an eclectic was a criticism that particularly annoyed Marshall. He was by temperament exceedingly sensitive and was inclined to react sharply against any faults found with him; but the notion that he was seeking simply to plaster together two incompatible elements without having the insight to realize their incompatibiltiy, seemed to him too much to be borne. For example, in a letter to John Bates Clark of Columbia in 1908 he said:

> One thing alone in American criticism irritates me, though it be not unkindly meant. It is the suggestion that I try to "compromise between" or "reconcile" divergent schools of thought. Such work seems to me trumpery. Truth is the only thing worth having; not peace. I have never compromised on any doctrine of any kind.[44]

As a matter of fact, in the *Principles* he gives an answer to the suggestion that the theorist can explain cost of production in terms

---

[44] Marshall to Clark, March 24, 1908, in *Memorials of Alfred Marshall*, p. 418. [For a discussion of the view that Marshall was an eclectic see R. S. Howey, *The Rise of the Marginal Utility School 1870-1889* (Lawrence, Kansas: University of Kansas Press, 1960) pp. 89-91.]

The addicts of utility analysis protested against Marshall's failure to treat cost analysis as merely a mechanism for showing how marginal utility explains valuation. (Outline, "Fifty Years as an Economist," talk before Columbia University Political Economy Club, May 11, 1943).

[They took the position that Marshall's central discussion of the "equilibrium of demand and supply" placed his work in the division of economic science devoted to "economic morphology," analogous to systematic zoology, and not in economic theory, analogous to "animal physiology," strictly speaking. "The morphology of economic science has the task of the classification of economic phenomena (according to classes, kinds and subkinds) and the description of their general nature (a description of the points possessed in common by different groups of phenomena of the same class). The theory of economic phenomena has to investigate and explain the laws governing the latter, the regularities in the coexistence and sequence of phenomena and the inner cause of these regularities." (Seager, "Lecture Notes on the History of Economic Thought," 1895, in editor's possession.) Henry R. Seager became a colleague of Mitchell at Columbia. It was Seager who successfully persuaded Mitchell to return to Columbia in 1922.]

of utilities foregone rather than in terms of actual sacrifices. It occurs characteristically in a footnote at a rather late stage of the book. As J. M. Keynes remarks in his sketch of Marshall's life, one of the characteristic features of the *Principles* is the absence of a controversial tone. Marshall went far to try to show that even his predecessors, who made formal errors, really knew better. He believed that they were betrayed by their words rather than mistaken in their fundamental thoughts. Particularly in any writer of the classical school, he could always see verities which are not to be found in the letter of his text. Consequently, when he felt called upon to dispose of some doctrine which he regarded as erroneous, he did it very quietly in a foot-note. This foot-note bears upon a point of fundamental importance, for it gives Marshall's justification for his fundamental position that the theorist must operate with two opposing sets of forces rather than try to operate only with the force of satisfaction or utility. He says:

> Recent discussions on the eight hours day have often turned very little on the fatigue of labour; for indeed there is much work in which there is so little exertion, either physical or mental, that what exertion there is counts rather as a relief from ennui than as fatigue. A man on duty, bound to be ready when wanted, but perhaps not doing an hour's actual work in the day; and yet he will object to very long hours of duty because they deprive his life of variety, of opportunities for domestic and social pleasures, and perhaps of comfortable meals and rest.

This is Marshall's statement of the theory that the sacrifice in labor is not so much the enduring of positive discomfort as the foregoing of other utilities or pleasures. He admits that this is the case in certain types of employment, but he goes on:

> If a man is free to cease his work when he likes, he does so when the advantages to be reaped by continuing seem no longer to overbalance the disadvantages.

This is what he does when he is free and can determine his own working hours. If he has to work with others, and that is the typical position of the modern workman, he is a member of some kind of crew, team or force.

> If he has to work with others, the length of his day's work is often fixed for him; and in some trades the number of days' work which he does in the year is practically fixed for him.

Not only the work that he does but the number of hours a day and the number of days in a week are practically determined for him without reference to his own individual desires.

> But there are scarcely any trades, in which the amount of exertion which he puts into his work is rigidly fixed. If he be not able or

willing to work up to the minimum standard that prevails where he is, he can generally find employment in another locality where the standard is lower; while the standard in each place is set by the general balancing of the advantages and disadvantages of various intensities of work by the industrial populations settled there.

That is, the theorist takes the situation as a whole, and while he may admit that the individual may be forced to work longer than if he were free, and would rather stop earlier and have lower earnings, or he may be forced to stop before he liked and might prefer another hour's work with its concomitant pay—while that may be true of individuals—still if the theorist takes communities he can say that the standard is set by the general balancing of advantages and disadvantages of various intensities of work by the industrial population, the whole of the workers.

The cases therefore in which a man's individual volition has no part in determining the amount of work he does in a year, are as exceptional as the cases in which a man has to live in a house of a size widely different from that which he prefers, because there is none other available. It is true that a man who would rather work eight hours a day than nine at the same rate of ten pence an hour, but is compelled to work nine hours or none, suffers a loss from the ninth hour: but such cases are rare; and, when they occur, one must take the day as the unit. But the general law of costs is not disturbed by this fact, any more than the general law of utility is disturbed by the fact that a concert or a cup of tea has to be taken as a unit; and that a person who would rather pay five shillings for half a concert than ten for a whole, or twopence for half a cup of tea than fourpence for a whole cup, may incur a loss on the second half.

Marshall is turning the tables on the utility theory. As Jevons pointed out the utility theory applied accurately only to commodities that are infinitely divisible. Pianos, say, cannot be taken for purposes of illustration. Jevons admitted that many commodities are of this indivisible sort, and the theory of utility does not precisely and accurately establish an equivalence between the satisfaction derived from the expenditure of the last unit of money upon goods of that sort and the satisfaction derived from the last unit that is bought. Take an obvious case, what Ricardo would have called a "strong case." Consider the purchase of an automobile. This is a large outlay, and it cannot be supposed that there is a nice balance established between the satisfaction derived from the last dollar spent on the car and the unit of satisfaction, the final degree of utility, of the car. Marshall is saying that there is no more inaccuracy in the application of the theory of increasing sacrifices in the course of a day's work because most people have to work as members of the team where someone else determines the length of the working day, there is no more inaccuracy in the application of the law of cost than in the applicability of the law of marginal utility to commodities which come in fairly large indivisible units. He says:

> There seems therefore to be no good foundation for the suggestion made by v. Böhm-Bawerk ("The Ultimate Standard of Value," sec. IV, published in the *Zeitschrift für Volkswirtschaft,* vol. III [1894, pp. 185-230]) that value must be determined generally by demand, without direct reference to cost, because the effective supply of labour is a fixed quantity . . . that is, fixed by other people than those who do the labor.[45]

There is still another way in which Marshall organizes economic theory more effectively than his predecessors. This has reference to the treatment of periods of different length. Marshall says in the preface to the first edition, which he reprinted in substance in all subsequent editions:

> . . . the element of Time, which is the centre of the chief difficulty of almost every economic problem, is itself absolutely continuous; Nature knows no absolute partition of time into long periods and short; but the two shade into one another by imperceptibe gradations, and what is a short period for one problem, is a long period for another.
>
> Thus for instance the greater part, though not the whole, of the distinction between Rent and Interest on capital turns on the length of the period which we have in view.

He goes on to say

> That which is rightly regarded as interest on "free" or "floating" capital, or on new investments of capital, is more properly treated as a sort of rent—a *Quasi-rent* it is called below—on old investments of capital.[46]

Marshall uses the conception of time as continuous and yet as being capable of division for purposes of economic inquiry into periods of different length as a device for seeing the relations between different types of price and distribution problems. It appears in the distinction between market price problems, those of determining the price as of a given moment, and the problems that are presented, when the time under consideration is long enough to permit of additions to the supply by new production. This comes in again when Marshall passes to periods which are long enough to permit the production of new means of production; that is, the birth and training of new laborers, the accumulation of new capital, perhaps of an increase of the amount of land, available as a source of supply through the extension of lines

---

[45] *Principles of Economics,* pp. 527-528. [A translation by C. W. Macfarland of the article is in *Annals of the American Academy of Political and Social Science,* supplement, September 1894; reprinted in Böhm-Bawerk, *Shorter Classics* (South Holland, Illinois: Libertarian Press, 1962) pp. 308-370.]

[46] *Principles of Economics,* pp. vii-viii.

of communication to areas which had not previously been drawn upon and finally the further development of business organization, the skill with which the whole procession of production is mastered.

In short, Marshall provides a thoroughly integrated scheme which permits the theorist to attack by a standardized method much the whole range of problems which Ricardo had treated in a series of more or less independent problems. Economics in Marshall's hands becomes in his own phrase "primarily an engine of inquiry." It was, as J. M. Keynes said, primarily in the creation of this engine that Marshall's peculiar genius shows itself. The results which he obtained by using it were in his eyes the things that we aim at, the things that have ultimate value. But he was a modest person, inclined to believe that those who came after him would be able to improve greatly upon the results which he had achieved. The thing that was important at the present stage was to find out how economic problems can most effectively be attacked; and his supply and demand engine served that purpose. It is itself nothing more than a framework but it is a valuable one in the sense that it tells the theorist what things he ought to inquire into, if he wants to understand the central problems of economics. On the one hand he must always inquire what gives rise to the demand for the goods under consideration; on the other hand what limits the supply of that good. This means that economic problems instead of being simple, as this framework may suggest at first sight, are complicated; because the theorist is bound to inquire into many factors when he engages in a serious study of the demand for any economic good, and bound to inquire into many other factors when he investigates the forces that limit the supply. He must recognize that the character of the forces that play upon demand on the one side and upon supply on the other side vary with the length of time under consideration.

The theorist must recognize also that particularly over the longer periods of time the factors of supply, demand, and the resulting price mutually determine one another, that the demand is influenced by the forces which dominate supply and the forces that regulate supply in turn are influenced by those of demand, and that both of these interacting forces bear upon the price, and the price bears upon both of them. Marshall's statements on this head are made with particular force in the discussion of the general problem of distribution which will be later discussed again.

Meanwhile, the discussion will turn to the set of problems which are presented by the relations between real forces and money forces.

The real forces that control human conduct are those set going by prospective satisfactions and sacrifices. In the last resort it is for them to determine what people shall do, what choices they shall make. The picture that Marshall gives of the individual's economic life is a picture drawn on these lines. Like Jevons he supposes that each individual is continually, so far as the forces in the environment make feasible, striving to maintain two sets of equilibria. As people making an income, just so far as conditions permit—and here should be recalled his discussion of the extent to which fixed working hours bear upon people's actions—people are supposed to carry their exertions in making income up to the point at which the sacrifices undergone in the last moment of working time is just equal to the satisfaction that will be derived from spending the earnings of that last moment for commodities. Second, as consumers people are supposed all the time, and once again just so far as conditions permit—and here recall his illustrations of the necessity of buying a cup of tea and a whole concert if one is to buy them at all—people are supposed to carry their expenditures for different types of commodities up to the point where the last penny laid out for different commodities will give them the same marginal satisfaction.

This is true of people as individuals according to Marshall. But turn to the market with which he is continuously concerned. In a market the equilibrium that the theorist can see plainly established is an equilibrium between demand and supply prices. In the first instance it is not the real forces of satisfactions and sacrifices but the amount of money. To illustrate, take the case of tea. The price is four shillings per pound. If that is the case, then it means that the marginal demand price and the marginal supply price are both measured by this amount of money. This is the suggestion which is commonly in mind, when an equilibrium is pictured by the diagrams which Marshall invented and freely used.

In short, first there is the equilibrium among the real forces constituted by the desire for satisfactions and the reluctance to undergo sacrifices in the lives of all individuals. This equilibrium has a double aspect: the efforts that all the people are supposed to make, in so far as the divisibility of the goods they buy does not interfere, to lay out their incomes in such a fashion that the satisfaction derived from the last shilling spent upon each thing that they buy is equal; and second, the corresponding tendency, in so far as it is not obstructed by the necessity of working a number of hours set by other people, for the individual to carry efforts to get income up to the point where the sacrifice undergone in earning the last shilling is just equal to the satisfaction that will be derived from spending that shilling upon some good from which he expects satisfaction. Then there is the objective equilibrium between the demand prices for and the supply prices of all the vast variety of goods that are offered for sale.

The question to discuss is what is the relationship between these two sets of equilibria; the equilibrium among real forces which exist in the life of every individual supposedly and the' market equilibria between supply prices and demand prices. One is a subjective equilibrium in the lives of individuals, the other an objective equilibrium found in the market place; the one an equilibrium between real forces, the other an equilibrium between prices which are sums of money.

To begin with, it is clear that there is no simple correspondence between a demand price and a supply price in the market and the sacrifices that are made by buyers who pay out money and the satisfactions that are gained by sellers or, if one likes, between the sacrifices that are made by sellers in producing the goods and the satisfactions that are derived by buyers in consuming.

Take a simple illustration, say the purchase of a morning paper from a newsboy for two cents. The fact that two cents is an equilibrium price does not mean the satisfaction the purchaser gets from the newspaper is just equal to the sacrifice undergone by the newsboy. That same newsboy may sell in the course of a morning to a hundred individuals. Some will be people with incomes perhaps as tiny as his own, and others, people with perhaps substantial incomes. On Marshall's showing there is every expectation that for people of very large incomes on the whole the marginal utility of money will be decidedly lower than will be the marginal utility of money to a corresponding number of individuals with substantially lower incomes. If that is the case, if the sacrifice represented by the various buyers of papers is unequal there cannot be an equilibrium.

Again consider the newsboy in his transaction in buying the newspapers as a little merchant. He is dealing usually with a big corporation and there cannot be established any satisfactory balance between the feelings on the part of the newsboy and the feelings of that artificial person the corporation! Also if the theorist tried to analyze the various items in the cost of the newspaper which are constituted by the sums paid in interest on capital, rent and the wages of the many different members of the staff who produce the paper, it would be still less possible to make accurate comparisons between the sacrifices of the individuals who make and sell and the satisfactions obtained by those who buy.

Marshall has no such notion that the relations between the equilibria that exist in the market and the equilibria that exist in people's individual lives are simple and direct. He is not one of those who argue, as some more superficial inquirers have sometimes seemed to argue, that there is a basis for assuming in a modern community that the sacrifices undergone by some members in working and the satisfactions obtained by those who purchase their product balance. Yet on Marshall's showing there is a series of indirect but important relationships between the two sets of equilibria.

In a modern society the goods that are produced are those from which a profit is expected; that is, the incentive to production is not the intensity or the importance of the wants of the community that must be satisfied. The inducement under the profit system is large profits—in a capitalistically organized country necessarily a profit in which all the calculations are made in terms of money prices and the differences between them. As Marshall points out, the business man thinks and by force of circumstances is compelled to think primarily in terms of money costs on the one side and money receipts on the other.

That being the case, the wants that will be satisfied in a modern community are the wants of people who are in a position to pay prices adequate to cover the costs of producing things and leave a margin for profits. It is also clear that out of the modern organization for producing things people get their incomes. To a certain limited extent people get satisfactions from things that they do for themselves. In the country particularly, a farm family is likely to raise no small part of its food. It may chop wood for fuel. And in almost every family a large and important part of all the satisfactions are the result of the work of the housekeeper. The housekeeper is commonly the wife or mother who does the cooking, makes the beds, looks after the internal organization of the family itself. But for the most part people satisfy their wants by making money incomes and then spending them. These incomes come out of that monetary organization in which all the computations run immediately in terms of money costs and money gain, instead of in terms of satisfactions and sacrifices. As all know, this monetary system pays out to different individuals incomes which are very different in amount. The consequence of these differences in incomes appears in the fact that money has differing marginal utilities to different members of the community. The economic system as it is organized at present will produce to satisfy the wants of people with very large incomes, and no matter how little profit-minded a business man is, he cannot afford to produce goods which would satisfy even the most important want to people who cannot pay. If he did, he would soon be put out of business; his losses would make it impossible for him to operate on that basis.

These are all patent facts and they might seem to indicate that the relationship between the equilibrium of the market and the equilibria that take place in people's private lives is non-existent. But that is not the fact. For the various incomes that accrue to people as producers in the process of making money are a very important element in determining the demand schedules expressed in money terms. The amount of money that people have to spend is a factor, along with their tastes, of critical importance in determining how much they are willing to pay for different types of goods. So, in a certain sense in this market based on profit, the real forces get translated into the cold terms of money costs, and money receipts react upon and even help to provide the schedules of money demand prices at which goods can be sold.

It also has a direct bearing upon the money supply prices at which the people who run the system of production can buy the labor and the use of capital and land that they need. For, needless to say, if out of the monetary mechanism a person derives an income that is very small he may be willing to labor hard in order to get an addition to the fund at his disposal. That fact has a bearing then upon the supply price at which the individual sells his services. So it helps to determine the cost to an organization of producing things which he is capable of aiding to make.

Thus the theorist can start if he likes with the two conceptions of equilibria and contrast them with one another. It is highly desirable to do so. But observe that the schedules of demand prices are built upon the price-paying dispositions of individuals. They reflect the tastes of consumers and also the amount of money that consumers have to spend. Similarly the schedules of money supply prices, which constitute the second set of facts that fix market prices in money, are influenced by the willingness of people to undergo exertion or to postpone enjoyment and so form the personal element in them. On the other hand, they are influenced frequently by the values that other members in the community will set in money on products of different sorts, and therefore on the prices of the contributions to the profits of production that any individual can make.

If the individual is in the unhappy position of having a very low income, that means in this money-making world that he does not happen to possess any quality for the use of which fellow-citizens are ready to pay more than a pittance. If on the other hand he is the fortunate possessor of a great deal of capital he has something for the use of which fellow-citizens are ready to pay a price that may seem to him low per unit but gives an income in proportion to the number of his units of capital. Also if he is a man possessing personal qualities that make an important contribution toward the production of goods for which people are ready to pay a high price he may find himself in possession of a handsome salary.

In a sense the individual and all his fellow-consumers, as consumers and producers, are determining their own economic position. The ultimate factors that fix prices in the market are from Marshall's viewpoint the individual's desire to get certain satisfactions together with that of all his fellows, his willingness to undergo the sacrifices of labor and waiting together with that of all his fellows. But the way in which these subjective qualities of the individual and all his fellows work out is conditioned in large part by the peculiar form of economic organization in which people today live, by the fact that in order to get the things he wants a man has to pay money for them, that in order to get the money he has to have something to sell that fellow-citizens want to buy. If the economic organization were set up on another basis, the whole structure of prices that prevail would presumably undergo important modifications.

An illustration will clarify the last point. It has often been observed of man that one of his leading traits is a desire for distinction. In the phrase of Thorstein Veblen, people get satisfaction out of drawing "invidious comparisons" between themselves and their fellows. Almost all people have what appears in others to be an almost malignant pleasure in finding ways of comparing themselves with others and in these comparisons appearing superior. A large part of people's day-dreaming consists of putting themselves in an advantageous position relatively to others. That presumably has been a trait of mankind since the beginning. The particular way in which this trait expresses itself in a society based on money-making takes the form of individuals wanting to seem to themselves and to others to be better off in a financial way than their fellow-citizens. So most people have, at least in some measure, an attitude of wanting to appear well off, of being able to disregard petty costs. It is expressed very largely in dress. It has a great bearing upon the places people are ready to live in, influences their choice of an automobile, and so on. In short, the particular form of economic organization presented by a money economy gives a pecuniary twist to this insistent human trait of desiring distinction above other people.

To go back to the early Middle Ages when society was organized in a different way, people were not so much concerned with comparisons in terms of money. They found equal satisfaction in comparisons in terms of status, or military prowess, or as in some circles of society, the type of accomplishments that were thought proper to a lady or a gentleman at the time.

The pecuniary twist which the prevailing form of economic organization presents expresses itself clearly in the price structure for different classes of commodities. Goods sell well when they cater to this desire to seem well off. People buy things very largely on the basis of their appearance, the impression that they are going to make on other people. It is a substantial element in the factor of style which is important in determining prices.

It is also true that pecuniary organization of society compels all to acquire certain habits which are far more highly developed among the denizens of the money economy than among people who dwell under a different social order, particularly the habit of accountancy in terms of dollars and cents. Living in a money economy means that at least part of the population which is engaged directly in the process of making money gets a thorough discipline in a certain type of rationality. There is not any more elaborate scheme for directing human activity in a methodical way than the scheme that modern accounting provides. Every business man has to learn and to follow that scheme. In comparison with the accountant engaged in the fine-spun calculations which are essential to the efficient conduct of a modern business, most people in their private lives are careless. They do not keep accounts in a methodical way. They do not commonly count costs in minor items very accurately or make precise discounts for futurity or for uncertainty. Yet in a broad and rough-and-ready fashion they are also controlled by the world in which they live into a habit of life that is at least more prudent in calculating than that which is characteristic of people who are not exposed to this discipline.

One of the things most commonly noted by so-called civilized people when they visit savage tribes is the extreme shiftlessness, carelessness, and wastefulness—disregard of future needs—which prevail among the lower orders. They are exceedingly unbusinesslike in their habits, as many of the denizens of modern states may be when judged by the severe canons of accountancy. But the latter are not permitted by the conditions of their lives to be so reckless.

Thus the type of life men live stamps its pattern upon their minds, indirectly influences their valuations, has its share in making up on the one side the demand schedules of money prices, offers for goods, and on the other side the supply schedules of the prices at which they are ready to sell whatever services they can contribute to production.

The particular prevailing form of economic organization exposes the community to certain dangers and conditions that are inherent in the scheme of organization and that are escaped by people who live simpler lives. In a money-making economy, men's fortunes are exposed to all the hazards that are peculiar to the type of life depending upon the maintenance of orderly relations between complicated sets of cost prices on the one side and selling prices on the other. The individual's fortunes are dependent upon an orderly flow of money incomes from business enterprise to him and the rest of the community and a reflow to the retail merchants and others who render services to consumers. This is a type of hazard from which people like the Mexican Indians in remote villages are substantially exempt at present. During recent years [meaning the early 30's] when most Americans have been having an exceedingly anxious time and many have undergone privations, life has flowed on much its accustomed course in little communities where they do not pursue their economic satisfactions through this highly complicated type of organization.

All these remarks are by way of leading up to a general statement. Remember that Marshall declares at the outset that money is "the center around which economic science clusters," and goes on to say that it is the center because it is the measure of the force of motives that control human behavior; that is, it is the center of economic influence; it is a tool of accounting. If the theorist really analyzes the relationship between the equilibrium of the real forces that Marshall regards as ultimately controlling conduct, and the equilibrium of the money forces, there is reason for believing that money is the center around which economic science clusters in a much more profound sense than Marshall implies. From this standpoint the importance of money is not in the technical sense that the economist must use money as a measure but that living in a society which is organized about the process of making and spending money incomes molds that life—molds the minds of people who live in that society, in a

large way, makes them as economic characters substantially different from the denizens of another type of economy. If the theorist
could take away the effect of the money economy from the modern
civilized nations, he would find that their inhabitants would be very
different creatures from what they are. Their lives would run on
different lines; the character of the goods that they consumed would
be different; the sort of occupations that they shun on conventional
grounds would be otherwise; their canons of valuation of their fellow-
citizens would be different. In other words, the behavior with which
the economist is dealing would be something substantially different
from what it is in fact. It is desirable to discuss some further points
that Marshall makes concerning the importance of money.

He notes that its use in practical life standardizes and, therefore,
simplifies the task of analysis. He shows (appendix F) that cases of
purchase and sale for money are much simpler to analyze than cases
of barter. Why? When the economist is dealing with a case of barter,
exchange of two things, it is practically necessary to assume, if he is
to remain within the realm of plausibility, that the marginal utility
of both commodities is subject to continual alteration, as a man parts
with more and more units of the commodities he is trading, and as
he acquires more and more units of the commodities he is buying;
that is to say, the problem of barter is a problem of two variables and
both are varying at a fairly rapid rate. When the theorist is thinking
about purchase and sale in money, however, he can within moderate
limits plausibly assume that no alteration takes place in the marginal
utility of money. In practice the occasions on which there is any
appreciable change in the marginal utility of small amounts of money
are comparatively rare. Of course, gradually as we get older and get
larger incomes, as we all do, on the basis of the economist's standard
treatment of human nature which Marshall adopts, we have to assume
that the marginal utility of the dollar and the cent gradually decline.

But in any given time, the economist can treat the marginal utility
of money as a constant without exceeding the permissible limits of
artificiality in the study of his cases. That means that the problem
of purchase and sale for money is a problem of one variable, and
therefore easier to handle. This is one of the points at which Marshall
has a better way of attacking problems than Jevons. Jevons, as noted
before, puts up as his first simple typical case the case of barter between two trading bodies. This is a problem of two variables. Marshall
says that to explain the theory of value the theorist better first take

purchases and sales for money and then he can go on with the more complicated notion of barter.

Second, and more important, Marshall points out that the use of money clarifies all sorts of economic relationships in the minds of economic men, and therefore facilitates the work of the theorist who is trying to give an account of their behavior. In particular he notes the distinction between prime and supplementary costs, a distinction of importance in practical business operations and therefore of considerable theoretical consequence; people are prone to overlook it until they have had a good deal of experience in that rather highly technical type of management which comes with business enterprise conducted for money profits. It has been observed by economists that European peasants, for example, commonly are willing to accept ruinously low prices for many of their casual products such as eggs, milk, or many of the things that they make in the winter. They accept those prices, because they think about the prime costs; that is, the immediate outlay required to get their chickens or cow or to buy the materials which they make up into knicknacks during the months when their farm work is less pressing. The prime costs are, however, only a minor part of the total expenses which a peasant family incurs in producing everything it turns out in the course of a year. A business enterprise running a manufacturing plant and producing toys for the market, for example, is not likely to overlook the fact that besides the prices it pays for materials and labor, it must also get recompense for overhead expenses.[47] Every sale has to be loaded with a small factor which is that item's contribution toward meeting the rent which the corporation has to pay, toward defraying the salaries of its general officials, toward paying interest on the capital that it employs in its business.

The use of money gradually teaches lessons of that kind to people. What is true of the European peasant seems to be true of the American farmer. If people go on a walking trip through the country and stop at a farmhouse to buy food supplies, especially in an out-of-the-way district, they will get them at prices which would ruin the farmers, if they spent all of their time in producing these articles. The farmers are in the position of the European peasant, charging a price which perhaps gives them a handsome margin over and above prime costs, but which may be far from covering both prime and overhead costs.

---

[47] "Overhead" is more or less the American business equivalent for Marshall's term—supplementary costs. "Variable" is generally the American equivalent for prime costs.

The distinction between prime and overhead costs is thus one of theoretical importance. People learn it in practice, when they get their affairs elaborately organized on a basis of dealing in money. The economist learns about it from observing behavior; and in this respect the development of the science of carrying on economic activities in the form of making and spending incomes contributes the basis of economic analysis. That is true not only of the instances cited above but in other cases. To sum up, the use of money is a factor of great significance in the study of economic theory, and from Marshall's viewpoint a fundamental instrument of economic analysis on whatever level of civilization the people whose behavior the economist is trying to explain are living.

Marshall has written that "It is this definite and exact money measurement of the steadiest motives in business life, which has enabled economics far to outrun every other branch of the study of man."[48] I should be inclined to say that it is the standardized systematic use of money with the form of rationalism which it inculcates that has made economic life easy to study and hence given economics an advantage over other social sciences.[49]

To recapitulate, economics is a study of behavior. "Money is the center around which economic science clusters." A novel view in orthodox economics. Why is it the center? 1. Because it measures force of motives, says Marshall. Why does that make money the center? As was said, he conceives economics as concerned with human behavior—what men do. Behavior is conceived as controlled by motives. These are numerous and frequently opposing. Action determined by resultant of these opposing forces. Hence to determine what men will do, we need measure of force of motives. Does equality of money measure mean equally strong feeling? For purposes of explanation of prices and distribution [it might be further asked] does it matter how strong are the feelings behind demand and supply prices? 2. Marshall also, as previously said, interested in satisfactions. Does money measure serve economists here? Does it serve as well as in case of motive? Yes; but satisfactions do not get objectified into money prices which become basis of further elaborations. 3. Marshall further interested in welfare. Does money measure *that?* 4. Money simplifies economic analysis—how? Subsequent lectures have generalized statement—study of economic behavior from outside and from inside. When studied from inside reasoned explanation of economic behavior. Money a means of systematizing and rationalizing behavior. Therefore an aid to economist.

How [the use of money] simplifies economic analysis. Take economics with Marshall as a study of human behavior. Human behavior can be investigated from outside, as animal behavior is. Biological analogy on which he lays emphasis, suggests this viewpoint of behavioristic psychology. Is actually adopted by certain investigators particularly students of economic history and economic statistics. Are generalizations to be found in this

---

[48] *Principles of Economics,* p. 14.
[49] "Marshall," APP 64-73, no. 61.

way, e.g., conclusions of Henry L. Moore's concerning relations between rainfall and economic cycles.[50]

Is materialistic conception of history another example? [Human behavior] can also be studied from inside, after fashion of introspective psychology. The common viewpoint among economists adopted by Marshall. Economic theory from this viewpoint is a reasoned account of behavior. At bottom, a statement of what it is to the economic interest of men to do. It passes as a statement of what men do do, if we assume the men whose behavior is explained to be themselves reasonable.

To economists working from this viewpoint money is the great instrument of theoretical analysis because it is the instrument for ordering practical economic behavior. Accounting is the method of economic control *par excellence*. It rests obviously upon the use of money throughout. The pecuniary calculus of accounting is much more definite, and more elaborate than the utility calculus. Much easier to show the gains and costs of a business enterprise than a household, because the gains of the former are gains in money and gains of the latter arè gains in well being, development. So far as men are systematic in control of their personal economic life, it is largely the application of habits learned directly or indirectly through the use of money. The fundamental reason why money helps the theorist to give a rational account of behavior, then, is that money helps the man in the street to behave in a rational fashion.

Resumé of previous discussion of Marshall. We have seen that: 1. He makes economics a study of economic behavior, and of satisfactions and welfare which result from it. 2. He holds money to be the center around which economics clusters. 3. His reason for this statement is that money enables the economist to measure the *force* of motives. 4. It is necessary to measure the force of motives, because economic behavior is the net resultant of many conflicting motives—none of which the economist is at liberty to neglect as long as they are regular in their action. 5. Further, money must be accepted as the only measure we have of amount of satisfactions, as well as of force of motives. 6. Finally the use of money simplifies economic analysis, because it systematizes economic action. Marshall points out that exchange at money price is simpler than barter. Money facilitates distribution of resources. Brings out distinction between prime and supplementary costs. Commutation increased economic freedom and latter makes "the line of division between the tenant's and the landlord's share" in product correspond with "the deepest and most important line of cleavage in economic theory"; namely, "the distinction between the quasi-rents which do not, and the profits which do, directly enter into the normal supply prices of produce for periods of moderate length." Theory of normal value applies with greater precision to actions of "city man" than to actions of others.

I generalize these various points into the contention that money is of greatest use in giving a rational theory of economic behavior because in practice it is the great instrument of exercising rational control over behavior.[51]

---

[50] Moore, *Forecasting the Yield and Price of Cotton* (1917). [Moore (1869-1958) was a pioneer in econometrics and a colleague of Professor Mitchell.]

[51] Outlines, January 10, 15, 17, 1917. Quotation is from *Principles of Economics*, p. 636.

I am inclined to go so far as to hold that the rise of pecuniary institutions, the whole set of practices which are concerned with making and spending money incomes, has controlled at least the larger stages in the development of economic theory. As noted almost at the beginning of these lectures, mercantilism, as a type of economic speculation, has arisen only in communities which were passing through the early stages in the development of a money economy. Mercantilism, to repeat, viewed the state in much the same way that people in the fifteenth, sixteenth and seventeenth centuries viewed the affairs of a merchant. They thought that just as a merchant grows powerful by growing rich, so does a state. They thought of the merchant's chief power as residing in the money which he controlled; consequently they viewed the state's power as primarily residing in the amount of money which it could get within its borders and keep. The mercantilists naturally endeavored to develop a scheme of statecraft which would serve a nation in much the same way that money-making methods served an individual. They planned to do everything they could to attract money into a country and to prevent it from leaving so that the nation would at all times have an abundant supply of the means by which it seemed to them that countries, like individuals, could get almost anything that they desired.

As the money economy became more fully developed, writers like Adam Smith and the physiocrats began to learn the difference between the real interests of the state and the economic interests of individuals. They began to see that states do not get rich by having an enormous amount of gold and silver inside their borders; that what is important to a state is a supply of useful commodities, large in proportion to its population. They came, just because they lived at a somewhat later stage of monetary development, to the insight that the mercantilists had in the flush of enthusiasm exaggerated the importance of money in statecraft. Adam Smith took the ground that countries get rich best, if everybody were allowed to choose that occupation in which he could make most money and to buy those things which best satisfied him at the most attractive price.

[Professor Mitchell was impressed with J. M. Keynes's *A Treatise on Money* and *The General Theory of Employment, Interest and Money* as a step in this direction, but he went on to say:] taking a broader view and utilizing conclusions reached by some very unorthodox writers, I incline to ascribe a much wider and much deeper importance to the fact that we live in what Keynes calls a monetary economy. (Outline, "Money and Economic Activities," discussion with the Banking Seminar, School of Business, Columbia University, October 5, 1939. See also Appendix VI, Professor Mitchell's comments on Keynes.)

At a somewhat later stage there is another advance. That comes
with Ricardo. Despite his advance upon the mercantilists, Adam
Smith had still accepted their main problem as central for economic
theory. Just as mercantilism was a system of statecraft aimed at
maximizing the wealth of nations, so Adam Smith's "obvious and
simple system of natural liberty" was a system of statecraft, or its
absence, aimed at maximizing the wealth of nations. But when the
money economy has been highly developed within a country, people
are likely to get to thinking less in terms of the general interest than
in those of individual interest. When that stage comes, they appreciate that the individual's interest is not nearly so much in the wealth
of nations as a whole as in what share of the wealth of a nation the
individual can get for himself. This is the stage at which appears
Ricardo, who laid so much stress upon the remark made in the
preface of his *Principles of Political Economy and Taxation* that the
central problem of economics is how the annual produce of the country
gets distributed among the several classes that contribute toward it.
That has continued to be the central issue down to the present.[51a]

We must give Marshall credit for the fruitful notion dawning somewhat late in English political economy that the use of money does
greatly facilitate the systematizing of economic behavior. It helps
in the discovery of important economic relations like that between
prime and supplementary costs, and therefore facilitates the work of
the economist indirectly; all this is beside the more fundamental fact
that from Marshall's viewpoint money is the economist's great means
for measuring the forces which control economic behavior. These remarks concerning the relations between the development of the money
economy and economic theory, however, are an interpellation, an
excursus; they have not much to do with the elucidation of Marshall's
economic theory which is my chief business at present. The way
back is not long if we return to the problem of the relationship between the two equilibria.

To repeat, the first significant characteristic of Marshall's type of
economic theory is that he makes economics explicitly a study of
human behavior. The behavior, however, he conceives in what seems
now a somewhat old-fashioned way as controlled by conscious motives.
The motives which the economist must take into account include all

---

[51a] [To convey more clearly his conception of money economy as a] "profits
economy" or "money making economy," [Professor Mitchell] in 1926 began to substitute "credit economy" [for "money economy"]. ("Diary," June 22, August 5,
1926).]

those which are regularly acting, which play an important role in deciding what people do in their efforts to get satisfactions. From Marshall's viewpoint that means that the economist's first requirement is to have some technique for measuring the forces which control behavior. The measure that he finds available is the amount of money which people will accept for their efforts or for sacrifices, and the amount that they will give for their satisfactions. Thus money, in his phrase, becomes "the center around which economic science clusters," not because he assumes that people want money above all other things, as the central focus of human desire, but simply because it is the economist's one available measure for the force of the motives which control conduct. It is critically important for the understanding of Marshall to be clear concerning this.

To see how Marshall builds up economic theory around this center, how he uses money to explain economic conduct, we should look at his *Principles of Economics* first in a broad way rather than following the abundant detail. This is difficult to do in Marshall's case, for as J. M. Keynes pointed out in his memoir, the book is written in a studiously low tone. Everything follows in orderly sequence. There is no heightening or lowering of the style; it is all on a level; the details are spread before the reader in a way which is persuasive, but it is difficult to see the woods on account of the trees. Let us see even at the cost of some repetition if we cannot survey the forest of Marshall's work as a mass.

He states that the central part of the *Principles of Economics* is Book V. "It sets out the theoretical backbone of our knowledge of the causes which govern value," so that value is the basic theme. Book V is led up to, first by a discussion of the theory of wants in Book III which treats the forces which lie behind demand. Book V is led up to, second by a discussion of the agents of production in Book IV, which is similarly a special study of the phenomena behind supply. Marshall goes from Book V to Book VI in which he applies his general survey of the "relations between demand, supply, and value" to the problem which he, like Ricardo, regarded as of most importance; namely, the problem of distribution.

To recapitulate, his treatise has a symmetrical character. He really gets started in Book III with a study of the factors which affect demand, and in Book IV with a study of the factors which eventuate in supply. Then in Book V he gives a general statement of the interrelations between "demand, supply, and value"; and he closes in Book VI with an application of this general theory of value to the value of human effort, that is, to the problem of wages; to the value of the use of capital, that is, the theory of interest; to the value of the use of land, that is, the theory of rent; and to the value of business organizing ability, that is, to the theory of profits.

In a certain sense, then, the volume is a treatise upon value. Incidentally, a great deal is said about production, because production is the agency for obtaining supply, which is one of the fundamental factors in controlling value. Also something, though not a great deal, is said about consumption, because it is, from Marshall's viewpoint, the desire to consume that stands behind demand. Much is said about distribution, but because distribution js, as he sees it, a series of value problems. The whole, to repeat, is a discussion of value, but it makes the theory of value shed light upon production and consumption as well as upon exchange and distribution.

In this way, Marshall is making another marked improvement upon Jevons's general scheme of developing economic theory. In the discussion of Jevons it was pointed out that he probably had glimpses of the way to organize economic theory more systematically than Ricardo, John Stuart Mill or any of the classical economists had unified it. Mill had begun with production and then came to distribution, which was followed by exchange, including value. Jevons began treating value and seems at least to have appreciated that certain problems of distribution might be handled as particular cases under the general theory of value. Marshall treats production and exchange and distribution and consumption almost as fully as does John Stuart Mill, but he takes Jevons's starting point and develops Jevons's insight into a systematic performance. He starts with the theory of value and elaborates it in such a fashion as to give an account of the problems of consumption, production and distribution, as well as of exchange.

It is important to realize sharply this increase in the integration among the various topics which had been discussed for a long while. Marshall's topics are very much like those of Ricardo; his broad theorems in numerous respects, though by no means in all, are more or less like Ricardo's. But whereas Ricardo presented a number of laws on different heads which he did not relate to each other, Marshall gives a finely integrated, subtly worked-out scheme which belongs in a single perspective. In this respect, he represents the modern view better than his predecessors. Few had gone further than he.

S. Was Marshall influenced by Jevons's ideas?

M. Not very much. He had been working on theory for some time before Jevons published *The Theory of Political Economy,* and seemingly he had discovered not a few of the matters which Jevons had turned up. His attitude toward Jevons was that of a careful, slow worker toward a brilliant hasty one. He seems to have felt that Jevons had set a bad example by premature publication of ideas that were not fully elaborated. He had at least a strong grip upon most of the important ideas advanced by Jevons, but he proceeded to elaborate them.

S. Was he influenced by Jevons's criticism?

M. By the criticism that was made of Jevons's work? He contributed toward that criticism as much as anyone. Whether he was influenced by criticism made by others I have no means of knowing. Marshall probably would have said that the people who had influenced him most were Johann Heinrich von Thünen, an early German theorist who worked on quasi-mathematical problems similar to those of Ricardo; Antoine Augustin Cournot, the early French mathematical economist, and later Gustav von Schmoller and the German historical school of whom he expressed hearty admiration.[52] Marshall was a man whose intellectual insight was wide enough to be impressed by the valuable suggestions found in the old French mathematical writer and in the contemporary German historical writers. He apparently was not much influenced by criticisms of his own work. If so, they confirmed him in the correctness of his opinion and gave him a very low opinion of the intelligence of those who were not able to understand him.

S. Does not Marshall's exposition and discussion of consumption mark an advance over his predecessors?

M. What he says on that head is fairly conventional. There had been an Australian economist, political scientist and anthropologist,

---

[52] Von Thünen is known for *Der Isolierte Staat in Beziehung auf Landwirtschaft und Nationalökonomie, oder Untersuchungen über den Einfluss den die Getreidepreise, der Reichthum des Bodens und die Abgaben auf den Ackerbau ausüben* ("The Isolated State in Relation to Agriculture and Political Economy, or Researches into the Influence on Agriculture of the Price of Grain, the Quality of Soil, and the Market"), 3 volumes (1826-1863).

For Marshall on historical school see *Principles of Economics,* p. 768. Opinion of the historical school is from "Marshall—Class Discussion I," APP 44-53, no. 73.

Marshall wrote of Schmoller's *Grundriss der allgemeinen Volkswirtschaftslehre,* ("Outline of Political Economy") that "it is especially notable for its breadth of view and its careful coordination of the material and psychical elements of progress." *Principles of Economics,* p. 684.

[The German edition of Marshall's *Principles of Economics,* which appeared in 1905, was supervised with Marshall's blessing by a member of the historical school, Lujo Brentano (1844-1931), professor of political economy at the University of Munich, who also supplied the introduction.]

William Edward Hearn who had made a very clever study of consumption, *Plutology, or the Theory of the Efforts to Satisfy Human Wants* (1863) which Jevons and Marshall highly praised.[53] Marshall applied to consumption the conventional notions which are derived in the last resort from the hedonistic view of human nature. On the whole he did a less valuable job in the part on consumption than in most other parts of his treatise; nor did he lay great stress upon it.

Treatment of the central problem of equilibrium of demand and supply. Marshall sees economic behavior concerned with establishing an equilibrium between demand and supply at each stage from the case of the boy picking and eating blackberries to the elaborate moving equilibrium of a nation's efforts at production and distribution of its national dividend. But the cases he is interested in are those presented by a modern community. In such a community the equilibrium is established in markets at money prices. Demand is the quantity which will be taken in a given market within a given time at a certain price. Supply is the quantity which will be offered within a given time in a given market at a given price. To determine what equilibrium price will be one needs schedules of demand and supply prices. The further problem is on what do these schedules of demand and supply prices depend? The role of money in the theory so far: 1. Money prices are the proximate phenomena to be explained—so to speak the subject matter to be dealt with. 2. The first step in explanation is to form demand and supply schedules. Here again uses his money prices—not actual prices but potential prices—as means of explanation. [So much by way of preliminary outline].[54]

Let us see how Marshall's general framework is developed in detail. As noted above the central part of the theory is Book V dealing with the relations among demand, supply and value. His general view of these relations is that there is a persistent tendency to establish an equilibrium between demand and supply at the marginal price. That equilibrium he likes to think of as characteristic of pretty much all economic behavior, from the simplest type to the most elaborate. To recall one of the former cases, he presents the picture of a boy picking and eating blackberries. In that bit of economic behavior there is an equilibrium established between demand and supply. The boy undergoes the labor of picking blackberries until his appetite for

---

[53] [Hearn (1826-1888) was a graduate of Trinity College, Dublin. He became professor of Greek at Queens College, Galway. In 1854 he was appointed to the chair of modern history and literature, logic and political economy at the University of Melbourne. His title later was simply professor of history and political economy. According to the University *Calendar* of 1857, the course on political economy was to consist primarily of "Lectures on the general principles of the science, as contained in Mr. Senior's treatise on political economy, and Adam Smith's *Wealth of Nations*." Cited in J. A. La Nauze, *Political Economy in Australia* (Melbourne: Melbourne University Press, 1949) p. 74. Later the textbook was that of Henry Carey's disciple E. Peshine Smith, *A Manual of Political Economy* (1853).]

[54] Outline, January 17, 1917.

more has been lowered to the point where the labor of picking an additional berry would equal or more than equal the satisfaction derived from eating another. An equilibrium is established.

Take a more complicated case: a housewife in arranging the expenditures of her family, aided by that wonderfully flexible medium of money, is able to approximate an equilibrium between the marginal satisfactions she gets upon the expenditure of money on all the different sorts of things that she buys; that is, the last shilling she lays out for clothing or for food, for music, for theatres—everything that she can buy in small amounts is supposed to give her the same amount of satisfaction.

Then go on to the most elaborate case. There is in Marshall's view a sort of rough and constantly moving equilibrium established between a whole nation's efforts at production and the satisfactions it enjoys in consumption. All through economic life, then, there is the tendency toward the establishment of an equilibrium. This view is in Jevons but it is stated far less broadly. It follows necessarily from Marshall's general conception of human behavior as controlled by two great sets of opposing forces, the forces that drive people to seek satisfactions and those that hold them back from making more than a certain amount of sacrifice in labor or in waiting. The individual will get the maximum satisfaction out of a situation when he continues his efforts at production up to the point where further effort will bring in goods that will yield a satisfaction just balancing the sacrifices. This is the condition of maximum satisfaction; the condition toward which rational economic behavior is always driving; it is the position of equilibrium.

Marshall's analysis is simple enough, but there are several questions not so simple that I must ask in order to make sure that the students get the full meaning of his general conception of economic behavior. While he deals occasionally, for purposes of illustration, with cases like the boy picking blackberries, the problems which concern him are better typified by the problem of the housewife laying out her income and still more by the complicated problem of the equilibrium of the nation's sacrifices in production and satisfactions derived from the consumption of what it puts out.

These are cases in which it is not easy to see how the equilibrium between satisfactions and sacrifices is achieved or where it is achieved, because the economic actors, and in turn the economic theorists, are dealing immediately with money. The equilibria are equilibria between demand prices and supply prices, not between satisfactions and sacrifices. It is necessary, therefore, to determine what the terms demand price and supply price mean, how they are constructed and how they come into equilibrium. What is demand from the point of view of the theorist?

S. Demand is the desire for a certain commodity and the ability to pay for it.

M. This is a good old-fashioned answer, which can be found in some of the classical economists. It is not different from John Stuart Mill's phrasing, but it is not the concept that Marshall offers. He does not find it adapted to effective analysis of the problem.

S. The amount of a commodity that will be taken at a given price.

M. That still is really indefinite.

S. At a certain time in a certain market.

M. That is, to get the thing in clear and objective form, Marshall wants to define demand as the commodities that will be taken in a given market, at a given time, at a given price. Why does he find it unsatisfactory to conceive of demand as intensity of desire? This is something that is indefinite. Why does he want to talk about the amount that will be taken in a given market? Because again the economist does not know how much will be taken, there are no measurable quantities, until the area is specified. He wants to say within a given time because the demand for cotton in the United States, for instance, taking the whole market, may be either two thousand bales if one is thinking of a day; or it will be billions of bales if one is thinking of a number of years. Why does he want to say— and this is a critically important question—the amount taken at a given price? It is obvious also, is it not, that one cannot gauge the amount of demand unless one speaks of not only a given time, but also of a given price. If the price is put low, a great deal more will be demanded than if the price is put high. That is specific. Similarly Marshall defines supply as the amount of the commodity that will be forthcoming for sale in a given market within a given time at a given price.

On the basis of these conceptions, he arranges what appears to be a somewhat elaborate apparatus of what he calls demand and supply schedules. What is a demand schedule?

S. It is the scale of prices a group in the community would pay rather than go without a particular commodity.

M. That is not quite specific enough.

S. A list of these prices can be represented in a diagram.

M. Yes, Marshall sometimes represents demand schedules by diagrams; he does so by preference. They are also capable of being represented by figures. A demand schedule shows the varying quantities of a commodity that will be taken within a given market and within a given time—we ought to put those conditions in again—at a series of different prices, which the theorist finds are more or less within the range of common experience. Similarly a supply schedule shows the varying amounts of a commodity that will be forthcoming for sale within a given market within a given time at differing prices. The characteristic feature of most demand schedules is that they show the amount which will be taken within a given market at a given time as increasing with the decline of prices. Similarly most supply schedules show that the amount of the commodity that will be forthcoming for sale within a given market within a given time increases as the price rises. Demand schedules as a rule are typically represented by a curve that slopes downward and the supply schedules by a curve that slopes upward. Consequently, Marshall is much interested to work out the broad conception in its details, in particular to discuss the difference between the form supply schedules have when thinking about short and long periods, and the difference between supply schedules of industries which have constant returns, diminishing returns and increasing returns.

Going on from this point I will want to ask the class shortly, in the first place, how an equilibrium is established between demand prices and supply prices on the basis of demand and supply schedules; and second and more important, whether these equilibria between demand prices and supply prices mean also equilibria between the real forces of satisfactions and sacrifices. But before going on with these problems I want to make clearer Marshall's treatment of the problem of price determination by the aid of demand schedules and supply

DEMAND SCHEDULES

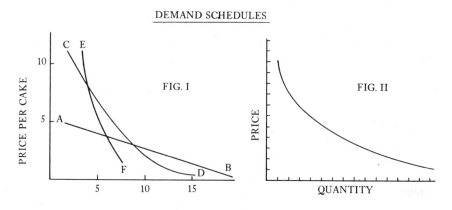

schedules which is one of the points at which his exposition marks a material advance over that of Jevons.

The general conception is that in say a large market like New York City there are a large number of people who want to buy at a given time articles of a given sort. In order to have a concrete case, suppose that the article in question is laundry soap of a certain type which is bought in cakes of a standard size. In the city there are perhaps a million households where the purchaser of family supplies is a customer for this particular commodity, and each customer presumably has her own demand schedule for laundry soap. The demand schedule might be represented as in Fig. I. The economist might find that one woman's demand schedule would be represented like line AB; that is, there might be one woman who at 10 cents would not be willing to buy even a single cake, but when the price got down to 5 cents she would be willing in the course of a month to buy four cakes. There might be another woman whose demand schedule had a different shape, perhaps like line CD. Then there might be a third whose demand schedule was like line EF—the price not having any bearing on the number of cakes she would buy. Thus there may be all sorts of curves. From a vast collection of demand curves of individuals the theorist can draw up a demand curve for the market as a whole which will have the same general form but in which the units of supply, instead of being one cake, would be, perhaps, thousands of cakes per month. There one might perhaps find a demand curve of that general character for the market as a whole (Fig. II). There is no telling what the shape of the curve would be except by actually finding out. It is an empirical question.

On the other side of the market there are supposed to be a considerable number of people who make and offer cakes of soap for sale, and for each of them the theorist can draw up a supply schedule showing the number of cakes which they will offer per month at various prices per cake. The characteristic feature of supply schedules for most articles is that the higher the price the more will be offered, whereas in the case of the demand schedules the higher the price the less will be the demand. Therefore, the curves for individual supply schedules are likely to have an ascending trend, and also may have a great variety of shapes. Conceivably some are very flat. From a considerable collection of supply schedules in this market the economist can compile a market supply schedule, similar in character to Fig. III, which will run in terms of, say, thousands of cakes, and the general shape of which will be presumably as in Fig. III.

Once the economist has these curves of the demand and supply schedules he can put the two curves on the same chart and he is in a position to argue that the selling price will be found at the intersection of the curves (Fig. IV). The reason is that if the price should at any given time be at point A, for instance, the supply offered at that point would be larger than the demand, and the result would be some of the cakes left on the market could not be sold and the sellers would offer concessions. Or, if the price offered at point B be taken, demand would exceed supply, which would tend to put the price up. In order to take advantage of that highly profitable demand more soap would be offered. If the inquirer considers what is going to happen, provided the price is at any given time either such that

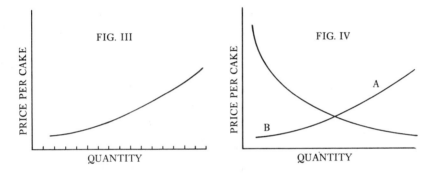

the supply will exceed the demand or the demand will exceed the supply, he will see that that price cannot maintain itself. The equilibrium price is the one at which the supply; that is, the quantity forthcoming for sale within the given market and the time we have in mind is just equal to the demand; that is, the quantity which in that market within the given time will be bought at the price in question.

All this has to do with the establishment of an equilibrium between quantity demanded and quantity supplied, or—to state the proposition another way—of an equilibrium between marginal demand price and marginal supply price. Demand price and supply price, quantity demanded and quantity supplied, are balanced at this point. But it is a matter of prices. How does Marshall know that at the equilibrium price there is an equilibrium between the real forces which he says control human nature, forces which we are merely measuring in our money prices? How does he know that in the case of soap the marginal sacrifices undergone in producing it just balance the marginal satisfactions derived from using soap?

S. It is an assumption.

M. Is it?

S. He says that money measures the forces of demand.

M. Does the class agree that Marshall does make the assumption that the equilibrium price measures on the one side the marginal sacrifice and on the other side the marginal satisfaction connected with soap?

S. Jevons said that each individual differed in the amount of sacrifices he is willing to give, but Marshall went ahead and said that within groups it is possible to have a general schedule of sacrifices.

M. That is, Jevons laid it down as one of his fundamental principles that the economist must not in his theory, undertake to compare the feelings of different people, did he not? Marshall says that there are certain circumstances under which theorists are justified in comparing the feelings of different people. That is, he says that a shilling represents about the same amount of satisfaction or sacrifice to the population of two different industrial towns in England. Can the proposition be applied to the buyers of soap as contrasted with the sellers, the makers of soap, and say that 25 cents represents about the same amount of satisfaction or sacrifice to the demanders that it represents to the suppliers?

To make that point a little clearer, suppose we drop soap as the example and take a different type of commodity; say, point lace. It is made primarily by poor women who get but a pittance for their work. Despite the fact that the price which they may receive for a yard is fairly high, they get only a small remuneration for every hour they put in, the work taking much time. Suppose also that this article is purchased only by women of large means. Would Marshall hold that 25 cents represents about the same amount of feeling to the makers and the consumers of point lace?

S. He would say that even in the first case the equilibrium price could not be reached unless other things were equal. He had to assume that the marginal utility of money in the two cases was the same.

M. The whole question is whether it must be assumed that the marginal utility of money is equal. Marshall would probably say it is just as possible to have the quantity of point lace forthcoming in the New York market in a given month substantially equal to the demand in New York City within the month—just as possible to have that situation in the point lace industry as in the soap industry— that is, a balance between supply price and demand price. But in the point lace industry the situation is such that it would be absurd to suppose that the marginal utility of money to the makers and users is equal. Does that mean that Marshall's theory of value breaks down in that industry?

S. This seems to be an extreme case. The theory might hold in normal cases in the long run.

M. It might be a difficult thing to go through a list of industries and see how many conform to the soap business which exemplified one type, and how many are closer to the point lace industry. Seemingly a general theory of value ought to explain the phenomena wherever they are met with. Has Marshall presented a theory that breaks down in a case in which the workers in the industry belong to a social class different from that of the consumers. Probably there are a good many cases of that sort. Take the men who work at making relatively expensive automobiles. Probably, if they have cars, they ride in Fords or Dodges. Very likely on the average they are not as well paid as the men employed in making the cheap cars. It might be possible to argue, if the economist is thinking of the consumers and purchasers of Ford cars, that he had, broadly speaking, groups in the same economic station, groups to both of which the marginal utility of money was about the same. But if the theorist shifted from Fords to Rolls-Royce cars, he might be confronted by a very different situation. Of course, it is not the rule that luxury goods are produced under circumstances which lead to the payment of high wages. He cannot assume anything of the sort. Does Marshall's scheme of explaining prices on the basis of real forces thus break down? It does not from his viewpoint. How do you say this? How could Jevons get away from the dilemma?

S. Jevons uses final degree of utility.

M. Yes, as opposed to marginal utility; but this is not the critically important point here.

S. It is an individual thing.

M. What is an individual thing?

S. People's sacrifices for pleasure. Each individual can decide whether he is going to work or stop working.

M. Is there an equilibrium between what Marshall calls "real forces" in Jevons's scheme of analysis?

S. No.

M. Yes, there is. And there is one in Marshall too.

S. In Jevons is it the ratio of exchange equalizing the forces?

M. What forces?

S. At the point where the price is determined, at the margin.

M. In the market?

S. Yes.

M. As between the buyers and sellers—the buyers as one trading body, and the sellers as another trading body on the other side; that is, does Jevons in talking about corn and beef state that the final degree of utility between the commodities is the same to the trading bodies at the end, that the sellers of beef get just as much satisfaction from the last unit that is left when the trading is over, as the buyers get from the last unit that they acquired?

S. Does he not equate the utility of one at the end in the disutility of the other party?

M. Jevons says that the final degree of utility and the final degree of sacrifices are equal to the sellers of beef and the buyers of corn, and they are equal to the buyers of beef and the sellers of corn, but he knows nothing as to whether they are equal or not as compared with the people who started out with the beef and those who began with the corn.

Can that analysis be applied to Marshall? All one has to say, is that the equilibrium of real forces is *in each individual economy.* That is all. Whether it is achieved in the market or not does not matter. The economist is seldom in a position to know with any certainty whether it is achieved in the market. Marshall is inclined to argue that he is justified, broadly speaking if he can get considerable groups of people in about the same economic situation, in saying that marginal utility of money will be the same to the two groups. He has a good reason for saying groups of people, and he has a good reason for saying groups in the same economic situation. If he takes individuals he would be as likely as not to get one highly sensitive person and one who is far less sensitive; he might have one person who is an excellent pleasure machine and get a lot of satisfaction out of a given good, and another who is a poor pleasure machine and whose satisfaction from the consumption of a certain commodity is relatively meagre. (But if the economist takes two considerable groups of people, Marshall argues the odds are that in both he will find all varieties of human beings, but the averages of those two groups will not differ very much.) Similarly, regarding the proposition that the two groups must represent more or less the same general average level of economic welfare, if one group such as is represented by the women who buy very expensive lace and another of very poor people who make the lace, no matter if he had thousands of both sets, Marshall would say the theorist is not justified in saying that the marginal utility of money will be equal. But provided he takes both conditions, he can assume that the marginal utility of money will be about equal.

This assumption, however, Jevons does not make. In that respect Marshall went a bit further than Jevons ventured in using the general measure of utility calculus. But so far as regards the fundamental problem of the balance of real forces, Marshall holds that the balance is attained, just as Jevons held, in the life of each individual concerned.

How does this work out with reference to prices? From Marshall's viewpoint every individual effects a sort of double equilibrium in the management of his affairs. In the first place, he effects an equilibrium between the sacrifices that he makes to get income and the marginal satisfactions the income brings. If he is a workingman he is supposed to work just up to the point where the increasing disutility of further labor will just offset the diminishing utility of the income that he obtains. Marshall is willing in effecting this balance to accept the modification which was suggested by Professor Simon N. Patten of the University of Pennsylvania, that among the sacrifices of labor ought to be reckoned the time used in producing which might be spent in enjoying. The reasoning is as follows: a characteristic of the nineteenth century was a shortening of the average working day. From the point of view of the economists who built on utility analysis, that means that as people's incomes become greater they become more and more loath to give up the time which is spent in enjoying good things in order by longer continued work to add more to the things they can enjoy. [In Patten's language, "When . . . the productive power of society has increased beyond a certain point the efficiency of the workman becomes so great that the time needed to consume what he has produced cuts into the time needed for production, he ceases to work before the pain of the last increment of production equals the utility of the last increment of consumption. There is for the efficient workmen a surplus at the margin of production equal to the pleasure that could be obtained in using their time in unproductive consumption. . . . In a highly civilized country the pain of the marginal increment of production is reduced absolutely as well as relatively. The labor becomes so mechanical that it is less painful, and the length of the working day is shortened through the influence of forces made active by the increase of consumption."][55]

---

[55] Patten "The Theory of Dynamic Economics," 1892; [reprinted in his *Essays in Economic Theory,* ed. by R. G. Tugwell (New York: Knopf, 1924) p. 75.]

Marshall, however, laid Patten's contention aside as a minor qualification. The substantial effect is that every individual is supposed
to work out an equilibrium between the sacrifices he makes in getting
income and the satisfactions the marginal increment of income brings
to him.

In the second place, the equilibrium has a great deal to do with
determining the size of the money income that a person will get.
If a man were willing to work longer, he might, from the point of
view of this type of economic theory, be expected on the average
to get a larger money return. The size of the income that he obtains
is one of the factors which is of great importance in determining his
demand prices for various goods. And when the economist turns from
the individual's activity as a producer to that as a consumer, he is
seen according to Marshall engaged all the time in working out a
second set of equilibria. He tries to carry his expenditure for each of
the many different types of goods that he buys to the point where
as nearly as possible an additional cent laid out in the purchase of
any one more of these things will give him the same amount of satisfaction as would the expenditure of an additional cent upon any other
goods that he might buy. Thus there is an equilibrium worked out
among his several demands.

As a result of the equilibrium between the individual's sacrifices as
a producer and his satisfactions as a consumer, a sort of double
equilibrium, there emerges a series of demand prices which that
individual will offer for all sorts of commodities. Those are the demand
prices which are pictured in the chart (Fig. I) on an individual basis.
If the theorist thinks about any one of the individual women who is
buying soap, or point lace, he is entitled, from Marshall's point of
view, to say that the last cent one of these women spends for the
common or rarer article will be just balanced with the satisfaction
she gets from using soap in one case and point lace in the other.
There is a real equilibrium within her individual economy. But when
the economist builds up, on the basis of the individual demand
curves, the demand curve for the market as a whole, he is not in a
position to lay down any proposition concerning an equilibrium between the satisfactions that will be derived from expenditures of the
whole body of buyers and the sacrifices they have undergone. He is
not entitled to lay down any proposition of the sort, according to
Marshall's analysis, if he has not the assurance that he is dealing
with a singularly homogeneous group of a considerable size.

The same is true of the supply situation. One of the effects of the individual producer's balancing between sacrifices in production and the gratifications from consumption is not only to determine the size of his money income but also to determine the supply price of his kind of productive effort. If the man is a spinner in a cotton mill, the equilibrium that he works out in his economy between the price he gets for his last hour of work and the last satisfaction which his wages bring, will have a bearing upon the price that he charges for a certain amount of labor.

Supply schedules for the general market can be constructed out of the individual supply schedules. When the theorist is dealing with the individual supply schedule he can say that there is an equilibrium between the real forces represented by the money prices, but when he is dealing with the market supply schedule he is not entitled to make any such statement unless the situation happens to be one in which he has a large, highly homogeneous group of people.

On Marshall's showing the theorist is seldom in a position to believe that the real forces are equalized in the market; that is, that the sacrifices undergone by the producers of a commodity at the margin are in equilibrium with the marginal gratifications derived by the consumers of the commodities in question. From his point of view there is in the market an equilibrium between the amount demanded and the amount supplied in physical terms, and also an equilibrium between marginal demand price and marginal supply price, but not an equilibrium between the real forces in the market as such. There is, however, an equilibrium of real forces within the economy of each individual. In fact, a sort of double equilibrium between sacrifices as a whole and satisfactions as a whole—marginal sacrifices and marginal satisfactions; and also an equilibrium between the marginal satisfactions that are derived from the expenditure of income in all sorts of different ways.

In sum: Ultimate basis of desire is desire for satisfaction. Ultimate limit upon supply is unwillingness to labor and to wait. Final equilibrium is between satisfactions and sacrifices. Where does this equilibrium of the real forces take place? Does Marshall hold that in the long run the marginal sacrifices involved in growing wheat and making bread equals the marginal satisfactions of eating bread? In a modern society where most of the bread is eaten by other than the growers, millers, bakers, etc., I am not sure that Marshall is altogether clear on that point—should re-read the *Principles* to find out; but I am sure that is not a necessary implication of the theory. As a clear case take point lace made by women who are poor and worn by women who are rich. Where does the equilibrium of real forces take place? In each individual economy, if anywhere. (Recall Jevons). Certainly not in the community where differences of wealth exist. Is there no new equilibrium in the market? Certainly there is. Supply and demand of point lace are as likely to be equalized as the supply and demand of any standard article in long run. What is it that is equalized in the market? Marginal demand price and marginal supply price. Or if it is preferred, quantity demanded and quantity supplied are equalized at equilibrium price.

But, to repeat, the equilibrium of marginal demand price and marginal supply price is no evidence whatever under existing social conditions of an equilibrium of sacrifice and satisfaction. Under modern conditions the sacrifices are made by one set of people, the satisfactions are gained by a different set, and there is not even a presumption of equality unless there be proof that the marginal producers and consumers belong to the same income class. In fact of course, the producers generally are made up of several different income classes—unskilled and skilled workers, employers and lending capitalists—so that the contrary can usually be proved. This is a point which subsequent analysis has made much clearer than Marshall did; e.g., Herbert Joseph Davenport's *The Economics of Enterprise* (1913).

Does it matter in fact what real forces stand behind the demand schedules and the supply schedules? Certainly not for the determination of money prices. In demand, my dollar counts for just as much and no more than any other man's dollar, be he very rich or very poor. In making up supply price, the dollar that has to be paid to me for a day's unskilled labor counts for just as much and no more than the dollar that has to be paid to a great lawyer for a moment's attention or to a great stockholder, or to anybody else who must be paid a dollar to get the supply in question. Why not say, then, that the demand price and the supply price are the real forces? Sacrifices and satisfactions seem to count in fixing prices only so far as they count in dollars and cents. Is there any connection between the equilibrium of marginal sacrifice and satisfaction and the equilibrium of marginal demand and supply price? In each individual's economy there is an equilibrium between sacrifice and satisfaction; i.e. individual establishes equilibrium between marginal sacrifice earning a dollar and marginal gratification of what a dollar will buy. This equilibrium is one factor in deciding size of his money income. Then he establishes equilibrium among satisfactions gained by each dollar spent in different ways. This equilibrium in conjunction with amount of income determines individual's demand prices of various things he buys. Market demand schedule is an aggregate made up of such individual demand prices. Similarly, market supply schedule is made up of aggregate of individual supply prices of factors needed. Further Marshall does not hold that the real forces control money prices completely in the sense just explained. Market prices of course are not so controlled, even normal prices are not so controlled in a world of change.

A student's objection to case of point lace makers. Suppose they earned 25¢ per day and that final buyers paid $1.00 for product of day's work; i.e., that gross profit of dealers equal 300 per cent of wages. Then to find out whether there is an equilibrium of real forces we must compare the 25¢ which the final buyers sacrifice to cover the wages with the real sacrifice which workers make, and the 75¢ which the final buyers sacrifice—to cover dealers gross profits with real costs to dealers, their employees, their creditors, etc. Case against an equilibrium of real forces becomes stronger on this analysis.

Marshall's view on this problem of equilibrium is not very clear, but I think my interpretation is substantially in accord with his logic. The market equilibrium which he presents is equilibrium between demand price and supply price. But he also thinks of the individual within his own economy as establishing a double equilibrium. First equilibrium between marginal sacrifice involved in getting his income and marginal utility conferred by unit of money. Second equilibrium between marginal expenditures on different lines. Effect of these two equilibria: First determines individual's supply price of the factors of production which the individual contributes, and limits his money income by limiting supply which he will sell at this price. Amount he sells times price equals income. Second (in conjunction with the amount of his income) determines his demand price for consumers goods and therefore indirectly for factors of production used for making these goods; and limits amount of such goods he will buy. Relation of the equilibrium of real forces within the individual economy to equilibrium of money prices in the market. Get supply prices and demand prices, based on these individual balancings. Add them together to make schedule of demand price and supply price and find tendency for those two sets of prices to balance at the price where amount demanded equals amount supplied. On basis of these money prices, business enterprise works out an equilibrium. Marginal dollar spent for each factor of production brings equal gain in money and this gain equals the outlay.

Why Marshall's view is not more clear. He does not attack the first problem, money price and then go into question what real forces are in the background. Instead he studies first wants and demand prices; second, factors of production and supply prices; third, equilibrium of demand and supply going back and forth between cases where money enters and where it does not; fourth, applies his general theory of equilibrium of demand and supply to special cases of labor, capital and organization ability. What he does say definitely: Shall find many limitations upon doctrine that cost price "represents" real cost (because of changes in conditions). Under certain circumstances money measure of costs corresponds to real costs. Efforts and sacrifices "underlie" money expences. Is perfectly clear that same amount of money represents different real costs and satisfactions to rich and poor. Business man takes money costs as he finds them without inquiring how far they measure real forces.

Marshall's conception is, I think, that real forces (sacrifices and utilities) are not in equilibrium themselves—and we should not know if they were—but that it is these real forces which establish the equilibrium of money forces—that they do not control money prices in any close and detailed fashion because of continual changes in the economic situation including the real forces themselves.[56]

S. Did Marshall go a step backward when he used this idea of final utility?

---

[56] Outlines, January 22, February 7, 1917.

M. Not from his viewpoint. You are thinking about the mere mathematics of his demonstration. But one of Marshall's characteristics is that he wanted to talk in terms of real forces. From his point of view satisfactions and sacrifices are genuine entities, substantially the matters that control behavior. They are quantities of feeling. He wanted to talk about them and not about mathematical formulae. He was, incidentally, a vastly better mathematician than Jevons.

Another question along this line is in order. In the market on Marshall's showing the intensity of a person's feeling about things does not count in the determination of prices, except as it does lead to the offer of money. Suppose that I am a very poor person and ardently desire a copy of some very expensive book; and suppose also that another member of this group possesses a large income and as a book collector rather fancies the book, although he does not care much about its contents. It does not matter in the determination of the price of the book, does it, whether I care much or little for it, if I am unable to make a bid? It does not matter to the very rich person who makes a bid of say a thousand dollars for a rare copy. His impact upon prices is not going to be affected by the fact that it is a mere passing whim. In other words, does it not look from this point of view as if intensity of desire or the sacrifices people undergo is almost beside the point as a matter of explaining prices? What counts is the price one can offer or the price one can demand.

Take an illustration from the other side of the game. Suppose a very poor man in bad health with a family depending on him and with comparatively little aptitude for work and a sensitive disposition is to take a job shovelling snow at an extremely low price, and he does it at terrible mental and physical cost. He undergoes an enormous sacrifice to get, say, 35 cents an hour, and the fact that he and many other people are ready to accept the job at this rate is the only fact that counts in determining the price; the agony which the work inflicts upon him is a matter of no consequence as a price-making factor.

On the other hand, suppose a skilful businessman who truly loves the game of business and who already has an abundant fortune and does not care much for more money. If he could not get a price for his services he would be glad to be in the business game just for the fun of it, but the fact that his particular type of ability is very rare, on the one side, and extremely valuable for making profits, on the other, enables him to command a salary of, say $75,000 a year. There are no sacrifices involved in his making the money, but he is in a position to set that supply price upon his services and he gets it.

Both examples are what Ricardo would have called strong cases. Do they not seem to show that when theorists are talking about the problem of price determination they might just as well throw overboard the whole machinery of satisfactions and sacrifices and say that the only thing that counts are demand prices and supply prices? No feeling that is not embodied in a price form seems to count, and any feeling that is embodied in a price form seems to count. Then why not toss feelings out of the window and talk about prices?

S. Marshall would say that there is a consumer's surplus and producer's surplus. The feelings of the group is what counts. The general feeling of the group is to work for 35 cents as snow shovellers and the feeling of the general group of highly expert business men is to work for $75,000.

M. That is, from Marshall's viewpoint these extreme cases are comparatively insignificant. What the theorist must concentrate attention upon are the positions of the marginal suppliers and demanders.

S. It would be all right to assume this on the hedonistic or utility conception.

M. Yes, you certainly do. If the theorist starts with Marshall's psychological basis then talk in terms of money price is empty. You have no explanation of what happens; that is, from his viewpoint in the determination of market price, it is the demand and supply schedules that count, and these run in terms of prices. It is the amount of money that people will offer or take that counts, and the feelings behind the schedules may be any magnitude you like; except in so far as they can affect the demand and the supply price of different quantities they will not have a bearing upon the market situation.

But Marshall holds that while this is all true, how is the theorist going to explain market prices, demand and supply prices? He has a very superficial explanation if he simply says the market price is determined by demand and supply schedules. He should ask what fixes them. The answer to this question from Marshall's point of view takes him back of the monetary forces to an analysis of the real forces; and the real forces are operating inside each individual's economy.

Take again the pitiful case of the snow-shoveller. From Marshall's viewpoint, exceedingly painful as the work may be to him, nevertheless the value of the money he gets is compensated for at the margin. He would not do it unless he had a desire for 35 cents an hour matching in intensity his repugnance to the work. There is a real balance at that point and he is neither a loser nor a gainer. As for the other extreme case, the business man who is able to command a very high salary for work which he loves to do, the theorist has to say also that, taking the situation as a whole, there is a kind of economic balance worked out, but, as was just pointed out by a member of the class, in order to see this it is necessary to bring into this analysis which so far has centered around what happens at the margin, the idea of consumer's surplus and the sister idea of producer's surplus.

These notions are a further illustration of how Marshall uses the conception of real forces, how in spite of the fact that he holds economic science to cluster around money, he nevertheless does try to get back of the pecuniary factors and show the effect on men's real interests. Consumer's and producer's surplus is an illustration of the difference between real and money forces. In short, the idea is important in his eyes as representing a point at which the economist can carry his analyses into the field of real forces.[57] We shall consider, first his conception of consumer's surplus and producer's or worker's surplus; and second, his brief but pregnant discussion of his justly celebrated pretty proposition that a community might conceivably increase its total satisfaction—by imposing a tax upon industries of diminishing returns and distributing the proceeds as a bounty among industries of increasing returns. As regards consumer's surplus, what is that quantity?

S. The saving people get by buying cheaper than they would be willing to pay.

M. It is the satisfaction they get;—that is it substantially. How do you measure it?

S. It depends upon the people. In some cases the individual would be willing to pay anything, no matter how much, to get a commodity; and the surplus would be quite large but in marginal cases it might be very small.

M. There are two cases for discussion: one is, say, that of a very rich person who is buying a player piano. Perhaps for the elegant type which he does buy he is asked, say $800. (I am quite at sea as to the price of such instruments and this may be absurdly low, but we will say $800.) As has just been suggested this person might

---

[57] Last two sentences from Outline, November 12, 1931.

have been willing to pay perhaps $5000 for the instrument if he had been compelled to do so. If it is offered to him at $800, then he gets a measure of surplus satisfaction which equals the difference between the price he would be willing to pay and the price he does pay. The second case Marshall regards as most typical. He supposes that most people, in buying the great bulk of the things they use, profit by consumer's surpluses. They have consumer's surplus upon the stock they buy, upon their soap, meals, even trifles, and upon all the common staple items which are sold at a very low price. How does this come about?

S. A person has a demand schedule of how many units of a given commodity he will buy at a certain higher price, and if the price is lower and he gets all the units that he wants to buy at that price, then there is a difference or surplus.

M. Yes. Marshall's favorite illustration is naturally an English one. It is cups of tea. Suppose a person for this indispensable pre-requisite of civilized life were compelled to pay 40s. for a single cup of tea. He might perhaps, if a person of considerable income, buy a cup. On the other hand, for a second cup he might not be willing to pay more than 20s. Then he would have a cup at lunch and one at tea time. For a third cup he might be willing to pay 5s. For a fifth, a sixth cup he would pay lower prices, until he would get down to what, say, is the market price. On Marshall's basis this individual in buying tea gets a consumer's satisfaction upon all the cups that he buys except the marginal one. He goes on buying tea until his expenditure upon the item is just sufficient to bring gratification from the consumption of the last cup into equivalence with the sacrifice imposed by the expenditure of the last outlay for tea.

The general idea was doubtless suggested to Marshall by the study of diagrams which, as was noted above, he began to make rather early in his experimenting with mathematics, more accurately the diagrammatic method in formulating economic theory.

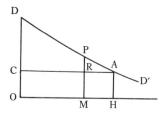

OH represents the amount sold in a large market at price AH.[58]
His habit of taking the geometrical approach to the study of these
problems and representing diminishing utility by the use of curves
and then drawing horizontals to show the point of marginal utility
left him an area of the curve far above the point of intersection, and
the question was: what does this area in the diagram represent?
It was easy to argue that it represented surplus satisfaction over and
above what the man actually has to pay. If he buys ten cups of tea
a day for which he pays 5d., and if he would be willing to pay 110d.
if necessary, he gets surplus satisfaction equal to 105d.

In one respect this runs counter to Jevons. Remember that Jevons
says that almost nothing is known about total utility. Does Marshall
think that very much can be known about total utility? His notion
of consumer's surplus looks as if it could actually measure in money
the amount of utility which a person would derive from the consumption of the first cup, the second, and so on down to the marginal
cup, and that by adding together all the satisfactions which successive cups yield the theorist gets at the total utility derived by the
individual from the consumption of tea measured in the money he
would be willing to pay. Does that mean that Marshall thinks economists know a great deal more about total utility than Jevons was
willing to admit they know? He says after going through this performance that theorists must not press it too hard; but he thinks
that economists know enough about consumer's surplus in the neighborhood of the marginal price to base upon the notion fairly important
conclusions regarding possible public policy; that is, he says that it
is schematizing things too much if the economist supposes that he
can get anything like a satisfactory measure of the surplus satisfaction upon the first cup or two of tea that a man buys; but when the
theorist gets down to the man's demand price for cups of tea in
the neighborhood of the marginal cup which he is in the habit of
buying, things begin to get fairly definite. The theorist has some
warrant in supposing that he can get tolerably reliable money measures of the consumer's surplus which people get from small changes
in the prices of their staple commodities occurring in the neighborhood of the prices which usually prevail.[59] That much is, in his eyes,

---

[58] Fig. 10, *Principles of Economics*, p. 128.

[59] [From his letters in 1889 on "Consumer's Surplus," which Marshall then called
"Consumer's Rent," it appears interestingly enough that he believed that Jevons
had confused "hedonics and economics." On November 26, 1889, he wrote to John
Neville Keynes, who was reading the proofs of the *Principles* that, "I regard Consumer's Rent as a sum of money not as an amount of utility. I hold that Jevons's
great error was that of applying to utility propositions that are only true of price. It

sufficiently definite, not only to be discussed by theorists but also to be taken into account in the plans of business men and of public officials.

What is relation of doctrine of consumer's and producer's surplus to Jevons? Development is along lines of marginal analysis. Idea not improbably suggested by diagrams such as Jevons used. But it was a development that went further than he was prepared to go. He held that we are in a position to know little about total utility. Marshall would admit that we may not know much about total utility but that we know something about utility in the neighborhood of the margin—market price—enough to suggest practical conclusions.[59a]

Marshall believes that whenever business men are led to a consideration of just where they should fix the price for almost anything they are offering for sale, they take into account the satisfaction that people get from the consumption of certain goods. A publisher, say, is considering whether to issue a forthcoming novel at $2.25 or $2.50 or $2.75. In thinking about that he tries to make the best guess that he can at what is going to be for him the maximum net revenue price; that is, the price that will bring him in the largest net receipts—not total receipts, but net receipts—over and above expenditures. To calculate the maximum net revenue price, first he has to consider how many copies people will buy at $2.25, $2.50 and $2.75, and to have any notion on this he has to have some opinions as to how strongly that book is likely to appeal to book buyers, and that is another way he has of saying he is thinking about the satisfaction, the gratification they will derive from using it.

is here that he thought himself most profound: and it is because I think that he was wrong in this one point in which he differed from his predecessors Von Thünen and Cournot that I consider his claims to greatness do not to any considerable extent rest on his *Theory of Political Economy*. I can see no connection between the loss of Consumer's Rent and the loss of Total Utility resulting from a tax, unless it is known whether the commodity taxed is one consumed by the rich, by the poor, or by all classes alike."

On December 2, he wrote Keynes: ". . . the very fact that my protest against Jevons's systematic confusion between the two—[hedonics and economics] has been (deliberately a silent one) makes me very anxious that my consumer's Rent should not be sewn up into his Total Utility. I had that prominently in mind when writing on the burden of a tax. I wanted to make clear that economic statistics had nothing to do with utility but only with its rough money measure."

In answer to Keynes's query "of the difficulty about the change of consumer's rent derived from other things consequent upon a diminished purchase of coals," he wrote, "If he spends less on coals, the marginal utility for other purchases will be affected to an *infinitesimal* degree—infinitesimal because the whole of this class of reasoning is strictly valid only on the assumption that the purchases under discussion are small relatively to the purchaser's whole wealth."

[The letters are in *Principles of Economics*, ninth (variorum) edition with annotations by C. W. Guillebaud, 2 volumes (London: Macmillan, 1961) I, pp. 260-261. Keynes's query is dealt with in *Principles of Economics*, p. 842.]

[59a] Outline, February 14, 1917.

So too, public officials who are considering such matters as the determination of postal rates, or are passing upon the rates for the service rendered by public utilities of all sorts, should always consider the sacrifices and satisfactions which are rendered to the communities which it is their duty to aid and direct. In imposing taxes such considerations are matters of great consequence. They should not be lost sight of in discussions of the tariff, property taxes, income taxes, etc.

[For clarification, the discussion of consumer's surplus can be presented in a slightly different way.] On Marshall's showing as already pointed out, the equilibria in the market established by business dealings result in paying out incomes to different individuals which are very unlike. That means that the marginal utility of money is different to different people. Meanwhile the prices that prevail in a market for a given kind of good at a given time may be taken as more or less uniform. Purchasers pay two cents for a newspaper; and the newsboy does not try to charge the first person more than the second because he knows that the second's income is five times the first's. There arises a nice problem about the relationship between the market prices that are uniform and the satisfactions which are derived by people who have incomes of different sizes.[60] That problem as previously noted, was doubtless brought to Marshall's attention when he began developing diagrammatic methods. Marshall in thinking about the diagram given above, concluded that the area, DCA represents something of considerable importance in modern life and he gave it the name, "consumer's surplus."[61] If a person buys twenty bags of peanuts in the course of a week and pays five cents for each, it represents the surplus of satisfactions that he gets from the consumption of peanuts over the sacrifices that he makes in laying out a dollar for twenty bags. In other words, it is an advantage that the buyer derives from living in a community where he can satisfy his

---

[60] Consumer's surplus according to Marshall would appear in an isolated economy. It becomes much greater for people of large incomes in a money economy because they can buy many goods at prices influenced by marginal demand of consumers of small incomes. (Outline, November 12, 1931.)

[61] *Principles of Economics*, Fig. 10, p. 128.

. . ."the price which a person pays for a thing can never exceed and seldom comes up to that for which he would be willing to pay rather than go without it. so that the satisfaction which he gets from the purchase generally exceeds that which he gives up in paying away its price; and he thus derives from the purchase a surplus of satisfaction. The excess of the price which he would be willing to pay rather than go without the thing, over that which he actually does pay, is the economic measure of this surplus satisfaction. It may be called *consumer's surplus.*" (*Principles of Economics*, p. 124) Quoted in Outline, "Marshall—Class Discussion II," no month, no day, 1917).]

desire for peanuts at a price which is less than he would be willing to pay if he bought only one bag.

The question is how much importance can he attach to the interpretation of this area in diagrams of the sort that are commonly used. The moment the economist begins to think about the reliability of the supposition that the buyer derives from the consumption of peanuts a degree of utility as indicated by the area, it becomes questionable. If a person is in the habit of buying twenty bags of peanuts a week, can he say, as a consumer of peanuts, that from any one of these bags he derives a satisfaction, the intensity of which is represented by the high point (D) of the curve? Perhaps if he could buy only one bag the satisfaction would be represented by the high point; but if he can eat peanuts to the extent of twenty bags a week, is he conscious at any time of so intense a degree of satisfaction? Is it not rather that the attitude the person has toward peanuts when he consumes this many, reacts upon and becomes characteristic of his attitude toward the first bag that he buys in the course of the week? That is, is not the whole shape of the curve altered by the fact that he carried his purchase to the point (D')? This is one difficulty with the diagram.

In the second place, the diagram will not mean a great deal to a socially-minded economist like Marshall unless he can use it to represent the feelings not only of a given individual but also of the people in the market. To a certain extent the reliability of the diagram becomes a little more genuine when the economist thinks of a large market in which there will be some people who can at a price of five cents get only a single bag. Those people perhaps get an intense satisfaction out of peanuts. If that is the case, then the economist might say that taking these people in the market all together it is proper to reckon that the surplus satisfaction that they get from peanuts corresponds to this area.

But Marshall points out that the theorist must remember that the marginal utility of money to different people is varying. If he tries to sum up the consumer's surplus that people in a whole market derive from the purchase of a certain commodity, he will be summing up satisfactions measured in money, but the common denominator has a different meaning to these different individuals. It is on the assumption that all the members of the group have incomes of the same amount that he can reckon up consumer's surpluses in that simple and direct fashion. That is, by neglecting "for the moment the fact that the same amount of money represents different amounts of pleasure to different people, we might measure the surplus satisfaction which the sale of tea affords, say, in the London Market, by the aggregate of the sums by what the prices shown in a complete list of demand prices for tea exceeds the selling price."][61a]

Even then Marshall says the notion of consumer's surplus is to be represented by conjectural diagrams. In his diagram, the demand curve is made to meet the vertical axis at the top. That is not common in drawing demand curves. It implies that there is a total limit to satisfaction derived, which can be measured by certain prices; and that the economist knows the rate at which the satisfaction to which he assigned a measure decreases. Those are facts which are not commonly known. Knowledge of the prices people will pay for successive units of goods and the amounts that will be sold, is limited then, to the area, of which there is actual experience; that is, to the area in which prices fluctuate in practice. In so far as the analysis is confined to areas along the demand curve within which there is some fairly definite knowledge of how prices are related to one another, the economist can make some practical use of the notion.

Just as Marshall believes that there is a measure of genuineness in the conception of consumer's surplus when considered with reference to points in the price scale not far from the prevailing rates, so he thinks there is validity in the sister conception of worker's or producer's surplus.

Producer's surplus. Labor ". . . if the price paid to him for doing any work is an adequate reward for that part which he does most unwillingly; and if, as generally happens, the same payment is given for that part of the work which he does less unwillingly and at less real cost to himself; then from that part he obtains a producer's surplus." (C. f., p. 527. Admitted here that man seldom thinks of himself as getting a producer's surplus. If so, is producer's surplus an important factor in determining wages? Patten's criticism [of Marshall's position] in "The Theory of Dynamic Economics." Is a surplus of pleasure over pain at the margin equal to sacrifice in spending time working instead of consuming? But does this criticism affect Marshall? Note his conception of what is involved in the "discommodity of labor," in Principles of Economics, p. 140 and especially p. 527.) Extra income earned by rare natural abilities may be regarded as a producer's surplus when one is analyzing the incomes of individuals, but not when one is considering the normal earnings of a trade, because high earnings of a few individuals affect the choice of that occupation by many, and therefore affect the supply of labor and therefore the long-period normal supply price of labor. Difficult to estimate worker's surplus because large part of his earnings are deferred payments for expense and trouble of his training.

[61a] [Principles of Economics, p. 128.]

"Nearly all his work may be pleasurable; and he may be earning a good wage for the whole of it; but in reckoning up the balance of human weal and endurance we must set off against this much effort and sacrifice endured by his parents and by himself in past time; but we cannot say clearly how much." (Marshall does not notice the theoretical difficulty involved here in setting off gratification derived by son from his earnings against sacrifice endured by his parents. Case of direct comparison between subjective sacrifices of different individuals.)

Saving. A capitalist "derives a saver's surplus through being remunerated for all his savings; that is, waiting, at the same rate as for that part which he is only just induced to undergo by the reward to be got for it."

Material appliances of production. Work and waiting by which they are provided yield their surpluses. In addition the appliances yield a surplus or quasi-rent of total money returned over direct outlay in *short periods*. But in *long periods* they yield no surplus over the surpluses of the workers and consumers who made them.

Land. True rent is a surplus in a sense in which the earnings from other agents are not. That is, land is not produced by labor and waiting; therefore its surplus cannot be analyzed into workers' and savers' surpluses. (Note that here we have a pecuniary surplus set side by side with a subjective surplus, in same way that Marshall gets total benefit of a monopoly by adding the consumer's surplus to monopoly net revenue. Also adds real cost of manufacturer to his money costs.)

Relation of producer's and consumer's surpluses. Not practically possible to reckon or add up consumer's surpluses and worker's and saver's surpluses. (Is this why Marshall makes little use of worker's and saver's surpluses?) What is case with producer's surplus from land? [See on land p. 832.][61b]

Marshall gets the basis of producer's surplus from studying the curve of increasing irksomeness of labor instead of the curve of diminishing utility derived from consumption. A man might be willing to work the first hour of a day for nothing just because it is more pleasant to work a little than to be idle. The second hour he might charge 1s., the third hour more, and so on until for the last hour he will perhaps insist upon a price of 10s. But in the market he will get for every hour the marginal price which he charges, just as in the market he buys all the units of the consumer's goods which he purchases at the marginal price. That means that the price for his first hour of work, 10s. represents a worker's surplus for him of 10s., because he would have been willing to work that hour for nothing. The second hour represents a worker's surplus of 9s., since he would have been willing to work for 1s. and gets 10s., and so on right through the day he gets a surplus upon every hour's work excepting the marginal hour. But he goes on working until the price that he receives is in equilibrium with the sacrifices that he undergoes.

[61b] "Marshall—Class Discussion II," no month, no day, 1917. Quotations from *Principles of Economics*, pp. 141, 830, 831.

S. Does not that seem to be an artificial distinction? Does the laborer ever think of his work in terms of hour units or total sacrifices. Is not the day the smallest unit he thinks of?

M. That may be. I am not able to meet the objection. It does seem to set the general artificiality of this conception of human nature in a clear light. I am inclined to take stronger exception to consumer's surplus on the ground that as far as experience goes no single box of matches that I consume yields the intense gratification which I would derive from a single box if I could not get the others. The first morsel of food I eat in a day, which might mean a difference of life and death if I could get no other, does not give me a world of bliss. Apparently the fact that I am well fed most of the time, probably over-fed, takes the edge off the kind of satisfaction in food which is imputed to one in these illustrations of the price that we would be willing to give for a single unit.[62] But to repeat, the facing of these things is serviceable because it helps us to realize the artificiality of the conception of human nature which underlies all such theorizing.

On the other hand it must be remembered that Marshall is willing to admit that comparatively little is known about consumer's demand prices or consumer's satisfactions save in the neighborhood of the prices at which people carry on their habitual dealings. It comes down to fairly close points. The business man and the economist know something about the quantity of goods people will take if the price is raised a little bit. The employer knows something about the more work he can get people to do if he gives them a little more wages. Down close to these points that are clear in people's minds because they are points with which they are continually dealing, people find it natural, not artificial, to believe that they get satisfaction at varying rates from increased or diminished stocks of commodities.

S. Is not that practically the same kind of feeling a person gets when he is getting a bargain?

M. That may be.

S. Is not that the basis of the feeling?

M. Maybe it is. Of course, that is not the kind of quantities Marshall has in mind. He seems to be thinking about the satisfaction from consuming the good. The satisfaction in a bargain might be separate.

---

[62] [Professor Mitchell's view has been developed in K. J. M. Tharakhan, "The Theory of Consumer's Surplus, A Defense," *Indian Journal of Economics,* January 1939, pp. 413-420, and "Consumer's Surplus, a Rejoinder," *Indian Journal of Economics,* January 1941, pp. 307-319; See also, H. E. Miller, "Utility Curves, Total Utility and Consumer's Surplus," *The Quarterly Journal of Economics,* February 1927, pp. 292-316.]

I do not know what a psychologist would say—whether the pleasure in the bargain is distinguishable from the consumption of the good or not. It might depend on what the good in question is. Maybe the buyer of rare books who never reads them gets most of the pleasure from the bargain.

S. How about the case of a man who would work for nothing for one hour but who would rather lose all the money he gets from the last hour rather than work that hour? That would set off the surplus in the beginning of his work.

M. Yes, Marshall mentions that case and admits that here and there the economist comes across a man who would much rather work eight than nine hours at the rate that is offered him but he is offered a job only on condition that he will work nine hours, and a man of that sort, says Marshall, suffers a producer's loss on his ninth hour.

S. A set-off in his surplus?

M. This would be for that individual. Marshall thinks that such cases are probably as rare as those of men who live in houses decidedly smaller or larger. Here and there is a man who would like to work longer at the rate of pay and another who prefers to work not so long at that wage, but both men have to fit into the scheme of work offered and one is robbed of the worker's surplus which he would get if he could work for another hour, and the other has imposed upon him a producer's loss.

There is another matter in this connection. Marshall warns of adding up a producer's surplus and a consumer's surplus for the same person under the same circumstance; that is, if the theorist computes that a certain man gets a producer's surplus of, say, 40s. on a day's work, the theorist is not in a position to figure up all the consumer's surplus the worker gets in spending the 40s. on different things and say that the total surplus is equal to the sum of the two. The producer's surplus includes the consumer's surplus and *vice versa;* that is, when a theorist sets up a producer's surplus of 40s. on the day's work, he arrives at that by thinking of the gratifications which the worker obtains by spending the 40s. over and above the sacrifices which are involved in the marginal interval of work. It is only because he can spend the money and get things that are going to give him gratification that the theorist can get a money estimate of the producer's surplus; that is, it is only by thinking of his position as a consumer that his surplus as a worker can be reckoned and *vice versa.*

[To use Marshall's words in the *Principles,* "These two sets of surpluses are not independent; and it would be easy to reckon them up so as to count the same thing twice. For when we have reckoned the producer's surplus at the value of the general purchasing power which he derives from his labour or saving, we have reckoned implicitly his consumer's surplus too, provided his character and the circumstances of his environment are given. This difficulty might be avoided analytically; but in no case would it be practically possible to estimate and add up the two series."]

To Marshall (let me add another comment of my own) it is obvious that these money measures of consumer's surplus and producer's surplus are the most individual of affairs. If a person has very large means, the theorist will have to figure out enormous money measures of his consumer's surplus because he would, if he had to, in order to get a single item, be willing to pay an extremely high price for it. On the other hand, if a man has slender means the largest consumer's surplus the theorist can figure out for his first morsel of food would be represented only by the little amount of money that he has. His money measure of consumer's surplus may be a thousand or a million times smaller than the measure of the consumer's surplus of a person of great wealth. This is another indication of the fact that the notion is of such a character that it can be given a real significance in the analysis of practical problems only in cases of small changes which take place in the neighborhood of the prices that people do in practice usually pay.

Could you supply data from which consumer's surplus of any commodity you habitually use could be constructed? Marshall, to repeat, admits that we can estimate it only in the neighborhood of actual prices. (What is consumer's surplus of air?) How much reality can we attach to those surpluses as representing conscious surplus satisfaction? Not very much it would seem. Our desires for first increments in supply do not have the keenness which the diagrams suggest. But see Marshall's footnote, p. 126. Marshall, to repeat, is aware of this difficulty and declines to press the interpretation. Holds that the idea of surpluses has real meaning only in the neighborhood of the equilibrium points. But even at that the idea is important in his eyes as representing a point at which the economist can carry his analysis into the field of the real forces; c. f., pp. 131-133, Bernouilli's suggestion, p. 130.

Idea difficult to use analytically, for we cannot add consumer's and producer's surpluses. Cannot even add consumer's surpluses on different goods: for if we had to pay much more for bread, we would have less to spend on tea, salt, etc., and our consumer's surpluses on latter would shrink. Cannot represent consumer's surplus of market by diagram unless we neglect difference of marginal utility of money to different people (see *Principles of Economics*, p. 128).[63]

The discussion will now turn to the second problem: Marshall's position on the tax and the bounty. Can some member of the class explain how it is that the satisfaction of the community can be increased, by levying a tax on industries of diminishing returns and giving the money to industries of increasing returns? How can a gain in satisfaction for the community be realized in that way?

The thing is argued out in this manner: If a tax be imposed on industries of diminishing returns the marginal supply price will rise because that will be the cost of production in the long run plus the tax. But just because it is an industry of diminishing returns the sum that is added to the marginal supply price will be less than the amount of the tax. Why? Because when the supply price is raised and the amount that people will buy is cut down, the supply which is still utilized can be produced under better conditions. If the industry in question is agriculture, then some of the poorer lands can go out of cultivation. The lands still under the plow need not be cultivated so intensively; that is, the marginal cost of producing the commodity which is still used does not rise by the amount of the tax. The net result of the operation is to increase the marginal supply price, but less than the tax by the amount of the saving effected by the production of the marginal units on lands which are very fertile and yield relatively larger return than that given by the marginal units when a larger supply was turned out. The increase in the supply price is less than the amount of the tax.

The tax is then distributed over industries of increasing returns. This effects a reduction in the price of these commodities which is greater than the amount of the bounty. By giving the bounty the cost is reduced. That increases the amount that people will buy, and now since a larger supply is being produced the cost of production drops more than the bounty. Therefore, the reduction of the satisfaction derived from the consumption of the commodity which is produced under the law of diminishing returns is substantially less than

---

[63] Outline, November 12, 1931; "Marshall—Class Discussion II," no month, no day, 1917.

["The Marshallian analysis is open to the criticism to which all cardinal utility analysis is subject, namely that it assumes the commensurability of utility. In addition, it is based on the objectionable assumption of a constant marginal utility of money; in modern terminology, it fails to account for the "income effect" resulting from price changes. This led . . . to its rehabilitation [in 1940] by Professor J. R. Hicks." (G. J. Malanos, "Early Cardinal Utility Theory," Georgia State College of Business Administration, *Bulletin*, no. 8, October 1960, p. 24. Sir John Hicks is Drummond Professor of Political Economy at Oxford.]

the increase of satisfaction from consuming of the amount produced under conditions of increasing returns. As for case of constant returns, the tax decreases consumer's surplus more than it increases the revenue of the state, for consumers lose consumer's surplus on part of supply interrupted. The gain in consumer's surplus from bounty is less than the cost to the state.[64]

S. Does the amount of the gain depend upon the elasticity of the demand for the commodity?

M. Oh, yes. It is supposed that the article produced under conditions of increasing returns will be one which people will want to obtain in decidedly increased quantities if they can get it at some lower price.

Marshall admits that complicated questions intrude upon anyone seriously considering this particular policy. He also points out that the cost of administering the scheme would have to be subtracted. He further states that it might divert the attention of business men from the industrial task of managing to influencing the officials who administer the bounty.[65] But this proposition again is worth considering, mainly because it helps to provide a clearer light upon the sort of uses to which Marshall's type of economic analysis can be put.

> or satisfaction. 2. Realistic? Taking the theory on its own terms, does it describe the facts of actual experience? Does the man rich enough to get all the tea he wants really derive more gratification from the consumption of tea than the same man would if he could afford but little tea? Does not the knowledge that he can have ten cups if he likes, and the practice of taking two or three react on his enjoyment of the first cup? i.e., is not this a clear case [to use John Stuart Mill's terminology] of chemical combination among elements in the situation instead of physical addition?
>
> Recapitulation of criticism of consumer's and producer's surpluses. 1. Hedonistic? Certainly a theory of what goods do to men, instead of what men do with goods. Makes man the passive element. This situation remains true whether one calls the effect which consumption produces pleasure

---

[64] Last two sentences from Outline, "Marshall—Class Discussion, II," no month, no day, 1917. [In recent terminology, Marshall's argument is as follows: a tax on a commodity produced under conditions of constant cost would yield less than the loss of consumer's surplus. If the commodity is produced under increasing costs, the tax might return more than the loss of consumer's surplus. In decreasing-cost industries, the loss to consumer's surplus would be greater than for constant-cost industries. The reverse would hold in the case of bounties.]

[65] [The authorities "would have to reckon up the direct and indirect costs of collecting a tax and administering a bounty; the difficulty of securing that the burdens of the tax and the benefits of the bounty were equally distributed; the openings for fraud and corruption; and the danger that in the trade that had received a bounty and in other trades which hoped to get one, people would divert their energies from managing their own businesses to managing those persons who control the bounties. Besides these semi-ethical questions there will arise others of a strictly economic nature, relating to the effects which any particular tax or bounty may exert on the interests of landlords, urban, or agricultural, who own land adapted for the production of the commodity in question." (Marshall, *Principles of Economics*, p. 473).]

Marshall would admit that those questions must be answered "yes"; but he would hold that his theory assumes everything to remain the same save that more units of tea are allowed to the man; that is, his appetite for tea must not be changed except in so far as its intensity is diminished by drinking successive cups. But that is exactly the point of the criticism. His initial appetite for tea on any afternoon is inevitably changed. We cannot keep the individual from feeling the reflex influence of his abundance on his appetite—not only at the margin where he stops drinking but all through his scale; c.f., what Marshall says about "the fulness of life." Is not this a case of breakdown of hedonism? i.e., units with which we deal change their quality under our hands because what man does reacts on his sensitiveness to pleasure; c. f., Marshall's remarks on activities and wants. This criticism then is not directed against the logical consistency of the conception but against its realism and hence its usefulness in accounting for economic phenomena. It makes the consumer static with a vengeance. Can we test the theory by supposing successive increments taken away from the consumer? Is the gratification he loses by deprivation of a habitual form of consumption equivalent to addition made to his gratification by addition of units earlier? Marshall would answer "not necessarily"; that is, would point again to limits of the concept in time, etc.

Theoretical use of doctrine of consumer's surplus: (1) To estimate roughly benefit which a person derives from his environment. (2) Suggestion of tax on industries of decreasing returns with proceeds providing bounties to industries of increasing returns; i.e., consumer's surplus is a factor of importance in welfare and therefore in public policy. (3) Total benefit of monopoly is sum of monopoly revenue plus consumer's surplus. Consumer's surplus must be considered by municipal monopolies and may be considered by business monopolies anxious to extend market; that is, monopolist while aiming immediately at maximum net revenue in money, may have occasion to consider consumer's surplus.

Addendum on the question of adding producer's and consumer's surplus. Marshall says they cannot be added. Tucker [a student] says they can, if we take a case free from money economy. Gives example of a lone fisherman under following suppositions:

	Disutility of labor	Number of fish caught	Utility of fish caught will be
1st hour	0	2	6
2nd hour	1	2	4
3rd hour	2	2	2
	3	6	12

Argues labor surplus at end of third hour is 3 (three what?). Consumer's surplus at end of third hour 6 (six what?). Total surplus at end third hour is 9.

Discussion: If we are to add these two surpluses they must be in similar units. In what units are we measuring each kind of surplus? In fish, or in units of feeling? Measured in fish, producer's surplus is indeed three fish; what is consumer's surplus in fish? The example does not afford data for answering, because the only utilities given are utilities of fish themselves, and of course we cannot say how many fish the utility of fish equal. Hence cannot solve the problem in terms of fish. Measured in units of feeling, producer's surplus clearly nine units. For three units of disagreeable feeling the fisherman gets twelve units of agreeable feeling. Consumer's surplus is also nine units. For fisherman gets first 6 units of agreeable feeling at a price of 0 units; second four units at a price of one unit; third two units at a price of two units; and summation of these differences equals nine. Now we are at liberty to reckon the fisherman's surplus in either way but not in both ways. Therefore conclude that we cannot add producer's surplus and consumer's surplus under these circumstances. What blocks Tucker's method of computation here is that the example does not permit measurement of consumer's surplus in fish. To test case further let us suppose that above schedule represents money values of disutilities and utilities as follows:

	Disutility of labor in $'s	Value of fish caught in $'s	Utility of fish caught each hour in $'s
First hour	$0	$2	$6
Second hour	$1	$2	$4
Third hour	$2	$2	$2
	$3	$6	$12

Now may we not say that his producer's surplus is equal to $3? and his consumer's surplus equals $6? Computation is as follows:

Producer's surplus	Money that he would take	Money that he does get	Measure of producer's surplus in $'s
First hour	$0	$2	$2
Second hour	$1	$2	$1
Third hour	$2	$2	$0
	$3	$6	$3

Consumer's surplus	Money that he would give	Money for which he could buy fish	Consumer's surplus in $'s
First hour	$6	$2	$4
Second hour	$4	$2	$2
Third hour	$2	$2	$0
	$12	$6	$6

Now may we not add these sums and say that his total surplus is $9? If we suppose that our fisherman is a sportsman with abundant supply of money from other sources than fishing, then the above suppositions are possible and the conclusion drawn from them is legitimate. But if we take case of man who is living from his exertions at fishing we (1) cannot draw up a statement of what he would give for fish without reference to the amount of his income and to the sacrifice at which each dollar is gained. That is, we cannot separate the consideration of the data from which consumer's surplus is computed from consideration of the data from which producer's surplus is computed; e.g., if above man earns only $6 per day we cannot assume that he could give $12 for his fish as food. Change supposition to following—that he would give for first hour's catch $3. (2) Similarly we cannot draw up a statement of what he would take for each hour of labor without reference to cost of what he consumes and utility of each increment of supply. That is, producer's surplus is involved in consumer's surplus and *vice versa*. If the two forms of surplus are thus dependent upon each other we cannot safely add them. In above addition we have implicitly assumed that producer's surplus equals $3 to a man with $6 income; that consumer's surplus equals $6 to a man with $12 to spend. Clearly we cannot properly compare these two men.

Can we change the suppositions so as to avoid this absurdity? That is, can we draw up a schedule of what the man would give for commodities bought under following conditions which are practically imposed by life? (1) Total sum he would give must not exceed total income (equals number of hours worked times wages per hour). (2) Sum offered for last unit of commodities bought must equal money value of last hour's disutility which also equals pay per hour. (If he would not give equivalent of last hour's pay for further commodities he would not undergo the corresponding disutility to obtain it.) Such a supposition cannot be drawn up; for sum offered for last unit of commodity bought must equal pay of last hour, the sums offered for earlier increments cannot be greater than that for the last, without being greater also than pay for last hour and therefore being greater than total income. Is this conclusion a *reductio ad absurdam* of whole notion of consumer's surplus? It does show that one cannot reckon consumer's surplus on whole of consumption when consumption practically equals income. But people may reckon consumer's surplus on single articles, for with reference to these men could devote a larger portion of money income to purchase, by withdrawing it from other uses, and hence by altering consumer's surplus income and consumer's surplus on other articles.[66]

Let us continue with Marshall by seeing what substantive results he finally reached. These conclusions are from the point of view of a great many students of economics, one finds on Ph. D. examinations, very puzzling and troublesome, for he does not sum up his conclusions in a form that can be memorized when cramming. On the contrary, he refuses to bind himself to any cut and dried propositions but insists continuously upon taking the view that economists are dealing with

---

[66] Outlines, February 7, 1917, "Marshall—Class Discussion II," no month, no day, 1917.

an enormously complicated situation in which the opposing forces are mutually determining one another; therefore, it is impossible to say that any one factor in a given situation causes any other factor. He will have none of the results such as Jevons gives in his *catena* that cost of production determines supply, that supply determines final degree of utility and that final degree of utility determines value. That very *catena,* to repeat, is one of Marshall's favorite targets of attack. He says it leads to an erroneous attitude toward the discussion of the central problem of economic theory. Economists to be considered such must accustom themselves to seeing the many in the one and the one in the many. A few of his definite statements make that proposition a little more specific. The first concerns the theory of value. He says:

> In this world therefore every plain and simple doctrine as to the relations between cost of production, demand and value is necessarily false; and the greater the appearance of lucidity which is given to it by skilful exposition, the more mischievous it is.[67]

Consequently the student must not expect to see Marshall giving a plain and simple doctrine on the subject of value or on any other subject in theory. If the student finds any such statements of plain and simple and lucid doctrine in any other authority he may be sure that in Marshall's eyes they are worse than useless; they are positively mischievous because they get the student into the habit of thinking of problems in a way which necessarily blinds him to the fundamental nature of economic activities.

In so far as the complexity grows out of a confusing conception of the problem, the fault is Marshall's. In so far as it grows out of the inherent difficulties of the problem the fault is that of the subject matter—or if you like the immaturity of the science. But an honest recognition of complexity is better than an elegant simplicity gained by glossing over difficulties. If you can, give by all means a simple explanation; but if you cannot reduce the phenomena to a simple orderliness in fact, do not pretend that you can. Be true to the facts as you see them first and elegantly simple (if you can) second.[68]

Here is another statement in which Marshall tries to make his position lucid, in a sense simple, by means of illustrations:

> The amount of the thing and its price, the amounts of the several factors or agents of production used in making it, and their prices— all these elements mutually govern one another, and if an external cause should alter any one of them the effect of the disturbance extends to all the others.
>
> In the same way, when several balls are lying in a bowl, they mutually govern one another's positions; and again when a heavy

---

[67] *Principles of Economics,* p. 368.
[68] Outline, January 9, 1918.

weight is suspended by several elastic strings of different strengths and lengths (all of them being stretched) attached to different points in the ceiling, the equilibrium positions of all the strings and of the weight mutually govern one another. If any one of the strings is shortened, everything else will change its position, and the length and the tension of every other string will be altered also.[69]

To repeat: as Marshall leaves the problem of value, it is a complex of forces which for convenience of analysis can be summarized in two great categories: demand and supply, equated at a price; but in which all the forces of demand and supply, and the price at which they are equated are continually determining one another. It will not do to say that cost of production determines price, even in the long run. To say that demand or marginal utility determines price, even in the short run, is incorrect. To say that the amount of the demand is controlled by price, whether in the short run or the long run will not do. No one of these plain, simple statements can be accepted. To attack the problem of value seriously, the student must work himself up to the point where he will face that problem in all its inherent complexity, and come out with an attitude toward it, rather with a set of conclusions concerning it—the attitude being that it is a problem in which there are a considerable number of factors, every one of which helps to determine every other factor.

The underlying logic of Marshall's work is much like that of Léon Walras, of whom a little was said in the discussion of Jevons, and more will be said later. His way of solving the problem of value at a given time was to set up a grand array of simultaneous equations and to demonstrate that the number of such equations that could be set up at any given time was equal to the number of unknowns presented by the problem and therefore the problem was theoretically solvable. This is a sort of mathematical variation of Marshall's view. The theorist has a set of simultaneous equations each one of which is capable of being solved in terms of all the others—not by itself but in terms of all the others. Here is Marshall saying the same thing in language that seems a little simpler but which leaves the reader with the same view of a situation in which there are many forces all of which are helping not only to solve the problem of price but also to determine each other.

Marshall's theory of distribution is an application of his theory of value to special cases: Putting a value upon the services of a man who works for another at wages; upon the uses of funds which one man

---

[69] *Principles of Economics*, p. 526.

lends to another for interest; upon the uses of land which one puts at the disposal of another under a lease; and finally upon the services of business organizers. All these problems which Ricardo treated as distribution problems and for which he laid down laws that had no organic connection with his laws of value, all the problems which John Stuart Mill continued to treat as separate in character from the laws of value, which he discussed before he expounded his theory of value—all these laws in Marshall's hands became special problems under the general head of value.

As regards the theory of distribution in the large, Marshall says that the problem of distribution concerns the way in which the national dividend is divided among the several factors of production. That notion of the national dividend is often treated as one of Marshall's important contributions to economic theory. By it he seems to mean substantially what Ricardo doubtless meant when he talked about the annual produce of the country's workers. It includes the sum total of the material and immaterial goods which a country produces in the course of a year.

The national dividend is on the one side the result of the coopera- tion of all the factors of production—land, labor, capital, business ability—and on the other side it is to be divided up among all these factors. The problem of distribution is how the shares in the national dividend are determined. They are determined through a process of putting a price on labor, on loans, on rent and on business ability— a price which in some cases is bargained for in the market, and in other cases is not. That is, if a person works his own farm he does not make any bargain about the rent value of the farm; if he uses his own capital, he does not make a bargain about the rate of interest; if he is a man in business on his own account, he does not make a bargain with anybody about his salary as a business organizer. But in society, as it is now, bargains are continually being made which put a price on the use of land, loans, business ability; and these prices provide tolerably clear information about the basis on which the shares of capitalists, the landlords and the business organizers are determined. Marshall presents this in good set terms:

> The net aggregate of all the commodities produced is itself the true source from which flow the demand price for all these commodi- ties, and therefore for the agents of production used in making them. Or, to put the same thing in another way, this national dividend is at once the aggregate net product of, and the sole source of payment for, all the agents of production within the country: it is divided up into earnings of labour; interest of capital; and lastly the pro- ducer's surplus, or rent, of land and of other differential advan-

tages for production. It constitutes the whole of them, and the whole of it is distributed among them; and the larger it is, the larger, other things being equal, will be share of each of them.[70]

So much on the problem of distribution as a whole. The discussion will now turn to particular factors—wages, to begin with. "Wages," says Marshall,

tend to equal the net product of . . . labour. They are not governed by that net product; for net products, like all other incidents of marginal uses, are governed together with value by the general relations of demand and supply.[71]

On the other side, wages tend to retain a close though indirect relation with the cost of rearing and sustaining the energy of efficient labor. Wages are governed neither by demand price, nor by supply price, but, to repeat, "are governed together with value by the general relations of demand and supply."

Note once again his insistence that the theorist cannot arrive at any simple statement concerning the fundamental economic problems which possesses any degree of validity. Most of the substantive contentions of theorists in the past concerning wages, on Marshall's showing, are justified in some degree. People who tried to demonstrate that wages are regulated by the cost of rearing, training and sustaining energetic and efficient labor have a part of the truth, but if they lay that down as the law of wages they are mistaken. Those who say that wages are regulated by the marginal productivity of labor are right in the sense that that is perhaps the most important factor in determining the demand price of labor; but if they stop with this proposition, they are far from showing anything like the whole truth. There are two great sets of forces which affect the price of labor: demand and supply prices. More than that, these two great forces keep affecting each other. And even more than that, what can go to any one of the sharers in production, such as labor, is dependent upon the size of the national dividend which is the cooperative work of all the factors of production together, and upon the various influences which determine the shares of capital and land and business ability. It is a faithful attempt, on the part of a man who had a strong realistic bent and a deep, serious ethical interest in these problems, to see them in all their complexity and not to indulge in simplifications which, though they may add to the elegance of a disquisition, are conducive to grave misunderstanding.

Thus in another passage on wages, Marshall writes

---

[70] *Principles of Economics*, p. 536.
[71] *Principles of Economics*, p. 538.

To conclude this part of our argument. The market price of every-thing, i.e. its price for short periods, is determined mainly by the relations in which the demand for it stands to the available stocks of it; and in the case of any agent of production, whether it be a human or a material agent, this demand is 'derived' from the demand for those things which it is used in making. In these rela-tively short periods fluctuations in wages follow and do not pre-cede, fluctuations in the selling prices of the goods produced.

But the incomes which are being earned by all agents of produc-tion, human as well as material, and those which appear likely to be earned by them in the future, exercise a ceaseless influence on those persons by whose action the future supplies of these agents are determined. There is a constant tendency towards a position of normal equilibrium in which the supply of each of these agents shall stand in such a relation to the demand for its services, as to give to those who have provided the supply a sufficient reward for their efforts and sacrifices.

By a sufficient reward is meant a reward sufficient to induce them to make the sacrifices and efforts to produce the supply in question. He continues:

If the economic conditions of the country remained stationary suffi-ciently long, this tendency would realize itself in such an adjustment of supply to demand, that both machines and human beings would earn generally an amount that corresponded fairly with their cost of rearing and training, conventional necessaries as well as those things which are strictly necessary being reckoned for. But conven-tional necessaries might change under the influence of non-economic causes, even while economic conditions themselves were stationary; and this change would affect the supply of labour, and would lessen the national dividend and slightly alter its distribution. As it is, the economic conditions of the country are constantly changing, and the point of adjustment of normal demand and supply in relation to labour is constantly being shifted.[72]

This is a warning that in addition to the complexity arising from the mutual determination of all the factors there is the complexity which consists in the different aspects which the problem wears with refer-ence to short or long periods. The analysis, if a thoroughgoing one, covers both aspects of how the price of a factor of production is determined at a given moment and over a long period, and also what is the character of the transition between these two types of problems.

On interest, Marshall says:

Thus then interest, being the price paid for the use of capital in any market, tends towards an equilibrium level such that the ag-gregate demand for capital in that market, at that rate of interest, is equal to the aggregate stock forthcoming there at that rate. . . .
An extensive increase in the demand for capital in general will there-fore be met for a time not so much by an increase of supply as by a rise in the rate of interest, which will cause capital to withdraw itself partially from those uses in which its marginal utility is lowest. It is

---

[72] *Principles of Economics*, pp. 576-577.

only slowly and gradually that the rise in the rate of interest will increase the total stock of capital.[73]

The increase in total stock of capital will react upon the going rate of interest, of course; that is, with reference to interest as with reference to wages, the price at any given time is the net resultant of two great sets of opposing forces: those concerned with demand and supply prices. Both forces are continually influencing each other. The elements in each which are practically important differ as one considers short periods or long periods. For long periods account must be taken of changes in the supply of capital which are produced at a cost, namely, the cost of waiting, involving sacrifices by savers. There is a tendency in the case of interest, as in the case of wages, towards an equilibrium in the long run between the marginal price received by those who save capital and the marginal sacrifices undergone in saving, at least in the case of the marginal saver.

In the case of rent, Marshall is inclined to hold, much more strongly than most modern theorists, to the classical position that rent is a category different in character from capital. A considerable number of writers, some of whom will be discussed later, say that to all intents and purposes in modern economic life all the durable material factors of production stand on substantially the same footing as a business proposition and should be treated in the same way in economic theory; that is, there is fundamentally no theoretical distinction between land on the one side and capital on the other. Marshall, however, says:

> Land is on a different footing from man himself and those agents of production which are made by man; among which are included improvements made by him on the land itself. For while the supplies of all other agents of production respond in various degrees and various ways to the demand for their services, land makes no such response. Thus an exceptional rise in the earnings of any class of labour, tends to increase its numbers, or efficiency, or both; and the increase in the supply of efficient work of that class tends to cheapen the services which it renders to the community.[74]

But an increase in the demand for land will not have such effect; it will not lead to an increase in the amount of land. Some modern economists would take a different view, as said before. For purposes of economic theory, land is not a certain area, it is an economic factor. If one is thinking about soil for agricultural purposes, differences in its quality become enormously important, and soils are made under modern conditions almost just as truly, the extremist would say, as factories are. Marshall holds that land does not increase that way:

---

[73] *Principles of Economics,* p. 534.
[74] *Principles of Economics,* pp. 534-535.

> While therefore the value of land, in common with the values of other agents of production, is subject to those influences which were discussed towards the end of the preceding chapter; it is not subject to those which have been brought into the reckoning in the present discussion.

It is subject to changes in demand, but not subject in the same way to changes in supply.

> It is true that land is but a particular form of capital from the point of view of the individual manufacturer or cultivator. And land shares the influences of the laws of demand and of substitution which were discussed in the last chapter, because the existing stock of it, like the existing stock of capital or of labour of any kind, tends to be shifted from one use or another till nothing could be gained for production by any further shifting. And, so far as the discussions of the last chapter are concerned, the income that is derived from a factory, a warehouse, or a plough (allowance being made for wear-and-tear, etc.) is governed in the same way as is the income from land.

In short, this holds, once those instruments of production are produced.

> In each case the income tends to equal the value of the marginal net product of the agent; in each case this is governed for the time by the total stock of the agent and the need that other agents have of its aid.
>
> That is one side of the question. The other is that land (in an old country) does not share the reflex influences, discussed in this chapter, which a high rate of earning exerts on the supply of other agents of production.[75]

There remains, therefore, from Marshall's point of view, an important element of truth in the old differential theory of rent that is ordinarily called the Ricardian theory.

To round out the discussion of distribution it is desirable to return to another and final statement of Marshall's position on the theory of distribution as a whole. The national dividend is distributed among the factors of production.

> Other things being equal, each agent is likely to increase the faster, the larger the share which it gets, unless indeed it is not capable of being increased at all.

The latter was a saving clause put in for the benefit of land. He continues:

> But every such increase will do something towards filling up the more urgent needs for that agent; and will thus lessen the marginal need for it, and lower the price at which it can find a market. That is to say, an increase in the proportionate share, or rate of remuneration, of any agent is likely to bring into play forces, that will reduce that share, and leave a larger proportionate share of the dividend

---

[75] *Principles of Economics*, p. 535.

to be shared among others. This reflex action may be slow. But, if there is no violent change in the arts of production or in the general economic condition of society, the supply of each agent will be closely governed by its cost of production; account being taken of those conventional necessaries, which constantly expand as the growing richness of the national income yields to one class after another an increasing surplus above the mere necessaries for efficiency.[76]

S. What was Marshall's chief contribution to economics? Was it the idea of the national dividend?

M. The term "national dividend" should not be regarded as one of his chief contributions. On the other hand, the general view of the necessity of taking into account the inter-relations among all the factors in any value problem and of knowing how a value problem changes its aspects as the inquiry shifts from short periods into long periods, is his chief contribution to economic theory. Put it this way: The general tendency of economists before Marshall was to take one of two grounds on the fundamental problem; to say value in the long run is determined by cost of production; or by final degree of utility (or in Austrian terminology, by marginal utility). He maintains that both theories help provide insight into the problem; each has a measure of truth, but neither contains the whole truth. The theorist must combine the two. Because of this notion a charge of eclecticism was brought against Marshall. He was very much annoyed by the charge. He felt that this is not eclecticism; it is simply being honest and looking at the situation as a whole.

S. What are the differences between the theories set forth by Marshall and those set forth in the ordinary college text; for instance, *Outlines of Economics* by Richard T. Ely, T. S. Adams, Max O. Lorenz and Allyn A. Young?[77]

M. I do not know. My guess is that inasmuch as the theoretical sequence in that treatise was composed by Allyn A. Young that they are very good Cantabrigian doctrines and follow Marshall. I do not know that I ever read that text.

S. Are modern economists holding the opinions of Marshall?

M. There are two or three different ways of looking at all these problems, so that one cannot make a valid statement about what modern theorists believe on the fundamental problems. That matter is at least as complex as the theory of distribution at which Marshall arrives.

---

[76] *Principles of Economics*, pp. 536-537.

[77] [This was the most popular textbook from the 1890's to the close of the 1920's.]

It may be said, that he has probably exercised more influence upon the formulation of systematic theory at the present time than any other writer. He has a large number of faithful followers, particularly in England, and a considerable number in other countries.

S. Isn't there a so-called Cambridge school?

M. Yes, Marshall succeeded to the place which was held by John Stuart Mill, earlier by Ricardo, and still earlier by Adam Smith as the great representative of orthodox theory; and people who have some questions in their mind about the adequacy of his discussion exhibit feelings regarding his influence similar to those of Jevons toward Mill.

S. Can you suggest a reference to a classification of economists such as classicists, neo-classicists, etc.?

M. I do not think anything has been worked out with special care that is particularly notable. In *The History and Prospects of the Social Sciences* that was edited by Harry Elmer Barnes (1925), the article on economics by K. W. Bigelow of Harvard offers a classification which is as interesting as any.[78] I use such labels myself, but it is not wise to tie too closely to classifications of that character for the reason that all who have any degree of original ability have been influenced by their great predecessors who approached the problem in different ways for different purposes in a different spirit. In the treatment of certain specific problems the student may occupy rather definitely a position, as a modern Ricardian, in other topics his views may be different. The classifier would have to pick out some particular problem in economic theory and study the specific attitude of writers toward it in order to make a classification that would hold, and then he would find that unless he is strongly commended by temperament to such schematic work he will have a good many reservations about the particular box into which each writer will fit.

S. Can anything be made of Marshall's practical applications?

M. Yes, he is right in saying that the economist in most economic problems continually deals with a somewhat vague notion concerning the effect of changes in price in the neighborhood of prevalent rates upon economic behavior. The theorist's speculations of what people will do as prices move up or down a bit imply, whether they are conscious of it or not, some sort of notion as to how important an article is in the minds of buyers and sellers; that is, they fall back upon what is equivalent to Marshall's notion of consumer's surplus.

---

[78] [Bigelow later left economics to enter the field of education at Teacher's College, Columbia University.]

S. Would you mind saying a few words about the way Marshall uses the levels of analysis [which you presented in the discussion of Ricardo, for example]?

M. Most of his theorizing moves on the monetary level, but he thinks his discussion in money terms is important, first with reference to its bearing upon such commodity concepts as the national dividend; and second, and more important, upon his concept of sacrifices and gratifications. Since he began work in economics with an ethical interest and maintained it to his closing days—the important thing, from his point of view, is not the sacrifices and the gratifications that people get—it is the fullness of their lives. The means of a good life is what he thinks should be the feature of the aim of every citizen, and in a sense the aim of the economist. But he is one of the people who hold that the theorist is much more likely to make a useful scientific contribution toward understanding the conditions under which a good life for the mass of the people can be obtained, if while he is carrying on the economic analysis he does not mix in ethical issues with his formulations.

Levels of analysis: Well being? Used as ultimate criterion of results achieved by economic activities but not as basis of explanation; c.f., criticism of working of pecuniary institutions. Money prices, commodities, or subjective feelings?

Have seen what Marshall means by declaring that "money is the center around which economic science clusters." Levels of economic analysis; common view in past: Money level superficial; commodity level more significant; psychic level fundamental. Difficulty with the commodity level: we need a common denominator for different commodities, only one available is money; in practice commodity level involves talk about "values"; money of unchanging purchasing power. Difficulties with psychic level: 1. Psychological—we have lost faith in hedonism. 2. Economic—does it not matter how much or how little feeling is behind a money demand of one shilling? "Money talks." These difficulties raise problem of relation between "real forces" and "money prices" in economic theory.

Marshall's discussion is largely realistic; i.e., concerned with actual processes by which prices are fixed and money incomes determined. In so far analysis runs on *monetary level;* e.g., discussion of prime and supplementary costs; effect of decline of demand on prices in short and long periods; prime and total costs in relation to joint products. (Commodity level: Effects of different forms of land tenure; general influence of economic progress, particularly in England since Industrial Revolution). In this realistic analysis the business man is the central figure and business man commonly takes money payments as guide to his actions. Still, even he has to consider real cost of his own labor, and in a measure of other things. And monopolist, while aiming immediately at maximum net revenue in money, may have occasion to consider consumer's surpluses. But after all, business man is only the medium through which the social forces work. These forces the business man feels in pecuniary form.

Real forces are to be found only by penetrating to a deeper level of analysis. Ultimate basis of demand and supply. Demand based on desire for commodities. Supply depends mainly on overcoming of unwillingness to labor and to wait. Note "fundamental principles of human nature which economists have to accept as facts." Real vs. money cost of production: Definitions: Where each one is appropriate; c.f., discussion of ultimate factors in supply price of labor. Must consider "net advantages" [of jobs] not mere money wages. Elements of real costs which are commonly neglected by men and disregarded by society; i.e., which can be taken into account not as explaining what happens, but as stating results in terms of welfare. True vs. nominal interest, [in this discussion] verbally Marshall here contents himself with the commodity level of analysis. Real income— distinctly a subjective magnitude, though he does not speak of psychic income. But do these real forces adequately explain actual pecuniary phenomena? No. Meaning of this passage not altogether clear. Let us analyze by taking, e.g., money prices of commodities as the pecuniary phenomena to be explained and consider them as Marshall does with reference to periods of different length.

1. Temporary equilibrium of demand and supply. Case of person satisfying one of his wants by his own effort. Are no pecuniary phenomena to be explained; is an equilibrium between real forces—desire and effort (sacrifice). Psychological criticism: Does boy stop picking berries because effort equals satisfaction, or because his attention is diverted? If reduced to hedonistic terms would not opportunity cost (sacrifice of doing something else) serve better than effort? Does not Marshall say this? Boy's "eagerness to play and his disinclination for the work of picking counterbalance the desire for eating."

2. Case of barter: There are prices resulting—though not in money. Generally is no true equilibrium of supply and demand; but usually a margin of satisfaction on either hand. Various prices are possible within a rather wide range. Therefore price phenomenon are not adequately explained by "real forces."

3. Case of corn market. True pecuniary phenomena. Demand schedules and supply schedules. Do they represent only "real forces"?—i.e., only balance of satisfactions against efforts: Marshall speaks in case of seller's schedules as "governed by his own need for money in hand, and by his calculations of the present and future conditions of the market." Both these factors contain pecuniary elements. (Note that influence of real or money costs of production in these cases is not mentioned.) Factors governing demand schedules of buyers are not explicitly stated beyond reference to marginal utility of the commodity. Implicitly there is also an assumption regarding the marginal utility of money—i.e., a pecuniary element. Thus the demand and supply schedules do not represent merely real forces. As for market prices on basis of these schedules, Marshall shows that these are not strictly determined. There is a true equilibrium—i.e., a price at which quantity demanded equals quantity supplied—price which is likely to be approximated in fact before market closes, but more or less corn

may change hands at other prices in process of bargaining and if these earlier prices be considered then certainly the "real" forces do not afford adequate explanation. Lest it be thought that the pecuniary elements in this case of corn market are superficial, that they may be resolved altogether into "real" forces, call attention to Allyn A. Young's point.

> In barter there is no efficient tendency toward a definite equilibrium. So far as the ratio of exchange between two commodities is concerned, an equilibrium point might conceivably be reached, but it would be only one of an indefinite number of possible points. And it would be quite unreasonable to expect that there should be any mutual consistency between the ratios of exchange thus accidentally reached.[79]

C.f., Joseph Schumpeter's contention in *Das Wesen und der Hauptinhalt der theoretischen Nationalökonomie* (1908) that use of money is a *logical* necessity and deducible from data assumed on basis of theory of static equilibrium. Without use of money there is no tendency to equilibrium; for exchange ratios between every pair of commodities are indeterminate within wide limits; and there is no ground to expect consistency among these ratios, as Marshall himself shows in Appendix F, "Barter." But recall contention that equilibrium might be reached by elaborate process of arbitrage.

Equilibrium of normal demand and supply. What is meant by equilibrium. Thus normal equilibrium rests upon normal supply and demand schedules which show quantities of the article in question which will be offered and taken in the given market within a given time at various money prices. Our problem is whether these normal prices so determined are fully reducible to real forces—sacrifices and satisfaction?

(1) Do normal supply schedules and normal demand schedules adequately explain pecuniary phenomena; i.e., the actual selling prices? Marshall of course thinks that they do not in world as it is, but would do so in a "rigidly stationary state." (Can Marshall consistently get a total real cost by adding "effort" and "waiting" if the classes by whom these sacrifices are made are not in the same economic position? Or does he not need to add them—would he compare amounts of effort required to make two commodities and also amounts of waiting? Or would he hold that they can affect market only in so far as they influence money costs? In any case he adds money cost to employer and his own personal "real cost."[80]

(2) Are normal supply and demand schedules themselves adequately explained by real forces? Again the answer is no in a world of change. Note that the schedules themselves consist of money prices for materials, labor, houses, etc.—money prices that are actual or supposed. The only actual prices are market prices, and in market prices we have shown above that other factors besides sacrifices and satisfactions affect the outcome; c.f.,

---

[79] "Some Limitations of the Value Concept," *The Quarterly Journal of Economics*, May 1911, p. 410.

[80] C.f., Henry W. Stuart, "Subjective and Exchange Value," II, *The Journal of Political Economy*, June 1896, pp. 378-379. See also, Marshall's addition of monopoly revenue and consumer's surplus to get total benefit of monopoly; and also discussion of surplus from land and producer's and saver's surpluses.

Marshall's remark that in temporary equilibrium cost of production (whether real or money cost of production) has little influence.

All this applies to the most general cases. If we take certain special cases we find other grounds for thinking that actual prices do not depend wholly on real forces; e.g., in monopoly prices normal supply price is a factor, but does not come as near determining selling price as under competitive conditions. Hence one set of the real forces gives even less adequate explanation here; i.e., there is no tendency here for normal supply price, real cost, to equal normal real value at the margin, but rather tendency for latter to exceed former. Problem of wages becomes indeterminate when both laborers and employers are organized; i.e., it is not controlled by real forces. Even in highly competitive trades, it is only at the margin that an equilibrium of sacrifices and satisfactions is attained. Away from this margin we get producer's and consumer's surpluses.

Conclusion concerning levels of economic analyses. We have seen that Marshall carries on his discussion of exchange and distribution largely in terms of money, but that he seeks to penetrate below the money surface of things to find real explanations. We have also seen that in his opinion the real forces do not adequately account for actual prices; i.e., he conceives the real forces to establish merely certain tendencies, which in a world of changes are continually interfered with. Interfered with by what? Partly by changes in the real forces themselves; i.e., demand schedules influenced by gratifications are not fixed. And supply schedules are similarly subject to changes from growth of population, changes in consumer taste, alterations in standards of living, etc. Real world in last resort is one of "organic growth." Interfered with also by the fact that men's anticipations of the material factors which men desire and the actual efforts which represent obstacles do not turn out as was expected. Hence the real forces suffice to explain only the general drift of economic life. And, may we add, they control even this general drift, only in so far as they affect money costs and money demand prices? That is, are not the latter phenomena the *real* causes—the effective causes? (Where real costs and real satisfactions do not explain money prices, the latter enter into new combinations, as ultimate elements; i.e., in these cases can we go back of money to a deeper level of explanation?)

Welfare. Nearest approach of Marshall to the subject is in his brief discussion of the ideals of life. No attempt to state its meaning definitely. (His disciple A. C. Pigou in *Wealth and Welfare,* 1912, on the first page states that "welfare cannot be defined"). But certain specific elements of welfare including "richness of character" are "the end of all our studies." Thus a rapid growth of population is an evil under some circumstances. Welfare is an end toward which material wealth is only a means. Would be promoted by decreasing inequality of distribution [provided it could be "attained by means that would not sap the springs of free initiative and strength of character." Welfare] concept more definitely stated when well being seems to be conceived as the "sum total of happiness." Present forms of expenditures are criticized on basis of their bearing on well being—they "do little or nothing toward making life nobler or truly happier." Is it measured? A nation's prosperity is better measured by "money income than by the money value of its stock [of wealth"]; but even this measure is unsatisfactory, [says Marshall]. To student of social science average income is generally more important than total national income. There is little direct connection between the aggregate stock of wealth of an individual and his aggregate happiness. Comes near being a connection between income and well being. But he accepts in accordance with Daniel Bernouilli's suggestion the position of regarding ["the satisfaction which a person derives from his income as commencing when he has enough to support life, and afterwards as increasing by equal amounts with every equal successive percentage that is added to his income; and *vice versa* for loss of income,"] and admits also that edge of enjoyment is blunted by familiarity. Whole conception of welfare in Marshall is vague and therefore cannot be used. It cannot be subjected to scientific treatment with the facility possible where money measures apply. But more than that this vague conception of well being is used as a criterion for criticizing actual situations and telling us what we ought to do.

Criticism of Marshall: All the above is merely by way of showing how Marshall himself conceives his analysis. It is not an objection. But is there anything to criticize? Of course we should like an adequate explanation of pecuniary phenomena among other things. But fact that he does not attempt to give it merely shows that economic theory as developed in his hands does not profess to be complete. And we are not sure that any other possible line of attack on the problem would enable us to complete the analysis or even to carry it farther than he has done.

But may we not object to Marshall's concept of the "real" forces in economic life? Of course we want to get back of money and the things which count in life, i.e., we want a psychological interpretation of economic life, a valid analysis of economic behavior; or rather to know how money along with other forces in the situation actually counts in economic activity— the use of money being one of the most important real facts in the whole situation. In seeking such an explanation are we to count effort of labor, sacrifice of waiting and satisfaction in commodities as the only real elements? Are there not other psychological factors in economic processes of moment in influencing prices; for example, just as real as those hedonistic quantities? What, for example, of differences in bargaining power which Marshall allows to play a role? Of differences in ability of entrepreneurs? Of forces which lead to formation of trade unions and employers' associations? Are not these psychological factors just as real as real cost? And do they not count in shaping economic life on Marshall's own showing? That is, I object that when he goes beneath the money level of things in search of the real forces, he speaks as if the only psychological factors were the hedonistic quantities. In fact, use of money is itself a psychological factor in the situation just as real as sacrifice or satisfaction.

But this is an objection to his language rather than to his analysis; and the misleading language he inherited from his hedonistic predecessors. This conclusion leads to the question as to whether Marshall's treatment of human nature is hedonistic? His real break with hedonism is confined to his occasional references to development—cumulative change, c.f., what he has to say about cumulative causes. And this process of development is in his eyes the "central idea of economics," but as he explained in preface [of 6th edition] most of his space is given to static and dynamic discussion in which no development takes place or no development which involves large cumulative changes. And here his difference from professedly hedonistic expositions is slight. Use of terms satisfaction or gratification for pleasure and effort or sacrifice for pain is of little significance.

Chief purpose of analysis of activity is to get a basis for the demand and supply schedules and these schedules have the same general form and are used for much the same general ends by Marshall as by hedonists such as Maffeo Pantaleoni or Jevons.

In short, in discussing the central problems of value and distribution he talks as a hedonist talks; e.g., "real" factors in price making contain as psychological elements only sacrifices and satisfaction; i.e., differences of bargaining power may affect prices, but they are not "real" elements—clearly a hedonistic view, except for different words for same ideas. But in verging on the treatment of practical problems in last section of *Principles* he talks much more realistically and has less hedonistic flavor. But so did most of the old hedonists.[81]

Note on Marshall and hedonism: Hedonism is not so much mistaken as it is inadequate. The psychological criticism that a desire cannot be roused by the anticipation of its own satisfaction seems to be primarily a logical objection and one that rests upon an over-sharp discrimination between desire and anticipation of satisfaction. A student has pointed out in the course of the discussion that the Freudian psychology represents even the most peculiar mental operations upon which it dwells as aiming at securing gratification. My conclusion was that we do not as yet know definitely and certainly the role which pleasure and pain play in directing behavior. The inadequacy of hedonism is, however, apparent even when the doctrine is reduced to as mild and common sense a basis as is found in Marshall. For if one follows the line of investigation pointed out by his conception of behavior as invariably controlled by two opposing sets of motives, one almost inevitably neglects the role that is played by habit, instinct and institutions. Marshall certainly neglects these factors most. He does not even raise, let alone solve the problems which they suggest. For example, advertising as a factor in demand, conspicuous waste in consumption, the social element in the irksomeness of labor, etc., do not appear in his *Principles of Economics*. It might be logically possible to make a place for such topics under a hedonistic framework, but the people who see hedonism as the savior of psychological theory have passed over such problems in silence. And of course a much better framework for including them can be had from a more modern viewpoint; one which

---

[81] Outlines, "Final Lectures" April and May 1914, February 12, 1917, November 1, 1927; "Marshall: Class Discussion II," no month, no day. 1917. Quotations are from *Principles of Economics*, pp. xv, 135, 141, 232, 461, 497, 714, 720. On Maffeo Pantaleoni, see Appendix V.

On Daniel Bernouilli (1700-1782), famous mathematician and early eighteenth century pioneer on marginal utility analysis, see Emil Kauder, *A History of Marginal Utility Theory* (Princeton, N. J.: Princeton University Press, 1965) pp. 32-35.

will set pleasure and pain in perspective, as two among a considerable number of factors of importance.[82]

S. Please explain Marshall's concept of quasi-rent?

M. In his terminology, as was explained in the discussion of his theory of rent, there is a difference between the principles which control the share in the national dividend that goes to land as such and the principles which control the share of capital or labor. But if the theorist takes rather permanent things that men have made, say a great bridge, or a durable building, or an instrument of production such as a lathe—he will see at any given moment that the supply of these commodities is somewhat analogous to the supply of land. It is not quite analogous, because the supply can be increased, given time enough; but it takes a considerable time to increase the supply, and so the principle which regulates the share of the owners of the fairly permanent objects are similar in character to the principles which regulate the share of the owners of land.

Then Marshall also talks about quasi-rents which go to certain people: a business man of exceptional ability or a lawyer of outstanding position, even an exceptionally skilled artist is the happy possessor of a factor of production the supply of which cannot be increased by human effort, so far as he is dealing with natural ability. A man of that sort is more or less in the same position as a man who owns a particularly fertile farm. He can get a return which is in excess of the marginal return for factors which have the same name, because of the exceptional quality of the factor which he controls, and that excess over and above marginal price which he commands may be called a quasi-rent.

Marshall's contribution: Created his engine of inquiry—the supply and demand framework that could be applied in uniform fashion to all his problems whether of value or distribution, whether of short periods or long ones. It was indeed by using this engine in uniform fashion that he gave unity to economic theory. He integrated economic theory more effectively than his predecessors. Demonstrated the logical continuity of theory of value and theory of distribution. Demonstrated also a method of using utility analysis and cost analysis in treating the two sets of problems. Demonstrated finally a method of treating the factor of time in such a fashion as to avoid a logical break in the analysis. Further, Marshall broke with the tradition of classical economics of imagining an abstract *homo oeconomicus*. He undertook to account for the behavior of real men in making their living and in that spirit he looked forward to development of what he called the "higher task" of quantitative analysis, an analysis that would supplement the qualitative analysis with which he stopped. Of

[82] Outline, January 7, 1920. [The student was Harry Elmer Barnes, the eminent historian and social scientist.]

course quantitative analysis requires use of statistical data and these data are observations of the behavior of real men—not of abstract men.[83]

Marshall, to repeat, provides an acute and realistic discussion of determination of money prices in modern life and regards it as economic theory. Does not explain the system and so falls short. So far as explanation is offered it is in hedonistic terms, no substantial improvement. Unanswered questions: How have the habits of the money economy grown up? What are the grounds of choice among men, and how have they developed? Advantage of Marshall's position. Discussion in pecuniary terms instead of in terms of subjective states of pleasure and pain, is less vague and more definite. But Marshall is continually explaining the prices people would pay or do pay by more fundamental facts of pleasure and pain. Takes some account of habit but does not attempt to account for either its rationalizing guidance of conduct by pecuniary calculation or the development of habit.

Summary and conclusion: His place in the development of English economic theory: Born in 1842, regular education, became a teacher. Trained in classical school; more sympathy with Ricardo than with John Stuart Mill. Developed utility analysis independently before Jevons published *The Theory of Political Economy*. Did not bring out his large treatise until impression made by the utility analysis had been deepened by Austrians. Controversy concerning relative importance of cost of production and marginal utility as factors affecting value was beginning to seem the decisive issue in economic theory.

What he stands for. In most economists' eyes, his treatise is an attempt at reconciliation on this issue—unison of cost and utility; that is, he crosses the classical type of analysis with the utility analysis. His simile of the [two blades of the] shears. Reason he is called an eclectic: Framework of theory—demand and supply equal utility and cost. Advantages: Clearness of arrangement. Continuity of theory from market to long run. More important contribution (I think) is his attitude toward use of money: Classicists concluded in John Stuart Mill that use of money made no difference save one of convenience. Jevons and his followers had more fundamental reason for dispensing with money. To them economic life was guided by utility not by money calculus. Marshall is true to the tradition in holding that the real forces which control economic action lie below the monetary level—are matters of pain and pleasure. But his analysis shows that the equilibria which he discusses are those between monetary magnitudes, that it is the monetary magnitude of a real force which counts not the amount of pleasure or pain as such. Residuum of hedonistic psychology seen in his conception of real forces as ruling the individual economy as a balance between pleasure and pain. (Marshall's hedonism was not aggressive even at the outset and has been recessive ever since. In later editions he has modified his hedonistic phrases. Has held that wants arise from activities as much as activities from wants.)

---

[83] Outline, "Current Developments in Economic Theory," remarks at luncheon at Political Economy Club, Columbia Faculty Club, April 5, 1936. Quotation from Marshall is in "Social Possibilities of Economic Chivalry," 1907; reprinted in *Memorials of Alfred Marshall*, p. 324.

General doctrinal results of Marshall's economic theory. 1. Theory of value: "In the real world a simple doctrine of value is worse than none." His theory is one concerning the relations between supply and demand and value. All these factors are supposed to be mutually determining—balls in a bowl. This process of mutual determination is continuous (in time) and so must be economic analysis from briefest market equilibrium to equilibrium in period long enough to allow for change in supply of the factors of production. 2. Theory of distribution: application of general theory of value to special cases.

Realism and seriousness of Marshall. Theory. His *Principles of Economics* stands in striking contrast with pure theory in general, with statics at large. Although a professor, Marshall has not wholly lost his sense of the real world of business and the purpose to show what really happens there. In this attitude also he is more like the classicists than like Jevons *et al.* The science is not a set of abstractions to be played on. It is not a field where anything may be true. It is not a field where truth or applicability to facts is of slight moment. But he goes beyond the classicists in bringing in the idea of cumulative change—Ricardo's laws of long period changes. Marshall's similar laws allow for alterations in the elements themselves; e.g., in labor. Proper analogy for economic theory is not physics but biology. When the Cambridge economic historian, William Cunningham, said that economics was a "pure science" Marshall retorted that he wanted not a "pure science" based on mathematics but a science of causation.[84]

Comparison of Marshall and John Stuart Mill.[84a] Marshall's definition of economics suggests a realistic science (but all of his analyses rest on some simplifying assumptions), while Mill insists that political economy must be highly abstract. Marshall insists that he is talking about real men, while Mill explicitly uses an artificial definition of man—a being animated solely by desire of wealth, aversion to labor and preference for present to future enjoyment. Marshall agrees with Schmoller that the economist must use both deduction and induction while Mill insists that political economy must rely upon the concrete deductive method although conclusions must be verified by "specific experience." Marshall holds that money is the center around which economic science clusters while Mill holds that "money is

---

[84] ["Dr. Cunningham refers us to an article in which he maintains that economics is not a science of 'cause' and effect but a pure science like logic or geometry, where this conception of 'cause' is not appropriate. I hold on the contrary that economics is a science akin to biology and not to logic; and that the conception of cause and effect is appropriate to it." (Marshall, "Reply," *The Economic Journal,* September 1892, p. 508. This was a reply to Cunningham, "The Perversion of Economic History," in the same issue of *The Economic Journal.* Among other things Cunningham complained that when critics speak of Marshall's *Principles of Economics* as "authoritative on points of history, or tell us that the historical school of economists made a useful protest but implicitly deny that they have necessary work to do in supplying a basis for positive economic doctrine, one cannot but feel that there is a time not only for silence but for speech; lest silence should be mistaken for acquiescence. At least, it is well to draw attention to the risks which even a very able man runs in attempting to construct history from general principles, instead of submitting to build it up bit by bit from definite data of fact" (pp. 497-498).]

[84a] "Spent most of the morning making notes for a series of comparisons between Mill's and Marshall's conceptions of economics and its methods." (Diary," January 5, 1943.)

a thing of indifference" that exercises no influence upon human behavior except when "it gets out of order."

Marshall and Mill differ also regarding the scope and organization of economics.

Marshall	Mill
(Book III): On Wants and Their Satisfactions.	A topic not treated apart from fact that utility is essential to value.
(Book IV): Agents of Production. Land, Labor, Capital and Organization.	Production treated systematically, Book I. Organization not given equal standing with land, labor and capital.
(Book V): General Relation of Demand, Supply, and Value.	[Marshall's Book V] a much improved version of Mill's Book III on exchange.
(Book VI): Distribution of the National Income. Application of the theory of value to the problems of distribution.	Book II on Distribution comes before theory of value in Book III.
(Mill's Book IV) represented only by incidental remarks.	Book IV. Influence of the Progress of Society on Production and Distribution.
(Mill's Book V) not treated systematically.	Book V. On the Influence of Government.

Presentation of some other comparisons. Statics and dynamics. Mill treats both although statics with more precision and more fully. Dynamics mainly in Books IV and V influence of progress and of government. Marshall likewise seeks to treat both, although he has nothing systematically corresponding with Mill's Books IV and V. Preface to sixth edition: "central idea of economics . . . must be that of living force and movement." But arrives there by degrees. Starts with statics and brings in dynamic forces by degrees. Importance of other things being equal. The usefulness and the risks of statics. Advances from mechanics to biology. Note that Marshall's statics is mechanical; his dynamics is biological in aim. Static analysis merely provisional; later to be thrown aside. Importance of cumulative effects.

Pure and applied theory. Mill seeks both—in very title of his book *Principles of Political Economy with some of their Applications to Social Philosophy*. Marshall likewise. His distinction between the two a matter of degree. Chief reason for study of economics a practical question. Dominant aim. J. M. Keynes's remark about Marshall being "too anxious to do good."

Marshall's methodological position seems to me fundamentally similar to Mill's. To him economics is a study of men in the actual business of life— men getting a living and apportioning what they get among different uses. Formally he is more realistic than Mill in that he does not use "an artificial definition of a man" but insists that he deals with real men. Admits that his real men differ in ability—ranging from "city men," who are adept calculators, to rustics. They range also from the very rich to the very poor, which makes a difference because the marginal utility of money cannot be assumed to be uniform. But this difficulty he surmounts by considering large groups of men as among which such differences in ability and wealth do not exist.

Marshall also proceeds primarily by deductive reasoning from assumed premises. Fundamental assumptions are desire to consume, dislike for labor and for waiting. These are the real forces that control economic behavior. These forces are measurable in money, at least in the vicinity of the margin where decisions to buy more or less and to produce more or less are continually being made. Accordingly Marshall's theory assumes the form of a study of the money measures of real forces; i.e., of prices, primarily in the neighborhood of the points at which prices are set by bargaining between buyers and sellers, but with some reference to the "surpluses" which men get as consumers or producers from the fact that they would have been willing to pay higher prices or to accept lower prices than they do for parts of the supplies they buy or sell. As said above, like Mill, Marshall reaches his conclusions primarily by setting up formal assumptions which in his book usually have the form of demand and supply schedules, and demonstrating that on these assumptions prices will settle at a certain point or points. Hardly more than Mill does he attempt inductive verification of his assumptions, or of the conclusions deduced from them. But he believes that his assumptions are substantially valid representations of prevailing practice and is at pains to point out wherein they do violence to the facts; e.g., his discussion of the non-divisibility of certain goods into small units; and of the impossibility of a man's stopping work in a modern factory when marginal sacrifice equals marginal satisfaction expected from further earnings. Also his start toward analyses of non-competitive prices. And if his assumptions are realistic he thinks well reasoned conclusions from them must be correspondingly valid in fact.

Marshall's standing among English economists of his generation. His pupils, e.g., [A. W.] Flux, [Sidney] Chapman, [A. C.] Pigou, [J. M.] Keynes.

[It might be noted here that] the classical attitude toward economics from Adam Smith to Marshall is an effort to gain understanding of actual economic behavior. But these masters wanted this knowledge primarily for a practical purpose—to improve economic organization. From Adam Smith who pleaded for economic freedom to Marshall who wanted to abolish poverty, the classical economists were at bottom reformers. They were critics of economic organization. To think of them as champions of capitalism is to reveal ignorance of their writings;—though I suppose all of them thought that private property as what a man "produced" as a worker, owner of capital, or business man, was necessary to stimulate labor and waiting as human nature now stands. Even so, Malthus, Ricardo, John Stuart Mill and Marshall are heartily dissatisfied with the outcome of the prevailing system of economic organization and hoped that their work would aid mankind to find better ways of carrying on the process of producing and distributing wealth. That they had to take an indirect route toward this end, they realized in part. But that was made clearer by criticism.

Broadly speaking, the following are the criticisms that have been brought against Marshall's type of economics: (a) Still infected by hedonism. (b) Economists have no competence for discussing valuation and no need of a theory of value. (c) Interrelations between economic forces cannot be adequately presented or analyzed in literary language. Should use the universal language of mathematics. (d) Economic behavior cannot be understood except in terms of the evolution of man's wants and means of satisfying them.

We shall take up in time types of theory that represent these several criticisms and attempt to supply what is lacking. 1. Economic psychology—Frank A. Fetter. 2. No theory of value necessary—price economics—H. J. Davenport. 3. Same plus mathematics—Gustav Cassel. 4. Factor of evolution—historical school and institutional economics—Marx, Schmoller, Veblen, John R. Commons.[85]

More specifically, one band of critics represented by Fetter proceeds to attempt to substitute for hedonism a psychology more in line with modern psychological views, with modern functional psychology. Another group sought to escape the same difficulty, by divorcing economics completely from psychology; that is, they said that the work of the economist and that of the psychologist do not overlap, and economic theories should be constructed in such a fashion that they do not rest upon any particular psychological foundation, so that they will remain valid whatever conclusions psychology ultimately obtains regarding the direct forces in human behavior. Then there are the writers who criticize neo-classical economics on the ground that it pays no attention to the institutional factor in behavior, that it does not give a competent account of the conditions which shape men's desires, which give rise to people's notions concerning what is worth while, concerning sacrifices as well as gratifications. There are a number of different lines of economic work, all of which aim more or less directly to fill this particular gap. When I say they aim to fill the gap, I do not mean that they regard themselves as simply supplementing such theory as is formulated by the neo-classical school. They consider themselves rather as making other lines of attack upon the problem, which do give effective attention to the institutional factor.[86]

Since Fetter is the first American economist we shall discuss in detail, a survey of the development of economics as a systematic study in the United States is appropriate before going on with him.

---

[85] Outlines, February 14, 19, 1917, March 17, 1936; "Seminar in Economic Changes and Economic Theory," January 5, 1943, May 2, 1944; "Economic Psychology: Marshall," APP 44-53, no. 3; "Marshall—Class Discussion I," APP 44-53, no. 73. Quotation from *Principles of Economics*, p. 368.

Marshall gave us not only a far more penetrating analysis of static equilibrium than Ricardo attained but supplements it with some discussions of changes over long periods of time. Yet I think J. M. Keynes is right when he says that Marshall's analysis is substantially static in character and that his wise and penetrating remarks upon dynamic problems have mostly the character of *obiter dicta—obiter dicta* which serve as a camouflage. Outline, "Lecture on Trade Cycles," Oxford University, June 2, 1932.

[86] Paragraph from "1918 Typescript."

CHAPTER XI

The Development of American Economics
and the Role of J. B. Clark

The history of American economic thought has not been worked up very systematically as yet, presumably for the reason that it has not seemed significant enough to attract the attention even of writers of doctoral dissertations. A great many monographs have been written about the development of various people as political economists and of various subjects and periods, but so far [Spring 1931] there is no very elaborate discussion of the history of economics in America.

The scholar who has made the most minute researches in this field is Professor E. R. A. Seligman of Columbia. In 1927, he published a very interesting comprehensive article on "The Early Teaching of Economics in the United States."[1] In it he sums up the general development of American economic theory in the following fashion:

The teaching of political economy in the United States may be divided into three stages. In the first, which comprises the eighteenth century and lasted until the War of 1812, the discipline was usually included under the general subject of moral philosophy, as had been customary in Great Britain. The industrial revolution, which began in the second quarter of the nineteenth century created practical problems of banking and production, and was responsible for the deep and widespread interest in economic topics, and for the introduction of a course in the subject as a regular part of the curriculum in many colleges. Independent chairs of political economy did not become common until the third period which began in the 1870's with the appearance of serious economic problems like the labor question, the railroad question and other indications of mature development.

---

[1] *Economic Essays, Contributed in Honor of John Bates Clark,* edited by Jacob H. Hollander (New York: Macmillan, 1927), pp. 283-320.

[Edwin R. A. Seligman (1861-1939) of Columbia University was a pioneer in the development of the field of public finance as well as a leading authority on the history of economic thought.]

Stated somewhat differently the increased interest in the subject as evidenced by the widespread creation of relatively independent chairs in the leading American institutions reflected the emergence of the important economic problems in active political life. Economic problems had been faced all along, but it was not until they became the subject of widespread discussion on a political basis that Seligman thinks that deep interest is taken in economics, interest keen enough to lead institutions of learning to recognize economics as a field which they should teach.

Consider the development of economics during the second of the periods which Seligman recognized; that is, from the beginning of the second war with England, a war which cut off commercial dealings with Europe for the most part and which led to a very rapid development of domestic manufactures and consequently started the United States vigorously upon its own industrial revolution. The development of economics during this period from the War of 1812 to the 1870's is interesting and obscure. There were a considerable number of books on economic theory published. The earliest that I have read is *Lectures on the Elements of Political Economy* (1826) by the president of South Carolina College (now the University of South Carolina), Thomas Cooper.[2]

Cooper (1759-1839) was one of those Englishmen of that generation who had taken all knowledge as his province.[3] He was a physician, physicist, chemist, lawyer; a man, the scope of whose learning is reminiscent of Benjamin Franklin. He was an active figure in public life, writing on a variety of topics.

As did most writers of the treatises in that day, Cooper saluted Ricardo as the great authority. But there was a significant difference. Ricardo and the philosophical radicals at large were skeptical folk who were definitely scientific in their interest. Ricardo, for example, seems to be a man who in his speculations is ready to face any conditions, however uncomfortable they may look for the future.

In the American colonies, for some time after independence was won, if political economy was taught at all, it was, as a rule, handled by the college president, who was almost certain to be a retired clergyman. In short, economics was taught as a division of moral philosophy by the heads of colleges which were definitely denominational. The moral philosophers were expounding a more or less philo-

---

[2] [The earliest comprehensive treatise that was published in the United States was *Thoughts on Political Economy* (1820) by Daniel Raymond (1786-1849).]

[3] [For biography of Cooper, see Dumas Malone, *The Public Life of Thomas Cooper; 1783-1839* (1926; 2nd edition, 1961).]

sophic conception of the universe. They were largely influenced by the common-sense philosophers[4] and they saw economic organization as a contrivance of the Creator for the benefit of humanity. They stressed harmony of relationships under the competitive system, indicating how precisely a man got what he merited, how much the institution of private property contributed to general well-being by giving everybody a strong inducement to produce more than he consumed himself in order that he might add to his own ownership, etc.

These people were at the same time drawing heavily upon the technical parts of the subject as developed by the classical writers on the other side of the Atlantic. The consequence is that attempting to read these books is a difficult task. To a modern reader they seem to have singularly little that is original. They were elementary—which they had to be for their purposes. They used ideas that had been expressed with greater vigor by men who developed them in England. They had most of the qualities that make text-books as dull as they are useful.

Even Cooper, who was born and reared in England [and was anti-clerical,] strikes one as singularly unobservant in this sense: that he wrote his treatise on British models and had nothing to say in a systematic way about the extraordinary difference between the economic organization of the community where he was writing and that of England. One would have thought that a person concerned with economic problems in South Carolina at the time would have felt it incumbent to show in his treatise what modifications in British views were necessary to take into account the great institution of slavery.[5] But the alterations are not found in Cooper's treatise. And in the other Southern writers so far as I have read them (and for the reason given above I have not read any of them thoroughly) little attention is given the differences between the English system from which

---

[4] [For the common-sense philosophy see Joseph Dorfman, *Thorstein Veblen and His America* (New York: The Viking Press, 1934) pp. 19-22.]

[5] [In his famous introduction to the English translation of Anton Menger's *The Right to the Whole Procedure of Labour* (1899), Herbert S. Foxwell of Cambridge and the University of London, praised the third edition of *Lectures on the Elements of Political Economy* (1831), particularly the addition which challenged the position of the Ricardian socialists as well as other radicals. He spoke of Cooper as "a very vigorous and independent thinker, of wide experience in both the old and new worlds. A Free Trader, he rejected the theory of Natural Rights; and he anticipated (Francis A.) Walker in the stress he lays on the value of business ability, genius and invention. His freedom from many of the narrowing dogmas of the English economists gave the greater effect to his answer to the socialists; and his arguments still remain forcible and pertinent."]

the theories they borrowed were derived and the system on this side
of the water.

If they had been writing about what they saw about them, if they
had been discussing the problems presented by contemporary life,
they would have been struck by the great difference between the
social institutions that Ricardo took for granted in England, where
slavery had not existed for some centuries, and the social conditions
under which they themselves were living. They were pure theorists,
and, to repeat, because primarily they were not talking about issues
that were growing out of American conditions, they were, broadly
speaking, a sterile set of people.

The attitude of the early American economists is reminiscent of the
attitude of the American poets who wrote many a verse to the skylark
without observing that the skylark is not an American species. It is
a sort of literary tradition carried on by men whose minds are not
primarily concerned with economics and people who are not thinking
hard about problems other than the formal ones which they found
in older books and which they reproduced and solved with their own
panegyrics upon the harmony of economic organization.

Then later from the end of the 1830's to the end of the 1870's
came a variety of text-books by such men as John McVickar, Francis
Wayland, Henry Vethake, Amasa Walker, Arthur Latham Perry,
Francis Bowen, George Tucker and others. These books are extraordinarily easy to obtain in second-hand bookstores. They are found
on the dustiest shelves in those little shops.[6] Very few have any distinctive spirit. They are extremely hard for me to read and I am a
most hardened consumer of such literature.[7]

Introduction of political economy occurred rather promptly; e.g., through
the text-books of John McVickar, Thomas Cooper, Henry Vethake, etc.
The translation of J. B. Say was extremely popular. Later, John Stuart
Mill's *Principles of Political Economy*. The subject made little mark in
colleges. Went with moral philosophy. Not very interesting to students or
teachers.[8]

[Towards the end of the period, the Frenchman Bastiat's *Economic
Sophisms* and *Economic Harmonies* enjoyed a considerable vogue in
the United States as they had in England. Two of the most popular text-
books, those by Amasa Walker and Perry, explicitly followed Bastiat.]

---

[6] [The situation has changed radically since Professor Mitchell said this in 1931.
These books now command the prices of rare Americana.]
[7] [The most popular text-book for the period as a whole and especially for the
pre-Civil War era was that of the Reverend Francis Wayland (1796-1865), president
of Brown University. His *Elements of Political Economy* (1837) sold over 40,000
before the Civil War and the abridged version over 13,000.]
[8] Outline, February 21, 1917.

There was at least one American economist, even before the 1870's, who made some impression outside his country. That was Henry C. Carey (1793-1879), a successful leading Philadelphia publisher, who was fond of social problems as a whole.[9] He was as much a sociologist as an economist and took advantage of his situation to publish his own books in considerable profusion. He became known primarily for his criticisms of the "Ricardian" theory of rent. Among other things, Ricardo said in discussing rent that the best lands in a country will be taken up first. Not until these lands came into cultivation will people resort to land of the second grade; and not until the lands of the second grade have been taken into cultivation, lands of the third grade; etc. Carey, however, saw things with his own eyes, and it occurred to him to test this British proposition by seeing how well it accorded with American experience; he concluded that it did not accord at all well. Lands which were first taken up when America was settled by Europeans were very far from the best farming lands. To attempt to wring a living from the stony soil of New England by farming was, from the point of view of agricultural technique, a stupid proposition when so much better land could have been found farther west. Carey pointed out, however, that the lands taken up first were those that were most accessible to the settlers; and that later on, as the country became more thoroughly built, they found far better farming country. The historical order of settlement was very different indeed from the theoretical order in Ricardo's view.

Carey generalized to the effect that the factor of most importance in settling a new land is likely to be accessibility to the seaboard, settling in a place where people can keep contact with the country from which they may expect new accessions to their ranks, the country upon which they are still depending for a supply of the fabricated commodities which they have not yet the facilities for developing, and the countries in which they may expect to find a market for those parts of the produce which they raise beyond the requirements of their own consumption. Somewhat later the American settlements tended to follow up the river courses, always of course paying some attention to the fertility of the soils. Even in New England, though the land as a whole is a particularly sterile part of the continent, there are places so stony that even the early settlers with their remarkable ignorance of farming, at least in the beginning, being people who

---

[9] [The principal works of Carey are *Essay on the Rate of Wages* (1835), *Principles of Political Economy*, 3 volumes (1837-1840) and *Principles of Social Science*, 3 volumes (1858-1859). A compact treatment is *The Past, the Present, and the Future* (1848).]

came from towns rather than from the countryside, people who were handicraftsmen rather than agriculturists—even they did not take into cultivation the worst lands. But fertility was here, Carey pointed out as an historical fact, not the basis of choice broadly speaking for first cultivation.

This criticism Ricardo's defenders could answer easily enough by pointing out that Ricardo was not taking into account actual historical circumstances; that his was a schematic, theoretical view of the subject; that the facts might be as Carey said, but none the less the Ricardian theory of rent remained true, in the sense in which Ricardo had enunciated it. It was even said from the point of view of the settlers the best lands were taken up first, for what constituted the best lands was not a matter of fertility; it was a matter of accessibility to European ports so that they could get supplies, and it was in part, a matter of safety.[10]

Much later than Carey, but beginning his work in the second period was Simon Newcomb (1835-1909). He is best known as an eminent astronomer, professor of mathematics in the United States Navy in charge of the Naval Observatory. He wrote extensively on economics and lectured especially on mathematical economics at Johns Hopkins. In his able treatise *Principles of Political Economy* (1886),[11] the man's native vigor of thought is abundantly revealed. It is an exposition of a system of political economy conceived much on English lines, but though he uses English materials he has really passed them through his own mind and they come out as something fresh and interesting.

Seligman's third period opens with the appointment of Charles F. Dunbar at Harvard in 1871, and the appointment the following year at Yale of William Graham Sumner and General Francis A. Walker. Arthur Latham Perry (1830-1905) of Williams College can be said to have had the first relatively separate chair of political economy in the United States.[12] [His *Elements of Political Economy*

---

[10] [Carey's line of argument was directed technically towards demolishing the "Ricardian" theory of rent, which found little support among most American economists. An interesting attempt to reconcile the rent doctrines of Ricardo and Carey is presented in Herr af Heurlin, *The Economic Theory of Agricultural Production* (Helsinki: Academiae Scientiarum Fennicae, 1954). See the summary in Ralph Turvey, "A Finnish Contribution to Rent Theory," *The Economic Journal,* June 1955, pp. 346-358.]

[11] [The treatise is particularly notable for its contribution to monetary theory.]

[12] Outline, January 20, 1920. [Perry was originally professor of history, political economy and German, but in 1868 he was simply professor of history and political economy and devoted most of his attention to the latter.

At Harvard Dunbar for a few years also taught a course in government. At Yale, Sumner was professor of political and social science and Francis A. Walker was professor of political economy and history.]

(1866) had twenty-two editions and a total sale of 19,000 copies.][13]
In addition, his *An Introduction to Political Economy* (1877) had
five regular editions plus a special edition for the blind. He also issued
Principles of Political Economy (1890).

The first three men had a considerably greater interest in economics,
one is tempted to say, greater intellectual vigor than their academic
predecessors in the United States. What one of them thought about
his predecessors was shown by Dunbar's article in the influential
The North American Review in 1876, in a series which was prepared for the Philadelphia Centennial Exposition, and which was
intended to set forth what the country had contributed to the advancement of civilization. Dunbar said that, "The United States
have done thus far nothing for the developing of the *theory* of
political economy."[14] He held a lower view of the work of his predecessors than I suppose the historians of American economics when
they come along will hold.[15]

Dunbar and Sumner, and still more, Walker, came to win the
regard of the economists of other countries in large measure. Walker
won a reputation, as noted in the discussion of Jevons, primarily
through developing in *The Wages Question* (1876), his ideas first
about the economy of high wages, and second about the place of

For a recent excellent study of the vigorous "third period," see John B. Parrish,
"Rise of Economics as an Academic Discipline," *The Southern Economic Journal,*
July 1967, pp. 1-16.]
    [13] [Frederick Rudolph, *Mark Hopkins and the Log* (New Haven: Yale University
Press, 1956) p. 55.]
    [14] "Economic Science in America 1776-1876," reprinted in his *Economic Essays,*
edited by O. M. W. Sprague (New York: Macmillan, 1904) p. 16.
    [Economics at Harvard until 1879 was in the department of philosophy. In that year,
Dunbar organized the department of political economy "as an area of study distinct
from that of philosophy. The new department offered the same two courses that the
philosophy department had offered—an elementary course covering Mill's textbook
and some financial history and an advanced course which studied Cairnes, Mill's
disciple, and . . . Henry C. Carey. (It also offered a third course, a very elementary
one for students not well enough prepared for the general introductory course). The
department dealt almost exclusively with Mill, more Mill and currency." Robert L.
Church, "The Economists Study Society at Harvard, 1891-1902," in *Social Sciences at
Harvard, 1860-1920,* ed. by Paul Buck (Cambridge, Mass.: Harvard University Press,
1965) pp. 25-26. The situation was broadly similar in the South; see Tipton R.
Snavely, *The Department of Economics at the University of Virginia 1825-1956,*
(1967).]
    [15] [Statement of 1945:] it is regrettable that in my college and graduate school
days in the 90's, little attention was paid to American writings before the 1890's.
Professor Joseph Dorfman's demonstration of the activity and ability of domestic
theorists, soon to appear, will be a revelation. Our professional economists in the 90's
worked in the British tradition for the most part. They held systematic theory in
highest esteem. A time when every ambitious economist wanted to write his own
treatise on principles of economics. (Outline, "Fifty Years As an Economist,"
talk before Political Economy Club, Columbia University, May 11, 1945. [Pro-
fessor Mitchell was referring to the first two volumes of Dorfman's *The Economic
Mind in American Civilization* (1946) which he read in manuscript.]

wages in distribution.[16] The exposition of the first he based on the difference between the price paid for labor and the cost of labor for the employer. He pointed out that what work costs to an employer does not depend wholly upon the price paid the worker; it depends upon the price which is paid in proportion to the efficiency of the worker. And if an employer could get a man who could do three times as much in a day as the common run of men, the employer could pay him twice the common wage and still make a very large extra profit. It had been frequently noted that the general rate of wages in the United States was higher than appeared to prevail in foreign countries for work of a similar sort; it was often said that this was the reason why the nation needed a protective tariff; that the American producer could not compete with the foreigner, because he had to pay higher wages. Walker undertook to show that when wages were high to the working man, they were nevertheless cheap to the employer. The explanation of the high rate of wages was the high degree of efficiency of Americans, working with the devices which they were in large part inventing and improving.

Walker's notions about the distribution of wealth were equally interesting. He set forth the view which was expressed by others a little earlier, including Jevons. The workingman gets the residual share in distribution in the sense that rent is determined in the definite way which Ricardo has explained; that interest is a charge which has its own law; that profits equalize risk and contain an element of wages. That means that, the other shares in distribution being fixed by independent laws, the amount that the wage-earner gets is determined by the size of the product after the necessary deductions have been made.

Walker would have been the first to admit that that seemed a little paradoxical; that at any given moment, profits is the residual share because a wage-earner is hired in advance and paid a stipulated price for his services, and if the product is larger than has been expected, the advantage goes to the man who hires him. But that is only a

---

[16] [Sir William Ashley later recalled that when he was a young tutor at Oxford in the 80's "the ordinary man was trained" on Henry Fawcett's *Manual of Political Economy* "though his reign was being threatened by the intensely American textbooks of General Walker." Ashley, *The Adjustment of Wages. A Study of the Coal and Iron Industries of Great Britain and America* (London: Longmans, Green, 1903) p. 6. Marshall used *The Wages Question* as a fellow at Cambridge.

Walker also acquired an international reputation as a statistician for his work as the Superintendant of the United States Censuses of 1870 and 1880. Marshall wrote him of the volumes of the census of 1880, "They are indeed a wonderful work and must fill all European statisticians with envy." Marshall to Walker, September 25, 1885, in J. P. Munroe, *A Life of Francis Amasa Walker* (New York: Holt, 1923) p. 198. See also Bernard Newton, *The Economics of Francis Amasa Walker* (1968).]

short run view. In the long run, he argues, people hire labor because of what labor can produce, and their efficiency increases in competition with each other, and then they find themselves continually bidding up the wages that they offer.

These ideas were not familiar to European economists. Walker was taking an independent line of his own and, as I said above, won considerable attention for his original ideas. In this respect he seems to have made more of a mark than that other extraordinary economist and colleague Sumner (1840-1910), a great teacher, but a man who, so far as economics was concerned, was content for the most part to expound the established doctrines. He wrote a large number of most penetrating essays and did a prodigious amount of highly original work in the sociological field. There he accomplished his most important results, notably the classic *Folkways; A Study of the Sociological Importance of Usage, Manners, Customs and Morals* (1907).[17] On economic theory he left comparatively little mark save that as the most effective teacher of his time, he interested pretty much all Yale men in the subject and did a good deal to stimulate thinking by others.

As for Dunbar (1830-1900), he was primarily a scholar. He published a most influential treatise on banking, *The Theory and History of Banking*.[18] Dunbar also brought out an admirable annotated edition of the nation's laws relating to money and banking, *Laws of the United States on Currency, Finance and Banking*, (1891). Furthermore he established in 1885 and maintained on a very high standard *The Quarterly Journal of Economics,* the enduring journal devoted exclusively to economics in the Anglo-American world. He did a great deal of work on the financial history of the United States, but he was not a man who made fundamental contributions to general economic theory.

Just about the time that Dunbar said that the United States had made no substantial contributions to economic theory, chairs were

---

[17] *Folkways* gives abundant illustration of the persistence of manners and customs. ("The Money Economy and Its Mechanism," September 1907, in uncatalogued papers.)

[18] [The book was influential in England as well as in the United States. It originally appeared in 1891 as *Chapters on the Theory and History of Banking.* After Dunbar's death, Oliver M. W. Sprague of Harvard brought out successive enlarged editions. The last, in 1929, contained a supplementary chapter on the Federal Reserve System by H. Parker Willis of Columbia.

Alfred Marshall privately wrote in 1901 that "on banking, Dunbar's book is much more widely read than any other except Bagehot's *Lombard Street.*" [Marshall to Richard T. Ely, October 28, 1901, in A. W. Coats, "Alfred Marshall and Richard T. Ely; Some Unpublished Letters," *Economica,* May 1961, pp. 192-193.]

being founded as was noted above in the more important institutions, and Simon Newcomb and General Francis A. Walker were elaborating their theories. What in the long run counted more, a considerable number of able young Americans were beginning to seek a better training in economics than could be had at the time within the nation's borders. Most of them went to Germany where training in economics had established itself more securely in the universities than anywhere else; where there was an abundance of courses and a larger number of distinguished men were professionally devoting themselves to teaching the subject.

[The first American economist who is known to have received a doctorate in Germany was Bernard Moses (1851-1930) Ph.D. Heidelberg 1873, the father of the department of political economy of the University of California.][19]

Among those who began their studies in Germany in the 70's were John Bates Clark, Richmond Mayo-Smith and Edwin R. A. Seligman of Columbia, Henry Carter Adams of the University of Michigan, Richard T. Ely of the University of Wisconsin, Henry W. Farnam of Yale, Arthur Twining Hadley, President of Yale, Frank W. Taussig of Harvard, Albion Small who achieved fame as a sociologist at the University of Chicago, and the three boyhood friends from Illinois who attended Halle together, Edmund Janes James, President of the University of Illinois, Joseph French Johnson of New York University, and Simon N. Patten who became such a remarkably successful teacher at the University of Pennsylvania.[20]

In the 80's and 90's some of those who joined the procession were Henry R. Seager of Columbia, Frank A. Fetter of Princeton, Carl C. Plehn of the University of California, Winthrop M. Daniels of Yale, Roland P. Faulkner [the pioneering statistician of the University of Pennsylvania], the economic historians, E. L. Bogart of the University of Illinois and Edwin F. Gay of Harvard. There was also A. Piatt

---

[19] [Probably the first American economist to study in Germany was the Reverend Arthur Latham Perry.

Perry was quite orthodox except in the matter of bank credit where he followed the views of the heterodox British economist and one time banker Henry Dunning MacLeod (1821-1902). In a letter to Walras, MacLeod asserted that "the most distinguished economist in America" has also adopted the view that "political economy is . . . the science of exchanges." MacLeod to Walras. February 18, 1875, *Correspondence of Léon Walras and Related Papers,* ed. by William Jaffé (Amsterdam: North-Holland Publishing Co., 1965) I, p. 47. The editor, Jaffé, commented that the American was probably General Francis A. Walker. Actually it was Perry who declared that the technical definition of political economy as "the science of exchanges" had been "adopted by the noted economist MacLeod in 1858 and by the present writer in the first edition of his larger book (*Elements of Political Economy*) in 1866." Perry, *Introduction to Political Economy* (1875; 5th ed., New York: Scribners, 1901) p. 24.]

[20] [The university posts given above are those last held.]

Andrew who went from Harvard to the secretaryship of the famous National Monetary Commission, then became assistant secretary of the treasury and finally went into Congress; [and Thomas Walker Page who went from the University of Virginia to the Brookings Institution and ended as vice-chairman of the United States Tariff Commission.][21]

When a *Festschrift* was prepared for Professor Gustav von Schmoller, entitled, "The Development of German Economics in the Nineteenth Century," Farnam (1853-1933) sent in a contribution in which he set forth the names and dates of attendance. This was based on a circular of inquiry he sent out in 1906 to American economists to find out how many had studied in Germany. These were men who made some mark on the subject. Of the 116 replies fifty-nine had been students in German universities—more than half.[22]

These men unquestionably were influenced by their German training and a large proportion did very well after they got back. Fetter (1863-1949), for example, said: "It would be hard to find anywhere in the history of scholarship a higher average of success and achievement than this little band of pioneers has achieved."[23] A similar opinion has been expressed by another member of the band, Carl C. Plehn.[24]

Ely, [James] and Seligman, three of the most vigorous among the returning Americans, thought it eminently desirable that there be on this side of the Atlantic some organization which would represent professional interest. They set about to do this very much in the German spirit. The English with their strong insistence upon *laissez faire* had found it possible to get on very nicely without an organization. They

---

[21] [Professor Mitchell also studied in Germany in the 90's, first at Halle under Johannes Conrad and then at Vienna under Carl Menger.

Emory R. Johnson of the University of Pennsylvania and another student in Germany in the 1890's wrote that the German universities "had more to offer" graduate students. Johnson, *Life of a Professor; and Autobiography,* (Philadelphia: Privately printed, 1943) p. 17. Johnson became a leading authority on transportation.]

[22] "Deutsch-amerikanische Beziehungen in der Volkswirtschaftslehre" in *Die Entwicklung der deutschen Volkswirtschaftslehre im neunzehnten Jahrhundert. Festschrift für Gustav Schmoller,* 2 volumes (Leipzig: Duncker & Humblot, 1908) I, pp. 25-29. [The information in the Farnam survey, with additions, is presented in J. C. Myles, "German Historians and American Economics: a Study of the Influence of the German Historical School on American Economic Thought," unpublished Ph.D. dissertation, Princeton University, 1956, appendices I and II. Myles found that almost a hundred had attended German universities. This does not include a goodly number whose specialty area was not economics but who wrote on the subject.]

[23] Fetter, "The Economist and the Public," *The American Economic Review,* March, 1925, p. 14; [see also Joseph Dorfman, "The Role of the German Historical School in American Economic Thought," *The American Economic Review,* May 1955, pp. 17-28.]

[24] "The Progress of Economics during the last Thirty-five Years," in *The University of California Chronicle,* July 1924.

had the Political Economy Club, centered in London, but little else in the way of a society. The Germans, however, had such a society, the *Verein für Sozial Politik* (Association for Social Legislation), which was established at a conference in Eisenach in 1872.

When the scheme was launched in 1885, it was looked upon askance by not a few of the older and more prominent teachers of economics, like Sumner. This was certainly the attitude of J. Laurence Laughlin and numerous others.[25] These representatives of the English tradition looked upon the scheme with suspicion, as something if not made in Germany, at least made on a German model and of a socialistic trend.[26]

Consequently, the young German-trained projectors found that in order to get in the eminent older men, whose membership they deemed indispensable to the success of the society, they would have to make some compromises. They set forth the net result of a good deal of deliberation in a definition of the objectives of the organization and a statement of its principles.

The objects were defined in Article II of the Constitution:

"1. The encouragement of economic research.

2. The publication of economic monographs.

3. The encouragement of perfect freedom in all economic discussion.

4. The establishment of a bureau of information designed to aid members in their economic studies."

The fourth represents a mild trace of German influence and it was one of the objects of the Association toward the realization of which it has made substantially no progress. There never has been set up a bureau of information connected with the American Economic Association.

---

[25] [Laughlin (1871-1933) held a Ph.D. from Harvard, where he began teaching in 1878. After an interval in the insurance business, he taught at Cornell, 1890-1892; and then became head professor of economics at the newly established University of Chicago. His favorite student at Chicago was Professor Mitchell, on whose monetary ideas he exercised considerable influence. He was the main promoter and secretary of the now defunct Political Economy Club, which was established in 1883 and which was dominated by economists of extreme *laissez faire* views. (See A. W. Coats, "The Political Economy Club; A Neglected Episode in American Economic Thought," *The American Economic Review,* September 1961, pp. 634-637. Some additional information on the club is in Joseph Dorfman, "The Background of Institutional Economics," in Dorfman *et al, Institutional Economics* (Berkley and Los Angeles: University of California Press, 1963) pp. 33, 36. On some relations of Mitchell and Laughlin see also Abraham Hirsch, "Wesley Clair Mitchell, J. Laurence Laughlin and the Quantity Theory of Money." *The Journal of Political Economy,* December 1967, pp. 822-843.]

[26] Sentence from Outline, January 20, 1920 and from Student Notes, March 12, 1924.

The organizers were personally eager that the association should take the general attitude toward economics which was dominant in the Germany of their time, an attitude that was commonly characterized as "Socialism of the Chair." At the time the historical school was growing up rapidly in Germany. It laid great stress upon the state as an institution, upon the role that it was destined to play in human life. Scarcely secondary to the state they ranked the church and the family as fundamental institutions. These people took a bold attitude regarding the duties of the economists to participate in the great tasks of the state of shaping culture into forms that were worthy of man's high destiny. Ideas of this sort cropped up in the third article in the Constitution called "Statement of Principles."

It begins as follows: "We regard the state as an agency whose positive assistance is one of the indispensable conditions of human progress." That was a view which had comparatively little in common with the *laissez faire* doctriness which had been taught by English economists and which were, perhaps, at no time more strictly held, more widely believed in as the ultimate gospel, than in the 1870's and 1880's. Adam Smith could hardly have used such language! If John Stuart Mill had been asked to subscribe to these words he might have acceded only on condition that he be allowed a small essay upon exactly what he meant. That principle was one of the stumbling blocks to older economists joining the association.

The statement went on: "We believe that political economy as a science is still in an early stage of its development." To people who held with Mill that nothing remains to be said on the theory of value, this also seemed a dubious proposition. The statement continued: "While we appreciate the work of former economists, we look not so much to speculation as to the historical and statistical study of actual conditions of economic life for the satisfactory accomplishment of that development." This again seemed to raise on American shores the great controversy over method which was exciting European economists. This was a challenge to the deductive method and an assertion that more progress would be achieved in the future by following the methodological principles of the Germans who were looking to the historical study of economic conditions as the necessary basis for building up the science on a foundation that would endure.

The next point was: "We hold that the conflict of labor and capital has brought into prominence a vast number of social problems, whose solution requires the united efforts, each in its own sphere, of the church, of the state and of science." People bred in the

British tradition would also shake their heads over this proposition. There were many of them who did not see much chance of a satisfactory working alliance between science and the church, and who thought that one of the chief principles of economic science was that things would go far better in human affairs if the state confined itself to the narrowest possible list of functions. That was a view being expounded at this time clearly and strictly as ever and possibly more forcibly than before by no less a person than Herbert Spencer, especially in his popular *Social Statics* and *Man Versus the State.*

The last point read: "In the study of the industrial and commercial policy of governments we take no partisan attitude. We believe in a progressive development of economic conditions, which must be met by a corresponding development of legislative policy." Once again like the Germans, the promoters were invoking the state as an important element in building up a satisfactory economic life. The English, Lord knows, had made sufficient and relatively skillful use of the state. They were beginning to do so in an increasing degree, just at this time, driven more or less by necessity. But every time that they invoked the powers of the state to regulate economic conditions they found some specific reason why this exception to the general rule should be made. As for subscribing to a general rule that there must be a development of legislative policy to create the basis of *laissez faire,* the Lord knows, no orthodox English economist or supporter of the English tradition could accede.

The last point in the statement of principles seems to mean that the people who founded this association anticipated mixing into the course of practical affairs in very considerable measure. They would "take no partisan attitude," but they did believe in a "progressive development of economic conditions" and "corresponding development of legislative policy." And that threatened again the meddling of the state in business affairs quite contrary to the general principles of *laissez faire.*

All this clearly indicates that the gentlemen who provided the "statement of principles" were at the time strongly under German influence, and it is not surprising that when they tried to secure members for the American Economic Association and turned to the men whose names had prestige value, they met with more than one refusal. Indeed, they found it so difficult to secure members that before they could get the association formed and the constitution adopted they found it necessary to subjoin to the statement of principles the following note: "This statement was proposed and accepted as a general indication of the views and purposes of those who founded the American Economic Association, but it is not to be regarded as binding upon individual members."[27]

The statement of principles, to repeat, was not binding. Anybody could join the association and not accept its creed unless that creed appealed to him; and on that understanding a good many of the older men, particularly the men whose accession was most ardently desired, came in; and the association was a going organization. The first president was Walker; the second was Dunbar, seven years later.[28]

The curious thing is that these young men, who turned out to have a high level of intelligence and vigor, who came back from Germany so thoroughly indoctrinated with the viewpoint of the German economists of the day, as they came in the course of years to face the problems of their positions as teachers of economics, as students of current problems, as writers of books, found themselves reverting from the German to the English tradition. The text-books that have been prepared by Seligman, and by Ely and younger colleagues who have worked with him under his banner, while making free and skillful use of a good deal of objective material, are still fundamentally organized on lines which were laid down by the writers of the classical school on the one side and by the Austrian school on the other side— lines one could more justly say derived from these two sources and blended after the fashion which Marshall had shown to be possible.

This is all the more remarkable because in the 70's and 80's the difference between the German and the English traditions seemed far more accentuated than it seems now. The period was the heydey of the younger historical school in Germany; that is, the time when Schmoller was carrying on his active controversy with Menger over method, and when, with his *protégés* he was exercising an enormous influence upon the minds and still more upon the perspective of the German economists, when the group of exceedingly vigorous, enterprising, marvelously industrious young Germans were thinking of themselves as laying the foundations for a new inductive science of economics. Few of the German professors whom the Americans heard were perhaps as extreme in insisting upon the sole righteousness of the inductive method as Schmoller himself, but most of them leaned very strongly in that direction.

---

[27] "Constitution, By Laws and Resolutions of The American Economic Association," in American Economic Association, *Publications,* 1st series (New York: Macmillan, 1887) volume 1, pp. 35-36.

[28] [Walker had been sympathetic to the organization from the start. Dunbar became a member shortly after the Council of the Association approved the dropping of the "Statement of Principles" in December 1887.]

Furthermore, those German-trained students who in later life had most to do with the development of economic theory in the stricter sense and who definitely devoted themselves to carrying on the theoretical side of economics, were working in the English rather than the German tradition. This refers primarily to J. B. Clark and Simon N. Patten, who long stood as the chief American theorists, with the possible addition of General Walker, so long as he lived.

If the student will read any of the numerous books of Patten (1852-1922), he will find that while they have a marked degree of originality, they are still quite clearly the output of a utilitarian philosopher, a man of great ingenuity, a man whose understanding of human nature, however, is not unfairly to be compared with that of Bentham. Patten was purely speculative but he was an inspirational teacher.[29]

Highly ingenious mind with quaint quirks. A utilitarian philosopher, concerned with problem of welfare in economics. Artificial and mechanical, much like James Mackaye in his *The Economy of Happiness* (1906) and *The Happiness of Nations* (1915). Patten's *Theory of Prosperity* (1902) treats of emergence from "pain" economy to "pleasure" economy. [Later he spoke of the development of society from a "deficit" to a "surplus" economy.] Patten's theory of consumption—sugar diet vs. liquor diet, 1884.[30]

["The rapid increase in the use of sugar is now worthy of special attention, because of its connection with the temperance movement. . . . The temperance people as a class live on a sugar diet, sugar being that part of their diet from which they derive the greater part of their pleasure. . . . With every reduction in the price of sugar, they gain an increasing advantage in the struggle for life over the drinking classes, and the day does not seem far distant when the cheapness of their diet will give them an industrial supremacy in the greater part of the field of employment."][31]

This topic is treated more elaborately in the monograph, *Consumption of Wealth*, four years later. Influence of cost of commodities upon consumption. Pains incident to consumption modify demand for commodities. We

---

[29] Last sentence from Student Notes, March 12, 1924.

[30] Outline, January 20, 1920.

[31] [Patten, "The Effect of the Consumption of Wealth on the Economic Welfare of Society," 1885; reprinted in his *Essays in Economic Theory,* edited by R. G. Tugwell (New York: Knopf, 1924) pp. 5-6.

Böhm-Bawerk said that "we see one of the most gifted of the younger investigators, Professor Simon N. Patten, who has drunk of the empiricism of Germany at its source, and carried it to America, nevertheless break a lance on behalf of the abstract-deductive method and its equal rights." ("The Historical vs. The Deductive Method," translated by Henrietta Leonard, *The Annals of the American Academy of Political and Social Sciences,* October 1890, p. 27.)

Joseph A. Schumpeter considered Patten along with Frank A. Fetter and Irving Fisher as "unconditional supporters of the marginal utility theory." See his *Economic Doctrine and Method,* translated by R. Aris (London: Allen and Unwin, 1954) p. 43.]

seek not greatest amount of happiness but greatest balance of happiness over pain. Example: Man at free feast as compared with man at a restaurant where he must pay for all. In latter case he would not eat many of the costly things which give much pleasure that he would eat at free dinner. This shows the two orders in which we choose commodities for consumption.

1. Natural order, i.e., order in which men choose commodities for consumption when influenced only by those ultimate psychological conditions which make consumption of some commodities more pleasurable than others.

2. Economic order, i.e., order of consumption when desires are modified by amount of labor required to produce articles of consumption. . . . Fall of price of sugar of great importance here. Ratio of pleasure to cost rises and therefore sugar comes into general use. It tends to take place of liquor which was formerly the pleasure giving portion of meals. Has thus great significance for the temperance movement.

The outlook for the future. "Cheap men" are those who will work hard for a little amount of food, because their appetites are so strong. Progress, it appears from above, comes through the destruction of the cheaper men due to their yielding to their appetites. Society's duty to these lower classes is to help them by making new pleasures—especially education—cheap to them.[32]

Anyone who gets into the profound treatises of J. B. Clark (1847-1938) will find himself walking in a world of the imagination which is built abstractly of set purpose and for a definite end. The whole technique of the discussion is of the sort that Ricardo provided and that Clark's German teachers would have repudiated [in part].[33]

How Clark's type differs from those heretofore discussed. Have noted that chief differentiating characteristic lies in central problem attacked. Adam Smith —how wealth of nations may be increased; Ricardo—problem of distribution; more specifically, the proportions in which income is distributed between labor, land and capital; Jevons—problem of exchange value; Marshall—value theory made the instrument for discussing distribution; Schmoller [to be discussed later]—historical evolution, statistical description, theoretical analysis and economic policy. Clark takes Marshall's neo-Ricardian view that distribution is the central problem; but he has a different way of stating the problem. An attack which makes his work widely diverge from Marshall's; practices the method of abstraction far

---

[32] Abstract of *The Consumption of Wealth* in "Patten," APP 74-83, no. 23. Another important work of Patten is *The Reconstruction of Economic Theory*, supplement to *The Annals of the American Academy of Political and Social Sciences*, November 1889. (Outline, January 20, 1920.)

[Two full length studies have been published on Patten: James Boswell, *The Economics of Simon Nelson Patten* (1934) and D. M. Fox, *The Discovery of Abundance and the Transformation of Social Theory* (1967).]

[33] On Clark see Paul T. Homan, "John Bates Clark: Earlier and Later Phases of His Work," *The Quarterly Journal of Economics*, November 1927, pp. 39-69. (Addition to Outline, January 20, 1920.)

more systematically than his predecessors. Analysis of the static state carried through elaborately, followed by analysis of dynamic factors to complete his system of political economy. Distinction between statics and dynamics in earlier writers—Clark's elaboration—he thought of statics as equivalent to discussion of natural or normal conditions by classical economists. He independently developed the same range of ideas as is found in Jevons, Menger and Walras. Like the latter two he did not impress hedonism on his disciples; in fact, he is the largest figure in the development of this type of economics in the United States.

Life: a typical New Englander of the philosophic, devout, reformist kind. Born, Providence, Rhode Island 1847. Educated at Brown and Amherst. A.B. 1872. Was among the earliest in the long procession of American students of economics to go to Germany. With Karl Knies at Heidelberg, and also a student at Zurich. Returned in 1875 to teach and write. Carleton College, Minnesota, 1877-1881; Smith 1881-1893; Amherst 1893-1895; Columbia 1895-1923 [and then emeritus]. In 1911 became director of the division of economics and history of the Carnegie Endowment for International Peace. As such, had a large share in organizing the foundation's History of the World War [I]. First book: *The Philosophy of Wealth: Economic Principles Newly Formulated*, (1886). [Origin:] In the later 1870's Clark began publishing a series of articles in *The New Englander*, which aim at "reformulating . . . certain leading principles of economic science." Chief defects which he found in traditional economics: "The traditional system was . . . defective in its premises. These were assumptions rather than facts, and the conclusions deduced from them were, for that reason, uncertain." In particular the conception of human nature was defective. "The better elements of human nature were a forgotten factor . . .; the man of the scientific formula was more mechanical and more selfish than the man of the actual world. A degraded conception of human nature vitiated the theory of the distribution of wealth." "The prevalent theory of value started with a misconception of utility and of the part which it plays in exchanges." "Economic science . . . made no important use of the fact that society is an organism, to be treated as a unit in the discussion of many processes affecting wealth." Clark was not aware of Jevons's work when he wrote.

Taking ten years for the task, Clark worked out these articles, revised them and published the volume above. This little book of less than 250 pages contains the germs of his later treatises; has a freshness of mind which the latter lack. But with all its power, the book is a collection of pregnant suggestions, not fully worked out. Shall confine myself to showing how Clark develops his leading criticisms of "the traditional system."

1. Assumptions regarding human nature must be replaced by study of facts. For them economists must go not to psychology, but to anthropology. What Clark himself tried to do in this direction: A man is not independent but an atom in a higher organization. Society is literally an organism and gradually makes man better—unselfish; thus opening the way to moral law, establishes non-competitive economics. With this process of moralizing economic life Clark is much concerned. Two elements in competition.

---

[34] Clark, *The Philosophy of Wealth* (Boston: Ginn, 1886) preface.

He dilates upon the evils of "predatory competition" of which workmen have been the chief victims. What we need for guidance is a clear standard of equity which we can apply. The preoccupation with the "honesty" of the social processes in distribution of wealth has dominated Clark's later work. The standard of equity in buying and selling commodities [is presented]. In fixing wages, best plan is cooperation, next best profit-sharing, next best arbitration. But we are likely to move through arbitration to full cooperation.

2. Clark's development of utility analysis. Later than Jevons but arrived at independently. "Effective utility," [which is Clark's term for marginal utility]. Definition of value. How it is measured. Social effective utility. The chief differences between Clark and the European formulators of marginal utility were two. First, he emphasized the part played by society as a whole in the organic process of the market. The other was finding fault with the English writers for their excessive individualism.[35]

As he went on with his teaching and reflecting, he elaborated his views. I strongly advise all members of the class to read *The Philosophy of Wealth* not only because of its originality, but because of its charm. It shows Clark as he was in his younger days when his vision of what economic theory might and ought to be was just beginning to dawn on him. It was before he had worked out the details and achieved an exposition so thorough that he became difficult to read.

He wrote many articles on economic theory, particularly in *The Quarterly Journal of Economics* and several technical monographs in *Publications of the American Economic Association* in 1888-1889. Had a series of discussions with Böhm-Bawerk on nature of capital and interest in *The Quarterly Journal of Economics* in 1895. Finally after fifteen years, published *The Distribution of Wealth: A Theory of Wages, Interest and Profits* (1899); his chief contribution to development of economic theory. Why not also rent [in title]? Because rent is merely another form of interest. Established his reputation as one of the leading economic theorists in a day when economic theory was vaguely thought of as something apart from and higher than factual investigation of economic conditions. [As Sir W. J. Ashley declared in 1907, "an independent theoretician of the first rank, Professor Clark already has carried most of the younger economists of the United States with him; and is beginning to make himself felt on this side of the ocean."][36]

Purpose: to show that distribution is controlled by "a natural law." This law is just in sense that it gives each factor what it contributes. But what is a "natural law"? The law which would prevail in a static state. What is a static state? Mobility of capital and labor without motion. Clark holds

---

[35] Outlines, January 20, 1920; January 19, 1932; "Ostensible Dropping of Hedonism in Economic Theory After Edgeworth," APP 44-53, no. 5. Last three sentences from Student Notes, March 12, 1924.

[36] ["The Present Position of Political Economy," *The Economic Journal,* December 1907, p. 47.]

that the best way to understand actual conditions in that rigorous scientific way which facilitates control is to begin with the simple and the fundamental forces—those found in the static state. Then admit the changes which differentiate static from actual conditions; see what modifications these changes introduce and so get dynamic theory. "One can hardly assert too emphatically the dominance of the static forces in real and dynamic societies."

Concept of human nature—hedonistic. Men pursue happiness. Men are controlled by forces in the environment. Man as consumer owns man as producer, etc. Ultimate aim of production is pleasure of consumption. Few no-rent men. Men can compare pleasures; also pleasures and pains; but they cannot measure them. Economists can "estimate" pleasure in terms of pain *at the margin,* which is all important. Balance between pain cost and pleasure won is found in each individual's economy. But not between different individuals as producers and consumers.

Outline of the argument: 1. A society in which production is organized in groups and sub-groups including transportation and merchandising; in which products of different groups are exchanged under free competition; in which each worker and each unit of capital can shift occupation freely and will shift if advantage can be gained thereby.

2. Static conditions. Population constant (number of laborers does not change, nor number of consumers). Capital constant (no new accumulation and no net loss, but constant renewal as with population). Methods of production constant (no technical discoveries introduced into industry). Forms of business organization constant (no new combinations of capital). Wants of consumers constant (no new consumers' goods). A static state inhabited by hedonists, organized for production in groups and sub-groups exchanging goods under free competition, perfect mobility of labor and capital. In this society there is perfect mobility but no motion, because adjustments among the several elements have been so perfectly worked out that no element has any inducement to change its place among the economic constellations.

3. Under these circumstances no distinction is to be drawn between land and capital. For old distinction between land as fixed and capital as variable does not hold in the static state, where capital is constant. And old distinction between rent as a differential income and wages and profits as fixed by laws of other types fails. In the static state one can apply differential methods of accounting for the labor income of any man, or the capital income for any enterprise quite as well as to the rent of any land; that is, there are no-rent margins for labor and capital as well as for land for which one may reckon. Lands are one form of capital goods in which capital can be invested and argument developed regarding return from capital applies to return upon capital invested in land in same way it applies to capital invested in machines. Rent and interest in a static state are the same income stated in different ways—net income in dollars is rent; that sum as a percentage of capital is interest.

4. Concept of capital. Clark's distinction between "capital" and "capital goods." Is a distinction between a fund of value invested in commodities and the specific commodities as such. "Capital consists of instruments of

production, and these are always concrete and material." Capital never "lives in a disembodied state." Capital goods also are concrete and material. Both can be valued in money. Difference lies in permanence of capital, perishability of capital goods; mobility of capital, immobility of capital goods. Now both capital and capital goods can be and habitually are valued in money, and we may speak of them in monetary equivalents. In this language "capital is a sum of productive wealth, invested in material things which are perpetually shifting—which come and go continually —although the fund abides. Capital thus lives . . . by transmigration." Capital earns interest; capital goods earn rent. Capital replaces itself; it provides a sinking fund, which must be allowed for before interest is calculated. New capital, however, is created by abstinence, by diverting income in money from purchase of consumers' goods to purchase of capital goods. "In the absence of disaster" the new capital will last forever. Abstinence and disaster are both dynamic phenomena. In the static state capital recreates itself without increment or diminution. It has "an inherent power to create wealth."

5. How distribution is effected. For production society organizes itself into industrial groups; e.g., producers of bread and of woolen clothing—and sub-groups; e.g., wheat growers, millers, bakers—wool growers, spinners and weavers, tailors. Distribution accordingly is effected by three stages: 1st division of total product fixes the income of industrial groups. 2nd division fixes the part of the total income of an industrial group which goes to each of its sub-groups. 3rd division "adjusts wages and interest within each of the innumerable sub-groups in the system." 1st and 2nd divisions depend entirely on the prices of goods." But these prices tend to be such that "labor and capital in one industry produce as much and get as much as they do in any other." In the static state these adjustments of prices to equalize wages and interest become perfect. "No further inducement to move"—"perfect mobility, no motion." "When the adjustment is complete, the income of . . . a group, if it be reduced to value, is its own virtual product." True also of each sub-group and each factor within it.

6. Wages. The unit of labor. How these units are allocated to different groups and sub-groups. The employer's role. Price of labor like that of any good, fixed by the marginal unit. Herbert Joseph Davenport's criticism [should say "at" instead of "by"]. To find what determines wages therefore, we must find what is the market on which marginal labor is sold. What final unit of labor gets in this market sets the standard for all labor. Find such a market on no-rent lands and no-rent capital goods. Under these circumstances men work "virtually empty-handed." No-rent uses of good instruments of production furnish a further and a larger market for marginal labor. This intensive margin runs through industry; that is, there is a zone of indifference in each employer's field of employment. If capital can change its forms there is no limit to number of men it can employ. These marginal men who work with no-rent instruments on the intensive or extensive margins get the product specifically attributable to their labor. The effective importance of *any man* to his employer is measured by seeing what he would lose if one man left—that loss is the loss of a marginal worker. When a man goes to another employment, what he adds is one

more labor unit which must be applied on the margin of employment in his new job. Competition equalizes effective productivity in all employments.

7. Interest. Similar reasoning leads to a conclusion about interest like that about wages.

8. Profits: Are residual incomes left after paying interest and wages as determined by final productivity. Are no such residuals in the static state. Note how Clark thinks of the entrepreneur's function: "includes no working and no owning of capital."

9. Reaction of these laws upon apportionment of labor and capital among industrial groups.

10. Reaction upon values. Note Clark's insistence upon regarding consumers' goods as bundles of different utilities tied together. Things sell according to their final utility to society. Every utility in a costly article is somewhere in the position of a final utility.

11. Unit for measuring values: Effective utility measured by pain. Effective social utility measured by marginal labor pain. Commodities exchange on basis of their effective social utility; these utilities are measured by marginal labor pains; every unit of labor and of capital gets what it has specifically added to the social product.

12. Outcome of the argument. Purpose of the whole investigation is "to show that distribution is controlled by a natural law, and that this law, if it worked without friction," would give each agent what it creates. The general thesis has been proved. The "right of society to exist in its present form" has been vindicated. Division of social income is "honest."[37]

Dynamics: Eight years more of work after *Distribution of Wealth* and Clark offered "a brief and provisional statement of the more general laws of progress," in the study *Essentials of Economic Theory as Applied to Modern Problems of Industry and Public Policy* (1907), a smaller and more elementary work but one which covers a large part of the field. Primarily a text book restating his system of static theory and adding his discussion of dynamics. Relation between a dynamic and a static state. Static forces at any given time dominant. But dynamic forces are always causing divergencies from static results and changing the static model itself. There may be any number of static "models," depending upon relative abundance of labor and capital (and technology?). Conformity to static model closer in highly dynamic societies. Five influences that disturb static equilibrium. "The grand resultant of all the changes that are going on" is a rise of wages. Technical progress. Increase of population tends to depress wages and interest. But is more than offset by technical progress and increase of capital. And a rise in standard of living tends to check increase of population. Accumulation of capital, of course, tends to accelerate economic well-being. Progress in accumulation of capital would be self-retarding if a low rate of interest checked saving, as has often been asserted. Such is not the case. On the contrary, a low rate of interest leads to greater savings. For primary motive of saving is to insure a given

---

[37] Outline, January 19, 1932. Quotations are from *The Distribution of Wealth* (New York: Macmillan, 1899) pp. v, 3, 15, 16, 67, 92, 116, 119, 120, 134, 135.

standard of living in future, and the lower the rate of interest the more saving is necessary to be sure of maintaining the standard in question. Savings further stimulated by the transience of large profits. A falling rate of interest even more conducive to saving than a low one. There is no danger that low interest resulting from large accumulations of capital will check further accumulation and so retard progress. "Influences which pervert the forces of progress." Changes in organization. Under operation of "natural forces," with no obstructions to competition, "progress will continue forever." Monopoly the antithesis of competition, the great perverting force. Necessity of regulation; potential competition as regulator. *Laissez faire* impossible, monopoly the gravest menace.

Conclusion: Public policy would be guided by "a knowledge of economic law."[38]

Clark's later books after *The Philosophy of Wealth* are more or less metaphysical in tone. He is one of the German-trained economists, who, when he began to think for himself, found it was important to consider what would happen in economic life under certain assumed conditions which he carefully defined. His marked logical power is shown by the subtle and powerful way in which he develops the consequences of the suppositions. In a certain sense, it is the Ricardian method of procedure carried on by a man whose intellectual talents are more or less those of a medieval schoolmaster, but who is also a very keen observer of the world about him.

His most important volume, from the theoretical point of view, *The Distribution of Wealth,* is confined to the discussion of static problems; that is, an imaginary situation in which no changes of what he calls the dynamic order are occurring, the theorist being aware, that his conclusions concerning what happens in the static state are incapable of direct application to the interpretation of the phenomena of experience, and is convinced that the only way of really achieving an understanding of the problems which concern the citizens of a modern community, is to subdivide the task of inquiry. First, set up a relatively simple imaginary problem in which the most difficult elements of reality are excluded, solve the problem in that form, then later bring in by way of added suppositions some at least of the important factors in the situation which were excluded in the first instance, and see what differences are caused in the conclusions by the introduction of these new elements, and so proceed by the method of approximation toward an understanding of what is actually going on.

---

[38] Outline, January 19, 1932. Quotations are from *The Essentials of Economic Theory as Applied to Modern Problems of Industry and Public Policy* (New York: Macmillan, 1907) pp. v, 308, 372, 374.

In *Essentials of Economic Theory* he makes some progress toward the ultimate goal of bringing into consideration factors other than static. Clark had grown up with an interest in ethical and moral issues at least as fervent as that which characterized Alfred Marshall. The problem that concerned him most, particularly in his earlier days, though his interest never waned perceptibly, was the question whether economic organization, as it exists, is justified. He set about getting an answer to the problem by studying the way in which economic organization actually operates. In order to find out how it works, he did not find it feasible to engage in laborious historical inquiries into the economic history of man in the United States or to undertake equally arduous statistical researches into the rates of wages, interest, rents and profits. Had he undertaken such investigations he might have spent a laborious lifetime in gathering materials which presumably would have had some pertinence to the question that he longed so deeply to answer; but he would never have gotten to the point where he would have had material which sufficed to give him his answer. Presumably long before his collection of data had reached anything like adequacy, he would have discovered that he could not utilize these materials for the solution of his problem.

Clark's way was to examine the matter in an analytic fashion. This seemed, as he thought matters out, to lead expeditiously to a set of conclusions which required no factual evidence to show their validity. His way of setting about the problem was to say that the inquirer must consider what is basic in present economic organization. When the theorist asks the question he will see that people are for purposes of production divided up first into industries; the industries that provide the people with clothing and so on. Then divide them up into sub-groups within the industries—special groups like the growers of wheat, the millers who grind flour, the bakers who make flour into bread, the retail dealers who sell bread; or again, like the men who grow cotton, the manufacturers who first spin and then weave the cotton into cloth, and the dealers who make the cloth up into clothing. This is the first characteristic to be observed in economic organization.

Then the theorist notices that each of the subdivisions is composed of people who perform various functions. There are the men who direct the process of production: employers. There are the people who provide capital: the investors. There are the people who do the bulk of the manual and clerical labor: the workers. And there are those who own the natural resources of one sort and another—notably including land which has to be used by every business enterprise.

If the theorist wants to find out whether this organization of society is justified, he must ask how does the distribution of wealth work itself out in an organization composed of industries and sub-groups of business enterprises in which there are employers, investors, owners of natural resources, and laborers? To discover how the distribution of wealth is carried on in this society is a task that is impossibly bewildering unless the theorist can simplify the problem. In practice changes keep occurring in so many different factors affecting the process, and the changes are so interrelated, that the theorist can never get a clear view of the fundamental controlling conditions unless he is willing for a while to set aside the obscuring flow of alterations.

So Clark said the problem is to be considered on the assumption that the society is one in which economic change is ruled out, that the number of the population and the number of laborers remain constant; that there is no alteration in the amount of capital available. It is also assumed that the forms of business organization do not alter; that is, the proliferation of new methods of business organization like the formation of trusts is precluded. Finally it is assumed that the habits of consumption do not change; that there is no incoming of new products like airplanes, electric refrigerators and radio sets. If we do this, then we have a problem which we can attack with a high degree of hope of getting substantial results, for the problem then is simple enough for the theorist to think about effectively.

Obviously this approach to the problem that commended itself to Clark's mind and which he had worked out with such extraordinary original acumen over a period of twenty-five years, is one of the general type to which David Ricardo set himself when he got in such quick order the conclusions that appeared in *The High Price of Bullion;* and which he followed again when he wrote on *The Principles of Political Economy and Taxation;* it was the method taken up by John Stuart Mill; it was the method too, after Clark had begun his work, which was so brilliantly exemplified by Marshall. By following this procedure through, Clark was able to get an answer to his question which satisfied his own mind. With this static society, it seemed to him possible to demonstrate that under the conditions of perfect competition which would prevail, every agent of production would get as a reward for participation in producing goods for society a value which was equivalent to the value attributable to his own service.

This was worked out in the fashion familiar to readers of Marshall, only Clark did the things on the basis of a static state, whereas Marshall was more realistic and considered many problems of change. It was worked out by showing that under these conditions the rates of pay for any kind of labor must be uniform in all business enterprises, in all sub-groups in all industries. For, given perfect competition, a man would be unwilling to labor in a place when for work of the same sort he could acquire higher pay elsewhere. Also the employer under the conditions of perfect competition will be unwilling to pay one laborer of a certain type more than the sum for which he could get another laborer of the same type.

Consequently the rate of wages for any given grade of labor must be uniform throughout the static society. The same remark would apply to capital. There could not be a higher rate of interest on capital in one business enterprise than another and there could not be a lower market rate prevailing anywhere. Clark went on to argue that natural resources in the modern state are to be regarded as goods in which capital has been invested. They are to be treated in exactly the same way as capital. Thus the rule of uniformity of return extends to the demand for the use of land and anything else.

What fixes the rate of return which will be paid for a given type of labor, remembering that the rate is going to be strictly uniform? It will be worthwhile for an employer to add additional men to his enterprises up to the point where the product that is due to the specific work of the added laborer is worth more than the wage he has to pay. It will not be worth an employer's while to increase the employment beyond that point; that is, he will not be willing to pay a person for producing things which have a value less than the wage that has to be paid. Wages must rise under these conditions up to the margin set by the value of service rendered, and will not rise above that point. In other words, the wages of every kind of labor equal the specific productivity of that labor.

The like remark applies to capital. Interest represents the specific addition which the use of things like machinery adds to the efficiency of the productive process. It cannot be less than the specific productivity of capital, for if it were then there would be a profit over and above the ordinary rate to be had by borrowing more capital, investing it in machinery, and turning out more products. Thus Clark was able to draw the comforting conclusion that in a society which works on the static model—observe—everybody gets an income which depends upon what he produces—and that is just.

To sum up the chief idea which Clark contributed to technical economic theory in *The Distribution of Wealth* is that every factor in distribution under static conditions is rewarded in accordance with its *specific productivity*. His analysis seems to show that under the given conditions it is possible to determine at the margin just what part of a product arising from the use of land, labor and capital can be attributed to each of these factors, and to show that the price which will be obtained by each of the factors under the conditions assumed will be equal to its specific marginal productivity.[39]

The only question that remains concerning the justification for society as now organized, is how far does the basic static law rule in a world of change? The problem is attacked in Clark's later, less well known *Essentials of Economic Theory*. He is able to show to his own satisfaction again, that the controlling forces in modern life are the static ones and that departures from the static model which are brought about by increase of labor, by changes in methods, etc., for the most part work to enhance the income of all participants in the process. The one set of changes which he viewed with great alarm were those which interfered with perfect competition.

From his point of view, the one serious departure in the practical operations of modern society from what prevails under static conditions, is found in the existence of monopoly; and like a good logician he became one of the most vigorous and great opponents of all practices that tended toward monopoly in any measure, whether those of business men and capitalists or those of laborers.

---

[39] [As regards his work in mathematical economics, Clark informed Walras in 1896 that "The little that I have myself done in that direction has not called for the use of algebraic formulas, though it has relied on diagrams. The articles have been published chiefly in *The Yale Review*, and *The Quarterly Journal of Economics*." His earliest statement of the marginal productivity doctrine, Clark continued, was in his monograph "Possibility of a Scientific Law of Wages," *Publications of the American Economic Association*, March 1889. "The statement of the law there given is mathematical in fact but not in form. In the later statements of the same law diagrams were used to express the variations of productivity involved. I suppose—though of course I cannot be quite certain—that the paper printed in the *Wages* monograph contains the earliest expression of the Final Productivity Theory of Wages and Interest. . . . I think we shall hereafter make a larger use of mathematical modes of thought and expression." (Clark to Walras, February 28, 1896, in *Correspondence of Léon Walras and Related Papers*, II, p. 669.) In the same letter Clark spoke of Wieser's "admirable" *Der natürliche Werth* (1889) "which has points of kinship with . . . [Clark's] theory, though it is not identical with it, [and] appeared almost at the same time." Clark presented an embryonic version of his theory in "Capital and Its Earnings" (*Publications of the American Economic Association*, May 1888). See Joseph Dorfman, *The Economic Mind in American Civilization*, 5 volumes (New York: The Viking Press, 1946-1959) III, pp. 196-198.]

Patten and Clark were subject to a great deal of criticism at the hands of another set of men who regarded themselves in a more especial degree as representatives of a sound classical theory. In the journals in the 1890's and the early 1900's, there were many articles criticizing the marginal analysis in economic theory at large, contrasting the ingenious and often beautiful speculations of Patten and Clark with the work of the great masters of classical economics and regarding the contrast to the disadvantage of the innovators. This meant that in the chairs of the leading universities there were many people who still felt that the model which had been set by John Stuart Mill, with some possible minor improvements introduced by his faithful disciple, J. E. Cairnes, represented the best that had been accomplished so far. Indeed, some of these men regarded even the temperate innovations introduced by Marshall, particularly the limited use that he made of marginal analysis, as moving in the wrong direction. People of this temper distrusted the bold originality of Patten and the subtleties of Clark, who represented at its best the type of theory which interested the most inquiring and constructive minds in the 1890's when economic theory began to be cultivated intensively and extensively in the United States.[40]

The older representatives of the classical tradition in economics, however, did not produce any important results in the science, for the reason that they did not see that innovations were called for. They were defenders of a system which so many seemed to regard, as did Mill himself, to be well rounded out. The duty of economists in their view was primarily that of teaching established doctrines, trying to apply them to problems of the day, to make the influence of economics felt in general public discussions, to guard the country against rash legislation which was contrary to the laws of political economy.

Despite these criticisms, Patten and Clark produced a considerable intellectual impression upon the younger people interested in the subject in the United States and became rather well-known abroad. Indeed, in so far as economic theory is concerned—and in those days there was a sharp distinction between economic theory and the rest of economics—the first important changes in the general character of the subject were introduced by these men.

If this were a systematic course on the development of economic theory; that is, if it were designed to trace the history of the subject in detail, it would be necessary to deal analytically and at considerable

---

[40] Outline, November 17, 1927.

length both with the somewhat quaint ideas of Patten and with the extraordinarily subtle system of economic theory excogitated by Clark. But, as the title indicates, it merely discusses representatives of various types of economic theory. Furthermore, since Patten's student, Professor R. G. Tugwell, likes to deal at length with his old teacher in the graduate course that he offers here at Columbia [in 1930] on contemporary economic theory and American samples, especially; and inasmuch as it is appropriate to deal with the contrasting work of Clark alongside that of Patten, I pass them over and take as a representative of the general line of inquiry which they may be said to have sponsored, a younger and later writer, Frank A. Fetter.[41] It is not that Fetter is in any strict sense a disciple either of Patten or of Clark, but he stands as the chief representative of what he himself has called the "American Psychological School" and it is in part, at least, another version of the conception of human nature that contributed to the originality of Clark and Patten.

---

[41] [The basic study of Patten is still Tugwell's "Notes on the Life and Work of Simon Nelson Patten," *The Journal of Political Economy*, April 1923, pp. 153-208. One of the most perceptive studies of J. B. Clark is by his son, J. M. Clark, "J. M. Clark on J. B. Clark," in *The Development of Economic Thought* edited by H. W. Spiegel (New York: Wiley, 1952) pp. 593-612.]

CHAPTER XII

Frank A. Fetter and the American Psychological School

Fetter's treatises seem to be fairly representative of the type of work which has been most characteristic of the American economists who have devoted themselves specifically to theoretical issues. A large proportion of the German-trained economists devoted themselves primarily to other matters. For instance, Seligman went into the broad field of public finance; Ely eventually specialized in land and public utility problems; Bogart in economic history; Seager largely in labor organization; Taussig in tariff and monetary questions. Fetter, however, like Clark and Patten was more concerned with developing a system of pure theory rather than with applied economic problems.[1] His studies are an admirable representation of some of the subtlest studies that Americans have done in that direction.

Fetter was born in Peru, Indiana, in 1863; he studied successively at Indiana University, at Cornell, at the Sorbonne, at the École de Droit in Paris, and at Halle where he received his doctor's degree in 1894. On returning to the United States he was an instructor at Cornell for a while, then after holding a professorship of political economy and social science at Indiana, he went to Stanford and then returned to Cornell in 1901 as professor of political economy and finance; in 1911 he transferred to Princeton as professor of political economy and chairman of the department of economics and social institutions.

Fetter is fond of referring to the "American Psychological School," a phrase which will be used to indicate the type of theory which he cultivated. The American Psychological School seems to have been largely influenced by Clark and Patten and by Austrian theorists,

---

[1] [Fetter became tremendously interested in the problem of monopoly, beginning in the early 1920's and was influential in the advancement of the treatment of that subject in both value theory and national policy. Clark and Patten likewise devoted considerable effort to the same question.]

particularly Böhm-Bawerk.[2] This so-called psychological school of economic theory, which Fetter represents, attempts to get down to fundamentals in giving an account of economic behavior. But particularly in his second treatise, *Economic Principles* (1915),[3] he recognized the urgent necessity of effecting what he regards as a basic change in the psychology which is employed to account for economic behavior.

In his attempt to provide a sounder psychological foundation, he represents an attitude which was gradually becoming common among the more alert theorists. In the discussion of the developments characteristic of the period between Jevons and Marshall, it was pointed out that there was a declining faith in hedonism. The doctrine which Bentham had propounded with so much confidence, which had seemed but common sense to the majority of his contemporaries, and which continued to be relied upon, broadly speaking, by most students of human behavior, was becoming less and less acceptable as people learned more about human behavior at large. The theory that men's actions are guided by an attempt to maximize pleasure and to minimize pain seemed incompatible with much that was being learned about mankind by biologists like Darwin as well as by people who were professionally engaged in psychological investigation.

We have seen that the broad pleasure-pain doctrine had not explicitly been made the basis of economic theorizing by the classical masters, but there is sufficient warrant for believing that their view of human nature was substantially the view that Jeremy Bentham drew up in meticulous detail. But not until Jevons does a major English economist take Bentham's exposition of the conventional psychology into economics and make it explicitly the foundation upon which economic theories were based. That happened just at the time that people were beginning to lose faith in Bentham's psychology,

---

[2] Sentence from Outline, January 20, 1920. [Böhm-Bawerk predicted that the utility school would be called the psychological school (see Chapter IX).]

[3] [His first book on theory was *The Principles of Economics with Applications to Practical Problems* (1904). There were three editions of this work plus reprintings of each edition. The second treatise was a two volume work in 1915-1916 with the general title *Economics;* volume I carried as the main title *Economic Principles* and volume II, *Modern Economic Problems.*]

Fetter, through his first book, was largely responsible at least in the United States for the revived use of the term "enterpriser." "Of the various aliases under which the man who is doing business on his own account passes in current economic literature (entrepreneur, undertaker, capitalist, employer, business man), the name enterpriser seems least objectionable. It is an old English word, recently brought back into current use at almost the same time by professors Frank A. Fetter (*Principles of Economics, . . .* 1904) and [W.Stanley Jevons's son] H. Stanley Jevons (*Essays on Economics, . . .* 1905)." Mitchell, *Business Cycles; The Problem and Its Setting* (New York: National Bureau of Economic Research, 1927) p. 90.

and this was one of Jevons's misfortunes. People at large lost faith in it gradually, and economists lagged behind the procession. Writers who cultivated the borderland between philosophy and economics warned economists of the passing of hedonism in psychology and raised the question, whether the utility analysis falls with hedonism.[4]

The matter was first discussed explicitly by James Bonar in 1888.[5] He pointed out that Menger, von Wieser and Böhm-Bawerk, unlike Jevons, did not explicitly build their theories upon a hedonistic foundation, but he was inclined to take a view that implicitly their utility analysis was an application of hedonistic notions. He pointed out to his brother economists that this view of conventional psychology was losing visibly among people who were making the examination of human activity their professional concern.

Presently another British writer, the philosopher John S. Mackenzie, in *An Introduction to Social Philosophy* (1890), pointed out the difficulties in accepting hedonism. He wrote:

> We may say, then, that the feeling of pleasure is simply the sense of *interest,* or of *value for consciousness.* . . . The *sense of value* presupposes *value.* . . . If value, or the sense of value, is to be estimated as more or less, we must have a standard of value, or a standard of the sense of value. . . . It will be important for us to determine whether it is value or the sense of value that we are seeking to estimate. . . . Our pleasures derive their whole colouring and content from the objects which afford pleasure—or rather from the totality of the consciousness which we feel to be agreeable . . .

> If pleasure is to be defined as a sense of value or of harmony within our consciousness, it may be allowed that there is this element in common in all particular pleasures. . . . Sense of value depends on the point of view from which value is estimated; and our point of view does not naturally remain constant throughout our conscious experience. . . . It is sometimes said that degree of pleasure means nothing more than degree of preference, . . . and since pleasure is a purely subjective experience, what is *for us* the greater *is* the greater. . . .

> When we prefer, we reflect. . . . We must . . . draw the distinction . . . between a *greater sense of value* and a *sense of greater value.* Our preference is a sense of greater value, and it does not imply that the pleasure which we prefer is in itself a greater sense of value, i.e., a greater pleasure.[6]

---

[4] Sentence from Outline, "Ostensible Dropping of Hedonism from Economic Theory after Edgeworth," APP 44-53, no. 5.

[5] Bonar, "The Austrian Economists and Their View of Value," *The Quarterly Journal of Economics,* October 1888, pp. 24-25. See also Bonar, *Philosophy and Political Economy* (London: Swann Sonnenschein, 1893) p. 236.

[6] John S. Mackenzie, *Introduction to Social Philosophy* (Glasgow: Maclehose, 1890; 2nd ed., 1895) pp. 242, 249-253. Quotations in "Pleasure and Value," APP 64-73, no. 57.

[Mackenzie at the time taught economics along with philosophy at the University of Manchester.]

Then "Thorstein Veblen made sport of the hedonistic psychology which was explicitly used by Jevons in his analysis of utility, and which was implicit in Marshall's tamer phrasing. Henry W. Stuart pushed the criticism home in more orthodox language,"[7] in several vigorous articles in 1895-1896, which clearly called the attention of American economists to the hedonistic element in most economic theorizing.[8] Stuart's viewpoint might well be called the instrumental viewpoint in economic theory, and especially pertinent is his criticism of the utility theorists for their analysis which implies a theory of what things do to men, instead of a theory of what men do to things.[9]

Many people interested in that side of economics were presently taking ground similar to that marked out by Bonar, Mackenzie, Veblen and Stuart. One of the most influential expressions of the skepticism of hedonism was the fact pointed out by Henry Sidgwick, when he said that he ate his dinner because he was hungry, not because he anticipated pleasure from food.[10] A definite positive formulation of anti-hedonistic views that had a great deal of influence upon economists was William McDougall's *Introduction to Social Psychology*, which appeared considerably later in 1908.[11] [In fact the concern of psychologists with "value" began during Professor Mitchell's years as a student at the University of Chicago in the 1890's, as indicated by his] synopsis of remarks of [Professor] James R. Angell on "Value as a Psychological Category," before the Philosophical Club of the university on February 15, 1899.[12]

I. Value is not, properly speaking, a psychological category. Word is not to be found in treatises on psychology. It is an affair rather of the special

---

[7] Mitchell, "Facts and Values in Economics," *The Journal of Philosophy*, April 13, 1944, p. 213.

[Stuart at the time was a fellow in the department of economics at the University of Chicago; later he was professor of philosophy at Stanford. He and Mitchell were close friends from their Chicago days, when both were students of Veblen and John Dewey.]

[8] "Hedonistic Interpretation of Subjective Value," *The Journal of Political Economy*, December 1895, pp. 64-84; "Subjective Exchange Value," March, June 1896, pp. 208-239, 352-385.

[9] Sentence from "H. W. Stuart," APP 84-91, no. 1a. [Professor Mitchell here used Stuart's criticism against A. C. Pigou's views as expressed in the latter's article "Some Remarks on Utility," *The Economic Journal*, March 1903, pp. 58-68.]

[10] Sentence from Outline, January 9, 1918.

[11] [McDougall was then at Oxford; later he made his home in the United States, teaching first at Harvard and then at Duke University.]

[12] [Angell taught psychology at the university; later he became president of Yale. He was a member of the Dewey school of "functional" psychologists. At a previous meeting of the club, November 27, 1898, Professor Mitchell spoke on "The Austrian Theory of Value."]

philosophical disciplines. Granted, then, that consciousness is selective, valuation is seen to be the fundamental fact of consciousness—for selection implies choice, preference of one thing over another, the valuation of one thing more than another. Basis on which this selection is made, this valuation, cannot here be discussed. It may be called "interest"; but then problem arises, what does interest imply, what makes one thing more interesting than another? Why psychologists have neglected valuation. If it be true that valuation is the fundamental fact of consciousness, question arises why value is not considered in treatises in psychology. Answer seems to be in the preponderant attention hitherto paid by psychologists to *structure* rather than *function*. Main interest had centered on the content of consciousness. Analysis has been static. Have found in mind at any given moment images and have investigated them at length. But less attention has been given to the process in which the images arise. William James, however, in his chapter on "The Stream of Consciousness" in *The Principles of Psychology* started to analyse the process rather than its content, and J. Mark Baldwin's late book—good, bad or indifferent as it may be—is an attempt in the same direction. Influence of later biology in paying more attention to function is likely to lead to similar development in psychology.

In the discussion that followed, Dewey said that the crucial point in the position taken by Angell was the explanation given of involuntary attention as after all the result of conscious selection. Also that psychologists, feeling the influence of biological thought, have come to explain selection by consciousness less on the single ground of the pleasure and pain accompanying an act; but economists seem to be accepting a theory [Austrian theory of value] which rests entirely on this basis. Asked if economic discussion had lately taken any note of biological considerations.[13]

Studies by economists for economists made the majority of the economic theorists aware of what was going on in psychology. It left them in an embarrassed and difficult position. A man like Alfred Marshall, for example, seems never to have known what to do about the issue. A comparison of the first edition of his *Principles of Economics* with later editions will reveal that without saying anything explicitly about the questionable character of the psychology upon which Ricardo, John Stuart Mill and Jevons had based their work, he modified the phrases which he employed in discussing the grounds of human action. In the first edition he talks unashamedly about pleasure as the thing which people want and about pain as that which they seek to avoid. In later editions he carefully avoided the words pleasure and pain and substituted what he seems to think were less offensive words like gratification and sacrifice, apparently

---

[13] Outline, Synopsis of James R. Angell, "Value as a Psychological Category," included in Mitchell, "Austrian Theory of Value," November 29, 1898. Brackets are Professor Mitchell's. [On Baldwin's genetic method see Joseph Dorfman, *Thorstein Veblen and His America* (New York: The Viking Press, 1934) p. 152.]

believing that by such modest changes in his choice of words he would clear his skirts of the taint of hedonism. Needless to say, the practical working conception which he entertained of human behavior remained unaltered to the day of his death. It was only the dress in which he clothed these ideas that was modified to suit the current psychological fashion.

Meanwhile other writers had tried to get rid of the taint of hedonism by more drastic methods. Irving Fisher (1867-1947) of Yale is an outstanding example. His very first publication in economics, his doctoral dissertation [in the department of mathematics at Yale], *Mathematical Investigations in the Theory of Value and Price* (1892) was such a notable performance that twenty-five years later it was thought valuable enough to be translated into French.[14]

In that book Fisher took the ground that Jevons and, in turn, Edgeworth had made a serious mistake in trying to connect economic theory with formal psychological notions. The economist, argued Fisher, should not attempt to explain why people act; for the theorist's purposes all that is necessary is to recognize that they choose. The simple fact or act of choice gives him a basis for building up demand and supply curves. It makes no practical difference to him on what their choices depend. If they do under certain circumstances choose to give certain prices for certain units in a supply of goods, or refuse to work an additional hour for less than a certain rate of pay, that is all the economist needs to know. He can take the data, make them into demand and supply schedules and then proceed to solve the problems of prices.[15]

S. The theorist cannot tell what people are going to do if he does not recognize psychological principles.

---

14 [The English original has been reprinted a number of times. There was a Japanese translation in 1933. For a complete bibliography of Fisher see Irving Norton Fisher's *A Bibliography of the Writings of Irving Fisher* (1961).]

15 [Edgeworth, who commended the work highly, pointed out that in fact Fisher was not so skeptical of the hedonistic calculus as might seem at first sight. He then went on to say, "At the same time he throws out some hints which will be valuable to the utilitarian. 'The statistician might begin with those utilities in which men are most alike—food utilities—and those disutilities in which they are most alike as the disutilities of definite sorts of manual labour. By these standards he could measure and correct the money-standard, and if the utility curves for various classes of articles were constructed, he could make rough statistics of total utility, total disutility, gain, and utility-value which would have considerable meaning. Men are much alike in their digestion and fatigue. If a food or labour standard is established, it can be easily applied to the utilities in regard to which men are unlike, as of clothes, houses, furniture, books, works of art, etc.'" (Edgeworth, review of Fisher, *Mathematical Investigations in the Theory of Value and Prices*, 1893, reprinted in his *Papers Relating to Political Economy*, 3 vols. (London: Macmillan, 1925) III, p. 41.)]

M. Yes, Fisher might admit this, but he would have said that more uncertainty is involved in passing upon psychological principles than statistical conclusions based on past behavior and accepting the belief that they will act somewhat in accordance with their past behavior in the future. If theorists do as Fisher recommended, then they are practically cutting themselves off from developing a theory of value, unless value is translated as merely equivalent to price; that is, they cut themselves off from the possibility of understanding why people attach importance to certain categories of goods. They deal with what Herbert J. Davenport has called the last mechanical stages in the process of determining prices, and they have on that basis no insight into the process of valuation as such. The theory of value for them, meaning something else than the theory of prices, gets thrown out of economics and is relegated to the tender mercies of psychologists.[16] That shift was tried, as said above, by people who were becoming uneasy concerning the compromising relations between past economic theory and hedonism.

Two other courses have been adopted: Fetter represents one and Veblen the other. After a word on Veblen by way of anticipation, the discussion will return to Fetter. Veblen beginning in 1898 published some extraordinarily subtle and penetrating criticisms of formal economic theory.[17] One of his grounds of attack was that no matter how far economists go in their ostensible efforts to get rid of hedonism they still keep on thinking about men substantially in the terms of Bentham; they still treat economic behavior as controlled by rational choice, whether they talk about pleasures and pains or sacrifices and gratifications they are practically regarding what men do as determined by a calculation concerning their advantage. This is a view of human activity, argues Veblen, which runs counter to substantially all that is known upon the subject. Whether we take the work of biologists or anthropologists or historians—and with all these branches of learning Veblen was vastly better acquainted than any but a few economic theorists—when the investigator takes any of

---

[16] Graham Wallas has pointed out in *Human Nature in Politics* (1908) that "An election (like a jury trial) will be, and is already beginning to be, looked upon rather as a process by which right decisions are formed under right conditions, than as a mechanical expedient by which decisions already formed are ascertained." Why not treat markets in similar fashion? Is not the bargaining a process by which valuations are formed under organized conditions rather than a mechanical scheme for registering the results of valuations alread arrived at. ("Graham Wallas," APP 84-91, no. 24.)

[17] "Why Is Economics Not an Evolutionary Science?," 1898; "The Preconceptions of Economic Science," 1899-1900; all reprinted in his *The Place of Science in Modern Civilisation and Other Essays* (1918). [For background of the book see preface to the fifth printing (1961) by Joseph Dorfman.]

these branches of learning or psychology itself, he comes to realize that a highly rationalized picture of human behavior is a caricature, not a faithful portrait.

Further, says Veblen, if economists study as they should the gradual evolution of human behavior, they come to see that it has changed enormously, with the progress of what he calls institutions. What a civilized man does in the course of the day is a world removed from what a savage does. This is so not because the brain of the civilized man is better organized than that of the savage, but it is vastly different, because he inherits a whole set of widely prevalent social habits of thinking, feeling and acting. If then we want a satisfactory account of economic behavior, the best hope lies not in deluding ourselves with some disinfected statement of how people make their economic conclusions, but in studying the gradual growth of the institutions that are the things which make all the difference between civilization and savagery, a view which was far more revolutionary in its implications than was Fisher's suggestion that we should drop all inquiry into the grounds of choice and center practically upon the problem of prices. Veblen would say that practically we must study human behavior as it is developing objectively, and for this purpose we must rely upon observation, supplemented at need with analysis, to find out how behavior changes from decade to decade.

S. Veblen, therefore, would change theories as frequently as institutions changed.

M. The fundamental theory would remain the same; but, his view would be that as institutions changed, new factors become of importance in affecting conduct and old factors, some at least, would become obsolescent. There will be a fuller view of Veblen when he is taken up for discussion. He is mentioned here by way of suggesting part of the pressure which Fetter as a man interested in developing the American Psychological School of economic theory felt in dealing with the problem of the hedonistic foundation.

That was more or less the situation with regard to this point when Fetter began to write. His first treatise on theory, *Principles of Economics,* was published in 1904 and, as he says in the preface of the second, which will be discussed, it was an imperfect attempt to modernize economic theory. With characteristic wit he remarks that "the ambition of successive writers has been to modernize [John Stuart] Mill rather than to modernize economics." His first effort went some way in that direction, but it did not satisfy him; in 1915 he took a second step. So far as the general standpoint of economics is con-

cerned, the most important feature of that book is that Fetter tries
to get rid of hedonism and to substitute a new and sounder psychological basis for his account of how men act. Speaking of himself in
the third person, he remarks in his foreword of *Economic Principles,*
that

> he presents here a quite new statement of the theory of value, one
> in accord with the modern volitional psychology, thus eliminating
> entirely the old utilitarianism and hedonism which tainted the terms
> and conceptions of value ever since the days of Bentham. The basis
> of value is conceived to be the simple act of choice and not a cal-
> culation of utility. Even the phrase "marginal utility" is definitely
> abandoned.

That sounds, perhaps, as though he was going to echo Fisher and
say that the economist should concentrate upon the theory of price.
But that turns out not to be the case; he does try to give in the
second chapter a theory of value. What is the new theory of value
that Fetter here propounds? How does it differ from what we find
in earlier writers?

S. Value comes before choice—subjective value.

M. What do you mean by saying subjective value?

S. Opposite to objective. He feels it gives a matter of choice—
valuing a thing in your own mind rather than objectively.

M. Of course, that is what the Austrians had been saying, and
they employed the term "subjective value"; so you hardly get the
differentiating characteristic of Fetter there. As for the remark that
value comes before choice, Fetter points out that in many cases
choice comes first and value second. Thus in the second chapter on
choice and value; he says:

> . . . choice is ruled fundamentally by instinct; one likes what he
> likes; *de gustibus non disputandum est.* . . . An expression of the
> importance of one object of choice in terms of another we may call
> *a valuation.* A comparison of this sort between things may take the
> form of a mere vague preference without any exact quantitative
> expression of the degree to which the one thing is more important
> to us than the other.

In other words, each comparison of the importance of one commodity
in terms of another "is a focus of many influences, a resultant of
many conditions, some in the environment, and some in the nature
and in the feeling of man." He continues:

> It is usual to speak of the valuation which a person has (or holds
> or makes) of an object as preceding choice; but evidently this is
> not so in the case of instinctive choice, and many choices have in a
> measure this impulsive character. In case of a choice of a thing by
> a person for his own use the valuation is simply the resultant of
> choice; it is the arithmetic expression necessarily involved in the

action and reveals to the person himself what he has done, how he values the object, rather than determines his action. . . .

Now as a choice is made and a valuation is thus expressed, the person choosing feels that there is a certain quality in the thing which evokes or determines his choice. This quality of importance which things have when they are the objects of man's choice is *value*. Broadly understood, value may be of many kinds: Moral (the quality in actions calling for approval or disapproval), religious (the quality in actions, sentiments, and beliefs reflecting what the persons believe to be the will of the deity), aesthetic (the quality in objects that accords with the canons of good taste in color, form, sound, etc.). Economic value is but one species of the larger genus of value. It is the quality in an object in the environment to influence a man's action in respect to the control and use of the object. We ascribe this quality to the object that motivates our choice. Bread, meat, dress, houses, land, gold, carriages, slaves, the labor of hired servants, each object is said by you to have (economic) value, just because you feel and know that it sways your behavior in relation to itself. Value in this sense is not inherent or intrinsic in anything; it goes and comes, it grows and wanes according to the intensity of the desire. It may have existence for one economic subject and not for another; it is not to be thought of as something in a thing before man makes it an object of choice. The logical order is: first, choice; secondly, a valuation by necessary implication; third, value—the quality imputed to the object. Yet in real life these are but three phases, absolutely contemporaneous, of the same thing. Value is but the abstract quality which we attach to the thing in our thought, because of the way it makes us behave in its presence.[18]

These citations sound different from the implications of the doctrines heretofore discussed. The old theory seemed to be that people value their feelings. They valued goods because of the feelings that these goods would produce in them; and on the basis of the values attributed to goods they made choices among them, which became the basis for demand and supply schedules. The fundamental thing was the feeling; then the value imputed to the object; then the choice. Fetter says this is all wrong. When the theorist looks at human behavior he sees in a large proportion of cases that we choose instinctively. It is not a calculation of pleasure and pain; it is instinct, or at least something impulsive that determines choices. And having made their choices, they may reflect upon them, and if they do they may discover value imputed to the commodity. But at best these three stages; first, choice; secondly, valuation by necessary implication; and third, value, are only three absolutely contemporaneous phases of the same thing or, he might have done better to say, of the same process. That looks like an attempt to bring the instinct-impulse psychology into economics and make it play the same fundamental

---

[18] *Economic Principles,* pp. 13, 15, 16, 18-19.

role that the hedonistic psychology had played. It is that which he feels justifies the statement in the Foreword.

S. Please explain how choice by instinct can explain economic behavior?

M. Why should not the instinctive tendencies express themselves sometimes with reference to goods? I am unwilling to be put in the position of defending an instinct psychology, but from Fetter's point of view I should say that for one who believes in instincts as psychological entities, it is not difficult to see that they may express themselves in choices with reference to goods; and if so, they become of economic interest. Hunger may be an instinct; it leads a person to choose foods; foods are one of the material means of maintaining life; the process of getting food is a matter that concerns the economist.

S. Does it enable one to select food?

M. From Fetter's point of view, yes.

S. What is the conflict between volitional psychology and the hedonistic?

M. From the hedonistic point of view the human being is a feeble sort of character; that is, what moves the individual is not anything inside himself but pleasures and pains that are, so to speak, free forces moving in the environment. A certain individual is set up in a given environment and the pleasures and pains in the environment push and pull him about according to their relative strength, very much as a pith ball attached to the end of a string is pushed and pulled about by any body charged with electricity and brought into its neighborhood.

From the volitional point of view the individual is conceived as a creature with inherent tendencies to do something. He is not passive but fundamentally active. There are things he wants, and he goes after them. His conduct is not to be explained in terms of what the environment offers as pleasures and pains but largely in terms of what he himself is striving for, recognizing that what he will do as an individual will depend largely upon the opportunities for action which his environment presents.

S. Do both the hedonistic and the volitional psychology recognize freedom of the will?

M. Perhaps neither does. Certainly that is a question that we must not begin debating. One can put up much the same type of arguments whether one is talking in terms of the Benthamite or the volitional view. From either point of view it can be said that in the last resort the individual's action is determined by forces surrounding him; or from either viewpoint the individual can be pictured as having at least a large measure of freedom.

S. Might it be that Fetter simply means not rational when he speaks about instincts?

M. The question as to what is rational, becomes a little uncertain in this interpretation from the volitional viewpoint. The important point is not that action becomes less rational but that it becomes less deliberate. It is not a matter of reflective choice. From the hedonistic viewpoint, all action is reflective choice.

S. Does Fetter stick to his ideas on instincts?

M. If his book was not put into stereotyped plates, I should expect him to modify the phrasing as Marshall did. I would not be surprised to find the word "instinct" occur less frequently. Instincts which were considered fairly good in 1915 are now apparently falling into disrepute.[19]

S. In Fetter's notion of choice he supposes that if a man chooses at all, he is going for some gratification, at least something that is good, otherwise it would be impossible to choose anything. Instinct tells him what must be good.

M. Fetter would say that in choosing food, for instance, individuals are not to be conceived of so much as going after something and then reflecting upon what they are doing, and discovering it is something good for them; but as first picturing a good to their minds and then concluding that they will go after that. It is a necessary implication that they choose what they prefer, and therefore something which at the moment they view as good.

A conception that at least many volitional psychologists have entertained part of the time is that people are acting more or less for the sake of acting and sometimes have the opportunity to consider the character of their actions. In the economic field people are largely dealing time after time with issues of substantially the same sort, so that they have a great opportunity to note the results of mistaken choices and keep improving their behavior, rendering it more and more adapted to what in the long run does seem to them a satisfactory course of life. Consequently there is a better opportunity in that field than in fields where they are always dealing with novel prob-

---

[19] Said in 1927. [There were no changes in the reprinting of Fetter's *Economics,* volume I, *Economic Principles,* but volume two, *Modern Economic Problems* was expanded in 1922.]

lems to make the results of their unreflecting choices agree with the deliberate reflections in which they may indulge.

S. Even then if the theorist accepts the view of the volitional psychologist, he can really make the hedonistic view a subdivision of it, because the volitional psychology will be somewhat calculated.

M. No, not everything will be impulsive. But to repeat, in slightly different form what I just said, if a good deal of an individual's early acts have an impulsive character, because he is faced by the same situation he has lots of chances of revising them. And if the results prove unsatisfactory, to alter his behavior on corresponding future occasions; so that his behavior does come to be stereotyped, it gets an habitual cast which may conform pretty closely to the sort of action that a man might recommend if he sat down and studied what he would do in certain circumstances. It is highly characteristic of economic behavior as a whole nowadays that at least the larger issues get subjected to a careful, methodical, meticulous study, not by the persons doing them but by other people who in the modern organization are put into positions where they are responsible for planning and control. Just think of all the study that is given to such matters as the drawing up of wills. There are professional experts upon the subject. Think of the vast amount of attention that is given by scientific management experts to determine exactly the best way to carry out trifling mechanical processes.

One of the things that does not come into Fetter's picture so far is the recognition of the role which social organization, that is, specialization in the task of planning what shall be done, plays in life as it is now lived. So far all this is an attempt to supply an analysis which is going to explain the behavior of every individual. Differences between individuals and the tasks they have to perform, which is an important part of the problem of how people behave today, is not taken up.

What change does Fetter's so-called shifting the psychological foundation of economic theory produce in the doctrines which he reaches concerning prices and the distribution of income, the two central problems of economic theory ever since the days of Ricardo? If theory rests fundamentally upon the theory of value—and that is Fetter's as well as Marshall's position and the position toward which Jevons was working—and if the theory of distribution is itself simply a case of the application of the theory of value to the various factors of production, then one would think an alteration in the theory of value would produce considerable changes in economic theory. Do Fetter's doctrines concerning the determination of prices, rents, wages, profits and interest differ in fundamental respects from his predecessors; and if they do, is it because of his underlying theory of value?

S. He forgets the beginning in his later chapters.

M. That is, he lays down a new theory of value at the outset and then forgets it?

S. At least he does not follow it very closely.

M. So that on your view Fetter has not made any very significant alterations in economic theory as a result of the change in his doctrine of value.

S. His theory of value is the main characteristic; all of the other parts—interest, profits, wages and rent—are based on value.

M. That was more or less true with Marshall, but Fetter tries to emphasize that more strongly.

To repeat the original question: What substantial difference does Fetter's theory of value have? What effect does it have on the economic doctrines of prices at large—for the prices which are paid for labor and the use of durable goods, for loans and for business organizing ability?

S. Nothing substantial except it puts them on a modern basis; it integrates them.

M. Yes, they are integrated. It appears that the students think that the revolutionary change of getting entirely rid of hedonism, which has tainted the conceptions of economists since the days of Bentham, has not made much difference in the bulk of the theorizing in Fetter's book. Suppose we accept that opinion. How can it be the case? If, as Fetter insists more than anyone else, economic theory is the theory of value and the application of the theory of value, how can an economist change his fundamental theory of value without effecting considerable alterations in the remainder of his economic theory?

S. It makes no difference because what Fetter does is to devote his explanation to how the demand schedule arises. He accepts the demand and supply schedules as though they determine price just as Marshall does.

M. Your explanation comes to this: the theory of value is a matter of comparatively slight consequence for technical economic doctrines. It is simply an undertaking to get behind certain notions—demand and supply schedules—with which the economist proceeds to operate and it does not matter much how one explains variations in demand or supply for the purposes of the economist.

S. It does not matter how the economist explains it; he gets the same result.

M. This is precisely the answer to the problem which has been given by certain of Fetter's more thoughtful reviewers; for example, by A. C. Whitaker of Stanford University.[20] He was one of J. B. Clark's ablest students at Columbia, a man thoroughly indoctrinated with the Clarkian type of economic theory, and a man of remarkable logical powers. He said that the new psychology that Fetter introduces

> . . . merely appears to impress one of Fetter's words, "innocuous." It is true that it seems to have interfered to a degree with a clear statement of the relation of value (in the sense of subjective value) to utility or usefulness, but apart from this you could seize upon it at the various points in the book where it may be found, and lift it out bodily, and leave the real argument unchanged.

> . . . it can be shown that neither Jevons' theory of final utility nor the similar Austrian theory of marginal utility rests on the technical hedonistic premises that pleasure is the end of life, or the object of desire, or that pleasures differ only in intensity, or what not. The utility theory remains unscathed by the new psychology. At least, a utility theory, containing what was and is the important contribution of the doctrine, framed in the same terminology as the Austrian teachings, can be defended without hedonistic premises . . .

> Of great importance the utility theory is not. The importance attaches to the empirical law of demand which it explains. But what can be the error of the theory? It states that men desire goods. Do they not? It has no doubt been made to say at times that men seek satisfaction, when it might have confined itself to saying that they seek goods. It speaks of the power of goods to satisfy desire as utility. This is a synonym for usefulness. Do not goods have usefulness, or does the anti-hedonist wish to run "usefulness" out of the language? Are desire and satisfaction myths? Fetter speaks of desire as "a mental reaching out for things." This is on a par for effectiveness with defining desire as a "feeling of incompleteness," suggestive of a man with a wooden leg. We give a definition in certain terms. We may in turn define these terms. But we cannot go on defining terms forever. In time we reach fundamental undefinables. Such are "desire" and "satisfaction." Their meanings are understood by all, but definition of them is futile.

> Does not the superior importance of scarce things as described by the utility theory exist? And do not men both fail to produce and

---

[20] [His doctoral dissertation was an outstanding study in the field of the history of economic thought], *History and Criticism of the Labor Theory of Value in English Political Economy* (1904). In this book, Whitaker had taken up a point that von Wieser raised in the preface to his *Natural Value.* "The confusion between the 'philosophical' theory of value and the 'empirical' theory of price in Adam Smith and Ricardo. . . . [Whitaker] has worked out this theme fully. . . . The result of these inquiries is a detailed demonstration that the classical writers from Adam Smith to Cairnes did not succeed in resolving all items of 'entrepreneur's cost' into labor costs— that is, they did not really get rid of pecuniary factors in their theory of exchange." (Mitchell, "The Role of Money in Economic Theory," 1916, reprinted in his *The Backward Art of Spending Money and Other Essays,* edited by Joseph Dorfman (New York: McGraw-Hill, 1937) p. 151.)

fail to demand the production of things, however useful as a general class of objects, when these things are superabundant and thus fail of this importance? This superior importance is called value. What is there in anti-hedonism which contradicts this use of the term? In searching further for what may be the psychological error of the theory, we shall have to make the fragmentary and rudimentary statement of it which has been given above serve our purposes. It is hardly feasible here to attempt to give it a fuller statement as a theory or part theory of market price and defend it against the various misapprehensions from which it has suffered. It is said that the conduct of men is governed by their instinctive impulses, or that what they desire is a matter of instinct. Of course. The utility theory has not denied or ignored this. It states that objective goods are necessary to satisfy desires and their usefulness is their capacity to satisfy desires. The utility theorist could say that goods are necessary for the *realization of instinctive impulses,* and then eliminate the word "satisfaction" and explain his points all over again. But to what end? It would be merely more pedantic and on the whole less intelligible. The fact that hunger is an instinct produces no modification in the proposition of the satiability of hunger and the consequent declining importance of successive increments of food. What advantages could be gained by saying that value (in the sense of subjective value) depends on *the marginal enabling power of goods to further the realization of instinctive impulses?* The utility theorist can readily admit that what man wants or the character of man's wants depends on his inborn nature. On what else in the world should they depend? No doubt they depend on the make-up of his instinctive impulses, however complex, or imitative, or socialized, however much influenced by advertisement or salesman's talk. The reviewer once attended a class in an American institution where the professor in charge, after chastising the classical political economy as being hedonistic, explained that the hedonistic conception of the mind was that of a mind without instincts or impulses and possessed of a reason only! Could a more stupid misapprehension be imagined? It is impossible to believe that even the purest hedonist proper ever held such a nonsensical conception of the mind.

Attacks on the importance of the utility theory would be more telling than the attacks of anti-hedonism on its truth. Errors in presenting it are not uncommon, especially in connection with the use of the term "marginal" as applied to goods which the consumer does not use in plural numbers or in stocks. . . .

In the reviewer's opinion, the more significant truths sought to be conveyed by the utility theory are not contradicted by the new psychology; but if they should be, it would be incumbent on the new psychology to square itself with these plain truths. Incidentally, no large number of professional psychologists have been showing an interest in the reform of economics in the name of their science. In Fetter's book the new psychology seems to exhaust itself in making the introductory exposition of the theory of value less clear.[21]

His point is that what the economist needs to operate with are demand and supply schedules; or, if one takes the strict Austrian

---

[21] Whitaker, "Fetter's Principles of Economics," *Political Science Quarterly,* September 1916, pp. 434-441.

viewpoint, demand schedules. For purposes of discussing problems of prices, of wages, interest, rent and profits it does not matter how the theorist explains the operations which go on inside people's heads and result in willingness to pay certain amounts of money for certain commodities, or accept certain amounts of a commodity for certain efforts. According to Whitaker all the psychologizing is really a matter of comparatively slight concern to the theorist. Therefore he can produce any individual fancy brand of psychology he likes without altering his economic theory for the reason that economic theory does not now or never has rested upon a psychological foundation. It takes the objective facts summed up in demand and supply schedules as its basis, and there is no reason why the economist should inquire as to what lies behind demand schedules. Jevons made a tactical blunder when he proposed to give a theory of valuation to account for people's willingness to pay certain prices for certain quantities of goods under certain circumstances. So too, Fetter makes a blunder when he presents his theory of value as a matter of fundamental concern to the economist, or, to put the same thing in slightly different, broader, and possibly less defensible terms, economics does not rest on psychology. To talk about an American Psychological School of economics is, maintains Whitaker, to suggest an unfortunate association of ideas. Are the students willing to accept Whitaker's interpretation or is there any other?

To repeat,[22] Whitaker in effect says Fetter's *Economic Principles* is a very good, sound work. He, however, makes a grave mistake in thinking that this economics had any necessary connection with psychology. The one thing which he ought to do is to try to free himself from dependence upon modern psychology. If he did that either his first book or his second book would be thoroughly acceptable. Is there any other way of treating the rather serious fact that a change in the alleged psychological foundation does not make any change in Fetter's economic theory? That what he has to say about the determination of prices, about the law of rent, the law of interest, the law of wages and the law of profits are already in line with his views on those subjects in 1904?

S1. You say it does not matter [according to Whitaker] which comes first, choice or value, but every increase in quantity affects the choice and lowers the value of what people choose.

M. I think that is saying what has already been said in a slightly different way, isn't it? That is to say, it does not make any difference

---

[22] Beginning of extract from "1918 Typescript."

to the demand schedule what your theory of the grounds of choice may be.

S1. Yes, it is very important if the law of choice is what it is.

M. Yes, that fact concerning the slope of the demand schedule is very important. That fact is represented in the choice. What has been previously suggested is that for economic purposes all you need are those demand schedules which have the characteristic declining form. You need those demand schedules for an economic basis, but Whitaker says for your purposes as an economist it makes not a whit of difference what views you may hold of the facts that lie behind the determination of those schedules. Start with them. That is all you need to concern yourself with as an economist. And leave the explanation of their origin to psychologists, or others whom it immediately concerns.

S2. I cannot agree with that, that it makes no difference as to what standpoint you take in your psychological reasoning, for I do think if you talk about value in economics, you are not any more in the field of real economics, you go already into another reasoning field, and if you go there, you have at least to take a standpoint in certain results, and you have to be clear what standpoint you take and it seems to be very fundamental if you change your psychological foundation. It seems very illogical that you can still have the same conclusions though you change your psychology. On Fetter's later view, I don't think it is at all possible to hold marginal utility.

M. That sounds like perfectly good logic, but naturally Fetter is not a man to stumble over simple fallacies. How do you suppose it happens that while he proceeds logically no change happens in his economic conclusions?

S3. His expression of functional psychology is pretty close to the hedonistic expression; that is, his theory of choice does not make the psychological process a very different one.

M. That is to say, it is possible that the explanation of the puzzle lies in this fact that the psychology has not been changed. It is possible, that is to say, that while writing introductory chapters which are very carefully framed in the phraseology of modern functional psychology Fetter still, when he comes to reasoning about economic behavior, tacitly assumes substantially the same kind of control and direction in the later book that he assumed in the early one.

S4. I still do not see why he says "choice." Is it instinct which makes us choose things? Why do we choose?

M. He does not undertake to explain choice except to say that we have instinctive choices, and that many choices share in a measure this impulsive character. He does not undertake to explain what controls our choices. His plan is, as he put it in the foreword, to erect his theory of value on the basis of the simple act of choice and not on the basis of calculation or utility.

S4. When he speaks of value by implication, does he mean that after we get the object we choose?

M. Do not say "after we get the object"; say "after we have chosen the object."

S4. Then it has value because it is ours?

M. In that act of choosing a valuation is implied, which we may or may not stop to reflect upon.[23]

S. What then does economics rest upon in Whitaker's view?

M. It rests upon demand and supply schedules. That is his argument. Those are the ultimate data with which the economist need concern himself. And if he inquires into what they rest upon, he is attacking the job which is really the psychologist's.

S. It is almost impossible to get good demand and supply schedules —schedules that mean anything. They are mostly imaginary, and therefore one ought not to use them as actual facts.

M. Yes, that is a very pertinent objection. The talk about demand and supply schedules, the objective foundation of economics, overlooks the fact that they are not empirically based. They are made to order in the theorist's imagination, and he takes such demand and supply schedules as happen to suit his convenience to draw up for an argument. If that objection is presented to him, his reply is that in his eyes it may be adequate; that the schedules which he draws up in elaborate form represent substantially broad factors which can be objectively observed. He can tell that if there is an overstock of shoes of a certain type in New York City in a certain season the price of the shoes is going to fall, and when the price falls it will be possible to dispose of a large number of pairs. If one wants to add materially to the working force, draw people into some branch of industry, they will have to be offered a higher price and this will induce an increased supply and so on.

S. As regards the instinctive element which Fetter emphasizes so much in the beginning, but much less later on, he confuses the way men's desires start. He speaks about the individual's instincts.

---

[23] End of extract from "1918 Typescript."

M. The suggestion is in other words that Fetter has changed his psychology only in the chapter on value, and then proceeds to reason about human conduct, or rather to discuss economic conduct, as reasoned behavior in his later chapters in precisely the same spirit as his predecessors. That is a different explanation of how he can change his theory of value and give substantially—I will not put it that way, for he does not arrive at quite the same theories as his predecessors; but so far as he makes changes in the theories, they are not based on alterations in his value theory; they are explanations of the same type. Is that way of looking at the puzzle more illuminating, more valid? Does it mean anything more than the first suggestion that economics does not have a psychological foundation and economists need not worry about the fact? Indeed psychological worries arise only in supposing that it is one of the psychological disciplines. Do you agree that Fetter operates through the greater part of his book with a conception of human behavior which is fundamentally not different from the classical conception; or do you not see any conception of human behavior in his later chapters?

From Whitaker's point of view the answer would be that Fetter is not using any special conception of human nature. Men want goods—we all know that. Their wants are satiable in various degrees —we all know that, too. They are unwilling to labor or save beyond certain limits—we all know that also; that is, the economist needs no psychology to know that—just observations which anybody can make by observing the way people act. Or, on the contrary, must the theorist take the ground that inasmuch as economics is patently a discussion of human behavior, inasmuch as every price problem is a problem concerning what people will do under certain circumstances, it is obvious that the economist who is not himself actually watching what people do and writing down the result of his observations, but is thinking about what people will do under certain conditions, must of necessity be operating explicitly, whether he knows it or not, with a certain conception of human nature?

The problem is made a little clearer by thinking of two different types of psychological work proper. A great deal of experimental work has been done by psychologists in recent years with animals. Most people have a happy faculty in dealing with animals of reading their own thoughts and feelings into the minds of the animals, and people will go through explanations as to why their pets do this and that. These explanations are in terms which we would apply to the explanation of anyone else. They are in terms we would employ in the explanation of some of our own behavior. More recently, however, many students of animal behavior have taken the ground that the only way to make progress in understanding animals is to watch and record what they do under given standardized situations. They will experiment with rats in a maze or with apes under certain conditions which they have arranged on purpose to discover what kind of reactions the beasts will make. They do not undertake to explain what goes on inside the animal's mind, but to determine what it does under specific circumstances.

A psychologist who operates that way may be said to be working almost without any implied notion concerning the beast's mental capacity. His question or problem is what is the beast's mental capacity. He does not take it for granted in the beginning and use his hazy notions to explain the animal's behavior, but studies its conduct and finds out what kind of physical and mental organism it has.

On the other hand, a great deal of human psychology is still written in introspective terms. A psychologist is acquainted with himself, so he believes; and he reads what is plausible to his mind concerning his own thoughts, feelings and actions into the minds of others and explains what they will do. He does not observe what they do. He has his notions of what constitutes human nature and he uses them to explain what people do.

Economists, even when they defined economics as the science of wealth, really have been talking about certain aspects of human behavior. They wanted to explain it. Each economist thought that he was acquainted with himself, that he could account for his own behavior. The theorists have in the past almost uniformly read their own feelings and attitudes into the behavior of others. Their problem has been to tell what people do under all sorts of economic circumstances. It is impossible to perform that task unless the economist takes some assumptions concerning human nature for granted.

Classical economics provides some simple illustrations. How did Ricardo know that wages in the long run were going to remain substantially stable or possibly shrink somewhat? Could one make a prophecy of that kind on the basis of what one knows about human nature? Presumably not. But he knew that the masses of the population have a definite behavior trait. When they get enough commodities to satisfy a meager standard of living they will take advantage of any further improvement in their condition to marry and to rear children. The increasing number of the population which results from this behavior trait will be always just that which is required to keep the standard of living down to the conventional level in a community. Is not there an assumption concerning how people behave which is applied as a decisive rule in determining the law of wages?

Today Ricardo's assumption and conclusion are not accepted because his assumption is no longer plausible. Theorists do not attribute to the workingmen a tropismatic longing to marry and rear children in large numbers. They attribute to workingmen a businesslike eagerness to better their condition by joining in associations, and to take advantage of improvements in their lot, not by enlarging their family, but by increasing their consumption. Theorists have some reason to believe that at least considerable numbers among the working class are even beginning to entertain ideas about the relation of pay on the one hand and efficiency as producers and money-makers for their employers on the other; that is, economists read thoughts into workingmen's minds different from those assumed by Ricardo; and on the basis of these different thoughts they come to entertain as plausible theories of the future course of wages which would have seemed to Ricardo preposterous. If he lived at present he would believe more or less as economists today do, but living when he did he did not entertain these notions.

Presumably he got his notions of the behavior of workingmen with reference to wages, marriage and children, not by way of deductions from the felicific calculus, but by watching what he supposed to be the characteristic behavior of most English workingmen in his day. Presumably we get our different notions of what people are going to do far less from a study of modern psychological doctrines than from such observations as we make concerning what workingmen do at the present time. The point, however, is that in thinking about these problems the theorist in large part makes the conclusions turn upon assumptions concerning human nature. This has been, and it always must be, a critically important point in many a fundamental issue of economics.

To say that the one point of junction between economics and psychology is the theoretical explanation given of demand curves and supply curves is an artificial and limited view. All through the discussion of what people will do, all through one's expectations, just so long as the theorist is not operating on a strictly objective basis, there must of necessity run assumptions which are not prominently present to his mind when he is doing his economic analysis. There must run through his mind assumptions of how people are going to make choices, the grounds which will control their actions. This is just as true in many practical business problems as in economic speculations. If the advertiser is wondering how to get people to buy goods, the odds are that he thinks the problem out in terms of what will be attractive to people. How does he know what will be? There are two ways. One is a perfectly objective way of studying statistics; the other is by letting his implicit notion concerning people's likes and dislikes, his implicit conception of human nature, give the answer.

The economists can in some measure carry on a discussion of economic behavior in a strictly objective spirit; that is, they can operate in the same way as do the modern psychological experimenters upon animals' behavior. The economists who come nearest to doing this are those who are working on problems of theory on a statistical basis. But a difficulty with that type of work is that there are many problems concerning which an adequate statistical summary of observations cannot be obtained. Of course, the statistics are simply observations taken in the main. If human beings were all nearly alike an objective type of economic theory would not be required. The investigator would have statistics of the workingman, the landlord, the capitalist and of the business man; then by seeing what they would do in certain circumstances he could tell what everybody else would do. But because people are diverse, the observations needed are of large groups of people, and these observations constitute statistics. So far as one can believe in statistics one can proceed in an objective way.

But there is very little economic theory, so called, at the present time which has this objective basis. Most of it is made by the more intimate way of reasoning what people are going to do; and that is true with practically all of Fetter's work. If the inquirer reasons about what people are going to do, he is shaping his discussion by his explicit notions concerning human behavior.

What was said about Fetter's change of psychological viewpoint is valid. In his chapter on value he attempts to achieve a statement different in its terms from that of Jevons; but through the remainder of the book in discussing problems of economic behavior, he relapses almost explicitly into the use of precisely the same opinions concerning human nature which his predecessors had entertained. I say almost explicitly—I want to show that verbally. Fetter says that "The aim of all human effort, whether work or play, is psychic income"; that is to be interpreted by finding what psychic income is. We search for a definition and we find it: "We may define the term psychic income as desirable results produced in the realm of feeling."[24] That sounds almost like saying in long words what Bentham said in shorter ones. Bentham said that pleasure and pain control what people do, and Fetter says that all human effort is directed toward getting pleasurable results in the realm of feeling. I gather that the desirable results in the realm of feeling are pretty close to pleasure!

S. Is there not a fundamental distinction between the methods of arriving at the values of consumer's goods and the value problem in commercial undertakings?

M. I think that there is.

S. That would give one type of explanation for Fetter's change. In his chapter on value he is trying to explain the value of consumer's goods, whereas in the chapters on wages, rents and things of that kind, he is talking more of value as determined in commercial undertakings.

M. Of course, from Fetter's point of view the value of these goods of higher orders, to use Austrian terminology, is based on the prices people will pay for consumer's commodities. Is it not?

S. Yes, but the methods by which the commercial entrepreneur arrives at the values, the prices of the various factors of production, are worked out from what the consumer will pay for the goods that he wants.

M. Let me put it this way. The commercial man is after desirable results in the realm of money; that is, profits. The consumer is after desirable results in the realm of feeling. What the merchant wants his money for according to the view of Fetter is in order to get desirable results in the realm of feeling—and the theorist is back pretty much at the old place.

That does, however, suggest another point which is worth mentioning in this connection; namely, that what presumably has made not only Bentham's felicific calculus but also the attenuated forms of that conception of human nature with which economists work today so plausible, is that in the modern economic organization with its continual use of money, its systematization of markets, people learn perforce a certain calculating type of behavior. The merchant must learn it if he is to be successful. It is an operation modern institutions force people to adopt, and it becomes second nature to a great many. So firmly established is that conception of how men operate, in the theorists' minds, that they carry it over with slight misgivings to

---

[24] *Economic Principles*, pp. 27, 174.

account for what people do outside the business world. In the last resort the theorists standardize this account of what they do in trying to satisfy their own personal desires and regard their own personal sacrifices so highly that they make this standardized caricature of their impulsive lives the basis on which they proceed to erect demand and supply schedules and get a basis for explaining men's calculating commercial conduct. This explanation of what people do as individuals is plausible enough to people who have learned a measure of rationality in business dealings. That will come out from time to time in future discussions.

S. All science is interested not only in finding out how things happen but why they happen. What Fetter is doing is to go back of the how and give the why, just as the physicist does.

M. Do you really think that the modern physicist is concerned with why? The question of the role that causation plays not only in science but also in philosophy is an old one and time should not be taken to discuss it in class, but I should like to point out a fact which is tolerably obvious. When the inquirer investigates a concrete problem, the more he knows about the given situation the more clearly he realizes that certain given effects are due not to any one factor in the situation which he can select as cause but to a whole combination of circumstances which, if he is thorough-going in his explanation, he will have to include. In view of that fundamental logical condition, and the great advantages of mathematical technique in presenting scientific results, the more perfect science, physics which you cited, is a beautiful case in point. Physicists are getting further and further away from dealings with the conception of cause and presenting their discussions primarily in a mathematical form.

Cause plays an important role in economics at the present day, presumably because economics is one of the backward sciences. As economists get more and more insight into their problems they are going to get away from that childish, simple habit of giving explanations of phenomena in terms of the influence that one factor in a situation exercises upon the second factor; that is, in terms which make large use of the words "cause and effect," and they will go increasingly in the direction of the sciences which are more mature in form. When they tell themselves that they have discovered a cause, the theorists are deceiving themselves or digging out some one factor in a situation for pragmatic reasons. It does no harm when a person's automobile stops to say that the cause was the fact that the gasoline tank had become exhausted. For practical purposes he can operate that way; and for many purposes in practical life that simple shorthand way of describing and accounting for things is eminently sensible. No doubt men will continue to follow this procedure indefinitely, but for scientific purposes there is need for something more thorough-going, which almost always assumes the guise of a descriptive analysis of an elaborate process.

As noted in *Business Cycles: The Problem and Its Setting,* "[T]he idea of causation has pragmatic, rather than scientific warrant. All the conditions which are indispensable to produce a certain result stand on much the same footing from the viewpoint of science. But there may be practical reasons why, from the many conditions indispensable to produce certain results, we should single out some one or more for special attention, and call them 'the cause' or 'the causes.' We stand a better chance of making a wise selection of factors for special attention, however, if we have already gained a scientific understanding of the process as a whole. In the progress of knowledge causal explanations are commonly an early stage in the advance towards analytic description. The more complete the theory of any subject becomes in content, the more mathematical in form, the less it invokes causations. ... Yet a stiff refusal to employ causal expressions in the details of our investigation[s] might often hamper us. In the present stage of our knowledge, we can make more rapid progress . . . by using the thought forms of daily life than by trying to express ideas at which we are grasping in the form which may ultimately prevail."

There is a technical feature of Fetter's *Economic Principles* which is of broad concern and at the same time is illustrative of the customary view of treating economic behavior;[25] namely, his view concerning interest which differs in certain respects from that of other contemporary writers. He sometimes refers to his theory as the capitalization theory of interest, and sometimes as the time discount theory. What is the novel feature of Fetter's view?

S. Biological interpretation of time preference. He says that people are animals and prefer immediate gratification in preference to gratification some time in the indefinite future.

M. If that is his view, why does he not agree with Irving Fisher's "impatience" theory of interest?[26] Fetter feels very distinctly that

---

[25] Clause from Outline, April 5, 1923.

[26] [Fisher's formulation at the time was well summed up in the proposition that "undervaluation of the future, rational or irrational, and differences in the provision for present and future are alone sufficient to explain the rate of interest." (Alvin S. Johnson, review of Böhm-Bawerk, *Kapital und Kapitalzins zweite abteilung: Positive Theorie des Kapitales,* in *The American Economic Review,* March 1914, p. 114.]

Fisher's view is not acceptable. He will not grant that the term "impatience" satisfactorily suggests the psychological basis upon which interest rests. You see why he dislikes to tie himself strictly to what you have been suggesting and what might be adequately covered by Fisher's term "impatience"?

S. There is no distinction between impatience and the desire for immediate gratification.

M. Fetter would hardly say that. He would assert that if that were the whole truth, "impatience" might as a catch-word satisfy theorists, but it distracts their attention from the fundamental explanation. The point at which Fetter would take exception to your suggestion regarding his view is a simple one. He states that in a modern community different people have all sorts of time discounts. There are some people who prefer future to present gratifications. But on the average, the time discount upon the future is in favor of the present. It is therefore, from his viewpoint, better to discuss the matter in terms of time discount and to recognize that time discounts are themselves highly variable from individual to individual. Does he tie up to impatience or simply to discount upon the future? The net effect is exactly the same on his showing, but he wants to be more circumspect in pointing out that it is merely on the average that the future is discounted.

S. Isn't it like Jevons's uncertainty?

M. Yes, as noted previously, certain passages of Jevons's *The Theory of Political Economy* can be interpreted in this sense. However, as was also stated before, other passages in Jevons's book seem to indicate what has been called a form of the productivity theory of interest; that is, the important thing is the fact that needing present goods to work with, a person can adopt roundabout methods of production and thus enhance the output of his efforts per unit and so get the surplus out of which it is feasible to pay interest, and this is why people are willing to pay interest.

How does Fetter get a theory of interest out of the notion of time discount or time value as he sometimes calls it?

S. Interest is the cost of the difference between the future price of capitalized income and the present price of the money people have on hand.

M. What do you mean by capitalized income?

S. Assuming that the income from given funds is a certain percentage.

M. When you talk about funds do you mean money?

S. Yes.

M. Fetter states very distinctly that rates of interest in money are derived from more fundamental factors. He would not be willing to have a reference to money funds brought in at this early logical stage in the development of the theory of interest. Yet there is a capitalized element in his theory. He does not offer a capitalization in money funds.

S. Durable goods.

M. What is the notion about durable goods?

S. In a period of time they bring in a certain amount of income satisfaction; and then the individual discounts this income for a series of years and this is his rate of interest.

M. We have not yet quite gotten to the rate of interest. Take any durable good, say the table in this room. That durable good is capable of yielding service for a period of time in the future day by day; and just because you presumably are an average person and will value the future service that table will render somewhat less highly than present service, when you are thinking about the value of the table as a whole, you will arrive at it by taking the present value to you of all the services you think it will render during its working life. That present value is considerably less than the value of the aggregate services as they are rendered. So you pay today a price less than you would be willing to pay through a series of future years for the aggregate services that the table will render. In other words, people are regularly buying durable and quasi-durable goods at present prices which are equal to values considerably less than the values of the services the quasi-durable goods are going to have in the future.

We have now reached the point for getting at the theory of interest. The individual gets all sorts of opportunities as a consumer or as a business man to purchase goods today—durable goods or quasi-durable goods—on these advantageous terms. If he has money in hand he can buy a table or a machine or a piece of land. Any one of these things will presumably give him in the end services which are worth much more in the aggregate than the price that he pays today. Thus command over present funds puts him in a position to get a series of surpluses over and above the present price he pays for such things. Fundamentally it is because he has money that he can exercise some of these advantageous options which the market offers on all sorts of durable goods; that makes him both able and willing to pay interest. The fundamental factor is time discount and the underpricing at the present moment of the services which durable and quasi-durable goods will render.

In a somewhat controversial paper in 1914, "Interest Theories Old and New," Fetter endeavored to sum up his capitalization theory of interest in a more succinct form than in his treatise and also meet the rival theories which have been suggested by Irving Fisher, the champion, to repeat, of the impatience theory, and by Henry R. Seager (1870-1930) of Columbia who in this particular discussion appeared as the advocate of a form of the productivity theory.[27]

> This, then, is the essence of the capitalization theory of interest as nearly as we can put it in a proposition: The rate of interest (contractual) is the reflection, in a market price on money loans, of a rate of capitalization involved in the prices of the goods in the community.

You see, fundamentally the rate of interest is found in the present prices of goods. He goes on:

> The price of durable agents is a capitalization which involves a discount of their future uses; and this is logically prior to the rate of contract interest. The logical order of explanation is from numberless separate acts of choice of goods *with reference to time,* to the value (and prices) of durable goods embodying future incomes, and finally to the market rate of interest. This interest theory was new in its *order of development* from elementary choice; in the *priority it assigned to capitalization* of all the phenomena of the surplus that emerges when undervalued expected incomes approach maturity, the surplus all being derived from the value of enjoyable (direct) goods, not by two separate theories, for consumption and production goods respectively; in the *integration* of the interest theory with the whole theory of distribution; and in a number of details necessarily related to these features.

This is a carefully drawn passage which suggests the specifications in the application for a patent! As opposed to Fisher's impatience theory Fetter says:

> Time-valuation or time-preference better expresses the complex of motives which at one time impels men to get goods earlier, and again leads them to postpone use by storing goods and by work-

---

[27] Seager, "The Impatience Theory of Interest," 1912; reprinted in his *Labor and Other Economic Essays* ed. by C. A. Gulick, Jr. (New York: Harper, 1931) pp. 175-199. Fisher replied and Seager made a rejoinder. Both statements are in *The American Economic Review,* September 1913, pp. 610-619.

See also an earlier champion of the productivity theory of interest, the Austrian, Friedrich von Wieser's "The Austrian School and the Theory of Value," *The Economic Journal,* March 1891, pp. 115-116. Strongly defending Fisher was Harry Gunnison Brown, "The Marginal Productivity versus the Impatience Theory of Interest," *The Quarterly Journal of Economics,* August 1913, pp. 630-650; (Brown's reply to Fetter's attack) "The Discount versus the Cost of Production Theory of Capital Valuation," *The American Economic Review,* June 1914, pp. 340-349; (Fetter's rejoinder) Fetter, "Capitalization versus Productivity. Rejoinder," *The American Economic Review,* December 1914, pp. 856-859. (Outline, March 5, 1917, and "Wieser," APP 84-91, no. 35.)

ing for the future in many ways. A prevailing rate of interest is the resultant of all kinds and degrees of time-preference in a community, *preference for goods in the future* in some cases as well as preference for goods in the present, and it seems a great straining of words to attribute the resulting rate of interest to impatience alone. Patience, self-denial, the quality expressed in the old term abstinence, have a no less important part in the explanation.

Then he criticizes the productivity theory of interest. This is a difficult matter with which Fetter must deal. [Consequently, an explanation of the productivity theory might be given before presenting Fetter's criticism.] One of the most commonly accepted, and most plausible theories of interest is that a person, say the business man, is ready to pay to the holders of money which would give him command of present goods, a sum over and above the value of the loan, because when he has present goods he can adopt highly efficient methods of production that take time. If I am developing a farm I must, if dependent solely upon the minute sum of capital which I possess, devote myself primarily to raising food enough to keep alive until I provide myself with some utensils with which to practice agriculture more efficiently. To take a long leap, it will probably be the case if I want to develop the farm almost to its highest possible efficiency, that the wise course is to start with a considerable outfit not only of means to live and maintain my efficiency—food, a comfortable house well-equipped and a good barn for the livestock—but also plows and perhaps tractors, certainly farm animals.

Maybe the soundest plan will be to put up fences and perhaps some drainage operation before beginning to farm. Maybe when I begin cultivating I had better turn in two or three clover crops to improve the fertility of the soil. Maybe this is the best policy but maybe I cannot pursue it—I cannot get the utensils, the house and barn, unless I have means in hand. If I can get them, however, I can pursue whatever policy my knowledge of farming indicates as most profitable in the long run. If there is a decided gain in efficiency in this time-consuming scientific method over and above the catch as catch can method, I shall be willing, in case I am dependent on very small amounts of capital, to pay interest to anyone who will advance capital to me.

This is the conception behind the productivity theory; to use whatever methods are most efficient, even though they take a long time. It is the idea that nowadays is becoming increasingly typical of industrial operations: to build large amounts of industrial equipment before turning out a single unit of goods. It is as characteristic of transportation, mining, lumbering, merchandising and warehousing on the modern basis as of manufacturing. In view of the great gains which can be achieved in the typical case by adopting round-about methods of production, business men are eager to control present purchasing power. They can well afford to pay interest on loans, and the rate is determined primarily by the demand for current loans by people who want the opportunity to exploit highly productive methods of operation as compared with the supply of loans forthcoming from those who are saving and wanting to get incomes without engaging in active business. This, broadly speaking, is the productivity theory of interest. Fetter disposes of all that:

> The productivity of which use is made when the explanation is really begun is not technical or physical productivity at all, but is the capacity which goods bought with judgment at *current prices* have, in the hands of enterprisers, of yielding a net surplus, sufficient not only to remunerate them, but to pay contract interest to lenders. The amount of interest which "enterprisers estimate" they can afford to pay (i.e., the maximum amount) is the difference between the discounted, or present, worth of products imputable to these agents and their worth at the time they are expected to mature. . . . Is it the productivity of agents that makes business men willing to borrow and pay interest? . . . Could they afford to pay interest varying with the time element, if the value of the productivity, however large or small, were not discounted in the price of the agents they borrow (or buy with borrowed money)? I think not. . . . It is the opportunity which the possession of ready money gives to the enterpriser to buy goods at a price involving a discount proportional to the futurity of the expected returns, that makes him willing to contract to pay interest. When these expected returns (the products) do appear in the course of time, their value-magnitude is, or should be, greater than was their investment magnitude, and it is out of this value-surplus, directly *conditioned on an antecedent discount of the value-productivity,* that contract interest is paid . . .
>
> My contention throughout has been that the productivity theory in any of the versions known to me, and specifically in the entrepreneur version, defended by Seager, involves a confusion between physical-productivity and value-productivity; that in the course of the reasoning there is a shift from the one idea to the other. Seager admits that this confusion "has sometimes occurred," but he believes that there is a "necessary or logical connection between physical productivity *as a general phenomenon of capitalistic production* and value-productivity". . .
>
> But is this not a recognition that technical productivity has *some* influence upon the comparison of present and future gratifications and hence upon the rate of interest? Surely, some influence it has, but the causal order of explanation is very different from that of the productivity theory. Technical productivity is one of the facts, physical, moral, intellectual, which go to make up the whole economic situation in which time-preference is exercised. That this, however, is not going over to the productivity theory of interest is shown by the fact that it points to an opposite conclusion as re-

gards the resulting rate. The greater provision for present desires
thus made possible leads us to expect a reduction of the preference
for present goods and a lowering of their valuation in terms of future
goods. This (other things being equal) would be reflected in a
lower rate of time discount and a lower, not higher, rate of interest,
as the productivity theorist believes.[28]

What does Fetter mean by saying that his theory of time discount
and the productivity theory of interest lead to different conclusions
regarding the effect which will be produced by an increase in physical
productivity? According to the productivity theories as commonly
expounded, it should be expected that when there is a marked increase in the average efficiency of time-consuming methods of production there will be an increased eagerness on the part of business
enterprisers to practice more efficient methods; therefore a greater
demand for loan funds, and therefore a rise in the rate of interest.
Fetter says, on the other hand, that a marked increase in the productivity of methods of production should lead to a decline in the
rate of interest. Why on Fetter's theory should improvements in
methods of production lead to a decline in interest?

Increased productivity of the standard methods of production promises a larger supply of goods for the satisfaction of current wants and
therefore reduces the rate at which people discount the future. The
more abundant the supplies at the present time the less pressing will
be present wants in comparison with future wants. Therefore the
lower will be the rate of time discount; and therefore the less will be
the discount at which people are valuing the future services of durable
goods. The prices which they are willing to pay for these goods will
contain higher amounts relatively of their future services as compared
with their present services, and therefore the business man who buys
durable goods at these higher capitalized figures has a lesser margin
of profit in prospect with the gradual maturing of their services; and
therefore finally the business man is ready to pay only a lower rate
of interest in order to obtain present possession of these profitable
agents.

S. Fetter explains the present prices for durable goods and not
necessarily the interest rate.

---

[28] Fetter, "Interest Theories, Old and New," *The American Economic Review*,
March 1914, pp. 77, 80, 84, 88.

Later criticism of Fetter's theory has been mainly on the ground that a real
psychological theory must be a descriptive analysis of the behavior of lenders and
borrowers, which Fetter's theory is not; see F. H. Knight, "Neglected Factors in the
Problem of Normal Interest," *The Quarterly Journal of Economics*, February 1916
[Knight referred to the "institution of lending at interest"]; see also G. A. Kleene,
Profits and Wages (New York: Macmillan, 1916) chapter 3 (Outline, April 5, 1923).

M. He would be pleased with that remark, because it would show at least his fundamental point. The essential thing in his eyes is the explanation of the present prices of durable goods. But he would go on to say that his theory affords an explanation of how people can pay interest and also the rate at which they are ready to pay, just because they can get these durable goods at prices that amount to less than their services when realized. The amount of interest you can pay depends upon the difference between the present value of those services and their future value; and that difference depends upon the amount of discount contained in present prices.

S. If business men want capital, it is to enable them to produce better because they see more profit in producing more. Fetter falls down on that point.

M. Yes, Fetter would say that is quite all right; you have gotten part of his case straight. But the chance they have of making any money by investment exists solely because they can today get at present prices goods whose services in the future are going to be worth more than the present price they pay for them. You could not make money by buying the best machine possible no matter how physically productive that machine was, if you had to pay at the present time the full value of the services that the machine is going to render. To say that the machine will be highly productive in the sense that it will enable the employer to dispense with the labor of two employees is not to the point, Fetter would say. It is to the point only in a vague and general sense. Whatever the value of those services is, if they be very great, you cannot make any money by owning the machine unless you get those services now for less than they would be worth when rendered.

S. That does not take into consideration the demand side of the picture, but only the supply side. And if the supply be increased and the price lowered, the demand might increase.

M. I suppose Fetter's answer would be that on this showing, the fundamental factor is the prevailing rate of discount—discount in the community as a whole. This is a rate which is determined by the actions of millions of people, some of whom have a considerable desire for the possession of future goods and others whose desire is less keen. There is a set of people who are offering a supply of future goods and a set of people demanding, and all the people are making choices with reference to time. Consequently the rate of time-discount is fixed in the community as a whole on the basis of the comparison of one set of comprehensive demand schedules for future goods and another set of comprehensive supply schedules. In other words, both demand and supply enter in determining the fundamental factor of time discount upon the services of durable goods. Once that has been settled, the rate of time discount gets embodied, crystallized in the market. And then when you think about the market prices for these durable goods you have again to think of it in terms both of demand and supply. There are people who are supplying these durable goods at prices which are affected by time discount, and there are people who want them.

S. Fetter has quite a bit to add to his 1914 theory.

M. Yes, I know he has. I had the pleasure of making some comments on a more elaborate statement of his position on the theory of interest at the last meeting of the American Economic Association [December 1926]. His paper "Interest Theory and Price Movements" is a much fuller and more carefully considered statement of his view upon this subtle problem than any that he advanced heretofore, but the paper was deficient in at least one respect; he omitted any specific referenec to the productivity theory. When I talked to him about the matter, he thought that a good many people believe that what he had said about productivity theory in 1914 was a peaceful surrender to the productivity theory and he did not want to be understood as having run up the white flag on that point; but I believe that he is going to think it over and discuss his views on productivity in the paper when published.[29]

S. Fetter maintains that the productivity theory takes a different view as to the course of the interest rate. How could one verify this matter?

M. We have a good opportunity to make a factual investigation on the basis of the extraordinary changes which took place in time discount during the [World] War [I]. It would seem obvious that under the extraordinary pressure for a vast increase in current supplies of many types of goods in all the belligerent countries, there must have been an increase of the rate at which people were discounting the future. People were ready to make far greater sacrifices of the future in 1914-1918, in order to get goods in the present, than had been the case in peace time. Does not that offer a nice opportunity to see whether rates of interest move in accordance with the changes in

---

[29] [In the published paper, Fetter added a few comments on the productivity theory. He dismissed its supporters as holding "two quite distinct theories of interest, one to cover the case of indirect goods (sometimes limited to those employed in commercial ways) and another to cover that of direct (i.e., enjoyable) goods." Fetter, "Interest Theory and Price Movements," *The American Economic Review*, March 1927, supplement, p. 72.]

prevailing time discount? Did they? You say not?[30] Market rates of interest obviously did not. That raises an important question to discuss in his paper as to whether economists in considering the interest problem must not subdivide the problem into market rates of interest on bank loans, for instance, in terms somewhat different from those in which they treat the general problem of interest at large; that is, there must be a recognition of "quasi-independent interest rates upon different types of loans."[31]

> Fetter's doctrine of interest. A time discount theory. Does Fetter admit that productivity of capital affects interest? Denies that it does so directly. On what ground? Productivity which he recognizes is the ripening of the series of rents which capital goods will yield. Present value of the capital goods is value of this series of future rents already discounted. Does Fetter explain? But what determines the rate of time discount? He does intimate the process by which rates of time discount are worked into a market rate. But he does not explain why the individuals discount the future. Nearest approach to such explanation seems to be the vague remarks on pp. 159-161.[32]

But we must not dwell too long on these refinements. Let us return to the broader problems of the school for which Fetter speaks. There have been two lines of interpretation and of criticism of the school.[33] The work has been taken in the first place simply as being what it purported to be—a psychological theory of economic behavior. From that point of view, the critics have argued that it is a theory which is unrealistic, which does not as a matter of fact account for

---

[30] "Professor Fetter thinks the recent war [World War I] brought for the time being a marked increase in our discount upon future goods. If so, and if time-preference is a factor of great significance in determining the present prices we are willing to pay for goods of unlike durability, then in 1914 to 1918 the prices of highly durable goods must have risen decidedly less on the average than prices of short-lived goods. Did that happen? I do not know the answer to my question. But it seems to me a question which Professor Fetter may well try to answer fully." (Mitchell, "Interest Theory and Price Movements—Discussion," *The American Economic Review,* March 1927, supplement, p. 110.)

[31] Clause is from Mitchell, "Interest Theory and Price Movements—Discussion," p. 109.

[Professor Mitchell enlarged on this point in his review of Lionel Robbins's *The Great Depression* (1934)]: "I wish that Professor Robbins and the Cambridge authorities whom he follows in stressing the importance of interest, would talk less about 'the' rate of interest. If we are ever to have a clear understanding of the relations between interest rates and business activity, we must recognize the different roles played by the various forms and kinds of interest; for example, in this country, by call money rates, the rates on commercial paper and short-time loans on collateral, the rates charged by banks to their own customers for lines of credit, Federal Reserve rates, mortgage rates, the yields on high-grade bonds, and the yields on second-grade bonds." ("Robbins, *The Great Depression,*" *The Quarterly Journal of Economics,* May 1935, p. 506.)

[32] Outline, March 5, 1917.

[33] Beginning of extract from "1918 Typescript."

what people actually do. The central difficulty that has been found in this respect lies in the theory of value which Fetter, in common with pretty much all the marginal analysts, presents. The criticism may be put in this form: The theory of value as commonly expounded in books like Fetter's supposes in the first place that people separate in their minds the idea of gratifications that they are going to get from commodities, from the idea of the commodities; then they set a value upon the feelings, the gratifications that those commodities will arouse in them; and then pass those values back to the commodities, and so determine what they are ready to give for the articles in question.

This is said to be a gross misrepresentation of the process of valuation; in short, "men value commodities, not feelings."[34] "For examples of such criticisms of the psychological school see Professor Veblen's reviews of Professor Fisher's *Capital and Income* and *The Rate of Interest,* in *Political Science Quarterly,* March 1908 and June 1909." If it is true that in thinking about values, the things that a person thinks about are the commodities, then the picture of the process of valuation which is implicit in an account like Fetter's is a caricature; for, as previously said, what Fetter's theory does imply—and in this respect it is simply representative of the whole school of marginal utility theorists—is that the individual separates the idea of the feelings, the gratifications, which the commodities are going to arouse, from the idea of the commodities themselves, that the value is something which he attaches in his mind to those feelings which are anticipated, and that, to repeat the process, you pass that idea of the value of the feeling to be aroused back and associate it with the idea of the commodities themselves.

Along the line of that criticism the critics say that this is an account of certain logical implications in men's feelings for commodities, not an account of their actual dealings with commodities. It is not an attempt to show what the process of valuation is. It is an attempt to outline what is logically implied in dealings with commodities, if the theorist ascribes men's interest in commodities to the hedonistic ground of anticipated pleasure or gratifications. A theorist like Fetter tries to escape the charge of hedonism by not talking about "pleasures," but about "gratifications" or "satisfactions." Obviously the change of the word does not change the substantial feature of his account of valuation. It still essentially assumes that man has a

---

[34] Mitchell, "The Role of Money in Economic Theory," 1916; reprinted in *The Backward Art of Spending Money and Other Essays,* p. 157.

motive consciously recognized for most of his economic actions, and that this motive is the attainment of certain pleasurable states of feeling. Just so long as the theorist supposes that people's interest in commodities is interest in feelings, the gratifications that they are going to produce, and works his theory of value out on that basis, he opens himself to this line of criticism.

S2. I did not quite understand the last sentence.

M. Let me go over the whole thing again. I will turn it around and state the positive contention first. The critics say positively that as a matter of actual fact men value commodities, not feelings; that is to say, while the person is thinking about an apple, he is not thinking of the taste or the sense of repletion which will come with eating it. Negatively they say this theory of value of the marginal analysts does violence to the facts, because it implies that people do not value commodities, but go through the following elaborate process: first they split up the idea of the commodities and separate from the other elements the idea of the feelings which the use of that commodity will arouse, the gratification. In the second place they put a value upon this anticipated feeling or gratification and then they pass the value set on the feeling back to the idea of the commodity and formulate their price offers on the basis of that value.

S4. Doesn't this line of criticism seem very general, indefinite? It seems to apply to other people beside Fetter.

M. Yes. It would apply to all economists who follow the ordinary marginal utility analysis. It would also apply to those who make use of cost as an important factor in determining values. They separate the idea of the pain from the idea of work, the disutility, the feeling that the work gives them. They set a value or a rating upon the idea of the sacrifice, then they pass that rating back to their idea of the work, and on this basis make up their minds what they would take to undergo the toil in question. You are quite right. It is a very general criticism. It is intended as a fundamental criticism of theories of value.

S5. What is the difference between wanting the good because people know it will benefit them some way or knowing that the good will benefit them in some way and wanting the good? People would not want it, if they did not think it would give them gratification.

M. The psychologist nowadays will almost always say that the causal relation is the other way around. A person first desires things. Because he desires them, possession gives gratification. But a person does not first have a notion of the gratification, and have that notion of the gratification awakening desire. Rather he wants the thing. That is a spontaneous act, and anything that he wants will gratify him when he gets it. That is to say getting it will be a gratification. Of course, afterwards it may have disappointing consequences. This is what the psychologists nowadays are inclined to say.

There is the wider and larger line of psychological criticism which was made about Marshall. If the theorist credits behavior with an instinctive rather than a rationalistic basis and control, he does not suppose that men are anticipating pleasures and pains, making net calculations as to how they can get the largest net amount of pleasure and guiding their conduct by that rational procedure. The view that is commonly taken nowadays is that man is born with a large number of instinctive propensities to act. He does not know why. Among his instinctive propensities are a set out of which arise the capacity of reasoning. Reason is, however, very imperfectly developed in the case of most people. For the great bulk of mankind it is true from first to last that their activity is determined for them by these instinctive impulses to act, of the source of which very little is known, and that being the case any account of human conduct, which makes man primarily a rational creature, pursuing a calculated course leading toward some given logical end, is not true to the facts. This is a particular working out of the general criticism.

S6. Wouldn't the theorist get more at the truth by analysing logically that way than by perhaps getting the actual psychological process, because whether a man does this thing instinctively, or whether he does it because he reasons, he does those things, and he has to analyse them, and the result of the instinct is that man has had certain experiences, and that has made the instincts into habits.

M. That is exactly the line that is taken in the second general criticism of Fetter's type of theory which I shall come to presently. Let us leave that aside for a moment. The first line of criticism takes the theory as being what it purports to be: a psychological account of human behavior in economic matters. From this point of view, beside that general psychological criticism another set of criticisms has been argued vigorously by writers like Thorstein Veblen and [the British economic historian] Sir William Ashley. They have said, taking the theory for granted, that it is all that it purports to be, waiving any questions as to its competence on its own grounds, still on its own grounds it is vague and an incomplete account of the determination of values. It leaves out the most important and the most interesting factors which shape conduct. How do they reach this conclusion? They say that in this so-called value theory people are supposed to have certain sets of desires. If the theorist is really interested in determining, in explaining, in understanding human conduct, he wants to know why a civilized man is different from a savage. If he wants to know why an Englishman is in some respects different from a Frenchman, why an occidental is in some respects different from an oriental, then he has to explain the factors which have given people different standard desires in these large communities; that is, the factors that have controlled the interests and formulated the conventional feelings.

The reader of a book like Fetter's gets the impression that human nature is a tolerably standard article, that men just do have certain desires for things like food, certain disinclinations such as the aversion to work, and nothing is given by way of accounting for these desires and disinclinations. But that assumption, say the critics, is an extremely violent one. If the inquirer will stop to think a moment, if he will get away from the small conventional limitations of the viewpoint such as is characteristic of these theorists, it may be true that man as man has certain physiological needs which are common to all the species, such as the need for food, the interest in reproduction; but if he takes any given act of people whose behavior he is studying, he will find there are great differences between the conditions under which they think it fitting to gratify their reproductive instincts, between the things which they consider good to eat, between the forms that their desires of every sort have actually taken.

The diet of no two nations is alike. Satisfactions regarding conventional necessities vary greatly, and the variations run through practically all the things that people do. Notions regarding what is and what is not a dignified form of work vary; so do the notions of what is a proper way for a human being to spend his time and what is an improper one. If the inquirer wants to understand the scheme of values that exists in a community at any time, he has to find out what has given the peculiar characteristics to the desires and the interests of men in that particular community, at that particular time. The marginal utility analysis leaves all those problems out of account, and the theorist can never succeed in getting an account of them if he confines himself to work with the types of theory which the marginal utility analysts represent. As Ashley, for instance, said, "Behind the workman's wife making up her mind on Saturday night whether to buy another loaf or a scrap more meat stands the whole of human nature and the whole of social history."[35] If the theorist wants to understand the fact that she is ready to pay certain prices for this particular article, he has to know the course of circumstances which has shaped the diet of the British working classes. As in effect Veblen put it "if you want to understand the makeup of a man's likes and dislikes at any particular time, you have to follow the cumulative development of the institutions under which those people have grown up."[36] Studying economic history in Ashley's sense, studying the cultural consequences of institutions, their development and changes, in Veblen's sense, is work that is as different as can well be imagined from the kind of speculation in a book like Fetter's *Principles*.[37]

These critics say further that it is the cumulative changes which are going forward in communities all the time that constitute the interesting and significant features of present life. To get a glimpse of what is likely to happen to the economic life of civilized society in the immediate future, the theorist cannot get it by speculations of the kind that the so-called American Psychological School supplies. The inquirer has to get it by studying the cultural consequences of the kind of work that people are doing, and the kind of things that they are getting to satisfy their wants. So that from this point of view even if the analysis of value which the American Psychological School and the other utility analysts give were satisfactory, it would leave out of account the most interesting and significant factors controlling human

---

[35] Quotation from "The Present Position of Political Economy," *The Economic Journal*, December 1907, p. 477, in Outline, March 5, 1917. [(This was Ashley's presidential address before Section F, Economic Science and Statistics, of the British Association for the Advancement of Science.) In the address the quotation is preceded by a critique of the marginalists. "I cannot help thinking that it takes us a very short way indeed. Instead of leading us to the very heart of the problem, the doctrine of marginal value seems to me to remain entirely on the surface; it is not much more than a verbal description of the superficial facts at a particular point of time. The intensity of demand varies inversely more or less rapidly, with the extent to which it is satisfied; for different commodities there are different scales of intensity; under certain circumstances one demand will be substituted for another. True doubtless. But *why* do people demand just those things? On what does the rapidity of satiation depend? Have their desires always been the same; or the possibilities of production in order to meet them? How are desires related to one another? What are they likely to become? What are the limits to demand set by the economic situation of the demanders? These are the things we really want to know. The problem is, in a wide sense of the term, an *historical* one, or if you prefer the phrase, a *sociological* one, both 'static' and 'dynamic.'" (pp. 476-477).]

[36] Professor Mitchell was referring to Veblen's "The Limitations of Marginal Utility," 1909; reprinted in *The Place of Science in Modern Civilisation*, pp. 231-251.

[37] Fetter is to be commended for giving some attention to the cumulative movement. His "theory also touches upon the historical process by which differences in the time-preference among the members of a group lead to the lending and borrowing of money, when a certain stage in the development of economic institutions has been reached. I am glad that Professor Fetter feels but slight misgivings at thus joining forces with the institutional theorists." (Mitchell, "Interest Theory and Price Movements—Discussion," p. 109.)

behavior. In short, from the standpoint of what may be called the historical criticism, the utility theorists have no explanation to offer of the crucial factor of human progress; namely, the development of institutions.[38]

S7. Why could not Fetter or the representatives of his school say "Yes, we agree with that. That's all true. No quarrel about that at all. We take these as given, and we will travel with our paraphernalia from one country to another, and take these as given, and our analysis will apply in the same way to these different conditions."

M. That is what they can say. They can admit the whole force of the criticism and still contend that for the analysis of the particular objects which they are dealing with, their type of theory is the proper one to try. If they make that reply then the only rejoinder is: "Your reply represents a misapprehension of how people really do value goods." The critic falls back on that first psychological criticism.

I pass to the second interpretation. That interpretation is to the effect that the utility theorists do not really realize the valuable part of their contribution. They have done work which if set in a proper perspective is genuinely significant, but it is not an adequate account of the valuation process. What is valuable in it is a study of the logical implications of one very important set of institutions. If taken as such, and put in its proper place in a general conception of the development of economic culture, then the theorist can make something constructive and valuable out of it.

More specifically, under this criticism the school is interpreted as "pecuniary logic," as having converted economics into "a system of economic accounting," "business economics." The transition to this status may be best seen in a review in 1914 by Alvin S. Johnson of the second volume of the revised edition of Böhm-Bawerk's *Kapital und Kapitalzins: Positive Theorie des Kapitales.* Johnson says: Böhm-Bawerk and his entire school which in a broad sense includes a man like Fetter "have erected valuation into what is essentially a logical process. Böhm-Bawerk's value theory has been described as a psychological theory, but as everyone now knows, this description is misleading." It is a study of the logical implications of value.[39]

---

[38] Outline, March 5, 1917.

[39] *The American Economic Review,* March 1914, pp. 115-116; see also Outline, March 5, 1917.

[Johnson concluded the review by saying that "Böhm-Bawerk's interest doctrine is the more likely to survive, when the logical theory gives way to a theory better grounded in psychology."

Johnson was one of J. B. Clark's outstanding students. He assisted Clark in the preparation of *The Distribution of Wealth* and *Essentials of Economic Theory.*]

Another formulation somewhat more definite in character states:

> The American Psychological School . . . has taken the habit of mind developed by business traffic, and imputed it to mankind at large in their dealings with goods in general. It has used the refined concepts of wealth, service, property, capital and income—concepts that are slowly elaborated products of the money economy—to frame an account of how men might behave if they were faultless products of the counting house . . . And in so doing the school has rendered a notable service, for the use of money and the pecuniary way of thinking it begets is a most important factor in the modern situation. To isolate this factor, to show what economic life would be if it dominated human nature, is to clarify our understanding of economic processes. It is regrettable only that these writers have not emphasized the monographic character of their work. Of these two interpretations, the second better accords with the trend of development within the school.[40]

The name "psychological school" is a misnomer.

This second interpretation says that in this modern civilization—in this modern cultural situation—which as Ashley and Veblen point out can be understood only as the result of an indefinitely long cumulation of institutional changes, the use of money is a factor of great consequence. The use of money in psychological terms means the habit of using money as a common denominator for all values. It means the organization of economic life largely in forms of business

---

The technical difference between Fetter's theory of interest and Böhm-Bawerk's theory of interest is a comparatively minor matter when such a broad issue is being discussed.

[40] Mitchell, "The Role of Money in Economic Theory," 1916; reprinted in *The Backward Art of Spending Money and Other Essays*, pp. 157-158. The American Psychological School turns into business economics according to John R. Commons and Alvin Johnson, [using Irving Fisher rather than Fetter as the example]. How? By standardizing feelings as basis of pecuniary logic. As business man learns to consider a forest with reference to number of board feet at so much per thousand, Fisher's economic man learns to look at commodities present and future in terms of "utils." ("Money in Economic Theory-Miscellaneous Notes," APP 84-91, no. 49.)

"Professor Fisher's text is fundamentally a translation of the whole economic world into terms of capital and income. It is a system of economic accountancy. . . . It would be more properly entitled 'Principles of Pecuniary Economics.' So far as practicable, all non-pecuniary elements in economic life are excluded from consideration. All the fruits of the earth become a homogeneous income, the earth itself becomes capital, and man an uncertain income." (Johnson, review of Fisher's *Elementary Principles of Economics* in *The Journal of Political Economy*, November 1913, p. 857, quoted in "A. S. Johnson," APP 64-73, no. 36.) For Commons's interpretation, see his "Political Economy and Business Economy. Comments on Fisher's *Capital and Income*," *The Quarterly Journal of Economics*, November 1907, pp. 120-125. For Fisher's reply to Veblen see "Capital and Interest," *Political Science Quarterly*, September 1909; and to Commons "A Reply to Critics," *The Quarterly Journal of Economics*, May 1909. For extracts of Fisher's replies, see "Fisher," APP 54-63, no. 77; see also E. H. Downey, "The Futility of Marginal Utility," *The Journal of Political Economy*, April 1910. (Outline, March 5, 1917.) [Downey, a student of Veblen, was a pioneer in the field of workmen's compensation legislation. See Joseph Dorfman, *The Economic Mind in American Civilization*, 5 volumes (New York: The Viking Press, 1946-1959) IV, pp. 112-116.]

enterprises which are conducted not to produce material goods that will meet human needs, but are conducted to make profits. It means that the people who are connected directly with the management of these business enterprises control them by means of more or less elaborate schemes of accounting. It means that somehow some habit of taking an accountant's view of economic life is forced upon other members of the community than those who would properly be called business men. In short it means that the rationalistic accountant's way of carrying on economic life, the pursuing of economic interest, is an extremely important factor in present economic activity.

In so far as the work of the marginal utility analysts in general, and the American Psychological School in particular, has significance it lies practically in showing how men might behave if they carried the logic of the money economy through remorselessly into all their economic calculations, if they acted on rules which would stand careful scrutiny by a certified public accountant, if they were thinking carefully about gratifications as separated from goods, if they were putting values on those things by comparing values to be obtained from other commodities, and then shaped their every act by the same degree of careful consideration which a business corporation might give to the study of the more important problems that come up in the conduct of its affairs. Anybody who considers this logical influence of pecuniary institutions and seriously follows out its implications, and shows what behavior would be if people obeyed those implications, is, as S7 put it, studying an important feature of the situation, and so is contributing toward the understanding of the situation as a whole, but if he thinks that he is giving an account of economic behavior, he is making a grievous mistake. He is practically attributing to men at large a type of behavior in which a comparatively small number of the population are more or less perfectly drilled by the exigencies of modern business life.

S1. In the great majority of cases I think that business houses on the one hand and the people who behave very much like them, housewives on the margin of starvation, have to behave in a very rational way. The recent investigation into family budgets in England proves that.

M. Have to behave in a very rational way?

S1. They do spend their money in the most rational way they can, and it seems to me that the poor housewife and the business houses are by far the greatest elements in determining the direction of economic activity.

M. Those contentions are all deserving of careful consideration. What is meant when it is said that housewives spend their money in a rational way?

S1. They know what is the cheapest way of driving starvation from their door.

M. Are they thinking, as a matter of fact, in conventional terms or in terms of food values?

S1. I should say always [in terms of food values].

M. That is to say in so far as the people who are on the ragged margin are concerned with satisfying the most fundamental of needs, rationality is more or less forced upon them, even if you test that rationality by a scientific standard, if you consider food values?

S1. I think you can link that up with the first question.

M. Wait a moment. Let us allow that contention to stand with reference to this particular class of consumers and their outlay on food. Of course, it would still remain true doubtless, if you went on that what seemed rational from the point of view of a poor English woman might not seem so to a Negro woman or to an American woman. There are considerable differences here, and to understand them the inquirer would have to resort to investigations of other than a physiological sort, but let us not go into that. Suppose you take any other class of consumers in the community and think not about their outlays in getting food exclusively, but about their expenditures as a whole. Can you consistently with the facts make the same claim that from other than a conventional point of view their expenditure is necessarily rational? The real point would be this: that what is rational for you and for me depends largely upon the conventional standards that we have. And those standards are derived by us from the communities in which we have grown up. They do not represent our reasoning. We do not know enough of course to find out what is the best way to satisfy our needs. We cannot go into that. They represent the net resultant of a long process of social development. Though you and I are both products of this situation, we probably have sufficient independence of judgment left after all the discipline to which we have been subjected to look around and to see that among all of the conventional standards, which have been ground into us, there is a large proportion which it is hard to justify. For instance why do we both wear the type of collar that we are wearing? If the inquirer gets away from the gratifications which have a comparatively narrow variety forced upon people by physiological needs which are common to the whole race of man, he will find, it is more and more difficult to contend that there is any rational basis of behavior which can be defended as against some other scheme of tastes. We think our tastes are good of course. They are. They are good for us. That is simply because men's minds have been given a particular bent by the communities in which they have lived, in which they have grown up. If we had had the good luck to have been born in Africa, we would have had another set of tastes, and they would seem just as good to us as the tastes we now have. We would still want children. We would need some kind of shelter from the weather. We would still need food. There are a few wants that are necessarily common to all mankind, just because he is an animal. If you can get away from these needs which are dictated by our physical constitution, any margin above what is necessary to fill people's stomachs and keep themselves warm and to beget children, you will find that the remaining elements present a very great variety, which is dictated by the tastes of the community in question, and these tastes are to be explained by studying the process through which this community has grown to whatever stage it is in when the theorist examines it.

S6. Are those special particular varieties so fundamental?

M. No, they are not so fundamental. That is what I say, but still they are present in the life of every community that has any margin above what is necessary to satisfy the creature needs.

S6. The question I was thinking about was would it be fundamental enough to require treatment in economic theory?

M. Yes. It does largely because we of course are interested in economic progress. We want to see mankind get further and further beyond the point where it has to give most of its working hours to the task of filling its stomach and keeping warm.

S6. What I thought was that if Fetter treated with general principles, that anyone could go on further with the problem to study the particular applications of it in the different communities and that a work that was more general; that is, just treated fundamentals would be more valuable because it would apply everywhere.

M. The reply is that if the economist wants to get an adequate account of how people value goods either those that are superfluous or prime necessities, it is much better to take the process of valuation as it goes on in people's minds than to impute to mankind at large the attitude of a careful accountant. The bulk of the people spending their money, even the very poor people, if they are following rational courses are doing so not because they have thought them out, but because there is a more or less recognized convention into which their community has fallen that saves them the necessity of thinking of prices. What the given individual does is to make minor adjustments inside the general conventional scheme which his time and place has made for him. That would be true of course of S5's example of an English housewife. English housewives as a class have learned a certain way to get along which may well be the best conceivable, granting their particular time, country and incomes, but no one English housewife has thought that scheme out for herself. They are like people everywhere, governed largely by habit, and their habits are somewhat different from people in similar situations in life in other countries. The habit, however, may well be rather rational in character.

S1. Couldn't dressing respectably be taken as a gratification?

M. What is dressing respectably if you go to China?

S1. Being like other people.

M. Being like other people, that is to say, abiding by the existing conventions, and those conventions, as this line of argument contends, you have to understand, and the way to understand them is to see how they have assumed their present form through a long period of development.

S1. There is no real contrast between custom and rationality. It is rational to try to be like other people. If one stops to think about it, he finds that conventional behavior is the best line.

M. I do not think you can maintain that thesis, because if you say that everybody is the same, then you are saying practically that people do not think things out for themselves, that they accept the current values.

S1. I do not wear sandals, because somebody might laugh at me. This is quite rational.

M. This is one of the conventions which applies in the kind of community in which we have grown up. It is better not to be erratic.

S1. It is rational.

M. I suppose that it is rational to find out in what points it is well not to be erratic.

S1. I do not think that irrational ought to be applied to something that satisfies.

M. I do not mean that at all. What "rational" seems to me to mean is studying carefully the problem which is before the individual in all cases, and making up his mind as to what is the best line of conduct for him. This is the attitude of mind that people like Fetter attribute to mankind at large, and the criticism is that it is not true. That is not the way people behave. They do not study out these things. People do as others do. You may be quite right in saying that by and large in most cases that is the conclusion that people would arrive at if they reasoned it out, but the fact remains that they do not; and if they did, they might come occasionally at least to a different conclusion.

Outline of theory as presented in *Principles of Economics* (1904). Subject is value. Definition of value (equals importance). Even production defined with reference to value. "[T]he unit of the complex problem of value being the simplest, immediate, temporary gratification." An advance on Jevons in extending the theory of value to cover all branches of economic theory. (But Marshall had set the example). "Part I. The Value of Material Things: Division A—Wants and Present Goods . . . Division B—Wealth and Rent . . . Division C—Capitalization and Time-Value . . . Part II. The Value of Human Services: Division A—Labor and Wages . . . Division B—Enterprise and Profits . . . Part III. The Social Aspects of Value: Division A—Relation of Private Income to Social Welfare . . . Division B—Relation of the State to Industry." 1. Value of present goods (material) the first problem. Wants—definition. Gratification—demand grows out of subjective valuations. Demand curves—the marginal law. Exchange grows out of demand (cost plays no part here). Barter—two parties. Effect of competition (pp. 33-34). (Discussion of monopoly deferred to pp. 302 ff.) 2. Value of uses of durable goods. Rent—the problem, diminishing returns applicable to other agents. Law of rent. Application to economic rent. On contract rent. On relation of economic rent and contract rent. 3. Value of durable goods—capitalization and interest. Present value of durable goods as sum of its expected rents discounted at some rate. How rate of discount is determined. Interest: Interest and time discount. Why Fetter rejects productivity as cause of interest. 4. Value of labor: Wages—economic and contract. Law of wages. 5. Value of enterpriser's services. Cost of production to enterpriser. Cost of production to economist. Profits. 6. Social aspects of value.

General characterization. American Psychological School is Fetter's own phrase, used in review of Herbert J. Davenport's *The Economics of Enterprise* in *The Journal of Political Economy,* June 1914. Desire to set off American writers from the Austrian school, its justification? Fetter speaks of himself as a psychological theorist. No elaborate acquaintance with psychology revealed. "Economics . . . the study of men earning a living." "Man is the center of economic reasoning." "The motive force in economics is found in the feelings of men." "The theory of distribution . . . a consistently subjective analysis of the relations of goods to wants." ". . . It is the attainment of pleasurable conditions in mind or soul that is the aim of all economic activity." "The objective income is sometimes called the 'real' income but certainly it is not income in the most essential sense." What Fetter really deals with is "psychic income" as the common denominator. "All things at last become comparable in terms of psychic income" in each individual's judgment. "Too often in economic reasoning they are looked at from the employer's point of view, etc." "Market values are built up on subjective valuations." "Gratification, afforded directly or indirectly, is the basis of all values." "In the last analysis the value of anything must be found in the power of affording psychic income." "In its last analysis a service is never a material thing, but a psychic effect on men and their wants." So too crises: "The fundamental cause of crises . . . is seen to be psychological." "The beginning and end of economic study is man." Conclusion: "Subjective" is a more accurate adjective than "psychological."

Recapitulation: General comments on first book. Simplicity. All problems are problems of value. Unit for all problems is "simplest, immediate, temporary gratification." Discusses once for all determination of price from facts relating to gratification, subjective value, demand and exchange. Assumes that the discussion is applicable in all later cases. Treatment of remaining cases is primarily analysis of what is valued; for method of valuation is always the same. Cost allowed no ultimate influence upon value. Enterpriser's cost is reflection of want—gratifying power of agents, and value cannot be related to psychic cost. Discusses economic, not contract, rent; difference in time value rather than interest; economic, not contract wages; economic, not actual, profits; functional, not personal, distribution; qualities of goods, not actual, goods; economic production not technical production. Fetter's contribution to economic doctrine. (1) Primarily in discussion of interest. Will allow no reliance upon productivity. (2) Extension of law of diminishing returns to every conceivable economic agent.

Profundity: Traces all problems back to the ultimate problem of human feeling. C.f., "The use made of the income is itself a kind of production in its last stage." It is the attainment of pleasurable conditions in mind or soul that is the aim of all economic activity. ("The motive force in economics is found in the feelings of men.") C.f., Edgeworth's conception of man as a pleasure machine; Fisher's conception of the body as a factory that makes pleasure out of commodities.

Questions for class discussion: Does American Psychological School as represented by Fetter undertake study of economic man? Anything corresponding to Jevons's quotations from Bentham? Is human nature conceived hedonistically? (Remember that hedonism is a psychology of action—an explanation of why men do or choose certain things). Means of attainment of "pleasurable conditions" is shrewd calculation of relative advantages of different lines of action. Sounds hedonistic. But Fetter hardly mentions pleasure and pain. Uses "gratification" instead of "pleasure." Insists that whatever motives make men desire things are in so far economic motives. Takes account of habits. Discusses rise of social institutions; e.g., history of contract rent; rise of the money economy, growth of trusts; history of crises, origin of private property. Recognizes existence of "a great system of social institutions that helps to determine what men will do." Defines capital as "economic wealth expressed in terms of the general unit of value." Rise of money economy has changed wealth from "crystalized" form in middle ages to "fluid" form in modern times. Led to clear recognition of problem of time value. Accountants' view of value of durable goods—admittedly a "logical" view of the situation. Reaction of interest rate on estimates of individuals. Welfare.

Conclusion: Conception of human nature is essentially hedonistic; for feeling is made the ground of action. Habits and institutions can be brought into the hedonistic psychology by virtue of doctrine of association of ideas. Is theory static or dynamic? Not merely static for it takes in development of above institutions; growth of population, effects of increase of savings, effects of introduction of machinery, etc. Is theory realistic? Does it deal with real men? Fetter says it must do so. Does it deal with real world? [To repeat], discusses economic, not contract, rent; differences in time value rather than interest; economic, not contract, wages; economic, not actual, profits functional, not personal, distribution; qualities of goods, not actual goods; economic, not technical, production. Yet Fetter would claim that his analysis of these strictly economic categories, combined with his analysis of how price is determined, gives real explanation of the actual categories. Does it merit to be called work of the American Psychological School?

Recent modifications of position of American Psychological School as expressed in Fetters second treatise, *Economics,* volume I, *Economic Principles* (1915). Important changes: "A quite new statement of theory of value." Connects value with choice, not with utility. Choice before and after valuation. Clear distinction between business economics and social economics. Fetter's characteristic doctrines are not greatly altered. Treatise changed by separation [of old volume] into theoretical part, now volume I, from practical part, now volume II, *Economic Problems in America.*[41]

[To emphasize and elaborate] the last point, the reason his economic theory did not change substantially in his second treatise is that the psychological base was unchanged. Let me read some passages. He says on page 174 of *Economic Principles* that the aim of all human effort, whether of work or play, is "psychic income." This is what he said in his earlier *The Principles of Economics,* is it not? [To continue with the latter work, he says,] that "The aim of all human effort . . . is psychic income." That looks like conscious motivation by some end you hold in view. To understand what that means you ought to be assured what psychic income is. You turn to page 27, and you find this statement: "We may define the term psychic income as desirable results produced in the realm of feeling by valuable objects or by valuable changes in the environment which accrue to or effect an economic subject, within a given period." Put those two statements together and what you get is this: The aim of all human effort is desirable results in the realm of feeling. Of course, this is good hedonism. In short, Fetter's economic theory does not change, because his working economic psychology, that is to say, his working conception of human nature is not altered, despite the strenuous efforts to restate the theory of value in the chapters that deal

---

[41]Outlines, February 26, 28, 1917; March 5, 1917; "Fetter," APP 54-63, no. 76. Quotations are from *The Principles of Economics,* pp. ix, xiv, 9, 15, 35, 43, 73, 122, 205, 354, 398, 412; *Economic Principles,* p. ix.

with the specific subject. In other words, so far as I can see, it remains questionable after all whether his conception of the driving forces of economic behavior has undergone any alteration. The explanation of the fact that his type of economic theory is not altered by an alleged new psychological foundation, is, or I think I ought to say, may be, that the psychological foundation had not been changed in fact. The work of the American Psychological School, however, can be considered valuable, if we take it not as a competent account of economic behavior as a whole but as particularly an analysis of the logic of one set of institutions; namely, the institutions which center around the use of money.[42]

The American Psychological School in a sense sought to carry on the work of the utility theorists (mechanics of utility). The older theorists had sought to penetrate to ultimate source of economic activity in feelings of pleasure and pain; also to give a more precise formulation to the classical problem of prices, particularly prices which constitute the distribution of income; that is, value and distribution as they exist at a given time. The American Psychological School systematized the discussion of distribution as a problem of value, distinguished sharply between statics and dynamics.

Bentham's table of the springs of action, hedonism at large, effort of writers like Adolf Wagner to include new motives, Marshall's insistence upon the money measure of motive, Fisher's basing of utility upon desire, etc., all imply that the important thing for economics is the *motive* to action. This is where we are to look for ultimate explanations. But does not this imply an over-rational concept of human nature? Is there any more useful way of conceiving activity? Does psychology of behavior accept this concept?

Psychological School at the outset stressed the subjective basis upon which desires and efforts are supposed to rest but it ran into pecuniary analysis by finding that the solid part of its work was logic instead of psychology, and into pure theory which puts emphasis upon the general problem of equilibrium of demand and supply under static conditions.

The former is represented by various types which in general would avoid the problem of hedonism by attempting to divorce economics completely from psychology. This view is represented most sharply and clearly by Herbert Joseph Davenport (1881-1931) of Cornell and is summed up in his *The Economics of Enterprise* (1913).[43]

---

[42] Paragraph from "1918 Typescript."
[43] Outlines, May 14, 16, 1917; "Types of Economic Theory," APP 44-53, no. 28; "Money in Economic Theory—Miscellaneous Notes," APP 84-91, no. 49.

CHAPTER XIII

Herbert Joseph Davenport and Pecuniary Logic

Davenport (1861-1931), who was born in Burlington, Vermont, is another of the American economists who received their professional training in considerable measure on the European continent. After two years at the Harvard Law School in 1882-1884, he went into business in South Dakota and made some money in land speculation. In 1890 he went to Europe to study, and spent some time in the University of Leipzig and L'École Libre des Sciences Politiques in Paris. [After his return, he registered at the University of South Dakota and within a year took all the examinations for the four year course] and received a Ph.B. in 1894. He took his Ph.D. at the University of Chicago in 1898. Meanwhile he had taught in and then became principal of high schools in Sioux Falls, South Dakota, and Lincoln, Nebraska. Four years after taking his doctorate, he was appointed an instructor of political economy at the University of Chicago, and he revealed remarkable powers as a college teacher. He was one of the best trainers in technical economic theory in the United States, a most skillful and stimulating expounder of his views. From Chicago, he went to the University of Missouri in 1908, where he also became dean of its school of commerce; in 1916 he moved to Cornell. In 1923-1924 he served as economic adviser to the Standard Statistics Corporation of New York. While at Chicago, he published his doctoral dissertation, *Value and Distribution* (1908), which exhibited his considerable abilities as a careful critic of past economic theory; while at Missouri, he wrote *The Economics of Enterprise* (1913), which will be the subject of discussion.[1]

The analysis of the present order of a money economy is the critically important thing. Davenport defines economics. Does any-

---

[1]Other books of Davenport are *Outlines of Economy Theory* (1896); *Outlines of Elementary Economics* (1897); *The Principles of Grammar* (with Anne M. Emerson, 1898); *The Economics of Alfred Marshall* (posthumous, 1936). See review of this book by C. W. Guillebaud, "Davenport on the Economics of Alfred Marshall," *The Economic Journal*, March 1937, pp. 21-43. (Outline, "Davenport," APP 44-53, no. 33).

one know exactly how? It is one of the shortest and neatest definitions there is. He says that economics is "the science that treats phenomena from the standpoint of price."[2]

This represents a position different from that of Jevons, for instance. If the economist deals only with "phenomena from the standpoint of price", he eliminates from economics the problem of valuation. He may treat the theory of value in the sense that he makes value equivalent to price; and the process of valuation which has made so much trouble, the study of pleasures and pains and utilities, drops out altogether. So too Davenport is genuinely different from Fetter, who says that economists not only can have a theory of value in the sense of valuation but also should have a theory of value which is based upon modern psychology. Davenport professes to hold that psychology is not of vital concern to the economist; certainly not with respect to the value problem, whereas Fetter discusses it elaborately. He also differs materially from Marshall. Marshall treats economics as concerned with man's behavior in trying to get a living; he discusses at considerable length wants and their satisfaction, and holds that money is the center around which economic science clusters. He says that this is the center because it is the means of measuring the force of motives. These motives are the ruling forces in economics and consist in men's desire to get satisfactions and avoid sacrifices.

Davenport wants to cut all this out and concentrate upon the problem of prices, which is objective and which in his eyes always had been the economist's chief concern. He can walk on firm ground and not get muddled up with the warring notions of a lot of psychological schools which are hard to understand and do very little for the economist but addle his brains. To repeat, the central characteristic of his type of theory is most clearly expressed in his definition of the science of economics: the science that treats phenomena from the standpoint of price. He recognizes that this type of economics, a discussion of phenomena from the standpoint of price, is applicable only to a given institutional situation, that of private property, individual initiative and production for exchange. If the theorist is discussing say, the economic behavior of the Australian black-fellows, or any community of men in which the scheme of economic organization differs widely from the one with which we are acquainted, then economics would not be the science that treats phenomena from the standpoint of price. It is a science, however, which has grown to maturity and which in its present shape does apply to the conditions presented by a society

---

[2] *The Economics of Enterprise* (New York: Macmillan, 1913) p. 25.

where the great majority of the people are getting their satisfactions largely by making and spending money; and money implies price.

Davenport explicitly points out that the particular institutional situation has a history, and one might think, therefore, that in order to formulate a science of economics it would be necessary to study the evolution of the scheme of institutions under which a discussion of phenomena from the standpoint of price becomes significant; that is precisely the viewpoint which Thorstein Veblen takes.[3] To Veblen the chief problem of the economist is to understand how the institutional scheme which gives such a peculiar character to men's economic behavior has arisen. Davenport, on the contrary, says that the "task before us is the study of the situation as it actually is, with small attention to its genesis, excepting so far as its past may throw light on its present."[4] Seemingly he thinks that the extent to which it is necessary to study the past of this institutional scheme in order to get light upon its present is not great.

That kind of work, I think he would say if he were questioned, is extremely valuable. It is a task that somebody ought to perform. He and his colleague Professor Veblen—when they were together at Missouri—have done a lot of work with that particular end in mind. But from Davenport's standpoint, that work is not economic theory.[5]

In other words, he proposes to treat economics distinctly as the science of the phenomena regarded from the standpoint of price with reference to a peculiar institutional situation widely prevalent among the more advanced countries, and without paying much attention to the way in which the scheme of institutions to be analyzed came into being and assumed its current shape.

Davenport undertakes to perform two tasks. The first is the scientific one of trying to understand phenomena from the standpoint of price. The other is a matter of appraisal. While pursuing the first objective, he goes ahead ruthlessly, but one cannot say that it was without regard to the question of the desirability of the types of behavior that he is discussing. On the contrary there is in *The Economics of Enterprise* frequent flaunting of the fact that much of the behavior in a money economy is seemingly undesirable. But that, he says, is no business of the economist as economist, [and he sets this discussion off in the book].

---

[3] [Davenport was a student of Veblen at Chicago. He brought Veblen to Missouri. He never ceased to insist, however, that "Veblen and I never could get together." (Davenport to Mitchell, no month, no day, 1908).]

[4] *The Economics of Enterprise,* p. 26.

[5] Paragraph from "1918 Typescript."

When he has performed the task of explaining to his satisfaction the situation as it now exists, he devotes the last two chapters to appraise the present scheme of institutions, and there he passes judgment upon them—a judgment which in many respects is very severe. He undertakes to show that a community of men organized upon the principles of private gain defeats the end of human welfare in many respects. To repeat, that appraisal of the present situation is from his viewpoint not a part of economic science. In his eyes, to think clearly, the economist must separate sharply the two tasks—undertaking first the understanding of how things go; and then, if he wishes, forming some kind of judgment as to whether it is satisfactory or not. In performing that task, the theorist can take without the slightest logical inconsistency a viewpoint altogether different from that which he followed in the effort to understand how things are.

For understanding the first of the tasks, Davenport states that it is indispensable to hold fast continuously to a particular point of view; which he calls the "private and acquisitive" viewpoint. He writes:

> It is, indeed, superlatively important, here and everywhere, to recognize that a complete acceptance of this private and acquisitive point of view is the only procedure possible, in the analysis and classification of the phenomena of a society organized upon lines of individual activity for private gain.[6]

Have the theorists with whom we have so far been dealing taken this private and acquisitive point of view which Davenport says is the only possible one? Are there any other people with whom we have so far dealt of whose procedure that remark is not true? Were Ricardo, Mill, Jevons proceeding from the private and acquisitive point of view? Were Marshall, Fetter? You have not heard any of these previous writers insisting upon this, have you? Is that simply because they were not explicit upon a procedure that they were nevertheless practicing; that they were working unconsciously with what this comparatively late critic of their work has come to see is inevitable in economics?

S. Adam Smith seemed conscious of doing it; he discussed welfare of the individual and it has been carried down the line.

M. What do you think about that? Is Adam Smith in opposition to the private and acquisitive point of view? He takes at least the national point of view, in his explanation of how things go.

S. Did he not say that the wealth of the nation is equal to the sum of the wealth of the individuals in it?

---

[6] *The Economics of Enterprise,* p. 517.

M. Yes, he defined the wealth of nations as consisting of the sum of the individual wealth of its citizens. Adam Smith was proceeding specifically from the private and acquisitive viewpoint. In a sense he was using it even more boldly than Davenport. From his critique of modern pecuniary organization, Davenport at least would have some reservations. Even Adam Smith pointed out certain cases in which he thought it was necessary for the government, as representing the interest of the whole, to intervene; it was desirable but those are from his viewpoint minor exceptions.

S. Bentham has the same viewpoint: private pain and pleasure.

M. Yes. What about Marshall? Is he proceeding from this viewpoint?

S. He is until he discusses the normal [representative] firm.

M. Certainly he is working with the individual viewpoint before that. But does he drop that individual viewpoint when he comes to consider the [representative] firm? Isn't that simply a device of his for getting at the critically important point of the supply curve? The representative firm is a firm that is in the "game" to make money, is it not? The theorist simply picks it out as a result of his analysis, as occupying a strategic point upon the supply curve.

S. Does not Marshall take the two points of view more than Davenport does? Davenport is strictly scientific without ever letting any utilitarian consideration come in, whereas Marshall does.

M. Yes, Marshall's *Principles of Economics* is full of incidental judgments about what is good and what is not. His interest in a full life for everybody is marked on many pages, and there are frequent appearances in a modest form all through his book of the kind of judgment which Davenport gathers together in his last chapter.

S. Does not the difference seem to be that Davenport always speaks in money terms while the others go from one level of discussion to another?

M. In that sense Davenport is developing the logic of the situation as a whole more clearly than had his predecessors. Remember that in discussing Ricardo and John Stuart Mill I referred to the different levels on which economic analysis can be and is conducted. The economist can think of economic life in terms of a process of making and spending money. This has commonly been regarded as the most superficial level. He can think of economic life also as a process of making and consuming commodities that satisfy man's wants. In this case he distinguishes between a man's money wages and his real wages, meaning by real wages how much in the way of desirable goods a man can buy with his money wages. Some writers have tried to push beyond, even below the commodity level of analysis to the level of what they like to call real forces, and to think of commodities as means of supplying what people really want. With Bentham, that was pleasure; with Marshall, it became gratification. Similarly those who try to get down to the ultimate forces think of men's efforts at making money or goods as counting as sacrifices; the pain of labor and the pain of abstinence; or, to take the revised phraseology of the later writers afraid of the terminology of hedonism, the sacrifices of labor and waiting.

Then there have been in these writers traces of discussion on still another level; that is, they talked frequently, not from the point of view of the individual as such, but of their valuation of the whole process in terms of welfare or some of its many equivalents. Few undertake to explain what people do in terms of welfare, but most of the writers on frequent occasions comment on whether a certain kind of action contributes to welfare or is inimical to it. The classical economists carried on their analysis in these different sets of terms, or different levels. They talked often in terms of money prices, very frequently in terms of commodities, occasionally in terms of pleasure and pain, and more or less promiscuously of welfare.

Davenport attempted to eliminate this constant shifting. In *Value and Distribution* he prepared himself for the task of constructive theory by careful and elaborate critical studies of previous writers. This is a series of very close, logical criticisms of the work of the more significant earlier economists on the problems which he regards as of fundamental importance to economic theory, particularly the problem of value and distribution. His way is to say that so long as economists are discussing the things that account for economic behavior, they must always suppose that men are animated by a desire for individual gain. They must draw all their distinctions with that factor in mind.

At the same time, as will soon appear at more length, they must realize that all their discussion of how men seek gain in terms of price is superficial; it leads round in circles; the economist must consider the problem of the relation of this pecuniary activity, carried on for individual gain, to the real forces. Thus, a fundamental question is how Davenport succeeds in relating his analysis on the money level to his notions of the underlying forces.

In a sense his efforts in this connection are an attempt to arrive at a satisfactory solution to the problem on which I have had to comment several times: what was an economist to do in view of the fact that he was becoming aware in the latter part of the nineteenth century that his implicit psychology was not valid in the eyes of psychologists? Marshall's way was to use new names for the old things and continue talking in the classical fashion of how people act. Fetter's procedure was to devise what he regarded as a completely new statement of the process of valuation, and to base his economic theory of price and distribution nominally upon the revised psychology. Davenport's method is different; it is to make economics from start to finish a discussion of price, and practically to toss the problem of valuation out of the window as something that the economist is not concerned with, though there does remain the shadowy problem of the relation of the discussion in terms of price to the real forces.

He[7] is particularly anxious to have theorists realize that supply price is made up of money costs to the entrepreneur, the enterpriser. In modern society, he says, in a particular case the analyst must not think of supply price as resting on subjective sacrifice. It rests on money costs to the business men who are engaged in buying raw materials, hiring labor, providing machinery, and then estimating what they can afford to sell the goods at, on the basis of the pecuniary costs which they have incurred. Further he dwells emphatically on the assertion that the money costs, to the enterprise of producing a particular good, are very largely what he calls opportunity costs. What are opportunity costs?

S1. I do not recall the particular term.

M. Opportunity costs? Does anyone?

S2. Davenport says that the entrepreneur could have engaged in other enterprises. He does not, however, and what he might have received from those enterprises are counted up as costs to him.

M. That is to say, the theorist, when he is thinking of the enterpriser planning his business arrangements, has to consider the other chances of making money which were open to him, and the foregoing of those other opportunities is among the necessary costs, money costs, for getting the article produced. For instance, for a man to go into the manufacture of structural steel at the present time [1918] for building, he must already know the price situation in other activities, to forego the tempting opportunity he has currently to make steel either for ship building or other military purposes; and the price, which is high enough to make him forego the other opportunities open to him, is among the necessary costs of getting steel produced for building purposes.

---

[7] Beginning of extract from "1918 Typescript."

The reason for dwelling on the fact is that it shows again how from Davenport's viewpoint the theorist cannot explain any part of the price system alone. To say that opportunity costs are among the most important money costs entering into supply price is to say that, in explaining the supply price of any given article like wheat or coal or steel, he must already know the price situation in those activities to which the producer of the commodities under investigation by the theorist might have resorted. That is to say, before the theorist can explain the price of a particular article, he has to know the whole price situation with reference to other opportunities open to the people who are turning out the article that he is investigating. To explain this price he has to know the existence of another big organized section of the price system, and here again, if he begins to follow out ramifications, it is quite conceivable that before he gets through with canvassing the prices that must be brought into the account before he can explain the supply price of wheat or steel, it may well be that he would have considered most of the other prices that he knows anything at all about before he is done. Given these two schedules of demand price and supply price the determination of market prices is a matter of "mere mechanical details."[8] The fixation of the market price is simply a mechanical process at the point where the demand price and the supply price schedules cross each other. It is in this connection that Davenport points out that price coincides with only the marginal price offers, or, as he states elsewhere, that prices are not fixed by the margins, but at the margins. In order to explain the determination of prices, the theorist has to have the whole array of facts summed up, the demand scales on the one hand, the supply scales on the other hand. To say that the marginal price offers fix the price is to use indefensible language. The fact is that the whole situation summed up in the two schedules, demand price and supply price, fixes the price, and the margins are merely the points at which the fixing takes place.

To recapitulate the discussion up to this point, Davenport says that he conceives economics as the science which views phenomena from the standpoint of price. This science, he holds, refers to a given institutional situation which is characterized by private property, individual initiative and the direction of economic activity toward the making of money profits. It is not, he holds, the business of economic theory to explain how this institutional situation developed. In trying to explain what does go on under this institutional situation he argues that the only possible viewpoint is what he calls the private, acquisi-

---

[8] *The Economics of Enterprise,* p. 141.

tive viewpoint; that is to say, since we are living in a society dominated by private property, individual initiative and profit making,
the only way to explain what people are going to do, or try to do,
is to credit everyone with the intent of making money for himself.
Accepting this viewpoint and carrying it out with rare consistency,
Davenport holds that the central problems are in the field of price.

The chief thing, therefore, is to explain price. To do so, the theorist
has to account for how much people are ready to give for goods, and
at how much they are ready to sell them. He has to account for
schedules of price offers [demand price] on the one hand, and supply
price on the other. To account for a schedule of price offers he has to
look at the price which given individuals each taken separately are
willing to pay.

He has to know what importance the individual attaches to the
article in question, as a consumer or as a producer or as an investor,
and then he also has to know what other things the individuals could
get as substitutes at specific prices. That is to say, before the theorist
can draw up any individual's demand scale for any article, he has to
know not only the importance of that article in his eyes, but also the
price at which he could get certain substitutes and the rating which he
puts on those substitutes; that is, to get the elements for the explanation of the price of any one commodity, the theory assumes the existence of many other prices. Similarly, in explaining the schedules of
supply price, he has to know the price which it costs an individual to
put on the market the article in which the individual is interested, and
before he can explain them, he has to understand the other opportunities for profit-making open to that individual; that is to say, he has to
count in many opportunity costs as the effective considerations in
making up the business man's decision as to what he can afford to sell
for.

When the schedules of demand price on the one side and supply
price on the other side have been explained, then the whole theory of
price has been substantially achieved; for, as Davenport puts it, the
explanation of price, once the two sets of schedules are known, is a
matter of mere mechanical detail. Given the two schedules, prices are
fixed at their intersection. In laying down this conclusion he warns
once again against the common fallacy that prices are fixed *by* marginal utilities. That, he says, is a misleading phrase. In the first place, it
always takes at least two marginal utilities to determine the price a
man will offer for anything; and in the second place even the marginal
utility, given two particular goods, will influence the price which a

man will offer for one in terms of the other. What one ought to say is: the prices are fixed *at* margins not *by* margins.

S3. I do not understand how he can come to that conclusion.

M. S4, can you explain?

S4. Davenport insists that the price is fixed mechanically by the balancing of all the supply forces against all the demand forces, and by an adjustment, an equilibrium is reached by that weighing of the forces on both sides. There will be of course at one side the marginal price which determines the basis from which price starts, but does not determine the market price; that is, the lowest price in the market, the lowest offer.

M. Is the lowest offer that is made in the market properly called the marginal price offer?

S4. It seems to me it is.

M. Is it then the price offer at which the price finally rests?

S4. No. The price at which the market price finally rests is the point of equilibrium.

Mr. That is ordinarily called the marginal price offer, the marginal supply price. It is not common to use the term "marginal price" for the lowest price offer.

S4. I was thinking of it in terms of the marginal buyer.

M. But the marginal buyer is by no means the man who offers the lowest price. The man who offers the lowest price may well be excluded from the bargain altogether. Suppose that S4 and S5 and I are in the market trying to buy a horse which belongs to S7. Suppose S4 at most could offer $75, S5 will offer $100 and I will offer $125. We three are there as competitors. Suppose S4 makes his offer first, and S5 raises the bid $25. I go up $25 higher. Neither of the others are ready to raise that bid, and the horse is knocked down to me. What is the marginal price offer under these circumstances? It is not the lowest. It is the highest.

S4. It happens to be the highest.

M. In advance could you have told what the marginal price was going to be?

S4. No. You could not tell his offer.

M. This is a simple illustration of one sided competition. There is one article for sale. To give a fairly representative illustration, it would be better to assume that there are three people with horses for sale. Say that S7 is willing to sell for $75, that S8 is ready to sell for $100 but no lower, and S9 is willing to sell for $125. There are three trying to buy horses, and three trying to sell. What is going to happen in the market?

S4. The strongest buyer will offset the weakest seller.

M. What will the price be? There are three would-be buyers with successive offers of $75, $100 and $125. There are also three willing to part with their horses successively at $75, $100 and $125.

S4. Probably there will be a buyer and a seller at each figure.

M. Let us suppose that you bid first $75, and S7 will be ready to sell to you if he cannot do better; and when S5 sees that there is that fine bargain going on, he bids it up to $80. He won't let you have that horse at $75. And then S8 and S9 will not be selling their horses for anything less than $100 in S8's case and $125 in S9's case. What will happen?

S4. It will strike about midway between the two extremes.

M. Let us see. Certainly that horse cannot be sold for less than $100—we are supposing the horses are to be all equally satisfactory to their purchasers. While S4 is willing to pay and S7 is willing to take $75 for a horse, S5 will not let S4 get such a bargain. Suppose that S5 bidding against S4 raises the price up to $100. S4 is out of the market when the price goes above $75. Then the bidding goes on between S5 and myself when he makes the bid of $100. Just one horse is offered for sale, and I am the only person who is willing to pay $125. There are two horses now offered for sale. S7 and S8 are both ready to sell for $100. At $100 both S5 and I can get horses. The price will not go above that, will it?

S4. $125 horses will be out of the market.

M. Yes, and also the $75 buyer. The marginal price offer will be $100 and the supply price will be $100. That will leave you and S9 out of the market. S8 is anxious to sell a horse and you are anxious to buy one. These two cannot effect a deal, and there is no reason why I who am willing to pay $125 should pay more than $100, and is there any reason why S7 who is willing to take $75 should take less than $100? Here is a marginal supply price in which the demand is two horses and the supply is two horses; that is the price at which the market will rest, the equilibrium price. The price is fixed *at* the margin. It is not fixed *by* that margin.

S9. Do you say the marginal price is $100? I should say it is $125, the marginal price offer.

M. Let us go back over the reasoning. Here at the start are three people all thinking about buying a horse, and there are three also ready to sell. Possibly S4 begins the bidding, saying he will give $50 for the horse. Two are ready to pay more than that and they raise the bid perhaps $5 at a time until they get up to $75. At that point when the bid is raised once more, S4 drops out, and then S5 and I are left bidding against each other, and there is only one horse that will be sold for less than $100. S7 will give it to that one of us who will offer the better price, and neither of us can get the horse for less than $100; but we do not go above that, because at this point S8 offers his horse for sale at $100 and we both get horses for $100. The price offer at $125 is never made. It just stands there as my original intent, the price I would pay if I had to.

S9. I do not understand whether Davenport is talking about subjective or objective phenomena.

M. Let us see what this means. Under Davenport's scheme the subjective phenomena are concerned with the factors which make people willing to sell horses at certain prices or to buy horses at certain prices. For each person that implies a comparison between his eagerness to get a horse or his willingness to dispose of a horse on the one side and a consideration of other things that he can get for the same money. That comparison with the other things implies, as Davenport reminds us, thinking about the importance of the other things that the individual can get, and also their money cost. Those are the subjective phenomena. People's price offers, the ones they make up their mind to, are subjective in the sense that they are people's decisions. But they are already in pecuniary form, are they not?

S9. I understand that they get to be objective.

M. They are more or less objective in people's minds, if they formulate them with definiteness as Davenport seems to imply that they do.

S4 has his particular demand schedule for a horse at $75 on the one side, S5 has his particular schedule by which he would give anything up to $100 and I have mine. I would give a price up to $125. There are three different demand schedules arising presumably from differences in our tastes, necessities, incomes perhaps.

S9. Could not you even go as far as to say that I would give the horse away for $75 even if someone else is offering me $100? The person could react—

M. Yes, but you would be a very unbusinesslike person. Davenport says that to explain what happens in the market, there must be attributed to all economic agents the private and the acquisitive point of view. We have to suppose that you will not give that horse up for less than the highest price you can get for it, under existing conditions.

Suppose S4 and S5 act in that same businesslike fashion; and under the circumstances S9 cannot make a sale. S7 makes a better bargain than he expected. S8 comes off with just what he is willing to take. S4 cannot buy. S5 comes off just as the marginal person with neither any marked gain or loss. I, on the other hand, have a marked gain. I get the horse for less than I would be willing to pay. There is a certain surplus which accrues to me as a buyer, and a certain surplus which accrues to S7 as a seller. S5 is a marginal person who neither loses or gains by the transaction. The same is true of S6. On the other hand S9 and S4 cannot do any business.

S4. I was thinking of a situation more like a stock market where there are sales at each of the figures. Union Pacific starts at 110 and works up and in the market remains around 115. The 115 market price is not fixed by the margin. I was thinking of the 110 as the marginal price. It starts with that. But the actual 115 price is established because the starting price could not equalize the buyers and sellers.

M. That is to say, you suppose that transactions actually do take place at different prices at succeeding moments.

S4. Under competition. You would say that the market price is the marginal price?

M. That is an assumption [S4's view] that implies that someone snaps up the bargain at 110 before the other people get a chance at it. That implies that there is not perfect competition; that implies in the case of the horse market that S7 closes with S4 at $75 before S5 had a chance to say "$80". S7 is a very weak holder of horses. He might agree to a sale before waiting for further buyers, but that is a case of imperfect competition.

S4. Davenport's argument would cover the stock market dealings even at those prices. The price starts at $110. That price is fixed in the same way.

M. If there are successive dealings as sometimes occurs as a matter of fact at different prices, it must be granted that this means that the people who are willing to pay more than $110 were not quick enough to get the chance. There was not a perfect market mechanism; that is, if you suppose that when the lower bid is accepted another man was ready to pay $111, why didn't he do it?

S3. If the thing is sold at $110 under the conditions, that very price comes about through the imperfect workings of the same forces that exist in the perfect market.

M. Yes, that is true.

S3. That is what I meant, but it is a case of an imperfect working out of these forces, if it is assumed that when the price was $110 there was another man ready to pay $111 or $112.

S10. So in the example of the horse market the price would lie somewhere between $75 and $100; anything over $75 or under $100 would cover that case.

M. According to the supposition the price could not be less than $100 because S8 is supposed to be unwilling to sell for less than that.

S10. As a matter of fact the two buyers and the two sellers would transact business at any of those prices.

M. They would if we do not hold to the rigid terms of our proposition. If we suppose that S8, when the price got up to $95 said, "I don't know—I would like the money, and there is something wrong with this horse anyway which they may find out about later," he might sell the horse at $95. Of course for purposes of presenting the theory it is much better to have a perfectly hard and fast supposition.

S3. If you start with the $125 horse and offer them one at a time, you may sell them all.

M. We are supposing that there is competition between the sellers and the buyers. Here comes S9 into the market and says, "I will sell this horse for $125." I am quite ready to pay $125 for a horse and should do it if it were not for the fact that here is S6 who says, "You can have my horse for $120," and there is S7 who offers a horse for $115.

S3. I am assuming that they are offering one horse at a time.

M. That does not give two sided competition.

S3. You have that situation in the stock market. You begin at the top and go down.

M. That is, this is the same kind of case presented in reverse. For example in dealings in Union Pacific, the market may open at 110, and a little later there may be transactions at 109, 108¾ and so on. The point is that there must also be a little lapse of time between dealings, in which the minds of the traders have changed concerning prices which they are ready to give, or that the mechanism of the market was imperfect, so that when a man was ready to sell at 110 before he could get his offer in, someone else had closed at 111, or a higher price.

S11. Is not the case of the man who would offer 111 the same as that of the man who would offer $125 in the horse case? Is it not rather that the supply was not adequate at 110 than the fact that the competition was imperfect, that supply increased as the stock went up?

M. The real complication in the stock market is this latter fact that S11 is suggesting, that a man's decision as to what he is ready to give for the stock is likely to undergo a change when he gets into the market. He looks the thing over, and even if he had made up his mind to a definite bid for any one specific thing at a certain price, he concludes that after all he would like to shade the price. Or he may conclude that the market looks pretty promising in the future, and that the stock will increase in value, so that it may be worth his while to give a little more. The assumption that the buyers and sellers come to market with hard and fast demand and supply prices, and that these do not change, is extremely artificial.

S3. I do not see that you have to suppose that people change their minds.

M. It may happen that someone is willing to bid 110, 109¾, and so on, all the way down. If you will cut out the supposition that there is any change in the willingness of people to buy, the question arises, why, when someone is ready to sell at 108 in the last resort, he would let other sellers get a better return by selling at 109 or 110?

S3. The same man may be willing to shade all the way down.

M. That is to say he will take more and more of the stock?

S3. If he is selling he will sell so much at a certain figure and something less at a certain figure, and shade down. If he is buying he will shade down the same way.

M. If you can represent those facts by definite schedules showing exactly what the willingness of the people to buy and sell would be at successive prices, I think you would find almost invariably that your schedules will give you just one particular price at which the transactions must take place at a given time if you hold to the original suppositions. Occasionally there are cases of what are known as multiple equilibria, where after a certain amount of trading has been done at a given price further trading is possible at a different price. I am saying this is what the theorist ordinarily finds if he applies himself at the outset with a definite set of demand scales on the one side, and supply scales on the other side. The phenomena of the stock exchange having different prices made in successive minutes are almost always due to the fact that the traders do not have definite hard and fast schedules of demand prices and supply prices in mind, or that the mechanism of competition in the market is not perfect.

S3. Then you have a series of margins at which prices are fixed from minute to minute or hour to hour or something like that, though you do not take your whole supply and demand and fix a price at the margin which covers the whole situation?

M. Let me say again how the thing is stated from a theoretical point of view. Of course price is supposed to be made within a given market at a given time. That time may be very short. For theoretical discussions of a perfectly definite sort, it is necessary to begin with suppositions concerning the amount of the commodity in question which people would be ready to sell at successive prices and with similar suppositions concerning the amount which they would be willing to buy at successive prices. Then the theorist has to assume once more, if he wants a perfect solution, that there is no interference whatever with competition; that it is to say, every would-be buyer and seller knows the offers which other buyers and sellers are making. If the theorist fits himself out with those assumptions, he will almost always find that there is one definite price at which selling has to take place. Suppose that is done. Then the whole business is swept out of the way. That changes the demand and supply schedules and some people have satisfied their needs. He will ordinarily find himself left with a situation like the one represented in the theoretical example of the horse market. There is one man who would like to buy and one also would like to sell, but they cannot do any business because S9 wants $125, and S4 would not pay more than $75. On the other hand, it sometimes happens that the situation after the bargains have been completed, makes it possible to have another bargain at a different price, but whether that is possible or not depends upon the particular character of the set of supply and demand schedules with which the theorist started out and it is a rare occurrence that the schedules make a second bargain possible. This is all by way of explanation of the theoretical discussion.

That analysis involves assumptions which are not perfectly realized in the market. There are in particular two assumptions which are ordinarily untrue. The first is the assumption of perfect competition, in other words that every buyer knows at every moment during the market what prices are being offered and what other sellers are willing to accept. Ordinarily that is not true. The second artificial assumption is that in the course of the bargaining people do not change their minds as to what they would be ready to give in the last resort; that is to say, the schedules remain fixed while the bargaining is going on. It is because there is not perfect competition; it is because supply and demand prices are subject to change during the process of negotiation and that the theory of price is not perfectly verified in most market transactions.

S9. It is not true that people are ready to change their minds?

M. They usually are.

S9. Davenport's conception of marginal utility is that through their knowledge they are influenced?

M. No. He is like the other theorists who are trying to explain the essence of the process in perfectly clear cut fashion. He assumes the fixity of demand and supply schedules. Like every other theorist, he is ready to admit that these assumptions are not representative of the facts in most markets.

S8. In what does his conception of marginal utility differ from that of Jevons and Marshall?

M. His conception does not differ from the ordinary Austrian conception. The one point in that connection which is a little peculiar to Davenport is the great stress he places on the proposition that prices are fixed not *by* margins but *at* margins, and what we started out to try to do today was to get the significance of that particular proposition.

S10. Still, what is the significance of saying not *by* but *at*?

M. What Davenport means is that the price is fixed by the demand schedules on the one hand as compared with the supply schedules on the other hand. The theorist has to know what those demand schedules and supply schedules are. He needs the whole array. If he can tell where the intersecting point is, the marginal price is that point of intersection. The point does not fix the price. It is the point at which the price is fixed. It is a little like the proposition about an arithmetical mean, for instance. If you know the form of different averages, it would be better to illustrate by the use of the median. The position of the median is fixed by the whole array of figures, of course, the whole array of data. The statistician has to have a whole array of data before he knows what his median is. Similarly if the theorist has not made his comparison of demand and supply schedules he cannot tell what the marginal price offer or the marginal supply price is going to be. The only way to tell is to compare them with each other. When he does so, he discovers the point of intersection. He finds out whether the demand equals the supply. That is to say whether the demand price will carry off a volume of goods just equal to the supply which will be forthcoming at that price; and when he has found that point, he has the point where the price will be fixed, granted perfect competition and no change in demand and supply schedules.

S9. Out of the few passages in Davenport which I have read, I think that his notion of marginal utility is what has just been explained, that there is free competition and no knowledge—

M. That is not a notion about marginal utility. We are now talking about marginal supply price and marginal demand price, and marginal utility has to do not directly with price but with the ratings that are put on particular goods. As Davenport explains, the theorist cannot get demand prices out of marginal utilities of particular commodities considered singly. He has to compare the utilities of two separate commodities; e.g., of money and of horses, before he can determine for any individual what his price offers will be; so that, while he is talking about this determination of prices, he is not talking directly about marginal utility. He is applying the concept "marginal" to price offer and the demand price.

S12. Please give a practical example showing what Davenport meant by "price fixed *by* the margin."

M. An example cannot be given because it is a non-existing thing.

S12. Why does he emphasize it?

M. Because people often use language implying that the price is fixed by the margin. As said previously, Davenport in his critical volume *Value and Distribution* has noted other passages in which that is said directly or implied, and he points out with reference to those theorists that they did not say what they mean. Obviously prices can not be fixed by the margins of any one particular commodity, that is to say, you cannot tell what price you would give for a commodity before knowing the relative importance of each article. You cannot even determine what you would give for successive [units of] commodities. You have to think of what importance a second article in which the price is reckoned is to you.

S3. Does this proposition take into account that each buyer and seller not only takes into consideration the value of the thing to himself, but also the probability of his getting a higher price by reason of the market conditions brought about by supply and demand?

M. In making up his mind what he would be willing to pay for the article in the last resort, I think that this is a fair statement; that everybody in the market tries to make the best guess he can as to his chances of getting something else or getting a satisfactory substitute.

S3. If that element exists in the market, that explains the reason why the marginal utility does not fix the price, does it not?

M. The reason why the marginal utility does not fix the price is explained by something more fundamental. The marginal utility of any particular commodity to the individual is a phrase almost without meaning. Suppose the theorist is thinking about apples. It is conceivable that he may attach varied importance to a supply of one apple, a supply of two, three, of four, of five and so on. He may think that the second apple is less important than the first, the third less than the second, the fourth less than the third and so on. That is just his scale of utilities for this particular consumption of goods. Out of that scale of utilities he cannot construct a market price. He cannot even tell what he, as one individual in the market, is ready to give for apples unless he compares this scale of importance of apples to himself with the importance to him of, say, successive pennies in which he is making up his bids. The array which is needed for price determination in the market is the aggregate of price offers which different individuals stand ready to make. Those price offers imply a comparison for every individual separately, the marginal utility of apples with the marginal utility of cents—it would be better not to have used the term "marginal utility"—the comparison of the utilities of successive apples with the utilities of successive cents. When he has that scale of utilities for the two articles for each individual, he can construct a scale of price offers for each individual. When he has a scale of price offers for all the individuals in the market, he can make up the scale of demand prices. Similarly he wants a schedule of supply prices which is an aggregate of prices which all the individuals who appear on the selling side of the market would take for apples, and to get those supply price schedules for each individual he has to go through an elaborate consideration of the importance that they attach to successive apples in that supply, and he has to consider directly the importance of successive cents which they might get by selling apples. Then in the long run he has to take account of how they get the money.

S1. The person's consideration of the valuation of others has a bearing on the price of that which he wants.

M. Thus Davenport's dictum about the price being fixed not *by* margins but *at* margins, is intended to emphasize the fact that prices are fixed by comparison of the whole situation with reference to supply as compared with the whole situation with reference to demand. It is a comparison of the aggregate demand schedule for the market which the theorist has under consideration at that given time with the aggrete supply schedule at that given time.

S10. Is it not another way of phrasing what Marshall and Fetter say, that the prices are fixed at the intersection?

M. Davenport is simply laying emphasis on a fact that the more careful writers have ordinarily brought out, though he found passages in Marshall's *Principles of Economics* in some of the early editions which slurred over that and suggested that prices are fixed by utilities, but Marshall never meant it any more than the other writers did.

What Davenport is trying to do is to help economists avoid a careless expression which does not state the meaning that anyone has seriously and consciously intended.

S9. Is that also the concept of the members of the Austrian School?

M. Yes, though they particularly have been careless in phraseology at all times.

S10. But theories of distribution like J.B. Clark's would require that price is fixed *by* the margin. Would not that be proving the productivity theory?

M. Even here, if you will look into the logic of the thing, you will find that this margin itself is determined by a complicated array of facts on two sides, and if you want to express Clark's meaning accurately you have to go back to these arrays which determine the crucial part, so that Davenport's dictum would hold even here, that the point is *at* which not *by* which prices are fixed.[9]

S. Is there not a process of valuation in his theory of opportunity costs?

M. Those are all price phenomena.

S. Yes, but it involves a valuation process between the two alternatives.

M. That is, a choice between two alternatives valued on a money basis. The fundamental question is, why are people ready to undergo painful efforts, why do they want goods? Opportunity costs do not have any direct bearing upon the ultimate psychological question concerning the real forces involved.

S. On p. 44, Davenport says, "We, as economists, have, in addition, to concern ourselves with the psychology of bargaining and with the influences that the different traders' limits have on the method by which the market equilibrium is reached or is disturbed." On p. 60 he says; "Purely as economists we are fortunately free from the neccesity of investigating the origin of choices or any of the psychological difficulties surrounding the question." How does he reconcile the two statements?

---

[9] End of extract from "1918 Typescript."

M. He would reconcile them by saying that when the theorist talks about the psychology of bargaining he is discoursing simply about the operations of business men intent upon pecuniary gain and that no matter how complete an account he gives of the arts of the bargainer, he is not going to arrive by that means at a fundamental explanation of why people, let us say, put a higher value upon pounds of wheat than pounds of potatoes.

S. He shifts his viewpoint then?

M. Davenport would say that he did not. It is, of course, phraseology that comes clearer at the surface, and if his attention was called to these two statements he would feel that it would be desirable to modify one of them in his new edition. But I think that he would say that there is nothing inherently incompatible in the two; that the economist may well be concerned with the arts of the bargainer, but that he is not concerned with the fundamental grounds of choice.

S. Does Davenport deny altruistic actions? How does he account for them?

M. He does not deny them. He says that when the theorist is trying to account for economic behavior he must stick to the private and acquisitive point of view. Let me give you an illustration of what he means. How does he define capital?

S. Anything that will yield income to an individual.

M. Yes, notably a burglar's jimmy. A burglar's jimmy is capital to Davenport. Burglary is most deplorable conduct, but since the jimmy is an implement belonging to the burglar by which he increases his private gain, it is just as much capital as the gas tank belonging to a public utility company. Any gain-bringing private property is capital. If a student, for instance, has come into the knowledge of some person's disgraceful secret and proceeds to blackmail that person and make money for himself by that process, that knowledge is as much capital as is the training he may have gotten in a law school in order to make a professional income by engaging in practice. That kind of thing Davenport insists upon.

What is productive labor? From his viewpoint there is only one answer: any labor by which a person makes money. Adam Smith seemed to have a feeling that some kinds of labor were more productive than others; they add more to the welfare of the country. From Davenport's viewpoint all that discussion is beside the point. The question is whether it brings gain to the individual; and if a person is a successful racetrack gambler, he is engaged in a productive occupation, producing income for himself. On matters of that sort Davenport is refreshingly logical. He follows from his own definition right straight from the start to the finish without lapses; he accepts the consequences of his view.

S. Does Davenport make any distinction between capital and labor? I cannot get his idea.

M. One of his definitions of capital is that "every property basis of private acquisition is by that very fact capital."[11]

If one can distinguish between what is a private property basis of acquisition and means of acquisition which do not involve property, one has a distinction between capital and labor. Broadly speaking that is the distinction economists draw. The economist distinguishes readily between a farmer's income due to his own labor and the income due to his capital, though Heaven knows it is hard enough for the economist to determine which is which when he begins to analyze the farmer's income!

S. He says production does not necessarily create.

M. No, it acquires; it does not create. It may acquire by creating. Take a nice agricultural illustration, say, one of the early cattle men who deserved a shady reputation. He was perhaps raising some cattle from his own stock; and he was acquiring others by rustling unbranded calves. Both enterprises are from Davenport's viewpoint productive acts, they bring him gain. From another viewpoint only one is productive: where the cattleman is looking after his own cattle, and through his efforts brings about an increase. The other, stealing cattle, is not productive from that viewpoint. But both are productive to Davenport. Take another illustration: I hold you up after you retire from this classroom and take $5 from you at the point of a pistol. That is productive labor from Davenport's point of view because it is private acquisition. To repeat, it is refreshing to find a person who takes a certain point of view and carries it through logically from start to finish. It does put the situation in a clearer light.

S. By his definition of capital and productive labor it would be impossible for him to have any social or welfare point of view.

M. In his economic theory the social or welfare point of view does not enter; but it is possible for him to think that this is in many respects a bad way of organizing people. He is a severe critic of this system.

Let us try and get a clearer appreciation of his whole point of view by seeing how it works out. This is comparatively easy, because Davenport is a thoroughly modern theorist in the sense that he gives

[11] *The Economics of Enterprise*, p. 519.

as much space to finding what is wrong with his predecessors as in establishing what is sound. He makes his position therefore very definite, he points out the differences between his views and those of others. Let us take what must be even more for Davenport than anyone else the central problem of economic theory. That problem is price determination. He approaches the problem by pointing out that every consumer has his individual scale of utilities.

Also every individual who is producing goods for sale has his individual scale of gain-bringing capacities, his own way of valuing goods as a means of making money. Furthermore every individual, whether he is in a given market for the moment as a consumer or as a producer, has his individual scale of discounting future services. Every individual on the basis of his peculiar scale of utilities for goods, or his peculiar scale of discounting the future, arrives at his own scale of what he will offer for every successive supply of a given good. On the other side of the market every individual has his own scale of what he will take in the way of price for the goods that he has to sell. The individual scales can be cast up into market demand and market supply schedules. When the offer price scales or the supply price scales of all the people on both sides of the market have been cast up, the materials are provided for determining where price will be set in the bargaining.

All this sounds familiar enough. But Davenport hammers again and again at the statement that these are scales that people have as individuals—it does not matter in the least what is the amount of feeling that stands behind any person's offer price or any person's supply price. The economist is not in a position to know much about the intensity of the feelings that lie behind offer prices and supply prices. For his purpose in trying to understand price determination, people's feelings, their desires are literally irrelevant. He cannot find out anything about them, and even if he could it would not contribute to his understanding.

Davenport, to repeat, particularly criticizes continuously the view that there is anything in the way of a real social process; thus the idea of social utility seems to him pure nonsense. The idea of specific productivity efficiency is also silly. So too is the idea of social time discount. The idea of a social organism as such is as lacking in foundation as the notions of social utility or specific productivity efficiency or social time discount. The writers who try to explain what goes on in terms of a social organism or of entities which belong to a society as such have been deluding themselves; in so far as they have allowed themselves to believe them, they have been deluding their readers.

He writes:

> Strictly speaking, there is no such thing as the comparison of the utility to one person with the utility to another. Men differ in desires and in the degree and manner in which things appeal or appear to offer service. Only so far as, in the general likeness of one man to another, human beings approach to a perfect similarity or only so far as for some purposes, the individual differences may safely be overlooked, is there room for talk of group aggregates of utility, or is there purpose or safety in the notion of social utility or of social sacrifices or of social pain. But for the problems of market price these individual differences will not down. Men are unlike, not only in tastes, in intensity and vividness of feeling and of desire, and in the relative strength of needs and desires, but even more in the pecuniary ability to command the appropriate satisfaction. Any homogeneity of utility, any attempt for the purpose of the price problem, to force different men into any other common denominator than this very obvious one of price-offer itself, is possible only at the sacrifice of all clear thinking. It is, indeed, worse than this; for it removes any problem to think about. As Pudd'nhead Wilson observed: "It were not best that we should all think alike; it is difference of opinion that makes horse races." And so of speculation; and so, in fact, of all trading. Abstracting from the differences between men in order to explain trade, all trade becomes impossible.[12]

This is vigorous insistence upon the fact that there are wide difference between individuals. The science has to be built up from the individual and acquisitive point of view, and that means these differences are vastly important. When the theorist begins putting all men into one heap as a sort of social unit, he gets completely away from reality and loses his problem.

Concerning particularly specific productive efficiency Davenport remarks:

> . . . the market price of each productive efficiency cannot express the quantum of that efficiency, is not equal to it, is not determined by it, does not measure it, and is not measured by it. And finally, with reference to productive efficiency, regarded as a specific or definite quality or quantity or attribute or power, it will be shown that there is no such thing.[13]

Regarding social time discount he remarks:

> . . . each seller or buyer has also his separate discount rate and his separate process through which he arrives at his individual present worth of any future income, and his maximum bid for it; that therefore individual capitalizing processes underlie both the demand and the supply schedules of the market process; and that thus the market process, if made both actual and intelligible, is not to be analyzed as a social or aggregate or organic process, but must instead be strictly and thoroughly individualized.

Regarding the social organism, he remarks succinctly: "There should

---

12 *The Economics of Enterprise,* p. 97.
13 *The Economics of Enterprise,* p. 136.

evidently be somewhere a social insane asylum in which to confine the social organism."[14]

To state these matters more simply: It is a great mistake to think that there is any such thing as social utility. There is only an infinitely numerous set of individual utilities. There cannot be a general social utility because there is not any general social organization [that is, a social organism]; but society is made up of individuals and the only utilities that exist in any other than a metaphorical sense are the utilities that things have for particular people. Similarly, Davenport contends with a great deal of emphasis that there is no such thing as productive efficiency. That term came into use in the writings of Professor J. B. Clark, and there have been theorists who have talked about the specific productive efficiency of particular things like coal or even of great classes of things like labor in the same sense in which a large number of theorists have talked about social utility. Again Davenport says this is nonsense. The rating which is put on the productive efficiency of different goods is put on them by different individuals one by one, and the only specific productive efficiency things have is in the ratings of these individuals. There is no social rating. So again he says that there is no such thing as social time discount. Each person has his own individual time discount, and until there is a society that can act as an organism to discount the future as a whole theorists are deluding themselves in talking about social time discount.

This is all by way of providing a foundation for his theory of prices. This foundation provides most of his general theory of prices, for he holds that prices are determined by schedules of price offers and similar schedules of supply prices. Once the theorist has determined the way in which the individual's set of price offers is made up, he has practically all that he needs for the problem. He must realize that there are other individuals with dissimilar scales of price offers. Some of the people who are in the market are offering goods for money instead of money for goods. The theorist's scale of supply prices is logically analogous with the scale of demand prices, taking society as a whole, or rather the market for any particular commodity at any particular time as a whole. The theorist finds the aggregate of the individual scales of price offers, and the market price is fixed at the intersection of the two scales in a familiar manner.[15]

Davenport, starting out to explain economic behavior from the private and acquisitive point of view, insists on operating all the time

---

[14] *The Economics of Enterprise,* pp. 233, 391.
[15] Last two paragraphs from "1918 Typescript."

with individuals, and insists upon the differences among them. He gets a method by which he can deal in prices by summing up the maximum price bids that different individuals in view of their individual circumstances are ready to make for successive units of a supply; and by summing up on the other side the minimum price offers that people will take for goods they want to sell. Then he uses the two summaries of demand schedules and supply schedules to solve the price problem.

To summarize briefly Davenport's type of theory up to this point: to him economics is "the science that treats phenomena from the standpoint of price." It is indispensable that it be studied from "the private and acquisitive point of view". The materials, therefore, come from individuals. From individuals the theorist gets on the one hand, and particularly when he regards them as buyers of consumer's commodities, their characteristically different schedules of the utilities of goods. Each individual, in view of his peculiar scales of the utility of different goods and the money that he has to spend makes up his mind what prices it is worth his while to offer for successive units of the supply of the commodities that he fancies. When the theorist is thinking about individuals as buying goods for business purposes he must get from each of them his scales of the gain-bringing value or profitableness to him of the types of goods he buys for use in his business. These scales differ among different business men just as individual scales of the utilities of goods to people as consumers differ. Also the business men have various amounts of money to spend and they make up their schedules of price offers for goods on the basis of computations of what goods are worth for profit-making purposes on the one hand, and the amount of money they have to spend on the other hand.

The theorist takes all the individual demand schedules or business demand schedules together and by summing them up gets for the market that he is considering, within the time he has in mind, a summation, a summary demand schedule for the goods in question. On the other hand, he can construct also a set of supply schedules, showing the amount of goods that will be offered within the market within a given time at given prices, the supply schedules being based on money costs to the people who have goods to offer, supplemented by considerations of what other opportunities they might find in which to invest their funds for profitable use. Thus demand schedules set against supply schedules, both running in terms of price, give the materials for determining what prices will prevail.

This problem is solved just as soon as the theorist gets for a given commodity a total demand schedule for it within the market and the time in question, on the one side, and a total supply schedule on the other side, because a price will be fixed at that point where the demand schedule just crosses the supply schedule; that is, the point where the quantity demanded at the price in question is just equal to the supply which will be forthcoming for sale at that price. The reason for believing that this is the point at which the price will fall is the old one that if some of the buyers should offer a higher price, they will find various competitors rushing in to meet that peculiarly advantageous offer, and as a result, the price will fall. If, on the other hand, people who have the goods to sell should make an offer of the goods at a lower price, then they would find that there were more buyers to get the goods at that price than they could supply and competition among the buyers would force up the price. Thus price tends to remain at the point indicated by the intersection of the demand and supply curves in the commodity market in the time in question.[16]

So far the discussion is familiar. But Davenport accompanies it with insistence upon several points which are not so well known. One is that every price offer presupposes the existence of two marginal utilities which are compared with each other; that is to say, in making up his mind what he will pay for shoes, the individual takes account on the one hand of the utility of shoes to him as a consumer, and on the other hand of the utility to him of a unit of the money which he is to spend. The utility of the units of money is ascertained by thinking of the utility of the other things that he might get with the funds he is going to spend on the shoes. The utility he is going to get from the amount of money that he spends on some alternative to the shoes depends in turn upon the price he has to pay for the other goods; that is, he cannot talk about the utility of matches to himself as compared with shoes in terms of money except if he knows how many matches he can get for a nickel. He has to know the prices of other goods before

---

[16] Davenport's reduction of the supply curve to a part of the demand curve was an interesting technical improvement. (See "Criticism of the Supply Curve," APP, 84-91, no. 34, which is concerned with Philip H. Wicksteed's similar approach.) "Professor Davenport is to be congratulated on the precision and effectiveness with which he has demonstrated the ruling fact that the usual cross curves of supply and demand, with their point of intersection determining the price, rests on a superficial and misleading analysis. The reservation prices of the sellers, are, in the ultimate analysis, demands, and are as important to the fixation of price, and important in *precisely the same way*, as the price paying dispositions of the sellers for goods. The tabular demonstration of principle on p. 51 ought to place it conclusively above challenge." Wicksteed, review of *The Economics of Enterprise*, 1914, reprinted in his *The Common Sense of Political Economy and Selected Papers and Reviews of Economic Theory*, 2 volumes, edited by Lionel [now Baron] Robbins (London: Routledge, 1938) II, pp. 823-824.

he can solve the problem of how to carry on his investment in shoes. This means, from the point of view of a consumer, the drawing up of his demand schedule is feasible only as he is acquainted with the market in which there are many prices already determined. To repeat, the basic element which Davenport uses in his theory of prices, the demand schedule of the individual, supposes an existing scheme of prices for a great many other goods. Thus if the theorist is trying to explain the demand schedule each individual has for shoes, he has to take into account as among his data the prices of other goods. Or, to put the whole thing still more simply, the price of shoes is determined by the prices of other things consumers may desire; one price is explained in terms of other prices.

So too with reference to the supply schedule. A man is making up his mind at what price he can afford to sell shoes in the market. From the private, acquisitive point of view, he wants to use his time and skill and individual capital to the best advantage; that is, to bring him in the largest profit. In considering what price he is to charge for shoes he has to consider not merely the outlay upon leather, the rent of the machinery which he hires or the cost of transportation, labor and the other things he buys, but he also must consider whether he could not make more money in the cotton sheeting business, or in farming, or in any one of a considerable number of other industries into which he might have gone. The price at which he is willing to supply shoes does bear upon the other gain-bringing opportunities aside from the shoe industry in which he might embark; that is, just as in wanting shoes, an individual must take account of the prices of other things in determining what he is ready to give for a pair of shoes, so from the point of view of the person who is supplying shoes, and therefore as a factor in the supply schedule of that commodity, it is necessary to consider the whole organized system of prices out of which profits might be made in other industries besides that of shoes. From the supply side too it thus appears that the price of one article depends upon the prices of other articles. When the theorist sets out to explain one price, the data he has to use is an organized system of prices. Hence it would appear that he explains prices in terms of prices. He walks around in a circle, a very large circle, but a circle out of which on this basis he cannot break.

Is Davenport wrong? Is it not something we find the earlier writers insisting upon? Is he pointing out a fact that others have seen less clearly? Or is the fact that he is regarding phenomena from the standpoint of price the reason why his discussion is condemned to this endless circle? Or has he a way of breaking out of the circle and of giving an explanation which is less circuitous? Davenport sets all this out with the most engaging candor.

> . . . it has also been made clear that, even with demand taken for granted, entrepreneur cost of production cannot stand as an ultimate explanation of price. Offered as such explanation it is, indeed, both circuitous and superficial; it purports to explain some prices by other prices—the price of the product by the prices of the costs.[17]

This is true when demand is taken for granted. If the theorist goes back to explain demand price, he explains demand price, the thing on which Davenport has to operate necessarily in part, in terms of the prices at which the consumer might get other things, because he must take the prices at which he can get other things into account in order to arrive at the marginal utility of different commodities, which is the consideration to the individual as a consumer. Davenport says: "The cost of production computation, however neglectful of ultimate bases and explanations, is entirely adequate for all the purposes of the entrepreneur."[18]

But he also holds that it is not altogether satisfactory to the theorist. For business purposes the individual does not have to get back to ultimate real forces. Here he is in a great big organized situation surrounded by a world of prices, and he can make his profits successfully without going behind those prices to anything that lies deeper by thinking about in what part of the business world the prices are such as to give the opportunity to make the most profit. That is all right. As business people, we are operating, individually we are all of us operating, on a minute scale; even the large business enterprise is doing a tiny fraction of the business of the country, and its business needs are met by finding out what changes in the price situation will be produced by its own operations.

Let me repeat the question. In sharply bringing out the fact that the theory of prices is circuitous, that it explains one price in terms of other prices, is Davenport revealing a superficiality in the theory which had been propounded by his predecessors?

S. Is not Marshall aware of the difficulty of seeing the logical consequences? Did he not speak about the simultaneous reactions?

M. That is, did not Marshall really take the same point of view, although never quite explicit about it? Remember that he expressed the view that any simple law concerning value, price or distribution must necessarily be wrong; that every factor in the situation helps to

---

[17] *The Economics of Enterprise*, p. 117.

[18] *The Economics of Enterprise*, p. 117.

determine, and is itself determined in part by every other factor in the situation. It is a problem of the simultaneous determination of each other by a host of factors, and all that the theorist does is to arrange the factors in some tolerable order so that in a given case he can canvass them with fair assurance of not omitting anything of great importance; that he is bound to make a mistake if he argues on simple and direct lines from one factor as a cause to the factors which it produces. Marshall does not talk about the superficiality of his explanation, and if some critic had done so don't you think that he would have been rather troubled? I fancy that he would have been.

S. Then Marshall would have said there are real forces?

M. There are real forces. Does Davenport admit there are real forces? His own comments on this situation are as follows:

> But the economist's problem is quite distinct; he must really explain; and part of his difficulty is in the fact that his explanations must be sought within the actual situation and must run in consistency with the actual entrepreneur process. He must accept the entrepreneur function and the entrepreneur analysis; but he must carry the analysis further than the entrepreneur is concerned to carry it in explaining what the entrepreneur does,—the situation conditioning his activity, the forces playing upon it, and the results that flow from it. Thus the economist must recognize that both the prices of the products and the prices of the bases of the product are equally results of the underlying and determining conditions; that neither does cost ultimately fix the price nor price ultimately fix the cost; that the outlays which the entrepreneur makes, the scarcity of the products which he produces, and the prices at which he must sell these products, are equally the results of the limited supply of the productive factors which he employs; and thus that, with the demand for the products taken for granted, the causal sequence on the supply side of the problem runs from the relative scarcity of the factors to the relative scarcity of the products, thence to the relative prices of the products, thence to the relative remunerations of the factors.[19]

M.[20] What are the real forces as Marshall see them?

S10. Exertions and desires. Davenport's ultimate forces are desires and scarcities which he subdivides into productive capacity and instrumental equipment. Is Davenport talking about the same thing as Marshall?

M. The exertions that Marshall is talking about as costs mean sacrifices. He is really balancing against each other in the last resort gratifications and sacrifices inside of each individual's economy. In Davenport we are told that the ultimate forces are desires and the

---

[19] *The Economics of Enterprise*, pp. 117-118.
[20] Beginning of extract from "1918 Typescript."

two factors which limit supply. You are not told that pain costs are one of the ultimate forces set over against desire.

S13. Doesn't he speak of the sacrifice of foregoing things?

M. When he talks about foregoing things you get the impression of foregoing another opportunity of enjoyment. You may represent your cost either as a sacrifice, the submission to some irksome exertion, or you may represent it as giving up the opportunity to do something else for the sake of doing what you prefer. Marshall of course in the last resort is inclined to talk about your actual sacrifices and exertions, although he is careful to point out that these may well involve the surrender of some other way of using your time. He says, for example, that what makes a person stop work when he does is not necessarily that he has come to the point where the actual pains of exertion itself balances the gratification of the return he gets from it. It may well be the accumulation of pain balances the growing desire to have an opportunity for some other pleasant use of his time. He may stop work, not because the exertion has become very painful, but because he wants so much to go to a baseball game.

S11. It seems to me that as an individual explanation these ultimate forces are objective forces.

M. The real difference between Marshall and Davenport is that Marshall carries the inquiry back to the ultimate solution; Davenport carries the analysis back to the institution that has reference to society at large, an institution where there are the people's desires for things on the one hand, and productive capacity and instrumental equipment on the other. He wants to understand economic life as it is lived under the present institutional order of private property and individual initiative.[21]

In short, Davenport says that his theory of prices is circuitous and superficial and though with all its circuitousness and superficiality it is adequate for the purposes of the business man, the economist must have some more fundamental explanation. What is Davenport's more fundamental explanation? How does he as a theorist break out of the circle of explaining prices in terms of prices?

S. He assumes demand. He has scarcity of goods and because of their scarcity there is a price for the goods, and then from the price of the goods [he goes] to the price of the factors.

M. But does Davenport more than temporarily take demand for granted? Does he not attempt to get a real explanation? In this par-

---

[21] End of extract of "1918 Typescript."

ticular passage he is talking about demand taken for granted. When
he comes face to face with this particular problem he says:

> The *ultimate* forces in the problem are, then: (1) the human
> desires for products affording motive for the aggregate social product
> of goods to be exchanged against one another, and expressing them-
> selves, also, in any one price-offer schedule, as the market demand
> in terms of money for that particular line of goods; (2) the pro-
> ductive capacities of human beings and the instrumental equipment
> at their disposal.[22]

The productive[23] capacity is men's knowledge of how to produce;
and instrumental equipment at their disposal includes not only machinery but also natural resources, everything of a material sort that
bears upon the possibilities of production.

S13. Does he not reduce the latter into one head—scarcity?

M. He sometimes does but when he does it is necessary to
recognize scarcity as depending upon the two factors—productive
capacity and instrumental equipment.

S13. Instrumental equipment and productive capacity depending
upon scarcity or determined by scarcity?

M. He would hardly say determined by scarcity.

S13. He always argues that on the supply side are real forces; on
the demand side, utility.

M. Yes, that is fair, but he carries his analysis of scarcity a little
further by inquiring into what limits the amount of certain goods
that we can turn out. The limit is established by our knowledge of
how to use the resources at our disposal or, to be a little more elaborate
—by our productive capacity on the one hand and by our instrumental equipment on the other.

S13. What is the difference between technology and productive
capacity? As I understand it these are two phrases for substantially
the same thing.

M. If by technology you mean peoples knowledge of how to handle
things, that is productive capacity. Our instrumental equipment is
made up of machines and natural resources already at our disposal.
For instance, if you send American railroad men to Russia at the
present time [1918] they will have productive capacity dependent
upon their scientific training and experience in this country. Over
there they will find that they have a very different instrumental
equipment at their disposal. They will not have machine shops with
which to repair their rolling stock, for instance. They may not have
as good means for getting coal and iron.

---

[22] *The Economics of Enterprise,* p. 143.
[23] Beginning of extract from "1918 Typescript."

S10. I was thinking equipment to be nothing more than working out of our knowledge of methods.

M. I do not think that it is. Take the present situation [1918] in the United States. We lack sufficient industrial equipment to turn out as much pig iron as could be used at the present time. Our productive capacity, that is, our knowledge, could be employed advantageously on a larger instrumental equipment than we now have.

S2. I do not see why Davenport lays so much stress on the fact that the first step is scarcity. If we go back and ask what makes supply— with larger remuneration there should be larger supply. By what right does Davenport take this stand?

M. I suppose that he would admit what you say with reference to any given commodity. You can increase the supply by offering better remuneration. When you talk about ultimate factors I think he would say that in the last resort what limits the amounts of goods as a whole at the disposal of the community is men's knowledge of how to produce and the natural resources with which they can operate, together with such machinery for production as has been produced in the past. Of course there is a certain justification for treating the matter in that way.

To repeat, as S2 says for any one commodity, you can increase the supply by increasing the remuneration in most cases; in some cases there may be a strict limitation of natural resources.[24] To return, we have, if you like, three sets of factors which represent the ultimate forces in the problem: human desires, the productive capacities of human beings and the instrumental equipment at their disposal; that is, not simply the natural resources which they control but also man-made industrial equipment. At any given time they may be regarded as one of the ultimate forces: the whole equipment with which they operate, including their own capacity and their desires.

S. If you have the desires, do you not still assume demand?

M. The desires can be regarded as the basis on which demand gets its intensity, its driving power. Davenport is using the word "power" to indicate whatever it is inside of man that makes him willing under given circumstances to buy one thing in place of other things.

S. Is not that almost the same thing as saying the ultimate forces of demand on the one hand and of supply on the other?

M. Yes, Davenport would even say that is what he means.

S. That is not much different from Marshall's view is it?

---

[24] End of extract from "1918 Typescript."

M. No. Davenport does not regard that as anything new. It does in a sense help to clarify the problem. See how sharply he recognizes the problem which is presented by Marshall's analysis. He says that the theorists get on swimmingly with their explanations of price; the only trouble is when they get them all done they see that while they have any one price very nicely, the explanation should be in terms of other prices. Behind the whole scheme economists must come definitely to see what are the real controlling forces; and these forces are catalogued under two headings, desires and productive capacities, including the capacities of the human beings and the equipment at their disposal.

It would seem that, if the real forces are matters to which economists resort in order to break away from the superficiality of their explanation of prices in terms of prices, then the theorist who wants to be thorough-going should investigate, on the one hand, human desires, and, on the other hand, capacities to produce, both man's capacities as a human being and the equipment he has at his disposal. Does Davenport give an analysis of desires? Does he present an analysis of the productive capacity of human beings? Does he make an elaborate inquiry into the natural resources at people's command? In the introductory chapter he does say something about the natural resources of the country and about how they have been exploited, but not very much. Here is what he says about these several matters. First about human beings:

> Purely as economists we are fortunately free from the necessity of investigating the origin of choices or any of the psychological difficulties surrounding the question.[25]

Human desires are one of the real forces, but fortunately economists do not have to investigate them.

> The present discussion will serve again to emphasize the fact that economic analysis need not attempt the solution of all, or of any of the difficult psychological problems connected with the theory of desire, and cannot safely commit itself to any particular school or method of solution. It is enough for all economic purposes that these desires exist, that these wants are with us, that these utilities *are*. We have merely to report the manner of their working as they effect the disposition to pay, and thereby effect the fixation of price.[26]

So, as far as this real force is concerned, Davenport's attitude is that the economists recognize that the analysis of the price problem is circuitous and superficial except as they go back to the real forces; and when they do so, they recognize that it is not the economist's busi-

---

[25] *The Economics of Enterprise,* p. 60.
[26] *The Economics of Enterprise,* p. 230.

ness to inquire into them. They must recognize their existence, and that is all that is necessary. About productive capacities of human beings he has practically nothing to say. Nor does he say anything specific about the instrumental equipment which men dispose of.

Thus Davenport recognizes more sharply than his predecessors the problem of the relation between the pecuniary phenomena and the real forces which are alleged to lie behind. He emphasizes most insistently the superficiality of the pecuniary phenomena as such, and then he says that the study of these real forces is not the economist's business. All this is strictly consistent with his definition of what economics is: The science that discusses phenomena from the standpoint of price. Just as soon as he leaves the ground of price he is off the ground which he holds that the economist is in duty bound to cultivate.

S. Does not Davenport emphasize the supply schedule more than the demand schedule?

M. He pays more attention to it. It is more interesting. Davenport would say that the theorist is forgetting one side if he leaves the demand schedules out of his discussion. They are logically just as important. When he gets back to the ultimate forces, he had desires as one side over against productive capacities as the other side.

S. Does he not give a fuller discussion of the demand for durable producers goods?

M. That is the business demand, of course. So in a sense it gets into the study of the factors which are involved in the supply schedules. Yes, it is worth observing the point that demand is not confined to the demand for the things people buy in order to satisfy future wants. Business demands, that is, demands for things which are bought as means of making money is a large element in the modern business world.

The service that Davenport renders is to point out in a sharp and effective fashion the difficulty which exists in the analysis of his predecessors. It is all the more a service because the way in which he leaves the matter seems unsatisfactory. It is provocative. Here theorists are told that they can explain price in terms of prices and the analysis Davenport carries on is beautifully worked out—an admirable piece of logical analysis. Then when that is done, he with his wonderful clear headedness and his admirable candor says, yes, he finds that it is all superficial and goes on to say that the economist ought not to be content with the superficiality; that will not do, as the economist ought to get back to the real forces. He goes to the length of telling what the real forces are; and finally leaves the problem in a way that cannot be regarded as intellectually satisfying.

We are told the economist cannot be content with the superficial price analysis. We must get back to the real forces; as economic theorists we should recognize their existence and then bow them out the door, turn them over, perhaps, Davenport would say, to the psychologists on the one hand and to the technical men, the engineering profession, on the other hand. It is a good plan for the division of labor. Our comprehension of the situation on the whole will be clearer if we see what the interrelations among these prices are, but the economist is not by his training adequately qualified to make a study of human desires or human productive capacities.

In the long run all the social sciences will get on better if the economist does the job he is fitted to do to the best of his ability, recognizing its narrow limitations, and then leaves to someone more skilled in psychological analysis on the one hand, and someone more skilled in the industrial arts on the other hand, the explanation of these ultimate forces. Is that one possible way of looking at it?

S. Does Davenport always adhere closely to his definition of economics? For instance, in analyzing demand I do not see any more reason for going to marginal utility than going back to the real forces.

M. No, there is some question there. But Davenport cannot be charged with having said a great deal about the analysis of desire. He has no such relatively full discussion of that subject as does Marshall.

S. Just as he lets this matter drop, he similarly drops the investigation of what lies behind supply and demand schedules.

M. That is what he is practically bound to do, after pointing out that it is part of his business to recognize what lies behind. The economist must see that his analysis in terms of price is superficial and see what it is that is fundamental. Having seen the promised land, it is not his to enter upon it. It is an interesting position for a person to take. Though Davenport may here and there have made some tiny slips, his standpoint is logically consistent throughout. I do not see how on the basis of his economics he is in a position to make these analyses, do you?

S. No, but he does go back in the one case and not in the other.

M. He would have been in a stronger position if he had left out the discussion of marginal utilities and tried to get rid of those words as Fetter tries to do in his second treatise. But to repeat, he has been very continent, for a person brought up in old-fashioned political economy, in his study of desires. Nobody of Davenport's generation can emancipate himself entirely from the influence of his early training. He has gone far in that direction and he may well hope that some of the students he has trained, not being saturated with the wrong kind of early teaching, will get rid of the last elements of impurity in his pecuniary logic.

A little more should be said of certain aspects of this interesting type of theory. Davenport is insistent that while the economist should recognize the existence of the real forces, he should not fall back into the old error of thinking that prices are measured, or determined, or equated in any sense, with utilities and sacrifices.

> . . . Market prices are not proportionate either to the labor or the pains or the feeling sacrifices of production on the one side, or to the service or utility or gratification in consumption on the other side, but are merely the equating point between the different reservation prices, based on costs in money terms, on the supply side, and the paying dispositions of consumers, as expressed in money terms, on the demand side. Costs cannot be reduced to any common denominator of pain, or price offers to any common denominator of utility. Nor do costs sum up or report the amount of labor, or even the amount of wages, incorporated in the product, but only the sum of marginal sacrifices reduced to the common denominator of price. And similarly on the demand side of the price equation: the fact that one will pay, at the maximum, say a dollar for a thing— in other words is marginal at this price offer—means only that at any higher price he would prefer to use his purchasing power for something else. A marginal price offer implies merely an equality of advantage between two competing lines of expenditure, without suggestion as to the absolute advantages of either.[27]

That is, he is trying to get all the old-fashioned machinery of pain cost and utility out of the theory of economics, still recognizing that desire is one of the ultimate forces and that also the amount of goods that men can produce, their capacities to produce, are the other real forces.

Another interesting feature of Davenport's treatise is his way of treating distribution. How many factors in distribution are there according to Marshall, how many shares of distribution? There are four: wages, interest, rent and profits. Davenport says that the costs of production are not four but legion and similarly the distributive shares are not four. So the factors in production are legion; and the interrelations among the factors in production are complex. All this means simply that he wants to break with another formally established tradition of economic theory and say that when the economist is

---

[27] *The Economics of Enterprise,* pp. 240-241.

thinking about individuals he ought to think about them as trying to acquire profits for themselves. Their ways of acquiring profits are most diverse. Every one of the people in question is going to use any way that seems for him most likely to lead to the desired end, and there is no particular sense in trying to classify all the different things that people use to make money into these intermixed categories of labor, capital, land and ability—categories it is impossible to use in practice because one cannot distinguish between land and capital. A good many theorists have given up trying to do so. One cannot differentiate any more between labor and business ability. Everyone who works with his hands has to put some intelligence into his work, and everyone who is managing a business enterprise has at least to sign his initials. He must do some work with his hands. We invest capital in ourselves. There is no use fussing with the old-fashioned categories. Everyone uses all the factors of production or, as Davenport likes to say, all the means of acquisition at his disposal, to the best advantage as he sees it. To repeat, the factors of production are for all intents and purposes legion; there are not four great categories of them, but an enormous number of things which differ significantly from each other.

To elaborate his theory of distribution, let us recall that Davenport insists that economic theory in the institutional situation in which we are living must be written from what he calls the "private and acquisitive point of view."[27a] The chief problem of this theory is to account for prices. He constructs his theory of prices by explaining that every individual as a purchaser of consumer goods has his own peculiar schedule of utilities. As a producer every individual has his own peculiar scale for discounting the future. Then he explains how individuals, on the basis of these peculiar scales, form their own schedules of price offers, both on the buying side of the market and on the selling side of the market. Finally, the market price is determined by a comparison between aggregates of individual price offers, both on the buying and on the selling side. That is so if the theorist conceives the market price to be dependent on an equation of demand prices and supply prices, each of these two schedules being demand prices of the individuals concerned.

This same scheme Davenport applies to the discussion of distribution. Likewise theorists make distribution a section of their discussion of value or prices. Most economists, like Fetter and Marshall, discuss distribution under the headings of wages, interest, rent and profits. These are regarded as the prices obtained for the four great

---

[27a] Beginning of extract from "1918 Typescript."

factors of production—labor, land, capital and business ability. Davenport says that this scheme of classifying the factors of production under four large heads is not justifiable. As he puts it, there are not four but a legion of factors of production. The fundamental classification into three or four factors, which we have inherited from the classical economists, he dismisses quite logically because he is stating the "private and acquisitive point of view." From this standpoint he argues that land is indistinguishable from capital as a means by which people get income. It does not make any difference to a person as a business man whether his funds are invested in land or in stock or invested in a mercantile enterprise that belongs to him exclusively or to him as one of a partnership. Similarly many things which have no tangible character Davenport insists are capital from a "private and acquisitive point of view"—such things as franchises, patent rights, all sorts of advantages which the person as a business man may have over other people in the same line of trade.

These things are capital just as much as a machine or a farm, because they are sources from which he gets income. The thing that counts is whether any kind of property will produce income for him. Anything that will produce income is capital. If the theorist begins to classify things which will produce income Davenport says that he is facing a practically impossible task. No classification possesses any great significance. It is foolish to talk about labor as a single commodity—it is so extremely diversified in character. The only sensible view to take is that there are as many different kinds of productive factors as work performed for gain. To repeat, in his view it is not wise to keep the traditional threefold or fourfold scheme of factors of production and make them bases. In every case the analyst should take specific commodities which are sold for the purpose of getting an income in his treatment of distribution, just as he takes specific commodities which are sold in his treatment of prices. Is that clear? Granted that viewpoint, the theory of prices gives the theory of distribution. All the theorist has to consider is the application of his general scheme of treating prices to cases of particular commodities from which different people are making gains.

If that is clear we are ready to go on to the final point that seems particularly worth while discussing in connection with Davenport. This point is with reference to the relation between the system of pecuniary logic which he sets up and the ultimate forces which he thinks control economic conduct. He points out very vigorously that his elaborate pecuniary analysis is superficial and circuitous in character. It is superficial because of the fact that money does not go to the heart of men's economic interests. Prices are symbols by which men have managed many different things but they are seldom interested in them for themselves. What concerns people is for what the symbols stand.

Similarly, all this price analysis is circuitous in the sense that the theorist cannot explain any one money price without supposing the pre-existence of a lot of other money prices. That point was brought out rather clearly in our first day's discussion of Davenport but it is so important a part of his analysis as a whole that I shall repeat the gist of it. The theorist cannot explain how much an individual will be willing to pay for any one unit of a commodity unless he knows how much of other commodities that appeal to that person he might be able to buy with the same amount of money. That is to say, before the analyst can set up his individual demand schedule for apples he has to understand not only the utility of successive apples to the individual but also the utility of the successive cents which he may spend on apples. When he has these two scales he can draw up a schedule of demand prices for apples. Before he can do this he must know the utility to him of successive cents; he has practically said that he must know the prices of many other things which money will buy. For money has no importance to him, or rather, it has little importance to him save as it represents possibilities of acquiring various desirable things besides apples that he has immediately in mind. If this be true it is obvious that the demand schedules of apples presupposes the existence of prices for many other things. The same would be true of the demand schedule of every individual for everything he was buying. It would be true of the business man's schedules of demand prices for producer goods as it would be true of the consumer's schedule for demand prices of consumer goods. What is true about the assumption of other prices to explain one schedule of demand prices is true likewise of assumptions involved in the explanation of any scale of demand prices.

Remember that Davenport says that among the factors the theorist must take into account in determining a business man's mind concerning the prices at which he can furnish any class of commodities are the other opportunities for profits that he must forego if he is to produce the article in question. That is to say, among the most important costs affecting the cost of a given article are opportunity costs. These costs are made up of prices. Hence when the theorist is talking about the supply price of any given article, such as wheat, as depending upon cost of production, he is saying in effect that the supply price of wheat depends upon prices of many other different things.

In other words, he supposes prices to exist for other articles in indefinite number in the very process of explaining the price at which any given article will be supplied. To repeat what I said at the beginning, the theorist finds his price analysis is itself circuitous—he explains prices by prices. The price of one thing is in very large measure explained by the prices of other things. If his pecuniary analysis is both superficial and circuitous, where does he stand? Let me read Davenport's statement of the matter:

> The cost of production computation, however neglectful of ultimate bases and explanations, is entirely adequate for all the purposes of the entrepreneur. It is no business of his to explain either the necessity of his outlays or the prices of his products, but only to arrive at the largest possible net gain from his efforts and his investment. But the economist's problem is quite distinct: he must really explain; and part of his difficulty is in the fact that his explanations must be sought within the actual situation and must run in consistency with the actual entrepreneur process. He must accept the entrepreneur functions and the entrepreneur analysis; but he must carry the analysis further than the entrepreneur is concerned to carry it in explaining what the entrepreneur does,—the situation conditioning his activity, the forces playing upon it, and the results that flow from it. Thus the economist must recognize that both the prices of the products and the prices of the bases of the product are equally results of the underlying and determining conditions; that neither does cost ultimately fix price nor price ultimately fix cost; that the outlays which the entrepreneur makes, the scarcity of the products which he produces, and the prices at which he must sell these products are equally the results of the limited supply of the productive factors which he employs; and thus that, with the demand for the products taken for granted, the causal sequences on the supply side of the problem runs from the relative scarcity of the factors to the relative scarcity of the products, thence to the relative prices of the products, thence to the relative remuneration of the factors. These remunerations are forthwith to be recognized as distributive shares.
>
> It thus appears that costs to the entrepreneur are merely the guise in which in an entrepreneur economy, the underlying and controlling situation of human needs on the side of demand, and of productive ability and productive equipment on the side of supply, present themselves to the entrepreneur and bear upon him in his process of placing a particular product upon the market. Costs are merely one point or aspect—but the central point or aspect—in the process of production and distribution in the competitive regime.

That is, the cost analysis while thoroughly adequate as applied to property by the business man is not a satisfactory solution of the economic problem to the economist. He must get behind this superficial talk about costs and prices. He must carry his analysis back to the ultimate forces and explain the terms of them. What are these ultimate forces? As those passages which I have already read to you imply, Davenport thinks of them as three: human desires, productive capacity—that is, man's knowledge of how to produce—and instrumental equipment are the ultimate forces.

I would like to say a final word or two on the subject [of the relation between pecuniary and real forces]. When *The Economics of Enterprise* came out I had occasion to review it in the September 1914 issue of *The American Economic Review*. I said in the course of the review that it was a keen analysis of the workings of our pecuniary institutions, that it amounted to a system of pecuniary logic with reference to the existence of certain ultimate forces, but that the relation between the ultimate forces and pecuniary analysis was not made clear. Davenport at once wrote me an extremely cordial note and said that that was perfectly true. He said that he did not see how to work the thing out; the only thing that seemed possible was to give a sort of genetic account of how the forces had reached their present shape.[28]

Summary: What is economics? "The science that treats phenomena from the standpoint of price." Has reference to a definite institutional situation. Leading features: An acquisitive society. Not task of theory to discuss its genesis. Cf., J. B. Clark's timeless static state and its universal truths and Joseph Schumpeter's static equilibrium. But Davenport thinks a few generalizations hold for all possible forms of organization. How does his pecuniary logic differ from Jevons's "mechanics of utility" and from Fetter's "psychological theory"? Two tasks: explanation and appraisal. Should be kept separate. (1) Explanation is economic theory—chapters 1-26. (2) Appraisal—economic welfare—chapters 27, 28. Cf., Harsh verdict on American wealth, pp. 519-521. Davenport does not keep all criticism out of chapters 1-26. See his strictures on American banking system in chapter 17, and remarks on good and ill of competition in chapter 26. Cf., definition of capital: "Anything . . . that earns rent or interest or that affords valuable service with passing time is capital. Capital and interest are correlative terms. The objective source of income is capital, the income from capital is interest. Thus, a credit against one's neighbor, or a bond against the government, is capital merely by the fact that either commands an interest income. So of good will, patents, trade marks, franchises, monopolies. Economic theorists will do well forthwith to recognize that rights of patent and royalty are capital; that police permits to rob passers-by after midnight are capital; that legislative authority to rob importers, both early and late, is capital; that royal patents for tax-farming the peasantry are capital; and that generally every property basis of private acquisition is by that very fact capital."

---

[28] End of extract from "1918 Typescript." Quotation from *The Economics of Enterprise*, pp. 117-118.

[Davenport referred affectionately to Professor Mitchell's "rebel mind." (Davenport to Mitchell, undated but around 1908).]

Viewpoint for explanation in economic theory. "Private and acquisitive point of view" is the only one possible. Does he explain what men do? Or show what their advantage is? He works from inside consciousness—on basis of motives—like Marshall *et al*. Applications: Every individual has his own peculiar (1) scale of utilities as consumer; (2) scale of gainbringing capacities of goods as producer; (3) scale of discounting future services as investor. From the above scales and from existing prices for other commodities he derives his peculiar scale of price offers for each article. There are no such things as social utility, specific productive efficiency, social time-discount, social organism. For example, note his definition of productivity. "[P]roductivity in the competitive society means merely serviceability for private income or private gain—means proceeds."

Theory of prices: Prices determined by above derived scales of price offers and similar scales of supply prices. Demand scales made up of different respective maximum price bids. Two marginal utilities necessary for a price offer. Cannot represent demand schedule as a schedule of social utility; for individual differences of sensitiveness and taste are of great importance. Strictly one cannot compare the utility of same good to different men. Supply price is made up of money costs to entrepreneurs. Largely opportunity costs. Cannot be reduced to pain. Given the two schedules of demand prices and supply prices, fixation of price is a matter of "mere mechanical details." Prices are fixed *at* margins not by margins. "Price . . . coincides with only the marginal price-offers." To buyers not on margin "there accrues a surplus advantage." Stated another way: 1. Prices fixed not by, but at margins; that is, prices are fixed by the *whole array* of conditions summed up in the schedules of demand prices and of supply prices. Further, price offer of each individual that is represented in either schedule rests upon *two* marginal utilities—or rather two total sets with reference to two commodities, from which a price offer results *at* margin. Not a novel doctrine; but often overlooked. Davenport has corrected the error in others so frequently (especially in *Value and Distribution*), that he thinks it is necessary to guard against it vigorously, on the part of his readers.

Relation of this system of pecuniary logic to the ultimate forces. Pecuniary analysis is indispensable, but "both circuitous and superficial." Demand schedule for any one good presupposes a whole system of prices for other goods. Supply schedule with its emphasis on opportunity costs presupposes a whole system of adjustments already made between costs and selling prices of other goods. Economists must seek some real explanation. Two attitudes toward this problem: Walras and literary economists. Does Walras really get any further than the latter writers? Does he not take real forces for granted? Davenport says that cost of production analysis is adequate for business man but not for economist. His explanation: The ultimate forces. Scarcity, with special reference to rents. The "ultimate income is psychic." The ultimate forces he does not analyze: (1) human desires he explicitly refuses to study, but he rejects hedonistic implications of marginal utility. Scarcity which rests upon limited (2) productive capacities and (3) instrumental equipment including all resources of environment, he hardly discusses. He says in "Cost and Its Significance":

"There is nothing possible here in the way of further explanation than fully and accurately to describe the process." But does he thus describe it? Relations between the ultimate forces and money prices. But note again that prices are not proportionate to sacrifices or utilities. Where Davenport leaves the problem: Keen study of inter-relations among money prices in a society where everyone is seeking his own gain, with all the fundamental factors in the problem taken for granted. A treatise upon pecuniary logic, without a theory of valuation and without an inquiry into the relations between pecuniary logic and human nature. Still, analysis of interrelations among prices has its value even though it is superficial and circular.

Other points: (1) Theory of distribution not separately discussed in a systematic order; but as a derivative of theory of prices. His chief peculiarity under this head is his view that there are not merely four factors of production and four shares in distribution, but a multitude of factors of production and shares in distribution; in short the theory of distribution is a problem of prices and the shares are legion. (2) Discussion of laws of diminishing and increasing returns (which he rechristens Law of the Proportion of Factors and Law of Advantage and Size). (3) Attitude toward psychology. What happens to the psychological school in Davenport's hands?[29]

---

[29] Outlines, March 14, 1917, "Davenport," APP 54-63, no. 53. Quotations from *The Economics of Enterprise,* pp. 25, 117, 119, 141, 145, 162, 488, 517, 519; "Cost and Its Significance," *The American Economic Review,* December 1911, p. 751.

[As of this writing (1967) there has been considerable recognition of the fact that many basic elements of current micro and macro economics are found in Davenport's *The Economics of Enterprise.* See Joseph Dorfman, *The Economic Mind in American Civilization.* III, pp. 375-389; Frank H. Knight, "Davenport, Herbert Joseph," *The Encyclopedia of Social Sciences,* fifteen volumes (New York: Macmillan, 1930-1934) V, pp. 8-9.

It should be noted that Davenport also divided his first book *Outlines of Economic Theory* (1896) into two parts "science" and "art." The "art" consisted, as the publisher stated, of discussions "of great practical value and . . . timely, touching on the competitive system, cooperation and profit sharing, state and municipal ownership, taxation, the eight hour day, the apprentice system, sweating shops, the labor of women and children, the unemployed, the currency, free coinage of silver, etc."

"There is a strong group whose members are fundamentally more in harmony with the Austrian school than with any other but who have worked more or less independently of the Austrian position or have modified theirs considerably. Among these we may mention in this country J. B. Clark of Columbia, H. J. Davenport of Cornell, Irving Fisher of Yale, T. N. Carver of Harvard and F. A. Fetter of Princeton. The main moot point of late with these men is that of interest and rent." (Robert F. Hoxie, "History of Political Economy," ms., 1915, copy in Joseph Dorfman's possession.)]

CHAPTER XIV

Austrian General Theory: Friedrich von Wieser

We now turn to the one great systematic comprehensive treatise produced by the founders of the Austrian School. This is *Theorie der gesellschaftlichen Wirtschaft (Social Economics)* which was published by Friedrich Freiherr von Wieser in 1914.

"[The] book does for the Austrian School what John Stuart Mill's *Principles* did for the Classical School. Written by perhaps the most original of the Austrian group after years of deliberation, it sums [up], systematizes and carries on the doctrine of Menger, Böhm-Bawerk and himself in a fashion which makes *Social Economics* a vastly better presentation of the Austrian viewpoint than any other book available in English, or in German for that matter."[1]

Friedrich von Wieser (1851-1926) came from a distinguished aristocratic Viennese family whose sons usually entered the public service. When he was in the *gymnasium* preparing for the University of Vienna, he became enamored of Homer, Virgil, the Niebelungenlied—in short of epic history at large—and dreamed of becoming an historian. That was his first intellectual ambition. But for the career in the government service which his birth had marked out for him, it was necessary that he devote himself to the study of law; and he dutifully pursued that course at the university.

While he was engaged in his studies, he came across some of Herbert Spencer's sociological writings, especially the opening volumes of the *Synthetic Philosophy,* the *First Principles,* which impressed Wieser

[1] Mitchell to Professor E. R. A. Seligman, April 15, 1924.
[Professor Mitchell first lectured on the book in 1918, when it had not yet been translated. A year before he had written a long review article, "Wieser's Theory of Social Economics," in the *Political Science Quarterly,* 1917, reprinted in *The Backward Art of Spending Money and Other Essays* edited by Joseph Dorfman (New York: McGraw-Hill, 1937) pp. 225-257. This seems to have been the only contemporary notice taken of the book in the English-speaking world. He arranged for the translation by his former student, A. Ford Hinrichs, which appeared in 1927. He wrote Wieser the following note on the need of a translation:]
"Your book ought to have a large influence upon the English-speaking economists and I regret to say it will not do so until it appears in translation. Twenty years ago a considerable percentage of American economists read German with some facility. Now-a-days, the percentage is considerably smaller and the chances seem to be that it will grow smaller yet in the near future as comparatively few of our graduate students are going abroad for their training." (Mitchell to Wieser, April 24, 1924.)

powerfully, because Spencer was dealing in a philosophical fashion with certain historical problems that had long interested him. In particular, Spencer had developed and defended the thesis that the "great-man theory" of history is a fundamental error; and that it is society which produces the hero. Hence, if the inquirer wants to understand the course of history, including the story of the great figures, he must understand society first, in order to gain insight into the great, silent, impersonal forces which determine the way in which human culture is developed. In reflecting on this set of problems, Wieser concluded that he would, so far as opportunity developed, direct his study toward the understanding of society. It seemed to him that the phase of social life which was most accessible to understanding was the economic aspect; and so he came to devote himself to economics.[2]

Wieser had not attended the lectures of Carl Menger at the University of Vienna[3] but it seems that shortly after he received the doctor of law degree (LL.D.) in 1872, he came across a copy of Menger's *Grundsätze der Volkswirthschaftslehre,* and his imagination was captivated by it.

While on a travelling fellowship from the Austrian government in 1876, he gave a report along Menger's lines in the seminar at the University of Heidelberg conducted by one of the leaders of the German Historical School, Karl Knies.[4] In that report on "The Relation Between Cost and Value," Wieser put forth the first sketch of the theory of imputation which is one of his basic contributions to the building up of the Austrian system of economic logic. It shows how the values of the means of production are derived from the values of their marginal contributions to the products made from them. Menger was [interestingly enough not very enthusiastic about the paper, but] sufficiently impressed with the author so that he helped Wieser get a renewal of the fellowship for further study in German universities. Meanwhile Wieser had accepted a post in the Tax Administration, he achieved a distinguished career in the civil service and was looked upon universally as one of the ablest as well

---

[2] [The courses in economics which Wieser attended at Vienna were given by Lorenz von Stein (1815-1890), "an indefatigable writer and zealous free trader." Arthur Latham Perry, *Elements of Political Economy* (New York: Scribners, 1866, 4th ed., 1868) p. 23. At Vienna, as at most continental universities, economics was taught in the faculty of law.]

[3] [Menger was then a *privatdozent.*]

[4] [The report was first published in 1929 in Wieser's *Gesammelte Abhandlungen* ed. by F. A. Hayek. Hayek studied with Mitchell in 1923]. "Call from von Hayek. Young Austrian economist, pupil of Wieser, now compiling annals of·business for use in Germany and Austria." Mitchell, "Diary," December 11, 1923.

as one of the most philosophic of the body of public officials who played a leading role in the government of the Austro-Hungarian Empire. The country was in those days one in which the crown still had great authority and the authority was exercised through the civil service. In the last two years of World War [I] Wieser was minister of commerce.

His academic career began in 1883 when he was appointed *Privatdozent,* one of those unpaid teaching positions which are the door through which people enter a career in a university in the German-speaking countries. As *Privatdozent,* he published the following year, *Über den Ursprung und die Hauptgesetze des Wirthschaftlichen Werthes* ("The Origin and Leading Principles of Economic Value") in which he treated the problem of how valuations are made by a single individual. That individual, however, is taken to represent a society. It is a curious conception, but one which Wieser thought necessary in order to get at the simple fundamentals of economic valuation. The book made a deep impression at once. He presently was appointed in 1884, with the help of Menger, *professor extraordinarius* (associate professor) of economics in the German University of Prague.

While at Prague, Wieser published in 1889 his second treatise, *Der natürliche Werthe (Natural Value).* When William Smart of the University of Glasgow was introducing the Austrian theory of value to English readers, he chose this book for a student to translate in preference to Menger's *Principles.*[5] It seemed to him then, as it has seemed to many since, to be the most competent presentation of the fundamentals of the Austrian theory available. The book led to his promotion as full professor the same year. In 1903 he returned to the University of Vienna as Menger's successor.

Wieser, so far as subsequent publications were concerned, then turned his attention primarily to matters of a practical sort. He dealt with the scientific side of economic problems which he had faced as an administrator: questions of money, of commercial intercourse, etc.

He always worked over the drafts of his books with great care; it was very difficult for him to be satisfied with their form. It may well be that he would never have published his general treatise on economic theory if it had not been for Max Weber. When the *Grundriss der Sozialökonomik* that great German cooperative project on social economics at large was being organized, Weber, who had a leading share in the planning, said that he would not participate unless Wieser would write the chief section on economic theory.

---

[5] It was translated in 1893 by C. A. Malloch.

Wieser consented reluctantly. He spent three years in perfecting further the system upon which he had been working so long. In 1914, *Theorie der gesellschaftlichen Wirtschaft* appeared in the first volume of the *Grundriss*.[6] Under ordinary circumstances, a treatise by one of the three men who were universally recognized as the leaders of the Austrian school and a work which for the first time undertook to expound not merely the theory of value but the whole range of economic theory from the Austrian viewpoint would have been seized upon most eagerly by people interested in economic theory the world over. But the [World] War [I] intervened, and it was not until after the war that the book began to make any impression. By and large it would have made comparatively little difference had Wieser's manuscript suffered the same fate that befell Gustav Cassel's treatise, which was simply set in type in 1914 and not printed until 1918.

"When the second edition was called for [1924], . . . the author declined to make any changes in his text. He had turned once more to the conflict between his youthful conceptions of epic history and Spencer's argument that heroes are by-products of culture— a problem of which his solution appeared last spring [1926] in *Das Gesetz der Macht* ["The Law of Might" (Power)]. As for his exposition of economic theory, he hoped others would find what is to be added, what is to be changed."[7]

To repeat, Wieser's *Social Economics* is a volume of considerable importance as far as theory goes, because it is the first comprehensive, systematic statement of the Austrian viewpoint. The number of theoretical books written by Austrian economists from their perspective is considerable, but up to the publication of Wieser's treatise they were more or less monographic in character, no matter how big their size finally became with successive editions, as, for example, Böhm-Bawerk's massive *Capital and Interest* and *Positive Theory of Capital*.[8] It is characteristic of the Austrian school that until the old

---

[6] [Wieser's treatise had much to do with the revival of interest in the Austrian school.] A. Landry, a French disciple of the school, had said in "L'École economique," *Rivista de Scienzia*, 1907, that "Today the Austrian School is somewhat played out." Quoted from Charles Gide and Charles Rist, *A History of Economic Doctrines*, first English translation from the French (Boston: Heath, 1915) p. 544, in "Changing Estimates of the Mechanics of Utility," APP 84-91, no. 48.

[7] Mitchell, "Forward," in Wieser, *Social Economics*, translation by A. Ford Hinrichs (New York: Greenberg, 1927) p. xi.

[8] Paragraph from "1918 Typescript."

[Böhm-Bawerk is known especially for his theory of interest which he said "was an attempt to explain all the different forms of the phenomenon of interest as arising from a difference in value between present and future goods, but to derive the difference itself from the interaction of a number of factors some of them psychological and some technological . . . That theory of the difference in value between present and future goods I should like to designate as the agio theory." He noted in the third and

age of Wieser none of their significant leaders had published a general treatise upon economic theory at large. Menger, their founder, had written his *Grundsätze,* a book which was abstract and as much confined to the analysis of value as Jevons's *The Theory of Political Economy*; in fact it was a comparatively fragmentary treatise on value, it had comparatively little to say even about price. Wieser's earlier work was concerned with further illustrations of the problem of value. Böhm-Bawerk had devoted himself primarily to the study of interest theory. That subject offered a considerable range of problems, but although his chief monograph became an enormous one in successive editions, it never purported to be a treatise upon economic theory at large. Other notable but specialized monographs by members of the school were Emil Sax's application of marginal utility theory to taxation in *Grundlegung der theoretischen Staatswirthschaft* (1887); and Robert Zuckerkandl, *Zur Theorie des Preises* (1889), a history of the marginal theory of value.

The one treatise by an Austrian economist that one is most likely to think of as systematic is the two volume treatise of Eugen Philippovich von Philippsberg (1858-1917), *Grundriss der politischen Ökonomie* (1893-1907). No other work is more comprehensive and systematic in its general outline, and Philippovich is one of the ornaments of the Austrian school. But nonetheless his book is not really organized on the Austrian basis. Rather the ideas of Menger, Wieser and Böhm-Bawerk are incorporated by a man who is essentially an eclectic and who borrowed from other sources considerable elements, which in the last resort were incompatible with Austrian ideas. Heretofore such attempts as have been made to incorporate the Austrian theory of value, interest, etc., with a general scheme of economics have been made by foreigners, particularly by American and French writers. It is particularly interesting, then, to see how one of the most eminent of the Austrians after having worked all his life in economic theory sums up the Austrian contribution to economics at large.[9]

Wieser's discussion still centers in value problems, but more or less as Alfred Marshall's theory does, for it brings into the value problem the whole theory of the distribution of income, and then Wieser goes on to discuss a variety of value problems which Marshall did not

---

fourth editions that "Similar concepts had appeared elsewhere, although less exhaustively worked out . . . I am thinking of a number of almost simultaneous pronouncements, especially among American economists such as Simon N. Patten, S. M. Macvane, and J. B. Clark." *Capital and Interest I. History and Criticism of Interest Theories.* 4th ed. Translation by George D. Huncke and Hans F. Sennholz (South Holland, Ill.: Libertarian Press, 1959) pp. 357-358.]

[9] The above paragraph from "1918 Typescript."

cover, i.e., the way in which value problems affect the state itself
and the value problems that turn up in the world economy.

Why economics is a theory of value: 1. Economic activity is the exercise of
rational control over the process of providing for wants. 2. Aim is to secure
maximum satisfaction possible under circumstances. 3. Its instrument is the
utility calculus.[10]

Social Economics has a simple and interesting outline. It is, to
repeat, a treatise on value from start to finish, and value is made to
comprehend practically all of the problems of economic theory. It
begins in Book I with what Wieser calls The Theory of the Simple
Economy; that is, with the problem of the valuations performed by
a single individual who himself represents the totality of a modern
community that practices division of labor. But there is no exchange
here. It is the valuation of a single person with a degree of power
immeasurably beyond that of any physical man. This is the problem
that Wieser discussed in his first treatise, *Uber den Ursprung und
die Hauptgesetze des Wirthschaftlichen Werthes*. It seemed to him
toward the end of his career, as at the beginning, that the logical
procedure was to discuss first the fundamental question of how an
individual conducts his economic planning to provide for the maximum satisfaction of his needs.

These fundamentals laid down, Wieser proceeds in Book II, Theory
of the Social Economy [Exchange Economy], to take account of the
fact that in modern society there are many people and that they do
not have like incomes. On the contrary, they differ enormously in
the wealth at their disposal. The problem, therefore, presents itself
of how exchanges are arranged. These exchanges are based on the
valuations of the millions of simple economies; it is necessary to take
account of the way in which out of the valuations of the simple economies there arises the enormously complicated system of prices.

Wieser then advances in Book III, Theory of the State Economy,
to deal with the peculiar problems of the public (or state) economy.
It considers the valuations made by the state as an entity in a sense
separate from the private individuals who are its citizens. The state
economy differs from that of the individual economies in the sense
that the state is not engaged so much in producing concrete goods
to satisfy people as in trying to make sure that there is as little interference as possible with the process of production on the part of
private individuals. It also has to take account of certain matters
touching the common welfare; and finally it obtains the means for

---

[10] Outline, "Wieser," APP 84-91, no. 35.

defraying the costs of its activities in a way altogether different from that possible to a private individual; namely, by levying compulsory taxes.

The last section of the treatise, Book IV, deals with the Theory of the World Economy. This again is a discussion of certain value problems; namely, those which arise from the interrelations among several states which are independent of each other and yet find themselves or their citizens carrying on extensive dealings with each other.

To repeat, each of the books is a treatise on a certain aspect of the value problem, so elaborated however as to bring into the problem practically all the topics which are ordinarily contained within an English or American treatise on economic theory. The difference between the books consists in the difference between the persons by whom and the circumstances under which the valuation is made. The Theory of the Simple Economy studies the valuations made by a single perfect economic man, just one subject. This is the foundation on which all the rest is built. The Theory of Social Economy studies valuations as made by individuals living together in a society where there is an unequal distribution of wealth. Wieser shows that the existence of competition and monopoly and inequality in distribution alters the conclusions which are drawn from the theory of the simple economy. He shows how far the theory of value must be modified when the theorist replaces the single person, who is a flawless economic man, with a horde of individuals living together under conditions of unequal distribution of income. The third book deals with valuations as made by a state which is seeking the economic welfare of its nationals, to use a word which is just coming into common parlance. The last book discusses the problem of valuation as it presents itself to one state among several states, taking up particularly the problems of national policy as they present themselves in international dealings among state governments—not international dealings between individual subjects of individual states, but among the governments themselves.[11] So much for the general outlines. In short, the treatise begins with the problems of value as presented in the simple economy; it advances to the value problems that present themselves to one state by differences of classes in "the economy of the state," and finally with the problems of value presented by the interrelations among independent states.

The first particularly interesting thing about *Social Economics* is to see how this scheme grows directly out of the fundamental Austrian

[11] Paragraph from "1918 Typescript."

idea. The method by which the discussion is carried on is described by Wieser at the outset as the "psychological" one.

> This investigation uses the method recently designated as the "psychological." The name is applied because the theory takes its point of departure from within, from the mind of the economic man. I myself once spoke of economic theory in this sense as applied psychology. The designation, however, is not a fortunate one. It may lead to the misunderstanding that the "psychological" economic theory starts from scientific psychology. This is by no means the case. It has still less to do with physiology, as an even more serious misunderstanding has tried to make it appear. The observations concerning the inner life of man, which our "psychological" theory of economics develops, have been made by it independently. They are psychological investigations that the economist makes, they are not borrowed from psychology. They are entirely independent of the result which scientific psychology might reach with regard to the psychical elements, the analysis of which are within its province.[12]

Wieser goes on to argue that economists should avoid "penetrating psychological analysis."

> Our theory finds in the consciousness of every economically active human being a wealth of experiences which are common property of all. These are experiences which every scientist shares with the layman, without resort to special scientific instruments. They are experiences concerning facts of the outer world, as for example, the presence of goods of various sorts; experiences concerning the source and current of the economic activity of mankind.

It is the business of the economist to make use of these common experiences without going into elaborate technical psychological studies of consciousness. He takes certain obvious features of experience known to all people relating to the goods in the external world, men's needs, and how they utilize the goods to supply their needs; and does not seek to go beyond that.

> The sphere of economic theory has the same limits as this common experience. The task of the theorist ends at the boundary of common experience; it ends where science feels constrained to collect its observations by historical or statistical investigation.[13]

In other words, the theorist as such must build on the experiences that all have continuously, without any reference to elaborate collections of an objective sort such as are provided by historical or statistical investigations. When he does make use of these materials, he is going beyond the task which it is his proper function to perform.

After this introduction the reader may be a little surprised to find Wieser say that "The method of economic theory is empirical. It is

---

[12] *Social Economics,* p. 3.
[13] *Social Economics,* p. 4.

supported by observation and has but one aim, which is to describe actuality." It is not that economics attempts to describe what actually happens in detail, Wieser hastens to add. The economist "endeavors to place before us the typical phenomenon, the typical development, and to eliminate whatever may be subordinate, accidental or individual."[14] That task is performed by two instruments at the economist's disposal. One is the instrument of isolation. He isolates the typical features of the economic experience that he wants to understand—in his own mind, more or less as the physicist may isolate certain phenomena that he wants to study by the use of clever contrivances in his laboratory. That is something the economist does not do with human experience, but he can accomplish the same end by a mental device. The second device is idealization, by which Wieser means thinking of pure cases.

> Isolation and idealization are his instruments, just as without demur they have always been the instruments of man pursuing other truly empirical sciences, for example, the exact physical sciences. Like the naturalist performing an experiment, the theoretical economist is bound to isolate, when making observations. It is even more necessary for him to do so because reflectively he will have to perfect his observation by the memory image of his experience. . . . Side by side with the isolating assumptions which embrace less than the entire truth, the theoretical economist then proceeds to form numerous idealizing assumptions which embrace more than the truth. In these he raises the empirical fact reflectively to the highest degree of perfection conceivable. But the most perfect state is at the same time the most simple and the most readily understood. Thus the theorist assumes the existence of a model man, a man such as actually has never existed, nor can ever exist.[15]

That is Wieser's statement of his methodological position. It is a view which he follows through with admirable consistency. In his Theory of the Simple Economy he is talking throughout about the valuations which are performed by a model economic man who has no weakness and no vices. Since this is the simplest case, it is the one which is most feasible to analyze and the one which shows substantial economic truth.

Proceeding this way, Wieser, though he started out by saying that economics aims to be an empirical science, almost of necessity finds himself developing economics less as an account of how men actually behave in valuing things than of how they ought to behave in order to attain maximum satisfaction; that is, economic science, as he treats it, is not a positive but a normative science. It shows what is

---
[14] *Social Economics*, p. 5.
[15] *Social Economics*, p. 5.

the proper line of action in order to gain in the great economic aim of attaining the greatest satisfaction possible under the circumstances instead of trying to show what people actually do in economic life. Wieser recognizes this fact explicitly. He says:

> Economic theory explains the laws of economic valuation and trade in a manner which differs conspicuously from that in which the natural sciences explain the laws of nature. The latter show a necessary connection of cause and effect, a compulsion (*Ein Mussen*). Economic theory presents a sequence arising under economic pressure, a desideratum (*Ein Sollen*). Economic valuation is that demanded by economic duty. Economic action is that demanded by economic necessity. . . .
>
> The theorist may easily seem to transgress the boundaries of his problem. He describes a theoretical obligation, a valuation which is demanded. In so doing, he may appear to establish a controlling force over the person of a man. The position of pharmacology is analogous. The latter discovers that certain remedies cater to the desire of the patient to regain health, that certain other agents induce death which he would escape. In the establishment of such relations as these, pharmacology is a descriptive science. With like purpose economic theory demonstrates that a certain process of valuation and action results in the greatest gain, that another process does not.
>
> Nevertheless it must be admitted that economic theory may not hold to this point of view at all times. No assurance can be given that it will not swerve from such purely descriptive character. This description of economic action is intended to lay down certain fundamental truths for the guidance of the science and art of politics.[16]

This conception would have pleased Jeremy Bentham most heartily. It is an undertaking to build the kind of science which is most useful. The interest in economics is not the interest of idle curiosity, to find out how things go or why they go as they do; but to expound the rational principles of economic life in order that they may be guides in the practical art of politics.

This is an aim which is different in character from that entertained at least by the later theorists of the English tradition. Deep as was Marshall's interest in ethical problems, though he presumably felt that the real justification for studying economics was the desire to throw light upon what ought to be done, still he seemed to conceive of economic theory as an explanatory science dealing with the actual processes of economic life, trying to show how things come about and why they come about as they do. And in his eyes that type of explanation is in the long run more germane to the science of politics in a broad sense than a statement of what ought to be done.

---

[16] *Social Economics*, p. 34.

Wieser belongs in this respect to the older tradition and with this aim in view he must not be expected to give an account of actual events. The discovery that certain of his theories yield results differing considerably from what actually happens is from his point of view not necessarily a criticism. He believes that there is substantial agreement in the long run between the statements concerning what valuations are demanded by the necessity of the situation and the valuations which are actually made. He takes pains to point this out now and then; the most notable instance will be discussed shortly. His aim is not to account for what is.

The great instrument that men have for maximizing their satisfaction is the utility calculus. That calculus is conceived by Wieser very much in the same way in which Jevons viewed it, save in the fact that Wieser makes no parade of a study of different dimensions of pleasures. The substantial similarity between his view of the calculus and that of Jevons lies in the fact that neither supposes that men have any capacity for measuring pleasures and pains, but rather that men are equipped with a balance which enables them to tell whether one pleasure is greater, less than, or equal to another pleasure; and to make similar comparisons among pains and between pleasures on the one side and pains on the other.

With this capacity Wieser credits his rational man; and that suffices for the individual to build up an elaborate series of plans for meeting his needs. If the individual can tell what need is the most pressing and from the satisfaction of what need he gets the greatest result and then can determine what are the needs greatest in intensity, he has all he requires for economic planning. He goes on to a computation of costs because when he knows what relative importance to attach to different products that might be made, he has the means of finding out what importance he should attach to the various things by means of which these final products can be made. Thus the individual's scheme of valuation which starts with the finished goods can be carried back into valuations of raw materials, of labor, capital, land and business ability, as agents of production.

That calculus Wieser works out in *Social Economics* in a beautifully symmetrical fashion. He introduces into it a modification of his earlier *Natural Value* which brings the whole discussion a little closer to the experience of ordinary life than was carried on by the first expositions of the Austrian value theory. This is the distinction which he draws between what he calls "specific goods" and "cost goods." A specific good is one which for some reason exists only in one particular example or can be applied only to the satisfaction of one particular want. A cost good, on the other hand, is one which is capable of subdivision; there are a great many examples of it, and it can be applied directly or indirectly to the satisfaction of many different wants. An example of a specific good would be the unique manuscript of some great literary light. The best example of the cost goods are materials, say, like pig iron which can be put to thousands of uses; or, better still, common labor, which can be employed for endless purposes.

The task of systematic planning can be carried out far more precisely with reference to cost goods than it can with reference to specific goods, because in the case of cost goods a good many different equations can be obtained showing how they fit into different processes of production and on the basis of the numerous equations the marginal utility of a unit of the cost goods can be determined; whereas in the case of the specific good there is no such opportunity of studying different applications. A definite value can be set on the specific good. If so, the satisfaction derived from its use can be measured. But since Wieser claims that all one can do is to say certain satisfactions mean more to him than others or mean less to him, that leaves the fundamental data on the basis of which the valuation of specific goods must be made rather vague. This is an original touch. Wieser is not trying to force the systematic marginal analysis in so rigorous a fashion as was undertaken by some of the earlier exponents of the Austrian doctrine.

[To repeat for clarification,] "Technically, the most important modification of his earlier work is the widening of the distinction between 'monopoly goods' and 'cost goods,' into a distinction between 'specific means of production' and 'cost means of production.' . . . The specific means of production in the strict sense are limited by physical scarcity or by peculiar quality to a single use, whereas cost means are sufficiently abundant and sufficiently adaptable to be used in many ways. A corresponding distinction is drawn between specific products and cost products. In general, lands are specific means, while most kinds of labor and capital goods are cost means."[17]

Lack of time precludes elaborating at this point his technical account of the distinction between cost means of production and specific means of production, and cost goods and specific goods. A feature of his discussion which is particularly significant turns up in the

---

[17] Mitchell, "Wieser's Theory of Social Economics," *The Backward Art of Spending Money,* p. 230.

part on economic society in Book II. The change in the problems presented when the theorist passes from the theory of the simple economy to the theory of social economy is that he has to take account now of exchange. In Book I Wieser was dealing with the valuations of a single ideal economic man but in Book II he has a great many different people exchanging with each other. He might have been expected to handle these problems by carrying forward his assumption that all the denizens of the social economy are perfect economic men, and that they meet on a par in the market where they exchange goods. That he does not do.

He begins by holding that if the economist wants to understand problems of exchange in a modern country he has to have as a basis for his economic theory a sociological theory, the chief point of which is to recognize that modern processes are shot through by differences in power. There are certain classes which are in a position of enormous advantage as compared with other classes, in the possession of wealth and prestige. (He lived in a society in which social prestige, as differentiated from wealth, counted for a great deal—much more than it does in the United States.) Those people who possess power of one sort or another exercise a potent influence upon the valuations of the other folks in the community. The result is that economic valuations in the social economy are warped most seriously from the model of economic rationality.

Three kinds of consumer goods must be considered. First, there is the mass of commodities which are used and bought in large measure by the working classes. The values of these goods are determined primarily by marginal valuations of poor people. At the other extreme are luxury goods for which Wieser takes diamonds as the illustration; they are not bought by poor people, and their valuations are fixed by their marginal utility to folks of larger means. Between the two extremes lies a third type of goods; those which are bought in some measure by the poor, but largely by the middle classes. There the valuations which count are those of the middle classes.

In short, in modern society there is always a stratification of demand which has a profound influence on prices. The theorist could not possibly, he says, understand the price paid for diamonds on the basis of a theory of value which does not take account of the fact that there is the enormous difference among people in purchasing power. He then goes on to say that the differences in purchasing power, the stratification of demand, warps all prices from the model of economic rationality. This makes it necessary that the state intervene in business affairs, in general economic life, in order to protect common interests which are threatened by inequalities in wealth.[18]

To repeat, the way to begin, according to Wieser, is to take the simplest cases first, and the simplest cases are those that represent the highest degree of abstraction and the most ideal purity. That is why he starts with the single economic subject, abstracting all other people, and with an economic subject who is a perfect economic man. That is the simplest case and therefore the one that is easiest to understand; a purely ideal situation, of course. Economics in this sense is really all a theory of value. It resolves itself into a theory of value for the further reason that economic activity is the exercise of rational control over the process of providing for men's wants. The aim of the rational control of course is to provide the maximum satisfaction that is possible under the circumstances. The instrument which men use for this scheme of rational control is the utility calculus. The whole subject is the exercise of rational control. The aim is the attainment of maximum satisfaction, and the method is the application of the utility calculus. That being the case, the theorist is concerned at every stage of his investigations with some phase or other of the application of the utility calculus. So that economics, to repeat, starts with the utility calculus as it is worked by a perfect economic man living in isolation. Then it advances one stage in complexity to the problem of the utility calculus as it is worked by many men living in a society where there are implications arising from lack of perfect freedom of competition and inequality of income. The analyst advances once more to the utility calculus as it should be worked by a state which aims at the welfare of all its subjects, and finally he considers the utility calculus as it should be worked by one state among several.

There are still several points that are of sufficient general importance to be worthy of further attention. The first of these is Wieser's peculiar way of defending the use of the utility calculus. This is nowadays [1918] particularly of interest because so many economists seem to be getting very much afraid of the idea of utility. Remember that Frank A. Fetter, for example, undertook to drop the use of the phrase "marginal utility" altogether. A considerable number of theorists, some of whom will be discussed in detail later, such as Joseph A. Schumpeter, have tried to transform economics practically into a theory of choice, starting with certain assumptions concerning what people will choose and not going into the fundamental question as to

---

[18] Remainder of discussion of Wieser is from "1918 Typescript," unless otherwise specified.

the grounds on which that choice rests. Even writers like Herbert J. Davenport say that economics is properly regarded as a theory of price, as the science which looks at phenomena from the viewpoint of price, and keep as clear as they possibly can from the notion of utility. Marshall attempts to avoid the same difficulty about comparisons of utilities by saying that he is going to use money measures of the force of motives, and is not going to illustrate the equivalence of feeling except in a certain restricted class of cases; that is to say, in cases where he can make comparisons between groups of people, not between individuals but between groups, such groups only as present substantially uniform economic conditions. Wieser appreciates the difficulties of the utility calculus that have been gradually developed by various critics.

To repeat, he says it is impossible to compare the feelings of different people, and the question is how, under these circumstances, can the theorist develop a scheme of rational control over the process of satisfying men's wants by the use of the utility calculus. The analyst cannot measure utilities directly. The enquirer has no unit by the application of which he can say that this particular entity has so many units, another entity has such another number. All that he can do is to make comparisons among utilities in terms of equality or in terms of greater or less. A person can tell whether the utility of another slice of bread to him, under given circumstances, would be equal to, greater or less than, the utility of a newspaper to him. He does not know how many units of utility there are in a newspaper, but he can make those comparisons by discriminating between their utilities, deciding whether one is greater or less than the other. That, Wieser says, is a sufficient basis for developing a scheme of rational control over the whole process of trying to provide for people's wants.

Let us see again how he works that out. We can do it best by taking a series of progressively more intricate problems. To start with the problem of a single good which you possess in a single unit, if you are going to have a rational control over the application of this good to the satisfaction of your wants, a rational control which will enable you to obtain the maximum satisfaction, you have only to determine what among the various wants that this good will satisfy is the greatest; that is to say, the ability to compare the utilities of the goods in various uses, and give decisions in terms of greater and less, will enable you to apply that particular commodity in a rational fashion so as to obtain maximum satisfaction. You do not need any calculations of units here. All you need to know is in which one of the various uses will it have the greatest utility, and of course you can tell that if you are able to compare its utility in one use with its utility in another and discriminate relative magnitude.

Let us go on to a slightly more complicated case. Suppose that you have several units of one and the same good. Your problem again is how to apply the means at your disposal in a rational fashion so as to get maximum satisfaction. Once more you can solve that problem by the simple method of considering the utility of the several units in succession as applied to the gratification of the various wants they serve, and getting your answer every time merely in terms of greater and less utility or equal utilities. Once again that limited power of analyzing utilities suffices to solve the problem of rational control.

We come to a more complicated problem. The economic goods which we are continually producing are not one, but many kinds, and the question is how can you arrange a rational disposition over the production of many different kinds of commodities. Wieser argues that, in the case of the great bulk of the goods which we produce nowadays, the theorist can employ what he calls the cost computation; that is to say, these goods are made up by using different combinations of certain staple factors of production, the great staple materials, the various kinds of ordinary and not very highly skilled labor and the various kinds of mechanical equipment. The theorist can run the analysis of most of the products back into terms of factors of production which are common to all these products and in that way get a sort of common denominator. Then an analyst can reckon in terms of the utilities of units of the common denominator, the cost goods. By deciding questions of greater and less with reference to the utilities of units of these common factors of production, he has a way of deciding problems relating to the utility of various units of all the different products which can be made from them.

S1: In that case does Wieser mean pain cost?

M: No, not pain cost, but he says with reference to labor that its importance to us is derived from the importance of the things which labor makes. There are a great many kinds of labor which are widely used for different things; that is to say, labor is one of these great staple factors of production. You attach a marginal utility of one unit of any common kind of labor by working backwards to the marginal utility of some one of the things that is made by it. Since labor enters into the production of a great many other different things, you can carry over the marginal utility derived from one of its products to any other of its products and in that way you have a way of comparing utilities straight down the line so far as the goods can be broken up into these common factors of production. There are, however, cases where you cannot break goods up in this fashion; that is to say, there are goods which are more or less unique in themselves (specific goods), or they are produced by factors of production which are more or less unique (specific means of production). In that case, says Wieser, there is another method of solving the problem of economic control. We find out to what among the goods which can be analyzed into common factors of production the particular unique good is equivalent in utility. For instance, a sable skin is a highly individual thing. It cannot be broken up in any genuine sense into a regularly organized set of costs. But you can tell whether the satisfaction of wearing a sable skin will be greater or less than the satisfaction of having a piano in your home. You can tell whether it will be greater or less than the satisfaction of sending your child to a fashionable school every year. You can make a series of comparisons in that sense and find some utility which is just the equivalent of the utility to you of that sable skin; if this other utility which is just about equivalent to it can be broken up into terms of cost, then you have a method of bringing the unique good itself into the general scheme of rational control.

The difficult problems begin to appear when you consider the complexity which an economic plan must assume in a situation where there are very many unlike goods to be considered. There the question arises as to how you can get any unit in terms of which you can apply the calculus, the goods themselves being qualitatively dissimilar. Wieser's answer to that problem is that in modern communities the great bulk of the products which people have to use, well or ill, are made by combining in different ways certain great cost goods such as coal, iron, labor, capital, all sorts of productive equipment and materials. He argues that whenever you have one and the same cost good, let us say pig iron, used in a considerable number of different productive combinations you can get enough equations by considering these different combinations to determine what productive value a unit of pig iron has. Then you treat all units of pig iron as having the same productive value. You can do the same thing with all kinds of common labor and with all kinds of materials which are at all widely used. The result is that people are able at the present time to analyze qualitatively different products into costs to arrive at a certain marginal utility. That makes it possible for people to plan with reference to their cost goods and to the bulk of products in such a fashion as to use every unit of their highly diverse supplies for the satisfaction of that want which yields the greatest utility.

A more serious difficulty, theoretically, appears in the case of those comparatively few goods which either because of their scarcity, their uniqueness or because of very important qualitative differences among them cannot be applied to more than one use. That makes trouble because it prevents you from breaking up these goods in terms of cost goods and carrying them into your general cost calculation. But Wieser says there is a way of surmounting that difficulty. Because of the fact that people can discriminate relations of equality among utilities, it is always possible for people, even in the case of an absolutely unique article, to relate it in a systematic fashion to the rest of their economic goods. That is to say, the individual can determine what utilities of the ordinary sort just balance the utility of the unique article. Then he ascribes to the unique articles a utility equal to that of the balancing goods and he is able accordingly to use even his unique articles as elements in a comprehensive economic plan.

Application of the proposition to different cases. (1) To a single good. (2) Different units in a stock of similar goods. The units taken separately. The units taken as a stock (value equals marginal utility times number of units). (3) Reduction of different units to comparable form. Two methods: (a) Resolution into equivalence with cost goods makes possible comparisons among products which are made by use of the common means of production. (b) Where we deal with unique articles not resolvable into equivalences with common means of production, we can find what articles thus resolvable are equivalent to them in utility at the margin. Thus [in both cases] we know little about total utility and where we have to reckon in terms of it; e.g., in considering the desirability of building strategic railways, our reckonings are vague. But we can order our usual economic affairs systematically by telling merely which utilities are greater, equal or less.

Three limitations: (1) When changes in methods of production occur they distort the relations between products and their cost goods. (2) Comparisons between different economies, and between times far apart for the same economy are not feasible because the utility units have not the same meaning. (3) The calculus becomes misleading when the fall in marginal utility outruns the increase in number of units. Then production must be guided by calculation of total utility and as said before total utility is vague.[19]

S2: What is the basis for the utility calculus on Wieser's analysis?

M: That is the next question that arises. Does all this mean, Wieser asks, that people do their economic planning in units of utility? He answers, "No." They do their economic planning in units of different

---

[19] Outline, "Wieser," APP 84-91, no. 35.

kinds of goods. They count in bushels of wheat, in tons of pig iron, in yards of calico, etc. But every unit of a commodity is at the same time a unit of utility, so that when people are counting in terms of bushels of wheat, they are at the same time counting in utility units.

When the person talks about tons of pig iron, he is at the same time talking about things that get their significance from their utility, about things that are not only physical units, but also utility units.

S3: Does the utility change in the process of production?

M: It may.

S3: The utility of the cost goods?

M: When you get a thoroughly organized situation Wieser would say that you impute to the cost good from the beginning of its entry into the process of production the utility which is derived from its contribution to the general product. That is to say, the pig iron which is made into watch springs has weight for weight, a much higher utility in watch springs than it had originally in the shape of crude pig iron, but the importance that you attach to the weight of pig iron entering into the watch spring depends upon the marginal utilities of pig iron itself, whether you make it into cooking ranges or cannon or watch springs. This is the utility that you attach to the pig iron throughout the whole process of its manufacture.

S3: Then the watch has no value of its own. If it does, then the cost value, the value of the cost good does not somehow or other affect it.

M: The reason why the watch spring has a much higher market value than the pig iron is that in order to convert pig iron into watch springs one has to use a great many other cost goods besides the pig iron itself and the final value of a watch spring is the sum of the values imputed to these several costs—all the labor, all the machinery, etc., that is required. Of course, that sounds like a reduction of values to the cost basis; that is to say, it sounds like a denial of the fundamental Austrian doctrine, but Wieser points out that this is, after all, only one step in the process of tracing value back to its original sources.

The next question to ask is what determines the value that is imputed to each of the cost goods whose sum makes the value of the watch spring; and he answers, the value of each of the cost goods depends upon its marginal utility, and to find that marginal utility you have to consider all the different uses to which pig iron is put, to which labor is put, to which the other elements which enter into the watch spring are put, and those marginal values are derived from the values of the products into which these things enter, so that you have to begin at the other end, a double process. The value of all kinds of cost goods is derived ultimately from the importance attached to the satisfying of wants, and then from the contribution which these cost goods make toward the satisfying of wants he establishes a standard value for each one of the cost goods. Then he simplifies the calculations from that point forward by allowing the cost goods to enter into his future proceedings on the basis of these standard unit values for them. You see, without reproach even from the Austrian viewpoint, that, taking any particular product, its value is equal to the sum of the values of the cost goods employed in making it.

S4: Does that sound like a circle? I don't see it.

M: Professor B. M. Anderson Jr. argues that there is circular reasoning involved here.[20] Let me go over it again and show where the circle is, if circle there be. The fundamental Austrian doctrine is that values are derived from the contributions that goods make to the gratification of people's wants. That is the ultimate source, this gratification. Pain cost does not count. How are you going to determine what contribution a given article that is used for many purposes makes to the gratification of our wants. You must examine its various uses and find out which among them is the marginal one. The marginal use will depend upon the applicability of the commodity in question to the gratification of different classes of wants together with the quantity of it available. If we had only half the amount of pig iron produced that we have at the present time, its marginal utility would doubtless be much higher. If we had double the quantity produced its marginal utility would fall much lower than it is. Its marginal utility is determined by the marginal contribution it makes to the gratification of wants. Let us suppose that the marginal use of pig iron is for making cooking ranges. Once that marginal utility is established and the price of pig iron is fixed on that basis, you count this marginal utility, or rather its representation in prices, as *the* value of pig iron for the time being and you use that value in guiding you in all other uses of pig iron. You will try not to use pig iron in the making of a product where the quantity involved at the price will not give a return which will be worth the outlay. You proceed in a similar way with all the other cost goods.

S2: How do you determine the amount that each factor of production contributes to the product?

---

[20]Anderson is discussed in chapter XVII.

M: That is done by the celebrated theory of imputation. Menger was the first of the Austrians to raise the particular problem in his *Grundsätze*. He did it by talking about the value of a horse and cart. He asked how the theorist can tell what is the value of a horse separately and of a cart separately, when the use that the individual wants to make of them requires both together? How can the theorist break up the joint article, horse and cart, into the value of its two components? He answered that the theorist should see first what he would lose if he broke the cart; secondly what be the loss if the horse died. Wieser taking up the same illustration said in effect, "Menger is wrong, because if you broke the cart, the whole combination for the uses that you have in mind would be gone." Then he would have to turn the horse that was left to some other use than that of dragging a cart so that if the original value of the two together was put at a hundred, and your cart was broken, the horse would have a value left, say, of only twenty. Its value in that other use would be less than its value in combination with the cart. On the other hand if the horse died and the individual had nothing but the cart left, he could not use it in the desirable combination of horse and cart; he would have to use it for some other purpose, say, a platform on which to build a henhouse roof, and in that case the cart by itself would have the value perhaps of only ten. On that basis the cart is calculated to have a value of eighty, because the horse which is left would have a value of only twenty, and the horse alone is calculated to have a value of ninety. That is to say, the value of each one separately added together is ninety and eighty, or one hundred seventy, whereas the two in combination was only one hundred. That, says Wieser, is an obvious absurdity.

How does the theorist meet the difficulty? He cannot avoid the absurdity if there is only one combined use from which the value of both factors must be obtained. To solve a problem of that sort the theorist needs as many equations as he has unknowns. If he had two combinations in which horses and carts entered then he would be able to figure out a rational solution by the theory of imputation. Wieser says in practice there is a long list of what, as said before, he calls "cost goods," a great many different combinations of combined utilities and costs as numerous as the unknown values of the costs which the theorist is seeking to discover. By setting up these equations and solving them, the theorist practically works out the value of each of the cost goods considered by itself.

This describes Wieser's central conception of economic planning, and how it is conducted by the means of the utility calculus, limited as it is essentially on his view, to ability to discriminate relations of equality and difference between utilities. On his argument the individual or theorist knows very little about such things as consumers' surplus and producers' surplus. To repeat, all that he can do is tell relations of equality, greater and less. How much greater one utility is than another, he is not in a position to say unless he can bring other terms into the comparison, and state that between two different objects, say, a grand piano and an apple he finds an indefinite number of things that have utilities greater than the apple, greater successively than earlier members in the series, but less than the grand piano; but the actual measurement of utility, and therefore of consumers' surplus is out of the question. This is the general doctrine which is propounded as the theory of the simple economy. In his view that is the essential foundation of economics upon which all the rest of the theory is built.

Supplementary note on "General Principles of Imputation" from *Natural Value*. Menger finds value of a production good by considering diminution of product which would result from its loss. But when heterogeneous elements which affect each other's working, cooperate, the injury by loss is greater than the gain by cooperation. Suppose three goods produced ten units of value and if any one is lost the other two alone will produce six units of value. Therefore by Menger's rule value of one good is four and of three is twelve—though together they produce but ten. "The Principle Solution": Production goods enter into many combinations producing different values. This gives a large number of equations from which we can deduce contribution of each factor. "The productive contribution . . . is that portion of return in which is contained the work of the individual productive element in the total return of production." The sum of the contributions equals the value of the total return. [Or to use Wieser's words, "The sum of all the productive contributions exactly exhausts the value of the total return."] Difference between Menger's and Wieser's solutions: Menger assigns to each factor the share dependent on its cooperation. Sum of these may exceed value of product. Wieser says he assigns to each factor its actual contribution in cooperation. Living horse adds less than dead horse deducts. Imputation of productive contribution assigns to each production good an effect greater than it could obtain alone, but less than might be expected from dependence of complimentary goods on its cooperation. Value of production good depends on share in production thus imputed to it. If our imputation is at fault, production would be injured for we will make an insufficient or excessive use of the given good corresponding to its too high or too low value. "Imputation and the Marginal Law": Where production goods are in stocks, imputation follows the marginal law. Though used to produce different values of product, the value of all similar productive items must be similar, and can only be that derivable from the least valuable product.[21]

When Wieser goes on to discuss the theory of the social economy, he is primarily concerned to show how differently the value problem is worked out in society from the way it is worked out by the single individual alone, whom we have so far considered. The difference between the simple economy and the social economy arises in his eyes primarily from the existence of inequalities between men. These inequalities he regards as a necessary result of the relations of leader and follower. It is characteristic of men that, in whatever group that they are found, they are not all equals. Some are in the lead, exercising domination, directing; others are following. More than that, in the large modern communities there is a certain hierarchy among the leaders; some are conspicuous personages exercising coercive authority. Others are so inconspicuous as to be more or less anonymous and influence their less energetic fellows merely by example. These relations of inequality which are characteristic of all human organization on all planes are represented on the economic plane by differences of income. This means that the utility units in different families do not have the same meaning. A pound of pig iron may mean a great deal more to a poor family than to a rich one, and if that is not obvious, it is obvious in Wieser's eyes that a pair of shoes means more to the poor than to the rich. The upshot is that in the social economy the same rational economic planning which is characteristic of the simple economy cannot be achieved.

Satisfaction cannot be maximised for society as a whole, because the wealthier people will be able to carry satisfaction of their several wants down to a much lower grade of intensity than the poorer people can, and that means that society in very large measure is expending its energy in producing commodities for the rich which satisfy wants of comparatively slight intensity, while large masses of poor people are left with intense wants not satisfied in any considerable degree. There is no possibility of working out a neat balance between marginal costs and marginal utilities, because the poor in their anxiety to increase their incomes are forced to incur costs much greater than the utilities which the commodities they produce will possess when these goods are consumed by people of large incomes.

Furthermore, Wieser points out that even competition under the modern relations of inequality does not give society the most effi-

---

[21] Outline, "Wieser," APP 84-91, no. 35; quotations from *Natural Value*, translation into English by C. A. Malloch (London: Macmillan, 1893) p. 88.

cient possible industrial leaders, for the reason that competition even when free is not equal. In business a man with large means has a conclusive financial advantage over an abler rival whose financial standing is much lower. It means in general that the whole system of prices is not fixed by social marginal utility. It represents rather a stratified social marginal utility running back to the difference of income per family possessed by the various social strata.

> In short, fundamental fact of social inequality which results from leadership and subordination results in inequality of influence on calculation. Hence: (1) Price is not fixed by social marginal utility, but by stratified social marginal utility. (2) Marginal costs do not tend to equal marginal utilities. (3) Competition does not assure most competent leaders, for competition is not equal.[22]

It is interesting to observe this, because the Austrians are sometimes represented as mere apologists of the present social order. Wieser distinctly is not an apologist. He does indeed hold the view that relations of inequality among men are inevitable, that men are not born equal and that dissimilarity is something that cannot be denied on the economic plane any more than in any other relation. Some people can sing better than others and that fact is not more patent than that some are better workers than others, can produce finer products or more of them.

Wieser also holds that the institution of private property is fundamentally a sound economic institution. He endeavors to support that view by a brief historical sketch of the rise of private property. It came about in the society in which he is interested by the breakdown of a thorough going system of governmental regulation which was characteristic of the medieval epoch. He goes back, of course, primarily to the German past, to the time when there was a wide-reaching system of governmental regulation for all branches of production and of all classes of prices. This system gradually gave way to one of private property and free enterprise, because the communities which practiced a larger measure of freedom flourished better than their regulated rivals. It was because of the inherent economic features of free enterprise and private property that that institution came to play the dominating role in modern economic life; and he says that one cannot deny that an institution which has thus arisen on its own merits is fundamentally sound.

But he goes on: the recognition that private property is beneficial does not involve the corollary that no governmental regulation is

---

[22] Outline, "Wieser," APP 84-91, no. 35.

desirable. Quite the contrary, because it is in accord with the philosophy of private property that the government should attempt to prevent this institution from developing its own characteristic series of abuses. A monopoly is an abuse. Anything which gives particular individuals a chance to get an advantage not due to their inherent superiority is questionable, and governmental authority may well intervene to keep that measure of freedom and equality in the economic sphere which is necessary in order that the institution of private property should work out its best social results. He gives a brief sketch of the general measures which he thinks desirable to check monopoly and other abuses.

Perhaps I ought to say again a word about the technical theory of distribution which Wieser inserts in the section on the social economy. His theory of rent is essentially the Ricardian one. Land on the whole is not to be regarded as a cost good, rather as a specific good; that is to say, different pieces of land differ so much in quality that a separate imputation of productive value has to be made to each particular farm or each particular field. The imputation of what the particular land produces as compared with other lands is practically what Ricardo gave in his differential theory of rent. Wieser's theories of interest and wages are both primarily productivity theories; that is to say, interest in the economic sense is that part of the marginal product which is imputed to the use of capital, and wages is the specific product which is imputed at the margin to the laborer. His theory of profits is primarily a residual claimant theory. Profits proper is the sum imputed to the capitalist's successful management. If his management is unsuccessful he loses, and the loss is imputed to his lack of skill in assuming the responsibility of production. So much for the chief points of Wieser's theory of the social economy.

His section on the economic theory of the state is again devoted primarily to the task of showing how the new problem differs from those which have already been solved. The point of crucial importance is that in its economic planning the state does not operate on the same basis as the private enterprise. The private enterprise is conducted primarily in terms of money profit and loss, and it considers commodities and labor on a pecuniary basis. The state, he argues, considers commodities on the pecuniary basis, but it does not consider labor purely on such a basis, for to the state the working man is himself a citizen whose welfare is of interest to the state itself.

Again, according to Wieser, the state economy differs from the private economy in that the state assesses the costs of its services on a different basis from that which is possible to a business enterprise. A business must meet its costs by selling at prices which consumers can be induced to pay. The state covers expenses primarily by assessing its subjects according to the rule of equal sacrifice, which is very different.

The state economy also differs from the private economy in that more often the state makes use of the idea of total utility instead of marginal utility in its calculations. For example, a business enterprise will seldom engage in any venture where the return will not cover the outlay as ordinarily computed. The business enterprise in figuring its return and its outlay can go on the basis of marginal costs and marginal receipts, but suppose that the building of a strategic railway in a nation is being considered. If the government has undertaken it and if the railway will pay not only strategically, but also as a business enterprise, then the state can do its accounting in ordinary terms, but it may well happen that the strategic railway will not pay commercially, and still it may be very desirable from the viewpoint of the national interest that it be constructed. In that case there cannot be effected a nice balance between the sums that are laid out for building the railroad, and the sums that come back from its operation. You have on the contrary to set off against the cost which is made up of the prices that are paid for iron, timber, land and labor, etc., the vague estimate of the total utility of the railroad after it has been constructed, a total utility that cannot be reduced to marginal terms. On the other hand there are a few additional cases where the costs themselves cannot be rated in marginal terms, but must be rated in terms of general disutility.

The last section dealing with the theory of the world economy brings out primarily two points. The first is that economic life in the world at large is not as highly organized as that within the several nations taken separately. The result is that there cannot be brought about as thorough and successful an economic utilization of the world's resources as is possible within the state, let alone as is possible within the limits of a single family. Within the single family one particular plan can be carried out which will secure a tolerably certain maximum satisfaction, for all its members can be counted as of equal importance by the member who is doing the planning. In the social economy this is not possible because of the inequalities among different members of society. The state cannot altogether reduce these differences and should not aim to do so; but it can, so far as its own economy is concerned, effect a tolerably complete and systematic plan by taking as its guide interest from the national viewpoint. When it comes to the world at large without any general authority, systematic economic planning in the common interest is not feasible. The possibility for planning insofar as it has a world basis is even more imperfect than planning inside the limits of a given state.

The second point that Wieser brings out in the section on the world economy is that there is economic justification for a policy of protection, on the ground that the development of a country's resources does not depend so much on natural as on human resources. It is much more a matter of what kind of people will constitute the nation, the diversity of knowledge and training that they shall acquire and practice, than it is a question of the differences in fertility of soils, abundance of mines, etc. Wieser says knowledge of technical processes, of industrial equipment, do not flow readily across international borders. It is desirable that each nation should adopt a commercial policy with reference to other nations aimed at producing the fullest utilization feasible of its human resources and that means getting diversified industry. The best way to accomplish that is to protect infant industries against the competition of more powerful foreign ones.

S4: What is the argument against that last point?

S5: Free trade tends to lead each nation to do what it can best do.

M: It does not necessarily follow that it is diversification within each nation but it is diversification for the world at large. For instance, if New Zealand were adapted primarily to grazing, the whole world would use all New Zealand for a pasture.

S5: I was thinking about the whole world.

M: Wieser was thinking about diversification within each country taken separately.

S5: If the human resources which were within the country were of one kind.

M: This is precisely what he says is not true; namely, that there are these diversifications in the country. He does not make this plain, it is true. That is my interpretation of his argument. The real point is the contention that differences of native ability in men are more important than differences in soils, mines, forests and other so-called natural resources.

S3: Does he hold that protection is needed, because there is no world government? If there were, would he still hold that protection would be desirable?

M: I do not know what he would say about that. If there were a central world government it is possible there would be a greater degree of fluidity among men, and in that case every man might move readily to the place where work for which he was adapted could be done to advantage. Possibly this is the line Wieser would take. I do not know.

Wieser's *Social Economics*, to repeat, is a discussion of what economic conduct ought to be, not what economic conduct is. It is normative not positive in kind. It is a logical scheme not a psychological account of behavior. To make a psychological account of how people behave, to get a positive science of economic behavior, it is necessary to use history, statistics and psychology as aids in accumulating and utilizing the materials. Wieser explicitly says that just as soon as the economist goes beyond the materials afforded by the treasury of economic experience in every man's mind and begins to collect additional data by historical or statistical methods, he ceases to be an economic theorist. That is to say, in Wieser's view, economic theory is strictly limited to the discussion of how effective economic planning can be conducted on the basis of economic experience which is common to every individual of the race. But if the economist really wants to know what people do, he cannot rely on speculation which he bases simply on his own economic experience.

No man's experience is broad enough to afford an adequate basis for showing what economic behavior is for large numbers of men. He has to have recourse to a collection of materials such as is afforded by history and statistics. Furthermore, if he wants to understand how people behave in any serious sense, it seems a great mistake to bar out, as Wieser explicitly does, recourse to psychology. For if the psychologists have accomplished anything of value, they should have something to contribute to all the sciences that are trying to understand human behavior in any of its aspects.

From this point of view then, it would seem that economic science, as Wieser presents it, is again an extremely limited type of theory. It is not so strictly limited in scope as is the "pure economics" of Joseph A. Schumpeter and some of the more famous mathematical economists such as Vilfredo Pareto, successor of Walras at Lausanne, but none the less, it has narrow limits and, so long as it stays within those limits, it cannot be developed into anything like an adequate account of economic processes. At most it contributes a keen and elaborate analysis of the logic of economic planning from a larger viewpoint. It would seem, in other words, that what Wieser undertakes is a part of the general task of economic science, but it is a very different part from what he himself thinks that it ought to be.

In his eyes the basis of all economics is planning in terms of the utility calculus by the single household, if not the single individual. This is the foundation of rational control in Wieser's view, and when the analysis leaves the single household, and goes into social relationships, the system becomes less definite. There is less possibility of securing the maximum utility in an organized community. From a more thoroughly psychological viewpoint, however, it appears that the systematic control over economic behavior is much less highly developed among single families, living more or less in isolation, as they do upon the frontier, than in modern communities.

The finest development of economic planning, of a systematic control over economic activity with a single aim in view, is found in great corporations conducted on the basis of accounting and insofar as we have succeeded in systematizing economic conduct it has been primarily in those places where there are great masses of people highly organized and working under very different institutional arrangements. In other words, the place where one finds the fullest development of a logical control over economic conduct is not, as Wieser thinks, inside the family, but it is precisely inside of organizations of a business character which have unified control on the basis of accounting. The modern man, that is to say, the man who lives in the modern community, who gets his training in economic life from business relationships, presumably carries over a considerable part of that systematic habit of thinking and planning into his family life. So far as a careful and elaborate control over the family expenditure, it is probably gotten primarily as a reflex from daily concern with business, with the use of money. In other words, if the theorist wants to find in a psychological sense the foundation for systematic economic control, he has to find it more or less along such lines as Thorstein Veblen has pointed out, in the habituation of a certain set of activities which have gradually grown up in modern communities, particularly the set of activities which center around the systematic use of money, as a means of guiding conduct.[23] That is one of the points, as was previously mentioned, on which Marshall lays considerable

---

[23] See below, chapter XX.

stress, though he does not develop this precise ground. He points out that money greatly facilitates the task of the economic theorist, precisely because it simplifies and systematizes the task of practical economic control. This is a bit of insight that the Austrians have never attained. They still fancy, in the spirit of Bentham and the whole set of hedonistic writers, that the basic element in control is a calculation of utilities, that this is something that the untrained man, the man who is not experienced in business affairs does for himself and his dependents, and that on the basis of calculations in terms of utility there is erected a more or less perfect social control.

Summary and conclusion: 1. Simple economy. The economic calculus. Basis— ability to discriminate greater, less and equal intensities of desire. Suffices to enable us to use economic goods wisely. This calculus gives us not equations but wavering boundaries of utilities. 2. Social economy. If society were made up of individuals all equal, pursuit of economic interest under rules of simple economy would maximise utility. But it is not. Instead we have social stratification which warps values. 3. State economy. Object is to promote general utility by checking monopoly advantages, yet maintaining private property and caring for common needs which are not commercially profitable. State takes social utility into account both in deciding on expenditures and in dividing the cost. 4. World economy. Less highly organized than state economy. Tendency to establish an equilibrium much weaker than within a state. Free trade not necessarily advantageous. Protection is justified.

Comments: Wieser claims to be psychological. But it is a queer psychology. In fact his theory is a logical rather than a psychological scheme. Tells not what behavior is but what it ought to be. It is to him a normative not positive science. What would happen if one took psychological viewpoint seriously? (1) Objective study of economic behavior: Statistical method; historical and comparative methods. (2) Subjective study of economic behavior: An analysis of institutional factors in behavior. Stated another way, the positive sciences we need: historical and statistical apparatus— which Wieser rejects. Also need serious psychological analysis. Wieser's attitude toward psychology. From this viewpoint the logic which he expounds is a part of the economic situation. But it is not a system of calculating utilities (at its best in the simple economy), as much as it is the disciplinary effect of use of money (at its best in accounting).[24]

The class will now deal with the foremost Austrian of the present generation, Joseph A. Schumpeter.

---

[24] Outline, April 20, 1920, and "Wieser," APP 84-91, no. 35.

[It has been claimed that Wieser's work appears to have been influenced by the "purists" on the one hand and the historical school, particularly Max Weber's "economic sociology," on the other hand. (F. O. Seth, "Wieser's Simple Economy," *The Indian Economic Journal*, January 1963) p. 245.]

CHAPTER XV

The Pure Economics of Joseph Alois Schumpeter and Vilfredo Pareto

Joseph A. Schumpeter[1] (1883-1950), while studying at the University of Vienna, was in the beginning a militant representative of the views of the German Historical School. ["His first serious work in economics seems to have been done in what we would now call a statistical research seminar conducted by the eminent economic historian and statistician, K. Th. v. Inama-Sternegg, in conjunction with Franz v. Juraschek."][2] Later he came under the influence of Wieser, who had succeeded to Menger's chair; and at the same time he read a good deal of the works of Léon Walras. He regarded himself as a pupil of these two masters, combining the mathematical method which Walras employed by preference with the general Austrian theory of value.[3]

After receiving his doctor of law degree in 1906 he practiced law for a period. In 1909 he accepted the professorship of political economy at the University of Czernowitz. Czernowitz was then the capital of the Austrian province of Bukowina but is now [1918] a part of Russia. Two years later he transferred to the University of Graz. In 1913-1914 he was exchange professor at Columbia University.[4] [He served as the first minister of finance of the Austrian Republic from March to October 1919. In 1921 he became president of a highly

---

[1] [Except where otherwise specified, the section on Schumpeter is from the "1918 Typescript."]

[2] Gottfried Haberler, "Joseph Alois Schumpeter, 1883-1950," 1950, reprinted in *Schumpeter: Social Scientist*, edited by Seymour E. Harris (Cambridge, Mass.: Harvard University Press, 1951) p. 26.

[3] Schumpeter thinks he stands nearest to Léon Walras and Wieser. See Schumpeter, *Das Wesen und der Hauptinhalt der theoretischen Nationalökonomie* (Leipzig: Duncker und Humblot, 1908) p. ix. (Outline, April 4, 1917.)

[4] [It was at this time that Mitchell and Schumpeter began their long friendship. Mitchell's diary at the time has such entries as:] "October 15, 1913 . . . Met Schumpeter at Columbia. He attended my lecture [in Types].... October 27, 1913. Schumpeter attended my lecture and then came home with me to talk over economic theory. . . . November 3, 1913. Schumpeter attended my lecture and went to lunch with him and he talked on economic theory."

Upon hearing that Mitchell had accepted the offer of a permanent appointment at Columbia in 1914, Schumpeter wrote him that the news was "gratifying to anyone who wishes well of Columbia University. . . . I rejoice in the thought that you will as a matter of course rise to a position of leadership in our science, and let us hope,

respected private banking house in Vienna, the Biedermann Bank. When the bank collapsed in 1924 in the stabilization crisis that followed the great inflation,] he returned to the academic world as a professor at Bonn in 1925, in order as he put it "to make up for lost time and to exploit his practical experience as well as new ideas."[5] After serving as visiting professor in 1927-1928 and in the fall term of 1930, he accepted a permanent post at Harvard.

He was a man of most extraordinary energy and while still under thirty published two books which are generally regarded as among the most important theoretical studies in German for the decade 1908-1918. The first, to which most attention will be devoted, is *Das Wesen und der Hauptinhalt der theoretischen Nationalökonomie* ("The Nature and Main Content of Theoretical Economics"), published in 1908. Four years later appeared a sort of supplementary volume, *Theorie der wirtschaflichen Entwicklung,*[6] which dealt with certain important economic problems for which he could find no place in "pure" theory, in the static equilibrium which he discusses in his first book.

Fortunately the gist of Schumpeter's pure theory can be put in comparatively brief compass. By and large the first book reminds one a little bit of some modern types of mathematics. There is a kind of mathematics which consists in giving logically impeccable proof of propositions of which the reader is convinced until he begins to question. Schumpeter develops substantially just one important thesis which is the most important result of Walras's speculations. What he adds to Walras is an elaborate methodological discussion of what he is going to do, the way in which he is going to do it, the limitations of what he has done, and finally the importance of the results which he sets forth. He states the starting point of the general problem before him in the following terms: "We observe the

---

leave it in a state different to what it is now. . . . The University affords really unsurpassed possibilities of creating a school of thought of your own, and believing as I do in personality, I am looking forward greatly to seeing you, from the other side of the Atlantic, having your own. . . . Please convey my felicitations to Mrs. Mitchell and tell her that we—she and I—ought to be proud of you." (Schumpeter to Mitchell, undated).

There was considerable difference of opinion on Schumpeter. "Some of my German correspondents think he is a great man; I am not so sure of this, but he certainly deserves attention." F. W. Taussig to Roswell C. McCrea, August 8, 1912, in Joseph Dorfman's possession.

[5] Schumpeter to Mitchell, April 30, 1926; quoted in Joseph Dorfman *The Economic Mind in American Civilization,* 5 volumes (New York: The Viking Press, 1946-1959) IV, p. 166.

[6] [The second revised edition (1926) was translated by Redvers Opie in 1934 as *The Theory of Economic Development.* This book will be referred to under its English title.]

group of concrete results which is commonly called pure economics, and ask ourselves how we can get possession of these results with the slightest expenditure of apparatus and principles." That is to say, the real task of pure economics is the task of finding how the essential results can be demonstrated with the utmost economy of intellectual means. Here again one is reminded of a characteristic of modern mathematical work. It is considered a great advance when a known truth can be demonstrated by some simpler method than that which has heretofore been employed. It is viewed as putting any branch of mathematics in better shape when the whole body of propositions that makes up that particular branch of mathematics can be established by a shorter intellectual road.

Schumpeter says his aim is to find out how a body of concrete results, known as pure economics, can be attained in the simplest fashion with the smallest number of assumptions and general principles. He starts out in this manner: "Let us observe any given economy"—meaning by "economy" a system within which economic behavior is going forward, where men have made plans, figure out the significance to them of various goods, and then carry out the plans. If "we observe any given economy, we find that every individual economic subject possesses certain definite quantities of definite goods. At the basis of our discipline there lies the knowledge that all these quantities, which for brevity we shall call economic quantities, stand in mutual dependence upon one another." It would be a little better and would make better English to say that all these quantities mutually depend upon each other—"in such wise that the alteration of any one of these quantities produces an alteration of all the others." "That," Schumpeter goes on, "is a simple fact of experience so obvious as scarcely to require investigation. We express this fact by saying that the economic quantities form the elements of a system." A system means some organized whole. We do not ordinarily lay stress on the meaning of system in our daily use of the word, but that idea is very distinctly implied. When you speak of things as making a system you imply that there is something systematic; that is to say, that these things are related to each other in certain definitely established ways. "This system as a whole may be perfectly arbitrary, but the various elements within the system cannot be arbitrary, because they have certain definite relations with each other." The economic subject may be in possession of any given mass of goods which the theorist has in mind. It is purely arbitrary what mass of goods the economic analyst supposes him to have, but the relations among the various goods in his possession are not an arbitrary matter.

Schumpeter then asserts that the task which the pure theorist has to perform is to study these relationships among the goods in possession of an economic subject. In particular he is anxious to determine the conditions under which the individual or the social economy may be in a position of equilibrium; that is, in a position in which there is no tendency to alter the relationships that exist at a given moment within the system. To repeat, he is particularly interested in discovering the condition of equilibrium; the condition under which the various goods will be so adjusted to each other that there is no tendency present in the economy to effect any further change. It is "our task when any given condition of a social economy is presented to us to deduce such alterations of the quantities as may be expected to occur the next instant if nothing unforeseen turns up. This deduction is what we call 'explanation.' It is accomplished by description of the relations of mutual dependence; that is, we may regard our task as the description of our system and its tendencies to change. This gives the whole discipline of pure economics. The conclusions which we deduce from our description are economic laws, at least they are so regarded when they have sufficient generality. The material of these laws makes up the discipline of pure or theoretical economics." Notice how carefully Schumpeter limits the task which he proposes to perform.

He goes on at considerable length to lay down further limitations. There are several important points in this discussion. In the first place he holds that all economic activity which is possible under conditions of static law may be regarded as agents of exchange. In a social economy the different economic subjects may exchange goods or services with each other; they may also produce, but producing goods may be regarded as exchanging, as trading the individual's productive efforts against the storehouse of nature, and getting in exchange for his work certain commodities that he desires. The general problem of describing the changes in his economy is that of describing conditions under which exchange will take place, and the amount of exchanging which will go forward, including the exchanging with nature which is commonly called production. With that view of the task of economic theory, the necessary basis is found in demand schedules. The schedules, Schumpeter says, are ascertained by asking each one of the individual economic subjects how much he would give for an additional unit of any of the economic goods in the possession of this social economy, and then how much he would give for another unit of the good. In other words, the theorist would keep questioning every individual as to what he would just be willing to part with in order to get another either by exchange or labor, and record his answers.

The answers will give a full picture of each individual's demand schedules, and from this full picture of each individual's demand schedule for every kind of good in possession of the social economy the theorist can if he so desires cast up average demand schedules for that economic society as a whole, the social economy. The one general characteristic of all demand schedules, says Schumpeter, is that the demand curves have a declining direction and toward the right. Further, [following Davenport and Wicksteed,] he holds the theorist can attain greatest simplicity by regarding what are ordinarily called supply schedules as simply another set of demand schedules. When a man comes into the market ready to sell certain goods at certain prices, the theorist is justified in saying that he is a man who is offering certain prices for certain other goods, so that the supply schedule is simply a disguised demand schedule. Among the things that are needed for the solution of the general problem of exchange then are demand but not supply schedules.

Schumpeter thinks that the theorist borrows unnecessary trouble in talking about supply schedules. He argues that the theorist makes himself grievous intellectual difficulties from a strictly logical point of view if he tries to reckon both the utilities and disutilities. The disutilities can be thrown out of the reckoning by treating supply schedules as demand schedules. "For we are treating the problem of exchanges on the basis of these demand schedules. We have further to assume a thoroughly static state." That is to say, the theorist must admit no changes in demand schedules themselves, no changes in methods of production, because such changes would alter what are ordinarily called supply schedules; that is to say, they would alter some of the demand schedules. We must consider primarily brief periods of time also for a logical end, for a practical reason.

Theory of prices: assumes free competition. Tendency to establishment of equilibrium. Costs. Cannot interpret them as disutility. Hence interpret supply curve as a second demand curve. This method enables us to discuss problem of prices of producers' goods.

General theory of prices or rather of exchange. The problem is determinate. Use of money is a logical necessity following from the supposed situation. A great triumph of abstract theory.[7]

As Schumpeter keeps reminding the reader, the entire apparatus of pure political economy is very abstract and unrealistic in its char-

---

[7] Outline, April 2, 1917.

acter, but the apparatus interests the theorist because it enables him to understand, better than he otherwise could, an important set of experiences. He sets up his assumptions solely for the purpose of getting insight into these experiences. He therefore forms his assumption, which logically he has a right to make in any way he likes, with a view of making them as useful in interpreting facts as he can. They become less useful, however, the more the assumptions themselves are contrary to fact. The necessary assumption that no changes take place in demand schedules collides seriously with the facts of the case, if the theorist applies the discussion to long periods. On the other hand it is substantially in accord with the facts if the theorist has very brief periods in view. So for that practical reason he assumes that the time which he considers is a brief period.

Furthermore, it is assumed that there is perfect competition. This means not only that everybody in the market knows what prices are being offered and accepted by other dealers for the goods that are being dealt in, but also that every person is at liberty to trade anything that he has just bought a minute before if he finds an opportunity of making a gain thereby.[8] These are the most important assumptions, and we are ready to see precisely how Schumpeter formulates the general problem of exchange, and the solution that he gives.

His formulation is, to repeat, a simplified version of the central discussion in Walras's treatise on pure economics. The theorist must observe a problem in definite form, have a perfectly definite list of data. Those things being given constitute his problem. Schumpeter says take a social economy made up of m individuals and n different kinds of goods. Then the theorist will have to know the value functions of each individual, for each kind of good, these value functions being what are ordinarily called demand curves. Schumpeter prefers the term "value functions." The theorist knows the demand curve of every individual for every kind of good, and finally he knows the quantity of each kind of good in the possession of each of the m individuals. Schumpeter says there is required by way of solution first the ratios of exchange between each of the n kinds of goods $(n-1)$; second the changes in the quantities of each kind of good in the possession of each individual (mn).

Let us stop a moment to see how this problem differs from the one which is ordinarily presented in the theory of prices.

---

[8] Assumes individualistic viewpoint because it is most prolific of valuable results. (Outline, April 2, 1917.)

S1: I did not understand the second point.

M: I will repeat the whole thing. There is required first the ratios of exchange between each of the different kinds of goods and second the changes which will occur in the quantities of each of the different kinds of goods in the possession of each individual in the economy.

S2: Please explain again just how he makes clear that a supply schedule is a demand schedule?

M: Suppose that a person is thinking of himself as belonging to Schumpeter's social economy and as having apples which he is willing to sell at different prices depending upon the amounts which he is considering parting with. When he says that he is ready to sell apples at certain prices that means that he is ready to buy other things by giving apples in exchange, so that one may regard the schedule of supply prices of apples as a demand schedule for the other things which he is ready to take in exchange for his apples.

To come back. Let me call your attention to the difference between Schumpeter's way of stating the problem of exchange and the way that is followed in the ordinary text books. In the latter, the expositor commonly begins the theory of prices by considering the market for some particular commodity, and asks what prices, what ratios of exchange will be established between this one commodity and the common medium of exchange. Schumpeter instead of taking a single commodity takes n commodities, any number that the theorist likes, and he asks, not what is the ratio of exchange between two commodities, but what is going to be the ratios of exchange between all the n commodities. It is a much more general problem. In the second place, in treating the theory of exchange theorists do not ordinarily concern themselves with the changes in the quantities of goods that are going to take place among the different individuals. Sometimes the assumptions are drawn in such a fashion as to show how much every individual will sell, and how much he will buy. That, however, is not always the case. Schumpeter on the other hand supposes that he knows in advance exactly how much of every commodity each individual in his market possesses. Among the things that he insists upon working out is the amount of each one of those goods that every individual will part with or receive. He supposes that certain of these individuals may at the outset possess none of certain kinds of goods. That is as definite an assumption concerning the quantities that they possess as if he supposes that each one had a certain quantity of each good. Further it is possible that the quantity of a certain kind of good that a certain individual may exchange will be zero, but that again is as definite a result as if it is supposed that he sold four horses or bought two apples.

The problem is of much wider scope than the usual one in the theory of prices. It undertakes to view the operations of a whole community of people at one time, and to treat those people as buying and selling not one commodity, but n commodities. Further it seeks to know not only the ratios of exchange among all these different commodities at the same time, but also what quantities will change hands.

Schumpeter demonstrates that this kind of problem is soluble by showing that the theorist can set up from his data a number of equations which is precisely equal to the number of unknowns. In mathematics a problem is theoretically soluble when this can be done. Let me show how Schumpeter works out the solution. To repeat, this is only another version of Walras's major performance. What are the number of unknowns? To find out the theorist in the first place takes the ratios of exchange among all the goods. If there are only two goods, there will be just one ratio of exchange. If there are three there will be two ratios. In general the number of ratios of exchange among n commodities is n minus 1.

S1: Are there not variations or combinations?

M: Those are all reducible to this n minus 1. For instance suppose three commodities, apples, pears and peaches. There is a ratio of exchange between apples and pears, between apples and peaches, and between peaches and pears, but the ratios of exchange between peaches and pears is deducible from the ratios of exchange between apples and pears and apples and peaches, so there are only two real equations represented in the data and if there be a fourth commodity, there would be three and so on. Then the second thing that the theorist would want to observe is the number of changes in the quantity of each commodity in the possession of each individual. The number of changes in the quantity is m individuals times n goods. That is to say, each individual may theoretically change the quantity of each one of the goods in his possession, therefore the total number of unknowns is mn plus n minus 1. He has n minus 1 ratios of exchange, and mn possible changes in quantity. This problem will be a determinate and soluble one if there are neither more nor less than mn plus n minus 1 equations.

Let us see how many equations the data enables the theorist to set up. The data consist of the supposition of m individuals and n different kinds of commodities, the value functions of each individual for each good, and the quantity of each of the different kinds of goods in the possession of each one of the different individuals. From these data the theorist establishes three different sets of equations. The first set is given by the fact that exchanging will stop when each individual has so altered his stocks that the marginal utility of increments of each of the different commodities is the same. In other words, the individual's motive for exchanging stocks is gone when another increment of a commodity would bring no more gain in utility than the individual would lose by parting with one increment of another commodity. The marginal utility of each good must equal the marginal utility of every other good for every individual.

How many of those equations are there? We have to take two individuals since we are supposing an exchange here. Suppose there are just two commodities in their possession. That number would be one equation for each person. If there are two people and the goods in their possession are apples and pears, then they will reach equilibrium in their exchanging when an additional increment of apples has the same marginal utility for A as an additional increment of pears, and the same is true of B. In general you get a number of equations which equals the number of individuals multiplied by the number of commodities minus one.

A second set of equations that can be set up is concerned with the necessary equality between the total amount of every one of the goods sold and the total amount of that same good bought. In the market under discussion where there are n commodities being exchanged, the total amount of goods sold by the original possessors must equal the total amount of the same quantities of goods bought. That is, the theorist can say for the good, apples, for example, that the whole amount of apples sold by people who sell will be just equal to the total amount of apples bought by another set of people. This is a truism. How many of these equations are there? Obviously there is one such equation for every kind of good. That is to say there are n of these equations.

S2: Why do you say the *total* amount is equal to the total amount? What is meant by "amount" here?

M: Suppose there are fifty bushels of apples sold by one set of people. You will also find if you cast up the purchases of apples that there are fifty bushels of apples bought by other people. That is true of apples. It is separately true of pears. It is separately true of any one of the other commodities.

S1: What kind of equations would they be?

M: They would be twenty-five bushels of apples sold by A plus eighteen bushels of apples sold by B plus thirty bushels of apples sold by C and so on, listing all the sales. Similarly I could put down all the apples bought by Z, by Y and by X. Cast up all these different sales and they will just equal the total amount of purchases.

S3: I am not quite sure about your mn there.

M: In the first one? Take one of the parties in this exchange. Before he stops trading, he must establish an equality of marginal utilities of additional increments of all the goods in the market. He will stop when he has attained such an equality. That means that the marginal utilities of different goods will be equal to his. How many equations of such equality of marginal utility can he set up? If the individual has two commodities he has one equation. If he has three commodities he has two. If he has four commodities he has three equations. That is to say, each individual will have a number of equations of marginal utilities for the different commodities at the close of the exchange equal to the number of commodities dealt in minus one. That will be true of each of the individuals. Therefore for the m individuals the total number of these equations will be m times n minus one.

S3: You have $mn + n - 1$.

M: This is the number of unknowns. What we are trying to do now is to see if the number of equations is equal to the number of unknowns. I explained at some length why we know that the number of unknowns is mn plus $n - 1$.

S3: That is the thing I am not clear on.

M: The things that we seek to know, that is the unknowns, are first the ratios of exchange among all the different commodities and in the second place the amount of each commodity in the possession of each individual. There will be changes in the possession of each commodity of each individual. How many of the ratios of exchange are there going to be? There are going to be one ratio of exchange for two commodities, two ratios of exchange for three commodities, three for four, and so on. That is to say there will be $n - 1$ ratios of exchange. How many changes are there going to be in the possession of commodities by each individual? There are m individuals. Each individual may make a purchase or a sale of each different commodity. Therefore there may be mn of those changes in the amounts of commodities possessed. Adding this mn to the $n - 1$ number of ratios of exchange we have as the number of unknowns, $mn + n - 1$.

Perhaps it would be better to start over again. Pure theory as Schumpeter sees it centers in the problem of exchange. The chief point in the book is showing how this particular problem can best be handled from the theoretical viewpoint. As I explained, his method of approach is peculiar as compared with the procedure that we have seen in other books, because he attacks the problem, not in detail, but as a whole. In the treatises with which we are familiar so far, you usually find the writer beginning his discussion of prices by taking up a market in which there is one article dealt in. What Schumpeter does is to take up a market in which there are a great many commodities being exchanged at the same time, and in which there are a large number of individuals. The point of his theory is to show that this particular kind of problem is theoretically soluble.

Let me go over the part presented at our last meeting, and then conclude the exposition very briefly. He says that if we are going to discuss the problem in a definite fashion, we must have definite suppositions; so we will suppose that we have the following data: a market including, first, m individuals, second n commodities, third, that we have what Schumpeter calls the "value functions" of each individual for each of the n commodities and, fourth, that we know the quantities of each of the n commodities in the possession of each of the m individuals. Given these data we have to show that it is possible to solve the problem of exchange, and the solution implies that we shall know the rates of exchange at which trading will cease for all of the n commodities—and that we shall know second what quantities of each of the n commodities are parted with and acquired by each of the m individuals. That is to say, we need to have the following results: Equations of exchange between each of the n commodities—the number of these equations is obviously equal to the number of commodities minus one; that is, we need n minus one equations. In the second place we must have equations which will show the quantities of all the commodities every individual has traded away or acquired, and these results are equal to the number of individuals multiplied by the number of commodities. That is to say, we need mn results of this sort. What we require then, in number, are the following results: $n - 1$ ratios of exchange; mn alterations in the quantities of commodities possessed by each individual; the total number of our unknowns. Adding these gives mn plus $n - 1$.

The solution consists in showing that we can set up a number of equations precisely equal to the number of the unknowns. What number of equations can we set up? In the first place, we know that trading cannot stop until the marginal utility of each commodity to each trader has been made equal to the marginal utility of every commodity to each trader. If you have just one individual and two commodities of course that means one equation of equivalence in marginal utilities. If you have two individuals and two commodities that means two such equations. If you have two individuals and three commodities that will mean two equations for each individual. In general you have as many of these equations of the equivalence of marginal utilities as there are individuals times commodities minus one. That is to say, you can set up m times n minus one equations of marginal utility. Then in the second place you know that the total amount of each one of the commodities sold by sellers must equal the total amount of those corresponding commodities bought by buyers. How many of these equations will there be? Obviously just as many as there are commodities. So we have n equations concerning the quantities bought and sold of each commodity. That is the point at which we arrived at our last meeting.

There is one other set of equations which the theorist can set up. We know that from the point of view of each individual the total commodities bought must equal the total amount of commodities sold. If the individual is in the market buying and selling he has to go on with the trading up to the point where everything that he parts with is equal to everything that he has gained. That will be true for every one of the individuals. Therefore there will be m of these equations.

$m(n-1)$ equations of marginal utilities.

n equations of quantities bought and sold.

m equations of commodities bought and sold by each individual.

S1: What is the difference between this and the other equations?

M: Here the theorist thinks in terms of the total transfer of goods and says that the sum of 500 apples, 4 horses, 25 ounces of gold, 100 yards of cloth, etc., all the things that are sold, when added together, will equal that same mass of commodities that is bought. To repeat, the theorist here is concerned with equations of total transfers of goods. In the other equations he takes the point of view of the individual, and having m individuals in the market he adds for each one of them all the commodities that he bought and all the commodities that he sold, asserting that these two quantities are equal.

S1: I understand in the second kind of equation four apples bought equals three pears sold.

M: Let me put it this way. Are you familiar with the system of bank clearings?

S1: No.

M: Then my illustration would not help. I will give it in another way. You have a great mass of different kinds of commodities being dealt with in the market and there are a good many different people who sell commodities. They sell them in very different lots. One man may sell ten apples, and another man 1,000 apples, and a third 25 apples. These commodities are bought by people in different quantities. One man will be buying 100 apples; another 75, and still another man 100. You know, however, that the total amount of these quantities of apples sold must equal the total quantity of the apples bought.

S1: Yes.

M: You know that is true for each of the n commodities. Take the point of view of each of the m individuals. When an individual trades five apples for four pears, if he is satisfied, that means that the five apples are equal to four pears for him. You can set up all the various things that a given individual sells on the one side and all the various things that the individual buys on the other side. The theorist can say that those purchases are equal to those sales. Then he has an equation for each individual's purchases and sales.

S1: I see just one equation. You say there are n equations.

M: This is true for every individual in the market and there are m individuals.

S1: With the n equations I saw just in that moment only one equation.

M: That is true for every one of the n commodities taken separately.

S3: Each individual sells only one kind of commodity.

M: No. The theorist starts out knowing the quantity of every commodity that is possessed by every individual. In a good many cases some individuals are without certain of the n commodities, but the theorist knows that they possess the quantity zero. The theorist can start with any kind of assumption he likes regarding the quantity of commodities possessed by any individual.

S3: In that case would not the theorist get more than one equation for each individual?

M: One equation of what?

S3: One equation of exchange for commodities bought and sold.

M: You mean under this caption? What the theorist does is to say with confidence at the end that the individual's total purchases and total sales must be equal, but the theorist cannot affirm with confidence that in every one of the exchanges that the individual makes there will be an equation from his point of view, for the reason that an individual may buy something that he does not want merely because with that something he can get something else that he does want. So all the theorist can be sure of is that when the market closes, when all the trading is done, the individual's total operations will represent an equivalence of purchases and of sales.

Let me go over that again. Suppose an individual in the market with a large stock of apples, and he wants to get an ounce of gold. At some point in the trading he may see a chance to get the gold by giving the man who has it some leather which he will take though he does not want any apples. Accordingly the apple-holder may take the apples to a third individual for some leather that the apple-holder does not want. That exchange really does not represent an equivalent to him. He is giving apples which have perhaps some slight value to him for leather that he does not want at all. But the leather he can afterward trade for the gold that he wants. When the operation is through the theorist can be sure, if competition has been perfectly free, if all the three suppositions are rigidly true, that what the individual parted with will be equal to what he has gained, in his eyes, and he cannot be sure until the individual is through. Therefore the theorist has only as many equations of that character as there are individuals in the market, one for each person.

S4: All those are taken care of in those two equations?

M: I do not see quite what you mean.

S4: I mean all those different steps of buying and trading.

M: Yes. They all take place in this market.

S4: All those equations cover all those intermediate cases?

M: Not necessarily. In the case which I discussed, giving apples for leather which he does not want, it is not true that the apples equal the leather.

S4: It is in the end.

M: Yes, in the end. Any other question?

S2: I do not quite see it. You say the apple-holder does not want the leather.

M: That is just my supposition.

S2: I am taking the supposition that he wants the gold, and to get it he has to get the leather. In that sense he wants the leather, because he needs it to get the gold.

M: He wants the leather, but regarded in and of itself it is not the equivalent of apples to him. That is a mere intermediate step which does not interest him for itself.

S3: Supposing I possess both the apples and the leather and exchange both those sets of commodities for two other different commodities, I will get two sets of commodities.

M: That is to say, it may be that in one of the separate exchanges that an individual makes a perfect equivalence is worked out. It might be possible for instance that the apples that he parted with for the leather just equalled the leather in his eyes. That is quite conceivable. But that is not something that the theorist knows in advance. The one equation that he can count on and therefore put into the demonstration is the ultimate equivalence of what the individual has parted with and what he has gained. There may be a lot of other equations as matters happen in this trading, but the theorist is not sure that they will be there.

There remains one more step. If the equations that have been obtained are added up the theorist finds that the problem is over determined, there is one too many equations. To demonstrate, multiply that through and the result is $mn - m$ plus n plus m. Cancelling minus m and plus m, there remains mn plus n equations, and the number of unknowns is mn plus $n - 1$. If a problem is over determined it means that it is not necessarily sound. The way out is this: Observe that the equations which are inserted from the point of view of the individual and the equations which are inserted from the point of view of the commodity overlap to the extent of one. That is to say if there are n equations of this sort, and the theorist has equations for every individual but one, he could get the equation for the nth individual by combining these equations for all the other individuals with the equations under n. That is, one of these equations may be deduced from the other equations, n equations for the commodities bought and sold. In other words, one of these equations is implicit in those equations, so that after all the number of independent equations is mn plus $n - 1$.

S4: I am not sure.

M: About that last point?

S4: I do not know whether you have a right to say that.

M: Let me restate that proposition.

S4: I mean, the last one about one of those being contained.

M: When the theorist is taking the point of view of the individual he is saying that all the commodities that every individual buys are just equal to all the commodities that that individual sells. When he takes the point of view of the commodity he says that all the different quantities of commodities bought are equal to all the different quantities of commodities sold. He has two totals which are equal to each other; that is to say, from one of the totals plus all of the equations but one that enter into the other total he can deduce the equality of the second set. In other words there is one equation overlapping.

S4: You have practically thrown one out.

M: It is thrown out, because it is already implicitly in the data that you have.

S4: Then what is the purpose of presenting it in the first place?

M: The answer is that it is easier to make the explanation in the other terms, just a matter of convenience in exposition, and then afterwards the theorist observes the implicit inclusion of one equation either in n or m, as he likes, in the data that he has already obtained. The question is: what is this scheme good for? What is the advantage of this way of presenting the theory of prices or, if one likes, are there any serious disadvantages attending this way of presenting the theory of prices?

S1: It wants to show on the one side that it is possible — if we would want to count all those things—to fix prices with those different equations. On the other side it just wants to give that absolutely decided answer on whether it is possible to fix it or not.

M: It is a demonstration that theoretically the problem of the determination of prices of many goods exchanged by many individuals in a single market is soluble.

S2: Herbert J. Davenport answers that in a non-mathematical form.

M: Does he? That brings up an instructive point. Remember that Davenport in his discussion of the price of any single commodity states that among his data the theorist has to include many other prices already determined; that is, he cannot explain the price of one commodity without reference to, without having knowledge concerning, a good many other commodities; so his theory of prices as he puts it is circuitous. He explains price by price, the price of one commodity by the prices of other commodities. Is Schumpeter's scheme open to the charge of being circuitous?

S2: When this man makes out his schedules the fact that he does not say that any one price is determined by the others does not make it the less true that each price is thereby determined.

M: Wait a moment. The data which Schumpeter assumes here are what he calls value functions. They are not prices; they are price offers. They show how much that individual, with reference to his own feelings, would be ready to give of any one commodity for successive units of any other commodity, and the theorist has to get for each one of the individuals as many value functions as there are commodities minus one.

S2: But Davenport in speaking of the same thing reminds the reader that it is an individual economy, and then he says that each individual is making up his mind as to the marginal utilities of all these different commodities in the market, and that includes sellers and buyers, and then when he has talked about that he says eventually there is a market price, and each individual has done his share. The present system [Schumpeter's] cannot get away from that.

M: What does this present system accomplish with reference to that point? Does it try to get away from the interdependence of prices?

S1: It shows that those different facts are determined through the mechanism of the market itself. When Davenport says that process is going on in every individual's mind, he is asserting a similar interdependence.

M: Schumpeter regards his theory as having an almost surpassing advantage in that it demonstrates the mutual dependence of prices on each other, also the dependence of quantities of commodities that are going to be exchanged. This is exactly one of the things that he wants to show, and he says his scheme shows it more clearly than ordinary expositions. Davenport more logically than anybody else that I know comes right out with the conclusion that his whole reasoning concerning prices is circuitous, and the only way that he sees to get behind the circuitous explanation of prices in terms of prices, that superficial pecuniary analysis, is to refer the theorist to the real underlying factors, and those factors are men's wants, productive capacities and technological equipment; but he does not succeed in establishing what the connection between these underlying factors and the pecuniary analysis is. His theory is weak just at that point. Schumpeter's procedure is one line of attack on the problem which demonstrates the interdependence of prices, at least as well as Davenport's way, but which does not suffer from the same defect of being circuitous in its reasoning. It takes all the prices at once and presents a scheme by which the theorist can conceive of their mutual determination in a single market—taking all the prices at a single time, and working out one problem of prices in such a fashion that the mutual interdependence of the process of determination is almost startlingly apparent, but not being open to the charge of being circuitous by explaining prices by prices.

S2: If he wants to take all the prices at one time, and then determine prices, how does he avoid ignoring what makes those prices what they are, which is after all the real forces?

M: You must remember what Schumpeter starts with, what his data are. He says what the theorist needs, in order to state the problem clearly, are assumptions concerning the number of individuals, the number of commodities, the quantities of each commodity in the possession of each individual and the value functions of each individual for each commodity. These value functions are obtained by going to each individual in turn and asking him concerning each one of the commodities in turn, "How much of some other commodity are you ready to give for another increment of the commodity we are talking about?" and the theorist records his answers. When he gets through he has that individual's value functions for every commodity in the market. He knows how much each individual will give for an additional increment to the stock which he already has on hand of any particular commodity the theorist chooses for any other commodity that the theorist is talking about. The theorist does not inquire what determines him to give just these quantities. That problem Schumpeter regards as lying outside the realm of pure theory. The theorist just takes the individual's answers to the questions as to what he would give as things with which the theorist is going to operate, but not investigate.

S2: But why is it a weakness for Davenport not to be able to make a connection between prices and real forces?

M: The theorist wants to get as much insight as he can into the processes of modern economic life. What Davenport gives is an elaborate analysis of these processes in pecuniary terms. But he announces with characteristic candor that the kind of explanation which he gives for any given money price involves a tremendous number of other money prices as necessary for an explanation; that is, the pecuniary analysis does not get back to anything else than other prices. The theorist explains one price by another price, and so clear around a circle. Davenport says that for purposes of the entrepreneur it is quite satisfactory to account for the selling prices of a product by the money cost of producing it, but the economist wants to do more. He wants to have an understanding which is less superficial, and the only way to do so, says Davenport, is to inquire into what lies behind this whole complicated set of interrelated mutually determining money prices. The answer to that question leads back to the underlying facts which are human wants, productive capacities and instrumental equipment. Further it is not satisfactory if the theorist merely says that the whole set of interdependent mutually determining money prices is fixed by these three factors. Davenport does not work out the relation between instrumental equipment and prices, between productive capacity and prices. He does not undertake to show what the relation is. He asserts that it is so, but does not explain it. Thus his *Economics of Enterprise* is, as he acknowledges, weak on that point.

S2: Schumpeter also says, if I understand you aright, that he does not go back of prices either. He says that does not belong to pure economics.

M: He goes back of prices. He shows what the theorist has to have in order to state and solve the problem; namely, the value functions of each individual for each object, the quantities of each object in the possession of each individual, and how many commodities and individuals there are. That is to say, he does not assume prices to explain prices. He assumes individuals, goods, stocks of goods in possession of individuals, and value functions of individuals for goods. Those data, however, he does not explain.

S5: The value of it is just a mental exercise, a very beautiful type, something entirely scholastic, and utterly devoid of any practical value, because, to repeat the things that you said last year [in the same class], a super-human intellect would be required to make use of this number of equations, if m and n are large, therefore the practical value is reducible to nothing. After all the only thing is the statement of the interdependence of prices. I do not see that we make any further advance. When we make this number of equations here, we cannot make use of them.

M: Let us see what your statement amounts to. Suppose that there are 1,000 individuals, which of course is not many for a modern community, and a thousand different commodities in which people are interested. How many equations would be needed?

S5: 1,000,999.

M: mn plus $n - 1$ or 1,000,999. It goes without saying that present [1918] mathematical technique is not sufficiently advanced to handle a set of 1,000,999 equations,[9] so that this scheme could not be worked

---

[9] [This was said in 1918, long before the day of modern computers, but Professor Mitchell's statement still stands.]

out in practice. That is granted. In general, attention is called to that limitation and a great deal of stress is laid on the fact by other pure theorists, although Schumpeter does not emphasize this particular defect. But if the theorist had all the data, could he solve his equations in complicated cases? In the second place can he get the data?

S5: This is another thing that I wanted to bring out. Schumpeter assumes that the value functions of each individual for each commodity are so clearly stated that he can put them into an equation.

M: Precisely. That is another difficulty with the practical application and Schumpeter lays a great deal of stress upon it. He explains that the theorist cannot really get these value functions, that if he should go around and ask these questions, no matter what sort of governmental authority he had behind his questions, he could not get out of the individual's consciousness anything like the knowledge that he would suppose necessary. Thus his scheme operates on the basis of data that cannot be had, and it is further a scheme that he cannot work through even if he had the impossible data. Does this mean that the scheme is of no value, no significance?

S6: It seems to me it carries through very clearly the orthodox way of attacking the problem, and I do not see that there is much difference between the people who say that actual market prices are determined by these schedules and people like Davenport. Schumpeter definitely says all this is not practical.

S1: This scheme has great theoretical value, although it has no practical value. It shows where the psychological school of Fetter leads, and where our limits are. Naturally no theory is in this regard to be applied. We never could, but just for the theory I regard this as one of the greatest achievements, because it is such a wonderful logical sort that shows us the end of the psychological school.

M: That is, a sort of *reductio ad absurdum.*

S1: But it is a wonderfully logical work, and it seems to me as if it were the end of that school, as if nobody could go further than that, because we see how little we could do with it further. Therefore I regard it as very valuable.

M: This achievement is not Schumpeter's at all. It belongs to Walras. Remember that when I discussed Jevons I took occasion to point out that Walras had a much better grip on the problem than Jevons ever obtained. Instead of treating single commodities one after another, he generalized the problem and treated all commodities at one time. He was the one man who tried to face the central difficulty of economic analysis: namely, the mutual interdependence of the quantities with which we are dealing, and this is the way of stating that. The criticisms which S5 has brought out clearly are valid. Their justice is recognized without dispute by the pure theorists themselves. If the thing has any value its value must be quite independent of immediate practical applications to anything on a large scale. What is claimed for it is substantially what S1 said, that better than any other way it helps us to see the problem of price determination as a whole, to appreciate the existence of mutual dependence among prices, and the baffling character of the situation which results from this mutual dependence. Are there any other questions or suggestions about it?

S7: Because it emphasizes the inductive method it tends to stimulate statistics and work in figures rather than abstractions and deductions.

M: I think that is fair.

S1: I see there is one other great achievement in Schumpeter's book besides the part which we took up. It has the other happy advantage that it shows exactly what the field for theory is, that it is in this sense pure theory.

M: Later I hope to bring out this aspect of Schumpeter's work a little more clearly.

S8: Is there any theory that can be applied practically?

M: That is one of the interesting points on which Schumpeter comments. As a matter of fact the characteristic value of Schumpeter's treatise lies, not in the presentation of the doctrine of Walras, but in discussing the limitations of economic theory of the pure type and what I want to do shortly is to show just what he thinks this kind of thing is good for, apart from the general survey that it gives of the mutual dependence among different prices.

I want to carry the exposition of Schumpeter's system of pure economics a little further before discussing the general significance and value of this line of attack on our problems. So far all that has been discussed is his central doctrine of prices. Out of this doctrine he proceeds to develop the theory of distribution. The idea that the theory of prices can be applied also to the theory of distribution is thoroughly familiar. All the theorist has to do is to include the factors of production, from the selling of which people get an income, among the goods which enter into the generalized markets, that is to say the theorist treats them as being among the n commodities that are being bought and sold, and theoretically the general scheme provides for the determination of their prices. Consequently it provides for the determination of the prices of commodities.

The unusual aspect of Schumpeter's analysis of distribution is his doctrine that in the static state—and his theory applies only to the static state—there are only two shares in distribution: wages and rent. There are no profits and there is no interest under static conditions. A considerable number of other theorists have excluded profits from the static state, for they have argued that the only element, belonging to what we call profits at the present time, that can remain in the static state would be the payment for the entrepreneur's services. That payment is often treated as wages. There would be substantially no risk; therefore there would be no payment for risk, and no profits in the narrower sense. Walras for instance, in presenting his general system of theory, took the ground that profits would be zero, and Schumpeter agrees with him. What is peculiar to Schumpeter, what he regards as his original contribution to pure theory, is an attempted demonstration that interest is not a static category, that in the static state no interest would be found.

This is a very difficult doctrine to understand. Schumpeter's way of demonstrating it is to show that neither of the two great explanations for the existence of interest would be valid in the static state; that is to say, either as arising from the productivity of capital or from time discount. Therefore there would not be any interest. Interest could not arise from the productivity of capital, because the full value of the product of any piece of capital such as a tool would be attributed to the tool itself. At the present time it is taken for granted that any instrument of production will have a value less than the value of what it contributes to the physical product. The difference is at least equal to interest on the value of the capital during the time when the capital is locked up, but, says Schumpeter, there is no ground for thinking that there will be a margin of undervaluation of tools. On that basis people could not discount them.

But why would there not be time discount in the static state? For the reason that there is no ground for thinking that people would undervalue future gratifications. The static state implies that production would run substantially the same round year by year; that is to say, it takes for granted that the supply of commodities for satisfying wants is going to be no greater in future years than at the present time, and no less. Under these circumstances people would lose marginal utility if they applied any part of what might be the supplies of the future to wants of the present and they would equally lose marginal utility if they applied any unusually large proportion of what might be present supplies to making provisions for the future. That is to say, saving would be a losing proposition on any considerable scale, for it would mean withdrawing commodities from present consumption. That would raise the marginal utility of commodities at the present time. The saving on the other hand increases the supply of commodities available for satisfying wants in the future. That would force down the marginal utility at the later period. Therefore, the man who interfered with the equilibrium of the distribution in the supply of goods as between the satisfaction of present and future wants would lose marginal utility.

This had better be restated because it is the crucial point of Schumpeter's argument. Suppose that in the static state where production does not vary substantially in volume from year to year there is an equilibrium attained in the uses of commodities as between different periods of time. The equilibrium on general logical grounds would be one that would keep the supply applied to each year's needs substantially constant, corresponding to the constant production. If under the circumstances the individual should begin to save, this would diminish the quantity of goods applicable to the present year's wants. That would mean that the marginal utility of the goods consumed this year would rise. On the other hand the increase in the amount of commodities applicable to wants in the future years, when used in those years, would diminish the marginal utility which goods would then possess so that the individual would in the long run be a loser by his saving. Conversely, he would be a loser by pursuing a spendthrift policy of increasing the amount of commodities which he consumed this year at the expense of the stock which he would have available for consumption in future years. On that basis Schumpeter says that there is no room for time discount, and a commodity is as valuable to the individual whether it is expected to be had next year or the year after, as if it were in his hand at the present time. Consequently in the static state there are only two shares in distribution: wages and rent.

Schumpeter points out a curious consequence of the denial of the existence of interest. If there is no interest, the value of every piece of land must be infinite, by logical necessity. Any permanent use-bearer will have a value equal to the total value of all the future uses which it may yield. If the use-bearer is really permanent then no matter how small the value of its present use, the value of the use-bearer itself becomes infinite.

S7: The interest is 100 per cent.

M: No. The interest is zero per cent.

S7: You can put it that way if you want to. That is to say the interest and the capitalization are synonymous.

M: Yes, that is to say the discount is zero. If time discount is zero there is no time discount. Is this demonstration that in the static state the price of every piece of land is infinite a *reductio ad absurdum*? How can Schumpeter deal with this apparent difficulty?

S7: If he does not recognize interest then he would not recognize zero interest either.

M: If you do not recognize zero interest that means that you do not recognize the future uses of land. Therefore to ascertain what is the value of a piece of land at the present time, you add all the future increments of value that it would yield, and since that is an indefinitely extended series, the sum is infinite.

S6: Is the static state of Schumpeter a time phenomena? It seems to me that it cannot handle any such thing at all. It seems to me instantaneous.

M: In a sense it is an instantaneous proposition. It also does not change with the lapse of time. It is instantaneous and also permanent. It is conceived in that way as a social state in which there are no substantial changes in methods of production, in population, in wants; in short, in any other of the vital factors.

S4: All the use-bearers then are permanent in such a state?

M: No, because some of them like tools get worn out. Then they are reproduced in precisely the same quantities. For example, at the very moment when a spade is so worn out that it goes on the scrapheap, at that moment in the well regulated organization of production another spade is forthcoming to take the place of the worn out one.

S9: Even in the static state things are not worn out at an even pace. They go to pieces more or less suddenly at the end.

M: I do not know that a theorist can hold quite to that, but to balance it he can say that the new one is being prepared, is coming on a little faster than the old one is wearing out. There is a perfect balance worked out. What can be done about the phenomenon of the infinite price of land?

S2: You would have to reckon it by the law of diminishing returns.

M: That law does not come into the scheme, for the reason that it is supposed that there is no increase in population, no change in methods of production and at any given moment land is cultivated up to a certain margin. Since that margin does not change, the question of diminishing returns is not considered. You might put this objection, that the fields are supposed not to be worn out, and the answer is quite right that they are not; but it is easier to conceive of the fields being maintained in a constant state of fertility than to think of tools of production being replaced just at the time when they are worn out.

S2: Will you explain again what you said about interest arising from productivity of capital?

M: It cannot arise from productivity, because the full value of what is produced by every piece of capital is attributed to the capital itself. For instance, if a person's possession of a spade will add ten bushels of potatoes to the crop that he is growing this year, then at the beginning of the year the spade is worth ten bushels of potatoes. The full value of the increment of production is imputed to the instrument of production itself.

S1: Individuals simply value the land as they would value other instruments of production.

M: No. If individuals value land at anything less than an infinite sum, then there would be a discount in their minds. That would be time discount and interest would arise.

S6: Does Schumpeter assume in the static state that people grow old and die, or that they remain always what they were at the beginning?

M: He conceives just as tools are worn out and reproduced, so people die and are reproduced. The population remains constant though the individuals keep changing.

S6: He could not value the other man's enjoyments, the man's whom he replaces.

M: At any given time, Schumpeter says, we have to conceive of this as the logical attitude for the population to take.

S6: He would have to treat land in exactly the same way as accumulated capital. How does he treat the value of capital in the static state?

M: The existing accumulated capital of course would have a value attributed to it on the basis of what that capital would produce. That does not make trouble, because the capital is going to be worn out, but among the accumulated things with which one starts are these pieces of land. Land has attributed to it the full value of what it will produce, but land will not wear out. It is not supposed to, and that means it will produce an infinite sum of values; therefore it is worth an infinite sum. Schumpeter's way out would be to say that land would never be bought and sold in the static state. What would be dealt in would be the uses of land.

Interest: Why interest does not exist in the static state. Tools, unlike land and laborers, are used up in process of production. Their value is the sum of values of their services. They are not a permanent source of income. But may not interest be involved in the prices of industrial equipment? No. Waiting and impatience play no role in the static state.

Criticism of interest theories: If future uses of land are undervalued, will not purchase of land at current prices yield a steady income which may be expressed as percent of outlay? Land itself will not be bought and sold in the static state but only its uses. Conclusion: Interest is not a static phenomenon.[10]

So much for Schumpeter's discussion of distribution. It is just an extension of his theory of prices. He develops the theory a little further by showing how his scheme could be used. The procedure is what he called the method of variations. The way to work it out is to start with any situation that the theorist likes; that is to say, with any given number of individuals having each of them different supplies of any number that the theorist wishes of different commodities, and the individuals having also definite value functions for each commodity. Then the theorist introduces a change in any one of these elements that he likes. He can change the number of individuals, the number of commodities, the stock that some individual has of a commodity, or the value function that some individual has for some commodity. After he has made the change in the data, he works out a new solution, and sees what alteration comes about in the results. In short, by the method of variations, the theorist varies his assumed data, one at a time, and ascertains what alteration that variation produces in the results. Schumpeter gives some examples of how this method may be worked out. The first, on pp. 478-479 reads:

> The simplest case is that of an isolated economic subject who produces only a single definite commodity with his means of production, this single commodity being applicable for nothing else than the satisfaction of his own needs. The demand curve here will be simply a function of his pain cost curve. Our man will produce so much that the marginal utility of the commodity will be just equal to the marginal pain of labor.

That is the supposition—a man producing one commodity applicable to a single use. Under the circumstances, working out the equations the theorist finds that the person has an equilibrium between the marginal utility of the last unit of the commodity that he can produce

[10] Outline, April 2, 1917.

and the marginal pain of his last moment of labor. That explains the method of variations. "Suppose that by some external power this isolated economic subject is required for the future to hand over a definite quantity of his product in each period of production to someone else." That is to say, suppose a tribute is levied upon him, a certain amount of his product. "What will happen? He will, under these circumstances, produce just so much that the marginal utility of the quantity of the good which remains to him after his tribute has been paid shall be just equal to the marginal pain of producing this quantity plus the quantity of the good that he has to hand over to somebody else. That is the precise answer."

On Schumpeter's basis if the man has to give away by tribute part of his product, he will then produce so much for himself that the marginal utility of the last increment which he consumes for his own satisfaction shall be just equal to the marginal disutility in terms of pain cost of producing what he consumes for himself plus what he has to give up by way of tribute. "We could," says Schumpeter, "if we had the necessary data prove that in general he will produce somewhat more under these circumstances than he was producing before the tribute was imposed upon him, but he would not necessarily produce the total amount of the tax in addition." That is to say, what was taken away from him would in part increase his pain cost, in part diminish the utility he enjoyed. This is an illustration of how to work the method of variations. The theorist starts with that very simple assumption, and he introduces a change in one factor, and then he finds how the result will differ from what he had in the beginning. That gives what Schumpeter calls a law of motion. Perhaps it is better to say a law of change. This is substantially the scope of Schumpeter's pure economics. The remainder of the book is an elaborate discussion of the logical characteristics of value; that is, of this type of economics. Discussion of that sort in general runs all through the book, and as S6 said at the last meeting one of the most characteristic things in the whole performance is Schumpeter's keen interest in *Erkenntniss Theorie*; that is, methodology, the way in which people get their results, what they really mean and what they are good for.

There are a number of important remarks that Schumpeter makes on that phase of the subject. In the first place, he points out that pure economic theory, as he regards it, is purely schematic in character. It simply provides a way of conceiving certain phenomena, a scheme of looking at them. He argues, however, that it is helpful in dealing with practical problems. We shall see that he is not extravagant in the claims that he makes for its practicability, but he wants economists to understand that a schematic way of conceiving phenomena is not necessarily a useless way, and may be the best way. For instance, in geometry the analyst neglects pretty much all the characteristics of bodies except extension, and yet for certain purposes that purely schematic way of handling materials is the best that mathematicians know. For certain purposes of the economists—the sordidly practical purposes—it is much clearer, much more effective, to proceed in a most unrealistic fashion, to fasten their eyes upon certain salient characteristics of the things that they have to handle and work out an elaborate analysis relating to them alone. The danger of such a proceeding is that the theorists may forget the limitations in the character, and therefore in the applicability of the results achieved; and Schumpeter is extremely anxious that no one shall overlook the limitations of the scheme which he has put forward.

In the second place, Schumpeter strenuously insists that pure economics has no dependence upon psychology or ethnology. It has nothing to do with these two branches of the science of human behavior. He says that pure economics is innocent of any dependence upon psychology, because it does not inquire into the forces which shape people's choices. It just starts with choice. That is a viewpoint that we already found developed in Davenport. It is the view that Irving Fisher stressed in the early 1890's. It is an attitude that has recently [1918] come much into favor among economists who are inclined to feel that there has been too much hedonism in economic theory in the past, and who do not know how to get any satisfactory substitute for hedonistic psychology. The common thing nowadays is to say that the theorist is going to start with choice, and it does not make the slightest difference what the factors controlling choice are. Schumpeter bears emphatically on that point. He holds that pure economics has no call to inquire into the psychological basis of valuation. The essence of the new theory lies in this, "*not* to analyze the definite scale of demand prices, but to accept it as the ultimate fact." The fact which we can observe is that after a certain point an individual will not offer so much for more units of a given commodity as he has offered for earlier units; "*why* he acts thus is not interesting from the viewpoint of economics."[11] In short, "Professor Schumpeter, following Walras, assumes as data for his general theory m individuals,

---

[11] Outlines, "Final Lectures," April, May, 1914. Quotations from *Das Wesen und der Hauptinhalt der theoretischen Nationalökonomie,* pp. 64, 72.

their respective value functions for each of n goods, and the quantity of each good in the possession of each individual, denying that the economist has any business with the psychological processes from which the value functions are derived."[12]

Similarly, he says that the theorist has no concern whatever with ethnology. His scheme is applicable to all men under all circumstances. Their state of civilization has nothing to do with the matter. Of course the concrete character of the theorist's data concerning wants, the number of different kinds of commodities that a given group would possess, the abundance with which every member of the group was supplied with these commodities, and the various sizes of the population group itself, all these factors would in concrete terms be very different at different levels of culture. If the theorist took a very rude type, he would find its members small in number, having few kinds of commodities that they produced and exchanged, and being scantily supplied with them. He would also find that they had a curious set of value functions for each of the goods. If he jumps from a savage state to the most advanced modern nation, he would find unlimited commodities, thousands of goods, enormous stocks, an altogether different set of value functions. Certain commodities that would be useless to the savage would be highly considered and some things that the savages set great store by would be out altogether. In Schumpeter's view, whether the theorist took the savage group or the modern community, it would still be true that if he could get the quantities of commodities in the possession of each individual and their value functions for each commodity, he could work out the results of pure theory.

Schumpeter asks: Is the developing of this type of economic theory worth the trouble? Yes, he answers, because in the first place it is intellectually interesting. The mainspring of science is curiosity. Men cultivate the sciences primarily because they like to do so; accordingly, to a person of an intellectual cast of mind the type of economics known as "pure" economic theory is peculiarly interesting because it can be put in such definite shape. It represents the possibility of rigorous thinking, instead of the vague process of general speculation

---

[12]Mitchell, "The Role of Money in Economic Theory," 1915; reprinted in his *The Backward Art of Spending Money and Other Essays* compiled and edited by Joseph Dorfman (New York: McGraw-Hill, 1937) p. 162. [It has been claimed that "Schumpeter changed his views in this respect later on. In his theory classes at Harvard and in conversations he often argued on 'psychological grounds,' using introspection in favor of cardinal utility or, occasionally, even for the possibility of inter-individual comparison of utility." (Haberler, "Joseph Alois Schumpeter, 1883-1950," *Schumpeter: Social Scientist,* p. 30.)]

which is typefied in the older treatises on economics. In the second place, says Schumpeter, his scheme is capable of certain practical applications. They are very few in number, but now and then there is a problem where the method of treatment is clarified by conceiving of it in his way; further there are for instance some simple cases of taxation where the theorist can conjecturally supply sufficient data, and can conjecturally limit the number of factors so as actually to work out something like a solution. In any case it is helpful practically, because his scheme gives a better way of conceiving the all important fact of interdependence than is provided by any other technique that economic theory has yet developed. But he admits that there are serious limitations upon its scope, and these are not confined to the matter of practical applications.

There are also theoretical limitations on its scope. In the first place, the theory applies to the static state alone. As Schumpeter explicitly says, the most important problems of economics are problems of dynamics and of cumulative change; and a man who wants to deal with them has to fall back upon very different and much vaguer lines of analysis. In the second place, he says that the restriction to the static state means a great deal more than most people realize, because it cuts out from pure economics not only profits, but also interest, savings, business cycles, etc.[13] No other theorist has limited his static state to so narrow a compass as has Schumpeter. No other treatise in economics professedly covers so slight a ground, and he recognizes, indeed emphasizes, that very strongly in his concluding pages, hoping that nobody will be misled into thinking his type of theory has a wider application than it actually possesses.

Finally he says that his line of approach will not explain even all static phenomena. It is quite possible that in the static state there may be interferences with perfect competition. There may be a condition of monopoly, and whenever that is the case this line of attack does not solve the problem. It is a little reckless to say "whenever that is the case. You can arrange certain problems in such a fashion as to get at least a start to the solution by this scheme, but in general such is not the case." Then, Schumpeter says, granted these limitations upon the scope of pure economic theory, what does economic science need and how does it progress? He says that there are several things that are perfectly clear. In the first place, pure economic theory needs no fundamental recasting; the foundation that Walras laid is solid.

---

[13] In his scheme, savings can be conceived in static equilibrium as exchange but they must be strictly limited or the situation will cease to be static. (Outline, April 2, 1917.)

The theorist's work is in the extension, the development of detail, not in the alteration of fundamentals. The way to develop the details is two-fold. In the first place, the theorist should elaborate the method of variations by setting up imaginary cases, altering one supposition after another and seeing what changes each alteration of the data will produce. The other line of advance for the theorist lies in the direction of trying to collect concrete data to be used inside the general scheme. He should try to find out the value functions that different individuals have for different goods; he should investigate stocks on hand, try to discover how many commodities are represented within the markets, etc., and then on the basis of the data, make theoretical examples which are not contrary to fact, but embody the results of his discoveries, and work out the results.

As for dynamic problems, Schumpeter points out that we have already concluded that no progress has been made by applying the general scheme to them. Here economists must use methods of economic history, statistics and description. I may add that this advice Schumpeter has himself followed in a measure in his later *Theory of Economic Development* [which he began while his first book was being printed.] This is devoted to certain dynamic problems.[14] It deals primarily with the problems of interest, profits and business cycles. It is based upon the assumption that there are two radically different types of economic men. In the first place there are the hedonistically minded men who are the proper inhabitants of the static state. In any modern population, Schumpeter asserts, the overwhelming bulk of people are not interested in change. They want to get their accustomed satisfactions, live their habitual lives. These are the people whose economic actions are adequately presented in pure economic theory. On the other hand in every great population there are a small number of peculiar individuals, innovators of one sort and

---

[14] In earlier periods [German theorists] applied British and Austrian theory; more recently have undertaken to recast and extend economic theory of prices, interest, crises, money, etc. Much influence exercised by Knut Wicksell and Gustav Cassel. Characteristic of the newer theoretical work in contrast to older is its interest in development. Classicists and early Austrians were static; so thoroughly so that when they treated a change, e.g., an increase in population, they supposed it to have taken place and then asked what alteration it would introduce into the pre-existing static condition. Newer men study the *processes* of change, primarily from viewpoint of enterprise. Dynamics is getting the upper hand. (From abstract of Julius Wolf, "Der Aufsteig der theoretischen Nationalökonomie," *Zeitschrift für Socialwissenschaft,* "Journal for Social Science", 1913 in "Types of Economic Theory Now Current in Germany," APP 84-91, no. 38). [Wolf was editor of the journal and professor of political economy at the University of Breslau. He had opposed Schmoller in the *Methodenstreit* and continued to attack the historical school. Schumpeter's work is referred to in the original German article.]

another, people who are making inventions, organizing new ways of doing things. They are not interested in satisfying their wants, but are driven by some inner devil which demands activity from them all the time at whatever cost. The innovators are the kind of people that in modern economic life make business enterprisers. To their activity is due the phenomena of profits, interest and business cycles. Because they see ways of changing methods of production they are ready to borrow and promise interest, and also to pay interest when they succeed. Because the result of the changes in methods exceeds the cost by margins larger than the interest they are called upon to pay, profits come into existence. Because of certain technical factors in the business situation that bring a dynamic alteration of ebb and flow in the changes of methods of production we have business cycles.[15]

The fundamental cause of business cycles Schumpeter finds in the innovations made from time to time by the relatively small number of exceptionally energetic business men—their practical applications of scientific discoveries and mechanical inventions, their development of new forms of industrial and commercial organization, their introduction of unfamiliar products, their conquests of new markets, exploitation of new resources, shiftings of trade routes, and the like. Changes of this sort, when made on a large scale, alter the data on which the mass of routine business men have based their plans. These plans doubtless involve a certain element of error; but business innovations produce a far graver situation.

Somehow, all enterprises must adapt themselves to the novel conditions now confronting them, or go to the wall. Considerable numbers do fail. A far larger number manage to work out new plans based on the new data concerning prices, costs, methods and markets. But this process of feeling out the novel conditions and making adjustments to them takes time. While the readjusting is under way, the making of innovations slows down; even the most restless of enterprisers cannot get the capital and cooperation required to carry out their schemes. This is the period of depression. It lasts until the readjustments have gone far enough to produce a fairly stable condition of affairs, stable enough to let men regain confidence in the future.

But the very restoration of quasi-stability makes it possible for the disturbers of the business peace to resume operations on a large scale. By borrowing for their new projects the innovators raise interest rates; by investing capital they raise the prices of industrial equipment and increase payroll disbursements. There follows an increase of demand and a rise in the prices of consumers' goods. The general activity thus initiated brings prosperity to the mass of enterprises—and stimulates further innovations. Prosperity continues until the unsettling consequences of the business changes begin to appear *en masse* in the shape of large supplies flooding the market, high costs of material and labor, shifting of demand to new

[15] Schumpeter's position is similar to that of J. B. Clark. But he develops a theory of business cycles out of the assumption that there is a special class of innovators. (Outline, March 17, 1937.)

products, the supersession of old sources of production by new sources, and so on. Then comes a new crisis and a new period of readjustments.

To complete this theory it is necessary to show why innovations themselves come in waves. Schumpeter explains that the combination of capacities required for conceiving new undertakings and carrying them through all obstacles and hazards is rare among men; but that when a few highly endowed individuals have achieved success, their example makes the way easier for a crowd of imitators. The rising prices, the increasing demand, the spread of optimism makes borrowers more eager and lenders less cautious. Men who do not have the capacity to originate new schemes may have the wit to profit by and even improve upon the work of the pioneers. So, once started a wave of innovation gains momentum—until it is checked by the consequences which it produces.[16]

But all this lies outside the scope of pure theory.[17]

Schumpeter's method of isolating monetary factors affecting price level. 1. Total incomes of given period equal total volume of goods produced times their prices. 2. Any change in volume of goods produced or of prices charged by one set of producers which produces a change in their money incomes must lead to a precisely compensating change in the sums of money spent by the body of consumers and savers upon other goods. 3. Hence the increase or decrease of money incomes of the first group is just offset by a decrease or increase of money incomes of some other group or groups. Hence no change in the left hand member of the equation implied by (1) can be produced by any change in goods or prices in the right hand member. 4. Therefore whatever changes occur in money incomes must be due to changes in the monetary factor. Thus if we could get adequate income statistics we should have reliable method of isolating the monetary factor in purchasing power of money.

To test Schumpeter's proposition: (1) Divide income receivers into three industrial groups, A, B, C. A and B represent specific industries. C represents remaining body of income receivers. Let A produce more goods, and sell at same prices so that income rises. Let income of C remain constant. Then what C spends for new goods made by A must be deducted

---

[16] "Dr. Schumpeter's first version of this theory was published in May, 1910: 'Ueber das Wesen der Wirtschaftskrisen,' *Zeitschrift für Volkswirtschaft, Sozialpolitik und Verwaltung,* vol. xix, p. 271. Successive revisions appear in his *Theorie der wirtschaftlichen Entwicklung,* Leipzig, 1912, chapter vi; "Die Wellenbewegung des Wirtschaftslebens," *Archiv für Sozialwissenschaft und Sozialpolitik,* July, 1914, vol. xxxix, pp. 1-32, and in the second edition of his *Theorie der wirtschaftlichen Entwicklung,* Munich and Leipzig, 1926, chapter vi. This latest version includes replies to several critics of the theory, and is written in the most emphatic tone." Mitchell, *Business Cycles: The Problem and Its Setting* (New York: The National Bureau of Economic Research, 1927) pp. 20-22.

[17] [While at Columbia University, Schumpeter called attention to another aspect of his doctrine which foreshadows modern theories of imperfect or monopolistic competition. He said in discussing railway rates at the meeting of the American Economic Association in 1913 that "if we pay proper attention to the theory of limited or imperfect competition and that of joint cost, and if we try to work out demand schedules for railroad services on the one hand, and to perfect cost accounting on the other, we shall be able to treat concrete cases and to render some practical service to the businessman." (Schumpeter, "Railway Rate Making—Discussion" *The American Economic Review,* March 1914, supplement, p. 81.)]

from what it spends on goods made by B. Then money income of B falls by same amount as that by which money income of A rises. (2) Suppose —as in change from depression to prosperity—that individual activity of great mass of producers increases and that prices rise at same time that output becomes greater. Then money income of great mass of producers becomes greater. They all practically have larger incomes to spend on each other's products. Why is not this a possible case? Indeed is it not a common one? If it does happen does it not represent an increase of money incomes not caused by monetary factors? There would of course have to be changes in monetary conditions to permit transactions of greater volume of business.[18]

I would like to ask the members of the class: How does Schumpeter's type of economics as a whole impress them? What value do they see in it? Do they find any difficulties with it?

S4: I can appreciate, I hope, the beauty of the economic theory but why make these two distinctions, and cut economics in two, and say, "This is economic theory pure and simple. It is good mental exercise, and we are making it, but if we want to find out what the situation is, we do not want that. We have to do something else."

M. From Schumpeter's viewpoint the answer is that to avoid confusion it is desirable to cut off that part of the subject matter of economics where exact thinking is possible from the other part where we have to proceed by looser methods. It is not that the economist is going to solve his problems by pure theory alone, but pure theory is a part of the problem and it is best to keep that part separate in which exact methods can be applied.

S4: I felt more confused. That is the reason I asked the question.

M: It does not seem to clarify the situation as a whole to your mind?

S6: It seems to me that in his method of variations there are very decided possibilities if he does not insist upon the single step.

M: Of course, he has to insist upon the single step for purely mathematical reasons. The problem is too complicated if the theorist introduces too many variations at one time.

S6: But the theorist can handle a complex situation by treating the single variations, and then combining them, can't he? So it seems to me it has possibilities of practical application.

S2: He is not very accurate in his illustrations when he brings in geometry.

M: I am afraid you must not cast that up against Schumpeter. That is an idea that occurred to me in talking.

---

[18] Outline, "Schumpeter's Method of Isolating Monetary Factor Affecting Price Level," APP 44-53, no. 60.

S2: The example of geometry does not quite apply, for geometry is definite in its results.

M: So is static theory. The difference is this: that in the case of geometry it is very simple to supply the concrete data, and put them into a formula. Schumpeter is aware of the difference. In his science it is extremely difficult to get the concrete data, and there is the further difference that the problem itself is such that if the theorist take any large number of cases, he cannot work the thing out, because his powers of computation are not sufficient.

S2: I was wondering just how much attention we ought to pay to what he says. It is intellectually interesting and satisfying. If we believe that men have wasted lots of time in thinking about something that does not amount to anything concrete—the old scholastics for instance were interested in futile speculations—does the indulgence of idle curiosity justify such waste of time?

M: I suppose the only answer to that is that there is no disputing tastes. If people like to do that sort of thing they like to do it. You might quarrel with the Esquimaux for eating whale blubber but they may enjoy it.

To summarize, the characteristic idiosyncracy of Schumpeter's way of treating economics is to begin with a careful review of what, in common with many others, he calls "static" problems. But instead of stopping with an analysis of what happens under static conditions he then attacks the problem of how change comes about in economic life. It is at this point, that he makes his most interesting contribution. Change occurs in modern economic life, on his showing, because there are two types of economic men. The great mass are routineers: these people follow along in customary ways. They are the people whose economic activity is caricatured by the picture of the mechanical man in most economic treatises; a person who calculates with some facility on the basis of data that are supplied to him and who makes his choices in the hope of securing the maximum net satisfaction of his wants. But there are, Schumpeter maintains, in every economy a relatively small number of people who are built on different lines. These are the innovators. They have a marked degree of energy as well as of imagination. They get their satisfaction not in the tame fashion of trying to make the best they can of established conditions but in inventing new schemes. Their minds are always teeming with projects of one sort or another which they strive to put into effect. This restless class of innovators is the group of folks who bring about what is vulgarly thought progress in economic life; they open up new stores of supply; they invent or, if they do not invent, apply in practice new methods of production; they organize business enterprises in ever new fashion. To the activity of these people the phenomena of interest, profits and business cycles are all due. In short, the basic idea is a psychological distinction between two types of human nature: the men who, quite content to do as their forefathers, dislike change, and the restless individuals, who are always striving to bring about change in the prevailing methods of operation.[19]

Resumé of Schumpeter's pure theory. Central problem of pure theory is exchange. Not only distribution but also production may properly be viewed as exchange. Central problem of exchange is theory of equilibrium price under free competition. What the theory of price does. Shows what data are necessary to definite solution of price problem—or, if you like, shows that a definite solution is possible granted certain data.

General problem of exchange.

Given: m individuals, n goods, value functions of each individual for each good, quantities of each good possessed by each individual, perfect competition. *Required:* Ratios of exchange between goods, changes in quantities of each good possessed by each individual. *Number of unknowns:* (1) Ratios of exchange. Number is = number of goods minus one; that is $n - 1$. (2) Changes in quantities of each good possessed by each individual; number is = number of individuals times number of goods; that is mn. Therefore, total number of unknowns is $mn + n - 1$. *Number of equations available for solution:* (1) Equations of marginal utility after completion of exchange of each good must = marginal utility of every other good for each person. For two goods with two persons this number would be one for each person. Generalizing it is $m(n - 1)$ or $mn - m$. (2) Equations of quantities of goods exchanged altogether; that is, equations of total transfer of goods; sales of each good must = purchases. Number of these equations = number of good, that is n. (3) Equations of quantities exchanged by each individual. Sales and purchases—payments and receipts—balance for each individual. Number of these equations; that is, purchases and sales by each individual = number of individuals, = m. So far we have in equations $mn - m$ plus $n + m = mn + n$; or one equation too many, i.e., one more than number of unknowns. But one equation of the last set is already implicit in the sum of the equations under (2); that is, it is implicit in difference between total of equations under (2) and all but the last under (3). Therefore it does not count as a new equation. Therefore number of equations is $mn + n - 1 =$ number of unknowns. Therefore problem is determinate.

Obvious disadvantages of this method of treating prices: It cannot be applied in practice. First because one cannot get the data. Second because number of equations would be too great to handle if one did get the data. Advantages: Handles all commodities at once (c.f., Davenport's demonstration that in any one price problem other prices must be assumed). Above all else it exhibits the interdependence of all the elements in the problem of prices. That is, it presents the problem in its full complexity. And if that complexity is real, this is the only proper presentation of the

---

[19] Paragraph is from the Myers Mimeograph.

fact. Perfectly generalized statement, applicable to all institutional situations. Independent of psychology. Assumes that individual has goods necessary to sustain life, and deals only with value of quantities of goods in excess of that minimum. Scope limited to "pure theory of exchange." Strictly static, essentially free from cumulative change. No theory of crises or of progress. Formal in character, having no reference to nature of goods valued, to development of institutions, to races of men, to peculiarities of environment, etc. Descriptive rather than explanatory; i.e., relies on theory of equilibrium in mathematical sense, not on cause and effect. Such theory does claim to set forth the general formula of the exchange relation which is applicable to every case of exchange (though admitting that it defines exchange only within wide limits when two monopolists face each other), but it makes no pretense to explain concrete economic phenomena in general.

How Schumpeter's pure theory differs from other types. 1. *Restricted scope.* Covers only problems of exchange under static conditions—or problems that can be cast into that form. 2. Most *abstract* because most highly generalized analysis of that central problem. Paradoxically, it is none the less *realistic* in one aspect—more realistic than any other type. Others abstract from the complexities of interdependence among economic phenomena. That complexity is part of the facts and Schumpeter's theory is realistic in holding to it. 3. Most self conscious. Schumpeter at least is fully aware of limitations upon scope of his theory. Does not present it as covering the whole ground of economic theory. Does not even claim that his methods are those that should be applied in covering other fields. Regards his doctrine rather as giving the theoretical gist of the central problem of economics; namely, exchange—treating rigorously that small part of the wide domain that is susceptible of exact scientific analysis. Requires to be implemented by looser treatment of the shadowy tracts (wastes) surrounding the oasis of white light.

Value of this type of theory. Most of us are likely to give this problem a temperamental answer. Few people who go in for economics find keen intellectual interest or emotional satisfaction in such a performance as Schumpeter's. But to give a valid answer to the question we should split it up [into two]: (1) Are the problems he considers a valid part of economic theory? (2) Is his method of treating these problems useful? First question one must answer "yes," if we understand by "problems" the broad issues on which he tries to throw light. Second question is not so simple. I cannot answer with equal confidence. Am inclined to think that the general scheme of conceiving the general problem of exchange which Schumpeter borrows from Walras is serviceable at a certain stage in the study of market phenomena. But what is serviceable in it can be very briefly put. And its chief serviceability lies in clearness with which it leads to other problems than those it professes to embrace. I do not see much advantage in working out the method of variations more elaborately and I am not sure that speculations confined to static regime are an indispensable stage in analysis of economic problems.[20]

"It is clear at once that this type of theory eliminates the problem of valuation from economics. That is, it does not concern itself with

[20] Outlines, "Final Lectures," April, May, 1914; April 2, 4, 1917; May 14, 16, 1917.

the way in which men find out what relative importance different goods have for their purposes . . . The [pure] theorist . . . does not, of course, profess to show what the market prices will be; for (1) the 'value functions' are as yet arbitrarily assumed, (2) the whole discussion presupposes static conditions and (3) when many men and many goods are introduced, the number of equations to be handled becomes too great for solution. But he does demonstrate more adequately than any other type of economist the complex interrelationships logically involved in the demonstration of prices in modern markets."[21]

Conclusion: Relation of pure theory to economics at large as represented by Schumpeter. Consciously static phenomena capable of being represented in terms of exchange. Interest and profit excluded. Methods appropriate to dynamics—history and description.[22]

Broadly speaking, Schumpeter's approach in his pure theory is representative of a type that sought a somewhat different way to eliminate hedonism than that attempted by Fetter's American psychological school. "The leader of this diversion is Professor Vilfredo Pareto," [the disciple and successor of Walras at Lausanne.] As his disciple, M. Zawadzki says, Pareto employed the hedonistic hypothesis in his earlier work. But since 1900 he has developed 'a new theory, which he calls the theory of choice, a theory which may replace the hedonistic hypothesis with advantage.'[23] Adopting a device invented by Professor Edgeworth in 1881,[24] he deduces everything necessary for his theory of equilibrium from 'curves of indifference.' Pareto's innovation consists in this: while Edgeworth derived indifference curves from the concept of utility, Pareto treats them as factual data.[25] Thanks to this procedure, 'The theory of economic science . . . acquires the rigor of rational mechanics; it deduces its results from experience, without requiring the intervention of any metaphysical entity.'[26] Pareto does not, however, wholly discard the concept of utility or ophelimity."[27]

Indifference curves: How Pareto's differs from Edgeworth's. Simply in that Pareto takes them as *data* instead of as results.

---

[21] Mitchell, "The Role of Money in Economic Theory," in *The Backward Art of Spending Money,* pp. 162-163.

[22] Outline, April 19, 1916.

[23] M. Zawadski, *Les Mathématiques appliquées à l'économie politique* (Paris: Riviere, 1914) pp. 142-143.

[24] *Mathematical Psychics* (London: C. Kegan Paul, 1881) pp. 28, 29.

[25] *Manuel d'économie politique* (Paris: Girard and Briere, 1909) p. 169.

[26] *Manuel d'économie politique,* p. 160.

[27] The above quotations and their footnotes are from Mitchell, "The Role of Money in Economy Theory," in *The Backward Art of Spending Money,* p. 161.

Use of indifference curves or surfaces in hyperspace: Systems of such curves with differing indices give a photograph of individual tastes. Can be employed as basis of pure theory of economic equilibrium; i.e., can render same services as Schumpeter's equations. Advantages [claimed]: Discussion becomes purely objective and yet in the *Manuel* Pareto continues to discuss ophelimities. As Zawadski remarks: it is possible to make a supposition concerning the *ground of choice,* but then the equations from which equilibrium is deduced become almost void of content. In what respect does one curve of indifference have a higher index than another? We continue to conceive the criterion as ophelimity, but we do not have to measure ophelimity accurately. Use an index not a measure.[28] Pareto lays down the basis of his economic theory in the *Manuel* as follows: "The notions of value in use, of utility, of ophelimity, of indices of ophelimity, etc., greatly facilitate the explanation of the theory of economic equilibrium, but they are not necessary in order to construct this theory. Thanks to mathematics, this whole theory, as we have developed it in the Appendix, is founded on nothing more than a fact of experience; that is to say, on the determination of the quantities of goods which constitute indifferent combinations for the individual. The theory of economic science thus acquires the exactness of rational mechanics; it deduces its results from experience, without the intervention of any metaphysical entity." Compare Pareto's procedure with Schumpeter's method of getting demand curves merely by asking each individual what he would give for each successive increment of supply. Compare with Fetter's dropping of marginal utility in new edition of his *Principles.* "The basis of value is conceived to be the simple act of choice and not a calculation of utility." Compare with Herbert J. Davenport's refusal to consider the grounds of choice; i.e., pure theory and psychological theory have come together.

Pareto's reasons for developing pure theory. Interpretation of cost of production:

"The literary economists, desiring to avoid at all cost the study of the *ensemble* of the conditions of economic equilibrium, have endeavored to simplify the problem by changing the sense of the term 'cost of production,' substituting for the monetary cost of production a cost of production expressed in sacrifices, which has only a vague and indeterminate meaning, lending itself to all sorts of interpretations.

How estimate the 'sacrifices' of the individual who grows his own strawberries? Is it the effort he makes plus his expenditures? We do not know how these heterogeneous quantities can be added. But let us assume that in some way the calculation is made. We have, so to speak, isolated from the rest of the economic phenomenon, the production of strawberries for our individual. Only, in this sense the proposition is false. The owner of the garden is a painter of talent. In one day's work he earns enough to buy more strawberries than he could produce by working six months in his garden. It is then to his advantage to paint and to buy strawberries at much more than they would 'cost' him.

To state our proposition accurately, we should change the sense of the

[28] [Professor Mitchell was aware that Irving Fisher had also worked with indifference curves in his *Mathematical Investigations in the Theory of Value and Prices* (1892).]

term 'cost' and say that our individual should not consider the trouble that he takes directly in order to produce the strawberries, but the advantages which he renounces in employing his time at cultivating strawberries, instead of being otherwise occupied. But in this case, the phenomenon of the production of strawberries is no longer isolated from the rest of the economic phenomenon, the proposition which we have stated no longer suffices to determine the price of the strawberries. It declares only that every individual endeavors to make the most advantageous use of his work and of the other factors of production at his disposal; which in this case conduces simply to the statement of a part of the conditions (equations) of economic equilibrium. . . .

The cost of production was conceived by the literary economists as a normal price around which should gravitate the prices determined by demand and supply, and so they came to take into account three categories of conditions. But they considered them independently of one another, and it seemed that the cost of production of a merchandise was independent of the prices of that merchandise and of others. It is easy to see how gross the error was. For example, the cost of production of coal depends on the price of machines, and the cost of production of machines depends on the price of coal, consequently the cost of production of coal depends on the price of the same coal. And it depends on it still more directly if we consider the consumption of coal in the machines employed in the mines."

Theory of general equilibrium: the proper type.

"It is the mutual dependence of economic phenomena which renders the use of mathematics indispensable to the study of these phenomena. Ordinary logic may very well serve to study the relations of cause and effect, but soon becomes pointless when relations of mutual dependence are to be considered. These in rational mechanics, and in pure economy require the use of mathematics. The chief utility derived from theories of pure economy is that they give us a synthetic notion of economic equilibrium, and for the time being we have no other means of arriving at that end."

Interpretation of general theory of economic equilibrium.

"Let us construct the hypotheses most favorable to such a calculation [of price]; let us suppose that we have triumphed over all difficulties to obtain knowledge of the data of the problem, and that we know the ophelimities of every sort of merchandise for each individual, all the circumstances attending the production of the merchandise, etc. We have already an absurd hypothesis, and besides, it still does not make possible the practical solution of the problem. We have seen that in the case of 100 individuals and of 700 kinds of merchandise, there would be 70,699 conditions (in reality, a larger number of circumstances which we have hitherto neglected would increase this number still more); we must then solve a system of 70,699 equations. This is practically beyond the power of algebraic analysis and will be still further beyond it if account were taken of the fabulous number of equations that would be given by a population of forty million individuals and some thousands of kinds of merchandise. In that case roles would be changed and it would no longer be mathematics that would come to the aid of political economy, but political economy that would come to the aid of mathematics. In other words, if we might truly know all these equations, the only means of solving them accessible to human attainments would be to observe the practical solution given in the market-place.

But if the conditions which we have enumerated cannot be of practical service to us in numerical calculations of quantity and of price, they constitute the only means known up to the present time of arriving at an idea of the way these quantities and prices vary, or, more precisely, in a general way, know how economic equilibrium is produced."

Is economic theory founded on a scale of preferences valid as explanation of economic phenomena? (1) Of course such a theory does not explain value. By dropping hedonism, by refusing to go back of the scale of preferences, all *analysis* of *process* of *valuation* of economic goods *is given up*. Perhaps the old explanation were unsatisfactory. But the new attitude abandons them without any effort to substitute something else in their place. The theory of distribution continues to rest on the theory of value and the theory of value rests on hypothetical schedules of unexplained choices. The problem of value is not solved but given up. Is this attitude satisfactory? Everyone admits that we are anxious both for scientific and for practical purposes to know what factors affect preferences for goods and preferences for different lines of action. Such topics belong among the accredited subjects of economic theory; e.g., relative attractiveness of different occupations. Surely these speculations are not devoid of practical importance or theoretical interest. We want not to drop but to develop them and to extend similar studies into new fields.

Idle to say that this part of problem is handed over to psychologists. They are not dealing with it except in a most general and formal way. What do they know or care about the relative attractiveness of different occupations, or the relative importances imputed to different goods? These are distinctly economic problems and if the economist does not work at them no one else will.[29]

The next writer will be Gustav Cassel, as a modern representative of the mathematical approach.

---

[29] Outlines, "Final Lectures," April and May 1914; April 19, 1916. The quotations are Professor Mitchell's translations from *Manuel d'économie politique,* pp. 160, 233-234, 236-238, 241, 247-248, in "Pareto," APP 74-83, no. 18. "Reading Pareto's *Manuel* where I left it last spring." Mitchell, "Diary," August 7, 1914.

"Finished reading Pareto's *The Mind and Society* (4 volumes). I had begun it in earnest on July 16th. Rather disappointed on the whole (Mitchell, "Diary," August 4, 1935.)

["The new treatise on *Principi di economia politica* which your friend Enrico Barone prepared . . . is an extremely able little work, resting for the most part on Pareto formulations. Barone, however, makes ridiculous claims for the mathematical method. Results are stated as having been discovered by means of that method which I learned from Prof. J. B. Clark fifteen or more years ago.

It was a surprise to me to find what extremely elementary teaching is done by Pantaleoni . . . at the University of Rome. The level is not higher than our own undergraduate standards." (Henry L. Moore to Seligman, May 21, 1910).

Mitchell had a similar experience with Menger at Vienna while on a travelling fellowship from the University of Chicago in 1897, 1898.]

CHAPTER XVI

The Mathematical Approach of Gustav Cassel

We now turn to Gustav Cassel who represents a modern simplified form of that exceedingly pure type of economic theory which was first effectively formulated by Léon Walras, who has already been mentioned several times.

Walras, at about the same time as Jevons and Menger, presented the idea of marginal or final degree of utility, in his *Pure Economics.* As Walras saw it scarcity—the French word is *rareté*—is the clue to obscure problems in economic theory, but his treatment of the general theme was, from the technical viewpoint, much more skillful. He was the first to face with complete frankness and in comprehensive fashion the fact that in a given market where many wares are being bought and sold continuously, every single price depends upon every other price. In short, he faced the fact that the theorist cannot explain the price for any given article until he has already explained the price of everything else.

Among the writers who have so far been discussed only one man has insisted vigorously upon that viewpoint in the English literature. To be sure, it is recognized in Alfred Marshall time and again, but not strongly insisted upon by him. On the other hand, Herbert J. Davenport has continually called attention to this fact. Remember his remarks about the circuitous, superficial character of price explanations, and remember also that he states that while such analysis is adequate for the purposes of the businessman, it is not satisfactory for the purpose of the economist; for the economist would like to get hold of something more fundamental. But recall also that while he mentions what he regards as the real forces underlying the determining of all the interdependent prices, he does not study them in an effective fashion.

Walras presented the view from the mathematical side and showed that the problem of the mutual determination of the prices of any number of commodities—n prices—at a given moment can be regarded as theoretically a determinate problem; that is, it can be solved, given adequate data. He showed that the theorist can set up on the basis of certain data such as economists ordinarily employ in price discussions a number of equations which is just equal to the number of the unknowns in the problem; that is, just equal to the number of prices which are to be ascertained. From the mathematical point of view, whenever the theorist can set up a number of simultaneous equations equal to the number of unknowns he has a determinate problem.

To a person with a mathematical cast of mind this is a satisfactory conclusion, though it must be admitted that from Walras's point of view the data which are required to set up the equations cannot be obtained; and even if this information were available, the number of equations which would have to be solved in order to show the mutual determination of all prices in a large, modern market, would be beyond the computing resources of mathematics. In other words, the theorist can see how it is conceptually possible that the prices of a very large number of goods can all be determined in a given market at a given time, but he cannot get the data necessary for the equations; and even if he could, he could not solve them, because they would be so numerous. In short, the problem is determinate in a purely formal sense.

The kind of data with which Walras wanted to operate was data that would show how much of each one of the n commodities in a market would be bought by every consumer at each one of the successive possible prices. By asking the consumers, the theorist is supposed to be able to draw up the demand schedule for each commodity of each individual in the market; and then by summing up the individual schedules, to draw up demand schedules for each of the commodities which will show the quantity of each commodity which will be bought by all the people in the market at successive prices. Similarly the theorist is supposed to know the amount of the commodity brought to market by each seller and the price each will take for each increment, and these give the supply schedules. The theorist is also supposed to know the stock of each commodity which each buyer and each seller has in his possession before the market opens.

Granted these facts, the theorist can set up equations which will show the total amount of each commodity—talking now from the commodity viewpoint—which will be sold and bought; and these equations will be equal in number to the number of prices which have to be determined. This means that the problem is soluble. When it is solved the theorist will have found not merely the price at which particular goods will change hands but also the amount of commodities which each individual will buy and the amount which each individual will sell; and combining these changes, these transfers of goods, and certain of the data with which he started, he determines what stocks of the commodities are in the hands of each individual at the end of the trading.

The analysis implicitly supposes a static situation. It takes the situation that exists at a given moment of time. There are certain stocks of commodities in existence and certain theoretically determinate demand and supply schedules for those commodities. All the participants are supposed to meet in a market where perfect competition exists. They are supposed to keep on buying and selling until the equilibrium price has been established for each article. All these are restrictive limitations of a very important order. That is to say, the theory, as Walras propounded it, was supposed to be applicable not to the conditions of real life but to certain imaginary conditions, and yet conditions which from the point of view of the mathematical theorist must be treated because they represent a critically important part of the market conditions which are prevalent wherever people are buying and selling together under conditions that admit, at least in some measure, of free competition.

Briefly, the Walrasian conception of general economic equilibrium, shown by system of simultaneous equations, in which supply and demand of all commodities, and all factors of production, and prices, are conceptually included in detail—the detail covering technical coefficients representing quantities of each factor required to make a unit of each commodity of which a supply is forthcoming. In this conceptual scheme of balance selling prices of all the n goods in the economy are so adjusted to one another that the physical volume of demand for each commodity during a unit period at its price equals the physical volume of supply of each commodity forthcoming during this period at that price. This proposition applies not merely to finished goods but also to raw materials and to factors of production; e. g., the selling price of bituminous coal is so adjusted to the price of pig iron, cattle hides, wheat, oak flooring, pick axes, labor of all varieties and 10,000 other goods that the aggregate demand for bituminous coal, which comes from business firms, railroads, gas companies, electric companies, factories, exporters, mines, etc., just equals the tonnage of bituminous coal currently produced by all the sources of supply. The like is true of pig iron, cattle hides, and all other goods including the factors of production. Also all prices are adjusted to cost of production. Implies an enormous number of adjustments among prices and x equations of form $D = S$. Since prices paid for goods come from incomes and these incomes are derived by selling factors of production—labor, use of property, management of business—the equations can be rearranged to show payments of income (after exclusion of all double counting), including profits as payment for management and risk = aggregate cost of production = aggregate selling prices = aggregate expenditures; profits as prices of services of the entrepreneur are costs of production and are adjusted to all other prices of factors and to all selling prices. Like is true of wages, interest, rents. All the innumerable adjustments of prices, physical demand, physical supply, income payments and expenditures, can be worked out and maintained only on the supposition that consumers are free to spend their money as they see fit, producers are free to engage in any income producing activity they see fit; that is, system presupposes private initiative in buying and selling, equality of prices of a given commodity on different markets, mobility of capital, labor, business enterprise: should be instantaneous, no long term bargains that interfere with mobility, free competition, static state, or evenly progressive state.

No one supposes that this vision of equilibrium is a realistic picture of actual conditions. It is used solely as a tool of analysis. As such it is useful to us [in the study of business cycles as well as general economic theory]. First, as suggesting the many ways in which changes in equilibrium may be caused: (1) Changes in tastes of consumers that influence allocations of income and therefore demand for different economic goods, their prices, profits, demand for factors of production and their prices, incomes disbursed to consumers, demand for consumers goods, consumers savings and investments. (2) Changes in methods of production that influence supply of goods and therefore selling prices, profits, demand for factors of production and their prices, income disbursed to consumers, demand for consumers goods, consumers savings and investments. (3) Interferences with freedom of the individual to buy what he pleases and use his labor or property as he pleases, whether these interferences come from government or from business developments, such as development of monopolies. (4) Random disturbances of the equilibrium system such as crop fluctuations, war. Second, [it is useful] as suggesting how so many explanations can be given of business cycles. If all the factors in an economy are adjusted to one another then marked departures from that equilibrium may be explained in terms of maladjustments of many types: overproduction, underconsumption, speculation, ill balanced production, bad business judgment under influence of optimism and pessimism, encroachment of costs upon prospective profits, lack of balance between savings and investment, errors of accounting, wrong monetary policies, innovations, mistaken adjustments of currency or credit to needs, interest rates that are not perfectly adjusted to changes in prices and profits, random perturbations, and so on through an interminable list; that is, if the economy is thought of as a system in which literally millions of adjustments must be maintained then any cause of maladjustment at any point will spread to other points and can be offered as an explanation of general disequilibrium. Can further be used as an explanation of the type of disequilibrium represented by business cycles, *if* it can be shown that the changes it sets in motion tend at least for a time to move in the direction of general expansion or contraction. This raises the question, to which we must go on, of differences between disturbances that do and do not have the tendency to produce cumulative expansions and contractions. Third as helping us to see how cumulative movements occur. If one price rises that is a reason why certain other prices must rise, *if equilibrium is to be maintained*. Rise in price of coal, e. g., tends to raise prices of all goods into which price of coal enters as a cost. Tends to raise demand for and therefore price of all goods that can be used instead of coal for any purpose. The latter price rises tend to spread to all goods in which these substitutes for coal are costs and to the demand for and therefore prices of all goods that can be used as substitutes for these coal substitutes. On the other hand, rise in price of coal tends (1) to reduce demand for coal and therefore employment at coal mines, and may or may not reduce profits of coal mines, dividends of mine owners, receipts of people who supply wants of those who derive incomes from coal mining; (2) reduce the demand for and therefore prices of other goods that would have been bought more freely if more money were not spent for coal. Which assumes that the elasticity of demand for coal is less than one. Similarly, if supply of one good increases, that increase tends to increase the demand for and therefore the supply of goods used in making the first, and of its by-products; (2) tends to reduce demand for and therefore supply of substitutes for the first good. Again, if income of any group in the economy rises, that rise tends to increase the incomes of those from whom the first group buys, tends to decrease the incomes of those to whom the first group sells—if the increase in income is due merely to changes in price.

Now it is not a foregone conclusion that a change of one type will tend predominately to call forth similar changes in relation of other factors. But neither is it a foregone conclusion that changes of an opposite sort will offset changes of similar sort. The one thing that will not occur in theory is that effect will be confined to the item that changes—a rise in prices merely calling forth an increase in supply which takes price back to original point. Thus the general theory of equilibrium, with its picture of the orderly ramifying interrelations among different factors in the economy is of help in building up a picture of how disturbances of the equilibrium may tend to spread and become general. Indeed, all theories of business cycles, explicitly or tacitly, make use of the conception that the economy is a congeries of interrelated processes, that a change in any one of the parts really affects others, some in one way, some in another and is affected by others. To get a tolerably clear picture of economic equilibrium in the strictest, most "theoretical," most unrealistic form is therefore of some use in understanding what actually happens—provided of course that we use the conception as it is designed to be used and not as representing the problem or as affording the actual solution. But all that we get, which is not a little, is a picture of what *may* happen. We are left with innumerable questions of fact: How close are the adjustments among different economic processes in fact? How promptly are effects of a shift in adjustment felt? Do they die out quickly as they spread from the center of disturbance? There are questions that can be answered only by drawing generalizations from many detailed investigations. And these generalizations have to be so discriminating that they may not be very sweeping. Effects in one market may depend on elasticity of demand, on the prospects of profits at the time changes occur, on the condition of inventories at the time, on the stocks of goods in the hands of consumers. Need of empirical investigation.[1]

---

[1] Outlines, "Lectures on Business Cycles," October 17, 1940, October 29, 1942.

It is not surprising, as previously noted, that Walras's exposition made even less impression upon his contemporaries than Jevons's did. Among other things, Walras wrote in French and it was unfortunate for him that the general trend of French economics had been far more strictly orthodox than even that of English economists, not to speak of the German or American. The faithful disciples of J. B. Say, who played much the same role in France as Adam Smith and Ricardo combined in England, would have none of this highly abstruse mathematical treatment, admittedly inapplicable to the discussion of conditions such as prevailed. Walras was for a long while a prophet without honor in his own country and with but little honor elsewhere —hard luck even for a prophet![1a]

Today, however, as the people, who have attacked economic problems by what the mathematical writers somewhat sneeringly call "literary" methods, have come to grasp more and more securely the interdependence of all economic phenomena—in particular interdependence of all prices—interest in Walras's method has revived. Scholars in different parts of the world have been endeavoring to develop his approach so as to make it more widely applicable. A number, notable amongst whom is Professor Henry L. Moore, think that it may be feasible to transform Walras's fundamental scheme of operating with simultaneous equations so as to put the price problem into a shape in which we can use statistical data and really operate the scheme to analyze dynamic problems. They think that, if this can be accomplished, it will turn out to be the most powerful tool for discussing the type of price problems that turn up in actual markets. Of these efforts to develop the technique Gustav Cassel's theory is the boldest. Let us examine Cassel's way of using this idea.

Cassel (1866-1945), a professor of political economy at the University of Stockholm, has long been interested in economic theory, and has been dealing with a wide range of problems for a long while. Incidentally, he seems to make a practice of publishing his books alternately in German and English. There have also been issued Swed-

---

[1a][Charles Dunbar in asking Simon Newcomb in 1886 to prepare an article on the mathematical method in political economy for *The Quarterly Journal of Economics* wrote the eminent astronomer and economist: "Professor Walras of Lausanne is the present representative of this of course and appears to have carried his use of it much further than Jevons ever did, but I have never seen . . . any really adequate discussion of the actual significance and promise of this method. The economists are seldom mathematicians and *vice versa*." (Dunbar to Newcomb, August 15, 1886, Newcomb Papers, Library of Congress.) Almost twenty years later, Dunbar's successor as editor after reminding Newcomb of Dunbar's request went on to say: "I do not know whether you have watched the recent developments of the mathematical literature of our subject, the usefulness of which I suspect is negligible." (Taussig to Newcomb, January 24, 1905, Newcomb Papers.)]

ish editions of them. In 1899 appeared his first important theoretical contribution, "Grundriss einer elementaren Preislehre" ("Outlines of an Elementary Theory of Prices") in *Zeitschrift für die gesamte Staatswissenschaft*. In this study he undertakes to develop Walras's scheme, directly acknowledging the fact that he is basing his work upon that of Walras. Then he returned to the problem of interest and published a monograph which has played a considerable role, *The Nature and Necessity of Interest* (1903). He also became much concerned with the theory of money because, of course, money is a factor of great consequence in price determination.

In July 1914 he had completed the manuscript of *Theoretische Sozialökonomie* and had it set up in type in German at Leipzig, but the outbreak of the war made the publisher doubtful of the market. It was not issued until 1918 when it was published without substantial alteration. It was afterwards translated into a number of languages including Swedish. In English it bears the title *The Theory of Social Economy*.[2]

There is one significant but little known fact concerning Cassel's training which is important for understanding his approach: he started as a student of engineering, earned his Ph.D. in mathematics in 1894 and at the comparatively advanced age of thirty-two turned to economics. He had developed certain intellectual habits to which he was more or less predisposed by the constitution of his mind, and which were further fixed by his engineering training. He states in the preface that:

> From the first beginnings of my study of this science I felt that it ought to be possible to do away with the whole of the old theory of value as an independent chapter of economics and build up a science from the beginning on the theory of prices and that we would be able to rid ourselves in this manner of a lot of unnecessary discussions, mostly of a rather scholastic nature, which had burdened earlier treaties on economics.[3]

His disinclination to accept what he refers to in the treatise as "the subjective theory of value" was natural enough in an engineer. And the way to construct economics as a theory of prices innocent of any contamination by psychological conceptions had been already indicated by Walras.

---

[2] [The first English translation, that of 1923, was used by Professor Mitchell in his lectures. The quotations given below are from the second and clearer translation by S. L. Barron (1932) from the fifth German edition. The book enjoyed a considerable vogue not only in Europe and the United States but also in Latin America. The Swedish translation appeared quite late.]

[3] *The Theory of Social Economy*, translated by S. L. Barron (New York: Harcourt, Brace, 1932) p. vii.

To make clear Cassel's particular approach to the problem of price determination resort will be made to the customary presentation of the theory of prices. Some one commodity is taken; suppose there is a market in which that commodity is being bought and sold. Then the theorist supposes that there are a number of would-be buyers, each one of whom will pay a certain price for successive increments of the commodity in question. On the other side of the market stand a number of sellers who are ready to part with their supply, at the prices which vary as the units in the stock become fewer. The theorist supposes too that there is free or perfect competition.

Under the assumed conditions he is able to show that the price of the article will be fixed between certain limits. He ordinarily arranges schedules of demand prices and supply prices so that the limits between which the competitive price has to fall are extremely narrow. One may, if he likes, make some definite point, at which the price must fall. The theorist can go on elaborating the discussion by saying "we have shown how prices are fixed for a certain commodity in a market at a given time. We now want to consider not simply this type of a not very remarkable problem, but problems which take into account variations in demand and variations in supply through time." Then, if the theorist is following the older model, he proceeds to discuss the conditions on which the demand for various commodities depends, developing presumably the ideas of variations in the utility of commodities and going as far as he likes into some realistic discussion of the way in which the demand schedules for different types of goods are likely to differ from each other.

He makes a similar analysis of the condition of supply and shows that the terms on which the commodities will be brought forward vastly differ according as he takes comparatively brief periods or long periods or very long periods, dividing the length of the period up on the basis of instantaneous dealings, periods long enough to permit fresh production, and finally periods long enough to allow for changes in the factors of production themselves: building of new factories, training of new workmen, the accumulation of new capital. This discussion runs along in a satisfactory fashion. A brilliant example of how it can be worked out is in Marshall's *Principles of Economics*.

But there is one condition connected with that method which is serious from the theoretical viewpoint; namely, that when the theorist thinks of treating the price of any one article in a market he has to realize that what people will be willing to pay for it will be affected by the prices at which they can get various other articles. For there is scarcely any commodity for which people will not substitute something else if the terms on which they can get the first or second article are very different.

A person's diet has a very great range. There is no single article of food on a commercial basis that is indispensable; there is a substitute for every one. That remark is even more true with reference to clothes, amusements, in fact to all the goods that we buy. It may even be that there is often for that matter a contest between different types of wants. People may vary the course of their life, the particular types of goods they consume, to a very considerable extent. Thus in recent years [1928] we have been told by people interested in clothing that consumers are buying less clothes, care less about their garments and are spending more on motor cars, radio sets, etc. This situation refers not simply to the case where one or two articles supply the same want, but also in the vague but still important cases of efforts to satisfy different wants. The consequence is that one cannot tell what the demand for any article will be unless one knows the terms on which other articles can be supplied.

That remark applies as well to supply. A business man, at least when he is considering the investment of his capital and his own organizing ability, has much the same choice among alternatives that the consumer has. If the market for steel in the years to come is taken into account and it does not look to him very promising, he may go into a wholesale trade or into copper production—any one of a considerable number of different things. Of course there are certain people whose opportunities for investment are limited, but if one takes the investment market as a whole the people who decide what articles are to be produced possess a wide range of choice.

The result is that the theorist cannot determine what sort of price for a given article will lead to the production of a supply unless he knows the profit; that is, the differences between the prices of finished goods and the cost of producing them, the prices that will prevail for other goods; in other words that is, the attempt to determine the price of any single commodity runs into the difficulty that the theorist cannot determine what is the demand for that commodity or what will be its supply until he knows the prices at which other goods can be had and the prices at which other goods will be supplied.

To avoid this difficulty Walras hit upon the plan, which at first sight seems impracticable, of viewing the problem of prices as that of the way in which the prices of n commodities, that is, of any number, are determined in a market at a given time. His way of solving it was to set up various sets of simultaneous equations, that is, equations all of which are supposed to be true at the same time. These equations show that the amount of a commodity sold in the market during a given time will be equal to the quantity offered within that time; that is, demand equals supply. They show, therefore, that under the stable conditions assumed, the supply of every commodity would be equal to the sum of the costs of producing it. They show further that the demand for every commodity would be a function of the price at which that commodity and all other commodities were sold. In this way, Walras demonstrated that it is possible to solve the problem of simultaneous determination of n prices in a market, in the sense that the theorist can set up a number of equations of the general types which have been mentioned and which will be just equal to the number of unknown prices that the theorist is trying to determine.

To repeat, the theorist had to admit, to be sure, that in the first place he could not get the data which would be necessary in practice to set up the equations which Walras's scheme called for. He could not determine, for instance, in practice just how many units of a given commodity any individual in the market would be willing to buy at successive prices. Nor could he determine the prices different sellers would be willing to take for successive units of their supply. Those are the fundamental data, and if the theorist could not determine them, then the Walrasian scheme had to be regarded as a solution of the general problem only in the most general sense. It did indicate, and that was its service, the conditions which bear upon the determination of the prices of commodities, and indicated them in a far more competent fashion, a far clearer scheme, than that which is indicated by approaching the problem through a consideration of how the price of a single commodity is determined. Indeed, in the latter problem the same difficulties in constructing the demand and supply schedules had to be faced; the theorist cannot get the actual data required.

A few statisticians have begun to try on the basis of past records to solve the problem for large groups of buyers and sellers. They attempted actually to construct (a) demand schedules which show how the prices of a certain number of commodities have varied with demand; and (b) supply schedules where there are records of volume sold or volume consumed and the prices and (c) finally how the two interacted, by means of mathematical formulae.[4]

---

4 [These people are now called econometricians.]

That was the general problem which was stated by Walras, the general type of solution which he offered; that was the type of inquiry which appealed to the mathematical mind of Cassel, and the scheme which he elaborated through years of labor into *The Theory of Social Economy*.

Like Wieser's *Social Economics* the treatise is divided into four books or sections. The first, General Survey of Economics, puts forward his fundamental ideas concerning the proper task of economic theory and the appropriate way to perform it. The most important proposition, as Cassel sees it, is the definition of what constitutes an economic situation; therefore the problem of economic theory

> the common element, which determines the specifically economic character of all economic activity, is the final condition of such activity—that is, the fact that there exists a definite limit to the satisfaction of wants as a whole. Some wants, it is true, can be satisfied to an unlimited extent; this for example, is normally the case with the desire for breathing. But the satisfaction of such wants must be excluded from the sphere of economic activity. Only those actions which are carried out on the condition of a limited possibility of the satisfaction of wants can be regarded as economic. Since, generally, only a limited quantity of means for the satisfaction of wants is available, and since the wants of civilised humanity as a whole are insatiable, the means for satisfying wants are generally *scarce* relatively to the wants themselves. Only scarce means are economic means. Every economic system thus labours under the condition of a scarcity of means for the satisfaction of wants; in this sense, economics is governed by the *"Principle of Scarcity."*[5]

The "principle of scarcity" is one of Cassel's constant catch phrases. It occurs again and again throughout the treatise. He goes on to say:

> Hence the special task of economy is to equate wants with the available means for their satisfaction in the way which is most advantageous. In so far as this task is completed successfully, the economic activity may be regarded as truly economic.
> The solution of this problem can be achieved in three different ways; first, by proportionately limiting wants and eliminating the less important ones; secondly, by using the available means for the defined ends in the best possible way; thirdly, by increasing, if possible, the productive power of the individual.[6]

To repeat, the fundamental feature of the definition of an economic situation is that people are faced with a condition under which the supply of goods is not sufficient to satisfy all their wants completely, making it necessary to economize in some sense. This is the principle of scarcity. Whenever the principle of scarcity does not prevail there is no economic situation, and thus such cases are outside the sphere

---

[5] *The Theory of Social Economy,* p. 5.
[6] *The Theory of Social Economy,* p. 5.

of economic science. There are three general ways in which people can meet the difficulties which the principle of scarcity puts before them, individually. They can either eliminate some of their less important wants; or face the problem of how best to utilize the supply in hand; or, third, exert themselves to increase the supply.

In dealing with a group of people the further problem of exchange necessarily comes to the fore. In these groups people do not as a rule consume the things that they individually produce; the individual does not produce the things he consumes for the most part. Each individual is dependent on others for the supply of the things he requires to satisfy his wants, and dependent on others also for a market for the things which he produces. This means that the exchange of what services they can render for the things which they require to satisfy their own wants is a matter of the first importance individually.

The extent to which they can satisfy their own wants depends in a real sense more on the rates of exchange between that which they contribute to production and the goods they desire to consume than it does on how many services they can render.

This also means that when people are thinking of the adaptation of the use of the limited supply of goods to the satisfaction of wants, the limit is found in the prices at which things can be had. The price factor comes in as the matter of chief concern to all members of the community. In Cassel's language:

> With the money which the individual households are prepared to give for the satisfaction of their wants they make certain demands upon the supply of goods in the society. As these goods are always limited in quantity, the demand on them must be restricted in some way, i.e. certain wants cannot be satisfied. This restriction is effected by fixing prices.[7]

The importance of prices in economic life, and hence in economic theory, is that they are the means by which the restriction in the satisfaction of wants necessarily imposed by scarcity is carried out. This means that the central feature of economic theory is the theory of prices—how these prices that play the all important role of restricting the satisfaction of wants are determined.

> As the restriction of consumption must be all the more vigorous, the greater the scarcity of goods in relation to the demands of consumers, and as, therefore, prices are largely determined by this scarcity, we see that the indicated purpose of pricing is an expression of the principle of scarcity which we outlined in the first section. *Thus, in the exchange economy, the principle of scarcity signifies*

---

[7] *The Theory of Social Economy*, p. 66.

the necessity, by the pressure of prices, to adjust consumption to a relatively scarce supply of goods.[8]

This puts all the emphasis upon the theory of prices. The most significant passages are those in which Cassel explains why it is unnecessary to have a theory of value as a basis for the theory of prices.

Human valuations are by their very nature relative, and man has always found it necessary in practice to reduce them to a common denominator—that is, express them in money. In practical economic life, the intensity of desire, as we shall see later, enters into consideration only in so far as it affects money valuations. This fact ought to define the limits of the science of economics; it can consider subjective economic factors only as they are manifested in pricing.

Consequently, it follows that a special theory of value is, to say the least, quite unnecessary in economics. Every attempt to frame such a theory without using a common measure to express estimates of value must encounter great difficulties.

That is, it will be hard to frame a theory of value without the use of a money unit; and since there is a monetary unit there are prices.

> But as soon as such a common measure is introduced, money in its essence is postulated. Values are then replaced by prices, valuation by pricing, and we have a theory of prices instead of a theory of value. From this we must conclude that the whole of the so-called theory of value ought to be discarded in economics. The theoretical exposition of the exchange economy must, from the start, take money into consideration, and thus be essentially a theory of pricing.
> This will show itself to be a great simplification. We shall be able to avoid completely a great number of contentious questions on which much useless trouble is now expended. We shall be in the position to free the science from discussions which only too often degrade it into scholasticism of the worst kind . . . Such a radical purging is absolutely necessary if we wish to concentrate as far as possible on the real and undoubtedly very important problems of economic theory.[9]

And then again:

> No further analysis of demand is needed in connection with the problem of prices. The extent of the demand at a given price is a tangible fact which has a quantitative and purely arithmetical expression, and in this form can be used directly by economic science as part of its structure. The psychological processes underlying this fact have, of course, a certain interest for the economist, inasmuch as a knowledge of them helps him to estimate correctly the influence of prices on demand; in so far as they can be elucidated, they are best studied from this standpoint. Such a study can only derive advantage from the fact that it is pursued in terms of a clear quan-

---

[8] *The Theory of Social Economy*, p. 74.
[9] *The Theory of Social Economy*, p. 49.

titative conception of the problem; the idea that the theory of prices discussed in his Book, in contradistinction to the so-called theory of value, would render more difficult, or even exclude, a psychologico-economic study, is therefore based on a complete misunderstanding. Such studies, however, lie outside the realm of economic theory proper.

These remarks are of special importance in relation to what is known as the *Marginal Utility Theory*. The first objection to this much discussed theory is that it is superfluous in economic science.[10]

One more brief citation will conclude this part of the discussion: "General social and economic policy covers a much wider area than theoretical economics proper. The task of the latter is to elucidate pricing."[11]

In this respect Cassel's viewpoint is identical with that of Davenport. There are other interesting relationships between their views of economic theory. Davenport also is continually calling attention to the fact that one cannot determine the price of any given commodity by itself. He was always reminding readers that the willingness of people to buy certain commodities took into consideration not only the price of that commodity but also the prices at which other commodities can be had. Similarly, in frequent discussions of what he called "opportunity costs" he stated that the supply of different commodities is as much an interdependent phenomenon as is the demand price for these commodities. He insisted that the discussion of prices as he presented it was "circuitous and superficial," although adequate for the purposes of the business man—and here comes this one difference: he said it was not adequate for the purposes of the economist. It remained "circuitous and superficial"—the explanation of one price in terms of other prices.

The difference is that Cassel says a discussion of prices which does not go into the theory of value is all that economics should profess to give. Davenport wants to go back of the phenomenon of the market to the real forces. His way of getting away from the circuitry and superficiality of price analysis was, to repeat, to point out what the real forces were. These consisted in the paying dispositions of people, in their willingness to labor and wait, and in the arts of production. Having pointed out the real forces, however, Davenport, like Cassel refuses to analyze them. To go back into an analysis of why people want things is, in his eyes, no business of the theory of economics. The theory should look at phenomena from the standpoint of price, and then further should point out the real forces which lie behind

---

10 *The Theory of Social Economy*, p. 80.
11 *The Theory of Social Economy*, p. 184.

the forces discussed in the theory of prices. Cassel also said there are real forces behind the price phenomena, among them the psychological attitudes of people, the psychological processes which lie behind demand; he says that they have a certain interest for the economist, but it is not the economist's business to inquire into this.

Both men present in this point a very marked contrast with Marshall who began with the real forces and took it for granted that the importance of money prices lies in the fact that they are the economist's only way of measuring the strength of the real forces. Yet the relationship between the real forces and demand and supply schedules—the factors that determine prices—is far from clear in Marshall. Cassel, however, wants to throw all that sort of analysis out of economic science. He is more radical than Davenport, because he does not even think it his duty to tell you, cursorily as Davenport does, what these real forces are. Unlike Davenport again, he does not admit, the circuity and superficiality of the mere price analysis.

S: Cassel's use of the word "scarcity" makes it necessary for him to use the idea of marginal utility—practically the same thing.

M: Wait until you see how he develops his theory of prices and then you will see just what role marginal utility plays there. This is not fully revealed yet in our discussion. He thinks he has ways of getting round it, though I am inclined to think that you will conclude that they are ways which admit the influence of the psychological process lying behind demand.

S: Why is it called *The Theory of Social Economy?*

M: Cassel says in the preface: "I call this work *The Theory of Social Economy*. The meaning of this is that I intend to treat the economic relations of a whole social body as far as possible irrespective of its extension, its organization, its laws of property, etc." That is, he will not consider all the differences of an institutional character which are found as between different nations or different stages of civilization. "The ultimate aim of economic science must be to discover those necessities which are of a purely economic nature and which cannot be arbitrarily mastered by the will of men." That means the necessities which result from the principle of scarcity. He sees in the necessities some of the august simplicity of the laws of physics.

> An intimate knowledge of these necessities is the first condition for Social Reformers being ever able to produce something more than cheap speculations on the economic organization of the future or costly disturbances of the very delicate machinery of present economic life.[12]

[12] *The Theory of Social Economy*, p. 111.

In his view, if you are interested very definitely as a social reformer, your duty is to master the fundamental necessities resulting from the principle of scarcity, that is to see how they work out.

S: How do Davenport and Cassel compare on the social organism concept?

M: Davenport states definitely that it is all nonsense, that there ought to be a social asylum somewhere in which to confine the social organism, and Cassel does not dignify it by mentioning it.

S: Is not Cassel's work rather deductive?

M: Yes, if you use the terms deduction and induction you can characterize *The Theory of Social Economy* as radically deductive.

S: It reminds one a little of David Ricardo.

M: Yes. It must be said, however, that Cassel is a man who makes considerable use of statistical materials. He likes to examine materials and go through a process of what he probably thinks of as inductive verification of his deductive theories.

S: Is his statistical material very good?

M: I do not think his statistical technique is of a very perfect sort.

Let me turn to the substantive value, in Cassel's eyes, of the central contribution that he makes. This consists in presenting in chapter IV of Book I what he calls "the mechanism of pricing." It consists of a modernized and doubtless somewhat improved version of the discussion of the Walrasian simultaneous determination of the prices of n commodities in a market. He approaches the problem by taking a succession of cases, starting with a relatively simple one and then introducing successive modifications.

He supposes that the supply of all the commodities whose prices are to be considered is known. He also supposes that the amount of money which every buyer in the market possesses is fixed in advance. He supposes, therefore, that people exchange their products; and whenever a man uses some part of the goods he has produced, he treats that man as himself purchasing a part of the supply.

The problem is to determine the prices at which the n goods in the market will be fixed under these conditions. Cassel points out that if the theorist takes an individual consumer it should be possible to ascertain by experiment what prices he would pay for successive units in the supply. As Cassel puts it: "If we . . . vary the price, we can determine how much of the particular commodity the individual will buy at any particular price, or in other words, how the individual demand varies with the price."[13] In more technical language, the theorist can treat the quantity of the article which the individual in question buys at a given price as a function of the price. The form of this function expresses the subjective valuation. He can treat demand measured in physical quantities of commodities bought in a given market at a given time as a function of the prices at which the articles sell.

Cassel, however, reminds theorists at once that in taking this view they cannot confine their consideration to a particular article in question. The demand of the individual consumer for a particular article is not determined until the prices of all articles that can be bought are fixed. Thus Cassel comes around to setting up as a starting point of his analysis a set of simultaneous equations which have the form:

$$D_1 = F_1(p_1, p_2 \ldots p_n)$$

D sub 1, that is, the demand for commodity 1, equals function sub 1, of p sub 1, the price of the particular commodity in question, of p sub 2, the price of the second commodity, etc.; for the prices of everything dealt with in that market until commodity n is reached. It states simply that the demand for commodity number one in this market can be regarded as a function of the prices at which all the commodities in that market sell.

Then there is a second equation:

$$D_2 = F_2(p_1, p_2 \ldots p_n)$$

There is a whole system of these equations until the theorist gets down to:

$$D_n = F_n(p_1, p_2 \ldots p_n)$$

In other words, the theorist sets up an equation of that form for every commodity in the market. These functions may or may not be alike. In every case the significant feature of the presentation is that the demand for a given article is the function not only of the price of that article but of all the articles in the market. The question is: how can the theorist find out what the unknown quantities are?

He can devise a set of equations which express the identity of the physical demand for each commodity with the physical supply of it under equilibrium conditions. Recall that Cassel said from the beginning that the basic proposition of economics is the principle of scarcity, that the fundamental service which price renders is to restrict demand to the limits of supply. So under equilibrium conditions, the theorist

---

[13] *The Theory of Social Economy*, p. 138.

knows that the demand for the first commodity reckoned in physical terms (D sub 1) must equal supply (S sub 1); and D sub 2 must equal S sub 2, etc., till the theorist gets down to D sub n equals S sub n:

$$D_1 = S_1; D_2 = S_2 \ldots; D_n = S_n$$

Then comes a third step. Inasmuch as the successive D's equal the successive S's, and inasmuch as the S's are known (they are given to the theorist in advance), he is in a position to write a series of equations in which he starts with the known quantity.

$$S_1 = F_1(p_1, p_2 \ldots p_n)$$
$$S_2 = F_2(p_1, p_2 \ldots p_n)$$
$$S_n = F_n(p_1, p_2 \ldots p_n)$$

The theorist has in this market to determine the prices of n commodities, the prices of the unknown quantities, and there are n of them. The supply is given in advance for n commodities. There are n of these equations. They can be used to determine the n unknown prices. That is to say, the first set of equations enables the theorist to ascertain what the prices of all the goods in the market will be. And the problem of the ascertainment of the price of n commodities at the same time in a market is solved under these conditions; that is, when the theorist has the supply given and when he supposes that the people in the market have fixed needs for which to buy.

S: How would you explain the relationship in those demand equations?

M: That is explained in the following passage:

> The relation between the demand for and the price of a commodity is most effectively shown where the price of the commodity chosen is an independent variable. If we then vary the price, we can determine how much of the particular commodity an individual will buy at any particular price, or in other words, how individual demand varies with price.[14]

S: That function is the sum of the prices?

M: It should not be described as the sum of those prices. It would be some sort of mathematical expression which would show how the supply in this set of equations varies as the prices of the various commodities vary.

S: Whatever the equation is, the p's will be the only unknowns in it?

M: Yes. These equations cannot be used at the start, because the p's as well as the D's are unknowns.

---

[14] *The Theory of Social Economy,* p. 138.

S: Are your S's known before the p's are known?

M: It is supposed that the S's are known.

S: What is the unit of measurement of the S's?

M: They run in physical terms.

S: How can you fit them into that equation in physical terms?

M: The character of the functions $F_1, F_2 \ldots F_n$ will vary according as the physical terms vary, but the theorist gets that element of elasticity so that he can express them in any kind of physical units he likes.

S: I should think you would want to have the units either in prices or physical terms.

M: No. These are just equations. I can say, for instance, that a certain number of bushels of wheat is the requirement of a given market within a given week and so many tons of steel is a requirement of that market for a week, and so many dozens of eggs. Or I can say that those three expressions represent the quantity available for sale fixed in advance, as is done in this case. Then I can say that the quantity of steel reckoned in tons, the number of tons of steel or fractions of a ton a given person will buy, will be some function of the prices that prevail for steel, wheat, eggs, and everything else that is bought and sold. If I reduce the unit of measure of the steel from tons to pounds, I would have exactly the same relation, only F would be in a somewhat different form.

S: I do not see how you could have equations of steel, eggs, and so on simultaneously.

M: Yes. It would still be true; let us say, 10,000 tons of steel (S) are here disposed of. The $S = D$ is all disposed of within the period and the way in which it is distributed among the different consumers is shown for each one of them by the quantities they buy being some function of the prices which are put on steel and everything else in the market. When you sum up the individual demands, each represented by an individual function of the whole array of prices, you can get a total expression which gives you functions representing the purchases of several markets. The F represents the relation between the purchases of steel in whatever units reckoned on the S side of the equation, and the prices of all the commodities given. Thus whatever unit is used on one side of the equations gets expressed on the other side.

S: What mathematical method would be used to find the p's?

M: Needless to say, if n is very large the resources of mathematics will scarcely enable the theorist to work it out. It is hardly a problem worth thinking about because the theorist cannot get the data. Quite apart from the question that the supplies are taken for granted it is absolutely impossible to find out by asking any individual, according to Cassel's requirement, when you vary the price how much he will buy of each one of the commodities in the market. The individual cannot tell. I ask you how many packages of cigarettes will you buy if the price for the brand you like is one cent, two cents, three cents, four cents and right on to a dollar. You cannot tell me. No one can give this data. If the theorist cannot get the data, then he cannot even begin the task of carrying out a computation. If he ever got to that point the resources of mathematics would enable him to arrive at a good many short cuts. But I do not know enough about mathematics to have any assurance that he could arrive at a solution which would give him an approximation of the actual result within any appropriate limit.

S: Have not Professor Henry L. Moore and others carried this further?

M: They have worked with single commodities; that is a very different story, is it not?

S: In a way, yet in actual practice it has yielded results.

M: That is so. When the economist comes actually to use statistical data he gives up this mathematically beautiful condition of the determination of all prices at one time and says, in terms of this operation, we will put all the p's but one or two equal to zero so as to get rid of them and then face quite a different problem. Yet it is true that under the circumstances several investigators have succeeded in getting functions which express the variations of the quantities of certain commodities which have been bought in certain areas year after year at given variations in price. The investigator can derive statistical formulae showing how, historically at least, quantities of commodities have varied with selling prices.

The simple stage of the problem has been given in the above discussion of Cassel and possibly suffices to give an impression as to the character of the theory. To go through the successive stages, making oral explanations to people, a good many of whom have not read the book would be futile. Those members of the class who are interested in seeing what mathematical economics is like in one of its best modern exemplars will turn to this particular chapter in Cassel and carefully consider how the argument is developed. I will present only a most general impression of the successive stages in the argument because it gets quite complicated. The equations which are used contain an increasing number of symbols. It is not, however, hard to understand.

In the second case Cassel drops the assumption that during the particular period the supply of commodities is fixed in advance and substitutes the assumption that the various factors of production are fixed but that the supply of the commodity which is sold is produced during the period. To treat this problem he supposes that there are r different means of production and these several means are indicated by $R_1, R_2 \ldots R_n$. Then he says that to produce any one of the articles which is supplied, that is to produce S_1, the supply of commodity number one which is produced within the period, will require a certain quantity of factors: quantities $a_1 \ldots a_{1r}$; for commodity number two, the quantities $a_2 \ldots a_{2r}$; and finally, for the unit-quantity of commodity n, the quantities $a_{n1} \ldots a_{n2}$.

The total supply of each commodity that will be forthcoming can then be written as S and will equal the sum of the quantities of each factor of production employed in manufacturing each particular commodity and he points out that for some commodities you will not have to use all the means at your disposal.[15]

He also points out that the price of a unit of S_1 will be equal to the prices of all the factors of production employed in making it. And prices of factors he treats as q's. Then he takes the problem of determining the q's after the same general fashion in which he attacks the problem of determining the p's. In other words, the elaboration involves specifically no new subject—but simply a recognition that the S's with which we started as taken for granted are produced from the factors of production which we now suppose to be taken for granted. And if these R's are taken for granted, there is only one step more of the same sort thrown into the procedure.

The third case which Cassel considers is that the amount of money which people have to spend upon goods during the period in view is not fixed in advance but is derived from their participation in the process of production during the period. A man gets his money income by selling a certain amount of whatever factor of production he owns. It is perhaps some kind of labor, perhaps some particular commodity, perhaps the use of some piece of property. The total incomes derived have to equal, of course, the total prices that are paid for the use of all the factors of production. Thus the theorist now derives, from a further analysis of the given elements a feature of the situation that

---

[15] ["Obviously several a's may be equal to zero since not all the factors of production are necessary for the production of any particular commodity." (*The Theory of Social Economy*, p. 142.)]

in the first case was taken for granted; he derives the amount of money income people will have available to spend.

The fourth case involves dropping the assumption so far maintained that the economy analyzed is a stationary one. He substitutes the supposition that in the broad group progress in the sense of increased production takes place from period to period. But it supposes that the advance is at a uniform or constant rate. That means only, in working out the conclusions, that in expressions of this sort there is added to the quantities of the factors of production which are employed, a certain percentage of the a_1's, a_2's, and so on down to a_n's. Instead of getting an a_1 the theorist has $a_1 + c$ (c standing for a fixed rate of increase). The equation can be worked out with as much facility after that is done as before.

In what might be called the fifth important case, Cassel points out that all that this analysis tells about prices is the relation which will exist among the prices of different commodities. It does not tell what any single price will be. It deals only with relative prices. But if the theorist can fix the price of any one commodity in the whole system then by implication the prices of all the others will be fixed. The general theory of pricing, in order to account for prices that exist in the world of actuality, has to be supplemented by a special theory dealing with the factors fixing the price of the particular article which is used in exchange: money. And he does in Book III Money give a long and particularly interesting analysis of the factors that determine the price of gold, the variations in its price, the variations in the general level of prices as shown by index numbers of wholesale prices. From his viewpoint, an advantage of his general scheme is that it provides an integrated theoretical connection between two subjects which in the hands of most theorists are not so well integrated: the general theory of prices and the theory of the value of money.

Up to this point Cassel has held to the supposition that the factors of production are fixed in quantity, or at most increased at a uniform rate. Of course that is not true. Thus it becomes necessary, if the theorist wants to make his general theory of prices applicable to the illumination of actual economic developments, to inquire into the processes which influence the supply of the great factors of production. These to Cassel, as to most of his predecessors, are land, labor and capital. Consequently Book I which culminates in the statement of the general theory of prices is followed by Book II which is entitled The Pricing of the Factors of Production. This book deals with the problem of wages, profits, rents and interest, more or less after the fashion in which they are treated by people who do not adopt Cassel's general approach.

S: He said something about saving not being saving. What is his conception of saving?

M: The point is that in the modern world there is presumably scarcely any hoarding going on. In a country like India, there is real saving in the sense that the word seems to connote to Cassel. There people hoard silver and gold and keep them until hard times come along, and then they have to spend their hoardings. But in the western world the man who in common parlance saves is merely spending part of his income for such forms of property as he thinks will yield him more income in the future. It is only a different form of spending.

S: Does Cassel make any contribution to the theory of interest?

M: Here is the central statement of his theory of interest: "The special theory of interest can therefore be nothing but a closer examination of the pricing process considered from the point of view of the price of capital-disposal."[16]

"Capital-disposal" means, in English-American usage, the use of loan funds; that is, his theory consists in a careful analysis of the peculiarities attendant on the process of putting a price on the use of loan funds. This price obviously has some peculiarities on its very face. We quote interest, for example, as a certain percent per annum on the principal. Markets for capital have a peculiar organization. In Cassel's eyes they have a very intimate connection with bank credit. Consequently his theory of interest turns into what is in considerable measure a lifelike analysis of the particular process of bargaining that goes on in the market where loans are made.

The most striking feature of his general statement, from the point of view of people brought up in the English tradition, is the argument that under ordinary conditions profits do not enter into cost; that, on the contrary, profits consist in positive differences between selling prices and costs. But this is a formal rather than a significant deviation from the usual methods of treatment. In the first place, Cassel states that economists should regard as part of cost, remuneration for the business man's time, interest for any capital that he uses, and compensation for whatever risks he encounters. If these three items are added to a sum which also contains the expenses which business men have incurred, Cassel thinks that in practice this sum generally equals the price. He says that the widespread prevalence of a

---

[16] *The Theory of Social Economy,* p. 210.

surplus of selling prices over costs thus computed is probably limited to the prosperity phase of business cycles. He thinks that it is probably true that during boom periods profits are common, in periods of depression losses are common. Profits also appear in many cases where some individual has been able to secure a specific monopoly, and probably he will be able to set selling prices at figures which cover all the sums paid out plus a return for his time, interest on his capital and remuneration for his risks. But business at large, Cassel would say, cannot be regarded as yielding profits, subtracting the good years from the bad, at least in competitive fields.

In a certain sense Cassel, by this discussion of profits and their variations in good times and bad, succeeds in hitching the last part of the treatise onto the proceeding ones. This part, Book IV, is devoted to the theory of business cycles.[17] His theory of business cycles, to which he has devoted a good deal of attention in a different fashion from that employed in his theory of pricing, is brought into relation to the general body of his theory by way of seeing at what times profits may be prevalent and at what times selling prices may commonly be below costs; costs including remuneration to the entrepreneur for his time, capital and risk.

S: Is his idea of profits far from classical theory?

M: That was the view that Walras developed more thoroughly than classical economists had done. It is one of the echoes of Walras to be found in Cassel. Warm admirers of Walras, like Henry L. Moore, feel discouraged, because Cassel does not recognize in this particular treatise the heavy debt which he owes to Walras. He does, at certain points, go beyond Walras and has stated the general theory of prices in simpler form than Walras had done. He does give not a little new light on the theory of money, and of course he attacks the theory of business cycles, but broadly speaking he is building on the foundation that was laid by Walras and he does not remember to mention this here. Doubtless he would say he made proper acknowledgements to Walras in his earlier studies.

S: Have any of his views been adopted in practical work?

M: On monetary phenomena Cassel has done a great deal of work and exercised a great deal of influence. There is probably no monetary theorist in the world who [as of 1933] has had more effect on practical policies since 1919 than he.

> No other writer on the subject [of money] commands a wider hearing. Internationally known as an economist before the war,

---

[17] [The second English translation contains a Book V, International Trade.]

publishing indifferently in Swedish, German and English, a delegate to all important monetary conferences in recent years, he has become an authority with whom everyone must reckon. Bank administrators find it necessary to answer his criticisms of their policies, statesmen ask him to prepare memoranda for their guidance, economists are eager to show where he goes wrong. . . .

Professor Cassel has not done much to improve the methods of monetary science. He is a theorist of the familiar type, dominated by a 'conception'; and using statistical data in an incidental rather than systematic way. But his conclusions rephrased as hypotheses to be tested, may help others to decide where to begin their analysis of the facts. It should not be long before discussions of the sort he produces are superseded by more exact and more conclusive demonstrations.[18]

Cassel has taken substantially the same course in *The Theory of Social Economy*. Starts the discussion of pricing with a schedule showing what different consumers are willing to pay for successive units of supply and goes on from that point. This course throws the theory of value—in the sense of an explanation of what people are ready to pay for goods—out of economic theory. In its place we have merely a theory of pricing which may seem to bring money back into heart of economics. He holds that it does in this sense: In the general theory of pricing "we must reckon all values in a unit of money." Hence, to complete the theory of pricing we must know how the purchasing power of this unit is determined. A theory of money is required to finish the general theory of pricing which means a theory of the general changes in the level of prices. The problem is simply solved by showing that the purchasing power of the monetary unit "is determined by the scarcity of the means of payment valid in the given monetary system."[18a]

In general, Cassel's type of economic theory has an interestingly close logical relationship to that of Davenport, a relationship to which the different dress in which the theory is presented ought not to blind the student. The fact that Davenport does not use a single mathematical symbol and that Cassel works with an elaborate apparatus of equations does not in the least prevent Cassel's *Theory of Social Economy* from being a discussion of substantially the same problems that Davenport treats in *The Economics of Enterprise,* or from leading to substantially the same range of conclusions. Both writers are endeavoring to make economics more scientific by circumscribing its undertaking in a severer fashion than their predecessors had done.

---

[18] Mitchell, review of Cassel, *Money and Foreign Exchange After 1914* in *Quarterly Publications of the American Statistical Association,* June 1923, pp. 2-4.

[18a] Outline, "Money and Economic Activities," discussion with Banking Seminar, School of Business, Columbia University, October 5, 1939.

The tremendous hold of Cassel on the able young Swedish scholars is illustrated by the following from Mitchell's "Diary." February 11, 1927, "[Erik] Lundberg, Swedish fellow of L[aura] S[pellman] R[ockefeller] Memorial came to talk of his perplexities of how to replace the economic theories in which Cassel had brought him up."

Both want to eliminate from economics discussions of production so far as that subject leads one to a study of resources or technical methods.

From their point of view the business of the economist centers in an analysis of the pricing process; and the analysis consists in explaining prices in terms of one another. Davenport sums up the situation most frankly when he says that the price analysis which he develops with such logical skill is circuitous, explaining one price in terms of other prices. He goes on to state that the circuitous explanation cannot be regarded as scientifically satisfactory; the economist must go behind it; but when he does so, his business is simply to recognize the kind of forces that exercise the ultimate control: the valuations which the economist is not competent to discuss; the relative abundance—Cassel says the relative scarcity—of natural resources and the technical knowledge which are matters not for the economist to investigate.

In a sense these developments in the direction of making economics a more technical and circumscribed science move far away from the ground that was occupied by the early classicists. Adam Smith, though a pioneer, covered an enormous range of topics. He was interested primarily in economic policy; and he had no conscientious scruples against discussing any factors that seemed pertinent to a treatment of his general question: on what did the wealth of nations depend? In the case of Ricardo the field of study is circumscribed in a certain sense. He discusses little beyond problems of value and distribution, plus certain problems of taxation that can be made to throw light upon value and distribution. But that was not because he thought that economics ought to be confined to that area; it was simply because he thought that these were the central problems of economics and problems that up to that time had been excluded. John Stuart Mill presents a fuller view of the classical conception of what economics ought to cover. To him it included production, distribution, exchange, the possible future development of economic institutions and the role of the state in economic life.

When we pass to Jevons, we find him like Ricardo, treating a restricted problem but he limited his scope for the same reason that Ricardo did: he believed that he had an important contribution to make to the fundamental problem of value and he pointed out most clearly that this was only a part of the whole field. Yet the general tendency of later economists who followed the classical tradition has been to take the view that the economist as such ought to throw whatever light he can upon not only technical problems of price formation and the distribution of income in the modern state, but also upon the real forces that control technical developments. This is the position that Marshall takes; and it has been characteristic of most economists who have been influenced primarily by the British tradition.

Davenport in this respect represents a distinct change, which is indicated by his feeling that what the economists as such are in a position to contribute to the understanding of the real forces amounts to very little. There are the tribes of investigators to deal with the ultimate forces, the psychologists, the people who know about natural resources of various sorts, geologists, economic geographers and the engineers who know about the technical methods of production. To them should be left the important problems of trying to delve into the types of questions which when they appeared pertinent had been discussed without much hesitation by people like John Stuart Mill or Alfred Marshall.

This is the line which mathematical economics as started by Walras and represented in later times by Cassel was taking. From one point of view the later developments may be regarded as the results of reflection of thoughtful minds upon the desirable scope of economics. Davenport was certainly fully and intimately acquainted with the work of his predecessors. Cassel has never spent anything like as much time as Davenport in studying the history of economic theory. His line of interest is not that which would lead him to be much concerned with the thoughts of other people. He has wanted to wrestle with problems as he saw them for himself, but his practical judgment leads him to the same conclusion that Davenport arrived at from his elaborate study on previous types of economic theory worked out in his *Value and Distribution;* namely, that the thing for economists to do if they want to make some substantial contribution to understanding is to focus attention upon a definite range of problems which belong to economists and to keep their layman's hands off problems for the solution of which they are not particularly equipped.

This has been one of the definite trends in the later development of economic theory. The exponents of this type which won most favor

> argue that the theory of prices . . . does not after all depend for its validity upon the underlying theory of valuation. Somehow men choose among goods. Their choices imply scales of preference, which can be represented by demand curves or schedules, or, more innocently by "indifference curves." Let the economist accept these schedules or curves as *data,* not to be inquired into, and build upon them his explanation of prices, including the prices of the factors of

production. The price theories will remain valid, whatever account may be given by others of the process by which men arrive at their valuations. This line was taken with variations in statement by Pareto, Cassel, Fetter, Davenport and others.[19]

Their disciples first of all "from my viewpoint . . . do not eliminate psychology from their doctrines by starting with the simple fact of preference. That device seems rather to lead in the direction of Walras and Pareto who, despite their protestations, are quite obviously working with a human nature that has fundamentally the characteristic attributed to it by Bentham."[20]

[Phrased somewhat differently]

Marshall's cornerstone is rejected by later builders. The theory of valuation is handed over to psychologists, philosophers, or any other group of workers who think themselves competent to deal with it. But while he discards his old theory of valuation, the economic theorist keeps finished valuations, as his basic "facts." They are facts only in a Pickwickian sense. The theorist does not himself ascertain men's preferences by empirical inquiry; he merely supposes them to have been ascertained. This practice saves a vast deal of labor. It also opens the door wide to interesting speculations. Supposed facts can be set up in a wide variety of patterns, which present a corresponding variety of problems in price determination. For example, by the use of assumptions fitted to the purpose, price theory has been extended since Marshall's day over the field of what is now tersely called "imperfect competition."

Convenient as is this modern fashion, it has serious disadvantages. First and most obvious, it means that economic theory moves on a more superficial level than in its more confident days. The theorist works with data he does not profess to explain. Of course, no science accounts for all the matters with which it deals; but each strives to delve ever deeper into its problems. To reverse this process and become more superficial is not pleasant.[21]

Perhaps more accurately it should be said that

knowledge of economic behavior remains exceedingly schematic, superficial, and technical when it rests on confessed ignorance of what men are striving to get and what they are striving to avoid. To say merely that men have scales of preference lays a foundation for speculations that apply logically to Esquimaux and London bankers, to men of the tenth and men of the twentieth centuries, to peoples at war and peoples at peace. The very generality of the conclusions that can be deduced from such assumptions prevents them from fitting the facts of any place and time. Pretty much all that economic historians try to learn is barred from economic theory of the current abstract type.[22]

---

[19] Mitchell, "Facts and Values in Economics," *The Journal of Philosophy,* April 13, 1944, p. 214.

[20] Mitchell to F. A. Hayek, December 21, 1923.

[21] Mitchell, "Facts and Values in Economics," pp. 214-215.

[22] Mitchell, "The Role of Money in Economic History," *The Journal of Economic History,* December 1944, p. 65.

In conclusion, it may be said that the founders of classical political economy, the mechanics of utility and the Austrian calculus were really engaged in studies of the logic of pecuniary institutions, while the representatives of pure theory, neo-classical theory and the American psychological school engaged in pecuniary analysis. The scientific defect of these theories— barring perhaps the last which as represented by Davenport is more self conscious—is that they do not see that they are developing the logic of an institution which has but partial sway over economic behavior.[23]

To fill the gap left by these schools in eliminating valuation, a new type of theory arose, best described as the social value type. We turn to this type, taking as its representative, Benjamin McAlester Anderson, Jr.[24]

---

[23] Outline, May 14, 16, 1914. [As for a theory of change, "Cassel puts a theory of conjuncture into his treatise but he did not see how to integrate it with his general theory of pricing. Schumpeter makes a more organic connection." Outline, "Lecture on Trade Cycles," Oxford University, June 2, 1932.]

[24] Outline, "Types of Economic Theory," APP 44-53, no. 28.

CHAPTER XVII

Social Value School:
Benjamin McAlester Anderson, Jr.[1]

To understand the social value type of economic theory, one should know something about the rise of social psychology, for this school sought to apply the lessons of social psychology to economics. Social psychology was at first generally regarded as a kind of supplement to individual psychology. Nowadays [1918], however, the social psychologists are ready to go much further. They say that theirs is the only psychology,[2] that there is no individual psychology, that the idea of an individual psychology over against a social psychology is a relic of the older individualistic conception of human nature which ran through the social sciences. Society was generally regarded by the exponents of the older view of human nature as little more than an aggregate of individuals who constituted a set of different units. The idea that society is something more than the mere aggregate of the people that comprise it was hardly met with. The economists were accustomed to hold the view that social wealth is simply the sum of property of the various individuals in society. Just as the economists implied that since the wealth of society is the total of the wealth of individuals, and that therefore the proper way to increase the wealth of the nation is to allow everyone to follow his own interests and thus to increase his property as freely as possible, so the economists and the writers on politics took the view that each individual is a sort of independent atom who is to be understood by himself, and added as an independent atom to get any social total in which the investigator is interested.

There is, however, no psychology but social psychology for the reason that every individual becomes what he is primarily under the

---

[1] This chapter is from the "1918 Typescript," unless otherwise noted.

[2] "One of [John] Dewey's favorite sayings, [is] 'There is no psychology but social psychology.'" Mitchell, "Research in the Social Sciences," 1919; reprinted in *The Backward Art of Spending Money and Other Essays,* compiled and edited by Joseph Dorfman (New York: McGraw-Hill, 1937) p. 79.

influence of the people among whom he grows up, the people who teach him what he knows, who form his habits of thinking, feeling and acting.

There were of course early applications of the ideas that were synthesized into the field of social psychology. Some of them have already been mentioned: Sir Henry Maine's *Ancient Law* and Bagehot's *Physics and Politics* emphasized a habit psychology[3] for the understanding of the differences of institutions. Auguste Comte stressed the factor of sympathy as a concern for the general welfare. There was also the French psychologist Gabriel Tarde who stressed imitation among other things.[4]

It was not, however, until the turn of the century that some kind of synthesis began to be made of the various ideas, and that social psychology proper came into existence. The social psychologists in their early days at least were animated largely by a reaction against certain aspects of the view of human nature and social policy entertained by the great line of utilitarian thinkers from James Mill to John Stuart Mill and Henry Sidgwick. They reacted against the hedonistic conception of man with its implications of extreme intellectualism and individualism.

The later writers are numerous. A few are particularly conspicuous for their influence on economists. Among these we certainly should count C. H. Cooley (1864-1929) of the University of Michigan, the author of *Human Nature and the Social Order* (1902) and *Social Organization* (1909). Recently [1912-1915] he published a series of

---

[3] [Mitchell also had in his notes the following quotation] from J. M. Keynes, "The Works of Bagehot," *The Economic Journal,* September 1915, p. 371: "Perhaps the most striking and fundamental doctrine in *Lombard Street* is, in a sense, psychological rather than economic. I mean the doctrine of the Reserve, and that the right way to stop a crisis is to lend freely." ("J. M. Keynes," APP 64-73, no. 41.)

[4] ["For more than a decade his work and that of his followers in France and the United States...dominated social psychology and almost sociology. I shall not rehearse the old discussions about Imitation as a psychological fact and a social force. I should assume with most of contemporary psychological critics that as a descriptive and explanatory conception it misplaced emphasis and tended to distort facts. But nevertheless we cannot minimize the immense power of this stage of social science in popularizing the idea of social psychology, and in bringing into recognition many facts, such as the importance of prestige, fashion, sensitiveness to the beliefs of others, the difficulties which innovation, no matter how reasonable, has to meet, etc., facts which are permanently imbedded in social science. . . . I do not think we shall ever outgrow some of his contributions, although to my mind they are found rather in logic than in psychology—such as the necessity for reducing the gross phenomena of social life into minuter events which may then be analyzed one by one. The most fruitful of his psychological conceptions was ahead of his time and went almost unnoted. It was that all psychological phenomena can be divided into the physiological and the social, and that when we have relegated elementary sensation and appetite to the former head, all that is left of our mental life, our beliefs, ideas and desires, falls within the scope of social psychology." (John Dewey, "The Need for Social Psychology," *The Psychological Review,* July 1917, p. 267.)].

articles which are of particular interest to the economist. This series is concerned particularly with pecuniary valuation and is the fore-runner of another carefully considered volume [*Social Process*, 1918].[5]

Cooley is primarily a sociologist who has become acquainted with modern psychology, and is trying to work out an account of certain prevalent habits of behavior in sociological terms—to explain why people believe in some things, why they appreciate certain things, how they love to be imposed upon by certain social factors that are detri-mental to their individual welfare, etc. His work is in great part responsible for "the high promise of that effort to frame an 'institu-tional theory' of value which certain of our colleagues have begun" (1914).[6]

Then there is William McDougall's *Introduction to Social Psy-chology* (1908). He is an Oxford psychologist[7] who thought it desir-able that workers in the social sciences should be provided with an elementary epitome of the psychology which was particularly impor-tant for them and he supplied it in the very readable book that has just been noticed. The sociological part of his speculations is for him an excursion into a foreign field just as the psychological part of the speculations of the older social psychologists was to them an adven-ture into an alien area. Another important participant was Graham Wallas (whom we have already met in connection with the philo-sophical radicals and Fabian Socialism). He was interested in political science rather than in sociology at large or in psychology. He was one of the best writers among the early Fabians and had a long experience of practical political life in London, on, of course, the unpopular side. Nevertheless he obtained considerable success in politics, success which was remarkable for a socialist leader. Then he began teaching in the London School of Economics and Political Science. His interest has

---

[5] The series was composed of "Valuation as a Social Process," *The Psychological Bulletin*, December 15, 1912, pp. 441-450; "The Institutional Character of Pecuniary Valuation," *The American Journal of Sociology*, January 1913, pp. 543-555; "The Sphere of Pecuniary Valuation," *The American Journal of Sociology*, September 1913, pp. 188-203; "The Progress of Pecuniary Valuation," *The Quarterly Journal of Eco-nomics*, November 1915, pp. 1-21.

[6] "See Cooley, 'The Progress of Pecuniary Valuation'; and the discussion of 'The Concept of Value' by Professors B. M. Anderson, Jr. and J. M. Clark, in *The Quarterly Journal of Economics*, August 1915, especially Professor Clark's remarks." (Mitchell, "The Role of Money in Economic Theory," 1915; reprinted in *The Backward Art of Spending Money and Other Essays*, p. 175).

[Speaking of Mitchell's *Business Cycles* Cooley wrote: Professor Mitchell's work is an excellent example of what a scientific study of social process in the economic sphere should be, and of the uses and limits of the statistical method." *Social Process* (New York: Scribner's, 1918) pp. 32-33.]

[7] [McDougall later came to the United States and taught first at Harvard and then at Duke.]

been primarily in investigating the psychological factors of modern political experience. He has two books both charming in detail, and illuminating in the large, *Human Nature in Politics* (1908) and *The Great Society* (1914).

John Dewey has probably had more influence than any other single person in the United States on the development of the newer viewpoint concerning man's nature and his relation to society. All who have taken his courses, under whatever topic, must realize that every one of them ought properly to be regarded as contributing to the field of social psychology in the large. He has in comparatively recent years published several articles bearing directly and explicitly upon certain topics in the field. He has delivered at least one course of lectures under the title, social psychology.[8] I hope the time will come when he will be publishing systematically in the subject. [Dewey has been critical of dominant economics as well as the social sciences in general.] He stated in a conversation:

1. Economists have not clearly distinguished between decline in intensity of wants through mere satisfaction of a want or appetite and the more general problem of relative importance of different goods.

2. One of great difficulties with present economic organization is that activities are directed not toward objects of interest, but toward intermediaries—e.g., making parts of a machine which workers will never see, learning things in school of which child does not appreciate the application.

3. Purposes are not found as objects of action, but we become conscious of what we are *doing* and then concentrate efforts on this aim more systematically.[9]

[To Dewey] empirical research has a pattern of growth unlike that of logical discourse. He hit off the difference by calling one retail, the other wholesale.[10] [As Dewey put it negatively] in *Democracy and Education*, "Men still want the crutch of dogma, of belief fixed by authority to relieve them of the trouble of thinking and the responsibility of directing their activity by thought. They tend to confine their own thinking to a consideration of what one among the rival systems of dogma they will accept."[10a]

---

[8] The series of lectures was delivered February and March 1914 in Schenectady, New York. [Professor Mitchell read over the lecture notes at Dewey's request.]

[9] "Talk with Dewey," March 19, 1914.

[10] Two sentences from Outline, "Seminar in Economic Changes and Economic Theory," May 9, 1944.

[10a] Quotation in "John Dewey," APP 54-63, no. 59. See for elaboration Vol. I, p. 147.

Again I may forewarn you that in a certain sense all of Thorstein Veblen's books may be regarded as constructive contributions to the understanding of the formation and development of social mind.[11] They are studies of a development, of the cumulative change of certain habits of thinking, feeling and acting. He does not go about his work with an elaborate critical commentary upon the shortcomings of earlier psychologists. He does not set himself the task of developing a systematic book, but he takes hold of certain immensely significant problems and undertakes a solution of them in what are substantially psychological terms. But this will be more clear when we come to discuss Veblen himself.

All this is by way of preparing for a discussion of the social value type of theory of economics. It is necessary, because this type is after all only an attempt to see the implications for technical economic theory of the change in the general conception of human nature and human behavior. The social value theory is one of the types that attempts to supply the absence of a theory of valuation in the pure theory of static equilibrium. More narrowly it represents one wing of the group which criticizes the work of the American psychological school on the ground that it pays no attention to the institutional factor in behavior, that it does not give a competent account of the conditions which shape men's desires, which give rise to men's notions concerning what is worthwhile, concerning sacrifices as well as gratifications. There are several different lines of work which aim to fill the vacuum. Their exponents consider themselves as making their particular lines of attack upon the problem by giving adequate attention to the institutional factor.

The first of these to be discussed is the social value type because it stands closer logically to the kind of theory that Frank A. Fetter represents. The particular problem that the theorists of this school have attacked is the problem of what determines men's valuations. As already noted, the utility theorists including the American psychological school as well as Jevons, make little attempt to explain why people attach significance to particular articles, to analyze the facts on which the demand schedules rest. The social value theorists attack the problem, and in so doing ascribe a large importance to the influence of institutions; that is to say, they regard men's desires as the outcome of widely prevalent social habits of acting, feeling; and these widely prevalent social habits are what they understand by institutions.

---

[11] Phrasing of sentence in part from Outline, March 11, 1918.

A second somewhat different line of attack is represented by the Historical School. This school has laid stress particularly upon the special ways in which existing economic institutions have attained their present shape in various communities. A still different line of attack, for which it is difficult to find a satisfactory name but which is often called the genetic type, is closely allied with the historical school but pays more attention to psychological analysis in the proper sense than the historical economists have been accustomed to do.[12]

We shall turn first to the work of B. M. Anderson, Jr. as an explicit representative of the social value school in the narrow sense. He is the most aggressive. He uses the label consistently concerning his own work, and has been probably the most systematic in his attempts to work out the viewpoint. But he by no means stands alone. Cooley was much earlier in the field and has covered a much wider range. There are a considerable number of other people who share at least in part the same notions; men like J. M. Clark and Walton H. Hamilton have for the most part been influenced more by other men than they have by their younger contemporary, Anderson, directly.[13]

[Anderson (1886-1949) came of a politically and culturally prominent Missouri family. He was a B.A. of the University of Missouri, an M.A. from the University of Illinois, and a Ph.D. of Columbia. After serving as an instructor at Columbia from 1911 to 1913, and as an assistant professor at Harvard until 1918, he accepted a position in 1918 as economic adviser of the National Bank of Commerce, New York. After the merger with the Chase National Bank two years later, he continued as economist of the new bank. In 1939 he returned to teaching at the University of California, Los Angeles. He was a pupil of Dewey at Columbia and he was an admirer of Cooley's work, particularly *Social Organization,* and of Veblen's various books.][14]

---

[12] [This "genetic" type represented in 1918 by Veblen became the "institutional" type represented by Veblen and John R. Commons in the mimeographed lecture notes. Earlier (1914) Professor Mitchell referred to Veblen's type as "evolutionary."]

[13] [Clark and Hamilton were influenced especially by Veblen and Cooley. For Hamilton (1881-1958) and J. M. Clark (1884-1963) see Joseph Dorfman, *The Economic Mind in American Civilization,* 5 volumes (New York: The Viking Press, 1946-1959) V, pp. 425-463.]

[14] [Anderson in his review of the original German edition of Schumpeter's *The Theory of Economic Development,* noted some similarities between Schumpeter and Veblen: "The psychology of Schumpeter's entrepreneur includes such elements as love of activity for its own sake, love of creative activity, love of distinction, love of victory over others, love of the game, and other traits which the newer psychology has been emphasizing, and with which such writings as those of Veblen . . . have made American students familiar. . . . The economist has too long been content with static theory, and work like that of Schumpeter and Veblen is full of significance for the better understanding of economic life." ("Schumpeter's Dynamic Economics," *Political Science Quarterly,* December 1915, pp. 645, 660.]

The discussion of Anderson will center first and primarily on his Hart, Schaffner, and Marx prize essay and Columbia University doctoral dissertation, *Social Value* (1911), and then on his extremely interesting *The Value of Money* (1917), a book which is more concerned with general theoretical issues than most treatises on money.[15] Of the latter book there are only two parts that particularly concern us: Parts I and IV. Parts II and III are rather highly technical criticisms of the quantity theory of the value of money. But Part I reviews and restates his general, theoretical scheme as represented by *Social Value* and Part IV makes a further advance by showing how, in Anderson's view, it is possible to reconcile statics and dynamics.

M: What seemed to be the outstanding features of Anderson's theory, the things that are significant about it as making it different from other types?

S1: The emphasis on the ethical point of view rather than any attempt to analyze. It seems to me it is rather an attempt to evaluate rather than to analyze. In *Value of Money* he does not attempt actually to analyze the social money as a tool. He wants to evaluate.

M: Evaluate what?

S1: Evaluate an existing system of institutions.

M: To tell whether it is good or bad?

S1: Yes, to tell whether it is desirable.

M: What is his criterion of what is desirable?

S1: I cannot see that it gets very far away from the good of the greatest number; from group benefit.

M: Is his interest in evaluation the chief distinguishing characteristic? Some of the other writers are much interested in telling what is good and what is bad, and having pronounced views on the subject.

S2: His chief interest is that he wants to grasp the value concept as an objective concept.

M: As an objective concept?

S2: As a concept which we could take in hand and measure in some way; therefore he opposes all the relativist value schools, all the earlier schools, and he thinks that through social psychology he will be able, or at least one would be able, to find such an objective measurement for value.

---

[15] [The prize provided for $400 in addition to publication.

Anderson wrote a third book which appeared shortly after his death in 1949, *Economics and the Public Welfare: Financial and Economic History of the United States, 1914-1946*. It was an outstanding study of the economic and financial history of the country, from the standpoint of a stringent critic of the policies identified with the New Deal.]

M: To put that in Anderson's own terminology, he lays heavy emphasis on the idea of absolute value, the contention that absolute value is prior to exchange. That certainly is one of his outstanding characteristics. What else is characteristic of him?

S3: He would not make a great distinction between economic value and ethical value and legal value.

M: That is where there is some justification for what S1 has in mind. That is true. He would have theorists say that economic value is not a species by itself, but that it is one of a larger genus, and that economic valuations are shot through with ethical and political and aesthetic interests. What else?

S1: Dynamic as opposed to static.

M: What leads you to that? *Social Value?* Do you mean that Anderson himself is developing a dynamic theory?

S1: He thinks that all other work is preparatory to the dynamic theory, and he is trying to show economists a way of developing it.

M: Has he any specific criticisms to advance of other types of economic theory?

S4: He charges that they took out, abstracted, in a sense they isolated the elements.

M: Before taking up Anderson's practical views, it would be well if the students bear these catch phrases in mind: First, "absolute value"; then what he calls "the vicious circle of the Austrians." And then "the social factors in valuation." If the student thinks of those three things, particularly trying to find out what they mean to Anderson, he will have the gist of his particular contribution or that of the school for which he stands.

To repeat, the best introduction to the characteristic doctrines of the social value school is the criticism which it makes of the Austrian theory of value, a criticism which is summed up in Anderson's phrase, "the vicious circle of the Austrians."

S5: Can you explain what "the vicious circle of the Austrians" is?

M: As Anderson presented it, a commodity according to the Austrians has value, because other commodities are acquired in exchange for it. The other commodities have value because they can be exchanged for the first one. In that way there is a circle. What is vicious about that circle?

S5: The theorist explains value in terms of value.

M: That is the way Anderson puts it. Let me read you one of the quotations which he presents as exhibiting this vicious circle in particularly clear form. It is from Wieser's *Natural Value,* one of the greatest classics of the Austrian school. The quotation runs as follows: "The relation of natural value to exchange value is clear." Notice, it is the relation of natural value, that is, the underlying concept, to exchange value, that Wieser is talking about. To continue with the quotation, "Natural value is one element in the formation of exchange value. It does not, however, enter simply and thoroughly into exchange value. On the one side, it is disturbed by human imperfection, by error, fraud, force, chance."[16]

Anderson is going to argue before he gets done with the quotation, that exchange value is already, on Wieser's showing, an element of natural value. There is one curious, characteristic feature of Wieser's conception of natural value. Natural value answers to the idea which would prevail regarding value in a community of men where nothing ever changed, that is to say, a static community, and where no mistakes were made. It is value as seen by the perfect economic man without any alteration or problem arising because of probable changes in his environment. Wieser says that natural value enters into the formation of exchange value, but it is "disturbed by human imperfection." Actual men are not perfect economic men. It is disturbed also by error—they make mistakes in calculation—by "fraud, force, chance." On the other hand it is disturbed in "the present order of society by the existence of private property, and by the differences between rich and poor."[17]

In the state in which natural value would appear in all its beautiful simplicity there would be no great difference between rich and poor, so that the substantial human value of things would stand out clearly to the community as a whole. Wherever some people are very rich and others very poor the theorist will find, on Wieser's showing, that certain rare commodities—one of the illustrations that he uses is the services of great medical experts—commodities of a rarity of this sort will be bid up in price by the richer members of the community, and they will not be utilized to the best human advantage. The medical specialists will spend most of their time in looking after nervous women who have nothing wrong with them except an undue personal vanity, whereas all their time ought to be given to alleviating cases of great suffering. To repeat: "On the one side, it is disturbed by human imperfection, by error, fraud, force, chance; and on the other, by the present order of society, by the existence of private property, and by the differences between rich and poor—as a conse-

---

[16] Quoted in Anderson, *Social Value* (Boston: Houghton Mifflin, 1911) p. 47.
[17] Quoted in *Social Value,* p. 47.

quence of which latter a second element mingles itself in the formation of exchange value, namely, *purchasing power.*"[18]

When Wieser arrives at this point Anderson says in effect in *Social Value* "Here you have it. He started out to show that natural value enters into the formation of exchange value, and here he is saying that natural value itself is affected by purchasing power." "What is purchasing power," Anderson goes on to say, "except another name for exchange value?" That is to say, argues Anderson, according to the theorist of the Wieser type here is exchange value entering into the formation of natural value and natural value entering into the formation of natural value. The theorist of the Wieser type goes back to exchange value, again. Again, he has no explanation.

S6: I thought Anderson's main objection was not so much that it was a vicious circle explaining value by value, but the fact that the individual utility curve and the individual demand price curve never coincided with the market prices, the exchange values. Market value is a thing quite independent of the tastes of the individual.

M: On the Austrian showing?

S6: In his opinion.

M: That is to say, in Anderson's opinion?

S6: The vicious circle which he presents is only an illustration to show that the Austrians could never explain the value in the market by what we call in this case the real forces behind it.

M: Suppose you go over that explanation once again, let us see if we can accept your version of the vicious circle.

S6: Anderson is not satisfied with the explanation of market values as given by the marginal utility theorists. They go back to real forces, that is human desires, or in Jevons's explanation, pain and pleasure, and he finds no actual relation, no explanation of the market values in the real forces that the marginal utility theorists present.

M: May I interrupt here to show that Anderson's criticism of the Austrians along that line is that their explanation of the values which individuals set on objects is a very imperfect one, because the Austrians seem to take account only of the individual's own feelings, and feelings, Anderson would say, with reference to economic situations alone. In contrast, Anderson would argue that the individual in setting values on goods himself is influenced by the whole social environment under which he has grown up, and that in particular, in setting values on goods, he does not separate economic from ethical, legal or other considerations.

---

[18] Quoted in *Social Value,* p. 47. Italics are Anderson's.

S6: Yes, this is the constructive side of his argument.

M: The critical side begins with the statement that the Austrians have made an illegitimate abstraction from the multiplicity of circumstances which influence men's valuations. Instead of seeing how many different factors there are that work in the minds of every person in the valuations set by individuals upon commodities, they keep too closely within the individual's skin, and on this basis they make another illegitimate abstraction cutting out all considerations which are not strictly and narrowly economic in character. That is the beginning of his criticism.

S6: But now he has to proceed to show how this explanation of the real forces does not give the explanation of the market values as they are.

M: Then he goes on with this demonstration, as he regards it, of how reasoning conducted on that plan runs in a circle.

S6: I miss a link. I have to put in one link. This link is in his book, but he did not make entirely clear that what he means is that real forces will give a proper explanation of market values.

M: On the Austrian showing?

S6: On the Austrian showing.

M: That is to say, that if the Austrians think that they account for market value in terms of real forces, they are mistaken. From one point of view he is making the same kind of criticism that was developed in class discussion on Marshall, though it is fairer to say simply that we were not so much criticising Marshall as trying to find out where the equilibrium was on his basis. If one accepts the logic of the Austrian analysis, market prices are not established by an equilibrium among the real forces, even in the Austrian sense of real forces. They are not, because Wieser points out that the working of the forces is interfered with by such factors as the unequal distribution of wealth. But the particular form in which Anderson meets that criticism is the alleged demonstration of the vicious circle, the explanation of value by value. That is to say, before the theorist can understand, on the Austrian basis, how market prices are fixed, he has to take for granted the existence of other price arrangements which are involved in an unequal distribution of wealth.

S6: This is the point where I do not agree with Anderson.

M: What is wrong with Anderson's criticism?

S6: Anderson's quotations from Wieser do not prove much. According to the marginal utility theory as put forth, say by Davenport, Fetter or Schumpeter, there is not a straight line between the real forces and the market equilibrium and the market values, exchange values, as they are. Therefore there is not necessarily a circle. If Anderson wants to be logical, he ought to take quotations from Wieser to show that as Wieser uses the phrase "purchasing power," the utility theorists do not explain adequately the forces in modern economic society. This is the thing which troubled Davenport. He said that there is no straight line from the real forces to the market values. Other theorists tried to do so. If Anderson wanted to be logical he had to show that a link is missing, that the real forces do not explain the market values. Instead he finds flaws in the expressions of Wieser, or somebody else, which is not convincing at all.

M: How does S6's criticism strike the other members of the class?

S7: The answer to the last thing S6 says is that all Anderson can go by is what these men say. In reference to the first part, what the Austrian school says is that there is a direct connection between market value and real forces. They either acknowledge it openly as Davenport does, or else evade it, as some of the others do by not showing where that connection comes in. He says that their theory is a connection between them, the real forces and market value. Anderson does not try to deny that there is a connection. His contention is that the Austrian School fails to show how valuations are made.

S1: Is not his criticism simply that in explanation of the real forces the Austrian school brings in an existing price situation, whereas Anderson insists that their mental makeup is extraneous to the prior value?

M: Are there other comments about it?

S2: I think that S6 is right.

S1: Is Mr. Anderson's absolute value really absolute value?

M: Let us carry the discussion forward by two stages. In the first place I would like to say a word or two about this circuitous reasoning you have represented in other lines, and in the second place it is quite clear that we have to form a definite notion as to what absolute value is in Anderson's conception.

About the circuitous reasoning. In the first place, remember that Davenport in setting up his prices said explicitly several times that all explanation of prices is circuitous; that in every one of the demand schedules employed for the explanation of the price of any given article, there is implicitly present a whole set of other pre-established prices. Here is a theorist who has in general the Austrian viewpoint, who has worked the thing out logically, to a finish, rather better than the rest of them, acknowledging frankly that price theory, as we have it, runs in terms of an endless circle. Davenport would not admit that it is vicious, but you do explain price in terms of other prices. Then back of that price discussion, remember Davenport says there is the play of three ultimate factors: people's desires for commodities, their instrumental equipment and their productive capacities. The point where his view of the matter is incomplete, is that the relationship between these ultimate forces and pecuniary factors is not explained. Again recall that on Schumpeter's showing all the factors in the market mutually determine one another. The way in which he argues the problem is by means of a large number of simultaneous equations, all of which are necessary for working out the solution; in other words, to have an explanation of any one of the prices or exchanges in Schumpeter's market, the theorist would have to bring in all the other prices in exchange in the course of his explanation.

S6: But they go back to the individual psychology.

M: What lies behind this circuitous price reasoning on Schumpeter's showing? It is slightly different from what lies behind the price reasoning on Davenport's showing. On Schumpeter's showing the things that lie behind market prices are the data upon which the theorist reasons, and the data consist of definite suppositions concerning the number of individuals, the number of commodities, the value functions of each individual for each commodity, and a statement concerning the stocks of each commodity in the possession of each individual. Those are the ultimate forces. Schumpeter explicitly refuses to go further back in his effort to get an explanation, saying that it is no part of the economist's task to try to account for value functions or for the stocks of goods on hand at a given time in the possession of each individual. Those are the data which the economist must take as given. Also bear this in mind as connected with Anderson's endeavor to show that the Austrians are guilty of reasoning in a vicious circle when they explain the relation between value and prices.

Let us go forward a little bit with the study of Anderson on constructive ideas, and see what his notion of absolute value is.

S4: I do not know that I get it entirely. There seem to be three factors in his absolute value. It forms two sides, the structural side and the functional side. He would say on the structural side that the three factors are first, feeling, second, a desire, and third what he called a residing in the commodity of some sort of force that attracts.

S6: Motivating power.

S4: Then on the functional side, the value of the commodity lies in its ability to make the individual want it; that is, its economic motivation. Then when he discusses social value, he says the value is a quantity socially valid, but I do not know what he means by that.

M: The first thing to do in trying to understand his doctrine of absolute value is to see why he is so sure that there is an entity to which he gives this name, absolute value. Why is he positive that the relative value concept is not adequate for purposes of economics, that we must have an absolute value behind our relative values? How does he work that out, S1?

S1: He discusses the prices as ratios between commodities and money is simply a commodity which must have an inherent value to balance against some inherent value in the other commodity against which it exchanges. In other words, price is simply an extra barter. It is simply an extra step in the process, and if you have commodities changing against each other, you do not have something changing against nothing, and you have to somehow provide for the value of money.

S6: I was surprised to find out how much he resembles Marx. Marx says two things exchange. Now it is not their color, their warmth, their tastes. It is not anything of that sort. They must have some substance. He says that substance is equality [of value]. But after all it amounts to the same.

M: The parallel is happily suggested.

The idea of the existence of absolute value is from Anderson's point of view a thing so simple that you can hardly discuss it. If you have an exchange value that must mean that there is a ratio between two quantities, and two quantities must have existence in your mind. They certainly must be quantities of value, that is to say, there must be those values in your mind before you can make comparison. You can not conceive of a conjectural price offer arising in your mind for anything unless you admit that there are two distinct quantities in your mind which are brought into comparison in that price offer. When the individual says that he will give two cents for an evening paper that implies logically that he must have two independent values there which he is equating. As S6 says, it is quite clear that they must be values on Anderson's point of view because you canvass the field in other respects in which these commodities are compared. They are not equal in any other respect. It is as factors which have motivating power over a person's economic conduct that they are equal. The absolute things are absolute values. These values, as Anderson sees things, must exist prior to exchange. This is a fundamental part of Anderson's notion; that is, as far as his own contribution is concerned, the notion of the necessity of the existence of absolute value prior to exchange.

S2: A student of logic would be able to oppose that, and it seems to me absolutely no argument.

M: Show us just how you get away from it. Here is a statement. You are ready to offer two cents for an evening paper. Anderson says obviously there must be in your mind two values which you are comparing in making that offer. Why isn't that right?

S2: Two values, and one relation between them.

M: I say that the price that you are ready to offer is a relation, but how can you have a relation unless there be two quantities between which the relation exists?

S2: Quantities, certainly. Quantities which already bring into relation something else.

M: That is to say you may put the same valuation on an apple that you do on two cents? That is quite possible.

S2: I do not understand that line of reasoning, but I feel this: If you have an absolute value, if you come with an absolute value, then you have to value in the following way. Let us say that the world has to go in the way of progress. I believe in radical progress and therefore I buy just a very radical paper, and I value that paper with so and so, but I would have that valuation altogether from the start. I would decide to value this paper just two cents. I mean only in this way could I get an absolute value.

M: That is to say an absolute value could not exist for any individual save as it were a deduction from a general scheme of life which had compelling power over that individual. Anderson would not admit that. He would say that the most foolish man that you can find attaches absolute value to things just as much as the wisest philosopher, that there is not any inherent logical necessity for consistency among these absolute values.

S2: I do not think that at all. A paper would have very great value if printing were much more scarce as in olden times than it is now, perhaps the value of many dollars, and now it has just the value of two cents. I do not see any absoluteness.

M: Anderson does not mean that these absolute values are unchanged.

S2: Then he should not call it absolute. He should call it objective.

M: He calls it absolute value to set it off from the term "relative value" just by way of getting a contrast to the idea of value as purchasing power. The term very likely is ambiguous, but that is distinctly the way in which he uses it.

S2: If he would use objective force he could say that he does not mean what the old classical school meant, but that he finds that objective value is explained by factors omitted from the other valuation. He should not use the word "absolute."

M: It is a misleading term. Let us try to understand it in his sense and discuss it and criticize it if we must, from his viewpoint.

S5: In one place he said positive value would be preferred, but he thought that could be contrasted with negative value.

M: Ricardo, remember, had a similar idea concerning value that was about as ambiguous and hard to understand as Anderson's. It is even more ambiguous, because he used "absolute value," "positive value," "real value," "value" without any adjective to convey his idea. Anderson probably looked over the list of Ricardo's terms, and selected the one which was the freest from objections. It certainly does suggest an immediate connection with an absolutist form of philosophy, but that connection Anderson would deny. He regards himself as very much of a pragmatist. I am not quite sure whether he has the right to regard himself so. Is there anything inherently objectionable or unsound in the term "absolute value" as Anderson interprets it?

S1: It does not seem to me that there is anything unsound. It simply is not sufficiently definite to have meaning. We are ready to admit, ever since biology has developed at all, that environment plays a part in determining man's action, and when you try to boil Anderson down that is as definite a conclusion as you can get from him. He simply says that economic value is a part of a general system of value, a product of evaluations in these other fields. They explain the different values as the result of man's education and surroundings, and all the other line of things that are brought into a man's education.

M: That is true to this extent: though we all find it easy to believe nowadays that personal valuations are influenced in vastly preponderating ways by social conditions, they are very much less so than people are likely to think. That is true, but it lies a little bit further along in the exposition of Anderson's ideas than we have reached so far and the thing is to try to find out whether the idea of the existence of absolute value in the mind of the individual is prior to exchange or not. An illustration may make this clear. In comparatively recent months [March 1918] we have had an enormous rise of prices over the whole western world. I have heard some discussions carried on in a committee appointed by the American Economic Association[19] between Fisher on the one side and Anderson on the other, concerning the causes of this rise of prices. Fisher is all for explaining that the rise of prices is caused by an increase in the volume of circulating media and the rapidity of its circulation. In the United States there has been an enormous influx of gold and a still greater expansion of bank credit, and during a part of the time there has been an increase in the rapidity with which the circulating medium has changed hands.

Anderson on the other hand says that to understand this rise of prices, one has to think about the value which attaches to money, that is, to gold, on the one side, and the value which attaches to commodities on the other side. Gold, he says, as far as he can see, has not diminished in value, that is, in absolute value. People attach about the same importance to it now that they did before the outbreak of the war, but there has been a great increase in the value of commodities. Absolute value again, you note. At the present time the people are in desperate need of fundamental staples like coal, iron, copper, wheat, hides. They are ready to mortgage their future in the most lavish way if they can by any shift increase the sum of these commodities that they have at the present time. They are ready through the government, and as individual contractors working for the government, to pay almost any price to control larger portions of the existing stocks of the indispensable commodities. They want the goods with an intensity that did not exist before the war. Their value has increased. That is to say, to understand the rise of prices the theorist has to contrast the value which at present attaches to gold with the value which attaches to commodities, and compare that with the value which attached to gold before the war and the value which attached to commodities before the war. You get the explanation of changes in the value of gold on the one hand, which has remained fairly stable, and commodities on the other hand which have become much more valuable. The rise of prices simply reflects the alteration in the ratios between the two sets of values. This is all by way of making clearer what he means by absolute value, and for what sort of purposes he employs the term.

S4: The way to understand Anderson's attitude is to say that absolute value precedes market price.

M. It must exist prior to exchange.

---

[19] [The Committee on the Purchasing Power of Money in Relation to War. Fisher was chairman. The other members besides Anderson and Mitchell were Royal Meeker, then United States Commissioner of Labor Statistics, E. W. Kemmerer of Princeton and Warren M. Persons of Harvard.

S4: The only way we can know what the absolute value is is by knowing what the market price is.

M: He has no means of stating absolute value in quantitative terms, but logically he knows it has existence prior to exchange. That is his reply. Logically it must be there before there can be such a thing as an exchange, simply because there cannot be a comparison unless there are some quantities between which the comparisons are to be made.

S2: I see in that the old fight between the subjective and the objective factions. What his contention amounts to is that the subjective side comes first.

M: Of course those values are subjective quantities.

S2: If we could account for those values we would have a basis for a theory of objective values.

M: Anderson thinks that he can account for them better than other people have, and that is where his emphasis on social factors comes in. He says if the theorist will go back to the study of their formation it may help him to see how these valuations are influenced by a host of social factors in existence: economic, ethical, political institutions.

S2: He perhaps could show this statistically. But if he really wants to give an account about the real forces he has to go back to the subjective side.

M: That is what he himself says. To understand ultimately how modern economic life actually develops, the theorist must go back behind prices to the antecedent absolute values, and to understand these values in the mind of the individual, he has to go back, or out, to the whole social situation of which that individual is a portion, so that he is plunging at once into a psychological study.

S5: Is there any connection between Anderson's absolute value and what Adam Smith means by value in use?

M: Absolute value in Anderson's eyes is much closer to what is meant by marginal utility among the Austrians, that is to say, it is the importance which the individual, under the circumstances, attaches to a particular increment of a particular commodity. That may be something very different from Adam Smith's value in use. For instance, diamonds to Adam Smith had less value than iron, less value in use. Diamonds to Anderson have a higher absolute value than a corresponding weight of iron.

S8: How does it differ from price plus the consumer's surplus?

M: It differs, directly, in that absolute value exists in the mind of the individual, whereas price is an objective factor.

S1: Scarcity is an objective factor.

M: Scarcity is an objective factor, too.

S8: How does it differ from what Marshall calls total utility?

M: Absolute values attach to increments, those being the quantities people are interested in setting values on. Total utility as a rule is concerned with a stock of goods, is it not?

S8: Considering everybody together, some men gain more from different prices than others.

M: The idea of total utility as Marshall employs it is usually concerned with a total stock of goods, and usually with a group of people, while Anderson's absolute values are thought of as in the minds of individuals separately, and there is not any necessary correspondence between your scheme of absolute values and the price a man would pay.

S8: But consumer's surplus is very much like this. I certainly would pay more for a newspaper than two cents.

M: From Anderson's point of view a newspaper has not any more absolute value to you than two cents, except fractionally perhaps. That is to say, if it had you would get more than one newspaper.

S8: Yes: but I may not like any but the one newspaper which I am in the habit of reading.

M: In that sense, that is simply an illustration of Anderson's general thesis that an individual's absolute value is determined by the whole social situation of which he is a part. The existence of a number of different newspapers is a factor in the situation from this standpoint, and so are peculiar tastes.

S2: Does that mean absolute value is different for each individual?

M: It may be different for each individual. That, as we shall see, is one of the points on which Anderson lays stress. There are good grounds for thinking that we are all the products of a somewhat similar situation. We probably do not differ very greatly.

To repeat: Anderson means by absolute value something simpler probably than the term connotes. His general thesis is that there must be a valuation prior to exchange, prior even to the formation of the idea of a price offer in the mind of any man. That is to say, a price offer is a sort of comparison, and there must be some things between which the comparison is made. A person says that he is ready to give two cents for a newspaper. That means that there are necessarily, logically must be, two values in his mind which he is equating;

on the one hand the value of the newspaper, on the other hand the value of the two cents. Is Anderson right about that? Is the notion one that possesses any importance for economic theory, is it a notion which helps us to understand the theory of price any better?

S4: Is that view any different when persons compare the margins of two utilities?

M: Anderson would say that there is this difference, that the Austrians, when they are expounding the theory of value, admit the idea of purchasing power among the factors that enter into the price bids. He says that this means that they are admitting the idea of value to the explanation of value; that is, they are reasoning in a circle. What he wants to insist on is that the comparisons implied in the price offers are comparisons between absolute values; that is to say, it is not purchasing power that is to be considered, but in the last resort two absolute values as they exist in the mind of the individual.

S2: I wanted to ask you last time about this—I don't remember whether those positive or absolute values differ with each individual.

M: Presumably. Wait a moment—I am speaking a little too quickly. One of Anderson's great points is that these absolute values in the mind of each individual are largely the product of the social situation in which he is brought up. He has the values that he has because he is himself, in a sense, a social product. In so far as individuals are members of the same community, they are more or less similar social products, therefore there is probability that their value schemes are very much alike, but the theorist deduces the conclusion that there is a general resemblance among these absolute values on the part of the individuals, not from anything that he knows directly, but from a theory of the way in which the absolute values are formed.

S2: I see in this only something much less definite than in any other value theory, especially since he does not construct any system. If he wanted to—

M: You mean any general philosophical system?

S2: Yes, and I also would say that we have to construct a sociological system.

M: Anderson would agree with you there, and say that the school which he represents is engaged upon that work. Cooley has gone much further in constructing a general sociological system than Anderson himself has, but Anderson accepted, in general, Cooley's results. What Cooley does is to offer an account of the way in which man's character and consciousness is socialized. That is a discussion of wide scope carried on in considerable detail. It may fairly be taken as a sort of general background for Anderson's particular economic theories.

S2: To me, it seems impossible to have a theory of value with this sociological basis or foundation.

M: Why can there not be a value theory resting upon a sociological foundation?

S2: Since sociology is investigating the phenomena which are so manifold in life, which tries to go into those manifold phenomena without reducing them in such a systematic way as economic theory wants to do, but tries to get them in an altogether different way. The method would be compared perhaps more to an artistic creation, something altogether different.

M: The social value sociologists and economists would not accept that verdict. They are inclined to say on the contrary that while they do take a great many different phenomena under consideration, it is necessary to do so in order to understand human consciousness on any level of civilization. As intelligence is for the most part a social product, man is born into the world with a lot of preformed connections among his neurones which represent his readiness even at birth to make certain definite responses. He is also born with the capacity to make new connections among his neurones. The kind of connections that he makes will be determined primarily by his experience as an organism, particularly as it relates to the formation of his intelligence in his experience with other people, so that everyone from the day of his birth is having his mind made in a very literal sense, even in a strictly physiological sense, by his relation with his mother and brothers and sisters and father, and then a little later with other children and grownup people with whom he comes in contact. In school he has a further widening of these contacts. That child at six or eight or ten years of age, whatever he is, is primarily what he has been made by the people among whom he has grown up. His value systems are among the products of intelligence, are part of the formation of his mind, and they bear the impress of the social factors which have worked upon him just as much as any other part of his intelligence.

Recently [1918] one of the younger representatives of this school, a young man named Clarence E. Ayres, at the University of Chicago, published a very diverting article, "The Epistemological Significance of Social Psychology."[20] This article shows how far the more militant members of the social psychology school are prepared to go. Ayres argues that in the past we have had epistemology of a metaphysical sort, an attempt to give a theory of knowledge based on various schemes of general reasoning, and that so far as one can see, the theory of knowledge has not been materially advanced by all of the elaborate metaphysical investigation. He says that social psychology offers a new kind of epistemology, which means something. Epistemology gives a theory of knowledge by showing how knowledge is actually formed, how minds are actually made. He says that a most brilliant and telling example of social psychology used for epistemological purposes is Thorstein Veblen's account of the incidence of the machine process. He says:

> Probably the work of the economist, Thorstein Veblen, is the weightiest contribution which has yet been made to the science of social psychology—as it is here defined. Not only might every one of his five books be classified as the systematic study of the social psychology beneath a selected group of social arrangements, but it will be some time before better social psychology is written than his discussion of "the cultural incidence of the machine process" in *The Theory of Business Enterprise* [1904], or his analysis of the nature and the sources of the spirit of belligerent patriotism which is both the cause and the result of the perpetuation of war, in *The Nature of Peace* [1917]. It is to work such as that of Veblen, therefore, that one must turn if one wishes to note the characteristics of social psychology as it is going to be written in the future.[20]

Veblen's discussion of the incidence of the machine process is an endeavor to show just what habits of thinking are inculcated by daily use of machinery, and by his account the man who does, day by day, have to do with machinery has formed in him a set of mental habits which are extremely different in character from those which are formed by the people whose daily life lies, say, in the counting house. There is one habit of thought, one type of mind, built up by doing work of a specific sort. This is real epistemology, says Ayres. This is a way of showing how people come to have the mental habits which are characteristic of them. It is a way of showing why they have different mental habits, why adults often find it extremely difficult to understand each other. If the social psychologists and the social value theorists are ready to go to the length of regarding their investiga-

---

[20] [Ayres's field at the time was philosophy but he always had a deep interest in economics. He has taught economics at the University of Texas since 1933. For a discussion of Ayres's views in the earlier period see Joseph Dorfman, *The Economic Mind in American Civilization*, IV, pp. 126-129.]

[21] Ayres, "The Epistemological Significance of Social Psychology," *The Journal of Philosophy, Psychology and Scientific Methods*, January 17, 1918, p. 40.

tions as giving an epistemology, surely it cannot be said that their work in intent at least is not wide enough, is not sufficiently radical and thoroughgoing.

S8: Anderson's books do not have anything more than the criticism that there is a value concept beside exchange value, which had been taken before, and he makes the point that this value has something to do with social thinking. But for any constructive problem, I find only one passage: "A valid price procedure . . . is essentially this: We take our quantitative value concept, summing up the multitudinous social forces which determine values,"[22] and then he assumes a given framework, and the rest is ordinary scientific method. How is he going to get a value concept out of such talk, for quantitative use?

M: The quantity value concept is implied in the idea of absolute value; that is to say, absolute values are definite quantities. Let me repeat again Anderson's way of explaining the rise of prices. That shows the concept at work in his mind more clearly than anything else. He says that since the outbreak of the World War [I] he sees no ground for thinking that there has been a fall in the value of gold. The value of gold before the war was a definite absolute thing, perhaps somewhat different in different minds—one does not know much about that—but it was a definite thing, and he says, so far as he can see, that definite quantity of absolute value attaching to the gold dollar has not altered much. On the other hand he says the values, that is the absolute values, which people set upon a great number of commodities have altered immensely. Because of the great change in the social situation which the war has brought about people attach very much higher absolute value to the present control over fundamental things like food, the necessary plain articles of clothing, steel, gun powder, ships and the necessary mechanisms for producing these absolutely essential things. The rise in prices is due to the fact that people are comparing at the present time the value of gold which has not changed much with the values of a large range of commodities, and these latter values have increased so much that people are now ready to give a much larger number of gold dollars unchanged in value for these commodities on which they set so much higher values than they formerly did. That is the way he uses the notion.

S8: How can he prove that?

M: It is difficult to prove. The kind of evidence which he suggests by way of proof is to point out—for instance—if the theorist will contrast the value of the gold dollar with the value of real estate,

---

[22] *Social Value,* p. 185.

he will not find evidence that the gold dollar has fallen in value. As a matter of fact, it will, he thinks, as a result of some inquiries that he has made, buy more real estate at the present time than it would have bought before the war. Similarly, he says if the theorist compares the value of the gold dollar with the value of securities, he will find in the great majority of cases that its purchasing power has increased; that is to say, there is no evidence there of any decline in the value of the gold dollar. There is, he says, only one class of commodities which gives any indication that might be construed as a diminished value of gold: the commodities which serve directly and indirectly the needs of war. Those things have increased greatly. Obviously, he says, it cannot be taken for granted that the great price people are willing to pay for these commodities has necessarily to do with a fall in the purchasing power of gold for other kinds of goods.

S8: Still a ratio.

M: Still a ratio. You are right.

S8: You cannot prove it.

M: He knows that perfectly well, but he says this is all evidence that the theorist ought to take into account. Anderson goes so far as to show that the theorist must not jump to the conclusion without more ado that the rise of prices is explained by the diminished value of gold. Then he would go on, if one argued a little further with him, to say that it is obvious that the western nations are eager to get gold at the present time. If the economist came to inquire into that procedure he would not get the impression that gold is a drug in the market, that the value of gold has fallen. Rather he would get the impression that the great banks and the governments behind them are more eager for gold than they were before.

S8: It is just because he uses the word "absolute value" that he gets into that mess. Other economists do not use the term.

M: The other economists do not use that term. I think that this is the best illustration of how he tries to use the concept of absolute value.

S6: I had the impression that in *Social Value* there was too much sociology and psychology, and everything, and too little political economy. I may be again a little too severe, when I say that the difficulty was that a great part of the problems that he was trying to explain were perhaps truths felt by this time by anyone who is more or less interested in social problems. No one thinks about the individual mind apart from all other minds, and no one thinks society nowadays is split up into independent and not interrelated individuals. For instance, in Gustav Schmoller's general treatise, in the introductory chapters, this problem is clearly explained and fully propounded, perhaps much better than in Anderson, though he does not lay so much stress upon it.[23]

As to the real economic problems, as to how theory works, as to the kind and amount of value, how can they say that there are two cents on one side and a newspaper on the other side, the amount of absolute value, that mysterious something that cannot be measured to such an extent. How it works when it comes to these problems, Anderson is extremely vague. As a matter of fact, he has nothing to contribute this way. He is again inferior to Marx who puts the labor problem into labor substance. As the substance of value, labor can be measured somehow or other, but Anderson's is a very vague conception.

M: It is clear that absolute value as Anderson sees the thing is a shadowy kind of logical abstraction. His test for it amounts simply to the statement that it must be there and it must be there before the idea of relative value can exist for the purely logical reason that relative value implies comparisons, and there must be something to be compared. But as S2 suggested, a logician would not be altogether convinced by that kind of reasoning, a little reminiscent of the talk about the necessity of there being some motive for action. One can easily get into a frame of mind in which one can say people must necessarily have a reason for doing something, otherwise why should they have done it. The modern psychologists find that that kind of logical inquiry is, from their view, beside the point. The literal fact is that is not the way that men's minds operate. Men do not very often perform an action with purposes in mind to guide their detailed behavior. On the contrary, for the most part, they do things, and afterwards become conscious of the purposes involved.

Similarly if a person begins to inquire rather carefully into the valuations which take place in his own mind, he will seldom find that he begins by thinking of two separate values, and then making a comparison between them. He will discover that his mental operation is that of thinking of two things together. If he actually can work out a definite notion of the absolute value of anything to him, he probably does it as a result of making a number of comparisons. Suppose that he sets himself seriously to determine what value a newspaper has to him. He has no notion of that save in so far as he compares newspapers with other things that interest him, and at the

---

[23] See chapter XIX on Schmoller.

end of an elaborate series of comparisons he probably can get some such result as that a newspaper means more to him than this, and more to him than that, through a whole list. But even so, he will hardly have any definite quantitative idea of the value of a newspaper, and without those comparisons a notion of the absolute value of the newspaper is almost meaningless; that is to say, the mind apparently does not operate in a strictly logical way in guiding behavior.

The logical point that the individual must have two quantities which he is comparing when he decides that he will give so much for a definite thing would be a legitimate point if human minds were as a matter of fact computing machines. That is not the sort of thing that mind is, and with minds constructed like ours, every value that comes in comes in as related to another set of interests; that is to say, relative values are prior to absolute values, if there is any such thing as an absolute value.

S6: I do not see in Anderson's concept the possibility of a sudden change in value for individuals or for groups. I have fresh in my mind now the value attached by a prisoner for a newspaper. It was one dollar for a newspaper and not a recent one either. According to Anderson I do not see any way of explaining value changes when sudden.

M: Sudden transformations could come about on his basis. For instance such increase of value as he says we now attach to munitions of war.

S6: The value of the munitions is social value, but here we have individual values.

M: Of course one of Anderson's great points is that all individual values are social products. We must not forget that.

S6: An individual in society would not attach as much importance to one newspaper as an individual situated in a particular situation.

M: An individual in a particular situation means an individual under pressure of certain social circumstances. Here again is the social factor.

S6: It would be in a roundabout way. It would not explain the thing. The same thing would apply to certain social classes. To one class the thing is more valuable than to another class. Then we have to split up society at large into social groups, and these into perhaps smaller ones, and then down to individuals, and so to the Austrian vicious circle which would be much more explainable than his social value.

M: He thinks that he is getting away from the Austrian vicious circle by holding that while we are all products of a common social process in this way and therefore are mutually dependent, still the social process produces in each person a whole host of absolute values which as data for price theory are independent; that is to say, they are the starting points.

S6: There is a vague indication in one of his chapters where he says he does not eliminate marginal utility and the demand curve, but he does not relate it with his other concepts, so the thing remains, to use his own phrase, "in the air."

M: He can perfectly well use the marginal curves with this idea of absolute value, can he not? That is to say he simply explains a curve of individual price offers by comparison between the absolute values of the successive increments of the commodities with which an individual is parting and the corresponding absolute values of successive increments of the commodity which the individual is thinking about purchasing.

S6: The element of scarcity?

M: No, scarcity would be among the elements which establish the absolute value in his mind. If you like you can say that these absolute values themselves are the products of an endless chain. Anderson does say that in a sense he is breaking the vicious circle of the Austrians by a margin. He would go with you (S6) there. Still from his point of view he enlarges it.

S6: You enlarge the circle so far as to bring in a whole organized system which stands by itself.

S1: Would Anderson agree that while the values are absolute in any particular instant, their amounts have been determined by considering a host of relative values? And does not the social environment work through relative values to produce absolute values?

M: In large part doubtless.

S1: It means simply that the two items which come into exchange at a particular moment have each been compared with the rest of the social atmosphere, and simply at that moment have a definite margin?

M: At that moment they have definite margins.

S1: That does not seem impossible.

M: That is what Anderson means by saying, if you like in regard to his criticism, that he is enlarging the circle, not getting rid of it, solely enlarging it.

S1: He demands that the process be taken up earlier, the process of the comparison of values.

M: That is to say, he does hold that these absolute values have been produced before the comparison which results in price offers can be instituted.

S2: The Austrians could analyze this by saying that if this entire group of people have the same value, which is a fixed one for them through the social environment, then it simply shows the demand schedule, the different marginal utilities in all those schedules, will be the same. It will show in the Austrian theory just in the same way. It will not explain it.

M: There is no necessary incompatibility between Anderson's view and the Austrian theory. It is something which the Austrians could accept if they like perfectly well.

Are there any other comments or questions or suggestions about absolute value? If not the discussion will pass on to some of the other points which Anderson raises. The idea of absolute value does not occupy as large or as essential a part in the social value theory as our discussion might suggest. The reason why we have paid especial attention to it is that it seems to be the one element in the system as a whole about which considerable difficulty arises in students' minds. It certainly is a point on which Anderson, as an individual representative of the school, has most that is original. With the general idea of the social value school, we need not concern ourselves at any considerable length, because incidentally we have also recognized just as readily that valuations are in large measure, if not altogether as many people would say, the product of social forces. Of course that is the leading thesis of the whole school, and it may be or may not be combined with the notion of absolute value, as one likes.[24] Then too

---

[24] ["Cooley's earlier books and the teachings of John Dewey have had an outstanding influence in spreading among the present generation of economists the notion that the human mind is essentially a social product, so that a really independent individual is impossible. From the same standpoint B. M. Anderson and Cooley have both attacked the problem of value and valuation. These writers demonstrate forcibly that economic values are dependent on the legal institutions of personal and property rights, and other legal regulations. The market gives prestige to the desires of certain classes, leading others to imitate them, and to some it gives the added weight of vast purchasing power, so that market values are different from what they would be without this institutional weighting. The evolution of these institutions, and others, results in profound changes in the character and meaning of market values and in the direction which they give to economic efforts.

As between the two men, Anderson is extremely preoccupied with the establishment of a concept of economic value as an absolute entity which shall be distinctively economic, and shall still embody the focussing of all these broader social forces. This quest leads him through paths of dialectic in which the present writer does not wholly follow him. Cooley's more realistic treatment avoids these difficulties, exhibiting the institutional character of the process underlying financial values in ways which hinge not at all on any particular definition of the tangible economic phenomena on which these forces take effect." J. M. Clark, "Recent Developments in Economic Science," in Recent Developments in the Social Sciences, ed. by E. C. Hayes (Philadelphia: Lippincott, 1927) pp. 274-275.]

there is the obvious corollary from the main proposition that since people's values are social products, presumably they bear a striking resemblance to one another.

Anderson has one other interesting suggestion, a suggestion of a way to reconcile statics and dynamics. What is Anderson's method of reconciling them?

S1: It is through the use of the money concept. That is, he feels that the exchange, that the time element that enters into business as it is actually carried on, the valuation that money by and large has, is constant. It is the most constant item in all our fluctuating values, and through it are reconciled the other fluctuating social values.

M: Is that clear to the members of the class?

S9: I don't understand it.

M: Will S1 labor with S9 once more?

S1: I don't know whether I remember it exactly, but I do remember that the value of money changes less than the value of any other item, that it is in the business man's eyes presumably constant, that through it, through comparison of other values with it, one can measure changes of values over periods of time.

M: You can state the thing in slightly different form, and perhaps make the meaning of it a bit clearer. Anderson holds that whenever the theorist can introduce the money measure as a common denominator for economic quantities, he has substantially a static problem. In economic theorizing as in business enterprise this measure can be taken for the time being as a constant, and when the theorist has a constant measure applicable to the quantities with which he is dealing, he can present the problem as one in statics. Anderson says that there are two ways of reconciling statics and dynamics. One is to say, as a number of writers, among whom he mentions chiefly Veblen, have shown, that the great important dynamic changing factors in economic life are themselves susceptible of expression in monetary terms. He argues that in so far as the dynamic factors themselves can be expressed in monetary terms, the theorist is assimilating dynamic to static problems. For instance he says Veblen has shown how money values can be set on such fluctuating quantities as prospects of profit, credit, gold—certainly dynamic factors—and once expressed in terms of dollars and cents they can enter into static analysis. That is one line of reconciliation.

The other is to recognize that among the factors which enter into ordinary static problems expressed in terms of dollars and cents are factors which themselves are subject to change; that is to say, factors which have a dynamic quality. So the two fields are by no means separated by an impassable gulf. The theorist can get the dynamic factors into shape for handling in static problems by putting money values on them, at least that is true of many of the factors; on the other hand, the theorist can find if he canvasses his static problems carefully that among factors stated in money terms are factors that change.

S1: I don't see, since he wanted to quote Veblen, just how he can omit reference to a passage which suggests that the money measure employed by static theory may not always remain constant. The static problems of money, Veblen says, distinctly are subject to change. While it is true that business men as a rule regard money, the money value, as not changing, it is not at all impossible that after a while they will get over that habit. It would be interesting to watch them and if they do it, then it means a complete wiping away of the base line, as he calls it. Veblen discusses this static notion of present social conditions, and does not say it is going to be so in the future.

M: Anderson would reply that it is clearly one of the ways of reconciling statics and dynamics.

In the static problem you have a factor which you realize is subject to change, so that the line of division is broken down. It is obvious of course that this achievement of reconciling statics and dynamics is one which is going to be important to a mind which has been thinking of economics in those fixed categories.

Anderson is a very interesting product. His mind, like those of the rest of us, has been formed by the circumstances of his upbringing. Among those circumstances were an introduction to economic theory at second hand, and then later at first hand through Professor J. B. Clark, who thinks of economic problems largely in terms of statics and dynamics.[25] These terms he borrowed, perhaps not too happily, from mechanics. They seem not only adequate but also helpful to people who have a distinctly mechanical conception of economic life and economic problems. If, on the other hand, a man happens to have what Alfred Marshall calls a biological view of economic problems he finds rather less service in the distinction, therefore, he finds less necessity for reconciliation between the two divisions, the significance of which he does not rate very highly. Anderson, after getting the habit of thinking in these terms definitely formed, came under the influence of people like John Dewey. He began to think in a some-

---

[25] [Anderson was first taught economics at the University of Missouri by a student of Clark, Jesse Pope.]

what different set of terms, and his advance under the recent influences appeared in the form of his desire to reconcile the old categories in which he was thinking with the new purposes which were gradually forming in his mind. That has left him in a curious half way house with some peculiar relics of his old viewpoint. These are, in particular, the notion of absolute value, hardly compatible with the pragmatic view which he has learned from Dewey, and also the idea that the thing that must be done to advance economics, is to find some way of reconciling the two great subdivisions of the subject: statics and dynamics.

S2: I do not understand the difference between the social value type of theory and the sociological type of theory.

M: I do not make any difference between them. The social value type of theory may fairly be called the sociological type.

S2: Is there anyone else who has tried to give a broader theory on the sociological basis?

M: Of value particularly?

S2: Of the social value theory.

M: Professor Cooley is the person to suggest.

S2: Could Veblen come into that school?

M: Veblen is not discussing the technical problem of value.

S6: Are there not other modern economists who have taken up the problem of social value, and tried to construct a theory on this basis?

M: This sociological viewpoint is common to most modern writers, at least to the younger ones, but it is common to them in such a thoroughgoing sense that few think it necessary to lay a great deal of stress upon it. It is one of the things that they take for granted. There have been a few who have made a special effort to work out in some detail what the view implies. Anderson is one; Cooley, to repeat, has done much the same sort of thing on a wider scale. But no one is interested to attack the general notion that a person's valuations are in large measure the outcome of social and sociological conditions.

S6: Is there not a prospect of eliminating that subjective element, the person's demand and supply schedule, and trying to construct an objective theory of value?

M: Along the lines of behavioristic psychology, you mean?

S1: The attempt Anderson has made is to construct an objective theory.

M: Objective theory?

S2: It means objective to the individual.

M: The individual is here conceived to be substantially the product of certain social conditions, and since that is true, his valuations among other characteristics of the individual are the product of social conditions. But valuations themselves remain subjective matters.

S6: They are more than subjective. They are objective in the sense that the individual takes them for granted, as given.

M: They are made in him. He does not so much take them for granted. They are made inside him. His mind is so formed by the set of conventions which he learns as to lead to these results, setting certain roughly uniform values upon different ranges of objects. The reason why I do not quite like to say that the theory is an objective one through and through is that Anderson, at least, lays so much stress upon absolute values, that is to say, once these products are in the individual mind, they stand, for his purposes, as fixed points upon which to construct a theory of prices. The absolute values, despite the fact that they are conceived as primarily social products, are themselves subjective quantities.

S6: As I interpret Anderson's procedure, he conceives of something as super, as above the individual mind. He says that there are some great social values and social conceptions. Of course they have no other way of manifesting themselves except through the individual mind. He thinks of them as something that is above the individual mind, as a thing of its own existence. He hates to become metaphysical, but he does when he speaks of these substances, these higher values, which are not within the individual mind. He constructs the individual mind as something that is only a portion, something of this social whole.

M: That is the case on his view in a sense, and yet what is the social mind apart from minds of the individuals that make it? The social mind even in the higher ranges is a sort of generalization from things that exist in the minds of the individual.

S6: That generalization also exists as something objective. He quotes Cooley as saying that it is the instruments and the orchestra that play—as the piece played by the orchestra. Each instrument contributes something to the whole, but the whole is not what is given by each instrument.

M: The whole is not given by each instrument any more than one nation is given by each individual, yet the valuations do take place inside individual minds, do they not? This is a whole that is made out of these individual scales.

S2: I also think with S6 the individual is simply supposed to have that valuation. So we can say it is an objective value with Anderson, if he should succeed in finding such a valuation.

M: The psychology of the group is something more objective than the psychology of the individual.

S6: I have been thinking of the state. The state is distinctly a thing that has no separate existence outside of the human mind. The theory of the state comes back to the individual mind, and in spite of this place of the state in the individual mind, the state has a value that is objective. It can compel individuals to act according to its way, which is supposed to be something for the individual also, above the persons constituting the state.

M: The state is distinctly an objective thing, is it not, in the sense that it has certain recognized forms of behavior that men are going to take in a standard way. This leads to what is the proper distinction between the subjective and the objective world in psychology and in economics. Nowadays there is a brand of psychology that is usually called "behaviorism," but which, rather recently, people have begun to speak of more properly as "objectivism." Objective psychology is a very different kind of thing from the sort of psychology that is suggested by Anderson's analysis. It differs in this important respect, that the behavioristic or objective psychologist refuses to inquire into what goes on inside the individual's mind. He observes his behavior; that is to say, he observes his muscular movements, things that can actually be seen to have a definite objective existence.

He goes so far as to believe that we have no mental processes which do not produce some kind of muscular movement as the bulk of the very subtle muscular movements which accompany certain mental processes, and which cannot be observed, possibly movements of the throat and palate. As opposed to this behavioristic viewpoint which is concerned merely with seeing what people actually do, you have Anderson's theory which insists that conduct is controlled in large measure by social factors, this is to say, by the behavior of other people among whom we grow up and with whom we are associated. Anderson uses the objective behavior forms to explain subjective processes inside people's minds, that is, absolute values, and then on the basis of those values he builds up his theory of prices; that is to say, the demand schedules are supposed to be gotten by comparisons between different absolute values. There is a subjective element in that, is there not? The thing is not purely objective.

S6: Yes, it is not objective. He says distinctly that he recognizes the usefulness of the marginal analysis as based on the social value structure, but I want to know whether it would not be possible to construct a purely objective theory, which would eliminate this subjective element.

M: That may well be feasible, but it has not been done, at least by economists. The behavioristic viewpoint has not yet been completely worked out in psychology; that is to say, there is a range of problems where it has not been applied, and where it is difficult to see that it can be applied, unless instruments can be devised for observing the alleged muscular movements accompanying any mental images, which so far as we know do not lead to action. There are behaviorists who think that it is going to be feasible to have instruments which would enable them to investigate, to see what behavior accompanies mental states which to our apprehension are passive so far as the body is concerned, instruments that will show for instance the slightest movement of the palate, the tongue, the throat muscles, but until that can be done, they are not in a position to observe all kinds of behavior.

That statement goes to show how thorough the radicals, at least, among the behaviorists, are in accepting their own viewpoint, in saying that the only scientific way to attack the psychological problem is the same objective way which we use in dealing with animals. That is to say, human psychology must in its method be put upon precisely the same plane as animal psychology. We have got to look upon man as a strange animal roaming around in our environment, that under certain circumstances we can put under controlled conditions and study. When we do that we will be in a position to draw up a series of results which are just as valid for the human species psychologically as the results that we have now obtained by this means for animals.

S7: If the behavioristic psychology could succeed in completing its investigations and positing results, wouldn't the economist, who believed in that, find his problem immensely simplified, because everyone we have studied is concerned with explaining the real forces which take the form of wants and desires, and if the economist could ignore that, and go by man's actions, would not this problem be simplified?

M: Presumably, the economist can scarcely ever resist the temptation to explain what the reasonable man will do, and what the economists do, the people who cultivate most of the social sciences do, the people who study politics and sociology at large. I am not going too far when I say the lawyers do it.

[Two letters from Professor Mitchell to Anderson on Anderson's work and in particular on methodology.]

March 26, 1918

I have read with much interest your discussion of the reasons why prices have risen so violently since the war began. In general I agree with your explanation more nearly than I do with Fisher's. There is, however, a third line of attack upon the problem which I prefer even to yours, though I suppose that in form at least, you and Fisher would each approve the other's better than either of you would approve mine.

What seems to me the illuminating way to handle such problems is to study the temporal processes concerned, that is, I should begin my attack on the factors in their whole complexity and make whatever abstractions proved necessary at a later stage of the game. Fisher begins by setting off the money factors from the commodity factors, and treating them as if they were more or less independent problems. You begin by setting off the absolute value of money from the absolute value of various commodities. Neither abstraction seems to me very helpful.

To come directly to the crucial point, I am unable to see anything substantial in "absolute value." You arrive at it, not by psychological analysis, but by a strictly logical inference. This inference would be valid provided the mind were thoroughly logical in its processes. I don't think it at all proved that in psychological fact, absolute value is prior to relative value. Henry W. Stuart has put the thing effectively in his contribution to the volume of essays which Dewey and Dewey's pupils published early last year [1917] under the title *Creative Intelligence*. . . .

Excepting the one contested point, I find myself in hearty agreement with the general argument of your *Value of Money,* and admiring greatly your constructive chapters. On the statistical side, you have made what seems to me highly significant contributions by demonstrating the enormous volume of speculative trade; by putting our foreign commerce in its proper statistical position, etc. Work of this sort comes so near having "absolute value" that I am almost tempted to believe in the term. . . .

April 10, 1918

You have done valuable service in insisting that "social values present themselves to the individual as opaque objective facts, largely beyond his control, to which he must adjust himself." [p. 43].

Further, I suppose that since this is a free country you are within your constitutional rights in calling the "opaque objective facts" referred to "absolute, social economic values." But I find the term "absolute" confusing. Its implications, for example, do not prepare the reader for what immediately follows on page 43. As illustrative of the "opaque objective facts," you use the "dollar and a half" which will induce one man to work all day in a ditch, but will not lure another man to that salutatory exercise. Now the power in motivation exercised by the "dollar and a half" depends largely on the price level, that is to say, it is mainly, if not exclusively, a matter of ratios of exchange.

I agree, of course, that there was a highly organized system of prices already in existence before any man living was born, and further that this established system of prices has exercised a powerful influence upon our economic behavior. In one sense, these "opaque objective facts" of price did exist prior to any exchange that we have made. I judge, from your criticism of [Ludwig] von Mises [*Theorie des Geldes und der Umlaufsmittel*], however, that this is not at all the sense in which you wish "absolute values" to be understood.

Indeed I cannot reconcile any acceptable interpretation of the term with such a passage as the following from page 7 of *The Value of Money*: "Values lie behind ratios of exchange, and causally determine them. The important thing for the present purposes is merely to note that value is prior to exchange relations, that it is an absolute quantity and not as many economists have put it, purely relative. The ratio of exchange is relative, but there must be absolutes behind relatives." So far as I can see, the "absolutes" which you put behind "relatives" are themselves organized relations.

When we come to individual valuations, I think that Stuart's criticism, which I referred to, amounts substantially to a different version of what I just said. That is to say, Stuart protests against setting off two "absolute values" in the individual's mind as *data* from which a definite ratio results. On the contrary, he sees in the actual process a continuous give and take between our feelings about any given object and our feelings about other objects. "Absolute values" existing prior to any exchange do not determine ratios of exchange. On the contrary, values of particular things do not get definite recognition except as *they are related* in the mental process to the values of other particulars. At any convenient pausing place in the recurring process of valuation, therefore, you must explain your "absolutes" by "relatives" just as much as your "relatives" by "absolutes."[26]

Leading points of social value theory: Criticism of Austrian theory of value: Austrians make two abstractions. The individual mind is isolated from society. Inside the individual mind, the economic interests stand isolated from other interests. Hence involve themselves in a vicious circle when they try to explain value in society. Start with desire for good A. Why has it "value"? Because of these desires? No, that is not enough—there must also be other goods to give in exchange; that is, there must be other *values*. Thus to explain value of good A, Austrians have to assume values of goods B, C, D, etc. Positive doctrine: How do we escape this vicious circle? By dropping the false abstractions on which it rests. 1. There is no individual mind but only a social mind. 2. In the social mind there is no separate set of economic values, they do not exist in isolation. What is value? "A quantity of motivating force, power over the actions of a man, embodied in an object." The quantity is a social product—especially influenced by social institutions of an economic, political and ethical order. How do we explain values then? By turning back "to the concrete whole of social-mental life, and especially to the moral and legal values of distribution." Absolute value must be back of relative value—values must exist before they can be compared. Hence we can compare the feelings of different men because social factors shape valuations.

[At this point the time has come to summarize:] How orthodox types differ in problems emphasized. Classical political economy centered interest in understanding of modern phenomena of prices, particularly prices which affect distribution of income. (As a body of technical doctrines is not as antiquated as are the cognate ideas—institutions—human nature, etc.). Orthodox descendants remained faithful to that central interest. Difference is that orthodox types primarily concerned with logic of the price system as now developed. Differences among the orthodox types: Mechanics of utility—Austrian theory-utility calculus—emphasized the analysis of demand which had been slurred over by classical political economy. Neoclassical doctrine seeks to restore due balance of emphasis by treating both cost and utility at length. Psychological school at the outset stressed the subjective basis upon which desires and efforts are supposed to rest; but it ran into pecuniary analysis, by finding that solid parts of its work was logic instead of psychology; that is, it presently finds that this subjective basis and reasoning based upon it is not psychological but pecuniary analysis; and then it also ran into pure theory [later called mathematical type]. It emphasizes the inter-relationships among all prices; that is, it emphasizes the general problem of equilibrium of demand and supply under static conditions.

The social value type thus falls roughly into the orthodox line as represented by the utility theory. It emphasizes the extent to which we are all the products of a given social regime and therefore have much that is common in all our scales of value.

---

[26] Mitchell to Anderson, March 26, April 10, 1918.

We now turn to the outlying [heterodox] types. These too are descendants of classical political economy, in that they remain faithful in part to the central interest of classical economics, that of understanding phenomena of prices, (John A. Hobson an exception, Veblen in chief measure, Gustav von Schmoller in part); but they differ from the orthodox types by being primarily concerned with social effects produced by workings of the price system (welfare economics); processes by which the price system has attained its present form and changes it is likely to undergo; namely, historical, institutional (or "exact type" of Richard Ehrenberg which studies particular business enterprises).[27]

---

[27] Outlines, May 14, 16, 1917, March 11, 1918, April 20, 1920. Quotations are from *Social Value,* pp. 106, 152.

[The discussion will now turn to Hobson's welfare economics.]

CHAPTER XVIII

John A. Hobson and Welfare Economics

In proportion as economic theory has taken the special and somewhat limited turn into the field of pecuniary economics represented by Davenport's *Economics of Enterprise* or Fisher's *Elementary Principles of Economics,* attention has been called to the need of supplementary discussions of certain topics that do not get covered in books like Davenport's and Fisher's. If theorists concentrate their attention primarily upon the effect of pecuniary factors, they leave out of account the whole set of problems concerned directly with public welfare, and so we have as another kind of investigation rather assiduously cultivated, perhaps more in England than elsewhere in recent years [1918], a line of investigation which is perhaps best called welfare economics. This is represented perhaps most simply by John A. Hobson's *Work and Wealth.*[1]

Preliminary survey of Hobson's work. How his type of theory differs from other types: Primarily in subject matter or rather in problem. Relation of economic life—both production and consumption—to welfare is of course no new subject. In one sense it has been the subject of interest to economic theorists from the beginning. But economists have usually pursued this most profound interest indirectly. They have sought to understand and to explain—at least to explain—the economic processes as they are, or as they would be under "normal" conditions. This understanding they assumed would promote efforts to establish welfare; but they have not directly treated the relation of production and consumption to welfare as the main, immediate problem.

Place of welfare (Hobson's main problem) in other books on economic theory. 1. Some writers, e.g., Schumpeter, are silent about it. Some, e.g., Marshall, make frequent references to it intermixed with their economic analysis. Some, e.g., Davenport, treat welfare, but keep the treatment quite separate from theory proper. Perhaps should add a fourth group who are telling how to establish welfare, or urging acceptance of certain specific measures to that end. But after all, these people are publicists rather than scientists. For that reason we have no example of their attitude

---

[1] Paragraph from "1918 Typescript."

in this course unless it be Schmoller. Welfare, it should be recalled, is the fourth level in the levels of analysis; it refers to some standard the appraiser accepts. It has been most elaborately worked out by Hobson, *Work and Wealth,* and A. C. Pigou, *The Economics of Welfare.*

Is Hobson's type of theory scientific? Does Davenport conceive his two final chapters [of *The Economics of Enterprise*] such? Does Marshall conceive his scattered reflections on courses which favor or injure well being as scientific? Is Hobson in a different position? What is his general method of attack upon the problem? Does he show what welfare consists in? Is that a scientific problem? Can one dispense with a criterion and still accomplish definite results? c.f., Pigou's ground; welfare cannot be defined. (Postpone consideration of Hobson's own answer. How Hobson arranges his attack on the problem: Analysis of costs connected with consumption. Human (plan) of redistributing the costs and utilities.[2]

Turning now to a detailed examination of the economics of John A. Hobson [1858-1940] as I have usually done, I should like to begin with a word about the man himself. He is an Englishman, born in Derby in 1858. He was educated in the Derby Grammar School and then went to Lincoln College, Oxford, where he devoted most of his time to the study of the classics.[3] After receiving his Oxford degree, he became a classical master in public schools, first in Faversham and then at Exeter.[4] He spent altogether eight years, 1880-1887, in teaching the classics in great boys' schools. He did not, however, find an adequate outlet for his energy in this work. He had decided gifts of exposition as well as lively interests and strong social feelings. So when he was about thirty he turned from teaching Greek and Latin to boys and for the decade 1887-1897 became an extension lecturer in English literature and economics under the programs sponsored by Oxford and London universities. Meanwhile he began to publish books dealing with economic problems, books which were well adapted to the kind of audiences that he met as an extension lecturer. The first of them was the very interesting *The Physiology of Industry* (1889) which he wrote with A. F. Mummery, a business man and famous mountaineer. In 1891 came *Problems of Poverty*; and in 1894 the book by which he is best known, *The Evolution of Modern Capitalism,* a very serviceable account of the way in which our modern capitalistic institutions grew up, particularly in England in the latter part of the eighteenth and the first half of the nineteenth century.

---

[2] Outlines, April 11, 1917; "Seminar in Economic Changes and Economic Theory," December 5, 1942.

[3] [His brother E. W. Hobson who became Sadleirian Professor of Pure Mathematics at Cambridge was J. M. Keynes's mathematics coach.]

[4] English public schools are equivalent to private schools in the United States.

It deals with the rise of finance as a dominating factor in English economic activity.[5] It was and is widely used in courses in economic history. In 1896 he published *The Problems of the Unemployed*; in 1898 came *John Ruskin, Social Reformer;* in 1900 *The War in South Africa* and also *The Economics of Distribution.* The latter is perhaps the closest approach to a conventional treatment of the technical problems of economic theory; it is a clever criticism of the general type of theory which is based upon marginal analysis. In 1901 he again published two books: *The Psychology of Jingoism* and *The Social Problem.* In 1902 came *Imperialism*; in 1904 one on *International Trade*; in 1906 one on *Canada Today.* In 1909 appeared *The Industrial System* which is another particularly effective account of modern industrial organization and its relation to financial organization. In 1911 he published *The Science of Wealth*[6] and *The Economic Interpretation of Investment.* In 1913 appeared *Gold, Prices and Wages,* in which he developed an extended criticism of the quantity theory of the value of money. In 1914 he published the book which will be discussed *Work and Wealth: A Human Valuation.*

I have not the full list of Hobson's publications since 1914. One needs an elaborate bibliography to keep track of him. [As of 1927] he has by no means given over his established habit of issuing a new volume on some social problem or economic topic every year or two, and sometimes two in a year. In the twenty-five years from his first book to *Work and Wealth,* he wrote twenty-four books; that is, in short he has been a very prolific writer.[7] His books do not by any means represent the whole of his literary productivity. For many years he was a journalist, connected with weekly papers. Especially he has been one of the most active members of the staff of the weekly *The*

---

[5] Sentence from Outline, October 14, 1919.

[6] [The posthumous fourth edition (1950), was revised with notes by R. F. (now Sir Roy) Harrod.]

[7] Some of Hobson's publications since 1914 and up to 1927 are: 1915, *Towards International Government;* 1916, *The New Protectionism;* 1917, *Democracy After the War;* 1918, *Richard Cobden, The International Man;* 1919, *Taxation in the New State;* 1921, *Problems of the New World;* 1922, *Incentives in the New Order* and *Economics of Unemployment;* 1926, *Free Thought in the Social Sciences.* [In 1938 came his last and fifty-third book, *Confessions of an Economic Heretic.*]

A full list of his books is in E. E. Nemmers, *Hobson and Underconsumption* (New York: Kelley & Millman, 1956) pp. 144-145.]

The three most important works of Hobson are (1) *Evolution of Modern Capitalism;* (2) the very valuable *The Industrial System;* (3) *Work and Wealth* ("1918 Typescript"). [Later Professor Mitchell added *The Economics of Distribution*].

[Professor Mitchell was largely responsible for the appearance of Hobson's "Neo-Classical Economics in Britain," *Political Science Quarterly,* September 1925, pp. 337-383. He wrote the editor that he should obtain a contribution from Hobson, and he urged Hobson to comply with the editor's request.]

Nation [and its successor *The New Statesman and Nation*]. For brief periods, Hobson wrote for the daily press.[8]

Hobson occupied in England a position in some respects—only in some respects—analogous to Thorstein Veblen's in the United States.[9] He never had even as much recognition from the orthodox economists as Veblen had. He never held an academic chair. And Veblen was assistant professor at Chicago, associate professor at Stanford and professorial lecturer at Missouri, not to speak of his work at the New School of Social Research in New York. Hobson had been from the start a gifted and steady dissenter from everything orthodox in the field of economics, rather the best of his generation among the economists who are not out and out Socialists like Sidney and Beatrice Webb and as such he has not found admirers among his university brethren.

His standing among orthodox economists is curious. He attracted attention first by a vigorous attack upon what he called the "over-saving fallacy" in *The Physiology of Industry*.[9a] Of course one of the great morals that the economists have been preaching since the days of Adam Smith and Jeremy Bentham has been the desirability of practicing thrift, and Hobson from the beginning has inclined to argue that a great deal of saving is made at excessive cost, that the community would be a great deal better off if people of moderate incomes tried to save less, and directed their lives in such a fashion that saving was not forced upon those who ought to be spending all their current income to meet current needs. [The work, in short, presented the heretical thesis that over-saving and underconsumption (in modern terminology "underspending") could exist and constituted a disease of the industrial system, a cause of recurrent periods of depression. According to his theory], "large incomes, which grow rapidly in prosperity, lead to oversaving and overinvestment in new plants, so that supply exceeds current demand. Depression follows, in which the large incomes are reduced, and oversaving ceases, so that consumption

---

[8] [The one notable episode in his work for the daily press was his activity for the *Manchester Guardian* on the eve of the Boer War. "In this experience lay the germ of Hobson's *Imperialism*, one of the most influential of his books." H. N. Brailsford, *The Life Work of J. A. Hobson*, L. T. Hobhouse Memorial Trust Lecture 17 (London: Oxford University Press, 1948) p. 8.]

[9] [Hobson was an admirer of Veblen, tried to interest publishers in a British edition of Veblen's *The Theory of Business Enterprise* (1904) and wrote a book about him—*Veblen* (1936).]

[9a] ["After Edgeworth's severe review of the book, the University of London authorities refused to allow him to lecture on economics but they could not refuse to pass 'John Ruskin,' heretic though he was, as a legitimate subject." J. H. Muirhead, *Reflections*, ed. by J. W. Harvey (London: Allen and Unwin, 1942) pp. 96-97.]

catches up with output and starts a revival."[10] [*The Evolution of Modern Capitalism* slightly restored his credit in academic quarters. It was received as a solid study and while it contained the germ for most of the author's disturbing ideas they were usually not generalized as laws and labelled as an attack on accepted theory.] But a little later, especially in *The Economics of Distribution,* he criticized severely the marginal analysis in general and in particular Alfred Marshall's doctrine of the "marginal shepherd," and expressed even graver doubts of the highly developed form of marginal analysis of Philip Wicksteed. All this of course was treated very ill in orthodox quarters. He has been, and still is in a measure a sympathetic disciple of John Ruskin, who felt that the business of the economists was not merely to understand the processes as they are going on at the present time and give accounts of what happens, but also to criticize the crudity of modern economic organization; to tell what ought to be done about it.[11] During the Boer War he was a vigorous anti-imperialist. Rather recently [1918] he has attacked the orthodox quantity theory of the value of money. And during the present [World] War [I] he has not

---

[10]Mitchell, *Business Cycles: The Problem and Its Setting* (New York: National Bureau of Economic Research, 1927), p. 52.

"Hobson holds that at any given time 'there is an exact proportion of the current income which, in accordance with existing arts of production and existing foresight, is required to set up new capital so as to make provision for the maximum consumption throughout the near future.' If in a period of prosperity, the rate of consumption should rise *pari passu* with the rate of production, there is no inherent reason why the prosperity might not continue indefinitely. But in modern societies, a large portion of the wealth produced belongs to a small class. In active times their incomes rise more rapidly than their consumption, and the surplus income is perforce saved. There results for the community as a whole a slight deficiency of spending and a corresponding excess of saving. The wealthy class seeks to invest its new savings in productive enterprises—thereby increasing the supply of goods and also increasing the incomes from which further savings will be made. This process runs cumulatively during the years of prosperity until finally the markets become congested with goods which cannot be sold at a profit. Then prices fall, liquidation ensues, capital is written down, and the incomes of the wealthy class are so reduced that savings fall below the proper proportion to spending.

During the period of depression, the glut of goods weighing upon the market is gradually worked off and the prospect of profitable investment slowly returns. Savings rise again to the right proportion to spending and good times prevail for a season. But after a while the chronic impulse toward over-saving becomes fully operative once more; soon or late it begets another congestion of the markets, and this congestion begets another depression.

Proximately then, the cause of alternating prosperity and depression is the tendency toward over-saving; ultimately it is the existence of the surplus incomes which lead to over-saving. . . . Hobson has presented his theory in several books, but most fully in *The Industrial System* and in *Economics of Unemployment* . . . The passage quoted is from p. 53 of the earlier volume." (*Business Cycles,* pp. 24-25.)

[11] [Ruskin created a tremendous furor especially with *Unto This Last* (1860) by his attack on the "bestial idolatry" of the political economists and his eloquent plea "that there is no wealth but life."]

been so hot and unreflecting a patriot as a great many people think it is desirable on the part of all Englishmen. In fact he is a gifted and sturdy dissenter from pretty much everything orthodox. Not unnaturally his writings have been regarded with some disfavor by the English academic economists.[12]

The expression of the average opinion of British economists concerning the value of Hobson's work is that given in a review of his *Gold, Prices, and Wages* by John Maynard Keynes in 1913. Keynes said: "One comes to a new book by Mr. Hobson with mixed feelings, in hope of stimulating ideas and of some fruitful criticisms of orthodoxy from an independent and individual standpoint, but expectant also of much sophistry, misunderstanding, and perverse thought."[13]

Hobson has not had severe technical training in economic theory. What he knows of theory does not command unmixed admiration by a long shot. He has always been at least as much interested in problems of the day, particularly when these issues have involved a strong ethical element, as he has been in economic problems. He is as much a publicist as he is an economic theorist, but with a special knowledge of and a set interest in economic abuse of one sort or another. Certainly Hobson's course of life is a little unusual for an economist nowadays. Most of the theorists with whom we have dealt were professors. In this respect they differ very widely from the men of the age of classical economics dealt with last term, none of whom except Malthus, and Adam Smith for a period of his life, were primarily engaged in teaching. They were men of affairs. Hobson has been primarily a publicist, more a journalist than anything else; in so far as he has been dealing with education, it had not been the

---

[12] All material above except the quotations from *Business Cycles* drawn from "1918 Typescript" and "Hobson," APP 54-63, no. 23.

[13] *The Economic Journal,* September 1913, p. 393.

[D. H. MacGregor, later of Oxford, declared in his review *Work and Wealth* "is a great contribution to sociology taking economics as a point of departure." (*The Economic Journal,* December, 1914, p. 563.) In 1936, Keynes in *The General Theory of Employment, Interest and Money* sharply reversed his original opinion of Hobson. At least as early as 1932, Keynes changed his attitude toward the heretic and engaged in a considerable correspondence with him to reconcile their views. Hobson with equal generosity declared by 1935 in a letter that he was trying to "correct my early presentation of over saving to bring it into accord with the financial analysis of Keynes. From my standpoint remedies for cyclical depression and unemployment are to be judged by the criterion: do they produce a more equal and equitable distribution of money and real income absorbing 'surplus' [unearned income] in a) wages and public services, b) public revenues for development of immediately non-remunerative activities such as education and roadmaking."]

technical education of graduate students,[14] but rather what is called "adult education," giving extension lectures. He is well read in technical economic theory, but when he comes to discuss a problem that seems to him of first rate social importance—and he never discusses any other types of problem—he approaches it from the attitude of a man writing for a weekly journal. In so far as he has made use of highly technical notions, he has done so with some reluctance and he employs always a notably skilful form of exposition.

In short, he is not a professional economist. All the men so far discussed in detail since the time of Jevons have been in that category. He belongs to the older type, like the masters of classical economics who were not professionally engaged in teaching economics. This is a comparatively recent development. Hobson who earned his bread and butter in other ways is a bit more like the great classical economists, but he has not been primarily a businessman.[15]

What is chiefly important as differentiating Hobson from the other people is the problem which he puts in the forefront of his investigations. Most of his predecessors have been interested ultimately in problems of social welfare. It was because he thought that the wealth of the nation contributed to its welfare that Adam Smith wrote his famous treatise with that title. The philosophical radicals were ultimately interested in welfare. That was the central part of their creed. The same remark doubtless applies to all the later writers who have been discussed. Alfred Marshall frequently introduces into his *Principles of Economics* observations of how certain factors which he is discussing bear upon the possibility of everybody living a full life. Even Davenport who makes economic theory such a highly technical matter, dealing solely with the price aspect of phenomena, spends a considerable amount of time, after he has finished his theory of economics, in showing how the institutional situation he is discussing bears upon the kind of life that men live.

All these people, however, have centered economics itself in the discussion of certain processes which have to do, in Adam Smith's case, primarily with the production of wealth, in the case of theorists since Ricardo, primarily with the process of exchange and distribution.

[14] [Hobson enjoyed giving a series of lectures in the 1920's at the Robert Brookings Graduate School of Economics and Government, Washington, D.C., an engagement he owed to his admirer Walton Hale Hamilton, who was dean of the faculty of this unfortunately short lived institution.

[Mitchell entertained him at the time]. "The John A. Hobsons dined with us [at Mitchell's home]. Pleasant talk about economic and social conditions in England and U.S." (Mitchell "Diary," March 29, 1925). [The "Diary" records that they first met on October 20, 1912, at Oxford.]

[15] Last two paragraphs from "1918 Typescript."

What they have to say about welfare is by way of incidental remarks that bear upon the subject which they are really discussing. It seems that the theme of welfare makes *Work and Wealth* of all Hobson's contributions to economic literature the one of greatest consequence. The book to be sure is singularly attractive, one very easy to read because Hobson does not trouble his readers with elaborate and difficult analyses.[16] But its importance lies in the fact that in it he develops and endeavors to treat, at least on a quasi-scientific basis, a problem which, while not altogether overlooked by his predecessors, has still not been taken up by them seriously for systematic examination. This is the grand problem of how far the prevailing methods of producing and distributing wealth are conducive to human welfare. A man like Marshall says a great deal on a subject of that sort, but incidentally only. Hobson makes that problem the center, treats it as the question above all with which the economist should concern himself.

In *Work and Wealth* he sets out to discuss welfare itself. It is in his view a human or humanistic conception of economics as opposed to the mechanized conception of the classical and so-called psychological theories.[17] His analysis concerns the way in which modern methods of producing and distributing wealth add to or subtract from the wealth of the community. This is a kind of discussion to which, as said before, one might suppose all of Hobson's predecessors would have felt that they should devote themselves, but they have not thought it feasible to discuss this interesting problem of economics on a scientific basis. Very often one of the previously discussed theorists, when he is dealing with the scope, the problems of economics, explains that while economics has its ultimate justification from the service it may render to society in deciding upon the kind of life it would like to live, it is after all only one of numerous sets of considerations which must be taken into account in passing upon the ultimate issues of public policy.

Hobson would not contest that well-established dictum that economic are only one of numerous sets of considerations which must be taken into account by anyone who is considering social welfare. Nevertheless he sees his way clear, as none of his predecessors have done, to develop a discussion of welfare as influenced by economic processes. In dealing with *Work and Wealth* our chief concern must be to see whether he has been successful in showing that these types

---

[16] Sentence from "1918 Typescript."
[17] Sentence from Outline, May 22, 1916.

of economic interest can be discussed in a satisfactory way; that is, in a way which shows something about the relations between present methods of producing and distributing wealth and economic welfare. Further, whether, if we do not believe that Hobson has gone very far in dealing with the problem, his methods nevertheless are capable of further development. If welfare is to be discussed as the central problem of economic theory, it would seem its exponents would have to begin by showing what welfare is. Does Hobson succeed in giving a satisfactory definition of welfare?

S: I have found none as yet.

M: How can welfare be discussed without defining it? Is it something we so well know, that is—that a definition is unnecessary? You might possibly make an investigation, say, of literacy without giving a definition. You know that any reader, himself literate, could look up a definition in the dictionary; and that presumably would meet your purposes as an investigator. Is the like true of welfare? Most economics text-books have careful definitions of fundamental concepts. People who deal with value tell what value is, give long chapters on the subject, explaining the ways in which the notions they intend to elucidate have been developed out of the earlier and, as they believe, cruder notions of their predecessors. You say that there is no definition of welfare in Hobson's book. How can he operate then?

S: He takes the consensus of opinion, the common opinion regarding welfare. There is no definite scientific measurement, but all agree that there is such a thing as welfare.

M: Does he not go a little further than that?

S: He does not make any very definite statement about what welfare is, but he seems to imply that welfare will center around two things: human cost in production and human utility from consumption, and these two things together give an indication of what welfare is.

M: Is there some other suggestion?

S: Does he not consider welfare from the standpoint that human society is an evolving organism and that we must think of the welfare of the individuals as taking place in this organism, just as we consider the individual cells of an animal organism as tied up with the welfare of the organism as a whole?

M: Hobson says:

> Our standard must be conceived in terms of a life that is good or desirable. This consideration might evidently lead us far afield. If we are to undertake a valuation of life as a preliminary to valuing

industry, it is likely that we may never approach the second undertaking. The best escape from this predicament is to start from some
generally accepted concept which indicates, even if it does not express fully, the desirable in life. Such a term I take to be "organic
welfare." Though in form a mere synonym for good life, it is by
usage more restricted and more precise.[18]

He says at the outset practically that he cannot define welfare
though he does not say it so explicitly as A. C. Pigou [1871-1959],
Marshall's successor at Cambridge, who has also written a book on
a similar range of problems, *Wealth and Welfare*.[19] Hobson says he
cannot define what constitutes the good life and it is obvious you
cannot; it is the central problem of ultimate existence.

But he thinks there is a way out. Welfare itself cannot be defined
in a comprehensive fashion, but there is a common agreement among
enlightened people concerning a good many things which are elements
in welfare. For example, few people will challenge the statement that
a high degree of literacy in a population is an element in welfare.
Few would question that other things being equal, a community
whose children are well nourished is one which in that respect has a
higher degree of welfare than one in which children are not as well
nourished. Thus there are a large number of aspects of modern life,
all of a rather humble sort, which can be subjected to some kind of
measurement, and which people have little difficulty in accepting,
at least in so far as they have relevance, as indicating the existence
of degrees of welfare.

Hobson proceeds to argue that the area of common agreement permits the possibility of making measurement, and is being expanded.
It is already wide enough to provide a basis for carrying on a significant series of discussions based upon partial glimpses of what
constitutes welfare, though there is no pretense to set up a comprehensive definition. His position is brought out more clearly in the
last chapter:

> The task of a human valuation of industry at the outset involved
> the arbitrary assumption of a standard of value. That standard con-

---

[18] *Work and Wealth, A Human Valuation* (London: George Allen and Unwin, 1914)
p. 12.

[19] "Welfare . . . cannot be defined, in the sense of being analyzed. . . . For the purpose of this volume, it is sufficient to lay down on the subject two propositions: first,
that welfare includes states of consciousness only, and not material things or conditions; secondly, that welfare can be brought under the category of greater and less."
Wealth and Welfare (London: Macmillan, 1912) p. 3.

[In the revision Pigou stated that "welfare . . . is a thing of very wide range. There
is no need here to enter upon a general discussion of its content." The first of the
two propositions is rephrased and reads "the elements of welfare are states of consciousness, and, perhaps, their relations." *The Economics of Welfare* (London:
Macmillan, 1920, 4th ed. 1932, reprint of 1938) p. 10.]

sisted in a conception of human well-being applicable to the various forms of human life, man as individual, as group or nation, as humanity. Starting from that conception of the health, physical and spiritual, of the individual human organism, which is of widest acceptance, we proceed to apply the organic metaphor to the larger groupings, so as to build up an intelligible standard of social well-being. This standard, at once physical and spiritual, static and progressive, was assumed to be of such a kind as to provide a harmony of individual welfares when the growing social nature of man was taken into due account.

With the standard of human well-being we then proceed to assign values to the productive and the consumptive processes of which industry consists, examining them in their bearing upon the welfare of the individuals and the societies engaging in them.

Now this mode of procedure, the only possible, of course involved an immense *petitio principii*. The assumption of any close agreement as to the nature of individual well-being, still more of social well-being, was logically quite unwarranted.

Economic values have, indeed, an agreed, exact and measurable meaning, derived from the nature of the monetary standard in which they are expressed. Now, no such standard of the human value of economic goods or processes can be established. Yet we pretended to set up a standard of social value and to apply a calculus based upon it, claiming to assess the human worth underlying the economic costs and utilities that enter into economic values.

Has this procedure proved utterly illicit? I venture to think not. Though at the outset our standard was only a general phrase committing nobody to anything, the process of concrete application, in testing the actual forms of work and wealth which make up industry, gave to it a continual increase of meaning. While the widest divergence would be found in the formal definitions of such terms as "human welfare" or "social progress," a large and growing body of agreement would emerge, when a sufficient number of practical issues had been brought up for consideration. The truth of our standard and the validity of our calculus are established by this working test. It is not wonderful that this should be so, for the nature and circumstances of mankind have so much in common, and the processes of civilisation are so powerfully assimilating them, as to furnish a continually increasing community of experience and feeling. It is, of course, this fund of "common sense" that constitutes the true criterion. The assumption that "common sense" is adequate for a task at once so grave and delicate may, indeed, appear very disputable. Granting that human experience has so much in common, can it be claimed that the reasoning and the feeling based on this experience will be so congruous and so sound as to furnish any reliable guide for conduct? Surely "common sense" in its broadest popular sense can go a very little way towards such a task as a human interpretation of industry.

There is no doubt a good deal of force in this objection. If we are to invoke "common sense" for the purposes of an interpretation or a valuation, it must evidently be what is termed an "enlightened common sense."[20]

This is setting up an ultimate criterion; that is, Hobson reserves the

[20] *Work and Wealth*, pp. 320-321.

right to decide what is "enlightened common sense" and what is not. But he thinks that even on that topic there is a comparatively wide range of agreement.

In a sense, the discussion is based upon a somewhat arbitrary set of assumptions. If the reader happens to be one of the people who have different ideas concerning welfare from Hobson's, then he has every reason not to accept Hobson's conclusions. But if his opinion of welfare in those aspects with which Hobson deals agree with his, the reader will be at least much interested in his conclusions. Therefore, let us see what conclusions Hobson arrives at, and how he attains to them.

He gives his plan of procedure in the third chapter; he proposes to estimate the human value of a given national income. To do this the investigator must first learn what the concrete goods and services are which constitute real income, and then he must trace the concrete goods and services backwards to the processes of their production and forward through the processes of their consumption in order to learn the human costs and utilities; that is, he attempts to treat the processes of producing and consuming goods in modern society from the standpoint of human welfare. This means, in practice, that he will analyze similarly the human utilities which are attained from producing goods. Then he will strike a balance as between these costs on the one side and utilities on the other side, and see where modern society comes out. He says:

> Our aim will be to set out, as well as we can, reliable rules for examining the productive and consumptive history of the various sorts of concrete marketable goods so as to discover the human elements of cost and utility contained in each, and by a computation of these positives and negatives to reach some estimate of the aggregate human value contained in the several sorts of commodities which form the concrete income of the nation and in this income as a whole.[21]

From one point of view, this is Jeremy Bentham's old problem, only Bentham talked in terms of pleasures and pains and Hobson is talking in terms of costs and utilities. Bentham employed the term "felicific calculus," and every now and then intimated at least that his method allowed one to calculate. So also Hobson, as the quotation shows. Needless to say, Bentham never really calculated; and Hobson never computes. Both compare quantities which are not capable of direct numerical expression, but about which the writers and presumably most readers agree that there are broad differences of a quantitative order.

---

[21] *Work and Wealth*, p. 34.

The matter becomes clearer as we learn exactly what Hobson believes he can accomplish in carrying out the plan. He must make a computation of costs; he must compare in human terms costs of production on the one side with the utilities derived from consumption on the other side. This means that he has to know first what his costs are, and then, second, what his utilities consist of; and he has to be able to make some, at least vague, quantitative statements concerning the magnitude of the costs and of the opposing utilities.

The first technical problem is what constitutes costs? Hobson accepts the standard economic categories, somewhat elaborated; that is, costs which consist of rent and interest and labor.[21a] But he sees at once that he can leave rent out, because rent represents no human cost. The landlords who let people live in their property or cultivate their land are not undergoing any human cost. Tenants have to pay for the privilege, but they are not compensating the landlord for any sacrifice he is making. Labor and waiting—in Hobson's terminology "saving"—are the forms of cost which must be considered.

Labor can be subdivided according to its type. In doing so Hobson elaborates the standard economic classification: "I propose to classify productive activities under the following heads: Art, Invention, Professional Service, Organisation, Management, Labour, Saving."[22] When he discusses human costs he is examining the human sacrifices involved in the work of the artist, the scientist and inventor, the professional man, the business organizer, the superintendent of industrial processes, and finally the manual worker, the operative.

The kind of conclusion at which he arrives is comparatively simple. To begin with artistic work, Hobson lays down the view that the artist is in the position of being paid handsomely (however not all artists would agree to that) for work which is in itself a pleasure to perform, and which he would do just as well if he were only paid his human keep. He makes a similar statement regarding the work of scientific people.

> The zest of the scientific student and the joy of discovery are emotions as vital and as valuable in themselves as the emotions of the artist. So far, then, as the scientist comes within our purview as a productive agent, his activity must rank with the artist's, as: yielding more human utility than cost.[23]

[21a] [Hobson early insisted on the importance of methodology, that the progress of a social science depended in good part on its having the instrument of a stable and fitting terminology to provide its own tools of inquiry. Hobson, "On the Relation of Sociology to the Social Sciences and Philosophy," in Proceedings of the Sociological Society, 1904, *Sociological Papers* (London: Sociological Society, 1905) p. 213.]

[22] *Work and Wealth*, p. 43.

[23] *Work and Wealth*, p. 49.

Much the same he believes holds true regarding the professional and managerial classes in business:

> For most of the productive energy given out by the artistic, inventive, professional, official, and managerial classes, which have passed under our survey, is seen to be in large measure creative, varied, interesting, and pleasurable.[24]

It is work which does not involve any net human costs. All that people who do it really need, to repeat, is their keep.

With the laborer the situation is different. After a long discussion Hobson sums up the result of the analysis of the human costs of labor as follows:

> So far as the merely or mainly physical costs are concerned, the muscular and nervous strain and fatigue, excessive repetition is a true description of the chief cause. Machine tending at a high pace for a long working-day is in itself the most "costly" type of labour.

In other words, the type of labor he believes the greatest strain upon the human organism is repetitive work of the type represented by machine tending. He continues,

> and, in so far as a machine controls the sort and pace of work done by a human being, these "costs" accumulate. But most work is not so directly controlled by machinery, and yet is so highly specialized that the routine constantly over-taxes with fatigue the muscles, nerves and attention. The duration and pace of such labour are usually such as to heap up heavy costs of physical wear and tear and of physical discomforts.[25]

I may say, by way of making this point clearer, that Hobson criticizes the general idea of scientific management on the ground that it is a scheme for organizing industry which concentrates pretty much all the considerable activity of thinking in the hands of a few and aims to turn the great bulk of the workers into a type of routine operators, people who will not have to think, but can devote all their energy simply to carrying out the specific tasks which have been assigned them. This is a vicious way of organizing work, he believes, because it robs the mass of operatives of even that remnant of varied interest in their work which was left them before the scientific managers got into power.

Note the contrast here between Hobson's view and one which is common among many writers. For example, those who have read the works of Sidney and Beatrice Webb will recall the phrase of which they are so fond: the "intolerable toil of thought."[26] There are many

---

[24] *Work and Wealth*, p. 61.
[25] *Work and Wealth*, p. 85.
[26] Quoted from Sidney and Beatrice Webb, *Industrial Democracy* (London: Longmans, Green, 1897; 2nd ed., 1920) p. 720.

people who maintain that thought is the most distasteful of human enterprises. Hobson takes the view that thinking, creating, is pleasurable and the task of performing merely routine work is necessarily a severe strain upon the organism. He is not in a position here to substantiate his view by any conclusive evidence. He takes the view that of the various costs which are usually included by economists under the general head of labor, all that have to do with the artistic, the scientific and even with the planning side of industry are relatively costless, but that the actual execution of the work, which includes the overwhelming majority of workers, is costly, for it involves strain.

Then Hobson turns to savings. In discussing this subject he classifies again, but in a different way. Some savings, in fact, a considerable fraction—are made by people of large incomes. For such savings there is neither an economic nor a human cost involved. Instead, it rests, in the economic sense, as much on surplus as the rent of land. People whose incomes are so large that it would be a bother to spend all of it are automatic savers. There is no sacrifice involved in what they put aside. The middle classes are in a somewhat similar situation, though one which is sufficiently different to make it necessary to treat the middle classes apart from the rich. Sacrifices ascribed to such saving, Hobson thinks, can for the most part not be regarded as involving any serious human costs. There is a certain satisfaction that the middle classes get out of the saving itself which is at least an adequate offset for the sacrifices involved. But, unfortunately a good deal of saving is done by the poorer classes, the working classes. That is unfortunate, not necessarily from the viewpoint of poor people who are trying to rise in the world, but from society's point of view that some of the saving is done by people of very small incomes. For when one's income is very small, any saving is necessarily done at heavy cost. Much saving of that sort "involves a stinting of the prime necessities or conveniences of life, or of some rise in present expenditure which would promote health or efficiency of the family."[27]

In particular Hobson thinks that saving by the poor is likely to be done at the expense of their children, in the sense that if the family could spend the money they put aside in having better medical and educational care for their children the children would profit greatly. To deprive children of that sort of attention in their growing years through saving means that the human cost involved in saving of this type is very great.

---

[27] *Work and Wealth*, p. 104.

To sum up, of the human costs of the three conventional costs recognized by economists, rent does not count. That is the mere payment
of a surplus. Labour by the bulk of the people who are directed does
count. The saving by the poor counts; but not the saving by the rich,
and probably not the saving by the middle classes.

So much for the human costs of production. There is no basis for
a computation here. Yet in the end one sees how Hobson comes to
put them together with the results of a similar character which he
draws concerning the utilities of consumption in such a fashion as
to arrive at a reasonable conclusion. But before looking at the conclusion the student ought to see what kind of results he gets when he
tries to estimate the human values of the utilities of consumption.

There are, Hobson maintains, for purposes of this discussion, two
situations which the economist should envisage. The first is that
presented by the consumption of those things which are necessary for
maintaining not merely life but efficiency. In so far as the community
has merely the amount of income which is adequate for food and
clothing and proper housing and adequate nourishment for its children, all the consumption stands on the side of utility. There is a
certain amount of waste in consumption of that sort, but it is comparatively meager. On the other hand, when a person's income is
rising above the point which will provide merely for meeting the
indispensable organic needs, the opportunity for wasteful consumption
becomes much greater, but it does not follow that all consumption
over and above what is required to meet creature needs is undesirable.
On the contrary, when the economist is dealing with a surplus of
income over what is necessary to maintain a decent standard of
comfort, he is going to discriminate and analyze. The way Hobson
attacks that problem is to classify again. He holds that there are three
factors in standards of consumption: these are concerned with meeting respectively physical, industrial and conventional needs. Physical
needs must be met. Industrial needs, by which he means the peculiar
demands of the kind of work a person does, must be met. Conventional
needs are another matter. Many of them, in Hobson's eyes, are
without human value. This represents the wide field of human vanity,
of human meanness, too; the satisfaction that people get out of consuming things just because the majority of their fellow-citizens cannot
consume them—the opportunity which they have to draw invidious
comparisons between themselves and others upon a pecuniary basis.

Hobson is very much a moralist and his blood boils with indigna-
tion when he thinks of the vulgar ostentation which is characteristic,

not merely, he points out, of the large part of the consumption of the wealthy but of a considerable fraction of the consumption of the middle class, and, he regrets to say, of an appreciable fraction of the consumption of the poor because the upper class standards seep down even to the lowest strata of society. He would damn tobacco, for instance, and a great many rather minor indulgences on which people spend money in harmful ways, money which ought to be devoted to giving their children an opportunity to learn how to live a better life than their parents.

An illustration of the character of the argument is Hobson's general summary of his results. He has a little scheme which runs as follows:[28]

WEALTH

"PRODUCTION		CONSUMPTION
Art & Exercise ⎱ Labour ⎰	Human Utility	⎰ Needs ⎱ Abundance
Toil ⎱ Mal-production ⎰	Human Cost	⎰ Satiety ⎱ Mal-consumption"

The headings are intended to sum up all the kinds of exertion which go into the production of goods that involve an element of personal expression. They count on the side of human utility, and Hobson, when he comes to the summing up, thinks also that it is good for everybody to do a certain amount of labor. Though perhaps done with a certain sense of strain it is nevertheless salutary. On the other hand, excessive labor which he calls "toil," and work in making things which the world would be better without, which he calls "mal-production," count on the side of human cost. Similarly, on the consumption side, all that is used to satisfy the people's needs and even to satisfy them abundantly, so that they are not continually left with painfully ungratified appetites, counts on the side of utility. When consumption is carried beyond that point so that men's appetites lose their edge and particularly when people consume goods which are positively noxious there is human cost.

Then the question is how ought our work and consumption be organized on a human basis? Hobson is clear that a considerable part of consumption falls in the category of human cost. He does not undertake to say how much; he is far more interested in the question of how life should be reorganized; on that head he is confident that he knows what should be done. The human law of distribution aims

---

[28] *Work and Wealth,* p. 159. [Hobson was emphasizing the point that the standard of living should not be interpreted merely in terms of consumption, but should also include "human costs."]

to distribute wealth in relation to its production on the one hand, and its consumption on the other hand, so as to minimize human costs and to maximize utilities. It is a good sound Benthamite conception with modernized phrasing. This means that each should contribute according to his abilities and receive according to his needs as a consumer, that is according to his capacity to derive utility.

Hobson argues that it is wrong to assume that all people are equally gifted as consumers. In this respect he is an offshoot of the utility school which agrees with Edgeworth who said in the clearer and more striking phraseology which the utilitarians used to employ, that some people are better pleasure machines than others and there will be a greater net pleasure in a community if more of the raw materials— commodities—are fed into better pleasure machines. The pleasure machines should be used to the best capacity to maximize pleasure. What Hobson says in vaguer terms comes to the same thing: to maximize utility, commodities should be distributed in society in proportion to capacity to derive utility from them.

He goes on to develop certain consequences which follow from his human law of distribution; consequences which relate to the position of the laborer in society, to the problem of leisure, to capitalistic organization of society, etc. A few passages will clarify these matters. The first concerns the demands which should be put forward on behalf of labor:

> The real demand of Labour is at once more radical and more human. It is a demand that Labour shall no longer be bought and sold as a dead commodity subject to the fluctuations of Demand and Supply in the market, but that its remuneration shall be regulated on the basis of the human needs of a family living in a civilized country.[29]

Concerning leisure, Hobson says:

> But from the standpoint of the individual worker the economy of a shorter work-day has a double significance. We have seen that it more than proportionately diminishes his personal cost, by cancelling the last and most costly portion of his work-day. But it also increases the human utility which he can get out of his wages.[30]

It does so by allowing him to consume in a more leisurely less hurried fashion.

Again, continuing this same theme, he writes:

> A community like that of Great Britain, with a population declining in its growth, will tend to take a continually increasing share of its real income in the shape of intellectual, moral, aesthetic, recreative, and other non-material services. These will absorb an ever-

---

[29] *Work and Wealth,* p. 190.
[30] *Work and Wealth,* p. 235.

growing share of the productive energy of the people. This demand for the satisfaction of higher economic needs will be likely to put a check upon the tendency towards an illimitable reduction of the work-day. For most of these higher non-material goods do not admit the application of those economies of capitalist production available in the making of material goods. Take one example, that of education.[31]

He goes on to argue that education is not a process which can be turned out on the principles of mass production.

Hobson points out what a destructive verdict one must pass on the capitalistic organization of society if one accepts the human law of distribution. For as the world works at the present time it cannot be said that there has been achieved a good approximation toward the principle of distributing the costs of production according to ability to bear them. Neither can it be said that the goods produced are distributed among consumers according to their capacity to get utility from them. Thus what I have just said in a most formal way, Hobson states in a very concrete fashion; it is a skilful exposure, full of moral zeal. He sums up the positive demands of the human law of distribution as he interprets them as follows:

> The humanisation and rationalisation of industry depend, as we recognize, upon reforming the structure of businesses and industries, so as to resolve these discords, to evoke the most effective co-operation, in fact and will, between the several parties, and to distribute the whole product, costs and surplus, among them upon terms which secure for it the largest aggregate utility in consumption.[32]

Then he returns to emphasize once more what he calls the "vital point":

> The substitution of direct social control for the private profit-seeking motive in the normal processes of our industries is essential to any sound scheme of social reconstruction.

Social control must be substituted for the private profit-seeking motive. "The pace of civilisation for nations, of moral progress for individuals, depends upon this radical reconstruction of common industry."[33]

Finally Hobson is much concerned to show that men have small likelihood of grasping the need of this fundamental reconstruction unless they learn to think of society as having in some sense personality; that is, he is taking precisely the opposite ground from Davenport. Remember Davenport's scornful remarks about the social organism: there is no such thing. Hobson says:

[31] *Work and Wealth,* p. 248.
[32] *Work and Wealth,* p. 283.
[33] *Work and Wealth,* p. 293.

> We are told indeed that "Society only exists in individuals."
> . . . I should rather say that society exists in the co-operation of
> individuals. . . . It is . . . of supreme and critical importance to
> obtain the widest possible acceptance of the conception of society
> as a living being to which each of us "belongs." . . . until we attribute
> to Society such a form and degree of "personality" . . . the social
> will will not be able to perform great works.[34]

I should like to ask the class how the whole performance strikes it.
Are we justified in regarding *Work and Wealth* as a contribution to
economic theory? I have ventured, at least tentatively, to speak of
it as representing the welfare type of economic theory. Can we put
it under that category or should we call Hobson a moral exhorter?
Is it a scientific analysis in any serious sense or is it a preachment?

S: The first half of the book deals with theory; he discusses value,
costs, consumption, production and so on. The second is more doubtful where he lays down the ideal of needs and capacities.

M: Yet, the second part in which he is drawing his conclusions, is
based, is it not, quite consistently on the same conception of human
nature that he employs in the first part, and comes like a set of more
or less necessary corollaries?

S: Economists have not agreed upon the object of the science of
economics; to explain what is or what ought to be. One cannot get
away from that.

M: Let us ask that question then. Does Hobson really explain
anything; if so, what?

S: In the first part of the book he discusses the organization of
society as it now is; later he goes on to theorize as to how that might
be modified.

M: In that part of the book does he explain anything?

S: He explains the costs of the workers.

M: Yes, he is there endeavoring at least to explain how what he
calls the human costs of industry are distributed on broad lines, and
also he undertakes to explain how utilities are distributed in society
at present; always with an eye to the discrepancies between the
existing institutions and that which would be nearer to his heart's
desire.

Please recall from the class discussion of Bentham last term that
the felicific calculus as Bentham used it had two sides. It afforded on
the one hand a means of explaining what people do; and on the other
hand, it afforded a means of judging what people ought to do. Of the
two sets of propositions which Bentham thought could be based upon

---

[34] *Work and Wealth*, pp. 308-309.

the felicific calculus the second set dealing with what people ought to do can be determined more rigorously, can be reasoned about on a more satisfactory basis. Having just granted the fundamental assumption that people pursue pleasure and that of necessity the great aim is to maximize pleasure, it is easier to tell how social affairs ought to be organized than it is to account for all the idiosyncracies of individual action, because while the inquirer assumes that everybody is pursuing pleasure he recognizes that this pursuit is in large part unenlightened: that people have all sorts of failures of the understanding.

Remember how much emphasis Bentham put on intellectual weakness, native and adoptive. Thus if the theorist wants to find out the actual course of human behavior in social matters, either he has to make a careful and extensive set of observations proceeding by statistical methods (which Bentham never [systematically] proposed); or he must at least set up the broad categories of the intellectual imperfections in the workings of people's minds which lead them to make wrong calculations concerning pleasures they receive. He has to take into account such traits of human nature, for instance, as the classical economists emphasized in their talk about the working classes; the misery they bring upon themselves, not because they do not want to get pleasure, but because their failing is not to realize the unhappy results that will come upon them from marrying early and begetting large families. This inquiry into what people actually do is a difficult kind of undertaking and leads to uncertain results. But to tell what people ought to do ought to be relatively a simple matter. One can reason about that with considerable confidence. Bentham himself says, for instance, in the earliest of his publications, the *Fragment on Government*, where he is criticizing the great mass of writers upon law in that they had given an account of legal institutions and neglected the most important of their tasks, that is, showing what legal institutions ought to be.

From anybody who has the Benthamite general approach to the discussion of social problems it must be expected that in his eyes the most important and the most certain of his conclusions will be that which deals with the ideal. Hobson is an attenuated example of utilitarian thought. He does not talk about pleasures and pains, but about sacrifices and utilities. To all intents and purposes his terms mean to this generation what Bentham's terms pleasure and pain meant to the generation that was flourishing between, say, 1800 and 1833.

Hobson, like Bentham, is giving an account of what happens, and gives it with a critical eye. He is not interested so much in showing actually how the costs of production are distributed, as in how far that distribution falls short of the one society ought to obtain. He is not so much interested in showing how utilities are distributed as he is in criticizing the present distribution of income and its use in purchasing goods. He does not come into his own until having gone through this criticism of existing institutions he sets up his large and yet simple scheme for reorganizing society, and proceeds to show how by this standard the fundamental economic institutions of the present age must be condemned; that is, how if we have a glimpse of the light, some intelligence and moral courage, we must undertake the task of revolutionizing the organization of industry.

Work and Wealth is the work of a man who is a sort of moral prophet, whose interest lies in welfare as primarily an ethical concept. He is longing for the good life, a trait that is characteristic of Marshall, though Marshall is more cautious in his suggestions for the betterment of economic institutions. Hobson is in many respects far more akin spiritually to Bentham than to any other writer previously discussed, not simply in his procedure, his methods of thought, but in his fundamental interest. There was, however, a decided temperamental difference between the two men. Bentham liked to play with ideas; he was a gay and happy sort of person; he cannot be said to have been filled with moral fervor. There was always an element of the free-funster about everything he did, he enormously enjoyed poking fun at British judges and institutions as a whole. Hobson, on the other hand, is a very serious person, giving little opportunity for humor in any of his discussions: still, to repeat, he is proceeding on the basis of a scheme of things with an apparatus which seems scarcely distinguishable from the utilitarianism that Bentham developed with such mechanical clearness.

The name of economic theory is not denied to the kind of analysis which Jevons built up. I do not see why we deny it to the type which Hobson constructs. Nor why, if economists can accept his fundamental principles, should they deny that, when he is drawing corollaries concerning the desirable state of affairs, he is proceeding on rational grounds to conclusions which must have whatever measure of value is guaranteed them by the premises. If they quarrel with these conclusions, it must be because for some reason or other they do not find Hobson's premises complete or satisfactory as a basis for treatment of social problems.

It is a common view that part of the task of the economist is to throw light upon the ultimate ends of life, not that any economist supposes that his science can exhaust the subject, but many people feel that economic theory has not performed its function fully until it has shown what contribution it can make toward the conception of the good, the desirable. Thus Hobson is by no means alone. On the other hand, it can be said that more courageously than any other writer he has undertaken this difficult task.

S: Do you agree with his criticism of marginal analysis?

M: The opinion that he develops in the last chapter particularly? It is very interesting. It is a sort of addendum to the book. There he develops substantially the thesis that in the marginal theory economists have undertaken to explain how economic behavior is rationalized by observing the expenditure of the last increments of income. According to the marginal theory, what people do on the margin is the systematizing element in all behavior. Hobson says, if a person actually considers his own behavior he knows that there is a minimum of system in the way in which he spends the marginal increments of income. That instead of basing his expenditures as a consumer upon a comparison of the satisfactions that he gets from the final pennies he spends on newspapers, theatres, beef steaks, etc., he has but the vaguest kind of notion concerning the returns from the final expenditures; as a matter of fact with that part of his income he plays, he experiments. This is a very penetrating and júst observation.

On the other hand, says Hobson, the part of the individual's expenditure which is more or less rationally controlled is the bulk of it lying well within the marginal limits. He can sit down today, if he kept accounts of the best order, and tell a good deal about the amounts of money that he lays out on clothing, food, and carfares. Most of his expenditures lie well within the margin, are regulated largely for him by social conventions and he adjusts the social conventions to his particular case on the basis of repeated experimentation. There is little of the whimsical in deciding whether or not to wear shoes, to pay carfares. The whimsical, uncertain, unpredictable part of the individual's expenditure is precisely the marginal element. Therefore since science can give rules only for the regularities, the part of expenditure which economic theory can give an account of is the part lying inside the margins; and the part on which the theorist can rely so little is the marginal portion. Hobson turns the tables upon the whole program of analysis which has come down to the profession from Jevons on the one hand and the Austrians on the other hand.

S: You said that we cannot deny the name of economic theory to Hobson's work.

M: One moment—if we accept his standpoint it seems difficult to deny it the name economic theory.

S: However, how would you compare this approach with the one Davenport suggests which is purely scientific?

M: You say purely scientific?

S: Yes.

M: Of course, it purports to be. As an effort to give a satisfactory account of what people do, Davenport's type is woefully deficient, because it leaves out the problem of value. It takes for granted the choices that people make concerning the character of different goods and the amount of money that they spend upon them, concerning the sacrifices involved in certain kinds of efforts. Any economic theory that takes this for granted has confined itself to a very technical, mechanical section of economic life. We are likely to get the best orientation to the problem of economics by dealing with it as an attempt to throw light on economic behavior. If the inquirer takes that viewpoint, then he simply cannot evade the fundamental problem of how people's likes and dislikes get into their current shape. If the economist is to attack that problem, then he has to proceed along the lines of marginal analysis or give up that procedure entirely and study by presumably more objective methods the development and changes in social tastes, using the word "social" there to indicate simply that he should deal with the development and changes in tastes which are characteristic of masses of people, not simply individuals.

S: I do not see why this whole problem of social reform is contingent on the metaphysical notion of social organization.

M: I suppose that Hobson's view is that economists will never get the mass of people alive to the great social problems unless they can put them in a form that comes home to individuals. The individual can feel sympathy with a personality. He is one. He can understand things in terms of a personality. He thinks of the United States not as consisting of one hundred and thirty million individuals, but as a nation. When people think about the nation, they readily get excited about it, it appeals to them, it has a hold upon their feelings. Hobson's notion is that if the economists can in this same effective fashion personify society, they can make it a genuine thing. They will make society mean something more than an abstraction to the great mass of people. I do not think this is, from his viewpoint, a necessary scientific conclusion, but society as a personality is a good slogan.

S: Ricardo is said to have used economics to solve specific problems. In Marshall it seems to me more of a general system. Does Hobson follow Ricardo more than Marshall?

M: Marshall has a far firmer grasp upon the unity of all economic problems than Ricardo. Ricardo lived in the comparatively early stage of the development of the science when people were beginning to see clearly separate parts of the field; outstanding problems appealed to them, became clearer in their field of vision. At that stage it was comparatively easy to think of the bits as in considerable measure independent of each other. Thus he lays down three laws of value, but they were not logically connected with each other. He developed laws of distribution which were neither logically connected with each other, nor were corollaries to the theory of value. Marshall, on the other hand, brings all the elements in the economic problem together. More than that, he has a firm grasp upon the proposition that all prices, all values mutually determine each other. One of the phrases he was particularly fond of in his later years, which occurs again and again in his letters, is "the one in the many, the many in the one." In that sense he was seeing all economic problems as part and parcel of each other.

Hobson, while not laying so much stress upon the unity of economic problems, would be inclined to say that Marshall's attitude was sounder in this respect than Ricardo's, that it represents later and more advanced insight. Is that pertinent to what the student has in mind?

S1: Yes.

S2: Isn't it finally a matter of the level of economic analysis which is considered? Hobson in his examination of welfare is not any nearer to the real forces than is Davenport in his price analysis.

M: The most satisfactory sort of discussion would be if the economist could develop the several levels and show their interrelations to each other.

S: Is that possible?

M: It may become feasible. That stage has not been reached yet in a satisfactory fashion; but I do not despair of it—not for myself but for you people and perhaps your children.

S: Until something actually workable is developed, isn't it an error to speculate about welfare—just in the air?

M: If you can accept Hobson's fundamental outlook on the world, welfare is something about which you can be pretty certain.

S: He has not proved anything; he just sort of talked.

M: If it is agreed—and this is a substantial "if"—that the aim of society should be to minimize costs and maximize utilities, then it seems that Hobson's general scheme of human distribution must be accepted. If you accept it, then you must agree with him that the present organisation of society is a bad one, and you must also agree with him about at least a considerable number of definite changes which we should strive to introduce.

S: He has not shown that any changes which he suggests are really going to make more welfare. He assumes that in this organic state, things will be so much better.

M: No, but from his point of view it simply must be better if what he says could be done. That is, if costs could be distributed in accordance with capacity to endure sacrifices, then human costs would be lessened. On the other hand, if you managed to distribute goods according to the capacity of people to get utility out of consumption, you have increased the amount of utility. Those are almost mathematical corollaries. The doubt is whether much of anything can be found out about the differences in human capacity to make sacrifices or to develop utilities out of consumption, and whether that kind of distribution can be effected. I agree that those are enormously big questions, and Hobson has made scarcely any effort to answer them.

S: He does not give a practical program in *Work and Wealth*.

M: No, that is true. But it remains also true, does it not, if one does try to follow up and apply this general scheme of analysis? It will require a great deal of careful investigating, thinking and analyzing concerning differences in the capacities of human beings and how the redistribution either of costs on the one side or of commodities on the other, can be effected.

M: [To repeat some of the questioning],[35] what is the outstanding difference between *Work and Wealth* and the other treatises which we have dealt with?

S1: The human element.

M: What does the book deal with primarily, S2?

S2: It deals in many generalities; in very unprecise thinking. It deals as the title says with work and welfare, primarily welfare, and the way the industrial situation affects—

M: That is what S1 means, that the book is distinguished by a

---

[35] The remaining questions and answers are from the "1918 Typescript."

human, perhaps it is better to say, a humanistic viewpoint. It is concerned primarily with what interests people most, about economics, namely welfare, instead of being concerned with means of obtaining welfare. Hobson does not concern himself so much about the production of wealth and valuation of commodities, as in what people get out of economic life and what it costs. That means, as S1 and S2 agree, that *Work and Wealth* differs primarily from the other books with which we have been concerned in its subject matter, the problem to which it addresses itself. I think they are right. Hobson sets himself primarily the problem of discussing the welfare which is obtained by different classes of the community under the present organization, the human costs which these people have to pay for what they get, and he indulges in some general discussion of how organization can be altered so as to increase the amount of welfare on the one hand and diminish the cost on the other.

I should like to ask the members of the class whether this is a scientific topic? S2 has been impressed with the amount of loose discussion in the book. Almost anyone who has been trained in orthodox economics would get a similar impression. Is the discussion loose, because the topic itself is not susceptible of scientific treatment? What would you say about that, S3?

S3: What he is dealing with is what we call the real forces, and he rather depends upon what real forces—

M: You would agree then, that in order to have a scientific treatment of welfare one would have to begin with knowing what welfare is. Most people would say that in a scientific treatment of welfare, the first requisite would be knowledge of what the writer is talking about. How does Hobson stand in reference to that matter?

S4: He says that we have to take it just as it is, as a conception which all reformers have of welfare. He does not try to go into it.

M: In other words he does not define it, does he? He says that there is a common agreement among intelligent portions of the community to the effect that this, that and the other change represents an increase in welfare. Welfare is increased when the death rate falls, when the morbidity rate falls, when children attain a certain age, or are found to be rather heavier, when the percentage of people who can read and write rises, when housing conditions are improved by providing a large number of cubic feet of air for every inhabitant, etc. All these different things together, on which we agree, constitute, says Hobson, our working notion of welfare, and he does not undertake to define welfare more definitely than that. Given that as the notion of welfare, is that an adequate basis for a scientific treatment?

S3: Only departmental.

M: What do you mean?

S3: If the investigator takes the infant death rate, he can treat all the causes that increase or decrease that death rate. There may be many elements that enter into it.

M: S3 is saying that with this sort of a working idea of what welfare is, the investigator can take up one aspect of welfare after another, and apply it to something like a quantitative standard as we have been doing. The census, for instance, throws some light on birth and death rates; on the health of the population; on the amount of crime in proportion to the population, etc. With each of these topics taken separately, the investigator has a basis on which there will be common agreement—he may say with some assurance—upon the direction in which welfare is changing, whether it is becoming greater or falling off; but there is no basis for a general conclusion. Unless the investigator has some common denominator to which he can reduce these different units of welfare, he has to treat the problem primarily as one of separate calculations. He has to split it up into the subdivisions, and operate within the subdivisions one at a time, but among these subdivisions he can get relations of greater or less. In some cases he can go further than that. He operates on a computation basis.

It is interesting to notice that this is the logical procedure which was characteristic of the hedonism of Jeremy Bentham and his disciples. Bentham started with the idea that the social sciences could be made real sciences by the introduction of a species of calculation. The felicific calculus which he developed was to perform the same sort of office for the social sciences that Newton's law of motion performed for physics and astronomy. But neither Bentham—nor any of his disciples—succeeded in making any social science a science of calculation. All they could do was to make out certain different aspects of pleasure which they could consider separately, and distinguish in these separate aspects of pleasure, relations of greater and less. For instance, in Bentham's scheme, the investigator must recognize pleasures have seven dimensions: intensity, duration, purity, fecundity, propinquity, certainty and extent. Bentham had on paper a plan for combining all these different elements in such a fashion as to get a different numerical value on different pleasures. But in practice all that he and his disciples ever accomplished was to carry on discussions in some such terms as these: A given act will increase the number of people to whom a certain pleasure is accessible. Another act will increase the intensity of pain which is suffered by certain people. Still another act will render certain pleasures or certain pains more uncertain than they now are. That is to say, they would take up the different dimensions separately and discuss them in terms of greater and less, and there the matter ended. Logically that is where Hobson stands today.

What is Hobson's own criterion of welfare?—no *unit* of welfare, treatment in terms of more and less—along separate lines, such as utilitarian treatment.[36]

He does not have a logical basis for any science of computing welfare. What he has is a series of agreements borrowed from the community at large and concerning certain aspects of welfare, and if each is taken separately relations of greater or less may be distinguished. Granted that that is what Hobson has in sum, let me repeat the question. Is discussion of his kind fairly to be called scientific? Before repeating the question, I ought to remind you how this matter of welfare stands in some other books with which we have dealt. Does Marshall have anything to say about welfare, S5?

S5: He does speak of the welfare of the community at large but he has no theory of social welfare.

M: No theory of social welfare? Interspersed among his discussions are certain references to social welfare. Are those remarks an integral part of economic science as he sees it?

S5: They are not an integral part of economic science, they simply come in as a by-product of his main discussion.

M: We are inclined to agree that welfare in the last resort interests him most, but he does not make a direct attack upon it, and what he has to say about welfare is merely by way of common sense comment as occasion arises.

S6: Does Davenport discuss welfare? Each section of his *The Economics of Enterprise* has specifically to do with questions of welfare, but it is not connected with the theoretical argument.

M: Precisely so. His book divides itself into two unequal parts; the first, much the longer part, is a discussion of economic science, and that science he writes has this distinguishing characteristic; it looks at phenomena from the viewpoint of price. It has nothing to do with welfare. He is fond of rubbing that remark in by reference to burglar's tools, houses of prostitution, etc., as capital investments on a par with flour mills. When he has finished his exposition of economic science he attacks the question of welfare as a separate problem and

[36] Outline, May 22, 1916.

as a problem which gives what interest it has to the preceding scientific exposition, but which is, after all, separate.

What about Schumpeter?

S4: He does not say anything.

M: He does not say anything. He has very strong principles against discussing welfare on the ground that it has nothing to do with pure theory. Judging by these examples, while the economists are all interested in welfare—primarily it is the great social problem—they do not find place for discussion of it inside the bounds of economic science. In so far as they comment on the subject these are primarily by way of *obiter dicta*. Hobson, however, is trying to make a social science of welfare. Can he do it? Or is the subject one which lies outside the bounds of scientific treatment?

S4: I don't think it should be outside the limit. Perhaps, it would not be pure economic theory, but with the help of sociology it would be larger, the larger field of sociology. It would mean that we would first have to define what welfare means as a conception for groups, for society at large, and perhaps we could treat that separately. It does not seem that Hobson's book treats it separately at all.

S5: Adding to S4's remarks first of all we ought to decide whether this book belongs to economic theory or not. I am afraid I disagree with Professor Mitchell. Economic theory is a theory which explains the laws operating in the existing economic organization, and in so far as this is not a teleological problem but a problem explaining the existing phenomena, it has no place within its scope for a theory of welfare.

M: Let us see, S5. Let us take your basis. Suppose that the aim of economics is to explain what goes in the present organization of society without any teleological aim whatever. Provided the economist can establish generalizations concerning the effects of present economic organization and processes on such things as the morbidity rate, the birth rate, criminality, hygiene, would that necessarily lie outside the realm of economics?

S5: I am afraid that all these things lie outside—the morbidity rate, the birth rate, criminality, hygiene—all the effects of the existing economic order would fall outside of the realm of pure theory. It would be applied economics, and would be perhaps on the theory of economics—

M: Wait a minute. You may not be interested at all in social welfare, yet you may study the problem of crime, being perhaps yourself a criminal and interested simply in the fluctuation that takes place in the field that is open to you.

S5: I mean the effect of economics on criminology and criminality. And still it would not be an economic investigation. It would be perhaps a sociological investigation or perhaps a legal investigation.

M: Why do you necessarily rule it out of economics?

S5: Because it does not give any laws concerning the workings of the existing economic organization.

M: If criminality is itself a product in considerable measure of the present economic organization, is not your knowledge of the working of that organization fuller after your criminal investigation?

S5: I will grant this also. One of the results of my investigation may be this; but the application of the finding or results would be not economic.

M: That is another story. The application may be another story, just as the application of investigations which you make into the banking organization may be cast out of your economics, but if they do throw light on the working of economic processes as they stand at the present time, then as a man who is interested in learning all you can about economic processes, why are you debarred from these studies?

S5: There is some flaw in it.

S6: Does the number of criminals in turn rest on the direction which economic development takes?

M: I would think rather decidedly, yes, it may. Certainly in such matters as morbidity it would act on the economic situation. Lines and occupations that are particularly conducive to sickness, for instance, are likely for that reason to have their rates of wages either higher or lower, perhaps lower rather than higher than the ordinary rate.

S3: It is interesting that both Davenport and Hobson include the same things, but they reverse the order. Hobson begins with social welfare, and then takes up the scientific discussion and Davenport does the reverse. The two do seem to go together.

M: That is a just and acute observation. They are substantially discussing the same field in reverse order. Hobson feels that this work is scientific or, if it is not scientific, that it is due to his own short-comings. A book in this field at the present time written by a busy journalist is likely to be far from giving a satisfactory discussion of the topics which it attacks, but he would argue that you have a perfectly solid basis here for scientific work, and all that is needed is the application of the same careful methods used by a large number of workers, that you have had in certain other branches of economics, to put this kind of work on a par with other types of economic theory. That is, he would say that this is a problem which you can discuss, not through its whole range but through a large part of its range, in quantitative terms and get very definite results. The question will of course remain, whether, granted that it can be done, you are going to call it economics when it is done.

S5: May we not make a distinction between theoretical economics and so called descriptive economics? I feel that an investigation of this kind cannot be included in the realm of theoretical economics. Must we not make a certain division between descriptive economics and theoretical economics?

M: If you are going to make that distinction, I do not think social welfare will fall into the descriptive field.

S5: Theoretical field?

M: Yes, it might. It seems to me logically conceivable that a theorist can concentrate attention primarily on the quantitative, ascertainable gauges of welfare as affected by present economic processes, and their reaction upon the continuation of those processes. He can concentrate attention on that just as readily as he can on the pecuniary side of those processes. Or, if one likes, he can concentrate directly on the specific, actual fields in price, industrial organization, welfare, and so far as the investigations can be conducted on the basis of definite materials by some approach to quantitative methods, this work is of a scientific character.

S7: Is the discussion of corporations and trusts theoretical economics or descriptive economics?

M: It depends upon how it is viewed. The discussion of the origin and development of the trust is a very important contribution to economic theory.

S5: And economic effects of course.

M: Yes. The further habits that they would engender in a community, but that is treating economic theory much in Veblen's sense, making a serious effort to understand economic behavior. If that is the thing that economists have in mind, if they want to understand how people act at the present time then they must regard the tracing out of the policy through which the trusts have arisen as a contribution to economic theory.

S4: There is a difference between economic theory and the fields which belong to social policy, where social reformers operate. The conceptions of morbidity and criminology and all those welfare conceptions in their relation to economics would be included in social policy but be excluded from economic theory.

M: I grant without any reservation that these matters have ordinarily been discussed by reformers who have had very little interest in scientific investigation, but I do not think that the association between investigations into morbidity, social activity, criminology, etc., on the one hand and an effort to change things is a necessary association. Those matters can be discussed on a purely scientific, impersonal basis by a man who is interested in the relation of cause and effect. In the long run that is the most desirable way to have them discussed. The reader of a book like Hobson's can at once feel its bearing on social reform. If he throws himself into the reformer's habit of mind, he is likely to overlook whatever process of social causation is there. But logically is it not quite conceivable that one can take up all those problems in a most objective fashion?

S4: Then they have to be treated very carefully. You have to state exactly what assumptions there are and define exactly the aims and purposes you have, and you have to define your ethics. You have to go to your last cause.

M: I am not so sure about that. The morbidity rate for instance does not have any ethical connotation. The investigator can take arbitrary statistical standards.

S4: Just in the morbidity rate I could imagine that an individualist, a man who has the absolute individualist standpoint could come to just the opposite conception to the social reformer. He thinks that it is much wiser if there were less human beings in the world.

M: That is another story. S4 is getting away from the study of what the morbidity rate actually is, and its connection with certain conditions, to the discussion of whether a high rate or a low rate is desirable. That discussion does not belong to the sort of thing that Hobson is discussing.

Resumé: Hobson's differentiating characteristic is the subject to which he assigns primacy—welfare. When discussed by other economists, it is not treated as part of economic theory. Is Hobson's work "scientific"? His criterion of welfare is vague, and restricted—consensus of opinion about matters of wealth which are rather simple. His analysis of costs is not closely quantitative; it is a classification of activities connected with production, accompanied by statements that much or some or no sacrifice is involved. His analysis of utilities is likewise a classification of factors in modern standards of consumption—organic, industrial and conventional—accompanied by statements that much or little waste is involved in each. His plan of reconstruction which he calls the human law of distribution—is based upon similar broad considerations of inequalities in men's capacity to work and "to get utility out of income." S1 suggested at the last meeting that a discussion cannot be scientific unless it involves measurement. If that be true then Hobson's discussion is not scientific. But is it true?

Issue concerning possibility of putting the social sciences on a definite
scientific basis by measurement has been prominently to the fore at least
since the day of Bentham. Recall his moral arithmetic or felicific calculus.
In fact Bentham did not compute sums of pleasure-pain but merely supposed men to compute them. The scientist did not make measures and
show what his material does or will do; but he claims that his material
itself will make measures and be guided by them. Bentham's lead we know
was not definitely followed up in economics until the day of Jevons. The
latter's own theory did not go beyond Bentham's limits in this respect.
Like Bentham, Jevons supposed men to do the measuring and used these
measures of theirs to account for their actions. But Jevons also dreamed
of the day when economists would themselves measure—compile elaborate
statistics which would show demand schedules, etc. Edgeworth took more
definite and firmer ground. "Where there are data which, though not
numerical, are quantitative—for example, that a quantity is *greater* or
less than another, *increases* or *decreases,* is *positive* or *negative,* a *maximum*
or *minimum,* there mathematical reasoning is possible and may be indispensable."[37] (Marshall's proposal to use money measures of the force of
feelings does not really take us beyond Bentham and Edgeworth. The
economist does not really measure; at most he announces conclusions of
greater or less derived from balancings which he supposes the individual
to make.) (C.f., also Friedrich von Wieser's position above: Men do not
measure their own feelings. All they can do is to determine which feelings
are stronger. They have not scales but a balance. The balance however
suffices to let them make rational choices.)

Is Hobson on any more doubtful ground in his analysis of the bearing of
economic processes upon welfare than Edgeworth, Marshall and Wieser
are in their analyses of price determination? They suppose men to balance
utility and sacrifice and to obey the stronger. They also suppose that by
observing these decisions the economist can tell what is deemed the greater.
Hobson does not suppose men to balance human cost against real serviceability, wealth against ilth; but he does suppose that the economists in
the cases treated by him can tell which predominates; that is, he develops
a non-numerical but nevertheless a quantitative analysis. And who differs
from any one of his specific propositions? Is not his type of welfare economic theory just as "scientific" as, say, Marshall's economic theory?
Hobson's discussions of "Social Science and Social Art" (last chapter)
concerns a different point. He takes possibility of quantitative analysis
in the social sciences for granted, and inquires whether this quantitative
analysis covers the whole ground required for direction of industrial or
social behavior. Answer is of course it does not. There is a qualitative
aspect of behavior not susceptible of reduction to quantitative terms.
With qualitative elements one cannot deal by means of science. This is
the realm of art.

Upshot. Hobson believes that his analysis is scientific and of practical value
in treating problems of welfare. But that after all living is a matter of art
even more than it is a matter of science and will always remain such.

Course taken by class discussion of April 16, 1917. We grant that a discus-

---

[37] *Mathematical Psychics* (London: C. Kegan Paul, 1881) p. 2.

sion may be quantitative although it is not numerical. Hobson's problems are such. Thus they answer to one requirement of scientific work. But if we are to decide whether work of Hobson's type is or can be scientific we must know what "scientific" means. S2 made this remark. I rejoined that in discussing what science means we face a problem like that faced by Hobson in discussing what welfare means. Our solution is like his, to fall back upon the admittedly vague consensus of opinion that certain things are characteristic of the sciences—as opposed say to philosophy. Among these characteristics we noted: 1) Experimental demonstration— not characteristic of Hobson's work or of much work in any type of social science. For that matter, it is not characteristic of any pure science— mathematics, e.g. 2) Ability to forecast—again, not more lacking in Hobson's work than in other types of social science. 3) Unanimity or difference of opinion among experts. Contrast between philosophers who seem to value themselves upon their divergencies and devotees of natural science who seem to believe that they all ought to think alike is striking. Scientific experts indeed differ on some points—those are mainly concerning small refinements (e.g., the decimal places in the determination of constants) or of fundamentals (e.g., the structure of the atom, vitalism vs. mechanism). But between these two regions of doubt lies a broad and ever widening tract of established conclusions which seem to be in no danger of reversal. Indeed this solid middle region is so well established that it affords the basis on which doubts concerning the fundamentals are debated—e.g., the vitalists and mechanists each try to show that their view interprets a larger part of the experimentally established facts than its rival, or that there are certain of these facts with which its rival is inconsistent.

Questions left with the class: Are the doubts to which Hobson's results are open like the doubts that prevail among the natural sciences? An example of doubts: Hobson holds that "excessive repetition" is chief cause of muscular and nervous strain and fatigue. I doubt validity of this remark as a generalization. There is a large number of workers, "morons" and a little higher grade, who find repetition gratifying and demand for initiative or creation very disturbing, e.g., Hugo Münsterberg's wrapper of electric bulbs who doubtless was a moron.[38]

Answer, April 18 (1918): They certainly are not like differences of opinion concerning the third place in decimals. Nor are they fundamentals, like the problem of the atom or of vitalism. The counterpart of such fundamentals in economics would be, e.g. What is welfare? What is ultimate basis of human behavior? Questions of this sort Hobson may sensibly refuse to discuss; he would get nowhere on another policy.

The doubts to which Hobson's results are open, are more like doubts about the middle scientific ground where investigation by established methods is feasible, and is rapidly extending the area of established conclusions.

Does the existence of doubts in this middle realm mean that Hobson's problem is not susceptible of scientific treatment; that Hobson himself is not scientific in procedure where scientific method is possible; or that

---

[38] In his *Psychology and Industrial Efficiency* (Boston: Houghton, Mifflin, 1913) pp. 195-196.

he is a pioneer surveying rapidly ground that may later be studied intensively and yield more compelling results?

Answer. *In so far as we can agree upon objective criteria of organic welfare*—e.g., morbidity rates, weight of children, literacy, regularity of employment, housing, etc., welfare economics presents problems susceptible of scientific treatment. As for Hobson, while his treatment may not be scientific, it is likely to promote interest in careful research among others. As compared with any other type of economics, it may well achieve as good scientific standing as any other—except pure theory. Logically pure theory is as impeccable as any branch of mathematics. It does not pretend to represent what is and therefore discrepancies with the results of investigation do not discredit it in the least. But as compared with this type of economics, Hobson's welfare theory type has the advantage of bearing directly upon great issues.

In so far as we cannot agree on what welfare is, investigations of the sort Hobson adumbrates may still be feasible though under another name, e.g., we may differ on the question whether an increase in the ratio of urban to rural population represents welfare or not—and perhaps this difference of opinion cannot be wholly resolved by scientific investigation of differences between the two modes of life—but we can seek by scientific methods answers to a long series of related questions which will probably alter our ideas about welfare although they may not bring us to agreement. But as Hobson points out in the last chapter, welfare economics can never be wholly a matter of science. It is quite as much a matter of art, or purpose or ideal. You may seek a scientific *explanation* of such standards, but scarcely a scientific *basis* for them.

It is in the concluding chapter on "Social Science and Social Art" that Hobson brings his criticism of orthodox economic theory to a head. Expenditure of income is an art as well as a science. Marginal expenditures are precisely those in which there is least regularity, most uncertainty. This fact destroys the logical basis for the type of economic theory which represents economic behavior as guided by marginal calculus. The marginalist type of theory is particularly mischievous because it is used to buttress the notion that everybody would get what he is worth as a producer under the existing organization of production, if only competition were free, etc. But this criticism of economic theory has been developed by S3 in the seminar and we have scanty time.

Hobson's criticisms of conclusions of marginal analysis. Argument runs: Expenditure of income is an art as well as a science. It is an art in that it involves an ideal which forms a general scheme into which qualitative as well as quantitative differences enter. Science can handle the quantitative differences but not the qualitative. It can only give rules for the regular [or the customary]. Statecraft is as much an art as the private expenditure of income. Involves qualitative differences which get their value from social ideals in which the personal equation of the statesman enters in large measure.[39]

---

[39] Compare H. W. Stuart, "The Phases of the Economic Interest," in John Dewey *et al, Creative Intelligence* (New York: Holt, 1917) pp. 282-353, especially section on "constructive comparison." The Outlines are of April 16, 18, 1917, April 20, 1920. For some additional comments on welfare see Appendix VII.

[However, it can be said that] "in becoming consciously a science of human behavior economics will lay less stress upon wealth and more stress upon welfare. Welfare will mean not merely an abundant supply of serviceable goods, but also a satisfactory working life filled with interesting activities."[39a] "Economists don't usually bring in these activities as an element of welfare. . . . I don't recall anyone who has tried to do that systematically except John A. Hobson and his success is not great."[39b]

[In so far as his theory of business cycles is concerned], it is a theory of overproduction of industrial equipment and hence of consumers' goods. Explained by automatic oversaving in prosperity which is due in turn to inequality of distribution of income. Has much in common with the theories of inadequate consumers' incomes. For industrial equipment is overproduced only in the sense that its product cannot be sold at a profitable price. And like those theories of inadequate consumers' purchasing power, this theory of overproduction of industrial equipment is not demonstrated. If there is gross over-investment in any line, business enterprises concerned will suffer losses, and in a strained credit situation their losses may start a process of liquidation. But does the trouble always come to a head first in this field?[40]

[Hobson in early days suggested two methods for abating the "maladjustment between the rate of possible production, and the rate of actual consumption. . . . A labor organization which increases the proportion of the general income that goes to the wage-earners and diminishes the proportion which goes in rent and profits, will thereby increase that proportion of the income which will be more largely expended in demanding commodities; thus will be brought about a rise of the general standard of consumption. That is one method, the method of the labor movement. The other method is one by which the state takes for public use, and expends in the public advantage, in raising public current consumption, an increasing proportion of the income of the community, taking that income away from the unearned incomes of private individuals in which it largely

---

[39a] Mitchell, "The Prospects of Economics," 1924; reprinted in *The Backward Art of Spending Money and other essays* (New York: McGraw-Hill, 1937) p. 81.

[39b] Mitchell to A. B. Wolfe, September 18, 1938, copy.

[40] Outline, "Lecture on Business Cycles," March 31, 1927.

[At this time Professor Mitchell classified Hobson's theory as the leading one among underconsumption theories along with those of the team of Foster and Catchings, and Emil Lederer. For Professor Mitchell's detailed examination of these other theorists, see *Business Cycles; The Problem and the Setting,* pp. 35-40.]

rests at present, claiming it as the unearned income of the community and spending it for public benefit."][41]

[The discussion will now turn to the foremost exponent of another of the outlying types, Gustav von Schmoller, leader of the most influential wing of the German historical school.]

---

[41] [Hobson, "The Problem of the Unemployed," Proceedings of the Sociological Society, 1906, Sociological Papers (London: Sociological Society, 1907) pp. 333-334.

In this same article Hobson explicity questioned "orthodox accepted analysis" that held that public works expenditures would not decrease "the aggregate of the unemployed" (p. 333).

He also spoke in the article of "leakages of employment" and of there being normally "more capital and labor in general than are able to find full employment."]

CHAPTER XIX

The German Historical School: Gustav von Schmoller

The discussion will turn to another trend in the direction of making the field of inquiry much larger than that which was occupied by the classical economists. This line is that taken by the historical school of economics and by certain other non-orthodox theorists who will be discussed later, the representatives of what is commonly called institutional theory. We shall first take up the historical school as represented by Gustav von Schmoller (1838-1917) of Berlin and his *Grundriss der allgemeinen Volkswirthschaftslehre* ("Outline of General Economic Theory"), of which the first massive volume appeared in 1900 and the second four years later.

[Schmoller was a graduate of Tübingen. He was professor of political science at Halle from 1864 to 1872. Then after a decade at the newly established University of Strasburg, he was called to Berlin University, the leading university in Germany. As one of his foremost American students said in 1900, "In addition to his work in the university, he has been active as a member of the Academy of Sciences, and of the House of Lords of the Prussian Diet. He was one of the founders and may still be described as the leading spirit of the *Verein für Sozialpolitik* [Association for Social Policy]. This association represents the scholarly side of recent social legislation in Germany. It has supplied much of the material on which that legislation is based; and has helped in no small degree to influence public opinion in favor of larger state activity. Professor Schmoller has also influenced public affairs as editor of his series of *Forschungen,* now in its twenty-third year, and of his *Jahrbuch,* which he has directed since 1881. He has had a peculiarly stimulating effect upon the production of monographic literature, while through his numerous pupils who now occupy public positions or university chairs, he has had a great influence upon thought. It would be safe to say that few, if any men in Germany outside of official life, have had a greater influence upon public affairs; few, if any, have had a more stimulating effect upon their pupils."][1]

It is not to be understood that the classical masters had no interest in the historical development of economics. It has often been observed that *The Wealth of Nations* is devoted in considerable part to a detailed study of the historical development of certain lines of policy which Adam Smith was interested in as bearing upon the wealth of nations. And his demonstration of the futility of a state's interference consists not simply in general argumentation but is supported by much detailed discussion of the precise way in which statesmen in different countries at different times tried to direct the enterprises of private people and demonstrations of the ill results that had followed from these efforts. Historical evidence, an appeal to past experience, seemed to him an important part of his task. This, however, was not the part which most impressed his successors nor did it shape larger issues of his theory.[2]

The same remark holds true in larger measure of Malthus. True, his fundamental argument about the principle of population took the form of a treatment of the two ratios; the arithmetic ratio in which food is supposed to grow in abundance, and the geometric ratio at which population is supposed to grow. He conceived the *Essay on the Principle of Population* in this formal way and did particularly in his first edition develop his argument on a speculative basis, but he at once undertook an appeal to experience. While use of experience in his first edition was of a sketchy sort, his mind was not satisfied until he had spent some years studying all the data that he could get, either by reading books in various libraries or visiting such countries as were open to an English traveller at the time and observing conditions at first hand. His was a temperament that while open to reasoning of a speculative sort was averse to accepting these speculatively derived conclusions until they had been substantiated by a careful factual survey in which there entered a study of the past; that is, historical investigation and studies of the present as shown by statistical materials. What Malthus did by way of studying past and present experience in dealing with the theory of population, he tried also to do, so far as he could, in studying other economic phenomena. His *Principles of Political Economy* had much more frequent and extensive reference to existing conditions or to previous experience than the substantially contemporary volume of Ricardo.

---

[1] [Henry W. Farnam, "Schmoller's *Grundriss*," *The Yale Review*, August 1900, p. 165.]

[2] Sentence from Outline, March 16, 1920.

Malthus was a factually-minded man who based his convictions just so far as he possibly could upon a knowledge of actual human experience.

Malthus had some contemporaries who took the same general line. His friend, the Reverend Richard Jones, was an early champion of historical method in England, more properly, the comparative method (historical and comparative evidence).[3] In *The Distribution of Wealth* he made, as previously noted, an extensive study of the way in which the use of land is paid for in different parts of the world by people who are not its owners; that is, the conditions surrounding the contract concerning the use of land. His volume gives an extraordinarily valuable and interesting mass of information upon rents as they are paid in different parts of Europe and Asia. Those areas in which the ancient manorial scheme of relations between landlord and tenant still continued in considerable measure; the partial transformation towards a system of free contract that existed in other parts of Europe; the system that prevailed under the regime of serfdom in Russia; and then the variety of methods of arranging relations between the actual cultivator and the owner of the land in different parts of British India. He wound up the broad survey with the observation that there were only two countries in which rents were paid on a commercial basis; namely, the Netherlands and England (and he might have added the United States). In these places the farmer was a small business man cultivating land in order to raise produce for sale and bidding against his fellows for the right to use certain farms in return for a money payment. It was only under this peculiar and limited institution, he argued, that the "Ricardian" theory of rent could be supposed to apply. In other words, he sharply differentiates the distribution of wealth under conditions prevailing in countries where the general wealth and political institutions were extremely different from those that prevailed in the Netherlands and England, the only countries which Jones would admit were in any sense adequately described by the Ricardian analysis.

About the same time the whole economic world was very much interested in the investigations that were being made by that curious, versatile and keen observer, the Swiss historian of the Italian republics, Simonde de Sismondi, who studied the current development of the Industrial Revolution in England and tried to show on the basis of his observations supplemented by analysis what the trends were.

---

[3] Sentence from Outline, March 16, 1920.

In his early years (as noted in volume I) he had distinguished himself by producing a French work, *De la richesse commerciale* (1803), in which he expounded the theories of Adam Smith for the benefit of the world at large, but after the Napoleonic Wars were over he had made a second visit to England in 1818-1819, and observed at first hand some of the results of the Industrial Revolution that was taking place. England was the country in which the "obvious and simple system of natural liberty" had made most progress in the early part of the century. When Sismondi was writing, England had not yet abolished the corn laws; it had not advanced as far toward *laissez-faire* as it did presently; but if one then compared the economic organization of life in England with that prevailing in any other country in Europe, the British system seemed to be a far closer approximation to the scheme which Adam Smith found desirable.

Having been a deep admirer and expounder of the merits of Adam Smith's "obvious and simple system of natural liberty," Sismondi came back to England expecting to find that the lives of people would be much better on the whole than on the continent. But he got there at a time of business depression and he found a large number out of work, who were in the most distressful circumstances. The employed were working exceedingly long hours at low wages. He received the impression that even the lives of employers were full of uncertainty. Business had frequent ups and downs. Losses of a ruinous character were accruing to employers at the same time that their hands were thrown on the street with not enough to eat, nor were they decently clothed or sheltered. These facts led him to engage in a series of close observations of the processes of economic life that were taking place in the early days of the Industrial Revolution. In the two volume work *Nouveaux principes d'économie politique* (1819), he set forth his findings concerning the way in which prices and the distribution of wealth were determined, findings that were based not upon speculatively formulated problems but upon what he saw with his own eyes as he moved around the financial centers and the industrial districts of Great Britain.

The treatise made an impression, but like the statistical work of Malthus and the historical sections of *The Wealth of Nations* the study seemed for many purposes for which men wanted to study economics less effective than theoretical considerations of the kind so brilliantly developed by Ricardo. For Ricardo's theories enabled one seemingly to understand in a general sense the basic phenomena of the time, and also enabled the theorist to discuss what would happen if such and such changes were introduced. He seemed to have hit upon a type of analysis that could be applied by a competent reasoner to a vast variety of problems. It exempted a person from the need of painful collection and analysis of statistics. It showed him the danger of depending upon personal observation in which the element of chance had so large a share, not to speak of the personal equation of the observer himself. It seemed to make economics much more like the subjects which were already recognized as established on a scientific basis than this troublesome work of dealing with actual experience at first hand. An historical investigation can expound only the particular case in hand; and everyone had known for a long while how exceedingly difficult, if not impossible, it was to establish generalizations successfully on the basis of historical researches. Statistical materials at that time were scanty; their quality was dubious; and the technical method of extracting valid generalizations from what data there were was still in its infancy.[4] As for personal observation, while anybody could go abroad and open his eyes, what was the use of doing that except in so far as he reflected systematically upon conditions? The high road to the study of economics seemed to be to select for discussion the critically important problems, to put them into shape for analysis by using assumptions that were simple and

---

[4] [The 1830's, a decade after Ricardo's death, witnessed the rise of serious systematic statistical inquiry. "The period saw the beginning of a new type of economics, realistic and inductive, based on what had formerly had been known as political . . . arithmetic . . . Institutions of various kinds . . . sprang up to develop the new study." In 1832 Lord Auckland and C. E. Poulett Thompson [later Baron Sydenham], M.P. for Manchester, established at the Board of Trade a Statistical Office, "Whose major task was to digest for the Board the mass of information in the Parliamentary reports and papers." At the 1833 meeting of the British Association for the Advancement of Science a statistical section was set up (Section F) and the following year the Statistical Society of London (now the Royal Statistical Society) was called into being. The period also saw the appearance of such handbooks of statistical information as J. R. McCulloch's *Dictionary of Commerce* (1832) and *Statistical Account of the British Empire* (2 vols., 1837), George R. Porter's *The Progress of the Nation in its Various Social and Commercial Relations from the Beginning of the Nineteenth Century* (3 vols. 1836-1843), and John Marshall's *A Digest of All the Accounts Relating to the Population, Productions, Revenues, Financial Operations, Manufactures, Shipping, Colonies, Commerce, etc. . . . of Great Britain and Ireland* (1833), of which 3,000 copies were purchased by the government for distribution to the reformed Parliament.

Technique advanced slowly. For example Porter, who headed the statistical office of the Board of Trade and was a pioneer in the use of index numbers, "contributed Section Fifteen, entitled 'Statistics' to Sir John F. W. Herschel's *Manual of Scientific Inquiry* (1849) which was prepared for the use of Her Majesty's Navy. His twenty-page treatment of statistics dealt with the taking of a census and suggests such subjects as population, manufactures, agriculture, mining, education, domestic and foreign trade, etc. He did not include any discussion of statistical method." T. S. Ashton, *The Manchester Statistical Society 1833-1933* (London: King, 1934) pp. 3-4, and Paul J. Fitzpatrick, "Leading British Statisticians of the Nineteenth Century," *The Journal of the American Statistical Association,* March 1960, pp. 38-39, 41-43.]

yet contained the essence of the situation, and then proceed to argue consistently as to what would happen under the conditions that were being set up in imagination; that is, the best method seemed to be that which is characterized by the phrase "imaginary experimentation."

It seemed as if the economist could in some measure overcome the fact that it was impossible for him actually to isolate certain phenomena for critical examination, as can be done to a very large extent in chemistry or physical experiments. It seemed as if he could overcome the difficulty by making the skillful arrangement not of actual substances and apparatus but by suppositions, "imaginary cases" that while simple enough for analytic discussion yet contained among their assumptions conditions which corresponded broadly to those which were known to intelligent observers.

The economists who continued to pursue the methods of Ricardo did not do so from laziness or reluctance to work hard, or from ignorance that it was possible to treat economic problems in different fashion. They had before them the highly honored examples of Adam Smith and Malthus and the brave strivings of Sismondi to make something of the tangled facts of their immediate situation. If they preferred to work after Ricardo's fashion it was because they believed that he had accomplished more in the direction of clarifying understanding than had been done by the people who made historical or statistical studies or took pains to collect facts at first hand by traveling.

Certainly when the British economists began to discuss the question of method as a formal object of inquiry, they commonly settled upon the opinion that the Ricardian method of procedure was the most efficient. They could argue that the historical studies of the past had proved to a practical certainty that of different historical episodes each has its own peculiar quality, and no two historical experiences are ever sufficiently alike. If it was difficult to get even two historical cases alike, then one certainly could not get a sufficiently large number to give such generalizations as were made any degree of validity.

These economists had observed that while many historians had generalized, the connections between the facts that they adduced and the conclusions that they drew were not of a demonstrable sort. It appeared that when they went to history with the idea of getting a generalization, they selected from historical knowledge those bodies of evidence that favored their case, and that another inquirer using the same general body of experience, if he happened to have a mind set in another direction, might draw conclusions of a different, not to say diametrically opposite, sort. As the British economists surveyed the resources of statistics they found them lacking. There were many problems that economists wanted to discuss about which one could get substantially no information of a definite quantitative sort. It was not possible at the time to discover by historical inquiry how the annual produce of the country was divided between the laborers, the capitalists and landlords even in England, which probably had better statistics than most other countries. It was only by the hazardous process of estimating that data of this sort could be put together. Frequent attempts were made to solve precisely this problem by the statistical approach, but the estimators commonly arrived at widely different results and they could scarcely prove one another wrong, because none of them had at his disposal anything more than a fragmentary basis on which he had to rest generalizations by applying magnifying factors of one sort and another and factors were determined largely as a matter of opinion.

On the other hand, it seemed to be demonstrated that the method of inquiry which proceeded by the making of imaginary experiments led to valuable results, valuable as a set of closely reasoned propositions which were mutually consistent one with another and valuable also—and this was a crowning proof—because they outlined a policy which when adopted by England proved in the long run to be conducive to the growth not only of the country's total wealth but also to the welfare of all the different sections of the population. There was no substantial doubt after the middle of the nineteenth century that the landlords who had feared they would be ruined by the abolition of the corn laws were better off than before. There was no question that the average real wages of the working classes, whose horrible condition at the period of depression had attracted the attention of Sismondi as well as other investigators, had reached a higher level than that which had prevailed in the eighteenth century. Consequently there was general agreement that the methods of working out economic theory which had been adopted by the conspicuous figures of the classical school were the most efficient methods available, and that their results deserved the name of scientifically established truths. This opinion was held more firmly in the latter part of the nineteenth century than before or since.

But just about the time that the English were convincing themselves that the best methods of developing economics had been found and that progress had been accomplished in applying them in obtaining reliable, scientifically valid results, the criticism of those methods, which had begun tentatively in Germany a generation before, reached a peak. There began to develop a program for making a different type of economics, a' type that would rest on carefully established knowledge of existing conditions. This was the work primarily of Germans but it had forerunners as previously noted among the classical economists of Great Britain, and at the time the great German historical school was getting under way it had close sympathizers in France, Great Britain and the United States.

The classical school, as represented in the writings of Adam Smith and Ricardo, produced a profound impression upon the minds of men interested in social, particularly economic, problems in other countries. It seems that here was a group of scholars who had worked out, in singularly finished and effective form, solutions for many problems which, as soon as they were systematically stated, appeared to be matters of concern quite as much in France, in Germany, in the United States, as in England. Quite naturally there appeared at first translations of the great English masters which seem to have been rather widely read, and then a bit later books written by men of other nationalities pretty clearly along the classical lines—treatises which were the reactions of faithful French and German and American disciples of Adam Smith, Malthus and Ricardo.

That happened in Germany as distinctively as anywhere. For a generation or two, the most widely read treatises dealing with economic problems in Germany were those produced by German scholars along the lines of the classical school. But within a generation or two, there arose in Germany criticisms of the classical procedure. There came efforts to do something which seemed, to certain German economists, more significant for their intellectual purposes than the work the English classicists had done.

The[5] English school of classical economics, to repeat, was for a considerable time dominant in Germany and the United States. Adam Smith was translated several times into German, finally with much success.[6] Ricardo was translated promptly, and intellectual Germans, with their aptitude for taking up fresh ideas wherever they were found, proceeded to make the classical economics their own. In so far as that

---

[5] Beginning of extract from "1918 Typescript."

[6] On Adam Smith's influence, see C. W. Hasek, *The Introduction of Adam Smith's Doctrines into Germany* (1925); [Wilhelm Treue, "Adam Smith in Deutschland. Zum Problem des 'Politischen Professors' zwischen 1776 und 1810," in *Deutschland und Europa; ... Festschrift für Hans Rothfels* (Dusseldorf, Germany: Droste-Verlag, 1951) pp. 101-133.]

was possible, under circumstances which will be discussed shortly, it left British economic theory something of an exotic in Germany. The most widely used textbook, particularly for training public servants, was that of John Stuart Mill's correspondent, Karl Heinrich Rau (1792-1870), professor of political economy at Heidelberg. His multi-volume *Lehrbuch der politischen Ökonomie* (of which the first volume appeared in 1826) dominated instruction in economics in German universities for almost fifty years; [it was translated into eight languages]. He later became a vigorous critic of historical studies on the ground that they did not show how to improve the present.[7]

[At the same time, he declared that "Some shocks to the economy are unavoidable whether they result from natural occurrences, or from stoppages of international trade; but just as the trees on the edge of a forest with their stronger roots can better withstand the storm's rages, so a freely growing economy can more easily weather periods of distress."[8] Like the British classical economists in general he strongly supported the English Poor Law Amendment of 1834, which in outlawing outdoor relief followed substantially the precepts of Malthus.

Rau should be credited with the establishment of most probably the first professional journal of some permanency in economics and related social sciences. He started in 1835 the *Archiv der politischen Ökonomie und Polizeiwissenschaft,* which he continued to publish until 1852, when it was merged with the *Zeitschrift für die gesamte Staatswissenschaft,* which was founded in 1844 by the professors of political economy of the University of Tübingen.][9]

The Germans not only assimilated the classical ideas, but they also had several capable men who developed more or less independent speculations of a similar type. The most notable was the landowner Johann Heinrich von Thünen, a powerful, original thinker, whose treatise, *Der Isolierte Staat in Beziehung auf Landwirtschaft und Nationalökonomie* ("The Isolated State in Relation to Agriculture

---

[7] Sentence from Outline, "Seminar in Economic Changes and Economic Theory," December 14, 1943.

[8] [Quoted from *Über Beschränkungen der Freiheit in der Volkswirtschaftpflege* (1847) in Donald C. Rohr, *The Origins of Social Liberalism in Germany* (Chicago: University of Chicago Press, 1963) p. 84.]

[9] [A much more extreme spokesman for free enterprise and free trade than Rau was the naturalized Prussian, John Prince Smith (1809-1874), who was born in London and attended Eton. (On Prince Smith see W. O. Henderson, "Prince Smith and Free Trade in Germany," *The Economic History Review,* 1950, no. 3, pp. 295-302).]

and National Economy," 1826-1863), deeply influenced Marshall.[10] Thünen's treatise contains a theoretical development of a doctrine of rent closely corresponding to Ricardo's and, with its ingenious elaborations, even more abstract in the form of its demonstration. A little later, Friedrich Benedikt Wilhelm von Hermann (1795-1868) published *Staatswirthschaftliche Untersuchungen* (1832).[11] This is an extremely penetrating piece of analysis of economic concepts, very much in the classical spirit; so much so that Hermann was often called the German Ricardo. [It was especially notable for its correction of the wages fund doctrine, and for the "doctrine that consumer's income is the real source of wages."][12]

The Germans took classical economics into the universities, because in a different sense from that in which it held true in contemporary England, the universities were the great centers of intellectual life, of research as well as of learning. In England in the first half of the nineteenth century the universities were perhaps the homes of learning but they certainly were not the homes of research. It is characteristic of England that economics like most other vigorous intellectual developments at the time, grew up outside the university walls, and did not gain admittance, to Oxford and Cambridge at least, until they were pretty thoroughly established among fairly intellectual people. In Germany, however, the universities were the homes of lively intellectual activity. They were not merely polite training schools for young gentlemen who were going to have a political and social career because of the accident of birth, and that was pretty nearly true of the English universities, if it is added that they were also the higher schools for training the clergy.

The German universities had, even before classical economics came in, been devoting a great deal of attention to the training of men for the service of the state. The work which was done in that line was largely in administration. It was designed primarily to provide the

---

[10] [A translation of a substantial part of von Thünen's treatise is in B. W. Dempsey, *The Frontier Wage* (Chicago: Loyola University Press, 1960) pp. 183-367; in 1966 under the title *Von Thünens Isolated State*, another abridged English edition appeared, translated by Carla M. Wartenberg, edited with an introduction by P. G. Hall.]

[11] [Hermann held the chair of cameral science at the University of Munich beginning in 1827. He was also director of the Bavarian Statistical Office. It seems that he was the only economist of the day who evidenced an appreciation in his *Staatswissenschaftliche Untersuchungen* of Daniel Bernoulli's pioneering 1738 formulation of the marginal utility doctrine. Bernoulli's essay, "Specimen Theoriae Novae de Mensura Sortis," was translated into English under the title of "Exposition of a New Theory on the Measurement of Risk," by Louise Sommer, *Econometrica*, January 1954.]

[12] [F. W. Taussig, *Wages and Capital; an Examination of the Wages Fund Doctrine* (New York: Appleton, 1896) p. 270.]

governments of the various states with efficient bureaucratic officials. The discipline in which these candidates for official positions were trained was known as *Cameralwissenschaft* (the science of public administration).[13] It was the forerunner of classical economics in Germany. Classical economics was a sort of generalized theory added to the training in administration under a science that came into a fresh field and existed independently of *Cameralwissenschaft*. It was in part the existence of this older line of work and its great vitality and importance in a country with such political institutions as Germany then suffered from, with a host of minor principalities, each one of them run more or less independently; it was, to repeat, partly the effect of the older type that led the Germans gradually to appreciate that classical economics did not satisfy their needs. That is to say, they found that classical economics with its insistence upon a thorough-going individualism, with its doctrine that it is best for the group to interfere very little in the affairs of the individual, that on the whole, society will be best off in a material sense if every man is left free to follow his economic interest as he sees it, they saw that these ideas were not compatible with the kind of social life which had produced as a home grown product *Cameralwissenschaft*. The same class of men were engaged in teaching the two subjects.

It is curious, in fact, nowadays to think that classical economics could have had so hospitable a reception by German minds, by

---

[13] ["Cameralism flourished in the German states in the late seventeenth and eighteenth centuries. The phrase *Cameralwissenschaft* came from the chamber (camera) in which the revenue and expenditure of the prince were administered and strictly speaking the 'science' referred to the effects of expenditure on the fund of wealth from which revenue might be drawn. In its narrowest sense, cameralism was apt to become a string of treatises on taxation. In its wider sense, it comprehended doctrines affecting the economic welfare of the state, the nature of the administration demanded to put those doctrines into effect, as well as the technical aspects of trade and industrial and agricultural production. . . . The first development of cameral science came after the Thirty Years War that ended with the treaty of Westphalia in 1648. Its immediate object was . . . to train a staff of competent officials to raise and manage the state revenues and foster the interests of the states ravaged by decades of war and destruction of life and resources. Here was the root of the German conviction . . . that the construction of a strong and prosperous economy demanded a partnership between the government and entrepreneurs. Waste lands had to be re-cultivated and re-populated, war debts liquidated, industry revived with the aid of new and borrowed skills. This cameral science became in its varied aspects a theory of agriculture, a theory of population, a theory of taxation. . . . The cameralist writers themselves frequently figured as entrepreneurs in action." C. H. Wilson, "Trade, Society and the State," in *The Cambridge Economic History of Europe*, volume IV, ed. by E. E. Rich and C. H. Wilson (Cambridge: Cambridge University Press, 1967) pp. 556-557, 561.

"Economic science has been taught at German universities for 240 years. In 1727, Friedrich Wilhelm I of Prussia established at the Universities of Halle and Frankfurt (Oder) the first chairs of economic science (chairs of fiscal science)". K. E. Born, "150 Years Department of Economic Science at the University of Tübingen," *The German Economic Review*, volume 5, no. 4 (1967) p. 326.

the minds of men who were already trained and were themselves training others, in the kind of public policy which then controlled the country, the general scheme of administration. The more that one thinks of the implications of classical economics, the general social situation which it presupposes, the more one's surprise grows that classical political economy could exist as an object of keen intellectual interest, more or less as an article of faith, among German university men. But after all the German is a man who has great powers of abstract speculation, of detachment. He can live, in a sense, a compartment life, perhaps as well as any specimen of the human race that one can find, and in taking up a foreign branch of learning, and speculating about it with a patient, thoroughgoing sort of spirit, the Germans seem to have taken perhaps twenty years or so to realize that the imported English doctrine was not the kind of explanation they wanted of the economic life of Germany.[14]

That development was inevitable, just as soon as people living in a country where the fundamental economic institutions differed substantially from the British undertook to work on economics not merely as a school subject taken up in academic fashion, but to work at it in a more vital way, as a manner of thinking about the problems of everyday life. It is possible to treat economics in the schools much as one treats geometry. It can be made an examination subject. Upon it lectures can be delivered which are concerned with the logical interrelations among propositions. That kind of strictly academic work, academic in the feeble sense, can be done anywhere in the world. But whenever the theorist tries to make use of certain economic concepts in order to explain what is going on round about him, he will find that a set of concepts that were predicated upon conditions differing from those about him will fail to be satisfactory. When he gets to that stage in using economics and realizes that the institutions under which he is living differ from those of the country which first excogitated the doctrines with which he is working, he runs into all sort of difficulties, and if he persist he finds himself trying to develop something new in the way of economic theory.

That realization was doubtless promoted a good deal by the protectionist agitation for which Friedrich List (1789-1846) was largely responsible. List wrote his great *Das nationale System der politischen Ökonomie (The National System of Political Economy,* 1842) on national economics, as a man who was interested in the unification of Germany, who believed in building up a strong nation,

---

[14] End of extract from "1918 Typescript."

and who thought that the application of protectionist principles was desirable in view of that larger political aim. Whether or not for the time being the country was better off under free trade or under protection, from a strictly material point of view it made comparatively little difference in List's eyes. To him the major controlling consideration was the ultimate construction of a powerful Germany. He had a large national idea. It seemed comparatively easy to sacrifice, if need be, the temporary material advantage of a generation or two. List's ideas captivated a large part of the German public, and did so the more readily because they fell in with the prevailing disposition to take distinctly a national viewpoint. That was only the economic expression of an ideal which was also freely expressed in German art, philosophy and politics by many different men. But the economic expression, through List, had a peculiarly intimate relation with the cultivation of an economic doctrine which looked directly toward free trade as one of the great national moral lessons. More and more as the century went on, at least for twenty years after Ricardo's death, economics came to mean in England insistence upon free trade. That was the great practical issue around which economic interest crystallized, and this development was clearly appreciated in contemporary Germany. So when economics seemed more and more to be running out to the practical conclusion of free trade in England, it was running more and more counter to the disposition of the Germans under the influence of such ideas as List represented.[15]

In a certain sense economic institutions were much alike all over Western Europe, including the British Isles. But the similarity does not mean anything like identity. In Germany, particularly before the foundation of the German Empire in 1870, there was a multitude of governments a large proportion of which were maintaining mercantilist institutions in great detail. In these states there was but a relatively small element of the freedom of enterprise, initiative and competition which the classical economists took for granted in the discussion of wages, prices, population and rent. In large part economic life was stabilized, crystallized according to certain forms and pro-

---

[15] Paragraph from "1918 Typescript."

[There have been two translations of List's work. The first was done in the United States by G. A. Matile (1856); the second in England by S. S. Lloyd (1885).

List was the original promoter of probably the first encyclopedia of the social sciences, at least in the western world, *Das Staatslexicon* ("Encyclopedia of Political Science"), of which the first volume appeared in 1834.

List developed his basic views in the United States. See Joseph Dorfman, *The Economic Mind in American Civilization*, 5 volumes (New York: The Viking Press, 1946-1959) II, 575-584.]

cedures which were dictated in good measure by political institutions and practices which had lasted for a long while.

In a country which was run in large part by a bureaucracy which felt as much concern with the regulation of the economic life of the citizens as it did with questions of public defense, economic questions had to be discussed largely from the administrative viewpoint. A country with a large bureaucracy required training for the members of the bureaucracy, and the more numerous and exacting their duties, the more elaborate the training they required in the discipline of *Cameralwissenschaft*. There were a large number of elaborate and learned, detailed eighteenth century treatises which were manuals for courses given by professors whose chief object was to see that the civil service of the coming generation understood what their duties were.

Cameralwissenschaft, to repeat, has a logical character quite different from that given, particularly by Ricardo, to political economy. It is not set up to be a science like Ricardo's; that is, it does not try to draw general conclusions on the basis of broad and simple assumptions. It is far more practical in character; it goes into enormous detail in telling what ought to be done. It is in spirit much more like army regulations than like the quasi-geometric type of science which, from one point of view, classical political economy in its severest form resembles.

Thus it was possible in one and the same place to teach *Cameralwissenschaft* and classical political economy. When they were taught that way they did not necessarily seem to be in conflict, because they did not have much to do with each other. Yet if one begins to think about economic problems constructively after Ricardo's fashion and then to ponder about them from the point of view of a man who is in an office that corresponds somewhat to the ministry of the interior and has to concern himself with the management of the state forests, the precise regulation of conditions under which a boy should be allowed to be trained as an apprentice, and the conditions under which men should engage in business as merchants, manufacturers, etc., if the same individual begins to reflect on these problems he will find himself in difficulties. One of the difficulties would be that the British theories were taking for granted a degree of individual freedom and initiative which was almost wholly lacking in German life.

If he observes this, he is likely to go on thinking more deeply about the subject and trying to account for the seeming conflict between British theories and German conditions, he is likely to ask where

British ideas came from. It was relatively easy to draw the conclusion that British political economy was an intellectual reflection of a certain institutional situation; that the theories, as Ricardo formulated them particularly, though seeming to apply to economic life at large, grew out of and apply to only that section of social life which was represented by British conditions after the industrial revolution had gotten well under way; that is, after there had developed a large element of private initiative in economic affairs, of competition for work and for business.

People who began to think of classical political economy in this way, if they felt that there was something natural and satisfactory about the German institutions, were likely to go on from what might be called historical criticism of the British doctrines, to contrast the comfortable organization of life in Germany with the harsh impersonal organization which was characteristic of Great Britain, and to feel in particular that in German life there existed a great institution of the utmost human significance which was left out of the account given by the British economists, except in so far as they had to deal with matters of taxation; namely, the state.

In *The Wealth of Nations* the grand argument put forward with such extraordinary skill is to the effect that the state should do comparatively little. As the classical school developed, the demand for *laissez-faire*, the withdrawal of the state from interference with economic affairs, was pushed further; more and more emphasis was laid on the fact that the economist should be concerned with the happiness of the greatest number and that meant that he should be talking in terms of the individual. Individualism was one of the cornerstones of the classical political economy, and it was an individualism which was extremely critical of the state. Few cultivated Germans, particularly those concerned about affairs, could reconcile themselves to such a view of human society. The state played an enormously important part in German life. They liked to develop the thesis that the state represented more than a mere aggregation of the citizens who belonged to it. It was something vitally significant added to the discrete individual citizens who constituted the body politic. But English political economy paid substantially no heed to the state except to preach to it the duty of non-intervention in economic affairs and to give some advice about how it could raise the necessary minimum of taxes in the least vexatious way.

Ideas about what came to be called the relativity of economic doctrine as against the extreme form of British individualism were favored by the fact that the German world of scholarship was thoroughly impregnated with a type of philosophy radically differing from the Benthamite type, which most of the British economists accepted explicitly or implicitly. In the early part of the nineteenth century Hegelianism was dominant among the German universities and Hegel put stress upon the state as an institution of overwhelming importance. He also laid emphasis upon historical study. The way in which to understand the development of human culture is by studying history in the philosophical fashion. All history is a certain unfolding, the significance of which can be grasped only by philosophy, but it is of the greatest importance to everyone who is concerned with social welfare. That historical view, which was radically different from the Benthamite view, was reinforced by the emphasis in Germany upon the study of jurisprudence at the time. It was and continued to be for a long period one of the subjects in which practically all the people who entered government service got their training.

The type of jurisprudence which attracted a large number of German university men was the historical jurisprudence represented by Friedrich Karl von Savigny of the University of Berlin. It was a way of thinking of the development of legal institutions which was as radically different from Bentham's way of building up a code of laws as could be imagined. Bentham built up his code on the basis of the felicific calculus; German scholars tried to expound and explain the legal institutions that prevailed in any country as the result of a long historical evolution.

In short, so far as German economists tried actively to work on economic problems, so far as they studied the relations between *Cameralwissenschaft* and the British political economy, so far as they came out of the university steeped in Hegelianism and so far as they had been trained in courses on jurisprudence, they were bound to find a great deal in classical political economy, which, however interesting, clear and logical it seemed on the basis on which one could take geometry, would nevertheless be unacceptable to them. The more earnest and vigorous the efforts to assimilate the foreign doctrine into their own thinking, the more thoroughgoing their protest was bound to become.

[It seems desirable to explain more elaborately.][16] As I said, classical economics had for a considerable period dominated in Germany somewhat in the same fashion as it did in England and France. The remarkable thing was, not that the influence of the classicists was

---

[16] Beginning of extract from "1918 Typescript."

after a while undermined, but that it lasted as long as it did. The reasons why it was undermined are several and rather patent. In the first place, as I explained, the whole institutional situation which is tacitly presupposed in the work of Ricardo and his contemporaries was different in Germany from what it was in England. Ricardo's presuppositions did not fit, and one of the chief reasons why the Germans for a while could accept classical economics in a rather academic fashion was that they did not perceive any more than contemporary Englishmen did how thoroughly the whole body of doctrines rested upon a particular kind of socio-economic organization. When, by getting away from a strictly academic treatment of the subject, they did come to appreciate that difference, they found that they had less use for the classical theory than they had supposed.

In the second place, as I pointed out, the teaching along lines somewhat similar to those traditionally established in Germany under the title of *Cameralwissenschaft* necessarily kept its place in institutions which were very largely devoted to the training of administrative officials for the government, and the whole spirit of *Cameralwissenschaft* was opposed necessarily, because of the difference in the institutional situation, to the spirit of classical economics. The attempts to blend the two never succeeded and they could not succeed for the reason that one was an endeavor to train bureaucratic officials for an institution, where governments were trying to control economic development in detail, while the other was a system in which it was supposed that every individual should be left to look after his own interest, and that government should do practically nothing; that there should be as few bureaucratic officials as possible and these should have a very limited range of activities and responsibilities.

In the third place, the rise of the nationalistic ideal in Germany, particularly as it was represented by List, the protectionist program in economics, made classical political economy many enemies, because it drew free trade as the moral lesson.

Fourthly, in a somewhat larger sense, the German school of jurisprudence, which counted among its students the bulk of the people who were also students of economics, was in the early part of the nineteenth century beginning to adopt an historical viewpoint, getting away from reasoning on all sorts of abstract bases. People who were working at jurisprudence of the type that Savigny and his disciples cultivated had very little use for jurisprudence of the kind that would find favor with Bentham. Bentham's jurisprudence was

readily amalgamated with classical economics. It was the outcome
of the same point of view. Savigny was as hostile to the general conception of the institutions that appeared in classical political economy
as Bentham was congenial to it.

Finally in a still larger sense, the whole philosophical background
of Englishmen of that generation of utilitarians particularly was
almost totally at variance with the philosophical background of the
corresponding generation of German scholars. The period when classical political economy was being founded in England saw the culmination of the great German school of metaphysics. It saw the long
reign of Hegel, and the Hegelian conception of society, of human
nature, of national destiny, etc. This was, it goes without saying to
any one who had the slightest acquaintance with it, radically different
from the conception of similar subjects which were held by Bentham,
James Mill and even John Stuart Mill. The utilitarians with their
hedonism, with their aim of obtaining the greatest possible amount
of happiness, with their notion that the greatest amount of happiness
was the average of happiness experienced by different individuals, had
a set of ideals which from the point of view of the men trained in
Hegelian philosophy seemed those of a set of cheap shopkeepers.

They were from the German point of view altogether unworthy
of mankind at large, for men, of course, should have realized that
betterment lies in realizing the development of spirit, and the destiny
of spirit is to be found, on the German Hegelian basis, through a
peculiar sort of philosophy of history. From the English point of view
that German set of ideas was a set of mystical nonsense. They had as
low an opinion of the Hegelians and their performance, or "Welt-
anschaung," as the Hegelians had of the philosophical radicals. The
two outlooks on life were worlds apart, and any body of doctrine
that was thoroughly congenial to the general English philosophy of
the day was sure, when it was fully understood and fitted into the
rest of their intellectual experience, to be as uncongenial to the
German minds of the day. So that it was only because the Germans
took the classical political economy in an academic, rather superficial sort of fashion at the beginning, that they put up with it.
The more they studied it and saw what its consequences were and
realized its spirit, the more they came to realize that it was not for
them. The wonder, to repeat, is that this realization was delayed so
long as it was.[17]

---

[17] End of extract from "1918 Typescript."

General acceptance of English theory on continent. Mainly a speculative acceptance; when continentals began to use the theory they found it would not work. Causes undermining dominance of classical political economy. 1. Inapplicability of tacit assumptions of classical political economy to the economic conditions of Germany. Interest in practical problems from bureaucratic viewpoint. 2. Increase of protectionist sentiment—Friedrich List. 3. Hegelian philosophy versus utilitarianism. 4. Historical jurisprudence opposed to Benthamite school; von Savigny versus John Austin.[18]

In short, the rise of the German historical school is to be traced primarily to efforts on the part of able, intellectually vigorous, Germans to use the British doctrines constructively, and to the resulting discovery that the account of human behavior which had been built up by British scholars did not apply very successfully as an account of economic behavior in Germany. As that conviction broadened and developed, people with a constructive bent turned to the task of developing something that was more satisfactory in the way of economics to take the place of the British doctrines. Trained as most of them were in Hegelian philosophy and in historical jurisprudence, the natural thing for them to undertake was historical studies in the evolution of economic institutions. Their conviction that the British doctrines were an outgrowth of historical conditions in Great Britain made this fresh attack seem all the more promising. As they began to develop this line of constructive work, they became increasingly critical of British doctrines; they adopted a more and more militant attitude. They thought that their approach was not only necessary in order to get a basis for understanding economic life in Germany but also that it was the proper way to attack problems of economic life anywhere.

Consequently in the 1840's and 50's there was the beginning of formal criticism of the classical doctrines, and in the 70's and 80's there is the gradual rise of a constructive school of workers, who described themselves as "historical economists." Their program called for an exhaustive systematic investigation of the development of economic institutions, not only in their own country but elsewhere, for as long a period as the necessary materials could be had. They planned the gradual accumulation of the data running far back in to the past and coming up to the present. When the necessary factual data had been assembled, they would then draw a new set of generalizations which would have enormous superiority over the generalizations of the classical economists, in that they would be valid in the sense of summarizing what human beings actually do. Instead of being a set

---

[18] Outline, March 16, 1920.

of speculations about what would happen under certain imaginary conditions that correspond but imperfectly to the real conditions of life, this program would give conclusions which were drawn from life itself. They would be applicable to life, because the new conclusions would have the validity of being derived from factual study and they would be a far safer guide to economic policy.

The task of the economist who wished to contribute to the development of the subject seemed to be that of devoting himself to factual research into conditions past or current. It was necessary that there should be many workers because the field was wide, and most of the members of the historical school utilized their rapidly growing seminar enrollments to set pupils at work on an innumerable array of dissertation subjects, all dealing with some particular phase or detail of economic life of some kind in some country. They quickly accumulated a large number of monographs which covered an enormous array of problems in time and in place. Of course they were more largely devoted to German historical and current conditions than to those of other countries, but the extent to which these ardent German investigators contributed to the knowledge of the economic history of Great Britain, France, Italy and Russia is remarkable.

The view was that when such investigations had been carried on to a sufficient extent—and in the early days of the movement that was commonly said to be a matter of two or three generations—then and not until then would the task of drawing conclusions begin. For the time being the duty of the scholar in economics was to devote himself, and all the time he could get from his pupils, to this patient task of accumulating materials systematically in the modest expectation that they were working for the benefit of the people who would come after them and be able to make use of their self-abnegating labors to establish a new economics which would rest upon bedrock, which would afford a genuine guide, because it represented actual, not hypothetical, conditions.

For this case, as for all the modern types which have been discussed, there are precedents, as said before. For example, Adam Smith pays a great deal of attention to a good many historical developments in *The Wealth of Nations*. Take, for instance, the long and exceedingly interesting chapters upon the history of banking, the references to mercantilist policy, the discussion of past English policy on shipping, the treatment of the indigent classes. While a good deal of space is devoted to these matters in *The Wealth of Nations*, the sections, which by contrast may be called theoretical, predominate, the ones which

influenced not only Adam Smith's contemporaries but the economists who followed in his footsteps and sought to develop the matter
further. Primarily, his argument that the wealth of nations can be
promoted most effectively by a policy of *laissez-faire* has been the
influential feature of his work. His argument for that type of policy
was not based primarily upon his historical researches, and it could
not be advocated primarily on historical grounds. It was an argument
which had to do with the future. It was a piece of speculation concerning how men would behave with reference to the production of
wealth.

The next great name, that of Malthus, represents again a strong
interest in historical research. In the second and later editions of the
Essay on the Principle of Population, and in the unduly neglected
Principles of Political Economy, he makes relatively even more elaborate use of historical materials than Adam Smith. Yet, once again,
what counted in his work was primarily his argument about how men
were going to behave with reference to getting married and rearing
families; he sought to support the argument on the basis of historical
and statistical evidence, which is merely a more precise form of the
historical record. But the argument was developed first on a speculative basis—recall Malthus's use of the two ratios. It was incorporated into economic theory, came to be tied in with the speculations
about the law of diminishing returns. In other words, it was primarily
his theory of population growth rather than his history that influenced
men's minds.

With Ricardo, this historical element in English political economy
is receding. Unlike Adam Smith and Malthus, he was far from being
a learned man. Probably he knew little history. Certainly he depended
hardly at all on the study of the past in developing his general ideas
concerning the problems about which he wrote, of value and distribution and the corollaries of those problems in the field of taxation
and money. His success in excogitating important conclusions concerning the distribution of income under modern conditions with
comparatively slight use of any but the most meager current observation and with practically no use of historical materials set the model
for later developments of economic theory in England and in the
countries where the English tradition was strong. It is true that in
the case of John Stuart Mill there is in a measure a recurrence to the
model set by Adam Smith. Yet what counted as influential in Mill's
Principles of Political Economy like what was influential in *The
Wealth of Nations* was not the use of historical materials, but the

theoretical discussion. Economists came to distinguish more sharply than they would be inclined to do nowadays between two elements; between the use of history in economics and the use of economic theory. It seems to have been doubted whether economic theory could rest upon an historical foundation.

There had been writers who had tried definitely to elucidate economic processes and behavior by a more thoroughgoing use of historical materials than is found in Adam Smith or Malthus; for example, to repeat, Sismondi and the Reverend Richard Jones. But they were regarded as unorthodox, their results were not believed to be of high value for the understanding of current conditions. As we have seen, the men who made a powerful impression upon their contemporaries, the men regarded as important figures in the development of economic theory were people who worked primarily by Ricardo's methods, men such as those we have dealt with in this course: like Jevons, Marshall, Wieser and several Americans.

The English model of political economy, as previously noted, was early introduced to the continent. It was followed in France even more faithfully than in England. In Germany it had a ready acceptance, particularly by the several generations which were interested in the social and political reforms which began to develop at the close of the eighteenth century in Prussia and which were enormously accelerated by the era of Napoleon's dominance, which brought many French reforms into German life. They were carried still further under Baron von Stein and Prince von Hardenberg in their efforts to revivify Germany and make her capable of resisting the French invader, but after the Napoleonic wars the Germans who continued to cultivate political economy began to find more and more difficulty in following the English tradition as they got away from the habit of repeating the foreign lessons and tried to do serious work with reference to German problems. In other words, the principal effect of studying English classical political economy was to persuade the Germans that it did not apply to their case. The net result was the emergence of a self conscious revolt against both the British conclusions and the methods by which they were established.[19]

In the middle of the nineteenth century there appeared in Germany, as noted before, vigorous critics of English political economy, who in later times came to be accepted as representatives of the early historical school. Accounts of their work are in all the histories of

---

[19] Last two sentences from Outline, "Seminar in Economic Changes and Economic Theory," December 2, 1943.

political economy and there is little need to do more than barely to recall their names and to note the comparatively modest changes in economic theory which they suggested at first. The outstanding figures were Roscher, Hildebrand and Knies.

The name that is always put first in the older historical school is that of Wilhelm Rocher (1817-1894). After teaching at Göttingen from 1840 to 1848 he was for many years professor of political and cameral science at Leipzig. He was the most influential of German economists, a man of wide learning and with considerable influence upon practical affairs, and with a very large following among students.

The break with classical political economy, that is to say, the rise of the German school of historical economics, is generally dated from the appearances of lectures of his in 1843, in which he set forth the advantages of the historical approach. He was at the time a comparatively young professor. He was destined in the next twenty years or so to become probably the most conspicuous economist of the day.[20] The volume bears the title, *Grundriss zu Vorlesungen über die Staatswirthschaft nach geschichtlicher Methode*, ("Outline of Lectures on Political Economy, following the Historical Method"). Here Roscher proposed to complete current economic theory by adding to it the study of current facts and opinions, to make the subject far more realistic than it had been, to take it down out of the air and show its direct applications to all sorts of issues of current importance. [He said that "The historical method . . . is remote (liegt fern) from the school of Ricardo, although in itself it by no means opposes it, and thankfully seeks to make use of its results. For that very reason it is nearer to the methods of Malthus and Rau. And, far as I am from holding that it is the only way to truth . . . I am equally far from doubting that it leads through districts of peculiar beauty and fruitfulness."][21] In his later writings, however, dealing with current issues, Roscher found himself proceeding much along the British fashion.[22]

Another leading member of the older historical school was Bruno Hildebrand (1812-1878), who taught at various universities—Breslau,

---

[20] [Interestingly, Menger's *Grundsätze der Volkwirthschaftslehre* is dedicated "with respectful esteem to Dr. Wilhelm Roscher, Royal Saxonian Councillor and Professor of Political and Cameral Science at the University of Leipzig." Roscher returned the compliment in his *Geschichte der Nationalökonomie in Deutschland* (1874) by speaking approvingly of Menger as a follower of Hermann and of his good grasp of the history of economic thought.]

[21] [Sir William Ashley's translation of the preface in "Roscher's Programme of 1843," *The Quarterly Journal of Economics*. October, 1894, p. 102.]

[22] Sentence from Outline, "Seminar in Economic Changes and Economic Theory," December 21, 1943.

Marburg, Zurich, Berne—before coming to Jena in 1861. One of his major contributions to economics was the establishment in 1862 of the *Jahrbücher für Nationalökonomie und Statistik,* which was generally referred to as *Hildebrands Jahrbücher.* [In 1872 Hildebrand associated with himself his son-in-law, Johannes Conrad of Halle, in the editorship of the journal; after his death, Conrad was the sole editor and the journal became popularly known as *Conrads Jahrbücher.*] Hildebrand was also director of the Statistical Bureau of Thuringia. In his famous *Die Nationalökonomie der Gegenwart und Zukunft* ("Political Economy of the Present and Future") in 1848, he went further than Roscher in criticizing the methods of classical political economy and suggesting other ways of working. He argued that what we need in economics is a law of the economic development of nations. English political economy is an analysis of a fictitious static state.[23] History, he held, ought to be used not merely to illustrate and to vitalize, as Roscher had proposed, but practically to recreate it; that is, economics should become the science of national development. This ambitious sketch, which he had drawn up in his younger years, he was never able to carry out in practice.

It should be noted that the term "money economy" was brought into vogue by Hildebrand. In 1864 he published a brilliant essay maintaining that there have been three stages in the economic development of communities: barter economy, money economy and credit economy. The essential feature of the money economy in this scheme is that most exchanges are conducted by payments in money, instead of by payments in kind or in instruments of credit. At present this narrow use of the term is obsolescent; for Hildebrand's three stages of economic development have not stood the exacting test of use as a framework for the study of economic history. But the term has fared better than the scheme which first gave it currency and content. For "money economy" is in constant use today—though with a broader and deeper meaning than Hildebrand grasped. It owes this survival to its fitness as a name for one of the fundamental features of our modern culture.[24]

[To return to Hildebrand's essay,] he states that the stages are not divided by hard and fast lines but arise gradually out of one another. While money

---

[23] Last two sentences from Outline, "Seminar in Economic Changes and Economic Theory," December 21, 1943.

[24] Paragraph from Mitchell, "Money Economy and Modern Civilization." Paper read before Cross Roads Club, Stanford University, May 6, 1910.
   The essay is titled "Naturalwirtschaft, Geldwirtschaft und Creditwirtschaft," *Hildebrands Jahrbücher* (1864), pp. 1-24.

economy prevailed at certain centers of exchange during the Middle Ages—particularly in towns—natural economy lingered long in certain social circles. Payment of tithes of product, and services in kind, e.g., were the rule in country districts of France to the time of the Revolution and their last remnants lingered on in many German states until 1848. Stress is laid in the article upon the social economic advantages of money over natural economy and of credit over money economy. Incidental remarks of interest in the essay: The whole feudal system was simply the political side of the barter economy. Money economy allowed rise of capitalist class. While the landlords formed a closed caste into which none could enter except by receiving property from those already members, the number of capitalists is not limited by anything. Hence made progress for poor far easier.[25]

Finally on the list of the great teachers and leaders of the older historical school was Karl Knies (1821-1898), who after a period at the University of Freiburg spent over thirty years at the University of Heidelberg beginning in 1865. His penetrating *Die politische Ökonomie vom Standpunkt der geschichtlichen Methode* ("Political Economy from the Standpoint of the Historical Method") of 1853 is a most thoroughgoing and destructive criticism of classical economics, though it offers nothing more in the way of constructive effort than is represented by Hildebrand. Knies questioned the existence of natural laws, and in those days people were still talking about the propositions of political economy as natural laws. He goes further and questions the existence of laws of development such as those to which Hildebrand thought economics should devote itself. From his viewpoint political economy is a history of the ideas which prevailed from time to time about economic development. The ideas bear deeply the impress of the times when the ideas were formulated. Economic theory in modern terminology is relative; it represents simply the reflection of the times in the minds of a succession of writers. The theorist can understand what people have had to say only by studying the circumstances under which their minds were formed. He can attribute value to what they said only as more or less enlightened opinions. Economists never have been able to arrive at natural laws.

The book is an acute analysis of classical economics which Knies holds to be an intellectual by-product of a certain stage in the historical evolution of economic organization. It is not a "science" in the sense that physics, chemistry, geology are sciences, but in the sense that it is a body of notions

---

[25] "Hildebrand," MPP 11-19, no. 72.

formed in the minds of certain time-bound speculators by the conditions under which their minds were formed.[26]

[It is incidentally the first comprehensive treatise on methodology.][27]

The[28] three early books of Roscher, Hildebrand and Knies have a curious definite character. They are almost wholly critical in so far as their aim and outcome is concerned. They call for a certain line of new policy but they do not show how that policy is to be followed. In general they develop their notions by pointing out the short-comings of classical economics. In the first place they declare what they call the relativity of economic doctrine. What finds favor at any particular time is necessarily related to the general institutional situation of the period, when it is written or when it is accepted. If we want to understand the mercantilists or the physiocrats or Adam Smith or Ricardo or the German *Cameralwissenschaft*, we must do it by seeing how the contemporary social conditions made the peculiar ideas in which these people believe possible to them and their genera-tion. This means that from another point of view none of these doc-trines have validity at large. None of them correspond in character to the scientific laws developed by subjects like physics. So far as their theories are true, they are true in relation to a social situation like that out of which they develop.

On the other hand, they declare that the classical economists sup-posed that their own doctrine was true somewhat in the same sense that physical laws were valid. They said that the classical writers believed that the doctrines which they had developed in the England of the 1820's held for the world at large and for all time. That is, they

---

[26] Outline, "Seminar in Economic Changes and Economic Theory," December 21, 1943.

[27] [One of the German-trained American students has claimed that the "first clear statement of the relation of value to utility was made" by Knies in 1855 in "Die Nationalökonomische Lehre vom Werth" in *Zeitschrift für die Gesammte Staatswissenschaft*, 1855, pp. 421-475.

"In this article he clearly shows that value and utility are related to each other as quantitative measure and the thing measured, that utility is a quality of which value is the quantity; that value signifies the degree (*Grad*) of utility; that there is the same logical distinction between value and utility as between height as a quantity and height as a quality, while at the same time there is the same inseparable relation between them. He shows clearly that value as such, is a generic term, and that 'value in use' and 'value in exchange' are but different species of the genus value. They both signify the quantitative measure of utility, and at the same time each is characterized by something which stands in direct contrast to that which characterizes the other. Thus Knies laid the logical foundation upon which Professor Clark and the Austrian economists have been building." (Charles A. Tuttle, "The Fundamental Economic Principle," *The Quarterly Journal of Economics*, February 1901, pp. 237-238).

Böhm-Bawerk and J. B. Clark were both students and admirers of Knies.]

[28] Beginning of extract from "1918 Typescript."

threw the reproach of what they called "cosmopolitanism" and "perpetualism" at the English classicists. The doctrine of relativity was perhaps the notion upon which they laid the most stress, but they also made great play with the consideration of the English conception of society, the critical notion, with which we are all so familiar nowadays; namely, that one leaves out the most important element of society, if one thinks of it as simply an aggregate of separate individuals. To these Germans with their own education, their historical and political background, the notion of society was obviously much more than the individuals taken separately and put together. To them, it was a grand scheme of organization, which the Englishman at large and the political economists in particular, failed to understand.

In the third place, they emphasized the necessity of historical study for the understanding of any kind of social activity. Savigny had already shown of course how historical study illuminates many of the problems of jurisprudence. These economists declared that it would in equal measure illuminate the problems of the economist when it was properly developed. This emphasis upon the necessity of historical study was carried in not a few cases to the length of declaring that no useful results can be obtained in economics by the use of what was then called deduction, deduction from assumed premises.[29]

The generation of students who were taught by Roscher, Hildebrand and Knies took their criticisms of classical political economy in a much more thoroughgoing fashion than their teachers had done and proceeded with greater earnestness to build a new type of economic theory according to these speculations. The men who embarked upon this high enterprise came to be known as members of the younger historical school, in which the dominating figure, almost from the beginning, was that of Gustav von Schmoller.

[He was long involved in controversy, first with the exponents of what might be called the old *laissez-faire* school and then with the exponents of the Austrian school. The first was more directly over social policy, in particular the problem of social reform looking toward a more equitable distribution of wealth. In 1871, the journalist Heinrich Oppenheim attacked the younger historical school and nicknamed its academic exponents *Kathedersozialisten* ("Socialists of the Chair"). Oppenheim, speaking as a defender of the "Manchester School," said that he regarded as a socialist "anyone who proposed a system of

---

[29] End of extract from "1918 Typescript."

state action to solve the social problem."[30] Those who were dubbed
Kathedersozialisten accepted the designation and termed their opponents reactionaries.]

Three years later another bitter phase of the battle broke out
between Schmoller and his future colleague at the University of
Berlin, Heinrich von Treitschke, who taught history and politics.
Treitschke began the fight with "Der Socialismus und seiner Gönner
("Socialism and its Patrons") in the *Preussische Jahrbücher* (1874).
Schmoller replied with "Offenes Sendschreiben an Herrn Professor
Dr. Heinrich von Treitschke Über einige Grundfragen des Rechts und
der Volkswirthschaft" ("Open Letter to Mr. Professor Doctor Hein-
rich von Treitschke on certain Fundamental Questions of Law and
Economy") in *Hildebrands Jahrbücher für Nationalökonomie und
Statistik* (1874-1875). Treitschke charged the professorial socialists
that "they proposed many a vague ideal which looked very much
like the phantasms of crude socialism and which, if carried out, would
destroy any social order." Schmoller informed Treitschke that "your
point of view is aristocratic or oligarchic, mine is democratic."[31]
[Among the keen observers at the height of the dispute was Andrew
D. White, the eminent historian and president of Cornell University,
then on leave as United States minister to Germany. He wrote, "I
began, and for a long time remained faithful in *laissez-faire* ideas of
political economy; but I am more and more convinced that they are
inadequate to the needs of modern society." He said that he did not
completely agree with Schmoller but "What society drifts into when
left entirely to *laissez-faire* ideas, whether in England or America,
is not altogether a pleasing picture to me.]"[32] That eminent historian
of utilitarianism, Sir Leslie Stephen commented that "John Stuart
Mill . . . would have sympathized, had he come to know it, with the
Socialism of the Chair, which was beginning at the time of his death
to make a mark in Germany."[33]

The rise of the younger historical school to influence under
Schmoller was accompanied by the development of the second and
later controversy in the 80's over method, the *Methodenstreit*, to
which occasional references have been made previously. Gustav

---

[30] [Quoted in James J. Sheehan, *The Career of Lujo Brentano: A Study of Liberalism and Social Reform in Germany* (Chicago: University of Chicago Press, 1960)
p. 59.]

[31] [Translations are from Jurgen Herbst, *The German Historical School in American Scholarship* (Ithaca, N. Y.: Cornell University Press, 1965) pp. 146-147.]

[32] [White to C. S. Fairchild, March 18, 1880, in Fairchild Papers, New York
Historical Society.]

[33] *The English Utilitarians*, 3 volumes (London: Duckworth, 1900) III, p. 231.
Quoted in "J. S. Mill's Political Economy," II, APP 44-53, no. 2.

Schmoller appeared as the champion of the historical school and Carl Menger as the self-appointed spokesman of the classical as well as the utility theorists; for he held that the people, who were analysing utility and deriving from it an explanation of the problem of value and distribution of income, were working by substantially the same methods that had been employed by Ricardo and John Stuart Mill.

Of the *Methodenstreit* I have already had occasion to say a word or two from time to time. Now I want to add a brief statement of the position Schmoller took in it. In his writings in the late 1870's and 1880's he occupied an extreme position, saying, practically, not only that economics if it is to amount to anything must be pursued by the historical method, but also that the economist could learn little of importance by what then was called deduction. The way to proceed is to collect enormous masses of material, most of which perforce will be of an historical character in the sense that it will come out of the record of the past, but part of which will be current history, will be observations of what men are doing in the present time. Only after such a vast collection of such materials has been made would it be possible for economists, by going over this systematized body of data, to draw by induction a series of generalizations. We cannot at the present time form any very clear idea of what generalizations will be possible because the material has not yet been assembled. That means that for the present, said Schmoller, there was no economic theory worthy of the name; we will remain destitute of any important economic theory until the program of the historical school has been carried out.

Consequently Schmoller and a considerable band of companions in various German universities set themselves and a rapidly growing body of seminar students to the collecting of historical materials, writing endless monographs, a considerable number of which are on the shelves of the Columbia University library. Most of them are disquisitions upon comparatively specific subjects; the aim was in most every case to present information in an orderly fashion, and in but few cases did the writers undertake to generalize. That was the program of the younger historical school on which they worked industriously for several decades.

Meanwhile it was necessary for the professional members of the school—and most of them were professors—to carry on the training of students; especially in connection with the civil service. Students had to pass the state examinations. Economics had long been one of the subjects in which members of the German civil service had been examined. Even before the days of Adam Smith, as noted previously, there had been a popular subject in the German Universities *Cameralwissenschaft,* which dealt with the methods of bureaucratic administration in economic affairs and all sorts of questions relating to economic regulation or cooperation in economic affairs. Doubtless the men who got this training were the better bureaucratic officials because of it. Certainly the German state could not dispense with that type of training, and the professors of political economy were concerned to participate in it.

That means that they had to give some general surveys of economics. The teacher cannot give such a survey without coming across all sorts of interesting problems that will have to be discussed. And unless the professor has not only completed an enormous collection of historical materials, but also digested the collection fully, he cannot treat many of the subjects according to the tenets of the historical school. The professors found themselves practically in their lecture rooms dealing with economics in a fashion not so different from that of their predecessors, of Roscher and Hildebrand, or even earlier instructors who had no particular scruples about following English models. They dealt with questions in part at least on a speculative basis, reasoning about what people would do much as Ricardo and John Stuart Mill had done.

They accompanied such discourses by a long introduction about deduction in economics, calling attention to the fact that in Germany there was gradually being provided a basis for a more adequate type of economics, but still they relapsed after the introduction had been delivered with full vigor, into in part a discussion of economic problems similar in character to the discussions which might at the same time be carried on in American or English or French classrooms. That was simply part of the situation. Either the economist could not discuss the problems concerning which all the relevant historical materials had not been gathered or he had to discuss them in some other way; and the only way to discuss them practically was the way in which they had been treated by the classical masters, with a larger use of such historical data as the professor knew was relevant, with a closer eye to current issues, but after all with a liberal allowance to speculation. In short, the professional economists were more deeply concerned than most other groups in constructive practical programs, as advisers (actual or would be) of government. Such problems betrayed them into theorizing more freely than their principles admitted.[34]

What concerns us at present is the change that came over Schmoller's views. He was, because of his extraordinary energy as well as his intellectual acumen, the natural leader of the so-called historical school. The older writers, Roscher, Hildebrand and Knies and their contemporaries seemed in the eyes of Schmoller, when he was a young man, to have done a very imperfect job in setting up a historical school. They had criticized the classical economists and its methods effectively, but when it came to the constructive task, they had failed according to Schmoller because in trying to write systematic books on economics they had themselves relapsed into the methods which they had formerly condemned.

This is clear in the case of Roscher. His great system of economics, published in many volumes, is a typical German work of erudition. It assembles a tremendous amount of information concerning actual economic processes—exactly the kind that is not in the typical English treatise; but the way in which that information is put together, the uses that are made of it, are practically all determined by the kind of economics that Roscher had learned in his youth, the economics of the classical school, the kind that he had repudiated in his lectures in 1843, but with which he could not dispense.

Roscher's five volume textbook, *System der Volkswirthschaft* ("Economic Science") which took forty years to complete (1854-1894), was widely used for a long period in the German schools. The first volume, *Grundlagen der Nationalökonomie,* [reached thirteen editions by 1878 when it was translated into English as *Principles of Political Economy* by the American John J. Lalor. The other four volumes were "Economics of Agriculture and Mining," "Economics of Trade and Industry," "Science of Finance" and "Poor Relief and Policy."] It conceived the subject very much after the English fashion. Hildebrand was not subject to quite the same kind of reproach because he never published a large, systematic work. Knies was, in a sense, in a worse way than Roscher. While finding grave difficulties, in accepting the economics of the classical school, he had nevertheless an extremely keen theoretical type of mind and interest. His interests seemed much more nearly akin to those of a great jurist than to those of an economist whether of the purely theoretical type or historical type, and things which he reproduced of a constructive sort, that is to say, his works other than his critical volume on the classical econo-

---

[34] Sentence from Outline, March 16, 1920.

mists had little to commend them from the historical point of view.

Schmoller and his colleagues in the heat of their youthful enthusiasm thought that it was necessary to adopt a constructive policy which was as radically different from that of the older generation of the historical economists as the critical policy of the latter had been different from that of the classical economists. So he began the publication of his great series of *Forschungen* in 1877, the series in which so many doctoral dissertations appeared. In that spirit he wrote his own early works in historical economics but by virtue of the fact that he was becoming, certainly one of the most, if not the most, conspicuous of German economists of the day, he gradually found it impossible to maintain the attitude that there can be no economics that claims to be a science until after the lapse of several generations.

For one thing he was continually consulted on matters concerning the state by high officials. They had to take action on many practical problems and they came to Schmoller as an eminent economist for advice. The only kind of advice that he could give them was advice based on analysis of the situation, on theorizing. More than that he was a teacher whose business it was to give lectures year by year on economics, "Volkswirthschaftlehre," and he found it practically impossible as a teacher not to satisfy the desire of his pupils, to have something in the way of a general survey of a certain field of great social interest. He gradually found himself developing a body of economic doctrine, and little by little he modified his old position in his articles on method and finally after 1900 was passed, he published the two great volumes of his major work which we will here consider as a type of economic theory.

I do not think Schmoller in his later years would have objected to any one using that phrase with reference to his treatise, because he had gradually admitted that he had gone too far in his controversy with Menger upon method, that we cannot wait for the future to supply generalizations which must be acted upon at the present, and that he had gone too far also in claiming that these generalizations can be framed by no other method than induction from a vast accumulation of historical and statistical materials.

Since the German teachers were bound by their positions not only to lecture but also to publish books, we can see what the members of the younger historical school were doing most clearly if we take the most important of the finished products of their work, Schmoller's *Grundriss der allgemeinen Volkswirthschaftslehre*, which was written toward the end of his life. It summed up the results of a full, vigorous and interesting experience. It shows that the writer himself, even when he was discussing methodological problems, had receded in no small measure from the extreme position he had taken in the controversy with Menger in the early 1880's. It also shows what a curious mixture there is of the older type of work with their new learning in the actual performance of the members of the historical school. Schmoller's treatise is a book at which it is infinitely easy to poke a good deal of fun, a game which is being played at the present time [1927] in Germany with a certain measure of levity.

Many members of the historical school were persons of considerable political influence, people who stood close to the center of German policy. They regarded themselves as exponents of the German system as a whole, felt that Germany had a great historical mission to perform and saw that mission in somewhat the same way that her political leaders did. These men suffered from the closeness of their connection with the old German policy; when Germany underwent a political and social revolution at the end of World War [I] their economic views were discredited along with the political system with which they had been allied. Since the war the German universities have been turning more and more for people to occupy the chairs to those who represent what is called in contrast to the historical interest the theoretical interest.

Joseph Schumpeter, one of the younger representatives of the Austrian school, pointed out in his history of economic doctrine in 1914, *Epochen der Dogmen- und Methodengeschichte* that the pupils of Menger, Wieser and Böhm-Bawerk for many years were excluded from the chairs in German universities.[35]

Scant attention, according to Schumpeter's sketch, was paid to theoretical work of that type. There were few among the prominent German professors who would be regarded as theorists. Heinrich Dietzel was perhaps the only important exception.[36] It is significant, however, that at the present time [1927] Schumpeter is himself professor at Bonn. After the war, in 1925 he was called to that important

[35] [Translation by R. Aris under the title, *Economic Doctrine and Method, an Historical Sketch* (London: Allen and Unwin, 1954) p. 184.

"A good deal of fighting was necessary before the right of the historical economist to a fair field was recognized in England and America. I should not be surprised to hear that in Germany some few years ago there was the opposite evil—a too complete exclusion of economic theorists from places of academic influence." Sir William Ashley, "On the Study of Economic History," 1893, introductory address before Harvard University on entering upon the professorship of economic history; reprinted in *Surveys: Historic and Economic* (London: Longmans, Green, 1900) pp. 8-9.]

[36] Dietzel (1855-1935) was professor at Bonn. His *Theoretische Socialökonomik* was included in [Professor Mitchell's] bibliography of the course in the early years.

chair, and he is by no means the only representative of the theoretical interest who has attained full academic recognition in Germany.

The German professional journals carry a great many articles which criticize in severe language the work of the historical school. It seems that the prevailing tone in professional circles in Germany is distinctly to undervalue the enormous amount of constructive work which the generations beginning in the 1870's performed. There is a decided tendency to put down Schmoller, for instance, as a man of comparatively minor consequence.

With this historical introduction and an historical introduction peculiarly appropriate to a discussion of this type of theory, let me call attention to certain ways in which Schmoller's treatise differs from those previously discussed in the course. In the first place it is a big work. The later editions have something like a thousand large pages, and including the edition of 1923 it has already had a relatively large sale, 15,000. It is larger than most treatises, not because it treats the problems of economic theory which are usually included in an Anglo-American treatise more extensively, but primarily because it regards as part and parcel of economic theory many topics which the English and American writers so far discussed leave out.

Schmoller in the introduction deals first with the concept of economics and then with the psychological and moral basis of economics, supplemented by a discussion of past economic literature and a disquisition upon the methods by which theory should be pursued. There is—and this has always interested me very much—a recognition that one of the things which an economist ought to give conscious attention to in his work is the treatment of the general character of human nature. When Schmoller writes about the psychological basis of economic theory he is giving a psychology of the springs of human action as he sees them. His psychology has, to be sure, an ancient cast. He is one of the people who begin by saying what men really want is to get pleasure and avoid pain. But he passes on at once to remark that the feelings about pleasure and pain are very conventional ones and they are most intimately connected with men's drives. Schmoller uses the work "triebe" which is most adequately rendered by the English word "drives," which has come into psychological use in recent years [1927], though what he has to say on this subject could be more properly described as a discussion of the instincts; that is, instincts that play a leading role in determining economic behavior. He cannot be regarded as making an important constructive contribution to the knowledge of the springs of action, to what controls human behavior, but he definitely brings a discussion of the subject into economics itself.

Then Schmoller passes on in his first section, by way of introduction—and the introduction covers over a hundred pages—to discuss land, population and technique. The discussion of land is a survey of natural resources. In dealing with population he treats not only the conventional topic of the rate at which men increase and the likelihood that this growth of numbers may be so rapid as to press uncomfortably on the means of subsistence, but he also discusses different races. Finally he has a very interesting discussion of changes in the technical methods of producing, transporting, storing and distributing goods. Thus, he regards it as part of the task of economic theory to understand the technical basis on which rests the enormous advances in providing real income which have been achieved throughout western Europe and in the lands that have derived their culture from western Europe within the last two centuries.

From the survey of land, population and techniques Schmoller goes on in the second section to discuss the social constitution of the national economy. He takes up first the family, then methods of settlement, urban and rural, the state and local organization, the social and economic division of labor, property and the principles of its distribution and finally the business enterprise as the modern unit in which people organize for getting income. In English economic theory "distribution" refers to the distribution of income; but Schmoller discusses also the distribution of property, the distribution of social classes.

Almost all these subjects are left out of economic theory as represented by Alfred Marshall, Frank A. Fetter, Herbert J. Davenport and practically all the writers who follow the old English tradition. Yet these topics are of great interest to a person who wants to understand current economic behavior.

In the third section Schmoller takes up the social process of circulation of goods and the distribution of income. Here he treats exchange, markets, commerce, competition, systems of weights and measurements, money, value and prices. Thus, well on in the second volume, he comes to the subjects with which most English and American discussions start: value and prices.[37] He goes on to deal with capital and credit, interest, organization of credit banks, condition of labor, wages, the more important modern institutions dealing

---

[37] "Der Wert und die Preise." *Grundriss der allgemeinen Volkwirthschaftslehre*, 2 volumes (Leipzig: Duncker und Humblot, 1900, 1904) II, pp. 100-173.

with the poor, insurance, unemployment, trade unions, etc., and finally with the distribution of income—profits and rents, income from property and income from labor.

In the fourth and last section he discusses what in the United States is usually called business cycles, then class conflicts, then economic relationships and conflicts among states, and finally the rise, the prime and the fall of nations.[38] All of these topics, to repeat, are part of economic theory in his eyes.

In short, the treatise starts with the development of man's means of communicating with man, the evolution of language and speech, and goes on through a discussion of psychological characteristics of the species to a treatment of natural resources, population, technological methods, social organization of economic life, the circulation of commodities, the distribution of income, business cycles, and finally the rise, ascendancy and decay of nations.

Schmoller covers not only an extraordinarily wide range of topics, but also so far as appropriate and the means exist he undertakes to treat each of the subjects from four viewpoints. He likes, first, so far as possible, to examine the historical evolution of an economic institution and this means in practice any condition which he finds it necessary to touch upon. That is what one expects from the leader of the historical school. Second, so far as the materials are available he likes to give a statistical picture of how matters stand with respect to the topic under discussion in recent times. Doubtless he would be glad to extend the statistical researches into the past and needless to say this is commonly not possible. He makes for wider use of descriptive statistical materials than is customary in economics treatises. Third, he regards it as part of his duty to give what would ordinarily be considered a theoretical analysis of the problem in hand. Lastly, he is seldom content to leave a subject without telling what ought to be done about the matter in question.

---

[38] [In attacking complete free trade Schmoller hails as his teachers Alexander Hamilton and Friedrich List.

Schmoller had changed his views on the tariff. At Halle, his first post, he was, wrote Ashley, "ready to risk his career to bring about freer trade in his native state," but by 1901 he had come to accept a protective tariff for Germany "for purposes of negotiation." Ashley quoted Schmoller as saying "The new era of Protection has arisen not because economists and statesmen have been unable to understand the beautiful arguments of Free Trade, nor because a few monopolists and manufacturers have dominated the government; it has arisen from the natural instincts of the peoples. It does not only rest—in many cases it does not primarily rest—on List's doctrine of educative tariffs (the 'productive powers' or 'infant industry' argument); it arises from a motive which is rather instinctively felt than clearly understood; viz., that tariffs are international weapons which may benefit a country, if skilfully used." Ashley, The Tariff Problem (London: King, 1903; 3rd ed., 1911) pp. 30, 31.]

In short, one finds in Schmoller an historical account, a statistical analysis, a theoretical explanation and a disquisition upon public policy on topic after topic. This is not uniformly so, because there are many topics concerning which he cannot get the materials and there are subjects which are not of a controversial order. But in a large part of his work he undertakes to weave together history, statistics, theory and discussions of policy.

Schmoller's book does not treat any of the subjects in a very detailed fashion. He presents so large a realm of the social sciences in a single treatise in attempting to combine history, statistics, theory and the discussion of public policy that the discussion on any one of these heads is necessarily limited. The treatise consequently has an encyclopedic character. It is valuable to consult whenever the economist is beginning the study of a particular problem; it will seldom tell him all that he wants to know about a subject, unless his interest in the subject is of the most casual order.

For example take his discussion of the development of economic technique. Scope of discussion indicated by paragraph headings. Discussion with reference to earlier stages of technical progress too brief to be of much value. Utilizes recent literature and furnishes good sketch. Again take his discussion of the population problem. Points out that under favorable conditions population always increases but that this increase encounters obstacles. Hence, the population problem. Three possible solutions: (1) Increase prevented by sickness, war, privation or by such practices as infanticide, etc.; points out that slavery is unfavorable to growth of population because conjugal relations of slaves are frequently interfered with. (2) Extension of boundaries by migration, conquest, colonization. (3) Greater density made possible by substantial technical, economic, ethical and legal progress. His discussion of the population problem employs ethnological material to a certain extent, but puts main emphasis on European situation. Too brief to be of much interest.[39]

Schmoller was somewhat conservative in his social ideas; that is, conservative in the political sense, but he had a peculiar kind of conservatism in discussing what is ordinarily thought of as social problems. His feelings were very warm. It was not a passive conservatism; it was primarily that of an ardent German patriot who believed most sincerely that the prosperity of the German Empire was in the interest of mankind, that the empire had a great historical mission properly to be regarded as belonging within the field of economics. In this respect Schmoller stands closer to the great classical masters than he does to most modern English and American writers. Nowadays the

---

[39] "Schmoller," APP 74-83, no. 54; "Population Problems," OPP 7-12, no. 93.

opinion is widely held that discussions concerning what ought to be done do not lie within the field of science. It is held that this is a matter which is often set for individual citizens as voters, it still more intimately and continuously concerns legislators and officials; it is a matter on which everybody who is called upon to make any decision, large or small, does well to consider the light which science may show; but it is never a question which can be decided on scientific grounds; what ought to be is not a scientific question.[40]

He was an ardent defender of that whole series of pioneering laws on social insurance which were enacted, Germany's unkind critics said, as a means of weaning the working classes away from the Social Democratic Party so far as possible; laws which, on the part of their sponsors and in the eyes of champions like Schmoller, were intended to maintain the vigor and creative capacity of the German nation.

As an economic politician (*Wirtschaftspolitiker*)—the phrase is just a little unfortunate; in German the term *politiker* does not have the invidious connotation that in this country is associated with the word "politician"—Schmoller was inclined to be a severe critic of many institutions which came into conflict with his ideals of promoting the greatness of Germany by means of the imperial government.

To repeat, Schmoller's treatise is an attempt to discuss history, statistics and theory in the narrower sense, and even economic policy, rather systematically carried out. When one thinks of the great range of topics covered and the effort to unite history and statistics, theory and policy, there is justification for the remark that Sir William Ashley made about the book. Ashley was one of the comparatively few English economists of his generation who were inclined to take the historical viewpoint. Those who know his charming and most famous works may recall that they are called *An Introduction to English Economic History and Theory* (2 volumes, 1888-1893). He was not in his own eyes merely an economic historian. In his view, the way to understand what was going on, was to get at it from the point of view of the evolution of these institutions. He was also one of the comparatively few English economists of his generation who was able to read German readily and kept fairly well abreast of the work

---

[40] Discussion of policy is always open to question for it is usually based largely on opinion rather than knowledge, involves many indeterminate elements, runs back ultimately to metaphysical foundations. (Outline, May 10, 1916).

Max Weber asserted that the neo-classical school confused politics and science as much as the members of the historical school. (Abstract of Julius Wolfe "Der Aufsteig der theoretischen Nationalökonomie," *Zeitschrift für Socialwissenschaft* 1913, p. 602, in "Types of Economic Theory Now Current in Germany," APP 84-91, no. 38.)

done by German economists.[41] He was the most competent critic that could have been found in his country and generation to review *Grundriss der allgemeinen Volkswirthschaftslehre* and he spoke of it as Schmoller's "Olympian survey." It is just that, in aim at least. That is a fitly chosen phrase. The treatise does impress one like the expanded view of a country which can be obtained by a man on a mountain top, a man who is intimately familiar with discussions of policy and is equipped with the telescope of history and statistics.[42]

Needless to say, most of the critics of the treatise found comparatively little difficulty in picking flaws in details, even on the historical

[41] [Ashley had gone from an Oxford fellowship in 1888 to the professorships of political economy and constitutional history at the University of Toronto. In 1892 he was brought to Harvard to occupy the newly established chair of economic history because of his contribution to "the social and economic side of mediaeval history, a field too little cultivated by American scholars." ("Editorial Notes and Memoranda," *The Quarterly Journal of Economics,* July 1892). In 1901 he returned to England as professor of commerce at the University of Birmingham.

Ashley later recalled that "when I was a young tutor in Oxford and began to talk about Gustav Schmoller, I suspect some of my friends almost supposed that I had invented him." *The Adjustment of Wages. A Study in the Coal and Iron Industries of Great Britain and America* (London: Longmans, Green, 1903) p. 6. Ashley wrote in 1900: "For a dozen years I have received more stimulus and encouragement from your writings than from those of any other; encouragement in the effort, which academic and popular opinion renders so difficult, to be an economist without ceasing to be an historian. You have shown me by your example how to carry the historical spirit into the work of the economist, and the economic interest into the work of the historian." (Ashley, Dedication in the form of a letter to Schmoller, *Surveys; Historic and Economic* (1900). In a course at Harvard in 1895-1896, Ashley attributed the expanding application of the historical method "to the romantic movement, the evolutionary philosophy of Hegel, Comte and Spencer, the evolutionary biology of Darwin and the anthropology of Edward B. Tylor. . . . Among the results of the new approach were the interest in the Middle Ages; the sense of uniformatism as opposed to catastrophism; the sense of relativism; and the view that regarded the present, the past, and the future as parts of a single development. Ashley mentioned that the historical movement had affected the study of law, theology, and of economics." Robert L. Church, "The Economists Study Society. Sociology at Harvard, 1891-1902," in *Social Sciences at Harvard 1860-1920,* ed. By Paul Buck (Cambridge, Mass.: Harvard University Press, 1965) pp. 72-73.]

[42] [The editor has been unable to find a review of the Schmoller treatise. The Ashley papers in the University of Birmingham contain no review. In a letter to Professor Seligman in 1900, he declared that he was not reviewing the first volume; but in letters and comments in books, such as the following one, it is clear that Ashley viewed the work as an "Olympian survey." Thus he wrote "I am glad you are going to review [it]. . . . You remark. 'It is fine, but it is not the Principles of Political Economy.' But does it profess to be? Indeed is not that very phrase one alien to the historical mode of thought? He calls it a *'Grundriss der allgemeinen Volkswirthschaftslehre.'* The analogy is rather to the plan of an edifice." (Ashley to E. R. A. Seligman, August 8, 1900, "The Seligman Correspondence," no. 4, edited by Joseph Dorfman, *The Political Science Quarterly,* December 1941, p. 586).

Ashley noted on the appearance of the second volume of Schmoller's *Grundriss* that "It is a splendid justification of the 'historical method' of which its author has been the leading champion; not that it gives us ultimate truth, but because it gives us a more living sense of the complexity of the historical movement, and a more patient and tolerant spirit in setting about our further enquiries." Ashley, *The Progress of the German Working Classes in the Last Quarter of the Nineteenth Century* (London: Longmans, Green, 1904) p. 57.]

side where Schmoller's knowledge was most extensive. It was possible for professional historians to demonstrate that here and there he had gone astray, that he did not know the whole field of human history with equal thoroughness; and that in dealing, say, with certain economic developments of the ancient world his knowledge was not abreast of current investigation. So too, people who were broadly familiar with statistical matters were able to show that now and then Schmoller did not have thorough knowledge of the data he was attempting to utilize. They could demonstrate that here and there he committed overt errors. [To be sure] his statistical discussion is imperfect; e.g., there is no adequate treatment of the method of index numbers, and he took Michael J. Mulhall at his own valuation.[43]

The people who were skilled in the refining of economic theory could point out similar flaws. To give an illustration: In his discussion of the theory of value he follows in general a supply and demand framework which according to the Marshallian tradition is an eminently wise procedure. But if one is to follow that framework, then seemingly supply and demand should be conceived as factors of a similar kind. Schmoller gives a definition of supply and a definition of demand. His definition of supply is that it consists of a quantity of goods which the people concerned know or estimate will be forthcoming for sale in a given market within a given time, or which they think will presently be offered in that market. He defines demand as the willingness of buyers to purchase goods supported by an offer of prices. One of these quantities—supply—is a quantity of goods; the other is a state of mind. Obviously one cannot compare a quantity of goods and a state of mind! When Schmoller went on to a detailed analysis of demand and supply he treats demand after all as being of the same nature as supply. This is the kind of flaw which the theorist-critics delighted to magnify. A man who is a professional theorist, in these later times at least, would scarcely be guilty of so reckless a form of phrasing. That phrasing Schmoller retained in the later editions.

People who were interested in public policy could be relied upon to differ from Schmoller. Not a few of the critics, among them Thorstein Veblen, took him to task somewhat severely on the ground that he let his wishes concerning what ought to be done interfere

---

[43] Last sentence from Outline, May 10, 1916. [Professor Mitchell was referring to Mulhall's famous *The Dictionary of Statistics,* 1892. A reviewer of the second volume of Schmoller's treatise, wrote: "one criticism of detail cannot be passed over, namely, that Mulhall should never be cited unless the sources from which his figures come are known." (C. P. Sanger, in *Journal of the Royal Statistical Society,* September 1904, p. 515.)]

with his analysis of what was actually going on. His dislike for social-ism led him, according to Veblen, into serious misapprehension con-cerning the inevitable operations of modern industry and prevented him from understanding the drift of these institutions. Veblen says that so long as Schmoller was dealing with the distant past he could be objective; when discussing current developments in Germany he saw them through spectacles colored by his strong predilections in favor of a powerful military state regulated through a more or less undemo-cratic government and following a policy of maintaining the vitality of the nation at the highest possible point.[44]

S: Is Veblen's work of a similar type to Schmoller's?

M: There are important differences between Schmoller and Veblen. Veblen is more of a theorist in the ordinarily accepted sense than Schmoller, and he has a much greater philosophic grasp. On the other hand, he is much less of an historian. He is inclined to treat his facts in rather masterful fashion. He has his own mental patterns, and he takes the materials more or less in the order which those patterns suggest. Schmoller's approach is more empirical; he is a man who is enormously industrious in collecting materials; he throws them together without cementing them. This is the greatest weakness of his book. All these things come between two covers. They are all relevant to the field of economics as Schmoller conceives it, but he has not so far mastered the enormous bulk of information which he has gathered so as to show the interconnection. The parts, for in-stance, on the history, the statistics, theory and public policy regard-ing a given topic, are likely to follow each other without being fused in any genuine sense. On the other hand, in reading any of Veblen's books one finds the fusing complete. In fact, it is so complete that anything that is not fused readily into the whole is likely to be omitted from the presentation.

S: Is Schmoller's analysis as far reaching as Veblen's?

M: In one sense. Schmoller goes outside the realm which Veblen proposes to cover, in that he devotes much attention to discussions of proper economic policy. That topic, at least, Veblen eschews. He has conscientious scruples against discussion of what ought to be done. In his eyes, men's notions of what ought to be done are part of the by-products of the ways they make their living. Such notions stand on the same basis as other economic institutions. Consequently they may come in for scientific discussion in the sense that the

---

[44] Veblen, "Gustav Schmoller's Economics," 1901; reprinted in his *The Place of Science in Modern Civilisation and Other Essays* (New York: Huebsch, 1918) p. 269.

inquirer may undertake to try to find out how people at a given stage of development have come to evolve, say, dynastic ideals, how they come to be patriots, how they come to be devout, how these same habits of thinking about the world as under divine guidance might be undermined and new ideals arise and take their place. This is relevant in an inquiry of what ought to be done, and Schmoller engages in that. So far as the logical implications of the two viewpoints are concerned, the chief difference is in the scope of the discussion. For if the theorist takes Veblen's institutional type of theory it would seem to make pertinent for his purposes almost every theme that Schmoller discusses and all the types of analysis in which Schmoller indulges.

S: Does Schmoller's theoretical work follow Marshall's type?

M: No, I should say that to anybody who is accustomed to such carefully elaborated analyses as he finds in people like Marshall, Fetter and Davenport, Schmoller's analytic parts seem crude and blurred; they are also weak. His theoretical passages, if lifted out and put by themselves in the way in which some modern editors have lifted out theoretical passages from *The Wealth of Nations* and put them by themselves, would present a scrappy and at points inconsistent body of analysis.

He borrows freely. When he gives the basic discussion of how prices are fixed, he takes from Böhm-Bawerk the case of the horse market, shows how prices would be determined then remarks that this is all right on the basis of the suppositions set up. But those suppositions, he continues, do not hold true in fact in actual markets, and then proceeds to indicate broadly how things would run.

Take another example: As part of his examination of value, he treats demand. He points out that the discussion of demand which has been most developed in theoretical treatises of the modern school [Austrian utility theory] commences with a logical scheme of dividing goods into categories of the first, second, third orders, etc., and then asks the reader to concentrate attention upon the importance men attach to successive increments of supply. All right, says Schmoller, but that does not cover the real ground. What the economist really wants to know about the man is something different. And Schmoller proceeds to tell something different. This consists, first, of an interesting disquisition upon the varied changes in the types of goods man has consumed in the course of history; a broad survey of changes in diet, methods of living, means of locomotion, etc.; second, in a statistical investigation of demand at the present time. This is concentrated primarily upon an inquiry into the class differences of demand characteristic of the very rich, the moderately well to do and the relatively poor.

From Schmoller's viewpoint these statistical facts, which are derived largely from German budgetary studies supplemented by some inquiries into the number of people in the three income classes that he distinguishes, these inquiries, these statistical studies are more significant, more important, to know than the modern, schematic view of variation in demand. Yet, he brings the latter in briefly and uses it simply as an introduction to his historical and statistical survey. Finally in the course of the survey of demand, he goes on to treat fluctuations in the demand for various classes of commodities of first rate importance, particularly fluctuations in the demand for food.

S: Has Schmoller any suggestions as to the causes of and remedies for the business cycle?

M: Yes, when Schmoller was working on his treatise he had as his secretary (assistant) the scholar who became his successor as editor of *Schmollers Jahrbuch*, Arthur Spiethoff.[45] He devoted much time to the study of business cycles. I do not know but fancy that the sections on business cycles were largely suggested or written by Spiethoff.[46]

S: How competent was Schmoller as an historian?

M: I am not competent to say. I did say that some of his critics in Germany took him severely to task for errors in detail. He knew the economic history of Prussia as few men, perhaps no other individual did. He was also a person who read very largely, and he read history. We must also remark that Schmoller was a very busy man; he was the most conspicuous economist of the chief university in the capital of Germany, and much of the time the closest adviser of the government. Nobody occupied so important a position in German society as Schmoller did without suffering from many distractions. He had many responsibilities to fulfill, social and public. He was a person of extraordinary industry. He must have been very systematic. He gave a great deal of time to the work of editing a great series of historical publications dealing with the sources of the history of Brandenburg and Prussia, *Acta borussica* and the *Forschungen Zur*

---

[45] The full title of the journal is the *Jahrbuch für Gesetzgebung, Verwaltung und Volkswirtschaft im Deutschen Reich* ("Yearbook for Legislation, Administration and Political Economy in Germany"); it was established in 1872. After Schmoller became the editor in 1881 it soon became known as *Schmollers Jahrbuch.*

[46] [Spiethoff (1873-1957) was later professor at Bonn University.]

brandenburgischen und preussischen Geschichte. Beginning in 1878 he also edited a distinguished series, *Staats- und sozialwissenschaft-liche Forschungen,* ("Investigations in Political and Social Science") which contained the monographs of his best pupils. His most notable piece of historical scholarship was *Das Merkantilsystem in seiner historischen Bedeutung (The Mercantile System in Its Historical Significance)* which appeared in his *Jahrbuch* in 1884. [Its impact has been well described by the statement that "It is to Schmoller that the mercantile system owes its rehabilitation."][47]

Presumably, if he had lived as quietly as Immanuel Kant he would have avoided some of the minor errors in his work. Whether that would have compensated for the more academic character that his work would then have had it is difficult to say. One of the characteristics of his treatise is that the reader feels that he was not only a great scholar very widely read and a person of strong understanding, but also a person who was in close and vigorous touch with what were in his day the guiding forces in German life.

S: Is his method the true historical method?

M: I do not know what the true historical method is. It is like the good at large; something that mankind is going to work out and keep changing opinions about till the end of time.

S: How does he treat the subject of capitalism? In the same way as Werner Sombart?

M: He has in the second section, which deals in general with the social organization of modern economic communities, a series of chapters which are concerned with the development of forms of business enterprise. But he does not make the same play with capitalism as an institution that Sombart does in *Der moderne Kapitalismus* (1902).[48]

His attitude toward it is very different from Sombart. He is primarily concerned with a strong Germany. He is at times as vigorous a critic of capitalistic institutions as he is of trade unionism and

---

[47] [S. P. Altman, "Schmoller's Political Economy," *The Journal of Political Economy,* December 1904, p. 87. The translation of Schmoller's essay was by Sir William Ashley in 1896.

Professor Mitchell said of the book in his reading list for the course on economic history at the University of Chicago that] Schmoller is particularly desirable for the class to read because discussion shows place of mercantile policy in historical evolution. Schmoller sketches rise of towns in northern Europe, then that of territories as larger units dominating town life, and finally the development of the state from several territories. Mercantilism is in this view the statecraft by which states were built up as coherent industrial, commercial and political organizations. ("Mercantile Policy," MPP 1-10, no. 106.) [The book was also on Professor Mitchell's reading list for the course on the history of economic thought at the University of California.]

[48] [For Professor Mitchell's view on Sombart see his "Sombart's *Hoch Kapitalismus,*" 1929, reprinted in *The Backward Art of Spending Money and Other Essays,* compiled and edited by Joseph Dorfman (New York: McGraw-Hill, 1937).]

Socialism. He thinks that whenever the pursuit of profit threatens to undermine the vitality of the population, business enterprise ought to be curbed by a strong government which stands securely in its power, above the capitalistic classes.

S: Which of the classical economists influenced Schmoller?

M: Schmoller would have been hurt if anyone suggested that the classical economists had exercised influence upon him. He was one of the most vigorous critics of the classical viewpoint. Probably he would have said the people who influenced him were his forerunners in Germany—like Knies; maybe he would have expressed gratitude to Roscher and Hildebrand; very likely he would have felt that he owed a great deal to Herbert Spencer, and to some of the eminent German historians.

S: What is his contribution to economic theory?

M: The attempt to see economic life as a whole and to bring the resources of history and statistics, as well as of analysis to promote an understanding. He has done the job on a large scale and with greater thoroughness than any other man.

It should, however, be repeated that he brought the various materials together without really fusing them into a unity. His successive sections on history, statistics and public policy are too discrete. In some of the modern American text-books which undertake to include a discussion of theory and a treatment of practical problems, the two parts do not have much to do with each other. The authors in their chapters on things like the tariff, the rise of trusts, or the organization of the Federal Reserve System, do not find a great deal of use for their preceding analysis of how prices are determined and how income is distributed. That impression is justifiably obtained from the writings of a man like Fetter who puts his theory in volume one and the practical problems in volume two. That is the same impression one gets upon reading Schmoller. He had not thought through his problems to the point which is attained by a writer like Veblen or Marx. Marx achieved a more thorough blending of economic analysis—what we ordinarily call theory—and historical investigation than Schmoller did. The same is true of Veblen.

S: Have any points been taken over by British economists from Schmoller?

M: Not to any great extent. Of course, there are English economists who dealt with the developments of institutions in an elaborate way. The most conspicuous example is Beatrice and Sidney Webb.

They made important investigations into the history of trade unions which appeared in the landmark, *The History of Trade Unionism.* Since then they have studied in a similar spirit the evolution of various other institutions on the grandest scale such as the development of local government in England. They not only treat these matters from the viewpoint of the ordinary historian, but they are also interested in showing interconnections. What they give is in large measure a blend of theoretical and historical discussion; that is, institutional economics.

Also the English economic historians have endeavored to show the interconnections among the institutions which they have dealt with. The man who has done this perhaps most successfully is Sir William Ashley. No one, however, has made as vigorous an attempt as Schmoller to combine the light that is shed upon economic problems by history and statistics and the evolution of politics as well as by theory in the narrower sense.

There was a variant developed by Richard Ehrenberg (1857-1921), who, however, thought that the members of the historical school were dilletantes. He was an economic historian who got interested in the history of the great Fugger family, especially under Jacob II ("Jacob the Rich") and Anton Fugger and their successors, a house of merchant princes who lived in Augsberg on the upper Rhine in Southern Germany and played a large role in the financial history of Europe in the sixteenth and seventeenth centuries. They were originally involved in the large, important overland textile trade in the fifteenth century between Italy and the rest of Europe. They made their great fortunes largely in mining, especially of silver and copper. They had extensive interests in other types of commerce and they became by all odds the leading capitalistic power in Europe and their day lasted at least for three generations.

Ehrenberg through his classic study of the rise and fall of this particular family, *Das Zeitalter der Fugger* (1896),[49] got the notion that the effective way to study economic life is to follow the history of business enterprises, especially the larger ones; and he thought this was particularly true of later days. He christened this method of work the "Exact Comparative Method." He set up a journal which was to be devoted to the presentation of what in the United

---

[49] [Translated into English in abridged form by H. M. Lucas as *Capitalism and Finance in the Age of the Renaissance* (1925).]

States would probably be called case histories—the histories of business enterprises.[50]

The characteristic of that line of work is to hold that if the economist wants to study the modern body economic he should concentrate on the economic cells of which that body is composed and the cell of the modern economic organism is the business enterprise—its internal organization and workings. He justified his presentation of studies of modern business enterprise similar to the one he had done on the powerful capitalistic house of the Fuggers on the ground that no one is in a position to understand the process of the modern community, until he knows intimately the problems, the organization and the procedures of the business enterprise. Until knowledge of this sort is known, no theoretical economics is possible. He thought, to repeat, that the most helpful method of studying economic phenomena is to study the fortunes of particular business enterprises; that is, to continue the same general type of work that he had done upon the most significant single circle of business enterprises at the close of the middle ages and the beginning of the modern era. It is only as economists come to look at problems as they present themselves in the experience of business enterprises that they get an understanding of what is characteristic of economic activity in the modern age. That work he carried on vigorously till the time of his death.

Evaluation of Ehrenberg's method. An important contribution to factual knowledge. But does not cover the whole field of economics by any means. Indeed summary statistical inquiries of sort represented by the United States Census of Manufactures are if anything more important than intensive studies of single enterprises.[51]

I do not know that Ehrenberg has any real successor in that line of endeavor, though, needless to say, work of that type has been done rather widely. It represents one of the leading points in the policy of *The Journal of Economic and Business History,* edited by Edwin F. Gay the Harvard historian (1867-1946), in endeavoring to get critical historical accounts of business enterprises prepared for publication.[52]

[50] He established the journal in 1904, with the title of *Thünen-Archiv* after the great economist, Johann Heinrich von Thünen, who had drawn support of his theories in good part from agricultural bookkeeping records of his estates. In 1906, it was changed to *Archiv für exakte Wirtschaftsforschung.*

[51] Outline, April 20, 1920.

[52] [*The Journal of Economic and Business History* was established in 1928. Another Harvard economic historian N. S. B. Gras who had become managing editor became editor in 1931, but the following year it "succumbed a victim of monetary malnutrition during the Great Depression." Herbert Heaton, *A Scholar in Action: Edwin F. Gay* (Cambridge, Mass.: Harvard University Press, 1952) p. 194. A sort of successor journal was started in 1941, *The Journal of Economic History,* by the Economic History Association of which Gay was the first president.]

S: How does Schmoller approach the problem of value?

M: That is an interesting question. As noted above he takes up the problem only when he gets to the third section, which is pretty well on in the second volume of his treatise. When he does take it up, it is after a discussion of the evolution of weights and measures and monetary systems. Then he comes to the subject and points out that economic valuation is only one of the various types of valuation with which men are concerned. Things can be valued for political, ethical, artistic and other purposes, in fact, economic valuation is subordinate in authority. All recognize that economic values are less significant than moral values.

Then he goes on to discuss the theory of market prices under free competition. This, of course, is a traditional problem of English economic theory; and Schmoller, to repeat, explicitly borrows his discussion of the topic straight from Böhm-Bawerk, including the illustration of the horse market.[53] He shows, if the economist supposes a considerable number of men coming to a market with a desire to buy and pay and another set of men willing to accept various prices for them, then under conditions of free competition the price will be set, or at least, the limits between which exchanges take place are set by a process of bargaining. This is a conventional analysis though Schmoller does add with more emphasis than most English or American writers would do, that the example is of an artificial sort; it does not represent the complicated processes in the markets in which men participate.

He then points out that the analysis of the prices for horses at any given time rests upon pre-existing market prices, that is, the prices at the present day, the prices people are willing to offer and accept for horses are largely determined by the prices which have prevailed for the particular commodity in the recent past. Then he breaks new ground by pointing out that aside from freely competitive prices in modern countries there is another large and important class of prices, called "regulated" prices. They are prices such as are set by governments, for instance, for carrying the mails, or such prices as governments allow public utilities to charge, or such prices as two big organized business interests may settle between themselves, not solely with an eye to the immediate profits they are going to make on the transaction, but with an eye to securing a satisfactory flow of goods and

---

[53] [See Böhm-Bawerk, "Grundzüge der Theorie des Wirtschaftlichen Güterwertes," *Jahrbücher für Nationalökonomie und Statistik* (Conrads), 1886. *The Positive Theory of Capital,* translation by William Smart (London: Macmillan, 1891) pp. 203-207.]

satisfactory outlet for products. These regulated prices, says Schmoller, are a feature of the present economic situation much the same as competitive prices. He discusses the principles followed in determining regulated prices in an illuminating fashion.

He links the discussion of regulated prices with the idea of the just price and sketches the history of attempts on the part of governments to secure just prices. The concept of the just price was a large element in the canon law and thus a factor of vital significance in the law of the Middle Ages. Schmoller regards the regulated prices of the present day as in a genuine sense the continuation of ideas which contain a large ethical element that prevailed in the era when economic affairs were much more definitely regulated by the law of the church than at the present time.

Then Schmoller passes on to a discussion of demand. English and American writers ordinarily discuss demand before they treat prices; that is, price making. Schmoller reverses the order. And when he treats demand he does not do it in a manner to which British and American economists are accustomed. He has little to say about the diminishing utility of things to consumers as the supply becomes greater; that is, he has little to say about the strategic importance of marginal utility in the process of price determination. What he discusses under demand is, first, the changing habits of consumers at different stages of culture, going back to ethnological evidence and coming down rapidly through the ages with a series of exceedingly interesting remarks about the increase of supplies of goods available for consumption by people of different classes from century to century.

Second, he deals with the effect of unequal distribution of income on the demand of the poor, rich and middle classes at the present time. He shows how different proportions of total consumption are devoted to matters like food, clothing, shelter, by people whose incomes are very large, people whose incomes are very small and people whose incomes are medium size. Finally he discusses the fluctuations in demand for particular classes of goods; what differences there are between the fluctuations of the demand for things like foods of the staple sort and foods in the nature of condiments, the demand for clothing or shelter or amusements, etc.

Having concluded the analysis of demand, he turns to a discussion of supply. Here his treatment assumes a more conventional cast. His analysis of supply is primarily a detailed study of costs of producing goods and how increasing costs limit the quantity which is made available to the market. That is, it is mainly an analysis of cost of production and its relation to market price. It is realistic in sense that it is primarily an analytic description of these relations in actual process of business.[53a]

He sums up his treatment of value by taking up the supply of and the demand for money, the article in terms of which all other prices are expressed. Then he passes on from the discussion of price-making to a discussion of distribution, showing how money incomes at the present time consist of aggregates of prices, and passes on to a detailed analysis particularly of income from human exertion, wages and salaries, with a less elaborate treatment of rents, interest and profits.

What Schmoller has to say about the process of price determination or even about costs of production and its bearing on prices is not comparable in fullness of subtle insight with what Marshall has to say on similar topics. But, on the other hand, one gets from his long discussion a far more realistic view of certain elements which the economists previously discussed take for granted, or at least have nothing to say about.

S: Is Schmoller's theory of distribution a theory of value?

M: It is a theory of prices rather than a theory of value. The connection between the two again is not brought out very sharply, as it is in say Cassel's *The Theory of Social Economy,* yet the one thing follows directly after the other, and there are incidental remarks which show that Schmoller understands that wage income consists of the prices paid for labor.

S: Is it a sort of bargain theory then?

M: It is a price theory: not necessarily a bargaining theory, at least not in the sense in which the bargaining theory of wages is ordinarily understood.

S: Is there much economic theory in Schmoller?

M: Perhaps not, if by theory is meant contributions to the generalizations concerning those topics which are commonly treated in English and American economics. But if by theory is meant a larger understanding of economic behavior at the present time, then one gets notable contributions from Schmoller.

As noted previously but worthy of repetition, the German historical school which in Schmoller's day seemed to dominate the university world in its own country at any event has recently fallen upon evil days. Time was when anyone who did not profess to represent, broadly speaking, the attitude toward economics which was most fully developed in Schmoller found it hard to get a chair in Germany. At the present time [1930] if one looks over the German magazines, sometimes even *Schmollers Jahrbuch,* one finds writers speaking of the

---

[53a] Last two sentences from Outline, May 10, 1916.

collapse of the historical school. They describe his magnificent effort as fundamentally a failure. It did not lead, they say, to any new scientific suggestions of significance comparable to those which had been drawn by economists like Ricardo and were refined by men like Marshall; and they say that the reason for the failure is that one cannot get historical materials of a sufficiently refined kind and sufficiently extensive to make it possible to carry out the program on which the historical school set forth so confidently in the 1880's. Even Schmoller, when he came to write his *Grundriss,* they point out, was forced to borrow from speculative discussions which in his militant days he would have represented as nearly valueless.

That condition, the critics insist, is due not merely to the fact that Schmoller compiled his treatise before the program of collecting historical materials had been carried out. It was not simply that this was a premature attempt at formulation. Experience shows, they say, the futility of expecting that at any time people are going to get material enough together to build up an economic science on a strictly inductive basis. In saying all that, of course, they are in a good dialectical position against the Schmoller of the *Methodenstreit* days when he was carrying on the heated controversy with Menger and trying at times to go to the extreme of claiming that only by inductive work could progress be had in the social sciences.

It does not follow that these critics are on strong ground if they imply—and they are careful in most cases not to go to the extreme— they are not on sound ground if they imply that the German historical school has made no contributions to the understanding of economic life. No one interested in economic affairs can read Schmoller without getting strong impressions that his comprehension of the modern situation has been rendered wider and more secure. He will not find any substantial addition to the theoretical analysis which is provided far more accurately in books that come from a different tradition. But unless a person thinks that the type of work he finds in Marshall is all there is in economics—and Marshall himself was far from holding that view—he will find also that if he will endeavor, as Schmoller did, in treating the problems which it falls to his lot to investigate, to look at them just so far as his capacity makes possible from the historical and statistical as well as the analytical viewpoint, that he will be a more competent economist and will render services of a greater value.

Those critics also overlook an important historical factor in the so-called collapse of the modern historical school; a factor that does not have much to do with the scientific merits of their discussions.

The historical school, like Schmoller himself, was, to repeat, intimately connected with the old regime in Germany and when the German empire collapsed in 1918 and a new social order came into being this whole group of quasi-official economic advisers suffered loss of prestige with the public at large. This factor colored very deeply the spirit in which younger economists now write about them. The members of the school were people who stood for the policy of a strong, militaristic empire, undemocratic in character; and, inasmuch as economic politics was part of their game, they suffered with the reaction against the sort of economic politics in which they believed so strongly.

As noted above, Schmoller and many of his less famous colleagues were vigorous champions of German nationalism at large, and of the monarchical Prussian regime in particular. Had a part in developing Bismarck's paternalistic policies toward labor. Collapse of the monarchy [in Germany's defeat in 1918] reacted disastrously upon the prestige they enjoyed at home. Inclination in Austrian circles and in those much influenced by the Austrians to regard the historical school as dead and buried under contumely.[54]

To repeat, Schmoller's *Volkswirtschaftslehre* is one of the great books on economics at the end of the nineteenth century which sums up in a most effective fashion an enormous amount of detailed work and has considerable substantive value. Yet it shows that the historical school by 1900 had not come through to the point where it had become master of the materials that had been collected. It could present an enormous bulk of data from different viewpoints, all exceedingly instructive, all valuable materials for use, but the material was presented in a way only less disconnected than material is put before the reader in an encyclopedia. One does well to turn to Schmoller's treatise for information in a compact form, for suggestions which very likely would not occur to one brought up in the good traditional American fashion, but one can seldom find in it what is likely to impress anyone as satisfactory illumination of any single problem. It is a treatise of beginnings, but as such enormously worthwhile and stimulating. It is a sad fact that the book has not been translated into English, and a still sadder fact that so few American students of economics nowadays are equipping themselves to make use in the original of this exceedingly valuable contribution, in which Schmoller insists on a connection between economic and other phenomena and on the study of economic development.[55]

[54] Outline, "Seminar in Economic Changes and Economic Theory," December 21, 1943.
[55] Clause from Outline, "Advanced Economics," August 1906.

M:[56] In what conspicuous ways does Schmoller's book seem to differ from the English and American books with which we have been dealing?

S1: I think it differs in that it does not recognize in its foundation any value theory, but starts out with the idea that economics can only be founded on a historical background, on the understanding of all the many other social factors which enter into economic life. It does not recognize any theoretical division of the whole matter as all those English books we studied are divided into. The only part which would be economics in the sense that Marshall would recognize is a very small part of the book. Most of it is on the many factors lying all around the whole science.

M: That is to say, the treatise differs in the first place in scope very greatly by taking into account a large number of factors which the conventional English works leave out.

A statement of subdivisions of the treatise will reveal how enormously wide is the field, as Schmoller conceives it. He begins, as S1 says, with an introduction which develops the concept of the national economy, and then examines what he calls the psychological, moral and legal foundations of the national economy, and of society in general—the psychological, moral and legal foundations of society as a whole, discussing, for instance, language, human impulses to action, the institutions in general which enable men to associate together and carry on their concerns in very large, organized bodies. That is just by way of introduction.

Schmoller proceeds to show how character of economic activity and organization has been interrelated at different stages of development. How can economic life be understood except as part of the larger social life. Hence necessity of undertaking study of leading phases of social life before entering into subject of economic life in general.[56a]

The treatise proper falls into four sections. The first is land, population and technique, an elaborate discussion of those three successive subjects—the characteristics of the earth from the economic point of view, the theory of population with reference to its changes (that discussion of population has long been a part of English economics, but it is the only topic so far that is currently recognized) and then in the third place an illuminating study of the development of methods of controlling the objective world for the satisfaction of wants, the rise of the basic arts and all that sort of thing.

---

[56] [The remainder of the discussion of Schmoller is from the "1918 Typescript," unless otherwise specified. S2 and S4 in the discussion were former students of Veblen, S3 a disciple of Marx.]

[56a] Outline, May 10, 1916.

The second section deals with the social organization of economic life. It takes up the family, the various changes that institutions have undergone, political organization both local and central, the division of labor—here again the one topic which has attracted a good deal of attention in English treatises—the institutions of property, the changes which it has undergone, the rise of social classes, the part they play in life today, the part they have played in various earlier forms of social organization and finally the business enterprise as a particular way for bringing together the various forces of production and directing their combined energy.

The third section, which opens volume two, is called the Social Process of the Circulation of Goods and the Distribution of Income— and here is the great bulk of what is ordinarily regarded as economic theory. There is a good deal more of it than S1's remarks might lead one to expect. If the student goes deeply into that second volume, he will find that Schmoller is developing theories upon practically all the topics that Marshall touches, although it is true that the theoretical discussion in Schmoller is not so elaborate as in contemporary English treatises.

S1: They always go back to his original grounds like the treatment of population which is altogether different from the ordinary treatment of the classical school. Population is treated with regard to race, an altogether different treatment. All the theories are treated in that historical realm, so that very little is left.

M: This third section covers a considerable range of topics. Schmoller begins with transportation, markets, commerce, economic competition, and he takes up weights and measures, coinage and monetary systems, and discusses these things in their own right as important economic institutions, the history of which economists ought to know as well as their present forms.

In the fourth part of this section he comes to the problem of value and price, and here as will later be discussed in greater detail he develops a theory of prices which he borrows directly from Böhm-Bawerk, though again he adds some elements that are not found in the Austrians. In the fifth part he discusses property, capital and credit, and income from capital and interest; that is to say, he brings in two of the shares of distribution. The next part deals with the organization of credit and its recent developments, the rise and peculiarities of various banking systems; part seven deals with conditions of labor, labor law, labor contracts, and what determines the rate of wages. After that there is a long part concerned with the more important and recent social institutions—poor laws, insurance, employment bureaus, trade unions, courts of conciliation and other forms of social machinery for handling particular problems.

The final part in the third section is on income and its distribution, profits, interest, rents and wages; and sums up the discussion relating to distribution that has appeared in some of the earlier parts and brings the whole together.

The concluding section deals with the general development of economic life, and here again the reader finds himself getting far away from what is generally regarded as the proper field of economic theory in other countries, except for the first part which deals with crises and depressions, with the general problems of business cycles. The second part is devoted to the theory of class struggles, class domination and its modification by the state, by law and reform. In the third he deals with economic relations among the states themselves and their struggles with each other and particularly commercial politics and policies. Finally he has a summary of the section entitled, Economic and Social Evolution of Mankind and of the Several Peoples, the Rise, the Prime and the Fall of Nations.

S2: Schmoller's two volumes cannot be regarded as a unit. The first volume is an institutional interpretation you may say, isn't it? The second is, as you say, probably more theoretical, but I should say that it is still more descriptive matter.

M: There is a great deal of descriptive matter in both volumes. Let me make one additional remark and come back.

The scope of the treatise is wide, not only in the sense that it maps out an enormous territory to be covered, but also in the sense that in dealing with the great majority of these topics, Schmoller had four different things in mind.

To repeat, in the first place he wants to give a description of the situation as it stands in the present time which may be, and generally is, a description of certain institutions as they are currently working. The description is, with reference to modern conditions, largely statistical in character. He wants to present a quantitative aspect of the situation. In the second place, whenever it is appropriate, he gives an historical sketch showing how this particular institutional situation has developed in the past so far as it is known. In the third place, and often quite apart from the preceding descriptive and historical portion, he puts in, where it is appropriate, a theoretical part in which he presents an account of the matter in hand from the viewpoint which originally is much like that of the English or the theoretical

Austrian economists. In the fourth place, again where appropriate, he is not content to drop the subject until he has outlined the proper social policy for dealing with it, and on this he lays a great deal of stress.

With reference to S2's suggestion that the book is not a whole, I should say that it does not so much fall into two parts represented by the first volume and the second volume, as into four parts in the sense that Schmoller's description and history have little to do with his theory. His theoretical notions are for the most part notions that he has gotten from others. This appears clearly, if S2 takes up what he has to say on particular problems that have been traditionally discussed in treatises on economic theory. Explicitly, as already mentioned, he borrows his exposition of the theory of prices from Böhm-Bawerk, and in other places, though not so explicitly, he is obviously giving conventional theory. That theory is not gotten out of his historical, statistical investigations to any large extent. Those two things exist side by side in Schmoller. They are not fused. In the third place there are the numerous wise parts on proper policy. These parts again make a unit very much to themselves.

Schmoller had decided views on the desirable line of growth for the German nation; it is a little more accurate to say for the development of Prussia and Germany through Prussia. As a man who views public policy [as paramount], he was not getting conclusions from the study of history on the one hand, or from theoretical considerations on the other.

In particular, the reader gets the impression if he notes with critical attention that Schmoller's chief interest was in public policies, and that in so far as there was a relationship between the main divisions of his work and his remarks on what ought to be done, it was established by the fact that he saw data, he saw present conditions, not so much as they were, but as he would like to see them. For instance take Schmoller's historical investigations into the present. One gets the impression that he writes in a rather colorless way. He has no particular ideas that he is trying to make out. When one comes to the descriptive parts of the treatise, those that are particularly concerned with modern social conditions in Germany, one is likely to feel, I think—I am quite sure that I feel so—that his hearty detestation of the Social Democratic Party blinds him to some patent aspects of modern German life. The thing that he thought ought to mark the line of development for the German state, was something he felt disturbed by, the line of development that the

German Social Democrats seem to be pointing toward. He could not see the Social Democratic Party and the role that it was playing in German life quite clearly.

I should now like to make some of the general remarks concerning Schmoller's treatise more specific by taking up his treatment of the topic that is generally regarded by theorists with whom we are best acquainted as the central one of economics, that is to say, value and price. The first thing to observe about his discussion about value and price is the place that it occupies in his treatise. English, American and French textbooks are expected to begin constructive work in economic theory with this particular problem. This is regarded nowadays as fundamental, as the one thing to start with, after a preliminary discussion of the general purpose of economic theory, a matter of a few chapters of definitions of fundamental concepts. Schmoller, on the contrary, does not get around to the subject of value and price until he is well started in the second volume. Please recall the general framework of the treatise. He starts with an introduction which gives what he calls the psychological and moral propaedeutic to the study of economics. Then there is the section on land, population and technique. The second section is on the social organization of the family, various governmental institutions, division of labor, the business enterprise. Not until the third section does he take up the social process of the circulation of goods. The first and second sections are sort of treatises on economic anatomy.

The third is called, not unfairly, a treatise on economic physiology, the processes which are going on inside the general economic body. What he has to say about value and prices comes in this section, the discussion of the social processes of the circulation of goods, but even here there is a considerable number of topics which Schmoller has to get out of the way before he comes to value and price. He begins with transportation, markets and commerce. Then he discusses competition. After an elaborate treatise on that subject he takes up weights, measures, coinage, monetary systems, and not until he has discussed all this part of the social machinery does he come to the subject of value and price, so that value comes in not as a basis on which all the theory rests, but as a discussion of one of the processes which is essential in the circulation of goods, and that part is developed after the reader is supposed to be familiar with much the whole of modern social organization and its historical development.

When he attacks the subject of value, however, he does so in a sweeping fashion. He begins by pointing out that value is a phenomenon much wider than one would think, if he were interested merely in economic problems. Valuation is a characteristic, he says, of all conscious life. It appears in all men's ethical and aesthetic considerations, in fact, in all people's interests, and he undertakes to explain in general the psychology of the valuation process. When he does this, he makes certain use of the psychological propaedeutic for the study of economics which had been provided in his introduction.

It is necessary to digress slightly for a moment to point out the peculiar characteristic of Schmoller's economic psychology. The key points are in two statements. The first is that the "basis of all individual consciousness and the ultimate starting point of all actions is found in feelings of pleasure and pain." That sounds familiar to a person who knows the older English treatises. It seems at once to put Schmoller in the class of the hedonists. But he holds the hedonistic view of human behavior with a difference that he probably got from Herbert Spencer. Spencer was, in a sense, a disciple of Bentham at the same time that he was the first of the great philosophers of evolution. He had a way of combining a hedonistic conception of human nature with a view that assigned considerable importance to the instincts.

Schmoller takes a similar neo-hedonistic position. The basic difference between his view and that of Bentham is that he does not lay much stress on calculations of how to maximize pleasures on a calculation of algebraic sum of pleasure and pain, but instead regards men's activity as very largely instinctive in character.[57] The student is inclined to think at first, of course, that these two views are mutually exclusive and contradictory. The way in which Schmoller gets from his statement that the ultimate starting point of action is found in feelings of pleasure and pain to the view that for the understanding of behavior the instincts are of fundamental importance, appears in the following sentence. "The important habitual feelings appear in their relation to the outer world as wants and in their active role of producing certain volitions and actions as propensities."

These are propensities or instincts, as Schmoller sees them, or the active side of men's feelings of pleasure and pain. Then he goes on to discuss the important human instincts. First, self preservation; second, sex; third, the instinct of general activity, to be active, to be doing something; fourth, the instinct of recognition; fifth, rivalry; sixth, acquisitiveness. Schmoller sets up this list of instincts, and then discusses it in the unilluminating way in which we expect to find lists

---

[57] [Professor Mitchell, as previously noted, preferred the term "drives" for a time— in the 20's. In the 40's he went back to instincts.]

of instincts discussed; that is to say, he has a series of comments on the ubiquitousness of his half dozen instincts and there drops the matter.

To return to his theory of value, he supposes that the general process of valuation which is characteristic of all human behavior, and which enters not only men's economic activity but also their moral, political, aesthetic and other activities, is to be run by those feelings which appear on the active side as propensities to definite kinds of behavior, as instincts. With that basis he proceeds to point out that people have a hierarchy of values and that the economic values rank fairly low in the hierarchy. In the conflict between economic and moral values, moral values have the right of way. The economist, in Schmoller's view, however, must not confine himself solely to the discussion of economic values, but must always keep an eye open for the most important moral values; this is a way of saying that it is part of the economist's business not only to get an historical understanding of how things have come to their present pass and a statistical examination of how they run, but he also must show what ought to be done in order to maintain the moral values as well as the strictly economic ones.

He then turns to an analysis of the moral values and begins with the theory of prices under conditions of free competition. The fundamental analysis of how price is determined, he borrows mainly as noted previously from an article which Böhm-Bawerk published in *Conrads Jahrbuch*. It contains the famous example of the horse market. Schmoller reproduced it, remarking, however, that the case presented is not typical of the actual process of price determination in modern life. He discusses the limitations, the differences between the assumptions which are here made for the purpose of facilitating the exposition and the conditions which are actually met with. There is not, in fact, he points out, the perfect knowledge on the part of everyone in the market which the example presupposes, etc.

Much more important than these obvious remarks on the limitations of the ordinary Austrian theory is his insistence that to understand price determination at any given point, one has to recall that the analysis proceeds on the basis of pre-existing prices. That point is important to remember if one is interested in understanding what happens, and it is a point on which the Austrians lay no stress, if they mention it at all. The fact is, however, as a writer like Davenport, for instance, recognizes clearly, that men's valuations at any given time, even before they enter a market, are necessarily affected profoundly by the prices that they have been accustomed to pay and to receive in the past, and what happens in any market is not so much the making of brand new prices as it is the alteration of some pre-existing prices. This is one of the most valuable parts of Schmoller's discussion of price determination.

Another interesting feature follows immediately. After the discussion of prices under terms of free competition in conventional Anglo-American treatises, we are never surprised to meet a discussion of price under monopoly. Schmoller has very little in this place to say about monopoly conditions. Instead he discusses at considerable length what he calls "regulated prices." He points out, as a student of the Middle Ages is likely to do, that the determination of the bulk of prices in what are supposed to be freely competitive markets is a comparatively modern phenomenon, that we have reached this stage by changing a form of price determination which persisted for several centuries in Europe, a form under which there was a definite attempt to determine by authority what prices shall be paid, an attempt which justified itself on the ground that it was setting up just prices. Schmoller explains the medieval ideas of just price and then goes on to show that in modern life we seem in a good many cases to be working back to that same conception, to a price which is regulated by public authority on a basis of social justice or social expediency.[58]

He also points out that even where government is not intervening for the purpose of regulating prices, the enterprises in a field frequently established regulations in their own interests, as when manufacturers, for instance, set a fixed price on trademarked products, or when big capitalistic interests meet and determine upon prices at which they will regularly hand over and receive certain commodities as they pass through the different stages of manufacture. He discusses "regulated prices" (regulated by public authority and by various forms of organized treaties between private parties) a feature of the present economic situation of much the same importance as competitive prices.[59]

The discussion is carried on with Schmoller's extraordinary learning. Very few economists would not, on reading these sections, find

---

[58] [The "just price" was not limited to a legally fixed price.

In discussion the role of justice in the distribution of wealth and income he said: "In custom, law, and existing institutions which rule economic life we have the outcome of all the struggles which history has seen for many thousand years." Schmoller, "The Idea of Justice in Political Economy," *The Annals of the American Academy of Political and Social Science*, May 1894, p. 736. This is a translation of his essay in *Schmollers Jahrbuch* (1881).]

[59] Sentence from Outline, May 10, 1916.

their knowledge of the actual situation considerably extended. From the excursus on regulated prices, Schmoller turns back to the general problem of price determination under the law of supply and demand, and gives an elaborate analysis, first of demand and second of supply, as a factor in fixing prices. His discussion of demand is different from the few and feeble remarks upon the subject by the Austrians, and most of the American and English theorists. He points out that about all the Austrians have to say on the subject of demand is by way of expounding the somewhat obvious law of the varying intensity of wants for successive units of goods.

He said that what the economists really ought to do, if they are seriously interested in demand, is analyze changes in people's wants for particular commodities, or the influence of social conditions as affecting demand. So he goes off on a long account of changes in the character of food which men use as their regular diet at different stages of their development, beginning with the kind of things that savages eat, coming down to the medieval diet and then showing the alterations which modern communications, modern techniques have made possible in the variety of food which is available particularly for Europeans at the present time.

The disquisition on food is followed by a discussion on the effect of unequal income distribution upon the demand of various classes of the community. Here naturally he analyzes family budgets, the statistics of family expenditure upon different classes of goods. That was a line of statistical investigation in which the famous German statistician, Ernst Engel, greatly distinguished himself, [especially as the author of "Engel's law."][60] Schmoller utilizes his figures, together with certain other foreign studies made at a later day, showing that the character of commodities for which they have an effective demand alters as their income increases. Then in another instructive part he deals with fluctuations in the demand for particular commodities, which we have discussed before.

Finally he returns to the subject of supply. What he has to say on that head is primarily the bearing of the cost of production upon prices, a study of what enters into the cost of production in monetary terms, and what are the relations between the price that exists at any time and the costs that business men are willing to incur in order to keep providing the market with what is in demand. This discussion

---

[60] [Ernst Engel (1821-1896) was a prominent member of the German historical school and director of the Royal Prussian Statistical Bureau. One of the most highly developed tools of current dominant economic analysis derives from Engel's "law"; namely, "Engel curves."]

is considerably less original, from the English and American viewpoint, than what he has to say upon demand and I am not sure that the student could not find a half dozen of such books as he has been reading that treat the same subject in greater detail and with greater acumen than does Schmoller. He ends the entire discussion with the rather loose conclusion: "we must content ourselves with the knowledge that in the long run cost of production regulates supply, and therefore value on the one side, while on the other side value is determined by demand and its causes," a statement the novelty of which will hardly shock anyone. A more interesting feature of Schmoller's theory of value is his treatment of supply and demand of money—fluctuations in the general price level—paper money episodes.[61] Taking the discussion as a whole, the reader will find that the material in the different parts is almost always interesting. I cannot say quite "always" because when Schmoller is just quoting Böhm-Bawerk's illustration of the horse market, or when he is giving his somewhat tedious analysis of cost, the English speaking reader, in any event, is not likely to be much diverted; but throughout most of the whole second part on value and price, he is talking about facts as they stand now, or as they have stood in the past.

But while the material is interesting and distinctly pertinent and while it throws light on the economic situation, it is difficult to trace the connection between various parts, that is to say, what Schmoller has done substantially is to fit a large amount of information into a thoroughly conventional framework, that provided by the notion of price depending upon supply and demand. At the end he comes out with a vague conclusion. What is worth while is not the general theoretical grasp upon the situation but the collection of interesting data.

What is true of this particular part of Schmoller's *Volkswirtschaftslehre* is true of the entire work; that is to say, the thing that is valuable in his treatise is the wide scope of the discussion as a whole, the attempt to look at the economic phenomenon from different viewpoints, to keep in line the development from the past, the quantitative situation as reflected today by statistics, the current theoretical explanation of how affairs are operating at the present time and finally his view of how the present problems ought to be handled. The difficulties with this particular part again seem characteristic of the book as a whole.

His critics, when the first edition appeared, pointed out many errors of detail in his facts. That was perfectly natural. He was a man

---

[61] Sentence from Outline, May 10, 1916.

of extraordinary learning with admirable facilities for getting help from other people, and yet when he tried to cover such a wide field it was almost inevitable that he should often have made errors through reliance on secondary authorities, or sometimes through carelessness or the mislaying of some of his notes, the sort of accidents which will happen to anyone who is trying to do so much that he cannot bring all his powers to bear upon every point. But the errors of detail are matters of subordinate significance.

The important defect is that Schmoller has not succeeded in blending what he brings together into anything like a synthetic whole. With his wide reading in many fields, he collected an enormous quantity of material. He presented this in orderly sequence; that is to say, he has it all neatly classified under heads and subheads, and that classification is as far as he has succeeded in going in the direction of giving anything like a general theory of the economic situation as a whole. To repeat, one respect in which the four different views of the subject which he keeps taking seem to have been most closely blended represents still another shortcoming; that is to say, he gets his views of public policy mixed up with the presentation of how things actually stand at the present time. There is a blending on that head but it is quite distinctly an unfortunate one. When one says that Schmoller despite the scope of his learning, the breadth of his viewpoint, has not succeeded in making it a single book, but rather has given a series of instructive chapters, one has merely said the sort of thing that is almost inevitably true of a man who is making so ambitious an attempt as he made in a comparatively novel field.

Schmoller was the first person who has tried to bring all the resources of the historical, descriptive and theoretical methods together. The kind of things which he has attempted no English or American writer is essaying on a systematic scale, nor has any other German economist made any like attempt.

The one man who seems to have led the way in this direction more truly than any other before Schmoller's time is Marx. In one way at least, he had much greater success than Schmoller. In writing *Das Kapital* he was not endeavoring to cover the whole field of economics. He was not even studying the ancient history of the part of the field which he was endeavoring to examine. Consequently in two important respects his aim was not so large as Schmoller's, but he did the sort of thing which, it is fair to say, the historical school must do if it is going to give what may fairly be called an historical type of theory.

That is to say, Marx made a penetrating examination of the development of capitalism, particularly in England, from the time of the industrial revolution to the years in which he was writing, and from that close study of historical and statistical materials, he did build a large theoretical view of the probable trend of economic organization. He may not have gotten his leading ideas out of his study of historical records, that is quite true, but no one does.

> [Take the case of Marx's] historical knowledge. His researches into current economic history had much influence on later developments. Helped to bolster up his theoretical economics. But it was not and could not be of decisive influence in shaping his theory. At bottom facts of history are unrelated except as the student organizes them by his ideas. At best one can approach history with some working hypothesis, seek to find whether the facts seem to agree with it, and make such modifications in the hypothesis as further reflection (guided by supplementary hypotheses) suggests. Process may continue until the investigator has got statement of the facts in a pattern that contents him. Marx worked more or less in this fashion. With him to a larger extent than with most later economic historians the working hypothesis ruled the facts. He took what facts suited him— they were real, significant. Other facts doubtless existed as exceptions— they did not deserve much attention because they were not in harmony with the inevitable trend of economic development.

> In short, Marx's theory of trend of social evolution did not rise from historical research—though it was authenticated—documented by much study of "blue books" after it had been formed. But is any historical theory likely to rest on historical research? Marx was first example of type of economics which we may call evolution of economic institutions. Marx, however, got his ideas of evolution from Hegel rather than Darwin.[62]

What happens in the case of the best historical investigators is that they construct a good many different imaginary pictures of how things that they are interested in have grown during the epoch with which they are concerned. These more or less imaginary sketches of how events have hung together serve the same purpose in their thinking that the hypothesis does in the work of the man who is dealing with some complicated problem in the natural sciences. Any worker in the physical sciences is likely to have a good many different guesses as to the solution of his problem before he finds the one that is brought out by the test of experiment. Similarly, the first-rate historical investigator with a desire to explain, to show how facts are collated, is likely to begin his work with ideas which he has not strictly derived from the facts, but with imaginary pictures. Yet the man who is really great at work of this type, keeps testing his imaginary pictures of how things have gone before, continually referring back to the materials with which he is acquainted, and seeking further

---

[62] Outlines, April 30, 1917, March 2, 1920.

materials on the points which his imaginary picture makes out to be crucial. Then he modifies his imaginary notions as he finds the early guesses were unsatisfactory and keeps working until he has a more or less satisfactory result.

That kind of work which Marx did, Schmoller cannot be said to have accomplished. The difference is one of original native aptitude. Marx was a superb theoretical intellect. Schmoller is a very industrious scholar, and the two things do not by any means lead to similar results. Marx, in the light of events that have happened since he was writing, was not correct on a considerable number of his anticipations. His theory of the direction in which economic organization would move seems, up to the present time at least [1918], to have been a mistaken one in several important particulars, though remarkably right in others. Probably that is a reproach that would not be very easy for future generations to bring against Schmoller.

He is not likely to be found guilty of great theoretical mistakes, but that is because he has not any strict theoretical ideas. The contrast between Marx and Schmoller is worth dwelling upon, to repeat, not for the purpose of belittling what Schmoller has done, but of pointing out the kind of theoretical result at which historical research might conceivably arrive, if it were conducted with good fortune. It helps us to see a little more clearly than we might otherwise what is lacking in the work of the historical school as represented by its best accredited academic exponent.

S3: I doubt whether Marx and Schmoller could be classed under one head in any respect. We could not even make the same requirements of Schmoller that we do of Marx. They are so opposite to each other, so extreme in their concepts and mental activities and mental aspirations. These two men are so different that they would spurn each other even if there was something on which they really agreed. Marx is not an historian even if he is the founder of the economic interpretation of history. Marx was not much interested in the facts of past history, but merely in the economic conditions of his time or a little in the future, and what he was primarily interested in was economic theory first and last.

M: Let us see, S3. It is not worth while to differ about the question of what is history and what is current material; that is to say, the sort of economic data that Marx was dealing with was very closely allied with the kind of material that is in Schmoller's descriptive parts applying to the present time, and those are a sort of cap upon his historical sketches. Marx, as I said above, may not have gotten his historical notions from his study of these conditions in the recent past and in his own life time, but he certainly utilized those materials on a large scale in *Das Kapital* in order to justify his general anticipations as to how economic organization is going to change.

S3: He uses them as illustrations.

M: He uses them as proofs, it is fair to say.

S3: Yes.

M: His theory is then as to what changes economic organization is undergoing and eventually will continue to undergo in the approximate future. It must be a theory in accordance with the facts.

S3: Not so much the facts, as the forces governing the facts.

M: But those forces will have to be exemplified in facts, that is to say, if the facts are patently in opposition to the theory, then the theory falls, does it not? It seems fair to say that Marx has constructed a very important system of economic theory out of the study of materials which if they are not historical, it is because S3 is using "history" with reference to what has happened in the past, and I am inclined to think that history is what happened yesterday as well as what happened one hundred years ago.

S3: As to Schmoller, he has nothing of this kind. He is not interested in these things. He really does not explain the mechanism of the economic order. He looks at it from various angles, and finds very interesting facts, and he goes on in a limited way to describe all sorts of factors that he sees without even caring to have a general view of the machinery. The entire machinery is an entity it seems to me.

M: That is what I was pointing out, that is exactly what one does not find in Schmoller, that attempt to put his whole body of material together into anything like a common result.

S3: Can it be said that Schmoller can be corrected, and can be improved on the basis of, or through a Marxian mind? I would not say so.

M: I do not suppose a Marxian mind would have any particular interest in correcting Schmoller. But it would have an interest in telling what is the significance of all the stuff that Schmoller has gotten together, telling what it means, interpreting it.

S3: And a lot of stuff that Schmoller did not give.

M: If you once had an interpretation in mind, you would have to supplement the collection of facts in a great many ways.

S2: It would be possible to have what is known as a Marxian system without history. The only difference between Schmoller and

Marx is simply the difference of the point of view, the use that they have made of the material. Schmoller started out in the first part of the volume practically the same way that Marx did, and ended like a pure historian, like Roscher for instance confining himself largely to description and classification, a book of classification.

M: That comes in also. He borrows sections of conventional economic theory and puts that in too.

S2: Yes, but, so far as we are dealing with historical facts, Marx takes his historical facts and data and uses them as a tool to construct a theory, to explain things, causal relations. It is a causal sequence. All that Schmoller does is to say, "We have this stage, and then we have that stage, now we have the family. If the present sort of thing goes on the family is going to break up, and I don't know what is going to become of this world." Marx is not interested in this. His interest is scientific. His theory is based on historical study.

S3: May I ask S2 a question: How much, if you exclude from the first volume the descriptions of child labor, English poor laws, etc.— about 120 pages—if you exclude this which is not connected with the entire theory, how much historical facts do you find in *Das Kapital,* and how much do you find in the second volume? That is almost wholly dialectical discussion.

S4: The difference is this: Marx is a disciple of Hegel and uses the Hegelian logic to explain his doctrine. He uses as illustration what economic history he can obtain which applies favorably to that viewpoint. Apparently Schmoller is not a philosopher, and he is not a disciple of Marx, and he does not use dialectic. That seems to be the difference. He is simply interested in historical facts.

M: I should not admit that Schmoller is interested in historical facts alone. He conceived himself as going a great deal further than that. He did not have so modest an idea of his pretensions.[63] On the other hand I do not think that Marx was merely using history to illustrate preconceived ideas. On the contrary, it is quite true that he made a careful study of what had been happening in England, and modified his preconceived ideas on the basis of the facts that he found, and tried to give an interpretation of actual conditions as they are running now, and as they are to continue to run in the future.

With that aid he constructed his economic system which, it seems to me, is perhaps the most intensely interesting contribution to economic theory that the nineteenth century produced, in the sense that

---

[63] [Schmoller said that "German (economic) science only attempted to find causal explanations." (Quoted in Herbst, *The German Historical School in American Scholarship,* p. 138.]

it bears directly upon the problem which concerns us all more than anything else; that is, the problem of changes in the general character of modern scientific work; namely that it can be tested by its agreement with what happens. That is one of its merits.

S2: The question is not how much historical fact is in this or that volume. It is a question of the use of these historical facts. What use is each one making of them? That is the point now. It may be that if you should count the pages, Marx might have thirteen and maybe Schmoller twenty six pages of such stuff.[64]

Recapitulation: The reader is impressed less by Schmoller's errors of detail than by the magnitude of his accomplishment as a whole. Range of his knowledge is extraordinary and even when the detail is lacking or is wrong, one is astonished by what Ashley calls "Schmoller's Olympian survey." Question of importance, however, is not so much the perfection or imperfection of Schmoller's discussion in detail as whether his treatise as a whole indicates that theorists can get a better understanding of economic life by restricting themselves to such theoretical work as the "pure theorists" do, or by including in addition to "pure theory" discussion of economic history, economic statistics and economic policy. The answer which the economist gives to this question depends partly on his metaphysical preconceptions, partly on his psychological ideas, partly on his bent toward mathematical habits of thought.

i-(1) One who goes back for his ultimate ideas to the plan of a divine providence, as did the physiocrats, will see little theoretical value in economic history, but will take kindly to discussions of economic statistics and economic politics. For the chief theoretical task to such a man is to discover what the plan of divine providence is; and the chief practical task is to find out whether the present situation harmonizes with that plan, and, if it does not harmonize at present, what policy can be adopted to establish harmony in the future.

i-(2) One who conceives things within the framework of evolutionary ideas as a process of cumulative change under the impetus of material causes— a process in which he can see no plan or aim except in the intelligences of the organisms which are themselves creatures of the process—must attach great importance to economic history. For he cannot understand the present situation except as a product of the past. The propensities of man, the character of common sense are to him not matters to be taken for granted as self evident, but phenomena to be accounted for. And his method for doing so is to trace as far back as he can the process by which they have been evolved. Economic statistics is also welcome to such a man for it affords him a method which promises—more than it accomplishes—to give him an exact quantitative knowledge of the situation as it stands at a given moment. Economic policy, however, is a matter

---

[64] "Class would not be persuaded to take Schmoller as seriously as I did." (Mitchell, "Diary," March 27, 1918.)

"Reading Schumpeter's essay on Schmoller with sidewipes at me." (Mitchell, "Diary," October 26, 1926.) [The essay was "Gustav Schmoller und die Probleme von heute" in *Schmollers Jahrbuch* (1926).]

about which he is likely to feel certain reservations. He will regard ideas as to aims of policy and means by which these ends are striven after as themselves interesting matters for investigation, and further as important factors in shaping the development of other features of the situation in which he is interested. But he may refuse to undertake to formulate what ought to be done himself, either because he does not possess full enough information, or because he regards his own ideas of what ought to be as themselves a product of the past process of events without any greater claim to recognition than those of other men. But he may also try to determine whither the process of events is now tending and advocate measures to facilitate the change. He probably would not like such a discussion as Schmoller's.

ii-(1) One who regards men as animated by careful reflection on their own interests—as primarily rational creatures—will not feel that economic history is indispensable to theoretical understanding of present situation. His explanation of economic phenomena consists in showing what the economic interests of different classes is, and perhaps of pointing out circumstances which obstruct clear knowledge of interests, or the way in which different interests of the same person conflict with each other. Economic history affords many interesting illustrations for his use, and is a subject which a scholar with abundant leisure may cultivate for its own sake; but it is pedantic to assert that it is indispensable to an understanding of the present situation. Economic statistics in his eyes is also a matter of secondary importance. It is a crude and imperfect way of showing the results of action which can be much better explained by analysis. Economic policy he is negatively interested in. It ought to be confined [he holds] to enlightening men concerning their own interests and preventing them from treading upon one another's interests. But extension of governmental control over a wider sphere of activity, which Schmoller seems to regard with complacency as the chief means by which economic prosperity is established, he regards as an evil.

ii-(2) One who regards men as organisms who have inherited a complicated set of appetites, instincts and emotions together with a moderate capacity for thought, one who regards early surroundings and education as exercising a deep influence on later life by the establishing of certain habits of thought and action, is logically bound to regard as fragmentary any explanation of human action which is not historical in character—i.e., which does not attempt to account for the peculiar character which men have today; i.e., economic history running a long way back is to him indispensable as a part of economic theory. Economic statistics also finds favor in his eyes as a convenient way of presenting certain broad features of a given situation. He does not know in advance what men will do and sometimes he can find out what as a rule they have done by the use of statistical methods. Economic policy to such a man is interesting as a subject for independent investigation, as one of the factors in shaping the situation and also perhaps as a means by which ends which the mass may regard as desirable may be promoted.

iii-(1) One who has a strong bias toward simple mathematical formulations of knowledge is likely to care little for economic history, economic statistics or economic policy. He explains by setting up a very simple imaginary situation in which relations are few and clear. On basis of this situation he may develop a highly elaborate theory, in which great nicety of formulation and refinement in the discussion of different cases is attained. That these theories are not immediately applicable to phenomena of economic life he will admit, but that fact does not disturb his faith in the theories. He sees their value clearly as an explanation of the essential features of economic life, admits that a process of modification is necessary to apply them to the complicated facts of life and advises people who are interested in such matters to make these applications in the light of their detailed concrete knowledge. Ordinarily he does not care to undertake the work himself.

iii-(2) One who has a more realistic bias, who wants to account for the factors he sees is temperamentally predisposed to attach more influence to economic history, economic statistics and economy policy. They present the phenomena which he desires to explain and the contribution of each is gratefully received.

Latter two contrasts less fundamental than first. Will not argue merits of any of the three sets of opposing points of view, but assuming that we take evolutionary standpoint, do not insist on regarding man as guiding action by light of reason only, and desire realistic explanations. Ask what help Schmoller gives us? Main defect of the discussion is that what we should expect from writer who is making one of the first attempts to combine economic history, economic statistics and economic policy with economic theory in narrow sense; *viz.,* that the different elements are not welded together. Different parts of the discussion have in considerable measure the connection of juxtaposition rather than of logical interdependence.

Discussion of value as an illustration of the defect. Begins with a modern psychological discussion of the process of valuation. Basis found in the feelings of pleasure-pain, esteem-disesteem, which accompany all states of consciousness. On basis of these feelings value judgments are built up. When Schmoller passes from this discussion of valuation to that of market price, however, he makes no effective use of his psychology but adopts as backbone of his exposition Böhm-Bawerk's horse market. True, he reminds us that supply and demand are not mechanisms but psychical forces; bargaining begins on basis of a previously existing price; all bargainers do not have full knowledge of market conditions, or equal financial power or equal skill in bargaining. But these remarks remain modifications added to a formal exposition of the old sort; they are not made an integral part of the whole. Much better results are attained by Sidney and Beatrice Webb in their discussion of the process by which price of labor is fixed.

To this discussion of market prices, Schmoller adds as further modification that idea of justice affects determination of many prices, and plays a particularly prominent role in public-fixed prices. This leads him to a discussion of the latter. Recognition of publicly fixed prices as a category to be discussed by economists besides prices fixed under conditions of market bargaining is perhaps the most valuable part of his treatment of value. But this discussion also stands much by itself; we are not given a clear idea of inter-relations between the two categories of prices. Analyses of demand and supply which follow are also rather detached. We are not shown a continuous process of valuations with their resulting market prices connecting our value-feelings with consumption goods, raw materials, machinery, labor, capital, land, business ability and business opportunities and organization. In this regard, discussion is distinctly inferior to that of Marshall or Fetter. Nor is historical continuity shown more effectively than logical continuity.

Discussion of wages affords a further illustration. Is made up of (1) economic history, (2) economic description, (3) economic theory. For most part the sections are independent of each other. Nearest approach to unified treatment found in his theoretical discussion of gradual fall of wages, 1500-1650; more rapid fall, 1750-1850; rise, 1850-1900. Shows how gradual change of economic organization by which class of free laborers was created affected situation, how mental characteristics of men aggravated difficulties of readjustment; how demand for labor varied with alternations of business prosperity; how development of new policy of government toward labor—such as, insurance against unemployment, accident, old age—has aided in advance of last half century. In this section, economic history, economic statistics, economic theory, economic policy are all utilized in intimate relation to each other.[65]

[One illustration of the fruitful use of Schmoller's work]: in discussing the rise of free labor in Germany (a process which had been proceeding slowly since 1500 but which was not completed until 1789-1870), he concludes that economic independence and economic responsibility were immediate blessings to perhaps a third of the laboring classes, a slowly developed advantage to another third and a disaster to the rest. Probably something of the sort was true of English laborers in earlier centuries. That is, the growing money economy favored the survival of those strains in the population which could acquire the pecuniary virtues of thrift and shrewd calculation, and the extinction of strains lacking such capacities, whatever virtues of loyalty, bravery or piety they may have possessed.[66]

Summary of discussion of Schmoller's *Grundriss der allgemeinen Volkswirthschaftslehre*. Two great defects: 1. Allows his interest in economic policy to interfere with his analysis of economic interrelations when dealing with present conditions. Would not object to his interest in policy were it not for this interference. 2. Does not succeed in welding together his discussions of economic history, economic theory, economic description and economic policy. Therefore does not give us a "theory" which represents the process of economic life as a whole. Over against these

[65] Outline, May 10, 1916.
[66] Mitchell, "Money Economy and Modern Civilization." The material is taken from Schmoller, *Grundriss*, II, pp. 263-268.

defects, we can set great merits. Carries out the evolutionary point of view in economic theory on a larger scale than any other economist. Thus gives a more scientific type of discussion—if by scientific we mean one written from point of view adopted in the sciences which are making the most rapid advances.

On the historical element in economics: Classical economics was interested in institutions in the sense that it criticized them from its own viewpoint and told what changes ought, and what others ought not, to be made. Not interested in the historical development of institutions. In Ricardian economics no specific reference to past historical development, no expectation of future change of institutions. Theory consisted of an account of economic behavior under present institutions—an account according to which the worker is supposed to subordinate other interests to seductions of early marriage while other classes follow their pecuniary interests. John Stuart Mill's stress on importance of institutions: distribution versus production dealt with desirable changes of considerable scope. In Jevonian mechanics of utility, no reference to evolution of institutions past or to come. A logic of behavior rather than account of actual behavior. Later orthodox types—much the same situation. Marx's *Das Kapital* made change of institutions central to his type of economics. Supported his theory of change by abundant documentary evidence but based his theory at bottom, not upon a study of history but on Hegelian metaphysics combined with utilitarian view of human nature and its concomitant political economy as worked out by Ricardo and the "Ricardian Socialists." Historical economics. Recent efforts to contract scope of economic theory explicitly cast out historical element in the problem; c.f., Herbert J. Davenport. Is there reason for having an historical economics? Are there two problems in the social sciences—"static" and "dynamic"? Anatomy of a cross section of social organization at one time? Physiology of growth of the body politic? Can one understand the situation at any given moment without reference to the past?

Conceive economics as dealing with behavior. Then we face problem of conceiving present organization of mind? That organization is obviously formed by past experience; e.g., conventions of elegance, of conspicuous waste, conventions of vulgarity of manual labor. State of the arts—how men make their living in any generation, how much of a living they can make. Demand curves, technical coefficients. Institution of property and its transmutations. Three-fold division of classes of Ricardo's scheme and four-fold division of today with problems of rent, interest, profits, wages. (Did not Turgot represent a four-class division and deal elaborately with interest as distinct from profits?) [He did.]

Granted that present cultural situation can be understood only as a result of historical evolution, still cannot one have a theory of present economic life with little reference to genesis of institutions—as Davenport, e.g., claims? Logic of institutions—what does that mean? Pecuniary logic, e.g. Is there not such a thing in as real a sense as there is a logic of our space perceptions, which can be worked out by taking careful thought? Yes. But such a logic is not an account of how men act, unless the institution has stamped its pattern unreservedly upon human nature. We do not, in fact, unreservedly obey pecuniary logic. If we did, we should seldom have strikes, never have wars. We should have fewer law suits, less philanthropy. Further, pecuniary logic does not conceptually set up ends of action that are acceptable. Money is only a means to an end. We cannot content ourselves with money-making. Even the most ardent money makers want money because it gives power, or because it is a mark of social distinction, or because. they like the activity of money making. Therefore the logic of institutions is a very incomplete form of social science at best, in that: (1) It does not show how men behave even at a given moment, (2) it does not explain the institutional situation to which it applies, (3) it throws no light on interesting problem of how institutions are changing.

Psychological scheme needed to give better perspective of problem of economics. Human nature: Inherited propensities—"instincts"; their indefiniteness. Supposed to change little. Institutions—acquired characteristics—subject to change—product of evolution. Adults in any generation a product of both. On this showing, obviously the social sciences must have a large historical element dealing with evolution of men's institutions. But that is not all: Varieties of human nature and capacity in every generation. A most important fact to which comparatively little attention has been paid, except by men who wish to justify an existing social situation on ground that the aristocracy of that day rests on solid ground of superior ability and is therefore socially serviceable (cf., Schumpeter's distinction between innovators and routineers). How can these varieties be managed? Only by statistical methods. Standard way of thinking of men should be not as all substantially similar, but distributed perhaps in accordance with curve of error [probability curve]. The individuals will have different ranking according to the quality in mind.

Conclusion: Historico-statistical investigations are necessary parts of the social sciences in general and certainly of economics. They supplement one another. Quantitative analysis, however, is difficult in part for lack of data. In so far historical investigation is necessarily imperfect. We shall never be able to make the social sciences on this side what we shall wish they might be. On the other hand, statistical analysis of recent past will doubtless expand greatly and be one of the most important elements contributing toward understanding of current institutional changes.

The collapse of the German historical school is to be taken, I think [1938], not as an indication that history is of no value in trying to understand modern economic life, but as evidence that the history needed for that purpose must be worked out more thoroughly than Schmoller, for example, did in the historical sections of his *Grundriss der allgemeinen Volkswirtschaftslehre,* and the history must be more informed by economic insight. Marshall himself evinced an appreciation of the value of such work in *Industry and Trade.* What is needed is an account of the evolution of economic organization at large, particularly of the money economy, that is of the scheme under which most families get most of their living by making money incomes and then buying with money most of the things that they consume.

How vast the influence of money upon economic behavior has been, we shall
not realize adequately until economic historians have recognized the importance of the topic and given us an account of the evolution of the
money economy at least since the middle ages. The account will start with
the long and gradual process of commuting knight's service, manorial
labor dues, payments in kind into services for money. Management of
landed estates for revenue instead of subsistence. Rise of trade from an
intermittent and minor process to a continual one, entering into most
transactions. Long series of experiments by which governments finally
learned how to maintain serviceable monetary circulation and standards.
Evolution of book-keeping; its gradual extension and refinement. Rise
of banking schemes for improving economic conditions by "money magic."
Analysis of the way in which the peculiar forms of monetary-banking system react upon production, distribution and consumption of wealth.
Effect that transition to money economy has upon forms assumed by
invidious comparison, esteem in which different human capacities are
held, criteria of public welfare, methods of waging war, etc.

In any event, one general advantage of historical studies is that they help
to emancipate us from the schematic and superficial view of human nature
that the early classical economists embodied in their *homo oeconomicus.*
That perfect product of the counting house is a plausible caricature only
of the human nature that develops in certain parts of a modern money
economy, the folk that Marshall called "City men." Though Marshall
abjured *homo oeconomicus* in good set terms, his ghost stalks the background of Marshall's analysis.

To repeat, we recognize that historical, statistical and theoretical studies
all contribute toward the understanding of economic phenomena, and also
that the final justification of economics lies in the contribution it may
make to wise public policy. But is all the historical and statistical material economic theory? Is not division of labor desirable? Monographic
work, rather than effort to bring so wide a field under single caption of
Volkswirthschaftslehre. Trouble with monographic work is that results of
tasks performed in severalty do not interpenetrate and illumine each
other. One of the troubles in Schmoller's own work—only much worse.
If all these kinds of knowledge are necessary to the economist's understanding then they should be brought together. And that not merely as
the mechanical assemblage of different parts between the covers of a
single treatise, but as parts whose relationship to one another is of mo-
mentous importance must be made clear. Only question is whether or
rather how far this desirable end can be attained in our present stage of
knowledge—or ignorance. That cannot be told except by trying. Schmoller
may not have succeeded very well, but those of us who plan to carry on
the work of economic investigation will not do our part except as we try
in whatever we do to the extent permitted by our mental capacity and
opportunities to utilize all the pertinent sources and kinds of knowledge
in the illumination of our problems; i.e., in our monographs themselves
can we not utilize all the different kinds of knowledge which Schmoller
brings together? Permits division of labor of a more fruitful kind than
that which divides off theory from history and statistics from both.

Veblen as a man who has done work of this character in one field of economics. Not the only one—Karl Marx and Sidney and Beatrice Webb—but one of the best to study.[67]

[So much for Schmoller. The discussion will now turn to Veblen's work, especially *The Theory of Business Enterprise*.][68]

---

[67] Outlines, May 10, 17, 1916, March 16, 1920; "Current Developments in Economic Theory," talk at Columbia Political Economy Club, April 5, 1938; "Seminar in Economic Changes and Economic Theory," December 16, 1940.

[68] [Ashley made Schmoller, one might say, the progenitor of both the institutional economics of Veblen and the economics of collective action of John R. Commons, even to the use of the designations. Thus in 1893 he declared at Harvard that "with this serious engagement [of Schmoller and his school] in historical inquiry has come a clearer perception of the nature of the generalizations towards which that inquiry must work. It is seen that these will not be mere corrections or amplifications of current economic doctrines. They will rather be conclusions as to the character and sequence of the stages in economic development. The point of view is here no longer that of a bargain between individuals in given social conditions, but of the life and movement of whole industries and classes, of the creation and modification of social mechanism, of the parallel progress and interaction of economic phenomena and economic thought. The studies of the school are no longer individualist and psychological but collectivist and institutional." Ashley, "On the Study of Economic History," 1893; reprinted in his *Surveys: Historic and Economic,* p. 7.

"Schmoller is recognized as leading representative of historical school since Roscher's death last year (1894). He is exceedingly conservative and evolutionary. (Henry R. Seager, "Lecture Notes — History of Economic Theories," University of Pennsylvania, April 30, 1895. Notes are in possession of Joseph Dorfman.]

CHAPTER XX

Thorstein Veblen's Institutional Approach

In the sketch on the development of the historical school in Germany an important feature of the growth of economics was left out of account. Little was said in a systematic form about the work of Marx, the most important of the "labor writers" who has not been considered in a detailed manner up to this point. His work had obviously significant intellectual relations to the ideas which the historical school was developing. He was like the historical school in several ways. He made much and effective use of historical material. An examination of the first volume of *Das Kapital* will reveal how thorough a student Marx had been of that great series of British Blue Books, those official papers in which the most authoritative record of successive stages and phases of the Industrial Revolution were laid down, and that his discussion was in considerable part a most acute and carefully documented account of certain changes in economic organization which were going on in his day, particularly in England.

He is ordinarily thought of simply as a Socialist; and the great majority of people who are interested in economic science think that it is not worth while to concern themselves with his views, except by way of refuting them. It may be an economist's duty to show from time to time how radically Marx misunderstood Ricardo, how absurd is his doctrine of surplus value. Anyone who reads him, however, not with the idea of trying to decide whether his analysis is right or wrong, but in the same spirit as one might read nowadays Jevons or Jevons's contemporary Walras will find that Marx is in many ways a modern type of economic theorist.

That thinker was concerned primarily with studying the workings of economic institutions as they existed, particularly in England during his lifetime; and he developed as subtle and clever an explanation of economic processes as they were then going on as anyone who has ever lived. He had a way of working which was in many ways decidedly superior to that of any of his predecessors and his orthodox contemporaries, for Marx based his work in large part upon the study of the Blue Books which were of extraordinary value to the economist, but to which the economists paid little attention.

The Blue Books were of particular value at the time Marx was writing, because the institutions which concerned him particularly were those characteristic of a society in which the Industrial Revolution had begun to affect a large part of the population and their economic activities. That Industrial Revolution had been accompanied by a period of social and economic phenomena which had forced themselves upon the attention of the Parliament, had led to many series of Parliamentary inquiries and official reports. In the Blue Books then, which naturally dealt primarily with social abuses, a person who was temperamentally a critic of the working English institutions found a congenial set of materials. They showed the dark side of English life during the period of active transition from an agricultural to a manufacturing community. They portrayed the unpleasant side in gloomy colors; and, to repeat, that made them congenial to Marx who was a critic of modern institutions. But he also made use of these materials as a means of explaining his observations of what was going on; and one finds him after the middle of the nineteenth century much the best informed economist of the time, a man who just because he had used great social documents far more thoroughly than any of the people who were recognized as economists proper had come to see far more clearly than any of his fellows, who were engaged in teaching the science of economics, what was going on. Finally he made more effective use of the materials for discussing economic problems than the members of the so-called historical school in Germany were making.

He was a person who was interested in the changes in institutions which he studied on the basis of factual materials instead of throwing away the reflective methods of classical economists, he tried to see what he could make out of these matters by thinking about them; that is, to avoid what now seems the stupid program of the historical school proper in its early days simply to collect materials over two or three generations and see what evidence they could establish. On the contrary, as an extremely active man of highly theoretical bent but with an eye for facts, he took the materials and tried to weave them together into an intelligent and illuminating account of the alterations which society was undergoing. Thus, he was in a real sense an institutional economist, not the first, but the greatest, certainly up to his time.

Marx came closer in a sense to accomplishing the aims which the members of the historical school set themselves more effectively than any member did. His work, taken on its own recognisances, is an account of the evolution of economic institutions, the changes in the fundamental features of organization among mankind for the purpose of getting a living. It differs from the work of the historical school mainly, to repeat, in the sense that he was as fundamental a theoretician as Ricardo and in the sense also that he was projecting the lines of development which he discovered in the past and present into the future. This projection made him the great intellectual leader of socialism. There are projections of a similar sort in other writers; prominently in Ricardo who had his ideas about the lines that were going to be followed by economic change. That element of the discussion remains of considerable importance in Marx.

The economists of the time did not commonly think of Marx as making important contributions to economic theory. They were so much concerned with combatting the conclusions he drew that they could scarcely be expected to be ardently trying to profit by the example of the methods that he practiced. But if the historical school had had, as a matter of fact, members sitting at the feet of Marx, learning as much as they could from him, they might, provided they had possessed the necessary intellectual acumen, have come nearer to blending their historical researches with their theory than they actually did. They accomplished little of this sort and they came out in the end, much where Schmoller did, having sections on theory and on historical development having little to do with each other's discipline. They certainly did not achieve their aim of trying to give an analytical account of human institutions in terms of their program. To that Marx came closer.

The man who will now be discussed, Thorstein Veblen, (1857-1929) achieved this end even more perfectly than Marx,[1] and he was enabled to do it largely because his approach towards economics was

---

[1] [Mitchell published the following articles on Veblen: "Thorstein Veblen 1857-1929," *The New Republic*, September 4, 1929, pp. 66-68; "Thorstein Veblen 1857-1929," *The Economic Journal*, December 1929, pp. 646-650; "Thorstein Veblen" in *What Veblen Taught; Selected Writings of Thorstein Veblen*, edited with an introduction by W. C. Mitchell (New York: The Viking Press, 1936) pp. vii-xlix. The last has been reprinted in Mitchell, *The Backward Art of Spending Money and Other Essays*, compiled and edited by Joseph Dorfman (New York: McGraw-Hill, 1937) pp. 279-312.]

[Veblen in 1920 attempted to persuade Mitchell to prepare and publish a book on "Types of Economic Theory" along the lines of "The Classical Economics" ms.]

"January 11, 1920: Spent working hours on making preliminary notes for two hour lecture on 'Prospect of Economics,' for course [on social sciences] by New School faculty. Went over collected materials on 'Types of Economic Theory,' read stenographic notes on 1918 lectures, etc. . . . January 12, Gave Veblen three ms.

somewhat akin to Marx. Marx's great problem was the evolution of fundamental institutions in economic organization. So, too, the important problem with Veblen was the evolution of economic institutions. But there was a very important difference between the two evolutionary approaches. The differences arose from the fact that Marx's idea of the evolutionary process was primarily the metaphysical concept which he derived from Hegel and Veblen's notions of the process were primarily the equally metaphysical ideas that he had derived from Darwin and Spencer.

Marx was thinking in terms of the thesis, antithesis and synthesis, which made the basis not only for Hegel's metaphysics but also for his philosophy of history; Marx had a philosophy of economic history written in Hegelian terms, but he insisted on the material factors as the controlling ones; in that history he showed one set of institutions acting as the thesis and a successive set as the antithesis, and he looked forward to socialism as the synthesis in which this great problem of humanity would find its ultimate solution.

Veblen, on the other hand, was thinking of humanity as a species of animal which got its substantial biological type definitely established thousands of years ago. He is inclined to think that all that is known upon the subject, which is not very much, favors the view that so far as man's physical and mental makeup, his body and brain are concerned, there has been no important step forward in human evolution at least since the days of the neolithic man, and that may be many thousands of years ago. But during the period while the race, this species of animal, has been keeping substantially the original type, there have been enormously large changes in the way in which the species has lived. The change, Veblen says, is due substantially not to any improvement in the human brain, but to the gradual accumulation of certain habits of thinking. The reason why the life that people live now is different from those of their ancestors in the river caves of France, for example, is that men have gradually through their minds acquired certain ways of utilizing the world around them

---

chapters on Bentham and Ricardo [from ms. of 'The Classical Economics'] to read. . . . January 15. Veblen who had been reading my early chapters advised me to complete book on 'Types of Economic Theory' on present scale. . . . April 15, 1920. . . . Set Mrs. Goodman [his secretary] to copying chapter on Ricardo's system of political economy for printer. . . . February 8, 1921. . . . lunch with Ben Huebsch to discuss publication of reports of the National Bureau of Economic Research, and my book on Classical Political Economy. . . . May 9. Make outline for Book on Classical Political Economy. But distractions. Call from Leo Wolman who will come to National Bureau of Economic Research if we get funds. President Wheeler [of University of California] came in. Talk with man to paint houses, etc." (Mitchell, "Diary").

to satisfy their needs. In that process there have been built up elaborate societies. People have developed arts and sciences. They have acquired queer tastes which their remote ancestors would not understand at all. They have become to all appearances a very different set of creatures with enormously vaster powers. It is all a matter of the evolution of culture.

That is, the economist, more than any other set of people working in the social sciences, is in a sense carrying forward the story of human evolution from the point where the biologist as such drops it, at least the biologists of the Darwinian type, the biologist who is interested in the evolution of the species, fixing certain more or less definite types. For most all types of animals, one may say without equivocation, for all of the species of animals, that may be the end of the story. But for humanity it is not much more than the beginning of the drama. It is the economist primarily who is concerned with carrying on the tale of human evolution, because it is a question of the evolution of mind; and the way in which mind evolves, on Veblen's lines, is controlled primarily by what men do.

Men acquire habits of thought unconsciously through the exercising of their powers, which means that the kind of thoughts that men get is shaped by their daily activities. Those activities in which the largest number of people are engaged most of the time will have more power in shaping minds. There is no other task which in the history of humanity has occupied the minds of so many people so much of the time as the task of getting food and shelter. That means that the mind of modern men has been shaped primarily by the exigencies of getting a living, has been shaped by their economic activities. In so far as men have managed to develop ideas which are not primarily derived in serviceable form in the economic realm, it is because they have acquired efficiency in getting a living, they have obtained a certain amount of leisure time which does not have to be devoted to obtaining food and shelter. Men developed societies in which a certain section of the population may be their life long emancipated from those simple tasks, and so it has been possible for them to amuse themselves in all sorts of ways, to develop arts, sciences and social distinctions of one kind or another.

Another way in which Veblen differs from Marx is that with this view of the evolutionary process he has naturally a different attitude toward the future character of evolution than the Marxian one. If the enquirer starts with the Darwinian conceptions of evolution and holds by them consistently he does not find it natural to see a term set to the process of change. He expects this evolution of species, so far as mankind is concerned, which has been going on for a millennium, to continue for millennia in the future, he expects nothing in the way of catastrophic change. That some fundamental alteration in methods of human organization is going to introduce a new world is not part of his logical outlook. It was, however, part of the forecast for anyone who started with Hegel's notions. His philosophy of history is as dramatic as Marx's anticipation of socialism. Marx could look forward to socialism as the great achievement and not be much concerned with what would come afterward. He gave readers the impression that this was the grand climax of the ages, because he was working within the range of Hegelian metaphysics.

Marx, somehow got it into his head not only that this process of institutional change which he was studying with such skill and acumen would change society, but also seemingly that once the socialist state was established that was the end of the process of institutional change; that is, he was looking forward to a definite consummation: the establishment of a scheme of institutions under which the proletariat, including the great mass of mankind, would come into control, would expropriate the expropriators, and which after that might continue no one knows how long. He was very definite about his conception, but his whole analysis gave the impression simply that society was going to work out a new institutional scheme which would be presumably permanent.

Veblen is just as much concerned as Marx with the process of evolution in institutions, but he is a Darwinian rather than a Hegelian in this respect. Instead of looking for some grand synthesis in which the processes of history would find their consummation, he looks toward a continuation of the process of cumulative change. The process has no end which we can foresee, but we can understand with some measure of correctness the changes which are in process, the fruits of which will be obvious to all mankind in the comparatively near future.

Take the case of the idea of the class struggle. Marx makes it a reasoned effort, first of the capitalists and later of the proletarians to promote their interests. Has an end when classes are all merged into one under socialism. [Veblen] sees no necessity that oppression of a class must produce class struggle. It may at times and at other times it may not. Depends on the effect which conditions of life produce on the given class of oppressed. May become patiently subservient. No proof either that proletariat will establish socialism or that if they do socialism will be permanent form of social organization.[2]

[2] Outline, March 2, 1920.

This attitude toward economics gives Veblen's writings a measure of vitality which is lacking in the discussions of the latter day representatives of the orthodox tradition. In the time of Ricardo and Malthus this was a matter which made an enormous difference to economists because they had a fashion of representing the shape the future was going to take. Economists came more and more to treat the subject on a professional basis; they doubtless perfected, purified the logic which was employed, but at the same time confined themselves more and more to highly technical problems. And the man on the street is inclined much less to dispute economics and the economists than he was in the days of Ricardo and Malthus but also less inclined to regard them as the great saviors of mankind. The subject stirs people decidedly less.

On the other hand with Marx, who thinks he has a way of showing the consummation of the process of change in which men are engaged now, one becomes at least as excited as in the days of Ricardo and Malthus. The same is true of Veblen. If Veblen is right, then the world in which our grandchildren grow up will be a world extremely different from that to which we belong. Somehow people get more excited over the pictures of what lies in store for them just over the horizon than over how the processes in which they are themselves engaged work out in a mechanical way. That shift in Veblen's problem is responsible in large measure for the enormous vogue which his work has had, a vogue much wider than that enjoyed by any other economist of his generation in the United States, a vogue which is none too wide in the universities where many an economist is wont to say that whatever Veblen may be he is not an economist, but which is enormous among the general reading public.

Veblen, who purports to tell a tale of how the gradual accumulation of small changes in man's habits of thought is responsible for all achievements of the race, was logically bound to look forward to a future of the same sort; it was a future in which external things might

---

[Professor Mitchell noted] that Marx was the one great writer who did incorporate or integrate the subject of business cycles into the general body of economic theory in the nineteenth century. Needless to say, his example was not one that professional economists sought to imitate. And what he had to say about the increasing severity of crises seemed to many of his critics one of his most obvious blunders. (Outline, "Lectures on Business Cycles," September 24, 1942.) [Mitchell felt that Veblen had also been a leader in integrating business cycles into a system of general theory but was free of Marx's "blunder." Professor Mitchell was deeply impressed by Veblen's views on Marx as the following "Diary" entries on Marx indicate.] "March 1, 1920. Preparing notes on Marx for lectures on Types of Economic Theory [at New School]—particularly Veblen's articles on Marx. March 2. Met class on Types, mathematical theory [Schumpeter's] and then Marx. March 9. Looked over my annotations on the three volumes of Marx's *Capital*. Made notes for afternoon lecture . . . Finished discussion of Marx." (Mitchell, "Diary.")

happen to the race which would produce important changes in their way of life—quite possible that climate would change, natural resources get exhausted; things with which man's scientific capacity might not be able to cope, but the outlook is for a continuation of change in culture, world without end—change of a gradual sort.

There is still another difference between the two thinkers: so far as the conception of human nature was concerned, Marx could not borrow very much from Hegel. Hegel was far more logician than psychologist. Marx got his ideas about human nature primarily where the English classical economists got them. A large part of his technical economic theory was borrowed from Ricardo directly or from the people who have come to be called the Ricardian Socialists, that set of good Benthamites who took Bentham's general approach toward the study of human problems, combined it with Ricardo's method of treating technical economic problems, and got a series of solutions to the problems which were far more sympathetic to Marx than to Ricardo. All these thinkers, in reasoning about what people are going to do, argued in terms of securing certain pleasures and avoiding certain pains. Marx did the same, his conception of human nature is fundamentally Benthamite.

The Benthamite conception of human nature does not fit satisfactorily into the conceptions arising from biological study. Darwin does not talk much in terms of calculations of advantage. It is not easy to impute such calculations to the lower species and hold them responsible for alterations in biological form. When Darwin goes on to treat the story of man, his discussion is more in terms of instincts and habits than of a calculation of advantage. The latter appears to be a capacity which arises late in the history of the species and can be accounted for in terms of the advantage it gives in the struggle for existence. It is an acquired characteristic and one which has a far more limited role to play in life fundamentally than it seemed to Bentham. The important things, the drives in human behavior, the things that determine what men are going to do, on this view, are instincts of self-preservation, of sex and the like.

In more mature forms of life the inborn instincts, getting developed under varying conditions, grow into certain habitual types of behavior which, as society becomes elaborate, may take distinctly different forms. The important psychological categories for a man who begins to ponder the evolution of society from the standpoint that Darwin started out with are instincts (Veblen would say tropisms and instincts)—and the habits which are outgrowths of instincts—among them the habit of calculation which in different classes gets developed to very different degrees.[2a]

From this viewpoint, it appears that if the theorist wants to understand modern economic life; that is, if he wants to have a scientific economics, the fundamental problems before him are those of accounting for the particular habits of thought which dominate any given period with which he is concerned. These habits of thought which prevail in a given period, the widely prevalent habits of thought, Veblen called institutions; that is, the fundamental task of the economist is to explain the institutions prevailing in whatever culture he is dealing with. Those institutions he has to regard as the current outcome of an age-long accumulation of human experience. Thus the theorist must approach his problems from the evolutionary viewpoint, and that means that the fundamental content of his economics will be something quite different from that in most treatises.

The basic defect of orthodox political economy, from this viewpoint, is that it is overlooking the fundamental problems. Really to understand, the inquirer has to know what the prevailing habits of thought are and account for them. He can put up a certain sort of apology for orthodox economics in terms of this scheme of thought and in doing so he is showing simply why the economics that is built on misconceptions has been of some service in trying to understand economic processes. Among those habits of thought which are characteristic of a modern age are the habits of business calculation. They are drilled into the part of the population which is engaged in the task of business management. They are, to a certain extent, enforced on all men. All have to live nowadays by making and spending money incomes; and to a modest extent most of us get disciplined in a crude kind of accounting calculation. The flower of this habit of thought appears in modern accounting which has come pretty nearly to the dignity of a branch of mathematics—a very exact type of thought on the whole.

What the orthodox economists following Bentham were doing substantially was to impute this particular habit of thought, this institution, to mankind at large, and to argue about how people would behave in case this was the only economic institution of consequence

---

[2a] "The human individual is born with a vaguely known equipment of tropisms and instincts. Instincts differ from tropisms in that they involve an element of intelligence. What modifications instincts will undergo, into what habits they will develop, depends upon the nature of the experience encountered, and that depends in turn upon the environment, especially the human environment, in which the individual grows up." (Mitchell, "Thorstein Veblen," 1936; reprinted in *The Backward Art of Spending Money and Other Essays*, p. 294.)

in modern culture. One may say therefore that orthodox economic theory can be regarded as a monographic treatment of the logical implications of one set of economic institutions.

Just to the extent to which that particular set of institutions plays a role in modern life, to that extent will a logic of the implications of pecuniary institutions prove enlightening to a person who wants to understand modern society. Business institutions, the pecuniary side of life, have become important enough in the last few generations, particularly in countries like England and the United States, to dominate people's whole lives to a considerable measure. Consequently, there is a certain plausibility in orthodox economic theories. They may indeed claim to have, from the strictly logical viewpoint, a high degree of certainty; but it is a certainty of the sort that is found in geometry. Geometry is like orthodox economics in that it is the working out of the logical implications of certain habitual ideas in man; such as ideas about space. The connections between elements of the ideas, the axioms with which the theorist starts, and the elaborate conclusions at which he may arrive can be made substantially logical.

Just so the investigator can start with certain axioms about the motives that control human behavior, and, if he reasons as accurately as geometers come to reason out their propositions, he can arrive at results that are just as certain as those of the modern text-books of the Euclidian sort. These conclusions will have a certain usefulness in interpreting the actual behavior of men much as Euclidian geometry has in mechanics, though there are no things in man's practical experience which correspond precisely to the points which have no breadth and thickness, the lines which have length only, the circles which are at all points actually equidistant from their center, etc. There are still little discrepancies between geometry and even the most exact practices that men can build upon it.

There must be far greater discrepancies between the logic of pecuniary calculation and people's actual economic lives simply because when talking about economic life the economist is talking about a set of activities in which a host of other habits of thought are playing their part side by side with the habits of pecuniary calculation.

What I have been saying about Veblen's approach to economics is the most important single thing by way of helping toward an understanding of his notions. His ideas of what constitutes the proper subjects of inquiry for economists are the views which the student should have in mind when he reads any of his books. They help the reader to understand why Veblen takes up certain problems for treatment and why certain others which one would expect to find adverted to in any book on economics simply are not there. It explains the basis for his critiques of economic theory. It accounts for the fact that when he began criticizing classical economic theory he wrote about what he called the "preconceptions" of economic science. The trouble with classical political economy and its derivatives, he holds, is that it set forth from certain naive notions about the nature of the world and mankind in the earlier days, of the relation of mankind to the deity, which are out of accord with later sciences and for which the model in Veblen's mind was evolutionary science of the Darwinian type. It also helps to explain why Veblen was so little understood by his contemporaries among the economists, why he was regarded as so queer a bird, why from the point of view of a large proportion of them he was not considered an economist.

If the student takes the definition of economic theory which is given by Veblen's close personal friend Herbert J. Davenport—"the science that treats phenomena from the standpoint of price"—there is no economic theory in Veblen. Veblen had his way of saying that work of the sort that Davenport did had a limited benefit in explaining the modern situation, and from Davenport's viewpoint Veblen might be regarded as throwing light on certain real forces, but his work could not be called economic theory from Davenport's viewpoint. From Veblen's viewpoint Davenport was concerned with certain trifling details, elaborated in shocking ignorance of the part that the habit of calculation plays in life, and without any understanding of the way in which this habit has grown up and come to play a certain part in the guidance of men's activities.

M: I should like to begin the discussion by asking what characteristic marks off Veblen's type of economics so sharply from the types with which we have heretofore been dealing?

S: He emphasizes institutions.

M: Are none of the writers which have already been discussed concerned with the influence of institutions? What about John Stuart Mill, for instance? Mill in his *Principles of Political Economy* says with much emphasis that there is a fundamental difference between the problems of production and those of distribution arising from the fact that distribution is a matter of human institutions. Distribution, therefore, is under social control, whereas in producing wealth man can never emancipate himself from certain natural conditions such as

Mill sums up under propositions concerning diminishing returns from land and the dependence of production upon capital.

In distribution Mill shows that people have perfected the present scheme and can in the future, if they are wise, bring to pass other schemes. Then, in the latter part of his treatise, in the celebrated chapter "On the Probable Futurity of the Laboring Classes," he explains at considerable length what changes in economic institutions seem to him desirable and what effects they would have. In particular he sets forth his favorite plan for co-operative workshops in which the workers themselves gradually become part and, in the end, sole owners, a scheme under which the distribution of income would be radically altered, because the average member of society would get an income composed of wages and profits, including interest. This is attaching great importance to institutions.

Would you say that a writer like Alfred Marshall pays comparatively slight attention to institution? Isn't there after all some other way of looking at the point that has been raised which comes a little nearer the mark than saying simply that Veblen lays great stress upon institutions and implying that the other writers previously discussed laid comparatively little stress upon them?

S: Veblen lays more stress upon instincts than his predecessors.

M: Yes. You would say that the chief differentiating characteristic of Veblen's work is another conception of functional psychology? You think it is more important than his attitude toward institutions. Yet Veblen is described as an institutional economist, by people who like to apply labels, and it is a useful practice, based on approximation, to call his work institutional theory.[3]

S: His theory is the outgrowth of all social forces. I do not think he allies himself to any particular school, psychological or other. He includes them all. It is an outgrowth of pre-existing institutions.

M: Are you proposing to combine the two suggestions and to say

---

[3] [Professor Mitchell originally referred to Veblen's work as evolutionary theory and then genetic theory; and around 1917-1918, finally, institutional theory.] Evolutionary theory is concerned with how things came to be as guide to how they may be changed. [This is combined] with functional theory as that which shows how things work out at present. ("Economic Man," APP 44-53, no. 66).

[This view was expressed by another student of Veblen in a slightly different manner. "Finally, another group seems to have in mind more or less clearly the establishment of economics on a new and evolutionary basis. In this they are allied to the historical school but are not to be thus technically classed. Among these men are Carl Bücher, Werner Sombart, Thorstein B. Veblen." (Robert Hoxie, "History of Political Economy," ms. 1915.)]

Even the classicists and marginalists in discussing practical problems are prone to forget their mechanics of utility and take the evolutionary point of view. (Outline, "Final Lectures," April and May 1914.)

that Veblen takes more account of institutions and also works with a more modern, more adequate conception of human nature? Is there any way of combining the two suggestions on Veblen's showing?

S: Habits; they are the dominant forces.

M: That does not give a definition which is different, it does not tell us specifically what their character is. Are they physical forces, political forces; what are they?

S: A combination of those things.

2nd S: There are two chief forces in institutional life: business and industry.

M: The "machine process" and "business enterprise" are the two phrases he employs in *The Theory of Business Enterprise* (1904). Another phrase that he has rung the changes upon in his later work is "absentee ownership." Those are samples of what Veblen means by institutions. The two things seem extremely different, and the whole purport of Veblen's investigation is to show how extremely different they are. They are both institutions. What are institutions?

S: Ways of doing things.

M: That is not quite adequate. There are all sorts of ways of doing things which may be personal.

S: Social ways. He considers institutions to be all social arrangements that are fashioned by the material environment.

M: Have you some addition to make to that?

S: The structure of human society.

M: The following is a definition that Veblen himself gave once. "An institution is of the nature of a usage which has become axiomatic and indispensable by habitation and general acceptance. Its psychological counterpart would presumably be anyone of those habitual addictions that are now attracting the attention of the experts in sobriety."[4] He has given on other occasions a briefer definition which is at least easier to carry in the memory: "Widespread social habit." Any widespread social habit is from Veblen's viewpoint an institution. With this definition of institution in mind, does the class see any close connection between Veblen's treatment of institutions as the central problem in economics and the conception of human nature which he employs, the difference between the view of human nature with which he approaches the discussion of economic theory and the conception with which it has been approached by economists more closely in the orthodox tradition?

---

[4] *Absentee Ownership and Business Enterprise in Recent Times: The Case of America* (New York: Huebsch, 1923) p. 101.

S: Does it not stand out in contrast to the volitional theory of psychology? Veblen seems to be of the opinion that human nature is the result of the actions and interactions of various institutions playing upon the human animal.

M: Is that satisfactory language from Veblen's viewpoint? Remember again that institutions are widespread social habits.

S: We are creatures of habit.

M: Yes, but in a sense we are the sum of our habits on Veblen's showing. This is the view of human nature, as he develops it; it contrasts sharply the almost infinitely varied capacities of development which a baby has at birth and the standardized forms of behavior which he acquires in the process of growing up. From the point of view of the individual, character is formed by the institutions, that is, the widely prevalent social habits prevailing in the community of which he is a member, the ways in which he is trained from the cradle. From the point of view of society as a whole I do not know whether one would like to say that people are formed by their habits. They are, from Veblen's point of view, the mass of these institutionalized ways of doing things; that is, their behavior is. Is it not clear that a man who has Veblen's conception of human psychology, of human nature, of human behavior, is bound to make institutions the focus of interest? And he is bound to do so, because institutions are the central feature of human behavior that concerns at least the social scientist.

This can also be approached from a little different point of view. Veblen is always thinking of the task of the economist as that of accounting for economic behavior. Of course, no theorist can account for all of economic behavior; he is not much interested in those aspects of behavior which are peculiar to different individuals. What concerns him are the mass phenomena of human behavior. Like any other scientific worker, he is interested in generalizations—what usually happens. What usually happens is almost by definition that behavior which is regulated by institutions, if one's further definition of institutions is that they are widely prevalent social habits, and habits are ways of acting, thinking and feeling which get expressed in objective actions.

To repeat, the economist who starts out with Veblen's conception of human nature necessarily makes the study of institutions the center of economics. Thus the two suggestions as to the differentiating characteristics of Veblen's work made above come to much the same thing. It is hard to say with which one the inquirer should start. He may perhaps take the view that Veblen originally had a glimmering of the importance of institutions and on the basis of his reflections as to what role they played, particularly in behavior, came to entertain his unusual view of human nature. Or the enquirer may say that Veblen started with a view of human nature that was different from that presented through various problems by the orthodox and as a result of reflections upon the conception of human nature came to the view that institutions are of primary consequence for the economist.

S: If the idea of ever changing institutions be accepted, can there be such a thing as economic law?

M: What do you mean by economic law?

S: Something that follows certain conditions, which is persistently true.

M: Give an illustration.

S: I do not know that it is a sound economic law, but economists speak of the law of joint costs.

M: Let us take that as an illustration without inquiring exactly what it means, hoping that we have more or less the same principles in mind. From Veblen's point of view it is conceivable that the law of joint costs may be a valid generalization concerning behavior of businessmen in practice as society is now organized. But equally from his viewpoint, it is a generalization which is not relevant to the life of savage peoples. So here would be a law—I do not recall that Veblen himself employs that phrase regarding his own work—which is applicable to one form of economic organization; that is, in terminology more akin to that which Veblen likes to use, a law which is applicable to a society with a certain set of economic institutions, which would not be applicable to other societies. Veblen would doubtless agree to some such statement. Would not Davenport do the same? Is not Davenport aware of the fact that the study of phenomena from the standpoint of price cannot be carried on with fruitful results when one is thinking about life, say, in America before the coming of Columbus?

In this respect there is no difference between Veblen's attitude and that of other theorists. Most of them have been interested in discussing the workings of economic institutions as they now prevail and, to quote Davenport's words, "with scant attention to the process by which they have assumed their present form." Veblen, on the other hand, is interested primarily in the way in which institutions have gotten into their present shape, what are the prevalent institutions, or rather what institutions give their special character to society as now organized; how did these institutions come to have their present form.

In short Veblen's work is differentiated from that of his predecessors by his dealing with institutions as a factor of the greatest consequence in determining economic behavior. He regards institutions as presenting a problem different in character from the problems of institutions which have been discussed by other economists. The economists who have followed along the lines either of Ricardo or of Jevons ought not to be charged with neglecting institutions. Certainly the philosophical radicals did no such thing; they talked a great deal about institutions, or rather "bad institutions," and their reform program was largely devoted to reform of institutions. Remember that John Stuart Mill laid such great importance upon the distinction between institutions which can be changed and natural conditions which presumably will always exist in much the same shape.

Most of the recent writers examined, while they say little about Veblen's problems, are becoming conscious, as Davenport is for example, that their discussions apply to a given institutional situation. But all the way along, the economists in so far as they have been conscious of dealing with institutions have tried to explain the workings of institutions which now prevail. They want to treat a mechanical type of problem; accordingly the theorist has a scheme of private property, one in which for purposes of making money people may be divided into a few classes: the wage workers, the merchants, the active employers and the investing public. Then the theorist wants to see how under this scheme with its elaborate markets prices are fixed in such a way as to distribute the products of industry among the participants both active and passive in production. It is a discussion of the workings of a more or less established scheme of social habits. Their explanations are concerned with the way in which prices are determined and how these prices determine distribution and, to a certain extent, how this scheme acts on the volume of goods produced in society as currently organized.

Veblen in most of his discussions evinces comparatively little interest in working upon the problems which have been the center of economic theory. But he says that, if the theorist wants to gain an understanding of this situation, he has to find out how these institutions have evolved; with what they started, through what transformations they have gone. How have people come to submit to this seemingly curious, and in some ways ineffectual way of organizing themselves to promote their fundamental economic interests? He also has a special, or rather malicious, interest in asking how can people actually come to believe that this is a desirable set of institutions. How is it that a group of shrewd people have come to approve the existing scheme as if it were one established by nature?

The questions which he discusses differ from the questions which are treated in orthodox economic theory less in that they are treating a different set of phenomena than that they are trying to throw light upon substantially similar phenomena from the other side. The orthodox theorist is concerned primarily with, say, the economic problems of how social institutions work at the present time, and Veblen with the problem of how these institutions evolved.

S: What relation does Veblen hold to the historical school?

M: The historical school, in its early days at any rate, treated the whole of the classical economics as a set of speculations spun out of a few assumed premises without much regard to the current experience of mankind. They argued that the proper way to understand economic life is to proceed not by the deductive process of reasoning on the basis of certain premises, but by the process of induction. The theorist should gather a great mass of information concerning economic facts from past history and from current experience. When he has assembled an adequate body of data, he should set himself down to establish generalizations by induction, to find out to what conclusions the enormous body of evidence that he has collected leads, what generalizations concerning economic behavior he establishes on the basis of his historical data and current statistics.

That involves a procedure extremely different from that of Veblen. Veblen is concerned primarily to gain a theoretical type of understanding. He is a born logician, just as definitely as Davenport is. He feels comparatively slight sympathy for the effort to throw away the whole body of economics on the basis of reasoning and to resort merely to observation and then to induction from observation.

S: Please discuss the relation of Veblen and Werner Sombart.

M: Sombart, [author of the classic *Der moderne Kapitalismus*], was deeply read in Marx and trained in the German historical school. He saw capitalism highly developed in Germany, he personified it as an institution and set to writing its history. This history he found mainly in German and Italian materials. Veblen was also a reader of Marx. He was trained not in history but in natural science and philosophy. That gave him insight into the significance of Darwin and facility in playing with systems of ideas. He too saw capitalism highly developed and became interested in its characteristics but to him capitalism was rather an English than a German institution in origin.

Differences between the two men: Sombart has more historical learning,
more patience with scholarly technique, more interest in system building.
Veblen has more philosophic grasp, and a peculiar satiric flavor. Also more
psychological insight and more anthropological lore. Sombart's chief theoretical defect is his lack of psychological knowledge, which results for example in his childish conception of different races. Veblen went in for
anthropology—sociology of the G. V. de Lapouge-Alfred Otto Ammon
type. To him races were, say, dolicho-cephalic blonds and brachy-cephalic
brunettes. All the people of modern Europe are mixtures of different races—
the mixtures differing only in the proportion of the whole made up by the
several types. Sombart, on the other hand, confounds races with nations
and talks arrant nonsense about the hero peoples and trading peoples. The
Romans, Normans, Lombards, Saxons and Franks are hero peoples. On
the other hand, the Etruscans (who settled largely in Florence), the
Frisians (who settled Holland and the lowlands of Scotland) and the
Jews are trading peoples. He had come to this idea before [world] war [I],
but he made great play with it during the war for propagandist purposes.[5]

If Veblen differs from the classical economists and their modern
representatives, it is not so much because he thinks their methods
as such were wrong as it is because he thinks they have applied their
methods in an unsatisfactory way. He holds that they were particularly led astray by an artificial conception of human nature.

S: If Veblen is really interested in the same set of problems, he did
not finish his task in *The Theory of Business Enterprise;* he should
show how these considerations bear on the technical problems of
value, wages, etc.

M: Veblen would probably say that there are lots and lots of
people working over those problems. They give a variety of solutions.
I do not care particularly about those problems. You can get their
conclusions from these people; but if you do you should keep a
wholesome skepticism in mind; their conclusions may be based on an
unfortunate conception of what controls human behavior.

S: Did not Veblen criticize orthodox theory in some of the essays
he published from time to time?

M: The first of his notable contributions was an essay in *The
Quarterly Journal of Economics* in 1898, "Why is Economics Not an
Evolutionary Science?", and it was quickly elaborated in three essays
in the same journal called "The Preconceptions of Economic Science"

---

[5] Outline, March 30, 1920; [the "S" in this case was the historian Harry Elmer
Barnes.

Professor Mitchell was not aware at the time that Veblen had courses in history
with Herbert Baxter Adams at Johns Hopkins, William Graham Sumner at Yale and
Moses Coit Tyler at Cornell.]

(1899-1900). In these essays and in a number of penetrating reviews which he published upon the books of several major writers, such as J. B. Clark, Schmoller, Irving Fisher and Werner Sombart, he developed certain technical criticisms of economic theory.[6]

To get the difference between Veblen's approach and the orthodox approach to economic theory most sharply I think the best procedure is to contrast Veblen's writings on "The Preconceptions of Economic Science" and Davenport's *Value and Distribution.* Davenport sets out to develop an elaborate criticism of the economic theory of his chief predecessors, and it is a wonderful piece of work. But he proceeds from the point of view of preconceptions which are exactly like those of his predecessors and his interest is in finding out at what points they were right and at what points wrong. Veblen also engages in a critical discussion of his leading predecessors, but he is not concerned with finding out whether they are right or wrong. His question primarily is what was it that led people to think their views plausible? He takes the successive writers apart to see how they work inside. He regards them not as constructive thinkers who were bound to be right or wrong, but as interesting museum specimens to be dissected and examined so far as possible. He has used the same attitude in treating his contemporaries. This has been responsible in good part for the discomfort which most of the economic fraternity experience in thinking about Veblen and his work. It is pleasanter for an economist to have his view vigorously disputed by someone who thinks he is wrong and that his mistakes ought to be corrected than it is to have someone take hold and say "well what a diverting and curious animal; how can you account for the fact that a man can think it was worth while to discuss this particular set of problems, and how does it happen that he comes to arrive at this particular set of conclusions, and what is it that makes the majority of his contemporaries think it is worth while and valid?"

---

[6] [The essays "Professor Clark's Economics" (1906) and "Gustav Schmoller's Economics" (1901) also appeared in *The Quarterly Journal of Economics* and were reprinted with the others in *The Place of Science in Modern Civilisation* (New York: B. W. Huebsch, 1919) pp. 180-230, 252-278.

On Fisher Veblen wrote, "Fisher's Capital and Income" (1907) and "Fisher's Rate of Interest" (1909) both of which appeared in the *Political Science Quarterly* and both of which are reprinted in *Essays in Our Changing Order,* edited by Leon Ardzroni (New York: The Viking Press, 1934) pp. 137-172. He reviewed Sombart's *Sozialismus und die soziale Bewegung im 19 Jahrhundert* in *The Journal of Political Economy,* March 1897, pp. 273-275, *Der moderne Kapitalismus* in *The Journal of Political Economy,* March 1903, pp. 300-305, and *Der Bourgeois* in *The Journal of Political Economy,* October 1915, pp. 846-848. There is also a review of Schmoller's earlier book dealing with method, *Über einige Grundfragen der Sozialpolitik und der Volkswirtschaftslehre,* in *The Journal of Political Economy,* June 1898, pp. 416-419.]

This is his general attitude because his approach to the whole problem has been so extremely different in character. What the economists have talked about is from his point of view not the chief scientific problem. The only way to explain economic life is to find out how this curious system has come into existence. To see the results that it is producing is, of course, interesting; but primarily because it gives rise to certain speculations of the future changes to which the existing set of institutions is probably going to be subjected. There again Veblen is concerned with the problem which the more orthodox economists have left severely alone.

The people who are engaged in trying to work out the mechanical results of institutions in their present form are likely to be as little concerned with alterations which economic institutions are undergoing as they are with the process by which these institutions got their current shape. On the other hand Veblen's approach, which makes the question of evolution of economic institutions the central feature of economic theory, leads naturally to the question how is this age-long process of evolution going to continue in the future, what changes are in progress and what kind of a society are they going to provide in the days to which we can look forward.

S: What was the reason for Veblen's attitude? He is difficult to understand for he is critical but not actively revolutionary.

M: That is a question concerning a man's personal equation, the sort of question that one must speculate about. The only people who answer questions of that sort with full confidence are psychoanalysts.

There are certain factors in Veblen's personal experiences, however, that throw some light on the matter and I will relate them for what they might be worth. He was born in Wisconsin in 1857 as one of the younger members of a large family of Norwegian immigrants. When he was only eight years old, his family moved to Minnesota which was then frontier country. The family lived a more or less lonely life. They kept speaking Norwegian at home; and it was not until Thorstein Veblen was pretty well in his 'teens that he came into sufficiently close contact with the English-speaking people to acquire a real command of English. Presently, in 1874, he went to the preparatory division of Carleton College, which was a Congregationalist institution dominated by the New England tradition. I think this means that Veblen got a very definite outlook from growing up on the farm in a small household community quite different from a modern culture. He was a person of almost insatiable curiosity who was interested in everything he encountered. He was much impressed by the difference between the sort of life that his family lived, which seemed to the end of his life quite admirable, engaged in making useful things for human betterment, and the life that had a decidedly modern cultural element of the sort that we have in mind when we are talking about cultured people. For although his people were of the farming class, they came from well-to-do peasant stock in the old country; they were more or less artisans, extremely fond of the old sagas which Veblen loved intensely, and they were clearly of intellectual capacity. One of his older brothers, Andrew Veblen, became a professor of physics at the University of Iowa, and a nephew, Oswald Veblen of Princeton University, later the Institute of Advanced Study, was a distinguished mathematician.[7]

He came out of that background and was thrown at Carleton into the midst of people who came from a money-making New England background. He also came from a Norwegian Lutheran family and was set down in a New England Congregational community. The contrast between the life seemingly devoted to making useful things and the life of money-making where it was not so easy to see that the activities of the shrewd businessman might really be contributing to the satisfaction of human needs struck him very forcibly, and interested him when he was young and impressionable in questions of cultural differences. He had to try to account in his inquisitive mind for the fact that such altogether different standards prevailed in the two communities, in general and in economic affairs. That gave him, according to his own theory, a very good advantage for scientific work. One of his most interesting essays is entitled, "The Intellectual Pre-eminence of Jews in Modern Europe" (1918)[8] and in that Veblen accounts for the extraordinary proportion of Jews among successful scientific inquirers on the ground that a Jewish boy is not to the manor born in the modern world, particularly if he comes out of an orthodox family. He gets one set of conventions impressed deeply upon him in the home and then he goes into the world where he carries on scientific work and that world he finds strange. He has the advantage of looking at things, which people who are to the manor born take as a matter of course, as strange novelties; and the result is that he is in a position to ask fundamental simple questions.

This is true, Veblen thinks, in pretty much all lines of scientific inquiry. That type of explanation is applicable to his own case, for

---

[7] [When Veblen was living in his last years in the environs of Stanford, Oswald Veblen asked a former student, the eminent mathematical statistician and economist Harold Hotelling then at Stanford, to keep him informed of his uncle.]

[8] Reprinted in Veblen, *Essays in Our Changing Order*, pp. 219-231.

the Norwegian culture out of which he came differs as strikingly from the modern world presented in the United States as does the Jewish tradition. In fact, in one way the difference is greater for the Norwegian background, a world of patient industry; the Jewish background, through force of historical circumstances, has been very largely a background of small business and bartering.

Veblen kept to the end of his life the feeling which he acquired so early that this whole matter of business enterprise has but a remote relation to the fundamental interests of mankind, and he looked at it as something strange that had to be accounted for. He saw the greatest contrast, which he pointed out most effectively in his "Industrial and Pecuniary Employments" (1901),[9] between what he called making goods and making money. This is the contrast which is dealt with in *The Theory of Business Enterprise,* which the class should read for the course. For his thought here is about the machine process on the one side and business enterprise on the other, the two features of modern life; in other words, industrial employments on the one side for making goods and pecuniary employments on the other for making money.

Veblen was, to repeat, a critic of modern life even more profoundly than a critic of modern economic theory, as criticism of economic theory grew out of criticism of life; the criticism of economic theory, as he saw things, was based on the fact that the economists were concerned primarily with the business arrangements by which people make their incomes. The whole felicific calculus, with its elaborate scheme of measuring, multiplying and discounting, seemed to him to be only a reflex of those habits of mind which are inculcated into people in the daily conduct of business traffic.

It ought to be added that when Veblen was a boy he was a great tease. That was purely an individual trait of his character; and to the end of his life—he was very much of a tease. He got a great deal of personal enjoyment out of his wickedly clever phrases. Nothing gave him more satisfaction, for instance, than to talk about "capitalistic sabotage" as a necessary practice in the modern world. His familiar phrase about "conspicuous waste" is a case in point. In *The Theory of Business Enterprise* he refers to philanthropy as "an excursion into pragmatic romance." That trait was not a necessary result of his up-bringing but a trait he happened to possess.

Of interest, too, is another feature of his individual traits and personal experience combined, which is important for explaining his

---

[9] Reprinted in *The Place of Science in Modern Civilisation,* pp. 279-323.

peculiarities. He was in his college days much interested in philology, which was natural in view of the fact that he had learned one tongue at home (actually two at home: the current Norwegian and the old language in which the sagas were written) and then at school he learned another language. He became much interested in this side of cultural development and thought for a time of devoting himself definitely to philological study. While at Carleton College he struck a deeper interest in philosophy.[10] When, after receiving his B.A. in 1880, he went on to Johns Hopkins the following year for graduate study, it was primarily to devote himself to philosophy. From Johns Hopkins, where he did not find what he wanted, he passed on to Yale and there continued to devote himself to philosophy as a major and political economy as a minor. He took his doctor's degree in philosophy in 1884 with President Noah Porter and wrote his dissertation under the title of "Ethical Grounds of a Doctrine of Retribution." One of the things that seemed to Veblen always amusing was the sanguinary character ascribed to the deity, with which he became so well acquainted in his own original circle and then among the New England people of stricter tradition.[11]

After he had received his Ph.D. Veblen sought an academic opening and for seven years he could not find any. In those days philosophy was a subject taught in most colleges by the president who was in more cases than not a clergyman by training and it was taught more or less as a system of Christian apologetics. Obviously, with his highly critical outlook particularly on current religious ideas, he was not acceptable to a philosophy department in which it was felt the chief duty of the philosopher was to justify the ways of God to man.

Veblen was greatly disappointed by this inability to get an opening and had to go back to Minnesota where he lived for four years on the family farm. After his marriage to an old college schoolmate in 1888, he lived on his father-in-law's farm in Iowa. He thus spent the seven years after his doctorate very largely in fresh independent study in a place where he had very little intellectual companionship. And that

---

[10] [At the same time Veblen became interested somewhat in economics. This was taught by J. B. Clark who spent five years (1875-1880) in Minnesota early in his career as a teacher.]

[11] [Professor Mitchell originally thought that Veblen's doctoral dissertation was on Kant and he] declared; I have never seen the document, but I have been told by philosophers that it reveals much of the same type of intellectual peculiarity that has become characteristic of his later economics work ("1918 Typescript"). [The document on Kant was later discovered to be the essay "Kant's *Critique of Judgment*" which appeared in *The Journal of Speculative Philosophy,* July 1884, pp. 260-274. It has been reprinted in *Essays in Our Changing Order,* pp. 175-193. Modern philosophers agree with the verdict that Professor Mitchell heard.]

period of hope deferred when he was living very much by himself, conscious as he was of very uncommon intellectual powers, had a considerable degree of influence in reinforcing all of his most marked individual traits. A person who lives very much to himself does not have his sharp corners rounded off. If he has a good deal of intellectual power he probably tends to become more fixed in whatever habits of thought appeal to him as an individual than would happen if he lived in a community where he had the opportunity to mix with his intellectual peers and to talk with men whose outlook on life differed very much from his own.

At the end of the seven years he returned to graduate study at Cornell and after a term won a fellowship. That was a very small appointment for a man who had a doctor's degree and a distinguished career as a graduate student. But it was the only thing he could get. He attracted the attention of Professor J. Laurence Laughlin, then head of the Cornell department of political economy, by writing an article criticizing certain views of Herbert Spencer regarding socialism, "Some Neglected Points in the Theory of Socialism" (1891).[12] The point of the article was that Spencer, whom he admired greatly, did not understand the real grounds for the social unrest that seemed to be growing in the modern world. The ground, Veblen thought, lay in the economic conditions of the time; the divorce of so large a proportion of the population from ownership of more than the most meager property; the fact that they were engaged in a type of mechanical organization which gradually inculcated only habits of thought which led them to test the modern conventions of society by material standards, to question what they themselves really were getting out of it and what the people of large means were contributing to the welfare of society that justified the incomes that they received.

Laughlin, as noted, was very much impressed by the essay, which I always supposed he had not understood very well; and when the following year (1892) he was called to the University of Chicago as head of the department of political economy, he took Veblen along with others from Cornell with him and that gave Veblen his first real chance. He stayed at Chicago fourteen years 1892-1906 and it was there that he did a large part of his important work. While at Chicago he wrote his early essays, "The Preconceptions of Economic Science," *The Theory of the Leisure Class* (1899) and *The Theory of Business Enterprise*. From 1906 to 1909 he was at Stanford and from 1911 to

---

[12] Originally it appeared in *The Annals of the Academy of Political and Social Science;* reprinted in *The Place of Science in Modern Civilisation*, pp. 387-408.

1918 the University of Missouri. Finally in 1918 he joined the staff of the New School for Social Research where he has been lecturing in recent years [1927] when he has lectured at all. The last two or three years his physical condition has not been such as to make it easy for him to lecture.

In short, Veblen's career was that of a student, a teacher and a writer of books. He indulged in only one other flight of fancy, being for a short time connected with the magazine *The Dial* in New York during and immediately after the war, in 1918-1919. Veblen was an editor and wrote not a little for it.

Veblen was highly trained, a subtle minded philosopher who turned to economics as his major interest. By virtue of his severe training in such work as that of commenting on Kant, he found no intellectual difficulties presented by economic theory. The amusing fuss made by some people about the technical refinements of theory and the difficulty of understanding such subtle notions did not impress him in the least. Also it must be said he was a philosopher in the sense that the orthodox economists themselves were philosophers; that is, he had greater inclination towards thinking things out systematically than he had toward the patient work of observation. He came to results in his attempt to think things out very different from those that the classical economists reached, not because his method differed from theirs but because his premises were different. They started primarily from the premise that man is rational, that the great factor in directing his behavior is calculation of advantage. Veblen started rather from the assumption that man is a creature of instinct and habit, that he does acquire in the modern world habits of calculation but they never come to be the chief directing feature of his life.

Among the instincts of outstanding importance for his purposes was the instinct of workmanship. Whereas the classical economists always talked about labor as representing pain, Veblen thought that the irksomeness of labor in modern society is a cultural problem. He set out in one of his most interesting essays "The Instinct of Workmanship and the Irksomeness of Labor" (1898)[13] to solve that problem and he solved it in cultural terms. Fundamentally people desire exercise and nothing is more painful to them than continued repose. They are always engaging in spontaneous activity and they take a particular satisfaction in the type of activity which results in the production of serviceable goods. Veblen attributed to mankind at large very much

---

[13] Originally published in *The American Journal of Sociology*, reprinted in *Essays in Our Changing Order*, pp. 78-96.

the attitude that his own father, his older brothers, and his mother had, that among the most satisfactory things a person can do is to do a good job in making serviceable things; he enjoys the things that he makes that way, he enjoys the process of making.

But in a society where the arts have become highly enough developed to make them decidedly productive, at that stage there are certain classes of people who through the force of circumstances have acquired an unusual proportion of property and they take a considerable degree of satisfaction in making their superior status known. Always men have been addicted to the making of invidious comparisons between themselves and their fellows; and when property begins to be accumulated, one of the most satisfactory invidious comparisons the man of property can make is between his possessions and the possessions of others. That means that people who have property are very desirous that this fact should be realized by others as well as themselves. It is another trait of human nature; that is, they get satisfaction from making invidious comparisons in which they rate themselves superior. People also get satisfaction from feeling that others are forced to make comparisons in which they seem inferior. They want their possession of considerable means recognized; and this leads to the whole set of practices which are characteristic of the leisure class in conspicuous waste of an indefinite number of forms. That characteristic of modern life runs definitely counter to man's instinct of workmanship and constitutes one of the drains to which modern society is exposed.

Veblen's first comprehensive publication of moment was in good part an elaboration of the article. This was *The Theory of the Leisure Class* in 1899, which remains his most widely read book. It is one of the ablest contributions on the role played by pecuniary institutions in social behavior.[14] In it he makes an analysis of the particular form which the desire for distinction takes in a society organized primarily for gain. One of his leading convictions about men, as noted previously, is that they are continually indulging in invidious comparisons between themselves and other people and they try to the very best of their ability to shape these comparisons in such fashion that they have the better of them.

This deep-set proclivity of mankind, he argues, expresses itself in every society. In societies where the economic organization takes the form of seeking gain, the great and most desired position of superiority

---

[14] Sentence from Outline, "Fifty Years as an Economist," address before Political Economy Club, Columbia University, May 11, 1945.

is the superiority in wealth; and the best way for the individual to demonstrate this is to be, or at least seem to be, so circumstanced that he can enjoy a large income and have leisure at the same time. From Veblen's point of view this is a very irksome way of living for most men, because he thinks men are active creatures always wanting to do something and are troubled if they have to live a life devoted to such futilities as sports. Hence, in societies where culture takes this form, men impose the duty of giving evidence of their capacity for a life of leisure upon their wives and daughters and commonly keep for themselves the pleasant life of activity at things which are regarded as reputable. Veblen works out this idea in the most engaging fashion, making use of the vast amount of ethnological material of which he had become master.

The Theory of the Leisure Class was written with considerable skill. Veblen's style was always a combination of qualities which attracted and repelled readers. He was addicted to a heavy form of sentence structure. But, on the other hand, he was a born phrase maker and his glittering phrases captured the attention and interest of readers to an extraordinary degree. Such phrases as "conspicuous waste," the great phrase of that particular book, have become almost a part of the language. The Theory of The Leisure Class was read by the intelligent public at large quite as much as by the economics fraternity. Indeed, many economists were inclined to take it as primarily a brilliant satire upon prevailing habits and not necessarily a serious contribution to an understanding of the modern phenomena of consumption. Veblen took it in the latter fashion. He was, to repeat, a born tease and greatly enjoyed the uneasy feeling which his discussion of current habits of thought produced in many of his readers.

The book was a highly satirical account of certain prevalent habits of mind characteristic of modern communities and their consumption of wealth. Veblen was interested in accounting primarily for the phenomenon of conspicuous waste, as he calls it, trying to explain how it comes about that we get so much satisfaction from using serviceable or dis-serviceable commodities in a wasteful fashion, when that waste can be known to all men. Of course, we all realize that great waste is a source of keen gratification to the average citizen of a modern community. I do not say it is a source of keen satisfaction to ourselves [in this class], simply because I want to spare your feelings; but, if I were telling the truth about myself, I would plead guilty to that feeling and I think that most of you, who think of your own attitude of mind in purchasing goods, find that it is a pleasant thing to spend recklessly. You get great gratification by being able to be a little wasteful in a way that other people will notice. You feel in a certain sense that it establishes a certain superiority on your part. That attitude of mind Veblen analyzed with extraordinary keenness and humor. The book made a good deal of a stir at the time [of its publication 1899] and is still kept in print.[15]

While he was preparing this book Veblen, as already noted, was also engaged in the earliest of his serious criticisms of economic theory. In these essays in 1898-1900 Veblen began with a critical onslaught upon orthodox theory. The general line he took was to the effect that economics as it stands is a pre-Darwinian science and in that sense scarcely a science at all. It had missed by all odds the most important problem of understanding how the economic organization of society had come to have its present form and devoted itself almost entirely to a subtle analysis of economic behavior which was based upon a radically imperfect conception of human nature.

That critical work was presently followed by *The Theory of Business Enterprise* dealing with a series of problems that current events had brought to the fore in public and technical economic discussion. In the late 90's and early 1900's the American public was much concerned by the development of giant trusts, schemes for controlling enormous business enterprises which were supposed to possess more or less monopolistic powers utilized to exploit consumers. Uneasiness was growing concerning this development and many schemes for putting a stop to it were being proposed. A large federal investigation was authorized by Congress in 1898 and organized under the title of the Industrial Commission. The commission began taking evidence concerning the practices of business enterprises, in particular concerning the financial structure of trusts, the way in which small companies were bought up and put together frequently at inflated values to form

---

[15] Paragraph from "1918 Typescript."

[As of 1968, *The Theory of the Leisure Class* is on the lists of five American publishers, and at least one British house.

"A hat, we hold, must be tall and shiny. Why? Because it is fragile and expensive so. Coats and trousers must never be shiny. Why? Because that is a condition to which all coats and trousers naturally aspire. Gloves must be white, dove-gray, fawn, because gloves of all things dirty quickly, and these colors will best advertise how little useful work we do and how often we can change our gloves. Automobiles must be capable of doing eighty miles an hour, although thirty-five is the limit fixed by law. As the advertisers tell us in their skilled promptings of our jealousy, it is the reserve power that counts—that is, the reserve pecuniary power. In their car we shall be able to show to all how much more we can afford to have than can be used by anyone. Thus, says Mr. Veblen, money sets the standard of our values and the touchstone of our goods is waste not taste." (C. E. Ayres, *Holier than Thou* (Indianapolis: Bobbs-Merrill, 1929) p. 75.]

new giant organizations of which the most conspicuous was the United States Steel Corporation.

This is the period of Mr. J. Pierpont Morgan's most spectacular activity: a long series of corporate organizations and reorganizations in the 1890's culminating in the establishment of the United States Steel Corporation. The commission gathered an enormous amount of factual material about a great many phases of business life in the United States and published it in nineteen volumes in 1900-1902. Of this material Veblen made considerable use in *The Theory of Business Enterprise.*

Veblen at the time began an inquiry into the relations between business enterprises and the industrial process of making goods. The inquiry is related in his *The Theory of Business Enterprise* which was much more definitely devoted to economic questions than *The Theory of the Leisure Class* had been.

I have selected it among his books for the course, because it is the one that comes closest to dealing with themes of the sort that the conventional theorist is concerned with. It is more constructive in its aim than several of his other books, which also makes it better for our purpose.[16]

The Theory of Business Enterprise is an institutional inquiry, for Veblen begins by showing that the modern cultural situation is dominated by two great institutions: the material framework of modern civilization is the industrial system and the directing force which animates this framework is business enterprise. The discussion is primarily concerned with the relation between these two institutions, between business enterprise, the art of making money, and the machine process which is characteristic of the distinctively modern art of making goods. Veblen's chief interest is to see how business enterprise, which most economists have regarded as the great means for the successful building up of modern industry, warps industrial efficiency at various points.

It does so, he argues, because the business man as the owner of industrial enterprise has an aim which does not run parallel with the industrial aim of turning out goods. In business enterprise the aim is money profits. Serviceable goods are frequently a by-product which men have to turn out in order to make money. This means, however, that business is not conducted with the object primarily of satisfying human needs. It is directed with the aim of making money and doing so for the specific individuals who run the business enter-

---

[16] Paragraph from "1918 Typescript."

prise. There are many circumstances under which, and ways in which, money can be made without enlarging the output of serviceable goods, the real income of people. When prices can be raised as is often possible—when business enterprise can through any device secure a monopoly, it is comparatively easy to increase profits without increasing, possibly even decreasing, the amount of serviceable goods which are produced in the course of social consumption.

So again, owing to the intricacies of modern business organization it may well be that people in actual control of the business enterprise find that they can make more money by speculating in the stocks of their enterprise than they can by running them for profit; that is, Veblen argues that the economist is not justified in taking for granted even that the interests of the people who run the enterprise are identical with the enterprise itself. He can cite a great deal of evidence of an authoritative sort, giving specific cases of that type of situation; for this book, written in 1904, is based largely upon a careful study of the voluminous reports issued by the federal Industrial Commission in 1900-1902.

Veblen studied the documents and it is particularly these reports which caused Veblen to justify the critical view of modern business enterprise which he preached in his writings. So you have in the book an argument which is documented much more fully than most of his treatises.

Veblen's bibliography kept increasing. There is time only to mention the chief ones. He published *The Instinct of Workmanship and the State of the Industrial Arts* (1914), a book in which he sets forth his conviction that one of the deepest traits of human nature is man's desire for activity of some serviceable sort, the conviction that had led him to take the ground in *The Theory of the Leisure Class* that most men find a life devoted to leisure irksome. They have to find some employment which they can at least regard as serviceable in order to be reasonably content.

The next year appeared *Imperial Germany and the Industrial Revolution* in which he dealt with the peculiar form the Industrial Revolution had taken in a country that was dominated by monarchical institutions and discussed also the relative staying power of Germany in World War I, forecasting that on the whole despite considerable technical advantages in certain respects the Germans would prove in the end scarcely a match for the powers against which they were arrayed. In 1917 he published *An Inquiry into the Nature of Peace and the Terms of its Perpetuation,* one of the keenest analyses of the obstacles which confront the efforts to limit armaments and maintain a policy of peace among nations. This is the volume that has been so misunderstood and so much discussed in very recent weeks [April 3, 1918].[17]

In 1918 came *The Higher Learning in America,* a critical account of the position of the higher institutions of learning, which look primarily to business men for endowment and that have boards of trustees drawn primarily from the business classes. In 1919 appeared *The Vested Interests and The State of the Industrial Arts,* in 1921 *The Engineers and the Price System.* That is a volume which in late 1932 came to the public attention again, because of the passing interest in the Technocrats, some of whom claimed that the scientific side of their program had been elaborated by Veblen. In 1923 he published his last book, *Absentee Ownership and Business Enterprise in Recent Times,* which in many ways sums up most effectively his economic analysis of how life runs in modern society.

In addition to these volumes, there appeared in 1919 a collection of his published articles under the title *The Place of Science in Modern Civilisation and Other Essays.*[18] In 1934 Ardzrooni edited another collection of essays under the title *Essays in Our Changing Order.*

The same year Joseph Dorfman of the department of economics of Columbia published an admirable biography of Veblen under the title, *Thorstein Veblen and His America,* a book that had been long in preparation and that gives a singularly complete account not only of the exciting life that Veblen lived so far as outward circumstances are concerned but also of the evolution of his scheme of thought,

The very titles of Veblen's books suggest that his interests have been different from those of the run of recognized economists. There is not a systematic treatise on political economy or economic theory or anything approaching that type of effort in the list. From a certain point of view every one of his books is a monograph. Yet in all of them the writer is dealing primarily with the economic aspects of his problem; whatever question he takes up for special investigation, he is first and foremost an economist, and an economist who asks questions different in character from those which are raised in the text books. How different they are, however, has previously been discussed. So we turn to the problems which come to the fore in the book which

---

[17] Sentence from "1918 Typescript." [For details of the episode see Joseph Dorfman, *Thorstein Veblen and his America* (New York: The Viking Press, 1934) pp. 382-383.]
[18] [The essays were selected by three former students: Leon Ardzrooni, Wesley C. Mitchell and Walter W. Stewart. The volume was issued by B. W. Huebsch who became Veblen's publisher.]

is the best sample of his work for our purposes, *The Theory of Business Enterprise*.

Possibly it would have been better to have made use of certain of the essays which were published in a single volume in 1919 under the title *The Place of Science in Modern Civilisation*. Or, if the students were well read in Veblen, his latest book, *Absentee Ownership*, might have been the best one to take as representative of his special method of approach, his peculiar interests. That is, however, a book which those who are not already fairly well accustomed to Veblen's idiosyncrasies are likely to read with difficulty. They find it hard to enter into sympathy with the writer, and the mood of irritation which he arouses in them is not conducive to getting the best results for themselves out of the treatise.

The Theory of Business Enterprise has, to be sure, its highly spiced passages. Nothing that Veblen ever wrote lacks them if he could help it, and he invariably could! But it deals primarily with a set of problems which, to repeat, were more in the forefront of the interest of the country at the close of the great period of trust formation during which the United States Steel Corporation and a large number of other scarcely less conspicuous business combinations had been effected. At the time the book was as difficult to read (without irritation) by one unaccustomed to Veblen's extraordinary approach as *Absentee Ownership* is today [1927]; presumably in ten or fifteen years more, if the students now have difficulty in reading *Absentee Ownership*, the drift of time will enable them to go through that volume with a considerable measure of sympathetic understanding.

In *The Theory of Business Enterprise*, Veblen undertakes an inquiry into the nature, causes, utility and further drift of business enterprise. [More accurately perhaps, the book] gives a brief study of the processes of cumulative changes which have established the present system of business enterprise, a descriptive analysis of the way in which those processes work at present; and a forecast of the probable course of cumulative changes which these processes and their contemporary cultural factors will probably follow in the future.[18a] He picks upon the mighty subject of business enterprise, because from his point of view it is the most important of modern economic institutions which does most to give the current period its peculiar characteristics. Veblen would not be concerned to deny that human wants, for instance, are far more basic as economic phenomena than business enterprise; he would not be concerned to deny that the question of price determination is in a sense more fundamental, but

---

[18a] Sentence from Outline, "Final Lectures," April and May, 1914.

he does hold that when a person wants to understand what is peculiar in the present age, what marks it off from the times that have gone before, what is peculiarly important to study, if the theorist is interested in the transitions that may be expected in the future, are not the things that have characterized human life from the beginning or at least from the period when men began to cooperate toward the satisfaction of their economic desires. It is not those features of economic life which presumably will continue to the end of time to characterize communities of men. It is rather those aspects which have come into prominence within comparatively recent times and a continuance of which is a matter of speculation. As he sees things, the modern age has two great characteristic institutions on the economic side: one, the machine process, he points out, is carried on in subordination to business enterprise. And so it happens that the second institution, business enterprise, is more characteristic of the age even than the machine process.

That from the beginning has been one of Veblen's favorite thoughts. Soon after *The Theory of the Leisure Class* was published he read in 1900—or rather had read, as he himself was not present, before the American Economic Association—the notable paper already mentioned called "Industrial and Pecuniary Employments" in which he called attention to the fact that the ways men have of making a living at the present time can be divided roughly, and yet to good scientific effect, into occupations which are concerned primarily either with making goods or with making money. In the one class belong the great mass of artisans, the people who are typified by the farmer, the operating railroad man, the machine tender, the civil engineer, a whole body of highly skilled technical experts who are applying the natural sciences to the regulation of the process of producing goods. In the other category, pecuniary employments, he throws people who are dealing with problems of price in various forms: the salesmen, the accountants and, most typically, the great business enterprisers.

That classification of employments is forecast and elaborated in *The Theory of Business Enterprise*. Veblen sees modern economic life as a fundamental process in which men are trying to get the material wherewithal for a comfortable life in a way which is like that which has always characterized the world in a sense, but also in a way that is somewhat different, because in the modern decades, the last two hundred years, men have been applying the natural sciences to the organization of production on an unexampled scale and with unexampled success: the Industrial Revolution and all that it implies. In the course of that process men have acquired the extraordinary range of knowledge represented by the engineering sciences. The high priests of this aspect of economic life are the engineers; they are the people who know how to make things. From Veblen's point of view if economic life were really organized for the purpose of satisfying people's wants, it would seem to be the sensible thing to turn the direction of labor and capital over to these experts, the men who are both best trained and best fitted to organize industrial processes, to make proper choices of materials on technical grounds, to understand the designing of machine processes; in short, the men who are great experts in making goods.

His criticism of modern economic life—I am not quite sure whether he would have called it a criticism, but let us put it in the more colorless language which he affects—the characteristic of modern life which looks strange is that instead of turning over the direction of the work producing the things people want to use to the men who have the native aptitude and training and are experts in production, we turn it over to another set of people and make the experts in production, the engineers, subordinate in authority to the business men. The business men of course are interested in making money and are acting as if their fundamental interest economically is to make money instead of to make goods, although one of the most patent and widely recognized facts concerning economic life is that it is not a country's money income that counts any more than does an individual's money income. It is what the nation or what the individual can get with his money income—a point of view which is particularly obvious with reference to the country at large; to multiply wealth a million fold in terms of money alone would add not one iota to the actual satisfaction of the people's wants. But the people continue to entrust the organization and routine conduct of economic activity to business people as if making money were their fundamental, deepest-seated economic interest!

Such a paradoxical situation greatly intrigues a person of Veblen's temper; it is exactly the kind of situation in which he is quizzically interested. He takes not a little time in elaborating the most paradoxical aspects of the results which are thus achieved. He is a person who is almost as much interested in the artistic side as in the scientific side of his work, and the peculiar dissonances which have often been represented as the harmonies of modern economic organization are delightful to his ear; he likes to ring the changes upon them. That is what he is doing in *The Theory of Business Enterprise*. He begins with a statement that there are two great institutions which are most characteristic of the age: the machine process on the one hand and business ownership on the other hand. He states that the extraordinary gains that people have made on the economic side in the last century or two are due wholly, so far as can be seen, to the advance of the machine process and what it implies. But modern society subordinates the use of machinery to business; and he goes on to investigate in what way business control over industry in part nullifies the economic advantages that might be gained if people set themselves to make full and unrestricted use of all applications of modern science.

How does business hamper industry? Veblen points out a number of ways. Here are only a few of them. He notes for one thing the business man is interested in the vendibility of his product rather than in its serviceability; a perfectly obvious and just remark. If what the individual wants to do is to make money, then as a business man he must produce things which will sell at the highest profit. As anyone can testify, the commodities which are highly vendible may not be goods which are highly serviceable. Thus the modern system of putting business in control of industry involves a constant bias in the direction of turning out goods which are fitted primarily to catch the purchaser's eye and appeal to his monetary desire rather than things which really gratify human wants. So too, he points out that advertising has become a branch of business which requires the use of a very large amount of capital and employs the efforts of thousands of men; and he asks of what use is advertising to satisfaction, to what human wants does it contribute? His answer is that advertising is a nuisance. Instead of satisfying men's wants it makes the world uglier than it need be, it presents all sorts of irritating nonsense in a blatant tone, interrupting one's peace. It is, however, very useful from the business point of view; that is, it helps people to get ahead of each other in competition. Veblen in his indictment does not pay perhaps sufficient attention to the defense of advertising which is sometimes advanced seriously on economic grounds; namely, that while it is not itself a means of satisfying wants it does contribute to an expansion of the market for certain types of goods and therefore makes it possible to produce them on a large scale and so to organize production at a lower cost.

Again, says Veblen, this trick we have of putting business men in control results in a continual striving to obtain monopolistic advantages which are highly profitable to the business man who gets them, but which are dangerous from the point of view of the community. Whenever a business man by the arts of advertising or in any other way succeeds in establishing a monopoly, then there is a patent contrast between the real interests of the community and the business interests of the successful monopoly, because monopoly means that the successful monopolist is in a position to exploit purchasers to his own advantage, charge what the traffic will bear and get for himself a large profit while he is preventing the community from getting anything like the supply of goods which modern industrial methods might turn out, at anything like the low cost for which these goods might be purchased were engineers in control.

Again, Veblen points out that modern industry is full of parasitic trades. He contends that the incomes of people who are making money by ways that do not really contribute to men's satisfaction are drawn by way of deduction from incomes of people who produce goods of real value. He observes that the scope of the waste of this sort which is possible at the present time is large, because of the extraordinary productiveness of the machine industry. The business class, he seems always to be on the point of saying, is a set of parasites who are living on the extraordinary productiveness of the engineers. Were it not for the triumphs of modern engineering skill, it would be impossible to support pyramids of business men drawing large incomes and still not themselves participating directly in large measure in the work of organizing production.

This kind of criticism is carried through in considerable detail. One of the most interesting, but also one of the most difficult, is the chapter on The Use of Loan Credit. There Veblen argues that under modern business conditions borrowing increases the volume of business that a business man can do. Thus it enhances his profits and is becoming necessary in competitive trade; everybody is compelled to borrow. He asks, what does borrowing contribute to the process of producing goods? He admits that, in so far as borrowing transfers the control of capital from the hands of people not able or willing to engage in active trade to the hands of people who are both willing and able to do so, borrowing may increase production. But he treats that as a rather minor qualification. For the most part on his view borrowing simply means that a tangled set of financial relationships is heaped on top of the industrial process. There is no addition made to machinery or to the volume of goods; that these interlocking credits produce a situation which every now and then leads to periods of forced financial liquidation.[19] Inasmuch as industry is run not for service but for profit, the periods of forced financial liquidation produce periods of industrial stagnation, unemployment, and so he turns to a theory of business crisis and depressions, one of the most ingenious and beautiful analyses of that fascinating problem which have been produced in recent years.

[Stated more explicitly] "prosperity works its own undoing. The substantial security behind the loans is prospective net earnings capitalized at the current rate of interest. When the rate of interest rises, as it does during prosperity, the capitalized value of a given net income declines, and the loan becomes less safe.[20] More than that, net earnings in many cases, prove less than had been expected in the optimistic days of the nascent boom. Prices cannot be pushed up indefinitely. The costs of doing business rise and encroach upon profits; bank reserves fall and it becomes difficult to get additional credit. When fading profits are added to high interest, creditors become nervous."[21]

Veblen's broad thesis on business cycles is that the value of business enterprise for business purposes is determined by prospective profits; also that the capital value of business enterprises becomes the basis on which credits are extended. Let us begin the analysis, say, at the time when profit margins are fairly liberal. There will be a rapid increase in the volume of borrowing. Hence there is built on the basis of the industrial process of making goods a financial pyramid which is secure so long as nothing occurs to reduce prospective profit margins. But if anything of that sort does occur—and Veblen argues that in the process of prosperity it is inevitable that conditions should be developed which will make something of that sort occur—then business capitalization is in the eyes of the business people revised down-

---

[19] Piercy Ravenstone in his *A Few Doubts as to the Correctness of Some Opinions Generally Entertained on the Subjects of Population and Political Economy* (1821) anticipated Veblen's theory of the loan fund. (Notes for Chapter 4 of "The Classical Economics ms," APP 84-91, no. 62). [The editor made use of Professor Mitchell's extracts in his introductory essay "Piercy Ravenstone and his Radical Tory Treatise," for the 1966 reprint of the work. The editor accepted the current view that "Piercy Ravenstone" is a pen name, but went on to suggest that the author is most likely the Reverend Edward Edwards.]

[20] [Professor Mitchell used the neglect of this point as one of his criticisms] of Lionel [now Baron] Robbins's, *The Great Depression* (1934) "I wish . . . , that Professor Robbins had thought to show how the rise of interest rates at the crest of the boom reacts upon the value of securities pledged as collateral for bank loans, and the capitalized value of prospective earnings. That familiar item of theory would strengthen his case." ("Robbins, *The Great Depression,*" *The Quarterly Journal of Economics,* May 1935, p. 506.)

[21] Mitchell, "Thorstein Veblen," 1936; reprinted in his *The Backward Act of Spending Money,* pp. 307-308.

ward. The prospective profits and therefore capitalization are reduced; that makes creditors uneasy and they proceed to reduce loans. That means starting a process of liquidation. In the process business men have to look primarily to avoiding bankruptcy; it becomes their chief concern for a while. While they are trying to ward off bankruptcy they restrict their commitments, reduce the volume of output, discharge working people and thus undermine the basis on which prosperity has rested. The result is a period of depression from which, on Veblen's view, business will not emerge until a fortunate circumstance from the outside comes along to start the wheels of industry going.

This is a most inadequate sketch of Veblen's criticism of the two institutions which he sees most characteristic of the modern age. It sounds by itself different from the kind of economic discussion with which the lectures heretofore have been dealing. But that is not the most peculiar and the most individual and original part of *The Theory of Business Enterprise,* for after having exploited through the greater part of the volume the lack of harmony between the fundamental economic interest in continuous industry and the process of making goods and the present institutional primacy of business enterprise, the process of making money—Veblen asks how long will the present curious institutional situation continue? That leads him to consider the cultural incidence of the machine process and of business enterprise. There again he finds diverting differences to exploit.

It is at this point that the novelty of Veblen's conception of functional psychology comes out most clearly. In talking about the future, speculating concerning how men are going to behave in reference to the making of goods and the making of money in generations to come, Veblen does not speak of the economic interests of the several classes, as do the writers we have so far examined when they face similar problems. Bentham or Jevons would have discoursed about the pleasures or pains which the wage-earning classes and the profit-making classes get from the situation as it is at present. If they thought that the wage-earning classes were dissatisfied they would explain their dissatisfaction on some such ground. Or if it were a Marshall or Fetter who is dealing with the matter, he would talk about gratifications and sacrifices. Veblen, however, talks about the habits of mind which are inculcated by the two great groups of occupations which he contrasts. His psychology is that of William James, who exploits the factor of habit far more than the psychology of Bentham or the people who tried to turn Bentham's view of human nature into language which is acceptable to moderns.

Veblen argues that the people who are continuously engaged in business traffic come to have a set of standards for judging what is right and proper in the world at large very different in character from the standards by which those who are engaged in the machine process judge the world. The people in pecuniary work are always inclined to think about their rights. It is a matter of human right, running back as a rule to notions about natural rights—such notions as Bentham and his particular group talk about freely at the time of the French Revolution and the American Revolution: the natural rights of man, and the whole system of legal practices and precedents built up upon the doctrine of natural rights; a view that appears frequently enough in the economics treatises, for instance in *The Wealth of Nations*.

On the other hand, says Veblen, the people who are engaged in working machinery come to think of things not in terms of natural rights but in terms of cause and effect. The machine tenders are a much more material set of people. They do not understand the fine-spun doctrines of natural rights because they get into a frame of mind where they cannot understand anything unless they are shown that it has a cause of a material sort behind it. For a person to talk to them about precedents is almost vain, because they have no background which fits them for understanding his opinion. They cannot enter into his preconceptions. It does not matter to them much what the fathers of the American Constitution wanted; the question is, is the present situation satisfactory; if not, why cannot some way be invented of making it meet the people's wants?

The difference in viewpoint is most clearly illustrated by the difference in the attitudes of a conventional lawyer on the one hand and a narrowly trained engineering specialist on the other. And you know how impractical a person an engineer is likely to be from the point of view of the lawyer; how impractical he is likely to be from the point of view of anyone not interested in mechanics; how little understanding he is likely to show of human nature! And you know also, of course, how troublesome and altogether futile a person a lawyer is likely to be in the eyes of an engineer who has a practical problem of reorganization of industry he wants to put over. The two do not understand each other; each shows primarily the effects of long addiction to a particular set of activities that have given his mind a certain way of looking at everything, a way which works beautifully for his purposes and badly for other purposes than his own. I will ask a few questions to bring out clearly the distinction.

M:[22] What are the psychological products of the use of machinery, S4?

S4: I haven't gone so far.

M: What are they S1?

S1: Calculating accuracy and the spirit of the scientific practice, putting together causes and effect to produce the economic product. Those are the two. Those really go together, the accuracy and the productivity.

M: Veblen thinks that a man who uses machinery day by day gets into the habit of asking in terms of cause and effect, of expecting very definitely that things are going to run in a regular fashion, not counting on all sorts of miraculous interventions to help out when things get into a fix, not taking a romantic view of life, but rather being a realist in the literary sense of the term in his attitude toward social questions at large. That habitual propensity to think in terms of cause and effect, Veblen holds, leads people to question a great many institutions which a large section of the community, and which particularly our grandfathers if not our fathers, took more or less on trust. The workingmen who have been most thoroughly exposed to the discipline of the machine process, Veblen says, are likely to be found skeptical, unmoral, undevout, questioning unreasoning patriotism, asking in general uncomfortable questions which those of us who live in a conventional world find it difficult to answer and still more emphatically find it very annoying to be asked at all. That then is the great outstanding cultural result of day-by-day use of machinery, according to Veblen: that it begets in the people who run it these habits of thinking rather exactly in terms of cause and effect, and doubting beliefs that cannot have a good causal explanation advanced for them. Over against this frame of mind Veblen puts the frame of mind begotten by business enterprise. What is the character of the daily concern with making money, S2? What influence does that have on the mind?

S2: Very decidedly a rationalistic point of view.

M: Rationalistic in what sense?

S2: In the sense of calculations for self interest. Similarly, it seems to me, cause and effect calculations but cause and effect in terms of money instead of in terms of sequence.

M: Yes, the great weapon of business enterprise of course is ac-

---

22 Beginning of extract from "1918 Typescript."

counting. That is the means by which we keep our business affairs in order. You employ people by paying them money. You get materials by purchase for money. You provide your plant by the investment of capital and capital is a pecuniary category, and you reckon success or failure by what appears on the balance sheet, profit or loss, don't you? What about cause and effect in accountancy? Is that in place there?

S2: There would be mathematical difficulties.

M: Accountancy is really a mathematical matter, isn't it? Primarily? Does cause and effect play an important role in mathematics?

S2: It depends upon what you mean by cause and effect. That's where I had difficulty with Veblen's analysis.

M: That is a very pertinent query. What does Veblen mean by cause and effect when he is talking about the cultural incidence of the machine process?

S2: The cause and effect in the machine process is simply interdependence, is the close connection between one phase and another phase of it, a matter of the relation between one machine and another machine and the various items of connection. That's something more than space and time connection, but is inherent in the situation, that gives something like interstitial connection.

M: You are thinking about interstitial adjustments. That is a slightly different matter. What Veblen has in mind here is characteristic of all of our thinking about mechanical processes, is a sort of physical causation. It is like the notion about one billiard ball moving because another billiard ball strikes it. That is an impact at which a certain effect follows. Veblen often speaks of opaque, mechanical causation. Is there anything corresponding to that present in accounting, in mathematics?

S2: No.

M: No, there is not really, is there? You speak of cause in geometry, for instance. Why is it that the sum of the angles of a triangle equal two right angles? Is there any cause at work there?

S2: Existing set of relationships.

M: Yes, it is a matter of consistency among a considerable number of logical propositions, isn't it, all deduced from certain axioms with which you start? Granted a certain number of original statements into the validity of which you will not inquire, these consequences follow by logical necessity. Our feeling about all that is something very different from our feeling about the kind of mechanical causation which appears in working machinery, isn't it? Accountancy is primarily mathematical and very little mechanical, isn't it? The relationships which appear in a series of accounts are much more closely analogous to the relationships that appear in one of the branches of mathematics than they are to the relationships which appear in any of the processes of manufacture. The people who are giving their days primarily to problems of business management, who are controlling things in terms of the balance sheet, accordingly fall into a very different habit of thinking from that which is characteristic of the man who works with machinery, a habit of mind which is characterised by thinking in terms of logical consistency, consistency with a few unquestioned propositions that stand as fundamental principles. What are the fundamental principles upon which modern accountancy, business enterprise in general, rest, S7?

S7: I don't know that I see just what you mean. Do you mean what is the basic principle?

M: What is the basic principle of business enterprise, S3?

S3: The basic principle would be a pecuniary calculus, the summing up of all values in pecuniary terms.

M: That summing up rests on one important underlying idea. What is that, S2?

S2: Private property.

M: The right of private property and its various corollaries such as the right to return on the investment of capital. What has begotten this curious notion of the right of property in modern life, S11? Why do we believe that property is a right?

S11: According to Veblen it is largely a matter of habit.

M: All our beliefs are a matter of habit according to Veblen. What has begotten this particular habit? How does he explain it?

S11: You mean how it has happened to be derived?

M: Veblen's explanation of the prevalence of any habit is in exactly those terms of how it has been derived. Where has it come from? What has produced it?

S11: I remember he goes into an historical explanation of how this idea of property was developed, through the idea of natural rights, and how the fundamental idea arose. In early times man makes goods out of his labor, and he is thus entitled to keep what he makes and do whatever he pleases with it. This is his original idea.

M: S11, whatever made people believe that curious thing that they are entitled to the proceeds of their labor, that that with which their labor is mixed is their own? How did Veblen account for that?

S11: Isn't that his belief?

M: Let us see if S3 has that account of the prevalence of the institution of ownership more clearly in mind.

S3: He accounts for this idea of private property a good deal in the same way that has been indicated. That is to say, there was a time in the simpler scheme of economic relationships between men in a given society where it was thought nothing out of the way to have what you made. In the rather simpler isolated economy where people earned their living by their own labor, the capital goods or the property was so insignificant an item in the productive process that nobody ever thought that it amounted to anything. The main productive factor was labor. Gradually, however, with the development of technology—at that time property was just recognized according to Veblen as a property right—with the gradual development of technology and ways and means of production, a control over the factors of production was taken over, simply carried over from the early time, in spite of the fact that property, the capital goods, became more and more important and labor became less and less important, so that now we are at a time when any control over these means of production has the laborer at its mercy, whereas in the first place it didn't count for a great deal.

M: That is, Veblen accounts, as S11 says, for the prevalence of this idea in terms of its origin, how it has been derived and he goes back to a certain starting point. The point where he starts with this particular account is the theory presented by John Locke, [in *Two Treatises Concerning Government*, 1690] not because this was the beginning of it all, but because that is as far back as it is necessary to push the inquiry. Locke explained property on the basis of labor, and what Veblen does is to show how that idea, as it prevailed in Locke's day, has undergone alterations until it has grown into the very different form that it has today. At our next meeting I shall want to come back to the discussion at this point.

In discussing further Veblen's disquisition on the cultural incidence of the machine process as contrasted with the cultural discipline of business enterprise, I should like, by way of introduction, to read again an excerpt from C. E. Ayres's article "The Epistemological Significance of Social Psychology." It shows how a social psychologist looks at precisely the bit of speculation which we have been discussing.

> Probably the work of the economist, Thorstein Veblen, is the weightiest contribution which has yet been made to the science of social psychology—as it is here defined. Not only might every one of his five books be classified as the systematic study of the social psychology beneath a selected group of social arrangements, but it

will be some time before better social psychology is written than his discussion of "the cultural incidence of the machine process" in *The Theory of Business Enterprise,* or his analysis of the nature and the sources of the spirit of belligerent patriotism which is both the cause and the result of the perpetuation of war, in *The Nature of Peace.*

It is to work such as that of Veblen, therefore, that one must turn if one wishes to note the characteristics of social psychology as it is going to be written in the future. For whatever the merits of that work may be, it represents an actual essay in the field which social psychologists are coming to recognize as their own, but which they themselves have not yet begun to work. An examination of this actual and accomplished social psychology reveals the fact that the great problems of society center about the major contradictions in the currents of thought and prejudice which are diffused through the minds of different groups and classes of people.

Then he goes on:

I want to read the last sentence again because it is particularly important.

An examination of this actual and accomplished social psychology reveals the fact that the great problems of society center about the major contradictions in the currents of thought and prejudice which are diffused through the minds of different groups and classes of people.

The great crises of history seem to be the points at which contradictory lines of influence, which have spread from incompatible phases of the social order to the different economic and political classes, have come into sharp conflict. Out of such conflict between groups whose whole way of thinking is antagonistic there come changes into the status of one group with respect to the others, or in the technique of production or of social observance, that alter the entire mental background of the members of those groups.

Ayres is saying that exactly the kind of conflict between habits of thought among different groups, which Veblen has analysed under the caption of the Cultural Incidence of the Machine Process and The Cultural Incidence of Business Enterprise, is responsible for the great crises in social history. That is to say, Ayres holds that this is material which is accounting for the factors which are of prime significance in determining the larger events in the history of societies. He goes on: "Take, as the most beautiful example available, the conflict between bourgeois satisfaction with the existing order of economic arrangements and the growing proletarian impatience with the whole system of private property and the private appropriation of interest and rent."

Then he quotes from *The Theory of Business Enterprise* (pp. 343-344) as follows:

The question of equity or inequity in the distribution of wealth presumes the validity of ownership rights on some basis or other, or at least it presumes the validity of some basis on which the claims of ownership may be discussed. Ownership is the major premise of any argument as to the equity of distribution, and it is this major premise that is being forgotten by the classes among whom socialistic sentiment is gaining. Equity in this connection seems not to belong to the repertory of socialist concepts. It is at this point—the point of a common ground of argument—that the discrepancy occurs which stands in the way, not only of an eventual agreement between the socialists and their conservative critics, but even of their meeting one another's reasoning with any substantial effect. In the equipment of common-sense ideas on the basis of which the conservatives reason on this matter, there is included the conventional article of ownership, as a prime fact; in the common-sense basis of socialistic thinking this conventional premise has no secure place. There is, therefore, a discrepancy in respect of the metaphysics underlying the knowledge and reasoning of the two parties to the controversy, and the outlook for a common understanding is accordingly vain. No substantial agreement upon a point of knowledge or conviction is possible between persons who proceed from disparate preconceptions.

Then Ayres resumes his own discourse:

Now the contribution of the social psychologist—in this case Professor Veblen—to the resolution of this controversy is the analysis of the social background of the conflicting groups for the causes of those "disparate preconceptions" which are the "common-sense basis" of the antagonistic convictions of the two parties. For we can never claim to control the reconstruction of our social arrangements until we understand something of the social nature of the main currents of thought and feeling which are the dynamic factors that are forcing reconstruction. That is to say, the function of social psychology (or of this type of social psychology under some other appellation) is to discover in the social environment of a given group or individual the causes and the limitations of "the peculiar acquired dispositions, sets and attitudes" which taken together constitute that group or individual. But this is the investigation of the sources and limits of knowledge—that is to say, it is epistemology.[23]

I read that passage primarily to show what a social psychologist sees in a discussion of the sort in which we have been engaged.

What use does Veblen make of his two analyses, one purporting to show the habit of mind which dealing with machinery begets, the other purporting to show the habit of mind which continual work in the counting house begets. Veblen discusses of course these two things separately. By themselves they would be interesting, but he does not stop with the discussion. He makes some use of it. He thinks that the difference in the two habits of mind is a matter of very great

---

[23] *The Journal of Philosophy, Psychology and Scientific Methods,* April 11, 1918, pp. 40-42.

consequence for the future of society. What use does he make of that analysis, S4?

S4: I am sorry I cannot tell.

M: Have you read the book, S8? What use does Veblen make of that contrast?

S8: He makes a sharp contrast between those two classes of people. His conclusion is that those engaged in the machine process are really deteriorating as far as thought is concerned, as far as mentality is concerned.

M: Is that the impression the discussion makes on you, S2?

S2: No. It makes exactly the reverse impression; that is, Mr. Veblen is contending that it actually makes for increased logical character of thought of the workman.

I would like to raise an objection right here in regard to that point because it seems to me that taking the whole discussion from the point of view of Mr. Veblen's method, his argument ought logically to lead to the reverse, because the director of industry is the dynamic factor that has control. Why should not that impress a consciousness on him of cause as agent instead of cause in mechanical terms? Why should not the machine process impose a mechanical habit of thought on the workingman, any workingman, for the static point of view rather than the dynamic point of view? In other words, Schumpeter spends a separate book on the entrepreneur as a dynamic factor. It seems to me that you get the same type of analysis. Using that same type of analysis you can set up those two possible different interpretations of the habits of thought that ought to result, and I don't see that Mr. Veblen actually proves that, for instance, the great mass are becoming unpatriotic, in particular more undevout.

M: Yes, materialistic, skeptical, unpatriotic, undevout. S2, your suggestion is a very interesting one. We will come back to it in a moment, but first let us try to make clear to ourselves what Veblen's notion of this contrast is. S8 got the impression from reading the book that in Veblen's eyes the cultural incidence of the machine process is to reduce the mental efficiency of the working people. You get the impression on the contrary that it is to train those people in more scientific habits of thought so that they, if I understand you correctly, become logically more capable than the people who are concerned with this trifling matter of business enterprise. Which one of these interpretations is correct, S5?

S5: Veblen says that there are those who believe that it makes the workman less efficient to fall into habits of standardization, more inefficient because of the mechanical nature of that habit of thinking. Veblen does not hold to that. It seems to me that what he was trying to prove was that the business men, because they were not under this rigid standardization, were getting more in the habit of thought than the others, were getting another habit of thought, and Veblen seemed to think unless something came in to change or merge the two, that in itself constitutes a great problem. But he thinks the mass of business enterprisers are not subject to all that rigid mechanical discipline. He proves that, in my judgment, from the first page where he says, for example, that these matters of business enterprise are thinking of profit in terms of rate per unit which is logical in itself.

M: You see that what Veblen is undertaking to argue is that a different habit of mind, of thinking, is produced in the two classes. Which class does he hold is turned out the better mental product?

S5: The masters of business enterprise.

M: That is to say, you agree with S8 that on his showing the intellectual discipline given by business enterprise is superior. Let us ask the class again how the matter stands in Veblen's eyes.

S9: It seems to me that he doesn't come to the final conclusion as to whether the machine process does or does not cause a deterioration in the workingman's mind. His discussion is pro and con. But what he does say is that by virtue of the turn of mind that they get in the machine process, they become antagonistic to the accepted order of things; that the business enterprise tends to conservatism, tends to rely upon pressure and convention and therefore is conservative, and that the machine turn of mind is in the opposite direction to the businessman's turn of mind, the basis on which society at present is constituted.

M: Does Veblen say anything about the relative superiority of one habit of mind to the other? Which does he think is the better?

S1: He discusses which of the two things is likely to win and considers that probably the machine process will win, because we must have its goods. He does not discuss which is the better.

M: Absolutely not, absolutely not. He tells you what the habit of mind is which each kind of daily vocation begets in the people who have to follow it. Readers may readily be misled, if they follow conventional habits of thought, into thinking that the adjectives which he applies connote superiority or inferiority. It may be in their eyes, for instance, a most unfortunate result that men who are using machinery tend to become sceptical, materialistic, unpatriotic, undevout.

Perhaps they do not like it. Veblen does not have anything to say as to whether it is commendable or unfortunate. It is simply there as one of the fundamental cultural results of the situation. You may think it unfortunate that the work of the counting house tends, if Veblen is right, to support all the conventional inherited ideas about property, etc., and in that case you may think, as apparently S2 does, that the people who are running the machinery get a better habit of thought. Again Veblen applies the notion, but he does not express an opinion whether one is better than the other or not.

S2: By "better" I don't mean superior except in the sense that Veblen seemed to conceive that the workingman's habit of thought was the more logical, the more effective, the more characteristic of the present situation.

M: It is more logical in terms of what? In terms of cause and effect. Is it more logical in the sense in which a lawyer reasons, for instance? Veblen says that the working classes have great difficulty in understanding the attitude of the courts. There they are mentally weak. Why are they mentally weak? It is because, according to Veblen, their type and habit of thinking runs in different terms. That habit of mind may be more scientific in the sense that it is rather more analogous to the habit of thought which is characteristic of men who deal with the physical sciences. It is probably less logical in the sense of the problems which are dealt with by the theologian and the lawyer. It has less sense for the nice differences between institutions, for the implications of broad institutional principles. It is not that one is better than the other in Veblen's eyes, but they are different in a way that produces an inevitable conflict between them.

Let us now take up the suggestion that S2 made. On Veblen's basis, the working classes who get disciplined by the machine process are the dynamic factor in society, whereas he represented the business man as conservative and therefore relatively static. What appears in fact, argues S2, if the investigator thinks the thing out for himself independently without being unduly imposed upon by the writer, is that he will find that the business man is, in modern society, as Schumpeter has undertaken to prove, the dynamic factor. He is the man who makes new combinations, who controls, so that Veblen ought to have represented the factor of business enterprise as dynamic, and the rather slow going cause and effect habit of mind, characteristic of the working class, as static. What is the class's reaction to that analysis?

S3: That is largely a question of fact, but Veblen has a very good case there, if one follows closely his analysis of the development especially of the business situation. Take a very common illustration of the development of banks. In their banking houses the larger investment bankers have had, in the last quarter of a century, to change and to modify their habits of mind to fit into the new industrial and technological development. They have to consult engineers, industrial chemists, etc. They have to take their advice. Of course they have to become dynamic, but they have been forced to become dynamic. They are not the original force. The original force is in the machine, perhaps it would be more accurate to say that it isn't so much the machine as the technological situation. That is a clear case of which comes first and which follows.

M: What would you say to that, S2?

S2: I question Veblen's identification of the technological advance with the great mass of workers. I don't see how he can claim it is the workingmen who have accomplished that advance.

M: Veblen does not make any such claim, does he? He does not declare that these machine workers are the people who have been primarily responsible for the fundamental technological improvements. On the contrary if he did discuss the thing in *The Theory of Business Enterprise,* one would expect to find him coming to the conclusion that the chief factor in the industrial advance has been scientific research, that this scientific research, however, the habit of mind which it represents, is itself, if traced back far enough, largely the result of a certain institutional development of an industrial order in England, that owing to the curious consequences of the English situation for a considerable period of time, there was an opportunity for people who had peculiar abilities in that kind of thinking to develop scientific interest and researches, and that this scientific habit of mind reacting on the industrial situation in the midst of which it arose, began that great process of technological improvement which is known as the Industrial Revolution.

Since that time the two things have grown together. The lead, particularly at present, in process of invention is with highly trained men who approach their tasks with the advantages not only of the native ingenuity which used to be typical, for instance of the Yankee backwoods farmer, but added to that a thoroughgoing training in mathematics, mechanics, chemistry and/or other sciences. They are the people nowadays who have charge of running the extremely elaborate machine process. It is the engineer type rather than the working man himself. So that if one understands Veblen's position correctly, he does not hold that the people who are operating the machines themselves are forcing the pace of advance so far as technological improvements are concerned. He mentions on the other hand that the habit of mind which is created in these operators is in itself a changing social factor of fundamental significance.

Veblen does not take the view that the business man is a passive factor in the present social situation. Quite the contrary, Veblen magnifies his role. I remember once asking him before *The Theory of Business Enterprise* was published, what he was going to call it and in his humorous way—this was a time when a series of new romantic novels had just been published and were selling by the hundred thousand, so that everybody was talking about the success of Mary Johnson and Winston Churchill[24]—Veblen said that he was going to call it "The Captain of Industry, A Romance." That represented the book. The hero was a captain of industry. He was writing about the deeds of this magnificent person. The captain of industry is, in Veblen's eyes, the man who determines the fortunes of society as matters go. He is the man who forms the organizations, who decides what shall be done. He may be conservative in a sense, but he runs society in the present day. In contrast with that viewpoint the workingman is a rather passive creature.

These are two different viewpoints. A moment ago I was talking about a certain habit of mind. Now I am talking about the activities of a certain class in the situation at the present time. The habit of mind begotten by handling machinery is, in Veblen's eyes, a factor which is particularly important because it is gaining at the present time in weight and extent. The business man on the other hand, despite all his activity, is a man who from the cultural point of view is holding to the past conventions of the order which we have inherited. That is to say, he is standing for a conservative social organization, whereas the fruits, or, if you like, the victims of the machine process are demanding social change. To talk of the problem in terms of statics and dynamics almost inevitably leads one to a misapprehension of the analysis. Those terms are in any case dubious metaphors when used in economics. They have been responsible for a great deal of confusion. The theorist will understand Veblen's point of view a great deal better if he keeps thinking of habits of mind as factors which are present in the situation and always undergoing some changes.

Even the habit of mind of the conservative class, as S2 remarks,

---

[24] [Not the English statesman].

are by no means fixed and stable. They are changing in the sense that the business situation which has to be managed is continually changing. The habit of mind of the working classes, as Veblen sees it, is changing, and the changes are of particular social significance for the immediate future, because ever larger proportions of the population are likely to become machine tenders as the years go on; that is to say, provided no other catastrophic changes come in to alter present tendencies; and not only will there be a larger number of these people who get the discipline of the machine process, but they also will get that discipline in a more unremitting fashion. That is to say, there will gradually form an increasing number of communities in a great country like the United States, that have the general character of the old machine districts in England, or the oldest seats of machine manufacture in Germany.[25]

Veblen, to repeat, thinks that modern society with its differentiating of the inhabitants into the classes that are making goods and those that are making money is building up two sets of people who are failing to understand each other, and the longer such a civilization continues, the further civilization is pushed along current lines, the deeper will become the rift within the body politic, the more serious the misunderstanding. The working classes, broadly speaking, are becoming incapable of understanding what to many of the more conventionally minded and thoroughly trained members of the community seem the finest flowers of past civilization; the working classes are becoming skeptical, unmoral, matter of fact, unpatriotic, materialistic. All the features of civilization which are not obviously to be justified upon a causal basis come to be hard for them to comprehend. Among the things which it is most difficult to understand from the viewpoint of cause and effect is the justification of the scheme of ownership, of

---

[25] End of extract from "1918 Typescript."

Economics remained vague and general as long as it assumed uniformity of human nature. Ricardo did not—his three classes; Marshall has "city men" and ordinary people; Schumpeter's innovators and routineers; Veblen's occupational differences; Marx's class differences. Is it not possible to substitute a classification based upon more fundamental differences established by scientific investigation? At least starting with that and then recognizing differences produced by culture, occupation, economic status and economic interest. For what purposes do these differences count? Demand schedule: if taken simply as statement of what people will buy remains unchanged. But if we try to explain those schedules, or discover their shifts, through advertising, etc., do not. Supply schedules do not on same understanding. But they do if we go back to the conditions which limit supply of different factors. ("Requirements of a Treatise on Economics," APP 44-53, no. 36).

What difference does Veblen see between psychology of business man and operatives? Contrast with Marshall's remarks in *The Principles of Economics* on "city man" [the man of the financial district of London] versus the mass of the population. ("Veblen," APP 44-53, no. 18).

exploitation of ownership for gain, in short, the institution of business enterprise.

Thus business enterprise is in a particular and a very interesting situation. It thrives on industry and can thrive only on industry of the machine process type, because that is the only way of organizing efforts which provide a sufficiently wide margin for business enterprise to waste. Business enterprise rests fundamentally upon the machine process; but the machine process turns its devotees into people who simply cannot understand the justification for business enterprise and they turn socialist; they question the legitimacy of the present organization of society and fall easily for the seductive words of any prophet who tells them he has invented some new method of social organization under which it will be possible for all men who are workers to work toward the satisfaction of each other's wants and to cut entirely out of the picture the supernumerary business man whose chief function is to obstruct the work of the engineer.

In Veblen's view business enterprise makes a very large class of industrial wage-earners indispensable. But also the duties of these people make it impossible for them to see things from the business man's viewpoint. The consequence is a state of things incompatible with the long continuance of business enterprise. Having brought that out, Veblen asks what is the remedy; and he considers, as noted before, philanthropy which he characterizes as "an excursion into pragmatic romance"—one of his lively phrases. Philanthropy may do a little bit to prevent the widening of the gulf between people who take the business and the industrial view of social problems, but only a little. What is needed is a business remedy; and Veblen discusses what business can do to offset the drift of the working classes toward socialism. He comes to the conclusion that this is not an enterprise which is likely to yield much profit consequently it cannot be operated on a business basis.

There is, he concludes finally, only one remedy which seems adequate to close the chasm that is opening in the ranks of modern society; namely, a program of warlike activity. But, he says, even that remedy is likely to prove dangerous, because countries which go in for warlike enterprise are awakening instincts which are far older even than the instinct of workmanship which is so characteristic of the modern industrial working classes, or the instinct of acquisition which prevails in the business ranks. More than that, war is likely to increase the economic wastes of social life to an extent which exceeds even those of the modern machine process under the prevailing system. It is likely to increase waste to such an extent as to be fatal to business enterprise itself. If that is the only adequate remedy and that remedy if adopted is likely to prove fatal, Veblen concludes that the prospects are that the regime of business enterprise will not be a long one. That interesting institution he thinks is doomed to pass in the not distant future, to be superseded by the development of industrial interests among the wage earners, unless it is sunk in the same type of general social ruin that followed the Thirty Years War, which he thought at the time not unlikely.

S: What are the prevalent opinions concerning Veblen?

M: It depends, to repeat, upon the quarters to which one goes. There is a set of opinions to the effect that Veblen is a dangerous kind of agitator who knows nothing about science. That represents one extreme. There is also the opinion that he is by all odds the most original and serious student of economics in his time. The majority of opinions lie somewhere in between. I am inclined to think that he has influenced the younger men much more than the older men. Many people think that the institutional viewpoint is one which promises very valuable scientific results. Whether Veblen's work will prove of permanent constructive value remains to be seen. He certainly has brought into the range of economics a set of problems which, though not entirely neglected by the more conventional writers, has never been exploited with anything like the skill which Veblen reveals. Of course his work is likely to be deprecated by people who are offended by some of his mannerisms—people who dislike some of his opinions. He has so little of the academic about him that he is *persona non grata* to a great many of his professional colleagues. Then too, he has such a queer alien approach to all these problems. He does not seem to be much interested in them except as intellectual puzzles.

I think that one difficulty in the way of Veblen's wider and prompter recognition by economists is his attitude as a critic—not disputing opinions, but taking people apart to see why they work as they do. He looks at his colleagues as curious museum specimens, wanting not to show that they are wrong but to give some plausible account of what has made them what they are. Of course temperamentally he is as much a man of letters as he is an inquirer; he is a satirist and has been called the greatest satirist since Laurence Sterne.[26] Some people are very much offended by his satirical attitude.

---

[26] [Sterne, a clergyman, is best known for the multi-volume *Tristram Shandy*.]

[Let me elaborate.][27] He was a man, who has been, I should say, more misunderstood than any other American economist of his day and misunderstood primarily because of his highly original temperament as well as because of his highly original turn of mind. The two things go together. Veblen is a great humorist and people who do not have a very keen sense of humor almost always misunderstand his books. He is the kind of humorist who gives no intimation aside from the genuine humorous contents of his remarks that he has intended to perpetrate a joke. Of course jokes are rare in American economic treatises. American economists have no expectation of meeting anything of that sort in each other's pages unless by way of some perfunctory remarks in an address to be read before the American Economic Association, so that even the unwary are not likely to be caught napping. But in his books there is a great deal of the satirical, the humorous, which a person, who is reading Veblen for the first time, stubs his toe against and feels correspondingly discomfited. The reader has to have really a very keen sense of humor himself to realize that a great many of his sesquipedalian sentences are really a peculiar way of presenting foibles of his own, or foibles which, if the reader cannot recognize in himself, he will recognize, after a little thought, in people whom he knows and does not like.

Beside this humor, Veblen has been misunderstood because of the very peculiar character of his interest in economic theory. Of course, we have in the United States, in fact in all countries where economics is cultivated, a great deal of controversy and theorists are very much in the habit of finding their particular doctrines disputed by other eminent authorities. No offense is taken by and large at the ordinary kind of technical criticism. Veblen as a critic has written in a way that is probably more formally courteous than the majority of the economists who have handled each other in a critical fashion. But his criticisms usually offended people because they puzzled them, and they have puzzled people because he has not been interested in the letter of economic doctrine. His general attitude has not been that of showing that this, that or the other point of doctrine was a mistake, but to show that it does not very much matter whether this, that or the other particular point of doctrine is right or wrong, that [much of current] economic theory as a whole is not so much right or wrong, as it is beside the point, that the real, the important economic problems, the things that are genuinely interesting from the intellectual point of view, had not been discussed. Of course, that is puzzling, par-

---

[27] Beginning of extract from "1918 Typescript."

ticularly to a person who does not feel the conviction of sin, who accepts current economic theory as a matter of very great practical importance, of great intellectual interest, and does not grasp the standpoint of the critic who is trying to show that, when we get a genuinely scientific interest in our socio-economic problems, we are going to concern ourselves with a range of inquiries which lie altogether outside the ordinary orthodox treatises.

What has been true about Veblen's critical studies also applies to his constructive work. He has dealt with problems which do not find a recognized place in pure theory, in such catholic conclusions as Marshall's economics or in such extremely wide reaching undertakings as Schmoller's sample of historical economics. He has found a group of problems which are more or less his own and his attempt to furnish solutions for them has not met with wide understanding or appreciation, just because people have not yet learned the importance of the problems themselves. Worst of all and most disconcerting is his uncanny attitude toward questions of ethics. Of course there are people in economics who take the ground that the economist, if he is going to be a scientific man, ought not to concern himself in the least with questions of right and wrong. This is a good orthodox viewpoint which is held by many people and disputed by many others and so stands in about the same position as most other points in economic theory. Veblen had a good deal to say about things that are right and wrong in the sense that he is much interested in what people think is right and wrong, in trying to display current notions of what is befitting or unbefitting, but he never takes these notions seriously except as problems; that is to say, he is not trying to show what is good or bad policy, but he is attempting to understand the curious notions that prevail among us regarding what had better not be done.

To most of us it is extremely uncomfortable, not to be contradicted, but to be taken apart in order to find out what makes us work in such a curious fashion, and that is substantially Veblen's attitude toward mankind. He regards modern civilized man as an extremely interesting product of a very complex situation and he wants to understand how this curious product has been made. To do that he studies primarily what he calls the cultural incidence of the great social economic institutions, tries to show what habits of mind those institutions beget among the people who practice them. That is to say, he is trying to account for ourselves, including even our most sacred and strongly held propositions of an ethical character. That means that he is dealing with problems that most of us do not recognize the existence of, and that even when we do we are in the habit of solving them in a radically different way. We do not think of our ideas of right and wrong ordinarily as having been made in us by any given set of causal factors, but we think of them as principles which we recognize by right of reason.

To look upon them after all as matters of the same sort as certain superstitions, for instance, that prevail among savage tribes, is, to people who have not had any experience in that kind of inquiry, often a very disagreeable one, so that many a person in reading one of Veblen's books has found himself, or herself, badly shocked, has gotten into a frame of mind where they either could not go on reading, or could not go on reading in a frame of mind which allowed them to understand what is being said. I think that more than anything else accounts for the fact that this extremely penetrating theorist has, until recent years [1918]—at least the last two or three, had comparatively little recognition outside a very small circle of people, who, largely for personal reasons, have understood what he is doing, better than the great majority.

In particular, I think it is fair to say that practically all the graduate students in economics who have come under Veblen's influence have felt his extraordinary power and have been inclined to attach a great deal of importance to the problems which he has seen more clearly than his contemporaries; also to the solutions, at least to some of the solutions which he has provided. But it is not until a man has had a considerable education of a rather unorthodox sort that he begins to see the real significance either of the problems or of the solutions that are offered, and it has only been recently that there has been any considerable number of people interested in economics who have gotten a sufficient glimmering of these problems and their importance to give Veblen anything more than a sort of esoteric recognition.

Veblen and his disconcerting insights. Taught us [at the University of Chicago] to look at [dominant] economic theory as a curiosity. Real problem is how reasonable men could think such notions plausible or important.[27a]

I hope that one of the things we may accomplish in our discussion is to help us all to understand clearly what Veblen is up to. Whether one agrees or not with this particular type of economic theory is, I suppose, not a matter of very profound significance, but as intelligent

---

[27a] Outline, "Prospects of Economic Theory," informal talk at University of Chicago, March 14, 1925.

students of present day economics, I think it is very desirable that we should all try to overcome the initial difficulties of understanding what the man is about, and try to view this very particular, highly flavored, intellectual product with calmness, not getting unduly excited over the writer's mannerisms or unduly frightened by the conclusions to which he seems to be conducting us.[28]

Veblen's standing among economists: His peculiar brand of satirical humor often misunderstood; what is with him a piece of fun is likely to be taken as a parade of long words. As critic he has dealt not with technical details of doctrine but with larger aspects of a more fundamental kind. Unfamiliar ground for economists. Knocks the underpinning from beneath much of current economic theorizing Has both puzzled and offended many. He has argued not so much that current economic theory is wrong as that it does not matter whether right or wrong. The really important problems of economic life lie outside the realm of orthodox theory. His constructive work lies largely outside the recognized beat of orthodoxy. Many economists have felt that it did not concern them whether true or false. His interest has widened to include "inquiry into the nature and cause of the growth of institutions," as he states in *The Instinct of Workmanship and the State of the Industrial Arts*. Institutions are prevalent habits of thought.

Veblen's treatment of questions of what ought to be done is disconcerting. His interest in such questions is not to discuss what is right and what is wrong, or what is expedient, but to account for the curious fact that we at the present time believe certain things to be right and to inquire how and why our beliefs are changing. When he takes us apart to see how we work, we do not enjoy the process. It is more pleasant to have our opinions disputed than explained as curiosities.

The Theory of Business Enterprise is an example of his constructive work. Monographic as contrasted with systematic character of other books that we have studied. But deals with what Veblen conceives to be the leading differential of modern economic situation. General aim of book as stated in preface is an "inquiry into the nature, causes, utility and further drift of business enterprise."

Digest of subjects treated in *The Theory of Business Enterprise:* Chapter I. Modern economic life characterized by machine process and business enterprise. Since latter controls the former, "the specifically modern economic phenomena" must be approached from the business man's viewpoint. (In 1923 he wrote in *Absentee Ownership* "absentee ownership has come to be the main and immediate controlling interest in the life of civilized men.") Chapter II. Machine process requires interstitial adjustments which are made by business transactions. Chapter III. Business enterprise does not secure management of industrial equipment in way most serviceable to community (making money and making goods). Chapter IV. Business principles are based on ownership which now has an impersonal

---

[28] End of extract from "1918 Typescript."

pecuniary cast. Ownership—property—valued in terms of money. Property is acquired not as much by labor as by investment at a profit. Chapter V. Loan credit does not increase productive equipment but does increase business capitalization. Corporation financiering has like effect. Chapter VI. Modern business corporation is capitalized at putative earning capacity. Puts control over industrial equipment into hands of men whose primary interest is traffic in capital, not prosperity of their corporation, let alone social serviceability of industry. Chapter VII. The Theory of Modern Welfare. Prosperity, crisis, depression are caused by modern business enterprise. Depression is chronic under the system. Only real remedy is ever wider coalition to control competition. Chapter VIII. Business Principles in Law and Politics. Law based on natural rights including free contract. Such "rights" no longer protect the working man. Politics managed for business prosperity. Popular consent obtained by patriotism and illusion that increase of property is increase of national wealth. Chapter IX. The Cultural Incidence of the Machine Process (an illustration of Veblen's working theory of human nature). Machine process inculcates habit of thought which is skeptical, matter of fact, materialistic, unmoral, unpatriotic, undevout. Chapter X. This influence undermines business enterprise. Only radical remedy is warlike politics. But that undermines natural rights—which are basis of business enterprise. Latter thus seems doomed.

What phases of economic theory does the book discuss? Primarily the activity of the larger business men in trying to make money out of the traffic in capital; i.e., reorganizing business enterprises, buying and selling securities. On what materials does Veblen base his work? Industrial Commission report most important.[29]

S: Is Veblen like Marx?

M: Marx was a person of more ordinary temper, a controversialist like other men. Veblen does not seem to have passions.

S: Has Veblen any predecessors?

M: If one takes people who have been critics of modern civilization at large there is, to repeat, a long line. Among the people working at institutions there are forerunners in men like Sismondi, the great Swiss historian and economist of the first part of the nineteenth century; people like Richard Jones who, it may be recalled, wrote an excellent book on rents as they are paid in societies organized on very different bases. Then there are the people whose work is generally summed up under the rubric of the historical school; and for that matter also the Marxian approach to the discussion of social problems, and the attempt to make out the lines of development characteristic of the present day and to form some kind of forecast

---

[29] Outline, May 17, 1916.

Veblen's theory of business cycles in the book based on the profit theory is of special value as showing the mechanics through which any of the changes analyzed by other theorists produces its effects. (Outline, "Lectures on Business Cycles," April 5, 1927.)

concerning the direction in which these lines of development will lead people if continued.

To see who are the people who have followed Veblen's lead is a still more difficult task. As I remarked before he seems to have made much more impression upon the younger than upon the older generation of his contemporaries. Probably twenty five years hence it will be easy to see his influence upon the work of a considerable number of men who by that time will have made their mark.[30]

S: Does he propose positive remedies of change?

M: No, he does not propose remedies. He discusses what remedies may be fashioned.

S: He does not believe in socialism?

M: I do not suppose he believes in socialism except that he believes in it as a movement; that is, it is one of these institutional changes which have been going on in human society since men began living together in organized groups. It is a passing phase. It comes to pass presumably in the minds of the people like the earlier forms of institutions, but that is the most that can be said for it. That is what has made it so difficult for so many people, particularly the conventionally-minded to see anything in Veblen's work. He does not say that socialism is worse than capitalism, but it is a movement that seems to be growing up in society as organized at the present time and it is interesting to speculate whether it will become dominant for a while.

S: That is what Marx said.

M: There is an important difference between Veblen and Marx. One gets strongly from Marx that when the socialist state is once accomplished we shall have become reasonably close to paradise on earth. That is the ultimate goal toward which evolution has been tending on the Marxian outlook. Of course, Marx is looking at history through the eyes of an Hegelian. When the synthesis is achieved the

---

[30] [There was a leading French economist and younger contemporary of Veblen, who [Mitchell] felt moved along Veblen's critique of orthodox economics as presented in "The Limitations of Marginal Utility" (1908, reprinted in *The Place of Science in Modern Civilisation*) pp. 231-251. This was François Simiand (1873-1933); his *La Methode positive en science economique* (1912) was on [Mitchell's] reading lists. Extracts from the book are under the following headings: "Criticism of Exchange Value," "Criticism of the Law of Diminishing Utility," "Criticism of Modern Theory of Interest," "Problem of Human Nature in Economics," "Pure Theory versus Positive Science." ("Simiand," APP 74-83, no. 62).]

"December 23, 1930. Conversation with [Maurice] Halbwachs, French sociologist [and admirer of Veblen, later at University of Strasbourg]. Talk about Simiand *et al.*" (Mitchell, "Diary.") There is a brief discussion of Simiand in Ben B. Seligman, *Main Currents in Modern Economics* (New York: Free Press, 1962) pp. 40-41.

process of change ends. Veblen, on the other hand, looks at the process of evolution through Darwin's eye and from the Darwinian point of view there is no discernible limit to the process of evolution. We can learn something about it at any moment. We can have some slight part in guiding the next steps. We may be able to determine what changes will take place in the near future. But it is not true that the process of evolutionary change will come to a rest. Thus, Veblen has a view that change will presumably be characteristic of the economic institutions for the whole of man's future existence just as it is for the whole of his past, so far as we know.

S4:[31] I know that there is a difference between Veblen and Marx because the conceptions of historic Marxism do not go into the methods of thinking of the various classes as Veblen does. But even here there is a close relation between the two.

M: You have put your finger on the vital difference. What Marx gave was an analysis of the material interests of different classes in modern society and he thought that these interests would necessarily shape the development of the future. Veblen does not limit himself to a discussion of the particular economic advantages of the business man, large or small, and of the proletarian working man in modern society, but he tries to go further, and to show that the way in which these people conceive their interests and the respect which they are likely to show to the interests of others are influenced by certain habits of thinking which their daily work begets in them. The relationship between Veblen's kind of analysis and the analysis in *Das Kapital* is close, and yet there is that very significant advance made by Veblen, an advance which, if one likes, means reading Marx through the eyes of William James.

S4: Eliminating the differences of possession, eliminating the fact that one is the owner of wealth and the other is not, and taking only the impress of thought as emphasized in Veblen, can't we agree with S2 who says that the leader of industry is by no means a conservative man—I imagine that the leader of industry has as much revolution in his methods of thinking and is as creative in his methods of thinking as the working man *en masse*. You can emphasize of course that the modern business man, the hero, the captain of industry of modern times controls the workers he uses as a tool. He uses the state as his tool. He uses the existing laws and institutions as tools, but he is superior to them, because he uses them as machinery, whereas he

---

[31] Beginning of extract from "1918 Typescript."

may be much freer in his thought than those whom he wants to exploit.

M: True. Take such a spectacular case as the late J. P. Morgan whose work was revolutionary in a sense. He was primarily an organizer of industry for financial ends. That is exactly the sort of thing that Veblen, instead of denying, is setting forth with great effectiveness. He sees just as clearly as anyone that as matters stand the organization and re-organization of social life as a whole is shaped more largely by business men and particularly by big business men; he sees this more clearly than anybody else. The fact remains, however, that when one is thinking whether our fundamental economic institutions will remain what they are or undergo a change, then one sees that the business men, the big business men in particular, are interested in maintaining the institution of ownership. They are interested in keeping business enterprise. In that sense they are conservative despite the fact that their work from one point of view is revolutionary, just as a general in the employ of an archaic community run by a despot may make absolutely revolutionary changes in the lives of thousands of people in order to maintain a mediaeval situation.

S4: Then again it is not merely a question of psychology or habits of thinking. It is a question of economic interest as propounded by Marx.

M: Veblen does not intend to deny the fact that economic interests are a very important factor in shaping economic behavior but he sees a problem about economic interest. One of the childlike things about Marx was that he imputed tacitly to men a clear conception of what it was to their economic advantage to do. He imputed to them the same conception of what it was to their economic advantage that he himself held. That is to say, in his economics he assumed practically the same type of social psychology that is found in the classical economists. In that way Marx is very close to Bentham and to Ricardo, and of course that is a perfectly natural habit of mind for people still to take when they are thinking about economic interest. It is the habit of mind that characterizes the bulk of modern socialists. For instance men like W. J. Ghent and William English Walling have hardly gotten away from that viewpoint.[32] But one of the things that people have been learning about human nature in the last generation, largely as a result of ethnological study and partly as a result of

---

[32] [William J. Ghent achieved prominence with his *Our Benevolent Feudalism* (1902), which drew on the "keen satire" of Veblen's *The Theory of the Leisure Class*. Walling (1877-1936), who inherited considerable wealth, was a former student as well as admirer of Veblen. Both later left the socialist ranks.]

straight psychological analysis, is that a man's interest as he sees it may be an extremely different thing from his interest as theorists see it, and if the theorists want to understand his probable behavior they have to find out what is his interest as he sees it. That is to say, they have to engage in the inquiry into his habits of thinking, which is exactly what Veblen attempts.

Along this line a reading of *The Theory of the Leisure Class* is particularly instructive, for here Veblen makes an analysis of the curious ways in which they see their interest. It is to their interest to appear to spend more than they have got. It is to their interest to be inanely foolish from anything like a rational human viewpoint. If the theorist sits down and thinks about it he will find that is what people are trying to attain, and, if he should approach the problem of the leisure class in ordinary economic terms of sacrifice for the sake of genuine gratification, he would make almost no progress. The theorist cannot explain behavior in terms of interest unless he knows how the interest appears to the people who are going to do the behaving.

S2: Would Veblen insist that those subject to the influence of the machine process had developed, or were developing, a habit of mind which would be against property as a whole, or simply against private property. Your whole pressure against private property has come largely through the state rather than the individual, autocratic states as well as democratic states, and you have had your attack on private property carried furthest in autocratic states. Moreover, to establish the fact of a habit of mind against any property would be a pretty difficult matter to do.

M: S2, there are two questions I want to ask. What is the distinction between private property and property?

S2: The only distinction I was using was state property as the only other conception that we can conceive.

M: I would say in Veblen's eyes it is the idea of private property which has lost ground. If ownership of private property has lost ground what remains? There remains the whole galaxy of serviceable commodities within the country. Very likely, if you have an institutional situation where private property was abolished, the limits of state [ownership] would make comparatively little difference. There would be this world of people in it engaged in producing the things that we require.

In the second place about the attacks on private property, you pointed out quite properly that the countries in which the most marked limitations have been put upon freedom of disposal of property have not been the countries under democratic control. How do you account for that on Veblen's grounds? Does he think that the habit of mind begotten by the machine process is the only enemy of business enterprise?

S1: Veblen considers these habits of mind precisely which are based on dynastic forms, and it is that habit of mind which would be represented by governments.

M: To discuss this intelligently, I would like to come back to the question I asked some time ago. What use does Veblen make of the analysis of the cultural incidence of the machine process and business enterprise? What is the point of it?

S5: He concludes that business enterprise faces a prospective inevitable decay.

M: His general conclusion is—let me read the very last sentences of the book—"It seems possible to say this much, that the full dominion of business enterprise is necessarily a transitory dominion. It stands to lose in the end whether the one or the other of the two divergent cultural tendencies wins, because it is incompatible with the ascendancy of either." What are the "two divergent tendencies?" One of them is the cultural incidence of the machine process. The other is the old inherited interest in national aggrandisement which is most fully preserved, Veblen thinks, in two countries at the present time [1918]—Germany and Japan.

On his analysis these two great dynastic powers are places where business enterprise has been allowed to develop within the limit set by the dominating dynastic control. The machine process has been utilized in both countries to a very great extent, very efficiently, again with the limit set by the interest of those who run the country; that is to say, within the limits set by people who have their eyes primarily on national aggrandisement, and in both cases business enterprise has not been allowed to control the situation in domestic and foreign relations to the same extent that it has prevailed in countries like England and the United States. So that is an answer to your second objection. In his eyes it has been the antagonism of one of the left-over forces of the Middle Ages which has been chiefly responsible for putting limitations on business enterprise in countries like Japan and Germany.

S2: But one could argue the fact as to whether the dynasty in Germany were a relic or whether it were a product of business enterprise.

M: I do not think the argument would last very long if one began looking into events. The dynastic situation in Germany for one thing is considerably older than the modern business enterprise.

S2: That is true, but modern German imperialism is so largely a product of the German business man's expansion.

M: Wait a moment. Is the imperialism a product of business expansion? The imperialism seems to be quite a legitimate product of the Prussian monarchy. It is the outcome of the expansion of this particular kingdom under its line of "hero kings." The thing that differentiates modern Germany from the Prussia of the eighteenth century is of course the acquisition of the immense productive advantage which came with the introduction of machinery and the efficient organization of this machinery on the basis of business enterprise. Modern Germany without business enterprise, of course, would be an altogether different thing. But it is rather that business enterprise and the machine process have been successfully utilized to give her strength in promoting the imperialistic policy that makes Germany what she is today.[31a]

S2: But the actual first attempts to raise a flag in foreign lands would be found to be part of German business expansion. The state might support the people who took the initiative in these various cases along the coast of Africa, in China, and in the islands of the Pacific, but it was the private business man followed by the state on pretext of defense and maintenance which was the order.

M: I think that may be true in a measure regarding her colonial empire, though even there I should want to know a little more about the actual relations between business men concerned and the gentlemen in Wilhelmstrasse before forming a conclusion. Of course the general imperialistic policy of Germany is not of recent origin and that policy has checked the development of business enterprise whenever it has seemed necessary in the national interest. The business man in Germany has not had so free a hand in Germany as he had in England or the United States, because there was a paternalistic government in Germany trying to preserve the strength of the people, and there has been no country in the world, of course, in which preservation of human resources has been managed with such scientific

---

[31a] Imperialism is a wholesome object for economists to study, because it helps us to check our predisposition to treat human behavior as directed by calculation of how to maximize economic gains. Another peculiarity of economic imperialism as a subject of study is that we have to treat the problem largely in terms of particular instances or episodes not in terms of overall analyses. (Outline, "Seminar in Economic Theory—Imperialism," May 23, 1939.)

care and with such zeal. The business man has not been allowed to use up masses of human material as he has been allowed to do in England and in the United States. He has been checked because men are necessary for military strength. In Veblen's eyes it has been this antagonism of one of the left over forces of the Middle Ages which has been chiefly responsible for putting limitations on business enterprise in countries like Japan and Germany.

Veblen thinks that business enterprise is not likely to remain a permanent feature of modern civilization on the ground that it is incompatible with two opposing tendencies, one or the other of which, he thinks, will probably control in the future. The first of these opposing tendencies is, to repeat, precisely the cultural incidence of the machine process; that is to say, the development in increasingly larger proportions of modern populations of a viewpoint, a habit of thought, from which the whole structure of business principles and aims appear more or less irrelevant, beside the point, a viewpoint from which it does not appear that business enterprise is a very serviceable institution.

The other opposing tendency is that of a blatant form of patriotism which Veblen sees particularly strong in dynastic countries, a frame of mind, an interest, which he thinks is derived from the past rather than reinforced by present conditions, but a frame of mind which prevails among populations which have recently, gradually increased their military powers by adopting modern methods of production. Veblen argues if the dynastic ideal dominates the modern world, then the control of civilization by business enterprise is likely to be comparatively limited because a society that is run in the interests of national aggrandisement is very different from a society that is run for the profit of the business classes. That is the general outcome of the discussion then, the probable brief duration of this institution which has developed with such extraordinary rapidity, which has played so great a role particularly in England, France and the United States within the last century.

Veblen's discussion of the permanence of business enterprise, however, is, to repeat, only one of the themes of *The Theory of Business Enterprise*. There are as a matter of fact two large questions which he analyzed here. The first of them relates to the bearing of business enterprise upon the process of producing serviceable commodities for satisfying men's wants. The second, to repeat, relates to the question as to how long this particular institution, business enterprise, promises to play its dominating role. It is characteristic of the impression that *The Theory of Business Enterprise* makes on the mind that, when I put both questions perhaps rather carelessly to the class, almost all the members of the class began to talk about the second instead of about the first theme. Thus, the class discussion of Veblen's type of theory has had an awkward, backhanded form given to it, given to it simply because the second theme is the one which is more out of the line of ordinary economic theorizing; it therefore makes probably a more striking impression on the reader's mind.

But before leaving this type of theory, I ought to call attention prominently to the argument of the first part of the book concerning the influence of business enterprise upon the economic process of providing serviceable commodities. This may be summed up as follows: In the first place Veblen argues that when the machine process is controlled, as it is in America for instance, by business enterprise, then the immense productive powers of machinery are utilized, not directly for producing serviceable commodities, but directly for producing profits. That is to say, the industrial revolution with the consequent rapid pace of improvements in methods of production has greatly enhanced modern man's ability to satisfy his economic needs, but at the same time, this growth of productive power has been controlled in a fashion which diverts the efficiency very largely from the primary aims of satisfying wants to the secondary artificial aim of piling up pecuniary profits. In other words, the people in modern civilization are very far indeed from getting the most service possible out of the methods of production, and they are far from it precisely because the managers do not even aim at making serviceable goods. That may sound like a startling proposition to the people who have never heard anything of the sort but to most of the class, I fancy, it will come more or less as a matter of course.

When one stops to think what the business enterprise is after, one realizes that what Veblen says here is literally true. A railroad is not managed to transport freight and passengers. It is managed to make money. What is true of the railroad is true of every other business enterprise which is run on good business principles, and the better the business management, the more strictly and uncompromisingly are serviceable goods a mere by-product and money-making the aim. It also goes without saying that there are many ways of making money without making serviceable goods. There are many ways for a man to increase his profits by diminishing the service that he renders to the community. So that the assumption which is implied more often than it is expressed in economic theorizing that modern productive efforts are efforts to produce goods that will satisfy man's wants, over-looks a very important fact, that the making of the goods is not the real aim which directs men's efforts.

The second impressive point that Veblen develops in the first part is that the whole modern structure of credit, which is so strictly a feature of modern business enterprise, does not add to the country's equipment for production. That again seems at first blush a most extraordinary statement. It is a view which, like the first one, runs counter to a common implication, if not to a common explicit conten-tion of modern theory. We take it for granted that credit is a neces-sary and serviceable part of the arrangements for producing goods. Veblen does not argue that credit is not necessary to modern business. On the contrary, he argues that it is precisely necessary to modern business not to modern industry as such. The business man in his effort to make profits is compelled practically to use borrowed funds, because thereby he can enhance his profits, and any opportunity applied to business enterprise for increasing the amount of business, thereby increasing the amounts of profits, is something which every business man under competitive conditions must take advantage of. That is to say, if a business man borrows and thereby increases the amount of business that he can do and thus the amount of profits he can make, he must enter into competition with all the other people who are trying to sell the same kind of goods in the same market. Veblen points out, however, that the heaping up of credits by itself does not increase either our knowledge of technical processes or stock of machinery. It is a fact of an altogether different order from the material facts and the knowledge which relate to productive efficiency.

Only one concession does he make to the claims that credit in-creases production. That admission, however, is, I am inclined to think, very important. He admits that in so far as credit transfers control over material factors of production from people who are not in a position to utilize them to advantage to people who can do so, just that far does credit increase productive resources,[33] but here again

---

[33] Relation [in Veblen] of borrowing to (1) profits—does increase individual's profits; that is why borrowing becomes universal. But when it becomes universal, it does not increase aggregate earnings of all enterprises except so far as it transfers funds to abler hands. (2) Material output of useful goods. Borrowed funds do not increase material equipment or efficiency of machine process. (Does not above exception count heavily here?) (3) Capitalization—Borrowed funds do not increase differential profits and therefore capitalization. Hence borrowing establishes a discrepancy between capital and industrial equipment. Increases the former without increasing the latter. (Excep-tion counts here emphatically.) When this discrepancy has become wide the profits

it increases productive resources not in a material sense, but as preventing certain uncomfortable consequences which would result from the institution of ownership. One of you may be an orphan quite destitute of any power to use property which has come into your hands by inheritance. In that case, under the institution of private property, this item of resource for production must remain unused unless some means can be found for transferring it to some person who does have the capacity for utilizing it. Credit does admit of such transfers, so that it prevents a restriction upon production which could result from the institution of property, of property getting into the hands of people who could not utilize it. That far, credit is productive, but only that far, on Veblen's showing.

In the third place he points out that the modern business enterprise with its machinery of credit is not run after all even for the profit of the enterprise as such, that particularly where enterprises have assumed the large form and the intricate organization which is particularly characteristic of recent years [1918], one is likely to find a management inside of any given enterprise, a management which, for practical business purposes, is quite different from the ownership. The ownership of modern corporations lies nominally with the stockholders. These in the typical cases are a very large number of people who hold shares. The business corporation is supposedly run by a committee of those shareholders, which committee is usually called the board of directors. These people are responsible. They in turn appoint the administrative officers who have direct control. Veblen's point is that the officers, usually supported by a majority of the directors, are likely to be found running the enterprise for their profit rather than for the profit of the shareholders. Of course they have to keep the majority of the shareholders substantially satisfied so that they will not insist upon a change in management, but in very many cases such corporations are effectively managed by people who directly are very far from controlling a majority of the stock, let alone the majority of the capital which is invested, for besides the stock of goods one has to remember the great mass of capital invested in bonds.

In other words, the modern business enterprise is in the typical case managed by people for their own profit, who do not represent the bulk of the property which is utilized for business purposes. So that Veblen's first proposition that our process of production is not

capitalized at current rate of interest may be less than the value at which capital has been taken as collateral. Begins a period of liquidation, in which ownership is distributed to advantage of creditors. (Outline, May 17, 1916.)

managed to make serviceable commodities, but to make profits has
to be supplemented by the addition that the profits which are aimed
at are less the profits of the owners of the enterprise than of the
particular people who happen to be in control at a given time, and
these people can oftentimes make profits for themselves by operations
which are greatly to the disadvantage of the corporation, a reflection
which is very familiar to anybody who has studied the scandals of the
old fashioned ways of constructing railroads by the managers giving
lucrative contracts to their friends or to corporations which really
represented the people in control under another name. We know that
even when scandals of that particular type are not practiced it is
again possible for "insiders," as they are popularly called, to make
considerable profit for themselves by stock exchange operations in
the securities of the corporation, utilizing their advance knowledge
of how the business stands to speculate in stocks, sometimes even to
speculate in bonds. All that range of facts is familiar enough. What
Veblen does is to generalize, set up this proposition that, on the whole,
in the typical case, I think he would say, the large corporation is
really run to make money primarily for the people who happen to be
in control.

Then Veblen presents his general thesis concerning the nature of
modern capital. Theorists are accustomed in their treatises to have
capital represented as primarily the aggregate of wealth used for
production of other wealth. That is to say, they usually think of
capital standing for machinery, buildings, land, etc. Veblen says that
if the theorist wants to understand the phenomenon, to think clearly,
he must distinguish sharply between the aggregate of material goods
which are used in production on the one hand and capital in the
business man's sense on the other hand. Capital in the business man's
sense is a pecuniary magnitude. It is a sum of dollars and cents.
On the one hand, it may represent the monetary equivalent of funds
which are actually invested in the business. On the other hand in the
typical case it does not represent that. It represents the putative
earning capacity of the business enterprise capitalized at the prevailing rate of interest. That is to say, the question always from the business standpoint is what is the enterprise worth. What it is worth is its
capital value for business purposes, capital value which of course
differs from its nominal capital value. What a business is worth for
business purposes depends primarily on profits, what it probably can
make, on its prospective profits. To determine the capital value on the
basis of prospective profits, profits must be capitalized at whatever

the rate of interest is for propositions of this kind, at the time when the calculations are made.

Finally, on the basis of the preceding analysis of credit and capital, Veblen develops his theory of modern prosperity.

S6: I don't understand the second division of capital that he makes. He makes two distinctions and he says we have to distinguish between capital—

M: Capital as the business man sees it is the aggregate of material goods which are used for production. That is to say, S6, if you have an establishment, say, for making corn into syrup, you will find the establishment owning certain plots of land, certain buildings, having certain machinery, perhaps having a considerable number of offices scattered around different parts of the country with a little equipment in each one of them. For productive purposes you have a certain amount of material goods, do you not? In the common sense use of the term, a sense that is very common in economic treatises today, that aggregate of material goods which is used for production is the capital. That is not the capital as it is understood by the business man. What he understands is the value of this productive material equipment.

If at the present time he happens to have an extraordinarily valuable market for syrup made from corn, the capital of that concern for business purposes will increase very rapidly, because its prospective profits will increase. This business capital is then a pecuniary magnitude, something in kind radically different from the material goods which are used in production. It is different from them in the basis on which it is calculated, for its value does not depend so much on what material equipment the business man actually has, as on his prospects of profits, and those prospects are influenced by many things beside the amount of machinery, land, etc., that he owns. Are there any other questions?

If not, then I will come back to the theory of modern prosperity which Veblen builds on his conception of business capital. This theory, as noted earlier, is his theory of business cycles; that is to say, it is his account of the fluctuations in the activity of the process by which the people are continually being provided serviceable commodities for their wants. One of the outstanding features of modern economic life is that men's activity in making useful goods is subject to more or less irregular, but recurrent alternations of activity and depression. There are years when the factories are being worked to practically the full extent of their capacities, pretty much all the available forces of labor and knowledge are being utilized. There are other years when a great many factories are standing completely idle, or working on short time, when a very appreciable proportion of the working people are standing idle.

Of course with modern economic life, all the organized processes of manufacturing things that the people want to consume, there would be no satisfactory reason for not making goods that they want unless there were some interference of a material kind which stood in the way, for instance, inability to get certain particular materials that might be wanted or distress brought about by act of God or human violence. But such interruptions of the work of supplying the wants of communities occur, as I say, regularly. They are a part of the expected order of things. Men count with a great deal of confidence in the future on periods of activity followed by periods of depression.

These regular oscillations of activity and depression are particularly characteristic of the economic life of the communities that are most thoroughly under the domination of business enterprise. More than that, they are particularly characteristic of those industries which are most highly organized on a business basis. The farmer, for instance, plants about the same number of acres so far as he can, year after year, working about as hard in the season of depression as in the season of activity. His business not having gotten into corporate form, not being dependent on the credit structure in a really great degree and not being dependent on a fluctuating market, runs in a much more stable way than that of the business of making even other necessities like cotton fabrics. The widest swings between depression and activity occur in precisely those industries which are making goods for business use, for instance, industries which manufacture machinery.

Veblen's account of these oscillations is too long and intricate to analyze in any detail, but his general idea is comparatively simple; that oscillations in business activity are brought about by a combination of complications due to increasing credits on the one hand and great capitalization on the basis of prospective profits on the other hand. He shows how, in every period of activity, the amount of borrowed credit increases very rapidly, on what for business purposes is a satisfactory basis of security, because during prosperity the increasing volume of trade brings an increase in profits. The increase is due partly merely to the larger output of business and partly to the fact that certain expenses of doing business rise less rapidly than the selling price; that is to say, profits gain at the expense of interest, rent and wages. There is a larger margin and a larger turnover on which that margin is realized. The increase of profits increases business capitalization and this in turn is a basis on which larger loans can be negotiated. The whole process is cumulative in Veblen's eyes. The larger profits enable the business men to borrow more money, the larger sums that they borrow allow them to extend their business operations still further, etc.

The result is that every period of prosperity is accompanied by a certain pyramiding of credit, and unless something interferes to check the process, there is no limit easy to see upon the extent to which the pyramiding might be carried. But, as Veblen points out, when there has been a substantial increase of loan credit on the basis of given productive equipment, anything that comes along to interfere with the profits of some important group of concerns is likely to make lenders somewhat nervous about the security of their enormous advances. The business people who have borrowed have to raise money in order to pay up. They call upon the people who are indebted to them in the way of business for settlement. That means trying to cash in. The result is that there is a certain pressure upon the market to realize on stocks of goods on hand.

That pressure is likely to check the rise of prices perhaps to produce a fall. Just as soon as there is any prospect of a fall of prices, prospective profits diminish and when prospective profits decline then the business capital represented becomes less, then the collateral behind all other loans becomes somewhat shaky in the eyes of the cautious banker. Then the pressure to realize is extended. Thus, once the process of liquidation is set going, it is cumulative and tends to produce a fall in prices which carries less prospective profits gradually over the whole field of highly organized business, and that means less inducement for activity. When business begins to restrict activity, one finds in particular that purchases of new equipment drop off. Then enterprises, which are engaged in building machinery and that kind of thing, find that they face a period of inactivity. That means unemployment for a certain number of their employees. Unemployment means, of course, restriction of buying power for the group of working people affected, and, if the businesss itself suffers considerably, there will be a certain group of investors and profit makers who will have less to spend. That will affect the demand for all other goods and spread gradually over the whole industry.

In a few months, sometimes in a very short period of time, there is a dramatic change from feverish activity to stagnation. Before, workmen could hardly think of anything except the next day's work, now all activities keep diminishing until a large part of the country's facilities for production are standing more or less idle. To repeat, in Veblen's eyes, the alternation of busy activity, of satisfying men's wants, with periods of idleness and distress, is due not to any inherent feature of the machine process or modern methods of production, but is due primarily to the fact that the machinery for production is operated through business enterprise and for profits. Is that clear?

S6: I didn't quite understand at the beginning when you said these oscillations are brought about by increasing credit on the one hand and on the other by recapitalization.

M: Let me repeat those two points. According to Veblen the period of prosperity is accompanied by a rapid increase of loan credit and people borrow to finance their increasing operations. This increase of credit is cumulative. It extends over pretty much all the field. It is supported by collateral which is represented primarily by the capitalized value of the borrowing business enterprise, but the capitalized value of the borrowing business enterprise is itself the capitalized prospective profits. If the value of the collateral shrinks, then the safety of the loans becomes dubious. Then people begin to restrict their loan credit, and that forces a general attempt to realize on stocks in hand. That brings down prices and makes the restriction of credit tighter. There is a period of liquidation in which business is much smaller in volume than it had been in the period of activity. Are there any questions about it?

S11: I would like to ask wherein his theory is original. That general proposition of the relation of speculative credit to prices is very well known.

M: Veblen is making very large use of ideas that are familiar but no preceding writer has put all these facts together in the same effective fashion. Many people have attempted to explain the alternation of activity and depression in business as a result of so-called speculative manias or as a result of a resort to so-called illegitimate credit. What Veblen is arguing is that these developments are all perfectly logical results of the institution of business enterprise. They come as necessary consequences in a community which is running its process of providing serviceable goods primarily for the profits of business men.[34]

Two major themes in *The Theory of Business Enterprise*. First is how business enterprise affects the process of supplying the community with serviceable goods. Second is the place and permanence of business enterprise

---

[34] End of extract from "1918 Typescript."

in modern culture. We have taken the second first. Now let us return to the first. 1. Under business control machine process run not to make goods but to make money. 2. Credit does not increase efficiency of equipment but does increase capital and capital is putative earning capacity. 3. Enterprises are not managed to make profits for the business, but rather for the business men in control, often by security manipulation, rather than by industrial operations. 4. The business cycle with its tendency to depression; that is, to checking of the process of supplying goods to meet men's wants, is a result of certain technical features of business enterprise.[34a]

M: Any more questions?

S: In regard to the collapse of the system of business enterprise, Veblen refers to the increase in the discrepancy between business credit and equipment of industry.

M: He regards that as an interesting, extremely characteristic, not unimportant, and still not a really vital element when it comes to summing up the probable future of the institution as a whole. In reading the chapter on The Use of Loan Credit you ought to observe a little exception which he makes rather early, incidentally, and then passes on, but an exception which must be taken seriously if the student tries from Veblen's viewpoint to figure what part loan credit is likely to have in further institutional development.

The exception is, as I recently discussed, namely, his remark that loan credit does not increase industrial productivity, except in so far as it transfers capital from the hands of people who are not in a position to use it effectively to the hands of those who are in a position to use it more effectively. From the point of view of the majority of economic theorists who have discussed loan credit as such, particularly from the point of view of the economists who dealt with the theory of bank credit, it is considered to be productive primarily for this very reason. It is the means by which society can redistribute the capital in its possession at any given time in such a fashion as to put it in the hands of those who will pay most for its use; and are, broadly speaking, assumed to be the people in the best position to make some gainful use of it.

To repeat, Veblen is careful to point out that his fundamental dictum that loan credit does not increase productivity is open to this exception, which the majority of writers on credit hold. He grants their chief contention, and then proceeds to argue in the most elaborate and diverting fashion that aside from this point credit has no serviceability from the industrial viewpoint and leads to a set of

---

[34a] Outline, April 8, 1918.

financial complications, the full results of which appear in his following chapter devoted to business cycles.

S: Is the psychology that Veblen develops in regard to the working class and the business class a new psychology that applies only to economics?

M: It is an economist's application of ideas concerning human nature which can be found set out in more systematic form in such books as William James's *Principles of Psychology*.

S: It is not anything new then?

M: The fundamental idea of human nature involved is not new. It is, however, novel to find an economist actually being fairly well up to date in modern psychology. Their practice is to be two generations behind.

S: Would it be fair to say that Davenport approaches economics from the individual standpoint and Veblen from the social standpoint?

M: Yes, it would be fair to say that, though the statement would not be an adequate characterization of the difference between the two. Further, in one sense the statement may even exaggerate the difference between them, because Davenport would be one of the first to admit that the characteristics of the modern individual are in a large measure due to the kind of social organization in which he lives; Veblen, on the other hand, is pointing out in the very book under discussion, *The Theory of Business Enterprise*, that modern society inculcates an acquisitive point of view in one class of the community.

To contrast the two economists most effectively it would have to be done on the basis of the problems they put into the forefront of their inquiries. Davenport sets a standard of price. Obviously economics is there something different from Veblen's. It is a science of human behavior in Veblen. And the part of human behavior which is significant to study is the development of the types of behavior which are common to large masses of the population and are themselves subject to change.

I might add a word about the reason for laying so much stress upon the study of institutions. Veblen is one of the people who accept the current modern notion that there is no reason to believe the human brain to have undergone any fundamental change, that it has achieved a substantial improvement, since the days of the later cave men. If, then, society at the present time is an enormously different concern from what society was in the days of the later cave men, if the kind of lives that we live today seems a world removed, it is not because of improvement in native intellectual capacity. It must be due to a change in man's knowledge, his ability to control the forces of nature. It is a difference of knowledge which sets off the citizen of an advanced, modern nation from those who lived in a society such as existed in France, for instance, ten thousand years ago. But the intellectual difference is not to be traced to improvement in the modern brain. It is due primarily to an accumulation of human experience, a very slow accumulative growth of insight into nature and of knowledge of how to apply such insight to the promotion of the interests of the human species.

The increased knowledge of natural processes and of how to apply knowledge for economic purposes is an institutional viewpoint. In other words, it is the growth of institutions that is the factor in human progress which is susceptible of change, susceptible of development. Therefore it is the factor upon which anyone who is interested in understanding the present situation or interested in making guesses as to the probable future fate of mankind should center his investigations.

S: Would Veblen hold that view if he were writing today [1927]?

M: If you compare his latest book *Absentee Ownership,* written in 1923, with *The Theory of Business Enterprise,* written nineteen years earlier, I think that you would feel that he had hardened in his earlier ways.

S: I am thinking in particular of the trust problem.

M: No, his viewpoint in dealing with these modern problems would not be fundamentally different. Perhaps in the later book he represents absentee ownership itself as the economic institution of fundamental importance at the present time, which on the face of things sounds very different from saying it is business enterprise. That is, he has shifted his standpoint a little bit, and instead of looking at the active business man he looks at the persons who have property claims as the people who are dominating the situation. There is a change there, but not one of a fundamental sort. The reader of the later book will find that the temper of it is much the same as that of the earlier one.

S: Do you think the applications of the behaviorist school have material effect now?

M: I do not know whether they would or not. The attitude of the behaviorist school is one which in many cases makes for a considerable difference in the words the investigator uses in describing, in accounting for a certain situation and not much difference in the general conclusions at which he arrives. For example, take Dr. John B. Watson who, as the high priest of the behaviorists, has been for some years engaged in the advertising business [as an executive of the J. Walter Thompson Co.]. As a leading expert in advertising it became necessary for him to find out what kind of appeals are likely to lead people to buy goods; that is, what is effective in motivating certain types of human behavior. Most men think of a problem of that sort as analyzing people's motives and saying what will happen. Behaviorists cannot talk of human motives in the usual sense; for that means dealing with people's consciousness. Yet, presumably, Watson finds himself sometimes in close agreement with colleagues concerning the possibility of certain definite advertising policies; though the colleagues have reached their conclusions by analyzing peoples' motives and he has supposedly reached them without having reasoned about individual subjective procedure.

To repeat, in many cases following the behaviorist's viewpoint leads to a different statement concerning what social scientists are actually doing; but a formulation of the latter's procedure in other words would not make much of an alteration in the conclusions at which he arrives. It may be that, if a strict behaviorist were editing this book of Veblen's, he might change the phraseology in a good many passages but he might come out at more or less the same conclusions regarding what behavior is to be expected of the two classes.

M:[35] You have something to say, S4?

S4: Yes, regarding Veblen's general theory. Where does the theory of goods satisfying wants come in his scheme. He seems to abolish it or does not think it very important.

M: On the contrary, Veblen thinks that the important thing is the production of serviceable commodities to satisfy our wants, and what he is pointing out is that that all-important process is distorted by the control which business enterprise has over production.

S4: That is, he takes for granted that if you want to find a market, you have to produce something that is to satisfy wants?

M: You are taking for granted the business situation as it exists. That is, the problem that you have to face, when modern industry is controlled by business enterprise, and so long as you are a producer for markets, you are in the modern business situation which is characteristic. Veblen does not try to sketch a scheme of social organization in which you could run production for the satisfying of wants,

---

[35] Beginning of extract from "1918 Typescript."

in which you could produce not for the market, but to meet the pressing needs of members of the community.

S4: Is he interested in the explanation of the equation of exchange?

M: I do not see that he is. He is interested in showing how our exchange operations get badly tangled and how those tangles bring upon the community periods of want and idleness.

S4: That would mean, putting it in a simple way, that the prices of commodities in a market are determined, not by desire for them and our wants, but by large business operations over which the individual customer has no control.

M: The small business man has much less control on Veblen's analysis than the big magnate.

S4: That would mean from Veblen's view that the theory of value including the theory of marginal utility has no bearing since those things are managed from above. The industries are run according to their prospects of profit.

M: I should not say quite that much, S4. What I should say is that Veblen would hold that the significant oscillations in price are due primarily to business operations and in a minor degree to changes in wants.

S4: But he does not look to the conventional side of the theory.

M: This is a book on business enterprise. He takes the price system as an established fact and analyzes the salient factors in producing oscillations.

S3: Would not S4 find the answer to that question in *The Instinct to Workmanship* where Veblen speaks of the "contamination of the instincts"?

M: He would find a good deal more bearing on that question in the later book than he would find in *The Theory of Business Enterprise,* but even there he would not find the conventional problems of the determination of prices worked out.

S3: Not for the general proposition of values, that is, not the economic value theory, but how it comes about that people value one thing as against another.

M: In *The Instinct of Workmanship* as well as in *The Theory of the Leisure Class* a good deal of attention is given to the problem of valuations. Veblen is particularly interested in anomalies; that is to say, some of the things which form the common sense point of view appear as anomalies; why is it that we attach a high degree of importance to certain things which, once you stop to think of them, are patently artificial.

I want to ask the class how Veblen's type of theory differs specifically from other types previously studied.

S4: Would it be correct to say that his theory is a specific outgrowth of American conditions more than European, because the business enterprises have been more influential in America than in any other country?

M: The phenomena which he discusses in *The Theory of Business Enterprise* have found their finest development in the United States. That certainly is true. But how does his type of theory differ from others? Does it differ primarily in conclusions or method? Or in problems treated?

S1: In method.

S6: In all three. In problems because it does not go into the problems of price, etc.; in method taking the phenomena as a whole; in conclusions also. He has altogether different conclusions which have more political bearing in my opinion on future prospects.

M: What does the class think? Are the members of the class correct who say that Veblen differs in all three of these points?

S5: He differs primarily in that he recognizes the goods market and the money economy, but he puts that in subordinate place in the larger credit market.

M: You are saying that he is attacking problems that are novel. It comes to that.

S5: Other economists have recognized their existence, but Veblen takes them as the starting point, as the governing factor.

M: That is a difference in the problems that he discusses.

S1: The problems are just the same, crises and that sort of thing as always.

M: Crises, you do not find them included in a book like Alfred Marshall's *Principles of Economics,* but certainly you will find a considerable number of problems in *The Theory of Business Enterprise* which you do not find discussed in ordinary treatises.

S1: That is, because of his method, he is not excogitating it out of his head. He is trying to see what other people would think.

M: That is to say, the problem which he sets himself is what are the prevailing habits of thought. In other words, it is a difference in problem.

S4: I call that method—the method of getting at the same problem.

M: That is a very interesting point, one which I cannot stop at present to discuss but which will come up in subsequent lectures. It is the point as to how far a difference in method necessarily implies a difference in problems and how far a difference in problems implies a difference in method. When the theorist comes to analyze the two things, can he really distinguish between them? Are there any further comments or questions concerning Professor Veblen's work?

S3: I don't know whether this is apropos or not, but previously a question was raised in regard to a comparison between Veblen's and Marx's interpretations. Do you suppose that there is a materialistic interpretation, putting it in the general terms of course of economic events or habits of thought, or whatever he calls them? Is it an economic interpretation in the most simple and elementary sense, or would you say it is a more complex interpretation of habits of thought?

M: I should say it is distinctly complex in the sense that as Veblen sees things the situation at the present, or for that matter, any situation that comes under our observation, is the result of an indefinitely long cumulative process of changes. That is to say, at the point at which we stand—and it is just as true at the point at which any savage race stands—the situation is the resultant of conditions and habits which come down out of an indefinitely remote antiquity. That means, of course, that, since there is a more or less continuous line of habits in a race, you cannot understand the situation simply on the basis of existing material conditions or even on the basis of what you know about past material conditions. That is to say, we in the present generation are primarily, I think it is fair to say that much, primarily what we have been made from the training we have received from our parents, and among the people with whom we have grown up and they are simply products of their grandparents and the people among whom they grew up, and so on indefinitely back. I should think it is very difficult, even speculatively, to present an explanation which runs purely in environmental terms, because it appears that the organism itself, once it is changed in the least, passes on the change to the organisms which follow after it in the next generation; that is to say, habits of thinking, feeling, and acting.

S3: Is one justified in characterizing what he says about the incidence of the machine process, as a spiritual rather than a material factor in civilization? For instance, the technology, the ways and means of doing things? I must admit I am sometimes puzzled whether he emphasizes one or the other. I know he has both of them. I was wondering if it would be a correct estimate to say that he imputes a good deal of influence to the so-called intangible spiritual factors, the technology which is really not a material thing.

M: If you trace the modern machine process back to its beginnings, of course you find it originating in certain thoughts. These thoughts get realized in certain tangible products. These tangible products, the machines, exercise a certain very definite and specific influence, if Veblen is correct, upon the people who work with them day by day. That is the influence of a factor which has become definitely materialized.

The influence itself, however, is an influence upon mind, upon people's daily habit of thinking, feeling, acting, and these habits, once they are begotten in members of a family, are passed on, not merely because the children of that family are likely themselves to become habituated to the use of machinery, but also because the parents will teach the children directly their own habits of looking at things. They may not do it formally but they do it informally. In processes like that, it is impossible to separate, in the long run, the influence of factors which seems to lie quite distinctly in the physical realm, from the factors which seem to lie in the psychical realm, and I do not see why one should attempt that rather old task.

Of course you can carry the whole thing back to the materialistic basis if you happen to take the materialistic view of physiology and psychology, and perhaps that is the sensible view to take, but you take it on other grounds than economic analysis. You can get such a conclusion, if you go with such a man as Dr. Jacques Loeb, who is connected with the Rockefeller Institute of Medical Research.[36] But his line of approach to the materialistic view comes from actual experimentation along physical and chemical lines, experimentation with animal forms.

S6: Does Veblen come to the conclusion that the all important process of producing serviceable goods is destroyed by business enterprise? Does he show at all any other line? Does he at all show anything that could take the place of business enterprise?

M: Not in this book.

S6: In any other book?

M: You will find a sketch bearing on that matter, suggestions rather than a constructive scheme, in the last chapter of *The Nature of Peace,* but that again is simply suggestions which, if you like, you can elaborate. He has not anything in the nature of an attempt to show what the future society is going to be like in detail.

S6: Does Veblen anywhere take up the national interference or the state interference with business enterprise in any other book?

---

[36] [Loeb who was a noted zoologist was a friend and admirer of Veblen.]

M: Of course in the theory of business enterprise itself he represents the possible conflict between the interests of the state and the interests of business enterprise. He also points out that in communities like the United States the conflict has not developed very much because business enterprise has in a large measure managed the state for its own interest. In *The Nature of Peace* you will find him laying a great emphasis on the contrast of state policy on the one side and business interests on the other side, with reference particularly to Germany of course.

S2: Does he put any emphasis on state policy, more than on business enterprise?

M: In discussing imperial Germany he does.

S6: Does he see any further line of development in state interference?

M: Veblen thinks that one of two things may happen if the policy of national aggrandizement which is the logical consequence of the scheme of the imperial German government should be successful, and there should be world peace on a German basis. Then presumably in the long run, the Germans would themselves have to be using, as all the subject populations would have used, modern machine methods. That would mean that there would be a gradual tendency toward undermining, even in Germany itself, the habits of thought which sustain the imperialistic organization. In the long run, there would be a gradual disintegration of that habit of mind which makes men good and loyal subjects, ready to be used for the purposes of national policy, and it would be very difficult, I am inclined to think on Veblen's analysis, to prevent the gradual undermining. It might possibly be managed by using the bulk of the German population for other than industrial purposes, and getting the support out of the subject population. That is, the only way it seems feasible is letting the subject population furnish the support for the bulk of the German nation. Then the Germans could be kept working as bureaucrats and soldiers. In this way they would be protected from the undermining influence of the machine process.

S7: Marx also says that capitalism in itself has to destroy itself in its consequences; so this imperialistic development would in itself, I think, destroy itself.

M: In that respect there is a similarity, but as S4 pointed out there is a very important difference between the Marxian analysis and Veblen's. According to Marx, the catastrophe to capitalism would be brought about in a rather direct and simple fashion through the following of their respective interests by the capitalistic and the proletarian classes. Veblen, instead of proceeding with this naive assumption that people will follow their economic interests, as the theorist sees them, undertakes to show the influence on the minds of the different classes in modern communities of the way of making their living. That is to say, the whole psychological part of his analysis has, so far as I know, no precedent in Marx. It is not by direct catastrophe that Veblen sees the situation overthrown. It is rather by the slow, cumulative effects of the methods of making a living upon the minds of people. When that cumulation has reached a certain point, however, there may occur, on his analysis, a sudden overturn.

Other questions?

S7: Veblen takes the attitude that the dynastic state cannot live under the machine process.

M: Not in the long run if it allows its subjects to work machines.

S7: It would not allow its subjects to use the machine process.

M: It can use the machine process indirectly by making the subject populations work.

S7: Assuming that premise then, and assuming the further premise, which I believe Veblen would stand for, that the modern democratic communities and democratic governments have been run primarily in the interests of the business man, does not that point to the fact that if the machine process continues and the dynastic state dies out, whatever state results will be a hand maiden to the industrial processes, to the business processes?

M: Not to the business processes because Veblen thinks that the discipline of the machine process is just as hostile in the last resort to business processes as it is to imperialism. It tends to undermine both of those cultural schemes on his showing.

S6: Does he say that the machine process tends to undermine the dynastic scheme?

M: Surely. How can a materialistic man who has become skeptical, unpatriotic, undevout, make good material for prosecuting dynastic aims?[37]

---

[37] End of extract from "1918 Typescript."

[Professor Mitchell was deeply concerned with the impact of business processes on business leaders. He explained in a private letter in 1911 that to complete his study of "The Money Economy," he wanted to be located in New York for] "I shall need a chance to come into contact at first hand with the workings of pecuniary institutions and to observe how the minds of the men who control the powerful business enterprises are formed by their daily tasks." (Mitchell to Lucy Sprague Mitchell, November 6, 1911. Quoted in Lucy Sprague Mitchell, "A Personal Sketch," in *Wesley Clair Mitchell: The Economic Scientist* edited by Arthur F. Burns (New York: National Bureau of Economic Research, 1952) p. 70.

I have endeavored to set forth the leading characteristics of Veblen's approach to the study of economics. He had, in the first place, a working conception of human nature very different in character from that which had characterized most of his predecessors, an approach which was founded primarily on the view of human nature propounded by biologists and the later psychologists, most of all by Darwin and William James, a view in which heavy emphasis is laid upon instinct and habit.

It was part of this view that the great changes that have taken place in human life are slowly cumulated results of man's experience with the world in which he lives, slowly cumulated results in the field of knowledge and its application to the facts of life. It is primarily because men have gradually learned more than they knew at the outset about materials and forces in nature that they have been able to turn them to their own advantage, to obtain for themselves a more secure and abundant livelihood than their remote ancestors enjoyed. Consequently the economic life of today is to be understood primarily as a cultural product. It follows that if the theorist wants to understand the modern economic situation he has to win his understanding by a genetic approach. It is the proper approach to understand, not only the past and the present, but also what man's life promises in the future. For just as the past history of the race consists significantly of a gradual accumulation of the lessons of experience, so the future will be shaped by the continuation of the accumulative process of learning. One can forecast it with a certain degree of accuracy, for a brief period at least in the future, by studying the trends in present development.

The trouble with the classical masters was that on the one hand they mistook men to be predominantly rational creatures who decided on their course of conduct by deliberate choice among alternative pleasures and pains. This makes them out to be a passive species of animal that is pushed and pulled about by those external stimuli in the environment whereas the truth is, on Veblen's showing, that they are active creatures born with propensities to follow certain lines of action. These propensities are modified in the course of learning; and the individuals of any generation get their pattern primarily from the culture of the people among whom they grow up.

Since the economists of the past have had this mistaken notion about human nature they have naturally been led to concentrate upon a problem of secondary interest. Since man is conceived as rational it was appropriate to study the forces in the environment that controlled his choices. That is what Veblen thinks the classical economists were primarily engaged in. They were concerned to make out how prices and distribution of income are determined in communities practicing division of labor and having arts already highly developed. They took this situation as a matter of course requiring no explanation, and the people were characterized by the supposedly human quality of rationality. It is even on their own showing, from Veblen's point of view, that the previous economists have dealt with merely mechanical ends of the great processes by which exchange is determined. They took their demand and supply schedules for granted, for they did not explain in any adequate way, even when they undertook the task at all, why it is that people put a certain valuation upon successive increments in a supply of goods. Veblen would have supported very heartily that criticism of this procedure made by Sir William Ashley[38] and quoted previously. If the economist really wants to understand the facts of the market he has to engage in a careful study of the valuation of men's desires for different classes of commodities. As he put it in his picturesque language: "behind the workman's wife making up her mind between a bit more tea and bacon on a Saturday night, whether to buy another loaf or a scrap more of meat, stands the whole of social history."

For the unsatisfactory formal dealing with problems of a superficial sort, Veblen proposes to substitute an account of economic phenomena in terms of the cumulative process of cultural growth. That is an undertaking that cannot be carried out in detail by a single investigator because no one man has time enough to master the materials available. Presumably it can be carried out but in the most sketchy fashion by a number of people working any length of time that is chosen, because the material cannot be assembled. But it is feasible from Veblen's viewpoint to take the cultural situation as it exists at a given time, any time about which the investigator's information is tolerably full, and inquire into the leading characteristics of some community of men at that particular time, see what are the dominant institutions of the age, and then inquire into the forces that have shaped these dominant institutions in the period preceding that in which the investigator is interested. He can inquire into the modifications that these institutions are undergoing during his period; and if the period is the present one, he can, to a certain extent, forecast the changes that are likely to come about in the future.

---

[38] "The Present Position of Political Economy," *The Economic Journal*, December 1907, p. 477.

It is common to speak of Veblen's economics as institutional, and this is an appropriate term. From his point of view, what the economist should be concerned with is primarily the effect of the great institutions upon the lives of men, the way in which these institutions have evolved, the changes they are undergoing at the present time and the further changes that they seem likely to undergo in the future.

The classical economists do not in most cases talk much about institutions. All of them were more or less concerned with what they thought of as bad institutions. Ricardo was a great radical reformer. He wanted to change certain bad institutions; he sought to alter the financial practices of the British government, change the constitution of the Bank of England and spread savings banks among the working classes. But these earlier economists of the classical school thought that no fundamental change could come about in the scheme of economic institutions without spreading havoc among mankind. Remember that, when Ricardo canvassed the scheme of Robert Owen for setting up a cooperative state, he came reluctantly to the conclusion that any weakening of the institution of private property would be socially disastrous, because if a man did not have full assurance that he could enjoy the wealth that he accumulated, then the growth of capital would be checked; and what society needed most of for advancement was a rapid accumulation of capital.

John Stuart Mill, however, attempted modifications even of that doctrine, with his distinction between the laws of production and the laws of distribution. The laws of production on his showing partake of the nature of physical truths; they are unalterable. The laws relating to distribution, on the contrary, are man-made contrivances; they have had different forms in the past, they may be given very different forms in the future. He based his temperate hopes for the amelioration of the lot of the mass of mankind upon progressive changes in the institutions relating to the distribution of income and wealth.

Veblen does not by any means depart altogether from the views of his predecessors concerning institutions; but coming after Darwin he was able to think more freely about institutions as undergoing gradual evolution than men like Adam Smith or Ricardo or even John Stuart Mill could. That habit of thought was characteristic of Veblen's time. He was one of the first economists to work out the implications for the science of economics of the view of human society as the product of ceaseless change.

Taken on his own terms, his view provides a certain place even for the severest types of economic theory. Take for example the pecuniary logic type that was excogitated by his friend and admirer, Herbert J. Davenport. Davenport, remember, worked explicitly upon the supposition that men are animated by the private and acquisitive point of view, and taking that as his basic premise, he elaborated fully the terms in which the theorist has to define concepts like capital, what must be regarded as production and the way in which prices are determined, etc.

From Veblen's viewpoint, Davenport was working out the logic of a certain set of institutions, taking them as they stood in a given time and seeing what they would mean for human behavior if they had unrestricted sway over mankind. That may be from Veblen's viewpoint an enlightening thing to do, just as it may be helpful in dealing with problems in mathematics to have such things as perfect circles and straight lines. Yet, no one set of institutions does fully stamp its pattern upon human nature. Even the most thoroughgoing money makers remain human beings. People have whims. They have those inherited impulses which cannot be completely suppressed by the habits of life in modern activities. Consequently an account of economic activity drawn even in terms of the dominant economic institution of a certain day, as Veblen would say Davenport's logic was drawn, cannot be a satisfactory system of economics. It may contribute to the economist's understanding but it covers only part of the ground. More than that, when the theorist undertakes to work out this logic, ignoring the way in which the institution got established and the way it is changing, he has dropped out of sight some of the most important and interesting problems that an economist might attack.

Veblen himself at times makes casual, implicit use of orthodox economic theory. For instance, if the theorist looks carefully at that brilliant chapter in *The Theory of Business Enterprise* on The Theory of Modern Prosperity in which he discusses business cycles, he will find Veblen explaining how a rise of prices at the beginning of the period of prosperity spreads from its source to other lines of industry, spreads from prices of commodities to the price of labor, the price of loans, etc. In that discussion he is taking for granted that the reader, as well as the writer understands the theory of prices as expounded in the ordinary text books, for the view that he gives of the process of the spread of a rise in prices is one which can be reinterpreted if the reader likes, in ordinary terms of supply and demand theory. In short, his theory of the expansion phase of business cycles runs in terms of rise of prices, of wages, etc., in terms of changes of conditions of supply and demand.

Are Veblen's conclusions in conflict with those of more orthodox theorists? Incidentally at certain points. For most part does not touch them. From Veblen's own viewpoint does *The Theory of Business Enterprise* cover the field of economics? Of course not. There are his other discussions of economic problems; e.g., *The Theory of the Leisure Class* and *The Instinct of Workmanship*. But admitting that, is the theory of cumulative change the whole of economics or of any social science? Current working of economic activity under institutions at any given moment is part of Veblen's own discussion; e.g., his theory of business cycles in chapter VII, The Theory of Modern Welfare of *The Theory of Business Enterprise*. Orthodox theory concerned with such current working in determination of prices particularly the prices that determine the distribution of income.[39]

Veblen's general method of work is closely akin to that of the classical economists in the sense that he reasons things out on the basis of his own suppositions and his general knowledge of the world and makes little effort to check his conclusions by direct observation or by a more elaborate procedure of mass observation which statistics makes possible. Take some of his most characteristic pronouncements in *The Theory of Business Enterprise,* such for example as his statement that the cultural influence of the machine process is in the direction of inculcating in people materialistic habits of thought, that the machine process is culturally inimical to such notions as those connected with patriotism and religion, that it undermines the conventional support for the institution of property, etc. Veblen knows all these things, knows them in much the same way that Ricardo knew about the factors that controlled the payment of rent for land. He has a body of observations in mind; so does Ricardo. Veblen has his scheme of ideas that makes all these observations fit into one another neatly, just as the Ricardian theory of rent owes its scientific interest, its immense prestige, to the neatness with which it coordinated men's observations about the fertility of different lands, their locations and the amount of rents that were paid for them in money.

Or take again Veblen's proposition that socialism does not spread far beyond the circle of machine tenders, that its scope is substantially the scope of the classes who are disciplined in the machine process. That proposition presumably was suggested to his mind by observations of the socialist movement in different parts of the world, though it did not seem to fit very well in the American conditions, because though the United States has a highly developed machine

---

[39] Outlines, May 2, 1935; "Veblen," APP 44-53, no. 18.

process it did not have a highly developed socialist movement. It is a proposition that Veblen makes no formal effort to prove beyond citing certain parts of the German evidence that is compatible with his notion. He was, in laying down rules of this sort, proceeding very much in the fashion in which the classical economists and their successors had done.

Consequently while Veblen's type of economics, this new institutionalism, does bring to the fore a range of problems which had not been recognized clearly by the classical economists, had been dealt with rather by people like Marx most effectively and to a considerable extent by the historical school, yet it does not differ in method and not fundamentally even in subject matter from the work which people had been accustomed to. It owes the impression of novelty largely to the introduction of a study of economic life among simpler people and still more to Veblen's fondness for playing up the features of economic life which almost all students find doubtful.

Classical economics, on the other hand, had tended to be at least a quasi-apology for the modern organization of society. Adam Smith had started economics as a grand attack upon the existing mercantilist framework, as an argument for a different type of economic organization: the "obvious and simple system of natural liberty." As that system came to be established it proved to be compatible with, presumably in large measure responsible for, the vast increase in wealth which the Industrial Revolution made possible in a technological sense. On the other hand, this "obvious and simple system of natural liberty" proved to be compatible with continued poverty among large numbers of mankind. The economists on the whole in their writing tended to present the bright side of the picture, to show how it is that in a system in which people are pursuing their own gain competition prevents the consumers from being exploited, how it is that the system of organization affords a strong inducement for industry and provides opportunities and incentives for the accumulation of capital upon which further progress depends.

Here and there one finds critics of this system, men like Thomas Carlyle and John Ruskin who developed vigorous onslaughts upon features of the modern economic organization with which the economist has comparatively little to do. Socialists preceded by the labor writers of Ricardo's generation point out the extent to which the working classes are exploited in a modern state and show how comparatively slight is the benefit that they derive from the remarkable increase in productivity which the Industrial Revolution brought with it. Here and there is a writer of the orthodox brand like John Stuart Mill facing the difficulties with candor. But the general trend has been in the direction rather of marveling at the intricacy of modern organization and the factor which it provides of making people industrious and frugal and proclaiming the rather obvious fact that in these modern centuries of capitalism the average standard of living has been higher than enjoyed in earlier ages.

Veblen, with his fondness for the simple life, with his interest in the material process of providing for men's wants, with his more than skeptical attitude toward the process of business and with his uncanny analytic skill, constructs largely out of materials provided by the industrial magnates who testified before the United States Industrial Commission of 1899-1902 a body of economic theory which is concerned in large part with the shady side of the picture, to show the way in which the pursuit of profit runs athwart the industrial process of producing serviceable goods, the extent to which business earnings may result not from the constructive efforts of the captain of industry but from the bargaining or skill of a man who makes his money by interfering with the process of supplying people with goods at reasonable prices.

Dissonance arising between economic welfare and business prosperity. What becomes of Adam Smith's unseen hand? of John Stuart Mill's doctrine that money makes no difference save one of convenience? To Veblen use of money is central feature of pecuniary institutions and this makes an enormous difference in outlook and character and outcome of economic behavior from leisure class to business cycles.

Veblen's theory. Quite a different type from those hitherto dealt with. Veblen differs far more from Jevons, Alfred Marshall, Fetter and Davenport than they differ among themselves. This difference rests upon a treatment of a different set of problems and on a different conception of human nature. Classical writers and their orthodox followers emphasize the rational calculating elements in human nature. Veblen emphasizes the element of habituation. Sees habits formed mainly by discipline of daily work. Widespread habits are *institutions*. "An institution is of the nature of a usage which has become axiomatic and indispensable by habituation and general acceptance. Its physiological counterpart would presumably be any one of those habitual addictions that are now attracting the attention of the experts on sobriety."[40]

Institutions are the most important factor in behavior to study, because they are the factor that changes. Men improve little in capaciy for reasoning, their instinctive propensities change little. But there is a cumulative

[40] "The Captain of Industry," *The Freeman,* April 18, 1923, p. 128, note; reprinted in *Absentee Ownership and Business Enterprise in Recent Times* (New York: Huebsch, 1923) p. 101, note.

evolution in institutions. The complex of institutions prevailing in any community at any time constitutes its culture. It is this complex which we must study if we would gain insight into economic behavior.

Antecedents. Treatment of economic institutions by orthodox political economy. Classical political economy took the fundamental institutions for granted as mature social achievements which would not change. Held private property to be necessary. More important than equality in ownership or income. With private property went use of money, investment for profit as guide of production. Sought to amend institutions not in line with these fundamentals; e.g., improve banking system, organization of labor market, check protective tariffs, maintain free competition, etc. Did not study evolution of institutions. That held not part of economist's task. Cf., Davenport, "the task before us is the study of the situation as it actually is, with small attention to its genesis, excepting so far as its past may throw light on its present, and entirely without attention to conjectural or probable future modifications."[41] The exception seems not to be taken as highly important by Davenport.

Thus Veblen puts into the center of economics a subject which writers of the classical school pushed to the edge and which Davenport, at least, pushed over the edge of economics. To repeat, study of economic institutions of course did not begin with Veblen. Richard Jones and his study of rents—*metayer*, ryot, peasant rents in Poland, etc., and the early critics of capitalism; Robert Owen and his new set of economic institutions; William Thompson, Thomas Hodgskin, Piercy Ravenstone and the other Ricardian socialists; Simonde de Sismondi, *Nouveaux principes d'économie politique;* Charles Fourier and St. Simon; John Stuart Mill and his emphasis upon importance of human institutions in distribution. German historical school: Roscher, Hildebrand and Knies; their criticism of classical political economy; their program for development of economics, their slight accomplishment; Schmoller and his mechanical juxtaposition of sections in economic history and theory. Marx and his theory of the trend of institutional change; his researches into current economic history and demonstration of way in which a *theory* of institutional change can be built up. Much more intimate blend of history and analysis than Schmoller effected.

Veblen's contemporaries in institutional economics: Mr. and Mrs. Webb, Sir William Ashley, *An Introduction to English History and Theory,* Werner Sombart—Richard Ehrenberg, John R. Commons *Legal Foundations of Capitalism* [and *Institutional Economics.*] How Veblen differs from these contemporaries. Firmer theoretical grasp, keener psychological insight. Less concern with technique of historical learning. Satirical temper.

Veblen's essays on "The Preconceptions of Economic Science." Differs from ordinary types of discussion of the history of economic theory. Of the latter there are two types which often merge into one another. 1. Tracing "the pedigree of the doctrines."[42] Implicit assumption is that one man's

---

[41] *The Economics of Enterprise* (New York: Macmillan, 1913) p. 26.
[42] See Veblen's [comments] *The Theory of Business Enterprise* (New York: Scribner's, 1904) p. 72 ft.

work is a logical elaboration and continuation of his predecessor's views. Example, Böhm-Bawerk, *Capital and Interest*. 2. Historical method. Views of any writer are dependent upon the circumstances of his time; e.g., Ricardo's theory of rent is result of economic situation of England in his day. Examples: usually worked out in conjunction with first type; e.g., Edwin Cannan's *A History of the Theories of Production and Distribution*.[42a]

Veblen's contribution: Not concerned to deny importance of either of preceding lines of explanation, but adds emphasis upon another factor generally overlooked; viz., preconceptions of the writers. What are they? Axiomatic assumptions. Usually unconscious. May not receive any explicit statement. If they do, it comes out incidentally. No effort made to justify them. They are the things which, in view of writers, have only to be stated to be perceived as true. Examples: natural order of the Physiocrats; guiding hand of Adam Smith; hedonism of Ricardo; meliorative trend of later classical writers. Whence do they come? Not reasoned out. Otherwise would not be preconceptions. Not lineally derived from writings of predecessors. Derived by group inheritance. They are the common sense of the day. Formed—according to Veblen's preconception—by disciplinary influence of prevalent habits of life. *Why they shift?* Relation to historical type of history of economic theory. Importance. From foundation of the systems of economics. These systems seem absurd when viewed from standpoint of other preconceptions, but are fairly consistent; e.g., logically valid when the preconceptions on which they are based are taken for granted.

Constructive results which follow from Veblen's discussion of preconceptions. We have no means of deciding the ultimate test of truth in economics; e.g., prevalent 'scientific' point of view relies on preconception of impersonal causal sequence. But we cannot prove validity of this assumption. According to the assumption itself its basis lies in the fact that our minds have been drilled by discipline of modern life into looking at things in this way. When we get a causal explanation we are satisfied. We know that causality is a gratuitous assumption on our part—as gratuitous as physiocratic law of nature. Hume proved as much in the eighteenth century. Our only logical defense is that this assumption *works; i.e.*, that it enables us to use things more effectively. Consequently what our generation wants in economics is a theory of causal process in human activity so far as it is concerned

---

[42a] Interestingly Cannan was anxious that Mitchell succeed him at the London School of Economics. "December 8, 1925. Discussed with Lucy [his wife] a tentative inquiry from Edwin Cannan whether I would consider a professorship in London School of Economics. . . . December 11, Lucy talked with Mrs. Stott about future of the [pioneering] school [which Mrs. Mitchell established in progressive education] —anent our possible transfer to London. . . . December 12. Lucy and I discussing the London question. . . . December 14 discussed National Bureau of Economic Research affairs and the London School of Economics matter with [Edwin F.] Gay [of Harvard, an old friend and collaborator] at the Century Club [New York City]. December 15. Dictated another large batch of letters—among them one to Cannan saying I cannot consider the London School of Economics if it is offered." (Mitchell, "Diary.") [Almost six years earlier he had been first approached by the London School of Economics for which there is only one brief diary entry.] "March 22, 1920. Received letter asking whether I would accept a professorship in London School of Economics."

with the material ends of life. Emphasis is on growth of habits and institutions—a process of cumulative change, primarily in men's way of doing and thinking. Prevailing type of economics—e.g., marginal utility does not satisfy this want. Takes an offhand solution of the most important problem —that of present human nature—for granted. Does not account for it. Nor is the solution in line with that worked out in causal terms by psychology and ethnology. But if evolutionary theory of economics is developed will it be true? That question cannot be answered—as said above. Will it continue to satisfy our successors? We do not know.

In short—we should not be the dupes of our preconceptions. We have them, whether we like it or not. Best to work them as explicitly as we can. Must make sure that details are logically consistent with them. But it is naive to fancy that what is common sense to us will appeal as common sense to later generations. This is the most dazzlingly disconcerting of Veblen's insights—the hardest to live with, but also the most enlightening.

Question on "The Place of Science in Modern Civilisation."[43] What is it that Veblen undertakes to do in these articles? What connection is there between the essays on "The Preconceptions of Economic Science" and this paper? What connection between discussion of this paper and our discussion of economic method with reference to economic man?

Essay an effort to explain how the scientific habit of thought has won its place of unquestioned authority in modern life. Ask a few questions to aid in understanding of the subject. What is the difference between pragmatic knowledge (in Veblen's use of the term) and the knowledge formulated under instinct of idle curiosity? What are the genetic relations between the two kinds of knowledge? What form does non-pragmatic knowledge assume at savage stage of culture? In terms of what are higher syntheses made? Apply same questions to barbarism. Note that early middle ages of Europe assumed to be barbarism. What was reason for change from principle of procreation to that of prescriptive authority as leading idea in formulation of non-pragmatic knowledge? What changes took place in formulation as transition was made from middle ages to early modern times? Why? What further changes on transition to latest phase? Why? In what fields does scientific habit of thought properly belong? Why not in law, theology and scholarship? Why has it begun to invade these other fields? Why are modern men restive under scientific habit of thought? How do men justify validity of principles on which their higher syntheses are based? Does this paper prove the superiority of scientific thought? Is it proper to ask whether scientific habit is better or worse than other ways of organizing non-pragmatic thought? What sort of evidence can be found bearing on question discussed? Has Veblen's method of discussion any relation to materialistic theory of history?

Veblen's *reductio ad absurdum* of hedonistic economics, in "Professor Clark's Economics."[44] This type is based on assumptions that (1) production

---

[43] Published in 1906, in *The American Journal of Sociology;* reprinted in the *Place of Science in Modern Civilisation*, pp. 1-31.

[44] Reprinted in *The Place of Science in Modern Civilisation*, pp. 203-214.

proceeds to margin where pain cost equals pleasure gain. (2) Total utility of product equals marginal utility times number of units. (3) Similarly total cost equals marginal cost times units of labor. On this basis no producer's or consumer's surplus can emerge. At best the hedonistic producer cannot gain. On the average he loses, because pleasure obtained is more often less than more pleasure anticipated. What is reply from hedonistic point of view? Drop second assumption? and third? Veblen's point that the *intensity* of labor in each hour should be taken into account. Seems to hold on any thorough hedonistic assumption.

Veblen summed up the criticisms of psychological preconceptions of economic theory more effectively than anyone else. I suppose he knew more than any other economist of the other sciences concerned with human behavior. To him the central problem of economics is the evolution of institutions— the prevalent ways of thinking about values. His technical papers on the preconceptions of economic theory were backed up by his studies of certain institutions—*The Theory of the Leisure Class; The Theory of Business Enterprise; The Instinct of Workmanship; Absentee Ownership;* and by his case studies of German and Japanese cultural evolution. Few professional economists liked to admit that Veblen's criticisms had much influence on their own works but I think he must have led many to think anxiously about their fundamental assumptions.

Spent some time on question: Could a writer with Veblen's psychological assumptions treat the problems of orthodox economic theory? Took Veblen's psychological assumptions to mean insistence upon the importance of instincts and habits. Took problems of orthodox theory to mean value and distribution. Discussion covered a wide range. Suggested that we can take instincts and habits as setting ends of desire and rational choice as concerned with means. Then Veblen's psychological assumptions help to explain value and distribution (in so far as the valuation of aims goes); but require to be supplemented by orthodox psychological assumption of rationality. Questioned whether a theorist with Veblen's assumptions would admit that the orthodox problems of value and distribution are genuine problems of economic behavior. Suggested on the other hand that the working out of Veblen's problem—the cumulative growth of institution—implies an understanding of how those institutions work at each successive stage, that in fact Veblen himself has thrown much light upon problems of value and distribution—though he has been most interested in illuminating corners of the field neglected by orthodox theorists; e.g., he has made business cycles an integral part of his economic theory; he has discussed the relation of profit making to industrial production; he has analyzed the effects of machine tending upon the valuations of the operatives, and the like. This suggestion I supplemented by throwing in the idea that the great economic institutions with which Veblen is concerned may have logical implications of their own not unlike the logical implications of our space perceptions, and consequently that orthodox theory may be regarded as a working out of these implications for economic behavior, much as Euclidian geometry is an elaboration of our space perceptions. Thus from Veblen's viewpoint orthodox economics may be regarded as having a certain use. It shows what economic behavior would be were it rational enough to be able to accept and be guided by all the implications of the institutions in question. This view derives a certain force from the fact that orthodox economics is plausible as an account of economic behavior under the money economy. Finally, I asked the class to turn our original question about and consider whether a writer with the orthodox conception of human nature could treat Veblen's problem of the cumulative change of institutions.

Procedure. (1) Ask for answers to question last posed. Expect answers to be that assumption of rationality is not of much use in discussing evolution of institutions—at least the kind of rationality which is assumed in economic texts. Rational explanations have been given in the past freely enough; e.g., the domestication of animals explained by foresight of advantages to be obtained; development of a priesthood explained by craft of the people who became priests. But such explanations do not fit in with later knowledge of savage life. And even in recent times it seems that our institutions have a way of taking us by surprise.

Rise of what Veblen calls machine process as an example: Inventions themselves involved a great deal of arduous thinking, contriving. Developed by rationally directed trial and error, taking advantage of happy accidents on occasion. Practical application of the inventions also involved a large amount of rationality. But the widespread use of machinery soon involved consequences which no one had foreseen: Decline in relative position of the landed interest in England; rapid increase in economic dependence of one nation on another; rise of trade unions; domestication of the business cycle; growth of urban population as compared with rural population; specialization of labor, repetitive work. These developments took England by surprise. Confounded Adam Smith's expectations relating to coming of free trade, importance of joint stock companies,[45] and Ricardo's expectations regarding shares of landlords in the distribution of income, profits, coming of the static state. If anyone doubts that the great changes in economic organization were unforeseen let him ask himself with what confidence he can foresee the economic changes which the further progress of the machine process will make in the next quarter century. Foresight and rational control over the process of cumulative change in institutions is an enlargement of rationality for which we are beginning to strive in detail. To increase such rationality is the greatest service the social sciences could render mankind.[46] But this is a bit of rationality in the making.

In short, it seems clear that whatever opinion we may hold about man's rationality in dealing with slight variations of customary routine problems—like the expenditure of money income for standard consumer's goods—we do not attribute to man's reason a prominent place in guiding changes in habits.[47]

---

[45] [Adam Smith held that it was utopian to expect free trade in the foreseeable future; he doubted that joint stock companies generally were useful, or could survive except by a legal monopoly.]

[46] C.f. W. F. Ogburn, *Social Change.*

[47] This is the great point made by H. W. Stuart, "The Phases of the Economic Interest," in John Dewey *et al., Creative Intelligence,* (1917).

(2) Some conclusions to which the discussion points. (a) Concerning the relation between Veblen's problem of cumulative growth [and change] and the orthodox problem of analysis of the *status quo*. Both problems are genuine and important whether one takes the orthodox or the Veblenian viewpoint. That a writer like Davenport refuses to regard Veblen's problem of cumulative change in institutions as part of economic theory does not mean that even he ignores its significance either for explaining the present, enlarging our measure of control or forecasting the future. (b) In our discussion of the differences between Veblen's psychological assumptions and those of orthodox economists have we not simplified an oversharp difference between instinct and habit on the one hand and rationality on the other? Picture of the function of thinking which John Dewey gives us shows it as a fumbling but nevertheless a tolerably efficient way of dealing with difficulties. Institutions have an enormous influence upon rationality—indeed they make the great difference between the thinking powers of a modern physicist and an exceptionally able cave dweller. For the modern man has at his disposal the net resultant of an enormous amount of past thinking, with its established techniques—mathematical and experimental —for dealing with problems of a certain type. (Bring in previous discussion about rationalistic explanations of savage and civilized life. In class I asked why we can still accept as plausible explanations of economic behavior posited on rationality while we have given up our rationalizing explanations of behavior of savages? Answer is that institutions of money economy play such a large role in our present behavior.) On the other hand these institutions are themselves in large part the result of past rational choices; e.g., John R. Commons's demonstration in *Legal Foundations of Capitalism* of the large role played by conscious judicial selection in building up our present economic institutions; that is, the extension of the notion of property in legal history. In short, what rationality we have is summed up for the most part in our institutions. The institutions represent successful adjustment. They are largely rational or once were so. And habits once established economize thought. Not necessary for a man to consider deeply what type of garments he shall use to protect himself against cold. His thinking can be confined to minor details. (3) So complex are these relations between institutions and reason indeed that we cannot disentangle them. No discussion of economic behavior can give objectively valid results which present man as guided solely by reason or solely by instincts and habits. Indeed neither Veblen nor the orthodox make that mistake. Even the classical economists laid heavy stress upon habit— note the role played in their theory of distribution by the standard of living and the habit of marrying and having children when at all possible. Just what role the two elements play no theorist has ever made out or probably can ever make out. The whole effort to explain behavior from the *inside*, by analysis of conscious mental processes, has serious limitations which we see no way of transcending.

(4). Is there not then some more effective way of treating human nature which will prepare us to attack both Veblen's problems and those of the orthodox theorist with hope of success? Behaviorism. Chief point for us is its objective attitude and methods—though perhaps we need not refuse all help from the hypothesis of consciousness as some behaviorists profess to do. Sidesteps the question about relative importance of instinct, habit and reason and concentrates upon the problem what men actually have done or now do. Since observation indicates wide variety of actions, behaviorism suggests resort wherever possible to quantitative methods of work—use of statistical description of mass phenomena and study of quantitative relations among our statistical series. (Suggests also that this observation be centered upon the mass phenomena. In this sense, the life of the peasant is more important to economic historian than life of the king.)

Where statistical material is not available—as in study of past economic history, in speculations about future or in treatment of many problems set by orthodox theory—there behaviorism suggests that our results, based as they must be upon relatively scanty and inexact observation supplemented by conjecture, are subject to a wide margin of doubt. Just what problems can be treated successfully in this objective fashion we do not know until we try, but we have a comfortable assurance that the range of problems will expand as collection of statistical data becomes wider and better. Very rapid progress of late [1924] in this direction.

(5). Effect of taking this viewpoint would have perhaps the same results upon our rating of Veblen's and orthodox work. Some, at least, of the conclusions are susceptible of quantitative treatment and are significant enough from the behaviorist viewpoint to merit treating. Some of these problems probably cannot be treated on an objective basis without rephrasing.

(6). Probably neither Veblen nor the majority of orthodox theorists would quarrel with the program for extending objective study of economic behavior on a quantitative basis wherever possible. A member of the class pointed out yesterday [April 1, 1924] Veblen now sets less store by instincts as a useful concept than he once did—for he keeps up with psychology. He prefers the behaviorist viewpoint. Orthodox theorists will probably take a similar view in most cases. It was Alfred Marshall who made the great plea for advancing from qualitative to quantitative analysis in the 1890's.[48]

Such discussions of methods as we have been indulging in may have a modest value. But that value depends upon the aid they give us in constructive work. Validity of our conclusion in favor of behaviorism, or objective psychology if we believe that better, is to be tested by the effectiveness of our efforts at constructive work.

Characteristics of Veblen's type of theory: As opposed to mechanics of self interest and price theory, study of actual world. As opposed to American psychological school, pecuniary logic, neo-classicism, study of process of cumulative change, in the sense that Veblen does not conceive of dynamic changes as always tending toward static adjustment. As opposed to Marxism, causal driving forces of change are the effects produced on men's minds by discipline of daily lives, or more specifically in the modern age what

[48] Marshall, "The Old Generation of Economists and the New," 1897; reprinted in *Memorials of Alfred Marshall* ed. by A. C. Pigou (London: Macmillan, 1925) pp. 301, 309-310.

brings on the changes is alterations of habits of thought caused by discipline of daily life working machinery. Marx on the other hand explained in terms of self interest of men under circumstances which themselves change from some inner necessity. What is it really? Cumulative—having no final goal like Marxian socialism. As opposed to historical theory of Schmoller's kind, intimate blending of historical research and analysis to explain evolution, current working and probable future of institution in hand.

What shall we call his type of theory? It is a study of the process of cumulative change by which an institution—business enterprise—conceived as a habit of thought—rose, worked for a time and may decay. Realistic historical, analytic. Shall we call it cumulative change, genetic, institutional? Answer: Institutional.

Veblen's concern with the evolution of institutions establishes a bond between his work and that of the historical school. But this bond is a loose one. His methods of work differ widely from those of the historian working with documentary methods on detailed problems. They have more in common with the procedures of a philosophic observer at large. Perhaps we can say that he was starting to build the science of ethology which Mill thought needed and possible. But that was also inexact; Mill's ethology was to be deductive science, which an account of evolution of habits of thinking was not. Veblen was a Darwinian and Mill came not too early to read, but too early to grasp the implications of *The Origin of Species* for the social sciences. A closer analogy is that to work of anthropologists and men interested in early practices out of which the law developed. Influenced by Herbert Spencer, Sir Henry Maine, Henry Lewis Morgan and other writers on the evolution of social institutions—the family, the clan, the state, the crafts and the arts of primitive societies. Veblen made an extensive and very free use of ethnological materials. His knowledge of later stages of economic history was wide—but it was not the knowledge of a specialist. And his way of dealing with these materials was to think about the mental attitude that different ways of getting a living will engender. Usually he had some observations upon actual practice to guide him, and often he would adduce citations of such material as confirmation of his views. But he did not go in systematically for "inductive verification" of his conclusions.[49] For the most part a reader must compare these conclusions with his own observations, and if he does not interpret them *a la* Veblen that is the end of the story for him. How uncannily right in some cases may be judged by reading H. T. Oshima, "Veblen on Japan," *Social Research,* November 1943. How wrong he could be in other cases may be judged from his forecast in 1904 in *The Theory of Business Enterprise* that business cycles would degenerate into a dragging depression from which only now and then would some extraneous happening produce a spurt of activity. Probably Veblen's chief influence on economic thinking has been to make economists more thoroughly aware of the fact that their work deals with a peculiar complex of institutions, that will presumably have its day

[49] "[Veblen's] work is on the whole like Darwin's—a speculative system uniting a vast range of observations in a highly organized whole . . . but waiting for its ultimate validation upon more intensive and tamer inquiries." Mitchell, "Thorstein Veblen," 1936, reprinted in *The Backward Art of Spending Money,* p. 302.

and then pass away. That fact Mill made tolerably clear without producing any notable change in economic theory. Perhaps Veblen's caustic critique will have more effect than Mill's serene hopefulness did. Certainly Veblen has annoyed many economists efficiently. The champions of orthodox theory think it part of their task to refute his criticisms and enlarge upon alleged futility of his approach.

Recapitulation: Criticism of classical economics. It has dealt with problems of secondary scientific interest and neglected the fundamental problems which concern the evolution of economic institutions. What institutions are —the habits of thought and action that prevail in a culture giving it its distinctive character. Leading institutions of current society in the more advanced nations: Business enterprise ([in margin] absentee ownership) and the machine process. These two institutions dominate the scene in Great Britain and the United States. They are coming to dominate the continent of Europe. They are making rapid headway in Japan. The only way they can be accounted for is on evolutionary grounds.

Current economics ought to be centered on way in which these two institutions have risen to dominance, their effects on the minds of men, the further changes they are now undergoing and the culture that will result in the calculable future. Instead of dealing with these problems, economics has devoted itself to working out the logical implications of business enterprise as if it were the natural habit of human thought, instead of a passing phase in the evolution of culture. In so doing economic theorists have imputed to all men the calculating habits a bookkeeper has to learn and by which a business enterprise is supposed to be guided. Bentham's felicific calculus is admirably fitted to their purpose. It supposes that men reckon in units of pleasure and pain, as bookkeepers reckon in terms of dollar income and dollar outgo. A most artificial view of human nature—one that is plausible only in a society so dominated by business enterprise that the technical methods of controlling business seem inherited instead of acquired characteristics. Economic theory of this sort is not sheer nonsense just because the institution of business enterprise is so firmly established. Since it is one of the two dominating institutions of modern life, it is worth while to work out its implications for conduct in detail. But the genuine value of this performance can be grasped only from the institutional viewpoint; that is, only by understanding that business enterprise is only one of the dominant institutions of the day, that it runs at cross purposes to the other great institution of our times—the machine process—and that its period of domination will be limited.

Genuine understanding of the current situation and its probable future development can be had only by working out the cultural incidence of the machine process as carefully as the economists have worked out pecuniary logic. Working with machinery tends to make men think of all processes in terms of material cause and effect. They tend to become undevout, unpatriotic, improvident, unromantic. They are not readily stirred by appeals to property, to loyalty, to natural rights. They do not feel that ownership of property gives the owner a right to dispose of that property in any way he sees fit. In short the drift of their thinking derived from habituation to machine tending makes it increasingly difficult for them to see the force of the arguments based upon the assumption of property rights. And their way of arguing is as unconvincing to the classes which are disciplined by business enterprise.

So modern society is breeding a conflict between two incompatible ways of looking at economic questions, and there is nothing effective that can be done to end the conflict. Business enterprise cannot dispense with the machine process, because it can flourish only as it disposes over the usufruct of that most efficient method of producing goods. But the machine process inevitably produces habits of thought that are incompatible with the continued dominance of business enterprise. Only cure is war, which harks back to and stands to revive more ancient habits of thought in the masses. But that cure means suicide for business. So the institution of business enterprise promises to have a relatively short life—either to perish through a revival of militarism or to be superseded by a scheme of organization that will suit the minds of the machine tenders.[50] Thus generalizing, where John Stuart Mill ran his theorizing on the basis of psychological assumptions of calculations of interest, Veblen operates with the cultural incidence of certain customs (to use Mill's word) and their evolution under the impact of cumulative changes in methods of getting a living.[51]

"The scientific character of Veblen's work. Is Veblen's work scientific? (a) His claim to scientific basis. Treats matters of fact susceptible to examination, to test truth or falsity; (b) effect of machine process on materialistic habits of thought of the masses. Based on German socialistic experience. Classes cherishing present order most strongly in districts not touched by modern process of life—agricultural. Cannot establish definitely for business men; (c) supplements view of modern cultural situation by knowledge of doctrine in past; (1) has no patience with statistics, or definite references to past documentary evidence; (2) considers obvious drift of situation as a whole; (d) not scientific in same rigid way of sta-

---

[50] ["It seems possible to say this much, that the full dominion of business enterprise is necessarily a transitory dominion." *The Theory of Business Enterprise,* p. 415. Note that Veblen says "the full dominion" not "the dominion."]

[51] Outlines, April 21, 1915; "Closing Lectures," May 14, 16, 1917, April 8, 1918, April 24, 1924, May 2, 1935; "Veblen's Preconceptions of Economic Science," discussion before economics seminar, University of California, May 5, 1911; "Seminar in Economic Changes and Economic Theory," March 30, December 21, 1943, January 11, May 2, 1944; "Fifty Years As An Economist," address before Political Economy Club, Columbia University, May 11, 1945; "Veblen," APP 44-53, no. 18; "Transition to Veblen," APP 44-53, no. 89.

[Some additional notes on Veblen:] I think "logical" is just the word Veblen would have applied to Davenport's work. That it leaves out so much that Veblen thought basic was due to the inadequate array of premises in Davenport's thought. The causes operating in different processes seem to be cumulative in different degree. To a certain extent I can treat the problem of cumulative changes in business cycles, but it is difficult: Also and this is important the cumulations in business cycles reverse their direction in a short time, and return in large measure to *status quo ante.*

Veblen points out efficiency of present order—without this high efficiency waste on a colossal scale would not be possible. The notion of crisis of constantly increasing

tistical investigations, but largely is so; it is a series of statements concerning matters of fact susceptible in broad way of proof or disproof."[52]

Whereas institutionalism was a name plastered upon Veblen and his disciples, one [leading economist of Veblen's generation boldly] accepted the designation. [The discussion will now turn to] John R. Commons who was very much a reformer.[53]

---

intensity belongs to Marx. Whereas Veblen thought business enterprise tended to establish a condition of chronic depression, interrupted by booms that will grow rarer.

For periods and processes illuminated by full records I can go a little further than Darwin and Veblen could go with their materials, but not much farther. I too study the evidence and select salient factors for special attention. The indefinite number of causes is an essential factor in my present stock of working ideas. (Mitchell's replies to Joseph Dorfman's comments on manuscript introduction for *What Veblen Taught* (1936).

[52] Notes taken in Professor Mitchell's course in Types of Economic Theory, Columbia University, by W. H. Steiner in 1917. In possession of Joseph Dorfman.

[53] Paragraph from Outline, "Seminar in Economic Changes and Economic Theory," December 21, 1943, January 11, 1944.

CHAPTER XXI

John R. Commons and the Economics of Group Action

Institutional economics has been much discussed since Veblen's first books were published. There are a variety of essays, some read before the American Economic Association, some in the critical reviews, that try to ascertain what institutional economics is and generally end with the complaint that institutionalists have done little except criticize economics of the standard sort and have not gotten round to the task of putting anything in its place. The most that the institutionalists give us, besides the criticisms, is discussions of certain aspects of economic processes like those of Veblen dealing with the machine process and business enterprise in modern life, but their work is of a monographic sort at best. They do not undertake to develop a body of institutional theory which can be regarded as anything like a substitute for the classical brand.

This general attitude lends a keen interest to the appearance in 1934 of a book by no less a person than John R. Commons (1862-1945) of the University of Wisconsin. *Institutional Economics*, a volume of 921 pages, covers a wide range of economic problems and certainly deserves consideration as a valiant attempt to provide the constructive contribution which had been demanded of institutionalists. Along with the volume should be read its companion piece, the earlier *Legal Foundations of Capitalism* (1924).

Even more than in most cases the comprehension of Commons's work is promoted by an understanding of the writer's own experience. He says in the first page of *Institutional Economics*: "My point of view is based on my participation in collective activities, from which I here derive a theory of the part played by collective action in control of individual action." That is, as he sees things, his institutional economics is derived primarily from his participation in collective activity. Indeed, that participation has been singularly varied, active and long continued.

701

Commons was born in 1862 near the small town of Hollandsberg, Ohio, on the border between Ohio and Indiana. His father was a Quaker who came from a family that lived in the South and because they hated slavery had moved north of the Ohio River. His mother was a woman of New England extraction who had graduated from Oberlin College; she was a fervent Presbyterian and an ardent Republican. His father had strong literary interests; he was a reader of Shakespeare, Darwin and Herbert Spencer. He was inclined toward atheism in middle life but turned in his later years when he became feeble, and after he had lost his favorite child, to psychic research and then to Christian Science for comfort. The father was engaged in newspaper work for a time but was an almost impossible business man. Consequently, the support of the family fell largely upon the capable shoulders of the mother. There were two boys who grew up: John and a younger brother, Alvin. They took up the printing trade in their father's country newspaper office and when through their mother's energy they entered Oberlin College they earned part of their expenses by type-setting on the student paper and by working during vacations in a printing office in Cleveland.

There Commons joined the Typographical Union and had his first experience in "collective action in control of individual action."[1] His college work was much impeded by the necessity of earning money and also by periodic attacks of ill health. It took him six years to obtain his B.A.[2] and in his senior year he decided to turn from his original plan of becoming a journalist to study economics. A lively interest in economics had been aroused in him through reading Henry George's *Progress and Poverty*. That volume, which made such a wide appeal to American working men as well as to European [and American] intellectuals, was put into his hands characteristically by a fellow printer. The lad at once got some of his fellows to join with him in setting up a political economy club.

His interest in economics was also fed through a young Japanese friend who was engrossed in social and economic matters; Commons assisted in his efforts to obtain money by helping him arrange lectures on Japanese economic questions and became more deeply concerned with economics. He decided to go to Johns Hopkins after taking his bachelor's degree in 1888 and for the purpose borrowed $1,000 from two friendly Oberlin trustees.

At Johns Hopkins he came in contact with Professor Richard T.

---

[1] [This is Commons's definition of "institution."]
[2] [The first year was spent in the preparatory division to make up deficiencies in his lower school education.]

Ely who had but relatively recently returned from his German experiences and who at that stage of his career was a most ardent advocate in the United States of the general viewpoint of the German historical school. Ely set this vigorous and eager young man who had been a practical printer, who knew working people and how to deal with them, to studying problems of charity organization and similar practical matters; Commons discovered, what he had not known before, that economics could be something more than a deductive discussion of the sort that he had heard from his teachers in Oberlin, of the sort that he found so brilliantly represented in *Progress and Poverty*. For this new type of work he developed extraordinary aptitude and fondness.

But his ordinary academic work did not prosper. He seemed to have what he himself called a stubborn curiosity. He very much wanted to find out things for himself. He did not believe things because he found them printed in books. He was of a skeptical turn of mind, skeptical even of scientific men. He always had to discover by personal investigation whether anything was true or not. And, if he could not find the muscles alleged to be in the heart by getting a heart from the butcher shop and cutting it up, he was not satisfied. That habit of mind impedes academic work as it is carried on. The person who proceeds smoothly and brilliantly through college and graduate work, alas can take in promptly and quickly what other people have found out and set down in books for his edification— and his mind raises no particular objections to believing what is in the books or is told him from lecture platforms.

Commons not being of that sort never got on well, particularly in examinations; after he had been two years at Johns Hopkins he made a flat failure, he recalls, in the history examination. This prevented him from getting a fellowship. So he could not go on in the usual fashion and obtain a doctor's degree. His teachers had considerable confidence in him, however, and they recommended him for a tutorship at Wesleyan where he received a salary of $1,000 and promptly got married. So he had not yet been able to repay any substantial part of the money that he had borrowed to study at Hopkins.

At Wesleyan he tried to teach in the orthodox, systematic fashion and scored so much of a failure that three months before the year was over the president of the institution told him he would not be wanted the following year. But, once again, his friends had confidence in him and at Oberlin they arranged an assistant professorship which paid the magnificent sum of $1,200. He stayed a year and then went to Indiana University, where his salary was increased again, this time to $2,000. There he succeeded his friend and Johns Hopkins classmate, Edward A. Ross [1866-1951], who was being taken by the former president of Indiana, David Starr Jordan, to the newly established Stanford University.[3]

Commons stayed at Indiana three years, which was in those days a long time in one place. There he became secretary of the American Institute of Christian Sociology of which Ely was president. The institute soon split and disappeared, according to Commons, on the issue whether "Christian Socialism meant Love of Man or Love of Woman."[4] That left Commons suspicious of love of any sort as the basis of social reform. He was increasingly convinced that the place to look for better conditions in the future, was not to the feelings and attitudes of the individual, but to social arrangements in which incompatible individuals could be induced to work together in some orderly and effective fashion.

While he was at Indiana, John S. Huyler, the gentleman who was known to an earlier generation as the maker of chocolate candy, created a chair of sociology and civics at Methodist-affiliated Syracuse University and Chancellor J. R. Day, its head, invited the versatile young man from the west to fill the post. The president of Indiana told Commons to accept the offer. Commons humorously told the chancellor that he was "a socialist, a single-taxer, a free-silverite, a greenbacker, a municipal ownerist, and a member of the Congregationalist Church." The Chancellor said it was all right so long as he

---

[3] [Jordan became the first head of Stanford. Ross eventually shifted his interests to sociology exclusively; he and Commons were later together at the University of Wisconsin.]

[4] Commons, *Myself* (New York: Macmillan, 1934) p. 51. ["*The Institute of Christian Sociology* is the organization founded by Ely and practically wrecked by Herron last year. The Herron faction imagines that the main reliance is the glorification of Christian sentiments." (A. W. Small to L. F. Ward, April 10, 1895 in "The Letters of Albion W. Small to Lester F. Ward," no. 1, edited by Bernard J. Stern, in *Social Forces,* December 1933, p. 171.) The Reverend George D. Herron (1862-1925) was at the time Professor of Applied Christianity at Iowa College (now Grinnell), and was prominent in the Socialist movement for a while. See Joseph Dorfman, *The Economic Mind in American Civilisation,* 5 volumes (New York: The Viking Press, 1946-1959) III, pp. 236-237; see also, B. G. Rader, *The Academic Mind and Reform; The Influence of Richard T. Ely* (Lexington, Ky.: University of Kentucky Press, 1966) pp. 132-135.

Commons continued to have very strong contacts in the movement to push reform through the churches (the Social Gospel Movement) at least until 1900. Thus he was active for a time in the influential Baptist dominated Brotherhood of the Kingdom, through its Boston chapter and spoke to the Eighth Annual Conference of that organization at Marlborough, New York, in August 1900 on "Evangelism and Social Economics." (See Frederic Miner Hudson, " 'The Reign of the New Humanity'; A Study of the Background, History and Influence of the Brotherhood of the Kingdom," unpublished Ph.D. dissertation, Columbia University, 1968, pp. 416, 420).]

was not "an obnoxious socialist." Commons went to Syracuse at a salary of $2,500.[5]

There he taught ethnology, anthropology, criminology, charity organization, taxation, political economy and city government. He investigated municipal ownership in various small towns around Syracuse and came to the conclusion that, excellent as it was in theory, it would not work unless those towns had a genuine civil service to insure for them the honesty and capacity of their employees. He took his students to visit penitentiaries, reform schools and factories. They also visited the George Junior Republic near Freeville, Tompkins county, which was founded by a New York business man and was attracting much attention as an illuminating experiment in the prevention and reform of juvenile delinquents. Commons, with the help of some of his students, wrote up the project in the *The American Journal of Sociology* in 1897. They also made a study with wide ramifications of a family of delinquents and defectives. They went into the question of real estate values, the relative relation between assessments in various parts of the town of Syracuse and the actual selling values of property. Commons helped the students to start a cooperative store against which the local merchants complained.

He had indeed a characteristically enjoyable time in engaging with his students in a great variety of first-hand investigations of social institutions. By this time he had learned to be a more interesting teacher, a teacher whose students were devoted to him, for he had given up the idea that he could accomplish anything by trying to organize lectures in the ordinary logical fashion and instead he made his courses a series of investigations of current matters, in which the students participated. He cared almost nothing about what was the subject indicated by the title of the course so long as they had a real problem to work at.

Commons had, however, after four years, serious difficulty at Syracuse. The issue arose over the subject of Sabbath baseball. He was asked to speak at a public meeting protesting against ball games in the public parks of Syracuse on Sundays. Instead he took the ground that so long as it was not professional baseball, but amateur play by workingmen who did not have even a Saturday half holiday, the whole procedure was socially desirable. Syracuse was a denominational college at the time and the chancellor when he went out on a money raising campaign came back with the report that several people refused to give money to the institution so long as that man Commons remained

---

[5] Commons, *Myself*, pp. 58-59.

upon the faculty. Later he reported to Commons—and this I am quoting from Commons's autobiography *Myself*—that "at a recent national meeting of college presidents which he attended, all had agreed that no person with radical tendencies should be appointed to their faculties." Commons says: "I began to draw some inferences . . . It was not religion, it was capitalism that governed Christian colleges." The authorities did not dismiss Commons because that would have raised an uncomfortable issue. What they did was to abolish his chair.[6]

The loss of his position, as it happened, did not harm him because a western friend, a businessman, George H. Shibley, the great bi-metallist and supporter of the presidential aspirations of William Jennings Bryan, asked Commons to assist him on a salary basis and publish news on "live questions." For this purpose they set up in New York the Bureau of Economic Research to investigate problems. Associated with them was [a specialist in public utilities] E. W. Bemis, who had been dropped from the University of Chicago.[7] With the aid of N. I. Stone, a well known statistician then and still better known in these days (1935), [Commons published two quarterly bulletins in 1900, primarily devoted to an index showing that prices were falling as the silverites contended.

A good summary of their contents appeared in the leading British statistical journal:

> This new publication is issued by an organization formed for practical investigation in economics, statistics and politics, which latter presumably means Political Science. The Bulletin will be concerned with index numbers, the department dealing with this subject being in charge of Professor John R. Commons. It is declared

---

[6] *Myself*, pp. 57-58. [The latest historian of the university writes: "Professor Commons utilised the city of Syracuse as a laboratory. His classes, therefore, visited factories, shops, and toured the city and county municipal offices and jails, wandered through distressed areas, analyzed the local newspapers, rang doorbells, and initiated a movement that led to the founding of a University Cooperative store. But 'that settled it.' Sensitive to criticism, especially when it stemmed from sources whose support of the University was not expendable, the Chancellor began to cramp these experiments in democracy and education. Soon Professor Commons found life increasing in complexity and annoyance. A crisis was reached during the winter of 1898-1899 . . . the Chancellor . . . in February, 1899, announced the retirement of Professor Commons effective early in May. No clear cut reasons were given . . . Although it may be contended that it was unfortunate for the University to have lost the services of one whose future academic career did much to enhance the reputation of the University of Wisconsin, there may be wider differences of opinion over his statement that 'it was not religion, it was capitalism' that governed Christian colleges." W. Freeman Galpin, *Syracuse University*, 2 volumes (Syracuse: Syracuse University Press, 1952, 1960) II, pp. 24-25.)]

[7] Sentence from Outline, May 7, 1935. [On Bemis at the University of Chicago, see Joseph Dorfman, *Thorstein Veblen and His America* (New York: The Viking Press, 1934) pp. 122-123.

that the Bureau will undertake, on application, an inquiry upon any point or subject within the range indicated above, which requires access to the greater libraries of the United States, or expert field work. . . . The two numbers received deal with index numbers of general prices and of water and railroad freights, of bank clearings, etc. The basis is the decade 1879-89, the years being reckoned from 1st July to 30th June. Annual results are given, covering 1878 to 1900 in the first number; and monthly results in 1896 to 1900, with quarterly figures for 1878 to 1882, in the second.

A noteworthy point is the comparison, of a simple average of the 66 prices used, with a weighted average, showing the result which previous comparisons of the same kind have shown, that the indications of price-movement are practically identical, i.e., that the variations between the two measures are quite small. The tabular results are also shown in a number of diagrams. Comparison is made too, with price-movements in Germany, Japan, India, and England, as also with those shown in the Aldrich report of 1893.

The introductory article by Professor Commons aims at explaining the nature and use of index numbers. The work of the Bureau, as we have already stated, is not to be confined to compiling index numbers . . . For its work on price-changes, of which alone we have as yet any specimens, we welcome its establishment. There is much interesting work on this subject for which the United States will provide material.][8]

But by the fall of 1900, Shibley, after a fruitless effort to secure financial aid for the Bureau which had already cost him $3,000, withdrew from the enterprisse and it soon collapsed.[9]

Commons was out of a job again, but once more he did not suffer. His former Oberlin student E. Dana Durand who was secretary of the United States Industrial Commission that had been recently organized—the commission out of whose evidence and reports Veblen got so much of his material for *The Theory of Business Enterprise*—asked Commons to join as an expert on immigration and labor questions on a salary of $3,000—once more a step up in the salary scale. He took charge of an investigation that gave him an opportunity to examine the working conditions of various immigrant communities in

---

[8] [Review of *Quarterly Bulletin of the Bureau of Economic Research,* no. 1, July 1900, no. 2, October 1900, in *The Journal of the Royal Statistical Society,* December 1900, pp. 675-676.

Professor Mitchell on the basis of Commons's autobiography, *Myself,* speaks of Commons issuing at the time a weekly index of wholesale prices. But there is no evidence of such an index. Commons writing of the event 35 years after its occurrence could easily have become confused.

In calculating the yearly and monthly indexes in the two Quarterly Bulletins, he and Stone did make use of the weekly quotations of articles subject to frequent fluctuations and of single monthly quotations of such articles as chemicals and building materials. Commons, it seems, confused in his recollections, his use of weekly quotations with the issue of a weekly index.]

[9] See Joseph Dorfman, *The Economic Mind in American Civilisation* III, pp. 288-289.

the United States, in such industries as clothing, steel, mining, etc., and to visit the headquarters of national trade unions to study the effects of immigration on unionism, as part of his endeavor to study trade unions in action.

One of his interesting associates in the investigation was a Russian Jewish immigrant named Abram Bisno whom he got to know at Jane Addams's famous settlement house in Chicago, Hull House. Commons, through discussions with Bisno, got a thorough drilling in the Marxian doctrines.[9a] When Commons finished his report on immigration he was asked to come to Washington and help in compiling the official report of the commission. That gave him a fine opportunity to study continuously over a considerable period of time the tremendous collection of materials regarding the general run of modern business, and particularly the conflict between labor and capital.

One thing which interested Commons in particular in that connection was to discover that there was a split in the ranks of capitalists between the big capitalists and the small capitalists who were merely millionaires. One of these small ones was T. W. Phillips, a congressman and an oil man from western Pennsylvania, who had been in good part responsible for getting the Industrial Commission established and was a member of the commission. He had found it his business to check up on the Standard Oil Co. and decided that he would publish a minority report. He asked Commons to draw it up. Commons had a hectic time with this political business magnate in presenting the case of the small or medium aristocratic business man against the great monopoly. From Phillips he got an insight into another type of problem of which theretofore he had known almost nothing.

When the work with the Industrial Commission was finished in 1902, Ralph M. Easley, the founder and secretary of the National Civic Federation, asked him to join the staff of his organization [at a salary of $4,000 to engage in labor conciliation and tax reform

---

[9a] [In his autobiography, Bisno recalled "Some time before I happened to have been introduced to Commons and spoke with him of the labor movement. I was known as a man well acquainted with the clothing trade and since a great many of the immigrants were in the clothing business Commons asked me to join him in the investigation, offered decent remuneration, and since I like the work better than tailoring, I accepted the offer and the appointment." They worked together for six months in 1900-1901. *Abraham Bisno: Union pioneer,* with a foreword by Joel Seidman (Madison, Wis.: University of Wisconsin Press, 1967) pp. 211-212.

Commons doubtless got a good deal of understanding of the Marxian system from Stone who translated Marx's *Zur Kritik der Politischen Oekonomie* under the title *A Contribution to the Critique of Political Economy* (1904).]

work.] The Federation, which was intended largely to assuage conflicts between labor and capital, was composed of prominent national figures representing employers, wage earners and the public. United States Senator Mark Hanna was the first president and Samuel Gompers was a vice president.

Commons developed considerable skill as a mediator in the settlement of labor disputes in some of the nation's leading industries, both with failure in steel as well as success in street car, coal and building trades. In the process he learned to know many of the chiefs of labor and learned "that the place of the economist was that of adviser to the leaders."[10]

Then at the end of 1903 Commons went to the federal Department of Labor for a few months to complete a project for its chief, Carroll D. Wright, on the restriction of output by capital and labor.[11] In this job, Commons had the help of Ethelbert Stewart [who was later United States Commissioner of Labor Statistics], Walter E. Weyl, who later became well known as one of the original editors of the *New Republic*, and of John H. Gray, later president of the American Economic Association.[12]

Finally in 1904 he was called to the University of Wisconsin where, as he says in *Myself*, Ely who had transferred from Hopkins to Wisconsin had worked up a position for him, a position that combined teaching with research and reform. It was at the University of Wisconsin that his varied activities came to their fruition. He promptly came into contact with Governor Robert M. La Follette and as much as any other man took part in shaping the long series of social and labor measures which have given Wisconsin its peculiar stand [as the great laboratory] among American states.

[Commons had been called by Ely to assist him in preparing a study for which Ely had raised $30,000 from some public spirited citizens; namely, a history of industrial democracy in the United

---

[10] Quoted in Outline, May 7, 1935, from *Myself*, p. 88.
Commons also thought that the group of young economists brought together by the Industrial Commission was the first "brain trust." Outline, May 7, 1935.

[11] [The Bureau of Labor was established in 1885 in the United States Department of Interior. Wright (1840-1909) was named as its head with the title of Commissioner of Labor. In 1898 the bureau was transformed into an independent Department of Labor without the status entitling its head to cabinet rank. In 1903, the Department of Labor became a bureau of the newly created executive division with cabinet rank, the Department of Commerce and Labor; (a separate Department of Labor with cabinet status was established in 1913.)]

[12] The study appeared as *Regulation and Restriction of Production,* prepared under the direction of Carroll D. Wright, U. S. Commissioner of Labor (1904). A somewhat revised version of the introduction appeared as Commons, "Restrictions by Trade Unions," *The Outlook,* October 27, 1906; reprinted as chapter IX in Commons, *Labor and Administration* (1913).

States. Commons soon had complete charge of the project which became a history of the American labor movement.] It was an investigation in which he had been interested since his boyhood days as a printer and upon which he had done a considerable amount of research in connection with his work with the National Civic Federation, the Department of Labor and other organizations. To carry out the project he organized a group of collaborators. They set themselves to ransacking the labor library which Ely had built up and which was lodged in the John Crerar Library in Chicago, and then they branched out to collections all over the country. The work proved to be much more extensive than they had realized and it was only slowly that the material accumulated for their purpose. In 1910, however, they were ready with a large collection of evidence obtained from old newspapers, local histories, monographs upon particular labor organizations, etc. In 1910-1911 they published *A Documentary History of American Industrial Society* in ten volumes, which constitutes the most important collection of sources for the history of labor in the United States. It is one of the notable contributions of American economic history and needless to say it is utilized by all specialists of the subject.

Commons and his collaborators also planned to use the great collection of documents for a history of labor, but this took a longer time still. Thanks in large part to the financial aid of Professor Henry W. Farnham of Yale, there appeared in 1918 the first two volumes of the *History of Labour in the United States*. And in 1935 volumes three and four were published.

While he was working at the tremendous task of accumulating and analyzing material relating to the history of labor, Commons was also continuing his study and participation in a variety of social movements. Hardly had he come to the University when he was promptly called upon by Governor La Follette to draft the civil service laws which were enacted. These he thinks have been basic in all later social reforms achieved by the state, because they provide Wisconsin with a set of state officers in whom the citizens at large can repose a high degree of confidence. It put Wisconsin in somewhat the same position that Great Britain is; that is, in undertaking elaborate attempts to benefit the community as a whole, Wisconsin has little fear of either incompetence or dishonesty on the part of officials.

Then in 1905 he was asked by the National Civic Federation to participate in a comparative study of municipal ownership in the United States and Great Britain. This project was precipitated by the sale of a huge municipally-owned public utility in Philadelphia—the gas works—to a private company. [Commons wrote later in *Myself* that "The politically managed municipal works had been the most disastrous failure of its kind in the country."] The transaction had shocked every one interested in public ownership and led the Federation to attempt to find out why municipal ownership succeeded so much better in Great Britain than in the United States.

The Federation set up a large and imposing committee of leading citizens. To quicken the inquiry, a smaller group of twenty-one— The Committee on Investigation of which Commons was a prominent member—did the actual work of visiting twenty-four American and British cities. The Committee spent five months in England studying both municipally and privately owned gas, electric lighting and power plants, street railways and water works. [Commons in the section of the report which he prepared, declared "My interpretation requires that at least for some time to come, both private ownership and municipal ownership be carried along side by side in the same country, that each municipality have full power and home rule to change from one to the other according to its judgment of which it is that offers the better results in the given case; and that in this way the defects of both municipal and private ownership in the United States may be gradually eliminated and both may be brought to the higher level occupied by both in Great Britain."[13]]   ,

On returning, he was asked by La Follette (then United States Senator) and Speaker Herman L. Ekhern of the Wisconsin Assembly to help the legislative committees to draft a bill which would extend the state's plan of regulating railroads to the regulation of municipal and inter-urban public utilities. It was in this connection, he states in *Myself,* that he had his first occasion to study legal precedents extensively, for the question of regulation involved a variety of nice legal points. There was no hope of securing a law unless it was so drafted that it would be held constitutional by the courts. Commons sought aid of lawyers and began with one of his characteristically thorough personal studies. He still continued to be a man who could not believe anything that was in the books until he had himself studied it first hand and passed it through his own mind. The result was the drafting of another fundamentally wise statute, the Public Utility Law of 1907.

Meanwhile, in 1906 he was asked to join the Pittsburgh Survey,

----

[13] Commons, "Labor and Politics"; reprinted under the title of "Labor and Municipal Politics" in his *Labor and Administration,* p. 160.

the first of the great investigations which made such a large addition to the factual knowledge of the social affairs in American cities. [This pioneering project which was financed by the Russell Sage Foundation was concerned with living conditions in the great industrial district at the headwaters of the Ohio.] Commons had charge of the labor end of the study, and as assistants he chose two of his graduate students, John A. Fitch [1881-1959] from the prairies of South Dakota and William M. Leiserson [1883-1957] from the sweat shops of New York. Both of these very able aides became prominent in later days. Fitch has been with the New York School of Social Work, [now the School for Social Work, Columbia University]. Leiserson is one of the most active and valuable labor economists.[14]

It was in this connection that Commons hit upon his first basic idea about accident prevention. From his study of the policy of certain of the younger officials of the United States Steel Corporation at Pittsburgh he learned that they thought the proper way to deal with an accident problem was not to aim at compensation merely but to set up a scheme which would make it in the interest of the companies to prevent accidents. That idea he took home with him and presently made use of in Wisconsin.

In 1910 he was asked by the socialist administration of Milwaukee to head an organization to investigate the municipality and devise a scheme for more efficient and economic city administration. On this he worked with several technical aides for a year and a half and devised an elaborate scheme for the management of the various departments of the municipality which was adopted and a large part of which is in use to this day.[15]

Meanwhile he had gotten the notion that it was desirable to codify all of Wisconsin's labor legislation and in doing so to extend it particularly with the idea to diminish accidents. This led to another elaborate economico-legal study and resulted in the law which established the Wisconsin Industrial Commission. Under The Workmen's

---

[14] "Spent most of morning talking with J. R. Commons and Leiserson—the favorite arbitrator of the clothing trade—about future trend of social organization." Mitchell, "Diary," December 29, 1921.

[15] Commons, *"Eighteen Months' Work of the Milwaukee Bureau of Economy and Efficiency,"* 1912; reprinted as "The Milwaukee Bureau of Economy and Efficiency," in his *Labor and Administration*, pp. 195-218.

[Specifically it was Victor Berger, the socialist newspaper publisher of Milwaukee and first socialist member of Congress, who brought about Commons's appointment. Commons commented in the introduction to the reprinted essay that "it is significant that the first official attempt on the part of an American municipality to install a complete system of business administration was made by the socialists of Milwaukee during their brief control of the city council and mayor's department in 1910-12."]

Compensation and Industrial Commission Act of 1911, in dealing with accidents particularly, a plan was arranged by which the cost of accidents was thrown in large part upon the employer with the object not so much of getting compensation for injured people as for inducing employers to put energy behind a safety-first campaign.

The act also went into considerable detail in providing safety codes for different industries. The general plan of operation was illustrated by the boiler code with which Commons seems to have had particularly intimate connection. It was drawn up by a small committee that had on it representatives of the three interested groups; the operators of boilers—the actual employees, employers—the factory owners and the manufacturers of boilers. They had a variety of citizens called before them. They investigated the work which had to be done with the boilers of different types in different parts of the state, and gradually developed a code which specified the kind of boiler that would be legal under the Wisconsin law, the mode of operating them and provisions for meeting the costs of accidents to operators.

The code, being drawn up on a cooperative basis, represented, Commons said, not ideal practice, but the best that could be attained under the circumstances. In executing it, the idea of the best practice that could be attained under existing conditions gradually changed until Wisconsin had stiffer and stiffer requirements. That was a type of change in existing practices which Commons liked very much, an arrangement in which groups of people whose interests were conflicting were induced to come together in order to draw up reasonable rules and then to operate them in the future through impartial officials chosen on a civil service basis in such fashion that the rules themselves were as the result of experience gradually raised to a more satisfactory level.[15a]

After the industrial code was enacted into law Commons was made a member of the Industrial Commission. He served two years on a salary of $6,000 but refused a reappointment in order to return to his professorship at a salary of $3,500. He says in *Myself* that he got a great deal of credit for this step but he did not deserve it because his friend Charles R. Crane gave him $1,000 per annum for himself and $1,500 for a secretary until his university salary was increased after World War [I] to $6,000.[16] He liked this situation which en-

---

[15a] [To Commons, "administration is legislation in action . . . ." Quoted in Arthur J. Altmeyer, *The Formative Years of Social Security* (Madison, Wis.: University of Wisconsin Press, 1966) p. vi].

[16] [Crane was an eminent philanthropist and diplomat; for a while he was an executive of one of the leading firms in the manufacture of plumbing supplies, the Crane Company.]

abled him to go on with his studies much better than that of simply administering a law with the details of which he was familiar.

In 1913 he was appointed by President Wilson to the United States Commission on Industrial Relations which was then set up to work out means of alleviating the increasing labor unrest. Commons gave such time as he could to the commission. He spent most of his vacations in Washington working on it and saw very reluctantly that a split was developing within the commission.[17] He claimed that a number of the members of the commission wanted to capitalize on labor unrest and make a political issue out of it, whereas he himself wanted to do on a national scale what he had been enabled to do in Wisconsin under the Industrial Commission; that is, set up a collective bargaining national labor board in which the various parties at interest would be represented. It would try to work out constructively a series of reasonable arrangements which would be accepted by all and which would bring order into an important area of human relations at the time characterized mainly by conflict. [Most disturbing to Commons was the fact that the commission by a vote of 7 to 1 upheld chairman Frank P. Walsh's order cancelling the continuation of the investigations by the research staff which was under Commons's supervision.][18] The result was from his point of view a serious disappointment.

He was also grieved by breaking with his old friend Senator La Follette over whether the United States should enter [World] war [I]. La Follette was a pacifist on this matter; Commons had a great fear of German aggression. He took the ground that American participation in the war was necessary in order "to make the world safe for America."

After the war he started an investigation of the money question. What called this particularly to his attention was the substantial rise in prices that occurred in 1919 and what seemed to him the demoralization of labor. It was a period in which prices were advancing rapidly, in which labor was scarce, and in which a large part of the laboring population and of a labor organizations seemed to him to be taking advantage of the situation. They jumped contracts whenever they found an advantage in so doing, just as many business men of the time sold goods to one set of customers and later shipped the same articles to others at higher prices, repudiated the first contract and

---

[17] [There was such a split in the commission that it issued what were in effect three final reports.]

[18] [See Graham Adams, Jr., *Age of Industrial Violence 1910-1915* (New York: Columbia University Press, 1966) pp. 208-214.]

accepted the more lucrative one. That to Commons's way of thinking was a most unfortunate effect that an ill-organized monetary system was exercising upon the working population. In May 1920 wholesale prices dipped downwards and there followed a catastrophic fall of prices even more rapid than the rise in 1919. Commons saw the working classes who had been demoralized by the rise pauperized by the fall. He came to the conclusion that the money question was the most important of all labor problems and began giving it his almost undivided attention. The remedy he insisted was price stabilization.

To oppose policies making for an "unstable" dollar he accepted the presidency of the National Monetary Association and served from 1922 to 1924. Later he collaborated with Congressman James G. Strong of Kansas on a banking bill which provided that the Federal Reserve Board use its powers to stabilize the price level. He had long talks with Benjamin Strong, Governor of the Federal Reserve Bank of New York, and spent a good deal of time in that bank making one of his patient studies of the new body of materials.

In 1923 he got into the Pittsburgh-Plus case [before the Federal Trade Commission on behalf of the interested western states] and brought in as associates Frank A. Fetter and William Z. Ripley [1867-1941] of Harvard. This was the case in which an attempt was made on the part of the users of steel to abolish what they thought was a discriminatory practice on the part of the steel trade at large, and the United States Steel Corporation particularly. Commons wanted collective bargaining between consumers and makers of steel and he won the legal fight to abolish Pittsburgh-Plus.[19]

In 1924 he was made administrator of a voluntary contributory scheme of unemployment insurance set up in the Chicago men's clothing industry by the employers and the union—the Amalgamated Clothing Workers of America. The union started that unemployment plan. Leo Wolman, who was then director of research of the union, asked Commons, as the economist in whom the laboring classes of the country felt more confidence than in any other man, to accept the headship of the administrative body as chairman of the Unemployment Reserve Funds, Chicago Men's Clothing Industry. That may have been thought of by some as primarily a window-dressing affair, but Commons never let himself be used as window dressing. He took

---

[19] Sentence from Outline, May 9, 1935. [On Commons and the Pittsburgh-Plus case, see Joseph Dorfman, *The Economic Mind in American Civilisation,* II, pp. 557-561; see also for the underlying philosophy, Dorfman, "Commons, John R.," *International Encyclopedia of the Social Sciences* (New York: Macmillan and the Free Press, 1968) III, pp. 22-23.]

active charge of the situation. That was another scheme which he liked, because the reserve funds were set up in such a fashion as to give the employers the inducement to stabilize employment so far as possible.

In 1932 he was the most active person in formulating the first unemployment insurance bill passed in the United States, the Wisconsin Unemployment Compensation Act. It extended the general principle of separate reserves for individual employers, the Chicago scheme, into a statewide commission to reduce unemployment. The idea was to treat unemployment on the same general principles on which accidents had been successfully treated by the Industrial Commission.[20]

Meanwhile he had become acquainted with the plan prepared by the Russell Sage Foundation for meeting the urgent social need for small loans at reasonable rates. One of its characteristically thorough studies on the subject dealt with the enormous levy upon poor people made by pawn brokers and others who provided small loans and charged fees which though slight in themselves often constituted a 100 per cent rate or more computed on an annual basis. The study showed that the actual cost of making these small loans of $100 or less was so great that to engage in this business and obtain a fair return on them lenders must charge far higher rates of interest than a bank lending thousands of dollars at a time. The Foundation advocated a standard law which provided for rates of interest not exceeding 3½ per cent per month. Commons successfully championed the proposal in Wisconsin, which became the Small Loans Act of 1927. After it was enacted, the measure was attacked and Commons was particularly abused for his pains.

It was pointed out that 3½ per cent per month amounted to 42 per cent per annum and he was charged with trying to exploit the poor people of the state, by legalizing these extortionately high rates. This time his opponents were on the Progressive side and they carried their opposition to his measure and to him personally to the extent of getting him investigated. It was possible for him to show that a small loan scheme that charged only 3½ per cent per month would be a substantial benefit to people who under the existing conditions

---

[20] Based on a separate fund for each employer with intention to give employers incentive to reduce unemployment. Like the Workmen's Compensation Law of 1911. (Outline, May 9, 1935).

[The act is popularly referred to as the Groves Act. Harold Groves, colleague and former student of Commons, introduced the bill into the Wisconsin Assembly, of which he was a member.]

would have to pay 100 per cent or more per annum. [Commons and Harold Groves collaborated on the preparation of a bill which allowed for flexibility in rates and was enacted in 1933.][20a]

Then in 1934 he published *Institutional Economics*.[21]

This is a most extraordinary record of personal activity. In his own account Commons sums up his general policy in this brief way: "I was trying to save capitalism by making it good . . . I wanted also to make trade unions as good as the best of them that I knew."[22]

One would have thought that a man who had worked so intensively in such a great variety of practical undertakings would have found these labors absorbing all his energies. It has been characteristic of Commons from the start, however, that while he was dealing with practical problems he was also thinking systematically about economic relations. From the time when as a journeyman printer he had read Henry George's *Progress and Poverty* down to the time he was finishing *Institutional Economics,* he tried always to think out a theory of his operations and also to see how this theory fits into the general body of economic doctrine. He has been not only one of the most effective in the general cause of social reform but also one of the most widely read students in the history of economic theory.

Among other things *Institutional Economics* contains a careful, critical account of the chief contributions which seem to him to have been made by an extraordinary number of writers upon economics from John Locke down to Gustav Cassel and even later writers. The concern with economic theory is as characteristic a part of his makeup as his interest in trying to better conditions. He explains at the beginning of the book why it is that this work in economic theory seems to him so important.

His point of departure is the statement previously quoted: "My point of view is based on my participation in collective activities,

[20a] [For Commons's role in the formulation and revision of the Small Loans Law, see Genevieve Townsend, *Personal Finance Companies* with a preface by John R. Commons, 1932.]

[21] [The posthumous *Economics of Collective Action* (1950) is a sequel volume. Commons had originally planned to call the sequel "Investigational Economics." (Commons to Mitchell, March 30, 1937, in Joseph Dorfman, "The Mutual Influence of Mitchell and Commons," in *The American Economic Review,* June 1958, p. 407).

For an account of Commons in the role of the "theorist as policy maker," see Mark Perlman, *Labor Union Theories in America* (Evanston: Row, Peterson, 1958) pp. 173-190.

Professor Jack Barbash of the University of Wisconsin has noted that "The academic specializations which Commons laid out—labor history, labor law, union government, collective bargaining, the labor market, personnel administration—are still viable today." "John R. Commons and the Americanization of the Labor Problem," *Journal of Economic Issues,* September 1967, p. 165.]

[22] *Myself,* p. 143.

from which I here derive a theory of the part played by collective action in control of individual action." Commons's experience had shown him a prevalent conflict of interests over a wide range of social affairs from small loans up to the relations between massive organizations of employees on the one side and great organizations of employers on the other side. There was conflict of interest between municipalities and private corporations in the management of public utilities. There was conflict of interest between ·immigrant workers and workers already domiciled in the United States. His whole life had been spent in studying conflict of interests.

The conflict of interests might reach to anarchy. Since such conflict keeps cropping up in almost all human relations and since the parties are also of necessity mutually dependent upon one another, it has been indispensable for society to find some way of controlling conflicts, of substituting at least formal harmony of interests between the parties. Society in its modern form cannot grow unless ways are found to induce the parties with conflicting interests to cooperate with one another; that is, there must be control by collective action over individual action. This control in modern society is exercised by the sovereign; that is, by the state; and the most important organ of the state in exercising collective control over individual action is the judiciary, the courts.

To understand modern economic life, we must start with a unit of investigation which is different from that in most economics treatises. In the ordinary textbook, says Commons, the unit is that of two people who are bargaining with one another for the exchange of a commodity. This is a very imperfect and partial view of what actually happens. The real unit of economic activity is a five-party transaction. There are three types of transactions. The first and the one with which the economists in the past have concerned themselves for the most part is the bargaining transaction. But in this type there are not two parties at interest, there are always at least five. There is a buyer who makes a certain offer and a seller who makes a certain offer; and also there is an alternative buyer and an alternative seller. And then as regulating the opposing interests of buyer against seller and of competing buyer against competing seller, there is always explicit or tacitly present in the transaction a court which sees to it that the existing rules of society in the regulation of such transactions are in force. Unless theorists get the idea of bargaining transactions as involving five parties instead of just two they have a most imperfect idea of what is happening in modern society.

In the second type, the managerial transaction, one party is a legal superior and the second is a legal inferior. It is typified by the relations between an employer and an employee in the workshop. There is a court in the background, an established system of labor law which sets up certain rights and duties which both the employer and the employee must observe.

Finally there is what Commons calls the rationing transaction. This is typified by the activity of a board of directors of a corporation in drawing up the budget. The board is a legal superior that has the right and the duty of appropriating the funds available for the business according to a certain scheme. And the employees, the legal inferiors of the board, have the duty of carrying out the allocations as made by the directors.

More specifically, in "rationing transactions there are three parties —a superior—an inferior—and a court—but here the superior is a collective body or its official spokesman, pro-rating burdens or benefits among inferiors. Examples are a government apportioning taxes, a trade-union collecting dues from and making disbursements to its members, the directors of a corporation levying assessments upon the stockholders or declaring dividends."[23]

To repeat, the unit of investigation for institutional economics as Commons sees it, is a transaction which may be a bargaining transaction or a managerial transaction or a rationing transaction, and it is the business of the theorist to consider the last two types as well as to study bargaining transactions.

This means, from Commons's point of view, that he is studying modern institutions. We may define an institution, as he says, as "collective action in control of individual action." This appears in the bargaining transaction whether the court is actually passing upon some bargain or whether the bargain is carried out in terms of existing rules of law laid down by the state in past cases. It also appears in considering a managerial transaction where both the employer and the employee, or legal superior and legal inferior, whoever they may be, are operating on terms of current rules developed by the courts in the past. And finally it apears in dealing with a rationing transaction, for in this case there are common rules enforceable by courts that regu-

---

[23] Mitchell, "Commons on Institutional Economics," 1935; reprinted in *The Backward Art of Spending Money and Other Essays,*" compiled and edited by Joseph Dorfman (New York: McGraw-Hill, 1937) p. 319.

Another example of a rationing transaction is a cartel apportioning output. (Outline, May 9, 1935.)

late the relations between the superior and the inferior. An institution, to repeat, "is collective action in control of individual action."

Contrast Commons's definition with the concept of an institution of the first of the great institutional economists, Thorstein Veblen. To Veblen an institution is a widely prevalent habit of thought and action In other words, habits of thought and action are ways of thinking and acting which as individuals people have learned in the process of growing up. In a genuine sense they represent "collective action in control of individual action," a control which on Veblen's showing is exceedingly intimate. It is exercised through the formation of men's minds, the establishment within people of certain standard ways of reacting in their own thinking, and reacting in their ways of getting a living to the situations presented by modern life. In form the two definitions are distinctly different but at bottom they are very much alike.

With his notion of institutions, Commons is in a position to state what the task of institutional economics is, what problem it should attack. The problem is twofold. On the one side it is necessary to study the general development of the common rules of action which have been laid down by the courts. This is part of the task which he has conceived in *Legal Foundations of Capitalism*. A large part of it is devoted to an historical survey of the development of the concept of property, the fundamental economic concept from the days of William the Conqueror down to the present day. In the time of William the Conqueror, maintains Commons, scarcely any distinction was made between property and sovereignty—one was the other. From that time down to the present, through a long line of unfolding precedents, the courts have gradually brought out the idea of private property in land as quite distinct from sovereignty over the land, and they have brought out the idea of a private property in movables, the rules of fair competition, the legal limit upon privilege, and the existence of property not only in material things but also in promises to pay, like bills of exchange and bank notes, and the right of property in expectations of profit.

The story of the unfolding of the concept of property at the hands of the courts is fascinating as Commons develops it. From his point of view it is not only a contribution to law, but also—and this is what interests him in it—a contribution to the understanding of modern economic life. For what he is studying in the *Legal Foundations of Capitalism* is the shaping of the rules of action which are observed today in all the bargaining, managerial and rationing transactions.

The economists have taken all this for granted without inquiring into the development of the institution of private property and have left out of account a vital factor in the actual knowledge of how the world goes at the present time.[24]

"In his *Legal Foundations of Capitalism*, Professor John R. Commons has shown how the English judges gradually reshaped the old feudal conceptions of suzerainty to fit the nascent conception of private property in land; how side by side with the law of prerogative they built up the common law to regulate the relations among individuals; how they legitimized property in promises to pay, in good will, in going concerns. The great development of mercantile law by Chief Justice Mansfield came in the middle of the 18th century."[24a]

The latest and exceedingly important step in the evolution of the notion of property is the appearance of the idea of intangible property. To use Commons's definition of intangible property, "the right to fix prices by withholding from others what they need but do not own."[25] This notion, Commons holds, the United States Supreme Court was gradually developing in the last quarter of the nineteenth century. He cites cases in the 70's in which the court is still confining the notion of property to corporeal property and only after 1890 do the decisions admit as property, rights of obtaining expected profits from business dealings.

These rights in prospective profits constitute intangible property. It is thus another stage in the long evolution of the fundamental economic concept at the hands of the courts, an evolution of an idea which has consisted in the gradual taking over by the courts of changing customs and practices on the part of the business community. It has been an evolution first of economic practices and second of lagging recognition by the courts of what practices are esteemed by

---

[24] C.f., Commons's extension of notion of property to legal history (comment appears under an addition dated April 15, 1924 to the Outline, April 8, 1918).

To understand collective action in control of individual action must study court decisions. That task performed in *Legal Foundations of Capitalism*. Important theme is the development of the concept of property by courts. See my review ("Commons on the Legal Foundations of Capitalism," *The American Economic Review*. June 1924, pp. 240-253) summarizing developments in England from days of William I when sovereignty was not distinguished from property, through gradual development of concept of property in land, development of rules for fair competition and enforcement of contracts, giving promises to pay legal validity, and thus recognizing that expected earning power is property—thus giving rise to intangible property. That step taken by United States Supreme Court after 1900. (Outline, May 9, 1935.)

[24a] *Business Cycles: The Problem and Its Setting* (New York: National Bureau of Economic Research, 1927) p. 71.

[25] *Institutional Economics* (New York: Macmillan, 1934) p. 3. Quoted in Mitchell, "Commons on Institutional Economics," *The Backward Art of Spending Money*, p. 328.

the business community at large as wholesome, [and are deemed at the same time for the public welfare].

The second task of institutional economics consists in reviewing the ideas of economists, starting with the modern concept of property as laid down by John Locke and then tracing the gradual way in which the economists have distinguished between property as material things and property as ownership. The final important step which he recognizes in this evolution is the taking by economists into their theory the idea of intangible property. That was, he says, the great service that was rendered by Veblen. Veblen's precise way of doing this, however, is different from his own.

Commons is concerned to show how the institutional economics that he is developing differs from that of Veblen. He grants that Veblen was really an institutionalist, because he grasped the idea of intangible property as a human arrangement of ownership of expected opportunities to make a profit and explored its workings in practice. The difference between his work and that of Veblen, Commons contends, was that Veblen obtained his case material from the testimony of financial magnates at the hearings before the United States Industrial Commission, the commission for which Commons himself had worked. Consequently his notion of intangible property ended in the Marxian ideas of "extortion and exploitation."[26]

In a sense that is a valid statement. Veblen does represent the case of the modern idea of property, to quote a definition he gave in his last book, as grounded in the "principle of Vested Interest" which "is a prescriptive right to get something for nothing."[27] It is a cynical sort of definition but he thinks that it is justified by the various strategic moves of business enterprisers who are exploiting industry in order to make money. Commons says: "my sources were my participation in collective action, in drafting bills, and my necessary study, during these participations, of the decisions of the Supreme Court covering the period; so that my notion of intangible property ends in the common-law notion of reasonable value."[28]

"[Commons] draws a lesson for economics from the two theories of intangible property. It ought to take the constructive, purposive attitude of the courts in its explanation of institutional growth, instead of the purely objective attitude of physical science that was professed by Veblen. In this connection, Professor Commons becomes momentarily

---

[26] *Institutional Economics*, p. 4.
[27] Veblen, *Absentee Ownership* (New York: Huebsch, 1923) p. 49.
[28] *Institutional Economics*, p. 4.

confused. Veblen, he says, considered that science is 'matter-of-fact' science, arising from the modern inventions of machinery, wherein the scientist eliminates all of the older ideas of purpose or 'animism' contained in the concepts of alchemy or divination, and adopts merely the idea of 'consecutive change' or 'process,' which has no 'causation' and no 'final end' or 'purpose.' If this is so [Commons comments], then there is no science of human nature. Science becomes only the physical sciences.

He proceeds to argue that institutional economics is concerned precisely with human purposes as summed up in 'worldly wisdom'— a mental attitude which Veblen regards as 'at cross purposes with the disinterested scientific spirit.'

Of course, Veblen did not conceive human beings as devoid of purpose. Commons himself presently recognizes that the 'instinct of workmanship' brings purpose into the foreground of behavior. That was not the only instinct with which Veblen endowed mankind, and all instincts are purposive. His chief criticism of hedonism is that it pictures men as passive creatures, controlled by the pleasure-pain forces which impinge upon them.

What Veblen was driving at is that science assumes no purpose in 'nature' or in 'the course of events' outside of man. In dealing with human behavior, he tries to give an account of human purposes in terms of an evolutionary process of natural selection. For those purposes are an evolutionary product and so can be explained in the same fashion as man's opposable thumb. The scientist should refrain, so far as is possible for such a purposeful creature as man, from mixing his own purposes into his explanations of cumulative changes in the purposes of others. That rule of intellectual honesty Commons accepts in principle and practises with indifferent success, like Veblen and the rest of us."[28a]

To resume the concrete point, where Veblen, thinking about the same fundamental phenomena of intangible property following the testimony that was given by financial magnates before the commission, sees it work out in exploitation of the community at large, Commons sees it as a series of conflicts that are submitted in typical cases to the Supreme Court, and there they get resolved in a run of decisions that are concerned with determining what is reasonable value and laying down rules to enable the parties at interest to work with one another without undue conflict.

[28a] "Commons on Institutional Economics," p. 333. The brackets are Mitchell's. The quotations are from Commons's *Institutional Economics*.

Institutional economics as thus conceived by Commons differs considerably in his eyes from the classical theory of Adam Smith, David Ricardo and their followers, and also from what he called the hedonic theory of W. Stanley Jevons and the Austrian School. The classical economists thought of two individuals bargaining with one another. They did not grasp the role of collective action in determining the working rules under which bargains are made and by which they will be enforced by the courts. To them, there were only the two individuals in every trade and they took for granted the elaborate institutional scheme that had been gradually developed by the courts.

Also the classical economists, he thinks, had scarcely any distinctions to make between property as consisting of corporeal objects and ownership. What happens in the ordinary transaction is that there is both a transfer of corporeal things and a shifting of ownership; on the one side a sort of engineering process of distributing goods, and on the other side the economico-legal process of getting legal titles to the goods in question. It is possible to have bargains in which there is no transfer of corporeal property but merely of ownership.

Further, the classical economists had scarcely anything to say of the managerial or the rationing transaction. Their concern began and practically ended in the bargaining transaction. As for the hedonic economists, they too failed to distinguish between ownership as a mass of corporeal goods owned and the legal right to use the goods. They also thought of individuals dealing with one another, each individual on the basis of an elaborate series of calculations regarding the pleasures and pains that will result from possible alternative lines of conduct. To work out institutional economics requires on the one hand the study of the evolution of the ideas of ownership, that is, the practical working rules of economic life; and on the other hand, it calls for careful review of economic theory to discover wherein economists in the past "have or have not introduced collective action."[29] The study of the evolution of court decisions was made in *Legal Foundations of Capitalism*, the study of the past work of economists is in *Institutional Economics*.

Commons finds that the fundamental notion of scarcity and the role that it plays in economic life was introduced by David Hume and then elaborated by Malthus. Hume and, still more, Malthus were also in advance of their time in that they did not make the error of most of the eighteenth and early nineteenth century writers in con-

---

[29] *Institutional Economics*, p. 5.

ceiving human nature as primarily rational. They recognized that the mass of mankind are rather stupid; that they are swayed by passions quite as much as by calculation. Scarcity and human stupidity give rise to conflict. It is only about scarce goods that conflicts occur. If all men were rational, conflicts would be relatively few, because they would recognize their mutual dependence and would not require the services of a third party to work out reasonable rules which make possible the orderly and efficient conduct of production and distribution. But since things are scarce and people are passionate and stupid, it is necessary, for the sake of order, to have supervision over economic conflict.

The heterodox economists from Henry Dunning McLeod (1821-1902), the British writer on banking, on to Karl Marx had some idea, Commons thinks, that ownership and corporeal property are not identical.[30] So that they made their contribution to the development of institutional economics. But not until the fact of intangible property had been evolved by economic experience and had been grasped by Veblen could the idea of institutional economics develop. Veblen's error, according to Commons, lay in the fact that he saw little but the conflicts of interest. What Commons does to complete the structure is to recognize the way in which the conflicts of interest that center in intangible property are resolved into the rules of reasonable value by court decisions, especially those of the Supreme Court of the United States.

The above outline covers broadly the general field of institutional economics, as envisaged by Commons. It starts with the recognition of scarcity, and the stupidity of human nature in not appreciating mutual interdependence, and consequently the necessity of collec-

---

[30] [Professor Mitchell had grave doubts as to Commons's view that Macleod should be called an institutionalist let alone the originator of institutional economics.] Macleod "was an acrid controversialist. . . . I do not see that he differed as an institutionalist from [John Stuart] Mill." (Mitchell, "Commons on Institutional Economics," *The Backward Art of Spending Money,* pp. 336-337.)

[Commons based his claim for Macleod on his famous theory of credit which Professor Mitchell] described as follows in an abstract of *The Theory of Credit* (3 vols., 1889-1891; 2nd ed. 1893-1897). Macleod's theory of credit is based on his peculiar "philosophy of economics." He makes economics "the science of Exchanges." Wealth includes everything that can be exchanged. Hence there are three species of wealth: (1) Material things; (2) personal qualities, both in form of labor and of credit; (3) abstract rights; for all these things and nothing else can be exchanged. A merchant's personal credit then is part of his wealth and the debts due him, his credits, are also a part of his wealth, for they are abstract rights to claim certain things from certain persons. The fall of prices since 1873 has not been due to a scarcity of gold, because of the lessened productivity of the mines, but primarily to the decrease of credit after the panic of 1873. ("Macleod's Theory of Credit," MPP 10.19, no. 83.)

tive action to control individual action. Its interest centers in transactions in which the court's role consists mainly of having formulated in the past rules that everybody at present takes for granted. It thinks of men not as primarily rational creatures concerned with calculations in terms of pleasure and pain, but views them essentially as originally stupid and passionate, as requiring control, and they are kept under control as the result of experience, of looking forward to the future, of conforming to decisions which are based upon a certain degree of foresight, of recognizing the collective rules which must be obeyed. For present economic action is always, from Commons's point of view, action which is concerned primarily with what will happen in the near future. Futurity thus becomes a fundamental concept of institutional economics.

In accordance with these basic ideas, Commons divided *Institutional Economics* into three parts. In the first, he presents an elaborate review of early economic theories in order to find how far the rule of collective action has been recognized by economists. Then he comes to an analysis of the idea of scarcity, and of efficiency as one of the great means for overcoming scarcity, efficiency here meaning efficiency in the production of the serviceable commodities which men require for satisfaction of wants. He passes to a still more elaborate study of the role of futurity in economic conduct and its applications. Then he takes up reasonable value, particularly the concepts of reasonable value that prevail in current times, the conditions that are attendant upon the effort to run society on the basis of the most recent Supreme Court decisions. That leads him to the question about the future of capitalism; whether it can be maintained or whether we must look forward to the supersession of a capitalistic organization of society by a more authoritarian form—communism or fascism.

Citation of a few passages from various parts of the book will give a clearer idea of the argument. The following sums up what he has to say about scarcity and efficiency. In the past, he contends, economics has been an absolutistic rather than a relativistic theory, and it is necessary for economics to pass from absolutism to relativity, as physics has done. "Scarcity and efficiency are thus two changing ratios with which the science of economics begins." But the classical economists got rid of one of the two ratios and the hedonic economists got rid of the other. Thus both schools operated with what was to all intents and purposes only one variable, they were absolutistic rather than relativistic in their work.

Smith and Ricardo eliminated the variability of *wants* of consumers (buyers) by assuming that they expanded or contracted equally with the supplies of materials or services offered by consumers in their function of producers (sellers). The decisive variables, therefore, in their conceptual schemes, were labor-pain with Smith, and labor-power with Ricardo and Marx.

In a genuine sense this is true. The classical economists did not present an elaborate study of variations in wants. It may be recalled that Ricardo touched upon this point and then put it aside on the ground that there is no scientific opening for a study of wants; they vary from individual to individual and he did not notice with any care the way in which the wants of a given individual for a given commodity vary. All that was cast aside and the central problems of economic theory were solved in terms of cost of production. To repeat, from Commons's viewpoint there was one variable.

The same was true of the Austrians:

> The Austrian school (Menger, Wieser) eliminated both labor-pain and labor-power of producers (sellers) by their assumption of a "pleasure" economy, equivalent to Smith's assumption of abundance. But this pleasure, for them, kept pace with the diminishing intensity of wants of consumers (buyers), so that wants were the decisive variables in their scheme.

In other words, just as the classical economists had taken wants pretty much for granted, so the Austrians practically eliminated cost from the analysis and centered their full force upon a study of the variability of wants. Once more the science was made one of a single variable.

> But Marshall co-ordinated the two schools by introducing the realistic concept of changing ratios between two opposite changing quantities—the quantities wanted by consumers (buyers) and the quantities supplied by producers (sellers)—both of which were variable independently on their own account.[31]

This is Commons's elaborate and strangely worded way of saying that Marshall combined in a single system the analysis of variable costs and the analysis of variable wants; and in that sense gives a discussion of the relation between costs and wants. It is a theory of relativity. But Commons goes on to say that Marshall was far from recognizing all the fundamental variables that ought to be taken into account by economists. He still treated as constants certain factors which in fact vary, hence his theory was much less thoroughgoing as

---

[31] *Institutional Economics*, p. 386n.
"Long chapter on Efficiency and Scarcity Schools is concerned mainly with clarification of concepts." Mitchell "Diary," January 27, 1935.

a treatment of relativity in economic life than the theories that are required.

One factor that Marshall viewed as a constant and not as a variable was ownership, for he continued the practice of thinking that everything valuable is owned, so that ownership and supplies of material goods were one and the same thing. Economists need to construct another relativistic concept, the concept of the transaction governed by working rules of collective action that transfer the ownership whether with or without exchanging material goods; that is, economists must recognize that under the general concept of ownership as connected with material goods there is the second concept of legal titles to the goods, and that it is a mistake to assume that in a transaction the only thing traded is the corporeal property. Titles may be exchanged though there is no actual transfer of tangible property.

The second independent variable that should be recognized is prices. Money and credit were eliminated from the classical and hedonic theories on the assumption of the stability of prices. That assumption is still used by Marshall to all intents and purposes in his *Principles of Economics*. He considers money as a constant whereas in practical life the relations between money and commodities are continually varying

A third variable, which Commons thinks Marshall treated inadequately, is the principle of futurity. "The concept of Time, in economic science distinguished from physical science, has shifted from the *past* time of classical . . . theory," where prices were accounted for by the cost of production that had been incurred, "into the *present* time of hedonistic theory," where people are supposed to be thinking about pleasures and pains, "until it is becoming the *future* time of waiting, risking, purpose, and planning."[32]

The problems of futurity, like the problems of legal titles to goods and of changes in the relations between money and commodities, constitute variables that ought to come into a general discussion of economic phenomena. The emphasis upon the neglect of futurity as a factor in economic life leads Commons to another long chapter in which futurity is made the primary object of investigation. In this connection he deals with debts, which are negotiable promises to pay in the future. It is this negotiability which makes debts a form of property. He deals likewise with interest and future discount, with profits and with the task of effecting payment for either goods that are exchanged at a given time or for the financial commitments that have

---

[32] *Institutional Economics,* p. 389.

been entered into as the result of past transactions. Thus he brings into the scheme of economic discussions the variables connected with futurity.

Whether in considering the problems that arise directly out of scarcity and efficiency or in viewing them as implied by man's attempts to look forward and plan for the future, it is necessary to understand the rules of reasonable value that prevail from time to time. This leads to a discussion of Veblen's contributions to economics and of the relations between natural rights and reasonable value. The doctrine of reasonable value is preceded by the older doctrine of natural rights. The latter prevailed from the eighteenth century and the French Revolution to the American Civil War and on to the opening years of the twentieth century. During this period, various philosophers have called in question the foundation of the doctrine. But the idea has continued to rule the thinking of courts, of business men and of economists. It is only since the World War [I], Commons holds, that it has been brought home to millions that such rights as people have proceeded from national and other collective action and are not natural. There are no such things as rights derived from nature in any other sense than the rights which are developed in communities of men through their authorities for deciding upon working rules of action. These working rules are the rules of reasonable value.

> Each economic transaction is a process of joint valuation by participants, wherein each is moved by diversity of interests, by dependence upon the others, and by the working rules which, for the time being, require conformity of transactions to collective action. Hence, reasonable values, are reasonable transactions, reasonable practices, and social utility, equivalent to public purpose.
>
> . . . during all these years of the Age of Reason, the common-law courts were developing an institutional idea of reasonableness and reasonable value, in the process of deciding conflicts of interest and bringing order out of incipient anarchy. This institutional idea of reason and reasonable value has been collective and historical, whereas the rationalistic idea was individualistic, subjective, intellectual, and static. The institutional idea undoubtedly reaches its clearest evolutionary change in the common-law method of making new law by taking over the changing customs of the dominant portion of the people at the time, and formulating them, by a rationalizing process of justification, into working rules for future collective action in control of individual action.
>
> Since this process has reached its pinnacle in the sovereignty of the Supreme Court of the United States, the evolution of the idea of reasonable value requires, as its institutional background, an understanding of the historic evolution from executive to legislative, and then to judicial sovereignty. . . . Reasonable value is the evolutionary collective determination of what is reasonable in view

of all the changing political, moral and economic circumstances and the personalities that arise therefrom to the Supreme bench.[33]

And finally: "The theory of reasonable value may be summarized, in its pragmatic application, as a theory of social progress by means of personality controlled, liberated and expanded by collective action."[34]

All this is because in the working rules that the court lays down, Commons sees a vast deal more than the inhibition of the warring impulses among men. It is only as rules of reasonable value are worked out that the individual personality can be genuinely elaborated and given its widest possible field of development.

> . . . It is not individualism, it is institutionalized personality. Its tacit or habitual assumptions are the continuance of the capitalist system based on private property and profits. It is fitted to a Malthusian concept of human nature, starting from the passion, stupidity, and ignorance whereby mankind does the opposite of what reason and rationality would prescribe and ending in an admiration for the individual who, by initiative, persistence, taking risks, and assuming obligations to others, rises to leadership.
>
> Unregulated profit-seeking drags the conscientious down towards the level of the least conscientious; yet a considerable minority is always above that level, no matter how high it may have been raised by collective action. These indicate the possibility of progress.
>
> The problem then, is the limited one of investigating the working rules of collective action which bring reluctant individuals up to, not an impracticable ideal, but a reasonable idealism, because it is already demonstrated to be practicable by the progressive minority under existing conditions.[35]

Reasonable value thus is a phenomenon that appears under capitalism. It is the fruit of a long process of evolution which one can take as beginning with feudalism—though its original start was far back from that—and evolving in three successive stages: merchant capitalism, industrial capitalism and finally banker capitalism. The United States has now reached the third stage according to Commons, that of banker capitalism in which great banking institutions exercise the chief economic control; and the question of the future is whether the working rules evolved by courts will make this latest form of capitalism really satisfactory. But recent events have shown that even the efficient banker capitalism of the United States, at times, is far from satisfactory in its working. That raises the question about the future evolution of economic institutions.

Commons holds that the economists of the world are forming a

---

[33] *Institutional Economics,* pp. 681-684.
[34] *Institutional Economic,* p. 874.
[35] *Institutional Economics,* p. 874.

new alignment which may be distinguished as the Bargaining School and the Managerial School of economists. He says that the one (the Bargaining School) "looks towards equality of Bargaining Power, the other towards rationing of Producing Power. The one looks towards Reasonable Capitalism, the other towards Communism or Fascism."[36]

In conclusion he says:

> . . . it is doubtful whether, under modern conditions, a decision can be reached as to which is the better public policy—the Communism of Russia, the Fascism of Italy, or the Banker Capitalism of the United States. In the two European systems and others that are copying them, liberty is suppressed and the intellectuals, who include artists, inventors, scientists, engineers, editors, professors, are eliminated, not merely because they are physically suppressed but because individual originality and genius cannot thrive in a nation of fear.[37]

Yet these suppressed classes are a small part of the population and the question about the future is about what will happen to the great mass of thrifty people who under the earlier forms of capitalism constituted the most considerable and the most efficient part of the population.

> The inflation and deflation of a twentieth century Banker civilization scrapes off the cream of that individual proprietorship which hitherto had induced individual wage earners and farmers to save, to economize, to take the risks which they had a chance to surmount, and to maintain the American Republic.[38]

That is, American banker capitalism is making it more difficult for small people to rise in the economic scale by the exercise of their own initiative and thrift. And that in Commons's eyes raises the most serious question as to whether capitalism of any type can long maintain itself.

> If these thrifty individuals are eliminated from the capitalist civilization by becoming a proletariat of wage and salary earners, then it is probable that, for the overwhelming majority, a communist or fascist dictatorship may be preferable to American Banker Capitalism. It will, no doubt, promptly eliminate academic liberty and a free press, but meanwhile the economists have, for the time being, a new equipment of experimental laboratories on three grand scales, in Russia, Italy and America, for a rough and tumble testing of their classical, hedonistic, and institutional theories.[39]

---

[36] *Institutional Economics,* p. 891.
[37] *Institutional Economics,* p. 903.
[38] *Institutional Economics,* p. 903.
[39] *Institutional Economics,* p. 903.

[J. M. Keynes who saluted Commons as "an eminent American economist" was especially impressed by his earlier discussion of the alternatives. See his "Am I a Liberal?", 1925, reprinted in his *Essays in Persuasion* (1931; reissue, London: Rupert Hart-Davis, 1952) pp. 334-336.]

Difference between orthodox economics and institutional economics: Earlier economists dealt with individuals supposed to be making voluntary bargains. Role played by social control through courts not recognized. It was about exchange of corporeal property (or services and corporeal property) on basis of calculations of pleasure and pain. Dealt with transfer of things rather than with transfer of ownership. Had little to say about managerial and rationing transactions. Institutional economics requires going through court decisions to trace development of collective action in controlling individual action, and similar review of writings of economists to see "wherein they have or have not understood collective action." Finds a slow development. Hume introduced scarcity and with it the conflict of interests. Followed by Malthus. Heterodox economists—Macleod to Marx—felt vaguely that ownership and physical goods were not the same thing.[39a]

In short, this discussion of Commons's *Institutional Economics* shows "only the skeleton of a living book. It shares the vitality of the author's career. His interest in economics has the driving force that characterized the work of Malthus and Ricardo and that declined as 'political economy' turned into an academic discipline. *Institutional Economics* is the fitting crown of a real investigator's life, and it should be an incitement to other investigators to follow the various leads that Professor Commons has given."[40]

General characteristics of *Institutional Economics:* Society gives rise to conflicts of interests, to necessity of collective action, to economic role of the courts and so "due process of law," through it to a new order among conflicting interests. Transactions—conducted by going concerns. Negotiational psychology. Volitional theory of consequences desired. Futurity plays dominant role. Layout of *Institutional Economics*. Review of earlier economic theories to find how far and how role of collective action is recognized. Efficiency and scarcity. Futurity brings debts, interest, profits, problems of payments, price levels, social control. Reasonable value. Communism, fascism, capitalism—evolution of capitalism.

[Not least of Commons's important contributions was the light he cast] upon the differences in the role of authority in determination of prices. Recall his statement that a market always has five parties potentially present: buyer and seller, alternative buyer, alternative seller, judge. Situation runs gamut from that in which the judge and alternative buyer and seller are shadows in the background to situation in which some public authority fixes the price.[41]

Speaking more broadly, "the problem now is not to create a different kind of economics, 'institutional' economics—divorced from preceding schools, but

---

[39a] Outline, May 9, 1935.

[40] Mitchell, "Commons on Institutional Economics," p. 341.

"Began reading John R. Commons's new book *Institutional Economics,* which shows remarkable vigor of thought." (Mitchell "Diary," October 12, 1934.)

[41] Outlines, May 9, 1935; "Current Developments in Economic Theory," talk before Political Economy Club, Columbia University, April 5, 1938.

how to give to collective action, in all its varieties, its due place throughout economic theory."[42]

Conclusion: Commons was not one of Veblen's pupils, but an original thinker whose work led him to adopt a somewhat similar approach. Thus Commons has been concerned with legal institutions much more than Veblen was. And his bent has been toward inventing institutions, rather than toward standing on the side lines and watching them develop. Also takes orthodox economic theory more seriously than Veblen did and seeks to show how it sustains his view of institutions.

Institutionalist criticism of classical economics: Veblen *et al.* Classicists treated man for purposes of economic theory as a calculating animal which guides its behavior by doing algebraic sums of pleasures and pains, or at least comparing satisfactions and sacrifices. This picture is a caricature. At bottom man is ruled by instincts and habits into which instincts are developed. The important controls are to be found in the habits of think-ing and acting that are the forms assumed by instincts under the pressure of the varying conditions under which men make their livings in different places at different times. The habits that prevail in any large group are its institutions. It is these institutions that make men sufficiently alike to understand one another and to work together. They form the basis for anticipating behavior—i.e., the basis for economic planning by individuals, business enterprises, governments, economists. They *are* economic gen-eralizations. They explain mass behavior. Consequently they should be the focus of economic investigation. This view is the more cogent because man's progress in culture is achieved primarily by cumulative change in institutions. Calculation of economic advantages and disadvantages, inso-far as it actually prevails among men, is a cultural reflex of the use of money, and the necessity of bookkeeping which that use compels when the arts of production develop to a point at which division of labor is advanced beyond its rudimentary stage and exchanges become frequent, i.e., economic calculation is an institution.

Habits are acquired not primarily by taking thought, but by the impact of experience on the individual's instincts. In this experience, teaching by elders is particularly important in youth. Elders try to pass on to youngsters the habits they have found good. The elders try to *rationalize* habits, rather than to explain how they were formed. Rationalization is concerned with the *effects* habits produce. They are valued as a means of harnessing instinctive impulses and so have a way of repressing certain instincts and channelizing others.

How can institutions be studied? Basic procedure is observation. To find out what institutions have prevailed in any group at any time and place one must examine records of what people believed and how they acted. For those records, Veblen goes to anthropology and history to get a wide view of cultural evolution. Uses his eyes and current documents to under-stand the present. Some records are even in quantitative form. To explain how the institutions prevailing came to prevail in any group or at any time,

---

[42] *Institutional Economics*, p. 5. Quoted in Mitchell, "Commons on Institutional Economics," *The Backward Art of Spending Money*, p. 339.

he uses hypothesis that chief factor in begetting habits of thought is the way men spend most of their time. Economic activities are most important agency because the bulk of mankind have had to direct more of their energy to getting a living than to any other activity. Not hypothesis that men follow their economic interests. For to Veblen what a man thinks to be his interest—what he will be interested in depends upon how his habits of thinking have been shaped by his dominant activities. Akin to psychological process of "conditioning." This view is a speculation, but one that Veblen can at times verify—as when he supports his analysis of the cultural incidence of machine technology by pointing out that the Socialist Party in Germany is recruited mainly from urban wage earners. (Other explanations of this fact by intimate observers.) Also he speculates about behavior of business men on the hypothesis that the abler among them follow the logic of money making remorselessly. And he projects future cultural change speculatively by supposing that different classes will act in accordance with the habits that have been drilled into them by experience.

Institutionalism is like classical economics in that it seeks to explain actual behavior. Differs from classical economics in that it emphasizes habits rather than calculation. Stresses evolution of institutions rather than working of present institutions. Professes (at least in Veblen's case) to have no reformist interests, but this may be protective coloring for it is not characteristic of institutionalism as such. Commons very much of a reformer.

Institutionalism relies more clearly on observation; must do so because interest in cultural evolution forces formal resort to sources not familiar to members of any one group of students, in any place or at any time. But also speculates freely about many things that cannot be tested. Is particularly addicted to forecasting. Done by extrapolating cultural trends it believes to prevail at a given time.[43]

---

[43] Outlines, "Seminar in Economic Changes and Economic Theory," December 21, 1943, May 2, 1944.

["The institutionalists were early advocates of empirical research and the use of quantitative measurement in the solution of economic problems. Wesley Mitchell and John R. Commons were both active in the early history of the National Bureau of Economic Research; and the Bureau itself, along with its many achievements such as the national income statistical series, are monuments to these efforts. . . . But the institutionalists were never interested in quantitative empirical research to the exclusion of all else. Commons and Mitchell also had a strong bent for qualitative empirical research which learns how institutions work by close observation especially from the inside and tests the significance of this knowledge against an historical background." (Harold M. Groves, "Institutional Economics and Public Finance," Land Economics, August 1964, p. 243.)

When Professor Paul T. Homan was assigned in 1930 the article on "Institutional Economics" for the Encyclopedia of the Social Sciences, he got in touch with Professor Mitchell for suggestions. Professor Mitchell replied:] "Like you, I entertain doubts whether one should use the word 'school' in this connection. Personally, I should not know whom to include under the heading apart from Veblen. The job would seem to me to consist primarily in showing how Veblen's viewpoint differs from that of Schmoller and that of Sombart, Weber and the economic historians at large. Also, of course, you will want to indicate how Veblen has influenced other people in this country. (Mitchell to Homan, December 22, 1930. Copy in possession of Joseph Dorfman.)

[Some interchanges on institutionalism: 1. Mitchell and Bonbright.] Mitchell's colleagues James C. Bonbright complained that he could not sympathize with let alone understand Commons's point of view although they both wrote essentially on the same subject "reasonable value"—and "despite the fact that I would suppose myself to be writing from the standpoint of an institutional economist. I wonder whether that term has not become a name for several entirely different points of view and whether we do not represent two of these divergent types." [Mitchell's reply:] "You seem to me to have as good a title to the name of institutional economist as anyone. But of course the fact that your approach to the study of economic behavior lies through institutions no more guarantees agreement in conclusions with another institutionalist, than did the fact that two men were classical political economists or historical economists guarantee that they would arrive at the same conclusion when studying a given topic."[44]

2. [Mitchell and Knight.] Frank H. Knight of the University of Chicago wrote [Mitchell] that his paper in the projected volume *The Trend of Economics* edited by Rexford G. Tugwell (1925) ["will be a presentation of the claims of old-fashioned theory as against institutional economics] . . . Of course I am the farthest in the world from having anything against the study of economic institutions. But . . . I am very skeptical about the development of any science in that field." [Mitchell's reply]: "I am glad that you are going to sum up the case of old-fashioned theory. Of course I think that this line of attack on economic problems has more than a historical justification. Its constructive value, as I see things, is that it contributes to our understanding of pecuniary institutions which are, as I have argued repeatedly, a factor of the very first moment in the situation, which it is important for us to understand. The scientific value of that contribution is really enhanced by taking the institutional viewpoint."[45]

Finally, it should be noted that institutionalism is primarily an American development though with affiliations or sympathisers in other countries, just as the historical school was primarily a German development with representatives scattered about elsewhere.[46]

[44] Bonbright to Mitchell, March 25, 1937; Mitchell to Bonbright, March 31, 1937.
[45] Knight to Mitchell, May 18, 1923; Mitchell to Knight, May 22, 1923.
"You make Knight a highly significant figure, and perhaps justly from a philosophical viewpoint—though I can't feel that his wistful harking back to ethical absolutes and an aristocracy of intellect contributes much toward the kind of understanding the world so desperately needs. WCM." Mitchell to Joseph Dorfman, undated, on back of Ms. chapter on Knight for Dorfman's study, *The Economic Mind in American Civilization*.
[46] Outline, "Seminar in Economic Changes and Economic Theory," January 11, May 2, 1944.

"Commons's contribution to economics . . . belongs to the institutional type represented in Germany by Sombart, in England by Mr. and Mrs. Webb, in America by Veblen and many of the younger men . . . [such as] John Maurice Clark's *The Economics of Overhead Costs* (1923), and the papers by Morris A. Copeland, Robert L. Hale, Summer H. Slichter and Rexford G. Tugwell in *The Trend of Economics* (1924."[47]

The time has come to sum up.

---

[47] Mitchell, "Commons on the Legal Foundations of Capitalism," *The American Economic Review*, June 1924, p. 253.

[Professor Crawfurd D. Goodwin of Duke University called attention in 1967 to the pioneering role of "institutional theory" in the development of economics in British West Africa. "Although the West African innovators in economic thought were not influenced significantly by outside thinkers, their work resembled most closely that of 'institutionalists' . . . in the United States." Professor Goodwin further notes that "many of their policy conclusions are remarkably similar to those of present day economists in developing countries, particularly in such matters as the economic value of education and social research, the role of the state in development, and the nature of stimuli to innovative and creative thought." ("Economic Analysis and Development in British West Africa," *Economic Development and Cultural Change*, July 1967, pp. 439, 451).]

CHAPTER XXII

Conclusion: Retrospect and Prospects

At the outset of the course, I said that its chief aim was constructive, to help young economists to decide how they can make their most effective contribution toward the development of economic theory, by working through the various types to a unified position.[1]

We have reviewed a number of "types of economic theory" or, perhaps slightly more accurately, "conceptions of what economic theory ought to be." We began with the classical political economy in the discursive form represented by its founder, Adam Smith. Then we passed on to see how that type of discussion was enriched by Thomas Robert Malthus, how it was reorganized by David Ricardo and how it got finally a masterly re-exposition at the hands of John Stuart Mill.

Then we turned to the second type which, following its author, we called the "mechanics of utility," the enormously suggestive but fragmentary work of W. Stanley Jevons. Next we took up what is most commonly called the neo-classical view of Alfred Marshall, that grand attempt to systematize efficiently in the body of economic theory not only the chief results attained by the classical masters but also the leading suggestions made by Jevons and his peers, particularly the Austrians, in the development of the marginal analysis.

Then, crossing to the American side of the Atlantic, there was first taken up the work of the American psychological school, as Frank A. Fetter has called the type of theory of which his own work made the leading example. From that we passed on to the pecuniary logic of Herbert J. Davenport, the economics which is constituted by looking at phenomena from the standpoint of price. We then passed to the European views, logically closely related to those of Davenport. After taking up the Austrian type of utility theory represented by Friedrich von Wieser, we passed to the theory of general equilibrium as propounded with the aid of mathematical apparatus by the Swedish economist Gustav Cassel [and with less mathematics by Schumpeter].

[1] Outline, May 14, 1931; "Diary," October 10, 1931.

We studied in some detail too [the social value theory of B. M. Anderson, Jr.] and the welfare economics of John A. Hobson. Also we surveyed briefly the net outcome of the aspirations of the historical school as represented by Gustav von Schmoller; then institutional theory as represented by Thorstein Veblen. And to complete the list we have studied the later trend of institutionalism of John R. Commons.

By way of conclusion I should like to discuss· first how the approaches differ among themselves. Needless to say, they differ in various ways. Ordinarily the differences are conceived to arise in good part from the employment of different methods. The old distinction between deductive and inductive reasoning still haunts the minds of economists and they are prone to mark off the types of theory which are considered more or less orthodox as developed by deductive reasoning from those other brands which in some other measure are characterized by a large use of induction.

There can be no question that the extent to which the different writers have endeavored to collect information about economic happenings varies greatly from case to case. Schmoller has made the most comprehensive attempt to present in his *Volkswirtschaftslehre* a view of actual conditions as they have developed through certain historical peculiarities in the past and as they exist at the present time. Veblen is another writer who makes much use of information— of a decidedly recondite sort. But on the other hand it was characteristic of Adam Smith that he was deeply interested in the realities of economic practice and that he expected his readers to take a similar interest. There is not a little of this sort of material in Malthus, especially in the second edition of his *Essay on the Principle of Population*. There is a good deal in John Stuart Mill and Alfred Marshall. There is more or less in almost all the writers discussed. But perhaps not all, for some take it for granted that the relevant factual information is at the disposal of the reader. In short the difference in practice in the extent to which economists utilize factual information—or rely upon imaginary conditions which may be far from conforming with reality—is one of degree and of a degree which does not control the differences.

". . . I do seriously think that our problems have to govern the methods we employ, in a broad sense. For example, if we wish to get an account of human behavior that applies to the world in which we live, we must at some stage of the proceedings make a large use of actual observations. If, on the other hand, we were trying to develop one of the geometries of hyper-space, I suppose observation would have no place in our operations. When you [J. M. Clark] were making your charming experiments with non-Euclidean economics it was not incumbent upon you to consider whether your reasoning checked with observations or not. There is, so far as I see, one element that is common to all sound methods of scientific investigation. Namely, obedience to the rules of logic. That is just as necessary in work with observation as it is with work confined to the implications of concepts.

Such being the case, the difference between the methods employed to solve different problems must be one of stress upon the formal and the factual elements in discussion. I hope no one got the impression that I think it possible in economic research to dispense with careful reasoning.

As for the influence of method on choice of problems, I suppose we would all say that an investigator's gifts and interests should have an influence upon the researches he undertakes. There are people who are extremely good observers but not adept at logical analysis. They would be ill-advised to attempt work in abstract analysis and, of course, this proposition can be reversed.

Of course it is true that statistical method does not enable one to handle all problems of the sort that nineteenth century economics posed. The important questions along this line seem to me to be, first, What of these problems remain significant? Second, Can they, by reformulation, be open to realistic attack? Third, How can we fit problems, about which we can do no more than speculate, into the corpus of results we can demonstrate empirically?"[1a]

Also of secondary importance is the similar difference between what is sometimes called the historical and the systematic approach to the discussion of economic problems. There is some "system" in all good history and all good systematic theorists realize that they are studying the situation as it exists at a given historical stage, but there is again a difference of degree.[2] If the investigator contrasts, say, Marshall and Schmoller he finds much less attention paid to what he might classify technically as historical materials in the first case and much more attention paid to them in the second case. The difference in the use of historical materials is thus again a matter of degree; it is not primarily responsible for the different ways of attacking economics which commended themselves to the two scholars.

[1a] Mitchell to J. M. Clark, January 19, 1944, copy.

[2] Last sentence from Outline, "Closing Lectures," January 19, 24, 1928.

The same conclusion must be reached for a variety of other differences which are sometimes alleged to exist among the various types
of economics, such as the great abstractness of some writers and the
more realistic or concrete character of the work done by others, or
what is sometimes mentioned as a difference between the relative
reliance upon qualitative and quantitative methods.

It should be again noted that mathematics is not confined to any single type
of theory and not excluded from any. Curiously Veblen uses mathematical
statements rather freely in his footnotes in *The Theory of Business Enterprise*. Conclusion: differences of method are of secondary importance and
arise chiefly from differences of problems attacked. In short all the alleged
differences of method stand on more or less the same ground. They are to
be explained in terms of a deeper line of difference.[3]

What are the central problems of economics represented by the
successive types? Classical political economy as represented by Adam
Smith was a discursive set of disquisitions upon the organization of
modern countries. It deserved its name *The Wealth of Nations* for
it dealt with whatever methods suggested themselves to the mind
of a singularly observant scholar in the eighteenth century as possible ways of adding to the annual income of a country, of maximizing
production.

That same discursive conception got definitely organized in the
hands of Ricardo. Living at a time when the problem of the relative
shares in the national income which might go to landlords, capitalists
and laborers was occupying the attention of practical politicians, he
viewed the distribution of income as the problem of central significance. But economics, as he treated it in *On the Principles of Political
Economy and Taxation*, had a necessary preliminary part. In a modern
community, the income that people get depends not so much on what
they produce themselves as on what share they can get of the income
produced by the community as a whole and the share they get
depends on the terms upon which they can exchange whatever they
have to contribute for the things that are contributed by others. That
problem of exchange was in Ricardo's terminology the problem of
value, and thus a discussion of the principles determining value was
a logically necessary introduction to the discussion of the terms on
which income was distributed into wages, profits and rent.

In the hands of John Stuart Mill, this organization of the subject
was still dominant. But he was not content in his *Principles of Political
Economy with Some of Their Applications to Social Philosophy* to

---

[3] Outline, "Closing Lecture," [May] 1915.

omit the problem which Adam Smith had stressed and Ricardo passed by with scarce a mention; that is, the problem of the production of wealth. As he sees the matter, the economist is still interested primarily in the distribution of income, and because he is interested in distribution he must understand the terms of exchange, but the welfare of the community depends in good part upon the total amount of income produced, consequently the first consideration is the laws of production; this is followed by distribution and that in turn by exchange.

With Jevons there is the beginning of a process of simplification through higher organization of the whole field. To him the central problem is exchange and he throws out the suggestion in *The Theory of Political Economy* that the theory of exchange when properly developed will cover the exchange of labor, or the use of capital or land, or the services of business men, for other goods; that is, the theory of exchange may itself come to include the theory of distribution.

The Austrian theory as exemplified by Friedrich von Wieser's *Social Economics* is concerned with the problem of the relation between the rational valuations of the individual and social phenomena, in other words, with isolated valuation, valuation in the market, valuation by the state and international problems.[4] Marshall carried out this idea of Jevons and the Austrians. He treats the principles of economics basically in terms of Ricardo's problems, but his *Principles of Economics* presents these problem inside a much more systematic framework. Economic theory in his hands becomes integrated whereas in Ricardo's *Principles of Political Economy* the discussion of the various successive problems is not closely knit together. Marshall accepts and develops further the analysis of cost which constituted the chief discussions of value in Ricardo and combines with it the analysis of utility which had been elaborated by Jevons and the Austrians, and this rounded theory of value he then proceeds to apply systematically to show the value of labor, the value of the use of capital and land, and the value of the services of the business organizer.

Much the same view of what constitutes the central problem of economic theory is held by the members of the American psychological school, but in working out the theory of value they perceived that the basic assumptions of rational choice among alternatives, which were made tacitly but unhesitatingly in Ricardo's generation

---

[4] Sentence from Outlines, May 14, 1931; "Closing Lectures," January 19, 24, 1928.

and explicitly by Jevons and Marshall, conceal a further problem which requires and gets consideration at their hands; namely, the problem of how the element of calculation which exists in most economic activity is related to the element of what they call instinctive choice or impulsive action, which is characteristic of all kinds of human behavior and has been stressed so much by modern psychological inquiry. The theory of value, as they represent things, leads the inquirer into an examination of how people make their choices, an examination which is found when followed up to include elements that are not adequately represented in the more or less mechanically formulated demand schedules of economists like Jevons or even Marshall.

Pecuniary logic, as exemplified in Davenport's *The Economics of Enterprise,* may be regarded as an attempt to set economic theory free from the metaphysical elements which the discussion of value seems to be bringing into it. A logically minded person like Davenport felt no intellectual satisfaction in the attempts of a psychologically minded economist like Fetter to rebuild the theory upon the basis of a new set of psychological assumptions. He was much impressed by the fact that the psychologists had by no means arrived at a consensus of opinion regarding the grounds of choice. He realized that fashions in psychology, if you like, types of theory in psychology, are at least as numerous as in economics. It seemed to him that after Jevons had made a serious error in trying to establish theory upon the basis of psychology borrowed from Jeremy Bentham, Fetter was making as great an error in trying to re-establish theory on the basis of his psychology of voluntary choice. The remedy was to exclude from economics one of the problems which Ricardo had tried to treat in a certain deductive fashion, which Jevons had regarded as fundamental, which Marshall included, and which Fetter also thought basic, though his formulation was somewhat different.

The question of why people like goods, how they make their valuations, was excluded by defining economics in such a fashion as to narrow its scope to a little group of central problems, which the economist as an economist is, according to Davenport, competent to deal with, and these were the problems of prices. It is true that having carried out the analysis, he recognized that his results were, in his own language, "circuitous and superficial," that he was explaining one price in terms of other prices. While that sort of explanation may be adequate for purposes of the entrepreneur, it was not adequate for purposes of the scientific inquirer. Therefore he held that the economist must recognize that behind the phenomena with which he deals there lie certain real forces. He pointed out what the forces were: the desires of men, natural resources over which they have control and the methods which they have devised of utilizing the resources. But having pointed them out, he stopped there, because he had reached the frontier of economic science proper. When he passed over into the study of desires he would be getting into the realm of the psychologist; to study the natural resources would get him into the realm of, say, the commercial geographer; when he passed over into the realm of the arts of production he would be entering the territory of the engineering professions.[4a]

The theory of general equilibrium, as represented by Cassel, proceeds like Davenport to make economics more "scientific," by throwing out the discussion of value and putting the process of pricing in the center of the picture. This is the only element of the value problem which on Cassel's showing can be treated in scientific terms without the use of metaphysical assumptions. Yet he too must assume that there are certain functions which can be taken to represent the relationship between the amount of goods that people will consume and the several prices at which the commodities can be had. Those functions are the carryover in Cassel of the old discussions of what value is and how people value different things. They represent in his analysis Davenport's few remarks to the effect that human desires are basic to the problem. But Cassel no more regards himself, as an economist, fitted to inquire into the precise character of the value functions —certainly not into their psychological basis—than does Davenport with regard to inquiries into human desires.

Cassel differs from Davenport only in the technical matter that in his eyes [as in those of his master Walras] the problem of pricing ought to be attacked all at once in the sense that it is hopeless to conceive of trying to show how the value of any one good is determined at one time, for then the discussion simply explains one price in terms of other prices, whereas if the economist starts with the problem of the determination of the prices of an indefinite number of goods in a market at the same time he can provide himself with

---

[4a] [In asking Mitchell to review *The Economics of Enterprise* for *The American Economic Review,* the editor said]: "I have a special interest in asking you to undertake this if not too uncongenial. Davenport seems to be a difficult person to interpret, and I think you are sufficiently sympathetic and at the same time critical, to present his thought fairly to our membership. There is also considerable in the book, as you are aware, in regard to variations (the ups and downs) of business." (Davis R. Dewey to Mitchell, July 12, 1914.)

the mathematical statement of the problem which shows that it is susceptible of a definite solution.[4b]

Cassel, like his predecessors, uses his particular form of the value discussion, his theory of pricing, to get light on the distribution of income and at this point, going further than Marshall, he uses his general picture of the pricing problem to show how the price of money is fixed; in other words, how variations in the general level of prices come about when a particular commodity is exploited as the monetary standard. Finally, again extending the scope of problems which belong in economics proper, he recognizes the inadequacy of his general scheme in the sense that it deals only with a static condition of affairs, or a situation where what is known as progress is going on at a uniform rate. It becomes a part of the theorist's task in his view to consider results which follow from inequalities in the rate at which economic activity is expanding. He is thus led to devote a section of *The Theory of Social Economy* to the theory of business cycles. Somewhat related is the social value school, as represented by B. M. Anderson, Jr. It sought to provide a rationale in social factors for the valuations that result in the demand schedules of the orthodox theory.

The general line of development, the main sequence in economics in a real sense represents a narrowing down from the start of Adam Smith in *The Wealth of Nations* to the problems which are taken up by people like Davenport, even people like Cassel. As opposed to this, there are a number of examples of how other folk want to broaden the field. These economists felt that the problem on which theorists centered their attention are not even the most important ones in the explanation of economic progress.

This view was true of the historical school. The immediate problem of inquiry on their showing should be into the developmental processes, which, running through an indefinitely long human past, have established the conditions under which men are now living, which have led to the growth of the present enormously intricate system of

---

[4b] "[I]n a system of private enterprise, all economic activities are interdependent. The intricacies of the crisscrossing relationships among the elements of such an economy have been schematically indicated by the system of simultaneous equations devised by Léon Walras and his successors. Fundamentally the same conception runs through Alfred Marshall's more concrete description of the integration of demand, supply and value in the operations of producing and distributing the national income." [In short], "economic activities are functionally related to one another in the numberless direct and indirect ways suggested in fancy by the equations of Walras and the analyses of Marshall." (*What Happens During Business Cycles. A Progress Report* (posthumous; New York: National Bureau of Economic Research, 1950) pp. 110-112.

producing goods, of organizing for carrying on business, which have given the people more or less standardized wants as consumers and which have led them to achieve such varied and often extraordinary capacities as producers. This modern situation which the classical school and their successors were inclined to take for granted is, from the point of view of the historical school, something which requires to be explained by the economist.

> [Stated somewhat differently,] the historical school sought to increase knowledge by bringing a wider range of problems into the discussion. It asserted that we ought not merely to assume that people will take certain quantities of certain commodities at certain prices as data and then discuss mechanics of price fixing. The important task is to inquire how the modern organization of society has come to exist; what goods, for example, people want; how much they can buy; what the arts of production really are; how they have changed, etc.[5]

Needless to say, the theorists of the main sequence agree that such an investigation is not primarily the task of an economist but of an historian as such.

Veblen's institutional approach has close relationships with that of the historical school; and yet the difference is of considerable importance. It arises primarily from the fact that Veblen has an analytic point of view of human nature which differed far more from the Benthamite tradition than did the view of human nature entertained by Schmoller; that is, the difference arises primarily from a different conception of human nature. Schmoller, despite his large list of the instincts important in economic behavior, continues to treat men's economic activity as dominated primarily by the effort to get pleasure. Veblen, as a student of modern biology and psychology, in his analysis of human nature distinguishes between the presumably unchanging original nature of man and his highly changeable habitual activities. From his viewpoint, one part of human nature is passed on from generation to generation with no perceptible alteration. On the other hand, men's habits of thinking and therefore their habits of acting have undergone enormous changes in the course of human history. Even in the decades which are covered by the century within which economic science has flourished, there have been extraordinary changes in men's social habits.

From Veblen's viewpoint the chief problem of understanding how men live today is the problem how the social habits of an economic character have been put into their present shape; his answer is to

---

[5] Outline, "Closing Lectures," January 19, 24, 1928.

show how the discipline of daily life in getting a living produces new habits as methods of obtaining a living change. Changes in methods of getting a living are themselves part and parcel of the process of alteration, and in turn may bring about far reaching changes in all men's habits. From Veblen's viewpoint the more traditional economics is an elaborate analysis of the way in which social habits operate, given a set of institutions which have come to dominate life within the last hundred years or so.

Institutional economics agrees with historical school that the important problem is how the present ways of organizing economic life have developed and what further changes they are undergoing. But it treats this problem more analytically. Makes analysis of human behavior definitely the central problem. Distinguishes between the supposedly unchanging "original nature" of man and his constantly altering "culture." Latter conceived to consist primarily of mass habits. Its concern is to see how these mass habits are formed by a process of cumulative change, in which characteristics of daily work are the factors of chief consequence.

Regards the more orthodox types of economic theory as having value in so far as they develop the logical implications of the current scheme of institutions for social behavior. Veblen's institutional theory holds that the central problem of economics is the evolution of men's habits of thinking, feeling and acting in getting along. Instead of assuming the competitive order as the sole object of interest and confining analysis to that, he seeks to find out how this mode of organization developed from very different forms that prevailed in the past by a process of cumulative changes; and what further modifications it seems to be undergoing in the present. Quantitative studies of economic life have reinforced this demand for insight into the evolution of economic activities. Even within the short period covered by most of our time series we found that secular and structural changes of great importance have occurred. Economic organization of today very different from that of Ricardo's day or even of 1890 when Marshall published the first edition of his *Principles of Economics*. One of the results of quantitative analysis is therefore to direct attention to the cumulative changes in economic institutions. To get light on these questions the investigator cannot confine himself to the relatively slender collection of statistical time series. He finds it necessary to appeal to consecutive accounts of the evolution of numerous economic institutions. Thus economic history and economic theory get drawn together.[6]

There remains one other type of theory: welfare economics. The problem of organic welfare which it puts into the forefront is different from that emphasized by any of the other types of theory, not that the writers of the latter have not thought that welfare was a matter of chief concern, but they have not seen how to give it scien-

---

[6] Outlines, "Closing Lectures," January 19, 24, 1928; "Current Developments in Economic Thought," remarks at Political Economy Club, Columbia University, April 5, 1938.

tific status. That is, the representatives of other types vaguely hoped their work might help them to deal with the problem of welfare, but they give little systematic attention to it, conceiving it to be a practical rather than a scientific issue.[7] Hobson thinks that he has found a way of treating in more or less scientific terms the relations between the activities of production on the one side and consumption on the other, and the welfare which is obtained by the mass of mankind.

In so doing he has not departed from the conception of human nature which was formulated for the classical masters by Jeremy Bentham. He has rather applied that conception with a simplicity and directness almost equal to Bentham's own. From Bentham's viewpoint the question of welfare under the head of maximising pleasure was a matter of far more concern than any other social problem; and those who adopted Bentham's conception of human nature consciously or unconsciously must have felt the same way about the situation, but, to repeat, they have not known how to subject this most important of all problems to a scientific analysis. Hobson thinks that can be done, at least in general terms. For he has faith that though theorists do not possess a generally acceptable criterion of what constitutes welfare, they do recognize the existence of a general consensus of intelligent opinion regarding what constitutes welfare in certain specific respects. And if the theorists will confine their analysis to the aspects of welfare about which there is agreement then they can carry on the discussion of these most fundamental economic, social problems in a satisfactory fashion.[7a]

To repeat, the problem of the economist has become much more highly differentiated with the passing of the years than it appeared to the classical economist; that is to say, the appearance of so many different types of economic theory is due primarily to the unfolding of new aspects of what was once conceived to be a comparatively simple and unified scientific problem. It may be anticipated that other types of economic theory will continue to make their appearance so long as we keep finding new aspects of economic behavior which seem susceptible of scientific treatment and important enough to engage the serious attention of scholars.[8]

---

[7] Sentence from Outline, "Closing Lectures," January 19, 24, 1928.

[7a] [In the orthodox view according to Mitchell], money is superficial. Below money lie goods. Below goods lie the real entities summed up in psychic cost and psychic income. And welfare is a blended psychic income in the long run. (Outline, "Price Economics in the Service of Welfare Economics," talk to Political Economy Club of Columbia University, February 18, 1921.)

[8] Last paragraph from "1918 Typescript."

So much for the brief review of the various types of economic theory which have been studied. Now comes the most interesting question of all. What use if any can students make of such acquaintance as they have gained with the different ways of conceiving the task of economic theory?

If I am right in holding that the chief difference among the several types consists in the emphasis upon different problems for investigation, then the question for one who is looking over the various types as possible helpful guides for his constructive work as an economist would seem to be what problems does he wish to attack? The answer must depend upon his personal equation, particular aptitudes and opportunities. But I do not see how it can be held that nothing can be learned from any of these types of theory which have been considered; that is, that we are in a position to say that any of the problems which are emphasized by the writers lack significance. Each and every one of the problems has some relevance for a person who wishes to understand economic processes as they run in the world. This applies as much to the highly abstract mathematical theory of general equilibrium as it does to Veblen's institutional theory or Hobson's welfare economics or the neo-classicism of Marshall. Every one of these problems is genuine in the sense that a person who studies it stands a chance of getting deeper insight into the lives that men lead today in producing and consuming income.

If that, however, is the case, economics requires a more definite framework than it seems to possess, there is need of some way of conceiving its task which will be capable of showing specifically what contribution the several types of economic theory are capable of making to economic life. I propose to suggest a framework that shows how each of the several types contributes to our understanding, that shows them not as rivals but as complements.

One of the characteristics of economists is that besides their concern with what they call economic theory they devote an enormous amount of time to the study of special problems. The latter work as a rule has no very close relationship to what is thought of as theory. It is represented by the many different lines of investigation that are carried on in schools of business, by the array of different courses that are given often under the title of applied economics, such as money and banking, insurance, marketing and tariff problems. There are special courses on price fluctuations and business cycles and commercial geography and a great many other subjects which keep increasing in number as time goes on. There are special courses on labor problems, social insurance and economic history at large.

All this investigation has some relevance to the problem of understanding economic activity. It should, one would think, have a clear and obvious relationship to economic theory, for theory is supposed to show the general underlying principles of economics which run through all the activities of men concerned in getting a living; and yet, as already noted, monographs upon these several subjects seldom start from the principles of economic theory as laid down in the treatises. The specialists have gone their own way in large part, seeming to derive little help or guidance from the theoretical treatises. Even the so-called theorists have often supplemented their expositions by separate chapters on "applied economics" which appears to have little relation to their general framework. For example, compare Marshall's *Principles of Economics* and his *Industry and Trade*.[9]

Many of the special investigators feel that they get comparatively little help from theory. Indeed not a few of them are disdainful of what they call "theoretical speculations." On the other hand, many of the people who are specially interested in what is called economic theory feel that there is great danger that economics is disintegrating, that it is losing its unity as a science and is running off into the sands of a widely dispersed factual investigation which may serve certain practical purposes but has comparatively little scientific significance.

It would seem that a conception of economics is needed which will be broad enough not merely to embrace all the various types of theoretical economics but also to include the infinite range of factual investigations into special subjects. If it is to be any good, it should be a framework which shows how every item that it includes bears upon the problem as a whole. It should show how any investigation of an economic order that a man may undertake makes its contribution, how it fits in with what other investigators are doing.

Such a framework is gradually emerging not only from the labors of the theorists of different brands but also from the work of many economic specialists. If the theorist can think of economics as a science which deals with economic behavior and get the implication of that phrase he will at last be on the high road to satisfy the need for a framework.

We should acquaint ourselves with the knowledge of human nature which psychology, ethics, history and biology has afforded since Ricardo's time,

---

[9] Last two sentences from Outline, May 14, 1931.

and then use all this knowledge, all the suggestions we can get from existing economic theory, all the materials put at our disposal by statistics,
and all our own wits to understand economic behavior. That phrase—
economic behavior—is probably the most suggestive name of the type of
economic theory that we should cultivate.[10]

I do not mean "behavior" in the technical and restricted sense
which it has come to have in psychology, in particular as employed
by John B. Watson.[11] How men act is what we wish to know, how
mass changes in action come about. We should not rule out in advance
any means of investigation which promise to throw light on that
problem.[12]

In other words, it would seem a grave mistake to rule out in advance
in dealing with economic phenomena any effort to consider what goes
on inside of people's consciousness, to confine investigations exclusively to a study of objective observations of what people do. That
method is doubtless extremely attractive and where it can be employed
yields results which may be regarded as uncontestable; but, as matters
currently stand, economists have not the possibility of observing in
a thoroughly objective fashion all types of economic activity that
may concern theory. In many cases economists still can with advantage employ the methods of analyzing the common ways of
thinking and acting which they practice themselves and of which
they can observe certain external objective evidences among their
fellows. It would be hard indeed to treat such problems as are offered
to the student of advertising, for example, if one confined himself to
thinking about objective evidence of activities, if he refused to consider what goes on in people's consciousness. I shall, therefore, use
the term economic behavior as indicating all the activities in which
men engage so far as they are seeking means to satisfy their wants
and suppose that the purpose of economics is to get such understanding as is possible of these activities.

That conception of economics embraces every one of the types of
economic theory that has been reviewed. Certainly it would include
historical investigations whether made by an economist or by an
economic historian. For in the study of how people in past generations have carried on their activities of producing and exchanging

---

[10] Outline, May 12, 1915.
[11] [Watson was the great pioneer in the formulation of the "behavior" psychology
which basically derived from the James-Dewey functional psychology. The movement was launched by Watson's series of lectures at Columbia University in 1913,
which were elaborated into the famous treatise, *Behavior, An Introduction to
Psychology* (1914).]
[12] Last two sentences from Outline, May 14, 1931.

and consuming wealth some addition to the knowledge of the general subject of economic behavior is being made. It includes not only the broad viewpoint of institutional inquiry that Veblen recommends but also what are ordinarily thought of as the more speculative ventures in economic thought; to take the most extreme example, that of the mathematical theory of the determination of prices.

An outstanding problem of economics at the present day [1927] is the role that is played in men's activities by prices. These prices are interconnected with each other; they constitute a system in which every part is modified ever and again by changes in certain other parts. There seems to be no end of the ramifications of the interrelationships of different prices. Just so far as the plan which Walras devised of exhibiting the interconnections among prices by the use of simultaneous equations illuminates the facts which are so clear in daily life, that type of theory may be regarded as contributing to the understanding of economic behavior.

Not only does the behavioristic general conception of what economics should be show that every one of the types of theory which have been discussed has some contribution to make, but it also shows how each contribution bears upon the problem as a whole. For all that the framework does is to put the general problem that concerns economists clearly and simply before their minds. Economic behavior turns out to be, on analysis, a most elaborate and complicated set of phenomena in which there are combined a myriad of influences coming from the past, ever renewed in the present, ever changing as men move forward. Highly systematic thinking plays a role in men's conduct, in their economic behavior; impulsive elements enter in; the so-called instincts or, as they are latterly called, inherent drives have a good deal to do with determining what men strive for and in shaping the habits which men gradually assume; their formal knowledge influences their technical processes and therefore influences the kind of work they do and reacts upon their habits and makes them into people a little different in each generation from their predecessors.

If the student begins to think in these terms he has a perspective in which he can arrange the contributions brought by the various types of theory and see in what fashion they supplement each other. Take once more the contribution of the mathematical theory of general equilibrium. This is a contribution to the understanding of the logical element in guiding economic life at the present time. It is a sort of outpouring of what I like to call pecuniary logic. All people are forced by the exigencies of modern life to acquire a certain acquaintance with this logic, to value goods in terms of money, to know something of the art of making exchanges, to get some slight acquaintance, at least, with the principles of investment, to have some share in that elaborate scheme of pricing which men have to utilize as denizens of the modern world. Anything which shows people more clearly the logical implication of these ideas about prices is giving a deeper insight into the organization of the society of which economists are a part.

Another marked advantage of the behavioristic conception is that it helps to solve what has been to theorists an increasingly difficult problem; that is, the problem of the relationship of economics to psychology. The story was previously told of how economics got its start in the days when the hedonistic view of human nature was accepted as common sense; how at a later stage the hedonistic scheme was represented as the logical function of economics and then how later still economists became aware of the inadequacies of this picture of human activity. In the eyes of psychology experts the question arose of what economics could do to get rid of the Benthamite foundation which was now proving so unstable.

Alfred Marshall tries to get away from it by substituting what seemed to him less dangerous terms for pain and pleasure. Frank A. Fetter tries to get rid of the hedonism of Bentham by applying what he thinks of as a new and more reliable scheme of psychology, "volitional" psychology. Gustav von Schmoller tried to make use of the instincts; Herbert J. Davenport and Gustav Cassel attempted to throw psychology out of economics by saying that it was not the business of the economist to inquire into the character of people's wants. Finally, Thorstein Veblen sought to explain what are to him the leading problems in terms of changes in habit, making habit the great category which economists must use, and thus borrowing largely from William James as W. Stanley Jevons borrowed from Jeremy Bentham.

If economics really must get a conception of human nature from another science, and if that other science is in the earlier stages of its development, as much as economics itself, if it has not yet solved the fundamental problems about how people act, then the economist's position is a difficult one. People are bound to borrow elements that are none too well accredited and it might be thought that the safe course is that commended by Davenport and Cassel: have no contact with psychology, carry on an analysis which is admitted to be superficial in character, but show that the explanations must be furnished, whenever that turns out to be feasible, by scientists who are not economists.

On the other hand, if economics is viewed as a science of behavior, an effort to explain a certain line or certain aspects of activities, then the relationship of economics to psychology becomes quite different at once. Economics does not have to borrow materials from psychology and proceed to erect a structure on that foundation. Rather the economist's task becomes itself psychological in character. The economist becomes one among the students of human behavior. And it is his business to borrow from others, to get all the light that he can upon a certain set of behavior problems. That makes the psychologist, to be sure, one of his allies. For, needless to say, the economist who begins the study of human nature as already familiar with what psychologists, students of human behavior have found out, is more likely to make satisfactory progress towards the solution of his own tasks than the man who comes devoid of all psychological studies.

Are economists in danger of getting entangled in psychological disputes? True that psychology is not a thoroughly harmonious science. True also that economists are not competent judges of technical differences among psychologists. But most of these differences do not affect the economist.[13]

In the same sense this behavioristic conception of what the task of economics really is makes several other sciences allies of economics. For, if economics is one science of human behavior, then sociology and political science and anthropology, engineering, law, history, mental hygiene, statistics are sister sciences just as much as psychology; all of them together have a common problem, they are concerned with the effort to explain how men in society carry on their myriad activities at the present time. It is not so much a different set of activities with which these several disciplines deal, as different aspects of activities which are running on in a society where people are not merely getting and making a living, but where they are also marrying and belonging to churches, where they are voting, where

---

[13] Outline, May 12, 1915.

"I beg to thank you for so kindly sending me a copy of your article ["The Rationality of Economic Activity"] in *The Journal of Political Economy* [1910], which I greatly appreciate. Your forcible statement of the case for psychology should do something towards answering the unbelieving, but I'm afraid it must be some considerable time before the principles you advocate are generally applied." William McDougall to Mitchell, April 2, [1910].

[John Dewey said of the article that it suggested to him the "mode of interpreting the hedonistic calculus of utilitarianism." *Human Nature and Conduct* (New York: Holt, 1922) p. 213.]

"Lucy and I dined with . . . the Sam Lewisohns [eminent mining magnate and philanthropist]. Lewisohn thinks literature on the manic-depressive type instructive to economists." Mitchell, "Diary," March 8, 1933.

they are educating their children, where they are all living a life that has many aspects beside that of obtaining money and spending money. One reason for thinking that this way of conceiving the task of economics is gradually spreading lies in the fact that the perception of the common interest of the social sciences has become clearer today. I well remember when I was a graduate student of economics at the University of Chicago that we people in the Department of Economics felt ourselves superior folk whenever we thought of our colleagues in sociology and political science, that we felt that we did not have anything to do with the anthropologists and we were advised by our tutors not to mess around with psychology. Few of us thought that the other departments had any real bearing upon the science that had been founded by Adam Smith and perfected by Alfred Marshall.

That view, needless to say, still has many exponents to this day. There are plenty of representatives of the several sciences who say that the way to promote knowledge is through specialization, and that the man who is giving his utmost energies to the pursuit of a particular subdivision of a particular science does ill to spend a considerable amount of his time in trying to learn a little of what is known by people in other branches of investigation. Such knowledge may be interesting, they contend, and it is as worth while to read treatises on other sciences in leisure hours as it is to read detective stories, but there is not much chance that what the economist learns will be of considerable value in his own work, and that if he messes around with those things he might prove the truth of the old adage that a little knowledge is a dangerous thing.

Recently [1930], however, there was a good deal of evidence that not a few people who are interested in the several social sciences have come to realize that the very nature of the problems which they are severally engaged in makes co-operation among the adepts of the various disciplines indispensable for the attainment of anything like adequate understanding. As such evidence note the half dozen books or more which have been published within the last ten years, dealing inside a single set of covers with all the different social sciences.[14]

Then there is the great venture represented by the *Encyclopedia of the Social Sciences* under the editorship of Edwin R. A. Seligman

---

[14] Perhaps the most interesting is the one that was edited by William F. Ogburn and Alexander Goldenweiser, *The Social Sciences and their Interrelations* (1927). It has contributions dealing with various branches of knowledge from people who covered not only economics, sociology, political science and psychology, but also education, history, social medicine and half a dozen other topics.

and Alvin Johnson, an undertaking which is aided by an advisory committee on which there are representatives of all the different social sciences. It is a tool which will be particularly valuable to the men in the different social sciences, not so much that it will tell each one what he does not know about his own subject, but that it is an easy means of forming some opinions upon ways of working that are engaging the attention of people in other fields.[15]

Then too, there have been such organizations formed as the Social Science Research Council and the Association of Learned Societies. These do not take the place of the American Economic Association, the American Historical Association, The American Psychological Association, The American Sociological Society, etc.; they are formed of representatives appointed by these several professional bodies with the explicit view that there are a host of interests common to all the associations concerned, interests which may be promoted by a definite organization of these associations on a national scale.

The two societies mentioned, The Association of Learned Societies and the Social Science Research Council, have been able to obtain funds for many investigations which in all cases are under the general direction of committees including representation from two or more of the social sciences. In not a few cases these studies are carried on co-operatively by staffs recruited from several disciplines.[15a]

What has been done on a national scale has been done within a number of American universities; for example, the Columbia University Council for Research in the Social Sciences. The people in the main affected departments are coming together, because the realization is spreading that each of the social sciences is concerned with understanding human behavior. The subject is so vast that it is only

---

[15] [The fifteen volumes of the *Encyclopedia of the Social Sciences* were published in 1930-1935.]

"To Columbia for meeting of advisory committee on Encyclopaedia of the Social Sciences. Representatives from ten disciplines, including education, jurisprudence, social work, history. Seligman presiding." Mitchell, "Diary," April 23, 1927.

[15a] [Mitchell was a leading member of the organizing group that in 1922-1923 formulated the plans for the establishment of the Social Science Research Council. He remained a dominant figure after it was chartered in 1924. The Council is comprised of representatives from the great variety of disciplines in the social sciences broadly conceived. Its object, he said in an address in 1930, was] to promote research in the social sciences—particularly to promote social research through cooperation of men representing different disciplines. Character of most social problems requires the joint attention of sociologists, political scientists, economists, psychologists, historians, the skill of statisticians and is often the better planned when anthropologists, lawyers, psychiatrists, physicians and others join in. (Outline, "Social Science Research Council," talk before American Association of University Professors, December 29, 1930). [For a perceptive account of Mitchell's role in the Social Science Research Council, see Barry D. Karl, "The Power of Intellect and the Politics of Ideas," *Daedalus,* Summer 1968, pp. 1012-1013, 1015.]

by cooperation of groups of workers each representing a large number of specialists that results of the best obtainable character can be had. In short, no one person can be expected to become thoroughly versed in all of these branches. But it is only by co-operation among men concerned with all of them that thorough understanding can be achieved.[16]

This behavioristic framework not only shows economists how their several types of economic theory recognized as such go together and how the several social sciences can cooperate effectively, but also a way of avoiding the conception of economic theory as some particular specialty which exists apart from the carefully detailed studies of economic activities as carried on in so many of the specialties. If one takes the view that economics is a science of human behavior, it follows that anybody who is making an intensive study, say, of the operations of a particular banking system in a country is learning something that is relevant to the general theme, something that has this general as well as a special interest. The man who is concerned with advertising and with insurance and with history and geography comes into the fold and a way is indicated for making use for general theoretical purposes of the contribution that the various specialist workers bring to the common fund of knowledge. Finally the assumption helps us with problems of methods of work.[17] An attempt to distinguish between speculations carried on more or less by themselves on a philosophical plane and factual investigation carried on intensively is a serious error. Men devote themselves to both types of activity. But for understanding the problem as a whole the economist needs to base his general ideas, just so far as he possibly can, upon factual knowledge of a great variety of processes. And the people who are gradually accumulating the factual knowledge are from this viewpoint laying the basis and actively contributing to economic theory at large.

There is, I think, very little use in criticising economic theories, save as an aid to the critic's own constructive efforts to improve economic theory. Practically then, the question is, what can one get from

---

[16] Last two sentences from Outline, May 14, 1931.

Anthropology and history and law enable us to conceive our problem more clearly. Not merely the present stage of culture has its problems. A science of economic behavior is as much needed for understanding the life of Australian blackfellows or ancient Egyptians as of contemporary United States. (Outline, "Closing Lectures," January 19, 24, 1928.)

[17] Sentence from Outline, May 14, 1931.

a survey of different ways of attacking the central problems of economics to assist in carrying on the work of his predecessors?

I think that such general familiarity with essays in economic theory of different sorts as the class has gained may be of very considerable assistance—assistance, in the first place, toward giving one a clearer conception of what the problems of economic theory are; what are the problems on which it is worthwhile to work, a conception which ought to be of some assistance in seeing where even the smallest piece of investigation that the theorist undertakes fits into a general pattern.

It seems to me that if one looks at the different types of theory from this viewpoint he sees that they are, after all, each one of them relevant in the sense that they do deal with economic problems on which we need light, problems which are interesting from the intellectual viewpoint, problems which are more or less important from the social viewpoint.

Is there, to repeat, no way in which we can define the general aim of economic theory in such a fashion as to provide a place for every one of the types of theory with which we have been acquainted, and in such a way as to get every one of these types into its proper place? I think—and here I am of course doing no more than expressing a personal opinion—I think there is a way of conceiving the field as a whole which renders us this service. If we view economics as a science which endeavors to give understanding of human behavior so far as that behavior is concerned with means of livelihood, then we have a general perspective which shows us where all of the problems treated by the several types of theory belong.

This behavior with reference to the means of livelihood includes what men do in producing wealth, and under production one includes not merely such things as the raising or extracting of raw materials and their manufacture, but also such activities as the storing, transporting and distributing of goods. This behavior includes what men do in producing the means of livelihood, in exchanging them, in consuming them. And in the modern process of producing, transporting, exchanging, the technical problem of distribution is likewise comprised; and obviously the technical problem of value comes in there. But the economist, in dealing with economic behavior with reference to the means of livelihood, is interested primarily, not in what the individuals do, but in the mass phenomena presented by society. And when one is talking about the behavior of men in the mass, one is by definition talking about institutional behavior, since we define institutions as widespread social habits of thinking, feeling and acting.

The thing which makes the behavior of the mass of men in economic matters at the present time very different from the behavior of men even two or three centuries ago is the fact that institutions of an economic sort have undergone great changes. Further, if the theorists have any well-grounded hope that the behavior of men in economic matters is going to alter in the future, that hope must rest upon the possibility of further cumulative changes in institutions. Consequently if they want to understand how the present situation has come to pass, if they want to understand what alterations are going on at the present time, if they want to get any light upon further changes in economic behavior that may be expected in the future, they must give close attention to institutional growth.

It is feasible, as the example of most of the theorists whom we have studied shows, to develop a certain analysis of the workings of economic institutions at the present time with very slight reference to their past. Work of that kind, however, is of a very fragmentary sort, and even the men who hold most strictly that economic theory should confine itself to dealing with economic behavior under an institutional organization such as prevails in the countries which concern most of us chiefly at the present time, are ready to admit that intellectually it is important to get some light upon how these institutions have come to have their present shape. But, like Jevons, they say it is better to proceed by a division of labor; the economic theorist should not mix himself up with investigations on the development of economic institutions; this is the proper task of economic historians.

From the point of view of a theorist who sees the institutional factors in current economic life as of large importance, that attitude is not altogether satisfactory. For if he wants to get light upon the changing character of our practices, if he thinks the changes in the character of economic behavior are so constant, so important that they constitute almost the center of his interest, then he cannot relegate to any other set of workers the task of finding out what men need to know regarding them. The economic historian who is not primarily concerned with understanding as best he may the behavior of men in economic matters at the present time is not going to put his results, is not going to conceive his problems in quite the way that is required for the economic theorist's purposes. The division of labor is certain to mean that while economic historians may provide many valuable materials for the theorist, they will still remain raw materials;

they have to be worked over for purposes of giving understanding regarding behavior as it goes on at the present time.

To repeat, it seems to me that the general conception of what economics is all about, the conception that it is concerned with economic behavior, leads one inevitably to stress the institutional type of work. That does not mean that one regards as of no utility whatever the kind of analysis that writers like Davenport or Cassel or Marshall provide. Quite the contrary. But these people again, like the economic historians proper, give the person who is interested in economic behavior a set of raw materials. From the viewpoint of economics as a science of behavior, the type of analysis in orthodox economic theory is monographic in character; that is, most of it deals primarily with how men would behave if they were all the time obeying implicitly the logic of our dominant pecuniary institutions which play a rather large role in our lives. But, to repeat, when the logical implications of our pecuniary institutions have been worked out, that constitutes only one element in the situation. It gives the theorist who takes the behaviorist viewpoint another set of raw materials, but one which he has to work over for his own purposes.

This viewpoint provides the considerable advantage of making economics most helpful in the wider sphere of social studies as they are being carried on at the present time. That is, if economics is a study of the behavior of men from one viewpoint, their behavior with reference to the means of livelihood, then the economist as a student of behavior is simply a fellow worker with men in the other social sciences who are trying to find out the other aspects of human behavior. If the other social scientists are achieving anything of substantial value, anything that really does contribute toward an understanding of human nature and human activity, then the economist is likely to find that an acquaintance with what the anthropologists, the psychologists, the sociologists, the students of political science, or history of jurisprudence are doing, is valuable for his purposes.

Certainly the man who is working at economics as a science of behavior does not think that he can borrow from any other sciences, not even psychology, a set of conceptions about human nature which he can apply to his particular problems. He realizes on the contrary that it is his task to find out about one aspect of human nature, about one type of human behavior; but in studying his aspect, since man is one being, [an organic] unit, and not a conglomeration of economic individual and political individual and social individual and emotional individual, the inquirer who is working at any aspect of man's character, any phase of his behavior, is more likely, I think, to work intelligently, to accomplish results that are significant, if he approaches his task well acquainted with the methods and the results that are achieved in the other social sciences.

Like economics, the other social sciences have relied upon one of two methods: they have tried to explain human behavior either on the basis primarily of introspection or observation. Orthodox economic theory has been built up on a peculiar type of introspection. The theorists have looked within themselves, have observed their own admirable calculating powers, have seen that they preferred a greater to a lesser gain, and have sought to account for the ratios at which goods exchange for each other, including the factors of production, but primarily by showing how men, no doubt more or less like themselves, will behave. This account has not been pushed to extremes, for at least the bulk of economists have been interested primarily in giving an explanation of how people do actually behave. And the most elementary of observations has shown that the mass of mankind are not quite so rational as themselves. So that the element of introspection, while predominant, has always been modified more or less by observation, such, for instance, as that old classical observation upon the stupidity of the working class with reference to marriage and the begetting of children.

The other great method pursued by the social sciences, that of observation, is carried on in two different ways. In some cases a social scientist is able to observe under controlled conditions; that is, he is able to carry on the type of work which we call experimental, to make careful measurements of how a person subjected to certain artificial conditions reacts—the type of work which is possible more in psychology than in any other social science. But it is also possible to observe, not under controlled conditions, but to observe behavior in the mass. And that type of observation, of course, leads to the collection and the analysis of statistical records. As one becomes acquainted with other social sciences, one gets the impression that the sciences which are accomplishing most valuable results are those which are getting away from an introspective type of work and toward a type of investigation which is based upon observation. Wherever the observations can be carried on under controlled conditions; that is, where experiment can be resorted to, the most exact and gratifying type of results can be achieved. But also in a great many cases it is possible to give work in the social sciences an objective basis by proper analysis of observations made in the mass by the application of statistical methods.

Economics will develop most fruitfully in the future upon the quantitative side. The economists of today stand the best chances of improving upon the work of their predecessors if they rely more and more upon the most accurate statistical recording of observations. That process of developing quantitative analysis in economics is likely to mean a considerable change, at least in the form in which we set many problems. For the problems of economics have in part been formulated primarily by men who were using an introspective type of method; and they were formulated in ways which are open to attack by that kind of method. If the theorist changes his method from the introspective to the objective type, if he tries to rely so far as possible upon the analysis of mass observation, then in many cases he must reformulate the problem before he gets it in shape for attack. So, if my anticipation [as of 1927] of rather active development of economics on the quantitative side be justified by the event, it is likely to mean a gradual alteration in the formulation of our problems. In other words, if the differentiating characteristic of the several types of economic theory in the past has been a change in the character of the problems that are put in the center of discussion, there are likely to develop still other types of theory if the forces of development take the turn which I anticipate. "Another [and related] change that will come over economics is the recession of the theory of value and distribution from the central position it has held ever since the days of Ricardo to make room for the theory of production."[18]

The objective approach is being greatly facilitated by the development of statistics. Gives students of today [1931] great advantage over predecessors, an advantage which they are pressing vigorously. Promises to make those advantages still greater in the future. This is one of the best hopes of progress of economics.

The failure of our predecessors to test their hypothesis by conformity to fact was due, primarily I think, to paucity of suitable observations. When they could readily ascertain facts relevant to their speculations, they used them as illustrations, or even essayed elaborate statistical

---

[18] Mitchell, "The Prospects of Economics" in *The Trend of Economics*, edited by R. G. Tugwell (New York: Knopf, 1924) p. 29.

[On the margin of a reprint of an article of 1949 in which this statement of Professor Mitchell was quoted, his eminent colleague J. M. Clark wrote "The prediction came true." (The reprint, which Joseph Dorfman possesses, is of George Schuller, "Isolationism in Economic Method," *The Quarterly Journal of Economics,* November 1949, p. 460.)]

demonstrations after the fashion of Malthus. But in few economic problems were the data so satisfactory as those Malthus could gather concerning population. Even when figures could be had, economists did not know how to use them effectively. The method of inductive inference was crude, and students of economics were not taught what methods had been developed.

Reason for slow advance of quantitative analysis. Primarily imperfections and lack of data. A secondary factor has been gradual development of skill and courage in use of statistical method. Social statistics is almost wholly new. Data accumulated and analyzed have given rise to a new conception of the uniformity of human behavior. We know now how to think of homogeneous groups and we are developing special techniques with which to deal with them. Difficulties are still formidable [1944]. Expensiveness of statistical inquiry is a serious difficulty, but it will diminish if the results are valuable. That they are being found valuable is demonstrated by the increasing extent to which business enterprises are developing statistical staffs. Much of the work these staffs now do has little scientific interest—like much of the work done by their staffs of chemists and physicists. But in economics as in the natural sciences, the research men employed by business do in the aggregate considerable work that has a general interest, and not a little of it gets published. Government's use of economic statisticians has a steeply rising secular trend. Has recently received a great random impetus from [World] War [II]. Secular trend promises to continue rising. The governmental work is largely in collecting and publishing data. In that respect it is fundamental. Provides raw materials for economics at large in this country and abroad. Analytic work of government statisticians was long of a very simple character. But even in that respect a marked change has occurred within the past generation and will continue. Universities and other research agencies have been giving and getting increasing support for scientific work. Rather remarkable in view of the strong appeal other types of research can make for philanthropic support. Economics has not, and does not deserve to have the prestige of research in astronomy, physics, chemistry or even biology. It does not have so assured a promise of relieving human suffering as medical research. Its results may be used in attacks upon the present distribution of wealth and the present organization of industry. Men who wish to maintain the *status quo* may well hesitate to support scientific inquiries into economic organization and its workings. Despite these handicaps economic research of a factual type has in the past generation found a modest place among the objects of private philanthropic support, and, if its results appear to be interesting and socially valuable, I suppose this type of aid will continue and expand.

In short, best outlook [as of 1925] is that of gradually making economics into a quantitative problem, i.e., introducing measurement. Notably sparse and vague in old theory. Possibility of the change rests on accumulation of statistical data. Advantages: gives more precision, more practical usefulness, and more touch between economic theory and practical problems. Effect on economic theory not limited to inductive verification of old theorems: leads to recasting of problems; e.g., distribution of income—farmers,

investors, workers; by enabling theory to attack problems of current importance in a realistic way will give increased vitality to economic theory.
Emphasis on objective behavior. Shifting in treatment of motives—[these
viewed not as] explanations but problems for investigation. Cooperation
with psychology—not mere borrowing from psychology. Cooperation with
other social sciences—not only psychology, but also political science, sociology, anthropology, law. Emphasis upon institutional factor in behavior,
especially study of pecuniary institutions.

Change in form of literature. Books will be less like philosophical treatises
and more like books on natural sciences. Discoveries will multiply. A great
literature of brief papers. Not an ignoring of logical reasoning on basis of
assumed premises. Just as much reason for qualitative analysis as ever.
Only qualitative analysis will deal with problems reformulated for statistical attack. Will cooperate with quantitative analysis. Possible illustrations for use in discussion: Quantity theory controversy; no definite answers.
Fresh attack in terms of phases of business cycle. Importance of problems
in science; what has made science grow is the grasping of problems from
which an issue is wanted. Example from history of economics: Ricardo's
new type rose from problem of distribution—came to front in course of
corn law controversy. Malthus's problem of population. In economic
theory these problems have in a measure been covered up by standardization in terms of systems of theory. Use of statistical measurement will
stimulate thought by its new formulations.[19]

The need for a science of economics, more powerful in technique, more
reliable, more applicable to actual experience, is becoming clearer each
decade. Current plight of the world a challenge to economists—a challenge
which we cannot meet at present [1931]. When depression passes, public
attention will be less keen perhaps, but the Russian, Italian and German
experiments with quite different forms of social organization promise to
keep us all critically interested in defects of the capitalist order.[20]

Increase of economic planning under Roosevelt regime will not wholly sub-
side. Engineering challenge—Ralph Flanders, for example.[21] The New
Deal was unlike the economic mobilization of 1917-1918 not only in that it
occurred during peace but also because it was designed to establish a
permanent order better than the old deal—one in which government would
give greater economic security, a higher standard of living and more
effective freedom to the mass of population who get their living by working
for employers or running little business enterprises. Seems that we have
good reason to take up again the problem that Adam Smith disposed of.

---

[19] Outlines, "Closing Lectures," May 14, 16, 1917; "Notes for Course on Distri-
bution of Income," February 10, 1921; "Seminar in Economic Changes and Economic
Theory," May 9, 1944; "Prospects of Economic Theory," talk at University of
Chicago, March 14, 1925; "Fifty Years as an Economist," address before Political
Economy Club, Columbia University, May 11, 1945.

[20] ["Italian and German" is pencilled in. It was added by May 14, 1937, when the
outline was last used, if not before.]

[21] [Flanders, an eminent engineer, industrialist and later U. S. Senator from Vermont, castigated economists for failure to meet problems of the depression, especially
the problem of orderly disposal of the great production that engineers had made
possible.]

Grave problem before mankind is whether we must continue to rely on the half-conscious process of social evolution to shape the social organization or whether we can design the social organization to promote human welfare as we design machines. Perhaps the social sciences have before them a century of achievement not unlike the nineteenth century in the natural sciences.[22]

Thus economic science remains primarily a discussion of public policies. *The Wealth of Nations* out of which modern economics grew is primarily a discussion of economic policies but a discussion that rests on analysis of economic organization and its workings. In a large measure economics still retains this fundamental character. It derives its claim to public attention, even its interest to its own votaries, primarily for its bearing on policies. And its critics are able to show that convictions about what ought to be done have often warped its supposedly objective analysis. This is a danger that even today [1942] we feel we must ourselves guard against as best we can in our own thinking. In the course of time, the analytic portion has become far more elaborate and has separated itself more clearly from discussions of policies. In some modern treatises there is hardly any practical advice, hardly any discussion of practical problems. Primacy of practical interest, however, is clearly revealed in its later development since Adam Smith. Appears when one thinks of the shift in the theoretical problems on which successive generations of theorists have centered their attention. Jevons, Austrians, Walras—value and price; Marshall—the persistence of poverty despite the industrial revolution, how value and distribution proceed in a system of free exchange; post-Marshallian—noncompetitive prices, business cycles. Shown also by the intensive study of practical issues on a monographic basis; slavery in the United States, free trade and protection, monetary standards, public utilities, transportation problems, particularly railroads, labor organizations and wages, trusts, merchandising and advertising, social security, full employment. Shown finally by the development of economic theory in non-orthodox types and most of all by Marxian socialism and its latter day variants.

The promise of economics lies largely in its ability to cope with economic change, more particularly with secular and structural changes. We shall examine a few areas: A. Population. Position of population problem in economic theory has undergone radical change. It had been treated by the classical economists as a dynamic factor. As economics became more rigorous and academic it became more static. Population changes had no place in a strictly static analysis. (Cf., J. B. Clark's *The Distribution of Wealth;* contrast with his *Essentials of Economic Theory*). They do not figure prominently even in Marshall. If we are to develop a dynamic economics, population must be restored as one of the basic factors in economic theory. Theorists must consider the implications of the prospect of an aging population in respect to character of demand, and also to available supply of labor.

---

[22] Outlines, May 11, 1931; "Seminar in Economic Changes and Economic Theory," October 1, 1940.

B. Problems of human nature: Idea of the "economic man" with which the earlier classical economists worked without stopping to think very carefully about what they were doing, and the idea that John Stuart Mill adopted as a conscious abstraction, has fallen into disfavor among many theorists. Marshall, e.g., proposed to consider actual economic men and to treat any motive that operates on a considerable scale, the force of which can be measured by money. Meanwhile biology and psychology have brought into prominence the factors of instinct and habit emphasized by people like Veblen, out of which they developed the concept of institutions as a changing factor in human nature opposed to the supposedly constant factor of biology and inheritance. Later still the rise of psychology of the unconscious has made investigators aware of factors that produce wide differences in the reactions of different individuals to the same stimuli. Throws further discredit upon the notion that economic behavior can be accounted for adequately in terms of calculation, even when that calculation is made in terms of some institutional setup. Present situation [1939] regarding ideas about human nature entertained by professional psychologists, psychiatrists, psychoanalysts, neurologists, etc., exceedingly confused. Perhaps the most important result for economics is awareness that economists cannot borrow a set of psychological principles from psychology and apply them to their special problems of how men get their livings, but must struggle with the problem either by observing behavior from the outside and presumably in the mass, or penetrating into the thinking of their subjects, but with insight more catholic than that of the earlier economists. In this fundamental task they may find statistics helpful in two ways: (1) It records human actions objectively in the mass. (2) It offers ways of grasping individual human reactions in an orderly fashion by means of frequency tables that may be useful in deciding what factors have large and what have small importance.

C. Technology is a factor that has undergone enormous changes and a factor concerning which economic notions have changed strikingly. Though the early classical economists lived during the middle stages of the industrial revolution they did not ascribe such great importance as we do to technological change; e.g., Ricardo's expectations of the future. Real wages would remain more or less constant, profits would form a shrinking fraction of national income, rents would form an increasing fraction of national income. What has upset these expectations is primarily technological changes. We have come to think of this as a factor that has not only changed greatly in the past but that would probably continue to change cumulatively in the future. Veblen, e.g., assumes that an industrial plant of later date would be more efficient than those already existing and on this assumption bases his expectation that business cycles will run out into long periods of dragging depression, alleviated occasionally by moderate expansions brought on by combinations of random factors that stimulate business activity. He also makes large use of this conception in his analysis of the economic positions and prospects of chief countries— Germany and Japan versus Great Britain. To us, continuing technological change poses such grave problems as technological unemployment, necessity for schemes of social security, public interest in utilization of technological improvement, possible efforts to protect investors against techno-logical obsolescence, suppression of patents, attempts to secure the benefits of modern technology for business enterprise by combination; also to avoid the losses that are threatening to vested interests, possible that social concern with this problem may be a large element in drive for state ownership or control; and finally there is the heady problem of the bearing of technological change upon national defense and offence. Thus in the economic theorizing that the coming generation is due to produce the continuing industrial revolution is certain to play a larger role than it did in classical political economy. Difficult to deal with because its inci-dence is uncertain. But as we review the time that has passed since *The Wealth of Nations* was published it seems that technological changes have been the most potent factor in altering economic life—both the kinds of activities men have engaged in and the results of these activities in human comfort. It seems probable that, in the future we can foresee dimly, this factor will continue to be of chief importance in its direct bearing upon man's work and consumption and upon the political fortunes of nations and so upon the economic fortunes of their peoples.

D. Changing aspects of uncertainty. This topic is of a different sort from the previous one. In a sense, we can say that the lives of a large part of the population of Great Britain in Adam Smith's time seemed more certain than the lives of people do now [1939] in the United States; that is, the bulk of the population looked forward to living much as their ancestors had done in country or town. Change in place of residence, kind of work, size of income less likely than today. But that stereotyped mode of life was one that involved great uncertainties. Men were more exposed to hazard from "acts of God" and perhaps quite as much exposed to hazards from acts of men. In India the rigidity of the caste system does not make life very secure. Instability, insecurity not prominent topics in economic theory of the past. It may prove to be in economic theory of the future. Reports [in the seminar] concerning conditions under which farmers, flour millers, employees in iron industry, lived and worked in 1820, 1900, 1938 in the United States have painted a picture of high degree of instability in all these occupations at all three periods. When we look forward, we have to anticipate continuation of economic change with the combination of somewhat better safeguarding of men against natural disasters and continuation in perhaps augmented degree of expo-sure to changes, both favorable and unfavorable, in conditions produced by human action. Sharp increase of effort to provide economic security to individuals by national organization for the purpose is probably an indication both of growing sense of insecurity and declining reliance on family and neighborhood in case of incapacity and increasing age of population. Presumably the effort to use government as defense against economic insecurity will continue and will give rise to experiments with which economists will be deeply concerned.

In any other field besides those we noted we should probably have found that changes have bulked large in recent past and appear likely to continue in the future. Hence that analysis limited to static conditions is of narrowly restrictive value at best; that if we want to develop an economics of use in dealing with actual problems, we must consider changes, that these changes present infinite detail calling for large amount of patient investigation and that we do not now see clearly just how to reshape economic theory to embrace the elements we consider important and still yield insights that we can use constructively.

We have two advantages over our predecessors that come to us not because of our merits but because we live at a later time than the hardy spirits in past generations who have tried to solve economic problems by taking thought: (1) better and fuller observations; (2) better analytic technique developed by workers called economic theorists, by workers called statisticians and by workers like the Webbs called historians. If we are not daunted by the difficulties before us, but are ready to work as earnestly and have capacity to work as intelligently as our predecessors, we may at the very least put our successors into a better position to solve economic problems than we are in. No need to abandon economic theory of the past. But there is need to use it critically. And using it means making fresh attacks on facts with all the insight the older writers afford. In short, economics is growing more realistic, more statistical, more allied with the other social sciences. New framework called for that will contain all the problems, encompass all the technical methods, facilitate cooperation with other social sciences, break down the separation between theory and research.[23]

"My own feeling is that, so far as possible, we should choose problems that the world needs to have answered, even if the answers are inexact and uncertain. But, if we take the world's needs as our criterion, it does not necessarily follow that we can meet them best by selecting a list of 'questions of the day.' By and large, I should say that scientific experience justifies belief that a systematic study of interrelations among concepts and among phenomena is requisite. After all the aim of science is to find uniformities and uniformities, when established, mean that there are elements pertinent to a good many issues or situations that may seem unrelated. To be more specific, I think our work at the National Bureau of Economic Research has profited from the fact that we have been dealing with a problem of exceedingly wide scope and that the results of our first studies have had a bearing upon all our subsequent undertakings. That is, we have been able to use what we learned in studying national income in what we have done with reference to wages and profits, business cycles, and so on. A program based solely on a rating of problems with reference to their seeming current importance would not, I think, yield results as valuable to society as one that pays careful heed to the interrelations among economic activities."[23a]

[23] Outlines, "Final Lectures," April, May 1914: "Closing Lectures," January 19, 24, 1928; "Seminar in Secular and Structural Changes in a Modern Economy," May 16, 1939, "Seminar in Economic Changes and Economic Theory," May 14, 1940.
[23a] Mitchell to J. M. Clark, January 19, 1944.

[For purposes of clarification, it seems desirable before entertain-
ing questions on the proposed framework, to review again the differences of the various types of economic theory and the constructive
suggestions in a slightly different way.][24]

We took a brief glance at the classical political economy which is,
I think it fair to say, the type from which all the other types that
we have discussed are descended. These descendants are, with some
justice, ranked in two classes: the orthodox and I,will not say the
heterodox, but the outlying types. We might think of them in perhaps more picturesque language as the legitimate and illegitimate
children of the mother classical political economy.

Among the orthodox types we have taken representatives of the
mechanics of utility—Jevons's *The Theory of Political Economy* being
the book we had here—and the Austrian form of the calculus of
utility, represented by Wieser's *Social Economics*. Then there comes,
as closely related in a logical sense and as a more generalized form,
pure theory which derives most directly from Jevons's contemporary,
Walras, but has been represented in the course by Schumpeter's book
[and later by Cassel's comprehensive treatise]. Then we have the
neo-classical economists represented by Marshall, the so-called American psychological school represented by Fetter, pecuniary logic represented by Davenport and finally, as the last of the orthodox variants,
the social value theory for which Anderson has stood.

The outlying types, include the historical economists, which
Schmoller represents; the genetic type of theory which Veblen represents, and finally, welfare economics which Hobson represents. Of
course that is a mere enumeration of the different types.[25]

The interesting question is what are the fundamental differences
between them. The primary difference is in the problems which have
been the chief interest of the various writers. There are, to be sure,
differences in methods. These have ordinarily been regarded as the
real differentiating characteristics. Certain types of theory are said
to rely primarily upon deduction and others upon induction. Some
are said to be primarily abstract and systematic; others historical
and concrete or descriptive. Those differences certainly exist, but the
differences in methods are for the most part the result of differences
in the problems which the writers have set themselves. If any man
had attacked Ricardo's particular problem, he would have found

---

[24] Remainder of chapter unless otherwise noted is from "1918 Typescript."

[25] [Professor Mitchell at this time, 1918, called Veblen's type "genetic or
evolutionary."]

it difficult, if not impossible, to treat it by any other than the speculative method which Ricardo used. If any one attacked Schmoller's problem, he would find it impossible to make any headway towards solving it, unless he relied largely upon historical and statistical research.

Again the different types of theory undoubtedly differ among themselves in respect to the conclusions at which the various writers arrive. Those conclusions are different again primarily because they are conclusions about different problems. I want to make that clearer by trying to show somewhat definitely the problems which are the chief concern of the various types of theory with which we have dealt.

To begin with classical political economy, the classical masters were primarily concerned with the problem of prices, particularly with explaining those prices which constituted incomes; that is to say, the prices which are the crucial factors in the problem of distribution of wealth inside of the money economy. The situation that they confronted was a fairly well developed capitalism, where men were pursuing their economic ends by trying to make money incomes and then buying with the money the things that they required. What the classical masters tried to explain was what determined the prices which give the working classes one share of the wealth produced, the landlord a second share and the capitalistic classes a third share. The problem of prices has in a large sense been the problem of the orthodox types of economic theory. On the other hand, if one claims that the outlying types have been concerned primarily with price theory, one will have to admit that they have studied price theory with other ends in view than either the classical masters or the orthodox disciples, and the other ends that they had in view so far as they have been concerned with prices at all have really made the problem in important aspects a new one. The aim, for instance, of Schmoller is not so much toward elucidating the determination of prices on which the distribution of wealth rests as it is to give a general account of how the present pecuniary organization came into existence and to show how the pecuniary institutions exist side by side with a number of other fundamental economic institutions. His problem, in other words, is a very much larger one than the problem which the classical economists faced. He not only tries to show how the whole group of institutions which constitute the modern social organization have reached their present form but also how from their combined workings the existing economic conditions result.

Take again a writer like Veblen in *The Theory of Business Enter-*

prise. He is a good deal concerned with the problem of prices, but what he is primarily interested in is tracing the origin, the present character and effect, and the probable future trend of our pecuniary organization, particularly as it bears upon the work of the business man. He is ready to take for granted a good deal of theory which is presented by the classical economists and their orthodox descendants, but the real point with him is quite a different problem. He regards these institutions as certain habits of mind, and he wants to show how these habits have been formed, how they differ among different classes in the community, what effect these habits have upon the production and distribution of serviceable commodities, and how these habits promise to change in the foreseeable future. Once again, Hobson's welfare economics is more or less concerned with the problem of prices, but what he is primarily interested in is social welfare, and prices come in as one among the factors which make for economic well- or ill-being of broad classes in the community.

Thus, the outlying types of economic theory differ from the classical type primarily in that they have a wider, and in part different set of problems, a different perspective which, in so far as they touch the classical problem proper, puts it in a very different status with respect to the task of economic theory at large. The orthodox theorists, to repeat, are closer to the classical prototype in the sense that they are more concerned with the price problem in the older sense, but they show considerable differences among themselves. The mechanics of utility, for instance as represented by Jevons on the one hand and Wieser on the other hand, while dealing with prices, lays the stress upon a problem which the classical masters passed by with very little attention, namely the problem of the factors lying behind demand. If the student reads James Mill or Ricardo or McCulloch, he gets the impression that there is no difficulty at all, that that is a part of the problem which it is not worth while to linger over. Jevons and the Austrians, however, with their utility analysis have discovered a very large and significant problem in that part of the field which the classical economists passed by so quickly.

The neo-classical writers are distinguished by trying to get a juster perception of the problem of prices than either the classical economists on the one side or the utility writers on the other side have had. To them the problem is one-sidedly treated, when attention is confined merely to the analysis of utility, as it was by Jevons and the Austrians.

Pure theory as represented by Walras and his disciple Schumpeter [and later Cassel] has still another problem in the foreground. With them the real task of economics is not to discuss the prices of separate commodities, but to discuss the greater problem of equilibrium as a whole. The student cannot, they say, get any adequate economic theory by making an approach from the side of one commodity inasmuch as there is such thoroughgoing interdependence among economic phenomena. The proper problem to set and the proper kind of solution to work toward is the problem of how all the prices for all commodities in the market are mutually determined at a given time and that is a different problem from that of the neoclassicists, or the utility writers, or the cost writers. It is a problem which has led to their employment of mathematics in economics inasmuch as it is only by a system of simultaneous equations that the student can, even speculatively, represent the problem of general equilibrium as soluble.

The American psychological school, once more, while interested primarily in prices, has another problem, or if one likes better, lays stress upon a different aspect of the same problem. With them, as represented by Fetter, at least in intention at the beginning, the real problem of economics is to go back to the psychological factors which lie behind people's willingness to purchase goods or to undergo exertions.

The representatives of pecuniary logic on the other hand have taken the ground that the theorists should concern themselves with the problem of prices in the narrow sense, and to leave out of economics all efforts in the direction of psychological analysis. They want to throw out not only such analysis as the reader finds in Fetter, but also the attempt to explain prices in terms of labor pain as in classical economics. The theory boils down with them to primarily a problem of money prices as formed in a society where the control is exercised by businessmen who are aiming at pecuniary profits.

The social value theorists have still another slant on the price problem; to them, the important and highly neglected problem is that of accounting for the similarity of men's valuations, showing that the importance that they attach to commodities, the disesteem in which they hold certain kinds of exertion are not primarily matters of individual tastes, but primarily matters of social standards which have been drilled into them from their childhood days, that just because their minds, their valuations are made for them by the training that they receive, both of formal and informal sort; by virtue of this fact, they are necessarily very much alike, and so to understand these valuations, the theorist has primarily to study social factors, and not individual tastes.

To repeat, the differences among the types of economic theory which have been discussed are primarily differences in the problems that seem of particular importance to the various writers.

I admit the differences of method and the differences of conclusion. About the latter differences, however, I want to say another word or two. The differences of conclusion that are discussed with liveliest interest, that are most often subject to controversy, are those between writers who prosecute one and the same type of economic theory, or who are interested in types of theory that are closely allied. One does not find, often, differences of conclusion between writers who represent types of theory which are distinctly divergent. When these theorists do fall foul of each other, it is not so much because they arrive at different conclusions as because they doubt the significance of what the other theorists are doing. A writer like Veblen, for instance, has not much of any quarrel with a writer like Fetter, so far as Fetter's technical conclusions are concerned. It is rather that Fetter's technical conclusions do not interest Veblen much, and a writer like Fetter returns the compliment with interest. Very likely, what Veblen has to say is correct enough from Fetter's standpoint, but it does not matter whether it is right or wrong. That is beside the point. Veblen's whole discussion [to him] is not economic theory. In other words the difference of opinion between the writers whose types of theory are far apart is primarily a difference of opinion concerning what is economic theory.

If I am right in saying that the primary differences among them are differences in the problems attacked, then the main reason for the development of so many divergent types must lie in the gradual proliferation of the problems of economics. It must be found in the fact that the problem, which the classical economists thought they had solved, but which has been attacked by successive generations of writers, turned out to be much more many-sided than Ricardo, James Mill, MacCulloch, Senior and even John Stuart Mill, dreamed. It is primarily because we found more in the problem, that there developed these various attempts to get something like a satisfactory form of economics, and we may anticipate that other types of economic theory will continue to make their appearance so long as we keep finding new aspects of economic behavior which seem susceptible of scientific treatment, and important enough to engage the serious attention of scholars.

Some of the most important factors in the unfolding of the problem of economics are the following: To begin with, a certain importance attaches to the forthright or direct logical development of economic theory itself. The problem has been developed in somewhat the same sense that a mathematical study can be developed by the coming of fresh people who see new logical possibilities in the older discipline. In short, one reason for the development of new types of economic theory is the unfolding of the economic problem through the study of past writers, but this factor has counted much less than the other factors.

In the second place, the problem has been enlarged through the transplanting of classical political economy to other lands. The classical economists had tacitly assumed the existence of a certain set of socio-economic institutions. As the subject, however, got transplanted into other countries, where the social-economic institutions were not built on the early nineteenth century English model, it became painfully obvious to people who were taking economics seriously and trying to account for the facts of their experience in terms of English theory, that the English explanations were less exhaustive than appeared upon their face, so that the problem broadened in their eyes and they found new features to attack.

The curious thing is not that the transfer of English economics led men to say that the problem was larger than the classical masters had supposed, but rather that it did not have this effect sooner and in a more vigorous way. The French economists, again, it is fair to say, never saw that point, or at least not until comparatively recent days. Similarly, the American economists were able to expound the English doctrines for two or three generations, to regard them as economic science *par excellence,* and not to appreciate that the problems presented by the life that they were living involved very important elements which were necessarily not covered by Ricardo because they were not presented by Ricardo's experience.

Transplanting of English political economy to other lands: Brought new problems to the fore in so far as foreign scholars really tried to account for domestic processes in terms of the English theories. No difficulty will be encountered and therefore no progress will be made in so far as economic theory remained purely academic, merely a discipline in "thinking"—as long as the institutions could be taken for granted by the foreigners also. The sacred books of the English economists were in part reprinted or translated in France, Germany and America. Further, new treatises on classical lines were turned out in each of these countries during the 1830's and 1840's. But no important reaction in the development of new types of theory appeared in either France or the United States.[26]

It was in Germany where this process of transplanting gave the most effective impetus to the enlarging of the circle of economic problems, and to the rise of new types of theory. The historical school, and Marx, owe not a little to the fact that they were familiar with a set of economic conditions to which Ricardo's analysis did not provide satisfactory solutions. They could see new problems largely because they saw new facts before them, and made a more or less vigorous attempt to give an account of them. In Germany no important change came until the 1840's. Then for thirty years more the German reaction remained negative.[27]

Another important factor in bringing new problems to light in economics has been the development of economic organization itself. Economic organization today, even in England, is substantially different from that of Ricardo's day. Let me mention a few outstanding differences. There has taken place a much sharper demarcation between the capitalist enterpriser and the investor than was characteristic in Ricardo's era. He thought of the capital engaged in business enterprise as being primarily provided by the capitalist employer. Nowadays economists think of there being two interested parties clearly differentiated in the business enterprise: the investors who provide the bulk of the capital and the business managers who are directing what shall be done in performing the so-called labor of management. Indeed the corporate form of organization draws a sharper line of demarcation between the two classes than exists as an actual matter of fact, so far as ownership is concerned. One result of the differentiation of the capitalistic system in the direction of a more elaborate organization has been that nobody nowadays can fail to see much more sharply than Ricardo did the necessity of admitting the existence of the two distinct problems, the problem of interest and the problem of profits.

Another outstanding feature of the development of economic organization has been that the system of free competition, which Ricardo naturally treated as typical of the business situation, has developed a great series of monopolistic and "monopoloidal" conditions. "Monopoloidal", a very convenient term which Wieser suggested, means quasi-monopolistic conditions. That has introduced a new series of

---

[26] Outline, "Closing Lectures," May 14, 16, 1917.
[27] Outline, "Closing Lectures," May 14, 16, 1917.

theoretical problems to solve; namely, the problem of price determination under varying conditions of monopoly. These problems are added to the series which the classical economists treated on the assumption of free competition. In short, the old assumptions of free competition are no longer regarded as covering the field even for theoretical purposes.[28]

Furthermore, the character of the population question has changed. The emphasis with which it is discussed has undergone a radical transformation because of an alteration in economic conditions. The great fear in the days of the classical masters was the fear of overpopulation. The fear nowadays [1918] is what president Theodore Roosevelt has called "race suicide" [in the western world]. The outstanding economic fact of the decline in the birth rate, particularly as affecting certain specially fortunate classes in the community, has given economists a set of problems which could not have occurred to Malthus and his contemporaries.

Again labor problems and the attitude of writers toward questions of wages has been enormously developed and fundamentally changed by the extension of the factory system, the tremendous increase in the size of the factories, the vast expansion of the area over which a factory can make its products and the consequent spread of the territorial base on which workers are organized on the one side and employers on the other side. That is another enormously large complicated problem with which theorists at present are concerned. It has come into economic theory because it has come into economic experience. Stated another way, class struggle has been made to stand out more clearly in economic life, at least by more definite organizing of the two classes, and by the greater difficulty of moving from one to the other. (Socialism).[29]

The importance of finance as contrasted with industrial operations and commercial routine in the narrow sense has become much more sharply differentiated than in Ricardo's day. It has given rise to a new series of problems which we are just beginning to define, and which probably will be as sharply marked off in the course of less than a generation unless the situation radically changes again—as sharply marked off in the minds of the next generation of students from other economic problems as the problem of profits has been separated in the economists' minds from the problem of interest.

The great [world] war [I] is bringing to the forefront a whole

---

[28] Sentence from Outline, "Closing Lectures," May 14, 16, 1917.
[29] Sentence from Outline, "Closing Lectures," May 14, 16, 1917.

series of new problems, or of old problems in perspectives so new as to make the problems themselves seem new, particularly the problems of governmental reorganization of industry and the direction of it not for the purpose of making money for anybody, but of supplying insistent social needs. There is also the problem of business cycles.[30] In short, the development of economic organization itself must have been in good measure responsible for the unfolding of the problems of economic theory and therefore the rise of different problems.

A final factor in the rise of new problems is the increased knowledge of human nature which has been acquired by investigators in various fields since Ricardo's day. It is at the disposal of economists, if they choose to use it, and it has been drawn upon in no considerable measure by certain types of economic theories and explains their appearance.

To begin with, anthropology including ethnology has practically been established as a science since Ricardo's time and the students doubtless have noted with a tolerant smile the funny references to the behavior of savages which are characteristic of writers of classical political economy. They apply their theories with confidence, to the terms of a bargain which would be struck between two savages altogether unacquainted with commerce and the use of money, and they professed to base their argument, in some measure at least, upon the natural procedure under these circumstances. In their day what was known of savage tribes went little further than a set of gossipy accounts given by travelers, missionaries and settlers in out of the way corners of the earth, who had come into casual contact with people of a low level of culture. Nowadays comparatively little is known about these simple cultures, but it is vastly more than people in Ricardo's generation knew. Economists can see part at least of the great story of the development of modern civilization, and they can get, if they so choose, not a little genuine light on the early stages of the development of certain economic institutions. History and jurisprudence are not new sciences since Ricardo's day, but they have undergone a revolutionary rewriting. Nowadays there is available a vast amount of classified information on the past history of legal institutions, and of economic and social organization in Europe among the cultivated races; and that account has been carried back by archaeology in a more or less speculative way to a stage where it can be hitched on, without any very glaring logical inconsistency, to early stages of culture given by modern ethnological research. In

---

[30] Sentence from Outline, "Closing Lectures," May 14, 16, 1917.

particular economic, social and intellectual history have been investigated.[31]

All this intimate knowledge of the development of economic and social institutions as a whole is particularly the product of the last century. Biology is even more emphatically than ethnology a new science, the base of which was hardly laid until Ricardo's day, when certain German scientists developed the cellular theory of physiological structure and extended it from botany to zoology. Biology is coming to exercise a profound influence upon all the social sciences, because it has given rise to the grand conception of an evolutionary development of different forms, a conception which promises to be more important and prove more valid in the social than in the biological sciences themselves. In other words, it has irradiated all social problems with the Darwinian theory of evolution.[32]

Next comes social statistics. It is in the same position as biology. Statistical work goes much further back than the beginning of the nineteenth century, but during that century the science greatly expanded the volume of reliable materials available for analysis and it has also gone a long way toward developing a new and powerful technique. It is interesting to notice that national censuses were just beginning to be taken when Ricardo was writing. The first such census was that of 1791 in the United States. England followed the example a decade later. Since that time all nations with any pretension to civilization have begun to take periodical stock of their resources in people and materials, with varying degrees of elaborateness; consequently there is available a vastly larger and better authenticated body of data concerning certain fundamental economic conditions. Index numbers had been invented before Ricardo's day, but it is interesting to note that he said that it was impossible to tell what the general trend of prices had been. The device was not known to him. It was not even known to Ricardo's friend Thomas Tooke whose elaborate *The History of Prices* made him one of the foremost authorities in that field in the early part of the nineteenth century in England.

It was while Ricardo was living that the great French mathematician the Marquis de Laplace [1749-1827] was developing the application of the theory of probability to social phenomena, showing that this particular device was an especially powerful instrument of analysis and was particularly applicable to the social sciences, because it made possible the handling of mathematical data which are not uniform

---

[31] Sentence from Outline, "Closing Lectures," May 14, 16, 1917.
[32] Sentence from Outline, "Closing Lectures," May 14, 16, 1917.

in character. Most of the applications of mathematics in the physical sciences are facilitated by the fact that the fundamental data are themselves treated, so far as we know with considerable justification, as almost entirely uniform. The data supplied by man presents a great many variations. Laplace shows that there are technical methods of representing those variations in a regular form which admit of mathematical analysis. He thereby laid the foundation for the modern methods of handling people in groups which can be described adequately for many purposes in mathematical· terms. Adolphe Quetelet (1796-1874), the great French statistician, on the other hand was not writing until a little after Ricardo's time. In other words, beginning in Ricardo's day and rapidly developing since then, there has been available a body of data and methods of analysis, which provide the possibility of effective treatment of many problems which the economists in Ricardo's time could hardly attack at all.

Data accumulated and analyzed have given rise to a new conception of the uniformity of human behavior. We know now how to think of the homogeneous group, and we are developing a special technique by which to deal with the phenomena.[33]

Sociology also began immediately after Ricardo's time. Auguste Comte is the first of the great thinkers in that science; and the first to make a serious beginning at a general survey of social phenomena in such a fashion as to allow the students of any social science to see where they belong within the larger scheme. Sociology as a comprehensive effort to draw together all that we know about society began with Comte.[34] Then came Herbert Spencer. True, even today sociology is in a much less organized stage than economics. If the economic theorist wants to envisage the problem of any one of the social sciences it is an immense service to have before him the general sketches of social science at large which different sociologists have provided. It is not that they have many positive results that are particularly instructive, but they help the economist in knowing where he stands, and telling in a large way in what part of the total problem of society he is engaged, and where he may hope to look for help on points that are not covered by his own narrow specialty.

Finally comes psychology. It is, in a sense, one of the old social sciences. The histories of psychology, written as they are primarily by people who are interested in the history of philosophy, almost always go back to the Greeks. But in a sense psychology has had a

---

[33] Outline, "Closing Lectures," May 14, 16, 1917.
[34] Outline, "Closing Lectures," May 14, 16, 1917.

development very much like statistics and biology. It has been practically made over. It has been constituted a separate discipline which does not have any close necessary dependence upon philosophy. It has begun to adopt scientific methods in the sense that it employs experiment and measurement. In Ricardo's time, his own friends were deeply interested in psychology. Bentham, it may be recalled, has a good deal to say about what he naively fancied explained the action of the human mind. James Mill in his *Analysis of the Human Mind* wrote one of the most important psychological treatises of the early nineteenth century. But in those days, psychology was almost entirely a speculative science. It consisted as far as the type of thinking with which the classical economists were acquainted primarily of an hedonistic theory of motive and of the analysis of the association among ideas together with some vague notions about the connection between the workings of the mind and the physiological processes within the body. Since then psychology has accepted from biology the conception of men as one of the animal species, as having an intelligence, such as it is, which serves primarily biological ends, an intelligence which is not qualitatively unlike in character that of the lower animals; that is to say, the psychologists nowadays accept substantially the biological view of man as an animal and endeavor to understand his behavior in somewhat the same way in which they study the behavior of other species. More than that, psychology has developed a substantial number of ingenious techniques of considerable importance in increasing the amount of data at its disposal and enabling it to put its analysis on a fairly definite foundation. The experimental type of psychology, the study of pathological cases, the application of comparative methods and then the development of the behavioristic viewpoint are the contributions which have added not a little to the knowledge of the human mind and its operations.

So much for the development of other social sciences. The point about them, to repeat, is that they have taught us a great deal more about man and his behavior than could have been generally known in Ricardo's day, and that it is in great part at least in the effort to make use of this new knowledge that we have been seeing more in the economic problems than Ricardo could. Because economists see more in the problems, they have developed new types of economics to try to understand the new questions.

I plan to discuss the way in which the problem of economics looks at the present time; that is to say, I am going to try to develop a viewpoint which will set in what purports to be systematic order the problems of economics as they exist for modern students. In other words, what I am professing to do is to sketch as before a sort of framework which will show the orderly relationships which exist among them, a framework which will give due place to the contributions that are brought by every one of the types of economic theory that have so far been discussed. A framework which will, moreover, help everyone who wants to devote himself to economics to find the particular place in the science as a whole where he can do most effective service.

One of the things we ought to learn from the development of the social sciences at large is that economics to be serviceable must be conceived as one among the numerous sciences of behavior. That is fundamental. It is unlike several of its sister sciences in that it is confined to the behavior of one particular species of animal, that gregarious species which is commonly called man. It does not even deal with the whole species but only with the variety of man inhabiting western Europe and its colonial offshoots including the United States and even here it limits itself to certain phases of behavior of very recent date.[35] It is conceivable that someday similar problems may be worked out for the behavior of other animal species.

If the viewpoint in economics that I am going to present is a valid one, it is one which does in a measure permit application to other forms of animals; that is, the enquirer can discuss in an objective way how animals have a social organization and pursue in common the task of getting a living. More than that, I think it is clear that while economics has been confined almost exclusively to the study of behavior of a comparatively small group of nations, in a comparatively recent time of their history, it is possible if the theorist takes the view that economics is a study of behavior that he can extend it to the study of peoples very much dissimilar from the civilized nations, and that he can carry the inquiry back on the basis of ethnological evidence to a much more remote period in the history of the Aryan races—for instance the Semitic peoples—than has ordinarily been thought feasible in the past.

In the first place, the differentiating characteristic of the behavior which economics deals with is that it is the behavior concerned with getting the material requisites of life. As a science economics is not primarily concerned with the technique of controlling nature. That is a matter rather for the technical branches. What it is concerned with is primarily man's behavior to man in the conjoint social enterprises

---

[35] Sentence from Outline, "Closing Lectures," May 14, 16, 1917.

of trying to carry on the struggle with nature. It deals not with the individual but with the group. It deals not with the technical activities of the group as much as with its organization. In laying down this proposition that economics is one of the sciences of behavior I do not think I am pronouncing anything that is radically new, rather I should say that such always has been the actual fact concerning economics, even among people who said that economics was the science of wealth. While they defined it in this way, they went on to discuss primarily social behavior of people in their endeavor to get the material requisites of life.

When I say that as a science of behavior it deals primarily with the group, and not with the individual, I think that is simply saying definitely what has always been the fact, even among the economists who have talked most frequently about Robinson Crusoe. Even among the economists who tried most definitely to build on the basis of the single individual satisfying his own wants, or on the basis of the isolated, independent family, it still has been true that the object that really concerned them was the behavior of men toward each other in their group struggle with nature. It has been really a problem of social behavior all the way through. This fact that economics always has been a science of social behavior, though the fact has not been admitted, explains why an increase in knowledge of human nature leads to further unfolding of the economic problem. If it were not for the fact that the economist really is dealing with how men conduct themselves, there is no particular reason why an expanding knowledge of human nature such as is given by ethnology, psychology and certain branches of statistics should mean anything to the economist. But if he is, and always has been dealing with human behavior, then any additions to knowledge of human behavior which comes within the economist's ken will lead to an expansion of his own problems if they are important enough. They will lead to the development of large new groups of problems and give rise to new types of economic theory.

Further, this view suggests that, if the economist is to carry on his task effectively, it is wise for him to be just as alert as he possibly can concerning developments in the other social sciences of human behavior. That is to say, if his science is one among several sciences, all of them devoted to the great task of understanding behavior, then it becomes part of his professional concern to know something at least about the results that the other social sciences are achieving instead of foolishly setting himself up as independent of psychology; instead of taking a haughty air of superiority toward the researches of statisticians; instead of complaining rather proudly of his ignorance of ethnology. The economist, just as far as his technical training, his time, his mental ability enable him to, should make it his business to follow what is happening in the other fields. Of course he is not in a position to know what is happening in subjects outside with the same authority that he knows what is happening inside his own field. Still he stands a much better chance of defining his own problems with accuracy and of getting suggestions toward effective handling of his own problems, if he tries to profit by what other social sciences are accomplishing, than he will if he tries to keep himself independent of them.

Once more this general proposition that the economist is trying to build up one among several different sciences of human nature shows that his relation to other social sciences is not merely the relation of what he wants to borrow from them. Economists who discuss particularly the relationship between economics and psychology almost as invariably assume tacitly that the economist is simply to borrow certain results that the psychologist puts before him. If the task of explaining human behavior is so large that it has to be split up into a considerable number of different sciences, then it ought to be just as true that the economist is contributing something toward the solution of that general problem, and something that should be of interest to wide-awake investigators in other sciences as it is true that he is borrowing something of other sciences. The relationship is not simply one of take. It becomes one of take and give, and the men in the other fields are, provided we do our work with any measure of success, just as likely in the long run to profit by our accomplishments as we are likely to profit by theirs. Finally it shows that economic theory should frame its own program in the light shed by general concepts of human behavior developed in biology, ethnology, history, statistics and psychology.[36]

If there is defensible ground for this general proposition that economics is one of the sciences of human behavior, it would seem to follow that before we can find exactly what our particular problem is, we ought to learn how human behavior looks at large from the standpoint of the social sciences in general. That is to say, we ought to have something like a definite understanding of what human nature is, of the factors by which this behavior is controlled.

In the second place, institutions represent the great variable ele-

---

[36] Sentence from Outline, "Closing Lectures," April, May, 1917.

ment in human behavior. From the point of view of our present notions regarding human nature our equipment of instincts is inherited in substantially the same shape by generation after generation. The brain of man today is about what it was in the ice age. What makes the man at the present time so extremely different from the man of the ice age is not at all that at birth he is superior, but that he has become accustomed to a different set of social institutions. These institutions are the factor which marks off one society from another. They are the forms of behavior in which acquisitions from the past are represented. That is to say, they are the part of human nature which not only represents what has been achieved in the past, but also which represents what possibility of further progress may come to the race in the future. Except so far as men may alter the native constitution of the race on the average by selective breeding, there does not appear to be much prospect of our improving the original nature of man. Our chances of getting on, our hopes that our children will be better and happier people than ourselves, our hopes that societies in the future will be less brutal organizations than the societies of which we are part and parcel, depend primarily on the institutions and the modifications which they can undergo. Thus it means that institutions are the liveliest subjects of interest to anybody who is interested either in the past or in the future progress of the race.

In the third place what rationality men have is summed up for the most part in their institutions; that is to say, these widespread social habits are the results of past thinking in a very large measure. What thinking does give to men of a valuable sort gets preserved in the form of widespread social habits. A great deal of excogitation of a valuable sort which goes on in every generation is not understood by contemporaries, does not affect their habits of feeling or acting in any perceptible degree, but in so far as the exercise of intelligence itself does carry the race forward in a secure fashion it accomplishes that by modifying old habits and establishing new ones. Thinking that is confined to individuals or small groups is not a factor of consequence. Thinking as it modifies the behavior of large groups is important. In other words, what intelligence we do have that is serviceable to us as a race is not going to come into our survey if we are directing our attention primarily to the subject of instincts.

What framework for economic theory is suggested by this view of human nature and of the task of economics? On the line of this argument economics is primarily an objective study of those standardized forms of behavior which we call economic institutions, and therefore everything that adds to our knowledge of these institutions or of the physical conditions under which they exist is properly part of economic science, and the chief business of the science is to analyze these institutions; to show what they are, what process they have gone through in assuming their present form, what changes they seem to be undergoing at the present time and perhaps what we may expect future changes to be.

If this is the central task of economics, the general field can be divided up in many different ways. For example, it is appropriate from this point of view to select particular institutions for monographic studies. To concentrate upon what one may call the logic of a given set of institutions; that is to say, to consider what are the forms of behavior to which the particular institution if it had free play would lead. Thus, it is appropriate then to engage in deep, speculative theorizing of a highly abstract sort. An economist ought to study the behavior of very simple tribes of men, to go through the past records of our race to see how the behavior of our ancestors differs from the behavior of the present generation. It is proper for the theorist to make the wisest and most effective use of statistics or any other method of observation which will give him data or help him forward in his analysis.

Practically all the types of economic theory discussed have some measure of justification, from the point of view of the framework. Each one gets some place assigned to it. The larger number of types studied, particularly those that are strictly orthodox in their reputation come in as more or less elaborate studies of the logic of pecuniary institutions. That is distinctly the case with classical political economy. It was primarily a statement of what is logical for people to do in the process of trying to get money incomes under the circumstances which face the various classes of the community. In one respect classical political economy was not working out the pure logic of pecuniary life because in its dealings with one class it relied upon what it supposed to be observations of human stupidity. The classical economists did not credit the working man with rationality in the conduct of his life. They always supposed that this man was too much subject to sexual passion to be a first rate economic man and that bit of observation was taken into their theory so that they were not by any means quite as unreserved and thoroughgoing in working out the logic of pecuniary institutions as some of their successors have been.

The mechanics of utility as represented by Jevons went further in this direction. He explicitly repudiated the theory of population as belonging to the central body of economic doctrine which he was expounding—a logical position for him to take. The Austrian theory, even in the form presented by Wieser in *Social Economics,* at the present time holds the position that the single family taken by itself obeys a form of logic which, so far as our institutions go, appears to be primarily characteristic of money making. The neo-classical theory too occupies substantially this ground. The work of the American psychological school as represented by Fetter belongs here, and so too does the pecuniary logic of Davenport.

All of these people so far as they have been working out a logical scheme of economic behavior have been making a contribution toward the understanding of economic behavior: the highly elaborated set of institutions which control our behavior in very large measure make us more rational than primitive men ever are. Those institutions are primarily the institutions connected with the making of money and the pecuniary logic finds its highest development in the control of very elaborate complicated undertakings through accounting. The fundamental difficulty with these various types of orthodox theory is that they have not realized really what they are doing. They attributed to man a highly logical method of control which as a matter of fact men in modern money-using societies have imperfectly learned.

The other types of economic theory discussed are superior to the orthodox types in that they have a clearer realization of what the problem of accounting for economic behavior is. They do not make the mistake of imputing to mankind at large complete obedience to the logic of any given institution. They are themselves studies of certain institutions, or of certain aspects of institutions in social life. The social value type of theory, for example, is a study of the influence of existing social institutions upon men's valuations. A man like Charles H. Cooley, for example, is concerned primarily to show how men's feelings regarding the worth of different commodities are generated in them by the experience which they have as members of modern societies. Welfare economics as represented by Hobson seems primarily a study of the effect of the whole group of economic institutions which make up the present economic organization upon the well being of different classes of the community. That is the point that he has in mind. He is not so much studying the institutions themselves and working out their logic as he is trying to show how the forms of behavior which these institutions standardize influence for good or ill the well being of the working classes, the professional classes, the capitalistic classes, the land owning classes, etc.

Finally historical economics professes to be devoted entirely to a study of institutions in their past form and their present working, but I think we would agree from what we have learned that the best that has been done by accredited representatives of the historical school in this direction does not go so far as or as deep as the work that has been done by people whom we have agreed to speak of as representing the genetic [institutional] type of theory. The object here is primarily to work out the effect in modern life of certain groups of economic institutions, how these institutions got their present form and what changes these institutions are undergoing.

To repeat, all the different types of economic theory that we have become acquainted with have a contribution to make, that contribution gains greatly in significance, gets set in proper perspective by taking the simple stand that the task lies primarily in understanding economic behavior, that the parts of behavior which are most open to scientific generalization, and the parts that are of chief interest to us as men as well as scientists are the institutional parts, and therefore the worthwhileness of any given piece of economic research depends primarily on how far it helps us to understand some part or other of institutional behavior.

In short, it can be said that human behavior rests upon a basis of inherited instincts; that behavior is standardized primarily by widespread social habits which we call institutions; it is subject, when need arises, in some limited degree to redirection by man's limited power of thinking. What thinking we do is very largely of a meritricious character. One way of getting out of trouble is not to think the trouble through but to pretend that it is not there. In recent years [1918], the psychoanalysts in particular have accustomed us to the notion that men in general build up a great many defenses, as they are technically called, with which they meet the disagreeable facts of the world; that is to say, the difficulties that face people, they often meet by thinking not how to solve the difficulty but by some trick of thought which enables them to evade it. And probably any person who really analyzes his procedure will find that a larger part of his intelligence was thus expended in trying to evade some difficulty than is honestly spent in trying to solve it. The normal persons are continually resorting to invidious comparisons as a source of power in the face of social difficulties that they encounter. They are continually thinking of ways that will make them appear rather stronger or more admirable people than others whom they have occasion to meet.

The charm that pure science has rests, it seems, quite distinctly in part at least upon this basis. People find themselves uncomfortable in the face of the brush-heap of experience. One way to meet the difficulty is to reconstruct the world in imagination, to smooth out the disagreeable features of it, to put it in such a proper shape that one can find his way around and at least in thought seem to achieve a mastery over it. In a similar way the power that many religions have for their devotees lies largely in the fact that they present the scheme of a world in which all the evils that are so patent here, if they look at the facts in any degree of honesty, are going to be smoothed out in some happier time or happier place to come. In other words, the thinking which we generally regard as the distinguishing characteristic is nevertheless a comparatively rare form of human behavior, a form of behavior which is not agreeable to the bulk of men, that is gone through with no more than is necessary and a form which is utilized in many ways to give a false and specious power instead of being utilized solely as a means of solving genuine problems.

In brief, summary form, it can be said: If thinking is primarily a form of behavior which men resort to in the face of necessity, one would expect that that type of activity which presents the most insistent problems would be of the most persistent character, would be the type of behavior that would come nearest to being rationalized. But while the way of developing economic theory on the assumption that economic behavior itself is rational is the easiest way to construct the theory, it is obviously a method that rests upon an assumption contrary to fact. Relatively great though the element of intelligence in economic behavior may be as contrasted with other forms, nevertheless anyone who will keep his eyes open in observing how people do get on with reference to economic matters can very readily convince himself that even in this field there is a much greater reliance upon rule of thumb, upon routine and habit, than there is upon initiative and intelligence. If that is the case, then it seems quite obvious that a much more scientific way of trying to give a satisfactory account of human behavior is to give up the assumption contrary to fact, that it is all planned out, and to approach the problem in an objective spirit, to observe the economic behavior of men both widely and closely, and try to discover, as the result of observations, what generalizations can be made; whether there are uniformities in behavior; what these uniformities are.

This is to apply to the behavior of men the methods to which the investigator resorts in studying the behavior of animals and it seems at least as probable that he can meet with success in studying economics on that basis as he can in accounting for animal behavior by applying objective methods. In the case of the animal man better facilities for observation are available than in the case of any other species, for ethnology, history, statistics, are all at the inquirer's service in dealing with man. They enable the theorist to extend his observations over a vastly wider field both in point of time and in point of numbers than is feasible in the case of dealing with other animals. On the other hand, there is the one serious drawback that one cannot experiment on man in the same sense that one can experiment on animals.

The only opportunity that people have to experiment very freely upon man is limited to their dealings with children and here their dealings are seldom guided simply and solely by scientific curiosity. Ordinarily, what the investigator does with a child, no matter how carefully he is observing him, is done not with the purpose of working out some specific problem that interests the investigator, it is done rather with the view to the child's benefit from some experience. In a limited degree, the inquirer can experiment in the narrower sense with children and with grown up people too. There are some simple things that anyone would submit himself to quite willingly on the assurance that by so doing he would please some other human being. But this is quite limited.

What the inquirer can do in economics then in applying these objective methods is not to experiment but to observe the facts in a systematic manner, and that observation that appears to be limited can be rendered extremely wide if he will have recourse to such devices as are available, by research among the simpler races, research in the records of our own past and careful quantitative study of what goes on at the present time. When the investigator has obtained the results of observation he must analyze; in fact, he must analyze before he observes. From the older point of view the task of analysis in economics is represented by deduction. From the more modern point of view the analysis is rather analogous to the formulation of a working hypothesis. The inquirer gets ideas as to what people would do under certain circumstances, and then he tries to test the validity of his notions by directing observations specifically to the points which the notions themselves mark out as crucially significant. Then he will ordinarily find as the result of the procedure that his original notions are not very well borne out by the facts in his observation. It will become necessary for him to modify his hypothesis as scientific workers in other lines are continually doing, to look in part at least for a new series of facts, and so he carries on researches by an almost inextricable mixture of analysis on the one side and observation on the other.

In the course of this observation and analysis of economic behavior, it seems fair to note that the point of chief interest for economists, for students in most of the social sciences, lies in the part of behavior which is institutional rather than instinctive. That is to say, the things which are of primary significance for the economist, for the student of jurisprudence, of politics, of sociology, of education, of a large part of psychology proper, etc., are the great social institutions themselves. The reason so much stress is laid upon the importance of institutions rather than upon the analysis of the instincts is, in the first place, institutions are themselves standardized behavior forms, and because they are standardized, they present generalizations such as the theorist does not get if he is directing his inquiry primarily to points peculiar to individuals. A good deal more in the way of formulating general results seems possible when he is thinking about forms of behavior that are common to large classes, if not to the entire population of a given country at a given time, than when he is directing his attention primarily to points in which individuals differ.

Economic institutions are the variable element in human progress, and since they are fundamental, the human race should direct what capacity of thought it has attained to putting its economic institutions into a shape which will serve its needs. To contribute toward that consummation is the task and opportunity of economic theory. Advantage of this viewpoint: Institutions being variable there is hope of progress. No natural law stands in the way. Economics can legitimately cultivate relations with practice. Need not be sterile and academic to be scientific. All the different types of economic theory fit into this framework. Indeed their real significance and interrelations are not to be grasped until they are so placed.

The following types are studies in the logic of pecuniary institutions: classical political economy, mechanics of utility and the Austrian calculus, pure theory, neo-classical theory, American psychological school, pecuniary analysis. The scientific defect of these theories—barring perhaps the last which as represented by Davenport is more self conscious—is that they do not recognize what they are doing. They do not see that they are developing the logic of an institution which has but partial sway over economic behavior. Most clearly seen in hedonism. The following types realize that they are dealing with institutions—with only a part of human nature and that part not the most fundamental. Social value type is a study of the influence of social institutions upon valuation; welfare economics is a study of the influence of social institutions upon the material well being of different classes of the population; historical economics and genetic [institutional] theory are studies of the evolution of institutions themselves. Thus all the different types of economic theory have something to contribute to the understanding of economic behavior.

The influence of statistical method. Resort to it suggested by the behaviorist viewpoint. The investigator's interest not in the individual case but in the average case, or better—in the whole group of cases. But how can we know the average with any definiteness, or the group, without statistics? Importance of measurement to knowledge, to control shown by the more advanced sciences. The means of measurement in the social sciences provided mainly by statistics. Experiment is not impossible perhaps, but far less easy to arrange in economics than in physical sciences. Growth of statistical data, improvements in their accuracy and refinement and in statistical technique, are the best way of overcoming this defect. Quantitative questions, such as: how much? how many? how soon? etc., involved in almost all economic problems. Men's knowledge is of little use until the inquirer can give at least approximate answers to social questions.

Finally, economic activities have continually a very important part in shaping all the various habits of thinking and acting that together make up culture. Political, legal, social, moral, religious and aesthetic institutions are the product of intelligence that found its first function and continually finds its chief function in dealing with fundamental economic problems—the problems of finding the material means for satisfying wants. On the other hand, it would appear that in proportion as institutions of the various sorts enumerated become well developed they assume a quasi independence and are able to react upon and modify in detail economic institutions themselves. Economic institutions are habits of thinking and acting and to understand them it is necessary to study the development of ideas. Further, this is not purposefully directed unfolding guided by a consciously pursued end, it is not even a logically consistent development of simple propositions, but a development that depends strictly upon practical exigencies of life. In other words, thinking or philosophy has never been the guide of life in the sense that men have selected some goal after due deliberation and then struggled toward it. It has been the guide of life only in the sense that men have used their capacity for thought as a method of discovering and adapting means toward ends that for the most part are not consciously understood. Maybe conscious appreciation of ends of life will be attained in the future.[26]

I now invite questions, remarks, and above all, criticisms of this

---

[26] Outlines, "Closing Lectures," May 14, 16, 1917; "Economic Origins," 1904, OPP 1-6, no. 94.

behavioristic viewpoint. I hope that they may be forthcoming with freedom.

S1: May I ask what definition you give the task of economics?

M: Economics should regard itself as one among several sciences of human behavior. The particular behavior with which it deals is the social activities of men in connection with their efforts to supply their needs.

S1: It seems to me that if you say that, you have included a much wider field. Because science at large, and the field altogether has widened so much, there is a great danger of losing ourselves. I think it is necessary to be clear about what the scope of economics is— the central economic point is the value problem, whether in price or whatever other problem.

M: I am inclined to agree with most of what S1 says. For example, I agree wholly with the general condition that the social sciences at the present time are marked off rather sharply from the natural sciences. It is possible that the line of demarcation will be somewhat less hard and fast as time goes on. It is to be hoped so. That is to say, we may gradually find that a great deal can be learned about human behavior, which is the chief problem of the social sciences as I see it, from researches carried on by biologists and psychologists and those researches in particular are at the present time being conducted more and more in physical and chemical terms. Thus, there seems to be the possibility of a bridge between physics and chemistry on the one side and the social sciences on the other side, a bridge that has its center pier on biology in general, and physiology in particular. Here I think there is no particular difference of opinion.

As to the danger of depending in the study of economics upon mistaken results in other sciences, I grant that the danger is there, but it is simply part and parcel of the situation. One of the characteristics of developing knowledge is that the sciences are spreading out more and more. As they reclaim larger and larger tracts from the great area of ignorance which surrounds mankind, they are likely to overlap at the edges, to become less distinct than they were when these sciences were first marked out. That is distinctly true in the case of physical science. In recent years [1918] one of the most important developments has been the rise of physics and chemistry. A generation ago those two sciences were much more restricted in the eyes of investigators than now. They have grown together, greatly to the power of both physics and chemistry. Nowadays the connection of geology with these two fundamental sciences is close and vital.

Thus it goes into the field of the natural sciences. Any student of physical nature, no matter what problem he is concerned with, is likely to gain by discoveries made in some other branches of the general study of physical nature, and the more alert he is to what is happening in the other branches, the more likely he is to profit by new knowledge.

To be sure, it happens in natural sciences all the time that mistakes are made. Plausible hypotheses are adopted, gain currency for a considerable time, direct investigation into certain lines and then are found to have been wrong in some important particular. The result is that the investigators have to get a new set of working hypotheses; in other words, a new specific set of problems. It may turn out later that they have gone off on another wrong tack, but they have carried the investigation further. This occurs in all sciences all the time. Doubtless many mistakes are made but in the present state of our ignorance a man who makes a mistake which sets interesting problems, which gives a point of investigation that adds to knowledge, is rendering a service even though it turns out ultimately that the lead which he started was not altogether correct. The economist is therefore, as S1 points out, in danger insofar as he is relying upon results reached in any other science, in so far as he is trying to get hints from what ethnologists or psychologists or from what students of jurisprudence or from what any other of the social sciences have turned up as a new discovery. That danger the economist will inevitably encounter provided he is trying to profit from what is done in the other sciences.

But let us see what price he would pay if he tried to guard himself very carefully against being misled by the results of the other sciences. He would pay the price of isolation by trying to carry on an investigation into one particular aspect of human behavior without knowing any aspect but his own. Just as much as natural processes possess a true unity although the science of nature is divided into physics, chemistry, etc., just so human nature, human behavior, possesses a true unity.

There is greater danger from isolation in the social sciences because in them even more than in the natural sciences, investigators get forward by expounding hypotheses that seem at a given time to be plausible, working them out, seeing to what consequences they lead and then modifying their hypotheses. That is to say, they go forward by the method of trial and error. The more things that they try that are at all plausible, the harder they try them, the more thoroughly they work them out, the faster they get through with their series of blunders and the more advanced lies the stage in which they are making their current blunders. From that point of view I think that the general science of economics does much better to seek stimulating ideas, even from sister sciences which are no further advanced than itself.

S1 says finally that it seems to her that the central problem of economics is the problem of value. I am inclined to agree with her on the whole, and not to find the remark at variance with what I have been saying. The difference would be primarily that the theorist has a distinctly more valuable approach to the study of the value problem, if he conceives valuation as one phase of economic behavior. He thereby sees economics devoted primarily to the intricate problem of human valuation, because it is through valuations that men arrange their behavior towards each other with reference to their control over the material universe.

S1: I never would say that the economist should not observe other sciences. Also I never would say that it is not profitable for an economist, but he has to be clear about his limits. A good example is set by a man like Schumpeter.

M: Here is a real difference of opinion between S1 and me. I think it is unwise on the whole to try to draw a hard and fast boundary around economics. Economists should define the problems on which they are working just as sharply as they can, because a sharp definition is an important aid to effective analysis, but it seems to me rather a mistake, after the investigator has defined the particular problem on which he is working, to say that he must also define sharply the limits of the economic field at large. The definition is just a bit presumptuous, because the problems of economics will doubtless multiply in the future as in the past, in proportion as man's knowledge of human behavior grows, and it will probably be as much a mistake for anyone in the present generation to say what the inherent and necessary limits of economics are as it would have been in Ricardo's day.

We are working nowadays with many problems that did not occur to Ricardo's mind; we regard them as fit and proper objects of economic interest, and our knowledge of economic behavior would at the present time be very limited if all the economists since Ricardo's day had confined themselves within the limits of the definition which would have appealed to him. To repeat, the economists ought to try to define the problems which they are specifically attacking in any investigation as sharply as they can but they ought to recognize that it is a vain effort to try to define the problem of economics at large further than to say that economics is one among several sciences of human behavior and the problem with which it is concerned is the cooperating dealing of men in their struggle with nature.

S1: I conceive of certain limits to our science or of defining the method in such a way that we look at it from a certain angle: the value problem.

M: You would want to say that economics is strictly confined to the value problem.

S1: I would not say that. I think it is rather the central problem.

M: I am inclined to agree. As matters have stood recently the value problem has been the central one. On the other hand, Professor Walton H. Hamilton [then at Amherst] in two extremely interesting papers[37] clearly demonstrates that the value problem was not the central one of economics in the days of the physiocrats; he points out that it was not the central problem with Adam Smith and he even goes so far as to say that it was hardly the central problem for Ricardo. I do not want to deny that the physiocrats were working at the problem of economics. Adam Smith was and yet the value problem was not the point about which their problem was focused. Furthermore in the future the value problem may fall out of the important place which it holds today [1918].

S1: Science is the only thing that we have to define, which one can define from different standards as different things. We may say that the physiocrats did not work directly on value. Why do we say Adam Smith was the founder of economic science? Because he was the one who brought out the central problem of value.

M: That is exactly what Hamilton contends that he did not do. You will find Hamilton's contention convincing if you will read what he has to say about Adam Smith, and then go back to *The Wealth of Nations*.

S1: Perhaps one could postpone the beginning of science, and start with Ricardo.

M: If you put up a hard and fast definition like that, it leads me to set up artificial restrictions to fit the definition. I think that most of us would be unwilling to deny that Adam Smith was working at economics. He certainly had a vast influence.

S1: Most of the writers in economics, most of the writers in all

---

[37] "The Place of Value Theory in Economics," *The Journal of Political Economy*, 1918; [on Hamilton see Joseph Dorfman, *The Economic Mind in American Civilization*, 5 volumes (New York: The Viking Press, 1946-1959) V, pp. 425-438, 752-753.]

the sciences are not at all clear about their method as Ricardo was.

M: About their method?

S1: About the method they use or the science. Only a very few bother about the methodology and most of these are not very clear. As soon as we begin to start a plan or program for a science we have to have in that very intricate field of science the theory of knowledge which is outside the scientific field proper.

M: I do not see that it is necessary to go far into epistemology when you are attacking the problem of how to lay out the field for a particular science. I know that that sounds like an unphilosophical remark, but suppose you go into epistemology, do you think that you would get a great deal from it that would profit you in your attempts to guide economic investigation into fruitful paths? Don't you think that the study of method that would profit you more would be the examination of the way in which such discussions have been made by economists? Don't you think that you would accomplish more by looking over the other social sciences, and seeing the logical and technical devices that they have employed? Don't you suppose, for instance, that a pretty careful study of modern statistical work would be more fruitful than the reading of epistemology?

S1: Yes. I also believe that, but if one begins to talk about that one has to know how far one can know something. I mean epistemology has to do with how far economic knowledge reaches; what are its limits; where we have to say to ourselves "we cannot answer that." We have to be definite about that.

M: It is impossible to be definite and clear on such matters. No one living knows how far economic problems may extend. That question the future alone can answer. It is a matter for the slow progress of economics to determine. We hope that its conquests will be vigorous, that it will enable economists in the future to solve many problems that they cannot attack nowadays. But to undertake to say now what problems they can pursue in economics as a whole with prospects of success is to try to anticipate what achievements the science may have to its credit in the future. I expect no gain in attacking a problem of that kind. The problems that economists should want to define specifically are those that are engaging their immediate attention.

S1: I see one practical side to [the need for epistemology] in economic investigation. Economics is always in danger of going into social politics, in giving plans for social politics, socialistic things and all that sort of thing. We have to be clear how far such things are purely scientific, and how far they have gone over the limit of science and are already matters of belief, of subjective opinion.

M: I believe heartily in the practical desirability of trying to draw a sharp line between what economists have succeeded in demonstrating and what is a matter of opinion. S1 is quite right in intimating that there is often a grievous confusion of ideas about that matter. But a question of that kind is one that has to be discussed with reference to particular points. Can economists as a matter of fact lay down general rules by which they can say that beyond this frontier in general, they are in the vague region of opinion, whereas inside this frontier they are within a region of well established truths? I do not see the possibility of such generalization, although, I do see the possibility—to agree with S1—of the desirability and importance of economists trying, when it comes to particular problems, to know whether they know or just believe, and this kind of problem economists have sorely neglected. The more attention paid to it in the future the better.

S2: With reference to the relation between the analysis of social evaluations on the subjective side and what is represented by such analysis as, for instance, Veblen's—he is analyzing attitudes of mind—its relation to the statistical survey of the actions that follow as result of these attitudes of mind, whether the statistics ought to bear out, ought to be proof of those attitudes of mind, or whether there is absolutely no possibility of connecting the two aspects of economic evaluations.

M: I should think there was an excellent possibility of connecting them, and that studies made for the purpose of testing such a hypothesis as Veblen's are feasible and important. Take, for instance, the general contention that the machine process tends to make people socialistic. That is not precisely the way in which Veblen puts the contention, but it is a form which I think is perhaps legitimate as a summary of his views. I do not see why it would not be feasible to make a detailed study of voting on the socialist and the other tickets with reference to the occupation of the voters. If you take a case in which a fair and square issue which can be treated on a socialistic or non-socialistic basis is presented to the voter, in a case where further you can get figures for sufficiently small election districts so as to make clear whether the bulk of the voters in each district had or had not been subject to the machine process, in a case like that you would have an opportunity to inquire into the validity of Veblen's hypothesis. That is a sort of work that has been neglected.

S2: Has not that interesting possibilities for the old question of the mechanistic interpretation of society compared with the vitalistic interpretation? You have the problem of social groups, using the will element and the arbitrary element in human nature, actually investigating that indeterminate element. Would not such an investigation have a bearing on the question of the effects of different kinds of work?

M: Yes, that probably has some bearing on the general question as to whether men's minds are made for them by their circumstances or whether men go off quite voluntarily and make up their own minds to anything they like. If you will allow that interpretation the issue is capable of statistical investigation.

S1: I want to oppose the example. If you should say that the socialistic view is due to the machine process, the machine process has the effect of socializing the minds of men, I would not accept that explanation.

M: By socializing the minds of men, you mean the same thing that Veblen does; that is, their work begets the habit of thought that makes socialism appeal to them.

S1: I would not accept the statistical proof. This proof would only mean to me, if I had the statistical proof—I would explain it introspectively by the fact that workmen do not have the same interest in property. Their interest, their subjective feelings, and everything is so much more bound together with the whole theory of socialism.

M: People who have suggested such ideas as Veblen puts forward have contrasted the industrial populations, particularly in Germany, with the populations of the agricultural districts. The former are so far as the voters are concerned pretty much made up of people who have no stake in property as do the population of the agricultural districts. So it is not the property interest which lies at the basis of the contrast. However, I will grant that the question might still remain as an open one as to the causal relation between the machine process and the socialistic vote. But on the other hand, if you found that there was a regular and high correlation between the population's devotion to the machine process and the socialistic vote, you probably would have to do a great deal of explaining to show there were not some causal connections.

S3: Might it not be possible in such cases as that that a socialistic trend was not caused by working on machines but by the close association that was caused with the machine process? Perhaps there is no contrast, but it seems so to me. You might have something like the cigar makers, an industry which is purely hand work, and you would have the close association which comes from the machine process.

M: I think that logically is quite true, just as what S1 has suggested is quite possible logically.

S4: Supposing that it could be pointed out that there were no objections to the statistical method.

M: You did not mean it was an objection to the statistical method did you S1?

S1: It was an objection against behaviorism altogether. You said that your view of economics was the study of human behavior. One could draw a parallel to behaviorism in psychology. We must make some use of introspective methods. So in economics I would not want to say that statistics is the only science of human behavior. This would exclude introspection. We would have only as method this experimental, this statistical method.

M: I agree that it would be rash for an economist to say that he is going to confine himself exclusively to objective methods in economics. It may be that the time is coming when the economists will think that this is the only safe way of working. It is a method that has great possibilities. It is one that has not been employed nearly enough in economics, and yet I am not prepared to say that it will displace the other method. In psychology the majority of investigators while conducting their investigations (like John B. Watson for example) have accomplished a great deal by purely objective methods, yet still they believe that the general method of introspection has and will long, perhaps always, keep a place. The question as to what is the proper method is a question that has to be decided by the results that the economist can obtain and it would be foolish to say in advance that he will confine himself to any one method, because that would mean that he is announcing in advance that satisfactory results cannot be obtained by applying other methods. Such a negative proposition is always a dangerous one.

S4: I would criticize Professor Mitchell's fundamental contention that it is a difference in problem and not in method that distinguishes the various types of economic theory. There is a fundamental difference in method and that explains why there is such controversy in economics. There is no such controversy about the scope of other sciences because the practitioners know there is only one method. Economics has two methods, and it can be studied by a sort of logical introspection, which has brought out just a few problems like that of price, but it has not been able to bring out other problems, therefore economics has been developed in certain parts and not in others. To repeat, the difference in methods has brought about a multiplicity of types. One man wants to study economics by the old scientific method, by the old static method which can be applied to every field, a way in which you can definitely map out the field between political science, economic science, technology, etc., but you cannot do that if you use the special economic method, and that seems to introduce new problems.

M: You see, what S4 is saying is that economics got started by the application of a peculiar method, that of balancing costs against gains, a method that is rather introspective in character, and that the appearance of new types of economic theory has been due to the fact that more recent workers have wanted to employ other methods; to do so, however, they have had to attack other problems because the particular problem of price is one that can be handled with some promise of success only by the method of balancing costs against gains. Do I interpret you correctly?

S4: Yes.

S2: Is there any reason why the newer problem should not have entailed a newer method rather than that the newer method should have entailed a newer problem?

S4: Actually in history people got a method and they used it to cover all the ground they could, and at the same time this explains the confusion which does not occur so much in other sciences. There are two methods which do not quite cover the same ground.

S2: Why did they start with that method in economics?

S4: The problem is primarily a matter of what the individual economist can do. If he has the ability to do a certain thing he will do it regardless of what it is. Ricardo found he was able to illuminate one kind of problem and he proceeded to do so. Malthus was one of the greatest economists who used both methods. His law of population is to a large extent based on numerical investigation, on what can be called statistics, but to a certain extent he used the other method.

M: In his political economy he tries to employ the same methods as Ricardo. He worked by both the statistical method and the introspective method.

S5: Is it so important whether the method itself first suggested the problem or whether the problem, after it has been suggested by the method, leads the method along? I think that on the whole the method is auxiliary to the problem because the method might first suggest the problem, but as soon as you have the problem, that is the important thing.

M: That is, you are reproving S4 and me—I believe that when one is confessing a fault one should put his own name first—you are reproving me and S4 for wrangling about the issue at all. I am not sure that you are not justified. Are there any other remarks on the point?

S2: Was not the fact that Ricardo did actually choose that particular method simply because he was not a scientifically trained man? It is only when men found an interest in different problems that they began to apply the same methods in economics. It is only when you get a different group of men that your new method is applied to the problems. It seems that it is not the method that develops the problem, but the problem that develops the method.

S4: Mathematics can actually be applied to certain problems. A man like Marshall who naturally uses mathematical reasoning will treat those problems which can be so handled. The problem is to find where the applicability of the method comes in. Marshall was astonishingly acute as a reasoner, but he did not take a statistical view.

M: You will recall that S4 is inclined to take the ground that the chief factor in the development of different types of economic theory has been a difference of method rather than the cropping up of new problems as I have been arguing. Whereas S5 pointed out in an ironic spirit, that this is after all not an issue that deserves to be discussed elaborately inasmuch as both factors presumably have counted. That is right in a sense, and yet there is an important difference in the way in which the two factors have operated on the development of different types of economic theory. As S4 said rightly, if you have men of a certain definite turn of mind, that turn of mind will mean that the particular method is especially native to them and they will always be found trying to solve problems that give scope to the method in which they are skilled. But I am inclined to insist upon the fact that these differences between different individual investigators, differences of interest, are characteristic of every generation of scientific workers.

It was just as true in the days of Ricardo that there were certain people who had a native preference for strictly analytical methods of procedure. There are some people to whom mathematical types of reasoning are so infinitely preferable that they will scarcely be found discussing problems to which those methods cannot be applied. On the other hand there are people with a distinctly statistical habit of mind who want to deal with concrete facts in a quantitative fashion by counting. Then there are also people who want to discuss types of situations and work out deductions by ordinary logical processes. Then there are the historical minded folk and so on. To repeat, these differences of aptitude are characteristic of every generation. True, certain of these methods seem to be inherently capable of greater elaboration than others, so that with the passing of generations the difference of method becomes pronounced. For example, statistics as a method of scientific work has undergone a much greater elaboration since Ricardo's day than has the straight form of logical argumentation on which Ricardo relied. Historical research is nowadays a more highly developed process on the technical side than it was among Ricardo's contemporaries.

But still the fact remains that there were even in Ricardo's day people who were working at economic problems by different methods which seem to stand out in S4's mind as the important differentiating characteristic of economists at the present time. The people who were working on other methods than Ricardo's had but comparatively little success. They attracted very little attention, primarily because the sort of problem that people of their special aptitudes naturally took hold of were not problems that were appreciated by the communities of their day as particularly worthy of scientific analysis. So the most important factor in leading to the differentiating of the types of economic theory has been the unfolding of the problem.

You see how skillfully I have finished the complete refutation of S4 just at the moment when he is entering the room.

S6: Do you think that there is any likelihood of economics becoming more vague by its basing itself on psychology? For instance, take sociology. There is a good deal in sociology that is vague, based on modern biology and psychology, or theories of survival, etc. I am wondering if economics would lose definiteness by reason of basing itself on the conclusions of psychology.

M: Economics would lose definiteness in certain parts of its structure and gain definiteness in other parts. It is feasible, taking the viewpoint that economics is the study of behavior, that the economist can, by a much more extensive application of statistical procedure than heretofore, get vastly more definite results than have yet been attained, and I do not see why from this same viewpoint economists should not work out the logic of institutions with even greater definiteness than they find outside of so-called pure economics. But the loss of definiteness which might occur in certain branches would occur primarily as a concession to the facts of the case, that is to say, economists would not profess to have definite knowledge where as a matter of fact the definiteness is all pretense.

S1: Do you regard economic values as high values? What value would you give to economic values in themselves? Questions like this are now being raised about the competitive system? Would you regard that the competitive system in itself brings about high values, I mean brings about such values which may not be brought about in another system where people would not have to strive at all for competition and all such things?—Where they would not have to struggle for an existence, where their existence would be assured by government or something like that. Would you regard that as very valuable?

M: I do not suppose anybody could answer that question with confidence who was not equipped with a scale of absolute values. Unfortunately that very valuable piece of mechanism was left out of my mental makeup. I have not any scale of absolute values, consequently it is rather difficult to say yes or no to a question of that sort.

S1: Does not Dewey see in the economic value high values?

M: I should expect Dewey, if a question of that sort were put to him, to admit just as I have, that he has not an absolute scale by which to rate values of different orders; perhaps he would go on to say that values are things which society is all the time creating. They are themselves subject to change as men's interests alter with changing conditions under which they live, and as they alter, the relative importance which they ascribe to different sorts of things undergo corresponding changes. At the present time our culture assigns a relatively higher importance to purely economic values than has been characteristic in the past. In the future it may reduce that rating. That would depend upon the way in which the conditions of life lead to changes in men's interests, and from a philosophical viewpoint there is perhaps no way of seeing whether the scale of rating adopted by one generation is a higher, nobler, finer and better one than that of another generation or not. The scale of each generation is the one that is appropriate to the generation in so far as it is not a relic from past generations that is undergoing change.

Are there any other remarks?

S7: Why do you lay so much emphasis on explaining institutional behavior? You said that ought to be the basis of the study perhaps even more than the pure instincts. I do not entirely agree that mainly because institutions change and instincts do not that that made institutions of more consequence. The fact that a thing is unchanging might not make it any the less important.

M: I did not intend that the recognition of the existence of instincts is not a matter of great significance. It was rather that I was inclined to think that institutions are matters of still higher importance. My argument on that head runs somewhat as follows: the instincts according to modern views are extremely numerous and specific. The behavior of adults is not to be accounted in terms of the instincts. The behavior of the person who is beyond his childish years is governed at all times by certain combinations that have been made among instincts. Your attitude in running away from dangers, your attitude in business, your attitude in family life, is never controlled by the instinct of fear, by the instinct of acquisition, by the instinct of sex love, taking those things in a radical sense, because what you are afraid of and run away from is something you are worrying about. For instance, you as a modern man are probably very much more afraid of a railway train. The things that you offer as a business man and try to acquire obviously are things which have been dictated to you by the community in which you have grown up. Your sexual instinct is not that of a primitive person. On the other hand it is highly sophisticated. That is to say, when it comes to accounting for the behavior of adults, and that is the task of economics, the theorist has to take into consideration not the instincts themselves, but the combinations that have been formed among the instincts as the result of the experience through which people have gone. This means in other words that the economist is concerned primarily with combinations of instinctive factors as controlling behavior and the combinations which are made are made primarily through man's intercourse with other people. Of these combinations, the most important for any student of society are the very prevalent ones, those which are characteristic of large masses of men, and that means that the institutions are the important things because "institution" is only another word for "prevalent social habits."

Then further I would say that there is something to make out of the statement that institutions are the factors in behavior which change. Our real interest of course in studying economics—at least I say "of course" since that is the ground I am taking—our interest in economics is derived from the possibility of improving social organization so as to make a larger number of people happier, to get a decent life for a bigger part of the population. If that is the case, then as previously noted what concerns us is precisely that part of the causes which regulate our behavior, which is itself susceptible of change, and here institutions enter. According to the current view, instincts in the proper sense are substantially unaltered. They are passed on from generation to generation presumably without any considerable alteration or modification. On the other hand there is a cumulative growth of institutions, and it is this cumulative growth that has raised the civilized races today from savagery. It is to a further cumulation of that sort that we must look for whatever hope we entertain for a better lot for mankind in the future.

To state the matter in a slightly different form: "Under this term [the institutional factor] there are included the socially prevalent habits which in any given group standardize the behavior of individual members. For the social sciences this factor is of peculiar importance, since it makes possible cumulative change. So far as these sciences can contribute to progress, they find their opportunity in purposive, intelligent control over institutions. One of the hopeful results of the present war is that it has demonstrated to all that our social economic institutions are far more malleable than has been supposed. Thus men like Professor [Carleton] Parker and like Professor Irving Fisher who see a conflict between man's inherited instincts and present living conditions are justified in pressing vigorously for such changes of our present institutions as will accord on the one hand with the original nature of man, and on the other hand with our present notions of productive efficiency."[38]

S7: Would you leave the study of pure instincts to sociology?

M: I should leave it primarily to psychology rather than to sociology, but I should say that the economists are very much interested in following that investigation.

S7: You would approach the problem from the other point of view?

M: I would say that our concern rather lies with the combinations that are made among inherent instincts than in instincts themselves.

Are there any other offerings?

S3: Assuming that it is proven that monopoly is really more eco-

[38] Mitchell, "Control of Wealth and Economic Life—Discussion," *The American Economic Review*, March 1918, Supplement, pp. 236-237.

"As the instincts constitute the first great factor in culture, so modifications of instinctive behavior through intelligence and habit constitute the second. Though secondary in origin, these modifications attain decisive importance because they are cumulative. They are passed on from generation to generation and each acquired element may become the basis of new acquisitions of this nature as usages, customs, conventions, preconceptions, canons of conduct, bodies of knowledge including the customary scheme of technology upon which workmanship proceeds." ([Part of Professor Mitchell's summary of Veblen's *The Instinct of Workmanship* in] "Human Behavior and Economics; A Survey of Recent Literature," *The Quarterly Journal of Economics*, November 1914, pp. 24-25.)

nomical so far as production is concerned than competition, is there anything in the discussions that we have had that either condemns or approves that situation?

M: Our work would point to this conclusion, that we would better try to get busy inventing some form of social organization that will give the community the enhanced efficiency in production, and avoid the loss of that efficiency to a few monopolists. That is to say, we would better try to invent a better set of institutions, and then see if we cannot set them going.

S3: This combination which is constantly occurring is usually approved upon the ground that it results in economy of production.

M: By all means let us try to maintain economy of production.

S3: If we have got to take the bad with the good—

M: That is the question. That is to say we ought to invent some way of not having to take the bad with the good. If we can arrange some organization no matter how large and complete the control, though it cover the whole field and exclude competition, if it combine with this features which will secure a share in the advantages to all members of the community it is desirable.

S3: So far we seem to have failed.

M: Precisely. That is a very important task awaiting the economic inventor.

S3: Some change in human nature will have to accompany it.

M: I do not know that it is necessary; or if you will let me talk in what seems to be a little more modern terms, a change in institutions is a change in human nature.

S3: There would be a difference between a change in laws?

M: No, laws are institutions.

S4: But they do not always change human nature.

M: In so far as laws represent established habits of thinking and acting, they represent human nature. On the other hand laws which are simply written on the statute book, but are not enforced, do not represent changes in human nature.

S3: I had in mind particularly the Sherman Anti-Trust Act which is sustained by public opinion, but the law has been constantly broken. I suppose the moral sense of the community has not gotten up to the point where that law makes a change in human nature.

M: There is a slight change, perhaps not one that has been very radical in its character. It is quite possible that the failure there has been largely due to the imperfections of the law and that the best thing to look for is not a more thoroughgoing enforcement of an imperfect statute, but an effort to invent some modification which would be more effective.

S3: Isn't the sentiment which is employed in the law a very old one that has been in existence as long as business?

M: Not so long as that, but it has been in existence for one hundred years or longer.

S3: In early times, whenever there has been an attempt at monopoly, hasn't there always been a feeling against it?

M: I should not venture in sustaining that generalization. There are two ways of taking monopoly. One is to damn it, which you are likely to do when you suffer by it; the other is to try to get a monopoly of your own. If you take the middle ages, the common opinion sustained the general idea of special privilege, only each man was trying to get special privileges for himself.

S2: Of course, years ago in England the monopoly was granted by the crown.

M: The Tudor monopolies encountered strong opposition, but at the same time there were many trade organizations which were enjoying monopolies which had come down from ancient times and were favored by public opinion. It was certain novel features of the Tudor monopolies that made trouble.

Are there any other remarks?

If not, I should like to say a few words in conclusion on the present [1918] status of economic theory, its future prospects and the special relation of this whole situation to the conduct of your lives. At the outset of the course I took the ground that the things which make economics worthwhile studying is the ardent desire for a better social organization, that as an object of mere intellectual curiosity economics as a science is very imperfect and if the student is animated simply by a desire to know as much as he can, to give free play to his intellectual faculties, he had better be devoting himself to other fields of learning. On the other hand there is no special subject where the need of greater knowledge than commonly possessed at the present time is clearer.

As [World] War [I] goes on and our experience in it comes a little closer home, economists ought to take an increasingly serious attitude toward their economics, and they are justified in taking a more optimistic view of the possibilities of utilizing what they know at the present time, and thereby increasing what they can learn in the future. One of the things that the war seems to have demonstrated beyond the peradventure of a doubt is the feasibility of considerable and rapid changes in economic organisation under the pressure of circumstances; that is, great and speedy changes in institutions under favoring conditions. We have been inclined in the last generation, particularly in the social sciences, to look upon civilization as an extremely slow moving concern. Outside the strictly technical branches of organization, outside of the natural sciences, they have been inclined to say that the people must trust to a slow evolution, to secular accretions, for the benefitting of society. Alfred Marshall for instance, prefaced his great *Principles of Economics* with the Latin motto that "Nature makes no leaps."

The war, on the other hand, has brought home to the economists the fact that when there is a situation where the eyes of the community are turned upon the attainment of one great goal, when there is some object which appeals to the masses of the people important beyond all others, then at least it is possible within a short space of time to bring about changes in social organization of a far and deep reaching character, and that lesson should mean for economists that the opportunities for putting in practice any hypotheses they may have regarding the possibilities of improving social organization are by no means as dim as they seemed in the days of peace. This experience in war shows too that the changes need not be left to blind chance, force and fraud, that nations are at a stage of civilization where it is possible to plan experimental alterations of economic socio-economic organization in advance, to keep track of them as they occur, in a definite quantitative fashion. That is to say, it looks as if nations could employ the method of trial and error in social organization in the way which makes trial and error effective.

In the past, a man argued quite rightly that civilization has made its advances by making trials, by finding which trials were mistaken, trying something else, and so going forward in proportion as people are able to learn promptly where their errors lie, to profit by them by lining up new trials that have a fairly good chance of success. That means that the greater the amount of intelligence which goes into running the process of trial and error, the better the prospects are for profit. European countries, as well as the United States, are learning something about the methods of carefully planning what they are going to do in advance, keeping track of what they are doing as they go forward, modifying their plans promptly as imperfections appear and preparing programs for the immediate future. That means again that the economist has a larger opportunity at the present time for doing something serviceable in the way of social reconstruction than has been granted to him in the past. But if the students are going to hold that rather optimistic view of the possibilities of economics at the present time, they must agree at least upon two or three general characteristics of the type of economic theory that they want to cultivate.

The first obvious characteristic of the type of theory which can be employed for social service is one which has constructive interest. In the past there has been a good deal of theory which was supposedly the exposition of certain "natural laws." Two generations ago, particularly in England, everybody who talked about economics talked about the laws of that science as being similar in character to the laws of physics and of chemistry. It was regarded as ridiculous to try to transcend the limits which nature herself had placed upon men's achievements, those limits being conceived to lie partly in the physical universe, partly in human nature itself. One ill-result of taking the view of economics merely as an exposition of "natural laws" is that it precludes the notion that economics is a science that can be utilized. It denies that economics belongs among the sciences which are of an experimental nature and consequently can be used by man, and puts it among the subjects in the serene body of the merely intellectually curious that must always be treated primarily as things simply to be known, but not to be acted upon. It makes the economist feel that there is something which so long as it is scientific must be kept free from the contagion of human endeavors to improve.

The present view that we take of human nature, substantiated in a sense by experience in this war, is that the real limits to the possibility of change are by no means as serious as has often been supposed. Doubtless there are limits upon man's endeavor to improve his condition. We live on this earth, so far as we know, our race will always be confined to this earth and must go forward by utilizing such limited opportunities as the earth offers. Doubtless again the instinctive equipment of human nature is something that is not subject to change, save in so far as we may some day eradicate the more vicious stocks by selective breeding. But people know that there is an immense possibility of increasing men's control over nature by the application of modern science, and we are inclined to think nowadays that there are immense possibilities for improving human nature, by improving institutions. Consequently there is ground for cultivating a type of economic theory that is characterized by highly constructive interest, a type that is not afraid to be made use of, that believes that the science is likely to learn faster if all the knowledge that it possesses is utilized to the full, provided always that that utilization is carried on in such a systematic fashion that experimenters know actually what does happen when they try to experiment. Again on this view, the type of economic theory that should be cultivated is one that deals with real, not with imaginary situations; not with an abstract human nature.

The possibility to deal effectively with real situations, with the behavior of real men, with what that behavior may be made as well as what it is, has been greatly enhanced by the advances in modern statistical technique. There was a time when the economist could scarcely handle a certain class of economic problems effectively for intellectual purposes except by making such a series of abstractions as was given by an altogether imaginary situation, as the object of intellectual curiosity. But through modern statistical devices economists have ways of handling large groups of social phenomena in such a fashion that they can analyze them effectively and establish relations among them through the process of sampling, which when legitimately deduced they may, with confidence, predict will hold, concerning the actions of other people than those of the group from which they are derived.

Once again the type of economic theory that ought to be cultivated is one which is not confined to what Marshall calls qualitative analysis. Most of the problems which the American people are facing in the partial economic reorganization which the war has brought are not problems of the existence or the non-existence of certain factors. They are problems of more or less. Only a science which can deal with quantities, which can reckon between smaller and larger quantities, which can at least, approximately, measure social phenomena, has something that can be readily put to use, something that people can experiment with, and learn from through the process of experiment. That possibility of quantitative analysis is due in large measure to the strides that statistical method has taken. There is no other technical device that is likely to prove of more importance to economics as a science—I will go so far as to say there is nothing else that will prove so important to economic theory as the application of statistical analysis to large groups of social phenomena.

If this is true, these are times that make extraordinary calls upon the economist, and times [1918] that offer him extraordinary opportunities. The need for scientific planning of changes in economic organization has never been greater than the present day. The chance of making these changes in an intelligent fashion, following them up with systematic study, and thus seeing what effects they give rise to, has never been so good as at the present, nor has there been a stage so favorable to intelligent efforts. This period of social-economic reorganization presumably will last for several years at least, perhaps longer, as long as the pressure of the present war rests upon the nations of the west they must, all of them, be endeavoring to perfect continuously not only year by year, but month by month and week by week, perfect their organization which is sustaining their enormous armies, and perfecting that organization means altering economic and industrial operations in such a fashion as to reduce waste and enhance the proportion of the people at home who are working for the armies in the field and the number of men who can actually be drafted into military service. That process of adapting the energies of the country to one superior object means that as long as the war is supported, there must be a continuation of efforts made by governmental authorities to change the people's established ways of acting today.

When the war is over, the one-time belligerents are going ot face another set of social problems which it seems almost impossible that the countries concerned will try to solve without utilizing the same sort of centralized direction which they are employing now for the purpose of killing their enemies, for the new purpose of reconstructing their own lives at home. Presumably that period of reconstruction will last for several years at least. It is possible that the people will never fall back quite to where they were. It seems possible that in the United States, and I speak only of the United States, because I know no other intimately enough to have even a hazardous opinion of the subject, that this nation will for a long time to come, perhaps always, continue to make more and more use of intelligence for the guiding of social economic forces, relying more and more upon trained people, to plan changes, to follow them up, to suggest alterations. If that is the case then the use that is going to be made of all the social sciences, of economics perhaps in larger measure than any other, will be greater in the future than in the past. You who are young, just beginning your work as economists, are entering the field under circumstances which offer a finer opportunity for developing the science and making it serviceable and entering opportunities which place upon you a heavier responsibility than any other generation of Americans which has ever studied the subject.[39]

---

[39] End of extract from "1918 Typescript." Use in the closing part has also been made of the Outline of the last lecture of the spring term, May 15, 1918.

The future of economics. 1. Increased vitality. Academic character of economics before World War I. War and economic mobilization. Economic mobilization and change of institutions. Economic exhaustion focuses serious problems on reconstruction. Character of economic work during war. Reconstruction more favorable to scientific work and still more to problem. Classical political economy arose during reconstruction and from a reconstruction problem. The social sciences flourish in troublesome times: excellent American literature on money and banking, at least excellent statistics. French literature on finance. 2. How economics will change as it grows. a. Will become far more a quantitative science. War work quantitative. How much? How soon? All practical problems quantitative. Recent improvements in and extension of statistical work. b. Production will become more prominent problem. Will result partly from quantitative studies of income. Many-sidedness of problems of production. Engineering and industrial technique. Organization of industry as a whole and elimination of systematic waste. Danger of new wastes through bureaucratic control. c. Problem of institutional change will come to the fore. Comparatively slow changes of economic institutions in the nineteenth century. Sudden changes forced by war. The present predicament promises further changes. Danger of light-headed changes of institutions vs. dangers of reaction. Obvious need of scientific study. d. Economics as a science of human behavior will come under study of institutional changes for institutions are habits. Prevailing delusions about psychology and economics: notion that economics needs light from psychology only on "motive." That when one is past that question, psychology is left behind and all the rest is plain economics. In fact if economics shows what men do it is a contribution to science of behavior and therefore a contribution to psychology. That is, economics contributes to psychology quite as much as it borrows from psychology. Problem of behavior is objective and can be studied by objective methods accessible to economist. e. Welfare will become more prominent in economics and more definite. How welfare will be made more definite by quantitative studies. Welfare will mean a satisfactory working life as well as sufficient supply of goods. Old conception of work and waiting as necessarily painful. And so aims must be to limit population and to enhance production not to make work satisfactory. Man is in fact active, capable of getting utmost satisfaction from his work, if it is adapted to his capacities. Task of analyzing men and analyzing jobs and then putting the two together. The work of the world today requires all sorts of workers, workers have great diversity of abilities, making work satisfactory is primarily a matter of selection and organization. 3. This generation of economic workers has a larger opportunity and a heavier responsibility than any of its predecessors since Ricardo at least. Gravity of problems is obvious: "the cake of custom"—to use Bagehot's phrase—is crumpled; new resources are offered by statistics, psychology, history, anthropology; instructive experiments have been tried by predecessors.[40]

[40] Outline, May 4, 1920.

Parent stock of modern economics—classical political economy as a body of technical economic doctrines is not so antiquated as are the cognate ideas—institutions—human nature. (Outline, "Closing Lectures," May 14, 16, 1917.)

Final summary: Economics like philosophy and the other social sciences is still in the stage of development marked by the existence of fairly distinct schools of thought, or, as I like better to say, "Types of Theory." These schools differ in method, but these differences arise from differences in problems which are taken as the central concern of economics. Orthodox economics: What it is to the economic advantage of men to do under the capitalistic organization. Concerns itself primarily with what I like to call pecuniary logic and the "purer" this theory becomes the more exclusive the concentration on that problem becomes. In dealing with pecuniary logic, the investigator employs the method of imaginary experimentation; that is, he sets up certain assumptions and seeks to think out what it is to the interest of men to do under the conditions supposed. The theory is developed by varying these assumptions with reference to such matters as the factors in the situation which are allowed to change—the length of the period considered in the problem, the degree of competition supposed, elasticities of demand, relations between unit costs and volume of output. How far the conclusions apply to the actual world depends upon the character of the assumptions made. The correspondence between these assumptions and actual conditions is seldom investigated. Hence the doubts about this type of theory are usually doubts, not about the correctness of the reasoning, but about how far it applies to the facts we want to under-stand. May have uncertain "operational" significance. Defence [by ortho-dox]: Tool makers; question about applicability not relevant. This de-scription applies less strictly to Marshall than to many of his pupils, to the later Austrians and to mathematical economists.

Institutional economics concerns itself primarily with the evolution of eco-nomic organization. To Veblen, this meant study of the widely prevalent habits of thought. To Commons, it means study of social controls over individual action—primarily through the courts. Methods employed: Combine ethnology and historical research with reasoning about how men act with a certain set of habits ingrained in them by the social circum-stances in which they have grown up and by the work they do, or how the social controls over individual behavior may be expected to work out. Again there may be doubts about how far the reasoning about economic behavior applies to actual conditions.

A third type of economics seems to be developing though not represented as yet by systematic theoretical treatises. It endeavors to learn by analytic studies of actual behavior how men conduct themselves. Its methods are closer kin to those of animal psychologists than to those of introspective psychologists, though these men show no reluctance to account for their observations by supposing that their subjects know the rules of the money-making and money-spending game. Here they go beyond the outlook of physical sciences—suppose men to have purposes; that they plan for the future. Large use of the mass observations afforded by statistics. Con-siderable emphasis upon mathematical analysis of these records. Not con-fined to statistics. Doubts here concern representative value of the data, trustworthiness of the mathematical analysis, extent to which features that are not recorded statistically may modify conclusions drawn. Work of this sort is primarily monographic. Since social phenomena are interdependent, the question concerning what is left out is highly important. Cannot be applied well except when mass observations are available. Promises to develop in the future because statistical observation is covering a wider range. Danger of "mere fact-finding"—John Dewey. Yes, but the facts may have deep operational significance. Relation to questions of policy.[41]

Let me conclude by saying that we should not be dismayed by the formidable character of our task, or by the admitted limitations of our knowledge and our methods of applying it. Economists often have given good counsel. As examples, let me mention two friends of my youth who are gone. I remember Allyn A. Young coming back from the peace conference at Versailles [after World War I] and predicting that the German indemnity never would be paid. About the same time T. S. Adams predicted that little beyond bad blood would come from efforts to collect the war debts from our Allies. Some years later [in 1930] a thousand American economists united in asking President Hoover not to sign the Smoot-Hawley tariff bill. Of course it would be easy to give equally striking examples of forecasts by economists that have gone wrong. It is salutary to recall these errors as reminders of our own fallibility. It is salutary to remember also that we have a very bad reputation with the public for always differing from one another. Certainly these differences are a sign of the immaturity of our science. But it is also well to recall that we have provided knowledge that is useful and learned ways of dealing with certain technical problems. Above all it is heartening to realize that we are in a position to accomplish more than our predecessors if we have intelligence, industry and seriousness equal to theirs. Now [1941] the country is calling for our services on a scale unparalleled in the past. We must answer this call with a deep sense of responsibility, determined to do our part as thoroughly as we can.

---

[41] Mitchell, "Position of Economics," address at Conference on Methods in Philosophy and the Social Sciences, New School of Social Research, May 22, 1932. [John Dewey was also a participant].

APPENDIX III

ADAM SMITH'S METHODOLOGY

How does Adam Smith reach his conclusions? Consider the following examples.

1. Thesis: Wages in Great Britain above subsistence minimum.
Proof: (1) Differences of summer and winter wages. (2) Wages do not vary with price of provisions. (3) Wages vary more from place to place than price of provisions. (4) Variations in wages often inverse of variations in price of provisions.

2. Thesis: Total advantages of different employments of labor are same except in so far as affected by policy of Europe. Necessary conditions: (1) Perfect freedom. (2) Employments must be well known and long established. (3) True only of ordinary or natural state of employments. (4) True only of primary and not of secondary employments. Proof: Conclusion is stated as self-evident. What psychological and sociological conditions are necessary to justify it?

3. Thesis: Monopoly price "is upon every occasion, the highest which can be got." Proof: Monopolists can keep the market understocked and so sell commodities above their natural price.

4. Thesis: High or low rent is result not cause of high or low prices. Proof: Rent is a monopoly price. Therefore proportioned not to what landlord can afford to take, but to what farmer can afford to pay. What farmer can afford to pay depends upon price of his products.

5. Thesis: Protection of home industries decreases wealth of nations. Proof. Wealth of nations equals summation of the wealth of citizens; each citizen is best judge of how to increase his own wealth; therefore wisest public policy is the obvious and simple system of natural liberty.

What is the method of proof adopted in these cases? 1. Wages in Great Britain above subsistence minimum. Conclusion drawn from careful observation of existing conditions.

2. Total advantages of different employments of labor equal. Deduced from assumed conditions only part of which are set out. Among tacit assumptions are: tastes of all men substantially alike; men weigh all advantages of occupations carefully before choosing; are free to choose among occupations they prefer, without reference to differences of natural aptitudes or opportunities to get necessary training.

815

3. Monopoly price always highest possible. Deduced from tacit assumptions, among which are: Monopolist guided by rational pursuit of pecuniary self-interest; his pecuniary self-interest found in charging maximum price.

4. Rent is determined by price of products. Deduced from observation that land is a monopoly and that limit of price farmer can pay is found in price of his product, and from thesis no. 3.

5. Protection of home industries decreases wealth of nation. Deduced from assumptions, partially tacit; among latter being assumption that men always follow their pecuniary interests.

Summary: Conclusions are derived chiefly by 1. logical deduction from premises which are supplied partly by 2. observation of contemporary fact, partly by 3. historical investigation, partly by 4. assumptions (usually tacit) regarding human nature. Smith aways assumes that there is a Scotsman inside of every man (Bagehot, *Economic Studies*). 5. Assumption about the "natural course of things." On this assumption we must dwell a little. Smith assumes that there is a natural course of events, apparently ordained by God, and working for man's felicity when not interfered with; c.f., physiocratic conception of natural law. Difference between Adam Smith and Quesnay: less insistence on the constraining power of this natural trend. More made of causal chain of events. God somewhat more remote; c.f., the "invisible hand." Examples of expression of this preconception are difficult to give because the preconception is usually tacit. Everywhere Smith is found appealing to the natural course of events, condemning all interference with it, and assuming things are well when it is allowed unrestricted sway.

Adam Smith's use of history is abundant—makes up greater part of the book but plays a very small role in theoretical work. Contrast with modern use of history in economic theory. What is sought is genetic account of institutions. So far as Smith uses history for the purpose he employs "conjectural history," the name given by Dugald Stewart. See *Essays on Philosophical Subjects by the late Adam Smith. To which is Prefixed an Account of the Life and Writings of the Author by Dugald Stewart* (London: Strahan and Cadell, 1795) p. xlii.

Smith's discussion of value and distribution is the first great body of theory which he contributed to economic theory. Much greater contribution is his theory of state policy: the "obvious and simple system of natural liberty."[1]

---

[1] "Adam Smith," APP 44-53, no. 1. [This outline seems to have been prepared some time before 1918.]

APPENDIX IV

THE CLASSICAL THEORY OF VALUE

Introduction: Two tasks in understanding a theory. 1. Understanding it logically as a consistent body of propositions having more or less relation to the facts. 2. Understanding how sensible men came to believe in it. In case of classical theory of value, the second task is now perhaps harder than the first. In fact the classical theory of value with all its variants is less subtle and less difficult than much modern theory even in the simple field of economics. But if we know the modern literature on value, the classical theory seems absurdly incomplete, to say the least. The modern expositions start with demand and supply. Proceed to investigating conditions on which both demand and supply depend in long periods and short, under various suppositions concerning limits imposed by physical and economic organization. Often end with effort to show that conditions limiting supply may in the last resort be resolved into terms of demand.

Exposition of classical theory: Limits demand and supply to market prices. Implies that there is a substantial difference between factors which regulate these prices and those with which economists are concerned. Normal value is determined by cost of production. Utility is assumed but not analyzed. Cost of production is made to mean labor alone (James Mill and J. R. McCulloch), capital outlay only (Colonel Robert Torrens) or a combination of labor and waiting (Ricardo indistinctly and Nassau W. Senior with aggressive confidence). Complications are set aside by 1. Law of rent—rent does not enter into cost of production. 2. Tacit assumptions of free competition, rationality and knowledge on part of bargainers, essential naturalness of the English division of classes and scheme of pecuniary institutions. 3. Treating differences of wages and profits in different occupations as constant factors which do not sensibly count in producing changes in natural value. How could a theory which neglected analysis of demand, which treated market price and normal value as subject to distinct laws and which made normal value depend on labor cost only or capital cost only—how could such a theory ever have seemed satisfactory to keen minds? The answer lies in understanding the development of the theory. Not its logical pedigree mainly, but the factors that influenced the minds of the men who made the classical political economy.

Conditions under which the classical theory of value was developed: 1. A *group* product. Not the work of Adam Smith, Ricardo and John Stuart Mill in orderly succession, but of a number of men in close intellectual touch

817

with each other, criticizing each other by letter and in conversation as well as in pamphlets. Organized for discussion in the Political Economy Club established in 1821. All of them interested in taking economic theory seriously. Leading members of the group: Ricardo, James Mill and Malthus —a little remote at Haileybury; McCulloch from Edinburgh—a rising light; Colonel Torrens, a retired military man who was trying to establish himself as an independent authority; J. B. Say, admiring and admired visitor from France; Hutches Trower, a correspondent of Ricardo and fellow [stock exchange member]; Sydney Smith, Maria Edgeworth [the novelist], Thomas Tooke, a merchant in the Russian trade who grew into a celebrated writer on prices. Younger men: Senior, George Grote, John Stuart Mill, John Austin, Francis Place. In the background, Jeremy Bentham. As part of the atmosphere—Cobbett, anti-Malthusians, Robert Owen, William Thompson, T. B. Macaulay—and a host of would-be reformers friendly and hostile. 2. Interest in economic theory was derived from interest in public questions. This group had only one professor of political economy—Malthus, and he was perhaps the most practical and muddle-headed man in the group. Others were in business, M.P.'s, philanthropists, semi-literary people, barristers, etc. All came to political economy to get or rather to defend their solutions of practical problems of the day. These were problems forced by internal economic development of industrial technology, growth of population or by wars with Napoleon. Dominating issues: Bank of England restriction; that is, [suspension of specie payments by the Bank as authorized by the government]. Was paper money depreciated? Ought the Bank be forced to resume payments in gold? Corn laws—England ceasing to export grain and beginning to import it. Ought landlord class to be protected by laws designed to keep up the price of grain? Taxation and funding: How raise revenue to pay interest on public debt increasing because of war? Ought public debt to be scaled down? [Other issues were] poor law reform, political reform, law reform, prison reform, public schools, church disestablishment, freedom of combinations of labor, restrictions on use of machinery. Ricardo wanted resumption of specie payments by Bank of England, abolition of corn laws, preservation of public faith with respect to debt but readjustment of taxation, etc. Malthus defended corn laws; McCulloch advocated scaling down of public debt. 3. How these questions involved theory of value. Bank of England notes—are they depreciated? Is there a stable standard of value by which to answer this question? What is stability in value anyway? What regulates value? Corn laws—what effect do these laws exercise on prices and therefore on cost of living of laborers? And on wages and profits? Would abolition raise real wages? [Would it] raise profits? What are in general the relations between wages, profits, rents and value, and *vice versa?* Taxation—a nest of complicated problems practically all centering in value.

Peculiarities of the theory determined by these conditions. 1. Separation between problem of market price and problem of normal value. To men who take a statesman's attitude toward these practical problems the point of interest is—not what is going to happen at once—but what will happen in the long run. 2. Neglect of analysis of utility. (C.f., Alfred Marshall's different opinion, [but note that] Ricardo felt that he could do nothing with utility). Thing which was changing was cost of production—under influence of industrial revolution. As practical men why go into subtleties of analysis of demand? We cannot do anything with marginal utility analysis after we have developed it in a practical sense (but c.f., advertising)—because the factual data are lacking. On the other hand, we can get factual data about costs and therefore can and still do use cost analysis in treating practical questions like the tariff. Dominance of practical over speculative interest particularly striking at this point, because Bentham laid stress on utility and provided the foundation on which Jevons built. Indeed in 1833 Longfield's *Lectures on Political Economy* called attention to fact of diminishing utility and might have become the cornerstone of a new theory of value, if there had been a set of professional scholars rating logically imposing ideas as the thing most to be desired. Exclusion of rent from cost of production. Peculiarity of agriculture at this time very striking. Law of diminishing returns contrasted with rapid advance in manufacturing. Landlord class, unlike employer class who were at this time particularly active, seemed to do little for process of production. If they were to be justified it was on other grounds from those which justified capitalist employers. Rent was not a payment for services of individuals or for sacrifices but for use of land. Price of grain obviously did not depend on what farm it came from. Therefore it did not depend on what rent the farmer paid. Rent must be determined by price instead of determining price. To reduce the price of grain by abolition of corn laws would therefore not hurt the farmer (save in the transition period which might be overlooked) and would benefit laborers (if they were wise enough not to increase population at once) and would benefit employers. 4. Reduction of cost of production to sacrifice. Money outlay the obvious form of cost, but to a generation which discussed the vagaries of the irredeemable paper currency and went through the violent price fluctuations of the Napoleonic wars, money costs could not be the costs that control in the long run. What did count on the basis of the prevalent common sense philosophy was pain and pleasure. Money was a symbol of pain and pleasure, but a symbol only, and we ought to get back of money to that for which it stood. Problem whether all sacrifices could be reduced to labor sacrifice alone was an interesting problem for debate within the school.

Element of science: All this interest in practical problems need not have led to establishment of political economy and would not have led to it, if it had not been that these men believed tacitly in the possibility of discovering laws in the social realm corresponding to those which had been discovered in physics—particularly in celestial mechanics. Certainly this faith was stimulated by constructive bent of these social reformers. They imagined what would happen under their happy schemes of social organization and got used to drawing broad and bold conclusions from hypothetical conditions. Applied this habit in seeking explanations of current economic phenomena. Prevalent conception of human nature fell in admirably with needs of economic speculation. Hedonism and bookkeeping are close akin. The economists could talk about what business men would do if they had full data and believe that they were really talking about human nature and real men. Finally, Ricardo was a genius at making abstractions shrewdly—abstractions that did simplify problems to manageable compass, and still left enough of reality in them to make the analysis and conclusions of great moment to himself and to other practical men.[1]

---

[1] Outline, "The Classical Theory of Value," talk before Political Economy Club of Columbia University, November 30, 1914.

APPENDIX V

MAFFEO PANTALEONI

[One of the few prominent continental writers who like Edgeworth followed Jevons's procedure of consciously basing economic theory on a hedonistic foundation was the Italian economist, Maffeo Pantaleoni (1857-1924). He had studied in Germany and took his doctorate at the University of Rome, where he became professor of economics. He was elected to parliament in 1900. In 1923 he was appointed a senator.] His principal work was *Principi di economica pura*. Not a work of striking originality, but the work of an ingenious and learned man who knows thoroughly and seeks to reproduce and harmonize the gist of English classical political economy with the work of Thünen, Hermann, Jevons and his forerunners—particularly Gossen and Jennings—and his contemporaries in marginal analysis—particularly Walras, Menger, Böhm-Bawerk, Wieser, Marshall's early work, recent representatives of the classical tradition—Cairnes, and the Americans, Simon Newcomb and Francis A. Walker. It represented one of the attempts, along with those of Heinrich Dietzel,[1] J. B. Clark and Marshall, to unite the two lines of thought—cost of production theory of value and utility theory of value.

Pantaleoni's treatise first published in 1889, after there had been time to criticize and evaluate the new departure of Jevons, Walras and the Austrians. Revised when undergoing translation into English in 1898 by T. R. Bruce under title of *Pure Economics*. Chief value for our purpose is that the book presents such a clear-cut specimen of an important type of the mechanics of utility. Accepts hedonistic postulate as basis of all economics and shrinks from no application. What are the problems of pure economics? Theory of value based on theory of utility and applied to theory of distribution. All these problems are treated as problems in statics for the most part. Dynamic theory is small in bulk, and like in character to John Stuart Mill's dynamics; i.e., Pantaleoni's dynamics does not seek to account for modern institutional framework, but taking all this for granted as in theory of statics, he lets one element in the situation change and considers results which follow; e.g., his dynamic theory of rent treats effect of increase of population, his dynamic theory of wages conceives of capital as a flow instead of a fund.

Pantaleoni's treatment of these problems does not call for detailed attention at our hands. Shall direct attention only to certain points of special interest.

---

[1] On Dietzel, see p. 555 above.

Logical character of economics: (1) The fundamental hypothesis—"hedonic premise." (2) The "premises of fact." (3) Hypothetical conditions under which forces work. Are conclusions deduced from these premises true? Yes, if reasoning is valid. Applicable to interpretation of experience? That depends on correspondence between the hypothesis and factual reality. Pantaleoni's interpretation of the hedonic postulate. Does it correspond with fact? An unsettled question, according to Pantaleoni. Three opinions [he says] are held on the subject: (1) Hedonism is a typical trait of human nature but one which admits concurrent action of other forces. Ascribed to John Stuart Mill, Cairnes, Wilhelm Lexis, Adolf Wagner.[2] (2) Hedonism is the entire truth in certain departments of human activity. Ascribed to Walter Bagehot. (3) Hedonism is the entire truth for human activity in general. Ascribed to Helvetius (Bentham). Pantaleoni accepts second view, but points out that men do not necessarily achieve end of maximizing pleasure. Men may be influenced by custom, morality, etc., in their estimates of pleasure. Unconscious and reflex action may be ruled out.

Pantaleoni's proof of hedonism: Evolutionary in character, based on Spencer's *Data of Ethics* (2nd ed., 1879); that is, he accepts Spencer's version of hedonism—"the equivalence of the instinct of self-preservation and the hedonic postulate." How this proof begs the question (see Warner Fite, *An Introductory Study of Ethics,* 1903).[3] But in what do people take pleasure? This question must be answered to give us a basis for economic theory. It is always tacitly assumed that men take pleasure in consumption of commodities and find pain in long continued labor. Some such facts as these must be assumed for purposes of reasoning. Pantaleoni has merit of seeing and bringing out the logical point. Note particularly in the book the necessity of assuming uniformity of human nature. Do men take pleasure in what benefits themselves as individuals alone? Or do they take pleasure also in what benefits their race? Pantaleoni proves on revoltionary ground that the latter is the proper view.

Commensurability of pleasures and pains. Hedonic calculation supposes that they are opposite but homogeneous sensations. Modes to be considered in the calculus: Intensity, duration, certainty, present or anticipated, approximate or remote. In Jevons the last two are united as propinquity or remoteness. Otherwise Jevons's and Pantaleoni's lists are alike. Treatment of anticipated pleasures and pains. Properly discounted for uncertainty but not for futurity. As a matter of fact men do discount for futurity through error; but such discounting cannot be adduced as explanations in pure economics. Pleasures and pains of different people: Pantaleoni does not explicitly discuss the possibility of comparing pleasures and pains of different people. He has, of course, pointed out that theorist must assume a

---

[2] [Wagner (1835-1917) was a leader of the moderate German historical school. Wilhelm Lexis (1837-1914) economist and statistician, who taught at a number of universities, finally ended up at Göttingen. He was much admired for his work in the theory of statistics especially by Edgeworth. Like Wagner, he was a member of the German historical school.]

[3] [Fite was a friend and colleague of Mitchell at Chicago. He became professor of philosophy at Princeton University.]

fundamental likeness among men in regard to what they take pleasure in. He also says that "tribal hedonists" are constantly comparing their own pleasures with the pleasures of others, "but with what admixture of error, we do not know." But in making constructive use of hedonic calculus for purposes of economic theory he seems careful to keep comparisons within the skin of one individual; c.f., the discussion of absolute scale of wants, particularly p. 50.

Two fundamental laws of men's sensibility to pleasure and plain "They are thus formulated by Gossen:—1st. Every enjoyment, as it is prolonged, decreases, and at length ceases altogether. 2nd. An enjoyment has, when repeated, a lesser initial intensity and a shorter duration than it had before; and its intensity and duration decrease the more, the shorter the intervals at which it is repeated." Note that these are "factual laws." Is use made of second for purposes of economic theory? Two theorems of hedonic maxima derived from (1) above "factual laws" and (2) hedonic postulate. Gossen's first theorem is: "Every enjoyment may be indulged in with such frequency that a greater or a lesser frequency will yield inferior hedonic results. . . . Gossen's second theorem is also an immediate consequence of the law of decreasing enjoyments. It is formulated as follows: Given the option of several pleasures, and at a time so limited as not to suffice for enjoying them all to the point of extinction, we obtain a hedonic maximum by enjoying each pleasure in such measure, that its intensity at the moment when the period of fruition expires is equal to that of every other pleasure. In other words: The final degrees of intensity of each kind of pleasure must be equal at the instant when the given time expires, whatever may have been the initial intensity of each kind of pleasure. . . . A first corollary . . . of . . . this second theorem is that, if several pleasures are available, and the time is insufficient to admit of their all being enjoyed to the point of satiety, the least of these pleasures should be partially enjoyed before it can be profitable to enjoy the greatest of them to the point of satiety. . . . A second corollary . . . is that: the possibility of increasing the sum of enjoyments is conditioned by the possibility of discovering a new pleasure, however small it may be, or by that of perfecting one already in existence."

Theory of wants. Note that above propositions from Gossen relate to variations in sensibility to pleasures and pains in general. The theory of wants is cut out of this broad field as a basis for economics. What are economic acts? To be economic, acts must be purposive. What are wants? Gets laws of marginal utility, etc., by applying to these peculiar economic feelings— wants—the above theorems concerning feelings in general. Absolute scale of wants; variety and progression of wants. Is any theoretical use made of these theorems? Relation of theory of value to theory of production. Production a form of exchange. Relation of theory of value to distribution—application of general laws to determinate categories. Relation of marginal analysis to doctrines of classical political economy: Pantaleoni declares that the two lines of analysis supplement one another and are in close harmony.

Doctrinal results: Little that is new or particularly striking aside from the eclectic fashion in which doctrines from many different sources are fitted together. Interest, he holds, cannot be due to time discount. He maintains wages-fund theory, but under "dynamic conditions," wages must correspond to productiveness of labor unaided by capital (when competition among laborers is free.) Conclusion: Edgeworth and Pantaleoni reveal the development of utility analysis consciously based upon hedonistic interpretation; that is, they follow Jevons consciously.[4] Most other writers have taken a different turn which we shall see exemplified by Fetter.

---

[4] Outlines, January 3, 1917; "Austrian Theory of Value," remarks before the Philosophical Club, University of Chicago, November 29, 1898; "Ostensible Dropping of Hedonism in Economic Theory after Edgeworth," APP 44-53, no. 5. Quotations from *Pure Economics* (London: Macmillan, 1898) pp. 16, 27, 28, 32, 36, 38, 44, 46, 48, 293, 307. Italics have been omitted.

APPENDIX VI

SOME NOTES ON J. M. KEYNES

[On December 13, 1913 Keynes as editor of *The Economic Journal* wrote to Mitchell for] "an article on the banking and currency legislation [the Federal Reserve Act]. The news on this subject which reaches us on this side is largely written by correspondents, who do not very clearly understand it, and it is not easy to get a coherent idea of events." [Professor Mitchell's article appeared as "The New Banking Measure in the United States," *The Economic Journal,* March 1914.]

From the "Diary": February 13, 1931, "Wrote up Keynes's explanation of recession and depression." September 3, 1931, [Aboard boat on way to be Eastman Professor at Oxford 1931-1932] "Resumed reading Keynes's *Treatise on Money,* which I began last spring when I got half way through volume I. Reviewed the chapter on fundamental equations and continued." September 5, 1931, "Finished Keynes's volume I, and read some seventy-five pages of volume II." September 6, 1931, "Read somewhat more than 100 pages of Keynes. Liking book better and better." September 11, 1931, [after landing] "I finished Keynes's *Treatise on Money,* which I found most stimulating." March 7, 1932, [at Kings College, Cambridge] "where I had an hour's talk with Keynes." March 8, 1932, "To D. H. Robertson's room for a talk."

[In an address at Columbia in the fall of 1932, Mitchell again voiced an appreciation of Keynes's *Treatise on Money* but to indicate its importance the summary of the outline will be given in full.]

Clear that economics has not only an established place but also an increasingly large place in English universities. The conception of economics which prevails (as exemplified by R. F. Harrod among others) is that of Marshallian theory (Austrian theory at London School of Economics). But the substantially static character of Marshall's analysis is more and more recognized, and various efforts are being made to develop dynamic theory. Of these efforts the one which is attracting the most attention at the moment is that represented by Keynes, especially in his theory of money. Like most of the best work done in the past by British economists this ambitious current work is inspired in large measure by interest in current problems. The fact that England faces such an abundance of pressing economic problems is perhaps the best augury of the current vitality of English economic theory.[1]

---

[1] Outline, "Economics in the English Universities," talk before the Political Economy Club, Columbia University, October 13, 1932.

Keynes represents a line of development which makes money a larger element in general economics [than in his orthodox predecessors]. In his contribution "Der Stand und die Nächste Zukunft der Konjunkturforschung", in *Festschrift für Arthur Spiethoff* (1933), he took the ground that we live not in a "Real-Exchange Economy," as Marshall's and Pigou's treatises seem to assume. It is a "Monetary Economy," and the difference is of great importance because changes in the volume of money exercise a marked influence. He concluded by saying "that to work out in some detail a monetary theory of production to supplement the real-exchange theories which we already possess, . . . is the task on which I am now working." Outcome of those labors was his *General Theory of Employment, Interest and Money* (1936). He describes it in the preface as "primarily a study of the forces which determine changes in the scale of output and employment as a whole." Shows that "money enters into the economic scheme in an essential and peculiar manner." Cassel and Keynes are best examples of men working in the orthodox tradition who have tried to show the role that money plays in economic behavior.[2]

Marshall was one of the greatest authorities of his day upon the theory of money, but he did not show how this specialty can be integrated with the general body of economic principles. Cassel, Keynes and others (including Knut Wicksell) have brought the theory of money into the general body of economic principles. The gradual change in the orientation of economists to the place of money in economic theory, typified best perhaps by the different place that money occupies in the work of Marshall who makes "money the center around which economic science clusters" merely in the sense that money is his instrument for measuring "the force of motives" and Keynes who knows how to cure depressions by governmental measures that alter the propensities to consume and to invest.[3]

Seminar's interest in the relation of monetary theory to general economic theory is a natural result of recent developments in economic speculation, especially the type cultivated by Keynes and his disciples. This is merely the latest phase in a long story that begins with the effort to throw money out of economic theory and general economic theory. To review the changing relation between monetary theory and general economic theory is not only to see the need of a new integration such as Keynes has attempted, but also the need to work on a deeper level than do Keynes and disciples.[4]

Marshall's discussion was mainly, though not exclusively, concerned with static problems. Since his time progress has been achieved in the direction of treating economic changes, not merely the long run problems with which Malthus, Ricardo and John Stuart Mill were concerned but also business cycles. Keynes's *General Theory of Employment, Interest and Money* is probably the best example of the effort from the orthodox

---

[2] Outline, "Money and Economic Activities," discussion with the Banking Seminar, School of Business, Columbia University, October 5, 1939.

[3] Outline, "Seminar in Economic Changes and Economic Theory," March 31, 1941.

[4] Outline, "Seminar in Economic Changes and Economic Theory," December 16, 1940.

standpoint to incorporate an analysis of these problems into a systematic treatise on economics.[5]

"Many a book on economics owes its effectiveness largely to trenchant criticism of abuses and moral fervor for reform. That these qualities are not necessarily incompatible with vigorous analysis is demonstrated by *The Wealth of Nations,* Mill's *Principles,* Marx's *Capital* and Keynes's *General Theory.*[6]

From the "Diary" November 24, 1944, "Read application by Keynes *et al* to Rockefeller Foundation for grant to set up a department of 'Applied Economics' at Cambridge and telephoned to Joe Willits [head of the Social Science division of the Foundation] about it."

[Apparently England's leading universities had been taking to heart the advice that Mitchell had offered, while Eastman professor at Oxford. In a letter from Oxford to Mrs. Mitchell dated October 25, 1931, he noted that after dinner one evening he had]

> talked with the economics tutors from six or eight colleges about what they are doing at present and what they would like to achieve in the future. Each one of these young dons is supposed to take complete charge of the work done by whatever students in his college are reading for honors in economics. They may send students to each other but only to a limited extent. Thus there cannot be much division of labor within the field, such as the departmental organization of our universities provides for. Also I learned that no psychology is taught at Oxford; that there is an anthropologist somewhere about, that political science is mainly dialectical discussion of theories; that sociology is not represented, and that while one of the economics tutors is interested in statistics he has no laboratory or library. And they want me to advise them how to build up a real center of economics work here on a post-graduate basis! Presumably they turn to me for advice because they have eyes on the Rockefeller Foundation as a source of funds, and fondly believe that I may have some influence in that quarter. What I can do for them I don't know. Perhaps help them to realize how much they must do for themselves before they can produce a program of work that should attract a donor. At any event, three of them are to dine with . . . me on November 8th and continue the discussion.

[This became a regular fortnightly conference with the tutors. Among the leaders initiating this was Harrod who was to become one of the foremost disciples of J. M. Keynes. In the last term of Mitchell's Oxford year ("fall term"), Harrod and two other dons (Bretherton and Phelps Brown) and five students took Mitchell's seminar in business cycles.]

---

[5] Outline, "Fifty Years as an Economist," address before Political Economy Club, Columbia University, May 11, 1945.

In general the serious critics of capitalist system paid more attention to crises than did orthodox theorists; notably Sismondi and Rodbertus. (Outline, "Lectures on Business Cycles," September 24, 1942.)

[6] Mitchell, *The National Bureau's First Quarter-Century* (New York: National Bureau of Economic Research, 1945) p. 35.

APPENDIX VII

COMMENTS ON WELFARE IN ECONOMICS

Welfare in economics: Can it be measured by use of market prices plus surpluses—producer's surplus and consumer's surplus? C.f., Marshall's *Principles of Economics* on value of income of £1000 in Africa and England. There is point in saying "that a person with a thousand a year there is not as well off as a person with three or four hundred here."[1] What we really want to get at in economics is bearing on welfare.

Can we measure it? Can we identify satisfaction with welfare and measure satisfaction by what a man does pay plus what he would pay if he had to? It is admitted that we cannot compute consumer's surplus for whole of a person's income or expenditure. Is this the fundamental difficulty in economics, or is consideration of welfare not part of our business? Ought we to talk about commodities in physical terms, money prices, objective economic activities, etc.? Can race vitality become such an ideal? Measurable to an extent in physical terms—units of muscular strength, reaction time, etc.? Can we rely upon measurements of such matters as an index of the things which are really worth while, whatever these things may be or may be given? If we work out such a standard, would it replace the pecuniary standard? Would we not rather continue to use the pecuniary calculus, but within a more closely defined sphere? Difficulty with pecuniary standard as gauge of public welfare. 1. Money in itself had no significance to man—save so far as it gratifies desire for distinction in some form. Does not represent adequately the gratification from eating any more than it represents the gratification derived from a picture. 2. Its availability as a guide to welfare of individuals is found in fact of organized markets where things can be had for a price—things which are significant. The limits of its use here are the limits of the market supply. The reliability of it as an index depends upon the stability and definiteness of prices. Thus it is a more certain index of the gratification from eating than of the gratification from pictures, simply because the prices of foods are more definite than those of paintings. 3. Its availability as guide to welfare of community is far less than in case of the individual precisely because one cannot count upon the market supply at a definite price in the same way. The whole population cannot count on finding bread enough in market at five cents a loaf as the individual can.[2]

---

[1] *Principles of Economics* (London: Macmillan, 1890; 8th ed., 1920) p. 127.
[2] Outline, "Welfare Economics," APP 44-53, no. 61. [The notes were made around 1910-1912.]

THE INTER-RELATIONS OF MONETARY PRACTICES, ECONOMIC THEORY AND BUSINESS CYCLES

[This appendix comprises a section that was discarded from the last draft of *Business Cycles: The Problem and its Setting* (1927). It is in the Mitchell Papers.]

As said in Chapter I, economics was assuming its modern form during the period when, and in the countries where, the recurrent character of crises became clear. This concomitance was not an accident. The evolution of pecuniary institutions had as much to do with producing economic theory as with producing business cycles. That fact merits consideration here, because it has a bearing upon our own procedure.

The reason why the growing use of money stimulates the development of economic thought may be stated schematically. Economics consists of generalizations about human behavior. Before the days of elaborate statistical work, these generalizations rest upon personal observations, broadened into reasoning concerning what men will do under given circumstances. The possibility of making generalizations about economic behavior in this way increases as behavior becomes standardized on a basis about which one can reason. Making and spending money requires and inculcates a calculating type of behavior—exactly the type about which a theorist can reason with confidence. The larger the fraction of a population that lives by making and spending money, the more thoroughly people become habituated to reckoning and following their pecuniary interests, the more significant are the generalizations about economic behavior which a theorist can draw from his personal observation and analysis of what it is to men's interest to do. Hence the development of monetary practices leads to the development of economic theory.

History confirms and enriches this bit of analysis. No system of economic doctrines has been produced by any community before it has organized much of its economic activity upon the basis of making and spending money. Nor do theorists who know something about anthropology and ancient histry now imagine, as did certain of their predecessors, that the modern generalizations apply to the behavior of peoples unaccustomed to pecuniary practices. Even the Greeks, with their considerable use of money and their genius for analysis, made but slight progress in economics. To these beginnings the scholars of the Roman Empire and the Dark Ages added little. But as the peoples of Western Europe began to re-acquire and greatly to extend the uses of money, they became involved in discussions which grew through a series of transformations into the political economy of Adam Smith, Sismondi and Ricardo.

In these discussions, the problems presented by the successive developments of money economy hold a dominant place:—abuses of the right of coinage; how coins of different denominations can be kept in concurrent circulation at a fixed ratio; the circumstances under which it is right to charge interest upon loans; what constitute just prices; the causes and consequences of fluctuations in prices; the proper regulation of markets; the advantages which a country derives from an abundant supply of the precious metals; how this supply can be increased by shrewd management of foreign commerce, colonial possessions, domestic resources, and the laboring population. Gradually there grew up in Europe that loose scheme of economic policies and doctrines which is fitly called mercantilism.

That the characteristic features of mercantilism were intellectual by-products of the rise of pecuniary organization seems clear. Men who were learning from experience the vast increase in efficiency which came from putting the exchequer, the army, estate management, trade and employment upon a monetary basis, might well think an abundant supply of gold and silver vital to the nation. Until further experience had made clear the difference, it was natural to conceive that a nation grew rich, and hence powerful, like a merchant. To acquire riches in this way, it seemed necessary that the statesmen at the head of a nation should direct all the activities of its citizens, just as a merchant must exercise a close and constant supervision over all the transactions involved in his ventures.

It is less obvious, but not less true, that the *laissez-faire* doctrine of the Physiocrats, and Adam Smith's "system of natural liberty," were intellectual by-products of a more advanced stage of pecuniary organization. In the transition from feudalism and the manorial system to the mercantilist state, and again in the transition from the mercantilist state to capitalism, money was the great liberator. Its use conferred a wider freedom of action upon individuals, forced them to think more, and gave larger rewards for successful innovations. Men of initiative and a calculating turn of mind kept discovering new opportunities for making money, which the business pioneers of the 16th and 17th centuries explored, and their successors of the 18th century developed more systematically. In grasping the new opportunities, the business innovators found themselves doing many things which conscience and the law condemned. They disregarded hampering regulations about prices, markets, methods of production, employment, exports and imports; they made more money than befitted their stations in life. Gradually, the classes which were doing violence to the established order shuffled off the feeling that they were doing wrong. They dropped subterfuges and apologies; they began to champion as legitimate exceptions to the rule of a regulated economy those practices by which they were profiting. The revolution in religious thought concerning economic life came earlier than the revolution in economic theory.[1] That is, after men had found a way of justifying business to their consciences, they had still to reconcile the conflicts which developed between the laws they had made in the supposed interests of the commonweal and the pecuniary requirements of their individual enterprises.

[1] See R. H. Tawney, *Religion and the Rise of Capitalism,* New York, 1926.

This movement toward a new order of thought can be traced in the later mercantilist writings. By the time of Quesnay and Adam Smith the changes in practice had gone far enough to demand a sweeping change in theory. Private enterprise in pursuit of gain was becoming a mass phenomenon. Its advantages in case after case were patent to many. Yet philosophic grasp and intellectual daring were needed to formulate and champion generalizations which would justify the new practices and discredit the entrenched faith. Writing a little later, and coming from a country farther advanced in pecuniary organization, Adam Smith succeeded better than Quesnay in rationalizing the new economic order which had been growing up within the old. Once expressed, his formula seemed to be obvious. Certainly it was more in harmony with the spirit of money making than were the doctrines of mercantilism. The wealth of a nation is the aggregate of the wealth of its citizens; each citizen can judge the most profitable use of his labor and capital better than can any statesman; therefore, the wealth of a nation will increase most rapidly when every citizen is left free to pursue his economic interest as he sees fit. Such was the new generalization. The cases in which governmental interference appeared to be proper were exceptions to the rule, each requiring a special justification.

This was the philosophy which Sismondi had learned in his youth from Adam Smith, and had expounded to continental readers with a disciple's zeal. And it was this philosophy which Sismondi came to doubt, when he returned to the study of economics at the close of the Napoleonic Wars. Accustomed now to the methods of historical research, he saw with realistic eyes the gravity of those crises and depressions which the unhampered sway of individual enterprise seemed to beget. Still a zealot—as historians sometimes are—Sismondi announced his new discovery to the world with eager eloquence, and found that the world was less interested in his criticisms of Adam Smith's philosophy than in a new variant of economic theory just produced in England.

On one vital point Adam Smith had not differed from the mercantilists— his central problem was their central problem; how to maximize the wealth of nations. But as the money economy came to dominate men's actions and men's thoughts more fully, a problem which Adam Smith had treated as subordinate pushed into the center of economic interest; how landlords, capitalists and wage-earners may increase their respective share in the wealth of nations. As pointed out above, the economic welfare of a family in a business economy depends primarily upon its money income and the money cost of living. That is, to every family taken *seriatim,* the relative size of the share it can get in the nation's output of serviceable goods is more important than the aggregate size of that output. Hence, when men take the extreme individualistic viewpoint in their treatment of economics, and that is the viewpoint which pecuniary organization inculcates at the stage which it had reached in England by 1800, distribution becomes the problem of chief concern.

Just before Sismondi announced that unfettered enterprise begets economic crises, the Corn Law struggle had brought the problem of distribution to the fore in British politics. Before the close of the 18th century, England had become a grain-importing country. But the long wars had interfered with shipments from the continent, and the high prices of grain had caused a marked expansion of cereal growing. By re-opening European ports to British ships, the fall of Napoleon threatened to cheapen foodstuffs, and to reduce the profits of British farmers and the rents of British landlords. Hence the landed interest in Parliament sought to protect its share in the national income by raising the import duties upon grains. On the other hand, the manufacturing and commercial interest contended that dear food meant high wages, and that high wages would disable them in competition with foreigners. Thus the proposed Corn Law would sacrifice business profits to increase rents. Both parties to the conflict contended that wage-earners had nothing at stake: as Alexander Baring put it, "whether wheat was 120s. or 80s. the laborer could only expect dry bread in the one case and dry bread in the other."

Reflection upon this class struggle led Malthus and West to develop a new theory of rent, which Ricardo incorporated with other elements into a general theory of distribution. The changed orientation of economics was expressed in the preface of Ricardo's *Principles of Political Economy:* "To determine the laws which regulate . . . distribution is the principal problem in political economy." To say that classical political economy was an intellectual reflex of pecuniary institutions may seem strange in view of the slight attention which the classical masters paid to money in discussing what they held to be the fundamental issues. John Stuart Mill expressed their views by saying that "There cannot . . . be a more insignificant thing in the economy of society than money, except in the character of a contrivance for sparing time and labor." But the economists achieved this explicit neglect of money only by reading the logic of pecuniary institutions into human nature itself. They reasoned as if men were endowed with the capacity of acting from calculated motives of self interest, which is really a habit that men who live by making money acquire in varying degrees.[2]

The logical character of the economic theory which Ricardo and his disciples excogitated was not well adapted to treating the problem of business cycles. A chain of reasoning about what men will do in pursuit of self interest requires that both the theorist and the men whose actions he is explaining shall be able to say where their interests lie. Knowledge of this sort, adequate for practical purposes, can plausibly be assumed to prevail under stable conditions. But if economic conditions keep fluctuating, the man of affairs is faced by uncertainty. His decisions become less a matter of calculation, more a matter of guesses and emotion. About behavior shaped by non-rational factors it is difficult to reason, unless the lapses from ration-

---

[2] Alfred Marshall presented the logic of the classical position more justly than Mill, when he said that, money "is the center around which economic science clusters." His explanation of this *dictum* shows that Marshall was making more intimate use of pecuniary factors in behavior than even he realized. Assuming that behavior is controlled by motives, he argued that the motives which concern the economist fall into two great categories, those which impel men to seek gratifications, and those which withhold men from sacrifices. In dealing with problems of human conduct, the economist therefore needs some way of measuring the force of opposing motives, and the one measure which social life now offers is money. This assumption, that economic behavior is determined by the net resultant of conflicting motive forces which a theorist can measure, is an attenuated version of Bentham's felicific calculus—a functional psychology which is plausible to perfectly trained pupils of the school which the money economy keeps for all of us, but in which few of us reach high grades.

ality can themselves be reduced to rule. Hence, political economy achieved its chief triumphs in dealing with what came to be called the "static state." Business cycles had no place in that changeless realm.

The "dynamic" problems which could be treated adequately by the classical theory were confined to problems in which the changes discussed proceeded at a steady pace in a fixed direction. Thus Ricardo considered the changes which the growth of population would produce, and supplemented his laws of distribution by a discussion of the "long-time tendencies" of rents (which he thought tend to rise), profits (which tend to fall), and wages (which tend to remain constant). Changes of this character are analogous to what we now call "secular trends," and quite different from what we call "cyclical fluctuations."

Yet commercial crises could not be wholly neglected. The simplest way of adapting the classical organon to the requirements of this problem was to classify crises as "abnormal" phenomena, and explain them by lapses from rationality. As suggested above, such lapses can be reasoned about, provided they are standardized. For example, the improvidence of the laboring classes in marrying early and rearing too many children was made the basis of a subsistence theory of wages. Similarly, the observation that good times beget over-confidence among investors converted another lapse from rationality into a rule of economic behavior, and afforded a simple theory of crises.

To deal effectively with the problem of business cycles, there was needed a more empirical approach than the classical economists were accustomed to—not less reasoning, but more comprehensive and more accurate observations upon which to reason. For economic measurements upon a considerable scale the time had not come in the generation of Ricardo, or of John Stuart Mill, or even in Alfred Marshall's youth. Realistic observers of social changes, like Sismondi, might offer plausible hypotheses, but neither they nor their critics could test the suggestions adequately. Early quantitative investigators, like Jevons and Juglar, had so limited a range of data that they too were forced to rely largely upon conjectures. Looking back from the vantage point which others have gained for us, we can see now that the nineteenth-century economists might have collected more observations than they did, had they grasped the promise of such work. But in that century, as in its predecessors, economics continued to be a series of reflections upon materials furnished by historical evolution. In due time the statistics which would help theorists to a more thorough type of work were provided. As money making became a more intricately organized process, carried on by larger units increasingly dependent upon each other for supplies and markets, accurate records grew in practical importance both to private enterprises and to governments. Gradually economists learned to utilize these records for scientific purposes. Once more it was the further development of monetary practices which pushed forward economic theory.

A sketch of the rise of statistics and of statistical methods in economics will be given in the next chapter. But here we may note the moral which the past development of economic theory points for present workers. Successive generations of economists have been able to better the analysis of their predecessors by using the fresh materials which a later day afforded. The long series of mercantilist writers, reflecting upon stage after stage in the growth of pecuniary institutions, paved the way for economic theory. It was by reflecting upon the achievements of private enterprise that Adam Smith's generation developed the philosophy of *laissez-faire*. It was by reflecting upon the Corn Law struggle that Ricardo's generation reached the classical theory of distribution. It is by reflecting upon the ever-growing body of statistical materials which the current phase of pecuniary organization offers, that our generation stands its best chance of making a further contribution to economic knowledge.

Of course this conclusion, though stated dogmatically, is merely another working hypothesis, the value of which must be judged by the results to which it leads. Following the line which it points out, we shall make use wherever possible of quantitative observations in analyzing that modern form of economic organization within which business cycles have reached their clearest form.

APPENDIX IX

CONCLUSION OF STEINER'S NOTES. 1917[1]

I. Various types of theory studied. A. Classical political economy—the great parent stock of which others are offshoots, of two kinds: 1. Orthodox types: (a) [Jevons's] "mechanics of utility" and Austrian analysis; (b) pure theory [Schumpeter], closely related to marginal analysis yet separate; (c) neo-classical [Marshall]; (d) "psychological" [Fetter]; (e) pecuniary analysis [Davenport]; (f) social value theory—Cooley and Anderson in United States. 2. Not quite orthodox: (a) welfare—Hobson; (b) historical [Schmoller]; (c) genetic—Veblen; (d) Ehrenberg and the German periodical *Archiv für Exaktewirtschaftsforschung*. Differs from historical in study of particular business enterprises; (e) Freiburg group, slightly different from (d), emphasizes private viewpoint to explain economic phenomena from standpoint of private individuals—more close here to English and Americans than to Germans.

II. Differences between types. A. Primarily in problems upon which they lay chief emphasis; (a) differences in methods in most part due to this; (b) conclusions differ in emphasis. B. Classicists—stress upon general problem of prices and particularly those concerning income, acquisitive viewpoint; (a) in a sense both derivative types true to this as central problem; (b) general difference between orthodox and outlying groups— (1) former concerned mainly with explaining actual prices as [they] run under present institutional situation; (2) outlying—trace social effects of economic processes as [they] run now (welfare)—or investigate how present institutions got their form and changes they are subject to (historical and genetic explanations). C. Orthodox writers differ among themselves chiefly as to subject emphasized; (a) classicists, cost of production; (b) Jevons and Austrians, emphasis on demand—supplement older views by treating neglected side of problem; (c) neo-classicists, try to restore just balance between the two sides of the problem of prices; (d) pure theory, does not deny validity of either side—emphasizes primarily problem of equilibrium in market under stable conditions [general economic equilibrium]; (e) psychological school, differs from utility analysis at outset—pays more attention to subjective basis on which utility is conceived to rest. Gradually realize logic more solid in their analysis than psychology, hence: (f) emphasize logical interrelations between various prices in place of psychology—Davenport; (g) social value theory, men's scales of value have much in common, as all people [in a community, etc.]

---

1 [Notes taken by W. H. Steiner in "Types of Economic Theory" 1917.]

are products of common environment. Consequences of uniformity stressed. D. Many differences of opinion among economists clearly seen in same type of theory: Fetter vs. Fisher on interest; while Fetter and Veblen hardly join issue at all—differ as to conclusions having scientific value. E. Day may come when we will think, not of different types of theory, but of different subdivisions of economic field: (a) bring all into general framework; (b) something like physics (highly specialized) presents today; day may come when established results in one field will not be genuinely inconsistent with those established in another field.

III. Which type is most promising? Partly personal equation. Abstractly considered, must consider question of what has led to assigning varying weights to subsidiary problems, which have cropped up as men thought more and more about central problem of prices. A. Quite possible this due to working out of past economic theory—logical evolution; (a) large attention paid to predecessors: (1) this view is much more position of philosopher than natural scientist; (2) learned economic theorist—[knowledge] of opinions of others; learned physicist—[knowledge of] physical processes, (b) work of this kind (monographs on past writers) not very fertile. New situation—fresh minds, rather than contemplation of old theories, leads to new standpoint. B. Counts for more than A—transplanting of old theories to other lands; (a) classical theory in America, France, Germany—early translations and reprints (in United States). Treatises along these lines in 1830's and 1840's; (b) might expect active intellectual reaction—leads to new problem, yet does not appear to great extent. United States minor reaction. France far worse than United States in lack of intellectual reaction; (c) why did domestication take place without more reaction? (1) can domesticate any economic theory provided it is used in academic work only—training of thought; United States, France, Germany subject in hands of professors—used primarily in university courses; then need no new thinking; (2) if institutional situation is like that from which the theory came; not case of United States, France and Germany; different institutional situation and problems confronting statesmen. Therefore due primarily to academic factor. C. Counts somewhat—further experience world has had with capitalistic organization—experience with pecuniary incomes; (a) sharper differentiation between class of business enterprises and class of investors, has opposed interest to profits; (b) competition has shown tendency to breed monopoly—by end of century did not answer to Ricardian situation—trusts, trade unions; (c) whole aspect of population question has changed since Malthus's day; now fear birth control, at most fear disproportionate growth of elements having weaker mentality; (d) change in social situation, at least change in emphasis on old problems; class struggle now drawn more sharply, though some differ on this point; (e) the above are representative elements—class struggle nearer to giving a total explanation of new theory, but cannot ascribe formation of new theories to anyone; draw differences more sharply. D. Most important—increasing knowledge of human nature; great expansion in this knowledge seen in development of various social sciences since Ricardo's time: (a) anthropology including ethnology—for the most part new creation since the time of Ricardo; (b) history and jurisprudence (1) not new but they have been rewritten to throw more light on man's nature than before,[2] (2) not related to individuals and military struggles but to efforts of man to adjust himself to changed environment; (3) economic history has made a new kind of history and taught economists much; (c) biological group of sciences has thrown much light on man himself—endless cumulative process of evolution—structure—methods of behavior—new; (d) social statistics—practically all new; (1) data concerning man and his activities; (2) conception of uniformity ture—methods of behavior new; (d) social statistics—practically all new; with respect to social phenomena in large groups and development of special technique—great promise; (e) sociology new—gives us wider conception of economics as well as hazy possibility of general science of society; (f) psychology.[3]

IV. Most fruitful to regard economics definitely as one among several sciences of behavior. A. Confined to one gregarious species—man. B. (a) does not treat all varieties of this one species—considers only western Europe; (b) considers only such as developed in recent times. B. Differentiating characteristic of economic behavior; (a) has to do with material requisites of well-being, to get material things men need.

---

[2] Outline, "Closing Lectures," May 14, 16, 1917, [reads]: Rewritten in a spirit which suggests continuation of the story as a part of the evolution of institutions from the point where ethnological evidence breaks off.

[3] [Details missing. Following is] from Outline, "Closing Lectures," May 14, 16, 1917. Psychology has definitely outgrown the simple stages of hedonism, association and separate faculties, is in a more modest frame of mind and is now ardently searching for a solid basis in measurement and experience. It has developed new types of work—experimental, pathological, comparative, etc. Objective viewpoint (behaviorism). It has accepted conception of man as an animal species whose intelligence such as it is serves primarily biological ends.